MW01090179

LEGAL ASPECTS OF CORPORATE FINANCE

LexisNexis Law School Publishing Advisory Board

LEGAL ASPECTS OF CORPORATE FINANCE

FIFTH EDITION

Richard T. McDermott
Adjunct Professor
Fordham University School of Law

ISBN: 978-0-7698-5945-3
LL ISBN: 978-0-7698-5946-0
eBook ISBN: 978-1-5791-1715-3

Library of Congress Cataloging-in-Publication Data

McDermott, Richard T.
Legal aspects of corporate finance / Richard T. McDermott, Adjunct Professor, Fordham University School of Law. -- Fifth edition.
p. cm.
Includes index.
ISBN 978-0-7698-5945-3
1. Corporations--Finance--Law and legislation--United States. 2. Securites--United States. I. Title.
KF1428.M33 2013
346.73'0666--dc23
2013010291

NOTE TO USERS
To ensure that you are using the latest materials available in this area, please be sure to periodically check the LexisNexis Law School web site for downloadable updates and supplements at www.lexisnexis.com/lawschool.

Editorial Offices
121 Chanlon Rd., New Providence, NJ 07974 (908) 464-6800
201 Mission St., San Francisco, CA 94105-1831 (415) 908-3200
www.lexisnexis.com

MATTHEW BENDER

(2013–Pub.440)

PREFACE

This book is the result of my experience in teaching a class in Corporate Finance at the New York University School of Law for 19 years and at the Fordham University School of Law for 12. That experience, in turn, is based upon the 37 years I spent practicing business law.

One of my objectives in the course has been to provide a forum in which terms and concepts pertaining to corporate finance and related matters can be discussed, defined, and explained in an atmosphere in which the students are not reticent to disclose that they have not yet completely mastered the field of business law. When I began to practice corporate and securities law, I was unfamiliar with the field, and began my education as a bag carrier and note taker at conferences, while trying to appear as if I actually knew what was going on. In some respects, my course and, to a certain extent this book, could be entitled "Everything You Wanted to Know About Corporate Finance but Were Afraid to Ask." Indeed, I make it a point to admonish my students that the only "stupid" question in my classroom is the one that is not asked. In addition to the cases, statutes, and textual materials, I have included excerpts from various corporate finance documents, such as debentures, trust indentures, preferred stock provisions, and acquisition agreements. It has been my experience that it is helpful for students to study the actual form of the documentation under consideration while they are also dealing with various explanatory secondary materials. I have inserted the documentation examples in the text, rather than as appendices, to encourage their being read with the other materials. I subscribe to the view, originally espoused by Christopher Columbus Langdell of the Harvard Law School (*see* Ames, *Professor Langdell — His Services to Legal Education*, 20 HARV. L. REV. 12 [1906]), that the most useful way of studying law is an analysis of legal opinions deciding actual cases or controversies. I believe that the principles of the case method can also be utilized to consider and analyze the corporate finance documents themselves. Their terms, often the product of complex and sophisticated negotiations and resulting in workable solutions to a myriad of business and financial issues, while at the same time being responsive to decisional and statutory law, are in a very real sense "the law of the case" with regard to a particular corporate finance transaction.

In the context of corporate finance and related transactions, the views of Professor Langdell were supplemented by Paul D. Cravath, who, nearly 100 years ago, advised young lawyers and general practitioners that:

> The provisions of the modern reorganization agreement and the modern corporate mortgage are the result of the experience and prophetic vision of a great many able lawyers. Every new provision is suggested either by some decision of the courts or by an actual experience or by some lawyer's conception of a possible exigency. Ordinarily in drafting a document a lawyer must draw chiefly upon his own experience and the results of his own observation, but corporate mortgages and reorganization agreements are public documents so that each lawyer can have the benefit of the experience of many others. . . . I advise you to adhere to precedent

> and, in most cases, you will find the long reorganization agreement based on precedent much safer than the agreement half as long drawn by your neighbor who scorns precedent.

CRAVATH, REORGANIZATION OF CORPORATIONS IN SOME LEGAL PHASES OF CORPORATE FINANCING, REORGANIZATION AND REGULATION 153, 178 (1917).

The materials in this book are those dealt with in my course in Legal Aspects of Corporate Finance. As the title suggests, this book is for the most part concerned with the legal aspects of corporate finance. Particular emphasis is placed upon the nature of the legal relationships created by corporate finance transactions. Indeed, the matters dealt with in this book and my course touch upon a number of areas of substantive law in addition to state corporation laws, including contracts, torts, antitrust, negotiable instruments, tax, securities, bankruptcy and creditors' rights, environmental law, constitutional law, and conflict of laws. It is important that students understand that outstanding corporate practitioners are versatile lawyers who apply their substantive knowledge to transactions. They are not technocrats engaged in some arcane subspecialty with little connection to the law. In a sense, these lawyers do their "litigating" by discerning and resolving issues at the negotiating table when transactions are being structured. The study of case law is important in corporate finance because it is essential that deal lawyers understand how judges approach disputes and construe documents in this area. Having a "judge's eye view" is thus of great value to one who is negotiating or drafting documents, and the cases in this book were selected with that in mind.

September 4, 2012

ACKNOWLEDGMENTS

I wish to express my appreciation for the contributions of my partners at Alexander & Green, Rogers & Wells, and Clifford Chance, particularly Klaus H. Jander. I also wish to thank Professor Jack Slain of the faculty of the New York University School of Law, and Michael Martin, Dean of the Fordham University School of Law. I also wish to acknowledge the outstanding administrative assistance, organizational skills, and editorial support of Randé L. DeGidio, Marge Oehler and my editor, Cristina Gegenschatz, the invaluable assistance of Frances Schoenfield (Reference Librarian) of Clifford Chance, as well as the contributions of Dave Thomas, Richard R. Howe, James Leyden, John Mark Zeberkiewicz, Robert Powel, Marissa Marco, Lawrence Lederman, Jack Porter, Nolan Welch, Jason Jones, and Palen McDermott.

I would certainly be remiss if I did not thank my children, Richard Bissell McDermott and Christina Henderson and their spouses, Martha Mary Rossi and Judson Roberts Henderson, who, in addition to their encouragement and support, contributed their names to the various entities which appear in the Problem and Example sections of various chapters, as do those of our grandchildren Palen, Carmel and Richard Peter McDermott and Maisie, Hutch and Mac Henderson. My wife, Mary Pat McDermott, has made the many sacrifices that the spouse of a lawyer necessarily and often inconveniently must endure. Her own participation in this process dates from her typing (and the now quaint use of carbon paper, cut and paste insertions and white-out) the countless drafts and revisions of my first legal publication: Note, *Taxation — Seller's Proceeds of "Bootstrap Sale" to Tax-Exempt Organization Held Taxable at Capital Gains Rates*, 34 FORDHAM L. REV. 358 (1965). Finally, I am most grateful to my father, Richard A. McDermott, with whom I first traversed the legal thickets.

TABLE OF CONTENTS

TABLE OF CONTENTS

Chapter 1

CORPORATE FINANCE AND THE PROCESS OF CAPITAL FORMATION

§ 1.01 CORPORATE FINANCE — GENERAL OBSERVATIONS

The term "Corporate Finance" as dealt with in this book involves an analysis of the legal aspects of how business corporations, particularly (but not exclusively) publicly traded ones, obtain and spend funds. They obtain funds principally from three sources: investors, institutional lenders (themselves a form of "investor"), and the net cash flow (*i.e.*, not mere financial statement "earnings") generated by the entity's operations. In the corporate finance context, business corporations spend money primarily by investments in new or expanded facilities or the acquisition from third parties of existing businesses, and by making distributions to their security holders in the form of interest and principal payments to holders of debt instruments and dividend distributions, stock repurchases or redemption payments to preferred or common stockholders.

Corporate finance involves a number of transactions to which a business corporation is a party. One category of such transactions is that of those between the corporation and those who become investors in it; they involve the transfer of funds from the investors, who have them, to the businesses, which need them, a process commonly known as "capital formation." Those transactions result in the establishment of contractual or statutorily imposed legal relationships between the investor and the corporation. They involve the issuance by the corporation to the investor of an instrument constituting the consideration for the delivery of the capital funds to the corporation. That instrument, which is called a security, may evidence either the establishment of a debtor-creditor relationship between the corporation and the investor, or the acquisition by the investor of shares of stock representing an ownership (or equity) interest in the corporation, which is referred to as the "issuer" of the security. One reason an ownership interest in a corporation is referred to as an "equity interest" is that, in accounting parlance, the term "equity" refers to an item on the corporation's balance sheet called owner's equity or stockholder's equity; that item consists of the aggregate consideration received by the corporation for the issuance of stock from time to time, and the aggregate amount of the corporation's profit and loss accounts.

The primary purpose of a business corporation's obtaining, utilizing, and distributing funds is to increase the worth of the corporate enterprise, which is reflected in the value of its securities. In the case of the publicly traded corporation, the value of its securities is, of course, reflected in their day-to-day trading prices.

The significance of the securities markets has been succinctly summarized as follows:

> For all their unpredictability, markets are nevertheless considered among the truest gages of the economy. The market is no more, and no less, than the sum of what thousands and thousands of people decide about it at any one time. The market is where all knowledge about the economy or individual enterprises — the surmises as well as the certainties, is brought to bear, almost instantly.[1]

There are various stock indices that measure how a particular group or segment of stocks are performing from time to time. The most well-known such index is the Dow Jones Industrial Average of 30 stocks, a list initially created in 1882 by Charles H. Dow who, with Edward Jones, started Dow Jones & Co. Although it is still referred to as the Dow Jones Industrial Average, the 30 companies presently making up the list include such non-industrial companies as McDonalds, Home Depot, Wal-Mart, and Walt Disney, thus reflecting the transformation of the U.S. economy from a primarily industrial one to one that is more service oriented. The term "Industrial," however, has been retained for tradition's sake. The list now includes a greater weighting from such sectors as services, healthcare, and technology. Also included are American Express and JPMorgan, which, of course, are banking and financial service companies. The importance of technology to the U.S. economy was further demonstrated by the addition in November 1999 of Microsoft and Intel. SBC Communications, of the telecommunications sector, also became a Dow company at that time. A detailed discussion of the purposes of and methodology used in the valuation of corporations is set forth in Chapter 2.

The parties' expectation is that ownership of the security acquired by the investor will result in income (through yield in the form of interest on debt securities and dividends on equity securities), and capital gain (through realized appreciation upon disposition). In the case of a debt security, there is, of course, the expectation of a return of capital through repayment of principal at maturity.

The primary purpose of the management of a business corporation is, of course, to increase the value of the enterprise and thus its common stock. With respect to the means of achieving that objective, there is presented the fundamental question as to whether the focus should be over the long term or the short term. Too much attention to the short term creates serious problems for the policy and decision makers. One commentator has recounted the following:

> I remember one lunch time conversation I had with the CEO of a well-known industrial company. He said, with great frustration, that the market's short-term focus made it impossible for him to adequately implement an exciting long-term strategy his company had developed. To make the point, he described how he had just met with a major institutional investor and had set forth his company's long-term strategy. "To accomplish this long-term purpose, we need to invest now," he had said, "and we'll have these wonderful benefits down the road." And the institution's response had been: "We don't want you investing for the future. Not because we disagree

---

[1] Arensen, *The New Trading Game*, N.Y. Times, Sept. 20, 1986, Sec. 1, p. 1, col. 2.

with you about the long-term benefits, but because we're not going to be there for the long-term. What we care about is your next quarter."[2]

The author also cites several developments which have fostered short term speculation by encouraging high trading volume: (i) the elimination in 1975 of fixed commissions for institutions and wealthy individuals, (ii) the advent of discount brokerage houses for middle-class investors in the early 1990s, and (iii) the establishment by the end of the 1990s of daily business and market news channels on cable television. Likewise, many of the 1980s debt financed "bust up" hostile takeovers succeeded September 4, 2012 because investors wanted "instant gratification" rather than steady growth. Long term investors became viewed by many as quaint relics of a bygone era.

One other observation regarding the securities markets: they are dependent upon the legal underpinnings of the various instruments representing the securities being traded. As Delaware Vice Chancellor Jacobs has stated:

> Corporate securities are a species of property right that represent not only a firm's fundamental source for raising capital, but also now a publicly traded commodity that is a critical component for creating both institutional and individual wealth that may affect the economic well-being of entire societies. Given the fundamental importance of such securities to our economic system, it is critical that the validity of those securities, especially those that are widely traded, not be easily or capriciously called into question. Otherwise, the resulting economic uncertainty to investors and institutions that relied upon the integrity of those securities would be destabilizing. Accordingly, our statutory scheme, elucidated by case law, has developed a clear and easily followed legal roadmap for creating these valuable instruments that represent claims upon an enterprise's capital. Under that model, if that roadmap is followed, the investment community will be assured that the corporate securities created by that process will not be vulnerable to legal attack. If, on the other hand, it is not followed, then the securities will become subject to possible invalidation.

Kalageorgi v. Victor Kamkin, Inc., 750 A.2d 531, 538 (Del. Ch. 1999), *aff'd*, 748 A.2d 913 (Del. 2000).

Students should not, however, be lulled into complacency by the phrase "easily followed legal roadmap." The importance of first class lawyering in corporate matters has been described by Sullivan & Cromwell partner, Benjamin F. Stapleton, as follows: "The educational experience my first three or four years was just staggering. I learned more about rigorous thinking, about people depending upon you to get it right and how serious it was if you didn't get it right." Julie Connelly, *He Handles the Big Ones*, The Daily Deal, Feb. 19, 2000.

The results of a failure to adhere to the standards articulated by Mr. Stapleton are illustrated by the slipshod manner in which many of the pre 2008 Credit Crisis mortgage backed securities were put together. As stated by Judge Cordy of the

---

[2] Robert E. Rubin, In An Uncertain World 335 (2003).

Supreme Judicial Court of Massachusetts in a decision voiding a foreclosure by the trustee for such a security:

> I concur fully in the opinion of the court, and write separately only to underscore that what is surprising about these [securitization] cases is not the statement of principles articulated by the court regarding title law and the law of foreclosure . . . but rather *the utter carelessness with which the plaintiff banks documented the titles to their assets* . . . the holder of an assigned mortgage needs to take care to ensure that his legal paperwork is in order. . . .

United States Bank Nat'l Ass'n v. Ibanez, 458 Mass. 637, 655–56 (2011) (emphasis added).

Finally, it should be borne in mind that: "Investor confidence in our capital markets depends, in part, on the certainty and predictability of corporate finance instruments and transactions." Joan MacLeod Heminway, *Federal Interventions in Private Enterprise in the United States: Their Genesis in and Effects on Corporate Finance Instruments and Transactions*, 40 SETON HALL L. REV. 1487, 1518 (2010).

§ 1.02 DEBT AND EQUITY SECURITIES

Economic and business conditions and the creativity and ingenuity of corporate lawyers have produced a myriad of corporate securities to deal with the vicissitudes of interest rates, economic conditions, and securities markets; however, as Professor Jack Slain, my colleague and mentor at the New York University School of Law would say, all securities, no matter how apparently esoteric and complex, are of only two types: an "IOU" or a "piece of the pie." The Credit Crisis of 2008, which is discussed in § 1.07 *infra*, was caused in substantial part by the use (and abuse) of toxic "IOUs," including mortgage-backed securities, collaterized debt obligations, and credit default swaps. Set forth below is a general description of the principal characteristics of debt and equity securities.

[A] Debt Securities

The security evidencing a debtor-creditor relationship sets forth the obligations of the corporation to pay to the holder of the instrument the borrowed money on a specific maturity date and, to pay interest as specified. Such a corporate "promissory note" may, depending upon its particular characteristics, be called a bond, a debenture, or a note, and in addition, may be in either registered or bearer form.

Today most corporate debt instruments are in registered form, which means that the name of the owner is registered with the issuer and the issuer remits to the holder the appropriate amount of interest when due. In the case of a bearer bond with coupon attached, the person who holds the bond or the coupons (which have a date and an amount of interest set forth thereon) is presumed to be the owner. Such coupons must be detached and submitted by the holder to the issuer for payment; hence the expression "clipping coupons."

[1] Bonds

The principal characteristics of a corporate bond are that the principal and interest payment obligations evidenced thereby are secured by a mortgage on property of the issuer. The term of a corporate bond is generally in excess of five years, meaning that the principal is due more than five years from the date of issuance of the bond. Where, because of the number of holders of a particular series of corporate bonds, it is impracticable for the issuer to enter into a direct contractual relationship with each while at the same time permitting transfers of the bonds by the holders thereof, the trust device is utilized in order to create and maintain the mortgage. A trust relationship is established with a financial institution which, in addition to contracting with the issuer and receiving a conveyance of the pledged property, also acts as a trustee for the holders of the corporate bonds, who are the beneficiaries of the trust. The terms of the contractual relationship between the issuer and the trustee, as well as the trust relationship between the trustee and the beneficiaries, are set forth in a document called an indenture, primarily because it is an instrument conveying the mortgaged property to the trustee. The various obligations of the issuer and the duties of the indenture trustee to the bond holders, in addition to those imposed by applicable law, are also set forth therein.

[2] Debentures

A debenture is an unsecured corporate obligation to pay principal at maturity and to make payments of interest and, like a bond, is generally for a term of more than five years. Debentures are also issued pursuant to an indenture; however, no conveyance is involved, and no security interest in property of the issuer is created. Rather, the indenture device is utilized to enable the issuer of the debentures to make certain contractual commitments to the indenture trustee for the benefit of the holders of the debentures and their transferees, without the necessity of the issuer entering into separate contractual relationships with each of the holders of the debentures and their transferees. Again, the relationships are twofold, that of promisor and promisee, and of settler, trustee, and beneficiary.

The contractual commitments of the issuer, which relate to the primary payment obligations and the conduct of its business while the debentures are outstanding, are set forth in the indenture and take the form of affirmative or negative covenants. These undertakings by the corporation to take, or to refrain from taking, certain actions with regard to the business or affairs of the issuer are intended to make it more likely that the issuer will be able to perform its central obligations with regard to the debentures, the payment of principal at maturity and interest when due. This special contractual protection for the holders of the debt instruments is often necessary because the protection afforded such holders under applicable state law (*i.e.*, the laws of the state under which the issuer is incorporated) are often minimal. The protection provided by such laws are generally prohibitions against fraudulent conveyances and prohibitions against distributions to stockholders that would, in effect, render the corporation insolvent or that would impair the corporation's legal capital. Legal capital in that context, however, generally includes only the par or stated capital of shares, not the amounts actually received by the corporation from the equity investors for the shares and certainly not the accumulated earnings of the issuer.

[3] Notes

Notes issued by the corporation may be either secured or unsecured, and may or may not be issued pursuant to an indenture. Corporate notes often have a maturity date of five years or less.

The definitional distinctions among bonds, debentures, and notes are not always recognized. For example, Section 102(a)(2) of the New York Business Corporation Law, *infra* § 1.08, provides that " 'bonds' includes secured and unsecured bonds, debentures, and notes."

[4] Subordinated Debentures

As stated above, bonds are secured obligations of the issuer and in the event of insolvency of the issuer; bondholders have the status of a secured creditor to the extent of their allowed claim and the status of an unsecured creditor with regard to the amount, if any, of their claim that is not allowed as a secured claim. A holder of debentures or notes is by definition an unsecured creditor, and in the event of insolvency, participates pro rata with the other general unsecured creditors of the corporation. Debentures and notes sometimes provide that in the event of insolvency of the issuer, the claims of the holder shall be subordinated to the claims of certain general creditors of the corporation; those other claims are treated as "senior indebtedness" insofar as the holders of the subordinated debentures or notes are concerned. "Senior" debt securities rank *pari passu* with all other unsecured and unsubordinated indebtedness of the issuer. In exchange for accepting the status of a subordinated creditor and assuming the economic risks thereof, the holder of such a debenture or note generally receives a higher interest rate than would normally be provided were the debentures or notes not subordinated. Such higher interest rate is designed to compensate the holder for the greater risks involved in being a subordinated creditor of the corporation. Additional compensation such as a conversion privilege, which is discussed below, is often afforded to the holder of a subordinated debenture or note.

The term "junk bonds" is another example of the varying terminology applicable to corporate securities. Junk "bonds" are actually unsecured, often subordinated, debentures. They are instruments rated by the rating agencies (principally Moody's Investors Service Inc. and Standard & Poor's Corp.) below investment grade. The term "junk bonds" came to prominence during the 1980s when those debt instruments were utilized to finance cash takeovers of publicly traded companies. At that time, the dominant market participant was the now defunct Drexel Burnham Lambert. Since then the junk bond business has grown from $200 billion to in excess of $600 billion, but the proceeds have been used by operating companies, particularly those in the telecommunications industry, for working capital purposes, as had been the case prior to the 1980s.

[5] Commercial Paper

This security is a short term debt instrument usually issued in denominations of not less than $100,000 by corporations with maturities of several months. Commercial paper is usually purchased by money market funds and institutional investors.

[B] Equity Securities

An ownership or equity interest in a business corporation is evidenced by two basic types of stock interests: preferred stock and common stock.

[1] Preferred Stock

The holder of a preferred stock interest is generally entitled to a preference with regard to dividends declared and paid by the corporation up to a fixed amount and the distribution of the assets of the corporation upon dissolution. The rights of the holders of preferred stock and the obligations of the issuer, including dividend and distribution rights, as well as covenants similar to those set forth in the indentures in the case of bonds and debentures, are set forth in the certificate of incorporation of the corporation or in resolutions the board of directors of the corporation adopted pursuant to specific authority delegated to the Board in the certificate of incorporation.

[2] Common Stock

Subject to the rights of holders of preferred stock, if any, owners of common stock are entitled to the entire equity interest in the corporation, either in the form of dividends, when and as declared by the board of directors of the corporation, or upon the dissolution of the corporation and the distribution of its assets.

[C] Convertible and Exchangeable Securities

Debt securities and preferred stock are sometimes referred to as "senior securities," because the holders thereof have priority over the holders of the common stock in the event of a dissolution of the corporation. Senior securities may, by their terms, be convertible, at the election of the holder, into junior securities or common stock of the corporation at a specified conversion rate or price. Exercise of the conversion privilege permits the holder of the senior security to change his interest in the corporation into that of the holder of the residual equity interest. The initial conversion price is generally higher than the market price of the junior securities or common stock at the time of the offering of the convertible senior securities. The difference between the then market price and the conversion price is sometimes referred to as a "conversion premium." Convertible securities generally have had premiums of approximately 20 percent; in some cases, however, the price was more advantageous to holders of convertible securities, with conversion premiums being as low as 10 percent. The conversion privilege is generally exercised by the holder of the senior security at a time when the market price of the junior securities or common stock is higher than the conversion price. Issuers are often able to market senior securities at a lower interest or dividend rate because of the possible economic benefits of the conversion feature to the holder. However, it must also be recognized that at the time of exercise, the corporation will receive the equivalent of less than the then current market price of value for its common stock. The statutory authority of business corporations to issue convertible securities has been utilized to create another of the newly developed "financial products," the "poison pill" preferred stock which is described in detail in Chapter 5, *infra*, dealing with convertible securities.

A convertible security is different from a warrant (which also provides the holder thereof with the right to acquire a security such as common stock) in that the consideration for the issuance of the junior shares upon a conversion of the senior securities is the relinquishment by the holder of the senior securities of the corporation. A warrant, on the other hand, generally provides the holder with the right to acquire shares for cash.

A senior security is often called an exchangeable security if equity or debt securities issued by another corporation or if securities other than the common stock of the issuer are receivable by the holder upon surrender of the exchangeable senior securities.

The terms of convertible or exchangeable securities usually include provisions intended to preserve the rights of the holder in the event that the issuer of the junior securities to be acquired upon conversion or exchange participates in a transaction prior to conversion or exchange that materially affects either the capital structure or the basic character of the corporation and causes a diminution of the value of the conversion privilege. These protective provisions, which are called anti-dilution clauses, are designed to place the holder of the convertible or exchangeable security in approximately the same position as it would have been had it exercised its conversion or exchange right and acquired the junior security immediately before the happening of such an extraordinary event.

[D] American Depositary Receipts (ADRs)

Many non-U.S. corporations enter the U.S. securities markets to access capital or to enhance their visibility. To facilitate trading in their securities they use ADRs, receipts that represent an ownership interest in a class of their securities. ADRs usually represent the common stock of a foreign corporation, although debt securities can also be so represented. ADRs are a more attractive U.S. investment than the underlying securities they represent because they trade in U.S. dollars; also, dividends paid on the underlying foreign securities are converted into U.S. dollars.

ADRs are created by the deposit of securities with a financial institution which acts as a depositary for the underlying foreign securities and the issuance by the depositary of receipts. Generally, the rights and obligations of the issuer, the depositary and the ADR holder are set forth in a Deposit Agreement.

[E] Debt-Equity Ratios

The capital structure of most business corporations consists of a combination of equity and debt securities of various types.

The term debt-equity ratio, is a commonly used financial measurement that generally compares a corporation's long-term debt to its stockholders' equity (the latter representing the corporation's assets less its liabilities).

A corporation is said to be "leveraged" if debt securities constitute a substantial proportion of its capitalization ("the total amount of a corporation's long-term financing, including stock, bonds and retained earnings").[3] If the corporation is profitable, however, the existence of leverage is attractive. "Among the reasons for the issue of senior securities . . . are the creation of 'leverage' the greater possible gain to the common shareholders on the total capital invested and the lesser investment necessary to obtain voting control."[4]

§ 1.03 REDEMPTION AND REPURCHASE OF DEBT AND EQUITY SECURITIES

Transactions resulting in a termination of the investor-issuer relationship are also included within the scope of corporate finance. They include the reacquisition by the corporation of the debt or equity securities previously issued by it, usually for cash. These reacquisitions may, in the case of senior securities, be pursuant to rights and options reserved by the corporation at the time of issuance of the securities: That right is commonly referred to as the corporation's "right of redemption." A right of redemption permits a corporation to reacquire the security at certain times and for certain prices, whether or not the holder of the security wishes to sell it to the corporation. For that reason, the redemption price includes a premium that is an amount in excess of principal and accrued interest and is intended to compensate the holder for having to sell it to the corporation involuntarily. The issuing corporation may also obligate itself to repurchase its security at the option of the holder thereof after several years but long before the redemption date. This "put" feature is designed to protect the holder of a debt security in the event that market interest rates rise, and it usually permits the issuer to save interest costs by initially issuing the security at a slightly lower interest rate than the investor would insist upon without the repurchase obligation and the consequent protection against a rise in interest rates.

The reacquisition by a corporation of a senior security can also benefit the holders of those senior securities that are not redeemed and thus remain outstanding. A reduction in the number of outstanding debt securities (and thus aggregate principal amount) increases the probability that the corporation will be able to pay the principal amount at maturity and make interest payments when due. Likewise, retirement of shares of a class of preferred stock reduces the aggregate amounts of dividend and liquidation preferences with the same beneficial effect upon the remaining preferred stock holders. For this reason, it is common to include in indentures and preferred stock terms provisions requiring the corporation periodically to reacquire those outstanding senior securities. They are called sinking fund provisions, because their effect is to lower or reduce the number of aggregate of senior securities that are outstanding.

---

[3] Bryan A. Sarner ed., A Handbook Of Business Law Terms 94 (1999).

[4] Ballantine, Corporations 501 (rev. ed. 1946).

There also are, of course, voluntary transactions between the corporation and the investor pursuant to which the corporation reacquires the security held by the investor.

The reacquisition by a corporation of its debt securities is attractive to it in a time of high interest rates and resulting depressed bond prices. When interest rates are high, debt securities that had been issued at lower rates are traded at a substantial discount from their principal amount. The reason for this is that the below market stated rate of interest together with the discounted sale price of the bond produces a "yield" or actual return that reflects current interest rates. If the issuing corporation were to acquire debt securities for less than their principal amount, the transaction would result in income to the corporation, since there is an economic gain to the issuer upon the repurchase of some of its bonds at a price less than the amount the corporation is obligated to pay at maturity.

In accounting parlance, transactions of this sort are often referred to as an "early extinguishment of debt," and for financial reporting purposes, the difference between the price paid by the corporation to reacquire a debt security and the principal amount thereof plus accrued interest is recognized in the period of extinguishment as either a loss or a gain.

In *United States v. Kirby Lumber Co.*, 284 U.S. 1 (1931), the issuer reacquired bonds in open market purchases at a cash price of $137,521.30 less than their principal amount. In holding that "the [issuer] had made a clear gain" and had thus increased federal income tax liability therefor, Justice Holmes observed that "as a result of its dealings, it made available $137,521.30 [of] assets previously offset by the obligation of bonds now extinct." (284 U.S. at 3.)

Prior to 1984, the acquisition of debt instruments that were the subject of an early extinguishment with shares of common stock of the issuer, although reportable as a gain or loss for financial reporting purposes, was not generally subject to federal income taxation. The reason that such a transaction was not generally taxable is that it is deemed to result in the continuation of the investor-issuer relationship, although in a different form. It was on the basis of these principles that the so-called "debt equity swap" was devised. In that transaction, an investment banking firm would acquire a large block of a corporation's outstanding debt securities, usually from an institutional investor such as a pension fund or a mutual fund and then sell the securities to the issuer in exchange for newly issued common stock. The investment banking firm would profit from the exchange transaction and from a public secondary offering by it of the common stock.

Section 108(e)(8) of the Internal Revenue Code of 1986 provides that in the event a corporation transfers its stock to a creditor in satisfaction of indebtedness, the debtor corporation generally may realize taxable gain from the discharge of indebtedness measured by the difference between the fair market value of the stock and the aggregate principal amount of the debt securities repurchased by the issuing corporation.

§ 1.04 ACQUISITIONS AND OTHER TYPES OF INVESTMENTS BY CORPORATIONS

Other types of transactions included in the study of corporate finance are those whereby the business corporation itself undertakes to make an investment in other business enterprises. The consideration paid by the corporation for such an investment often is securities issued by it or cash; the source of the investing corporation's funds may be either borrowings from financial institutions, funds received from investors through the issuance of securities, or funds derived from the conduct of business operations, or a combination thereof. Those types of corporate investments include mergers and other types of acquisitions. Consideration of these transactions includes an analysis of both the obligations of the investing or acquiring corporation and the rights of the holders of various types of debt and equity securities of the corporation being acquired. These matters are dealt with in Chapter 7, *infra*.

§ 1.05 PARTIES TO AND BASIC STRUCTURE OF CAPITAL FORMATION TRANSACTIONS

The following is a general description of capital formation transactions involving the transfer to the corporation of investment funds and the issuance by that corporation of securities to the investors. Those transactions are basically of two types.

One involves the purchase of debt or equity securities directly from the issuer by a relatively small number of investors.

The other involves a sale by the issuer of securities to a purchaser who acquires securities with a view toward, and for the purpose of, reselling them at a profit to the investing public. The person, firm, or corporation making the purchase and subsequent resale is referred to as an underwriter, because by paying cash to the issuer for the entire offering, the purchaser in effect underwrites such offering and the financing transaction.

The structure and form of those two basic types of capital formation transactions result in some respects from the provisions of the Securities Act of 1933, regulating public and private offerings of securities.

The Securities Act of 1933 and the Securities Exchange Act of 1934 were enacted following the commencement of the economic depression in the United States and were designed to prevent fraudulent practices in securities transactions. At the time, there were various state laws proscribing such conduct. Because the misrepresentations of promoters and the like were so blatant that the securities they were peddling might as well have been as worthless as those that purported to represent shares of the blue sky, these laws thus became known as "blue sky" laws. They did not, however, effectively deal with the problem because of their limited scope and a lack of uniformity.

A series of national laws were passed, requiring, among other things, full disclosure of information relevant to the making of an informed investment decision as to whether to buy or sell a security, particularly in the case of an initial offering.

An agency of the federal government, the Securities and Exchange Commission, was created to administer and enforce those laws and to adopt rules to clarify them and facilitate their implementation.

The Securities Act of 1933 thus governs the initial issuance and distribution by a business entity, such as a corporation, of securities. For capital formation purposes, the principal requirements of the Securities Exchange Act of 1934 (i) deal with the reporting and disclosure obligations of corporations that have outstanding securities held by the public and (ii) prohibit fraud in connection with trading of securities, subsequent to their original issuance.

The Securities Act of 1933 provides that no public interstate offering of securities may be made unless a document called a Registration Statement is in effect. A Registration Statement contains business and financial information about the offering company, which is intended to permit a potential investor to make an informed decision whether or not to invest in the corporation. Such information is set forth in a separate document called a Prospectus, which forms the principal part of the Registration Statement. A Prospectus provides information concerning the issuing corporation. The Commission has historically insisted that a Prospectus contain past information upon which an investor may form assumptions regarding the future prospects of the corporation. Certain projections as to future prospects are permitted but not encouraged. Under the administrative framework that has developed under the 1933 Act, the Registration Statement becomes effective when the Commission issues an administrative order so declaring. Generally, such an order is not issued by the Commission until it is satisfied that the Registration Statement and the documents included therein, particularly the Prospectus, comply with the applicable rules and regulations of the Commission as to form and content.

Under the 1933 Act, a private offering transaction is exempt from the Registration Statement and Prospectus requirements. Section 4(2) of the Act provides that the registration requirements "shall not apply to . . . transactions by an issuer not involving any public offering."

The terms "public" and "private" offering are not defined in the 1933 Act. Consequently, they have been the subject of numerous administrative regulations and interpretations, court decisions, and an abundance of legal commentary. As a general proposition, an offering is considered to be private when the number of offerees and ultimate purchasers is relatively small, the investment is prudent in the light of the investor's financial condition, and the investor or someone acting on its behalf has been provided with information similar to that required to be set forth in a Registration Statement of the type described above. The SEC's administrative regulations relating to non-public offerings of securities are set forth in the Commission's Regulation D. In 1990, the SEC adopted Rule 144A, which provides a more efficient way to resell privately placed securities without registration under the 1933 Act. The Rule increased the liquidity of the secondary private placement market and thus made private placements of securities in the United States a more attractive option for capital-raising. Also in 1990, the SEC adopted Regulation S that clarified the circumstances under which the 1933 Act does not apply to offerings of securities made by a domestic issuer to foreign investors.

In a public offering, the economic and business terms of the transaction are generally arrived at as a result of negotiations between the issuer and the underwriter and its representatives. Included in the negotiations are such matters as (i) the interest or dividend rate of the security (which is often not fixed until the time of the actual offering in order to reflect the then prevailing market conditions); (ii) the maturity date of a debt instrument; (iii) whether and under what terms the debt instrument or preferred stock is to be redeemable by the corporation; (iv) whether the senior security is to be convertible into common stock of the issuer or exchangeable for another security; (v) sinking fund provisions; and (vi) whether the indenture or charter provision relating to the senior security is to contain any affirmative or negative covenants on the part of the issuer designed to render it more probable that the issuer will meet its payment obligations. When these matters have been agreed to by the issuer and the underwriter, they are often set forth on a piece of paper called a "term sheet." Counsel for the parties utilize that document in preparing the transaction documents.

In a private offering, those matters are determined by the issuer and the investors or their representatives.

As stated previously, the Securities Exchange Act of 1934 regulates post distribution trading. In the case of publicly traded securities, the 1934 Act mandates the public filing of periodic Reports containing SEC required business and financial information concerning the issuer. These Reports, which must be filed annually (on Form 10K), quarterly (on Form 10Q), and shortly after the occurrence of certain specified events (on Form 8K), are intended to permit an investor to make an informed decision as to whether to purchase or sell securities of a particular issuer. The 2004 amendments to the Form 8K requirements, which mandate an 8K filing within four days of certain newly specified events, were adopted by the SEC pursuant to the post Enron enacted Section 13(1) of the 1934 Act which authorizes the SEC to require "real time" disclosure of material information. As a result, 8K Reports are no longer occasional; they have become routine.

Section 408 of the Sarbanes Oxley Act of 2002, another post Enron statute, requires the SEC to review the filings of 1934 Act reporting issuers at least once every three years. The 1934 Act proxy rules require that an investor have the information necessary to make an informed decision regarding voting on various corporate matters, ranging from the election of directors to merger proposals.

Other SEC Rules under the 1934 Act are intended to create a level playing field for investors by prohibiting, in connection with the purchase or sale of a security, the use of material non public information concerning the issuer by an insider thereof or another person where such use would constitute a breach of a duty to refrain from such use. Those prohibitions also apply to the issuer itself when it repurchases its securities.

§ 1.06 INVESTMENT BANKING

Generally speaking, investment banking activities involve the rendering of two basic services to business corporations, the underwriting or placement of securities offerings and the rendering of advice with respect to such matters as corporate investments, mergers and acquisitions, divestitures, and reorganizations. In many investment banking firms, however, advisory business came to be overshadowed by another source of revenue, proprietary trading. Since substantially more capital was needed to support those operations than could be raised from the partners of those partnerships, the firms were converted into publicly traded corporations through stock offerings which raised the necessary capital, and also made the partners multi-millionaires based on the market value of their ownership of the shares of those newly minted public corporations. The transformation from partnership to corporation was possible because, in the aftermath of the 1960s back office crises on Wall Street (which financially decimated a number of venerable brokerage firms and their partners) the Rules of the New York Stock Exchange (until then an unincorporated association) were changed to allow member firms to be corporations. Consequently, it was no longer the case that "partners had personal liability for the [financial] exposure of the firm, right down to their homes and cars." Peter Weinberg, *Wall Street Needs More Skin in the Game*, WALL ST. J., Oct. 1, 2009, at A23.

The investment banks' business model of advisory service and trading profits became so successful that the large commercial banks decided to enter those same lines of business; however, they faced a significant legal obstacle. For more than 65 years, the Banking Act of 1933, commonly known as the Glass-Steagall Act, severely restricted the authority of commercial banks (*i.e.*, those that receive deposits and make loans) and their affiliates to engage in investment-banking activities. The Glass-Steagall Act's "design reflect[ed] the congressional perception that certain investment banking activities are fundamentally incompatible with commercial banking." *Securities Industry Ass'n v. Board of Governors of Federal Reserve System*, 468 U.S. 137, 147 (1984). For historical reference, and because of their continuing relevance, excerpts from that opinion are set forth below. The Gramm-Leach-Bliley Financial Services Modernization Act of 1999 effectively repealed the Glass-Steagall Act, and permits the establishment of so-called "universal banks," financial institutions with affiliates engaging in banking, insurance, and securities businesses.

There were two principal reasons for the scuttling of Glass-Steagall: (1) Congress became convinced that the safeguards perceived to have been realized from the separation of commercial banking from investment banking activities were no longer required; (2) it was thought that U.S. banks should be permitted to compete with their European counterparts, which for years had been engaged in universal banking activities.

A significant aspect of that permitted "competition" was that the newly consolidated commercial and investment banks became able to obtain investment banking business by making loans to prospective clients in order to obtain their business provided they structured the client relationship to avoid a banking law prohibition against banks utilizing so-called "tying" arrangements. One result of that practice has been reported to be the following:

> Citigroup and J.P. Morgan Chase, two of Enron's biggest financial backers, each earned tens of millions of dollars in fees from the company for a variety of banking and investment-banking services in recent years.

> Now, each is likely to be writing off hundreds of millions of dollars in losses from loans to Enron and related entities that the company can't pay back in full.
>
> This sort of situation was why the Glass-Steagall Act was passed in 1933: to keep separate the business of lending from investment-banking services such as handling the issuance of securities. And in the wake of the Enron disaster, Congress, which repealed the law in 1999, could face new pressure to reestablish some restrictions or oversight on mixing commercial banking and investment banking.[5]

The Enron debacle brings to mind an earlier observation that Felix Rohatyn, then Senior Partner of Lazard Freres & Co., made to the financial community some years prior thereto: "If you need to commit capital to advisory business, maybe you ought to improve your advisory business."[6]

It is interesting that, in the view of one commentator, the success of U.S. investment banking firms in Europe prior to the repeal of Glass-Steagall was in fact attributable to the existence of that law, which had "prevented U.S. investment banks from subsidizing their activities with large retail banking bases as Europe's big banks do. It 'forced U.S. institutions to work harder than their counterparts in other countries to make money.' "[7]

The following excerpt is from one of many cases in which the Securities Industry Association, representing the investment banking community, locked horns with the commercial banks and their regulators over the permissible scope of commercial bank involvement in securities prior to the enactment of the 1999 Modernization Act. It is commonly known as "Bankers Trust I" to distinguish it from the numerous other cases of the period with the caption "Securities Industry Association v. Board of Governors." In "Bankers Trust I," the Supreme Court overturned a ruling by the Federal Reserve Board of Governors that short-term commercial paper was not a "security" for purposes of applying the Glass-Steagall underwriting prohibition. The Board had determined that since commercial paper was short-term in nature and was similar to Bank Commercial loans, in enacting Glass-Steagall Congress did not intend to prohibit banks from underwriting such commercial paper. However, the Court held that, given the broad proscripted purposes of Glass-Steagall and the similarity of commercial paper to other types of securities, the Board exceeded its discretion in finding that it was not a security. In so holding, the Court took the occasion to go into the background and history of Glass-Steagall as follows.

---

[5] *Enron Lessons*, WALL ST. J., Jan. 15, 2002, at A4.

[6] WALL ST. J., Mar. 27, 1986.

[7] Sesit, *U.S. Financial Firms Seize Dominant Role in the World Markets*, WALL ST. J., Jan. 5, 1996, at A1, col. 4.

SECURITIES INDUSTRY ASSOCIATION v. BOARD OF GOVERNORS

United States Supreme Court
468 U.S. 137 (1984)

JUSTICE BLACKMUN delivered the opinion of the Court.

. . .

In [*Investment Co. Institute v. Camp*, 401 U.S. 617 (1971),] this Court explored at some length the congressional concerns that produced the Glass-Steagall Act. Congress passed the Act in the aftermath of the banking collapse that produced the Great Depression of the 1930's. The Act responded to the opinion, widely expressed at the time, that much of the financial difficulty experienced by banks could be traced to their involvement in investment banking activities both directly and through security affiliates. At the very least, Congress held the view that the extensive involvement by commercial banks had been unwise; some in Congress concluded that it had been illegal. Senator Glass stated bluntly that commercial-bank involvement in securities had made "one of the greatest contributions to the unprecedented disaster which has caused this almost incurable depression." 75 Cong. Rec. 9887 (1932).

Congressional worries about commercial-bank involvement in investment-bank activities reflected two general concerns. The first was the inherent risks of the securities business. Speculation in securities by banks and their affiliates during the speculative fever of the 1920's produced tremendous bank losses when the securities markets went sour. In addition to the palpable effect that such losses had on the assets of affected banks, they also eroded the confidence of depositors in the safety of banks as depository institutions. This crisis of confidence contributed to the runs on the banks that proved so devastating to the solvency of many commercial banks.

But the dangers that Congress sought to eliminate through the Act were considerably more than the obvious risk that a bank could lose money by imprudent investment of its funds in speculative securities. The legislative history of the Act shows that Congress also focused on "the more subtle hazards that arise when a commercial bank goes beyond the business of acting as fiduciary or managing agent and enters the investment banking business." *Camp*, 401 U.S., at 630. The Glass-Steagall Act reflects the 1933 Congress' conclusion that certain investment banking activities conflicted in fundamental ways with the institutional role of commercial banks.

The Act's legislative history is replete with references to the various conflicts of interest that Congress feared to be present when a single institution is involved in both investment and commercial banking. Congress observed that commercial bankers serve as an important source of financial advice for their clients. They routinely advise clients on a variety of financial matters such as whether and how best to issue equity or debt securities. Congress concluded that it was unrealistic to expect a banker to give impartial advice about such matters if he stands to realize a profit from the underwriting or distribution of securities. *See, e.g.*, 75 Cong. Rec. 9912 (1932) (remarks of Sen. Bulkley). Some legislators noted that this conflict is exacerbated by the considerable fixed cost that a securities dealer must incur to build and maintain a securities-distribution system. Explaining this concern, Senator Bulkley, a major sponsor of the Act, described the pressures that commercial banks had experienced through their involvement in the distribution of securities:

> In order to be efficient a securities department had to be developed; it had to have salesmen; and it had to have correspondent connections with smaller banks throughout the territory tributary to the great bank. Organizations were developed with enthusiasm and with efficiency. . . . But sales departments were subject to fixed expenses which could not be reduced without the danger of so disrupting the organization as to put the institution at a disadvantage in competition with rival institutions. These expenses would turn the operation very quickly from a profit to a loss if there were not sufficient originations and underwritings to keep the sales departments busy.

Id., at 9911 (1932).

Congress also expressed concern that the involvement of a commercial bank in particular securities could compromise the objectivity of the bank's lending operations. Congress feared that the pressure to dispose of an issue of securities successfully might lead a bank to use its credit facilities to shore up a company whose securities the bank sought to distribute. See Operations of the National and Federal Reserve Banking Systems: Hearings Pursuant to S. Res. 71 before a Subcommittee of the Senate Committee on Banking and Currency, 71st Cong., 3d Sess., pt. 7, p. 1064 (1931) (1931 Hearings). Some in Congress feared that a bank might even make unsound loans to companies in whose securities the bank has a stake or to a purchaser of securities that the bank seeks to distribute. *Ibid.* Alternatively, a bank with loans outstanding to a company might encourage the company to issue securities through the bank's distribution system in order to obtain the funds needed to repay bank loans. 75 Cong. Rec. 9912 (1932) (remarks of Sen. Bulkley). Congress also faced some evidence that banks had misused their trust departments to unload excessive holdings of undesirable securities. *Camp*, 401 U.S., at 633; 1931 Hearings 237.

The Act's design reflects the congressional perception that certain investment-banking activities are fundamentally incompatible with commercial banking. After hearing much testimony concerning the appropriate form of a legislative response to the problems, Congress rejected the view of those who preferred legislation that simply would regulate the underwriting activities of commercial banks. Congress chose instead a broad structural approach that would "surround the banking business with sound rules which recognize the imperfection of human nature that our bankers may not be led into temptation, the evil effect of which is sometimes so subtle as not to be easily recognized by the most honorable man." 75 Cong. Rec. 9912 (remarks of Sen. Bulkley). Through flat prohibitions, the Act sought to "separat[e] as completely as possible commercial from investment banking." *Board of Governers v. Investment Company Institute*, 450 U.S. 46, 70 (1981) (ICI). Such an approach was not without costs in terms of efficiency and competition, but the Act reflects the view that the subtle risks created by mixing the two activities justified a strong prophylaxis. *Camp*, 401 U.S., at 630.

Sections 16 and 21 of the Act are the principal provisions that demarcate the line separating commercial and investment banking. Section 16 limits the involvement of a commercial bank in the "business of dealing in stock and securities" and prohibits a national bank from buying securities, other than "investment securities," for its own account. 12 U.S.C. § 24 Seventh. In addition, the section includes the general provision that a national bank "shall not underwrite any issue of Securities or stock." Section 5(c) of the Act, 12 U.S.C. § 335, makes § 16's limitations applicable to state banks that are members of the Federal Reserve System. It is therefore clear that Bankers Trust may not underwrite commercial paper if commercial paper is a "security" within the meaning of the Act.

Section 21 also separates investment and commercial banks, but does so from the perspective of investment banks. Congress designed § 21 to prevent persons engaged in specified investment banking activities from entering the commercial banking business. The section prohibits any person engaged in the business of issuing, underwriting, selling, or distributing stocks, bonds, debentures, notes, or other securities" from receiving deposits. . . .

. . .

The 1933 Congress also was concerned that banks might use their relationships with depositors to facilitate the distribution of securities in which the bank has an interest, and that the bank's depositors might lose confidence in the bank if the issuer should default on its obligations. See *id.*, at 631; 1931 Hearings, pt. 7, p. 1064. The concern would appear fully applicable to commercial-paper sales, because banks presumably will use their depositor lists as a prime source of customers for such sales. To the extent that a bank sells commercial paper to large bank depositors, the result of a loss of confidence in the bank would be especially severe.

By giving banks a pecuniary incentive in the marketing of a particular security, commercial-bank dealing in commercial paper also seems to produce precisely the conflict of interest that Congress feared would impair a commercial bank's ability to act as a source of disinterested financial advice. Senator Bulkley, during the debates on the Act, explained:

> Obviously, the banker who has nothing to sell to his depositors is much better qualified to advise disinterestedly and to regard diligently the safety of depositors than the banker who used the list of depositors in his savings department to distribute circulars concerning the advantages of this, that, or the other investment on which the bank is to receive an originating profit or an underwriting profit or a distribution profit or a trading profit or any combination of such profits. 75 Cong. Rec. 9912 (1932). This conflict of interest becomes especially acute if a bank decides to distribute commercial paper on behalf of an issuer who intends to use the proceeds of the offering to retire a debt that the issuer owes the bank.

A leading contemporary commentator on the subject has observed that:

> Ironically, just as [the questionable activities of the securities business affiliate of] City Bank had created the final impetus for Glass-Steagall, its successor created the final impetus for its repeal more than six decades later. Separation of commercial and investment banking officially remained in place until 1999, when President Clinton signed the law repealing those provisions of Glass-Steagall. Unofficially, strict separation had already slowly begun to erode in the 1980's and 1990s. The financial industry and a chorus of academic critics attacked it an ill-conceived, anachronistic, and unnecessary restriction standing in the way of financial institutions trying to diversify their businesses and compete on the global stage. In response, federal banking regulators and the courts slowly began to permit commercial banks to engage in securities-related activities and then allowed bank holding companies to acquire investment banking subsidiaries.
>
> Those trends culminated in the 1998 merger of Citibank, as it was then known, and the Travelers Group. Citigroup was immediately the world's largest financial services company, a full-service firm that combined consumer, commercial, and investment banking with insurance and investment management.

Michael Perino, The Hellhound of Wall Street 290 (2010).

§ 1.07 THE CREDIT CRISIS OF 2008

Capital formation in the United States came to an abrupt halt as a result of the Credit Crisis of 2008. Banks stopped lending (particularly to other financial institutions) because many such borrowers lacked the apparent ability to repay. By this time, their "assets" consisted in large part of mortgage backed securities and their even more complex cousin, collateralized debt obligations, both of which suddenly had an actual value substantially less than that reflected on their financial statements; many of the underlying mortgages had been granted to home owners who were unable to repay the mortgage loan. It soon became apparent that the true value of the assets of a number of financial institutions was less than their liabilities. Such entities were thus insolvent, or at least required additional capital. As Felix Rohatyn, of Lazard Freres & Co. prophetically stated more than 20 years before, "[t]he word 'credit' derives from the Latin *credere* to believe. The belief in the integrity of our securities market is a national asset that we should not dissipate carelessly." *Junk Bonds and Other Securities Swill*, Wall St. J., Apr. 18, 1985.

Two other principal culprits of the credit fiasco were (i) a peculiar sounding financial instrument called a credit default swap (an IOU type contractual obligation to make a payment to the holder of the "swap" in case a particular debtor fails to perform its own financial obligation)[8] and (ii) credit ratings (a prediction by a purported expert of the likelihood of a party being able to perform a specified financial obligation). Such ratings play an important role in the determination of the market value of debt securities. The Crisis could not have occurred to the extent it did without both of these devices being essentially free of legal oversight. Federal

---

[8] Many non-securities based swap transactions serve a valid business purpose by providing protection against fluctuations in the value of certain assets, commodities, currencies, and interest rates.

legislation had been enacted which made the use (and abuse) of swaps and the dissemination of credit ratings generally free of regulatory constraints. In the case of credit default swaps, the U.S. Congress enacted and President Clinton signed an innocent sounding law called the Commodity Futures Modernization Act of 2000. That law added amendments to the Securities Act of 1933 and the Securities Exchange Act of 1934 which exempted swaps from their regulatory coverage and literally *prohibited* the SEC from regulating swaps, including credit default swaps, thus paving the way for their unbridled, irresponsible use in the absence of transparency and margin/capital requirements. In describing the enactment of this so-called "Modernization" law, Professor Frank Partnoy of the University of San Diego School of Law observed:

> Anyone who imagined that members of Congress, or their staffs, drafted laws regarding derivatives would have been surprised to peek inside the offices of the House Agriculture Committee during the time Congress was considering the [law]. Instead of seeing members of Congress at work, you would have seen [a] lobbyist . . . writing important pieces of the legislation . . . the role of Congress was simply to look over the shoulders of the finance lobby and nod.

FRANK PARTNOY, INFECTIOUS GREED 295 (2003).

In addition to being debt securities under any common sense definition of the term, swaps can be viewed either as (i) an insurance policy against the possibility of a payment default or (ii) enabling a wager on the likelihood of such a default. To avoid state insurance regulation, in 2000, the financial industry obtained a ruling by the New York Insurance Department that was understood to exempt all swaps from such regulation. (Testimony of Eric Dinallo, Superintendent, New York Insurance Department to the United States House of Representatives on November 20, 2008 [testifying as to the action of a prior Insurance Department administration]). State gaming regulation of credit default swaps was precluded by the Modernization Act itself.

By 2006 it was becoming apparent that in many cases the work product of the credit rating agencies was often unreliable, if not worthless. In a purported response to calls for regulation, the euphemistically named Credit Agency Reform Act of 2006, which became Section 15E of the Securities Exchange Act, was enacted. Although the law requires the major credit rating agencies to *register* with the SEC, it *prohibits* the SEC (and any state) from regulating "the substance of credit ratings or the procedures and methodologies" used by them. Yet the preamble of the law recites that "credit rating agencies are of national importance" and that the SEC "needs statutory authority to oversee the credit rating industry."

The Credit Crisis was thus preceded by the: (i) conversion of investment banks from conservatively managed private partnerships to well capitalized publicly held corporations and (ii) emergence of "invest to play" competition from the large, publicly traded commercial banks recently freed from the restraints of Glass-Steagall. This, in turn, led the publicly held investment banks, which historically were allowed to do business with less oversight than the commercial banks, to engage in (i) proprietary trading as well as (temporarily) highly profitable, risk intensive, real estate securitizations (not only allegedly "risk free" owing to their credit ratings, but also purportedly "insured" by credit default swaps) as well as (ii) traditional investment banking activities. Because this strategy seemed to work so well, the newly minted "universal" commercial banks quickly followed suit. Disaster was not far behind. *See* GRETCHEN MORGENSON & JOSHUA ROSNER, RECKLESS ENDANGERMENT 109 (2011).

The legislative response to the Credit Crisis, which can be viewed as closing the barn door after the horses have run out, was the Dodd-Frank Wall Street Reform and Consumer Protection Act ("Dodd-Frank") which became law on July 21, 2010. The law was touted as the most comprehensive set of securities market reforms since those enacted in the 1930s. Dodd-Frank, however, is, to put it generously, not self executing. Instead, it requires the SEC to issue hundreds of regulations and conduct a number of studies. Similar obligations are imposed by Dodd-Frank on other federal agencies. (One can easily imagine the type of lobbyists referred to above by Professor Partnoy working overtime.) Fourteen months after the passage of Dodd-Frank less than 10 percent of the approximately four hundred required administrative regulations had been adopted. Moreover, political objections to many Dodd-Frank provisions prompted legislators to propose rolling back portions of the law.

The law consists of 16 Titles, three of which are particularly relevant to the matters discussed herein.

Title VI, Improvements to Regulation of Bank and Saving Association Holding Companies and Depositary Institutions, contains, in Section 619 of Dodd-Frank (which is Section 13 of the Bank Holding Company Act of 1956), the Volcker Rule (named after former Federal Reserve Chairman Paul Volcker) which prohibits proprietary trading by commercial[9] banks. Section 619, which became effective on July 21, 2012, but provides for a subsequent "conformance period." It does not, however, prohibit market making and risk management hedging. Those two last-mentioned activities, which resemble proprietary trading, are not defined in the statute; instead, the law requires the SEC and other federal regulatory agencies to issue regulations defining those terms. As would be expected, the commercial banking interests urged the adoption of definitions of market making and risk management hedging so broad that they would nearly emasculate the statutory proprietary trading prohibition.

To supplement the Volcker Rule and further "mitigate the risks derivatives pose to the [commercial] banking industry," the Swaps Push-Out Rule was a last minute addition to Section 619. That Rule in effect "forces [commercial] banks to spin off their derivative trading desks into separately capitalized affiliates." Kristine Antoja, *The Dodd-Frank Act's One-Year Anniversary: Evaluating the Volcker Rule and the Swaps Push-Out Rule*, 15 N.Y. BUS. L.J. 7, 8 (2011).

Title VII, Wall Street Transparency and Accountability, provides, *inter alia*, for the regulation of the credit default swaps market. Like the rest of Dodd-Frank, Title VII is conceptual in nature; it is dependent upon SEC regulations to provide substance for its legislative gloss. Dodd-Frank grants to the SEC sole authority over securities based credit default swaps. Title VII amends Sections 2A and 3A of

---

[9] Section 619 does not apply to investment banks that are not also commercial banks.

the 1933 and 1934 Acts discussed above which since 2000 had excluded credit default swaps from the definition of a "security" and also had prohibited the SEC from regulating them. Dodd-Frank repealed those excluding provisions of the Commodity Futures Modernization Act of 2000 by (i) amending Sections 2(a) and 3(a) of the Securities Act and the Exchange Act, respectively, to include "security-based swaps" within the definition of a "security" and (ii) by adding Section 3(a)(78) to the Exchange Act which changed the definition of the 1933 and 1934 Acts *exempt* "security based swap agreement" by *excluding* "any security based swap."[10]

> The legislative intention was to provide the security-based swaps market with greater transparency, as well as to install margin, capital and reporting requirements, which would be achieved through the use of clearing agencies. On March 30, 2012, the SEC issued Releases which exempted transactions in such swaps by clearing agencies meeting certain conditions "from all provisions of the Securities Act, other than the Section 17(a) anti-fraud provisions, . . . [the] Exchange Act registration requirements and . . . the Trust Indenture Act. . . ." Exemptions For Security-Based Swaps Issued By Certain Clearing Agencies, Securities Act Release No. 33-9308, Exchange Act Release No. 34-66703, Trust Indenture Act Release No. 2484 (March 30, 2012).

Sub Title C of Title IX of Dodd-Frank, Improvements to the Regulation of Credit Rating Agencies, amends Section 15E of the Exchange Act by adding subsection (r) thereto; it directs the SEC to prescribe rules to ensure that credit ratings are determined using procedures adopted by the board of the organization issuing the rating and that they comply with the issuing organization's policies and procedures. Untouched by Dodd-Frank, however, is the prohibition in Exchange Act Section 15E(c)(2) against SEC regulation of "the substance of credit ratings or the procedures and methodologies" used in determining them.

Among the casualties of the Credit Crisis was the U.S. commercial paper market. During the nadir of the Crisis in the autumn of 2008, the per share net asset value of the Reserve Primary Fund, a money market mutual fund, fell below $1.00 and became only the second such fund to thus "break the buck." The reason for that diminution in value was that the Reserve Fund's holdings of $64 billion in commercial paper included $785 million issued by Lehman Brothers Holdings Inc. which filed for bankruptcy in September 2008. This caused the Fund's investors to seek to recover their investment by exercising their right to redeem their shares, thus prompting "a run in the bank." Because the amount of redemptions exceeded the Fund's ability to make the required cash payments, only 80 percent of the Fund's shares had been redeemed as late as a year after the Lehman bankruptcy. It is expected that the shareholders will eventually receive approximately 99 percent of the value of their investment.

Money market funds, such as the Reserve Fund, are significant purchasers of commercial paper and, as those funds and other investors stopped purchasing

[10] Section 17 of the 1933 Act, however, prohibits fraudulent trading of "any securities (including security based swaps) or any security based swap agreement as defined in section 3(a)(78) of the [Exchange Act]."

commercial paper as a result of the Reserve Fund experience, the short term credit needs of U.S. businesses could not be met. It was for this reason that in October 2008 the Federal Reserve Bank of New York, acting pursuant to its emergency powers under Section 13 of the Federal Reserve Act, established a Commercial Funding Facility which created a purchaser of last resort for commercial paper issuers. The purchases were made through a special purpose vehicle funded by a loan from the New York Fed, thus providing a market for commercial paper and enabling U.S. businesses to satisfy their short term credit needs. In addition, in September 2008, the U.S. Treasury guaranteed for one year the shareholder balances of money market funds.

§ 1.08 PERTINENT STATUTORY MATERIAL

Set forth below are certain provisions of the Business Corporation Law of the State of New York, including definitional terms, all of Article 5 thereof (entitled Corporate Finance), all of Article 8 thereof dealing with amendments to a corporation's certificate of incorporation, and all of Article 9 thereof dealing primarily with mergers and consolidations. The following statutes are presented for purposes of illustration and not for the purpose of emphasizing New York law in any particular respect. The Business Corporation Law of New York has been chosen for this purpose, because it has been structured in such a fashion so as to lend itself to analysis of the type to be undertaken in connection with the study of the matters covered in this book.

Effective February 22, 1998, a number of provisions of Articles 1, 5, 8, and 9 were amended to liberalize the corporate finance and related sections of the New York Business Corporation Law. The New York State Senate Memorandum in Support of the Amendments stated that they are intended to "provide substantial additional flexibility in equity financing" and to "provide a New York corporation with greater latitude in determining its appropriate capital structure in connection with future financings."

Also set forth are certain corresponding provisions of the Delaware General Corporation Law and the Pennsylvania Business Corporation Law.

Certain of the sub-sections, or portions thereof, of the statutes set forth below, as well as other statutes and corporate finance documentation reproduced in this book, have been italicized to facilitate class discussion and review and consideration of certain documents.

NEW YORK BUSINESS CORPORATION LAW

ARTICLE 1. SHORT TITLE; DEFINITIONS; APPLICATION; CERTIFICATES; MISCELLANEOUS

§ 101 Short title

This chapter shall be known as the "Business Corporation Law".

§ 102 Definitions

(a) As used in this chapter, unless the context otherwise requires, the term:

(1) "Authorized person" means a person, whether or not a shareholder, officer or director, who is authorized to act on behalf of a corporation or foreign corporation.

(2) *"Bonds" includes secured and unsecured bonds, debentures, and notes.*

(3) "Certificate of incorporation" includes (A) the original certificate of incorporation or any other instrument filed or issued under any statute to form a domestic or foreign corporation, as amended, supplemented or restated by certificates of amendment, merger or consolidation or other certificates or instruments filed or issued under any statute; or (B) a special act or charter creating a domestic or foreign corporation, as amended, supplemented or restated.

(4) "Corporation" or "domestic corporation" means a corporation for profit formed under this chapter, or existing on its effective date and theretofore formed under any other general statute or by any special act of this state for a purpose or purposes for which a corporation may be formed under this chapter, other than a corporation which may be formed under the cooperative corporations law.

(5) "Director" means any member of the governing board of a corporation, whether designated as director, trustee, manager, governor, or by any other title. The term "board" means "board of directors".

(6) [Repealed]

(7) "Foreign corporation" means a corporation for profit formed under laws other than the statutes of this state, which has as its purpose or among its purposes a purpose for which a corporation may be formed under this chapter, other than a corporation which, if it were to be formed currently under the laws of this state, could not be formed under this chapter. "Authorized", when used with respect to a foreign corporation, means having authority under article 13 (Foreign corporations) to do business in this state.

(7a) "Infant" means a person who has not attained the age of eighteen years.

(8) "Insolvent" means being unable to pay debts as they become due in the usual course of the debtor's business.

(9) "*Net assets*" means the amount by which the total assets exceed the total liabilities. Stated capital and surplus are not liabilities.

(10) "Office of a corporation" means the office the location of which is stated in the certificate of incorporation of a domestic corporation, or in the application for authority of a foreign corporation or an amendment thereof. Such office need not be a place where business activities are conducted by such corporation.

(11) "Process" means judicial process and all orders, demands, notices or other papers required or permitted by law to be personally served on a domestic or foreign corporation, for the purpose of acquiring jurisdiction of such corporation

in any action or proceeding, civil or criminal, whether judicial, administrative, arbitrative or otherwise, in this state or in the federal courts sitting in or for this state.

(12) "*Stated capital*" means the sum of (A) the par value of all shares with par value that have been issued, (B) the amount of the consideration received for all shares without par value that have been issued, except such part of the consideration therefor as may have been allocated to surplus in a manner permitted by law, and (C) such amounts not included in clauses (A) and (B) as have been transferred to stated capital, whether upon the distribution of shares or otherwise, minus all reductions from such sums as have been effected in a manner permitted by law.

(13) "*Surplus*" means the excess of net assets over stated capital.

(14) "Treasury shares" means shares which have been issued, have been subsequently acquired, and are retained uncancelled by the corporation. Treasury shares *are issued shares, but not outstanding shares*, and are not assets.

ARTICLE 5. CORPORATE FINANCE

§ 501 Authorized shares

(a) Every corporation shall have power to create and issue the number of shares stated in its certificate of incorporation. Such shares may be all of one class or may be divided into two or more *classes*. Each class shall consist of either shares with par value or shares without par value, having such designation and such relative voting, dividend, liquidation and other rights, preferences and limitations, consistent with this chapter, as shall be stated in the certificate of incorporation. The certificate of incorporation may deny, *limit or otherwise define* the voting rights and may limit or otherwise define the dividend or liquidation rights of shares of any class, but no such denial, limitation or definition of voting rights shall be effective unless at the time one or more classes of outstanding shares or bonds, singly or in the aggregate, are entitled to *full voting rights*, and no such limitation or definition of dividend or liquidation rights shall be effective unless at the time one or more classes of outstanding shares, singly or in the aggregate, are entitled to *unlimited dividend and liquidation rights*.

(b) If the shares are divided into two or more classes, the shares of each class shall be designated to distinguish them from the shares of all other classes. Shares which are entitled to preference in the distribution of dividends or assets shall not be designated as common shares. Shares which are not entitled to preference in the distribution of dividends or assets shall be common shares, even if identified by a class or other designation, and shall not be designated as preferred shares.

(c) Subject to the designations, relative rights, preferences and limitations applicable to separate series and *except as otherwise permitted by subparagraph two of paragraph (a) of section five hundred five of this article*, each share shall be equal to every other share of the same class. With respect to corporations owning or leasing residential premises and operating the same on a cooperative basis, however, provided that (1) liquidation or other distribution rights are substantially equal per share, (2) changes in maintenance charges and general assessments pursuant to a proprietary lease have been and are hereafter fixed and determined on an equal per-share basis or on an equal per-room basis or as an equal percentage of the maintenance charges, and (3) voting rights are substantially equal per share or the certificate of incorporation provides that the shareholders holding the shares allocated to each apartment or dwelling unit owned by the corporation shall be entitled to one vote in the aggregate regardless of the number of shares allocated to the apartment or dwelling unit or the number of shareholders holding such shares, shares of the same class shall not be considered unequal because of variations in fees or charges payable to the corporation upon sale or transfer of shares and appurtenant proprietary leases that are provided for in proprietary leases, occupancy agreements or offering plans or properly approved amendments to the foregoing instruments.

§ 502 Issue of any Class of Preferred Shares in Series

(a) *If the certificate of incorporation so provides,* a corporation may issue any class of preferred shares in *series.* Shares of each such series when issued, shall be designated to distinguish them from shares of all other series.

(b) The number of shares included in any or all series of any classes of preferred shares and any or all of the designations, relative rights, preferences and limitations of any or all such series *may be fixed in the certificate of incorporation,* subject to the limitation that, unless the certificate of incorporation provides otherwise, if the stated dividends and amounts payable on liquidation are not paid in full, the shares of all series of the same class shall share ratably in the payment of dividends including accumulations, if any, in accordance with the sums which would be payable on such shares if all dividends were declared and paid in full, and in any distribution of assets other than by way of dividends in accordance with the sums which would be payable on such distribution if all sums payable were discharged in full.

(c) *If any such number of shares or any such designation, relative right, preference or limitation of the shares of any series is not fixed in the certificate of incorporation, it may be fixed by the board, to the extent authorized by the certificate of incorporation.* Unless otherwise provided in the certificate of incorporation, the number of preferred shares of any series so fixed by the board may be increased (but not above the total number of authorized shares of the class) or decreased (but not below the number of shares thereof then outstanding) by the board. In case the number of such shares shall be decreased, the number of shares by which the series is decreased shall, unless eliminated pursuant to paragraph (e) of this section, resume the status which they had prior to being designated as part of a series of preferred shares.

(d) Before the issue of any shares of a series established by the board, a certificate of amendment under section 805 (Certificate of amendment; contents) shall be delivered to the department of state. Such certificate shall set forth:

(1) The name of the corporation, and, if it has been changed, the name under which it was formed.

(2) The date the certificate of incorporation was filed by the department of state.

(3) *That the certificate of incorporation is thereby amended* by the addition of a provision stating the number, designation, relative rights, preferences, and limitations of the shares of the series as fixed by the board, setting forth in full the text of such provision.

(e) Action by the board to increase or decrease the number of preferred shares of any series pursuant to paragraph (c) of this section shall become effective by delivering to the department of state a certificate of amendment under section 805 (Certificate of amendment; contents) which shall set forth:

(1) The name of the corporation, and, if it has been changed, the name under which it was formed.

(2) The date its certificate of incorporation was filed with the department of state.

(3) That the certificate of incorporation is thereby amended to increase or decrease, as the case may be, the number of preferred shares of any series so fixed by the board, setting forth the specific terms of the amendment and the number of shares so authorized following the effectiveness of the amendment.

When no shares of any such series are outstanding, either because none were issued or because no issued shares of any such series remain outstanding, the certificate of amendment under section 805 may also set forth a statement that none of the authorized shares of such series are outstanding and that none will be issued subject to the certificate of incorporation, and, when such certificate becomes accepted for filing, it shall have the effect of eliminating from the certificate of incorporation all matters set forth therein with respect to such series of preferred shares.

§ 503 Subscription for shares; time of payment, forfeiture for default

(a) Unless otherwise provided by the terms of the subscription, a subscription for shares of a corporation to be formed shall be irrevocable, except with the consent of all other subscribers or the corporation, for a period of three months from its date.

(b) A subscription, whether made before or after the formation of a corporation, shall not be enforceable unless in writing and signed by the subscriber.

(c) Unless otherwise provided by the terms of the subscription, subscriptions for shares, whether made before or after the formation of a corporation, shall be paid in full at such time, or in such installments and at such times, as shall be determined by the board. Any call made by the board for payment on subscriptions shall be uniform as to all shares of the same class or of the same series. If a receiver of the corporation has been appointed, all unpaid subscriptions shall be paid at such times and in such installments as such receiver or the court may direct.

(d) In the event of default in the payment of any installment or call when due, the corporation may proceed to collect the amount due in the same manner as any debt due the corporation or the board may declare a forfeiture of the subscriptions. The subscription agreement may prescribe other penalties, not amounting to forfeiture, for failure to pay installments or calls that may become due. No forfeiture of the subscription shall be declared as against any subscriber unless the amount due thereon shall remain unpaid for a period of thirty days after written demand has been made therefor. If mailed, such written demand shall be deemed to be made when deposited in the United States mail in a sealed envelope addressed to the subscriber at his last post office address known to the corporation, with postage thereon prepaid. Upon forfeiture of the subscription, if at least fifty percent of the subscription price has been paid, the shares subscribed for shall be offered for sale for cash or a binding obligation to pay cash at a price at least sufficient to pay the full balance owed by the delinquent subscriber plus the expenses incidental to such sale, and any excess of net proceeds realized over the amount owed on such shares shall be paid to the delinquent subscriber or to his legal representative. If no prospective purchaser offers a cash price or a binding obligation to pay cash sufficient to pay the full balance owed by the delinquent subscriber plus the expenses incidental to such sale, or if less than fifty percent of the subscription price has been paid, the shares subscribed for shall be cancelled and restored to the status of authorized but unissued shares and all previous payments thereon shall be forfeited to the corporation and transferred to surplus.

(e) Notwithstanding the provisions of paragraph (d) of this section, in the event of default in payment or other performance under the instrument evidencing a subscriber's binding obligation to pay a portion of the subscription price or perform services, the corporation may pursue such remedies as are provided in such instrument or a related agreement or under law.

§ 504 Consideration and payment for shares

(a) Consideration for the issue of shares shall consist of money or other property, tangible or intangible; labor or services actually received by or performed for the corporation or for its benefit or in its formation or reorganization; a binding obligation to pay the purchase price or the subscription price in cash or other property; a binding obligation to perform services having an agreed value; or a combination thereof. In the absence of fraud in the transaction, the judgment of the board or shareholders, as the case may be, as to the value of the consideration received for shares shall be conclusive.

(b) [Repealed]

(c) Shares *with* par value may be issued for such consideration, *not less than the par value thereof*, as is fixed from time to time by the board.

(d) Shares *without* par value may be issued for such *consideration as is fixed from time to time by the board* unless the certificate of incorporation reserves to the shareholders the right to fix the consideration. If such right is reserved as to any shares, a vote of the shareholders shall either fix the consideration to be received for the shares or authorize the board to fix such consideration.

(e) *Treasury shares* may be disposed of by a corporation on such terms and conditions *as are fixed from time to time by the board.*

(f) Upon distribution of authorized but unissued shares to shareholders, that part of the surplus of a corporation which is concurrently transferred to stated capital shall be the consideration for the issue of such shares.

(g) In the event of *a conversion* of bonds or shares into shares, or in the event of *an exchange* of bonds or shares for shares, with or without par value, *the consideration* for the shares so issued in exchange or conversion shall be the sum of (1) either the principal sum of, and accrued interest on, the bonds so exchanged or converted, or the stated capital then represented by the shares so exchanged or converted, plus (2) any additional consideration paid to the corporation for the new shares, plus (3) any stated capital not theretofore allocated to any designated class or series which is thereupon allocated to the new shares, plus (4) any surplus thereupon transferred to stated capital and allocated to the new shares.

(h) Certificates for shares may not be issued until the amount of the consideration therefor determined to be stated capital pursuant to section 506 (Determination of stated capital) has been paid in the form of cash, services rendered, personal or real property or a combination thereof and consideration for the balance (if any) complying with paragraph (a) of this section has been provided, except as provided in paragraphs (e) and (f) of section 505 (Rights and options to purchase shares; issue of rights and options to directors, officers and employees).

(i) When the consideration for shares has been provided in compliance with paragraph (h) of this section, the subscriber shall be entitled to all the rights and privileges of a holder of such shares and to a certificate representing his shares, and such shares shall be fully paid and nonassessable.

(j) Notwithstanding that such shares may be fully paid and nonassessable, the corporation may place in escrow shares issued for a binding obligation to pay cash or other property or to perform future services, or make other arrangements to restrict the transfer of the shares, and may credit distributions in respect of the shares against the obligation, until the obligation is performed. If the obligation is not performed in whole or in part, the corporation may pursue such remedies as are provided in the instrument evidencing the obligation or a related agreement or under law.

§ 505 Rights and options to purchase shares; issue of rights and options to directors, officers and employees

(a) (1) Except as otherwise provided in this section or in the certificate of incorporation, a corporation may create and issue, whether or not in connection with the issue and sale of any of its shares or bonds, rights or options entitling the holders thereof to purchase from the corporation, upon such consideration, terms and conditions as may be fixed by the board, shares of any class or series, whether authorized but unissued shares, treasury shares or shares to be purchased or acquired or assets of the corporation.

(2) (i) In the case of a domestic corporation that has a class of voting stock registered with the Securities and Exchange Commission pursuant to section twelve of the Exchange Act, *the terms and conditions of such rights or options may include, without limitation, restrictions or conditions that preclude or limit the exercise, transfer or receipt of such rights or options by an interested shareholder or any transferee of any such interested shareholder or that invalidate or void such rights or options held by any such interested shareholder or any such transferee.* For the purpose of this subparagraph, the

terms “voting stock”, “Exchange Act” and “interested shareholder” shall have the same meanings as set forth in section nine hundred twelve of this chapter;

(ii) Determinations of the board of directors whether to impose, enforce or waive or otherwise render ineffective such limitations or conditions as are permitted by clause (i) of this subparagraph shall be subject to judicial review in an appropriate proceeding in which the courts formulate or apply appropriate standards in order to insure that such limitations or conditions are imposed, enforced or waived in the best long-term interests and short-term interests of the corporation and its shareholders considering, without limitation, the prospects for potential growth, development, productivity and profitability of the corporation.

(b) The consideration for shares to be purchased under any such right or option shall comply with the requirements of section 504 (Consideration and payment for shares).

(c) The terms and conditions of such rights or options, including the time or times at or within which and the price or prices at which they may be exercised and any limitations upon transferability, shall be set forth or incorporated by reference in the instrument or instruments evidencing such rights or options.

(d) The issue of such rights or options to one or more directors, officers or employees of the corporation or a subsidiary or affiliate thereof, as an incentive to service or continued service with the corporation, a subsidiary or affiliate thereof, or to a trustee on behalf of such directors, officers or employees, shall be authorized by a majority of the votes cast at a meeting of shareholders by the holders of shares entitled to vote thereon, or authorized by and consistent with a plan adopted by such vote of shareholders. If, under the certificate of incorporation, there are preemptive rights to any of the shares to be thus subject to rights or options to purchase, either such issue or such plan, if any shall also be approved by the vote or written consent of the holders of a majority of the shares entitled to exercise preemptive rights with respect to such shares and such vote or written consent shall operate to release the preemptive rights with respect thereto of the holders of all the shares that were entitled to exercise such preemptive rights.

In the absence of preemptive rights, nothing in this paragraph shall require shareholder approval for the issuance of rights or options to purchase shares of the corporation in substitution for, or upon the assumption of, rights or options issued by another corporation, if such substitution or assumption is in connection with such other corporation's merger or consolidation with, or the acquisition of its shares or all or part of its assets by, the corporation or its subsidiary.

(e) A plan adopted by the shareholders for the issue of rights or options to directors, officers or employees shall include the material terms and conditions upon which such rights or options are to be issued, such as, but without limitation thereof, any restrictions on the number of shares that eligible individuals may have the right or option to purchase, the method of administering the plan, the terms and conditions of payment for shares in full or in installments, the issue of certificates for shares to be paid for in installments, any limitations upon the transferability of such shares and the voting and dividend rights to which the holders of such shares may be entitled, though the full amount of the consideration therefor has not been paid; provided that under this section no certificate for shares shall be delivered to a shareholder, prior to full payment therefor, unless the fact that the shares are partly paid is noted conspicuously on the face or back of such certificate.

(f) If there is shareholder approval for the issue of rights or options to individual directors, officers or employees, but not under an approved plan under paragraph (e), the terms and conditions of issue set forth in paragraph (e) shall be permissible except that the grantees of such rights or options shall not be granted voting or dividend rights until the consideration for the shares to which they are entitled under such rights or options has been fully paid.

(g) If there is shareholder approval for the issue of rights and options, such approval may provide that the board is authorized by certificate of amendment under section 805 (Certificate of amendment; contents) to increase the authorized shares of any class or series to such number as will be sufficient, when added to the previously authorized but unissued shares of such class or series, to satisfy any such rights or options entitling the holders thereof to purchase from the corporation authorized but unissued shares of such class or series.

(h) In the absence of fraud in the transaction, the judgment of the board shall be conclusive as to the adequacy of the consideration, tangible or intangible, received or to be received by the corporation for the issue of rights or options for the purchase from the corporation of its shares.

(i) The provisions of this section are inapplicable to the rights of the holders of convertible shares or bonds to acquire shares upon the exercise of conversion privileges under section 519 (Convertible shares and bonds).

§ 506 Determination of stated capital

(a) Upon issue by a corporation of shares with a par value, the consideration received therefor shall constitute stated capital to the extent of the par value of such shares.

(b) Upon issue by a corporation of shares without par value, the entire consideration received therefor shall constitute stated capital unless the board within a period of sixty days after issue allocates to surplus a portion, but not all, of the consideration received for such shares. No such allocation shall be made of any portion of the consideration received for shares without par value having a preference in the assets of the corporation upon involuntary liquidation except all or part of the amount, if any, of such consideration in excess of such preference, nor shall such allocation be made of any portion of the consideration for the issue of shares without par value which is fixed by the shareholders pursuant to a right reserved in the certificate of incorporation, unless such allocation is authorized by vote of the shareholders.

(c) The stated capital of a corporation may be increased from time to time by resolution of the board transferring all or part of the surplus of the corporation to stated capital. The board may direct that the amount so transferred shall be stated capital in respect of any designated class or series of shares.

§ 507 Compensation for formation, reorganization and financing

The reasonable charges and expenses of formation or reorganization of a corporation, and the reasonable expenses of and compensation for the sale or underwriting of its shares may be paid or allowed by the corporation out of the consideration received by it in payment for its shares without thereby impairing the fully paid and nonassessable status of such shares.

§ 508 Certificates representing shares

(a) The shares of a corporation shall be represented by certificates or shall be uncertificated shares. Certificates shall be signed by the chairman or a vice-chairman of the board or the president or a vice-president and the secretary or an assistant secretary or the treasurer or an assistant treasurer of the corporation, and may be sealed with the seal of the corporation or a facsimile thereof. The signatures of the officers upon a certificate may be facsimiles if: (1) the certificate is countersigned by a transfer agent or registered by a registrar other than the corporation itself or its employee, or (2) the shares are listed on a registered national security exchange. In case any officer who has signed or whose facsimile signature has been placed upon a certificate shall have ceased to be such officer before such certificate is issued, it may be issued by the corporation with the same effect as if he were such officer at the date of issue.

(b) Each certificate representing shares issued by a corporation which is authorized to issue shares of more than one class shall set forth upon the face or back of the certificate, or shall state that the corporation will furnish to any shareholder upon request and without charge, a full statement of the designation, relative rights, preferences and limitations of the shares of each class authorized to be issued and, if the corporation is authorized to issue any class of preferred shares in series, the designation, relative rights, preferences and limitations of each such series so far as the same have been fixed and the authority of the board to designate and fix the relative rights, preferences and limitations of other series.

(c) Each certificate representing shares shall state upon the face thereof:

(1) That the corporation is formed under the laws of this state.

(2) The name of the person or persons to whom issued.

(3) The number and class of shares, and the designation of the series, if any, which such certificate represents.

(d) Shares shall be transferable in the manner provided by law and in the by-laws.

(e) The corporation may issue a new certificate for shares in place of any certificate theretofore issued by it, alleged to have been lost or destroyed, and the board may require the owner of the lost or destroyed certificate, or his legal representative, to give the corporation a bond sufficient to indemnify the corporation against any claim that may be made against it on account of the alleged loss or destruction of any such certificate or the issuance of any such new certificate.

(f) Unless otherwise provided by the articles of incorporation or bylaws, the board of directors of a corporation may provide by resolution that some or all of any or all classes and series of its shares shall be uncertificated shares, provided that such resolution shall not apply to shares represented by a certificate until such certificate is surrendered to the corporation. Within a reasonable time after the issuance or transfer of uncertificated shares, the corporation shall send to the registered owner thereof a written notice containing the information required to be set forth or stated on certificates pursuant to paragraphs (b) and (c) of this section. Except as otherwise expressly provided by law, the rights and obligations of the holders of uncertificated shares and the rights and obligations of the holders of certificates representing shares of the same class and series shall be identical.

§ 509 Fractions of a share or scrip authorized

(a) A corporation may, but shall not be obliged to, issue fractions of a share either represented by a certificate or uncertificated, which shall entitle the holder, in proportion to his fractional holdings, to exercise voting rights, receive dividends and participate in liquidating distributions.

(b) As an alternative, a corporation may pay in cash the fair value of fractions of a share as of the time when those entitled to receive such fractions are determined.

(c) As an alternative, a corporation may issue scrip in registered or bearer form over the manual or facsimile signature of an officer of the corporation or of its agent, exchangeable as therein provided for full shares, but such scrip shall not entitle the holder to any rights of a shareholder except as therein provided. Such scrip may be issued subject to the condition that it shall become void if not exchanged for certificates representing full shares or uncertificated full shares before a specified date, or subject to the condition that the shares for which such scrip is exchangeable may be sold by the corporation and the proceeds thereof distributed to the holders of such scrip, or subject to any other conditions which the board may determine.

(d) A corporation may provide reasonable opportunity for persons entitled to fractions of a share or scrip to sell such fractions of a share or scrip or to purchase such additional fractions of a share or scrip as may be needed to acquire a full share.

§ 510 Dividends or other distributions in cash or property

(a) A corporation may declare and pay dividends or make other distributions in cash or its bonds or its property, including the shares or bonds of other corporations, on its outstanding shares, except when currently the corporation is insolvent or would thereby be made insolvent, or when the declaration, payment or distribution would be contrary to any restrictions contained in the certificate of incorporation.

(b) Dividends may be declared or paid and other distributions may be made either (1) out of *surplus*, so that the net assets of the corporation remaining after such declaration, payment or distribution shall at least equal the amount of its stated capital, *or (2) in case there shall be no such surplus, out of its net profits for the fiscal year in which the dividend is declared and/or the preceding fiscal year*. If the capital of the corporation shall have been diminished by depreciation in the value of its property or by losses or otherwise to an amount less than the aggregate amount of the stated capital represented by the issued and outstanding shares of all classes having a preference upon the distribution of assets, the directors of such corporation shall not declare and pay out of such net profits any dividends upon any shares until the deficiency in the amount of *stated capital* represented by the issued and outstanding shares of all classes having a preference upon the distribution of assets shall have been repaired. A corporation engaged in the exploitation of natural resources or other wasting assets, including patents, or formed primarily for the liquidation of specific assets, may declare and pay dividends or make other distributions in excess of its surplus, computed after taking due account of depletion and amortization, to the extent that the cost of the wasting or specific assets has been recovered by depletion reserves, amortization or sale, if the net assets remaining after such dividends or distributions are sufficient to cover the *liquidation preferences* of shares having such preferences in involuntary liquidation.

§ 511 Share distributions and changes

(a) A corporation may make pro rata distributions of its authorized but unissued shares to holders of any class or series of its outstanding shares, subject to the following conditions:

(1) If a distribution of shares having a par value is made, such shares shall be issued at not less than the par value thereof and *there shall be transferred to stated capital at the time of such distribution an amount of surplus equal to the aggregate par value* of such shares.

(2) If a distribution of shares without par value is made, the amount of stated capital to be represented by each such share shall be fixed by the board, unless the certificate of incorporation reserves to the shareholders the right to fix the consideration for the issue of such shares, and there shall be transferred to stated capital at the time of such distribution an amount of surplus equal to the aggregate stated capital represented by such shares.

(3) A distribution of shares of any class or series may be made to holders of the same or any other class or series of shares unless the certificate of incorporation provides otherwise, provided, however, that in the case of a corporation incorporated prior to the effective date of subparagraph (4) of this paragraph, then so long as any shares of such class remain outstanding a distribution of shares of any class or series of shares of such corporation may be made only to holders of the same class or series of shares unless the certificate of incorporation permits distribution to holders of another class or series, or unless such distribution is approved by the affirmative vote or the written consent of the holders of a majority of the outstanding shares of the class or series to be distributed.

(4) A distribution of any class or series of shares shall be subject to the preemptive rights, if any, applicable to such shares pursuant to this chapter.

(b) A corporation making a pro rata distribution of authorized but unissued shares to the holders of any class or series of outstanding shares may at its option make an equivalent distribution upon treasury shares of the same class or series, and any shares so distributed shall be treasury shares.

(c) A change of issued shares of any class which increases the stated capital represented by those shares may be made if the surplus of the corporation is sufficient to permit the transfer, and a transfer is concurrently made, from surplus to stated capital, of an amount equal to such increase.

(d) No transfer from surplus to stated capital need be made by a corporation making a distribution of its treasury shares to holders of any class of outstanding shares; nor upon a split up or division of issued shares of any class into a greater number of shares of the same class, or a combination of issued shares of any class into a lesser number of shares of the same class, if there is no increase in the aggregate stated capital represented by them.

(e) Nothing in this section shall prevent a corporation from making other transfers from surplus to stated capital in connection with share distributions or otherwise.

(f) Every distribution to shareholders of certificates representing a share distribution or a change of shares which affects stated capital or surplus shall be accompanied by a written notice (1) disclosing the amounts by which such distribution or change affects stated capital and surplus, or (2) if such amounts are not determinable at the time of such notice, disclosing the approximate effect of such distribution or change upon stated capital and surplus and stating that such amounts are not yet determinable.

(g) When issued shares are changed in any manner which affects stated capital or surplus, and no distribution to shareholders of certificates representing any shares resulting from such change is made, disclosure of the effect of such change upon the stated capital and surplus shall be made in the next financial statement covering the period in which such change is made that is furnished by the corporation to holders of shares of the class or series so changed or, if practicable, in the first notice of dividend or share distribution or change that is furnished to such shareholders between the date of the change of shares and the next such financial statement, and in any event within six months of the date of such change.

§ 512 Redeemable shares

(a) Subject to the restrictions contained in section 513 (Purchase, redemption and certain other transactions by a corporation with respect to its own shares) and paragraph (b) of this section, a corporation may provide in its certificate of incorporation for one or more classes or series of shares which are redeemable, in whole or in part, *at the option of the corporation, the holder or another person or upon the happening of a specified event.*

(b) No redeemable common shares, other than shares of an open-end investment company, as defined in an act of congress entitled "Investment Company Act of 1940", as amended, or of a member corporation of a national securities exchange registered under a statute of the United States such as the Securities Exchange Act of 1934, as amended, or of a corporation described in this paragraph, shall be issued or redeemed unless the corporation at the time has outstanding a class of common shares that is not subject to redemption. Any common shares of a corporation which directly or through a subsidiary has a license or franchise to conduct its business, which license or franchise is conditioned upon some or all of the holders of such corporation's common shares possessing prescribed qualifications, may be made subject to redemption by the corporation to the extent necessary to prevent the loss of, or to reinstate, such license or franchise.

(c) Shares of any class or series which may be made redeemable under this section may be redeemed for *cash, other property, indebtedness or other securities of the same or another corporation, at* such time or times, price or prices, or rate or rates, and with such adjustments, as shall be stated in the certificate of incorporation.

(d) Nothing in this section shall prevent a corporation from creating sinking funds for the redemption or purchase of its shares to the extent permitted by section 513 (Purchase, redemption and certain other transactions by a corporation with respect to its own shares).

§ 513 Purchase, redemption and certain other transactions by a corporation with respect to its own shares

(a) Notwithstanding any authority contained in the certificate of incorporation, the shares of a corporation may not be purchased by the corporation, or, if redeemable, convertible or exchangeable shares, may not be redeemed, converted or exchanged, in each case for or into cash, other property, indebtedness or other securities of the corporation (other than shares of the corporation and rights to acquire such shares) if the corporation is then insolvent or would thereby be made insolvent. *Shares may be purchased or redeemed only out of surplus.*

(b) When its redeemable, convertible or exchangeable shares are purchased by the corporation within the period during which such shares may be redeemed, converted or exchanged at the option of the corporation, the purchase price thereof shall not exceed the applicable redemption, conversion or exchange price stated in the certificate of incorporation. Upon a redemption, conversion or exchange, the amount payable by the corporation for shares having a cumulative preference on dividends may include the stated redemption, conversion or exchange price plus accrued dividends to the next dividend date following the date of redemption, conversion or exchange of such shares.

(c) No domestic corporation which is subject to the provisions of section nine hundred twelve of this chapter shall purchase or agree to *purchase more than ten percent of* the stock of the corporation from a *shareholder for more than the market value thereof* unless such purchase or agreement to purchase is approved by the affirmative vote of the board of directors and *a majority* of the votes of all outstanding *shares* entitled to vote thereon at a meeting of shareholders unless the certificate of incorporation requires a greater percentage of the votes of the outstanding shares to approve.

The provisions of this paragraph shall *not apply* when the corporation offers to purchase shares from all holders of stock or for stock which the holder has been the beneficial owner of *for more than two years.*

The terms "stock", "beneficial owner", and "market value" shall be as defined in section nine hundred twelve of this chapter.

§ 514 Agreements for purchase by a corporation of its own shares

(a) An agreement for the purchase by a corporation of its own shares shall be enforceable by the shareholder and the corporation to the extent such purchase is permitted at the time of purchase by section 513 (Purchase or redemption by a corporation of its own shares).

(b) The possibility that a corporation may not be able to purchase its shares under section 513 shall not be a ground for denying to either party specific performance of an agreement for the purchase by a corporation of its own shares, if at the time for performance the corporation can purchase all or part of such shares under section 513.

§ 515 Reacquired shares

(a) Shares that have been issued and have been purchased, redeemed or otherwise reacquired by a corporation shall be cancelled if they are reacquired out of stated capital, or if they are converted shares, or if the certificate of incorporation requires that such shares be cancelled upon reacquisition.

(b) Any shares reacquired by the corporation and not required to be cancelled may be either retained as treasury shares or cancelled by the board at the time of reacquisition or at any time thereafter.

(c) Neither the retention of reacquired shares as treasury shares, nor their subsequent distribution to shareholders or disposition for a consideration shall change the stated capital. When treasury shares are disposed of for a consideration, the surplus shall be increased by the full amount of the consideration received.

(d) Shares cancelled under this section are restored to the status of authorized but unissued shares. However, if the certificate of incorporation prohibits the reissue of any shares required or permitted to be cancelled under this section, the board by certificate of amendment under section 805 (Certificate of amendment; contents) shall reduce the number of authorized shares accordingly.

§ 516 Reduction of stated capital in certain cases

(a) Except as otherwise provided in the certificate of incorporation, the board may at any time reduce the stated capital of a corporation in any of the following ways:

(1) by eliminating from stated capital any portion of amounts previously transferred by the board from surplus to stated capital and not allocated to any designated class or series of shares;

(2) by reducing or eliminating any amount of stated capital represented by issued shares having a par value which exceeds the aggregate par value of such shares;

(3) by reducing the amount of stated capital represented by issued shares without par value; or

(4) by applying to an otherwise authorized purchase, redemption, conversion or exchange of outstanding shares some or all of the stated capital represented by the shares being purchased, redeemed, converted or exchanged, or some or all of any stated capital that has not been allocated to any particular shares, or both. Notwithstanding the foregoing, if the consideration for the issue of shares without par value was fixed by the shareholders under section 504 (Consideration and payment for shares), the board shall not reduce the stated capital represented by such shares except to the extent, if any, that the board was authorized

by the shareholders to allocate any portion of such consideration to surplus.

(b) No reduction of stated capital shall be made under this section unless after such reduction the stated capital exceeds the aggregate preferential amounts payable upon involuntary liquidation upon all issued shares having preferential rights in the assets plus the par value of all other issued shares with par value.

(c) When a reduction of stated capital has been effected under this section, the amount of such reduction shall be disclosed in the next financial statement covering the period in which such reduction is made that is furnished by the corporation to all its shareholders or, if practicable, in the first notice of dividend or share distribution that is furnished to the holders of each class or series of its shares between the date of such reduction and the next such financial statement, and in any event to all its shareholders within six months of the date of such reduction.

§ 517 [Repealed]

§ 518 Corporate bonds

(a) No corporation shall issue bonds except for money or other property, tangible or intangible; labor or services actually received by or performed for the corporation or for its benefit or in its formation or reorganization; a binding obligation to pay the purchase price thereof in cash or other property; a binding obligation to perform services having an agreed value; or a combination thereof. In the absence of fraud in the transaction, the judgment of the board as to the value of the consideration received shall be conclusive.

(b) If a distribution of its own bonds is made by a corporation to holders of any class or series of its outstanding shares, there shall be concurrently transferred to the liabilities of the corporation in respect of such bonds an amount of surplus equal to the principal amount of, and any accrued interest on, such bonds. The amount of the surplus so transferred shall be the consideration for the issue of such bonds.

(c) A corporation may, *in its certificate of incorporation, confer* upon the holders of any bonds issued or to be issued by the corporation, *rights to inspect* the corporate books and records *and to vote in the election of directors and on any other matters* on which shareholders of the corporation may vote.

§ 519 Convertible or exchangeable shares and bonds

(a) Unless otherwise provided in the certificate of incorporation, and subject to the restrictions in section 513 (Purchase, redemption and certain other transactions by a corporation with respect to its own shares) and paragraphs (c) and (d) of this section, a corporation may issue shares or bonds *convertible into or exchangeable for*, at the option *of the holder, the corporation or another person, or upon the happening of a specified event*, shares of any class or shares of any series of any class or cash, other property, indebtedness or other securities of *the same or another* corporation.

(b) If there is shareholder approval for the issue of bonds or shares convertible into, or exchangeable for, shares of the corporation, such approval may provide that the board is authorized by certificate of amendment under section 805 (Certificate of amendment; contents) to increase the authorized shares of any class or series to such number as will be sufficient, when added to the previously authorized but unissued shares of such class or series, to satisfy the conversion or exchange privileges of any such bonds or shares convertible into, or exchangeable for, shares of such class or series.

(c) No issue of bonds or shares convertible into, or exchangeable for, shares of the corporation shall be made unless:

(1) A sufficient number of authorized but unissued shares, or treasury shares, of the appropriate class or series are reserved by the board to be issued only in satisfaction of the conversion or exchange privileges of such convertible or exchangeable bonds or shares when issued;

(2) The aggregate conversion or exchange privileges of such convertible or exchangeable bonds or shares when issued do not exceed the aggregate of any shares reserved under subparagraph (1) and any additional shares which may be authorized by the board under paragraph (b); or

(3) In the case of the conversion or exchange of shares of common stock other than into other shares of common stock, there remains outstanding a class or series of common stock not subject to conversion or exchange other than into other shares of common stock, except in the case of corporations of the type described in the exceptions to the provisions of paragraph (b) of section 512 (Redeemable shares).

(d) No privilege of conversion may be conferred upon, or altered in respect to, any shares or bonds that would result in the receipt by the corporation of less than the minimum consideration required to be received upon the issue of new shares. The consideration for shares issued upon the exercise of a conversion or exchange privilege shall be that provided in paragraph (g) of section 504 (Consideration and payment for shares).

(e) When shares have been converted or exchanged, they shall be cancelled. When bonds have been converted or exchanged, they shall be cancelled and not reissued except upon compliance with the provisions governing the issue of convertible or exchangeable bonds.

§ 520 Liability for failure to disclose required information

Failure of the corporation to comply in good faith with the notice or disclosure provisions of paragraphs (f) and (g) of section 511 (Share distributions and changes), or paragraph (c) of section 516 (Reduction of stated capital in certain cases), shall make the corporation liable for any damage sustained by any shareholder in consequence thereof.

ARTICLE 6. SHAREHOLDERS

§ 623 Procedure to enforce shareholder's right to receive payment for shares

(a) A shareholder intending to enforce his right under a section of this chapter to receive payment for his shares if the proposed corporate action referred to therein is taken shall file with the corporation, before the meeting of shareholders at which the action is submitted to a vote, or at such meeting but before the vote, written objection to the action. The objection shall include a notice of his election to dissent, his name and residence address, the number and classes of shares as to which he dissents and a demand for payment of the fair value of his shares if the action is taken. Such objection is not required from any shareholder to whom the corporation did not give notice of such meeting in accordance with this chapter or where the proposed action is authorized by written consent of shareholders without a meeting.

(b) Within ten days after the shareholders' authorization date, which term as used in this section means the date on which the shareholders' vote authorizing such action was taken, or the date on which such consent without a meeting was obtained from the requisite shareholders, the corporation shall give written notice of such authorization or consent by registered mail to each shareholder who filed written objection or from whom written objection was not required, excepting any shareholder who voted for or consented in writing to the proposed action and who thereby is deemed to have elected not to enforce his right to receive payment for his shares.

(c) Within twenty days after the giving of notice to him, any shareholder from whom written objection was not required and who elects to dissent shall file with the corporation a written notice of such election, stating his name and residence address, the number and classes of shares as to which he dissents and a demand for payment of the fair value of his shares. Any shareholder who elects to dissent from a merger under section 905 (Merger of subsidiary corporation) or paragraph (c) of section 907 (Merger or consolidation of domestic and foreign corporations) or from a share exchange under paragraph (g) of section 913 (Share exchanges) shall file a written notice of such election to dissent within twenty days after the giving to him of a copy of the plan of merger or exchange or an outline of the material features thereof under section 905 or 913.

(d) A shareholder may not dissent as to less than all of the shares, as to which he has a right to dissent, held by him of record, that he owns beneficially. A nominee or fiduciary may not dissent on behalf of any beneficial owner as to less than all of the shares of such owner, as to which such nominee or fiduciary has a right to dissent, held of record by such nominee or fiduciary.

(e) Upon consummation of the corporate action, the shareholder shall cease to have any of the rights of a shareholder except the right to be paid the fair value of his shares and any other rights under this section. A notice of election may be withdrawn by the shareholder at any time prior to his acceptance in writing of an offer made by the corporation, as provided in paragraph (g), but in no case later than sixty days from the date of consummation of the corporate action except that if the corporation fails to make a timely offer, as provided in paragraph (g), the time for withdrawing a notice of election shall be extended until sixty days from the date an offer is made. Upon expiration of such time, withdrawal of a notice of election shall require the written consent of the corporation. In order to be effective, withdrawal of a notice of election must be accompanied by the return to the corporation of any advance payment made to the shareholder as provided in paragraph (g). If a notice of election is withdrawn, or the corporate action is rescinded, or a court shall determine that the shareholder is not entitled to receive payment for his shares, or the shareholder shall otherwise lose his dissenters' rights, he shall not have the right to receive payment for his shares and he shall be reinstated to all his rights as a shareholder as of the consummation of the corporate action, including any intervening preemptive rights and the right to payment of any intervening dividend or other distribution or, if any such rights have expired or any such dividend or distribution other than in cash has been completed, in lieu thereof, at the election of the corporation, the fair value thereof in cash as determined by the board as of the time of such expiration or completion, but without prejudice otherwise to any corporate proceedings that may have been taken in the interim.

(f) At the time of filing the notice of election to dissent or within one month thereafter the shareholder of shares represented by certificates shall submit the certificates representing his shares to the corporation, or to its transfer agent, which shall forthwith note conspicuously thereon that a notice of election has been filed and shall return the certificates to the shareholder or other person who submitted them on his behalf. Any shareholder of shares represented by certificates who fails to submit his certificates for such notation as herein specified shall, at the option of the corporation exercised by written notice to him within forty-five days from the date of filing of such notice of election to dissent, lose his dissenter's rights unless a court, for good cause shown, shall otherwise direct. Upon transfer of a certificate bearing such notation, each new certificate issued therefor shall bear a similar notation together with the name of the original dissenting holder of the shares and a transferee shall acquire no rights in the corporation except those which the original dissenting shareholder had at the time of transfer.

(g) Within fifteen days after the expiration of the period within which shareholders may file their notices of election to dissent, or within fifteen days after the proposed corporate action is consummated, whichever is later (but in no case later than ninety days from the shareholders' authorization date), the corporation or, in the case of a merger or consolidation, the surviving or new corporation, shall make a written offer by registered mail to each shareholder who has filed such notice of election to pay for his shares at a specified price which the corporation considers to be their fair value. Such offer shall be accompanied by a statement setting forth the aggregate number of shares with respect to which notices of election to dissent have been received and the aggregate number of holders of such shares. If the corporate action has been consummated, such offer shall also be accompanied by (1) advance payment to each such shareholder who has submitted the certificates representing his shares to the corporation, as provided in paragraph (f), of an amount equal to eighty percent of the amount of such offer, or (2) as to each shareholder who has not yet submitted his certificates a statement that advance payment to him of an amount equal to eighty percent of the amount of such offer will be made by the corporation promptly upon submission of his certificates. If the corporate action has not been consummated at the time of the making of the offer, such advance payment or statement as to advance payment shall be sent to each shareholder entitled thereto forthwith upon consummation of the corporate action. Every advance payment or statement as to advance payment shall include advice to the shareholder to the effect that acceptance of such payment does not constitute a waiver of any dissenters' rights. If the corporate action has not been consummated upon the expiration of the ninety day period after the shareholders' authorization date, the offer may be conditioned upon the consummation of such action. Such offer shall be made at the same price per share to all dissenting shareholders of the same class, or if divided into series, of the same series and shall be accompanied by a balance sheet of the corporation whose shares the dissenting shareholder holds as of the latest available date, which shall not be earlier than twelve months before the making of such offer, and a profit and loss statement or statements for not less than a twelve month period ended on the date of such balance sheet or, if the corporation was not in existence throughout such twelve month period, for the portion thereof during which it was in existence. Notwithstanding the foregoing, the corporation shall not be required to furnish a balance sheet or profit and loss statement or statements to any shareholder to whom such balance sheet or profit and loss statement or statements were previously furnished, nor if in connection with obtaining the shareholders' authorization for or consent to the proposed corporate action the shareholders were furnished with a proxy or information statement, which included financial statements, pursuant to Regulation 14A or Regulation 14C of the United States Securities and Exchange Commission. If within thirty days after the making of such offer, the corporation making the offer and any shareholder agree upon the price to be paid for his shares, payment therefor shall be made within sixty days after the making of such offer or the consummation of the proposed corporate action, whichever is later, upon the surrender of the certificates for any such shares represented by certificates.

(h) The following procedure shall apply if the corporation fails to make such offer within such period of fifteen days, or if it makes the offer and any dissenting shareholder or shareholders fail to agree with it within the period of thirty days thereafter upon the price to be paid for their shares:

(1) The corporation shall, within twenty days after the expiration of whichever is applicable of the two periods last mentioned, institute a special proceeding in the supreme court in the judicial district in which the office of the corporation is located to determine the rights of dissenting shareholders and to fix the fair value of their shares. If, in the case of merger or consolidation, the surviving or new corporation is a foreign corporation without an office in this state, such proceeding shall be brought in the county where the office of the domestic corporation, whose shares are to be valued, was located.

(2) If the corporation fails to institute such proceeding within such period of twenty days, any dissenting shareholder may institute such proceeding for the same purpose not later than thirty days after the expiration of such twenty day period. If such proceeding is not instituted within such thirty day period, all dissenter's rights shall be lost unless the supreme court, for good cause shown, shall otherwise direct.

(3) All dissenting shareholders, excepting those who, as provided in paragraph (g), have agreed with the corporation upon the price to be paid for their shares, shall be made parties to such proceeding, which shall have the effect of an action quasi in rem against their shares. The corporation shall serve a copy of the petition in such proceeding upon each dissenting shareholder who is a resident of this state in the manner provided by law for the service of a summons, and upon each nonresident dissenting shareholder either by registered mail and publication, or in such other manner as is permitted by law. The jurisdiction of the court

shall be plenary and exclusive.

(4) The court shall determine whether each dissenting shareholder, as to whom the corporation requests the court to make such determination, is entitled to receive payment for his shares. If the corporation does not request any such determination or if the court finds that any dissenting shareholder is so entitled, it shall proceed to fix the value of the shares, which, for the purposes of this section, shall be the fair value as of the close of business on the day prior to the shareholders' authorization date. *In fixing the fair value of the shares, the court shall consider the nature of the transaction giving rise to the shareholder's right to receive payment for shares and its effects on the corporation and its shareholders, the concepts and methods then customary in the relevant securities and financial markets for determining fair value of shares of a corporation engaging in a similar transaction under comparable circumstances and all other relevant factors.* The court shall determine the fair value of the shares without a jury and without referral to an appraiser or referee. Upon application by the corporation or by any shareholder who is a party to the proceeding, the court may, in its discretion, permit pretrial disclosure, including, but not limited to, disclosure of any expert's reports relating to the fair value of the shares whether or not intended for use at the trial in the proceeding and notwithstanding subdivision (d) of section 3101 of the civil practice law and rules.

(5) The final order in the proceeding shall be entered against the corporation in favor of each dissenting shareholder who is a party to the proceeding and is entitled thereto for the value of his shares so determined.

(6) The final order shall include an allowance for interest at such rate as the court finds to be equitable, from the date the corporate action was consummated to the date of payment. In determining the rate of interest, the court shall consider all relevant factors, including the rate of interest which the corporation would have had to pay to borrow money during the pendency of the proceeding. If the court finds that the refusal of any shareholder to accept the corporate offer of payment for his shares was arbitrary, vexatious or otherwise not in good faith, no interest shall be allowed to him.

(7) Each party to such proceeding shall bear its own costs and expenses, including the fees and expenses of its counsel and of any experts employed by it. Notwithstanding the foregoing, the court may, in its discretion, apportion and assess all or any part of the costs, expenses and fees incurred by the corporation against any or all of the dissenting shareholders who are parties to the proceeding, including any who have withdrawn their notices of election as provided in paragraph (e), if the court finds that their refusal to accept the corporate offer was arbitrary, vexatious or otherwise not in good faith. The court may, in its discretion, apportion and assess all or any part of the costs, expenses and fees incurred by any or all of the dissenting shareholders who are parties to the proceeding against the corporation if the court finds any of the following: (A) that the fair value of the shares as determined materially exceeds the amount which the corporation offered to pay; (B) that no offer or required advance payment was made by the corporation; (C) that the corporation failed to institute the special proceeding within the period specified therefor; or (D) that the action

of the corporation in complying with its obligations as provided in this section was arbitrary, vexatious or otherwise not in good faith. In making any determination as provided in clause (A), the court may consider the dollar amount or the percentage, or both, by which the fair value of the shares as determined exceeds the corporate offer.

(8) Within sixty days after final determination of the proceeding, the corporation shall pay to each dissenting shareholder the amount found to be due him, upon surrender of the certificates for any such shares represented by certificates.

(i) Shares acquired by the corporation upon the payment of the agreed value therefor or of the amount due under the final order, as provided in this section, shall become treasury shares or be cancelled as provided in section 515 (Reacquired shares), except that, in the case of a merger or consolidation, they may be held and disposed of as the plan of merger or consolidation may otherwise provide.

(j) No payment shall be made to a dissenting shareholder under this section at a time when the corporation is insolvent or when such payment would make it insolvent. In such event, the dissenting shareholder shall, at his option:

(1) Withdraw his notice of election, which shall in such event be deemed withdrawn with the written consent of the corporation; or

(2) Retain his status as a claimant against the corporation and, if it is liquidated, be subordinated to the rights of creditors of the corporation, but have rights superior to the non-dissenting shareholders, and if it is not liquidated, retain his right to be paid for his shares, which right the corporation shall be obliged to satisfy when the restrictions of this paragraph do not apply.

(3) The dissenting shareholder shall exercise such option under subparagraph (1) or (2) by written notice filed with the corporation within thirty days after the corporation has given him written notice that payment for his shares cannot be made because of the restrictions of this paragraph. If the dissenting shareholder fails to exercise such option as provided, the corporation shall exercise the option by written notice given to him within twenty days after the expiration of such period of thirty days.

(k) The enforcement by a shareholder of his right to receive payment for his shares in the manner provided herein shall exclude the enforcement by such shareholder of any other right to which he might otherwise be entitled by virtue of share ownership, except as provided in paragraph (e), and except that this section shall not exclude the right of such shareholder to bring or maintain an appropriate action to obtain relief on the ground that such corporate action will be or is unlawful or fraudulent as to him.

(l) Except as otherwise expressly provided in this section, any notice to be given by a corporation to a shareholder under this section shall be given in the manner provided in section 605 (Notice of meetings of shareholders).

(m) This section shall not apply to foreign corporations except as provided in subparagraph (e)(2) of section 907 (Merger or consolidation of domestic and foreign corporations).

ARTICLE 7. DIRECTORS AND OFFICERS

§ 717 Duty of directors

(a) A director shall perform his duties as a director, including his duties as a member of any committee of the board upon which he may serve, in good faith and with that degree of care which an ordinarily prudent person in a like position would use under similar circumstances. In performing his duties, a director shall be entitled to rely on information, opinions, reports or statements including financial statements and other financial data, in each case prepared or presented by:

(1) one or more officers or employees of the corporation or of any other corporation of which at least fifty percentum of the outstanding shares of stock entitling the holders thereof to vote for the election of directors is owned directly or indirectly by the corporation, whom the director believes to be reliable and competent in the matters presented,

(2) counsel, public accountants or other persons as to matters which the director believes to be within such person's professional or expert competence, or

(3) a committee of the board upon which he does not serve, duly designated in accordance with a provision of the certificate of incorporation or the bylaws, as to matters within its designated authority, which committee the director believes to merit confidence, so long as in so relying he shall be acting in good faith and with such degree of care, but he shall not be considered to be acting in good faith if he has knowledge concerning the matter in question that would cause such reliance to be unwarranted. A person who so performs his duties shall have no liability by reason of being or having been a director of the corporation.

(b) In taking action, including, without limitation, action which may involve or relate to a change or potential change in the control of the corporation, a director shall be entitled to consider, without limitation,

(1) both the long-term and the short-term interests of the corporation and its shareholders and

(2) the effects that the corporation's actions may have in the short-term or in the long-term upon any of the following:

(i) the prospects for potential growth, development, productivity and profitability of the corporation;

(ii) the corporation's current employees;

(iii) the corporation's retired employees and other beneficiaries receiving or entitled to receive retirement, welfare or similar benefits from or pursuant to any plan sponsored, or agreement entered into, by the corporation;

(iv) the corporation's customers and creditors; and

(v) the ability of the corporation to provide, as a going concern, goods, services, employment opportunities and employment benefits and otherwise to contribute to the communities in which it does business.

Nothing in this paragraph shall create any duties owed by any director to any person or entity to consider or afford any particular weight to any of the foregoing or abrogate any duty of the directors, either statutory or recognized by common law or court decisions.

For purposes of this paragraph, "control" shall mean the possession, directly or indirectly, of the power to direct or cause the direction of the management and policies of the corporation, whether through the ownership of voting stock, by contract, or otherwise.

ARTICLE 8. AMENDMENTS AND CHANGES

§ 801 Right to amend certificate of incorporation

(a) A corporation may amend its certificate of incorporation, from time to time, in any and as many respects as may be desired, if such amendment contains only such provisions as might be lawfully contained in an original certificate of incorporation filed at the time of making such amendment.

(b) In particular, and without limitation upon such general power of amendment, a corporation may amend its certificate of incorporation, from time to time, so as:

(1) To change its corporate name.

(2) To enlarge, limit or otherwise change its corporate purposes.

(3) To specify or change the location of the office of the corporation.

(4) To specify or change the post office address to which the secretary of state shall mail a copy of any process against the corporation served upon him.

(5) To make, revoke or change the designation of a registered agent, or to specify or change the address of its registered agent.

(6) To extend the duration of the corporation or, if the corporation ceased to exist because of the expiration of the duration specified in its certificate of incorporation, to revive its existence.

(7) To increase or decrease the aggregate number of shares, or shares of any class or series, with or without par value, which the corporation shall have authority to issue.

(8) To remove from authorized shares any class of shares, or any shares of any class, whether issued or unissued.

(9) To increase the par value of any authorized shares of any class with par value, *whether issued or unissued.*

(10) To reduce the par value of any authorized shares of any class with par value, whether issued or unissued.

(11) To change any authorized shares, with or without par value, whether issued or unissued, into a different number of shares of the same class or into the same or a different number of shares of any one or more classes or any series thereof, either with or without par value.

(12) To fix, change or abolish the designation of any authorized class or any series thereof or any of the relative rights, preferences and limitations of any shares of any authorized class or any series thereof, whether issued or unissued, *including any provisions in respect of any undeclared dividends, whether or not cumulative or accrued, or the redemption of any shares, or any sinking fund for the redemption or purchase of any shares, or any preemptive right to acquire shares or other securities.*

(13) As to the shares of any preferred class, then or theretofore authorized, which may be issued in series, to grant authority to the board or to change or revoke the authority of the board to establish and designate series and to fix the number of shares and the relative rights, preferences and limitation as between series.

(14) To strike out, change or add any provision, not inconsistent with this chapter or any other statute, relating to the business of the corporation, its affairs, its rights or powers, or the rights or powers of its shareholders, directors or officers, including any provision which under this chapter is required or permitted to be set forth in the by-laws, except that a certificate of amendment may not be filed wherein the duration of the corporation shall be reduced.

(c) A corporation created by special act may accomplish any or all amendments permitted in this article, in the manner and subject to the conditions provided in this article.

§ 802 Reduction of stated capital by amendment

(a) A corporation may reduce its stated capital by an amendment of its certificate of incorporation under section 801 (Right to amend certificate of incorporation) which:

(1) Reduces the par value of any issued shares with par value.

(2) Changes issued shares under subparagraph (b)(11) of section 801 that results in a reduction of stated capital.

(3) Removes from authorized shares, shares that have been issued, reacquired and cancelled by the corporation.

(b) This section shall not prevent a corporation from reducing its stated capital in any other manner permitted by this chapter.

§ 803 Authorization of amendment or change

(a) Amendment or change of the certificate of incorporation may be authorized by vote of the board, followed by vote of a majority of all outstanding shares entitled to vote thereon at a meeting of shareholders; provided, however, that, whenever the certificate of incorporation requires action by the board of directors, by the holders of any class or series of shares, or by the holders of any other securities having voting power, by the vote of a greater number or proportion than is required by any section of this article, the provision of the certificate of incorporation requiring such greater vote shall not be altered, amended, or repealed except by such greater vote; and provided further that an amendment to the certificate of incorporation for the purpose of reducing the requisite vote by the holders of any class or series of shares or by the holders of any other securities having voting power that is otherwise provided for in any section of this chapter that would otherwise require more than a majority of the votes of all outstanding shares entitled to vote thereon shall not be adopted except by the vote of such holders of class or series of shares or by such holders of such other securities having voting power that is at least equal to that which would be required to take the action provided in such other section of this chapter.

(b) Alternatively, any one or more of the following changes may be authorized by or pursuant to authorization of the board:

(1) To specify or change the location of the corporation's office.

(2) To specify or change the post office address to which the secretary of state shall mail a copy of any process against the corporation served upon him.

(3) To make, revoke or change the designation of a registered agent, or to specify or change the address of its registered agent.

(c) This section shall not alter the vote required under any other section for the authorization of an amendment referred to therein, nor alter the authority of the board to authorize amendments under any other section.

(d) Amendment or change of the certificate of incorporation of a corporation which has no shareholders of record, no subscribers for shares whose subscriptions have been accepted and no directors may be authorized by the sole incorporator or a majority of the incorporators.

§ 804 Class voting on amendment

(a) Notwithstanding any provision in the certificate of incorporation, the holders of shares of a class shall be entitled to vote and to vote as a class upon the authorization of an amendment and, *in addition* to the authorization of the amendment by a majority of the votes of all outstanding shares entitled to vote thereon, the amendment shall be authorized by a majority of the votes of all outstanding shares of the class when a proposed amendment would:

(1) Exclude or limit their right to vote on any matter, except as such right may be limited by voting rights given to new shares then being authorized of any existing or new class or series.

(2) Change their shares under subparagraphs (b) (10), (11) or (12) of section 801 (Right to amend certificate of incorporation) or provide that their shares may be converted into shares of any other class or into shares of any other series of the same class, or alter the terms or conditions upon which their shares are convertible or change the shares issuable upon conversion of their shares, if such action would adversely affect such holders, or

(3) Subordinate their rights, by authorizing shares having preferences which would be in any respect superior to their rights.

(b) If any proposed amendment referred to in paragraph (a) would adversely affect the rights of the holders of shares of only one or more series of any class, but not the entire class, then only the holders of those series whose rights would be affected shall be considered a separate class for the purposes of this section.

§ 805 Certificate of amendment; contents

(a) To accomplish any amendment, a certificate of amendment, entitled "Certificate of amendment of the certificate of incorporation of . . . . (name of corporation) under section 805 of the Business Corporation Law", shall be signed and delivered to the department of state. It shall set forth:

(1) The name of the corporation and, if it has been changed, the name under which it was formed.

(2) The date its certificate of incorporation was filed by the department of state.

(3) Each amendment effected thereby, setting forth the subject matter of each provision of the certificate of incorporation which is to be amended or eliminated and the full text of the provision or provisions, if any, which are to be substituted or added.

(4) If an amendment provides for a change of shares, the number, par value and class of issued shares changed, the number, par value and class of issued shares resulting from such change, the number, par value and class of unissued shares changed, the number, par value and class of unissued shares resulting from such change and the terms of each such change. If an amendment makes two or more such changes, a like statement shall be included in respect to each change.

(5) If any amendment reduces stated capital, then a statement of the manner in which the same is effected and the amounts from which and to which stated capital is reduced.

(6) The manner in which the amendment of the certificate of incorporation was authorized. If the amendment was authorized under paragraph (d) of section eight hundred three of this chapter, then a statement that the corporation does not have any shareholders of record or any subscribers for shares whose subscriptions have been accepted and no directors.

(b) Any number of amendments or changes may be included in one certificate under this section. Such certificate may also include any amendments or changes permitted by other sections and in that case the certificate shall set forth any additional statement required by any other section specifying the contents of a certificate to effect such amendment or change.

(c) In the case of a change of shares, the shares resulting from such change, shall upon the filing of the certificate of amendment, be deemed substituted for the shares changed, in accordance with the stated terms of change.

§ 805-A Certificate of change; contents

(a) Any one or more of the changes authorized by paragraph (b) of section 803 (Authorization of amendment or change) may be accomplished by filing a certificate of change which shall be entitled "Certificate of change of . . . . (name of corporation) under section 805-A of the Business Corporation Law" and shall be signed and delivered to the department of state. It shall set forth:

(1) The name of the corporation, and if it has been changed, the name under which it was formed.

(2) The date its certificate of incorporation was filed by the department of state.

(3) Each change effected thereby.

(4) The manner in which the change was authorized.

(b) A certificate of change which changes only the post office address to which the secretary of state shall mail a copy of any process against a corporation served upon him or the address of the registered agent, provided such address being changed is the address of a person, partnership or other corporation whose address, as agent, is the address to be changed or who has been designated as registered agent for such corporation, may be signed, verified and delivered to the department of state by such agent. The certificate of change shall set forth the statements required under subparagraphs (a) (1), (2) and (3) of this section; that a notice of the proposed change was mailed to the corporation by the party signing the certificate not less than thirty days prior to the date of delivery to the department and that such corporation has not objected thereto; and that the party signing the certificate is the agent of such corporation to whose address the secretary of state is required to mail copies of process or the registered agent, if such be the case. A certificate signed, verified and delivered under this paragraph shall not be deemed to effect a change of location of the office of the corporation in whose behalf such certificate is filed.

§ 806 Provisions as to certain proceedings

(a) The department of state shall not file a certificate of amendment reviving the existence of a corporation unless the consent of the state tax commission to the revival is delivered to the department. If the name of the corporation being revived is not available under section 301 (Corporate name; general) for use by a corporation then being formed under this chapter, the certificate of amendment shall change the name to one which is available for such use.

(b) The following provisions shall apply to amendments and changes under this article, except under section 808 (Reorganization under Act of Congress):

(1) The stated capital in respect of any shares without par value resulting from a change of issued shares shall be the amount of stated capital in respect of the shares changed or, if such stated capital is reduced by the amendment, the reduced amount stated in the certificate of amendment. No corporation shall change issued shares into both shares with par value and shares without par value unless the stated capital in respect of the shares so changed or, if such stated capital is reduced by the amendment, the reduced amount of stated capital stated in the certificate of amendment, exceeds the par value of the shares with par value resulting from such change; and the amount of such excess shall be the stated capital in respect of the shares without par value resulting from such change.

(2) No corporation shall increase the aggregate par value of its issued shares with par value, unless, after giving effect to such increase, the stated capital is at least equal to the amount required by subparagraph (a) (12) of section 102 (Definitions).

(3) No reduction of stated capital shall be made by amendment unless after such reduction the stated capital exceeds the aggregate preferential amount payable upon involuntary liquidation upon all issued shares having preferential rights in assets plus the par value of all other issued shares with par value.

(4) Any changes that may be made in the relative rights, preferences and limitations of the authorized shares of any class by any certificate of amendment which does not eliminate such shares from authorized shares or change them into shares of another class, shall not for the purpose of any statute or rule of law effect an issue of a new class of shares.

(5) No amendment or change shall affect any existing cause of action in favor of or against the corporation, or any pending suit to which it shall be a party, or the existing rights of persons other than shareholders; and in the event the corporate name shall be changed, no suit brought by or against the corporation under its former name shall abate for that reason.

(6) A holder of any adversely affected shares who does not vote for or consent in writing to the taking of such action shall, subject to and by complying with the provisions of section 623 (Procedure to enforce shareholder's right to receive payment for shares), have the right to dissent and to receive payment for such shares, if the certificate of amendment (A) alters or abolishes any preferential right of such shares having preferences; or (B) creates, alters or abolishes any provision or right in respect of the redemption of such shares or any sinking fund for the redemption or purchase of such shares; or (C) alters or abolishes any preemptive right of such holder to acquire shares or other securities; or (D) excludes or limits the right of such holder to vote on any matter, except as such right may be limited by the voting rights given to new shares then being authorized of any existing or new class.

§ 807 Restated certificate of incorporation

(a) A corporation, when authorized by the board, may restate in a single certificate the text of its certificate of incorporation without making any amendment or change thereby, except that it may include any one or more of the amendments or changes which may be authorized by the board without a vote of shareholders under this chapter. Alternatively, a corporation may restate in a single certificate the text of its certificate of incorporation as amended thereby to effect any one or more of the amendments or changes authorized by this chapter, when authorized by the required vote of the holders of shares entitled to vote thereon.

(b) A restated certificate of incorporation, entitled "Restated certificate of incorporation . . . . (name of corporation) under section 807 of the Business Corporation Law", shall be signed and delivered to the department of state. It shall set forth:

(1) The name of the corporation and, if it has been changed, the name under which it was formed.

(2) The date its certificate of incorporation was filed by the department of state.

(3) If the restated certificate restates the text of the certificate of incorporation without making any amendment or change, then a statement that the text of the

certificate of incorporation is thereby restated without amendment or change to read as therein set forth in full.

(4) If the restated certificate restates the text of the certificate of incorporation as amended or changed thereby, then a statement that the certificate of incorporation is amended or changed to effect one or more of the amendments or changes authorized by this chapter, specifying each such amendment or change and that the text of the certificate of incorporation is thereby restated as amended or changed to read as therein set forth in full.

(5) If an amendment, effected by the restated certificate, provides for a change of issued shares, the number and kind of shares changed, the number and kind of shares resulting from such change and the terms of change. If any amendment makes two or more such changes, a like statement shall be included in respect to each such change.

(6) If the restated certificate contains an amendment which effects a reduction of stated capital, then a statement of the manner in which the same is effected and the amounts from which and to which stated capital is reduced.

(7) The manner in which the restatement of the certificate of incorporation was authorized.

(c) A restated certificate need not include statements as to the incorporator or incorporators, the original subscribers for shares or the first directors.

(d) Any amendment or change under this section shall be subject to any other section, not inconsistent with this section, which would be applicable if a separate certificate were filed to effect such amendment or change.

(e) Notwithstanding that the corporation would be required by any statute to secure from any state official, department, board, agency or other body, any consent or approval to the filing of its certificate of incorporation or a certificate of amendment, such consent or approval shall not be required with respect to the restated certificate if such certificate makes no amendment and if any previously required consent or approval had been secured.

(f) Upon filing by the department, the original certificate of incorporation shall be superseded and the restated certificate of incorporation, including any amendments and changes made thereby, shall be the certificate of incorporation of the corporation.

§ 808 Reorganization under act of congress

(a) Whenever a plan of reorganization of a corporation has been confirmed by a decree or order of a court in proceedings under any applicable act of congress relating to reorganization of corporations, the corporation shall have authority, *without action of its shareholders or board*, to put into effect and carry out the plan and decree and orders of the court relative thereto, and take any proceeding and any action for which provision is made in any statute governing the corporation or for which provision is or might be made in its certificate of incorporation or by-laws and which is provided for in such plan or directed by any such decree or order.

(b) Such authority may be exercised, and such proceedings and actions may be taken, *as may be directed by any such decree or order*, by the trustee or trustees of such corporation appointed in the reorganization proceedings, or if none is acting, by any person or persons designated or appointed for the purpose by any such decree or order, *with like effect as if exercised and taken by unanimous action of the board and shareholders of the corporation.*

(c) Any certificate, required or permitted by law to be filed or recorded to accomplish any corporate purpose, shall be signed, and verified or acknowledged, under any such decree or order, by such trustee or trustees or the person or persons referred to in paragraph (b), and shall certify that provision for such certificate is contained in the plan of reorganization or in a decree or order of the court relative thereto, and that the plan has been confirmed, as provided in an applicable act of congress, specified in the certificate, with the title and venue of the proceeding and the date when the decree or order confirming the plan was made, and such certificate shall be delivered to the department of state.

(d) A shareholder of any such corporation shall have no right to receive payment for his shares and only such rights, if any, as are provided in the plan of reorganization.

(e) Notwithstanding section 504 (Consideration and payment for shares), such corporation may, after the confirmation of such plan, issue its shares, bonds and other securities for the consideration specified in the plan of reorganization and may issue warrants or other optional rights for the purchase of shares upon such terms and conditions as may be set forth in such plan.

(f) If after the filing of any such certificate by the department of state, the decree or order of confirmation of the plan of reorganization is reversed or vacated or such plan is modified, such other or further certificates shall be executed and delivered to the department of state as may be required to conform to the plan of reorganization as finally confirmed or to the decree or order as finally made.

(g) Except as otherwise provided in this section, no certificate filed by the department of state hereunder shall confer on any corporation any powers other than those permitted to be conferred on a corporation formed under this chapter.

(h) If, in any proceeding under any applicable act of congress relating to reorganization of corporations, a decree or order provides for the formation of a new domestic corporation or for the authorization of a new foreign corporation to do business in this state under a name the same as or similar to that of the corporation being reorganized, the certificate of incorporation of the new domestic corporation or the application of the new foreign corporation shall set forth that it is being delivered pursuant to such decree or order and be endorsed with the consent of the court having jurisdiction of the proceeding. After such certificate of incorporation or application has been filed, the corporation being reorganized shall not continue the use of its name except in connection with the reorganization proceeding and as may be necessary to adjust and wind up its affairs, and thirty days after such filing, the reorganized domestic corporation shall be automatically dissolved or the authority of the reorganized foreign corporation to transact business in this state shall cease. To the extent that the adjustment and winding up of the affairs of such dissolved corporation is not accomplished as a part of the proceeding or prescribed by the decree or order of such court, it shall proceed in accordance with the provisions of article 10 (Non-judicial dissolution).

(i) This section shall not relieve any corporation from securing from any state official, department, board, agency or other body, any consent or approval required by any statute.

ARTICLE 9. MERGER OR CONSOLIDATION; GUARANTEE; DISPOSITION OF ASSETS; SHARE EXCHANGES

§ 901 Power of merger or consolidation

(a) Two or more domestic corporations may, as provided in this chapter:

(1) Merge into a single corporation which shall be one of the constituent corporations; or

(2) Consolidate into a single corporation which shall be a new corporation to be formed pursuant to the consolidation.

(b) Whenever used in this article:

(1) "Merger" means a procedure of the character described in subparagraph (a)(1).

(2) "Consolidation" means a procedure of the character described in subparagraph (a)(2).

(3) "Constituent corporation" means an existing corporation that is participating in the merger or consolidation with one or more other corporations.

(4) "Surviving corporation" means the constituent corporation into which one or more other constituent corporations are merged.

(5) "Consolidated corporation" means the new corporation into which two or more constituent corporations are consolidated.

(6) "Constituent entity" means a domestic or foreign corporation or other business entity that is participating in the merger or consolidation with one or more domestic or foreign corporations and domestic or foreign limited liability companies.

(7) "Other business entity" means any person other than a natural person, general partnership (including any registered limited liability partnership or registered foreign limited liability partnership) or a domestic or foreign business corporation.

(8) "Person" means any association, corporation, joint stock company, estate, general partnership (including any registered limited liability partnership or foreign limited liability partnership), limited association, limited liability company (including a professional service limited liability company), foreign limited liability company (including a foreign professional service limited liability company), joint venture, limited partnership, natural person, real estate investment trust, business trust or other trust, custodian, nominee or any other individual or entity in its own or any representative capacity.

(c) One or more domestic corporations and one or more other business entities, or one or more foreign corporations and one or more other business entities may as provided by the limited liability company law and this chapter:

(1) Merge into a single domestic or foreign corporation or other business entity which shall be one of the constituent entities; or

(2) Consolidate into a single domestic or foreign corporation or other business entity which shall be a new domestic or foreign corporation or other business entity to be formed pursuant to the consolidation.

§ 902 Plan of merger or consolidation

(a) The board of each corporation proposing to participate in a merger or consolidation under section 901 (Power of merger or consolidation) shall adopt *a plan* of merger or consolidation, setting forth:

(1) The name of each constituent entity and, if the name of any of them has been changed, the name under which it was formed; and the name of the surviving corporation, or the name, or the method of determining it, of the consolidated corporation.

(2) As to each constituent corporation, the designation and number of outstanding shares of each class and series, specifying the classes and series entitled to vote and further specifying each class and series, if any, entitled to vote as a class; and, if the number of any such shares is subject to change prior to the effective date of the merger or consolidation, the manner in which such change may occur.

(3) The terms and conditions of the proposed merger or consolidation, *including the manner and basis of converting the shares of each constituent corporation into shares, bonds or other securities of the surviving or consolidated corporation, or the cash or other consideration to be paid or delivered in exchange for shares of each constituent corporation, or a combination thereof.*

(4) In case of merger, a statement of any amendments or changes in the certificate of incorporation of the surviving corporation to be effected by such merger; in case of consolidation, all statements required to be included in a certificate of incorporation for a corporation formed under this chapter, except statements as to facts not available at the time the plan of consolidation is adopted by the board.

(5) Such other provisions with respect to the proposed merger or consolidation as the board considers necessary or desirable.

§ 903 Authorization by shareholders

(a) The board of each constituent corporation, upon adopting such plan of merger or consolidation, shall submit such plan to a vote of shareholders in accordance with the following:

(1) Notice of meeting shall be given to each shareholder of record, as of the record date fixed pursuant to section 604 (Fixing record date), whether or not entitled to vote. A copy of the plan of merger or consolidation or an outline of the

material features of the plan shall accompany such notice.

(2) The plan of merger or consolidation shall be adopted at a meeting of shareholders by (i) for corporations in existence on the effective date of this clause the certificate of incorporation of which expressly provides such or corporations incorporated after the effective date of subclause (A) of clause (ii) of this subparagraph, a majority of the votes of the shares entitled to vote thereon or (ii) for other corporations in existence on the effective date of this clause, two-thirds of the votes of all outstanding shares entitled to vote thereon. *Notwithstanding any provision in the certificate of incorporation, the holders of shares of a class or series of a class shall be entitled to vote together and to vote as a separate class if both of the following conditions are satisfied:*

(A) such shares will remain outstanding after the merger or consolidation or will be converted into the right to receive shares of stock of the surviving or consolidated corporation or another corporation, *and*

(B) the certificate or articles of incorporation of the surviving or consolidated corporation or of such other corporation immediately after the effectiveness of the merger or consolidation would contain any provision which, is not contained in the certificate of incorporation of the corporation and which, if contained in an amendment to the certificate of incorporation, would entitle the holders of shares of such class or such one or more series to vote and to vote as a separate class thereon pursuant to section 804 (Class voting on amendment). In such case, in addition to the authorization of the merger or consolidation by the requisite number of votes of all outstanding shares entitled to vote thereon pursuant to the first sentence of this subparagraph (2), the merger or consolidation shall be authorized by a majority of the votes of all outstanding shares of the class entitled to vote as a separate class. If any provision referred to in subclause (B) of clause (ii) of this subparagraph would affect the rights of the holders of shares of only one or more series of any class but not the entire class, then only the holders of those series whose rights would be affected shall together be considered a separate class for purposes of this section.

(b) Notwithstanding shareholder authorization and at any time prior to the filing of the certificate of merger or consolidation, the plan of merger or consolidation may be abandoned pursuant to a provision for such abandonment, if any, contained in the plan of merger or consolidation.

§ 904 Certificate of merger or consolidation; contents

(a) After adoption of the plan of merger or consolidation by the board and shareholders of each constituent corporation, unless the merger or consolidation is abandoned in accordance with paragraph (b) of section 903 (Authorization by shareholders), a certificate of merger or consolidation, entitled "Certificate of merger (or consolidation) of .... and .... into .... (names of corporations) under section 904 of the Business Corporation Law", shall be signed on behalf of each constituent corporation and delivered to the department of state. It shall set forth:

(1) The statements required by subparagraphs (a) (1), (2) and (4) of section 902

(Plan of merger or consolidation).

(2) The effective date of the merger or consolidation if other than the date of filing of the certificate of merger or consolidation by the department of state.

(3) In the case of consolidation, any statement required to be included in a certificate of incorporation for a corporation formed under this chapter but which was omitted under subparagraph (a) (4) of section 902.

(4) The date when the certificate of incorporation of each constituent corporation was filed by the department of state.

(5) The manner in which the merger or consolidation was authorized with respect to each constituent-corporation.

(b) The surviving or consolidated corporation shall thereafter cause a copy of such certificate, certified by the department of state, to be filed in the office of the clerk of each county in which the office of a constituent corporation, other than the surviving corporation, is located, and in the office of the official who is the recording officer of each county in this state in which real property of a constituent corporation, other than the surviving corporation, is situated.

. . .

§ 905 Merger of parent and subsidiary corporations

(a) Any domestic corporation owning at least ninety percent of the outstanding shares of each class of another domestic corporation or corporations may either merge such other corporation or corporations into itself without the authorization of the shareholders of any such corporation or merge itself and one or more of such other corporations into one of such other corporations with the authorization of the parent corporation's shareholders in accordance with paragraph (a) of section 903 (Authorization by shareholders). In either case, the board of such parent corporation shall adopt a plan of merger, setting forth:

(1) The name of each corporation to be merged and the name of the surviving corporation, and if the name of any of them has been changed, the name under which it was formed.

(2) The designation and number of outstanding shares of each class of each corporation to be merged and the number of such shares of each class, if any, owned by the surviving corporation; and if the number of any such shares is subject to change prior to the effective date of the merger, the manner in which such change may occur.

(3) The terms and conditions of the proposed merger, including the manner and basis of converting the shares of each subsidiary corporation to be merged not owned by the parent corporation into shares, bonds or other securities of the surviving corporation, or the cash or other consideration to be paid or delivered in exchange for shares of each such subsidiary corporation, or a combination thereof.

(4) If the parent corporation is not the surviving corporation, provision for the pro rata issuance of shares of the surviving corporation to the shareholders of the

parent corporation on surrender of any certificates therefor.

(5) If the parent corporation is not the surviving corporation, a statement of any amendments or changes in the certificate of incorporation of the surviving corporation to be effected by the merger.

(6) Such other provisions with respect to the proposed merger as the board considers necessary or desirable.

(b) If the surviving corporation is the parent corporation, a copy of such plan of merger or an outline of the material features thereof shall be given, personally or by mail, to all holders of shares of each subsidiary corporation to be merged not owned by the parent corporation, unless the giving of such copy or outline has been waived by such holders.

(c) A certificate of merger, entitled "Certificate of merger of. . . . . into . . . . (names of corporations) under section 905 of the Business Corporation Law", shall be signed and delivered to the department of state by the surviving corporation. If the surviving corporation is the parent corporation and such corporation does not own all shares of each subsidiary corporation to be merged, such certificate shall be delivered not less than thirty days after the giving of a copy or outline of the material features of the plan of merger to shareholders of each such subsidiary corporation, or at any time after the waiving thereof by the holders of all of the outstanding shares of each such subsidiary corporation not owned by the surviving corporation. The certificate shall set forth:

(1) The statements required by subparagraphs (a) (1), (2), (4) and (5) of this section.

(2) The effective date of the merger if other than the date of filing of the certificate of merger by the department of state.

(3) The date when the certificate of incorporation of each constituent corporation was filed by the department of state.

(4) A statement that the plan of merger was adopted by the board of directors of the parent corporation.

(5) If the surviving corporation is the parent corporation and such corporation does not own all the shares of each subsidiary corporation to be merged, either the date of the giving to holders of shares of each such subsidiary corporation not owned by the surviving corporation of a copy of the plan of merger or an outline of the material features thereof, or a statement that the giving of such copy or outline has been waived, if such is the case.

(6) If the parent corporation is not the surviving corporation, a statement that the proposed merger has been approved by the shareholders of the parent corporation in accordance with paragraph (a) of section 903 (Authorization by shareholders).

(d) The surviving corporation shall thereafter cause a copy of such certificate, certified by the department of state, to be filed in the office of the clerk of each county in which the office of a constituent corporation, other than the surviving corporation, is located, and in the office of the official who is the recording officer of each county in this state in which real property of a constituent corporation, other than the surviving corporation, is situated.

(e) Paragraph (b) of section 903 (Authorization by shareholders) shall apply to a merger under this section.

(f) The right of merger granted by this section to certain corporations shall not preclude the exercise by such corporations of any other right of merger or consolidation under this article.

§ 906 Effect of merger or consolidation

(a) Upon the filing of the certificate of merger or consolidation by the department of state or on such date subsequent thereto, not to exceed thirty days, as shall be set forth in such certificate, the merger or consolidation shall be effected.

(b) When such merger or consolidation has been effected:

(1) Such surviving or consolidated corporation shall thereafter, consistently with its certificate of incorporation as altered or established by the merger or consolidation, possess all the rights, privileges, immunities, powers and purposes of each of the constituent corporations.

(2) All the property, real and personal, including subscriptions to shares, causes of action and every other asset of each of the constituent entities, shall vest in such surviving or consolidated corporation without further act or deed.

(3) The surviving or consolidated corporation shall assume and be liable for all the liabilities, obligations and penalties of each of the constituent entities. *No liability or obligation due or to become due, claim or demand for any cause existing against any such constituent entity, or any shareholder, member, officer or director thereof, shall be released or impaired by such merger or consolidation.* No action or proceeding, whether civil or criminal, then pending by or against any such constituent entity, or any shareholder, member, officer or director thereof, shall abate or be discontinued by such merger or consolidation, but may be enforced, prosecuted, settled or compromised as if such merger or consolidation had not occurred, or such surviving or consolidated corporation may be substituted in such action or special proceeding in place of any constituent entity.

(4) In the case of a merger, the certificate of incorporation of the surviving corporation shall be automatically amended to the extent, if any, that changes in its certificate of incorporation are set forth in the plan of merger; and, in the case of a consolidation, the statements set forth in the certificate of consolidation and which are required or permitted to be set forth in a certificate of incorporation of a corporation formed under this chapter shall be its certificate of incorporation.

§ 907 Merger or consolidation of domestic and foreign corporations

(a) One or more foreign corporations and one or more domestic corporations may be merged or consolidated into a corporation of this state or of another jurisdiction, if such merger or consolidation is permitted by the laws of the jurisdiction under which each such foreign corporation is incorporated. With respect to such merger or consolidation, any reference in paragraph (b) of section 901 (Power of merger or consolidation) to a corporation shall, unless the context otherwise requires, include both domestic and foreign corporations.

(b) With respect to procedure, including the requirement of shareholder authorization, each domestic corporation shall comply with the provisions of this chapter relating to merger or consolidation of domestic corporations, and each foreign corporation shall comply with the applicable provisions of the law of the jurisdiction under which it is incorporated.

(c) The procedure for the merger of a subsidiary corporation or corporations under section 905 (Merger of parent and subsidiary corporations) shall be available where either a subsidiary corporation or the corporation owning at least ninety percent of the outstanding shares of each class of a subsidiary is a foreign corporation, and such merger is permitted by the laws of the jurisdiction under which such foreign corporation is incorporated.

(d) If the surviving or consolidated corporation is, or is to be, a domestic corporation, a certificate of merger or consolidation shall be signed, verified and delivered to the department of state as provided in section 904 (Certificate of merger or consolidation; contents) or 905 (Merger of parent and subsidiary corporations), as the case may be. In addition to the matters specified in such sections, the certificate shall set forth as to each constituent foreign corporation the jurisdiction and date of its incorporation and the date when its application for authority to do business in this state was filed by the department of state, and its fictitious name used in this state pursuant to article thirteen of this chapter, if applicable, or, if no such application has been filed, a statement to such effect.

(e) If the surviving or consolidated corporation is, or is to be, formed under the law of any jurisdiction other than this state:

(1) It shall comply with the provisions of this chapter relating to foreign corporations if it is to do business in this state.

(2) It shall deliver to the department of state a certificate, entitled "Certificate of merger (or consolidation) of . . . . and . . . . into . . . . (names of corporations) under section 907 of the Business Corporation Law", which shall be signed on behalf of each constituent domestic and foreign corporation. It shall set forth:

(A) If the procedure for the merger or consolidation of a constituent domestic corporation was effected in compliance with sections 902 (Plan of merger or consolidation) and 903 (Authorization by shareholders), the following:

(i) The statements required by subparagraphs (a) (1) and (2) of section 902.

(ii) The effective date of the merger or consolidation if other than the date of filing of the certificate of merger or consolidation by the department of state.

(iii) The manner in which the merger or consolidation was authorized with respect to each constituent domestic corporation and that the merger or consolidation is permitted by the laws of the jurisdiction of each constituent foreign corporation and is in compliance therewith.

(B) If the procedure for the merger of a subsidiary corporation was effected in compliance with section 905, the following:

(i) The statements required by subparagraphs (a) (1), (2), (4) and (5) of section 905.

(ii) The effective date of the merger if other than the date of filing of the certificate of merger by the department of state.

(iii) If the surviving foreign corporation is the parent corporation and such corporation does not own all the shares of a subsidiary domestic corporation being merged, either the date of the giving to holders of shares of each subsidiary domestic corporation not owned by the surviving foreign corporation of a copy of the plan of merger or an outline of the material features thereof, or a statement that the giving of such copy or outline has been waived, if such is the case.

(iv) That the merger is permitted by the laws of the jurisdiction of each constituent foreign corporation and is in compliance therewith.

(v) If the parent domestic corporation is not the surviving corporation, a statement that the proposed merger has been approved by the shareholders of the parent domestic corporation in accordance with paragraph (a) of section 903 (Authorization by shareholders).

(C) The jurisdiction and date of incorporation of the surviving or consolidated foreign corporation, the date when its application for authority to do business in this state was filed by the department of state, and its fictitious name used in this state pursuant to article thirteen of this chapter, if applicable, or, if no such application has been filed, a statement to such effect and that it is not to do business in this state until an application for such authority shall have been filed by such department.

(D) The date when the certificate of incorporation of each constituent domestic corporation was filed by the department of state and the jurisdiction and date of incorporation of each constituent foreign corporation, other than the surviving or consolidated foreign corporation, and, in the case of each such corporation authorized to do business in this state, the date when its application for authority was filed by the department of state.

(E) An agreement that the surviving or consolidated foreign corporation may be served with process in this state in any action or special proceeding for the enforcement of any liability or obligation of any domestic corporation or of any foreign corporation, previously amenable to suit in this state, which is a constituent corporation in such merger or consolidation, and for the enforcement, as provided in this chapter, of the right of shareholders of any constituent domestic corporation to receive payment for their shares against the surviving or consolidated corporation.

(F) An agreement that, subject to the provisions of section 623 (Procedure to enforce shareholder's right to receive payment for shares), the surviving or consolidated foreign corporation will promptly pay to the shareholders of each constituent domestic corporation the amount, if any, to which they shall be entitled under the provisions of this chapter relating to the right of shareholders to receive payment for their shares.

(G) A designation of the secretary of state as its agent upon whom process against it may be served in the manner set forth in paragraph (b) of section 306 (Service of process), in any action or special proceeding, and a post office address, within or without this state, to which the secretary of state shall mail a copy of any process against it served upon him. Such post office address shall supersede any prior address designated as the address to which process shall be mailed.

(H) (i) A certification that all fees and taxes (including penalties and interest) administered by the department of taxation and finance which are then due and payable by each constituent domestic corporation have been paid and that a cessation franchise tax report (estimated or final) through the anticipated date of the merger or consolidation (which return, if estimated, shall be subject to amendment) has been filed by each constituent domestic corporation and (ii) an agreement that the surviving or consolidated foreign corporation will within thirty days after the filing of the certificate of merger or consolidation file the cessation franchise tax report, if an estimated report was previously filed, and promptly pay to the department of taxation and finance all fees and taxes (including penalties and interest), if any, due to the department of taxation and finance by each constituent domestic corporation.

(f) Upon the filing of the certificate of merger or consolidation by the department of state or on such date subsequent thereto, not to exceed ninety days, as shall be set forth in such certificate, the merger or consolidation shall be effected.

(g) The surviving or consolidated domestic corporation or foreign corporation shall thereafter cause a copy of such certificate, certified by the department of state, to be filed in the office of the clerk of each county in which the office of a constituent corporation other than the surviving corporation is located, and in the office of the official who is the recording officer of each county in this state in which real property of a constituent corporation, other than the surviving corporation, is situated.

(h) If the surviving or consolidated corporation is, or is to be, formed under the law of this state, the effect of such merger or consolidation shall be the same as in the case of the merger or consolidation of domestic corporations under section 906 (Effect of merger or consolidation). If the surviving or consolidated corporation is, or is to be, incorporated under the law of any jurisdiction other than this state, the effect of such merger or consolidation shall be the same as in the case of the merger or consolidation of domestic corporations, except in so far as the law of such other jurisdiction provides otherwise.

§ 909 Sale, lease, exchange or other disposition of assets

(a) A sale, lease, exchange or other disposition *of all or substantially all the assets of* a corporation, if not made in the usual or regular course of the business actually conducted by such corporation, shall be authorized only in accordance with the following procedure:

(1) The board shall authorize the proposed sale, lease, exchange or other disposition and direct its submission to a vote of shareholders.

(2) Notice of meeting shall be given to each shareholder of record, whether or not entitled to vote.

(3) The shareholders shall approve such sale, lease, exchange or other disposition and may fix, or may authorize the board to fix, any of the terms and conditions thereof and the consideration to be received by the corporation therefor, which may consist in whole or in part of cash or other property, real or personal, including shares, bonds or other securities of any other domestic or foreign corporation or corporations, by vote at a meeting of shareholders of (A) for corporations in existence on the effective date of this clause the certificate of incorporation of which expressly provides such or corporations incorporated after the effective date of this clause, a majority of the votes of all outstanding shares entitled to vote thereon or (B) for other corporations in existence on the effective date of this clause, two-thirds of the votes of all outstanding shares entitled to vote thereon.

(b) A recital in a deed, lease or other instrument of conveyance executed by a corporation to the effect that the property described therein does not constitute all or substantially all of the assets of the corporation, or that the disposition of the property affected by said instrument was made in the usual or regular course of business of the corporation, or that the shareholders have duly authorized such disposition, shall be presumptive evidence of the fact so recited.

(c) An action to set aside a deed, lease or other instrument of conveyance executed by a corporation affecting real property or real and personal property may not be maintained for failure to comply with the requirements of paragraph (a) unless the action is commenced and a notice of pendency of action is filed within one year after such conveyance, lease or other instrument is recorded or within six months after this subdivision takes effect, whichever date occurs later.

(d) Whenever a transaction of the character described in paragraph (a) involves a sale, lease, exchange or other disposition of all or substantially all the assets of the corporation, including its name, to a new corporation formed under the same name as the existing corporation, upon the expiration of thirty days from the filing of the certificate of incorporation of the new corporation, with the consent of the state tax commission attached, the existing corporation shall be automatically dissolved, unless, before the end of such thirty-day period, such corporation has changed its name. The adjustment and winding up of the affairs of such dissolved corporation shall proceed in accordance with the provisions of article 10 (Non-judicial dissolution).

(e) The certificate of incorporation of a corporation formed under the authority of paragraph (d) shall set forth the name of the existing corporation, the date when its certificate of incorporation was filed by the department of state, and that the shareholders of such corporation have authorized the sale, lease, exchange or other disposition of all or substantially all the assets of such corporation, including its name, to the new corporation to be formed under the same name as the existing corporation.

(f) Notwithstanding shareholder approval, the board may abandon the proposed sale, lease, exchange or other disposition without further action by the shareholders, subject to the rights, if any, of third parties under any contract relating thereto.

§ 910 Right of shareholder to receive payment for shares upon merger or consolidation, or sale, lease, exchange or other disposition of assets, or share exchange

(a) A shareholder of a domestic corporation shall, subject to and by complying with section 623 (Procedure to enforce shareholder's right to receive payment for shares), have the right to receive payment of the fair value of his shares and the other rights and benefits provided by such section, in the following cases:

(1) Any shareholder entitled to vote who does not assent to the taking of an action specified in clauses (A), (B) and (C).

(A) *Any* plan of merger or consolidation to which the corporation is a party; *except that* the right to receive payment of the fair value of his shares *shall not be available*:

(i) To a shareholder of the parent corporation in a merger authorized by section 905 (Merger of parent and subsidiary corporations), or paragraph (c) of section 907 (Merger or consolidation of domestic and foreign corporations); or

(ii) To a shareholder of the *surviving* corporation in a merger authorized by this article, other than a merger specified in subclause (i), *unless* such merger effects one or more of the changes specified *in subparagraph (b) (6) of section 806* (Provisions as to certain proceedings) in the rights of the shares held by such shareholder; or

(iii) Notwithstanding subclause (ii) of this clause, to a shareholder for the shares of any class or series of stock, which shares or depository receipts in respect thereof, at the record date fixed to determine the shareholders entitled to receive notice of the meeting of shareholders to vote upon the plan of merger or consolidation, *were listed on a national securities exchange or designated as a national market system security on an interdealer quotation system by the National Association of Securities Dealers, Inc.*

(B) Any sale, lease, exchange or other disposition of all or substantially all of the assets of a corporation which requires shareholder approval under section 909 (Sale, lease, exchange or other disposition of assets) other than a transaction wholly for cash where the shareholders' approval thereof is conditioned upon the dissolution of the corporation and the distribution of substantially all of its net assets to the shareholders in accordance with their respective interests within one year after the date of such transaction.

(C) Any *share exchange* authorized by section 913 in which the corporation is participating as a subject corporation; except that the right to receive payment of the fair value of his shares shall not be available to a shareholder whose shares have not been acquired in the exchange or to a shareholder for the shares of any class or series of stock, which shares or depository receipt in respect thereof, at the record date fixed to determine the shareholders entitled to receive notice of the meeting of shareholders to vote upon the plan of exchange, *were listed on a national securities exchange or designated as a national market system security on an interdealer quotation system by the National Association of Securities Dealers, Inc.*

(2) Any shareholder of the subsidiary corporation in a merger authorized by section 905 or paragraph (c) of section 907, or in a share exchange authorized by paragraph (g) of section 913, who files with the corporation a written notice of election to dissent as provided in paragraph (c) of section 623.

(3) Any shareholder, *not entitled to vote* with respect to a plan of merger or consolidation to which the corporation is a party, whose shares will be cancelled or exchanged in the merger or consolidation for cash or other consideration other than shares of the surviving or consolidated corporation or another corporation.

§ 912 Requirements relating to certain business combinations

(a) For the purposes of this section:

(1) "Affiliate" means a person that directly, or indirectly through one or more intermediaries, controls, or is controlled by, or is under common control with, a specified person.

(2) "Announcement date", when used in reference to any business combination, means the date of the first public announcement of the final, definitive proposal for such business combination.

(3) "Associate", when used to indicate a relationship with any person, means (A) any corporation or organization of which such person is an officer or partner or is, directly or indirectly, the beneficial owner of ten percent or more of any class of voting stock, (B) any trust or other estate in which such person has a substantial beneficial interest or as to which such person serves as trustee or in a similar fiduciary capacity, and (C) any relative or spouse of such person, or any relative of such spouse, who has the same home as such person.

(4) "Beneficial owner", when used with respect to any stock, means a person:

(A) that, individually or with or through any of its affiliates or associates, beneficially owns such stock, directly or indirectly; or

(B) that, individually or with or through any of its affiliates or associates, has (i) the right to acquire such stock (whether such right is exercisable immediately or only after the passage of time), pursuant to any agreement, arrangement or understanding (whether or not in writing), or upon the exercise of conversion rights, exchange rights, warrants or options, or otherwise; provided, however, that a person shall not be deemed the beneficial owner of stock tendered pursuant to a tender or exchange offer made by such person or any of such person's affiliates or associates until such tendered stock is accepted for purchase or exchange; or (ii) the right to vote such stock pursuant to any agreement, arrangement or understanding (whether or not in writing); provided, however, that a person shall not be deemed the beneficial owner of any stock under this item if the agreement, arrangement or understanding to vote such stock (X) arises solely from a revocable proxy or consent given in response to a proxy or consent solicitation made in accordance with the applicable rules and regulations under the Exchange Act and (Y) is not then reportable on a Schedule 13D under the Exchange Act (or any comparable or successor report); or

(C) that has any agreement, arrangement or understanding (whether or not in writing), for the purpose of acquiring, holding, voting (except voting pursuant to a revocable proxy or consent as described in item (ii) of clause (B) of this subparagraph), or disposing of such stock with any other person that beneficially owns, or whose affiliates or associates beneficially own, directly or indirectly, such stock.

(5) "Business combination", when used in reference to any domestic corporation and any interested shareholder of such corporation, means:

(A) any merger or consolidation of such corporation or any subsidiary of such corporation with (i) such interested shareholder or (ii) any other corporation (whether or not itself an interested shareholder of such corporation) which is, or after such merger or consolidation would be, an affiliate or associate of such interested shareholder;

(B) any sale, lease, exchange, mortgage, pledge, transfer or other disposition (in one transaction or a series of transactions) to or with such interested shareholder or any affiliate or associate of such interested shareholder of assets of such corporation or any subsidiary of such corporation (i) having an aggregate market value equal to ten percent or more of the aggregate market value of all the assets, determined on a consolidated basis, of such corporation, (ii) having an aggregate market value equal to ten percent or more of the aggregate market value of all the outstanding stock of such corporation, or (iii) representing ten percent or more of the earning power or net income determined on a consolidated basis, of such corporation;

(C) the issuance or transfer by such corporation or any subsidiary of such corporation (in one transaction or a series of transactions) of any stock of such corporation or any subsidiary of such corporation which has an aggregate market value equal to five percent or more of the aggregate market value of all the outstanding stock of such corporation to such interested shareholder or any affiliate or associate of such interested shareholder except pursuant to the exercise of warrants or rights to purchase stock offered, or a dividend or distribution paid or made, pro rata to all shareholders of such corporation;

(D) the adoption of any plan or proposal for the liquidation or dissolution of such corporation proposed by, or pursuant to any agreement, arrangement or understanding (whether or not in writing) with, such interested shareholder or any affiliate or associate of such interested shareholder;

(E) any reclassification of securities (including, without limitation, any stock split, stock dividend, or other distribution of stock in respect of stock, or any reverse stock split), or recapitalization of such corporation, or any merger or consolidation of such corporation with any subsidiary of such corporation, or any other transaction (whether or not with or into or otherwise involving such interested shareholder), proposed by, or pursuant to any agreement, arrangement or understanding (whether or not in writing) with, such interested shareholder or any affiliate or associate of such interested shareholder, which has the effect, directly or indirectly, of increasing the proportionate share of the outstanding shares of any class or series of voting stock or securities convertible into voting stock of such corporation or any subsidiary of such corporation which is directly or indirectly owned by such interested shareholder or any affiliate or associate of such interested shareholder, except as a result of immaterial changes due to fractional share adjustments; or

(F) any receipt by such interested shareholder or any affiliate or associate of such interested shareholder of the benefit, directly or indirectly (except proportionately as a shareholder of such corporation) of any loans, advances, guarantees, pledges or other financial assistance or any tax credits or other tax advantages provided by or through such corporation.

(6) "Common stock" means any stock other than preferred stock.

(7) "Consummation date", with respect to any business combination, means the date of consummation of such business combination, or, in the case of a business combination as to which a shareholder vote is taken, the later of the business day prior to the vote or twenty days prior to the date of consummation of such business combination.

(8) "Control", including the terms "controlling", "controlled by" and "under common control with", means the possession, directly or indirectly, of the power to direct or cause the direction of the management and policies of a person, whether through the ownership of voting stock, by contract, or otherwise. A person's beneficial ownership of ten percent or more of a corporation's outstanding voting stock shall create a presumption that such person has control of such corporation. Notwithstanding the foregoing, a person shall not be deemed to have control of a corporation if such person holds voting stock, in good faith and not for the purpose of circumventing this section, as an agent, bank, broker, nominee, custodian or trustee for one or more beneficial owners who do not individually or as a group have control of such corporation.

(9) "Exchange Act" means the Act of Congress known as the Securities Exchange Act of 1934, as the same has been or hereafter may be amended from time to time.

(10) "Interested shareholder", when used in reference to any domestic corporation, means any person (other than such corporation or any subsidiary of such corporation) that

(A) (i) is the beneficial owner, directly or indirectly, of *twenty percent or more* of the outstanding voting stock of such corporation; or

(ii) is an *affiliate or associate* of such corporation and at any time within the *five-year* period immediately prior to the date in question was the beneficial owner, directly or indirectly, of *twenty percent or more* of the then outstanding voting stock of such corporation; provided that

(B) for the purpose of determining whether a person is an interested shareholder, the number of shares of voting stock of such corporation deemed to be outstanding shall include shares deemed to be beneficially owned by the person through application of subparagraph four of this paragraph but shall not include any other unissued shares of voting stock of such corporation which may be issuable pursuant to any agreement, arrangement or understanding, or upon exercise of conversion rights, warrants or options, or otherwise.

(11) "Market value", when used in reference to stock or property of any domestic corporation, means:

(A) in the case of stock, the highest closing sale price during the thirty-day period immediately preceding the date in question of a share of such stock on the composite tape for New York stock exchange-listed stocks, or, if such stock is not quoted on such composite tape or if such stock is not listed on such exchange, on the principal United States securities exchange registered under the Exchange Act on which such stock is listed, or, if such stock is not listed on any such exchange, the highest closing bid quotation with respect to a share of such stock during the thirty-day period preceding the date in question on the National Association of Securities Dealers, Inc. Automated Quotations System or any system then in use, or if no such quotations are available, the fair market value on the date in question of a share of such stock as determined by the board of directors of such corporation in good faith; and

(B) in the case of property other than cash or stock, the fair market value of such property on the date in question as determined by the board of directors of such corporation in good faith.

(12) "Preferred stock" means any class or series of stock of a domestic corporation which under the by-laws or certificate of incorporation of such corporation is entitled to receive payment of dividends prior to any payment of dividends on some other class or series of stock, or is entitled in the event of any voluntary liquidation, dissolution or winding up of the corporation to receive payment or distribution of a preferential amount before any payments or distributions are received by some other class or series of stock.

(13) [Repealed]

(14) "Stock" means:

(A) any stock or similar security, any certificate of interest, any participation in any profit sharing agreement, any voting trust certificate, or any certificate of deposit for stock; and

(B) any security convertible, with or without consideration, into stock, or any warrant, call or other option or privilege of buying stock without being bound to do so, or any other security carrying any right to acquire, subscribe to or purchase stock.

(15) "Stock acquisition date", with respect to any person and any domestic corporation, means the date that such person first becomes an interested shareholder of such corporation.

(16) "Subsidiary" of any person means any other corporation of which a majority of the voting stock is owned, directly or indirectly, by such person.

(17) "Voting stock" means shares of capital stock of a corporation entitled to vote generally in the election of directors.

(b) Notwithstanding anything to the contrary contained in this chapter (except the provisions of paragraph (d) of this section), no domestic corporation shall engage in any business combination with any interested shareholder of such corporation for a period of five years following such interested shareholder's stock acquisition date unless such business combination or the purchase of stock made by such interested shareholder on such interested shareholder's stock acquisition date is approved by the board of directors of such corporation prior to such interested shareholder's stock acquisition date. If a good faith proposal is made in writing to the board of directors of such corporation regarding a business combination, the board of directors shall respond, in writing, within thirty days or such shorter period, if any, as may be required by the Exchange Act, setting forth its reasons for its decision regarding such proposal. If a good faith proposal to purchase stock is made in writing to the board of directors of such corporation, the board of directors, unless it responds affirmatively in writing within thirty days or such shorter period, if any, as may be required by the Exchange Act, shall be deemed to have disapproved such stock purchase.

(c) Notwithstanding anything to the contrary contained in this chapter (except the provisions of paragraphs (b) and (d) of this section), no domestic corporation shall engage at any time in any business combination with any interested shareholder of such corporation other than a business combination specified in any one of subparagraph (1), (2) or (3):

(1) A business combination approved by the board of directors of such corporation prior to such interested shareholder's stock acquisition date, or where the purchase of stock made by such interested shareholder on such interested shareholder's stock acquisition date had been approved by the board of directors of such corporation prior to such interested shareholder's stock acquisition date.

(2) A business combination approved by the affirmative vote of the holders of a majority of the outstanding voting stock not beneficially owned by such interested shareholder or any affiliate or associate of such interested shareholder at a meeting called for such purpose no earlier than five years after such interested shareholder's stock acquisition date.

(3) A business combination that meets all of the following conditions:

(A) The aggregate amount of the cash and the market value as of the consummation date of consideration other than cash to be received per share by holders of outstanding shares of common stock of such corporation in such business combination is at least equal to the higher of the following:

(i) the highest per share price paid by such interested shareholder at a time when he was the beneficial owner, directly or indirectly, of five percent or more of the outstanding voting stock of such corporation, for any shares of common stock of the same class or series acquired by it (X) within the five-year period immediately prior to the announcement date with respect to such business combination, or (Y) within the five-year period immediately prior to, or in, the transaction in which such interested shareholder became an interested shareholder, whichever is higher; plus, in either case, interest compounded annually from the earliest date on which such highest per share acquisition price was paid through the consummation date at the rate for one-year United States treasury obligations from time to time in effect; less the aggregate amount of any cash dividends paid, and the market value of any dividends paid other than in cash, per share of common stock since such earliest date, up to the amount of such interest; and

(ii) the market value per share of common stock on the announcement date with respect to such business combination or on such interested shareholder's stock acquisition date, whichever is higher; plus interest compounded annually from such date through the consummation date at the rate for one-year United States treasury obligations from time to time in effect; less the aggregate amount of any cash dividends paid, and the market value of any dividends paid other than in cash, per share of common stock since such date, up to the amount of such interest.

(B) The aggregate amount of the cash and the market value as of the consummation date of consideration other than cash to be received per share by holders of outstanding shares of any class or series of stock, other than common stock, of such corporation is at least equal to the highest of the following (whether or not such interested shareholder has previously acquired any shares of such class or series of stock):

(i) the highest per share price paid by such interested shareholder at a time when he was the beneficial owner, directly or indirectly, of five percent or more of the outstanding voting stock of such corporation, for any shares of such class or series of stock acquired by it (X) within the five-year period immediately prior to the announcement date with respect to such business combination, or (Y) within the five-year period immediately prior to, or in, the transaction in which such interested shareholder became an interested shareholder, whichever is higher; plus, in either case, interest compounded annually from the earliest date on which such highest per share acquisition price was paid through the consummation date at the rate for one-year United States treasury obligations from time to time in effect; less the aggregate amount of any cash dividends paid, and the market value of any dividends paid other than in cash, per share of such class or series of stock since such earliest date, up to the amount of such interest;

(ii) the highest preferential amount per share to which the holders of shares of such class or series of stock are entitled in the event of any voluntary liquidation, dissolution or winding up of such corporation, plus the aggregate amount of any dividends declared or due as to which such holders are entitled prior to payment of dividends on some other class or series of stock (unless the aggregate amount of such dividends is included in such preferential amount); and

(iii) the market value per share of such class or series of stock on the announcement date with respect to such business combination or on such interested shareholder's stock acquisition date, whichever is higher; plus interest compounded annually from such date through the consummation date at the rate for one-year United States treasury obligations from time to time in effect; less the aggregate amount of any cash dividends paid, and the market value of any dividends paid other than in cash, per share of such class or series of stock since such date, up to the amount of such interest.

(C) The consideration to be received by holders of a particular class or series of outstanding stock (including common stock) of such corporation in such business combination is in cash or in the same form as the interested shareholder has used to acquire the largest number of shares of such class or series of stock previously acquired by it, and such consideration shall be distributed promptly.

(D) The holders of all outstanding shares of stock of such corporation not beneficially owned by such interested shareholder immediately prior to the consummation of such business combination are entitled to receive in such business combination cash or other consideration for such shares in compliance with clauses (A), (B) and (C) of this subparagraph.

(E) After such interested shareholder's stock acquisition date and prior to the consummation date with respect to such business combination, such interested shareholder has not become the beneficial owner of any additional shares of voting stock of such corporation except:

(i) as part of the transaction which resulted in such interested shareholder becoming an interested shareholder;

(ii) by virtue of proportionate stock splits, stock dividends or other distributions of stock in respect of stock not constituting a business combination under clause (E) of subparagraph five of paragraph (a) of this section;

(iii) through a business combination meeting all of the conditions of paragraph (b) of this section and this paragraph; or

(iv) through purchase by such interested shareholder at any price which, if such price had been paid in an otherwise permissible business combination the announcement date and consummation date of which were the date of such purchase, would have satisfied the requirements of clauses (A), (B) and (C) of this subparagraph.

(d) The provisions of this section shall not apply:

(1) to any business combination of a domestic corporation that does not have a

class of voting stock registered with the Securities and Exchange Commission pursuant to section twelve of the Exchange Act, unless the certificate of incorporation provides otherwise; or

(2) to any business combination of a domestic corporation whose certificate of incorporation has been amended to provide that such corporation shall be subject to the provisions of this section, which did not have a class of voting stock registered with the Securities and Exchange Commission pursuant to section twelve of the Exchange Act on the effective date of such amendment, and which is a business combination with an interested shareholder whose stock acquisition date is prior to the effective date of such amendment; or

(3) to any business combination of a domestic corporation (i) the original certificate of incorporation of which contains a provision expressly electing not to be governed by this section, or (ii) which adopts an amendment to such corporation's by-laws prior to March thirty-first, nineteen hundred eighty-six, expressly electing not to be governed by this section, or (iii) which adopts an amendment to such corporation's by-laws, approved by the affirmative vote of a majority of votes of the outstanding voting stock of such corporation, excluding the voting stock of interested shareholders and their affiliates and associates, expressly electing not to be governed by this section, provided that such amendment to the by-laws shall not be effective until eighteen months after such vote of such corporation's shareholders and shall not apply to any business combination of such corporation with an interested shareholder whose stock acquisition date is on or prior to the effective date of such amendment; or

(4) to any business combination of a domestic corporation with an interested shareholder of such corporation which became an interested shareholder inadvertently, if such interested shareholder (i) as soon as practicable, divests itself of a sufficient amount of the voting stock of such corporation so that it no longer is the beneficial owner, directly or indirectly, of twenty percent or more of the outstanding voting stock of such corporation, and (ii) would not at any time within the five-year period preceding the announcement date with respect to such business combination have been an interested shareholder but for such inadvertent acquisition; or

(5) to any business combination with an interested shareholder who was the beneficial owner, directly or indirectly, of five percent or more of the outstanding voting stock of such corporation on October thirtieth, nineteen hundred eighty-five, and remained so to such interested shareholder's stock acquisition date.

§ 913 Share exchanges

(a) (1) Two domestic corporations may, as provided in this section, participate in the consummation of a plan for binding share exchanges.

(2) Whenever used in this article:

(A) "Acquiring corporation" means a corporation that is participating in a procedure pursuant to which such corporation is acquiring all of the outstanding shares of one or more classes of a subject corporation.

(B) "Subject corporation" means a corporation that is participating in a procedure pursuant to which all of the outstanding shares of one or more classes of such corporation are being acquired by an acquiring corporation.

(b) The board of the acquiring corporation and the board of the subject corporation shall adopt a plan of exchange, setting forth:

(1) The name of the acquiring corporation and the name of the subject corporation, and, if the name of either of them has been changed, the name under which it was formed;

(2) As to the acquiring corporation and the subject corporation, the designation and number of outstanding shares of each class and series, specifying the classes and series entitled to vote and further specifying each class and series, if any, entitled to vote as a class; and, if the number of any such shares is subject to change prior to the effective date of the exchange, the manner in which such change may occur;

(3) The terms and conditions of the proposed exchange, including the manner and basis of exchanging the shares to be acquired for shares, bonds or other securities of the acquiring corporation, or the cash or other consideration to be paid or delivered in exchange for such shares to be acquired, or a combination thereof; and

(4) Such other provisions with respect to the proposed exchange as the board considers necessary or desirable.

(c) The board of the subject corporation, upon adopting the plan of exchange, shall submit such plan, except as provided in paragraph (g) of this section, to a vote of shareholders in accordance with the following:

(1) Notice of meeting shall be given to each shareholder of record, as of the record date fixed pursuant to section 604 (Fixing record date), whether or not entitled to vote. A copy of the plan of exchange or an outline of the material features of the plan shall accompany such notice.

(2) (A) The plan of exchange shall be adopted at a meeting of shareholders by (i) for any corporation in existence on the effective date of subclause (ii) of this clause, two-thirds of the votes of all outstanding shares entitled to vote thereon and (ii) for any corporation in existence on the effective date of this sub-clause the certificate of incorporation of which expressly provides such and for any corporation incorporated after the effective date of this subclause, a majority of the votes of all outstanding shares entitled to vote thereon. Notwithstanding any provision in the certificate of incorporation, the holders of shares of a class or series of a class shall be entitled to vote together and to vote as a separate class if both of the following conditions are satisfied:

1. Such shares will be converted into shares of the acquiring corporation, and

2. The certificate or articles of incorporation of the acquiring corporation immediately after the share exchange would contain any provision which is not contained in the certificate of incorporation of the subject corporation and which, if contained in an amendment to the certificate of incorporation

of the subject corporation, would entitle the holders of shares of such class or such one or more series to vote and to vote as a separate class thereon pursuant to section 804 (Class voting on amendment).

In such case, in addition to the authorization of the exchange by the proportion of votes indicated above of all outstanding shares entitled to vote thereon, the exchange shall be authorized by a majority of the votes of all outstanding shares of the class entitled to vote as a separate class. If any provision referred to in subclause 2 of this clause (A) would affect the rights of the holders of shares of only one or more series of any class but not the entire class, then only the holders of those series whose rights would be affected shall together be considered a separate class for purposes of this section.

Notwithstanding shareholder authorization and at any time prior to the filing of the certificate of exchange, the plan of exchange may be abandoned pursuant to a provision for such abandonment, if any, contained in the plan of exchange.

(B) Any corporation may adopt an amendment of the certificate of incorporation which provides that such plan of exchange shall be adopted at a meeting of the shareholders by vote of a specified proportion of the holders of outstanding shares, or class or series of shares, entitled to vote thereon, provided that such proportion may not be less than a majority and subject to the second sentence of clause (A) of this subparagraph (2).

(d) After adoption of the plan of exchange by the board of the acquiring corporation and the board of the subject corporation and by the shareholders of the subject corporation entitled to vote thereon, unless the exchange is abandoned in accordance with paragraph (c), a certificate of exchange, entitled "Certificate of exchange of shares of . . . . , subject corporation, for shares of . . . . , acquiring corporation, or other consideration, under section 913 of the Business Corporation Law", shall be signed on behalf of each corporation and delivered to the department of state. It shall set forth:

(1) the statements required by subparagraphs (1) and (2) of paragraph (b) of this section;

(2) the effective date of the exchange if other than the date of filing of the certificate of exchange by the department of state;

(3) the date when the certificate of incorporation of each corporation was filed by the department of state;

(4) the designation of the shares to be acquired by the acquiring corporation and a statement of the consideration for such shares; and

(5) the manner in which the exchange was authorized with respect to each corporation.

(e) Upon the filing of the certificate of exchange by the department of state or on such date subsequent thereto, not to exceed thirty days, as shall be set forth in such certificate, the exchange shall be effected. When such exchange has been effected, ownership of the shares to be acquired pursuant to the plan of exchange shall vest in the acquiring corporation, whether or not the certificates for such shares have been surrendered for exchange, and the acquiring corporation shall be entitled to have new certificates registered in its name or at its direction. Shareholders whose shares have been so acquired shall become entitled to the shares, bonds or other securities of the acquiring corporation, or the cash or other consideration, required to be paid or delivered in exchange for such shares pursuant to the plan. Subject to any terms of the plan regarding surrender of certificates theretofore evidencing the shares so acquired and regarding whether such certificates shall thereafter evidence securities of the acquiring corporation, such certificates shall thereafter evidence only the right to receive the consideration required to be paid or delivered in exchange for such shares pursuant to the plan or, in the case of dissenting shareholders, their rights under section 910 (Right of shareholder to receive payment for shares upon merger or consolidation, or sale, lease, exchange or other disposition of assets, or share exchange) and section 623 (Procedure to enforce shareholder's right to receive payment for shares).

(f) (1) A foreign corporation and a domestic corporation may participate in a share exchange, but, if the subject corporation is a foreign corporation, only if such exchange is permitted by the laws of the jurisdiction under which such foreign corporation is incorporated. With respect to such exchange, any reference in subparagraph (2) of paragraph (a) of this section to a corporation shall, unless the context otherwise requires, include both domestic and foreign corporations, and the provisions of paragraphs (b), (c), (d) and (e) of this section shall apply, except to the extent otherwise provided in this paragraph.

(2) With respect to procedure, including the requirement of shareholder authorization, a domestic corporation shall comply with the provisions of this chapter relating to share exchanges in which domestic corporations are participating, and a foreign corporation shall comply with the applicable provisions of the law of the jurisdiction under which it is incorporated.

(3) If the subject corporation is a foreign corporation, the certificate of exchange shall set forth, in addition to the matters specified in paragraph (d), the jurisdiction and date of incorporation of such corporation and a statement that the exchange is permitted by the laws of the jurisdiction of such corporation and is in compliance therewith.

(g) (1) Any corporation owning at least ninety percent of the outstanding common shares, having full voting rights, of another corporation may acquire by exchange the remainder of such outstanding common shares, without the authorization of the shareholders of any such corporation and with the effect provided for in paragraph (e) of this section. The board of the acquiring corporation shall adopt a plan of exchange, setting forth the matters specified in paragraph (b) of this section. A copy of such plan of exchange or an outline of the material features thereof shall be given, personally or by mail, to all holders of shares of the subject corporation that are not owned by the acquiring corporation, unless the giving of such copy or outline has been waived by such holders.

(2) A certificate of exchange, entitled "Certificate of exchange of shares of . . . . , subject corporation, for shares of . . . . , acquiring corporation, or other consideration, under paragraph (g) of section 913 of the Business Corporation Law" and complying with the provisions of paragraph (d) and, if applicable, subparagraph (3) of paragraph (f) shall be signed, verified and

delivered to the department of state by the acquiring corporation, but not less than thirty days after the giving of a copy or outline of the material features of the plan of exchange to shareholders of the subject corporation, or at any time after the waiving thereof by the holders of all the outstanding shares of the subject corporation not owned by the acquiring corporation.

(3) The right of exchange of shares granted by this paragraph to certain corporations shall not preclude the exercise by such corporations of any other right of exchange under this article.

(4) The procedure for the exchange of shares of a subject corporation under this paragraph (g) of this section shall be available where either the subject corporation or the acquiring corporation is a foreign corporation, and, in case the subject corporation is a foreign corporation, where such exchange is permitted by the laws of the jurisdiction under which such foreign corporation is incorporated.

(h) This section does not limit the power of a domestic or foreign corporation to acquire all or part of the shares of one or more classes of another domestic or foreign corporation by means of a voluntary exchange or otherwise.

(i) (1) A binding share exchange pursuant to this section shall constitute a "business combination" pursuant to section nine hundred twelve of this chapter (Requirements relating to certain business combinations) if the subject corporation is a domestic corporation and the acquiring corporation is an "interested shareholder" of the subject corporation, as such term is defined in section nine hundred twelve of this chapter.

(2) With respect to convertible securities and other securities evidencing a right to acquire shares of a subject corporation, a binding share exchange pursuant to this section shall have the same effect on the rights of the holders of such securities as a merger of the subject corporation.

(3) A binding share exchange pursuant to this section which is effectuated on or after September first, nineteen hundred ninety-one is intended to have the same effect as a "merger" in which the subject corporation is a surviving corporation, within the meaning of any provision of the certificate of incorporation, bylaws or other contract or instrument by which the subject corporation was bound on September first, nineteen hundred eighty-six, unless it is apparent on the face of such instrument that the term "merger" was not intended to include a binding share exchange.

§ 105 Certificates; corrections

Any certificate or other instrument relating to a domestic or foreign corporation filed by the department of state under this chapter *may be corrected* with respect to any informality or error apparent on the face, incorrect statement or defect in the execution thereof including the deletion of any matter not permitted to be stated therein. A certificate, entitled "Certificate of correction of . . . . (correct title of certificate and name of corporation)" shall be signed, verified and delivered to the department of state. It shall set forth the name of the corporation, the date the certificate to be corrected was filed by the department of state, a statement as to the nature of the informality, error, incorrect statement or defect, the provision in the certificate as corrected or eliminated and if the execution was defective, the proper execution. The filing of the certificate by the department of state shall not alter the effective time of the instrument being corrected, which shall remain as its original effective time, and shall not affect any right or liability accrued or incurred before such filing. A corporate name may not be changed or corrected under this section. The provisions of this section shall apply to all instruments and certificates heretofore and hereafter filed with the department of state.

GENERAL CORPORATION LAW OF THE STATE OF DELAWARE

Certain of the subsections, or portions thereof of the Delaware statutes set forth below, have been italicized to facilitate class discussion.

§ 151 Classes and series of stock; redemption; rights

(a) Every corporation may issue 1 or more classes of stock or 1 or more series of stock within any class thereof, any or all of which classes may be of stock with par value or stock without par value and which classes or series may have such voting powers, full or limited, or no voting powers, and such designations, preferences and relative, participating, optional or other special rights, and qualifications, limitations or restrictions thereof, as shall be stated and expressed in the certificate of incorporation or of any amendment thereto, or in the resolution or resolutions providing for the issue of such stock adopted by the board of directors *pursuant to authority expressly vested in it* by the provisions of its certificate of incorporation. Any of the voting powers, designations, preferences, rights and qualifications, limitations or restrictions of any such class or series of stock may be made dependent upon facts ascertainable outside the certificate of incorporation or of any amendment thereto, or outside the resolution or resolutions providing for the issue of such stock adopted by the board of directors pursuant to authority expressly vested in it by its certificate of incorporation, provided that the manner in which such facts shall operate upon the voting powers, designations, preferences, rights and qualifications, limitations or restrictions of such class or series of stock is clearly and expressly set forth in the certificate of incorporation or in the resolution or resolutions providing for the issue of such stock adopted by the board of directors. The term "facts," as used in this subsection, includes, but is not limited to, the occurrence of any event, including a determination or action by any person or body, including the corporation. The power to increase or decrease or otherwise adjust the capital stock as provided in this chapter shall apply to all or any such classes of stock.

(b) Any stock of any class or series may be made *subject to redemption* by the corporation at its option *or at the option of the holders* of such stock or upon the happening of a specified event; provided however, that immediately following any such redemption the corporation shall have outstanding 1 or more shares of 1 or more classes or series of stock, which share, or shares together, shall have full voting powers. Notwithstanding the limitation stated in the foregoing proviso:

(1) Any stock of a regulated investment company registered under the Investment Company Act of 1940 [15 U.S.C. § 80 a-1 et seq.], as heretofore or hereafter amended, may be made subject to redemption by the corporation at its option or at the option of the holders of such stock.

(2) Any stock of a corporation which holds (directly or indirectly) a license or franchise from a governmental agency to conduct its business or is a member of a national securities exchange, which license, franchise or membership is conditioned upon some or all of the holders of its stock possessing prescribed qualifications, may be made subject to redemption by the corporation to the extent necessary to prevent the loss of such license, franchise or membership or to reinstate it. Any stock which may be made *redeemable* under this section *may be redeemed for cash, property or rights, including securities of the same or another corporation, at such time or times, price or prices, or rate or rates, and with such adjustments, as shall be stated in the certificate of incorporation or in the resolution or resolutions providing for the issue of such stock adopted by the board of directors pursuant to subsection (a) of this section.*

(c) The holders of preferred or special stock of any class or of any series thereof shall be entitled to receive dividends at such rates, on such conditions and at such times as shall be stated in the certificate of incorporation or in the resolution or resolutions providing for the issue of such stock adopted by the board of directors as hereinabove provided, payable in preference to, or in such relation to, the dividends payable on any other class or classes or of any other series of stock, and cumulative or noncumulative as shall be so stated and expressed. When dividends upon the preferred and special stocks, if any, to the extent of the preference to which such stocks are entitled, shall have been paid or declared and set apart for payment, a dividend on the remaining class or classes or series of stock may then be paid out of the remaining assets of the corporation available for dividends as elsewhere in this chapter provided.

(d) The holders of the preferred or special stock of any class or of any series thereof shall be entitled to such rights upon the dissolution of, or upon any distribution of the assets of, the corporation as shall be stated in the certificate of incorporation or in the resolution or resolutions providing for the issue of such stock adopted by the board of directors as hereinabove provided.

(e) Any stock of any class or of any series thereof may be made *convertible into, or exchangeable for, at the option of either* the holder or the corporation or upon the happening of a specified event, shares of any other class or classes or any other series of the same or any other class or classes of stock of the corporation, at such price or prices or at such rate or rates of exchange and with such adjustments as shall be stated in the certificate of incorporation or in the resolution or resolutions providing for the issue of such stock adopted by the board of directors as herein above provided.

(f) If any corporation shall be authorized to issue more than 1 class of stock or more than 1 series of any class, the powers, designations, preferences and relative, participating, optional, or other special rights of each class of stock or series thereof and the qualifications, limitations or restrictions of such preferences and/or rights shall be set forth in full or summarized on the face or back of the certificate which the corporation shall issue to represent such class or series of stock, provided that, except as otherwise provided in § 202 of this title, in lieu of the foregoing requirements, there may be set forth on the face or back of the certificate which the corporation shall issue to represent such class or series of stock, a statement that the corporation will furnish without charge to each stockholder who so requests the powers, designations, preferences and relative, participating, optional, or other special rights of each class of stock or series thereof and the qualifications, limitations or restrictions of such preferences and/or rights. Within a reasonable time after the issuance or transfer of uncertificated stock, the corporation shall send to the registered owner thereof a written notice containing the information required to be set forth or stated on certificates pursuant to this section or § 156, 202(a) or 218(a) of this title or with respect to this section a statement that the corporation will furnish without charge to each stockholder who so requests the powers, designations, preferences and relative participating, optional or other special rights of each class of stock or series thereof and the qualifications, limitations or restrictions of such preferences and/or rights. Except as otherwise expressly provided by law, the rights and obligations of the holders of uncertificated stock and the rights and obligations of the holders of certificates representing stock of the same class and series shall be identical.

(g) When any corporation desires to issue any shares of stock of any class or of any series of any class of which the powers, designations, preferences and relative, participating, optional or other rights, if any, or the qualifications, limitations or restrictions thereof, if any, shall not have been set forth in the certificate of incorporation or in any amendment thereto but shall be provided for in a resolution or resolutions adopted by the board of directors pursuant to authority expressly vested in it by the certificate of incorporation or any amendment thereto, a certificate of designations setting forth a copy of such resolution or resolutions and the number of shares of stock of such class or series as to which the resolution or resolutions apply shall be executed, acknowledged, filed and shall become effective, in accordance with § 103 of this title. Unless otherwise provided in any such resolution or resolutions, the number of shares of stock of any such series to which such resolution or resolutions apply may be increased (but not above the total number of authorized shares of the class) or decreased (but not below the number of shares thereof then outstanding) by a certificate likewise executed, acknowledged and filed setting forth a statement that a specified increase or decrease therein had been authorized and directed by a resolution or resolutions likewise adopted by the board of directors. In case the number of such shares shall be decreased the number of shares so specified in the certificate shall resume the status which they had prior to the adoption of the first resolution or resolutions. When no shares of any such class or series are outstanding, either because none were issued or because no issued shares of any such class or series remain outstanding, a certificate setting forth a resolution or resolutions adopted by the board of directors that none of the authorized shares of such class or series are outstanding, and that none will be issued subject to the certificate of designations previously filed with respect to such class or series, may be executed, acknowledged and filed in accordance with § 103 of this title and, when such certificate becomes effective, it shall have the effect of eliminating from the certificate of incorporation all matters set forth in the certificate of designations with respect to such class or series of stock. Unless otherwise provided in the certificate of incorporation, if no shares of stock have been issued of a class or series of stock established by a resolution of the board of directors, the voting powers, designations, preferences and relative, participating, optional or other rights, if any, or the qualifications, limitations or restrictions thereof, may be amended by a resolution or resolutions adopted by the board of directors. A certificate which

(1) states that no shares of the class or series have been issued,

(2) sets forth a copy of the resolution or resolutions and

(3) if the designation of the class or series is being changed, indicates the original designation and the new designation, shall be executed, acknowledged and filed and shall become effective, in accordance with § 103 of this title. When any certificate filed under this subsection becomes effective, it shall have the effect of amending the certificate of incorporation; except that neither the filing of such certificate nor the filing of a restated certificate of incorporation pursuant to § 245 of this title shall prohibit the board of directors from subsequently adopting such resolutions as authorized by this subsection.

§ 160 Corporation's powers respecting ownership, voting, etc., of its own stock; rights of stock called for redemption

(a) Every corporation may purchase, redeem, receive, take or otherwise acquire, own and hold, sell, lend, exchange, transfer or otherwise dispose of, pledge, use and otherwise deal in and with its own shares; *provided, however*, that no corporation shall:

(1) Purchase or redeem its own shares of capital stock for cash or other property when the capital of the corporation is impaired or when such purchase or redemption would cause any impairment of the capital of the corporation, except that a corporation may purchase or redeem out of capital any of its own shares which are entitled upon any distribution of its assets, whether by divided or in liquidation, to a preference over another class or series of its stock, or, if no shares entitled to such a preference are outstanding, any of its own shares, if such shares will be retired upon their acquisition and the capital of the corporation reduced in accordance with §§ 243 and 244 of this title. Nothing in this subsection shall invalidate or otherwise affect a note, debenture or other obligation of a corporation given by it as consideration for its acquisition by purchase, redemption or exchange of its shares of stock if at the time such note, debenture or obligation was delivered by the corporation its capital was not then impaired or did not thereby become impaired;

(2) Purchase, for more than the price at which they may then be redeemed, any of its shares which are redeemable at the option of the corporation; or

(3) Redeem any of its shares unless their redemption is authorized by subsection (b) of § 151 of this title and then only in accordance with such section and the certificate of incorporation.

(b) Nothing in this section limits or affects a corporation's right to resell any of its shares theretofore purchased or redeemed out of surplus and which have not been retired, for such consideration as shall be fixed by the board of directors.

(c) Shares of its own capital stock belonging to the corporation or to another corporation, if a majority of the shares entitled to vote in the election of directors of such other corporation is held, directly or indirectly, by the corporation, shall neither be entitled to vote nor be counted for quorum purposes. Nothing in this section shall be construed as limiting the right of any corporation to vote stock, including but not limited to its own stock, held by it in a fiduciary capacity.

(d) Shares which have been called for redemption shall not be deemed to be outstanding shares for the purpose of voting or determining the total number of shares entitled to vote on any matter on and after the date on which written notice of redemption has been sent to holders thereof and a sum sufficient to redeem such shares has been irrevocably deposited or set aside to pay the redemption price to the holders of the shares upon surrender of certificates therefor.

§ 170 Dividends; payment; wasting asset corporations

(a) The directors of every corporation, subject to any restrictions contained in its certificate of incorporation, may declare and pay dividends upon the shares of its capital stock, or to its members if the corporation is a nonstock corporation, either (1) out of its surplus, as defined in and computed in accordance with §§ 154 and 244 of this title, *or (2) in case there shall be no such surplus, out of its net profits for the fiscal year in which the dividend is declared and/or the preceding fiscal year.* If the capital of the corporation, computed in accordance with §§ 154 and 244 of this title, shall have been diminished by depreciation in the value of its property, or by losses, or otherwise, to an amount less than the aggregate amount of the capital represented by the issued and outstanding stock of all classes having a preference upon the distribution of assets, the directors of such corporation shall not declare and pay out of such net profits any dividends upon any shares of any classes of its capital stock until the deficiency in the amount of capital represented by the issued and outstanding stock of all classes having a preference upon the distribution of assets shall have been repaired. *Nothing in this subsection shall invalidate or otherwise affect a note, debenture or other obligation of the corporation paid by it as a dividend on shares of its stock, or any payment made thereon, if at the time such note, debenture or obligation was delivered by the corporation, the corporation had either surplus or net profits as provided in clauses (1) or (2) of this subsection from which the dividend could lawfully have been paid.*

(b) Subject to any restrictions contained in its certificate of incorporation, the directors of any corporation engaged in the exploitation of wasting assets (including but not limited to a corporation engaged in the exploitation of natural resources or other wasting assets, including patents, or engaged primarily in the liquidation of specific assets) may determine the net profits derived from the exploitation of such wasting assets or the net proceeds derived from such liquidation without taking into consideration the depletion of such assets resulting from lapse of time, consumption, liquidation or exploitation of such assets.

§ 242 Amendment of certificate of incorporation after receipt of payment for stock; nonstock corporations

(a) After a corporation has received payment for any of its capital stock, it may amend its certificate of incorporation, from time to time, in any and as many respects as may be desired, so long as its certificate of incorporation as amended would contain only such provisions as it would be lawful and proper to insert in an original certificate of incorporation filed at the time of the filing of the amendment;

and, if a change in stock or the rights of stockholders, or an exchange, reclassification, subdivision, combination or cancellation of stock or rights of stockholders is to be made, such provisions as may be necessary to effect such change, exchange, reclassification, subdivision, combination or cancellation. In particular, and without limitation upon such general power of amendment, a corporation may amend its certificate of incorporation, from time to time, so as:

(1) To change its corporate name; or

(2) To change, substitute, enlarge or diminish the nature of its business or its corporate powers and purposes; or

(3) To increase or decrease its authorized capital stock or to reclassify the same, by changing the number, par value, designations, preferences, or relative, participating, optional, or other special rights of the shares, or the qualifications, limitations or restrictions of such rights, or by changing shares with par value into shares without par value, or shares without par value into shares with par value either with or without increasing or decreasing the number of shares, or by subdividing or combining the outstanding shares of any class or series of a class of shares into a greater or lesser number of outstanding shares; or

(4) To cancel or otherwise affect the right of the holders of the shares of any class to receive dividends which have accrued but have not been declared; or

(5) To create new classes of stock having rights and preferences either prior and superior or subordinate and inferior to the stock of any class then authorized, whether issued or unissued; or

(6) To change the period of its duration.

Any or all such changes or alterations may be effected by 1 certificate of amendment.

(b) Every amendment authorized by subsection (a) of this section shall be made and effected in the following manner:

(1) If the corporation has capital stock, its board of directors shall adopt a resolution setting forth the amendment proposed, declaring its advisability, and either calling a special meeting of the stockholders entitled to vote in respect thereof for the consideration of such amendment or directing that the amendment proposed be considered at the next annual meeting of the stockholders. Such special or annual meeting shall be called and held upon notice in accordance with § 222 of this title. The notice shall set forth such amendment in full or a brief summary of the changes to be effected thereby, as the directors shall deem advisable. At the meeting a vote of the stockholders entitled to vote thereon shall be taken for and against the proposed amendment. If a majority of the outstanding stock entitled to vote thereon, and a majority of the outstanding stock of each class entitled to vote thereon as a class has been voted in favor of the amendment, a certificate setting forth the amendment and certifying that such amendment has been duly adopted in accordance with this section shall be executed, acknowledged and filed and shall become effective in accordance with § 103 of this title.

(2) The holders of the outstanding shares of a class *shall be entitled to vote as a class upon a proposed amendment*, whether or not entitled to vote thereon by the certificate of incorporation, if the amendment would increase or decrease the aggregate number of authorized shares of such class, increase or decrease the par value of the shares of such class, *or alter or change the powers, preferences, or special rights of the shares of such class so as to affect them adversely*. If any proposed amendment would alter or change the powers, preferences, or special rights of 1 or more series of any class so as to affect them adversely, but shall not so affect the entire class, then only the shares of the series so affected by the amendment shall be considered a separate class for the purposes of this paragraph. The number of authorized shares of any such class or classes of stock may be increased or decreased (but not below the number of shares thereof then outstanding) by the affirmative vote of the holders of a majority of the stock of the corporation entitled to vote irrespective of this subsection, if so provided in the original certificate of incorporation, in any amendment thereto which created such class or classes of stock or which was adopted prior to the issuance of any shares of such class or classes of stock, or in any amendment thereto which was authorized by a resolution or resolution adopted by the affirmative vote of the holders of a majority of such class or classes of stock.

(3) If the corporation has no capital stock, then the governing body thereof shall adopt a resolution setting forth the amendment proposed and declaring its advisability. If a majority of all the members of the governing body shall vote in favor of such amendment, a certificate thereof shall be executed, acknowledged and filed and shall become effective in accordance with § 103 of this title. The certificate of incorporation of any such corporation without capital stock may contain a provision requiring any amendment thereto to be approved by a specified number or percentage of the members or of any specified class of members of such corporation in which event such proposed amendment shall be submitted to the members or to any specified class of members of such corporation without capital stock in the same manner, so far as applicable, as is provided in this section for an amendment to the certificate of incorporation of a stock corporation; and in the event of the adoption thereof, by such members a certificate evidencing such amendment shall be executed, acknowledged and filed and shall become effective in accordance with § 103 of this title.

(4) Whenever the certificate of incorporation shall require for action by the board of directors, by the holders of any class or series of shares or by the holders of any other securities having voting power the vote of a greater number or proportion than is required by any section of this title, the provision of the certificate of incorporation requiring such greater vote shall not be altered, amended or repealed except by such greater vote.

(c) The resolution authorizing a proposed amendment to the certificate of incorporation may provide that at any time prior to the effectiveness of the filing of the amendment with the Secretary of State, notwithstanding authorization of the proposed amendment by the stockholders of the corporation or by the members of a nonstock corporation, the board of directors or governing body may abandon such proposed amendment without further action by the stockholders or members.

§ 251 Merger or consolidation of domestic corporations and limited liability company

(a) Any 2 or more corporations existing under the laws of this State may merge into a single corporation, which may be any 1 of the constituent corporations or may consolidate into a new corporation formed by the consolidation, pursuant to an agreement of merger or consolidation, as the case may be, complying and approved in accordance with this section.

(b) The board of directors of each corporation which desires to merge or consolidate shall adopt a resolution approving an agreement of merger or consolidation and declaring its advisability. The agreement shall state:

(1) The terms and conditions of the merger or consolidation;

(2) the mode of carrying the same into effect;

(3) in the case of *a merger*, such *amendments or changes* in the certificate of incorporation of the surviving corporation as are desired to be effected by the merger, or, if no such amendments or changes are desired, a statement that the certificate of incorporation of the surviving corporation shall be its certificate of incorporation;

(4) in the case of a consolidation, that the certificate of incorporation of the resulting corporation shall be as is set forth in an attachment to the agreement;

(5) the manner, if any, of *converting* the shares of each of the constituent corporations into shares or other securities of the corporation surviving or resulting from the merger or consolidation, or of cancelling some or all of such shares, *and, if any shares of any of the constituent corporations are not to remain outstanding, to be converted solely into shares or other securities of the surviving or resulting corporation or to be cancelled, the cash, property, rights or securities of any other corporation or entity which the holders of such shares are to receive in exchange for, or upon conversion of such shares* and the surrender of any certificates evidencing them, which cash, property, rights or securities of any other corporation or entity may be in addition to or in lieu of shares or other securities of the surviving or resulting corporation; and

(6) such other details or provisions as are deemed desirable, including, without limiting the generality of the foregoing, a provision for the payment of cash in lieu of the issuance or recognition of fractional shares, interests or rights, or for any other arrangement with respect thereto, consistent with § 155 of this title. The agreement so adopted shall be executed and acknowledged in accordance with § 103 of this title. Any of the terms of the agreement of merger or consolidation may be made dependent upon facts ascertainable outside of such agreement, provided that the manner in which such facts shall operate upon the terms of the agreement is clearly and expressly set forth in the agreement of merger or consolidation. The term "facts," as used in the preceding sentence, includes, but is not limited to, the occurrence of any event, including a determination or action by any person or body, including the corporation.

(c) The agreement required by subsection (b) of this section shall be submitted to the stockholders of each constituent corporation at an annual or special meeting for the purpose of acting on the agreement. Due notice of the time, place and purpose of the meeting shall be mailed to each holder of stock, whether voting or nonvoting, of the corporation at the stockholder's address as it appears on the records of the corporation, at least 20 days prior to the date of the meeting. The notice shall contain a copy of the agreement or a brief summary thereof, as the directors shall deem advisable. At the meeting, the agreement shall be considered and a vote taken for its adoption or rejection. *If a majority of the outstanding stock of the corporation entitled to vote thereon* shall be voted for the adoption of the agreement, that fact shall be certified on the agreement by the secretary or assistant secretary of the corporation. If the agreement shall be so adopted and certified by each constituent corporation, it shall then be filed and shall become effective, in accordance with § 103 of this title. In lieu of filing the agreement of merger or consolidation required by this section, the surviving or resulting corporation may file a certificate of merger or consolidation, executed in accordance with § 103 of this title, which states:

(1) The name and state of incorporation of each of the constituent corporations;

(2) That an agreement of merger or consolidation has been approved, adopted, certified, executed and acknowledged by each of the constituent corporations in accordance with this section;

(3) The name of the surviving or resulting corporation;

(4) In the case of a merger, such amendments or changes in the certificate of incorporation of the surviving corporation as are desired to be effected by the merger, or, if no such amendments or changes are desired, a statement that the certificate of incorporation of the surviving corporation shall be its certificate of incorporation;

(5) In the case of a consolidation, that the certificate of incorporation of the resulting corporation shall be as set forth in an attachment to the certificate;

(6) That the executed agreement of consolidation or merger is on file at an office of the surviving corporation, stating the address thereof; and

(7) That a copy of the agreement of consolidation or merger will be furnished by the surviving corporation, on request and without cost, to any stockholder of any constituent corporation.

(d) Any agreement of merger or consolidation may contain a provision that at any time prior to the time that the agreement (or a certificate in lieu thereof) filed with the Secretary of State becomes effective in accordance with § 103 of this title, the agreement may be terminated by the board of directors of any constituent corporation notwithstanding approval of the agreement by the stockholders of all or any of the constituent corporations; in the event the agreement of merger or consolidation is terminated after the filing of the agreement (or a certificate in lieu thereof) with the Secretary of State but before the agreement (or a certificate in lieu thereof) has become effective, a certificate of termination or merger or consolidation shall be filed in accordance with § 103 of this title. Any agreement of merger or consolidation may contain a provision that the boards of directors of the constituent corporations may amend the agreement at any time prior to the time that the agreement (or a certificate in lieu thereof) filed with the Secretary of State becomes effective in accordance with § 103 of this title, provided that an amendment made subsequent to the adoption of the agreement by the stockholders of any constituent corporation shall not

(1) alter or change the amount or kind of shares, securities, cash, property and/or rights to be received in exchange for or on conversion of all or any of the shares of any class or series thereof of such constituent corporation,

(2) alter or change any term of the certificate of incorporation of the surviving corporation to be effected by the merger or consolidation, or

(3) alter or change any of the terms and conditions of the agreement if such alteration or change would adversely affect the holders of any class or series thereof of such constituent corporation; in the event the agreement of merger or consolidation is amended after the filing thereof with the Secretary of State but before the agreement has become effective, a certificate of amendment of merger or consolidation shall be filed in accordance with § 103 of this title.

(e) In the case of a *merger*, the certificate of incorporation of the surviving corporation *shall automatically be amended* to the extent, if any, that changes in the certificate of incorporation are set forth in the agreement of merger.

(f) Notwithstanding the requirements of subsection (c) of this section, unless required by its certificate of incorporation, no vote of stockholders of a constituent corporation surviving a merger shall be necessary to authorize a merger if

(1) the agreement of merger does not amend in any respect the certificate of incorporation of such constituent corporation,

(2) each share of stock of such constituent corporation outstanding immediately prior to the effective date of the merger is to be an identical outstanding or treasury share of the surviving corporation after the effective date of the merger, and

(3) either no shares of common stock of the surviving corporation and no shares, securities or obligations convertible into such stock are to be issued or delivered under the plan of merger, or the authorized unissued shares or the treasury shares of common stock of the surviving corporation to be issued or delivered under the plan of merger plus those initially issuable upon conversion of any other shares, securities or obligations to be issued or delivered under such plan do not exceed 20% of the shares of common stock of such constituent corporation outstanding immediately prior to the effective date of the merger. No vote of stockholders of a constituent corporation shall be necessary to authorize a merger or consolidation if no shares of the stock of such corporation shall have been issued prior to the adoption by the board of directors of the resolution approving the agreement of merger or consolidation. If an agreement of merger is adopted by the constituent corporation surviving the merger, by action of its board of directors and without any vote of its stockholders pursuant to this subsection, the secretary or assistant secretary of that corporation shall certify on the agreement that the agreement has been adopted pursuant to this subsection and, (1) if it has been adopted pursuant to the first sentence of this

subsection, that the conditions specified in that sentence have been satisfied, or (2) if it has been adopted pursuant to the second sentence of this subsection, that no shares of stock of such corporation were issued prior to the adoption by the board of directors of the resolution approving the agreement of merger or consolidation. The agreement so adopted and certified shall then be filed and shall become effective, in accordance with § 103 of this title. Such filing shall constitute a representation by the person who executes the agreement that the facts stated in the certificate remain true immediately prior to such filing.

(g) Notwithstanding the requirements of subsection (c) of this section, unless expressly required by its certificate of incorporation, no vote of stockholders of a constituent corporation shall be necessary to authorize a merger with or into a single direct or indirect wholly-owned subsidiary of such constituent corporation if:

(1) such constituent corporation and the direct or indirect wholly-owned subsidiary of such constituent corporation are the only constituent corporations to the merger;

(2) each share or fraction of a share of the capital stock of the constituent corporation outstanding immediately prior to the effective time of the merger is converted in the merger into a share or equal fraction of share of capital stock of a holding company having the same designations, rights, powers and preferences, and the qualifications, limitations and restrictions thereof, as the share of stock of the constituent corporation being converted in the merger;

(3) the holding company and the constituent corporation are corporations of this State and the direct or indirect wholly-owned subsidiary that is the other constituent entity to the merger is a corporation or limited liability company of this State;

(4) the certificate of incorporation and by-laws of the holding company immediately following the effective time of the merger contain provisions identical to the certificate of incorporation and by-laws of the constituent corporation immediately prior to the effective time of the merger (other than provisions, if any, regarding the incorporator or incorporators, the corporate name, the registered office and agent, the initial board of directors and the initial subscribers for shares and such provisions contained in any amendment to the certificate of incorporation as were necessary to effect a change, exchange, reclassification, subdivision, combination or cancellation of stock, if such change, exchange, reclassification, subdivision, combination or cancellation has become effective);

(5) as a result of the merger the constituent corporation or its successor corporation becomes or remains a direct or indirect wholly-owned subsidiary of the holding company;

(6) the directors of the constituent corporation become or remain the directors of the holding company upon the effective time of the merger;

(7) the organizational documents of the surviving entity immediately following the effective time of the merger contain provisions identical to the certificate of incorporation of the constituent corporation immediately prior to the effective

time of the merger (other than provisions, if any, regarding the incorporator or incorporators, the corporate or entity name, the registered office and agent, the initial board of directors and the initial subscribers for shares, references to members rather than stockholders or shareholders, references to interests, units or the like rather than stock or shares, references to managers, managing members or other members of the governing body rather than directors and such provisions contained in any amendment to the certificate of incorporation as were necessary to effect a change, exchange, reclassification, subdivision, combination or cancellation of stock, if such change, exchange, reclassification, subdivision, combination or cancellation has become effective); provided, however, that

(i) if the organizational documents of the surviving entity do not contain the following provisions, they shall be amended in the merger to contain provisions requiring that

(A) any act or transaction by or involving the surviving entity, other than the election or removal of directors or managers, managing members or other members of the governing body of the surviving entity, that requires for its adoption under this chapter or its organizational documents the approval of the stockholders or members of the surviving entity shall, by specific reference to this subsection, require, in addition, the approval of the stockholders of the holding company (or any successor by merger), by the same vote as is required by this chapter and/or by the organizational documents of the surviving entity; provided, however, that for purposes of this clause (i)(A), any surviving entity that is not a corporation shall include in such amendment a requirement that the approval of the stockholders of the holding company be obtained for any act or transaction by or involving the surviving entity, other than the election or removal of directors or managers, managing members or other members of the governing body of the surviving entity, which would require the approval of the stockholders of the surviving entity if the surviving entity were a corporation subject to this chapter;

(B) any amendment of the organizational documents of a surviving entity that is not a corporation, which amendment would, if adopted by a corporation subject to this chapter, be required to be included in the certificate of incorporation of such corporation, shall, by specific reference to this subsection, require, in addition, the approval of the stockholders of the holding company (or any successor by merger), by the same vote as is required by this chapter and/or by the organizational documents of the surviving entity; and

(C) the business and affairs of a surviving entity that is not a corporation shall be managed by or under the direction of a board of directors, board of managers or other governing body consisting of individuals who are subject to the same fiduciary duties applicable to, and who are liable for breach of such duties to the same extent as, directors of a corporation subject to this chapter; and

(ii) the organizational documents of the surviving entity may be amended in the merger to reduce the number of classes and shares of capital stock or other equity interests or units that the surviving entity is authorized to issue; and

(8) the stockholders of the constituent corporation do not recognize gain or loss for United States federal income tax purposes as determined by the board of directors of the constituent corporation. Neither subdivision (g)(7)(i) of this section nor any provision of a surviving entity's organizational documents required by subdivision (g)(7)(i) shall be deemed or construed to require approval of the stockholders of the holding company to elect or remove directors or managers, managing members or other members of the governing body of the surviving entity. The term "organizational documents", as used in subdivision (g)(7) and in the preceding sentence, shall, when used in reference to a corporation, mean the certificate of incorporation of such corporation, and when used in reference to a limited liability company, mean the limited liability company agreement of such limited liability company.

As used in this subsection only, the term "holding company" means a corporation which, from its incorporation until consummation of a merger governed by this subsection, was at all times a direct or indirect wholly-owned subsidiary of the constituent corporation and whose capital stock is issued in such merger. From and after the effective time of a merger adopted by a constituent corporation by action of its board of directors and without any vote of stockholders pursuant to this subsection:

(i) to the extent the restrictions of § 203 of this title applied to the constituent corporation and its stockholders at the effective time of the merger, such restrictions shall apply to the holding company and its stockholders immediately after the effective time of the merger as though it were the constituent corporation, and all shares of stock of the holding company acquired in the merger shall for purposes of § 203 of this title be deemed to have been acquired at the time that the shares of stock of the constituent corporation converted in the merger were acquired, and provided further that any stockholder who immediately prior to the effective time of the merger was not an interested stockholder within the meaning of § 203 of this title shall not solely by reason of the merger become an interested stockholder of the holding company,

(ii) if the corporate name of the holding company immediately following the effective time of the merger is the same as the corporate name of the constituent corporation immediately prior to the effective time of the merger, the shares of capital stock of the holding company into which the shares of capital stock of the constituent corporation are converted in the merger shall be represented by the stock certificates that previously represented shares of capital stock of the constituent corporation and (iii) to the extent a stockholder of the constituent corporation immediately prior to the merger had standing to institute or maintain derivative litigation on behalf of the constituent corporation, nothing in this section shall be deemed to limit or extinguish such standing. If an agreement of merger is adopted by a constituent corporation by action of its board of directors and without any vote of stockholders pursuant to this subsection, the secretary or assistant secretary of the constituent corporation shall certify on the agreement that the agreement has been adopted pursuant to this subsection and that the conditions specified in the first sentence of this subsection have been satisfied. The agreement so adopted and certified shall then be filed and become effective, in accordance with § 103 of this title. Such filing shall constitute a representation by the person who executes the agreement that the facts stated in the certificate remain true immediately prior to such filing.

§ 271 Sale, lease or exchange of assets; consideration; procedure

(a) Every corporation may at any meeting of its board of directors or governing body sell, lease or exchange all or substantially all of its property and assets, including its goodwill and its corporate franchises, upon such terms and conditions and for such consideration, which may consist in whole or in part of money or other property, including shares of stock in, and/or other securities of, any other corporation or corporations, as its board of directors or governing body deems expedient and for the best interests of the corporation, when and as authorized by a resolution adopted by the holders of a majority of the outstanding stock of the corporation entitled to vote thereon or, if the corporation is a nonstock corporation, by a majority of the members having the right to vote for the election of the members of the governing body and any other members entitled to vote thereon under the certificate of incorporation or the bylaws of such corporation, at a meeting duly called upon at least 20 days' notice. The notice of the meeting shall state that such a resolution will be considered.

(b) Notwithstanding authorization or consent to a proposed sale, lease or exchange of a corporation's property and assets by the stockholders or members, the board of directors or governing body may abandon such proposed sale, lease or exchange without further action by the stockholders or members, subject to the rights, if any, of third parties under any contract relating thereto.

(c) For purposes of this section only, the property and assets of the corporation include the property and assets of any subsidiary of the corporation. As used in this subsection, "subsidiary" means any entity wholly-owned and controlled, directly or indirectly, by the corporation and includes, without limitation, corporations, partnerships, limited partnerships, limited liability partnerships, limited liability companies, and/or statutory trusts. Notwithstanding subsection (a) of this section, except to the extent the certificate of incorporation otherwise provides, no resolution by stockholders or members shall be required for a sale, lease or exchange of property and assets of the corporation to a subsidiary.

§ 103 Certificates; corrections

. . .

(f) Whenever any instrument authorized to be filed with the Secretary of State under any provision of this title, has been so filed and is an inaccurate record of the corporate action therein referred to, or was defectively or erroneously executed, sealed or acknowledged, the instrument may be corrected by filing with the Secretary of State a certificate of correction of the instrument which shall be executed, acknowledged and filed in accordance with this section. The certificate of correction shall specify the inaccuracy or defect to be corrected and shall set forth the portion of the instrument in corrected form. In lieu of filing a certificate of correction the instrument may be corrected by filing with the Secretary of State a corrected instrument which shall be executed, acknowledged and filed in accordance with this section. The corrected instrument shall be specifically designated as such in its heading, shall specify the inaccuracy or defect to be corrected, and shall set forth the entire instrument in corrected form. An instrument corrected in accordance with this section shall be effective as of the date of the original instrument was filed, except as to those persons who are substantially and adversely affected by the correction and as to those persons the instrument as corrected shall be effective from the filing date.

PENNSYLVANIA BUSINESS CORPORATION LAW

§ 1523 Pricing and issuance of shares

Except as otherwise restricted in the bylaws, shares of a business corporation may be issued *at a price determined by the board of directors* or the board may set a *minimum price or establish a formula or method* by which the price may be determined.

§ 1524 Payment for shares

(a) GENERAL RULE. — Consideration for shares, unless otherwise restricted in the bylaws:

(1) May consist of money, obligations (including an obligation of a shareholder), services performed whether or not contracted for, contracts for services to be performed, shares or other securities or obligations of the issuing business corporation, or any other tangible or intangible property or benefit to the corporation. If shares are issued for other than money, the value of the consideration shall be determined by or in the manner provided by the board of directors.

(2) Shall be provided or paid to or as ordered by the corporation.

(b) ISSUANCE WITHOUT CONSIDERATION. — Except as otherwise restricted in the bylaws, upon authorization by the board of directors, the corporation may issue or distribute its own shares pro rata to its shareholders or the shareholders of one or more classes or series, if the relative rights of the holders of any class or series are not adversely affected thereby, to effectuate stock dividends or splits *and any such transaction shall not require payment of consideration.*

(c) STATUS OF ISSUED SHARES. — Except as provided in subsection (e), all issued shares of a business corporation shall be deemed fully paid regardless of failure to pay in full the agreed consideration therefor. Except as otherwise provided by a regulatory statute controlling under section 103(c) (relating to structural provisions in regulatory statutes controlling), all issued shares of a corporation shall be nonassessable. This subsection shall not affect the personal obligation of a subscriber for shares of a corporation to pay the agreed consideration for the shares.

(d) RIGHTS OF SUBSCRIBING SHAREHOLDER. — Notwithstanding any other provision of this subpart, the right to vote, to receive dividends and to have and exercise the other rights of a shareholder prior to payment in full of the agreed consideration for the shares of a shareholder who has acquired his shares by subscription may be denied or limited as provided in the subscription agreement. Any such denial or limitation of rights shall be noted conspicuously on the face or back of the share certificate, if any, or in the notice provided by section 1528(f) (relating to uncertificated shares). Unless so noted, such denial or limitation (even though permitted by this section) shall be ineffective except against a person with actual knowledge of the denial or limitation.

(e) TRANSITIONAL PROVISION. — A corporation may enforce calls on partly paid shares outstanding on September 30, 1989, in the same manner and to the same extent as if this subpart had not been enacted. (Last amended by Act 169, L. '92, eff. 2-16-93.)

Subchapter C. Corporate Finance

§ 1551 Distributions to shareholders

(a) GENERAL RULE. — Unless otherwise restricted in the bylaws, the board of directors may authorize and a business corporation may make distributions. A provision in the articles setting forth a par value for any authorized shares or class or series of shares shall not restrict the ability of a corporation to make distributions.

(b) LIMITATION. — A distribution may not be made if, after giving effect thereto:

(1) the corporation would be unable to pay its debts as they become due in the usual course of its business; or

(2) the total assets of the corporation would be less than the sum of its total liabilities plus (unless otherwise provided in the articles) the amount that would be needed, if the corporation were to be dissolved at the time as of which the distribution is measured, to satisfy the preferential rights upon dissolution of shareholders whose preferential rights are superior to those receiving the distribution.

(c) VALUATION. — The board of directors may base its determination that a distribution is not prohibited under subsection (b)(2) on one or more of the following:

(1) the book values of the assets and liabilities of the corporation, as reflected on its books and records;

(2) a valuation that takes into consideration unrealized appreciation and depreciation or other changes in value of the assets and liabilities of the corporation;

(3) the current value of the assets and liabilities of the corporation, either valued separately or valued in segments or as an entirety as a going concern; or

(4) any other method that is reasonable in the circumstances.

In determining whether a distribution is prohibited by subsection (b)(2), the board of directors need not consider obligations and liabilities unless they are required to be reflected on a balance sheet (not including the notes thereto) prepared on the basis of general accepted accounting principles, or such other accounting practices and principles as are used generally by the corporation in the maintenance of its books and records and as are reasonable in the circumstances.

(d) DATE OF DISTRIBUTION. — The effect of a distribution shall be measured:

(1) as of the date specified by the board of directors when it authorizes the distribution if the distribution occurs within 125 days of the earlier of the date so specified or the date of authorization; or

(2) as of the date of distribution in all other cases.

In the case of a purchase, redemption or other acquisition of its own shares by a corporation, the distribution shall be deemed to occur as of the date money or other property is transferred or debt is incurred by the corporation or as of the date the shareholder ceases to be a shareholder of the corporation with respect to the shares, whichever is earlier.

(e) REDEMPTION RELATED AND SIMILAR DEBT. — Indebtedness of a corporation to a shareholder incurred by reason of a distribution made in accordance with this section shall be at least on a parity with the indebtedness of the corporation to its general unsecured creditors except to the extent subordinated by agreement.

(f) CERTAIN SUBORDINATED DEBT. — Indebtedness of a corporation, including indebtedness issued as a distribution, *shall not be considered a liability for* purposes of determinations under subsection (b) *if its terms provide that payment of principal and interest are made only if and to the extent that payment of a distribution to shareholders could then be made under this section.* If such indebtedness is issued as a distribution, each payment of principal or interest shall be treated as a distribution, the effect of which shall be measured on the date the payment is actually made.

. . .

Chapter 2

VALUATION OF THE CORPORATE ENTERPRISE — PURPOSES AND METHODOLOGY

§ 2.01 INTRODUCTION

There are a number of instances in which an ongoing business entity or the ownership interests thereof must be evaluated in a manner that conforms to the requirements of applicable corporate law. These include (i) certain transactions whereby the corporation acquires or sells business assets, and (ii) transactions in which the shares of stock of the corporation are acquired by its management or a third party. With regard to category (i), the overarching applicable legal principle is the prohibition of a "waste" of corporate assets. The law generally requires that category (ii) transactions be carried out in a method that achieves a standard referred to as "entire fairness" and is often said to be composed of "fair dealing" and "fair price." All of those legal requirements are predicated upon the fiduciary duties of loyalty and due care owed by a board of directors to the corporation and its stockholders.[1]

In *Cede & Co. v. Technicolor, Inc.*, 2003 Del. Ch. LEXIS 146, at *6 (Dec. 31, 2003), *rev'd on other grounds*, 875 A.2d 602 (Del. 2005), the Chancery Court stated:

> The value of a corporation is not a point on a line, but a range of reasonable values, and the judge's task is to assign one particular value within this range as the most reasonable value in light of all of the relevant evidence and based on considerations of fairness.

A working knowledge of the terminology utilized in connection with the valuation process is essential to the understanding of the process itself and the materials that follow in this chapter. Set forth below is a set of definitions formulated by the American Society of Appraisers and set forth in Mahler, *Decisions Have Set Parameters for Establishing "Fair Value" of Frozen-Out Shareholder Interests*, 71 N.Y. St. B.J. No. 6, 21, 25 (July-Aug. 1999).

§ 2.02 VALUATION TERMINOLOGY

The Business Valuation Committee of the American Society of Appraisers (hereinafter "ASA") has adopted the following definitions of terms to be used for the valuation of businesses, business ownership interests or securities by all ASA members:

---

[1] *See, e.g.*, Robert J. Giuffra, Jr., Note, *Investment Bankers' Fairness Opinions in Corporate Control Transactions*, 96 Yale L.J. 119, 124 (1986).

Adjusted Book Value: The book value which results after one or more asset or liability amounts are added, deleted or changed from the respective book amounts.

Appraisal: The act or process of determining value. It is synonymous with valuation.

Appraisal Date: The date as of which the appraiser's opinion of value applies.

Appraisal Method: A specific procedure applied to determine value.

Appraised Value: The appraiser's opinion or determination of value.

Book Value:

1. With respect to assets, the capitalized cost of an asset less accumulated depreciation, depletion or amortization as it appears on the books of account of the enterprise.

2. With respect to a business enterprise, the difference between total assets (net of depreciation, depletion and amortization) and total liabilities of an enterprise as they appear on the balance sheet. It is synonymous with net book value, net worth and shareholders' equity.

Business Appraiser: A person who by education, training and experience is qualified to make an appraisal of a business enterprise and/or its intangible assets.

Business Enterprise: A commercial, industrial or service organization pursuing an economic activity.

Business Valuation: The act or process of arriving at an opinion or determination of the value of a business enterprise or an interest therein.

Capitalization:

1. The conversion of income into value.

2. The capital structure of a business enterprise.

3. The recognition of an expenditure as a capital asset rather than a period expense.

Capitalization Factor: Any multiple or divisor used to convert income into value.

Capitalization Rate: Any divisor (usually expressed as a percentage) that is used to convert income into value.

Capital Structure: The composition of the invested capital.

Cash Flow: Net income plus depreciation and other non-cash charges.

Control: The power to direct the management and policies of an enterprise.

Control Premium: The additional value inherent in the control interest as contrasted to a minority interest, that reflects its power of control.

Discount Rate: A rate of return used to convert a monetary sum, payable or receivable in the future, into present value.

Economic Life: The period over which property may be profitably used.

Enterprise: *See* **Business Enterprise.**

Equity: The owners' interest in property after deduction of all liabilities.

Fair Market Value: The amount at which property would change hands between a willing seller and a willing buyer when neither is acting under compulsion and when both have reasonable knowledge of the relevant facts.

Going Concern: An operating business enterprise.

Going Concern Value:

1. The value of an enterprise, or an interest therein, as a going concern.

2. Intangible elements of value in a business enterprise resulting from factors, such as having a trained workforce; an operational plant; and the necessary licenses, systems and procedures in place.

Goodwill: That intangible asset that arises as a result of name, reputation, customer patronage, location, products and similar factors that have not been separately identified and/or valued, but which generate economic benefits.

Invested Capital: The sum of the debt and equity in an enterprise on a long-term basis.

Majority: Ownership position greater than 50 percent of the voting interest in an enterprise.

Majority Control: The degree of control provided by a majority position.

Marketability Discount: An amount or percentage deducted from an equity interest to reflect lack of marketability.

Minority Discount: The reduction from the pro rata share of the value of the entire business, to reflect the absence of the power of control.

Minority Interest: Ownership position less than 50 percent of the voting interest in an enterprise.

Net Assets: Total assets less total liabilities.

Net Income: Revenues less expenses, including taxes.

Rate of Return: An amount of income realized or expected on an investment, expressed as a percentage of that investment.

Replacement Cost New: The current cost of a similar new item having the nearest equivalent utility as the item being appraised.

Reproduction Cost New: The current cost of an identical new item.

Valuation: *See* **Appraisal.**

Working Capital: The amount by which current assets exceed current liabilities.

§ 2.03 METHODS USED IN THE VALUATION PROCESS FOR BUSINESS CORPORATIONS

With respect to the methodology of valuation, set forth below are excerpts from a Memorandum from Counsel discussing generally the three primary methods of valuing a business entity.

[A] Market Value

There are several commonly accepted criteria that are utilized for the purpose of valuing shares of a business corporation. One of these is market value, which can be utilized where the stock in question is actively traded on a national stock exchange or in the over-the-counter market. That criteria, of course, is not applicable in the case of Woodstock Widget Corporation ("Woodstock").

However, there are instances where the market value of shares of stock in a corporation that is engaged in the same industry as the business being evaluated may be useful. The value of such comparisons is limited however, since no two businesses are identical, even though their products may be similar. Differences in other areas such as plant, patent and market position, and management (as well as negative factors such as increasing product liability exposure and resulting insurance and litigation costs) will result in a substantial difference in value between any two corporations.

[B] Net Asset Value

Another method used to measure the value of a business corporation is its net asset value, which is an amount equal amount to the excess of the fair market value of the corporation's assets over its liabilities, and is also sometimes referred to as liquidation value. That number is usually much higher than the amount derived from the calculation of book value, because, for the purposes of determining net asset value, assets are measured by fair market value rather than by historical cost less depreciation. Net asset value, however, is usually not considered to be an appropriate standard for measuring the value of a business that is to be continued as a going concern, rather than one that is being liquidated.

[C] Capitalization of Earnings

The most commonly used, and probably the most realistic method of approximating the value of the shares of a corporation such as Woodstock is the capitalization of earnings technique. Capitalization of earnings (which is also sometimes referred to as investment value) involves the determination of two items of measurement. First, a reasonable estimate of future earnings must be made. Second, such estimated future earnings must be in turn multiplied by a figure, sometimes referred to as a times-earnings factor, which represents the value of such estimated future earnings in the light of the risks and uncertainties involved in the business. The Woodstock times-yearly earnings factor (which is also referred to as a multiplier) would be large in the case of a business with a future subject to relatively few risks; it would be correspondingly low in the case of a business subject to greater risks.

The formulation of a reasonable estimate of future earnings is generally based upon an analysis of the past earnings of the business. This is generally done through the formulation of an average of earnings over a period of years, usually ranging from three to ten. Such past earnings have to be adjusted for any known abnormal factors that affected them. Such year by year comparisons may be employed to determine what the past profit trend has been; such comparisons include those relating to (i) gross sales (which indicate volume trends) and (ii) the cost relationship to gross sales (which will indicate cost trend). Two particular trends that should be considered in this respect are litigation fees in respect of product liability cases, which have doubled in the past two years, and related insurance costs that also are expected to increase.

There are other factors that should be taken into account in appraising Woodstock's shares. Woodstock is presently a one-product company and there is always the risk of market saturation.

§ 2.04 APPLICATION OF VALUATION TECHNIQUES; FAIRNESS OPINIONS

A fairness opinion is expressed in a letter usually addressed to the Board of Directors of the corporation, the shareholders of which are participants in the transaction or a special committee thereof. The opinion letter generally states that the consideration proposed to be paid to such stockholders is "fair" to them "from a financial point of view." Those words are understood to limit the scope of the opinion to financial considerations.[2]

> The purpose of valuations of publicly held companies, therefore, is to determine the difference between the market price of a company's shares and the value of the shares in a transaction where corporate control is being sold.
>
> . . .
>
> The "fairness" of the consideration offered in a merger or tender offer is both a legal and financial question. When rendering fairness opinions, investment bankers evaluate the financial fairness of transactions, namely, would a rational buyer and seller, assuming that each had knowledge of relevant facts, purchase or sell the shares in question at the offered price. Modern valuation techniques do not permit an investment banker to determine whether a price is fair with absolute precision. A fair price is not the highest value attainable for the firm or a single value but a range of reasonable values.[3]

The following excerpts from an Offer to Purchase relating to a cash tender offer illustrate the application by an investment banking firm of commonly used valuation

[2] Michael W. Martin, Note, *Fairness Opinions and Negligent Misrepresentation: Defining Investment Bankers' Duty to Third-Party Shareholders*, 60 Fordham L. Rev. 133, 137–38 (1991).

[3] 96 Yale L.J. 119, 122, 123–24. (Footnotes omitted).

techniques to determine whether an acquisition transaction is fair from a financial point of view to the stockholders of the target company.

Opinion of investment banking firm ABC. The Company engaged ABC to act as financial advisor to the Company in connection with the Offer and the Merger. On June 8, 1999, at a meeting of the Company's Board (at which only the Unaffiliated Directors were present) and Special Committee held to evaluate the proposed Offer and Merger, ABC rendered an oral opinion, which opinion was subsequently confirmed by delivery of a written opinion dated June 8, 1999, to the effect that, as of that date and based upon and subject to matters stated in its opinion, the $37.00 per Share cash consideration to be received in the Offer and the Merger by the holders of Shares (other than Parent and its affiliates) was fair, from a financial point of view, to such holders.

The full text of ABC's written opinion dated June 8, 1999, which describes the assumptions made, matters considered and limitations of the review undertaken, . . . is incorporated herein by reference. ABC's opinion is directed to the Company's Board and Special Committee, addresses only the fairness of the cash consideration to be received in the Offer and the Merger by the holders of Shares (other than Parent and its affiliates) from a financial point of view, does not address the merits of the underlying decision by the Company to engage in the Offer and the Merger, and does not constitute a recommendation to any shareholder as to whether or not such shareholder should tender Shares in the Offer or how such shareholder should vote with respect to matters relating to the proposed Merger. The summary of ABC's opinion described below is qualified in its entirety by reference to the full text of its opinion.

In connection with ABC's role as the Company's financial advisor, and in arriving at its opinion, ABC:

- reviewed publicly available financial and other information concerning the Company and internal analyses and other information furnished to or discussed with ABC by the Company and its advisors;
- held discussions with members of the senior management of the Company regarding the business and prospects of the Company;
- reviewed the reported prices and trading activity for the Shares;
- compared financial and stock market information for the Company with similar information for other companies whose securities are publicly traded;
- reviewed the financial terms of recent business combinations which ABC deemed comparable in whole or in part;
- reviewed the terms of the Merger Agreement; and
- performed other studies and analyses and considered other factors as ABC deemed appropriate.

ABC did not assume responsibility for independent verification of, and did not independently verify, any information, whether publicly available or furnished to ABC, concerning the Company, including, without limitation, any financial information, forecasts or projections considered in connection with the rendering of its opinion. For purposes of its opinion, ABC assumed and relied upon the accuracy and completeness of all information it reviewed. ABC did not conduct a physical inspection of any of the properties or assets, and did not prepare or obtain any independent evaluation or appraisal of any of the assets or liabilities, of the Company. With respect to the financial forecasts and projections made available to ABC and used in its analyses, ABC assumed that they were reasonably prepared on bases reflecting the best currently available estimates and judgments as to the matters covered thereby. In rendering its opinion, ABC expressed no view as to the reasonableness of the forecasts and projections or the assumptions on which they are based. ABC's opinion was necessarily based upon economic, market and other conditions existing on, and the information made available to ABC as of, the date of its opinion.

For purposes of rendering its opinion, ABC assumed that, in all respects material to its analysis, the representations and warranties of the Company, Parent and Purchaser contained in the Merger Agreement are true and correct; the Company, Parent and Purchaser will each perform all of the covenants and agreements to be performed by it under the Merger Agreement; and all conditions to the obligations of each of the Company, Parent and Purchaser to consummate the Offer and the Merger will be satisfied without any waiver. ABC also assumed that all material governmental, regulatory or other approvals and consents required in connection with the consummation of the Offer and the Merger will be obtained and that in connection with obtaining any necessary governmental, regulatory or other approvals and consents, or any amendments, modifications or waivers to any agreements, instruments or orders to which either the Company, Parent and Purchaser is a party or is subject or by which it is bound, no limitations, restrictions or conditions will be imposed or amendments, modifications or waivers made that would have a material adverse effect on the Company or materially reduce the contemplated benefits of the Offer and the Merger to the Company. In connection with its opinion, ABC was not requested to, and did not, solicit third party indications of interest with respect to the acquisition of all or a part of the Company. No other instructions or limitations were imposed by the Unaffiliated Directors or Special Committee upon ABC with respect to the investigations made or the procedures followed by it in rendering its opinion.

The following is a summary of the material analyses performed by ABC in connection with its opinion to the Company's Board and Special Committee dated June 8, 1999. The financial analyses summarized below include information presented in tabular format. In order to fully understand ABC's financial analyses, the tables must be read together with the text of each summary. The tables alone do not constitute a complete description of the financial analyses. Considering the data set forth below without considering the full narrative description of the financial analyses, including the methodologies and assumptions underlying the analyses, could create a misleading or incomplete view of ABC's financial analyses.

Analysis of Selected Public Companies. ABC compared financial and stock market information for the Company and the following seven selected publicly held companies in the distribution industry:

ABC reviewed adjusted market values, calculated as equity market value, plus debt, less cash, as multiples of latest 12 months earnings before interest, taxes, depreciation and amortization, and earnings before interest and taxes, and equity market values as a multiple of latest 12 months and estimated calendar year 1999 and 2000 net income. All multiples were based on closing stock prices on June 4, 1999. Estimated financial data for the selected companies were based on publicly available research analysts' estimates and estimated financial data for the Company were based both on publicly available research analysts' estimates and internal estimates of the management of the Company. This analysis indicated the following implied adjusted market value and equity market value multiples for the selected companies, as compared to the following implied multiples for the Company based on the cash consideration in the Offer and the Merger of $37.00 per Share:

	Implied Multiples of Selected Companies Mean		
	Mean	Range	Multiples for the Company Implied by Cash Consideration
Adjusted Market Values:			
Latest 12 months earnings before interest, taxes, depreciation and amortization	10.0x	7.9x-13.8x	12.9x
Latest 12 months earnings before interest and taxes	12.2x	9.5x-15.3x	17.0x
Equity Market Values:			
Latest 12 months net income	18.3x	13.2x-25.1x	32.2x
Estimated calendar year 1999 net income (research analysts' estimates)	16.0x	12.0x-21.4x	27.0x
Estimated calendar year 2000 net income (research analysts' estimates)	13.1x	9.6x-19.2x	22.9x
Estimated calendar year 1999 net income (management estimates)	16.0x	12.0x-21.4x	22.5x
Estimated calendar year 2000 net income (management estimates)	13.1x	9.6x-19.2x	16.2x

Analysis of Selected Precedent Transactions. ABC reviewed the purchase prices and implied transaction multiples in the following eight selected transactions in the distribution industry:

ABC reviewed adjusted market values in the selected transactions as multiples of latest 12 months earnings before interest, taxes, depreciation and amortization, and earnings before interest and taxes, and equity market values as a multiple of latest 12 months net income and forward net income. All multiples were based on publicly available information at the time of announcement of the relevant transaction. This analysis indicated the following implied adjusted market value and equity market value multiples for the selected transactions, as compared to the following implied multiples for the Company based on the cash consideration in the Offer and the Merger of $37.00 per Share:

	Implied Multiples of Selected Transactions			
	Mean	Ranges	Implied Multiples of XYZ Transaction	Multiples for the Company Implied by Cash Consideration
Adjusted Market Values:				
Latest 12 months earnings before interest, taxes, depreciation and amortization	12.7x	8.9x-18.7x	8.9x	12.9x
Latest 12 months earnings before interest and taxes	16.5x	9.7x-24.0x	12.8x	17.0x
Equity Market Values:				
Latest 12 months net income	31.5x	16.6x-44.2x	23.4x	32.2x
Forward net income (research analysts' estimates)	23.7x	15.4x-36.9x	17.2x	25.1x
Forward net income (management estimates) .	23.7x	15.4x-36.9x	17.2x	19.3x

Discounted Cash Flow Analysis. ABC performed a discounted cash flow analysis to estimate the present value of the unlevered, after-tax free cash flows that the Company could generate for the fiscal years 1999 through 2003, based both on internal estimates of the management of the Company and on publicly available research analysts' estimates. The range of estimated terminal values for the Company was calculated by applying terminal value multiples ranging from 8.0x to 10.0x to the Company's projected fiscal year 2003 earnings before interest, taxes, depreciation and amortization. The present value of the cash flows and terminal values were calculated using discount rates ranging from 12.0% to 14.0%. This analysis yielded the following implied equity reference ranges for the Company, as compared to the cash consideration in the Offer and the Merger of $37.00 per Share:

Implied Per Share Equity Reference Range for the Company	Per Share Cash Consideration
$24.75 – $34.75 (research analysts' estimates)	$37.00
$28.72 - $39.90 (management estimates)	

Premiums Analysis. ABC reviewed the premiums paid in 96 selected transactions, including eight selected transactions discussed above in "Analysis of Selected Precedent Transactions," 24 selected transactions effected since January 1, 1995 in which the acquiror had a 20% to 50% ownership in the target company prior to the transaction and increased its ownership to 90% or greater following the transaction, and 64 selected transactions effected since January 1, 1994 having transaction values of between $1.0 billion and $1.5 billion. ABC analyzed the premiums in these transactions based on the target company's stock price one day, one month and three months prior to public announcement of the transaction as compared to the implied premiums for the Company in the Offer and the Merger based on the stock price for the Shares as of June 4, 1999 and one month and three months prior to June 4, 1999. This analysis indicated the following premiums in the selected transactions, as compared to the premiums implied for the Company in the Offer and the Merger:

	Premium One Day Prior to Public Announcement		Premium One Month Prior to Public Announcement		Premium Three Months Prior to Public Announcement	
		Range	Mean	Range	Mean	Range
Selected Transactions (8)	28.6%	8.0%-67.2%	36.4%	13.3%-66.2%	32.7%	(28.3)%-84.6%
Selected Transactions (24) ...	30.8%	3.2%-118.6%	32.4%	4.2%-104.0%	42.6%	(9.7)%-201.9%
Selected Transactions (24) ...	29.5%	(13.9)%-118.5%	41.2%	(9.7)%-130.7%	46.1%	(27.7)%-164.9%

	Premium One Day Prior to Public Announcement	Premium One Month Prior to Public Announcement	Premium Three Months Prior to Public Announcement
XYZ Transaction	27.4%	30.8%	5.8%

	Premium as of June 4, 1999	Premium One Month Prior to June 4, 1999	Premium Three Months Prior to June 4, 1999
Premium Implied for the Company in the Offer and Merger	23.1%	41.0%	57.0%

Other Factors. In rendering its opinion, ABC also reviewed and considered, among other things:

- historical and projected financial data for the Company;
- historical market prices and trading volumes for the Shares and the relationship between movements in the Shares, movements in the common stock of selected companies and movements in the S&P 500 Index;
- selected published analysts' reports, including analysts' estimates as to the earnings per share of the Company; and
- a shareholder profile of the Company and business and financial profile of Parent.

The above summary is not a complete description of the opinion of ABC to the Company's Board and Special Committee or the financial analyses performed and factors considered by ABC in connection with its opinion. A copy of ABC's written presentation to the Company's Board and Special Committee in connection with its opinion has been filed as an exhibit to the Rule 13e-3 Transaction Statement on Schedule 13E-3 filed by Parent and Purchaser with the Securities and Exchange Commission and will be available for inspection and copying at the principal executive offices of the Company during regular business hours by any interested shareholder of the Company or representative of such shareholder who has been so designated in writing and may be inspected and copied, and obtained from the EDGAR Database accessible through the Commission's Website (www.sec.gov/index.html) or by mail, from the Commission.

The preparation of a fairness opinion is a complex analytic process involving various determinations as to the most appropriate and relevant methods of financial analyses and the application of those methods to the particular circumstances and, therefore, a fairness opinion is not readily susceptible to summary description. ABC believes that its analyses and the summary above must be considered as a whole and that selecting portions of its analyses and factors or focusing on information presented in tabular format, without considering all analyses and factors or the narrative description of the analyses, could create a misleading or incomplete view of the processes underlying ABC analyses and opinion.

In performing its analyses, ABC considered industry performance, general business, economic, market and financial conditions and other matters existing as of the date of its opinion, many of which are beyond the control of the Company. No company, transaction or business used in such analyses as a comparison is identical to the Company or the Offer or Merger, nor is an evaluation of the results of those analyses entirely mathematical; rather, the analyses involve complex considerations and judgments concerning financial and operating characteristics and other factors that could affect the acquisition, public trading or other values of the companies, business segments or transactions being analyzed. The estimates contained in ABC's analyses and the ranges of valuations resulting from any particular analysis are not necessarily indicative of actual values or future results, which may be significantly more or less favorable than those suggested by its analyses. In addition, analyses relating to the value of businesses or securities do not purport to be appraisals or to reflect the prices at which businesses or securities actually may be sold. Accordingly, ABC's analyses and estimates are inherently subject to substantial uncertainty.

The type and amount of consideration payable in the Offer and the Merger was determined through extensive discussions between the Company and Parent. Although ABC provided financial advice to the Company during the course of discussions, the decision to enter into the transaction was solely that of the Unaffiliated Directors and Special Committee. ABC's opinion and financial analyses were only one of many factors considered by the Unaffiliated Directors and Special Committee in their evaluation of the Offer and the Merger and should not be viewed as determinative of the views of the Unaffiliated Directors, Special Committee or management with respect to the Offer or the Merger or the consideration payable in the Offer and the Merger.

As stated above in the Memorandum From Counsel, net asset value is generally not a relevant valuation factor when the corporation is to continue operations as a going concern. There are, however, instances in which fairness opinions at least consider net asset or liquidation value, particularly where the net asset value may possibly exceed the value of the consideration being offered to the target's stockholders. Set forth below are excerpts from a fairness opinion which dealt with this issue.

As part of our analysis, we have also considered possible net values, which might be realized in a hypothetical liquidation of each of the operating businesses of Target and of the other, non-operating, assets of Target over an assumed period not exceeding two years. The analysis of the liquidation of the operating businesses was considered both in terms of possible sales as on-going businesses and in terms of an orderly disposition of individual assets. This analysis, which was intended only as a reasonable estimate of the net proceeds which might be derived from such a liquidation if informed prospective buyers were available, resulted in a hypothetical liquidation value in the range of approximately $23.70 to $24.50 per Target Common Share. Such value might differ substantially from the net proceeds per Target Common Share which would be derived from an actual liquidation because of market conditions existing at the time of sale, the underlying motivations and assumptions of a given buyer, and the uncertainties of national and international economic and political conditions. Such factors could result in net proceeds from any actual liquidation which would be significantly higher or lower than our above estimate.

In addition to the foregoing, we have made such other analyses and examinations as we have deemed necessary in arriving at our opinion expressed below. In connection with such opinion, we have considered the [Acquisition Consideration] to have a per share value in the range of $20.50 to $21.25 (which is not necessarily the range within which the [Acquisition Consideration] will initially or ultimately trade).

. . .

In arriving at our opinion we have considered as significant the uncertainties and time involved in an asset liquidation. We did not make or obtain independent evaluations of the physical assets, mineral reserves or rights, or real properties of Target. Furthermore, because of the nature of many of the assets and investments of Target, data with respect to recent sales of similar properties was generally not available. We have not undertaken physical inspection of properties outside the United States and our inspection of other properties was limited by time and other factors. Although, as noted above, we have engaged in various discussions and other activities with respect to the business, operations and prospects of Target and Purchaser, and we have made certain analyses, we have assumed the accuracy and completeness of the financial and other information furnished to us, including that contained in the Registration Statement, and of the other information used by us which we obtained from published and other sources. Our opinion herein is based upon circumstances existing as of the date hereof.

CAWLEY v. SCM CORP.

Court of Appeals of New York
530 N.E.2d 1264 (1988)

Simons, J.

The issues presented in this stock appraisal proceeding under Business Corporation Law § 623(h)(4) are: (1) whether, in assessing the fair value of SCM Corporation stock, the courts below abused their discretion by disregarding the tax deduction that SCM became entitled to upon the consummation of its merger with HSCM Merger Company, Inc. and, if so, (2) whether the value of this postmerger factor should have been distributed equally among all of SCM's stockholders or solely to those stockholders whose shares were responsible for this tax advantage. We hold dissenting shareholders are entitled to receive fair value for their securities as determined by a consideration of all relevant factors, including the prospective, nonspeculative tax benefits accruing to the acquired corporation from the merger. Furthermore, because each share of stock within a given class must be treated equally, the tax advantages attendant to corporate actions must be distributed proportionately among all shareholders in calculating fair value and the dissenters (in this case petitioner is the only dissenter) given their aliquot share of the benefit. Accordingly, we reverse the Appellate Division order and remit the matter for a hearing.

The present dispute arises out of the March 31, 1986 merger between SCM and HSCM, two New York corporations, whereby SCM became an indirect wholly owned subsidiary of Hanson Trust PLC.[4] SCM is a multinational company engaged in the production of chemicals, coatings and resins, paper products, foods and typewriters whose common stock, prior to the merger, was traded on the New York and Pacific Stock Exchanges. Through its subsidiaries, Hanson renders various services, and manufactures and supplies a diverse line of products, including bricks, building materials, construction equipment, food processing and footwear. Its ordinary shares are traded on the London Stock Exchange.

Hanson began a hostile tender offer for all outstanding shares of SCM common stock (par value $5 per share) on August 26, 1985 by offering $60 per share in cash,

---

[4] [1] HSCM Merger Co., Inc., was an indirect wholly owned subsidiary corporation of Hanson Trust PLC and was a corporate shell used by Hanson to facilitate the merger with SCM.

over $14 per share higher than the preannouncement market price for SCM's stock. SCM's board of directors had previously recommended that such an offer be rejected as inadequate. On September 3, 1985, SCM announced it had executed a merger agreement with Merrill Lynch Capital Markets, providing for the leveraged buyout of SCM by Merrill Lynch and senior members of SCM's management for $70 per share in cash and subordinated debentures (junk bonds) on a fully diluted basis. SCM's financial advisor, Goldman, Sachs & Company, informed the SCM board that in its opinion this price was fair.

In response to the agreement between SCM and Merrill Lynch, Hanson raised its takeover bid from $60 to $72 per share in cash, conditioned upon SCM's granting any lock-up devices. SCM and Merrill Lynch, in turn, ended their prior agreement and executed a new one, providing for a leveraged buyout of SCM at $74 per share in cash and junk bonds on a fully diluted basis. Goldman, Sachs & Company approved this price as fair. SCM granted Merrill Lynch an option to purchase two of SCM's "crown jewels," its consumer foods and pigments divisions, for $80 million and $350 million respectively, thereby attempting to discourage Hanson from seeking control of SCM. On October 8, 1985, however, Hanson increased its tender offer price for SCM shares to $75 per share in cash, contingent upon the termination or judicial invalidation of this lock-up option. Following a Federal court order preliminarily enjoining SCM and others from exercising the lock-up option (*See Hanson Trust PLC v. ML SCM Acquisition*, 781 F.2d 264 [2d Cir]), Hanson completed the first step of the merger by purchasing over 50% of SCM's outstanding shares at the $75 tender offer price. At that time, Hanson having wrested control of SCM's board of directors, SCM and HSCM entered into a merger agreement under which the remaining common stock of SCM including exercised and unexercised stock options, would be purchased at $75 in cash. At a special shareholders' meeting on March 27, 1986, the "squeeze out" merger was approved, effective March 31, 1986. In connection with the merger, Goldman, Sachs & Company again expressed its opinion that the $75 per share price was fair.

At the time of the merger, the sale of shares acquired through the exercise of stock incentive options, referred to as ISO shares, was taxed as follows. If ISO shareholders transferred their securities within one year of the exercise of their incentive stock options (or within two years of the grant of these options), the transaction constituted a "disqualifying disposition" under Federal tax law (*see*, 26 U.S.C. § 421[a], [b]; § 422A[a][1]; § 425[c][1]). As such, the difference between (1) the exercise price and (2) the lesser of the fair market value on the date of exercise and date of sale was treated as ordinary income to the ISO shareholder, and the remaining profit (if any) was treated as a capital gain (long-term gain if the shares were held more than six months, and short-term gain otherwise (*see*, 26 U.S.C. § 1222; F. Tax Regs § 1.421.5[b][2], [3] [26 CFR]). If ISO shareholders held their stock beyond the holding period, the entire difference between the exercise price and fair market value on the date of sale was taxed more favorably as a long-term capital gain (*see*, Fed Tax Regs § 1.421-5[a]). Concomitantly, to the extent ISO shareholders recognized ordinary income because of "disqualifying dispositions," the issuing company was entitled to take a tax deduction in the nature of trade or business expense (26 U.S.C. §§ 162, 421[a], [b]).

At the time of the merger, petitioner Cawley had worked at SCM for 23 years and was its treasurer. He owned 9,539 shares of SCM common stock, 7,000 of which he had bought in January 1986 by exercising his incentive stock options. Cawley rejected the $75-per-share price and commenced this proceeding, alleging the merger's tax consequences made his 7,000 ISO shares worth much more. Cawley pointed out that the Hanson-SCM merger, which, in effect, forced him to sell his stock, entitled SCM to take a $354,437.50 tax deduction for Cawley's ISO shares, and a $3,852,031.77 tax deduction for the remaining ISO shares because the stock was sold before the end of the requisite holding period. Given the 46% corporate tax rate, SCM thus obtained a substantial posttax benefit of $163,041.25 and $1,771,934.60 respectively. Cawley asserts that these tax consequences should have been weighed in assessing fair value; and, specifically, that his ISO shares were worth $43 per share more than SCM's common stock because SCM derived this tax benefit directly and exclusively from the ISO shares. He also asserts, that because he was forced to sell his stock prematurely, his profit from the sale of his ISO shares was subject to tax as ordinary income (not more favorably as capital gains) thereby requiring him to pay $107,100 in excess taxes.[5] Cawley urges that this too should have been considered in valuing his ISO shares. Supreme Court, New York County, dismissed Cawley's petition seeking a determination of the fair value of his shares; the Appellate Division unanimously affirmed, without opinion.

As a threshold issue, we note that a court's appraisal of dissenting shareholders' interests, "to the extent that it is confined to issues of fact, rests largely within the discretion of the lower courts" (*Matter of Endicott Johnson Corp. v. Bade*, 37 N.Y.2d 585, 588 [citing Cohen and Karger, Powers of the New York Court of Appeals § 148, at 589-590 (rev. ed.)]). Our decision here is confined to whether the courts below abused their discretion in disregarding the tax consequences of the Hanson-SCM merger.

Under the Business Corporation Law, two or more domestic corporations in New York can merge into a single corporation, with one of the constituent corporations surviving (Business Corporation Law § 901 [a][1]). The board of directors of a corporation that participates in a merger must follow certain procedures in adopting a plan of merger (Business Corporation Law § 902) and in submitting it to the shareholders for their approval by a two-thirds vote (Business Corporation Law § 903). Shareholders who do not assent to the merger have the right to receive payment for the "fair value of their shares" (Business Corporation Law § 910[a]). The remedy available to those who have perfected their status as dissenting shareholders — through compliance with the various procedures set forth in section 623 — is to enforce this right through an appraisal proceeding (Business Corporation Law § 623 [h][4]). As we noted in *Alpert v. 28 Williams St. Corp.* (63 N.Y.2d 557), this remedial mechanism protects minority shareholders "from being forced to sell at unfair values imposed by those dominating the corporation while allowing the majority to proceed with its desired merger" (*id.*, at 567-568; *see also, Matter of Endicott Johnson Corp. v. Bade*, 37 N.Y.2d 585, 590, *supra; Anderson v. International Mins. & Chem. Corp.*, 295 N.Y. 343, 349-350). Where, as here, equitable relief based upon unlawful or fraudulent corporate action is not pursued, the appraisal

---

[5] [2] Individual income derived as capital gains is now taxed at the same rate as ordinary income (*see*, 26 U.S.C. former § 1202, repealed by Pub. L. 99-514, tit. III, § 301 [a], 99 U.S. Stat 2216).

proceeding is the dissenting shareholders' exclusive remedy (see, Business Corporation Law § 623[k]; *Breed v. Barton*, 54 N.Y.2d 82, 85-87; *cf.*, *Alpert v. 28 Williams St. Corp.*, 63 N.Y.2d 557, 558, *supra*).

Prior to 1982, Business Corporation Law § 623(h)(4) prevented courts from considering postmerger factors in assessing "fair value" by expressly excluding from the calculus "appreciation or depreciation directly or indirectly induced by [the] corporate action or its proposal" (L 1982, ch. 202, § 9; *see, Matter of Endicott Johnson Corp. v. Bade, supra*, at 587, 590-591). Case law held that fair value was determined by considering, as of the date of merger, net asset value, investment value and market value, and according weight to each as the facts and circumstances of a particular case dictated (*Matter of Endicott Johnson Corp. v. Bade, supra*, at 587; *Klurfeld v. Equity Enters.*, 79 A.D.2d 124, 137). To assure that fair value determinations reflected the business realities of a given corporate action, the Legislature in 1982 amended paragraph (4) of Business Corporation Law § 623 (h) to provide a more expansive and flexible case-by-case approach to the valuation of shares (*see*, L 1982, ch. 202, § 1; Bill Jacket, L 1982, ch. 202, at 18-19). In fixing fair value under the statute as amended, courts must examine "the nature of the transaction giving rise to the shareholder's right to receive payment for shares and *its effects on the corporation* and its shareholders, the concepts and methods then customary in the relevant securities and financial markets for determining fair value of shares of a corporation engaging in a similar transaction under comparable circumstances and *all other relevant factors*" (Business Corporation Law § 623[h][4] [emphasis added]). By including the phrase "all other relevant factors" and deleting the phrase "excluding any appreciation or depreciation directly or indirectly induced by such corporate action or its proposal," the Legislature evinced its intent that postmerger factors enter valuation computations (*see*, Bill Jacket, L 1982, ch. 202, at 20; *cf.*, Business Corporation Law § 1118 [fair value of interest in a close corporation excludes any element of value arising from the filing of the judicial dissolution petition under Business Corporation Law § 1104-a]). However, in amending section 623(h)(4), the Legislature was not encouraging the abandonment of the three basic methods of valuation delineated in *Endicott.* Rather, it intended courts to supplement these approaches by also considering "[e]lements of future value arising from the accomplishment or expectation of the merger which are known or susceptible of proof as of the date of the merger and not the product of speculation" (*Alpert v. 28 Williams St. Corp.*, 63 N.Y.2d, at 571, *supra; see, Weinberger v. UOP, Inc.*, 457 A.2d 701, 713 [Del.]).

Here, pursuant to CPLR 409(b), Supreme Court made a summary determination, based upon the parties' submissions, that no issue of fact existed regarding the fairness of the $75 price per share, basing its conclusion on the recommendations of SCM's financial experts, the active bidding contest between Hanson and Merrill Lynch centering on a price in the low 70's, and the trading history of the stock in the years immediately prior to the merger. The factors discussed by Supreme Court were plainly significant. The letter from Goldman, Sachs & Company demonstrated that the $75 figure was comparable to an amount that would have been set by arm's length negotiations (*see, Alpert v. 28 Williams St. Corp.*, 63 N.Y.2d 557, 572, *supra*) while the other two factors were an excellent indication of the market value for SCM stock on the day the merger was approved (*see, Matter of Behrens*, 61 N.Y.S.2d 179,

183, *aff'd without op'n* 271 A.D. 1007). In that SCM and Cawley contest only the relevancy of the tax consequences of the merger, it is law of the case that the $75-per-share figure is otherwise a fair amount (*see, e.g., Martin v. City of Cohoes*, 37 N.Y.2d 162, 165-166). Accordingly, we reach only the questions whether the tax deductibility of ISO shares was improperly disregarded and, if so, how an aliquot valuation of this tax benefit should be accomplished upon remittal.

Citing *Matter of Endicott Johnson Corp. v. Bade* (37 N.Y.2d 585, 587, *supra*), Supreme Court stated that the tax consequences of the acquisition were a postmerger factor not subject to valuation. Business Corporation Law § 623(h)(4), enacted after our decision in *Endicott*, authorizes courts to consider and accord weight to relevant postmerger factors, however, including the prospective tax benefits of a given transaction. Thus, the court should have addressed the tax benefits from the transfer of ISO shares. The deduction for acquisition of the ISO shares was, as the dissent concedes, a corporate asset of SCM, admittedly susceptible to precise calculation before the merger, that represented value to SCM and arose from the accomplishment of the merger. However, the record is silent on whether the tax deductibility of ISO shares was considered in arriving at the $75-per-share figure (*cf., Matter of Endicott Johnson Corp. v. Bade*, 37 N.Y.2d 585, 591, *supra*). In fact, SCM's director of taxes, William V. Meltzer, averred that "this future tax benefit . . . is not properly considered an element of fair value," indicating the tax deductibility of ISO shares was not considered at all. Upon remittal, Supreme Court should determine, among other things, whether the $75-per-share figure included consideration of the tax deductibility of ISO shares.

The next issue raised is whether the value of the tax deduction should be spread among ISO shareholders, their securities solely being responsible for the tax advantage, or should be spread equally among all shareholders of SCM common stock. Business Corporation Law § 623 does not resolve this question. On the one hand, section 623(g) promotes uniformity of treatment by requiring the surviving corporation of a merger to offer to pay all dissenting shareholders of the same class the same price per share when that corporation takes its fair value offer. On the other hand, in support of Cawley's position, this subdivision allows a corporation and an individual dissenting shareholder to agree upon a price for his or her shares after the former has made its fair value offer. This conflict is resolved, however, by Business Corporation Law § 501(c) which provides that "[s]ubject to the designations, relative rights, preferences and limitations applicable to separate series, each share shall be equal to every other share of the same class." Because the record indicates ISO shares were identical in all respects to SCM common stock held by the investment public, section 501(c) mandates that ISO shareholders be treated no differently from other SCM common stockholders (*see also, Fe Bland v. Two Trees Mgt. Co.*, 66 N.Y.2d 556, 568-569). Thus, if Supreme Court concludes that the $75 price per share did not include consideration of the deductibility of ISO shares, the tax benefits that accrued to SCM are to be spread among all of its common stockholders, for calculation purposes, and petitioner is to be awarded his proportionate share of this corporate asset.[6]

---

[6] [3] The relief granted is consistent with the relief demanded in petitioner's pleading although the incremental increase in the value of petitioner's shares after a new hearing may be less than petitioner

Finally, petitioner contends that his personal income tax situation should have been considered. However, personal income tax liability is not an element of future value to SCM arising from the merger (*Alpert v. 28 Williams St. Corp.*, 63 N.Y.2d 557, 571, *supra; see, Weinberger v. UOP, Inc.*, 457 A.2d 701, 713 [Del.], *supra*). As the Supreme Court of Delaware stated in defining fair price: "The basic concept of value under the appraisal statute is that the stockholder is entitled to be paid for that which has been taken from him, viz., his proportionate interest in a going concern. By value of the stockholder's proportionate interest in the corporate enterprise is meant the true or intrinsic value of his stock which has been taken by the merger" (457 A.2d, *supra*, at 713 [quoting *Tri-Continental Corp. v. Battye*, 31 Del. Ch 523, 74 A.2d 71, 72]). Manifestly, Cawley's $107,100 increased tax liability had no bearing on the value of SCM's common stock and thus was properly disregarded below.

The dissenter questions the "purpose to be served" by this decision. He concedes, however, that the tax benefit respondent corporation derived from repurchasing ISO shares constituted a corporate asset. Indeed it did. Because of the tax treatment of respondent's cost of repurchasing the ISO shares, the corporation was entitled to a deduction of more than four million dollars and a tax benefit of almost two million dollars. Petitioner contends that the statute contemplates that the fair value of his shares should reflect this corporate asset and that courts below erred interpreting the 1982 statute and a decision of this court superseded by the 1982 amendment when they failed to consider it. Although the dissenter would ignore this claim as merely an attempt to "sweeten" a "windfall,"[7] we believe petitioner's proceeding represents an appropriate request for judicial intervention to resolve a legal question of importance to New York's business community. The dollar benefit to petitioner in the end, may be relatively small or even nonexistent, but the fact does not reflect the importance of the underlying statutory question presented by the case and could not justify our failure to answer it.

Nor have we, by our decision, unduly complicated these proceedings. Nothing in the statute or its legislative history supports the dissenter's claim that the Legislature, in amending section 623, was concerned with a need to make the statutory remedy "fast and summary." On the contrary, section 623(h) gives the court plenary powers to adjudicate fair value issues and gives the parties broad pretrial disclosure rights to assist them in the presentation of their claims. We assume jury trials are not permitted in these proceedings because corporate matters are traditionally equitable in nature and because difficult and technical

---

requests. That is not a determination to be made by this court, however, and the speculative computation of the increase and its amount, recited in the dissent, is unsupported by evidence in the record or statements in the briefs.

Finally, in answer to the dissent, this proceeding is not in any sense a class action or the functional equivalent of a class action. Petitioner was the only shareholder to perfect his right to a fair valuation determination, as provided by statute, and thus he will be the only shareholder entitled to a value greater than $75 if the court finds the shares have a greater value after considering the tax benefit to the corporation.

[7] [4] We would note that the exercise of stock options, earned long before merger was contemplated, and the valuation of shares purchased under them, has nothing to do with "golden parachutes" and the trial court did not so characterize this transaction.

valuation problems are commonly addressed by the court without a jury.

Accordingly, the order of the Appellate Division should be reversed and the matter remitted to Supreme Court to determine whether a summary determination was appropriate, and to reassess the fair value of SCM's stock, in light of this decision.

Bellacosa, J. (dissenting).

I dissent and vote to affirm the order of the Appellate Division which affirmed the judgment of Supreme Court fixing the fair value of petitioner Cawley's stock at $75 per share. My particular disagreement with the reversal is that it effects as a matter of law an asset-specific accounting in what is supposed to be simply a fair value appraisal of a minority shareholder's stock. It would then necessitate a pro rata calculation of this minuscule asset relative to the 22,000 other shareholders.

The legal issue that separates us in this complex billion dollar corporate-financial merger is narrow. Did both lower courts correctly apply the fair value appraisal criteria of Business Corporation Law § 623(h)(4), or must a *sui generis* tax factor of the kind implicated in this case be expressly considered I would say "yes" to the first question and "no" to the second.

My difficulty is discerning a sufficient legal basis to disturb as a matter of law the lower courts' determinations. Moreover, on a practical basis, there is no manifestation on the record and no purpose to be served in concluding that the Appellate Division did not weigh all the "relevant factors" in arriving at its fair value determination under the statute.

Cawley was the treasurer of SCM at the time that Hanson Trust PLC initiated its two-step merger acquisition of SCM (*see, Alpert v. 28 Williams St. Corp.*, 63 N.Y.2d 557, 563; Brudney & Chirelstein, *A Restatement of Corporate Freezeouts*, 87 Yale L.J. 1354, 1356, 1358 [1978]). At the time of the merger, Cawley owned 9,539 shares of SCM *common stock*. All Cawley's stock was purchased pursuant to incentive stock options ("an option granted to an individual for any reason connected with his employment by a corporation," Internal Revenue Code § 422A[b] [26 USC]). Seven thousand of his shares were acquired five months after the initiation of the takeover, three months before Hanson sought to freeze out minority shareholders, and two days *after* Hanson acquired greater than a 50% controlling interest in SCM. There is no difference in class or in character between Cawley's common stock and the over 12 million other outstanding shares of SCM common stock. The factors which Cawley parlays into a personal enhancement of his valuation treatment are the manner in which he purchased the shares and the tax consequences that emerged solely from the timing of his liquidation of his common stock.

An employer is not entitled to a trade or business expense deduction (Internal Revenue Code § 162 [26 U.S.C.]) for employee profit realized from an incentive stock option if the employee holds the shares for more than one year from the exercise of the option and more than two years from the grant of the option (Internal Revenue Code § 421[a]; § 442[a] [26 U.S.C.]). If the time periods are not satisfied, the employer becomes entitled to a tax deduction equal to the ordinary income *compensation* realized by the employee (Internal Revenue Code § 421[b] [26 USC]; F. Tax Regs § 1.421-5[b] [3]; [e] [26 CFR]). By reason of forced buyout of 7,000 shares of Cawley's common stock before he had held them for a year, Hanson-SCM acquired a pro rata tax deduction. That is the nub of this case.

As the sole remaining dissenting shareholder in this appraisal action, Cawley through careful crafting of his legal argument, argued that the fair value of his common stock is greater than the fair value of all other stock in his class because of the tax deduction which inured to the acquiring corporation. The majority acknowledges that Cawley does not otherwise contest the $75 common stock fair value determination, calling it "law of the case" (majority opn, at 472). There is no dispute that the SCM's independent financial advisor, Goldman, Sachs & Company, advised the SCM board of directors that the common stock offerings at $70, $74 and, finally, $75 all represented fair value offers. In fact, the tender offer price of $75 per share was $29 per share more than the pretakeover announcement market price. The record reveals not a hint of contradiction of Hanson-SCM's cogent argument before the trial Justice that its $75 freeze-out offer was fair value because it far exceeded the market value of the stock preceding the active bidding contest, that the offer exceeded the investment value of the stock, and that net value is not an appropriate measure of fair value of an ongoing concern (record on appeal, at 40-42).

Cawley was recipient of a most generous special stock preference (option price of $21 for 5,000 shares and $32.12 for remaining 2,000) owing to his status as an insider corporate treasurer (indeed a fully informed senior management officer). He was afforded in the midst of a corporate takeover battle a guaranteed substantial profit at 350% (the option price was $53 below market price on the day he exercised it and his over-all buyout from the corporation was characterized by the trial court as a "golden parachute"). He now argues that the successor to his benefactor, Hanson-SCM should not incidentally benefit from the tax deduction accruing as a consequence of his special treatment, and that the fair value of his common stock should be different from the $75 uncontested "law of the case," appraiser certified, common stock fair value, and should be sweetened by the value of the corporate deduction. Business Corporation Law § 623 gives dissenting minority shareholders like Cawley a fair value appraisal remedy, not the equivalent of an accounting and a windfall to boot.

The implementation of an appraisal proceeding requires that "shares of the same class be equal in all respects to every other share of the class" (*Fe Bland v. Two Trees Mgt. Co.*, 66 N.Y.2d 556, 569; *see, Katowitz v. Sidler*, 24 N.Y.2d 512, 518). Business Corporation Law § 623(h)(4) provides that in appraising stock value of a dissenting shareholder, "the court shall consider the nature of the transaction giving rise to the shareholder's right to receive payment for shares and its effects on the corporation and its shareholders, the concepts and methods then customary in the relevant securities and financial markets for determining fair value of shares of a corporation engaging in a similar transaction under comparable circumstances and all other relevant factors." "[I]t is well established by case law that, in our State, the elements which are to enter into such an appraisal are net asset value, investment value and market value . . . [but] the weight to be accorded to each varies with the facts and circumstances in a particular case" (*Matter of Endicott*

Johnson Corp. v. Bade, 37 N.Y.2d 585, 587 [citations omitted]).

No rigid rule exists for determining the fair value because the appraisal will necessarily have to be flexible to the "existence of a state of facts peculiar to the situation" (*Matter of Fulton*, 257 N.Y. 487, 494). "It follows that all three [appraisal methods] do not have to influence the result in every valuation proceeding. It suffices if they are all considered" (*Matter of Endicott Johnson Corp. v. Bade*, 37 N.Y.2d 585, 588, *supra*). Additionally, "[e]vidence that an independent investment firm was retained to render a fairness opinion the price offered to the minority" is one means of demonstrating the price was proper (*see, Alpert v. 28 Williams St. Corp.*, 63 N.Y.2d 557, 572, *supra*). "The ultimate valuation to the extent that it is confined to the issues of fact, rests largely within the discretion of the lower courts" (*Matter of Endicott Johnson Corp. v. Bade, supra*, at 588, citing Cohen and Karger, Powers of the New York Court of Appeals § 148, at 589-590 [rev. ed.]).

The record here amply demonstrates that the trial court was cognizant of the fact that the tender offers made throughout these takeover proceedings far exceeded the market value of the stock prior to the initiation of the buyout. The court also had Hanson-SCM's uncontested arguments before it regarding the investment and net asset value of the stock. Heavy reliance was placed on the fair value appraisals of the independent financial advisors Goldman, Sachs & Company. It is of no legal consequence that the Trial Justice refused to engage in tax asset accounting, because there is no error in discounting such tax consequences as "particularizations of a conscientious step-by-step analysis of relevant income account factors rather than as added aliquot valuations" (*Matter of Endicott Johnson Corp. v. Bade*, 37 N.Y.2d 585, 591, *supra*). The tax consequences of Cawley's option exercise and freeze-out-compelled distribution, together with those of the two other senior executive officers privileged to own incentive stock option shares, were among the myriad of factors that produced a merger price of $75 per share, which was by all accounts fair and generous as far as Cawley was concerned. By this analysis, I do not propose that the courts "ignore" or "refuse" to answer the key question; rather I say the lower courts have answered it — correctly for the parties and for New York's business community.

Alternatively, even if we were to assume, however, that the tax factor is a mandatory relevant factor under the Business Corporation Law § 623 "catch all" — cogent legislative history and close analysis of the law and evidence here suggest that is not necessarily so — and even if we were to assume further that the lower courts did not consider that factor at all, I still arrive at the same result. A remittal for what is likely to be a relatively fruitless exercise should produce no or de minimis effects in this case. The tax asset acquired by Hanson-SCM from the buyout of Cawley's stock must be given specific recognition under the majority's holding and must be spread equally among all common stock shareholders. This would result in an increase in value of 1.3 cents per share ($163,041/12,172,340 shares = 1.3 cents [this calculation is made, of course, on the only shares for which appraisal is sought — Cawley's — and will no doubt be the subject of proof by the contending accountants at the trial]). The holding that the corporate tax benefits, derived from the freeze out of all incentive stock option shares, be accounted for and then calculated pro rata as among all of SCM's former shareholders with Cawley being awarded his proportionate share grants relief never requested by Cawley and also necessarily deals with the fair value of common stock of nondissenting shareholders. This was not within the purview of Cawley's Business Corporation Law § 623 fair value proceeding and functionally grants a kind of class action relief.

Only Cawley's shares (7,000 out of 12 million) are really involved, and not all stock and shareholders, as is required, are really affected by Cawley's "red herring," "relevant" factor. Individualization of this kind of tax consideration could not have realistically been intended by the Legislature and it seems to me may be fraught with mischief and impracticality. The holding in this case may flip like proceedings into full scale accountings, with all the delay, uncertainty and speculation of such matters (*see, Johnson v. Manhattan & Bronx Surface Tr. Operating Auth.*, 71 N.Y.2d 198; *Matter of Lanzano v. City of New York*, 71 N.Y.2d 208). The Business Corporation Law § 623 remedy is supposed to be relatively fast and summary, which is why jury trial is forbidden. That procedural goal will be negated or at least frustrated by the interpretation given the statute in this case as applied to the numerous vexatious cases sure to be generated.

I agree with the majority that Cawley is not entitled to an increase in the fair value of his common stock equal to the difference between the ordinary income tax treatment of the profits from his stock and the capital gains treatment he would have received had he held the stock for more than the six-month capital gains period.

Both irrelevant tax factors were correctly excluded or discounted from this fair value determination by the courts below, and I would affirm.

CHIEF JUDGE WACHTLER and JUDGES KAYE, ALEXANDER, TITONE and HANCOCK, JR., concur with JUDGE SIMONS; JUDGE BELLACOSA dissents and votes to affirm in a separate opinion.

Order reversed, with costs, and matter remitted to Supreme Court, New York County, for further proceedings in accordance with the opinion herein.

FRIEDMAN v. BEWAY REALTY CORP.

Court of Appeals of New York
661 N.E.2d 972 (1995)

LEVINE, J.

Petitioners are minority stockholders in nine family owned close corporations, each of which had as its sole asset a parcel of income-producing office, commercial or residential real estate in New York City. In 1986, the board of directors and the requisite majority of stockholders of each corporation voted to transfer all of its property to a newly formed partnership. Petitioners voted their shares against the transfers and, pursuant to Business Corporation Law § 623, timely elected to exercise their appraisal rights and receive the "fair value" of their shares in each corporation. When the corporations failed to offer to purchase their shares, petitioners commenced this proceeding to have a judicial determination of the fair value of the shares (*see*, Business Corporation Law § 623[h]).

In the first phase of a bifurcated valuation trial, Supreme Court determined the net value of the leasehold interest in an office building held by one of the family corporations, a decision not now disputed. The parties then stipulated to the net asset values of the remaining corporations. It is undisputed that, based on the percentages of each petitioner's stockholdings in the nine corporations, her proportionate share of the aggregate net asset values of all nine corporations was $15,200,833.

The second phase of the trial was devoted to a determination of the fair value of petitioners' shares in the nine corporations, given the net asset values previously fixed. At the conclusion of the trial, Supreme Court rejected the testimony of petitioners' expert, who had essentially arrived at his opinion of fair value by simply applying petitioners' fractional corporate stock ownership to the aggregate corporate net asset values. The court reasoned that this approach ignored the effect of the lack of marketability of the corporate stock and "valued these shares as if petitioners were co-tenants in the real estate rather than corporate shareholders."

Instead, Supreme Court adopted the net asset-based valuation methodology employed by Kenneth McGraw, the corporations' expert. McGraw's technique was, first, to ascertain what petitioners' shares hypothetically would sell for, relative to the net asset values of the corporations, if the corporate stocks were marketable and publicly traded; and second, to apply a discount to that hypothetical price per share in order to reflect the stocks' actual lack of marketability. As to the first step in this valuation process, Supreme Court accepted the comparability of one group of publicly traded shares suggested by McGraw, that is, of real estate investment trusts (REITs). McGraw suggested that REITs shares traded primarily in direct relation to each REIT's net asset value and, hence, the mean discount between REIT net asset values per share and REIT stock prices (which McGraw found was 9.8%) could be applied to determine what petitioners' stocks were worth if they were marketable. Thus, McGraw opined that the hypothetical value of the dissenters' shares here, if marketable and publicly traded, would be 9.8% less than their net asset value per share.

For the second step in McGraw's valuation process he applied a discount to reflect the illiquidity of petitioners' shares, i.e., that a potential investor would pay less for shares in a close corporation because they could not readily be liquidated for cash (*see, Matter of Seagroatt Floral Co. [Riccardi]*, 78 N.Y.2d 439, 445-446). The primary unmarketability discount recommended by McGraw was 30.4%. According to McGraw, that figure represented the mean reduction in price per share when ordinarily publicly traded shares in "comparative" corporations became unregistered and thus, restricted shares, which could only be sold in private placements. The corporations' expert then exacted an additional 14.6% discount in the value of the shares, which he based upon the existence of restrictions on transfer contained in stockholder agreements covering the shares of all nine corporations.

Although Supreme Court approved of the net asset valuation methodology of the corporations' expert as a generally valid approach to determining the fair value of petitioners' shares, it found various flaws in McGraw's evaluation and modified the values accordingly. First, the court eliminated the initial 9.8% discount from each petitioners' share in the aggregate net asset value of the corporations. The court based this upon McGraw's testimonial concession that the discrepancy between net asset value per share and price per share in REITs actually represented for the most part the minority status of the REIT shares traded. Thus, the court reasoned, to reduce petitioners' share of net asset value by 9.8% would in effect impose a discount based upon petitioners' status as minority stockholders, a result the court concluded violated New York precedents (citing *Matter of Raskin v. Walter Karl, Inc.*, 129 A.D.2d 642; *Matter of Blake v. Blake Agency*, 107 A.D.2d 139, *lv denied* 65 N.Y.2d 609).

Second, Supreme Court rejected McGraw's rationale for the imposition of a second unmarketability discount of 14.6% based upon stockholder agreement restrictions, as factually "unpersuasive." Finally, the court found that McGraw's 30.4% unmarketability discount actually included "a minority interest factor which is implicit in any minority stock holding." Consequently, the court considered it necessary to eliminate that factor from the value equation. It did so by reducing the 30.4% discount by 9.4%, which the court regarded as the discount McGraw had testified reflected the minority status of the shares traded in comparable REITs.[8] Thus, Supreme Court only applied a 21% discount for unmarketability against each petitioner's proportionate share of the aggregate net asset value of the corporations, resulting in a fair value determination of each petitioner's total stock interests of $2,008,682.

The Appellate Division affirmed for the reasons stated by Supreme Court.

I

The corporations' primary argument for reversal is that Supreme Court erred as a matter of law in refusing to take into account in its fair value determination the financial reality that minority shares in a close corporation are worth less because they represent only a minority, rather than a controlling interest. Although the corporations' argument may have validity when corporate stock is valued for other purposes, it overlooks the statutory objective here of achieving a *fair* appraisal remedy for dissenting minority shareholders. Mandating the imposition of a "minority discount" in fixing the fair value of the stockholdings of dissenting minority shareholders in a close corporation is inconsistent with the equitable principles developed in New York decisional law on dissenting stockholder statutory appraisal rights (a position shared by the courts in most other jurisdictions), and the policies underlying the statutory reforms giving minority stockholders the right to withdraw from a corporation and be compensated for the value of their interests when the corporate majority takes significant action deemed inimical to the position of the minority.

Several principles have emerged from our cases involving appraisal rights of dissenting shareholders under Business Corporation Law § 623 or its predecessor statute. (1) The fair value of a dissenter's shares is to be determined on their worth in a going concern, not in liquidation, and fair value is not necessarily tied to market

---

[8] [1] As earlier described, the actual mean minority discount McGraw derived from his REIT study was 9.8%, not the 9.4% the court applied to reduce McGraw's recommended unmarketability discount. None of the parties to this appeal has raised any objection based upon this discrepancy.

value as reflected in actual stock trading (*Matter of Fulton*, 257 N.Y. 487, 492). "The purpose of the statute being to save the dissenting stockholder from loss by reason of the change in the nature of the business, he [or she] is entitled to receive the value of his [or her] stock for sale *or its value for investment*" (*id.*, at 494 [emphasis supplied]). (2) The three major elements of fair value are net asset value, investment value and market value. The particular facts and circumstances will dictate which element predominates, and not all three elements must influence the result (*Matter of Endicott Johnson Corp. v. Bade*, 37 N.Y.2d 585, 587-588). (3) Fair value requires that the dissenting stockholder be paid for his or her *proportionate* interest in a going concern, that is, the intrinsic value of the shareholder's economic interest in the corporate enterprise (*Matter of Cawley v. SCM Corp.*, 72 N.Y.2d 465, 474). (4) By virtue of the 1982 amendment to Business Corporation Law § 623(h)(4) (L 1982, ch 202, § 9), fair value determinations should take into account the subsequent economic impact on value of the very transaction giving rise to appraisal rights, as supplemental to the three basic value factors (net asset, investment and market values). (5) Determinations of the fair value of a dissenter's shares are governed by the statutory provisions of the Business Corporation Law that require equal treatment of all shares of the same class of stock (*Matter of Cawley, supra*, at 473).

Further, contrary to the corporations' contention here, there is no difference in analysis between stock fair value determinations under Business Corporation Law § 623, and fair value determinations under Business Corporation Law § 1118. The latter provision governs the rights of minority stockholders when the corporation has elected to purchase their interests, also at "fair value," following their petition for corporate dissolution under Business Corporation Law § 1104-a for oppressive majority conduct. The corporations' opposing argument is that considerations of the oppressive conduct of the majority stockholders enter into fair value considerations conducted under Business Corporation Law § 1118; therefore, the cases decided under that section are distinguishable and not authoritative for fair value considerations under Business Corporation Law § 623. The corporations' position in this regard is untenable because their basic underlying assumption-that oppressive majority conduct enters into the court's fair value equation under section 1118-is in error. As we stated in *Matter of Pace Photographers (Rosen)* (71 N.Y.2d 737), once the corporation has elected to buy the petitioning stockholders' shares at fair value, "the issue of [majority] wrongdoing [is] superfluous . . . [f]ixing blame is material under [Business Corporation Law §] 1104-a, but not under [Business Corporation Law §] 1118" (*id.*, at 746; *see also, Matter of Seagroatt Floral Co.*, 78 N.Y.2d, at 445, *supra).*

Thus, we apply to stock fair value determinations under section 623 the principle we enunciated for such determinations under section 1118 that, in fixing fair value, courts should determine the minority shareholder's proportionate interest in the going concern value of the corporation as a whole, that is, " 'what a willing purchaser, in an arm's length transaction, would offer for the *corporation* as an operating business' " (*Matter of Pace Photographers [Rosen]*, 71 N.Y.2d, at 748, *supra*, quoting *Matter of Blake v Blake Agency*, 107 A.D.2d, at 146, *supra* [emphasis supplied]).

Consistent with that approach, we have approved a methodology for fixing the fair value of minority shares in a close corporation under which the investment value of the entire enterprise was ascertained through a capitalization of earnings (taking into account the unmarketability of the corporate stock) and then fair value was calculated on the basis of the petitioners' proportionate share of all outstanding corporate stock (*Matter of Seagroatt Floral Co.*, 78 N.Y.2d, at 442, 446, *supra*).

Imposing a discount for the minority status of the dissenting shares here, as argued by the corporations, would in our view conflict with two central equitable principles of corporate governance we have developed for fair value adjudications of minority shareholder interests under Business Corporation Law §§ 623 and 1118. A minority discount would necessarily deprive minority shareholders of their proportionate interest in a going concern, as guaranteed by our decisions previously discussed. Likewise, imposing a minority discount on the compensation payable to dissenting stockholders for their shares in a proceeding under Business Corporation Law §§ 623 or 1118 would result in minority shares being valued below that of majority shares, thus violating our mandate of equal treatment of all shares of the same class in minority stockholder buyouts.

A minority discount on the value of dissenters' shares would also significantly undermine one of the major policies behind the appraisal legislation embodied now in Business Corporation Law § 623, the remedial goal of the statute to "protect[ ] minority shareholders 'from being forced to sell at unfair values imposed by those dominating the corporation while allowing the majority to proceed with its desired [corporate action]' " (*Matter of Cawley v. SCM Corp.*, 72 N.Y.2d, at 471, *supra*, quoting *Alpert v. 28 William St. Corp.*, 61 N.Y.2d 557, 567-568). This protective purpose of the statute prevents the shifting of proportionate economic value of the corporation as a going concern from minority to majority stockholders. As stated by the Delaware Supreme Court, "to fail to accord to a minority shareholder the full proportionate value of his [or her] shares imposes a penalty for lack of control, and unfairly enriches the majority stockholders who may reap a windfall from the appraisal process by cashing out a dissenting shareholder" (*Cavalier Oil Corp. v. Harnett*, 564 A.2d 1137, 1145 [Del]).

Furthermore, a mandatory reduction in the fair value of minority shares to reflect their owners' lack of power in the administration of the corporation will inevitably encourage oppressive majority conduct, thereby further driving down the compensation necessary to pay for the value of minority shares. "Thus, the greater the misconduct by the majority, the less they need to pay for the minority's shares" (Murdock, *The Evolution of Effective Remedies for Minority Shareholders and Its Impact Upon Evaluation of Minority Shares*, 65 NOTRE DAME L. REV. 425, 487).

We also note that a minority discount has been rejected in a substantial majority of other jurisdictions.[9] "Thus, statistically, minority discounts are almost uniformly viewed with disfavor by State courts" (*id.*, at 481). The imposition of a minority discount in derogation of minority stockholder appraisal remedies has been rejected as well by the American Law Institute in its Principles of Corporate Governance

---

[9] [2] *E.g., Brown v. Allied Corrugated Box Co.*, 91 Cal. App. 3d 477, 486, 154 Cal. Rptr. 170; *Cavalier Oil Corp. v. Harnett, supra*, at 1144 (Del); *Hickory Cr. Nursery v. Johnston*, 167 Ill. App. 3d 449, 521 N.E.2d 236, 239-240; *Eyler v. Eyler*, 492 N.E.2d 1071 (Ind); *Woodward v. Quigley*, 257 Iowa 1077, 133 N.W.2d 38, 43, *mod* 257 Iowa 1104, 136 N.W.2d 280; *Matter of McLoon Oil Co.*, 565 A.2d 997, 1004-1005 (Me.); *Rigel Corp. v. Cutchall*, 245 Neb. 118, 511 N.W.2d 519.

(*see*, 2 ALI, Principles of Corporate Governance § 7.22, at 314-315; comment *e* to § 7.22, at 324 [1994]).

II

We likewise find no basis to disturb the trial court's discretion in failing to assign any additional diminution in value of petitioners' shares here because they were subject to contractual restrictions on voluntary transfer. As we noted in *Matter of Pace Photographers (Rosen) (supra)*, a statutory acquisition of minority shares by a corporation pursuant to the Business Corporation Law is not a voluntary sale of corporate shares as contemplated by a restrictive stockholder agreement and, therefore, "the express covenant is literally inapplicable" (71 N.Y.2d, at 749). Nor is there any reason to disturb Supreme Court's award of prejudgment interest.

III

While we have concluded that Supreme Court correctly applied the legal doctrines respecting fair value determinations of dissenting minority stockholders' shares in the instant case, we find error in the court's calculation of the unmarketability discount which must be applied here. As previously explained, Supreme Court, generally adopted the net asset valuation approach of McGraw, the corporations' expert, and his two-step evaluation process. However, the court added back the 9.8% discount McGraw took in the first step of that process because the court concluded that it actually represented a minority discount. Then, when it reached the second step of the evaluation process, the court removed what it regarded as the same minority discount from the 30.4% unmarketability discount McGraw applied at that stage. Thus, Supreme Court added back McGraw's minority discount twice, once in each of the stages of the process. Apparently, this was based upon the court's erroneous finding that McGraw arrived at the 30.4% discount by analyzing privately transacted sales of stock "with restrictive sale provisions and [McGraw] found that they exhibited a median discount of 30.4 percent *relative to net asset value*" (emphasis supplied). Supreme Court further reasoned that, because the sales McGraw analyzed were of minority shares, his unmarketability discount also must have contained an element of reduced value because of their minority status. The evidence in the record does not support the foregoing conclusions. In actuality, McGraw did not arrive at the 30.4% discount by comparing shares with "restrictive sale provisions" to their net asset values. He calculated the unmarketability factor by comparing the purchase prices of registered, publicly traded *minority* shares in comparative corporations, to the purchase prices of *the same class of minority shares* in the same corporations that were unregistered and, therefore, not publicly traded but purchased under trading restrictions in private placements. Because McGraw in his calculations always compared the prices of a marketable set of minority shares to the prices of a set of minority shares when the same stock was unmarketable, the difference in prices of the shares did not contain any additional minority discount element, and the discount was solely attributable to the difference in the marketability of the shares in the same stock.

Thus, Supreme Court erred in removing a nonexistent minority discount element from the reduction in value of petitioners' shares McGraw attributed to their lack of marketability. It is unclear, however, as to whether Supreme Court would have accepted in full McGraw's 30.4% discount as a proper reflection of diminution in value due to unmarketability had the court been aware that it did not also reflect a reduction in value due to the shares' minority status. Because of this uncertainty, the matter must be remitted to Supreme Court for a new determination of the appropriate discount for unmarketability of petitioners' shares and a recalculation of fair value when that discount is applied to the proportionate net asset value of petitioners' stockholdings in the nine corporations.

Accordingly, the order should be reversed, without costs, and the matter remitted to Supreme Court for further proceedings in accordance with this opinion.

M.G. BANCORPORATION v. LE BEAU

Delaware Supreme Court
737 A.2d 513 (1999)

HOLLAND, JUSTICE:

This appeal is taken by Respondents-appellants, M.G. Bancorporation, Inc. ("MGB"), and Southwest Bancorp, Inc. ("Southwest"), Delaware corporations, from a final judgment of the Court of Chancery. The proceeding arises from a cash-out merger of the minority shareholders of MGB on November 17, 1993 (the "Merger"). MGB was merged into Southwest, which owned over 91% of the outstanding shares of MGB's common stock, pursuant to 8 Del. C. § 253. The Petitioners-appellees were the record owners of 18,151 shares of MGB common stock as of the date of the Merger. The Merger consideration was $41 per share.

The Petitioners initiated an appraisal proceeding, in accordance with 8 Del. C. § 262 ("Section 262"), to determine the fair value of MGB's common stock. Following a three-day trial, the Court of Chancery concluded that the fair value of MGB's common stock as of the Merger date was $85 per share. The Respondents were ordered to pay that sum, together with interest, compounded monthly, at the rate of 8% from November 17, 1993.

This Court affirms that portion of the judgment by the Court of Chancery that awarded the Petitioners $85 per share. That portion of the judgment that awarded compound interest to the Petitioners, however, is remanded for further consideration.

APPELLANTS' CONTENTIONS

On March 30, 1998, the Respondents appealed from the final judgment. The Respondents have raised four issues. First, the Respondents submit that the Court of Chancery erred, as a matter of law, by improperly placing the burden of proof on the Respondents and accepting the "comparative acquisitions" appraisal of the Petitioners' expert witness. Second, the Respondents contend that the Court of Chancery's rejection of other valid valuation methods (e.g., the discounted cash flow method) was contrary to its statutory responsibility to appraise the fair value of the

Petitioners' shares independently. Third, Respondents argue that the Court of Chancery violated 8 Del. C. § 262(h) and Delaware case law by appraising the fair value of MGB stock on the basis of merger and acquisition transactions which, according to the Respondents, contained acquisition premia unrelated to the fair value of MGB as a going concern. . . .

FACTS

The Petitioners are shareholders who owned 18,151 shares of common stock of MGB before the Merger. The Respondents are Southwest and its subsidiary, MGB. Before the Merger, MGB was a Delaware-chartered bank holding company headquartered in Worth, Illinois. MGB had two operating Illinois-chartered bank subsidiaries, Mount Greenwood Bank ("Greenwood") and Worth Bancorp, Inc. ("WBC"). Both banks served customers in the southwestern Chicago metropolitan area. MGB owned 100% of Mount Greenwood and 75.5% of WBC.

Before the Merger, Southwest owned 91.68% of MGB's common shares. On November 17, 1993, MGB was merged into Southwest in a "short form" merger under 8 Del. C. § 253. Because the Merger was accomplished unilaterally, neither MGB's board of directors nor its minority shareholders were legally required to, or did, vote on the transaction.

Southwest engaged Alex Sheshunoff & Co. Investment Bankers ("Sheshunoff") to determine the "fair market value" of MGB's minority shares for the purpose of setting the Merger price. Sheshunoff determined that the fair market value of MGB's minority shares was $41 per share as of June 30, 1993. Accordingly, MGB's minority shareholders were offered $41 per share in cash as the Merger consideration. The Petitioners rejected that offer, electing instead to pursue their statutory rights, and this appraisal proceeding was commenced.

A stockholders class action based on breach of fiduciary duty was also filed challenging the Merger. On July 5, 1995, the Court of Chancery issued a decision in that companion class action, holding that Sheshunoff had not performed its appraisal in a legally proper manner.[10] The basis for the Court of Chancery's conclusion was that Sheshunoff had determined only the "fair market value" of MGB's minority shares, as opposed to valuing MGB in its entirety as a going concern and then determining the fair value of the minority shares as a pro rata percentage of that value.[11]

Petitioners' Valuation

At the December 1996 trial, the Petitioners' expert witness was David Clarke ("Clarke"). He testified that as of the Merger date the fair value of MGB common stock was $58,514,000, or $85 per share. In arriving at that conclusion, Clarke used three distinct methodologies to value MGB's two operating bank subsidiaries: the comparative publicly-traded company approach, yielding a $76.24 to $77.50 per

[10] [1] *Nebel v. Southwest Bancorp, Inc.*, Del. Ch., C.A. No. 13618, [1995 Del. Ch. LEXIS 80], 1995 WL 405750 (July 5, 1995) Mem. Op. at 4.

[11] [2] *Id.*

share value; the discounted cash flow ("DCF") method, yielding a $73.96 to $72.23 per share value; and, the comparative acquisitions approach, yielding an $85 per share value.

In performing his analysis, Clarke added a control premium to the values of the two subsidiaries to reflect the value of MGB's controlling interest in those subsidiaries. He then added the value of MGB's remaining assets to his valuations of the two subsidiaries. Clarke arrived at an overall fair value of $85 per share for MGB.

At the trial, the Petitioners also introduced evidence of what MGB's fair value would be if Sheshunoff's prior determination were revised as of the Merger date and if its minority discount were eliminated.

Respondents' Valuation

The Respondents relied upon the expert testimony of Robert Reilly ("Reilly") at trial. He testified that, as of the Merger date, the fair value of MGB common stock was $41.90 per share. Reilly arrived at that conclusion by performing two separate valuations: the discounted cash flow method and a "capital market" analysis. Reilly did not add any control premium to the values of MGB's two subsidiaries, because he determined that a control premium was inappropriate in valuing a holding company such as MGB.

The Respondents did not call anyone from the Sheshunoff firm as an expert witness at trial, even though Sheshunoff's valuation had served as the basis for setting the $41 per share Merger price consideration.

COURT OF CHANCERY'S DECISION

At the conclusion of the trial, the Court of Chancery had before it: three per share values from Clarke; two per share values from Reilly; and a revision by the Petitioners' witness of the Sheshunoff $41 per share computation. The parties' experts' respective valuation conclusions and the revised Sheshunoff valuation were summarized by the Court of Chancery in the following chart:

Valuation in $'000's:	WBC	75.5% of WBC	Greenwood	Other Assets	Total	Per Sh.
Petitioners (Clarke)						
Comparative Publicly-Traded Method:	33,059	24,960	20,952	6,814	52,726	76.59
With Control Premium:	43,300	32,692	27,100	6,814	66,606	96.76
DFC Method:	32,075	24,217	20,079	6,814	51,110	74.25
With Control Premium:	44,800	33,824	28,300	6,814	68,938	100.15
Comparative Acquisitions Method:	38,100	28,800	22,900	6,814	58,514	85.00 =fair value
Respondents (Reilly)						
Capital Market Method:					28,400	41.26
						42.45
DCF Method:					29,220	41.90 =fair value
Sheshunoff (Updated) (Without Control Premium)						
Adjusted Book Value:						64.13
Adjusted Earnings Value:						76.80

The Court of Chancery concluded that $85 per share was the fair value of MGB's stock on the date of the merger.

BURDEN OF PERSUASION

COLLATERAL ESTOPPEL DOCTRINE

The Court of Chancery's written analysis in its valuation determination contained the following statement:

The fact that Reilly's per share value determination serendipitously turned out to be only 90 cents per share more than Sheshunoff's legally flawed $41 valuation, cannot help but render Respondents' valuation position highly suspect and meriting the most careful judicial scrutiny. As a matter of plain common sense it would appear evident that a proper fair value determination based upon a going concern valuation of the entire company, would significantly exceed a $41 per share fair market valuation of only a minority block of its shares. If Respondents choose to contend otherwise, it is their burden to persuade the Court that $41.90 per share represents MGB's fair value. The Court concludes that the Respondents have fallen far short of carrying their burden, and independently determines that the fair value of MGB at the time of the Merger was $85 per share.[12]

. . .

In the context of this Merger, the breach of fiduciary duty damage action was adjudicated first. In writing the decision in the statutory appraisal action that is now before this Court, the Court of Chancery specifically noted that it had previously "issued an opinion in the companion class action holding that Sheshunoff had performed its appraisal in a legally improper manner."[13] The Court of Chancery also noted the basis for its "conclusion was that Sheshunoff had determined only the 'fair market value' of MGB's minority shares, as opposed to valuing MGB in its entirety as a going concern and determining the fair value of the minority shares as a pro rata percentage of that value."[14]

"Pursuant to the doctrine of collateral estoppel, if a court has decided an issue of fact necessary to its judgment, that decision precludes relitigation of the issue in a suit on a different cause of action involving a party to the first case."[15] Accordingly, the Court of Chancery's prior holding in the breach of fiduciary duty damage action collaterally estopped the Respondents from relitigating the factual finding which rejected Sheshunoff's opinion that the $41 per share was the fair value of MGB's stock as of June 30, 1993. The record reflects that the Respondents did not even attempt to present an expert witness from the Sheshunoff firm during the statutory appraisal proceeding.

In a statutory appraisal proceeding, both sides have the burden of proving their respective valuation positions by a preponderance of evidence.[16] Nevertheless, the Respondents were collaterally estopped from arguing in the statutory appraisal action that Sheshunoff's $41 determination represented MGB's fair value per share, given the entry of the Court of Chancery's prior final judgment in the breach of fiduciary duty damage action involving the same Merger. Consequently, it was entirely appropriate for the Court of Chancery to require the Respondents to demonstrate how Reilly's purportedly proper statutory appraisal valuation resulted

---

[12] [3] *LeBeau v. M.G. Bancorporation, Inc.*, Del. Ch., C.A. No. 13414, [1998 Del. Ch. LEXIS 9], 1998 WL 44993 (Jan. 29, 1998) Mem. Op. at 7.

[13] [10] *LeBeau v. M.G. Bancorporation*, Inc., Del. Ch., C.A. No. 13414, [1998 Del. Ch. LEXIS 9], 1998 WL 44993 (Jan. 29, 1998) Mem. Op. at 1.

[14] [11] *Id.*

[15] [12] *Messick v. Star Enterprise*, Del. Supr., 655 A.2d 1209, 1211 (1995).

[16] [13] *Gonsalves v. Straight Arrow Publishers, Inc.*, Del. Supr., 701 A.2d 357 (1997).

in only a 90 cents (approximately 2%) per share increase over the legally improper Sheshunoff valuation that had included a minority discount. In doing so, the doctrine of collateral estoppel was correctly applied by the Court of Chancery in the statutory appraisal proceeding.

EXPERT TESTIMONY REJECTED

GATEKEEPING ROLE PROPERLY EXERCISED

. . .

Reilly's "Capital Market" Approach

The qualifications of the Respondents' expert witness, Reilly, were undisputed at trial. The parties were in sharp disagreement, however, about whether Reilly's "capital market" approach was "generally accepted" within the financial community for valuing banks and bank holding companies. Reilly's capital market analysis used a number of pricing multiples related to the market value of invested capital ("MVIC"). Reilly computed the ratios of MVIC to: earnings before interest and taxes ("EBIT"); earnings before interest, depreciation and taxes ("EBIDT"); debt free net income ("DFNI"); debt free cash flow ("DFCF"); interest incomes; and total book value of invested capital (TBVIC").

The Petitioners' expert, Clarke, testified that Reilly's capital market approach was not generally accepted in the financial community for valuing banks and bank holding companies. According to Clarke, the financial community focuses upon the ratio of price to book value and price to earnings for purposes of valuing banks and bank holding companies. The Court of Chancery concluded that the Respondents had failed to establish that Reilly's capital market methodology is generally accepted by the financial community for purposes of valuing bank holding companies, as distinguished from other types of enterprises.[17]

The Court of Chancery also determined that Reilly's capital market valuation approach included a built-in minority discount. The Court of Chancery noted that the valuation literature, including a treatise co-authored by Reilly himself, supported that conclusion.[18] The Court of Chancery concluded that because Reilly's capital market method resulted in a minority valuation, even if it had concluded that Reilly's capital market approach was an otherwise acceptable method of valuing a bank holding company, the use of Reilly's capital market approach is improper in a statutory appraisal proceeding.

. . .

---

[17] [25] *See Security State Bank v. Ziegeldorf*, Iowa Supr., 554 N.W.2d 884 (1996).

[18] [26] *See* S.P. Pratt, R.F. Reilly & R.P. Schweis, *Valuing a Business* 194-95, 210 (ed. 1996) (explaining that comparative publicly traded companies produce a minority discounted valuation); *See also* C.Z. Mercer, *Valuing Financial Institutions* 198-200 and Chapter 13 (1992) (explaining that comparative publicly traded company valuation technique produces a minority valuation that requires adding a control premium to be accurate).

The record reflects that the Court of Chancery rejected Reilly's capital market approach for two independent and alternative reasons. First, it concluded that the Respondents had failed to establish that Reilly's capital market approach is generally accepted in the financial community for valuing banks and/or bank holding companies. Second, it concluded that Reilly's capital market approach contained an inherent minority discount that made its use legally impermissible in a statutory appraisal proceeding. Both of those conclusions are fully supported by the record evidence that was before the Court of Chancery and the prior holdings of this Court construing Section 262.[19]

DISCOUNTED CASH FLOW

BOTH EXPERTS OPINIONS REJECTED

Both parties' experts also gave valuation opinions using the same discounted cash flow methodology. The qualifications of each parties' expert witness were accepted by the Court of Chancery. The propriety of using a discounted cash flow analysis in a statutory appraisal action was also acknowledged. The discounted cash flow methodology has been relied upon frequently by parties and the Court of Chancery in other statutory appraisal proceedings.

Although Reilly and Clarke used the same discounted cash flow methodology, each applied different assumptions. The Court of Chancery determined, for example, that "the difference between Clarke's 12% discount rate and Reilly's 18% discount rate [was] attributable primarily to their different estimates of MGB's cost of equity capital, and their different assumptions of the company specific risks confronting MGB at the time of the merger."[20] The Court of Chancery disagreed with certain of the other assumptions applied by both of the parties' experts. The Court of Chancery ultimately concluded that it could not rely on the DCF valuation opinion of either parties' expert.[21]

The Respondents submit the *only* significant concern raised by the Court of Chancery with respect to Clarke's DCF analysis involved his use of a 12% discount rate, i.e., it incorporated a 1% small stock premium based on a 1996 study that may contain post-merger data. The Respondents contend that particular error could have been corrected through a mathematical adjustment, i.e., the addition of a 5.2% small stock factor based on a 1992 study (which Clarke had used in several other bank appraisals) results in a 15% discount rate. The Respondents have calculated that the substitution of the 15% discount rate for Clarke's 12% rate produces a fair value for MGB of $57 per share. The Respondents argue the Court of Chancery erred by rejecting their adjusted Clarke discounted cash flow valuation of $57 as a reliable indication of fair value.

---

[19] [30] *See, e.g., Rapid-American Corp. v. Harris*, Del. Supr., 603 A.2d 796 (1992); *Weinberger v. UOP, Inc.*, Del. Supr., 457 A.2d 701 (1983).

[20] [31] *LeBeau v. M.G. Bancorporation, Inc.*, Del. Ch., C.A. No. 13414, [1998 Del. Ch. LEXIS 9], 1998 WL 44993 (Jan. 29, 1998) Mem. Op. at 10.

[21] [32] *Id.*

Having accepted the qualifications of both parties' experts and the propriety of using a discounted cash flow model in this statutory appraisal proceeding, the Court of Chancery was not required to adopt any one expert's methodology or calculations *in toto.*[22] Similarly, by recognizing the discounted cash flow model as *one* proper valuation technique, the Court of Chancery was not *required* to use that methodology to make its own independent valuation calculation by either adapting or blending the factual assumptions of the parties' experts. The ultimate selection of a valuation framework is within the Court of Chancery's discretion.[23]

HOLDING COMPANY VALUATION

CONTROL PREMIUM FOR SUBSIDIARY PROPER

The comparative acquisition approach used by Clark included the value of MGB's controlling interest in its two subsidiaries. In conducting his comparative acquisition analysis, Clarke identified three specific transactions involving community banks in the same geographical area as MGB's subsidiaries, and which had occurred within a year of the merger. Clarke also considered data published by The Chicago Corporation in its September 1993 issue of *Midwest Bank & Thrift Survey*, which reflected an analysis of 137 bank acquisitions announced from January 1, 1989 and June 1, 1993.

The Respondents contend that Clarke's comparative acquisitions approach was erroneously relied upon by the Court of Chancery because that valuation analysis is proscribed by the statutory directives in Section 262, as construed by this Court. The interpretation and application of the mandates in Section 262 to this appraisal proceeding presents a question of law. Therefore, the Court of Chancery's construction of Section 262 must be reviewed *de novo* on appeal.[24]

This Court has held that in valuing a holding company in a statutory appraisal proceeding, pursuant to Section 262, it is appropriate to include a control premium for majority ownership of a subsidiary as an element of the holding company's fair value of the majority-owned subsidiaries.[25]

In *Rapid-American*, this Court stated:

Rapid was a parent company with a 100% ownership interest in three valuable subsidiaries. The trial court's decision to exclude the control premium at the *corporate level* practically discounted Rapid's entire inherent value. The exclusion of a "control premium" artificially and unrealistically treated Rapid as a minority shareholder. Contrary to Rapid's argument, Delaware law *compels* the inclusion of a control premium under the unique facts of this case. Rapid's 100% ownership interest in its subsidiaries was clearly a "relevant" valuation factor and the trial

---

[22] [33] *Cede & Co v. Technicolor, Inc.*, Del. Supr., 684 A.2d 289, 299 (1996).

[23] [34] *Id.*

[24] [35] *Cede & Co. v. Technicolor, Inc.*, 684 A.2d 289, 294-95 (1996).

[25] [36] *Rapid-American Corp. v. Harris*, Del. Supr., 603 A.2d 796, 806 (1992).

court's rejection of the "control premium" implicitly placed a disproportionate emphasis on pure market value.[26]

Based upon the foregoing statements from *Rapid-American*, the Court of Chancery concluded that Clarke's comparative acquisition approach, which includes a control premium for a majority interest in a subsidiary, was a relevant and reliable methodology to use in a Section 262 statutory appraisal proceeding to determine the fair market value of shares in a holding company. The Respondents argue that this Court's holding in *Rapid-American* turned on the "unique fact" that its subsidiaries were involved in three different industries. The Court of Chancery rejected the Respondents' construction of *Rapid-American* as "too narrow." We agree. The fact that the holding company being valued in *Rapid-American* owned subsidiaries engaged in different businesses was not the dispositive basis for our holding.

"The underlying assumption in an appraisal valuation is that the dissenting shareholders would be willing to maintain their investment position had the merger not occurred."[27] Accordingly, the corporation must be valued as a going concern based upon the "operative reality" of the company as of the time of the merger.[28] Therefore, *any* holding company's ownership of a controlling interest in a subsidiary at the time of the merger is an "operative reality" and an independent element of value that must be taken into account in determining a fair value for the parent company's stock.[29]

The Court of Chancery properly concluded that the rationale of this Court's holding in *Rapid-American* applied to the MGB appraisal proceeding. Because MGB held a controlling interest in its two subsidiaries, it was necessary to determine the value of those controlling interests in order to ascertain the value of MGB, as a whole, as a going concern on the Merger date.[30] We hold that the Court of Chancery acted in accordance with the statutory parameters of Section 262 by making a per share fair value determination of MGB on the basis of the comparative acquisitions approach applied by Clarke, using the premia that he attributed to MGB's controlling interests in Greenwood and WBC.

---

[26] [37] *Rapid American Co. v. Harris*, 603 A.2d at 806-07 (emphasis added).

[27] [38] *Cede & Co. v. Technicolor, Inc.*, Del. Supr., 684 A.2d 289, 298 (1996), *citing Cavalier Oil Corp. v. Harnett*, Del. Supr., 564 A.2d 1137, 1144 (1989). *See also Tri-Continental Corp. v. Battye*, Del. Supr., 74 A.2d 71, 72 (1950).

[28] [39] *Cede & Co. v. Technicolor, Inc.*, 684 A.2d at 298.

[29] [40] *Rapid-American Co. v. Harris*, 603 A.2d at 606-07.

[30] [41] *Rapid-American Co. v. Harris*, 603 A.2d at 806-07; *In re Appraisal of Shell Oil Co.*, Del. Supr., 607 A.2d 1213, 1218 (1992). *See also Hintmann v. Fred Weber, Inc.*, Del. Ch., C.A. No. 12839, [1998 Del. Ch. LEXIS 26], 1998 WL 83052, Steele, V.C. (Feb. 17, 1998) Mem. Op. at 25; R.F. Balotti & J.A. Finkelstein, *The Delaware Law of Corporations and Business Organizations* § 9.57, at 9-117 (3d ed. 1999 Supp.); R. Ward, Jr., E. Welch, A. Turezyn, *Folk on the Delaware General Corporation Law* § 262.9 (4th ed. 1999).

COURT OF CHANCERY

INDEPENDENTLY APPRAISED SHARES

The Respondents contend that the Court of Chancery failed to discharge its statutory obligation to function as an independent appraiser. The record does not support that argument. In its appraisal opinion, the Court of Chancery stated:

> The Court is mindful that $85 per share is more than double the Merger price. The Court is also aware of its role under § 262, which is to determine fair value *independently.* In discharging that institutional function as an independent appraiser, the Court should, where possible, test the soundness of its valuation conclusion against whatever reliable corroborative evidence the record contains. On that score the record falls far short of perfection. Limited corroborative evidence is available, however, in the form of Sheshunoff's 1993 fair market valuation, (i) adjusted by Clarke to exclude Sheshunoff's minority discount and (ii) updated by Clarke to reflect value data as of November 17, 1993, the date of the Merger.[31]

In discharging its statutory mandate, the Court of Chancery has the discretion to select one of the parties' valuation models as its general framework or to fashion its own.[32] The Court of Chancery's role as an independent appraiser does not necessitate a judicial determination that is completely separate and apart from the valuations performed by the parties' expert witnesses who testify at trial. It must, however, carefully consider whether the evidence supports the valuation conclusions advanced by the parties' respective experts. Thereafter, although not required to do so, it is entirely proper for the Court of Chancery to adopt any one expert's model, methodology, and mathematical calculations, *in toto*, if that valuation is supported by credible evidence and withstands a critical judicial analysis on the record.[33]

In this case, the Court of Chancery carefully evaluated the valuation testimony and evidence proffered by the parties' experts. It determined that Reilly's capital market approach is legally impermissible, but even if valid, was improperly applied, thereby requiring the rejection of the values Reilly derived by that method. The Court of Chancery found that both Clarke's and Reilly's DCF analyses were improperly applied, thereby requiring the rejection of the values both experts derived by that approach.

The Court of Chancery concluded that Clarke's comparative acquisition approach was a legally valid method to value MGB and that the credible record evidence supported Clarke's $85 per share determination of MGB's fair value as of the Merger date. In making its independent appraisal valuation, the Court of Chancery could have relied entirely upon Clarke's comparative acquisitions approach. Instead, it critically tested Clarke's comparative acquisition approach by

---

[31] [42] *LeBeau v. M.G. Bancorporation, Inc.*, Del. Ch., C.A. No. 13414, [1998 Del. Ch. LEXIS 9], 1998 WL 44993 (Jan. 29, 1998) Mem. Op. at 12.

[32] [43] *Cede & Co. v. Technicolor, Inc.*, 684 A.2d 289, 299 (1996); *Gonsalves v. Straight Arrow Publishers, Inc.*, Del. Supr., 701 A.2d 357, 362 (1997).

[33] [44] *Cede & Co. v. Technicolor, Inc.*, 684 A.2d at 299. See also *Gonsalves v. Straight Arrow Publishers, Inc.*, 701 A.2d at 361-62.

using its own judicial expertise to make corrective adjustments to Sheshunoff's legally improper valuation determination and found corroboration for Clarke's result.

The determination of value in a statutory appraisal proceeding is accorded a high level of deference on appeal.[34] In the absence of legal error, this Court reviews appraisal valuations pursuant to the abuse of discretion standard.[35] The Court of Chancery abuses its discretion when either its factual findings do not have record support or its valuation is not the result of an orderly and logical deductive process.[36]

In this case, the findings of fact upon which the Court of Chancery predicated its decision are supported by the record. The analysis that preceded the Court of Chancery's valuation of MGB's shares exemplifies an orderly and logical deductive process. Consequently, the portion of the Court of Chancery's judgment that concluded that $85 per share was the fair value of MGB stock on the date of the Merger is affirmed.

Appraisal actions are highly complicated matters that the Court of Chancery is uniquely qualified to adjudicate in an equitable manner. Since *Weinberger*,[37] this Court has eschewed choosing any one method of appraisal to the exclusion of all others.[38] Today, we reinforce the substance of this philosophy and support methods that allow the Court of Chancery to perform its statutory role as appraiser, based on a solid foundation of record evidence, independent of the positions of the parties.[39]

. . .

CONCLUSION

The portion of the Court of Chancery's judgment that appraised the fair value of the Petitioners' stock at $85 per share is affirmed. . . .

---

[34] [45] *Rapid-American Corp. v. Harris*, Del. Supr., 603 A.2d 796, 802 (1992); *In re Appraisal of Shell Oil Co.*, Del. Supr., 607 A.2d 1213, 1219 (1992).

[35] [46] *Rapid-American Corp. v. Harris*, 603 A.2d at 802.

[36] [47] *Id., citing Alabama By-Products Corp. v. Neal*, Del. Supr., 588 A.2d 255, 259 (1991).

[37] [48] *Weinberger v. UOP, Inc.*, Del. Supr., 457 A.2d 701 (1983).

[38] [49] *Id.* at 713-14.

[39] [50] *Rapid-American Corp. v. Harris*, Del. Supr., 603 A.2d 796 (1992); *Gonsalves v. Straight Arrow Publishers, Inc.*, Del. Supr., 701 A.2d 357 (1997).

GLOBAL GT LP v. GOLDEN TELECOM, INC.

Delaware Chancery Court
993 A.2d 497 (2010)

Strine, Vice Chancellor.

I. INTRODUCTION

This is an appraisal action. The petitioners Global GT LP and Global GT Ltd. owned nearly 1.4 million shares of respondent Golden Telecom, Inc. ("Golden"), a Russian-based telecommunications company that was listed on the NASDAQ. The petitioners claim that Golden was undervalued in a 2007 merger in which Golden was purchased for $105 per share by Vimpel - Communications ("VimpelCom") — a major Russian provider of mobile telephone services whose two largest stockholders were also the largest stockholders of Golden.

As is typical, the outcome of this appraisal proceeding largely depends on my acceptance, rejection, or modification of the views of the parties' valuation experts. Both experts were well qualified to testify about the appropriate inputs to use in valuing a public company; but neither had a deep knowledge of the Russian telecommunications market or of Golden itself. Both these men of valuation science purported to apply the same primary method of valuation — the discounted cash flow ("DCF") method — but the expert for the petitioners came up with a value of $139 per share and the expert for Golden came up with a value of only $88 per share — a modest $51 per share value gap.

In this decision, I reach a valuation of Golden using the DCF methodology, which is the method that both experts viewed as the most reliable. I eschew any reliance on methods based on analogizing to comparable companies or transactions because the experts themselves had even less knowledge of the comparables than they did of Golden and both viewed it difficult to find a good sample of comparables. Thus, I focus on coming up with a solid, if necessarily imperfect, valuation using the DCF method that both experts embraced as the technique most susceptible to useful application.

In focusing on a DCF valuation, I reject Golden's argument that I should give weight to the merger price itself on the grounds that the merger reflected a market-tested price. I reject that proposition for several reasons. First of all, the Special Committee that negotiated the merger never engaged in any active market check either before or after signing the merger agreement with VimpelCom. Second and most important, the passive market check that is supposed to instill confidence in me required market participants to assume that Golden's two largest stockholders, Altimo Holdings and Investments Limited ("Altimo") and Telenor ASA ("Telenor"), would both sell their Golden stake to another bidder, despite the fact that they had an economic interest in VimpelCom that was far more substantial than their stake in Golden — an unlikely prospect made even more doubtful by Altimo's public announcement that it did not intend to sell its 26% stake in Golden in another transaction. Given these market realities, it is not surprising that Golden's Special Committee chairman admitted that the Committee had focused on getting the best deal they could from VimpelCom. There was no open market check that provides a reliable insight into Golden's value.

After rejecting that argument, I wade through the discrete differences that explain the experts' differing DCF valuations, which primarily involve Golden's terminal growth rate, and the appropriate equity risk premium and beta to use in calculating a discount rate. After making my determinations as to these disagreements, I plugged them into the petitioners' DCF model and generated a per share value of $125.49 per share, which I supplement with an award of interest at the applicable statutory rate.

II. FACTUAL BACKGROUND

The trial record was largely dominated by the testimony of the experts. For their part, the petitioners presented the testimony of Paul Gompers, a Professor of Business Administration at Harvard Business School. Golden offered Marc Sherman, a Managing Director of Alvarez & Marshal, to respond.[40] Both experts are well qualified generally in the literature of valuation. Although Sherman has a bit more practical telecommunications experience, having done some valuation work involving other telecommunications firms, neither struck me as anything close to an industry expert. Moreover, neither had a deep knowledge of Golden itself or the Russian telecommunications industry.

Golden has tried to impress me with the fact that Sherman spoke with management for Golden *after* the merger and *during* the litigation, and therefore supposedly gained a deeper sense of the firm and industry than did Gompers, who did not do so. Of course, the managers for Golden working for the VimpelCom corporate empire had an incentive to cooperate with Sherman, and doubtless Golden would not have given Gompers unfettered access to them. In that respect, the testimony of the two fact witnesses who testified about Golden was not particularly helpful in terms of conveying a good sense of Golden's prospects.

Fortunately, the experts did agree that there were a reliable set of projections prepared by Golden's management that existed for the first five years beyond the merger. Given the existence of those projections and the general evidence in the record regarding the telecommunications industry both in Russia and internationally, and the predicted future of the Russian economy, there is a rational, if far from fully satisfying, record from which to resolve the discrete areas of opinion where the experts differ.

What precedes my resolution of those issues is my distillation of the record, such as it is, regarding Golden and its prospects.

---

[40] [3] Sherman graduated from the University of Baltimore, and received his J.D. from the University of Maryland School of Law. Before joining Alvarez & Marshal, Sherman was a Managing Director at Huron Consulting Group, and a partner at KPMG. He has also authored or co-authored several books. He is a certified public accountant, an attorney, a Certified Insolvency and Reorganization Advisor, a Certified Fraud Examiner, and is certified by the American Institute of Certified Public Accountants in Financial Forensics. Sherman has served as a valuation expert for businesses in a variety of industries, including communications, and has worked on a number of valuation projects involving the telecommunications industry. *See* JX 730 (Expert Report of Marc B. Sherman) ("Sherman Report") at 4–5, Ex A.

A. Golden's Business And Plans For Expansion

Golden, a telecommunications company, operated in the former Soviet Union, and was publicly traded on the NASDAQ.[41] Its initial public offering took place in September 1999 and, after that time, Golden grew primarily through self-financed acquisitions of regional-based telecommunications companies in Russia and other countries in the Commonwealth of Independent States (the "CIS").[42] Although Golden was, at first, predominately focused on providing long-distance services, its acquisitions of local telephone companies throughout Russia and certain CIS countries gave Golden the capacity to provide local service to homes and businesses.

Golden traditionally focused on providing fixed-line services, meaning that it provided telephone services through fiber or copper wiring, and derived its revenues primarily from corporate customers and from services provided to other telecommunications and mobile operators. By 2006, Golden had begun to expand its focus to include Wi – Fi, which was in the early stages of development in Russia and the CIS, and broadband internet, which was available only in major Russian cities. By the end of 2007, Golden had completed approximately thirty acquisitions of smaller companies, and had become a leading facilities-based provider of integrated telecommunication and internet services in the most populated areas of Russia and other countries of the CIS, and the largest independent telecommunications operator in Russia. In particular, Golden acquired a 51% stake in Corbina, a telecommunications service provider that offers broadband internet in several Russian cities, which allowed Golden to offer bundled services including broadband internet, voice over internet protocol, internet protocol television, and mobile virtual network-based services.

B. Golden's Management Creates A Five Year Plan

Despite its expansion into other areas of the internet and telecom market and its goal to sell a wide variety of related services to the customers on the ends of its cables, Golden remained primarily a fixed-line telecommunications provider for the business sector. Golden's Board of Directors established a five-year business plan for Golden (the "Five Year Plan") in October 2007 to chart the company's continued expansion. The Five Year Plan established a three-pronged strategy for Golden. First, Golden would continue to widen its corporate customer base in large cities, such as Moscow and St. Petersburg. Second, Golden would continue regional expansion to become a "national market player in both corporate and retail market segments." Third, Golden would enter the emerging broadband market, and seek to become a "leading provider of broadband access in Russia and the CIS." Although Gompers contends that Golden's strategy reflected a marked move away from its prior consistent involvement in mergers and acquisitions activity, my reading of the

[41] [4] Before it was incorporated, Golden was a majority-owned subsidiary of Global TeleSystems, Inc., which was among the first foreign telecommunications operators in the former Soviet Union. *See* JX 16 (Golden 2007 10-K (Mar. 17, 2008)) ("2007 10-K") at 4.

[42] [5] The CIS includes: the Azerbaijan Republic; the Republic of Armenia; the Republic of Belarus; Georgia; the Republic of Kazakhstan; the Kyrgyz Republic; the Republic of Moldova; the Russian Federation; the Republic of Tajikistan; Turkmenistan; the Republic of Uzbekistan; and the Ukraine. See Commonwealth of Independent States: CIS States, http://cis.minsk.by/main.aspx?uid=3360.

record suggests that to accomplish this three-pronged strategy, Golden would be required to continue to engage in M & A activity to enter additional markets (which are comprised of cities smaller than Moscow but still far larger than, say, Wilmington, Delaware) and to gain scale in the product markets it wished to enter.

The Five Year Plan projected revenue to grow annually at a declining rate:

2007	47.8%
2008	34.8%
2009	20.2%
2010	19.5%
2011	13.0%
2012	8.5%

The Five Year Plan also estimated that Golden's EBITDA margins would grow for three years, and then level off:

2007	25.9%
2008	31.8%
2009	32.1%
2010	32.6%
2011	32.6%
2012	32.5%

The projections of Golden's management were based on Golden's business plan of expanding its corporate customer base, broadband service, and regional expansion throughout Russia and the CIS. The Five Year Plan considered the increased competition that Golden would face in all segments of its business as the Russian telecom market continued to grow, and a variety of potential risks, including political risk.

The predictions in the Five Year Plan are reasonable when considering the trends in the Russian market generally, and the telecom industry in particular. For example, the projected compound annual growth rate ("CAGR") of the Russian nominal GDP was expected to be 14.6% from 2007 to 2012, which is consistent with the average projected CAGR predicted for Golden in the Five Year Plan of 14.5%. The projected CAGR of the Russian nominal GDP of 8.5% from 2012–2017 is in line with Golden's projected revenue growth in 2012 of 8.5%. And, the decline in Golden's growth rate is consistent with the decline in the (still healthy) growth rate of Russia's overall telecom sector since 2004.

C. Russia's Expanding Telecom Market And Golden's Predicted Growth

Golden's Five Year Plan was based, in part, on the reasonable expectation that the Russian telecommunications market would continue to expand. Russia was one of the few remaining growth markets in Europe, and its telecom industry was predicted to grow rapidly, particularly the broadband retail market. Golden was particularly well-poised to grow with the Russian market because it was the only operator present in all segments of Russia's fixed-line market in 18 of Russia's 20 largest cities. Renaissance Capital, for example, opined in February 2007 that Golden was "well positioned to maintain its leadership in the corporate [telecom] segment," and Golden's residential internet market would become Golden's "second-largest contributor to operating income in 2010" largely because Golden's "fiber-to-the-home" internet service was "the best option on the market." Golden was also in a position to expand because it had very low levels of debt compared to other telecom companies.

D. Golden And VimpelCom Agree To Merge

Of course, just as Golden hoped to become a major competitor in the Wi – Fi and broadband markets, so too did other industry players have their eye on Golden's space. One industry player in particular had box seats from which to contemplate Golden. That was VimpelCom.

Golden's two largest stockholders, Altimo and Telenor, also happened to be the largest stockholders of VimpelCom. Indeed, Altimo and Telenor's combined stake in VimpelCom was larger in both percentage terms and value. Specifically, Sunbird Limited, which owned 26% of Golden's outstanding common stock, and Eco Telecom Limited, which owned 44% of VimpelCom's outstanding voting capital, are both subsidiaries of Altimo. And, Nye Telenor East Invest AS, the beneficial owner of 18.3% of Golden's outstanding common stock, and Telenor East Invest AS, the beneficial owner of 33.6% of VimpelCom's outstanding common stock, are both subsidiaries of Telenor. Moreover, Altimo and Telenor not only had board representatives on the VimpelCom board, but also had appointed members of the Golden Board. Four nominees of Eco Telecom Limited served on the VimpelCom board, including Oleg Malis and Alexey Reznikovich, who also served on the Golden Board. Four nominees of Telenor East Invest served on the VimpelCom board, including Kjell Morten Johnsen, who also served on Golden's Board. Together, Altimo and Telenor appointed a majority of the nine-member VimpelCom board, suggesting how deep their interest in VimpelCom was.

Given the cross-holdings and the reality that Golden was strong in fixed-line services and weak in mobile capabilities, and VimpelCom had just the opposite qualities, it was perhaps inevitable that a merger of the two firms would be considered. At first, in February 2007, Golden's CEO, Jean-Pierre Vandromme, and VimpelCom's CEO, Alexander Izosimov, began to discuss the possibility of the two companies working together by, for example, cross-selling their services. Discussions between senior management of Golden and VimpelCom continued throughout 2007 and, in furtherance of those discussions, the two companies entered into a confidentiality agreement and exchanged non-public information.

In April 2007, Izosimov met with Vandromme, and suggested that the two companies explore a transaction whereby VimpelCom would acquire 100% of Golden. Golden's Board met on May 17, 2009 to discuss VimpelCom's proposal and decided to establish a Special Committee made up of the four Golden non-management directors who were not affiliated with Altimo or Telenor.

The Special Committee retained Skadden, Arps, Slate, Meagher & Flom, LLP as outside counsel, and Credit Suisse Securities (USA), LLC as its financial advisor.

On July 3, 2007, VimpelCom gave Golden a summary sheet of proposed terms for a combination of the two companies. But because the summary sheet did not specify an offer price, the Special Committee decided not to respond until a more detailed proposal was presented. Around this time, the news of VimpelCom's interest in Golden leaked into the market. In early September 2007, VimpelCom proposed to pay $80 per share of Golden's stock, which the Special Committee rejected, and, in late September 2007, VimpelCom changed its proposal to a range of $80 to $95 per share. The Special Committee felt that the upper end of the range was "sufficiently attractive" to justify continuing the negotiations process and entered into a second confidentiality agreement with VimpelCom, which gave VimpelCom access to Golden's non-public information and Golden's management.

VimpelCom raised its offer price again to $100 on November 12, 2007. But the Special Committee felt that this amount was inadequate, and rejected the offer on November 15, 2007. On November 28, 2007, VimpelCom raised its offer to $103 per share, and the Special Committee again rejected the offer. Although VimpelCom initially told the Special Committee that $103 per share was its final offer, VimpelCom raised its offer to $105 per share on December 1, 2007, which the Special Committee agreed to accept provided that all other material terms for the merger were fully resolved.

According to Patrick Gallagher, Chairman of the Special Committee, Vimpel-Com's offer of $105 per share represented the "highest per share consideration reasonably obtainable" when considering the inherent risks in Golden's business plan, such as the increased competitiveness in Golden's key markets, political uncertainty in Russia, adverse changes in the global credit markets, and Vimpel-Com's intention to directly compete with Golden in the broadband market. The Special Committee recommended that the full Board accept the merger and, on December 3, 2007, the Board unanimously approved the merger. Credit Suisse completed a fairness opinion for the $105 per share price (the "Fairness Opinion") and, at a December 20, 2007 meeting of the Special Committee, opined that the price was fair.

The discounted cash flow ("DCF") analysis conducted by Credit Suisse came up with a range of $85–$128, and a median value of $102. Importantly, this valuation was premised on a nominal GDP growth rate for the Russian economy of 5.6%. That was supposedly taken from an Economist Intelligence Unit ("EIU") forecast for 2013 to 2017. The number used, however, does not track the December 2007 EIU data, which forecasted nominal GDP growth of 7.4%. If the figure in the December 2007 EIU data was used in Credit Suisse's model, its DCF value for Golden would have had a median value of $110 per share.

The merger agreement between Golden and VimpelCom (the "Merger Agreement") was executed the next day, on December 21, 2007. The Merger Agreement required that at least 63.3% of Golden's outstanding shares be tendered before the merger could close. Additionally, the merger provided for: (1) an $80 million termination fee, which represented 2% of the $4 billion transaction; (2) a $120 million fee for Golden if VimpelCom's financing fell through; and (3) a matching right for VimpelCom to address superior offers. But Altimo, which owned 26% of Golden, publicly indicated that it did not intend to sell its Golden stake to another bidder. Telenor was more coy, but gave no affirmative indication that it would sell to another bidder, and its representative on the Golden Board had voted for the merger. Unsurprisingly, given the objective facts regarding Altimo and Telenor's ownership interest in VimpelCom, no third party came forward after the Merger Agreement was signed to express an interest in buying Golden.

E. The Market Reacts Negatively To The Merger Price

After the merger price was announced on December 21, 2007, market analysts commented that the $105 per share price was very favorable to VimpelCom and, perhaps most important, VimpelCom's stock price rose substantially.[43] Morgan Stanley, for example, downgraded Golden on the day that the price was announced, and expressed its concern that although "Golden offer[ed] attractive organic growth and prospects . . . the net realizable value for [Golden's minority stockholders] may [have been] limited only to the level of the bid price." Renaissance Capital also commented that the transaction was favorable to VimpelCom shareholders, stating that "even purely taking the difference between [Renaissance Capital's] valuation of Golden Telecom ($136/share) and the tender offer ($105 per share) add[ed] about $1.2 per VimpelCom share."

F. Shareholders Overwhelmingly Tender Their Shares At The $105 Price

Although the movement in VimpelCom's stock price suggested that the market believed that VimpelCom was getting a good deal, an overwhelming majority of Golden's shareholders tendered their shares at the $105 price. Under the terms of

---

[43] [56] After rumors about the proposed VimpelCom/Golden merger were leaked, the price of VimpelCom stock steadily increased until a few days after the Merger Agreement was announced. VimpelCom stock traded at $22.12 on July 5, 2007, increased slightly to $22.31 on July 6, 2007, the day that the first rumor of the merger was leaked, rose to $41.98 on December 21, 2007, the day that the merger was announced, and peaked three days later at $44.98 on December 24, 2007. *See* Google Finance, Vimpel – Communications (ADR), *available at* http://www.google.com/finance?q=NYSE:VIP (last visited Apr. 18, 2010); Yahoo Finance, Vimpel – Communications (VIP), http://finance.yahoo.com/echarts?s=VIP#chart2:symbol=vip (last visited Apr. 18, 2010). In fact, VimpelCom's stock price increased from $37.73 on December 19, 2007, to $39.38 on December 20, 2007, before reaching $41.98 on the day of the merger announcement. *See id.;* Business Week, Historical Stock Quotes for VimpelCom, http://investing.businessweek.com/research/stocks/snapshot/historical.asp?ticker=VIP:US (last visited Apr. 18, 2010); *see also* Sherman Cross Examination Demonstratives 7–9; Tr. at 1052–54 (Sherman). The rise in VimpelCom's price per share is difficult to attribute to general market trends. The DOW Jones Industrial Average, for example, was at 13,611 on July 6, 2007, and a bit lower at 13,450 on December 21, 2007. *See* Yahoo Finance, Dow Jones Industrial Average Index Chart, http://finance.yahoo.com/echarts?s= ^DJI (last visited April 10, 2010). Similarly, the NASDAQ closed at 2,666.51 on July 6, 2007, and at 2,691.99 on December 21, 2007. *See* Yahoo Finance, NASDAQ Composite Historical Prices, http://finance.yahoo.com/q/hp?s= ^IXIC (last visited April 10, 2010). Nor can the rise in VimpelCom's stock price be easily attributed to the performance of the global telecom industry, which remained stable from early July 2007 to late December 2007. *See* Yahoo Finance, iShares Dow Jones U.S. Telecom Historical Prices, http://finance.yahoo.com/q/hp?s=IYZa=05b=26c=2007d=11e=30f=2007g=dz=66y=0 (last visited April 22, 2010) (showing that the Dow Jones U.S. Telecom index fund traded at $31.98 on July 6, 2007, and at $28.03 on December 21, 2007); Yahoo Finance, iShares S & P Global Telecommunications Historical Prices, http://finance.yahoo.com/q/hp?s=IXPa=06b=1c=2007d=11e=30f=2007g=dz=66y=0 (last visited April 22, 2010) (showing that the S & P Global Telecommunications index fund traded at $65.56 on July 6, 2007, and at $71.18 on December 21, 2007).

the Merger Agreement, Lillian Acquisition, Inc., a wholly owned subsidiary of VimpelCom, was to acquire 100% of Golden in a two step transaction. First, VimpelCom would commence a cash tender offer of $105 per share for the outstanding shares of Golden common stock. Second, a back-end merger would convert all Golden shares not tendered — other than those Golden shares subject to the exercise of appraisal rights — into the right to receive $105 per share in cash.

VimpelCom commenced the tender offer on January 18, 2008. Altimo had already indicated that it intended to tender its shares and did so, but Telenor decided to first conduct its own analysis to determine whether the price was adequate, and finally tendered its shares on February 5, 2008. A total of 94.4% of Golden's shareholders tendered at the $105 price before the offer expired on February 26, 2008. The merger closed on February 28, 2008, and Golden became a wholly-owned subsidiary of VimpelCom.

G. The Petitioners Request An Appraisal

The petitioners filed their request for an appraisal on April 18, 2008. Following extensive expert discovery, a trial was held on October 14–15, 19, and 30, 2009. This is my opinion on the fair value of Golden.

III. LEGAL FRAMEWORK

Under 8 Del. C. § 262(h), this court must, upon finding that a stockholder is entitled to an appraisal, "determine the fair value of the shares exclusive of any element of value arising from the accomplishment or expectation of the merger or consolidation, together with interest, if any, to be paid upon the amount determined to be the fair value." The entity must be valued as a going concern based on its business plan at the time of the merger, and any synergies or other value expected from the merger giving rise to the appraisal proceeding itself must be disregarded.

IV. ANALYSIS

In addressing the question of fair value, I proceed in two steps. First, I explain why I reject Golden's argument that the merger price is itself a reliable indication of fair value. Then, I grapple with the contending positions of the parties' experts about the value of Golden, in particular regarding the valuation of Golden in light of its future expected cash flows.

A. Deference To The Merger Price

As an initial matter, I find the price that VimpelCom paid for Golden in the merger to have no reliable bearing on my appraisal valuation. Golden argues that deference should be given to the merger price of $105 per share because the Special Committee, assisted by outside advisors, was able to determine for itself the fair price of Golden, and because no other interested bidders came forward despite rumors of the potential merger that leaked to the market in July 2007. It is, of course, true that an arms-length merger price resulting from an effective market check is entitled to great weight in an appraisal. For example, in *Union Ill. 1995*

Inv. Ltd. P'ship v. Union Fin. Group, Ltd. [847 A.2d 1137 (Del. 1989)] this court held that the merger price was the best indicator of fair value for appraisal purposes because the merger "resulted from a competitive and fair auction, which followed a more-than-adequate sales process and involved broad dissemination of confidential information to a large number of prospective buyers." But, as Gallagher, the Special Committee chairman, admitted at trial, the Special Committee did not engage in any sales efforts at all and instead concentrated solely on getting as good a deal as it could from VimpelCom. In essence, the Special Committee treated the context as one closer to a merger proposal by a controlling stockholder, given the reality that Golden's two largest shareholders — Altimo and Telenor — owned more of VimpelCom, the buyer, than Golden, the seller. Now, in appraisal, Golden acts as if the Special Committee was simply locking in a floor, and creating the perfect conditions for an effective passive market check. That after-the-fact litigation argument is without any factual foundation.

The reality is that any bidder peering in from the outside was confronted by a merger agreement that did not contain an active go-shop provision, and by a public statement by Golden's largest stockholder, Altimo, that it would not sell its 26% stake in another transaction. Although Golden argues that Telenor was more equivocal about whether it was willing to sell its 18% stake, equivocation in this context does not help Golden. The idea that a rational third-party bidder would make a blind expression of interest in a situation where the economic interests of Golden's largest stockholders was more heavily weighted toward doing what was best for VimpelCom — a corporation on whose board they had seated eight designees — and each stood to gain hugely if the merger generated synergy gains for VimpelCom is not one that I accept. In a situation such as this, to actually entice bids, the Special Committee, if it was relying on a market check to obtain the highest value, should have affirmatively sought guarantees from Altimo and Telenor that they would support a higher bid and used those guarantees to attract bidders. Instead, the Special Committee created a situation where other market players would rationally infer that the merger was the deal supported by Golden's two largest stockholders (and the three directors that Altimo and Telenor appointed to Golden's Board) whose interest in VimpelCom gave them special reasons to support that deal and not to sell into another transaction.

Golden also makes a more novel argument. It contends that the fact that only a single investor has brought an appraisal claim demonstrates the fairness of the merger price. But analyzing a deal price based on the size of the appraisal class is not supported by the appraisal statute itself, and would require this court to speculate about the reasons for the size of the appraisal class. Investors may choose to forego appraisal for any number of reasons. Appraisal claims are expensive to pursue, and the petitioners get none of the merger consideration during the pendency of the case, making such claims beyond the means of some investors to fund. And, certain institutional investors may be happy to take a sizeable merger-generated gain on a stock for quarterly reporting purposes, or to offset other losses, even if that gain is not representative of what the company should have yielded in a genuinely competitive sales process.

Critically, if market evidence were to be considered, the weight of the evidence suggests that the market believed that VimpelCom was getting a bargain. As discussed earlier, a number of market analysts felt that the $105 price undervalued Golden, and downgraded Golden after the merger was announced. For example, Alfa Bank suggested that VimpelCom's offer undervalued Golden, and estimated that $129 per share would have been a more appropriate price. More importantly, VimpelCom's stock rose substantially from $22.31 per share at the time that rumors about the proposed merger were leaked in July 2007 to $41.98 on December 21, 2007, the day that the Merger Agreement was announced, although the overall market remained relatively stable. When the definitive terms of the merger were announced on December 21, 2007, VimpelCom's stock rose $2.60 for a price of $41.98 per share, and continued to rise in the immediate days following the merger announcement to $44.98. These realities are noteworthy given that the stock price of an acquiring company will generally drop when it announces that it intends to merge with another company.

For all these reasons, I reject Golden's argument that the merger price is a reliable indication of value.

B. The Experts' DCF Analyses

The petitioners argue that the fair value of Golden as of February 28, 2008 (the "Valuation Date") was $138.37 per share. Golden, on the other hand, argues that the $105 merger price is generous because $88.14 is the fair value of Golden as of the Valuation Date. The parties' assertions are based on the reports of their valuation experts — Gompers and Sherman. As I noted earlier, neither Sherman nor Gompers is an expert in Russia or in the telecom industry generally, although Sherman has more experience in conducting valuations of telecom companies in the context of litigation.

Both experts conducted a DCF analysis, a comparable companies analysis, and a comparable transactions analysis. But, both give little weight to the latter two analyses. Sherman weighted his comparable companies and transactions analyses at only 20% of his conclusion. Gompers did not give those methods any actual weight in his valuation, using them only as a check on his DCF findings. Both experts admitted that there were few, if any, appropriate comparables for Golden and the Golden – VimpelCom merger. As important, neither of the experts convinced me that he really knew Golden deeply as a company, much less that he knew anything substantial about the sparse number of potential comparables, and their expert reports and the information they use to support them do not, in my view, provide me with any reliable basis to come up with a sound group of comparable companies or transactions myself. The lack of confidence I have in this aspect of the experts' analyses is confirmed by the slight weighting they gave these methods. I am also not going to pretend that I am personally qualified or have the time to engage in a from-scratch construction of comparable companies and transactions analyses using such public resources as I could obtain.

Therefore, rather than engage in a speculative exercise based on tinkering with analyses that the two experts themselves essentially do not stand behind, I concentrate my valuation analysis on deploying the method that each expert believed was the most reliable and pertinent — the discounted cash flow method — and use that as the basis for my award.

The components of a DCF analysis are familiar, and do not require repetition.[44] Both experts largely adopted the projections of Golden's management, including the Five Year Plan, which I have already found to be reasonable. This provides the court with a largely-agreed upon projection of Golden's estimated cash flows for the period from 2008 to 2012.

The major area of disagreement between the experts about Golden's cash flows is the terminal growth value to be used in applying the Gordon growth model version of the DCF, which has been employed by both experts. The smaller argument about the cash flows is the tax rate to be applied to them.

After resolving those arguments, I then address the two critical differences the experts have that are relevant to determining the rate at which Golden's expected future cash flows are to be discounted back to present value. Both experts purport to apply the capital asset pricing model ("CAPM"). The weighted average cost of capital they derive, however, is different because the equity risk premium and beta they use in coming up with their cost of equity diverge markedly.

1. Terminal Growth Rate

In a DCF analysis, future cash flows are projected for each year during a set period, typically five years. After that time, a terminal value is calculated to predict the company's cash flow into perpetuity. Generally, once an industry has matured, a company will grow at a steady rate that is roughly equal to the rate of nominal GDP growth. In this case, the experts had access to assumptions by Golden's management as to its growth rate for a full ten years. The first five years (2008 to 2012) of those assumptions were quite specific projections of future cash flows in the Five Year Plan, and the next five years were based on an assumption that Golden would grow at the rate of Russia's overall GDP. That is, the management projections assumed that Golden would keep up with Russia's overall growth during that period, even though, as I shall note, that is a conservative assumption. A viable company should grow at least at the rate of inflation and, as Golden's expert Sherman admits, the rate of inflation is the floor for a terminal value estimate for a solidly profitable company that does not have an identifiable risk of insolvency.[45] Sherman argues that the growth rate of the Russian economy will decline significantly in 2017 and beyond, and that Russia will reduce its inflation rate to a level below that which the United States has experienced in the last century.

---

[44] [81] For the standard description, see RICHARD A. BREALEY & STEWART C. MYERS, PRINCIPLES OF CORPORATE FINANCE 75–80 (7th ed. 2003).

[45] [86] *See Lane v. Cancer Treatment Ctrs. of Am., Inc.*, 2004 WL 1752847, at 31[, 2004 Del. Ch. LEXIS 108] (Del. Ch. July 30, 2004) (rejecting a terminal growth rate below inflation as unreasonable because "it must be assumed that [the company] would continue to grow at least at the rate of inflation"); PETER A. HUNT, STRUCTURING MERGERS & ACQUISITIONS: A GUIDE TO CREATING SHAREHOLDER VALUE 51 (2009) ("As a proxy for long-term growth, inflation assumes a company can pass along increases in its costs, but cannot necessarily increase its volume."); SHANNON P. PRATT & ALINA V. NICULITA, VALUING A BUSINESS: THE ANALYSIS AND APPRAISAL OF CLOSELY HELD COMPANIES 248 (5th ed. 2008) ("If the company is in an industry subject to vigorous competitive pressure, with little prospect for real growth without large capital expenditures, then perpetual growth at the rate of expected long-term inflation may be reasonable (i.e., zero real growth)."); *see also* Gompers Report at 42; JX 731 (Rebuttal Report of Marc B. Sherman) ("Sherman Rebuttal") at 14.

Nowhere in his report or at trial did Sherman explain the basis for his prediction, which also tends to conflict with his suggestion that the risk of revolutionary changes in Russia that could put Golden out of business hangs over Golden. In other words, Sherman somehow suggests that Russia will whip inflation now and have a very low inflation, low growth economy, and that, despite the world-wide popularity of telecommunications-related products, Golden will grow only at that whipped rate of inflation.

But Sherman's position does not translate, in my view, into a reasonable approach to developing a terminal growth rate. Although Golden was a well-positioned, low-leverage firm that had a demonstrated history of profitability and above-average growth in an industry with above-average growth prospects in a market (the former Soviet Union) with above-average growth prospects, Sherman adopted a terminal growth rate for Golden based on his assumption about the rate of inflation. That is, Sherman assumed that as soon as the ten-year projection period ended, Golden would only grow with the rate of inflation in Russia. That is an unduly pessimistic assumption.

Not only that, Sherman used a 3% estimate for inflation, an estimate that he largely made up himself with no rational basis. Notably, data from the EIU in February 2008 estimates Russian inflation to be an average of 3.9% from 2018 to 2030. For some unexplained reason, Sherman's terminal rate is below the floor. If Sherman is correct, it is not clear why VimpelCom was interested in buying Golden in the first place, as it was buying a firm that was not expected to even keep pace with Russia's overall growth, much less provide the above-market returns that, if the projected growth rate of the Russian telecommunications industry was consulted, might have been expected. If the telecom industry in the United States, which grew at an annualized real rate of 9.3% from 1963 to 2003 while the annualized real growth rate of the U.S. GDP was just 3.3%, is any indication, the Russian telecom industry will exceed GDP growth for quite some time. Thus, I believe is unduly pessimistic and reject it.

Although Gompers, perhaps even more than Sherman, had a less than ideal understanding of Golden itself, Gompers knew enough about Golden and the telecommunications industry in Russia and worldwide to come to a much more responsible estimate than Sherman did. Sherman gave too slight a weight to Golden's good financial health, solid record of growth, and to the growth prospects of the Russia telecommunications industry. By contrast, Gompers came to a measured conclusion that gave responsible, but not overenthusiastic, weight to each of these factors. Although the relevant factors might have supported a terminal growth rate equal to the long run growth rate of Russia's GDP, Gompers used a 5% terminal growth rate. Gompers' rate is the mid-point between the forecasted long-term Russian nominal GDP growth of 6.2%, and a forecasted inflation rate to 2030 of 3.9%.

Gompers' use of a 5% terminal growth rate is based on a respected source of such projections, the EIU. That approach was measured and realistic given that the Russian telecom industry was expected to grow at a rate significantly exceeding the Russian GDP. The reasonableness of expecting the Russian telecommunication sector to outpace the overall Russian economy is buttressed by actual history in the

United States, where the telecom industry has grown at nearly three times the rate of the United States GDP. Gompers' estimate accounts for the fact that the Russian telecommunications market is continuing to grow and that, with the increase of the broadband and Wi – Fi markets, companies such as Golden would have the opportunity to reach new customers and offer bundled services to existing customers. By choosing the average of the Russian GDP and inflation rate, Gompers accounted for the very real possibility that Golden will be close to (or in my view, likely exceed) the GDP rate for a period of time, but then, as the telecom market matures, settle closer to the inflation rate. I therefore adopt a 5% terminal growth rate.

2. Golden's Tax Rate

Sherman and Gompers also disagree about the tax rate to use. The tax rates in the Five Year Plan for 2008 to 2012 ranged from 30.1% to 35.3%, and the tax rate Credit Suisse used in connection with the DCF analysis undergirding its Fairness Opinion was 30%.Gompers adopted the tax rate used by Credit Suisse in the Fairness Opinion. He also reasoned that a 30% tax rate was "consistent with the numbers forecasted by [Golden's] management." Sherman, on the other hand, selected a tax rate of 31.6% based on the predictions of Golden's management, and on Golden's average historical tax rate for 2004 to 2006,which ranged from 23.7% to 32.4%. Gompers simply adopted Credit Suisse's calculations without explaining convincingly why those calculations are reasonable. By contrast, Sherman adjusted management's projections to reflect the average of Golden's historical tax rate, a rate that is at the conservative end of management's predictions, which called for tax rates ranging from 30.1% to 35.3% for the period from 2008 to 2012. I therefore adopt Sherman's tax rate of 31.6% for purposes of my DCF analysis.

3. Equity Risk Premium

To figure out the cost of capital by which to discount Golden's future cash flows, both Sherman and Gompers had to come up with a cost of equity. One of the two major sources of disagreement between the experts was over what equity risk premium ("ERP") to use.[46] Sherman relied on an ERP of 7.1%. The ERP Sherman selected is from the 2008 Ibbotson SBBI Valuation Year Book, which is based on long-term historical data from 1926 to year-end 2007.[47] Gompers used an ERP of 6.0%, which he selected based on his teaching experience, the relevant academic and empirical literature, and the supply side ERP reported in the 2007 Ibbotson Yearbook.

In a theme that will be continued when I next examine the debate about beta, the parties spar about the approach to take, with the petitioners portraying themselves

---

[46] [101] The ERP is the premium an investor should receive for the risk associated with investing in equities versus riskless assets, such as U.S. government short-term bonds. *See* Shannon Pratt & Roger Grabowski, Cost of Capital: Applications and Examples 89, 91 (3rd ed. 2008); Sherman Rebuttal at 14; Gompers Report at 37.

[47] [102] JX 501 (Ibbotson Assoc., SBBI: 2008 Yearbook Valuation (2008)) ("Ibbotson Yearbook"); Tr. at 938 (Sherman).

as using the most reliable, market-accepted method because their method is "forward looking" and thus consistent with the purpose of this valuation, which is to determine the value of Golden based on its prospects in a future, not past, market. For its part, Golden portrays the petitioners as advancing novel, unaccepted approaches that are more speculative and less reliable than the more traditional approaches it advances.

In reality, the debate is not nearly so stark. Although the petitioners, through Gompers, advance techniques that are designed to be forward-looking, those techniques are of course entirely based on using past data to predict the future, just like the techniques advanced by Golden, through Sherman. Each technique depends to a certain extent on taking some combination of past data and using it to predict a necessarily uncertain future.

In the case of their debate about the ERP, that reality can easily be discerned. For its part, Golden uses the most traditional estimate of the ERP, the historic ERP published by Ibbotson. That estimate is based on Ibbotson's consideration of stock returns from 1926 to the present (or as relevant to this case, to year end 2007). Sherman testified that the Ibbotson historic ERP (the "Historic ERP") is the best estimate of predicting long-term future performance because it relies on a long period of history, while a predictive ERP is "an attempt at predicting the future as opposed to just letting history be the guide. . . ." Golden buttresses its reliance upon the Historic ERP with three primary sources. First, Golden cites an article by Peng Chen and James Harrington which explains that "the historical equity risk premium estimate is a very solid estimate, and should continue to serve as a starting point for applying the equity risk premium in portfolio optimization and business valuation."[48] Second, Golden cites an article by James Hitchner and Katherine Morris which states that "[i]n practice, valuation analysts rarely rely on predictive models to forecast equity risk premiums. Risk premium components based directly on historical stock market return data are widely accepted and relied upon by the valuation community."[49] Finally, Golden relies on Ibbotson's 2008 Valuation Yearbook, pointing to a section where Ibbotson states that both Ibbotson's supply side and Historical ERP estimates are "from actual market statistics over a long historical period of time."[50] Crucially, all three of these sources include both historic and supply side ERP models.[51]

The petitioners, through Gompers, say that continued rote use of the Historic ERP will lead to unreliable results. Speaking most directly to that point, Gompers

---

[48] [106] JX 724 (Peng Chen & James Harrington, *Ibbotson Authors Discuss Historical and Supply Side Estimates of ERP* (Jan. 2008), *available at* http://www.bvlibrary.com/BVUpdatePlus/bvuPlusArticles3Print.aspx?docRef=9543).

[49] [107] JX 801 (James Hitchner & Katherine Morris, "*Cost of Capital Controversies: It's Time To Look Behind the Curtain,*" (Jan. 2008), *available at* http://bvlibrary.com/BVUpdatePluls/bvuPlusArticles3Print.aspx?docRef=5089).

[50] [108] Ibbotson Yearbook at 98.

[51] [109] *Id.* at 92 (explaining the benefits of a supply side ERP); JX 724 (Chen & Harrington, *supra* note 106) at 4 (noting that the historic and supply side "models do not conflict" and will "converge over time"); JX 801 (Hitchner & Morris, *supra* note 107) at 5 (describing a variety of approaches to ERP, including supply side risk premiums).

notes that Ibbotson and his co-authors have themselves developed an alternative model to forecast the long-term expected equity return because of their view that the historic approach wrongly assumes that the relationship between stocks and bonds observed in the past would remain stable into the future. As Gompers notes, Ibbotson indicates "[o]ver the long run, the equity return should be close to the long-run supply estimate."[52] The supply side estimate that Ibbotson publishes uses the Ibbotson historical sample from 1926 to the present, but estimates which components of the equity risk premium are driven by the price-to-earnings ratio of a stock, and which components are driven by expected earnings growth.[53] The supply side rate assumes that actual returns to equity will track real earnings growth, not the growth reflected in the price-to-earnings ratio.[54]

In arguing that continued use of the simple Historic ERP is unjustifiable, Gompers has substantial support in the professional and academic valuation literature.[55] Shannon Pratt, for example, has urged his readers who still use an ERP of 7% to "immediately make a downward adjustment to reflect recent research results,"[56] and has written that the "ERP as of the beginning of 2007 should be in the range of 3.5% to 6%."[57] Gompers also cites to a survey of finance professors, which found that the mean ERP taught by 369 professors is 5.96%,[58] and a report of JP Morgan estimating the ERP to be in the range of 5% to 7%.[59] Although the surveys cited by Gompers are not so compelling as to be conclusive, they suggest that current academic thinking puts the ERP closer to 6.0% than to 7.1%.

The question is not free from doubt, but I believe that Gompers has the better of the argument for the following reasons. First, to cling to the Ibbotson Historic ERP blindly gives undue weight to Ibbotson's use of a single data set. 1926 might have been a special year because, for example, that was the year when Marilyn Monroe was born, but it has no magic as a starting point for estimating long-term equity returns. If one is going to use an approach that simply involves taking into

---

[52] [111] JX 109 (Robert G. Ibbotson & Peng Chen, *Long – Run Stock Returns: Participating in the Real Economy*, FIN. ANALYSTS J. (Jan./Feb.2003)) at 88, 94; Ibbotson Yearbook at 92 (stating the same principle).

[53] [112] Ibbotson Yearbook at 95–96, 98 (discussing how the supply side model is structured); Tr. at 420–22 (Gompers).

[54] [113] *Id.* at 96 ("[T]he main difference between the historical and forecast equity returns is the exclusion of growth in P/E ratio in the forecasted earnings model.").

[55] [114] *See, e.g.*, JX 113 (Jeremy Siegel, *Perspectives on the Equity Risk Premium*, FIN. ANALYSTS J. (2005)) at 62–64, 70 (setting forth the "persuasive reasons [that] support a lower forward-looking real return on equity than the return found in the historical data").

[56] [115] JX 319 (Shannon Pratt, "Valuers Should Lower Equity Risk Premium Component of Discount Rate," *Business Valuation and Resources*, BUSINESS VALUATION UPDATE (Nov.2003)).

[57] [116] JX 318 (PRATT, COST OF CAPITAL, *supra* note 101).

[58] [117] JX 114 (Ivo Welch, *The Consensus Estimate For the Equity Premium by Academic Financial Economists in December 2007* (Jan. 2008), *available at* http://ssrn.com/abstract=1084918) at Table 2. Of the professors who responded to the survey, the middle 50% of respondents teach an ERP between 4% and 6%. Of the other fifty percent of respondents, five percent teach an ERP of 2–4%, twenty percent teach 4–5%, twenty percent teach 7–8.5%, and five percent teach 8.5–20%. *Id.*

[59] [118] JX 112 (JP Morgan, *The Most Important Number in Finance: The Quest for the Market Risk Premium* (May 2008)) at 2.

account historical equity returns, then one has to consider that very well-respected scholars have made estimates in peer-reviewed studies of long-term equity returns for periods much longer than Ibbotson, and have come to an estimate of the ERP that is closer to the supply side rate Ibbotson himself now publishes as a reliable ERP for use in a DCF valuation.[60] For example, Professor Jeremy Siegel has examined the period from 1802 to 2004 and come up with an ERP of 5.36%.[61] Likewise, Professors Eugene Fama and Kenneth French considered the period from 1872 to 2000, and calculated an average ERP of 5.57%.[62]

Relevantly, the literature also suggests that the ERP for companies operating in foreign markets is, if anything, lower than the Historic ERP for a domestic company.[63] Importantly, these studies reach results that are consistent with the actual logic used by Ibbotson in recent volumes. Although it is true that Ibbotson does not disavow the use of the Historic ERP as a basis for valuing corporations on a going forward basis, the text is utterly devoid of any explication of why the Historic ERP should used. By contrast, the 2003 article by Ibbotson and Chen explains that "investors' expectations for long-term equity performance should be based on the supply of equity returns produced by corporations" because "[t]he supply of stock market returns is generated by the productivity of the corporations in the real economy."[64] And, Ibbotson's 2008 Valuation Yearbook makes a strong argument for the supply side method by stating that "over the long run, equity returns should be close to the long-run supply estimates."[65]

---

[60] [119] *See* JX 828 (Michael Devaney, *Will Future Equity Risk Premium Decline?*, J. of Fin. Planning (Apr. 2008)) at 47 (finding that a mean equity risk premium of 5.5% covers the period from 1870–2002).

[61] [120] JX 113 (Siegel, *supra* note 114) at 63.

[62] [121] JX 833 (Eugene Fama & Kenneth French, *The Equity Premium*, 57 J. of Fin. 637, 638 (Apr. 2002)) (considering different measures of the expected ERP utilized by the market, such as the dividend growth model, and comparing those measures to the historical ERP). Golden argues that, because Fama and French advocate a three-factor model that differs from the CAPM in determining the cost of equity, their ERP findings cannot be compared to those of Ibbotson. But, whatever differences may exist between the CAPM and Fama – French models for calculating the cost of equity, those differences do not affect the applicability of Fama and French's ERP estimate, which is an input to both models. *See* Brealey & Myers, *supra* note 81 at 208–09; *see also* Pratt, Cost of Capital, *supra* note 101 at 102 (discussing the ERP calculated by Fama and French from 1951 to 2000 and comparing it to other ERPs calculated by, among others, Ibbotson). Nothing suggests that the ERPs derived by Fama and French are only appropriately used in the Fama – French, and not the CAPM, model.

[63] [122] *See, e.g.*, JX 318 (Pratt, Cost of Capital, *supra* note 101) at 109 (noting that equity returns and historical equity premiums for foreign companies should be adjusted *downward* to account for the fact that corporate cash flows in most foreign countries typically exceed investors' expectations (citing Dimson, Marsh & Stauton, *Global Evidence on the Equity Premium; The Worldwide Equity Premium: A Smaller Puzzle*, EFA 2006 Zurich Meetings Paper, April 7, 2006; Global Investment Returns Yearbook 2007)); JX 113 (Siegel, *supra* note 114) at 63 (explaining that due to the "survivorship bias," ERPs based on the United States market typically overstate the returns on equities, particularly in markets "where stocks have faltered or disappeared outright, such as they did in Russia"); *see also* Aswath Damodaran, *Equity Risk Premiums (ERP): Determinants, Estimation and Implications* at 12, *available at* http://ssrn.com/abstract=1274967 (describing a view "backed by a study of large equity markets over the twentieth century" that "[t]he historical risk premium obtained by looking at U.S. data is biased upwards because of a survivor bias").

[64] [123] JX 109 (Ibbotson and Chen, *supra* note 111) at 94.

[65] [124] Ibbotson Yearbook at 92.

Ibbotson's reasoning comports with the strong weight of professional and academic thinking, which is accurately represented by Gomper's view that the most responsible estimate of ERP is closer to 6.0% than 7.1%. I come to this conclusion with full realization that any estimate of ERP is just that, an estimate of something that is highly uncertain, and that the relevant academic and professional community — and not this court — should develop the accepted approach. Sherman's approach has met with the approval of this court on prior occasions,[66] but, when the relevant professional community has mined additional data and pondered the reliability of past practice and come, by a healthy weight of reasoned opinion, to believe that a different practice should become the norm, this court's duty is to recognize that practice if, in the court's lay estimate, the practice is the most reliable available for use in an appraisal.[67] Here, there is solid academic and professional thinking that supports the view that 6.0% is the most responsible ERP to deploy, and I do so. In reaching this conclusion, I give heaviest weight to the published literature, but also find the admittedly squishier academic survey data supportive. Although that data is far from perfect, it does reveal that the weight of academic thinking at our nation's finest finance departments places the ERP much nearer to Gomper's estimates than Sherman's. For all these reasons, I adopt Gompers' ERP of 6.0%.

4. Beta

In round two of their theoretical debate, Gompers and Sherman spar over what beta [a statistical measurement of a stock's volatility risk, with a number greater than 1.0 representing some element of risk] to use in calculating Golden's cost of equity capital. As in the prior debate, Gompers claims that he is using the best forward-looking, academically and professionally sound approach while Sherman is using a backward-looking, outdated approach. Again, the petitioners overstate their case and, in this instance, also fail to put forward reliable academic and professional support for their position.

It is true that Sherman uses a more traditional approach to beta. Sherman uses the Bloomberg five-year weekly historic beta for Golden of 1.32. The Bloomberg

---

[66] [125] *See In re PNB Holding Co. S'holder Litig.*, 2006 WL 2403999, at 30 (Del.Ch. Aug. 18, 2006) (choosing to adopt a historical ERP of 7% because a long-term supply side ERP had not yet gained "universal acceptance").

[67] [126] *See Weinberger v. UOP, Inc.*, 457 A.2d 701, 713 (Del. 1983) (interpreting 8 Del. C. § 262 to require that appraisal actions "include proof of value by any techniques or methods which are generally considered acceptable in the financial community and otherwise admissible in court"); *Union Ill.*, 847 A.2d at 363 (adopting the Fama – French approach to cost of capital over the more widely accepted CAPM approach because the court determined the former approach to be more reliable and more appropriate for use in that valuation of a regional bank). As in any complex area involving the prediction of future human events, one can expect that academic and professional thinking on the expected ERP will not remain static but will evolve as more data and additional thinking is done. That is the nature of things. What, of course, makes the use of such thinking of piquancy in this context is that ideas that academics and professionals throw around to create ranges of value are used by a law-trained judge to come to a single point estimate of value that could require a party to pay another party millions of dollars. The law-trained judges who must perform such analyses are more conscious than anyone of the inherent risk of error in such an endeavor, and indeed of the reality that no one can really tell if an error was made. That is why many of us eschew the hoary term "intrinsic value," a term best reserved for judgments of the divine than ones made by human judges.

beta is based on a publicly-available regression calculation, and is computed in the standard way by examining the co-variance of a company's stock performance with that of the stock exchange on which the firm's shares are listed. Although there is a fairly substantial amount of imprecision and a general disagreement in the finance industry and academia over the proper way to select a beta value,[68] the Bloomberg historic beta is considered to have a fair amount of predictive power, and to be a reliable proxy for unobservable forward-looking betas.

Sherman argues that his use of a historic beta is appropriate because Golden's operating and capital structure would have remained substantially the same going forward as it had during the five years captured in the Bloomberg historical beta. Sherman also accurately points out that the Bloomberg historical beta for Golden remained relatively stable during the five year period, suggesting that the market had a good bead on its systematic risk.

By contrast, Gompers eschews reliance on Golden's historical beta and advocates a lower beta of 1.2, based on a so-called predictive beta from the financial consultancy MSCI Barra ("Barra"). Gompers argues that his approach is forward-looking and more reliable because beta estimates are not stable over long periods of time, and thus the use of a historical beta is not the best basis for predicting the future, especially because there is some evidence that the betas of companies tend to eventually revert towards the mean. Gompers also claims that because Golden was seeking to evolve its business strategy from one heavily reliant on acquisitions for growth toward one that was less dependent on M & A and more on organic growth, Golden's historical beta is not a good predictor of its future beta.

The petitioners ask that if this court declines to adopt the Barra beta, a Bloomberg adjusted beta of 1.17 be used, but it is not clear why they advocate the Bloomberg adjusted beta as an appropriate alternative to the Barra beta. Aside from the fact that the Bloomberg adjusted beta produces a value close to 1.2, the methodology used by Bloomberg to adjust the beta value bears no apparent relationship to that used by Barra. Unlike the 13-factor Barra model, Bloomberg uses only two factors for its adjusted beta, giving 66% weight to a corporation's historic beta, while taking into account the possibility of later mean reversion by giving 33% weight to 1, or the average market beta.

This battle of the experts is one that I am poorly positioned to resolve, and it appears unlikely that a finance professor would fare any better. Even after asking the parties to go back and submit relevant literature on beta, and even after doing an independent review, I admit to finding no literature that sheds reliable light on this question of whether to use a historical or the supposedly forward-looking Barra beta. The standard texts do not explore the reliability of different approaches to calculating beta in any useful depth.[69] I suppose that is not surprising because most

---

[68] [130] *See* JX 106 (Robert Bruner et al., *Best Practices in Estimating the Cost of Capital: Survey and Synthesis*, FIN. PRACTICE AND EDU. (Spring/Summer 1998)) at Ex. 4 (showing that beta values for a sample company given by Bloomberg, Value Line, and Standard and Poor's range from a mean beta of 1.03 to 1.24).

[69] [137] *See, e.g.*, BREALEY & MYERS, *supra* note 81 at 173–75, 232–34 (defining beta, and giving a cursory discussion of how beta reflects market sensitivity, and how beta is calculated relative to foreign markets for foreign investments in the United States); PRATT, VALUING A BUSINESS, *supra* note 86

practitioners who use beta are not looking for precision but for a reasonably reliable tool to make range of value estimates. But, whatever the reason, the reality is that the available literature is far from helpful, and does not aid Gompers or his client, the petitioners.

Gompers touts the Barra beta as one that has been relied upon by the financial community for equity valuations.[70] I accept that that is the case, although I also recognize, as Gompers does, that the use of the Bloomberg historical beta is also a common, indeed probably more common, practice. But for several reasons that I now explain, Gompers has not given me the confidence to embrace the Barra beta technique as reliable one.

For starters, the Barra forecasting model is proprietary, and cannot be reverse-engineered. The Barra predictive beta, which is a forecast of a stock's future looking beta using past data, is based on a thirteen-factor model,[71] but the weight given to each of the factors is not publicly available. In fact, Barra has used three different versions of its model without explaining why or what changes have been made, and it is not apparent whether Barra retroactively updates its past beta calculations as it tinkers with? improves? changes for changes' sake? or lessens? the reliability of its model. Consistent with these realities, Gompers himself does not fully understand the details of how the Barra model works and, thus, I cannot rely on his advocacy of it. The only thing Gompers knows about the model is that it lists certain valuation-relevant factors, including factors relevant to the historical beta such as volatility, leverage, and trading activity, and throws them in a stew pot in undisclosed proportions to come up with an outcome. Put simply, despite his impressive academic credentials, Gompers himself could not cook me up a Barra beta of Golden, Microsoft, or any other company if I asked him to do so.

In a critically important difference from the ERP controversy I just decided, the Barra beta's reliability is not buttressed by the weight of any reliable academic or professional literature. The only evidence that the petitioners have produced showing that the Barra beta has a greater reliability than other beta providers such as Bloomberg or Morningstar is a quarter-century old paper authored by Barr Rosenberg, the creator of the Barra beta.[72] No neutral academic support for the predictive power of the Barra beta has yet been published. And, as discussed, the

(discussing beta as a measure of systematic risk, extreme betas that are above and below the average beta of 1.0, beta measurement problems, and listing problems that arise when applying betas estimated for guideline companies to the valuation of the subject company); Bradford Cornell, Corporate Valuation: Tools for Effective Appraisal and Decision Making 219–22 (1993) (noting that certain analysts adjust beta toward 1.0, or toward the industry average, but stating that a more detailed discussion was "beyond the scope of [the] book").

[70] [138] Tr. at 351–52; *see also* JX 106 (Bruner, *supra* note 130) at 20 (stating that "[t]he best known provider of fundamental beta estimates is the consulting firm BARRA"); JX 115 (Scott Widen, *Delaware Law, Financial Theory and Investment Banking Valuation Practices*, 4 NYU J. of L. & Bus. 579, 585–86 (2008)) (citing numerous sources for the notion that "[m]any investment banks now use predicted Barra betas in their fairness opinion analyses").

[71] [140] The thirteen factors used in Barra's model include: volatility, momentum, size, size nonlinearity, trading activity, growth, earnings yield, value, earnings variability, leverage, currency sensitivity, dividend yield, and a non-estimation universe indicator. *See* JX 117 (Barra, Risk Model Handbook United States Equity: Version 3 75–76 (1998)).

[72] [144] *See* JX 111 (Barr Rosenberg, *Prediction of Common Stock Betas*, J. of Portfolio Mgmt.,

undisclosed recipe for the Barra beta has changed several times since the Rosenberg paper was published.

Finally, Gompers' advocacy of the Barra beta is inconsistent with a DCF valuation that Gompers submitted to this court in *Doft & Co. v. Travelocity.com Inc.*[73] Tellingly, in that valuation, Gompers utilized a historic raw beta similar to Sherman's approach covering various time periods during the two-year period before the relevant merger, which was lower than the Barra beta that would have applied to Travelocity at that time. Gompers testified in this case that his opinion in *Travelocity* was in line with what he taught and understood about beta at that time and, since 2006, he has switched to using a Barra beta or an adjusted beta. But, oddly, he cannot point to an epiphanic moment or any academic or other studies that prompted him to change his approach. In fact, the Barr Rosenberg article that Gompers predominantly relies on was published in 1985 — nineteen years before Gompers used a raw historic beta in *Travelocity*. This is in strong contrast to the ERP question, where Gompers is able to cite a wealth of recent academic and professional writings that supports a lower ERP estimate.

I wish to emphasize that I do not reject the Barra beta for use in later cases. Rather, I decline to adopt the Barra beta for purposes of this appraisal, given both Gompers' inability to shed light on the inner workings of the Barra beta model and his unexplained shift from advocating the historical beta in *Travelocity* to the Barra beta in this case. If the Barra beta is to be used in appraisal proceedings, a more detailed and objective record of *how* the Barra beta works and *why* it is superior to other betas must first be presented. To this point, it is more persuasive to a judge to know that a testimonial expert who is an academic has written about the reliability of a valuation methodology in an academic study in a peer-reviewed journal than to be among those first privileged in the world to hear from the academic about that issue in his expert reports and seat-of-the-pants testimony in a valuation assignment for a self-interested litigation client.

Although I reject Gompers' use of a Barra beta, I am persuaded that the simple use of historical beta is not the best method to use in calculating Golden's cost of equity. Although beta is a somewhat metaphysical concept, the literature does tend to suggest that, as a matter of theory anyway, companies that are more unstable and leveraged, less established and financially and competitively secure, and in colloquial terms "riskier," should have higher betas.[74] Betas can also take into account considerations like political risk to the extent they are priced by the

Winter 1985) at 5–14 (discussing the overall predictive performance of the first Barra beta model).

[73] [146] [2004 Del. Ch. LEXIS 75 (May 21, 2004)]. The court in *Travelocity* declined to conduct a DCF analysis in determining the fair value of the company because the underlying management projections were unreliable. *Id.* at 5.

[74] [151] *See, e.g.*, Pratt, Cost of Capital, *supra* note 101 (explaining that companies with higher levels of debt are "riskier" than the equity of companies with less leverage); Pratt, Valuing a Business, *supra* note 86 ("Securities that have betas greater than 1.0 are characterized as aggressive securities and are more risky than the market."); JX 312 (Pablo Fernandez, *Are Calculated Betas Worth for Anything?*, IESE Business School, Working Paper (Oct. 16, 2008)) at 13 (pointing out a problem with historic betas that high-risk companies often have smaller historical betas, although riskier companies should have higher betas).

market.[75]

Given these realities, a more substantial, if still less than ideal, part of the valuation literature comes into play. As even Golden admits, there is support for the notion that more extreme betas tend to revert to the industry mean over time.[76] The historical beta of Golden is quite high, especially given its low leverage, and might reflect, among other things, its geographic concentration in an emerging market with some higher risk of political instability, its high growth strategy and its position in the telecom sector.

But Sherman has premised his valuation of Golden on the notion that its growth will slow, its domestic market will become a place friendly for those desirous of Volcker-style inflation policing, and that Golden will become a steady, staid company. To my mind, this view is consistent with the notion that Golden will, over time, revert toward the telecom industry's typical beta.

Unlike Gompers, however, I do not believe the immediate use of a lower beta is in order. The record supports the conclusion that Golden will continue to engage in a good deal of M & A activity, will enter new product markets, and continue to operate in a market with some political risk.[77] Rather, the more balanced approach is to give the predominant weight to Golden's historical beta, while giving some substantial weight to the industry beta.[78]

---

[75] [152] Tr. at 685 (Gompers) (explaining that, by accounting for the "historical correlation of the stock return with the market," the beta values account for political risk).

[76] [153] *See* JX 318 (Pratt, Cost of Capital, *supra* note 101) at 130 (stating that "[o]ver time, a company's beta tends toward its industry's average beta").

[77] [154] Although Golden had a substantial presence in the largest Russian cities as of the valuation date, there were substantially-sized markets it still wished to enter and new product markets it hoped to join. *See* JX 416 (Transcript of Golden's Third Quarter Earnings Release Conference Call, *supra* note 18) (announcing that Golden's growth strategy included expansion into thirty additional cities); Tr. at 814, 816–17 (Svetlichny) (explaining that Golden was exploring a number of smaller acquisitions before it was acquired by VimpelCom). The likelihood is that to do so, M & A activity would have remained an important element of its growth strategy, as would risky product launches. Even if Gompers were correct that Golden was shifting its strategy to one of predominantly organic growth, Gompers fails to explain why such a strategy would result in a lower beta. Beta values measure systematic risk, and it is not clear that organic growth is less risky than M & A. Furthermore, Gompers' argument that the Barra, and not historical beta, would better account for this supposed strategy shift is belied by the fact that Gompers selected a Barra beta from June 2007 while Golden's Five Year Plan announcing its strategy is from October 2007. *See* Gompers Report at 37.

[78] [155] The petitioners argue that it is not appropriate to use an historic beta because such a beta gives weight to political risk, which was already accounted for by Golden's management in estimating Golden's future cash flows. But, although the Proxy explained that the Special Committee based its recommendation that Golden's shareholders accept VimpelCom's tender offer on factors that included "political uncertainty in the Russian market," and noted that risks inherent in the forward-looking statements in the Five Year Plan included "the political, economic and legal environment in the markets in which [Golden] operate[d]," Golden's cash flow projections did not incorporate any specific value for political risk. *See* Proxy at 27, 46; Tr. at 828–29 (Svetlichny) (explaining that the Five Year Plan's projected cash flows did not account for political risk because such "risks are . . . binary in nature" and could not "be predicted and incorporated"). Moreover, it is difficult to estimate what value to place on political risk; in the case of Russia, the only real concern in the record seemed to be about some radical change in which companies like Golden might be expropriated. Management could not really price that risk, but it may be, I cannot say for sure, that the reported beta does capture some of that risk and, if the market does that, I cannot see why this court should not consider that real-world valuation factor.

In doing so, I reject Gompers' argument that if I decline to adopt the Barra beta, I should instead adopt a Bloomberg adjusted beta of 1.17, which begins with the historic beta used by Sherman and adjusts it towards 1.0 on the theory that "extreme" betas eventually revert toward the overall average market beta of 1.0.[79] As an initial matter, Gompers' advocacy of the Bloomberg adjusted beta is not convincing because he simply suggests it as an alternative to the Barra beta, without any rational linking of these two disparate methods. Moreover, he offers no explanation as to why adjusting the Bloomberg beta to 1.0 makes more sense for Golden — a company with low leverage, fast growth, and consistent performance in the telecom sector — than the raw five-year beta or, to the extent there is a reversion, an industry-based beta.

In my view, no reliable literature or evidence was presented to show that the beta of a telecom company like Golden, which operates in a risky market, will revert to 1.0. Instead, it makes more sense that companies in emerging markets will become more like their industry peers in more mature markets.[80] That intuition is also linc with the views of both Gompers and Sherman that Russia's growth rate will slow, its telecom industry will approach maturity, and that Golden's growth rate will eventually settle closer to the Russian rate of inflation.

According to the Ibbotson telecom (SIC 4813) beta, which gives the beta values for approximately 50 telecom companies that are traded in the United States including Golden, the median industry beta as of December 2007 was 1.45, and the SIC composite beta was 1.24. Similarly, the Bloomberg CUTL Index, which is a telecommunications index of companies traded on the NASDAQ, including Golden, puts the five year weekly industry beta at 1.249. Golden was a much larger, less levered company than the median company on the Ibbotson SIC 4813 list and, therefore, the composite beta of 1.24 is more appropriate than the median beta of 1.45.[81] I adopt it as the industry beta for purposes of this analysis.

I find that a beta that gives 2/3 weight to the Bloomberg historic raw beta of 1.32 and 1/3 weight to the 1.24 industry beta is the best approach to this DCF analysis. By predominantly adopting the historic raw beta, I give weight to the fact that

---

I also think it odd that the petitioners would have courts, and I suppose all those performing valuations, parse betas for factors that might have also been accounted for (e.g., leverage or the riskiness of certain industries) in management estimates of cash flow. The petitioners have not explained how or why one would do that. By giving weight to the industry beta, I also take into account the idea that Sherman embraced, which is that Russia is becoming more, not less, like markets such as the United States in terms of inflation and other relevant factors. Thus, I am confident that I am not giving some undue weight to political risk by relying heavily on Golden's historical beta.

[79] [156] *See* JX 311 (Marshall Blume, *Betas and Their Regression Tendencies*, 30 J. of Fin. 785, 794 (1975)) (explaining that "extreme" betas "tend to regress towards the grand mean of all betas over time"); Tr. at 626 (Gompers).

[80] [158] *See* Pratt, Cost of Capital, *supra* note 101 at 130 (stating that "[o]ver time, a company's beta tends toward its industry's average beta").

[81] [162] The median company listed by Ibbotson in the SIC 4813 industry code has median sales of $141 million and median total capital of $389 million. Golden had sales over $1 billion and its total capitalization was over $4 billion. Tr. at 1135–36 (Sherman) (citing Sherman Cross Examination Demonstrative 18). And, the median company in the SIC 4813 had debt equal to 30% of its total capital, while Golden had debt equal to only 5% of its total capital. Sherman Cross Examination Demonstrative 18; 2007 10-K at 34; Tr. at 1137–38 (Sherman).

Golden presently operates in a riskier, emerging, high-growth market, while tempering that number to account for the evidence that Russia is normalizing and that Golden is a stable company that would eventually have had a beta closer to its more mature, NASDAQ-traded peers. I thus apply a beta of 1.29 to the DCF analysis for a cost of equity of 12.3%.

V. CONCLUSION

For the reasons I have explained, I adopt a terminal growth rate of 5.0%, a tax rate of 31.6%, an equity risk premium of 6.0%, and a beta of 1.29. I applied those inputs to Gompers' DCF model, and came up with a value of $125.49 per share. The parties should confer and make sure that I used the model correctly. Assuming that I did, they should present a final judgment using an amount of $125.49, plus interest from the Valuation Date to the date of payment at the legal rate, compounded quarterly.[82] If the dollar figure is different, they should explain why they use the different figure and submit the corrected amount. The parties shall submit an order within five days.

NOTE

In affirming *Golden Telecom*, the Delaware Supreme Court noted Vice Chancellor Strine's expertise in appraisal cases. 11 A.3d 214, 218 (Del. 2010).

---

[82] [163] 8 Del. C. § 262(h) (setting the interest rate for appraisal cases at the legal rate at 5% over the Federal Discount Rate, compounded quarterly, unless there is "good cause" to deviate from that rate).

Chapter 3

DEBT SECURITIES

§ 3.01 INTRODUCTION

Long-term debt financing, or, as it is commonly referred to, the bond market, has historically been an important source of capital for U.S. business corporations. It has been observed that "long-term financing built this country and fueled its economy . . ." and that "for half of America's history those corporations and local governments have been able to build factories, bridges, roads — whatever they needed — by borrowing large sums of money for thirty or more years from the millions of investors who have bought long-term corporate and municipal bonds."[1]

§ 3.02 LEGAL AUTHORITY FOR ISSUANCE

A business corporation is a creature of statute and thus it only possesses those powers and has that authority which applicable law has provided to it. It is imperative, therefore, that, in considering the legal aspects of any proposed corporate finance transaction, it be verified that the corporation is authorized to enter into and carry out the transaction. For this reason, it is customary in a corporate finance transaction to obtain an opinion of legal counsel for the issuer as to the validity and legality of the transaction. In the case of an offering of debentures, for example, the opinion of counsel usually states that: (i) the indenture has been duly authorized, executed, and delivered by the parties thereto and constitutes a valid and legally binding instrument, enforceable in accordance with its terms except as the same may be limited by bankruptcy, insolvency, reorganization, moratorium, or other laws of general applicability relating to or affecting the enforcement of creditors' rights; and (ii) the debentures have been duly authorized, legally and validly issued and outstanding, and will constitute binding obligations of the Company, enforceable in accordance with their terms, except as may be limited by insolvency, reorganization, moratorium, or similar laws relating to or affecting generally the enforcement of creditors' rights. The reason for the "except" clause in those legal opinions has been explained as follows:

> A legal opinion is often an essential part of an agreement for the sale of property or the creation of an obligation. One party to a transaction will customarily demand an opinion from the other party's lawyer stating that the agreement is "valid, binding, and enforceable in accordance with its terms" — an enforceability opinion. But while an obligation may remain

[1] Julia Vitullo-Martin, *First Things First: Save the Bond Market*, N.Y. Times, Jan. 2, 1982, Sec. 1, at 17.

> valid" and "binding," a party may be released from performance, or may otherwise have the enforceability of the obligation drastically limited, by its subsequent bankruptcy and by the actions of the trustee in bankruptcy. As a result, an enforceability opinion is usually qualified by the proviso "except as enforceability may be limited by bankruptcy, insolvency, reorganization or similar laws affecting the rights of creditors generally" — the "bankruptcy out." This limitation on the scope of the enforceability opinion is particularly important if the language "enforceable in accordance with its terms" is taken to mean that the agreement is specifically enforceable by the party to whom the opinion is addressed.
>
> The traditional understanding of the bankruptcy out as a qualification which "relates to the availability of remedies and the collectibility of debt" clearly limits the enforceability opinion by excluding from its scope a wide range of the effects of bankruptcy under the new Bankruptcy Code (the Code). For example, the filing of a petition in bankruptcy acts as an automatic stay-preventing the commencement or continuation of lien enforcement proceedings as well as other lawsuits, against the debtor and his property.

Harter & Klee, *The Impact of the New Bankruptcy Code on the "Bankruptcy Out" in Legal Opinions*, 49 FORDHAM L. REV. 277, 278 (1980).

For useful information concerning legal opinions, see the various Reports of The TriBar Opinion Committee (of which the author is a member). TriBar has been commenting on legal opinion issues for more than 30 years. Recent Reports include *Third-Party "Closing" Opinions*, 53 BUS. LAW. 591 (1998); *Special Report of the TriBar Opinion Committee: The Remedies Opinion — Deciding When to Include Exceptions and Assumptions*, 59 BUS. LAW. 1483 (2004); *Third Party Closing Opinions: Limited Liability Companies*, 61 BUS. LAW. 679 (2006); Special Report of the TriBar Opinion, *Duly Authorized Opinions on Preferred Stock*, 63 BUS. LAW. 921, 925 (2008). *See also* Richard T. McDermott, *Legal Opinions on Corporate Matters in* LEGAL OPINION LETTERS CH. 3 (M. John Sterba ed., 3d ed. 2009); and *Supplemental TriBar LLC Opinion Report: Opinions on LLC Membership Interests*, 66 BUS. LAW. 1065 (2011).

Set forth below is the text of a form of legal opinion that would be rendered by counsel for the issuer of debentures in a public offering of debt securities. The opinion is addressed to the underwriter of Bissell's public offering in order to permit the underwriter to assert, in the event of a claimed legal infirmity of the debentures or the registration statement, the due diligence defense provided by Section 11(b)(3) of the Securities Act of 1933 which states that an underwriter shall not be liable for a misstatement or omission in a registration statement if the underwriter is able to establish that it had "reasonable ground to believe and did believe" that the statements in question were true. Section 11(c) provides, in turn, that "in determining, for the purposes of paragraph (3) of subsection (b) of this section, what constitutes reasonable investigation and reasonable ground for belief, the standard of reasonableness shall be that required of a prudent man in the management of his own property." Obtaining a legal opinion along the lines of the one set forth above contributes to compliance with that standard. *See generally* ABA Section of

Business Law, Report of the Subcommittee on Securities Law Opinions Committee on Federal Regulation of Securities, *Negative Assurances in Securities Offerings*, 64 Bus. Law. 395 (2009).

It is to be observed that the last sentence of paragraph 7 of the opinion states that the Underwriting Agreement has been duly executed and delivered but, unlike the Debentures and the Indenture, no opinion is expressed as to the enforceability of that Agreement. The reason for this distinction is that there is a legal question as to whether provisions in an agreement purporting to indemnify an underwriter for liabilities relating to the accuracy of a registration statement are contrary to public policy and thus unenforceable. *See* Thomas Lee Hazen, The Law of Securities Regulation 390 (4th ed. 2002).

August 24, 2011

Harmon & Hempstead
Investment Bankers
299 Wall Street
New York, New York 10128

Re: Bissell Corporation

Ladies and Gentlemen:

We have acted as counsel to Bissell Corporation, a Delaware corporation (the "Company"), in connection with the issuance by the Company to you of $62,270,000 aggregate principal amount at maturity of its Zero Coupon Senior Convertible Debentures due 2026 (the "Debentures"). This opinion is given pursuant to Section 6(b) of the Underwriting Agreement, dated August 24, 2011 (the "Underwriting Agreement"), by and between the Company and you. *Except as otherwise indicated, terms used in this letter have the meanings given to them in the Underwriting Agreement.*

In rendering the opinions expressed below, we have examined originals or copies, certified or otherwise identified to our satisfaction, of such documents, corporate records and other instruments as we have deemed necessary, including executed counterparts of the Underwriting Agreement, the Indenture and the Supplemental Indenture.

We have relied as to matters of fact which we could not confirm independently, upon certificates and written statements of public officials and of officers, directors, employees and representatives of, and accountants for, the Company (including, without limitation, the representations made in the Underwriting Agreement).

In examining documents, we have assumed the genuineness of all signatures, the authenticity of all documents purporting to be originals, and the conformity to the respective originals of all documents purporting to be copies.

Based on the foregoing, and such examination of law as we have deemed necessary, we are of the opinion that:

1. The Company has been *duly organized* and is validly existing as a corporation in good standing under the laws of the State of Delaware, with corporate power and authority to own or lease its properties and conduct its business as described in the Prospectus; each of the Designated Subsidiaries has been duly organized and is validly existing as a corporation or partnership, as applicable, in good standing under the laws of the jurisdiction of its incorporation or formation, with corporate or other power and authority to own or lease its properties and conduct its business as described in the Prospectus; the Company and each of the Designated Subsidiaries are duly qualified to transact business in all jurisdictions in which the conduct of their business requires such qualification, except where, to the best of our knowledge, the failure to qualify would not have a materially adverse effect upon the business of the Company and the Subsidiaries taken as a whole; and the outstanding shares of capital stock of each of the Designated Subsidiaries have been duly authorized and validly issued and are fully paid and non-assessable and are owned by the Company or a Subsidiary; and, to the best of our knowledge, the outstanding shares of capital stock of each of the Designated Subsidiaries are owned free and clear of all liens, encumbrances and equities and claims, and no options, warrants or other rights to purchase, agreements or other obligations to issue or other rights to convert any obligations into any shares of capital stock or of ownership interests in the Designated Subsidiaries are outstanding.

2. The Company has authorized and outstanding capital stock as set forth under the caption "Capitalization" in the Prospectus; the outstanding shares of the Common Stock have been duly authorized and validly issued and are fully paid and non-assessable; the Debentures are convertible into Common Stock in accordance with the terms of the Indenture and the Debentures; the shares of Common Stock issuable upon conversion of the Debentures have been duly reserved for issuance upon such conversion and, if and when issued upon such conversion, will be validly issued, fully paid and non-assessable and will conform to the description thereof contained in the Prospectus; and no preemptive rights of stockholders exist with respect to the capital stock or any other securities of the Company or the issue or sale thereof.

3. Except as described in or contemplated by the Prospectus, to our knowledge, there are no outstanding securities of the Company convertible into or exchangeable for or evidencing the right to purchase or subscribe for any shares of capital stock of the Company and there are no outstanding or authorized options, warrants or rights of any character obligating the Company to issue any shares of its capital stock or any securities convertible into or exchangeable for or evidencing the right to purchase or subscribe for any shares of such stock; and except as described in the Prospectus, to the best of our knowledge, no holder of any securities of the Company or any other person has the right, contractual or otherwise, that has not been satisfied or effectively waived, to cause the Company to sell or otherwise issue to them, or to permit them to underwrite the sale of, any of

the Debentures or the right to have any shares of Common Stock or other securities of the Company included in the Registration Statement or the right, as a result of the filing of the Registration Statement, to require registration under the Act of any shares of Common Stock or other securities of the Company.

4. The Company has all requisite corporate power and authority to execute, deliver and perform its obligations under the Debentures and the Indenture.

5. The Indenture has been duly qualified under the Trust Indenture Act; the Indenture has been duly and validly authorized, executed and delivered by the Company, and (assuming the due authorization, execution and delivery thereof by the Trustee) constitutes the valid and legally binding agreement of the Company, enforceable against the Company in accordance with its terms, *subject to (i) bankruptcy, insolvency, reorganization, fraudulent conveyance, moratorium or other similar laws relating to creditors' rights generally and (ii) general equitable principles.*

6. The Debentures are in the form contemplated by the Indenture. The Debentures have each been duly and validly authorized, executed and delivered by the Company and, when paid for by the Underwriters in accordance with the terms of the Underwriting Agreement (assuming the due authorization, execution and delivery of the Indenture by the Trustee and due authentication and delivery of the Debentures by the Trustee in accordance with the Indenture), will constitute the valid and legally binding obligations of the Company, entitled to the benefits of the Indenture, and enforceable against the Company in accordance with their terms, *subject to (i) bankruptcy, insolvency, reorganization, fraudulent conveyance, moratorium or other similar laws relating to creditors' rights generally and (ii) general equitable principles.*

7. The Company has all requisite corporate power and authority to execute, deliver and perform its obligations under the Underwriting Agreement and to consummate the transactions contemplated thereby; the Underwriting Agreement and the consummation by the Company of the transactions contemplated thereby have been duly and validly authorized by the Company. *The Underwriting Agreement has been duly executed and delivered by the Company.*

8. The Indenture and the Debentures conform as to legal matters in all material respects to the descriptions thereof contained in the Prospectus as supplemented or amended.

9. The Registration Statement *has become effective* under the Act and, to our knowledge, no stop order proceedings with respect thereto have been instituted or are pending or threatened under the Act.

10. The Registration Statement, the Prospectus and each amendment or supplement thereto and document incorporated by reference therein *comply as to form in* all material respects with the requirements of the Act or the Exchange Act, as applicable, and the applicable rules and regulations

thereunder (except that we express no opinion as to the financial statements and related schedules incorporated by reference therein). The conditions for the Company's use of Form S-3, set forth in the General Instructions thereto, have been satisfied.

11. The statements under the captions "Description of Debentures," "Certain Federal Income Tax Considerations," "Description of Debt Securities" and "Description of Capital Stock" in the Prospectus and Item 15 of the Registration Statement, insofar as such statements constitute a summary of documents referred to therein or matters of law, fairly summarize in all material respects the information called for with respect to such documents and matters.

12. We do not know of any contracts or documents required to be filed as exhibits to or incorporated by reference in the Registration Statement or described in the Registration Statement or the Prospectus which were not so filed, incorporated by reference or described as required, and such contracts and documents as are summarized in the Registration Statement or the Prospectus are fairly summarized in all material respects.

13. We know of no material legal or governmental proceedings pending or threatened against the Company, any of the Subsidiaries except as set forth in the Prospectus.

14. The execution and delivery of the Underwriting Agreement, the Indenture and the Debentures and the consummation of the transactions therein contemplated do not and will not conflict with or result in a breach of any of the terms or provisions of, or constitute a default under (or an event that with the giving of notice or lapse of time or both would constitute a default under) or result in the imposition or creation of (or the obligation to create or impose) a lien on any property or assets of the Company, of any Designated Subsidiary with respect to, the Charter, By-Laws or other comparable documents of the Company, of any Designated Subsidiary, or any agreement or instrument known to us to which the Company, or any of the Designated Subsidiaries is a party or by which the Company, of any of the Designated Subsidiaries may be bound, or any order, rule or regulation known to us to be applicable to the Company, or any Designated Subsidiary of any court or of any regulatory body or administrative agency or other governmental body having jurisdiction over the Company, of any Designated Subsidiary.

15. No approval, consent, order, authorization, designation, declaration or filing by or with any regulatory, administrative or other governmental body is necessary in connection with the execution and delivery of the Underwriting Agreement, the Indenture and the Debentures and the consummation of the transactions therein contemplated (other than as may be required by the NASD or as required by State securities and Blue Sky laws, as to which we express no opinion), except for the filing of the Registration Statement and the Prospectus under the Act and the qualification of the Indenture under the Trust Indenture Act, all of which have been made or occurred.

16. The Company is not, and will not become, as a result of the consummation of the transactions contemplated by the Underwriting Agreement, and application of the net proceeds therefrom as described in the Prospectus, required to register as an investment company under the Investment Company Act.

We have participated in the preparation of the Registration Statement and the Prospectus and participated in discussions with certain officers, directors and employees of the Company, representatives of Judson & Henderson LLP, the independent accountants who examined certain of the financial statements of the Company included or incorporated by reference in the Registration Statement and the Prospectus, and the Underwriters and we have reviewed certain corporate and partnership records and documents. While we have not independently verified and are not passing upon, and do not assume any responsibility for, the accuracy, completeness or fairness of the information contained in the Registration Statement and the Prospectus (except as set forth in paragraph (11) above), on the basis of such participation and review, *nothing has come to our attention that leads us to believe that the Registration Statement* (except for the financial statements and schedules and any other financial or statistical data therein, as to which we do not express any belief), at the time the Registration Statement became effective, contained any untrue statement of a material fact or omitted to state any material fact required to be stated therein or necessary to make the statements therein not misleading, or *that the Prospectus* (except for the financial statements and schedules and any other financial or statistical data contained or incorporated by reference therein, as to which we do not express any belief) as of its date or the date of this letter included or includes any untrue statement of a material fact or omitted or omits to state a material fact necessary in order to make the statements therein, in light of the circumstances under which they were made, not misleading.

We are a firm of attorneys licensed to practice in some, but not all, states in the United States of America. The opinions set forth in this letter relate only to the federal securities laws of the United States of America, the laws of the State of New York and the general corporate statutes of the states in which the Company and the Designated Subsidiaries are incorporated.

The phrase "to our knowledge" and similar expressions as used herein refer to the actual knowledge of the individual lawyers in the firm who have participated directly and substantially in the specific transaction to which this opinion relates.

This opinion is effective as of the date hereof. No expansion of our opinion may be made by implication or otherwise. We express no opinion other than is herein expressly set forth. We do not undertake to advise you of any matter within the scope of this letter that comes to our attention after the date of this letter and disclaim any responsibility to advise you of any future changes in law or fact that may affect the above opinion.

This letter is given solely for your benefit and may not be relied upon by any other person for any purpose without our prior written consent in each instance.

Very truly yours,
(Signature)

§ 3.03 DEBENTURE FORM

[FORM OF DEBENTURE]

[FACE]

NO . . . . $ . . . .

FSC CORPORATION

15 3/4 percent Senior Sinking Fund Debenture Due 1995

FSC CORPORATION, a Delaware corporation (herein called the "Company," which term includes any successor corporation under the Indenture hereinafter referred to), for value received, hereby promises *to pay to . . . . or registered assigns*, the principal sum of . . . . Dollars on August 1, 1995, at the principal office of the Trustee maintained for such purpose in the City of Pittsburgh, Pennsylvania, in such coin or currency of the United States of America as at the time of payment shall be legal tender for the payment of public and private debts, and to pay interest on said principal sum until payment of said principal sum has been made or duly provided for at the rate of 15 3/4 percent per annum, at said office or agency, in like coin or currency, *semi-annually* on February 1 and August 1 of each year, until payment of said principal sum has been made or duly provided for, from August 1, 1980, or if interest to any February 1 or August 1 has been paid, from the February 1 or the August 1, as the case may be, next preceding the date hereof to which interest has been paid, unless the date hereof is a date to which such interest has been paid, in which case, from the date hereof (except that so long as there is no existing default in payment of interest on the Debentures, if this Debenture was authenticated by the Trustee after the close of business on January 15 or July 15, as the case may be, and prior to the next succeeding February 1 or August 1, it shall bear interest from such February 1 or August l, provided, however, that if the Company shall default in the payment of interest due on such February 1 or August 1, then this Debenture shall bear interest from the next preceding February 1 or August 1 to which interest has been paid, or if no interest has been paid on the Debentures, from August 1, 1980). The interest so payable on any February 1 or August 1 will, subject to certain exceptions provided in the Indenture referred to on the reverse hereof, be paid by check via mail to the order of the person in whose name this Debenture is registered at such person's registered address at the close of business on the January 15 or July 15, as the case may be, next preceding such February 1 or August 1. Any interest not so punctually paid or duly provided for shall be payable as provided in said Indenture.

The provisions of this Debenture are continued on the reverse side hereof, and such continued provisions shall, for all purposes, have the same effect as though fully set forth at this place.

This Debenture shall not be entitled to any benefit under the Indenture or any indenture supplemental thereto or become valid or obligatory for any purpose until the certificate of authentication hereon shall have been signed by the Trustee under the Indenture referred to on the reverse hereof.

This Debenture shall be governed by and construed in accordance with the laws of the State of New York.

In Witness Whereof, FSC CORPORATION has caused this Debenture to be executed in its corporate name, manually or by facsimile, by its President or one of its Vice Presidents and by its Secretary or one of its Assistant Secretaries, and a facsimile of its corporate seal to be printed hereon.

Dated:

FSC CORPORATION

By. . . . .

President

Attest:

By. . . . .

Secretary

NOTE

With reference to the governing law clause providing that the Debenture is to be governed by New York law, the enforceability of such clauses is sometimes dependent upon whether the transaction bears a reasonable relation to the jurisdiction selected. The State of New York has enacted a statute specifically providing for the enforceability of governing law clauses. Section 5-1401 of the New York General Obligations Law provides as follows:

§ 5-1401. Choice of Law

1. The parties to any contract, agreement or undertaking, contingent or otherwise, in consideration of, or relating to any obligation arising out of a transaction covering in the aggregate not less than two hundred fifty thousand dollars, including a transaction otherwise covered by subsection one of section 1-105 of the uniform commercial code, may agree that the law of this state shall govern their rights and duties in whole or in part, *whether or not such contract, agreement or undertaking bears a reasonable relation to this state*. This section shall not apply to any contract, agreement or undertaking (a) for labor or personal services, (b) relating to any transaction for personal, family or household services, or (c) to the extent provided to the contrary in subsection two of section 1-105 of the uniform commercial

code.

2. Nothing contained in this section shall be construed to limit or deny the enforcement of any provision respecting choice of law in any other contract, agreement or undertaking.

In *IRB – Brasil Resseguros, S.A. v. Inepar Investments, S.A.*, 2012 N.Y. LEXIS 3665, at **3, the New York Court of Appeals explained the rational for the statute as follows:

> The Legislature passed the statute in 1984 in order to allow parties without New York contacts to choose New York law to govern their contracts. Prior to the enactment of § 5–1401, the Legislature feared that New York courts would not recognize "a choice of New York law [in certain contracts] on the ground that the particular contract had insufficient 'contact' or 'relationship' with New York" . . . . Instead of applying New York law, the courts would conduct a conflicts analysis and apply the law of the jurisdiction with " 'the most significant relationship to the transaction and the parties' " (Zurich Ins. Co. v. Shearson Lehman Hutton, 84 N.Y.2d 309, 317 [1994] [quoting Restatement (Second) of Conflict of Laws § 188(1)]). As a result, parties would be deterred from choosing the law of New York in their contracts, and the Legislature was concerned about how that would affect the standing of New York as a commercial and financial center . . . . The Sponsor's Memorandum states, "In order to encourage the parties of significant commercial, mercantile or financial contracts to choose New York law, it is important ... that the parties be certain that their choice of law will not be rejected by a New York Court . . . . The Legislature desired for parties with multi-jurisdictional contacts to avail themselves of New York law if they so designate in their choice-of-law provisions, in order to eliminate uncertainty and to permit the parties to choose New York's "well-developed system of commercial jurisprudence" . . . .

Although a student law note, Barry W. Rashkover, *Title 14, New York Choice of Law Rule for Contractual Disputes: Avoiding The Unreasonable Results*, 71 Cornell L. Rev. 227 (1985), asserts that the New York statute may be constitutionally infirm because in certain instances it might require a New York court to decline to apply the law of another state, and thus deprive that other state's law of the "full faith and credit" to which it is entitled by Article IV, Section 1 of the U.S. Constitution, such an assertion would appear to have no applicability to a commercial transaction involving the delivery of legal opinions. A choice of law by a state court is violative of the full faith and credit clause when it is "arbitrary" or "fundamentally unfair." *See Allstate Ins. Co. v. Hague*, 449 U.S. 302, 308 (1981). It is difficult to imagine a court making such a finding where the parties were represented by counsel and legal opinions were delivered. *But cf. Lehman Bros. Commer. Corp. v. Minmetals Int'l Non-Ferrous Metals Trading Co.*, 179 F. Supp. 2d 118, 137 (S.D.N.Y. 2000) (dictum).

[FORM OF TRUSTEE'S CERTIFICATE OF AUTHENTICATION]

TRUSTEE'S CERTIFICATE OF AUTHENTICATION

This is one of the Debentures described in the within-mentioned Indenture.

ABC BANK, N.A., as Trustee

By . . . .

Authorized Signature

[FORM OF DEBENTURE]

[REVERSE]

FSC CORPORATION

15 3/4 percent Senior Sinking Fund Debenture Due 1995

(Continued)

This Debenture is one of a duly authorized issue of Company, designated as its 15 3/4 percent Senior Sinking Fund Debentures Due 1995 (herein called the "Debentures"), limited to $7,000,000 aggregate principal amount, all issued or to be issued *under and pursuant to an indenture* dated as of August 1, 1980 (herein called the "Indenture"), duly executed and delivered by the Company to ABC Bank, N.A., Trustee (herein called the "Trustee," which term includes any successor trustee under the Indenture), to which Indenture and all indentures supplemental thereto reference is hereby made for a description of the rights, limitations of rights, obligations, duties and immunities thereunder of the Trustee, the Company and the holders of the Debentures and of the terms upon which the Debentures are, and are to be, authenticated and delivered.

In case an Event of Default, as defined in the Indenture, shall have occurred and be continuing, the principal hereof may be declared, and upon such declaration shall become, due and payable, in the manner, with the effect and subject to the conditions provided in the Indenture. As provided in the Indenture, the holders of a majority in aggregate principal amount of the Debentures at the time outstanding may rescind any such declaration upon payment of all amounts then due otherwise than by acceleration. Such holders may also, prior to any such declaration, on behalf of the holders of all of the Debentures, waive any past default under the Indenture and its consequences, except a default in the payment of the principal of or premium, if any, or interest on any of the Debentures. Any such waiver or any consent by the holder of this Debenture (unless revoked as provided in the Indenture) shall be conclusive and binding upon such holder and upon all future holders and owners of this Debenture and any Debenture issued in exchange herefor or in place hereof, irrespective of whether or not any notation of such waiver or consent is made upon this Debenture.

The Indenture contains provisions permitting the Company and the Trustee, with the consent of the holders of not less than a majority in aggregate principal amount of the Debentures at the time outstanding, evidenced as in the Indenture provided, to execute supplemental indentures adding any provisions to or changing in any manner or eliminating any of the provisions of the Indenture or of any supplemental indenture or modifying in any manner the rights of the holders of the Debentures; provided, however, that no such supplemental indenture shall: (i) extend the fixed maturity of any Debenture or reduce the principal amount thereof, or reduce the rate or extend the time of payment of interest thereon, or reduce any premium payable upon the redemption thereof, or make the principal thereof or any premium or interest thereon payable in any coin or currency other than that hereinbefore provided, without the consent of the holder of each Debenture so affected, (ii) reduce the aforesaid percentage of Debentures, the holders of which are required to consent to any such supplemental indenture, or the consent of whose holders is required for any waiver (of compliance with certain provisions of the Indenture or certain defaults under the Indenture or their consequences) provided for in the Indenture, without the consent of the holders of all Debentures then outstanding, or (iii) impair the right to institute suit to enforce the payment of principal, premium, if any, and interest on the Debentures when due, without the consent of the holders of all Debentures then outstanding.

No reference herein to the Indenture and no provision of this Debenture or of the Indenture shall alter or impair the obligation of the Company, which is absolute and unconditional, to pay the principal of and premium, if any, and interest on this Debenture at the respective times, at the place, at the rate and in the coin or currency herein prescribed.

The Debentures are issuable only as registered Debentures *without coupons* in denominations of One Thousand Dollars ($1,000) and any integral multiple thereof. Upon due presentment for registration of transfer of this Debenture at the principal office of the Trustee, in the City of Pittsburgh, Commonwealth of Pennsylvania, a new Debenture or Debentures, of authorized denominations, for a like aggregate principal amount, will be issued to the transferee as provided, and subject to the limitations, in the Indenture. No service charge will be made for any such transfer, but the Company may require payment of a sum sufficient to reimburse it for any tax or other governmental charge that may be imposed in relation thereto; and this Debenture may in like manner be exchanged without service charge for one or more new Debentures of other authorized denominations but of the same aggregate principal amount; all subject to the terms and conditions set forth in the Indenture.

The Debentures are *subject to redemption* at any time after August 1, 1985 prior to maturity, as a whole or from time to time in part, at the option of the Company, at the redemption prices equal to the percentages of the principal amount set forth below if redeemed during the 12-month period beginning August 1 of the years indicated:

Year	Percentage of Principal Amount	Year	Percentage of Principal Amount
1985	115.750%	1990	107.875%
1986	114.175%	1991	106.300%
1987	112.600%	1992	104.725%
1988	111.025%	1993	103.150%
1989	109.450%	1994	101.575%

Together in each case with accrued interest to the date of redemption.

The Debentures are also redeemable through operation of the *sinking fund* provided in the Indenture, which provides for the redemption on August 1 in each year beginning with 1983 to and including August 1, 1985 of Debentures in the aggregate principal amount per year of $117,000 and on August 1 of each year beginning with 1986 to and including August 1, 1994 of Debentures in the principal amount of $665,000. The Debentures are subject to redemption through the sinking fund at a redemption price of 100 percent of the principal amount being redeemed together with interest accrued to the date fixed for redemption. The Company may elect to take credit against sinking fund requirements for any Debentures acquired or redeemed (other than Debentures called for redemption pursuant to the sinking fund).

As provided in the Indenture, the notice of redemption to the holders of Debentures to be redeemed, in whole or in part, shall be given by mailing a notice of such redemption not less than 30 days before the date fixed for redemption to such holders at their addresses as they shall appear upon the registration books.

If this Debenture (or, if this Debenture is of a larger denomination than $1,000, any portion hereof which is $1,000 or an integral multiple of $1,000) is duly called for redemption and payment duly provided, this Debenture (or such portion hereof as aforesaid) shall cease to bear interest from and after the date fixed for such redemption.

Upon any partial redemption of this Debenture, this Debenture shall be surrendered to the Trustee in exchange for one or more new Debentures in principal amount equal to the unredeemed portion of this Debenture.

The Indenture provides that under the circumstances specified therein funds may be deposited with the Trustee or with any paying agent (other than the Company) in advance of the maturity or redemption date of any of the Debentures, in trust for the payment or redemption of such Debentures, and the interest due or to become due thereon, and that thereupon all obligations of the Company in respect of such Debentures shall cease and be discharged and the holders thereof shall thereafter be restricted exclusively to such funds for any and all other claims on their part under the Indenture or with respect to such Debentures.

This Debenture is transferable by the registered holder hereof in person, or by his attorney duly authorized in writing, at the principal office of the Trustee, but only in the manner, subject to the limitations, and upon payment of the charges provided in the Indenture and upon surrender and cancellation of this Debenture. Upon any such transfer a new registered Debenture of the same denomination, subject to the limitations provided in the Indenture, will be issued to the transferee in exchange for this Debenture.

Prior to due presentment of this Debenture for registration of transfer, the Company, the Trustee, any paying agent and any Debenture registrar may deem and treat the registered holder hereof as the absolute owner of this Debenture (whether or not this Debenture shall be overdue and not withstanding any notation of ownership or other writing hereon made by anyone other than the Company or any Debenture registrar), for the purpose of receiving payment hereof or on account hereof or interest hereon or for all other purposes, and neither the Company nor the Trustee nor any paying agent nor any Debenture registrar shall be affected by any notice to the contrary. All payments made to or upon the order of such registered holder shall to the extent of the sum or sums paid, effectually satisfy and discharge the liability for moneys payable on this Debenture.

As more fully provided in and subject to the terms and conditions of the Indenture in the event of the death of a natural person who is the registered holder of this Debenture, or of a natural person who is a co-registered holder with one or more other natural persons (whether as tenants in common or as joint owners with or without right of survivorship), either or both of the surviving co-registered holder, or the executor or personal representative of the deceased holder or his assignee, successor in interest or joint tenancy survivor (hereinafter referred to, whether such surviving co-registered holder or such successor to the interests of the deceased register holder, as the "successor holder") shall have the option to sell to the Company, and the Company shall be obligated to purchase, this Debenture (or portion hereof in denominations of $1,000 or any integral multiple thereof) for cash at a purchase price equal to the principal amount of this Debenture or such portion thereof to be sold, plus unpaid interest thereon accrued to the date of payment. To exercise such rights, the successor holder must notify the Company in writing by registered or certified mail not later than 12 months after the death of the deceased registered holder hereof of the exercise of such option as provided in the Indenture, accompanied by this Debenture duly endorsed for transfer. Payment for this Debenture or portion hereof to be sold, and delivery of any reissued Debenture for the balance hereof not being sold, shall be made by the Company on or before the March 1 immediately following the end of the calendar year in which the Company received such notice and this Debenture duly endorsed. As more fully provided in the Indenture, the Company shall not be obligated to so purchase this Debenture (or portion hereof) by any such March 1 if the principal amount to be purchased, together with the principal amount of all other Debentures to be so purchased by such date, would exceed the sinking fund payment, if any, by the sinking fund redemption date immediately following such March 1. Accordingly, the Company shall not be obligated to make payment for any such purchases prior to March 1, 1983. Purchases of Debentures shall be made in the order of receipt by the Company of notices from successor holders exercising their rights to sell, and the Company's obligation to purchase Debentures not required to be purchased by any such March 1 shall cumulate in order of receipt to March 1 of the following calendar year or years. Upon receipt of the successor holder's notice to sell this Debenture (or portion hereof), the Company shall notify the successor holder of the priority and latest date of purchase of this Debenture (or portion hereof). The successor holder shall have the right to withdraw his election to sell all or any portion (in integral multiples of $1,000) of this Debenture tendered for sale by so notifying the Company in writing by registered or certified mail not later than 30 days prior to such latest purchase date, and the Company shall return to the successor holder this Debenture (or withdrawn portion thereof).

No recourse shall be had for the payment of the principal of or premium, if any, or interest on this Debenture, or for any claim based hereon, or otherwise in respect hereof, or based on or in respect of the Indenture or any indenture supplemental thereto, against any incorporator or against any past, present or future stockholder, officer or director, as such, of the Company or of any successor corporation, whether by virtue of any constitution, statute or rule of law, or by the enforcement of any assessment or penalty or otherwise, all such liability being, by the acceptance hereof and as part of the consideration for the issuance hereof, expressly waived and released by every holder or owner hereof, as more fully provided in the Indenture.

[FORM OF ASSIGNMENT]

FOR VALUE RECEIVED the undersigned hereby sell(s), assign(s) and transfer(s) unto ______________ the within Debenture and all rights thereunder, hereby irrevocably constituting and appointing ______________ attorney to transfer said Debenture on the books of the Company, with full power of substitution in the premises.

Dated:

Notice: The signature to this assignment must correspond with the name as written upon the face of the within Debenture in every particular, without alteration or enlargement or any change whatever.

NOTES

(1) The Debenture provides for registration of ownership thereof. Interest is to be paid to the registered holder by check mailed to such holder's registered address. Nearly all corporate debt instruments are registered today. Formerly, many corporate debt securities were bearer instruments; the owner of such a debt instrument received a large, sturdy piece of paper, part of which was divided into small segments, called coupons, each of which reflected the obligation of the issuer to pay a fixed amount of interest on a particular date, with one coupon for each interest payment date. The owner of the bond collected interest by delivering the appropriate coupon to a paying agent of the issuer of the debt security, usually a bank. It is from that procedure that the phrase "clipping coupons" is derived. The following is a form of coupon bond:

> On the first day of May, 20 ____ unless the Bond hereinafter referred to shall have been called for redemption before the first day of May last preceding said date and payment thereof duly provided for, the Company will pay to the bearer, upon surrender hereof, at its office or agency in the Borough of Manhattan, City and State of New York, in such coin or

currency of the United States of America as at the time of payment shall be legal tender for the payment of public and private debts, such amount, if any, as may be payable on said date as interest on its 8% Income Bond No. under the provisions of the Indenture referred to in said Bond.

The "coupon" or "contractual" rate of interest is to be distinguished from the "yield" of a debt instrument. The distinction between "yield" and "coupon rate" is illustrated by the following example:

> Corporation XYZ issues a ten year $1,000 Debenture that according to its terms pays interest annually at the rate of ten percent (the coupon rate), or $100 per year. Ten percent is also the market rate of interest for that type of instrument at the time it is issued. Thereafter, such market rate of interest declines to nine percent. The holder of the Debenture will not sell the Debenture at par ($1,000) because the purchaser would be entitled to receive interest in excess of the then market rate. Instead, the Holder will sell the Debenture for $1100 which, given the *contractual* annual interest payment of $100, will yield nine percent to the purchaser. Likewise, if market interest rates increase to eleven percent, a purchaser will pay only $900 for the Debenture which, again given the $ 100 *contractual* annual interest rate, will produce a yield of 11 percent.

The term "coupon rate" is still widely used and denotes the annual amount of interest the issuer of a debt instrument is required to pay.

(2) Transfer of a registered debt security is by assignment rather than by negotiation.

(3) The Sinking Fund Provisions set forth in the Debenture are to be effected pursuant to the terms of the Indenture. The pertinent Indenture sections are as follows:

> *Notice of Redemption: Partial Redemption.* In case the Company shall desire to exercise such right to redeem all, or, as the case may be, any part of the Debentures in accordance with the right reserved so to do, it shall fix a date for redemption and shall mail by first-class mail a notice of such redemption not less than 30 nor more than 60 days prior to the date fixed for redemption to the holders of Debentures to be redeemed as a whole or in part, at their last addresses as they shall appear upon the registry books, but any defect therein or failure of the addressee to receive such notice shall not affect the validity of the proceedings for the redemption of any of the Debentures. Failure to give such notice to the holder of any Debenture shall not affect the validity of the proceedings for the redemption of any other Debenture. The Trustee, on behalf of the Company, will give all notices required by this Section to be given by the Company.
>
> Each such notice of redemption shall specify the date fixed for redemption and the redemption price at which Debentures are to be redeemed, and shall state that payment of the redemption price of the Debentures to be redeemed, together with accrued interest to the date fixed for redemption, will be made at the principal office of the Trustee or at such office or agency to be maintained by the Company in accordance with the provisions of

§ 4.02 upon presentation and surrender of such Debentures and that on and after said date interest thereon will cease to accrue. If all the outstanding Debentures are called for redemption, the notice of redemption shall so state. If less than all the Debentures are to be redeemed, the notice shall identify the serial numbers of the Debentures to be redeemed. In case any Debenture is to be redeemed in part only, the notice which relates to such Debenture shall state the portion of the principal amount thereof to be redeemed and shall state that on and after the redemption date, upon surrender of such Debenture, the holder thereof will receive the redemption price in respect of the portion of the principal amount thereof called for redemption and a new Debenture or Debentures of authorized denominations in principal amount equal to the unredeemed portion of such Debenture will be issued without charge to the holder.

In the case of redemption of Debentures other than through the operation of the Sinking Fund provided for in Article III, at least one business day prior to the redemption date specified in the notice of redemption given as provided in this Section, the Company covenants and agrees that it will deposit with the Trustee an amount of money sufficient to redeem on the redemption date all the Debentures outstanding on such date so called for redemption at the appropriate redemption price, together with accrued interest to the redemption date.

If less than all the Debentures then outstanding are to be redeemed, the Company shall give the Trustee not less than 60 days notice prior to the redemption date as to the aggregate principal amount of the Debentures to be redeemed, *and thereupon the Trustee shall select, in such manner as it shall deem appropriate and fair in its sole discretion, the numbers of the Debentures to be redeemed in whole or in part and shall thereafter promptly notify the Company thereof.* For purposes of redemption of Debentures, each Debenture of a denomination more than $1,000 shall be deemed to be such number of Debentures of a denomination of $1,000 as is obtained by dividing its denomination by $1,000.

Payment of Debentures Called for Redemption. If the giving of notice of redemption shall have been completed as above provided, the Debentures or portions of Debentures specified in such notice shall become due and payable on the date and at the place stated in such notice at the redemption price, together with interest accrued to the date fixed for redemption and on and after the date fixed for redemption (unless the Company shall default in the payment of such Debentures or portion thereof at the redemption price, together with interest thereon to the date fixed for redemption) interest on the Debentures or portions of the Debentures so called for redemption shall cease to accrue at the close of business on said date. If the Company shall have deposited with the Trustee sufficient cash, as provided in Section 2.02 or Section 3.01 hereof, for the payment of the redemption price, together with interest accrued to the date fixed for redemption of the then outstanding Debentures called for redemption, then on and after such date of redemption interest on the Debentures or portions of Debentures so called for redemption shall cease to accrue, and such Debentures or portions of Debentures shall be deemed not to be outstanding hereunder and shall not be entitled to any benefit under this Indenture except to receive payment of the redemption price, together with accrued interest to the date fixed for redemption. Upon presentation and surrender of such Debentures on or after said date at said place of payment in said notice specified, the Trustee shall make payments of the amounts deposited with it with respect to the redemption of such Debentures so surrendered. All Debentures redeemed and surrendered for cancellation under Articles II and III shall be forthwith cancelled by the Trustee pursuant to Section 1.10. Installments of interest due on or prior to the date fixed for redemption shall continue to be payable to the holders of such Debentures on the relevant record dates according to their terms and the provisions of Section 1.03.

Upon presentation and surrender of any Debenture which is redeemed in part only, the Company shall execute and the Trustee shall authenticate and deliver to the holder thereof, at the expense of the Company, a new Debenture or Debentures of authorized denominations in principal amount equal to the unredeemed portion of the Debenture so presented.

§ 3.04 THE INDENTURE

"The corporate indenture is needed for mechanical and administrative reasons whenever there are multiple public holders of the same issue of debt securities. Historically, use of the indenture arose in the early 19th century in the railroad mortgage context because of the need to name the mortgagee in the mortgage as recorded. Mortgages could not normally be recorded as being granted to 'the holders of the bonds, from time to time.' If the initial holders were named as mortgagees, it might then have been necessary to amend the public recording documents every time a bond changed hands. This was obviously impractical. Designation by the issuer of a trustee to hold the liens in trust for the constant flux of holders was the simple and obvious 19th century solution to this problem. Today, other arrangements might suffice for that purpose, but in the 19th century when the need arose the trust was the only available, widely understood and suitable device. Early trust indentures used an officer of the issuer as trustee, and use of individuals as trustee persisted into the late 19th century. Later, however, use of trust companies became prevalent.

By the 1920s, use of the mortgage in public offerings began to decline, and the unsecured debenture emerged as the predominant medium for public investment in corporate debt securities. This obviated the lien-recording need for a single trustee. However, other mechanical reasons favored retaining the trust device. Primary were the conveniences in predefault services relating to payments and transfer; *i.e.*, the trustee usually performs the functions for bonds that a transfer agent, registrar and dividend paying agent performs for stocks. However, also important among these were the functions of central control of postdefault litigation, pro rata distribution of postdefault payments and adequate representation of all bondholders in litigation. Otherwise, postdefault races to the courthouse could be encouraged, and the more diligent holders might recover a greater portion of their claims than the less fleet."[2]

BROAD v. ROCKWELL INTERNATIONAL CORP.

United States Court of Appeals, Fifth Circuit
642 F.2d 929 (1981)

RANDALL, CIRCUIT JUDGE

. . .

II. CONSTRUING THE INDENTURE

A. The Nature of the Contract

Because the construction of the Indenture is basically a question of contract law, it is perhaps worthwhile to discuss briefly the way in which this type of contract operates, and the reasons why such contracts must be so long and detailed. . . . In part because of the differing treatment of debt and equity securities both by statute and at common law, debt securities are, to a much larger degree than is true of equity securities, creatures of contract law.[3] As a result, the written contracts that govern the rights and obligations of debt securities are often long and complex, for

---

[2] Steven H. Case, *The Trust Indenture Act Needs No Conflict of Interest Revisions*, 35 BUS. LAW. 161, 163–64 (1979) (footnotes omitted).

[3] [10] The American Bar Foundation's Commentaries on Indentures make the following comments on the distinctions between long-term debt financing and equity financing:

> In general, funds needed for financing private corporate enterprises are obtained in exchange for interests of two essentially different kinds: (l) those of the "equity" owners or shareholders, whose securities represent certain rights of ownership, control and profit accompanied by a relatively greater risk of loss, and (2) those of the "lenders," who classically forego control and profit in return for periodic payments (interest and often sinking fund) without regard to profits and for repayment of principal at a fixed date, ahead of the equity owners.
>
> The most obvious and important characteristic of long-term debt financing is that the holder ordinarily has not bargained for and does not expect any substantial gain in the value of the security to compensate for the risk of loss. This is not true of a debt security which is convertible into an equity security, and it is not entirely true of a debt security purchased for much less than its principal amount. With these exceptions, however, the significant fact, which accounts in part for the detailed protective provisions of the typical long-term debt financing instrument, is that the lender (the purchaser of the debt security) can expect only interest at the prescribed rate plus the eventual return of the principal. Except for possible increases in the market value of the debt security because of changes in interest rates, the debt security will seldom be worth more than the lender paid for it, provided he bought it at approximately its face amount. It may, of course, become worth much less. Accordingly, the typical investor in a long-term debt security is primarily interested in every reasonable assurance that the principal and interest will be paid when due.
>
> The second fundamental characteristic of long-term debt financing is that *the rights of the holders of the debt securities are largely a matter of contract*. There is no governing body of statutory or common law that protects the holder of unsecured debt securities against harmful acts by the debtor except in the most extreme situations. Short of bankruptcy, the debt security holder can do nothing to protect himself against actions of the borrower which jeopardize its ability to pay the debt unless he takes a mortgage or other collateral or

those contracts attempt to anticipate and deal with in advance all possible contingencies that might call into question the operation of those rights and obligations. In the case of debentures, those contractual rights are set forth in a document that is separate from the debt instrument itself. That document, whose terms are incorporated by reference on the face of the debt instrument, is commonly called an indenture.[4]

The debt represented by the debenture is typically not secured by specific assets of the issuer,[5] and is frequently subordinated to senior indebtedness of the issuer.

> establishes his rights through contractual provisions set forth in the debt agreement or indenture.
>
> Finally the long-term debt may be held by many holders, all of whom expect to be treated on a parity. Here, again, there is no body of law governing the procedures by which the holders of debt securities may take collective action. These procedures, as well as the mechanics of transfer and exchange of the securities, are matters of contract which are usually set out in the indenture and sometimes in the debt instrument. Thus the situation is quite unlike that involved in the issuance of stock where various substantive rights and procedural matters are in effect incorporated in the certificate of incorporation of the issuer by operation of the applicable corporation laws.

American Bar Foundation, Commentaries on Indentures 1-2 (1971) (emphasis added).

[4] [11] The modern form of debenture indenture was originally adapted from a different form of negotiable security:

> The first debt securities termed "debentures" did not involve a trustee. They were, in effect, promissory notes issued in quantity with no underlying indenture or comparable agreement. Prior to World War I, draftsmen were challenged with the task of creating debentures as to which all holders would be on a parity and protected by adequate covenants and which would nevertheless be negotiable. The solution was to take the corporate mortgage indenture form, delete the conveyancing and other provisions relating to the collateral, and insert covenants designed to protect the debentureholders. These protective covenants were designed to prevent the borrower from placing other creditors in a position senior to the debentureholders, indulging in excessive borrowing or otherwise jeopardizing its ability to meet the obligations on the debentures. Other provisions of an administrative nature remained much the same in a debenture indenture as those in a mortgage indenture. The result is a form of instrument which offers great flexibility for adaptation to a particular transaction.

Id. at 7 (footnote omitted).

[5] [12] This feature distinguishes debentures from corporate bonds:

> There is no inherent or clearly established distinction between "bonds" and "debentures." . . . The terms "bond" and "debenture" came into use in the United States without any definite or consistent legal connotation and to some extent are still inter-mingled. Financial men refer to the "bond market" as including all forms of long-term debt securities. . . . [Under preferred usage], *"debenture" means a long-term debt security which is not secured,* and "bond" (except with respect to governmental or other public corporation securities) means a long-term debt security which is secured by a lien on some or all of the assets of the borrower. Most recent issues conform to this usage.

Id. at 7 n.3 (emphasis added). Debentures are also distinguishable from long-term notes:

> There is no basic or historically established distinction between "debentures" and "notes." There has emerged, however, a clear and useful distinction in modern usage. According to this usage, in the area of long-term debt securities, a security is properly termed a "note" when it is not issued pursuant to an indenture and there is no indenture trustee. However, it may be, and usually is, issued to one or a few purchasers pursuant to a purchase or loan agreement which, in addition to provisions dealing with the terms of purchase, includes many of the contractual rights found in an indenture. In today's nomenclature *the security is properly termed a "debenture" when it is issued pursuant to an indenture and there is an indenture trustee.*

Id. at 8 (emphasis added). These distinctions are, of course, merely generalizations; as such, they do not hold true in all cases. For example, long-term notes may be issued pursuant to an indenture, but without

It is usually the case that the debentures of a given issue are held by a great number of parties, and for this reason it was found desirable, as the modern concept of debentures developed, that the indenture designate a corporate trustee to protect the rights of the many holders of the debentures and to perform certain ministerial tasks connected with the normal operation of the debentures. Thus, although the debts created by the debentures run directly from the issuer to the holders, the contractual rights conferred by the indenture run from the issuer to the trustee for the benefit of the holders of the debentures.[6] In today's usage, then, a security is generally termed a "debenture" when it is a long-term unsecured debt security, issued pursuant to an indenture and with an indenture trustee.

Not all debentures are "straight debt securities." The Debentures at issue in this case are examples of "convertible debentures," which exhibit characteristics of both debt and equity securities:

> A convertible debenture is one which gives the holder the right to exchange his debenture for other securities of the [issuing] Company, usually for shares of common stock and usually without payment of further consideration. The conversion right, although set forth in the debenture and in the indenture, is separate and distinct from the debt evidenced by the debenture. As a separate right it has its own ascertainable value.

American Bar Foundation, Commentaries on Indentures 522-23 (1971) (footnotes omitted) (hereinafter cited as *Commentaries*). The fact that a debenture is convertible into equity securities is an important feature, and therefore the terms under which the debenture may be converted are usually summarized on the face of the debenture itself. All convertible debentures, however, purport only to summarize the salient provisions of the conversion terms on the face of the instrument; as is the case with the other complicated provisions that govern the duties of the issuer and trustee, the terms of redemption, and so forth, many of the details concerning the debenture's convertibility must be set forth instead in the governing indenture.

---

a trustee because they are to be purchased by a comparatively small number of institutional investors.

[6] [13] The function of the trustee is explained by the historical context through which debentures developed:

> Even though the debenture indenture creates no lien, it was found desirable to retain the trustee. In fact, since 1939 a trustee has been required by the Trust Indenture Act for issues subject to registration under the Securities Act of 1933. The fact that the debenture indenture trustee does not hold title to, or have possession of, any property has caused some persons to regard its position as an anomaly and the title "trustee" a misnomer. As a matter of law, however, it is well established that the corpus of a trust may consist of contractual rights and that one who holds contractual rights for the benefit of others may be a trustee. Accordingly, the title "trustee" is appropriate in this situation because, although the debts created by the debentures run directly from the issuer to the holders, the contractual rights conferred by the indenture run from the issuer to the trustee for the benefit of the holders.
>
> Apart from legal semantics, the role performed by the debenture indenture trustee is a practical necessity whenever there are any substantial number of holders of the debt securities. Some of the most useful functions customarily performed by the trustee are not performed in its capacity as trustee, but rather as transfer agent and paying agent. Nevertheless, the protection to debentureholders accorded by the pure trustee functions is of significant value.

Id. at 7-8.

The indenture will specify a rate at which the debentures can be converted into equity securities (usually common stock). This is often expressed in terms of a "conversion price," which may be conceptualized as the price at which a share of stock may be "purchased" by the holder of the debenture in exchange for the surrender of indebtedness under the debenture. For example, if the conversion price for a debenture in the principal amount of $1000 is $50, the holder of the debenture is entitled to convert his $1000 debenture into a total of 20 shares of common stock.

The discussion above only briefly describes the manner in which convertible debentures function. Given this,

> it is not surprising that corporate indentures are lengthy and complex. There is much that must be covered by the contract set forth in the indenture. But it is also true that much of what has to be covered is, or could be, virtually the same for all indentures. These are the provisions that are commonly referred to as "boiler-plate," *e.g.*, provisions regulating the issuance, authentication, transfer and exchange of securities; provisions establishing the procedures for collective action by the security holders; and provisions prescribing the duties of the trustee. These, and certain others, are provisions which have been stated in many different ways in various indentures. Since there is seldom any difference in the intended meaning, such provisions are susceptible of standardized expression. The use of standardized language can result in a better and quicker understanding of those provisions and a substantial saving of time not only for the draftsmen but also for the parties and all others who must comply with or refer to the indenture, including governmental bodies whose approval of authorization or the issuance of the securities is required by law.

Commentaries at 3. Not least among the parties "who must comply with or refer to the indenture" are the members of the investing public and their investment advisors. A large degree of uniformity in the language of debenture indentures is essential to the effective functioning of the financial markets: uniformity of the indentures that govern competing debenture issues is what makes it possible meaningfully to compare one debenture issue with another, focusing only on the business provisions of the issue (such as the interest rate, the maturity date, the redemption and sinking fund provisions and the conversion rate) and the economic conditions of the issuer, without being misled by peculiarities in the underlying instruments.

CONCORD REAL ESTATE CDO 2006-1 v. BANK OF AM. N.A.

Delaware Chancery Court
996 A.2d 324 (2010)

LASTER, VICE CHANCELLOR.

* * *

The Common Law Rule That Governs Absent a Controlling Provision In The Indenture

The Indenture [in this case] does not explicitly address the surrender of Notes for no consideration with an instruction that they be canceled. No provision expressly allows it. No provision expressly prohibits it. Unable to cite a provision directly on point, the parties have joined issue over two boilerplate provisions that speak indirectly to cancellation in general. I therefore first determine the common law rule that will apply to the surrender of the Subject Notes absent a governing contractual provision. I look to the common law because this body of jurisprudence provides a backdrop of standard default rules that supplement negotiated agreements and fill gaps when a contract is incomplete, whether by inadvertence or design. Parties can contract around virtually all common law rules. In a lengthy and sophisticated agreement like the Indenture, the terms of the agreement and not the common law will control many issues. But unless contradicted or altered by the parties' agreement, the common law rules form an implied part of every contract.

NOTES

(1) As explained by the court in the *Broad* case, a trust indenture is often a "long and complex" contract. The following is the cover page heading and the table of contents of a fairly standard trust indenture.

FSC CORPORATION
AND
BANK, Trustee
Indenture
Dated as of August 1, 1980[7]

15 3/4 percent Senior Sinking Fund Debentures
Due 1995

INDEX[8]
to
INDENTURE

FSC CORPORATION

Dated as of August 1, 1980

---

[7] Reprinted by permission of the Trilos Corporation.

[8] This Index is not part of the Indenture and does not have any bearing upon the interpretation of any of its terms or provisions.

	(c) Debentureholders to whom reports shall be transmitted
	(d) Filing of reports
SECTION 7.04	Reports by Company
	(a) Company to file SEC reports with Trustee
	(b) Company to file additional reports with Trustee pursuant to SEC rules and regulations
	(c) Company to transmit reports to Debentureholders pursuant to SEC rules and regulations
ARTICLE VIII	Concerning the Debentureholders
SECTION 8.01	Evidence of Action Taken by Debentureholders
SECTION 8.02	Proof of Execution of Instruments and of Holding of Debentures
SECTION 8.03	Registered Holders of Debentures May Be Treated as Owners
SECTION 8.04	Debentures Owned by Company Deemed Not Outstanding
SECTION 8.05	Right of Revocation of Action Taken
ARTICLE IX	Debentureholders' Meetings
SECTION 9.01	Purpose for Which Debentureholders' Meetings May Be Called
SECTION 9.02	Call of Meetings by Trustee
SECTION 9.03	Company and Debentureholders May Call Meeting
SECTION 9.04	Persons Entitled to Vote at Meeting
SECTION 9.05	Determination of Voting Rights; Conduct and Adjournment of Meeting
SECTION 9.06	Counting Vote and Recording Action of Meeting
ARTICLE X	Supplemental Indentures
SECTION 10.01	Supplemental Indentures Without Consent of Debentureholders
	(a) Successor corporations
	(b) Further covenants, etc., for the protection of Debentureholders
	(c) Curing of ambiguities
	(d) Providing for Debentures in coupon form
SECTION 10.02	Supplemental Indentures With Consent of Debentureholders
SECTION 10.03	Effect of Supplemental Indentures
SECTION 10.04	Supplemental Indenture Shall Conform to Trust Indenture Act of 1939
SECTION 10.05	Notation on Debentures in Respect of Supplemental Indentures
SECTION 10.06	Trustee May Receive Opinion of Counsel
ARTICLE XI	Consolidation, Merger, Sale, Conveyance or Liquidating Distribution
SECTION 11.01	Company May Consolidate, etc., on Certain Terms
SECTION 11.02	Successor Corporation to be Substituted

(2) The Section on Developments in Business Financing of the American Bar Association's Section of Corporation, Banking and Business Law has prepared a form of indenture called the Model Simplified Indenture. Its primary purpose is to provide a "model" as a starting point for the preparation of trust indentures. The form and accompanying explanatory materials are set forth in 38 Bus. Law. 741 (1983).

(3) As its cover sheet and index indicates, the FSC Indenture provides for the issuance of only one type of debt security, its 15 3/4 percent Senior Sinking Fund Debentures Due 1995. The Indenture relates only to that security, and specifically provides, as set forth below, that the aggregate principal amount of those Debentures shall not be more than $7 million. Relevant portions of the FSC Indenture in this regard are as follows:

> WHEREAS, for its lawful purposes, the Company has duly authorized the issuance of its 15 3/4% Senior Sinking Fund Debentures Due 1995 (herein called the "Debentures") in an aggregate principal amount not to exceed $7,000,000; and
>
> WHEREAS, the form of the Debentures is to be substantially in the form annexed hereto as Exhibit "A"; and
>
> WHEREAS, the Company represents that all acts and things necessary to make the Debentures, when executed by the Company and authenticated and delivered by the Trustee as in this Indenture provided, the valid, binding and legal obligations of the Company, and to constitute this instrument a valid indenture and agreement according to its terms, have been done and performed, and the execution and delivery of this Indenture and the issuance hereunder of the Debentures have in all respects been duly authorized, and the Company, in the exercise of each and every legal right and power in it vested, executes this Indenture and proposes to make, execute, issue and deliver the Debentures;
>
> NOW THEREFORE:
>
> In consideration of the premises and of the purchase and acceptance of the Debentures by the holders thereof the Company covenants and agrees with the Trustee, for the equal and proportionate benefit of the respective holders of the Debentures from time to time, as follows:
>
> ARTICLE I
> Designation, Issue, Execution, Registration and Transfers of Debentures
>
> SECTION 1.01. *Designation, Authentication and Delivery.* The Debentures shall be designated as the Company's "15 3/4% Senior Sinking Fund Debentures Due 1995." Debentures for an aggregate principal amount *not exceeding $7,000,000* at any time outstanding, except as provided in Section 1.08, may be executed by the Company and delivered to the Trustee for authentication upon the execution of this Indenture or from time to time thereafter, and the Trustee shall thereupon authenticate and deliver said Debentures to or upon the written order of the Company, signed by its President or any Senior Vice President or Vice President and by its

Secretary or an Assistant Secretary under its corporate seal, without any further action by the Company.

Other types of indentures are not limited to a single debt security, but instead authorize the corporation to issue various types of such securities *in unlimited amounts*. This type of indenture, portions of which are set forth below, provide the corporation and its board of directors with a type of "blank check" authority to issue debt instruments. This general authority is exercised by the board of directors setting the terms for issuance of debt securities from time to time. This procedure is similar to that often employed in the case of preferred stock discussed in Chapter 4, *infra*. Pertinent portions of a form of such indenture are set forth below.

WHEREAS, for its lawful corporate purposes the Issuer has duly authorized the issue from time to time of its unsecured debentures, notes or other evidences of indebtedness to be issued *in one or more series* (the "Securities") *up to such principal amount or amounts as may from time to time be authorized in accordance with the terms of this Indenture*; and to provide, among other things, for the authentication, delivery and administration thereof, the Issuer has duly authorized the execution and delivery of this Indenture; and

WHEREAS, all things necessary to make this Indenture a valid indenture and agreement according to its terms, have been done;

Now, THEREFORE, THIS AGREEMENT WITNESSETH:

That in consideration of the premises and the purchases of the Securities by the holders thereof, the Issuer and the Trustee mutually covenant and agree for the equal and proportionate benefit of the respective holders from time to time of the Securities as follows:

. . . .

ARTICLE TWO
Securities

SECTION 2.1 *Forms Generally.* The Securities of each series shall be in the form (not inconsistent with this Indenture) as shall be established by the Board of Directors or pursuant to a Board Resolution or in one or more indentures supplemental hereto, in each case with such appropriate insertions, omissions, substitutions and other variations as are required or permitted by this Indenture and may have imprinted or otherwise reproduced thereon such legend or legends, not inconsistent with the provisions of this Indenture, as may be required to comply with any law or with any rules or regulations pursuant thereto, or with any rules of any securities exchange or to conform to general usage, consistently herewith, all as may be determined by the officers executing such Securities, as evidenced by their execution of the Securities.

The definitive Securities shall be printed, lithographed or engraved on steel engraved borders or may be produced in any other manner, all as determined by the officers executing such Securities, as evidenced by their execution of such Securities.

SECTION 2.2 *Form of Trustee's Certificate of Authentication.* The Trustee's certificate of authentication on all Securities shall be in substantially the following form:

This is one of the Securities of the series designated therein referred to in the within-mentioned Indenture.

THE CHASE MANHATTAN BANK
as Trustee
By
authorized officer

SECTION 2.3 *Amount Unlimited; Issuable in Series.* The aggregate principal amount of Securities which may be authenticated and delivered under this Indenture *is unlimited.*

The Securities may be issued *in one or more series.* There shall be established by the Board of Directors or in or pursuant to a Board Resolution and set forth in an Officers' Certificate, or established in one or more indentures supplemental hereto, prior to the issuance of Securities of any series,

(1) the title of the Securities of the series (which shall distinguish the Securities of the series from all other Securities);

(2) any limit upon the aggregate principal amount of the Securities of the series that may be authenticated and delivered under this Indenture (except for Securities authenticated and delivered upon registration of transfer of, or in exchange for, or in lieu of, other Securities of the series pursuant to Section 2.8, 2.9, 2.11 or 13.3);

(3) the date or dates on which the principal of the Securities of the series is payable;

(4) the rate or rates, or method by which the rate or rates are determined, at which the Securities of the series shall bear interest, if any, the date or dates from which such interest shall accrue, the interest payment dates on which such interest shall be payable and the record dates for the determination of Holders to whom interest is payable;

(5) the place or places where the principal and any interest on Securities of the series shall be payable;

(6) the price or prices at which, the period or periods within which and the terms and conditions upon which Securities of the series may be redeemed, in whole or in part, at the option of the Issuer, pursuant to any sinking fund or otherwise;

(7) the obligation, if any, of the Issuer to redeem, purchase or repay Securities of the series pursuant to any sinking fund or analogous

provisions or at the option of a Holder thereof and the price or prices at which and the period or periods within which and the terms and conditions upon which Securities of the series shall be redeemed, purchased or repaid, in whole or in part, pursuant to such obligation;

(8) if other than denominations of $1,000 and any multiple thereof, the denominations in which Securities of the series shall be issuable;

(9) if other than the principal amount thereof, the portion of the principal amount of Securities of the series which shall be payable upon declaration of acceleration of the maturity thereof pursuant to Section 5.1 or provable in bankruptcy pursuant to Section 5.2;

(10) any other terms of the series (which terms shall not be inconsistent with the provisions of this Indenture); and

(11) any trustees, authenticating or paying agents, warrant agents, transfer agents or registrars with respect to the Securities of such series.

All Securities of any one series shall be substantially identical except as to denomination and except as may otherwise be provided by the Board of Directors or in or pursuant to such Board Resolution and set forth in such Officers' Certificate, or as may be otherwise provided in any such indenture supplemental hereto.

[A] Express Covenants

RIEVMAN v. BURLINGTON N.R. CO.

United States District Court, Southern District of New York
618 F. Supp. 592 (1985)

Carter, District Judge

This action concerns two series of bonds issued in 1896 by the Northern Pacific Railway Company ("Northern Pacific"). The first, 4 percent Prior Lien Railway and Land Grant Gold Bonds ("Prior Lien Bonds"), were issued pursuant to a mortgage dated November 10, 1896. The Prior Lien Bonds pay 4 percent annual interest and mature on January 1, 1997. They were issued in a face amount of $121.6 million, of which approximately $69.9 million remained outstanding as of April 22, 1985. The second series of bonds, 3 percent General Lien Railway and Land Grant Gold Bonds ("General Lien Bonds"), were issued pursuant to a second mortgage dated November 10, 1896. The General Lien Bonds pay 3 percent interest and mature on January 1, 2047. They were issued in a face amount of $60 million, of which approximately $47.8 million remain outstanding. Neither issue of bonds is callable by the issuer before maturity. Both mortgages were executed in New York and the bonds were issued in New York.[9]

---

[9] [1] The parties agree that New York law applies in this diversity action.

Northern Pacific was merged into the Burlington Northern Railroad Company ("Railroad") in 1970, and Railroad is now obligor of the bonds. Since 1981, Railroad has been a wholly-owned subsidiary of Burlington Northern Inc., a holding company. Bankers Trust Company is the successor trustee of the Prior Lien Bonds, and Citibank, N.A., is the successor trustee of the General Lien Bonds (collectively, "trustees").

The bonds are secured by two types of collateral/first, by railroad property owned by Northern Pacific as of November 10, 1896 ("Railroad Properties"). The Railroad Properties include the lines of railroad and related rights of way, all extensions and branches and any improvements and appurtenances thereto. Railroad Properties also include all equipment (including after-acquired equipment) used on the mortgaged railway lines, as well as locomotives and other rolling stock, and the buildings, stations and shops pertaining to the mortgaged railway lines. Second, the bonds are secured by millions of acres of land in the northwestern United States (the "Resource Properties") originally granted to Northern Pacific's predecessor by Congress to encourage construction of the railroad. Today, the Resource Properties remaining subject to the mortgage liens comprise approximately 1.9 million acres of land in fee simple, and 2.4 million acres of mineral rights.

Plaintiffs are bondholders, who collectively hold $439,000 par value of the bonds. They are supported in this suit by other individuals and institutions holding or representing holders of more than $43 million par value, out of a total of $117.7 million par value, of the bonds outstanding. Plaintiffs bring this suit as a class action on behalf of all bondholders.

All the parties to this litigation agree that the Resource Properties are now worth many times the $117.7 million face value of the bonds they secure; plaintiffs estimate the land's current value at "billions of dollars" (Plaintiffs' brief at 6). So long as the Resource Properties remain subject to the mortgage liens, however, the Railroad cannot benefit from the development or sale of the properties. That is because the mortgages do not provide for the withdrawal of excess collateral, or for the substitution of collateral. Further, in the event of sale of Resource Properties, the mortgages require the Railroad to deposit all the proceeds with the trustees, as collateral. Thus the Railroad would reap no benefit from the sale or development of the properties. Since the bonds are not callable before maturity, the bondholders can effectively block or "hold up" the Railroad from exploiting the Resource Properties until all the bonds mature in 2047.

Precisely because they have this "hold up" value, the bonds (which are traded over the counter on the New York Stock Exchange (NYSE)) have commanded prices far above their value as debt obligations alone. For instance, on April 19, 1985, the Prior Lien Bonds traded at 3 percent above their value as debt obligations, and the General Lien Bonds at 66 percent above such value (Batkin Aff. ¶¶ 7-8). Bondholders speculated that the Railroad would be so eager to release the land from the mortgage liens that it would some day offer to buy back the bonds at a premium/perhaps even above par (Railroad's brief at 24).

The Railroad wishes to have the Resource Properties released from the mortgage liens. It has attempted to accomplish this without buying back the bonds from the holders. Instead, on April 19, 1985, it entered into agreements with the trustees (the "Letter Agreements") whereby the trustees will release the Resource Properties from the mortgage liens on June 22, 1985, provided that certain conditions are met to protect the bondholders. The central condition is the so-called Deposit Plan, under which the Railroad will deposit in irrevocable trusts sufficient United States securities to satisfy fully all future financial obligations of the bonds as they become due. In essence, the government securities would substitute for the Resource Properties as collateral for the bonds and would guarantee timely payment of all bond obligations.

The Railroad has already purchased a portfolio of government securities for $63.4 million, containing bonds with varying maturity dates totaling $184,315 million in principal amount. This is sufficient to meet all outstanding bond obligations as they become due. For instance, the portfolio will yield $4,815,205 in 1986, when the Railroad's obligations under the bonds will not exceed $4,814,752. In 1997, the year in which the Prior Lien Bonds mature, the Railroad's total obligations will be approximately $67.5 million. The portfolio that year will yield $67.56 million in interest and principal amount. The longest-term securities will mature in 2014 and 2015. The yield then will be sufficient, without reinvestment, to pay the principal and all future interest payments due on the General Lien bonds, which mature in 2047.

With government paper securing every dollar of bond interest and principal, the plaintiffs certainly cannot argue that the Deposit Plan would impair their security. On the contrary, the Deposit Plan would give plaintiffs an iron-clad guarantee of timely payment of interest and principal. *See, e.g., Taxpayers and Citizens of Shelby Co. v. Shelby Co.*, 246 Ala. 192, 20 So. 2d 36, 39 (1944) (United States securities are "uniformly regarded as a perfectly safe . . . investment"); Financial Accounting Standards Board, Statement of Financial Accounting Standards No. 76 (1983) (government securities are "essentially risk free as to the amount, timing, and collection of interest and principal"). Nevertheless, plaintiffs oppose the plan, because it would eliminate the hold up value of their bonds. If the Letter Agreements are implemented, the Railroad will not be required to offer plaintiffs large premiums to buy back the bonds in order to free up the Resource Properties for sale and development. The bonds would then be valuable only as debt obligations, and it is anticipated that their value on the market will plummet.

To protect the bondholders against this sudden drop in bond value, the trustees included a tender offer at current market prices as a second condition for the release of the Resource Properties. Pursuant to the Letter Agreements, the Railroad is currently offering to buy back all outstanding bonds at $53.50 per $100 par value for the Prior Lien Bonds and $39 per $100 par value for the General Lien Bonds, a price slightly above their market price on the day before the Letter Agreements were made public. The bondholders thus have the opportunity to sell their bonds back to the Railroad at slightly above current market price. Since the market price is expected to fall precipitously once the Resource Properties are released and the bonds lose their hold up value, prudent bondholders will feel compelled to accept the Railroad's price.

Plaintiffs oppose the agreement between the trustees and the Railroad, even though it includes the tender offer. They hope to block the plan to substitute collateral and force the Railroad to negotiate with them for the release of the

Resource Properties. Presumably, plaintiffs believe they will be able to hold out for prices higher than those now offered by the Railroad in its tender offer.

The case is currently before the court on plaintiffs' motions for class certification and for a preliminary injunction.

. . . .

II. PRELIMINARY INJUNCTION

To obtain a preliminary injunction in this circuit, "a movant must make a "showing of (a) irreparable harm and (b) either (1) likelihood of success on the merits or (2) sufficiently serious questions going to the merits to make them a fair ground for litigation and a balance of hardships tipping decidedly' in its favor." *Rockwell International Systems, Inc. v. Citibank, N.A.*, 719 F.2d 583, 586 (2d Cir. 1983), quoting *Jackson Dairy, Inc. v. H.P. Hood & Sons, Inc.*, 596 F.2d 70, 72 (2d Cir. 1979). The court turns first to the question of irreparable harm.

1. Irreparable harm

Plaintiffs offer three reasons why they would suffer irreparable harm if implementation of the Letter Agreements is not enjoined. First, they argue that what is at stake in this case is plaintiffs' interest in land. Plaintiffs note, quite rightly, that it is a well-settled principle of equity jurisprudence that every tract of land is considered unique, "so that a remedy at law which does not secure to plaintiff the interest in land to which he is equitably entitled, or does not prevent substantial injury thereto, is not adequate." H. McLintock, Handbook of the Principles of Equity § 44 at 105 (1948).

Strictly speaking, however, plaintiffs do not have any direct interest in the land qua land. What they have is a mortgage on the land; "[a] mortgage is merely an interest by way of security for debt, and a mortgagee has no title, but only a lien upon the land." In re Braddock Ave., 251 A.D. 669, 672, 297 N.Y.S. 301, 305 (1st Dept. 1937), aff'd, 278 N.Y. 163, 15 N.E.2d 563 (1938). Even if the Railroad were to default, plaintiffs would not take title to the land; rather, they would be entitled to the proceeds from the sale of the land to the extent of the unsatisfied debt. Consequently, the mere fact that land is involved is not sufficient to render the threatened harm irreparable.

Second, plaintiffs argue that they will suffer irreparable harm if implementation of the Letter Agreements is not enjoined because the amount of money damages would be difficult to ascertain in a subsequent trial. The law is settled in this circuit "that a remedy at law may be considered inadequate when the amount of damages would be difficult to prove[.]" Rockwell International Systems, Inc. v. Citibank, N.A. supra, 719 F.2d at 586. See also Gerard v. Almouli, 746 F.2d 936, 939 (2d Cir. 1984) (affirming the District Court's finding of irreparable harm on the basis that "it would be impossible to produce an accurate money damages figure"); Danielson v. Local 275, Laborers International Union of North America, AFL-CIO, 479 F.2d 1033, 1037 (2d Cir. 1973) ("[i]rreparable injury is suffered where monetary damages are difficult to ascertain or are inadequate"); Foundry Services, Inc. v. Beneflux

Corp., 206 F.2d 214, 216 (2d Cir. 1953) (Hand, L., J., concurring) ("impossibility of ascertaining with any accuracy the extent of the loss . . . has always been included in [the] meaning" of the phrase, irreparable harm).

The Railroad argues that damages would not be difficult to ascertain. According to the Railroad, if the release of property and tender offer buy-back are not enjoined now but are subsequently adjudged to have been illegal, plaintiffs can be made whole by receiving the difference between the tender offer bond price and whatever would have been a fair price, as determined by expert testimony. At maximum, the Railroad argues, it will be obligated to pay the difference between the tender offer price and par value ($100). Since money damages would be available, the Railroad asserts, the harm cannot be considered irreparable, and an injunction should not issue.

The problem with the Railroad's argument is that if the release and tender offer go forward, it will be exceedingly difficult to ascertain after the fact what a "fair price" would have been. The Railroad's reliance on expert testimony is misplaced. This case is unlike most other tender offer or merger and acquisition cases, where experts can be relied on to estimate what the market would have done had a disputed act not been performed. As the Railroad's own investment banker explained: "In a normal merger situation, when I am asked as an investment banker to give a 'fairness' opinion, I can value the assets being acquired by, for example, evaluating the earnings stream produced by those assets and comparing the premium or multiple of those earnings being offered to premiums that have been offered in similar transactions. Thus, objective standards are obtainable and can be applied. In this case, however, the purpose of the offer was to provide liquidity to the bondholders at the current market prices. . . . For the purposes of a 'fairness' opinion . . . , *it is impossible to value objectively the 'hold-up' premium*" (Batkin Aff. ¶ 15) (emphasis added).

If the Letter Agreements are implemented, it will be difficult, if not impossible, to determine what price the bondholders and the Railroad would have finally agreed on in a buy-back to release the properties. The appreciation in value of the Resource Properties may be viewed as a pie to be divided between the bondholders and the Railroad. There is no objective way to determine how big the respective slices would or should be. Nor is it true, as the Railroad urges, that the outside limit of the Railroad's liability would be par. It is possible that the Railroad would ultimately agree to pay more than par in order to obtain early release of the valuable properties (See Railroad's brief at 24).

This is a case where, if an injunction does not issue, it will be "difficult, and sometimes virtually impossible, for a court to "unscramble the eggs."" *Sonesta International Hotels Corp. v. Wellington Associates*, 483 F.2d 247, 250 (2d Cir. 1973) (citations omitted). The opportunity for doing equity is thus considerably better now than it would be later on. *Electronic Specialty Co. v. International Controls Corp.*, 409 F.2d 937, 947 (2d Cir. 1969). The court is satisfied that the money damages would be difficult to assess. Accordingly, the threatened harm is irreparable.

Even if that were not the case, plaintiffs have made a third argument — that the harm would be irreparable because the bondholders are threatened with the imminent delisting of their securities. The bonds are currently listed on the NYSE. But as the tender offer's offering circular warns, the bonds may be delisted by the exchange upon completion of the offer. Rule 802.00 of the NYSE provides that bonds may be delisted if the aggregate market value of principal amount of the outstanding bonds falls below $1 million, or for various other reasons inapplicable here. If a significant number of bonds are tendered pursuant to the tender offer, there may not be enough bonds outstanding to meet Rule 802.00's requirements.

In *Norlin Corp. v. Rooney, Pace Inc.*, 744 F.2d 255 (2d Cir. 1984), the Second Circuit explicitly held that NYSE delisting constitutes irreparable harm. The court affirmed the issuance of a preliminary injunction, noting:

> Listing on the "Big Board" protects the liquidity of shares, and reassures shareholders and potential purchasers that the extensive NYSE listing requirements are being met. See *Sonesta Int'l Hotels Corp. v. Wellington Associates*, 483 F.2d 247, 254 (2d Cir. 1973). Moreover, as we noted in *Van Gemert v. Boeing Co.*, 520 F.2d 1373 (2d Cir. 1975), cert. denied, 423 U.S. 947 [96 S. Ct. 364, 46 L. Ed. 2d 282] (1975), the investing public places great stock in these protections:
>
>> . . . [L]isting on the New York Stock Exchange carries with it implicit guarantees of trustworthiness. The public generally understands that a company must meet certain qualifications of financial stability, prestige, and fair disclosure, in order to be accepted for that listing, which is in turn so helpful to the sale of the company's securities. Similarly it is held out to the investing public that by dealing in securities listed on the New York Stock Exchange the investor will be dealt with fairly and pursuant to law.

Id. at 1381. Cf. *United Funds, Inc. v. Carter Products, Inc.*, [1961-64 Transfer Binder] Fed. Sec. L. Rep. (CCH) ¶ 91,288 (Balt. Cir. Ct. May 16, 1963) (enjoining stock issuance that would lead to loss of NYSE listing, which constituted "valuable corporate asset").

The Railroad's attempts to limit and distinguish Norlin are unpersuasive. The law in this circuit is clear: the threat of NYSE delisting — as candidly set forth in the Railroad's tender offer in the instant case — constitutes a threat of irreparable harm sufficient to support the issuance of a preliminary injunction.

2. Likelihood of success on the merits

As the Railroad concedes in the tender offer's offering circular, "[t]he Mortgages, which were signed in 1896, do not provide by their terms for the modification thereof, or a release of collateral in the manner contemplated by the Deposit Plan, without the consent of the holders of all outstanding Bonds." Plaintiffs argue that in the absence of language providing for the release or substitution of collateral, the trustees and the Railroad may not agree to the substitution of collateral contemplated in the Deposit Plan. The bonds, plaintiffs point out, are a contract between the Railroad and the bondholders. The contract included the provision that a particular collateral — the Resource Properties — would secure the debt, and it did not provide for the substitution or release of that particular collateral. Bondholders entered into the entire contract, plaintiffs assert, purchasing the right to interest and principal payments, as well as the right to insist that the collateral not be substituted without their consent. If the Railroad now wishes to substitute collateral — if it wishes to vary the terms of the contract — it cannot do so without obtaining the consent of the bondholders.

The plaintiffs cite *Hollister v. Stewart*, 111 N.Y. 644, 18 N.E. 782 (1889), in which the New York Court of Appeals voided a plan of reorganization that was contrary to the terms of a railroad mortgage. The court held:

> The plaintiff had a clear right to stand upon his contract, and the trustees had no power or authority to compel him to make a new and different one. We are not concerned with his motives but only with his rights. Without his consent, the company and the trustees, the other parties to the contract could not vary its terms. . . . The proposition is almost too plain for argument. Unless the railroad syndicates or committees are to be put above the Constitution, the trustees cannot set aside and change their contract with plaintiff of their own volition, without his consent.

Id. at 659-60, 19 N.E. 782. See also *St. Louis & San Francisco Railroad Co. v. Guaranty Trust Co. of New York*, 205 N.Y. 609, 99 N.E. 162 (1912).

A case even more closely on point is *Colorado & Southern Railway Co. v. Blair*, 214 N.Y. 497, 108 N.E. 840 (1915), where the court held that trustees under a railroad mortgage did not have the power to sell or otherwise release the property securing the mortgage. As in the case at bar, the railroad wishes to sell some property that was under a mortgage lien. The court held: "We think it plain that a trustee in such a case as this has no power to change or compromise the security pending a default, unless such power was conferred by the instrument creating the trust." *Id.* at 512.

The Railroad, on the other hand, argues that despite the absence of any provision for the substitution of collateral, the trustees and the Railroad may substitute collateral where, as here, the bondholders' security would not be impaired by the substitution. The Railroad argues strenuously that the only legally protected right the bondholders have is to payment of the dollar amounts of principal and interest on the bonds when due. See *Prudence Co. v. Central Hanover Bank & Trust Co.*, 237 A.D. 595, 600, 262 N.Y.S. 311, 317 (1st Dept.), *aff'd*, 261 N.Y. 420, 185 N.E. 687 (1933) (the purpose of the mortgage is "to assure payment of the bonds when due by keeping sufficient funds with the trustee to accomplish that end"). The Railroad notes that the relationship between a corporate bondholder and the corporation is one of creditor and debtor only; the bondholder is not granted any interest in the corporation's assets. *Cass v. Realty Securities Co.*, 148 A.D. 96, 100, 132 N.Y.S. 1074, 1078 (1st Dept. 1911), *aff'd*, 206 N.Y. 649, 99 N.E. 1105 (1912); *Marx v. Merchants' National Properties, Inc.*, 148 Misc. 6, 7, 265 N.Y.S. 163, 165 (Sup. Cit. N.Y. Co. 1933). The Railroad argues that where the bondholders' only right — the right to payment — is not harmed by the substitution of collateral (and a fortiori where, as here, that right is absolutely guaranteed by the substitution), bondholders have no cause of action.

The Railroad asserts that *New York State Railways v. Security Trust Co. of*

Rochester, 135 Misc. 456, 238 N.Y.S. 354 (Sup. Ct. Monroe Co. 1929), *aff'd*, mem., 228 A.D. 750, 238 N.Y.S. 887 (3d Dept. 1930), is dispositive of plaintiffs' claims. In that case, the court allowed the release and abandonment of a portion of the railway system covered by a mortgage agreement, even though the agreement did not provide for such abandonment. The court emphasized that the abandonment and release should be allowed because circumstances had changed — advances in competing modes of transportation had rendered unprofitable the portion of railway in question. "Neither mortgagor nor mortgagee can change the tide of events or alter new conditions arising in the course of time, and both should be prepared to meet new situations and to adjust the properties covered by the mortgage to the changed circumstances." *Id.* at 357. The Railroad argues that changed circumstances justify the release of the Resource Properties in this case, as well. See also *Central Railway Col. of New Jersey v. Central Hanover Bank & Trust Co.*, 29 F. Supp. 826 (S.D.N.Y. 1939) (Woolsey, J.) and *T.J. Moss Tie Co. v. Wabash Railway Co.*, 11 F. Supp. 277 (S.D.N.Y. 1935) (Woolsey, J.), two cases in which this court allowed the abandonment and release of unprofitable railroad property subject to mortgages that did not provide for such abandonment and release.

The Railroad also relies on several cases from outside this jurisdiction, most notably, *Beaumont v. Faubus*, 239 Ark. 801, 394 S.W.2d 478 (1965). In that case, State of Arkansas bonds had been issued with the contractual provision that they were to be serviced by "highway revenues." The state, however, needed such revenues for construction of new highways and bridges. To free the highway revenues, the legislature authorized their release in return for the deposit of United States government securities in an amount sufficient to cover the state's payment obligations under the bonds. The State Supreme Court affirmed the dismissal of a class action complaint attacking the substitution of security, holding:

> The real obligation, from the standpoint of impairment of contractual considerations in the case of bond issues, is the obligation of the issuing authority to pay the bonds, principal and interest, when due. This is the matter that is of vital significance to the bondholders. Bondholders necessarily expect and have a right to be paid, but payment does not always have to be made from a particular fund or source. . . . *It follows, therefore, that any change involving a substitution of security which does not diminish the prospects of, or adversely interfere with, expected payment does not constitute a contractual impairment.* . . . This substitution will leave the bondholders with government securities backed by the faith and credit of the United States, which is the foundation of all money values and without which there would be no financial security. The bondholders' prospects of payment are not diminished.

394 S.W.2d at 482-83 (citations omitted) (emphasis added).

The Railroad also cites *Van Wyck v. Alliger*, 6 Barb. (N.Y.) 507 (1849), an old Appellate Division case which rejected a mortgagee's request for an injunction restraining the commission of waste — specifically, the cutting of timber — on mortgaged premises, on the ground that the mortgagee had failed to show that the injunction was necessary to preserve his security. In response to the mortgagee's argument that the waste should be enjoined even if it would not impair his security, the court stated:

> If this doctrine — that the land is a security for the mortgage debt, and as the whole estate is a security, the court should enjoin any cutting of timber or other waste, without reference to the sufficiency or insufficiency of the security — is to prevail, great wrongs could be perpetrated under the rule. Suppose A has a mortgage of $300 upon timbered land belonging to B worth as many thousand dollars, and B goes on to cut timber and clears the land, without any design or even probability of impairing A's security, still he shall be enjoined if the doctrine of some of these cases is to be sustained. I am not prepared to sanction such a doctrine.

Id. at 513. Apparently, this remains the rule today. *See, e.g., Band Realty Co. v. North Brewster, Inc.*, 59 A.D.2d 770, 771, 398 N.Y.S.2d 724, 725 (2d Dept. 1977) ("foundation of an action for waste by a mortgagee is the impairment of the security of the mortgage with knowledge of the lien"). The Railroad argues that the rule that applies to enjoining waste should apply, by analogy, to enjoining substitution of collateral.

The Railroad also argues that the cases bondholders cite for the proposition that a mortgagor may not substitute collateral without the mortgagees' consent are inapposite, because they deal with substitutions of collateral that would have impaired the mortgagees' security. *Hollister v. Stewart, supra*, for example, involved a diversion to new securities of the collateral pledged by the mortgagor to secure payment of the plaintiffs' bonds. And in *Colorado and Southern Railway v. Blair, supra*, the mortgagor sought a release of property that it had purchased for over $1 million in order to sell it for only $150,000.

On balance, plaintiffs have the better argument. First of all, many of Railroad's key cases may be distinguished from the case at bar. For instance, the trilogy of *New York State Railways v. Security Trust Co. of Rochester, supra; Central Railway Co. of New Jersey v. Central Hanover Bank & Trust Co., supra*; and *T.J. Moss Tie Co. v. Wabash Railway Co., supra*, differs from the instant case in crucial respects. First and foremost, none of those cases permit what the Railroad and trustees propose to do in the instant case. None holds that when circumstances change, the mortgagor and the trustees may, on their own, substitute collateral. Rather, the cases hold that when circumstances change, the mortgagor may petition a court of equity to direct the trustees to take actions not particularly provided for in the trust instruments. The cases contemplate prior court approval, after a hearing at which all interested bondholders can be heard — not the sort of independent agreement between Railroad and trustees involved in the instant litigation. *See, e.g., T.J. Moss Tie Co. v. Wabash Railway Co., supra*, 11 F. Supp. at 285.[10]

---

[10] [2] The Railroad suggests that the court consider the merits of the proposed release and tender offer now, and exercise its equity power to instruct the parties to go forward (Railroad's brief at 67). Though the court has the power to do this, it does not believe it is able to make a final determination on the fairness of the proposed transaction now, with the speed called for on a motion for a preliminary injunction.

Further, all three of those cases involve the release and abandonment of unprofitable property, not the release for sale or development of highly valuable property. In the latter case, it may be legitimate to require the Railroad to negotiate with bondholders for the release, as a way of splitting the windfall from the appreciation of the Resource Properties between the Railroad and the bondholders. In the former, it seems unfair for a court of equity to require a railroad to bargain for the privilege of cutting its losses.

Beaumont v. Faubus, supra, is also not on point. In that case, the defendant was the governor of Arkansas and the issue was not whether the substitution of collateral constituted *breach* of contract (as it is in the instant case), but rather whether the substitution of collateral constituted a constitutional *impairment* of collateral by the sovereign. The court stated explicitly that an action that was not an impairment could nevertheless be a breach. *Id.* 394 S.W.2d at 482 ("[e]very unilateral change in a contract may amount to a technical breach of that contract, but not every breach is an impairment of the contractual obligation").

In addition, at least one of the key cases relied on by plaintiffs cannot be effectively distinguished by the Railroad, and appears to govern this case. The Railroad argues that *Colorado & Southern Railway v. Blair, supra*, is inapposite because the proposed transaction would have impaired the mortgagees' security — the mortgagor sought to sell for only $150,000 collateral it had purchased for over $1 million. But the inference that the proposed substitution would have been an impairment is without basis. In *Colorado & Southern Railway*, the mortgagor proposed to deposit the $150,000 proceeds as substitute collateral. There is no evidence that the mortgagor was planning to sell the land for less than its then-market value; on the contrary, it is reasonable to assume that the mortgagor would not have sold the land for $150,000 if it could have gotten a better price. If the land was worth only $150,000 at the time of the proposed sale — no matter what it was worth when the railroad first bought it — then a deposit of $150,000 as cash collateral would not have compromised the security, but only changed it. There would have been a substitution of cash for land, much like the substitution proposed in the instant case's Deposit Plan, but no impairment of security.

More importantly, the *Colorado & Southern Railway* court assumed that the release would have been in the interest of the bondholders, and nevertheless reached its decision that the trustees could not release the mortgaged property without the bondholders' consent. 214 N.Y. at 511, 108 N.E. 840. The New York Court of Appeals seemed to be laying down a per se rule: because of the "vast sums invested in railroad bonds" and the need to insure investor confidence, railroad mortgage trustees may not "sell, change, or in any manner compromise the security except as authorized in express terms or by necessary implication" — even where the sale or change would not harm the bondholders' interests. *Id.* Note that the court forbids the trustees to "sell, change, or . . . compromise" the security. The ruling applies not only to cases where security would be "compromised" (*i.e.*, impaired), but also to cases where the security would merely be "sold" or "changed."

Plaintiffs have made out a good case. Though not absolutely certain that plaintiffs would prevail on the merits at trial, the court is persuaded that plaintiffs have made a sufficient showing of the likelihood of success on the merits to warrant preliminary relief.

3. Serious questions going to the merits and a balance of hardships tipping decidedly in movants' favor

However, even if the court's analysis of the law is flawed as to plaintiffs' likelihood of success on the merits, it is clear that this is a difficult, complex case, fitting the alternative standard in this circuit for preliminary relief if on balance the movant will be harder hit if the motion is denied. Able counsel for all the parties have advanced interesting and well-supported arguments. It is beyond dispute that serious questions on the merits have been raised that need to be litigated.

The Railroad argues that even if there remain serious questions on the merits, the balance of hardships does not tip decidedly in movants' favor. It asserts that an injunction would cause greater hardships for the Railroad in three ways. First, the exploration and development of the Resource Properties would be delayed. Second, the Railroad would be exposed to market risk, because it would be left holding a portfolio of government securities whose market value fluctuates inversely with general interest rates in the economy. Third, an injunction would cast a "speculative cloud" on one of the Railroad's securities, and would "inevitably raise[ ] questions in the market concerning [the Railroad's] other securities" (Railroad's brief at 83). On the other hand, the Railroad asserts, plaintiffs would not suffer a hardship if the Letter Agreements are implemented. Plaintiffs' only legal right — the right to payment of interest and principal — would be guaranteed, and plaintiffs could cash in their bonds at the current market price if they so desired. The Railroad urges: "[E]quity will withhold as oppressive an injunction when the injury is not serious or substantial and the injunction would subject the other party to great inconvenience and loss." *Michelsen v. Leskowicz*, 55 N.Y.S.2d 831, 836 (Sup. Ct. Suffolk Co. 1945), *aff'd*, 270 A.D. 1042, 63 N.Y.S.2d 191 (2d Dept. 1946).

The Railroad cites *Abell v. Safe Deposit & Trust Co. of Baltimore*, 192 Md. 438, 64 A.2d 722 (1949), as a similar release-of-mortgaged-property case, in which the court refused to nullify an unauthorized release of collateral because to do so would have harmed the mortgagor greatly, but would not have benefited the mortgagee in any meaningful way. The Maryland Supreme Court found that maintenance of the mortgage lien would "harass or injure the Company and [was] not necessary to protect bondholders against any actual threatened impairment of security." 64 A.2d at 727.

Abell is inapposite. There the court was concerned with post hoc relief, not with a preliminary injunction. Significantly, the court held that "the release of the mortgage by the Trustee to the Company was a violation of the contract between the Company and the bondholders, and a breach of duty by the Trustee." *Id.* at 726. Though the court refused to nullify the release after the fact, it is not clear whether it would have preliminarily enjoined it to prevent it from occurring in the first place. Perhaps more importantly, in *Abell*, the plaintiffs apparently were not interested in negotiating for a hold up premium, but rather in blocking the development of the encumbered land. *Id.* Thus they were not losing any hold up premium, but rather just the technical right to prevent development. The plaintiffs in this case are interested in negotiating for release of the properties, and they would lose their ability to do so if the Letter Agreements are implemented. Plaintiffs' position is clear: "We are not here to kill any possibilities of there being a development of these resources. We are not a dog in the manger. That's not the point. We are just saying, "When you have a deal, if you want to change it, come to us, let's talk about it, let's negotiate it. You've got to live by your deal. If you want to vary it, then do it, but don't do it unilaterally. You don't have the legal right to do it. The trustees don't have the right as fiduciaries to permit it. You can't do it'" (Hearing transcript at 23).

The Railroad's recitation of the harms it would suffer if implementation of the Letter Agreements is enjoined is unconvincing. The Railroad has waited ninety years to develop the Resource Properties; surely it can wait but a few more weeks. Indeed, the Railroad's own vice-president and treasurer admitted that he does not "believe anything terrible" would result from delay of the proposed transaction (Boyle dep. at 51). The potential harm from market fluctuation is de minimis, and the fear of a "speculative cloud" over all the Railroad's security is groundless. Further, it is not true that withholding an injunction would not harm any of their protected legal rights; plaintiffs appear[11] to have a legal right to insist that the collateral will not be substituted without their consent. Realistically, this means that the bondholders have a right to bargain for the release of the property; if the property is released now, that right will be irretrievably lost. I find the balance of hardships clearly tips in movants' favor.

Accordingly, plaintiffs' motion for a preliminary injunction is granted. Defendants Railroad and trustees are hereby enjoined from: (a) implementing the Letter Agreements dated April 19, 1985; (b) releasing any or all of the Resource Properties; and (c) proceeding with the tender offer commenced by Railroad to purchase any and all outstanding bonds.

IT IS SO ORDERED.

NOTES

(1) As the *Rievman* court stated, the United States Congress had granted to the railroad millions of acres of land and mineral rights "to encourage [its] construction," and thus created an early example of what has come to be referred to as "corporate welfare."

(2) Very long term corporate debt instruments, such as those in *Rievman* have not gone completely out of style. In 2010, Norfolk Southern Corp. issued $250 million of 100 year debentures, and Goldman Sachs Group Inc issued $250 million of 50 year debentures. Unlike the *Rievman* bonds, however, these debt instruments were not secured and were redeemable.

---

[11] [3] The court is not now willing to hold with finality that plaintiffs have this right, but only that plaintiffs have shown a likelihood of establishing this right at a trial on the merits/that they appear to have this right.

AFFILIATED COMPUTER SERVICES. v. WILMINGTON TRUST CO.

United States District Court, Northern District of Texas
2008 U.S. Dist. LEXIS 10190 (Feb. 12, 2008)

Sidney A. Fitzwater, Chief Judge.

This lawsuit requires the court to interpret a provision of an indenture agreement that obligates the issuer of notes to timely file certain reports with the indenture trustee. The court must decide whether the provision requires the issuer to timely file the reports with the Securities and Exchange Commission ("SEC") or merely obligates the issuer to timely file with the indenture trustee the reports that it files with the SEC, even if the SEC filings are themselves untimely. For the reasons that follow, the court agrees with the plaintiff issuer's interpretation: the provision merely requires the issuer to timely file with the indenture trustee the reports that the issuer has filed with the SEC.

I

Plaintiff-counterdefendant Affiliated Computer Services, Inc. ("ACS") sues defendant-counterplaintiff Wilmington Trust Company ("Wilmington") in Wilmington's capacity as indenture trustee ("Trustee") of two series of senior notes issued by ACS. ACS asks the court to declare that ACS is not in default under an indenture agreement ("Indenture") entered into between ACS and the Bank of New York Trust Company ("Bank of New York"). Wilmington is Bank of New York's successor as Trustee. Wilmington counterclaims for a declaratory judgment that ACS breached the Indenture by failing to timely file a Form 10-K with the SEC and by failing to furnish a Form 10-K to Wilmington as Trustee, and that ACS breached its covenant of good faith and fair dealing. Wilmington also counterclaims alleging that ACS violated § 314(a) of the Trust Indenture Act of 1939 ("TIA").

The parties essentially agree on the relevant facts. In 2005 ACS conducted a public offering of two series of senior notes ("the Notes") under the Indenture: (1) $250 million in 4.70% notes, due 2010 (the "4.70% notes"), and (2) $250 million in 5.20% notes, due 2015 (the "5.20% notes"). The Notes added two supplement agreements to the Indenture.

ACS was later investigated for backdating stock options. In response to an inquiry from the SEC and a subpoena from the Department of Justice, ACS announced in May 2006 through an SEC Form 8-K that it was initiating an internal investigation of its stock option practices. In September 2006 ACS announced through an SEC Form 12b-25 that, due to the ongoing internal investigation, it would not be timely filing its Form 10-K with the SEC for the fiscal year ending June 30, 2006. The Form 10-K was due the day before ACS made this announcement.

In response, Cede Company ("Cede"), the registered holder of record of the 5.20% notes, notified ACS and Bank of New York, the Trustee, that ACS was in default under the Indenture due to its failure to timely file the Form 10-K with the

SEC. The notice of default cited § 4.03 of the Indenture as the basis for ACS's affirmative contractual duty to make timely filings with the SEC according to §§ 13 and 15(d) of the Securities Exchange Act of 1934 ("Exchange Act"). Section 4.03(a) of the Indenture provides:

> The Company shall file with the Trustee, within 15 days after it files the same with the SEC, copies of the annual reports and the information, documents and other reports (or copies of those portions of any of the foregoing as the SEC may by rules and regulations prescribe) that the Company is required to file with the SEC pursuant to Section 13 or 15(d) of the Exchange Act. The Company shall also comply with the provisions of the TIA 314(a).

D. App. 33. The notice of default also cited § 6.01 of the Indenture, which makes the failure to comply with certain Indenture covenants or agreements an "Event of Default." *Id.* at 36 (Indenture § 6.01(3)). Section 6.01 also provides, however:

> A Default under clause (3) of this Section 6.01 is not an Event of Default until the Trustee notifies the Company, or the Holders of at least 25% in principal amount of the then outstanding Securities of the series affected by that Default, or, if outstanding Securities of other series are affected by that Default, then at least 25% in principal amount of the then outstanding Securities so affected, notify the Company and the Trustee, of the Default, and the Company fails to cure the Default within the period of days specified in the applicable indenture supplement after receipt of the notice. The notice must specify the Default, demand that it be remedied and state that the notice is a "Notice of Default."

Id. at 37–38. The parties agree that although the Indenture contemplates a cure period to be spelled out in the indenture supplements, the two indenture supplements are silent on a cure period for this type of breach. Once the cure period elapses, and the breach of the Indenture under § 6.03(3) ripens into an "Event of Default," the Indenture permits the Trustee or the holders of notes who have a right to give notice of default under § 6.01 to accelerate the Notes upon proper notice. Indenture § 6.02. Cede's notice satisfied the Indenture's notice of default provision.

ACS, in turn, filed suit against Bank of New York as Indenture Trustee seeking a declaratory judgment that ACS is not in default under the Indenture. Bank of New York, in a notice similar to Cede's, also notified ACS that it was in default on the 5.20% notes. Then Cede, and later Bank of New York, invoked § 6.02 of the Indenture and demanded from ACS acceleration of the 5.20% notes.

Thereafter, the holders of 25% of the 4.70% notes sent ACS and Bank of New York notices of default alleging the same ground of default as had been asserted regarding the 5.20% notes. These notices complied with the Indenture's requirements for notices of default. Cede followed by delivering to ACS letters demanding acceleration of the 4.70% notes in conjunction with the earlier notices of default.

After completing a lengthy internal investigation, in January 2007 ACS finally filed its Form 10-K with the SEC for the fiscal year ending June 30, 2006. ACS also filed its belated Form 10-Q with the SEC for the first quarter of the following fiscal year ending September 30, 2006. On January 25, 2007 ACS delivered both SEC filings to the Trustee.

Wilmington moves for summary judgment dismissing ASC's declaratory judgment action and establishing its right to recover on its counterclaims. ACS moves for summary judgment on its request for declaratory relief and for dismissal of Wilmington's counterclaims.[12]

II

The Indenture's choice-of-law provision specifies that New York law controls this contract dispute. . . .

III

A

Section 4.03(a) of the Indenture unambiguously requires ACS to file with the Trustee copies of its SEC reports within 15 days of filing them with the SEC. The question is whether § 4.03(a) itself imposed on ACS the obligation to file such reports with the SEC.

The court finds persuasive the analysis of *Cyberonics, Inc. v. Wells Fargo Bank Nat'l Ass'n*, 2007 WL 1729977[, 2007 U.S. Dist. LEXIS 42779] (S.D. Tex. June 13, 2007). *Cyberonics* involved a declaratory judgment action focusing on an almost-identical indenture provision as is contained in § 4.03(a) of the Indenture. The provision read:

> Reports. The Company shall deliver to the Trustee within 15 days after it files them with the SEC copies of the annual reports and of the information, documents and other reports (or copies of such portions of any foregoing as the SEC may by rules and regulations prescribe) which the Company is required to file with the SEC pursuant to Section 13 or 15(d) of the Exchange Act. . . . The Company shall also comply with the other provisions of Section 314(a) of the TIA.

Id. at 1.[13] Just as Wilmington argues that § 4.03 of the Indenture creates an independent covenant to make timely filings with the SEC, the indenture trustee in *Cyberonics* argued that the "Reports" covenant affirmatively obligated the issuing company, Cyberonics, Inc. ("Cyberonics"), to file with the SEC the reports required by §§ 13 and 15(d) of the Exchange Act. *Id.* at 4. Because Cyberonics filed its Form 10-K report with the SEC late, the indenture trustee maintained that Cyberonics

---

[12] [1] In its summary judgment response, Wilmington moves to strike the declarations of William Jacobs. In its reply, ACS moves to strike the declarations of Robert Lamb. Because in deciding these motions the court has not relied on the testimony in these declarations, the court denies the motions to strike as moot.

[13] [2] The only differences between the "Reports" provision in Cyberonics and § 4.03(a) of the Indenture are the use of "deliver to" instead of "file with," "them" instead of "the same," and "which" instead of "that."

was in default under the "Reports" covenant. *Id.* at 3–4. The court disagreed, holding that the "Reports" covenant unambiguously required only that Cyberonics deliver copies of the annual reports and other documents to the indenture trustee within 15 days after filing them with the SEC. *Id.* at 4. Therefore, unless Cyberonics filed documents with the SEC, it was not obligated to deliver any SEC-related documents to the indenture trustee. Although the provision referred to "reports and of the information . . . which the Company is required to file with the SEC pursuant to Section 13 or 15(d) of the Exchange Act," the court noted that the phrase "which the Company is required" merely identified the types of reports that Cyberonics was required to deliver to the indenture trustee, and did not independently obligate Cyberonics to make any SEC filings. *Id.* The court concluded that had the parties intended to impose a filing, rather than a delivery, obligation, they could easily have done so. *Id.*

The court finds further support for the reasoning of *Cyberonics* from the Indenture's treatment of covenants generally. Section 4.03 is found in Article IV of the Indenture, which focuses on the covenants of ACS, the issuing company. Article IV clearly designates its other covenants by beginning an independent clause with language such as, "[t]he Company shall" (used nine times), "[t]he Company will" (used five times), and "[t]he Company covenants" (used two times). Consistent with this approach, § 4.03(a) begins, "[t]he Company shall file with the Trustee[.]" Considering Article IV's other covenant language, there is no reasonable basis to conclude that the parties intended § 4.03's modifying phrase — "that the Company is required to file with the SEC" — to affirmatively obligate ACS to timely file with the SEC those reports and documents that it is already statutorily obligated to file under § 13 or § 15(d) of the Exchange Act. If the parties had intended that the Indenture obligates ACS to timely file reports with the SEC, it would have done so with the same clear language employed by the balance of Article IV's covenants.

Instead, properly interpreted, § 4.03(a) simply obligates ACS to file with the Trustee copies of the reports that ACS in fact files with the SEC, and to do so within 15 days of filing.

E

Wilmington maintains that ACS's construction of the Indenture cannot be correct, because ACS would then be able to escape its duty to provide financial information to the Trustee by not filing anything with the SEC at all. ACS is statutorily obligated, however, to file continuing reports with the SEC under the Exchange Act. Although ACS's failure to file with the SEC may not subject it to penalties under the Indenture, a late filing exposes ACS to other potential sanctions that are surely adequate to prevent ACS from attempting to take advantage of the note holders. Accordingly, the court's interpretation of § 4.03(a) does little to encourage ACS or other indenture obligors to attempt to skirt their statutory and contractual filing obligations.

F

Wilmington insists that the court follow *Bank of New York v. Bearingpoint, Inc.*, 824 N.Y.S.2d 752 (N.Y. Sup. Ct. 2006) (unpublished table decision). In *Bank of New York*, a New York County trial court interpreted an Indenture provision substantially similar to § 4.03 as requiring the indenture obligor to timely file periodic reports with the SEC. *Bank of N.Y.*, 2006 WL 2670143, at 7. But *Bank of New York* is an unpublished decision of a trial court that is not binding on this court.

> In order to determine state law, federal courts look to final decisions of the highest court of the state. When there is no ruling by the state's highest court, it is the duty of the federal court to determine as best it can, what the highest court of the state would decide.

Transcon. Gas Pipeline Corp. v. Transp. Ins. Co., 953 F.2d 985, 988 (5th Cir.1992) (citing *Comm'r of Internal Revenue v. Estate of Bosch*, 387 U.S. 456, 464–65, 87 S. Ct. 1776, 18 L.Ed.2d 886 (1967)); *see also O'Neill v. City of Auburn*, 23 F.3d 685, 689–90 (2d Cir.1994) ("Our task is to predict how the state's highest court would rule on this issue"). The court finds *Bank of New York* unpersuasive. First, the court held that the indenture provision equivalent to § 4.03(a) incorporated the Exchange Act, thus making § 13 of the Exchange Act a part of the indenture contract. *Bank of N.Y.*, 2006 WL 2670143, at 3. The court also held that § 314(a)(1) of the TIA and the indenture provision largely restating § 314(a)(1) obligated the indenture issuer to timely file with the SEC. *Id.* For the reasons set forth above, the court respectfully disagrees with both of these conclusions.

Under § 4.03(a) of the Indenture, ACS was not obligated to file timely reports with the SEC according to §§ 13 and 15(d) of the Exchange Act. Because ACS filed its belated Forms 10-K and 10-Q with Wilmington within 15 days after filing them with the SEC, ACS is entitled to judgment declaring that it is not in breach of § 4.03(a) of the Indenture.[14] The court therefore grants ACS's May 7, 2007 summary judgment motion, denies Wilmington's March 27, 2007 motion, and today files a judgment in ACS's favor.

RACEPOINT PARTNERS, LLC v. JPMORGAN CHASE BANK, N.A.

New York Court of Appeals
928 N.E.2d 396 (2010)

Pigott, J.

On February 7, 2001, the energy company Enron executed an indenture agreement with Chase Manhattan Bank (Chase), naming Chase as the indenture trustee for the holders of certain Enron notes. The agreement contained, in section 4.02, a standard provision setting forth a covenant by Enron

---

[14] [5] Because ACS is not in default under § 4.03(a) of the Indenture, the court need not address the parties' arguments as to the cure period and the acceleration of the Notes.

"[to] file with the Trustee [i.e. Chase], within 15 days after it files the same with the SEC [Securities and Exchange Commission], copies of its annual reports and of the information, documents and other reports . . . which the Company [i.e. Enron] is required to file with the SEC pursuant to Section 13 or 15(d) of the [Securities] Exchange Act. Delivery of such reports, information and documents to the Trustee is for informational purposes only and the Trustee's receipt of such shall not constitute constructive notice of any information contained therein or determinable from information contained therein, including the Issuer's compliance with any of its covenants hereunder (as to which the Trustee is entitled to rely exclusively on Officers' Certificates). The Issuer also shall comply with any other provisions of Trust Indenture Act Section 314(a)."

The agreement also set forth various circumstances or events that would constitute default by either party, including failure by Enron to comply with this provision, if not corrected within 60 days of notification by Chase.

In December 2001, in the wake of the major accounting fraud scandal with which it has become synonymous, Enron filed for bankruptcy. Thereafter, plaintiffs Racepoint Partners, LLC, and Willow Capital — II, L.L.C., bought approximately $1 billion of the notes from their holders. Plaintiffs, which, as secondary holders of the notes, are vested with the claims and demands of the sellers, then brought this common-law action against Chase alleging, among other things, breach of contract. Plaintiffs claim, first, that Enron defaulted under the indenture agreement and, second, that Chase had actual knowledge of this default and that its failure to notify Enron and the noteholders of the default constituted breach of the agreement.[15] The issue in this appeal is the allegation of contractual default by Enron in filing reports that were false.

Plaintiffs point to the fact that Enron agreed in section 4.02 to file with Chase copies of all reports that it was "required to file with the SEC pursuant to Section 13 or 15(d) of the [Securities] Exchange Act." Section 13 of the Act requires publicly traded companies to keep records accurately reflecting their transactions and assets, and to file annual and quarterly reports with the Securities and Exchange Commission (see 15 USC § 78m). Plaintiffs argue that because the financial reports filed by Enron with Chase were inaccurate and did not comply with federal securities law, they were not the reports Enron was "required to file with the SEC." Plaintiffs posit that, by filing these same fraudulent reports with Chase, Enron failed to satisfy its section 4.02 covenant, and thus defaulted.

Chase moved to dismiss the complaint under CPLR 3211. Supreme Court denied Chase's motion. The Appellate Division reversed, granting the motion. . . . We granted leave to appeal . . . and now affirm.

Section 4.02 of the indenture agreement is a mandated provision based on the requirements of section 314(a)(1) of the Trust Indenture Act of 1939:

[15] [*] On a similar theory, plaintiffs also allege that Chase breached its fiduciary duty to the noteholders. Plaintiffs concede that the dismissal of their breach of contract cause of action is fatal to the breach of fiduciary duty cause of action.

> "Each person who, as set forth in the registration statement or application, is or is to be an obligor upon the indenture securities covered thereby shall . . .
>
> > "file with the indenture trustee copies of the annual reports and of the information, documents, and other reports (or copies of such portions of any of the foregoing as the [Securities and Exchange] Commission may by rules and regulations prescribe) which such obligor is required to file with the Commission pursuant to section 13 or section 15(d) of the Securities Exchange Act of 1934 [15 USC § 78m or § 78 *o* (d)]; or, if the obligor is not required to file information, documents, or reports pursuant to either of such sections, then to file with the indenture trustee and the [Securities and Exchange] Commission, in accordance with rules and regulations prescribed by the Commission, such of the supplementary and periodic information, documents, and reports which may be required pursuant to section 13 of the Securities Exchange Act of 1934 [15 USC § 78m], in respect of a security listed and registered on a national securities exchange as may be prescribed in such rules and regulations" (codified at 15 USC § 77nnn [a][1]).

Plaintiffs concede that the parties' intent in section 4.02 may be equated with congressional intent with respect to section 314(a) of the Trust Indenture Act of 1939. In drafting the Trust Indenture Act, Congress intended simply to ensure that an indenture trustee was provided with up-to-date reports on a company's financial status, by requiring the company to send the trustee a copy of filed financial reports. In the 1930s, when section 314(a) was drafted, computer-based technologies, whereby copies of SEC reports can now be obtained, did not exist.

The legislative history of section 314(a) suggests that Congress intended to create a delivery requirement and no more. The 1939 House Report highlighted the legislators' concern that trustees and bondholders at the time did not receive periodic reports from companies issuing bonds.

> "In a substantial portion of the indentures . . . the issuer was under no obligation to file an annual report with the indenture trustee. None of the indentures . . . required the transmission to the bondholders of periodic reports, such as stockholders customarily receive. None of them established machinery for the transmission of such reports. . . ." (HR Rep. 1016, 76th Cong., 1st Sess., at 35 [1939].)

It is apparent that section 314(a) was designed to mandate such a mechanism of delivery of reports to indenture trustees. The same House Report, observing that in many cases a company "will already be required to file periodic reports with the [Securities and Exchange] Commission under section 13 or section 15(d)," stated that the bill under consideration "merely requires that copies of such reports . . . be filed with the indenture trustee" (HR Rep. 1016, 76th Cong., 1st Sess., at 35).

As federal courts have observed, when considering indenture agreement provisions very similar to the one at issue here,

"[T]he provision merely requires the company to transmit to the trustee copies of whatever reports it actually files with the SEC . . .

"[A]ny duty actually to file the reports is imposed 'pursuant to Section 13 or 15(d) of the Exchange Act' and not pursuant to the indenture itself. The provision does not incorporate the Exchange Act, it merely refers to it in order to establish which reports must be forwarded.

"[It] impose[s] nothing more than the ministerial duty to forward copies of certain reports, identified by reference to the Exchange Act, within fifteen days of actually filing the reports with the SEC" (*UnitedHealth Group Inc. v. Wilmington Trust Co.*, 548 F.3d 1124, 1128–1130 [8th Cir. 2008]; *see also e.g. Affiliated Computer Servs., Inc. v. Wilmington Trust Co.*, 565 F.3d 924, 930–931 [5th Cir. 2009] . . . .

It is clear therefore that indenture agreements containing the required delivery provisions pursuant to section 314(a) refer to the Securities Exchange Act only to identify the types of report that should be forwarded to indenture trustees. They do not create contractual duties on the part of the trustee to assure that the information contained in any report filed is true and accurate. That is simply not the mission or purpose of the trustee or the contract under which it undertakes its duties.

Of course, companies have a duty to file accurate reports with the SEC. That obligation, however, derives from the Securities Exchange Act, not from indenture agreements.

Our holding that section 4.02 of the indenture agreement simply embodies a delivery requirement, and does not imply a duty on the part of the trustee to assure the filing of accurate reports or risk default, is consistent with the limited, "ministerial" functions of indenture trustees (AG Capital Funding Partners, L.P. v. State St. Bank & Trust Co., 11 N.Y.3d 146, 157, 866 N.Y.S.2d 578, 896 N.E.2d 61 [2008]), and with the plain language of section 4.02, which states that "[d]elivery of such reports, information and documents [filed with the SEC] to the Trustee is for informational purposes only." Plaintiffs' proposed interpretation, on the other hand, would require indenture trustees to review the substance of SEC filings, so as to reduce the risk of liability, greatly expanding indenture trustees' recognized administrative duties far beyond anything found in the contract.

NOTE

What was Enron?

In 1985, Enron was born of the merger of Houston Natural Gas with Internorth, creating the first nationwide natural gas pipeline network . . . . An extremely ambitious company, Enron pushed the envelope and shifted from the regulated transportation of natural gas to the unregulated energy trading markets, under the impression that there was more money in buying and selling financial contracts linked to the value of energy assets than in actual ownership of physical assets. . .At its zenith, Enron was named the "most innovative" company in the United States by Fortune

> magazine every year between 1996 and 2001. In mid-August 2000, Fortune magazine named Enron as one of the top ten stocks that would last the decade because Enron had so successfully transformed itself from a stodgy gas utility into the largest online broker of energy . . . . Over time, Enron developed a veritable buffet of financial strategies to skirt and sometimes defy the boundaries of the law, all of which created the façade of profitability . . . . Several issues contributed to Enron's downfall, although two in particular sealed its fate: 1) Enron lived and died by the "deal" – and many of its deals went horribly wrong, losing millions of dollars; and 2) when Enron's sham accounting schemes came to light, the company collapsed, virtually overnight, as people sought to distance themselves from the company and its stock . . . .

NANCY B. RAPOPORT & BALA G. DHARAN, ENRON: CORPORATE FIASCOS AND THEIR IMPLICATIONS 11-12 (2004) (footnotes omitted). See also the references to Enron in § 1.06, *supra*.

[B] Implied Covenants

METROPOLITAN LIFE INS. CO. v. RJR NABISCO, INC.

United States District Court, Southern District of New York
716 F. Supp. 1504 (1989)

WALKER, DISTRICT JUDGE:

I. INTRODUCTION

The corporate parties to this action are among the country's most sophisticated financial institutions, as familiar with the Wall Street investment community and the securities market as American consumers are with the Oreo cookies and Winston cigarettes made by defendant RJR Nabisco, Inc. (sometimes "the company" or "RJR Nabisco"). The present action traces its origins to October 20, 1988, when F. Ross Johnson, then the Chief Executive Officer of RJR Nabisco, proposed a $17 billion leveraged buy-out ("LBO") of the company's shareholders, at $75 per share.[16] Within a few days, a bidding war developed among the investment group led by Johnson and the investment firm of Kohlberg Kravis Roberts & Co. ("KKR"), and others. On December 1, 1988, a special committee of RJR Nabisco directors, established by the company specifically to consider the competing proposals, recommended that the company accept the KKR proposal, a $24 billion LBO that called for the purchase of the company's outstanding stock at roughly $109 per share.

---

[16] [1] A leveraged buy-out occurs when a group of investors, usually including members of a company's management team, buy the company under financial arrangements that include little equity and significant new debt. The necessary debt financing typically includes mortgages or high risk/high yield bonds, popularly known as "junk bonds." Additionally, a portion of this debt is generally secured by the company's assets. Some of the acquired company's assets are usually sold after the transaction is completed in order to reduce the debt incurred in the acquisition.

The flurry of activity late last year that accompanied the bidding war for RJR Nabisco spawned at least eight lawsuits, filed before this Court, charging the company and its former CEO with a variety of securities and common law violations.[17] The Court agreed to hear the present action — filed even before the company accepted the KKR proposal — on an expedited basis, with an eye toward March 1, 1989, when RJR Nabisco was expected to merge with the KKR holding entities created to facilitate the LBO. On that date, RJR Nabisco was also scheduled to assume roughly $19 billion of new debt.[18] After a delay unrelated to the present action, the merger was ultimately completed during the week of April 24, 1989.

Plaintiffs now allege, in short, that RJR Nabisco's actions have drastically impaired the value of bonds previously issued to plaintiffs by, in effect, misappropriating the value of those bonds to help finance the LBO and to distribute an enormous windfall to the company's shareholders. As a result, plaintiffs argue, they have unfairly suffered a multimillion dollar loss in the value of their bonds.[19]

On February 16, 1989, this Court heard oral argument on plaintiffs' motions. At the hearing, the Court denied plaintiffs' request for a preliminary injunction, based on their insufficient showing of irreparable harm.[20] An exchange between the Court and plaintiffs' counsel, like the submissions before it, convinced the Court that

---

[17] [2] On December 7, 1989, this Court agreed to accept as related all actions growing out of the RJR Nabisco LBO. On January 4, 1989, the Court consolidated with the present suit an action brought by three KKR affiliates — RJR Holdings Corp., RJR Holdings Group, Inc., and RJR Acquisition Corporation — against the Jefferson-Pilot Life Insurance Company. KKR established those entities to effect the buyout of RJR Nabisco. Throughout this Opinion, these entities and their parent will be referred to collectively as "KKR." When this action was filed, those entities and KKR were not formally named as parties. However, in its January 4 Order, the Court granted KKR's request to participate fully in the present action. Pursuant to that Order, KKR filed joint briefs with RJR Nabisco and participated in oral argument before the Court on February 16, 1989.

[18] [3] The Court set January 12, 1989 as the close of the expedited discovery period for these motions, which were filed the next day.

[19] [4] Agencies like Standard & Poor's and Moody's generally rate bonds in two broad categories: investment grade and speculative grade. Standard & Poor's rates investment grade bonds from "AAA" to "BBB." Moody's rates those bonds from "AAA" to "Baa3." Speculative grade bonds are rated either "BB" and lower, or "Ba1" and lower, by Standard & Poor's and Moody's, respectively. *See, e.g.*, Standard and Poor's Debt Rating Criteria at 10-11. No one disputes that, subsequent to the announcement of the LBO, the RJR Nabisco bonds lost their "A" ratings.

[20] [5] In their papers, plaintiffs had argued that the LBO "should be Preliminarily Enjoined Unless Provision is Made to Ensure That Funds for Redemption will be Available after Trial." P. Mem. at 59 (capitalization in original). The preliminary injunction requested "is not intended to stop the transaction, but only to enjoin any substantial encumbrance on the [c]ompany until the [c]ompany posts a bond or otherwise provides security to ensure its ability to redeem Plaintiffs' bonds after trial." P. Mem. at 60. References throughout this Opinion are as follows: Transcript of February 16, 1989 Argument ("Tr."); Amended Complaint ("Am. Comp."); [Name of affiant] Affidavit ("[Name of affiant] Aff."); [Name of affiant] Response Affidavit ("[Name of affiant] Resp. Aff."); [Name of affiant] Reply Affidavit ("[Name of affiant] Reply Aff."); Exhibit ("Exh."); Plaintiffs' Exhibit ("P. Exh."); [Name of deponent] Deposition ("[Name of deponent] Dep."); Plaintiffs' Memorandum in Support of Summary Judgment ("P. Mem."); Plaintiffs' Answering Brief [in Opposition to Defendants' Motions] ("P. Opp."); Plaintiffs' Reply Brief ("P. Reply"); Defendants' Memorandum in Support of their Motion for Judgment on the Pleadings [and Partial Summary Judgment and Partial Dismissal] ("D. Mem."); Defendants' Memorandum in Opposition to Plaintiffs' Motion ("D. Opp."); Defendants' Reply Memorandum ("D. Reply").

plaintiffs had failed to meet their heavy burden:

> THE COURT: How do you respond to [defendants'] statements on irreparable harm What we're looking at now is whether or not there's a basis for a preliminary injunction and if there's no irreparable harm then we're in a damage action and that changes . . . the contours of the suit. . . . We're talking about the ability . . . of the company to satisfy any judgment.
>
> PLAINTIFFS: That's correct. And our point . . . is that if we receive a judgment at any time, six months from now, after a trial for example, that judgment will almost inevitably be the basis for a judgment for everyone else. . . . But if we get a judgment, everyone else will get one as well. . . .
>
> THE COURT: [Y]ou're . . . asking me . . . [to] infer a huge number of plaintiffs and a lot more damages than your clients could ever recover as being the basis for deciding the question of irreparable harm. And those [potential] actions aren't before me.
>
> PLAINTIFFS: I think that's correct. . . .

Tr. at 39. *See also* P. Reply at 33. Plaintiffs failed to respond convincingly to defendants' arguments that, although plaintiffs have invested roughly $350 million in RJR Nabisco, their potential damages nonetheless remain relatively small and that, upon completion of the merger, the company will retain an equity base of $5 billion. *See, e.g.*, Tr. at 32, 35; D. Opp. at 48, 49. Given plaintiffs' failure to show irreparable harm, the Court denied their request for injunctive relief. This initial ruling, however, left intact plaintiffs' underlying motions, which, together with defendants' cross-motions, now require attention. The motions and cross-motions are based on plaintiffs' Amended Complaint, which sets forth nine counts.[21] Plaintiffs move for summary judgment pursuant to Fed. R. Civ. P. 56 against the company on Count I, which alleges a "Breach of Implied Covenant of Good Faith and Fair Dealing," and against both defendants on Count V, which is labeled simply "In Equity."

For its part, RJR Nabisco moves pursuant to Fed. R. Civ. P. 12(c) for judgment on the pleadings on Count I in full; on Count II (fraud) and Count III (violations of s 10(b) of the Securities Exchange Act of 1934 and Rule 10b-5 promulgated thereunder) as to most of the securities at issue; and on Count V in full. In the alternative, the company moves for summary judgment on Counts I and V. In addition, RJR Nabisco moves pursuant to Fed. R. Civ. P. 9(b) to dismiss Counts II, III and IX (alleging violations of applicable fraudulent conveyance laws) for an alleged failure to plead fraud with requisite particularity. Johnson has moved to

---

[21] [6] Count I alleges a breach of an implied covenant of good faith and fair dealing (against defendant RJR Nabisco); Count II alleges fraud (against both defendants); Count III alleges violations of Section 10(b) of the Securities Exchange Act of 1934 (against both defendants); Count IV alleges violations of Section 11 of the 1933 Act (on behalf of plaintiff Jefferson-Pilot Life Insurance Company against both defendants); Count V is labeled "In Equity," and is asserted against both defendants; Count VI alleges breach of duties (against defendant Johnson); Count VII alleges tortious interference with property (against Johnson); Count VIII alleges tortious interference with contract (against Johnson); and Count IX alleges a violation of the fraudulent conveyance laws (against RJR Nabisco).

dismiss Counts II, III and V.[22] Although the numbers involved in this case are large, and the financing necessary to complete the LBO unprecedented,[23] the legal principles nonetheless remain discrete and familiar. Yet while the instant motions thus primarily require the Court to evaluate and apply traditional rules of equity and contract interpretation, plaintiffs do raise issues of first impression in the context of an LBO. At the heart of the present motions lies plaintiffs' claim that RJR Nabisco violated a restrictive covenant — not an explicit covenant found within the four corners of the relevant bond indentures, but rather an implied covenant of good faith and fair dealing — not to incur the debt necessary to facilitate the LBO and thereby betray what plaintiffs claim was the fundamental basis of their bargain with the company. The company, plaintiffs assert, consistently reassured its bondholders that it had a "mandate" from its Board of Directors to maintain RJR Nabisco's preferred credit rating. Plaintiffs ask this Court first to imply a covenant of good faith and fair dealing that would prevent the recent transaction, then to hold that this covenant has been breached, and finally to require RJR Nabisco to redeem their bonds.

RJR Nabisco defends the LBO by pointing to express provisions in the bond indentures that, inter alia, permit mergers and the assumption of additional debt. These provisions, as well as others that could have been included but were not, were known to the market and to plaintiffs, sophisticated investors who freely bought the bonds and were equally free to sell them at any time. Any attempt by this Court to create contractual terms post hoc, defendants contend, not only finds no basis in the controlling law and undisputed facts of this case, but also would constitute an impermissible invasion into the free and open operation of the marketplace. For the reasons set forth below, this Court agrees with defendants. There being no express covenant between the parties that would restrict the incurrence of new debt, and no perceived direction to that end from covenants that are express, this Court will not imply a covenant to prevent the recent LBO and thereby create an indenture term that, while bargained for in other contexts, was not bargained for here and was not even within the mutual contemplation of the parties.

II. BACKGROUND

. . .

Both sides now move for summary judgment on Counts I and V. In support of their motions, the parties have filed extensive memoranda and supporting exhibits.

---

22 [7] Johnson has not filed memoranda in support of his motions but instead incorporates the arguments set forth in the papers filed by RJR Nabisco and KKR. Johnson has not moved with respect to Counts IV, VI, VII or VIII. Counts VI, VII and VIII apply only to Johnson. Count IV is the only count with respect to which RJR Nabisco has not moved.

23 [8] On February 9, 1989, KKR completed its tender offer for roughly 74 percent of RJR Nabisco's common stock (of which approximately 97% of the outstanding shares were tendered) and all of its Series B Cumulative Preferred Stock (of which approximately 95% of the outstanding shares were tendered). Approximately $18 billion in cash was paid out to these stockholders. KKR acquired the remaining stock in the late April merger through the issuance of roughly $4.1 billion of pay-in-kind exchangeable preferred stock and roughly $1.8 billion in face amount of convertible debentures. *See* Bradley Reply Aff. P. 2.

Having carefully reviewed the submissions before it, the Court agrees with the parties that there is no genuine issue as to any material fact regarding these counts, and given the disposition of the motions as to Counts I and V, the Court, as it must, draws all reasonable inferences in favor of the plaintiffs.

A. The Parties

Metropolitan Life Insurance Co. ("MetLife"), incorporated in New York, is a life insurance company that provides pension benefits for 42 million individuals. According to its most recent annual report, MetLife's assets exceed $88 billion and its debt securities holdings exceed $49 billion. Bradley Aff. P. 11. MetLife is a mutual company and therefore has no stockholders and is instead operated for the benefit of its policyholders. Am. Comp. P. 5. MetLife alleges that it owns $340,542,000 in principal amount of six separate RJR Nabisco debt issues, bonds allegedly purchased between July 1975 and July 1988. Some bonds become due as early as this year; others will not become due until 2017. The bonds bear interest rates of anywhere from 8 to 10.25 percent. MetLife also owned 186,000 shares of RJR Nabisco common stock at the time this suit was filed. Am. Comp. P. 12.

Jefferson-Pilot Life Insurance Co. ("Jefferson-Pilot") is a North Carolina company that has more than $3 billion in total assets, $1.5 billion of which are invested in debt securities. Bradley Aff. P. 12. Jefferson-Pilot alleges that it owns $9.34 million in principal amount of three separate RJR Nabisco debt issues, allegedly purchased between June 1978 and June 1988. Those bonds, bearing interest rates of anywhere from 8.45 to 10.75 percent, become due in 1993 and 1998. Am. Comp. P. 13.

RJR Nabisco, a Delaware corporation, is a consumer products holding company that owns some of the country's best known product lines, including LifeSavers candy, Oreo cookies, and Winston cigarettes. The company was formed in 1985, when R.J. Reynolds Industries, Inc. ("R.J. Reynolds") merged with Nabisco Brands, Inc. ("Nabisco Brands"). In 1979, and thus before the R.J. Reynolds-Nabisco Brands merger, R.J. Reynolds acquired the Del. Monte Corporation ("Del Monte"), which distributes canned fruits and vegetables. From January 1987 until February 1989, co-defendant Johnson served as the company's CEO. KKR, a private investment firm, organizes funds through which investors provide pools of equity to finance LBOs. Bradley Aff. PP 12-15.

B. The Indentures

The bonds[24] implicated by this suit are governed by long, detailed indentures, which in turn are governed by New York contract law.[25] No one disputes that the holders of public bond issues, like plaintiffs here, often enter the market after the

---

[24] [9] For the purposes of this Opinion, the terms "bonds," "debentures," and "notes" will be used interchangeably. Any distinctions among these terms are not relevant to the present motions.

[25] [10] Both sides agree that New York law controls this Court's interpretation of the indentures, which contain explicit designations to that effect. *See, e.g.*, P. Mem. at 26; D. Mem at 15 n. 23. The indentures themselves provide that they "shall be deemed to be a contract under the laws of the State of New York, and for all purposes shall be construed in accordance with the laws of said State, except as

indentures have been negotiated and memorialized. Thus, those indentures are often not the product of face-to-face negotiations between the ultimate holders and the issuing company. What remains equally true, however, is that underwriters ordinarily negotiate the terms of the indentures with the issuers. Since the underwriters must then sell or place the bonds, they necessarily negotiate in part with the interests of the buyers in mind. Moreover, these indentures were not secret agreements foisted upon unwitting participants in the bond market. No successive holder is required to accept or to continue to hold the bonds, governed by their accompanying indentures; indeed, plaintiffs readily admit that they could have sold their bonds right up until the announcement of the LBO. Tr. at 15. Instead, sophisticated investors like plaintiffs are well aware of the indenture terms and, presumably, review them carefully before lending hundreds of millions of dollars to any company.

Indeed, the prospectuses for the indentures contain a statement relevant to this action:

> The Indenture contains no restrictions on the creation of unsecured short-term debt by [RJR Nabisco] or its subsidiaries, no restriction on the creation of unsecured Funded Debt by [RJR Nabisco] or its subsidiaries which are not Restricted Subsidiaries, and no restriction on the payment of dividends by [RJR Nabisco].

Bradley Resp. Aff., Exh. L at 24.[26] Further, as plaintiffs themselves note, the contracts at issue "[do] not impose debt limits, since debt is assumed to be used for productive purposes." P. Reply at 34.

1. The relevant Articles

A typical RJR Nabisco indenture contains thirteen Articles. At least four of them are relevant to the present motions and thus merit a brief review.[27]

Article Three delineates the covenants of the issuer. Most important, it first provides for payment of principal and interest. It then addresses various mechanical provisions regarding such matters as payment terms and trustee vacancies. The Article also contains "negative pledge" and related provisions, which restrict mortgages or other liens on the assets of RJR Nabisco or its subsidiaries and seek to protect the bondholders from being subordinated to other debt.

Article Five describes various procedures to remedy defaults and the responsibilities of the Trustee. This Article includes the distinction in the indentures noted above, see *supra* n. 11. In seven of the nine securities at issue, a provision in Article

may otherwise be required by mandatory provisions of law." Bradley Aff., Exh. L, § 12.8.

[26] [11] While nine securities are at issue in this suit, the parties agree — and the Court's review confirms — that the separate indentures mirror one another in all important respects, with one exception that is discussed herein. Indeed, plaintiffs have submitted a helpful Addendum in which they outline what they term "[t]ypical RJR Nabisco [i]ndenture [t]erms." See P. Reply, Addendum. Thus, the prospectus statement quoted above has its counterpart in each of the other prospectuses. *See* Bradley Aff. P. 9.

[27] [12] For the following discussion, see generally, Indenture dated as of October 15, 1982, between R.J. Reynolds Industries, Inc., Issuer, and Bankers Trust Company, Trustee, included as Bradley Aff. Exh. L, and Plaintiffs' Exh. 1.

Five prohibits bondholders from suing for any remedy based on rights in the indentures unless 25 percent of the holders have requested in writing that the indenture trustee seek such relief, and, after 60 days, the trustee has not sued. *See, e.g.*, Bradley Aff. Exh. L, ss 5.6, 5.7. Defendants argue that this provision precludes plaintiffs from suing on these seven securities. *See* D. Mem. at 22-25. Given its holdings today, see *infra*, the Court need not address this issue.

Article Nine governs the adoption of supplemental indentures. It provides, inter alia, that the Issuer and the Trustee can

> add to the covenants of the Issuer such further covenants, restrictions, conditions or provisions as its Board of Directors by Board Resolution and the Trustee shall consider to be for the protection of the holders of Securities, and to make the occurrence, or the occurrence and continuance, of a default in any such additional covenants, restrictions, conditions or provisions an Event of Default permitting the enforcement of all or any of the several remedies provided in this Indenture as herein set forth. . . .

Bradley Aff. Exh. L, § 9.1(c).

Article Ten addresses a potential "Consolidation, Merger, Sale or Conveyance," and explicitly sets forth the conditions under which the company can consolidate or merge into or with any other corporation. It provides explicitly that RJR Nabisco "may consolidate with, or sell or convey, all or substantially all of its assets to, or merge into or with any other corporation," so long as the new entity is a United States corporation, and so long as it assumes RJR Nabisco's debt. The Article also requires that any such transaction not result in the company's default under any indenture provision.[28]

2. The elimination of restrictive covenants:

In its Amended Complaint, MetLife lists the six debt issues on which it bases its claims. Indentures for two of those issues — the 10.25 percent Notes due in 1990, of which MetLife continues to hold $10 million, and the 8.9 percent Debentures due in 1996, of which MetLife continues to hold $50 million — once contained express covenants that, among other things, restricted the company's ability to incur precisely the sort of debt involved in the recent LBO. In order to eliminate those restrictions, the parties to this action renegotiated the terms of those indentures, first in 1983 and then again in 1985.

MetLife acquired $50 million principal amount of 10.25 percent Notes from Del Monte in July of 1975. To cover the $50 million, MetLife and Del Monte entered into

---

[28] [13] The remaining Articles are not relevant to the motions currently before the Court. Article One contains definitions; Article Two contains mechanical terms regarding, for instance, the issuance and transfer of the securities; Article Four concerns such mechanical matters as securityholders' lists and annual reports; Article Six addresses the rights and responsibilities of the Trustee; Article Seven contains mechanical provisions concerning the securityholders; Article Eight concerns procedural matters such as securityholders' meetings and consents; Article Eleven deals with the satisfaction and discharge of the indenture; Article Twelve sets forth various miscellaneous provisions; and Article Thirteen includes provisions regarding the redemption of securities and sinking funds. *See, e.g.*, Bradley Aff. Exh. L.

a loan agreement. That agreement restricted Del Monte's ability, among other things, to incur the sort of indebtedness involved in the RJR Nabisco LBO. See promissory note §§ 2.6-2.15, attached as Exhibit A to Bradley Aff. Exh. E. In 1979, R.J. Reynolds — the corporate predecessor to RJR Nabisco — purchased Del Monte and assumed its indebtedness. Then, in December of 1983, R.J. Reynolds requested MetLife to agree to deletions of those restrictive covenants in exchange for various guarantees from R.J. Reynolds. *See* Bradley Aff. P. 17. A few months later, MetLife and R.J. Reynolds entered into a guarantee and amendment agreement reflecting those terms. *See* Bradley Aff. P. 17, Exh. G. Pursuant to that agreement, and in the words of Robert E. Chappell, Jr., MetLife's Executive Vice President, MetLife thus "gave up the restrictive covenants applicable to the Del Monte debt . . . in return for [the parent company's] guarantee and public covenants." Chappell Dep. at 196.

MetLife acquired the 8.9 percent Debentures from R.J. Reynolds in October of 1976 in a private placement. A promissory note evidenced MetLife's $100 million loan. That note, like the Del Monte agreement, contained covenants that restricted R.J. Reynolds' ability to incur new debt. *See* Bradley Aff., Exh. H, §§ 2.5-2.9. In June of 1985, R.J. Reynolds announced its plans to acquire Nabisco Brands in a $3.6 billion transaction that involved the incurrence of a significant amount of new debt. R.J. Reynolds requested MetLife to waive compliance with these restrictive covenants in light of the Nabisco acquisition. *See* D. Mem. at 45; Bradley Aff. P. 18.

In exchange for certain benefits, MetLife agreed to exchange its 8.9 percent debentures — which did contain explicit debt limitations — for debentures issued under a public indenture — which contain no explicit limits on new debt. An internal MetLife memorandum explained the parties' understanding:

> [MetLife's $100 million financing of the Nabisco Brands purchase] had its origins in discussions with RJR regarding potential covenant violations in the 8.90% Notes. More specifically, *in its acquisition of Nabisco Brands, RJR was slated to incur significant new long-term debt, which would have caused a violation in the funded indebtedness incurrence tests in the 8.90% Notes.* In the discussions regarding [MetLife's] willingness to consent to the additional indebtedness, it was determined that a mutually beneficial approach to the problem was to (1) agree on a new financing having a rate and a maturity desirable for [MetLife] and (2) modify the 8.90% Notes. The former was accomplished with agreement on the proposed financing, while the latter was accomplished by [MetLife] agreeing to substitute RJR's public indenture covenants for the covenants in the 8.90% Notes. In addition to the covenant substitution, RJR has agreed to "debenturize" the 8.90% Notes upon [MetLife's] request. This will permit [MetLife] to sell the 8.90% Notes to the public.

MetLife Southern Office Memorandum, dated July 11, 1985, attached as Bradley Aff. Exh. J, at 2 (emphasis added).

3. The recognition and effect of the LBO trend:

Other internal MetLife documents help frame the background to this action, for they accurately describe the changing securities markets and the responses those changes engendered from sophisticated market participants, such as MetLife and Jefferson-Pilot. At least as early as 1982, MetLife recognized an LBO's effect on bond values.[29] In the spring of that year, MetLife participated in the financing of an LBO of a company called Reeves Brothers ("Reeves"). At the time of that LBO, MetLife also held bonds in that company. Subsequent to the LBO, as a MetLife memorandum explained, the "Debentures of Reeves were downgraded by Standard & Poor's from BBB to B and by Moody's from Baal to Ba3, thereby lowering the value of the Notes and Debentures held by [MetLife]." MetLife Memorandum, dated August 20, 1982, attached as Bradley Reply Aff. Exh D, at 1.

MetLife further recognized its "inability to force any type of payout of the [Reeves'] Notes or the Debentures as a result of the buy-out [which] was somewhat disturbing at the time we considered a participation in the new financing. However," the memorandum continued, "our concern was tempered since, as a stockholder in [the holding company used to facilitate the transaction], we would benefit from the increased net income attributable to the continued presence of the low coupon indebtedness. The recent downgrading of the Reeves Debentures and the consequent "loss' in value has again raised questions regarding our ability to have forced a payout. *Questions have also been raised about our ability to force payouts in similar future situations, particularly when we would not be participating in the buy-out financing.*" *Id.* (emphasis added). In the memorandum, MetLife sought to answer those very "questions" about how it might force payouts in "similar future situations."

> A method of closing this apparent "loophole," thereby forcing a payout of [MetLife's] holdings, would be through a covenant dealing with a change in ownership. Such a covenant is fairly standard in financings with privately-held companies. . . . It provides the lender with an option to end a particular borrowing relationship via some type of special redemption. . . .

Id., at 2 (emphasis added).

A more comprehensive memorandum, prepared in late 1985, evaluated and explained several aspects of the corporate world's increasing use of mergers, takeovers and other debt-financed transactions. That memorandum first reviewed the available protection for lenders such as MetLife:

> Covenants are incorporated into loan documents to ensure that after a lender makes a loan, the creditworthiness of the borrower and the lender's ability to reach the borrower's assets do not deteriorate substantially. *Restrictions on the incurrence of debt*, sale of assets, mergers, dividends,

[29] [14] MetLife itself began investing in LBOs as early as 1980. See MetLife Special Projects Memorandum, dated June 17, 1989, attached as Bradley Aff. Exh. V, at 1 ("[MetLife's] history of investing in leveraged buyout transactions dates back to 1980; and through 1984, [MetLife] reviewed a large number of LBO investment opportunities presented to us by various investment banking firms and LBO specialists. Over this five-year period, [MetLife] invested, on a direct basis, approximately $430 million to purchase debt and equity securities in 10 such transactions. . . .").

> restricted payments and loans and advances to affiliates are *some of the traditional negative covenants that can help protect lenders in the event their obligors become involved in undesirable merger/takeover situations.*

MetLife Northeastern Office Memorandum, dated November 27, 1985, attached as Bradley Aff. Exh. U, at 1-2 (emphasis added). The memorandum then surveyed market realities:

> Because almost any industrial company is apt to engineer a takeover or be taken over itself, *Business Week* says that investors are beginning to view debt securities of high grade industrial corporations as Wall Street's riskiest investments. In addition, *because public bondholders do not enjoy the protection of any restrictive covenants*, owners of high grade corporates face substantial losses from takeover situations, if not immediately, then when the bond market finally adjusts. . . . [T]here have been 10-15 merger/takeover/LBO situations where, *due to the lack of covenant protection, [MetLife] has had no choice but to remain a lender to a less creditworthy obligor*. . . . The fact that the quality of our investment portfolio is greater than the other large insurance companies . . . may indicate that we have negotiated better covenant protection than other institutions, thus generally being able to require prepayment when situations become too risky. . . . [However,] a problem exists. And *because the current merger craze is not likely to decelerate* and because there exist vehicles to circumvent traditional covenants, the problem will probably continue. Therefore, *perhaps it is time to institute appropriate language designed to protect Metropolitan from the negative implications of mergers and takeovers.*

Id. at 2-4 (emphasis added).[30]

Indeed, MetLife does not dispute that, as a member of a bondholders' association, it received and discussed a proposed model indenture, which included a "comprehensive covenant" entitled "Limitations on Shareholders' Payments."[31] As becomes clear from reading the proposed — but never adopted — provision, it was "intend[ed] to provide protection against all of the types of situations in which shareholders profit at the expense of bondholders." *Id.* The provision dictated that the "[c]orporation will not, and will not permit any [s]ubsidiary to, directly or

[30] [15] During discovery, MetLife produced from its files an article that appeared in The New York Times on January 7, 1986. The article, like the memoranda discussed above, reviewed the position of bondholders like MetLife and Jefferson-Pilot:

> Debt-financed acquisitions, as well as those defensive actions to thwart takeovers, have generally resulted in lower bond ratings. . . . Of course, a major problem for debtholders is that, compared with shareholders, they have relatively little power over management decisions. *Their rights are essentially confined to the covenants restricting, say, the level of debt a company can accrue.*

Bradley Reply Aff. Exh. H (emphasis added).

[31] [16] *See* Bradley Resp. Aff. Exh. F. That exhibit is an August 5, 1988 letter from the New York law firm of Kaye, Scholer, Fierman, Hays & Handler. A partner at that firm sent the letter to "Indenture Group Members," including MetLife, who participated in the Institutional Bondholders' Rights Association ("the IBRA"). The "Limitations on Shareholders' Payments" provision appears in a draft IBRA model indenture. *See* Bradley Resp. Aff. PP 3, 7.

indirectly, make any [s]hareholder [p]ayment unless . . . (1) the aggregate amount of all [s]hareholder payments during the period [at issue] . . . shall not exceed [figure left blank]." Bradley Resp. Aff. Exh. H, at 9. The term "shareholder payments" is defined to include "restructuring distributions, stock repurchases, debt incurred or guaranteed to finance merger payments to shareholders, etc." *Id.* at i.

Apparently, that provision — or provisions with similar intentions — never went beyond the discussion stage at MetLife. That fact is easily understood; indeed, MetLife's own documents articulate several reasonable, undisputed explanations:

> While it would be possible to broaden the change in ownership covenant to cover any acquisition-oriented transaction, *we might well encounter significant resistance in implementation with larger public companies.* . . . With respect to implementation, we would be faced with the task of imposing a non-standard limitation on potential borrowers, *which could be a difficult task in today's highly competitive marketplace. Competitive pressures notwithstanding, it would seem that management of larger public companies would be particularly opposed to such a covenant since its effect would be to increase the cost of an acquisition* (due to an assumed debt repayment), a factor that could well lower the price of any tender offer (thereby impacting shareholders).

Bradley Reply Aff. Exh. D, at 3 (emphasis added). The November 1985 memorandum explained that

> [o]bviously, our ability to implement methods of takeover protection will vary between the public and private market. In that public securities do not contain any meaningful covenants, it would be very difficult for [MetLife] to demand takeover protection in public bonds. Such a requirement would effectively take us out of the public industrial market. A recent *Business Week* article does suggest, however, that there is increasing talk among lending institutions about requiring blue chip companies to compensate them for the growing risk of downgradings. *This talk, regarding such protection as restrictions on future debt financings, is met with skepticism by the investment banking community which feels that CFO's are not about to give up the option of adding debt and do not really care if their companies' credit ratings drop a notch or two.*

Bradley Resp. Aff. Exh. A, at 8 (emphasis added).

The Court quotes these documents at such length not because they represent an "admission" or "waiver" from MetLife, or an "assumption of risk" in any tort sense, or its "consent" to any particular course of conduct — all terms discussed at even greater length in the parties' submissions. *See, e.g.*, P. Opp. at 31-36; P. Reply at 16-17; D. Reply at 15-16. Rather, the documents set forth the background to the present action, and highlight the risks inherent in the market itself, for any investor. Investors as sophisticated as MetLife and Jefferson-Pilot would be hard-pressed to plead ignorance of these market risks. Indeed, MetLife has not disputed the facts asserted in its own internal documents. Nor has Jefferson-Pilot — presumably an institution no less sophisticated than MetLife — offered any reason to believe that its understanding of the securities market differed in any material respect from the description and analysis set forth in the MetLife documents. Those documents, after all, were not born in a vacuum. They are descriptions of, and responses to, the market in which investors like MetLife and Jefferson-Pilot knowingly participated.

These documents must be read in conjunction with plaintiffs' Amended Complaint. That document asserts that the LBO "undermines the foundation of the investment grade debt market . . . ," Am. Comp. P. 16; that, although "the indentures do not purport to limit dividends or debt . . . [s]uch covenants were believed unnecessary with blue chip companies . . . ," Am. Comp. P. 17;[32] that "the transaction contradicts the premise of the investment grade market . . . ," Am. Comp. P. 33; and, finally, that "[t]his buy-out was not contemplated at the time the debt was issued, contradicts the premise of the investment grade ratings that RJR Nabisco actively solicited and received, and is inconsistent with the understandings of the market . . . which [p]laintiffs relied upon." Am. Comp. P. 51.

Solely for the purposes of these motions, the Court accepts various factual assertions advanced by plaintiffs: first, that RJR Nabisco actively solicited "investment grade" ratings for its debt; second, that it relied on descriptions of its strong capital structure and earnings record which included prominent display of its ability to pay the interest obligations on its long-term debt several times over, Am. Comp. P. 14; and third, that the company made express or implied representations not contained in the relevant indentures concerning its future creditworthiness. *Id.* P. 15. In support of those allegations, plaintiffs have marshaled a number of speeches made by co-defendant Johnson and other executives of RJR Nabisco.[33] In addition, plaintiffs rely on an affidavit sworn to by John Dowdle, the former Treasurer and then Senior Vice President of RJR Nabisco from 1970 until 1987. In his opinion, the LBO "clearly undermines the fundamental premise of the [c]ompany's bargain with the bondholders, and the commitment that I believe the [c]ompany made to the bondholders . . . I firmly believe that the company made commitments . . . that require it to redeem [these bonds and notes] before paying out the value to the shareholders." Dowdle Aff. PP 4, 7.

III. DISCUSSION

At the outset, the Court notes that nothing in its evaluation is substantively altered by the speeches given or remarks made by RJR Nabisco executives, or the opinions of various individuals — what, for instance, former RJR Nabisco Treasurer Dowdle personally did or did not "firmly believe" the indentures meant. *See supra*,

---

[32] [17] Due to a typographical error, the Amended Complaint contains two paragraphs numbered "17." The passage above refers to the first such paragraph.

[33] [18] *See, e.g.*, Address by F. Ross Johnson, November 12, 1987, P. Exh. 8, at 5 ("Our strong balance sheet is a cornerstone of our strategies. It gives us the resources to modernize facilities, develop new technologies, bring on new products, and support our leading brands around the world."); Remarks of Edward J. Robinson, Executive Vice President and Chief Financial Officer, February 15, 1988, P. Exh. 6, at 1 ("RJR Nabisco's financial strategy is . . . to enhance the strength of the balance sheet by reducing the level of debt as well as lowering the cost of existing debt."); Remarks by Dr. Robert J. Carbonell, Vice Chairman of RJR Nabisco, June 3, 1987, P. Exh. 10, at 5 ("We will not sacrifice our longer-term health for the sake of short term heroics.").

and generally Chappell, Dowdle and Howard Affidavits. The parol evidence rule bars plaintiffs from arguing that the speeches made by company executives prove defendants agreed or acquiesced to a term that does not appear in the indentures. *See West, Weir & Bartel, Inc. v. Mary Carter Paint Co.*, 25 N.Y.2d 535, 540, 307 N.Y.S.2d 449, 452, 255 N.E.2d 709, 712 (1969) ("The rule in this State is well settled that the construction of a plain and unambiguous contract is for the Court to pass on, and that circumstances extrinsic to the agreement will not be considered when the intention of the parties can be gathered from the instrument itself.") In interpreting these contracts, this Court must be concerned with what the parties intended, but only to the extent that what they intended is evidenced by what is written in the indentures. *See, e.g., Rodolitz v. Neptune Paper Products, Inc.*, 22 N.Y.2d 383, 386-7, 292 N.Y.S.2d 878, 881, 239 N.E.2d 628, 630 (1968); *Raleigh Associates v. Henry*, 302 N.Y. 467, 473, 99 N.E.2d 289 (1951).

The indentures at issue clearly address the eventuality of a merger. They impose certain related restrictions not at issue in this suit, but no restriction that would prevent the recent RJR Nabisco merger transaction. *See supra* at 1510 (discussion of Article 10). The indentures also explicitly set forth provisions for the adoption of new covenants, if such a course is deemed appropriate. *See supra* at 1510 (discussion of Article 9). While it may be true that no explicit provision either permits or prohibits an LBO, such contractual silence itself cannot create ambiguity to avoid the dictates of the parole evidence rule, particularly where the indentures impose no debt limitations.

Under certain circumstances, however, courts will, as plaintiffs note, consider extrinsic evidence to evaluate the scope of an implied covenant of good faith. *See Valley National Bank v. Babylon Chrysler-Plymouth, Inc.*, 53 Misc. 2d 1029, 1031-32, 280 N.Y.S.2d 786, 788-89 (Sup. Ct. Nassau), *aff'd*, 28 A.D.2d 1092, 284 N.Y.S.2d 849 (2d Dept. 1967) (Relying on custom and usage because "[w]hen a contract fails to establish the time for performance, the law implies that the act shall be done within a reasonable time. . . .").[34] However, the Second Circuit has established a different rule for customary, or boilerplate, provisions of detailed indentures used and relied upon throughout the securities market, such as those at issue. Thus, in *Sharon Steel Corporation v. Chase Manhattan Bank, N.A.*, 691 F.2d 1039 (2d Cir. 1982), Judge Winter concluded that

> [b]oilerplate provisions are . . . not the consequences of the relationship of particular borrowers and lenders and do not depend upon particularized intentions of the parties to an indenture. There are no adjudicative facts relating to the parties to the litigation for a jury to find and the meaning of boilerplate provisions is, therefore, a matter of law rather than fact. Moreover, uniformity in interpretation is important to the efficiency of capital markets. . . . Whereas participants in the capital market can adjust

---

[34] [19] In support of this proposition, plaintiffs also rely on *Reback v. Story Productions, Inc.*, 15 Misc. 2d 681, 181 N.Y.S.2d 980, modified and *aff'd*, 9 A.D.2d 880, 193 N.Y.S.2d 520 (1st Dept. 1959). The court in that case, however, was presented with an ambiguous written agreement. See 181 N.Y.S.2d at 983. Plaintiffs similarly rely on *Van Gemert v. Boeing Co.*, 520 F.2d 1373 (2d Cir.), cert. denied, 423 U.S. 947, 96 S. Ct. 364, 46 L. Ed. 2d 282 (1975) ("*Van Gemert I*"). In that case, however, the right asserted was addressed by an express provision which provided a framework for determining the scope and effect of the implied covenant. See *infra*.

> their affairs according to a uniform interpretation, whether it be correct or not as an initial proposition, the creation of enduring uncertainties as to the meaning of boilerplate provisions would decrease the value of all debenture issues and greatly impair the efficient working of capital markets. . . . Just such uncertainties would be created if interpretation of boilerplate provisions were submitted to juries sitting in every judicial district in the nation.

Id. at 1048. *See also Morgan Stanley & Co. v. Archer Daniels Midland Co.*, 570 F. Supp. 1529, 1535-36 (S.D.N.Y. 1983) (Sand, J.) ("[Plaintiff concedes that the legality of [the transaction at issue] would depend on a factual inquiry. . . . This case-by-case approach is problematic. . . . [Plaintiff's theory] appears keyed to the subjective expectations of the bondholders . . . and reads a subjective element into what presumably should be an objective determination based on the language appearing in the bond agreement."); *Purcell v. Flying Tiger Line, Inc.*, No. 82-3505, at 5, 8 (S.D.N.Y. Jan. 12, 1984) (CES) ("The Indenture does not contain any such limitation [as the one proposed by plaintiff]. . . . In light of our holding that the Indenture unambiguously permits the transaction at issue in this case, we are precluded from considering any of the extrinsic evidence that plaintiff offers on this motion. . . . It would be improper to consider evidence as to the subjective intent, collateral representations, and either the statements or the conduct of the parties in performing the contract.") (citations omitted). Ignoring these principles, plaintiffs would have this Court vary what they themselves have admitted is "indenture boilerplate," P. Reply at 2, of "standard" agreements, P. Mem. at 14, to comport with collateral representations and their subjective understandings.[35]

---

[35] [20] To a certain extent, this discussion is academic. Even if the Court did consider the extrinsic evidence offered by plaintiffs, its ultimate decision would be no different. Based on that extrinsic evidence, plaintiffs attempt to establish that an implied covenant of good faith is necessary to protect the benefits of their agreements. That inquiry necessarily asks the Court to determine whether the existing contractual terms should be construed to preclude defendants from engaging in an LBO along the lines of the recently completed transaction. However, even evaluating all facts — such as the public statements made by company executives — in the light most favorable to plaintiffs, these plaintiffs fail as a matter of law to establish that the purported "fundamental basis" of their bargain with defendants created a contractual obligation on the part of the defendants not to engage in an LBO. It is first worth noting that plaintiffs have quoted selectively from certain speeches and remarks made by RJR Nabisco executives; in some respects, those public statements are more equivocal than plaintiffs would have this Court believe. *See, e.g.*, P. Exh. 3 at 25. ("[W]e believe our strong balance sheet and our debt capacity . . . provide us with the flexibility to pursue any conceivable strategy or financial option we choose.") More important, those representations are improperly raised under the rubric of an implied covenant of good faith when they cannot properly or reasonably be construed as evidencing a binding agreement or acquiescence by defendants to substantive restrictive covenants. Moreover, nothing like the mutual understanding plaintiffs now advance has been shown; in fact, as far as these parties are concerned, quite the opposite is true. *See infra* at 39-40. Thus, as a matter of law, and accepting all extrinsic evidence offered, the "implied covenant of good faith" does not serve these plaintiffs in the way they represent. As explained more fully below, by relying on extrinsic evidence and the familiar implied covenant of good faith, plaintiffs do not seek to protect an existing contractual right; they seek to create a new one, and thus to obtain a better bargain than originally agreed upon. Therefore, even if the parole evidence rule did not block plaintiffs' path, their course would not be followed.

The parole evidence rule of course does not bar descriptions of either the background of this suit or market realities consistent with the contracts at issue.

A. Plaintiffs' Case Against the RJR Nabisco LBO

1. Count One: The implied covenant

In their first count, plaintiffs assert that [d]efendant RJR Nabisco owes a continuing duty of good faith and fair dealing in connection with the contract [i.e., the indentures] through which it borrowed money from MetLife, Jefferson-Pilot and other holders of its debt, including a duty not to frustrate the purpose of the contracts to the debtholders or to deprive the debtholders of the intended object of the contracts — purchase of investment-grade securities.

In the "buy-out," the [c]ompany breaches the duty [or implied covenant] of good faith and fair dealing by, inter alia, destroying the investment grade quality of the debt and transferring that value to the "buy-out" proponents and to the shareholders. Am. Comp. PP 34, 35. In effect, plaintiffs contend that express covenants were not necessary because an implied covenant would prevent what defendants have now done.

A plaintiff always can allege a violation of an express covenant. If there has been such a violation, of course, the court need not reach the question of whether or not an implied covenant has been violated. That inquiry surfaces where, while the express terms may not have been technically breached, one party has nonetheless effectively deprived the other of those express, explicitly bargained-for benefits. In such a case, a court will read an implied covenant of good faith and fair dealing into a contract to ensure that neither party deprives the other of "the fruits of the agreement." *See, e.g., Greenwich Village Assoc. v. Salle*, 110 A.D.2d 111, 115, 493 N.Y.S.2d 461, 464 (1st Dept. 1985). *See also Van Gemert v. Boeing Co.*, 553 F.2d 812, 815 ("*Van Gemert II*") (2d. Cir. 1977) Such a covenant is implied only where the implied term "is consistent with other mutually agreed upon terms in the contract." *Sabetay v. Sterling Drug, Inc.*, 69 N.Y.2d 329, 335, 514 N.Y.S.2d 209, 212, 506 N.E.2d 919, 922 (1987). In other words, the implied covenant will only aid and further the explicit terms of the agreement and will never impose an obligation " "which would be inconsistent with other terms of the contractual relationship."' *Id.* (citation omitted). Viewed another way, the implied covenant of good faith is breached only when one party seeks to prevent the contract's performance or to withhold its benefits. *See Collard v. Incorporated Village of Flower Hill*, 75 A.D.2d 631, 632, 427 N.Y.S.2d 301, 302 (2d Dept. 1980). As a result, it thus ensures that parties to a contract perform the substantive, bargained-for terms of their agreement. *See, e.g., Wakefield v. Northern Telecom, Inc.*, 769 F.2d 109, 112 (2d Cir. 1985) (Winter, J.)

In contracts like bond indentures, "an implied covenant . . . derives its substance directly from the language of the Indenture, and "cannot give the holders of Debentures any rights inconsistent with those set out in the Indenture.' [Where] plaintiffs' contractual rights [have not been] violated, there can have been no breach of an implied covenant." *Gardner & Florence Call Cowles Foundation v. Empire Inc.*, 589 F. Supp. 669, 673 (S.D.N.Y. 1984), vacated on procedural grounds, 754 F.2d 478 (2d Cir. 1985) (quoting *Broad v. Rockwell*, 642 F.2d 929, 957 (5th Cir.) (en banc), cert. denied, 454 U.S. 965, 102 S. Ct. 506, 70 L. Ed. 2d 380 (1981)) (emphasis added).

Thus, in cases like *Van Gemert v. Boeing Co.*, 520 F.2d 1373 (2d Cir.), cert. denied,

423 U.S. 947, 96 S. Ct. 364, 46 L. Ed. 2d 282 (1975) ("*Van Gemert I*"), and *Pittsburgh Terminal Corp. v. Baltimore & Ohio Ry. Co.*, 680 F.2d 933 (3d Cir.), cert. denied, 459 U.S. 1056, 103 S. Ct. 475, 74 L. Ed. 2d 621 (1982) — both relied upon by plaintiffs — the courts used the implied covenant of good faith and fair dealing to ensure that the bondholders received the benefit of their bargain as determined from the face of the contracts at issue. In *Van Gemert I*, the plaintiff bondholders alleged inadequate notice to them of defendant's intention to redeem the debentures in question and hence an inability to exercise their conversion rights before the applicable deadline. The contract itself provided that notice would be given in the first place. *See, e.g., id.* at 1375 ("A number of provisions in the debenture, the Indenture Agreement, the prospectus, the registration statement . . . and the Listing Agreement . . . dealt with the possible redemption of the debentures . . . and the notice debenture-holders were to receive. . . ."). Faced with those provisions, defendants in that case unsurprisingly admitted that the indentures specifically required the company to provide the bondholders with notice. *See id.* at 1379. While defendant there issued a press release that mentioned the possible redemption of outstanding convertible debentures, that limited release did not "mention even the tentative dates for redemption and expiration of the conversion rights of debenture holders." *Id.* at 1375. Moreover, defendant did not issue any general publicity or news release. Through an implied covenant, then, the court fleshed out the full extent of the more skeletal right that appeared in the contract itself, and thus protected plaintiff's bargained-for right of conversion.[36] As the court observed,

> What one buys when purchasing a convertible debenture in addition to the debt obligation of the company . . . is principally the expectation that the stock will increase sufficiently in value that the conversion right will make the debenture worth more than the debt. . . . Any loss occurring to him from failure to convert, as here, is not from a risk inherent in his investment but rather from unsatisfactory notification procedures.

Id. at 1385 (citations omitted).[37] I also note, in passing, that *Van Gemert I* presented the Second Circuit with "less sophisticated investors." *Id.* at 1383. Similarly, the court in *Pittsburgh Terminal* applied an implied covenant to the indentures at issue because defendants there "took steps to prevent the Bondholders from receiving information which they needed in order to receive the fruits of their conversion option should they choose to exercise it." *Pittsburgh Terminal*, 680 F.2d at 941 (emphasis added).

The appropriate analysis, then, is first to examine the indentures to determine "the fruits of the agreement" between the parties, and then to decide whether those "fruits" have been spoiled — which is to say, whether plaintiffs' contractual rights have been violated by defendants.

---

[36] [21] Since newspaper notice, for instance, was promised in the indenture, the court used an implied covenant to ensure that meaningful, reasonable newspaper notice was provided. *See id.* at 1383.

[37] [22] *See also id.* at 1383 ("An issuer of [convertible] debentures has a duty to give adequate notice either on the face of the debentures, . . . or in some other way, of the notice to be provided in the event the company decides to redeem the debentures. Absent such advice as to the specific notice agreed upon by the issuer and the trustee for the debenture holders, the debenture holders' reasonable expectations as to notice should be protected.").

The American Bar Foundation's Commentaries on Indentures ("the Commentaries"), relied upon and respected by both plaintiffs and defendants, describes the rights and risks generally found in bond indentures like those at issue:

> The most obvious and important characteristic of long-term debt financing is that the holder ordinarily has not bargained for and does not expect any substantial gain in the value of the security to compensate for the risk of loss. . . . [T]he significant fact, which accounts in part for the detailed protective provisions of the typical long-term debt financing instrument, is that the lender (the purchaser of the debt security) can expect only interest at the prescribed rate plus the eventual return of the principal. Except for possible increases in the market value of the debt security because of changes in interest rates, the debt security will seldom be worth more than the lender paid for it. . . . It may, of course, become worth much less. Accordingly, the typical investor in a long-term debt security is primarily interested in every reasonable assurance that the principal and interest will be paid when due. . . . Short of bankruptcy, the debt security holder can do nothing to protect himself against actions of the borrower which jeopardize its ability to pay the debt unless he . . . establishes his rights through contractual provisions set forth in the debt agreement or indenture.

Id. at 1-2 (1971).

A review of the parties' submissions and the indentures themselves satisfies the Court that the substantive "fruits" guaranteed by those contracts and relevant to the present motions include the periodic and regular payment of interest and the eventual repayment of principal. *See, e.g.*, Bradley Aff. Exh. L, § 3.1 ("The Issuer covenants . . . that it will duly and punctually pay . . . the principal of, and interest on, each of the Securities . . . at the respective times and in the manner provided in such Securities. . . ."). According to a typical indenture, a default shall occur if the company either (1) fails to pay principal when due; (2) fails to make a timely sinking fund payment; (3) fails to pay within 30 days of the due date thereof any interest on the date; or (4) fails duly to observe or perform any of the express covenants or agreements set forth in the agreement. *See, e.g.*, Brad. Aff. Exh. L, § 5.1.[38] Plaintiffs' Amended Complaint nowhere alleges that RJR Nabisco has breached these contractual obligations; interest payments continue and there is no reason to believe that the principal will not be paid when due.[39]

---

[38] [23] Plaintiffs originally indicated that, depending on the Court's disposition of the instant motions, they might seek to amend their complaint to allege that "they are not equally and ratably secured under the [express terms of the] "negative pledge' clause of the indentures." P. Reply at 12 n. 7. On May 26, 1989, shortly before this Opinion was filed, the Court granted defendants' request to assert a counterclaim for a declaratory judgment that those "negative pledge" covenants have not been violated by the post-LBO financial structure of RJR Nabisco. This counterclaim was advanced in response to notices of default by plaintiffs based on matters not raised in the Amended Complaint. The Court of course will not now determine whether an alleged implied covenant flowing from a "negative pledge" provision has been breached. That inquiry necessarily must follow the Court's determination of whether or not the "negative pledge" provision has been expressly breached.

[39] [24] The Court here incorporates by reference its earlier discussion not only of plaintiffs' failure to demonstrate sufficiently a risk of irreparable harm on their motion for a preliminary injunction, but also

It is not necessary to decide that indentures like those at issue could never support a finding of additional benefits, under different circumstances with different parties. Rather, for present purposes, it is sufficient to conclude what obligation is not covered, either explicitly or implicitly, by these contracts held by these plaintiffs. Accordingly, this Court holds that the "fruits" of these indentures do not include an implied restrictive covenant that would prevent the incurrence of new debt to facilitate the recent LBO. To hold otherwise would permit these plaintiffs to straightjacket the company in order to guarantee their investment. These plaintiffs do not invoke an implied covenant of good faith to protect a legitimate, mutually contemplated benefit of the indentures; rather, they seek to have this Court create an additional benefit for which they did not bargain. Although the indentures generally permit mergers and the incurrence of new debt, there admittedly is not an explicit indenture provision to the contrary of what plaintiffs now claim the implied covenant requires. That absence, however, does not mean that the Court should imply into those very same indentures a covenant of good faith so broad that it imposes a new, substantive term of enormous scope. This is so particularly where, as here, that very term — a limitation on the incurrence of additional debt — has in other past contexts been expressly bargained for; particularly where the indentures grant the company broad discretion in the management of its affairs, as plaintiffs admit, P. Mem. at 35; particularly where the indentures explicitly set forth specific provisions for the adoption of new covenants and restrictions, *see, e.g.*, Bradley Aff. Exh. L, § 9.1(c); and especially where there has been no breach of the parties' bargained-for contractual rights on which the implied covenant necessarily is based. While the Court stands ready to employ an implied covenant of good faith to ensure that such bargained-for rights are performed and upheld, it will not, however, permit an implied covenant to shoehorn into an indenture additional terms plaintiffs now wish had been included. *See also Broad v. Rockwell International Corp.*, 642 F.2d 929 (5th Cir.) (en banc) (applying New York law), *cert. denied*, 454 U.S. 965, 102 S. Ct. 506, 70 L. Ed. 2d 380 (1981) (finding no liability pursuant to an implied covenant where the terms of the indenture, as bargained for, were enforced).[40]

---

defendants' proof concerning the financing of the LBO and the company's current equity base. *See supra* at 4-5. Consequently, the Court rejects plaintiffs' general assertion that the LBO "subjects existing debtholders to dramatically greater risk of non-payment, and the Company to a significant risk of insolvency." Am. Comp. P. 26. In brief, there is no implied covenant restricting any action that might subject plaintiffs' investment to greater risk of non-payment. What plaintiffs have failed to allege is that an interest or principal payment due them has not been paid, or that any other explicit contractual right has not been honored.

[40] [25] The cases relied on by plaintiffs are not to the contrary. They invoke an implied covenant where it proves necessary to fulfill the explicit terms of an agreement, or to give meaning to ambiguous terms. *See, e.g., Grad v. Roberts*, 14 N.Y.2d 70, 248 N.Y.S.2d 633, 636, 198 N.E.2d 26, 28 (1964) (court relied on implied covenant to effect "performance of [an] option agreement according to its terms"); *Zilg v. Prentice-Hall, Inc.*, 717 F.2d 671 (2d Cir. 1983), *cert. denied*, 466 U.S. 938, 104 S. Ct. 1911, 80 L. Ed. 2d 460 (1984). In *Zilg*, the Second Circuit first described a contract which, on its face, established the publisher's obligation to publish, advertise and publicize the book at issue. The court then determined that "the contract in question establishes a relationship between the publisher and author which implies an obligation upon the former to make certain [good faith] efforts in publishing a book it has accepted notwithstanding the clause which leaves the number of volumes to be printed and the advertising budget to the publisher's discretion." 717 F.2d at 679. In other words, the court there sought to ensure a meaningful fulfillment of the contract's express terms. *See also Van Gemert I, supra; Pittsburgh*

Plaintiffs argue in the most general terms that the fundamental basis of all these indentures was that an LBO along the lines of the recent RJR Nabisco transaction would never be undertaken, that indeed no action would be taken, intentionally or not, that would significantly deplete the company's assets. Accepting plaintiffs' theory, their fundamental bargain with defendants dictated that nothing would be done to jeopardize the extremely high probability that the company would remain able to make interest payments and repay principal over the 20 to 30 year indenture term — and perhaps by logical extension even included the right to ask a court "to make sure that plaintiffs had made a good investment." *Gardner*, 589 F. Supp. at 674. But as Judge Knapp aptly concluded in *Gardner*, "Defendants . . . were under a duty to carry out the terms of the contract, but not to make sure that plaintiffs had made a good investment. The former they have done; the latter we have no jurisdiction over." *Id.* Plaintiffs' submissions and MetLife's previous undisputed internal memoranda remind the Court that a "fundamental basis" or a "fruit of an agreement" is often in the eye of the beholder, whose vision may well change along with the market, and who may, with hindsight, imagine a different bargain than the one he actually and initially accepted with open eyes. The sort of unbounded and one-sided elasticity urged by plaintiffs would interfere with and destabilize the market. And this Court, like the parties to these contracts, cannot ignore or disavow the marketplace in which the contract is performed. Nor can it ignore the expectations of that market — expectations, for instance, that the terms of an indenture will be upheld, and that a court will not, sua sponte, add new substantive terms to that indenture as it sees fit.[41] The Court has no reason to believe that the market, in evaluating bonds such as those at issue here, did not discount for the possibility that any company, even one the size of RJR Nabisco, might engage in an LBO heavily financed by debt. That the bonds did not lose any of their value until the October 20, 1988 announcement of a possible RJR Nabisco LBO only suggests that the market had theretofore evaluated the risks of such a transaction as slight.

The Court recognizes that the market is not a static entity, but instead involves what plaintiffs call "evolving understanding[s]." P. Opp. at 21. Just as the growing prevalence of LBO's has helped change certain ground rules and expectations in the field of mergers and acquisitions, so too it has obviously affected the bond market, a fact no one disputes. *See, e.g.*, *Chappell Dep.* at 136 ("I think we would have been extremely naive not to understand what was happening in the marketplace."). To support their argument that defendants have violated an implied covenant, plaintiffs contend that, since the October 20, 1988 announcement, the bond market has

Terminal, *supra*. In the latter two cases, the courts sought to protect the bondholders' express, bargained-for rights.

[41] [26] *Cf. Broad v. Rockwell*, 642 F.2d at 943 ("Not least among the parties "who must comply with or refer to the indenture' are the members of the investing public and their investment advisors. A large degree of uniformity in the language of debenture indentures is essential to the effective functioning of the financial markets: uniformity of the indentures that govern competing debenture issues is what makes it possible meaningfully to compare one debenture issue with another, focusing only on the business provisions of the issue. . . .") (citation omitted); *Sharon Steel Corporation v. Chase Manhattan Bank, N.A.*, 691 F.2d. 1039, 1048 (2d Cir. 1982) (Winter, J.) ("[U]niformity in interpretation is important to the efficiency of capital markets. . . . [T]he creation of enduring uncertainties as to the meaning of boilerplate provisions would decrease the value of all debenture issues and greatly impair the efficient working of capital markets.").

"stopped functioning." Tr. at 9. They argue that if they had "sold and abandoned the market [before October 20, 1988], the market, if everyone had the same attitude, would have disappeared." Tr. at 15. What plaintiffs term "stopped functioning" or "disappeared," however, are properly seen as natural responses and adjustments to market realities. Plaintiffs of course do not contend that no new issues are being sold, or that existing issues are no longer being traded or have become worthless. To respond to changed market forces, new indenture provisions can be negotiated, such as provisions that were in fact once included in the 8.9 percent and 10.25 percent debentures implicated by this action. New provisions could include special debt restrictions or change-of-control covenants. There is no guarantee, of course, that companies like RJR Nabisco would accept such new covenants; parties retain the freedom to enter into contracts as they choose. But presumably, multi-billion dollar investors like plaintiffs have some say in the terms of the investments they make and continue to hold. And, presumably, companies like RJR Nabisco need the infusions of capital such investors are capable of providing. Whatever else may be true about this case, it certainly does not present an example of the classic sort of form contract or contract of adhesion often frowned upon by courts. In those cases, what motivates a court is the strikingly inequitable nature of the parties' respective bargaining positions. *See generally*, Rakoff, *Contracts of Adhesion: An Essay in Reconstruction*, 96 Harv. L. Rev. 1173 (1982). Plaintiffs here entered this "liquid trading market," P. Mem. at 17, with their eyes open and were free to leave at any time. Instead they remained there notwithstanding its well understood risks. Ultimately, plaintiffs cannot escape the inherent illogic of their argument. On the one hand, it is undisputed that investors like plaintiffs recognized that companies like RJR Nabisco strenuously opposed additional restrictive covenants that might limit the incurrence of new debt or the company's ability to engage in a merger.[42] Furthermore, plaintiffs argue that they had no choice other than to accept the indentures as written, without additional restrictive covenants, or to "abandon" the market. Tr. at 14-15.

Yet on the other hand, plaintiffs ask this Court to imply a covenant that would have just that restrictive effect because, they contend, it reflects precisely the fundamental assumption of the market and the fundamental basis of their bargain with defendants. If that truly were the case here, it is difficult to imagine why an insistence on that term would have forced the plaintiffs to abandon the market. The Second Circuit has offered a better explanation: "[a] promise by the defendant should be implied only if the court may rightfully assume that the parties would have included it in their written agreement had their attention been called to it. . . . Any such assumption in this case would be completely unwarranted." *Neuman v. Pike*, 591 F.2d 191, 195 (2d Cir. 1979) (emphasis added, citations omitted). In the final analysis, plaintiffs offer no objective or reasonable standard for a court to use in its effort to define the sort of actions their "implied covenant" would permit a corporation to take, and those it would not.[43] Plaintiffs say only that

[42] [27] *See, e.g.*, MetLife Memorandum, dated August 20, 1982, attached as Bradley Reply Aff. Exh. D, at 3; MetLife Memorandum, dated November 1985, attached as Bradley Resp. Aff. Exh. A, at 8.

[43] [28] Under plaintiffs' theory, bondholders might ask a court to prohibit a company like RJR Nabisco not only from engaging in an LBO, but also from entering a new line of business — with the attendant costs of building new physical plants and hiring new workers — or from acquiring new

investors like themselves rely upon the "skill" and "good faith" of a company's board and management, *see, e.g.*, P. Mem. at 35, and that their covenant would prevent the company from "destroy[ing] . . . the legitimate expectations of its long-term bondholders." *Id.* at 54. As is clear from the preceding discussion, however, plaintiffs have failed to convince the Court that by upholding the explicit, bargained-for terms of the indenture, RJR Nabisco has either exhibited bad faith or destroyed plaintiffs' legitimate, protected expectations.

Plaintiffs argue that defendants have sought to blame plaintiffs themselves for whatever losses they may have incurred. Yet this Court need not address whether plaintiffs are at fault, or whether they assumed a risk in any tort sense, or whether they should never have agreed to exchange the specific debt provisions in at least two of the covenants at issue for alternative benefits and public covenants. Instead, it concludes that courts are properly reluctant to imply into an integrated agreement terms that have been and remain subject to specific, explicit provisions, where the parties are sophisticated investors, well versed in the market's assumptions, and do not stand in a fiduciary relationship with one another. It is also not to say that defendants were free willfully or knowingly to misrepresent or omit material facts to sell their bonds. Relief on claims based on such allegations would of course be available to plaintiffs, if appropriate[44] — but those claims properly sound in fraud, and come with requisite elements. Plaintiffs also remain free to assert their claims based on the fraudulent conveyance laws, which similarly require specific proof.[45] Those burdens cannot be avoided by resorting to an overbroad, superficially appealing, but legally insufficient, implied covenant of good faith and fair dealing.

2. Count Five: In Equity:

Count Five substantially restates and realleges the contract claims advanced in Count I. Compare, *e.g.*, Am. Comp. PP 33, 35 ("The transaction contradicts the premise of the investment grade market and invalidates the blue chip rating that [RJR Nabisco] solicited and took the benefit from. . . . In the 'buy-out,' [RJR Nabisco] breaches the duty of good faith and fair dealing . . .") with Am. Comp. PP 51-52 ("The 'buy-out' was not contemplated at the time the debt was issued, contradicts the premise of the investment grade ratings that RJR Nabisco actively solicited and received, and is inconsistent with the understandings of the market. . . . The 'buy-out'. . . is contrary to the implied representations made by RJR Nabisco . . . that it would act consistently with its obligations of good faith and fair dealing.") Along with these repetitions, plaintiffs blend in allegations that the transaction "frustrates the commercial purpose" of the parties, under "circumstances [that] are outrageous, and . . . it would [therefore] be unconscionable to allow the 'buy-out' to proceed. . . ." *Id.* PP 52-53. Those very issues — frustration of purpose and unconscionability — are equally matters of contract law, of course, and plaintiffs could just as easily have advanced them in Count I. Indeed, to some extent plaintiffs did advance these claims in that Count. *See, e.g.*, Am. Comp. P. 34

businesses such as RJR Nabisco did when it acquired Del Monte.

[44] [29] The Court, of course, today takes no position on this issue.

[45] [30] As noted elsewhere, plaintiffs can also allege violations of express terms of the indentures.

("RJR Nabisco owes a continuing duty . . . not to frustrate the purpose of the contracts. . . ."). For present purposes, it makes no difference how plaintiffs characterize their arguments.[46] Their equity claims cannot survive defendants' motion for summary judgment.

In their papers, plaintiffs variously attempt to justify Count V as being based on unjust enrichment, frustration of purpose, an alleged breach of something approaching a fiduciary duty, or a general claim of unconscionability. Each claim fails. First, as even plaintiffs recognize, an unjust enrichment claim requires a court first to find that "the circumstances [are] such that in equity and good conscience the defendant should make restitution." *See, e.g., Chase Manhattan Bank v. Banque Intra, S.A.*, 274 F. Supp. 496, 499 (S.D.N.Y. 1967); P. Mem. at 56. Plaintiffs have not alleged a violation of a single explicit term of the indentures at issue, and on the facts alleged this Court has determined that an implicit covenant of good faith and fair dealing has not been violated. Under these circumstances, this Court concludes that defendants need not, "in equity and good conscience," make restitution.

Second, in support of their motions plaintiffs claim frustration of purpose. Yet even resolving all ambiguities and drawing all reasonable inferences in plaintiffs' favor, their claim cannot stand. A claim of frustration of purpose has three elements: First, the purpose that is frustrated must have been a principal purpose of that party in making the contract. . . . The object must be so completely the basis of the contract that, as both parties understand, without it the transaction would make little sense. Second, the frustration must be substantial. It is not enough that the transaction has become less profitable for the affected party or even that he will sustain a loss. The frustration must be so severe that it is not fairly to be regarded as within the risks that he assumed under the contract. Third, the non-occurrence of the frustrating event must have been a basic assumption on which the contract was made. Restatement (Second) of Contracts, 265 comment a (1981). In *The Murphy Door Bed Co., Inc. v. Interior Sleep Systems, Inc.*, 874 F.2d 95 (2d Cir. 1989), defendants argued that the contract was void ab initio since its purpose, allegedly the conveyance of trademark rights, was frustrated because the mark was generic. However, the Second Circuit concluded, "there is no indication that a transfer of trademark rights was the essence of the distributorship agreement. . . ." *Id.* at 102-03. Similarly, there is no indication here that an alleged refusal to incur debt to facilitate an LBO was the "essence" or "principal purpose" of the indentures, and no mention of such an alleged restriction is made in the

---

[46] [31] For much the same reason, the Court rejects defendants' reliance on cases like *In re Kemp & Beatley, Inc.*, 64 N.Y.2d 63, 70, 484 N.Y.S.2d 799, 803, 473 N.E.2d 1173, 1177 (1984), for "the ancient principle that equity jurisdiction will not lie when there exists a remedy at law." *See, e.g.*, D. Mem. at 26. That case contemplated a classic equitable remedy — the dissolution of a corporation. And in that respect, it accurately set forth a rule of law; no court will, for instance, enter an injunction or order specific performance or dissolution if an adequate legal remedy remains available. The Court has already denied plaintiffs' request for an injunction. To the extent that Count V does in fact merely restate plaintiffs' prayer for injunctive relief — "it would be unconscionable to allow the 'buy-out' to proceed until defendants make restitution to the debtholders," Am. Comp. P. 53 — it is of course inappropriate. As far as the Court can determine, however, and reading plaintiffs' "In Equity" Count as charitably as possible, the claims advanced by plaintiffs in Count V do not necessarily seek such an exclusive remedy. In general, remedies based on claims of unjust enrichment or frustration of purpose are certainly quantifiable and subject to money damages, and would thus support a legal remedy.

agreements. Further, while plaintiffs' bonds may have lost some of their value, "[d]ischarge under this doctrine has been limited to instances where a virtually cataclysmic, wholly unforeseeable event renders the contract valueless to one party." *United States v. General Douglas MacArthur Senior Village, Inc.*, 508 F.2d 377, 381 (2d Cir. 1974) (emphasis added). That is not the case here. Moreover, "the frustration of purpose defense is not available where, as here, the event which allegedly frustrated the purpose of the contract . . . was clearly foreseeable." *VJK Productions v. Friedman/Meyer Productions*, 565 F. Supp. 916 (S.D.N.Y. 1983) (citation omitted). Faced with MetLife's internal memoranda, *see, e.g.*, Bradley Resp. Aff. Exh. A, plaintiffs cannot but admit that "MetLife has been concerned about "buy-outs' for several years." P. Opp. at 5. Nor do plaintiffs provide any reasonable basis for believing that a party as sophisticated as Jefferson-Pilot was any less cognizant of the market around it.[47]

Third, plaintiffs advance a claim that remains based, their assertions to the contrary notwithstanding, on an alleged breach of a fiduciary duty.[48] Defendants go to great lengths to prove that the law of Delaware, and not New York, governs this question. Defendants' attempt to rely on Delaware law is readily explained by even a cursory reading of *Simons v. Cogan*, 549 A.2d 300, 303 (Del. 1988), the recent Delaware Supreme Court ruling which held, inter alia, that a corporate bond "represents a contractual entitlement to the repayment of a debt and does not represent an equitable interest in the issuing corporation necessary for the imposition of a trust relationship with concomitant fiduciary duties." Before such a fiduciary duty arises, "an existing property right or equitable interest supporting such a duty must exist." *Id.* at 304. A bondholder, that court concluded, "acquires no equitable interest, and remains a creditor of the corporation whose interests are protected by the contractual terms of the indenture." *Id.* Defendants argue that

---

[47] [32] At least one of Jefferson-Pilot's directors — Clemmie Dixon Spangler — not only was aware of the possibility of an LBO of a company like RJR Nabisco, but he also in fact proposed an LBO of RJR Nabisco itself, a fact plaintiffs do not dispute. See Bradley Aff. P. 28, Exh. R. Spangler apparently never mentioned his unsolicited bid for RJR Nabisco to his fellow Jefferson-Pilot directors.

[48] [33] While the Court reads plaintiffs' Amended Complaint and submissions as charitably as it can, it nonetheless has trouble with assertions such as this: "The right of unsecured creditors [like plaintiffs] against having the [c]ompany's assets stripped away is not in the nature of broad fiduciary duty, but rather a specific charge, founded in principles of equity and tort law of New York and other jurisdictions. . . ." P. Mem. at 51-52. Any such "charge" — beyond a potential fiduciary duty the Court now addresses, see *infra* — is not, however, so "specific" as to have been stated with any clarity by any one court. Indeed, cases relied upon by plaintiffs to support their "In Equity" Count focus on fraudulent schemes or conveyances. *See, e.g., United States v. Tabor Court Realty Corp.*, 803 F.2d 1288, 1295 (3d Cir. 1986) (explaining lower court's findings in *United States v. Gleneagles Investment Co.*, 565 F. Supp. 556 (M.D. Pa. 1983)); *Pepper v. Litton*, 308 U.S. 295, 296, 60 S. Ct. 238, 84 L. Ed. 281 (1939) ("The findings by the District Court, amply supported by the evidence, reveal a scheme to defraud creditors . . ."); *Harff v. Kerkorian*, 347 A.2d 133, 134 (Del. 1975) (bondholders limited to contract claims in absence of "'fraud, insolvency, or a violation of a statute.'") (citation omitted). Moreover, if the Court here were confronted with an insolvent corporation, which is not the case, the company's officers and directors might become trustees of its assets for the protection of its creditors, among others. *See, e.g., New York Credit Men's Adjustment Bureau v. Weiss*, 278 A.D. 501, 503, 105 N.Y.S.2d 604, 606 (1st Dept. 1951), *aff'd*, 305 N.Y. 1, 110 N.E.2d 397 (1953). If not based on a fiduciary duty and the other equitable principles addressed by the Court, plaintiffs' claim, in effect, asks this Court to use its broad equitable powers to fashion a new cause of action that would adopt precisely the same arguments the Court rejected in Count I.

New York law is not to the contrary, but the single Supreme Court case they cite — a case decided over fifty years ago that was not squarely presented with the issue addressed by the Simons court — provides something less than dispositive support. *See Marx v. Merchants' National Properties, Inc.*, 148 Misc. 6, 7, 265 N.Y.S. 163, 165 (1933). For their part, plaintiffs more convincingly demonstrate that New York law applies than that New York law recognizes their claim.[49] Regardless, this Court finds *Simons* persuasive, and believes that a New York court would agree with that conclusion. In the venerable case of *Meinhard v. Salmon*, 249 N.Y. 458, 164 N.E. 545 (1928), then Chief Judge Cardozo explained the obligations imposed on a fiduciary, and why those obligations are so special and rare:

> Many forms of conduct permissible in a workaday world for those acting at arm's length, are forbidden to those bound by fiduciary ties. A trustee is held to something stricter than the morals of the market place. Not honesty alone, but the punctilio of an honor the most sensitive, is then the standard of behavior. As to this there has developed a tradition that is unbending and inveterate. Uncompromising rigidity has been the attitude of courts of equity when petitioned to undermine the rule of undivided loyalty. . . . Only thus has the level of conduct for fiduciaries been kept at a level higher than that trodden by the crowd.

Id. at 464 (citation omitted). Before a court recognizes the duty of a "punctilio of an honor the most sensitive," it must be certain that the complainant is entitled to more than the "morals of the market place," and the protections offered by actions based on fraud, state statutes or the panoply of available federal securities laws. This Court has concluded that the plaintiffs presently before it — sophisticated investors who are unsecured creditors — are not entitled to such additional protections.

Equally important, plaintiffs' position on this issue — that "A Company May Not Deliberately Deplete its Assets to the Injury of its Debtholders," P. Mem. at 42 — provides no reasonable or workable limits, and is thus reminiscent of their implied covenant of good faith. Indeed, many indisputably legitimate corporate transactions would not survive plaintiffs' theory. With no workable limits, plaintiffs' envisioned duty would extend equally to trade creditors, employees, and every other person to whom the defendants are liable in any way. Of all such parties, these informed plaintiffs least require a Court's equitable protection; not only are they willing participants in a largely impersonal market, but they also possess the financial sophistication and size to secure their own protection.

Finally, plaintiffs cannot seriously allege unconscionability, given their sophistication and, at least judging from this action, the sophistication of their legal counsel

---

[49] [34] The indenture provision designating New York law as controlling, see *supra* n. 10, would, one might assume, resolve at least the issue of the applicable law. In quoting the relevant indenture provision, however, plaintiffs omit the proviso "except as may otherwise be required by mandatory provisions of law." P. Mem. at 52, n. 46. Defendants, however, fail to argue that the internal affairs doctrine, which they assert dictates that Delaware law controls this question, is such a "mandatory provision of law." Nor do defendants respond to plaintiffs' reliance on *First National City Bank v. Banco Para El Comercio*, 462 U.S. 611, 621, 103 S. Ct. 2591, 2597, 77 L. Ed. 2d 46 (1983) ("Different conflicts principles apply, however, where the rights of third parties external to the corporation are at issue.") (emphasis in original, citation omitted). Ultimately, the point is academic; as explained below, the Court would grant defendants summary judgment on this Count under either New York or Delaware law.

as well. Under the undisputed facts of this case, see *supra* at 13-20, this Court finds no actionable unconscionability.

. . .

NOTES

(1) RJR Nabisco was the last and most noteworthy[50] contested leveraged acquisition in the 1980s, a decade marked by a number of such transactions. Because underlying asset values had appreciated substantially more than share prices, so-called financial (as opposed to strategic) buyers could finance premium acquisition prices by borrowing against the target's asset base and amortizing the acquisition debt by selling various business segments of the target. In many instances, the new owner thus acquired the remaining "core" business at no out-of-pocket cost, or sold the entire acquired enterprise for a monetary profit.

Such transactions were not without their critics. Felix Rohatyn, whose views on related subjects are noted in Chapter 1, *supra*, has posed the question as to whether substantial publicly held corporations should "be treated as artichokes and simply torn apart without regard for employees, communities, or customers, solely in order to pay off speculative debt," quoted in BRUCE WASSERSTEIN, BIG DEAL 134 (1998).

(2) As the court notes in the text preceding footnote 17 of its opinion, the rating agencies' evaluation of the RJR Nabisco bonds largely determined the market value thereof.

(3) In the light of decisions such as *Metropolitan Life*, indentures written after leveraged buy-out transactions came into vogue, often contain so-called "poison put" provisions requiring an issuer, which was the subject of a leveraged buy-out, to redeem debentures at the election of the holder thereof. An example of such a provision follows.

Redemption at Holder's Option

Right to Redemption.

> (a) After the occurrence of a Redemption Event, each Holder of Securities shall have the right, at the Holder's option, to require the Company to redeem on the Redemption Date all or any portion (equal to $1,000 or any integral multiple thereof) of the Holder's Securities for cash at the Redemption Price specified in the fourth paragraph on the reverse side of the form of Security hereinbefore set forth together with accrued interest, if any, from the last Interest Payment Date to which interest has been paid or duly provided for (or if no interest has been paid or duly provided for, from, 1999) thereon to the Redemption Date.
>
> (b) A "Redemption Event" shall be deemed to have occurred upon the occurrence of either of the following events:

[50] The RJR deal was the subject of the best seller BARBARIANS AT THE GATE, by Bryan Burrough and John Helyer, published in 1990 by Harper & Row, and of a movie with the same title.

(i) Any Person or any Persons acting together which would constitute a "group" for purposes of Section 13(d) of the Securities Exchange Act of 1934, as amended (the "Exchange Act") (a "Group"), together with any Affiliates thereof, shall beneficially own (as defined in Rule 13d-3 of the Exchange Act) at least 50% of the total voting power of all classes of Capital Stock of the Company entitled to vote generally in the election of directors of the Company; or

(ii) Any Person or Group, together with any Affiliates thereof, shall succeed in having sufficient of its or their nominees elected to the Board of Directors of the Company such that such nominees, when added to any existing director remaining on the Board of Directors of the Company after such election who is an Affiliate of such Group, shall constitute a majority of the Board of Directors of the Company.

(4) Another form of contractual protection against a ratings downgrade is the "Step-Up Coupon," which provides in effect that if the credit rating of a particular debt instrument deteriorates, the contractual (or coupon) interest rate automatically increases.

§ 3.05 REDEMPTION PROVISIONS

Set forth below is a form of Notice of Redemption relating to Debentures.

CHRISTINA COSMETICS, INC.
10% SUBORDINATED DEBENTURES

NOTICE OF REDEMPTION ____________

To: All Holders of 10% Subordinated Debentures of Christina Cosmetics, Inc.

Ladies and Gentlemen:

This notice is delivered to you by Christina Cosmetics, Inc., a Wisconsin corporation (the "Company"), in connection with *the exercise* of the Company's *right to cause the optional redemption* (the "Redemption") of the Company's 10% Subordinated Debentures (the "Debentures") pursuant to the terms of the Debentures and Section 4.02 of the Indenture, dated as of December 22, 2002 (the "Indenture"), between the Company and The Hobart State Bank, Geneva, N.Y., a national banking association, as Trustee (the "Trustee").

On December 5, 2010 (the "Redemption Date"), all of the Debentures issued and outstanding under the Indenture shall be redeemed at a redemption price (the "Redemption Price") equal to one hundred percent (100%) of the principal amount of Debentures being redeemed, together in each case with interest accrued to the Redemption Date.

Payment of the Redemption Price, together in each case with interest accrued to the Redemption Date, shall be made to the registered holders thereof, payable on the Redemption Date, after presentation and surrender of the Debentures at the offices of the Trustee, 100 Main Street, Geneva, N.Y. 07095 Attn: Corporate Trust Department, Room 105.

Interest on the Debentures accrued to the Redemption Date together with the Redemption Price shall be payable on the Redemption Date as aforesaid, and NO INTEREST SHALL ACCRUE ON THE DEBENTURES ON AND AFTER THE REDEMPTION DATE, in accordance with the terms of the Debentures and the Indenture. Debenture holders should deliver all Debentures to the Trustee at the foregoing address as soon as possible in advance of the Redemption Date, and in accordance with any instructions delivered herewith by the Trustee.

UPON DEPOSIT BY THE COMPANY WITH THE TRUSTEE OF FUNDS SUFFICIENT TO REDEEM THE DEBENTURES ON THE REDEMPTION DATE, TOGETHER IN EACH CASE WITH INTEREST ACCRUED TO THE REDEMPTION DATE, ALL OBLIGATIONS OF THE COMPANY IN RESPECT OF THE DEBENTURES SHALL CEASE AND BE DISCHARGED, AND THE HOLDERS OF THE DEBENTURES SHALL THEREAFTER BE RESTRICTED EXCLUSIVELY TO SUCH FUNDS FOR ANY AND ALL CLAIMS OF WHATEVER NATURE ON THEIR PART UNDER THE INDENTURE, OR IN RESPECT OF THE DEBENTURES. In accordance with the Indenture and subject to applicable law, any moneys so deposited with the Trustee, and not applied to such payment within six (6) years after the date that the Indenture shall be satisfied and discharged, by such deposit together with payment of any and all fees and expenses of the Trustee and other sums payable by the Company under the Indenture, shall be repaid to the Company on its written demand. Thereafter the Trustee shall be released from all further liability with respect to such moneys, and any holder of Debentures entitled to receive such payment shall thereafter look only to the Company. In any event, as aforesaid, no interest shall accrue on the Debentures on and after the Redemption Date.

Dated: November 5, 2010

Very truly yours,
CHRISTINA COSMETICS, INC.

MORGAN STANLEY & CO. v. ARCHER DANIELS MIDLAND CO.

United States District Court, Southern District of New York
570 F. Supp. 1529 (1983)

SAND, DISTRICT JUDGE

This action . . . arises out of the planned redemption of $125 million in 16% Sinking Fund Debentures ("the Debentures") by the defendant ADM Midland Company ("ADM") scheduled to take place on Monday, August 1st, 1983. Morgan Stanley & Company, Inc. ("Morgan Stanley") brings this suit under § 10(b) of the Securities Exchange Act of 1934, 15 U.S.C. § 78j, § 17(a) of the Securities Act of

1933, 15 U.S.C. § 77q, §§ 323(a) and 316(b) of the Trust Indenture Act of 1939, 15 U.S.C. §§ 77www(a), 77ppp(b), and other state and federal laws, alleging that the proposed redemption plan is barred by the terms of the Indenture, the language of the Debentures, and the Debenture Prospectus. Plaintiff contends, in addition, that the failure on the part of ADM to reveal its intention to redeem the Debentures, as well as its belief that such redemption would be lawful under the terms of the Indenture Agreement, amounts to an intentional, manipulative scheme to defraud in violation of federal and state securities and business laws. Morgan Stanley seeks a preliminary injunction enjoining ADM from consummating the redemption as planned, and, after full consideration on the merits, permanent injunctive relief barring the proposed transaction and damages. Both parties have pursued an expedited discovery schedule and now cross-move for summary judgment.

FACTS

In May, 1981, Archer Daniels issued $125,000,000 of 16% Sinking Fund Debentures due May 15, 2011. The managing underwriters of the Debenture offering were Goldman Sachs & Co., Kidder Peabody & Co., and Merrill Lynch, Pierce, Fenner & Smith, Inc. The Debentures state in relevant part:

The Debentures are subject to redemption upon not less than 30 nor more than 60 days' notice by mail, at any time, in whole or in part, at the election of the Company, at the following optional Redemption Price (expressed in percentages of the principal amount), together with accrued interest to the Redemption Date . . . , all as provided in the Indenture: If redeemed during the twelve-month period beginning May 15 of the years indicated:

Year	**Percentage**	**Year**	**Percentage**
1981	115.500%	1991	107.750%
1982	114.725	1992	106.975
1983	113.950	1993	106.200
1984	113.175	1994	105.425
1985	112.400	1995	104.650
1986	111.625	1996	103.875
1987	110.850	1997	103.100
1988	110.075	1998	102.325
1989	109.300	1999	101.550
1990	108.525	2000	100.775

and thereafter at 100%; provided, however, that prior to May 15, 1991, the Company may not redeem any of the Debentures pursuant to such option from the proceeds, or in anticipation, of the issuance of any indebtedness for money borrowed by or for the account of the Company or any Subsidiary (as defined in the Indenture) or from the proceeds, or in anticipation of a sale and leaseback transaction (as defined in Section 1008 of the Indenture), if, in either case, the interest cost or interest factor applicable thereto (calculated in accordance with generally accepted financial practice) shall be less than 16.08% per annum.

The May 12, 1981 Prospectus and the Indenture pursuant to which the

Debentures were issued contain substantially similar language.[51] The Moody's Bond Survey of April 27, 1981, in reviewing its rating of the Debentures, described the redemption provision in the following manner:

> The 16% sinking fund debentures are nonrefundable with lower cost interest debt before April 15, 1991. Otherwise, they are callable in whole or in part at prices to be determined.

The proceeds of the Debenture offering were applied to the purchase of long-term government securities bearing rates of interest below 16.089%.

ADM raised money through public borrowing at interest rates less than 16.08% on at least two occasions subsequent to the issuance of the Debentures. On May 7, 1982, over a year before the announcement of the planned redemption, ADM borrowed $50,555,500 by the issuance of $400,000,000 face amount zero coupon debentures due 2002 and $100,000,000 face amount zero coupon notes due 1992 (the "Zeroes"). The Zeroes bore an effective interest rate of less than 16.08%. On March 10, 1983, ADM raised an additional $86,400,000 by the issuance of $263,232,500 face amount Secured Trust Accrual Receipts, known as "Stars," through a wholly-owned subsidiary, Midland Stars Inc. The Stars carry an effective interest rate of less than 16.08%. The Stars were in the form of notes with varying maturities secured by government securities deposited by ADM with a trustee established for that purpose. There is significant dispute between the parties as to whether the Stars transaction should be treated as an issuance of debt or as a sale of government securities. We assume, for purposes of this motion, that the transaction resulted in the incurring of debt.

In the period since the issuance of the Debentures, ADM also raised money

---

[51] [1] The May 12, 1981 Prospectus announcing the issuance of the Debentures provides, in relevant part:

The Sinking Fund Debentures will be subject to redemption, upon not less than 30 nor more than 60 days' notice by mail, (1) on May 15 in any year commencing with the year 1992 and ending with the year 2010 through operation of the sinking fund at a Redemption Price equal to 100% of the principal amount, and (2) at any time, in whole or in part, at the election of the Company, at a Redemption Price equal to the percentage of the principal amount set forth below if redeemed during the twelve-month period beginning May 15 of the years indicated:

. . .

and thereafter at a Redemption Price equal to 100% of the principal amount, together in each case with accrued interest to the Redemption Date, provided, however, that the Company will not be entitled to redeem any of the Sinking Fund Debentures prior to May 15, 1991 as part of a refunding or anticipated refunding operation by the application, directly or indirectly, of the proceeds of indebtedness for money borrowed which shall have an interest cost of less than 16.03% per annum.

The Indenture provides, in relevant part:

The Debentures may be redeemed, otherwise than through the operation of the sinking fund provided for in Article Twelve, at the election of the Company, as a whole or from time to time in part, at any time, subject to the conditions and at the Redemption Prices specified in the second paragraph on the reverse side of the form of Debenture hereinbefore set forth; provided, however, that prior to May 15, 1991, the Company may not redeem any of the Debentures pursuant to such option from the proceeds, or in anticipation, of the issuance of any indebtedness for money borrowed by or for the account of the Company or any Subsidiary or from the proceeds, or in anticipation, of a sale and leaseback transaction (as defined in Section 1008), if, in either case, the interest cost or interest factor applicable thereto (calculated in accordance with generally accepted financial practice) shall be less than 16.08% per annum.

through two common stock offerings. Six million shares of common stock were issued by prospectus dated January 28, 1983, resulting in proceeds of $131,370,000. And by a prospectus supplement dated June 1, 1983, ADM raised an additional $15,450,000 by issuing 600,000 shares of common stock.

Morgan Stanley, the plaintiff in this action, bought $15,518,000 principal amount of the Debentures at $1,252.50 per $1,000 face amount on May 5, 1983, and $500,000 principal amount at $1,200 per $1,000 face amount on May 31, 1983. The next day, June 1, ADM announced that it was calling for the redemption of the 16% Sinking Fund Debentures, effective August 1, 1983. The direct source of funds was to be the two ADM common stock offerings of January and June, 1983. The proceeds of these offerings were delivered to the Indenture Trustee, Morgan Guaranty Trust Company, and deposited in a special account to be applied to the redemption. The amount deposited with the Indenture Trustee is sufficient to fully redeem the Debentures.

Prior to the announcement of the call for redemption, the Debentures were trading at a price in excess of the $1,139.50 call price. At no time prior to the June 1 announcement did ADM indicate in any of its materials filed with the Securities and Exchange Commission or otherwise that it intended to exercise its redemption rights if it felt it was in its self-interest to do so. Nor did it express any contemporaneous opinion as to whether it was entitled under the terms of the Indenture to call the Debentures when it was borrowing funds at an interest rate less than 16.08% if the source of such redemption was other than the issuance of debt.

Plaintiff's allegations can be reduced to two general claims: First, plaintiff contends that the proposed redemption is barred by the express terms of the call provisions of the Debenture and the Indenture Agreement, and that consummation of the plan would violate the Trust Indenture Act of 1939, 15 U.S.C. § 77aaa *et seq.* and common law principles of contract law. The plaintiff's claim is founded on the language contained in the Debenture and Trust Indenture that states that the company may not redeem the Debentures "from the proceeds, or in anticipation, of the issuance of any indebtedness . . . if . . . the interest cost or interest factor . . . [is] less than 16.08% per annum." Plaintiff points to the $86,400,000 raised by the Stars transaction within 90 days of the June 1 redemption announcement, and the $50,555,500 raised by the Zeroes transaction in May, 1982 — both at interest rates below 16.08% — as proof that the redemption is being funded, at least indirectly, from the proceeds of borrowing in violation of the Debentures and Indenture agreement. The fact that ADM raised sufficient funds to redeem the Debentures entirely through the issuance of common stock is, according to the plaintiffs, an irrelevant "juggling of funds" used to circumvent the protections afforded investors by the redemption provisions of the Debenture. Plaintiff would have the Court interpret the provision as barring redemption during any period when the issuer has borrowing at a rate lower than that prescribed by the Debentures, regardless of whether the direct source of the funds is the issuance of equity, the sale of assets, or merely cash on hand.

The defendant would have the Court construe the language more narrowly as barring redemption only where the direct or indirect source of the funds is a debt instrument issued at a rate lower than that it is paying on the outstanding Debentures. Where, as here, the defendant can point directly to a non-debt source of funds (the issuance of common stock), the defendant is of the view that the general redemption schedule applies.

Plaintiff's second claim, brought under federal and state securities laws and state business law, is based on the alleged failure on the part of ADM to reveal three material facts in any of the documents with the Securities and Exchange Commission or otherwise: (1) that ADM held a "highly restrictive" view of the redemption language that prohibited it from calling the Debentures only where such redemption was funded directly from an account holding the proceeds of a prohibited borrowing; (2) that ADM contemplated redemption when it deemed it to be in ADM's self-interest despite contemporaneous borrowing at rates below 16.08%; and (3) that ADM intended to use the proceeds from sale of the Debentures for speculation in long-term government securities in conjunction with a plan to call the Debentures if and when interest rates dropped. Morgan Stanley contends that the failure to disclose these facts amounted to a deceptive, misleading, and manipulative course of conduct because it fostered what it describes as the prevailing view among investors that ADM could not and would not call its Debentures in the near future.

According to Morgan Stanley, the fact that the Debentures were trading at levels above the call price prior to the redemption announcement bolsters the argument that the investing public thought it was protected against early redemption. The plaintiff asserts that it would not have bought the Debentures without what it perceived to be protection against premature redemption.

ADM contends that plaintiff's allegations of securities fraud stem in the first instance from its strained and erroneous interpretation of the redemption language. Defendant argues that the redemption language itself — a boilerplate provision found in numerous Indenture Agreements — was sufficient disclosure. Moreover, defendant asserts that it had no plan or scheme at the time the Debentures were issued to exercise its call rights in conjunction with speculation in government securities or otherwise and that the provision existed solely to offer the issuer "financial flexibility." More important, defendant contends that its view of the Debenture language was the one commonly accepted by both bondholders and the investing public. In support of this contention, defendant points to the only case directly to address the issue, *Franklin Life Insurance Co. v. Commonwealth Edison Co.*, 451 F. Supp. 602 (S.D. Ill. 1978), *aff'd, per curiam on the opinion below*, 598 F.2d 1109 (7th Cir.), *rehearing and rehearing en banc denied, id., cert. denied*, 444 U.S. 900, 100 S. Ct. 210, 62 L. Ed. 2d 136 (1979). *Franklin* held, with respect to language almost identical to that contained in the ADM Debentures, that a redemption directly funded through equity financing was not prohibited despite contemporaneous borrowing by the issuer.

Defendant contends that it first seriously contemplated redemption in the Spring of 1983 upon the suggestion of Merrill Lynch, one of its investment bankers. Merrill Lynch had received legal advice that a redemption transaction of the sort contemplated was proper under the language of the Debenture and the analysis of the Court in *Franklin*. Moreover, the defendant asserts that Morgan Stanley itself was fully aware of this interpretation of the redemption language, although it may have disagreed with it. ADM explains the high price at which the Debentures were trading prior to the redemption announcement not as a reflection of investors' belief that the Debentures were not currently redeemable, but rather as a reflection of the belief that ADM itself, or some other interested buyer, might seek to purchase the Debentures through a tender offer or other financial transaction.

DISCUSSION

. . .

Despite what plaintiff's counsel characterizes as the "monumental importance" of the ultimate ruling in this action, this dispute involves a specific quantity of fixed-term financial debentures bearing interest rates and call prices governed by a detailed Indenture. Given this detailed financial information, we can discern no reason why plaintiff could not, should it prevail on the merits, present expert testimony on the present value of debentures with similar characteristics or such other financial data necessary to calculate an income stream comparable to the redeemed Debentures. The ADM Debentures are traded nationally and while the market is rather limited, there appears to be no impediment to introducing historical data on market trends in these or similar securities for purposes of ascertaining damages. Moreover, should this task prove too difficult or imprecise, it is within the power of the Court to order ADM to reissue Debentures for the same term containing the same interest rates, as counsel for ADM conceded at oral argument.

Plaintiff's assertion that the Debentures are somehow "unique" financial instruments for which there are no comparable substitutes is unconvincing. This argument is based on two propositions: first, that the ADM Debentures are "A" rated long-term bonds issued by a financially sound company that pay a high rate of interest. Second, that the present value of the future income stream yielded by the Debentures is a function of each bondholder's subject perceptions of the market and is therefore not capable of quantification.

The fact that the Debentures are "A" rated and pay a high rate of interest over a significant period of time does not in any sense make them unique. The record reveals a number of financial instruments that are arguably comparable to the ADM Debentures with respect to interest rate, maturity and risk. To be sure, bonds of superior quality may very well be hard to come by in today's market. Nevertheless, this fact does not prove they are unique, but merely that they represent an excellent investment; should plaintiff prevail, its damages would accordingly be greater than they might be were the bonds of a lesser quality.

Plaintiff's second argument is equally unconvincing. Indeed, were the Court to accept the proposition that these Debentures were unique because of the varying subjective evaluations of the individual bondholders, we would be hard pressed to deny preliminary relief in any securities case on the grounds of a failure to show irreparable harm.

Regardless of the strength of plaintiff's claims on the merits, the lack of a colorable showing of irreparable harm would require the denial of preliminary relief on this basis alone. Even if we were to assume, arguendo, that Morgan Stanley had made out a claim for irreparable harm, it has failed to meet the additional criteria necessary for the issuance of a preliminary injunction.

With respect to the likelihood of success on the merits, defendant's interpretation of the redemption provision seems at least as likely to be in accord with the language of the Debentures, the Indenture, and the available authorities than is the view proffered by the plaintiff. We first note that the one court to directly address this issue chose to construe the language in the manner set forth in this action by the defendant. *Franklin Life Insurance Co. v. Commonwealth Edison Co.*, 451 F. Supp. 602 (S.D. Ill. 1978), *aff'd, per curiam on the opinion below*, 598 F.2d 1109 (7th Cir), *rehearing and rehearing en banc denied, id., cert. denied*, 444 U.S. 900, 100 S. Ct. 210, 62 L. Ed. 2d 136 (1979). While plaintiff is correct in noting that this Circuit is not bound by this decision, and while this case can no doubt be distinguished factually on a number of grounds, none of which we deem to be of major significance, Franklin is nevertheless persuasive authority in support of defendant's position.

Defendant's view of the redemption language is also arguably supported by The American Bar Foundation's Commentaries on Model Debenture Indenture Provisions (1977), from which the boilerplate language in question was apparently taken verbatim. In discussing the various types of available redemption provisions, the Commentaries state:

> [I]nstead of an absolute restriction [on redemption], the parties may agree that the borrower may not redeem with funds borrowed at an interest rate lower than the interest rate in the debentures. *Such an arrangement recognizes that funds for redemption may become available from other than borrowing*, but correspondingly recognizes that the debenture holder is entitled to be protected for a while against redemption if interest rates fall and the borrower can borrow funds at a lower rate to pay off the debentures.

Id. at 477 (emphasis added). We read this comment as pointing to the source of funds as the dispositive factor in determining the availability of redemption to the issuer — the position advanced by defendant ADM.

Finally, we view the redemption language itself as supporting defendant's position. The redemption provision in the Indenture and the Debentures begins with the broad statement that the Debentures are "subject to redemption . . . at any time, in whole or in part, at the election of the company, at the following optional Redemption Price. . . ." Following this language is a table of decreasing redemption percentages keyed to the year in which the redemption occurs. This broad language is then followed by the narrowing provision "provided, however . . . the Company may not redeem any of the Debentures pursuant to such option from the proceeds, or in anticipation, of the issuance of any indebtedness" borrowed at rates less than that paid on the Debentures.

While the "plain meaning" of this language is not entirely clear with respect to the question presented in this case, we think the restrictive phrasing of the redemption provision, together with its placement after broad language allowing redemption in all other cases at the election of the company, supports defendant's more restrictive reading.

Morgan Stanley asserts that defendant's view would afford bondholders no protection against redemption through lower-cost borrowing and would result in great uncertainty among holders of bonds containing similar provisions. In its view, the "plain meaning" of the redemption bondholders of these bonds and the investment community generally, is that the issuer may not redeem when it is contemporaneously engaging in lower-cost borrowing, regardless of the source of the funds for redemption. At the same time, however, the plaintiff does not contend that redemption through equity funding is prohibited for the life of the redemption restriction once the issuer borrows funds at a lower interest rate subsequent to the Debenture's issuance. On the contrary, plaintiff concedes that the legality of the redemption transaction would depend on a factual inquiry into the magnitude of the borrowing relative to the size of the contemplated equity-funded redemption and its proximity in time relative to the date the redemption was to take place. Thus, a $100 million redemption two years after a $1 million short-term debt issue might be allowable, while the same redemption six months after a $20 million long-term debt issue might not be allowable.

This case-by-case approach is problematic in a number of respects. First, it appears keyed to the subjective expectations of the bondholders; if it appears that the redemption is funded through lower-cost borrowing, based on the Company's recent or prospective borrowing history, the redemption is deemed unlawful. The approach thus reads a subjective element into what presumably should be an objective determination based on the language appearing in the bond agreement. Second, and most important, this approach would likely cause greater uncertainty among bondholders that a strict "source" rule such as that adopted in *Franklin, supra.*

Plaintiff's fear that bondholders would be left "unprotected" by adoption of the "source" rule also appears rather overstated. The rule proposed by defendant does not, as plaintiff suggests, entail a virtual emasculation of the refunding restrictions. An issuer contemplating redemption would still be required to fund such redemption from a source other than lower-cost borrowing, such as reserves, the sale of assets, or the proceeds of a common stock issue. Bondholders would thus be protected against the type of continuous short-term refunding of debt in times of plummeting interest rates that the language was apparently intended to prohibit. *See Franklin, supra*, 451 F. Supp. at 609. Moreover, this is not an instance where protections against premature redemption are wholly absent from the Debenture. On the contrary, the Debentures and the Indenture explicitly provide for early redemption expressed in declining percentages of the principal amount, depending on the year the redemption is affected.

At this early stage of the proceedings, on the record before us, and for all the reasons outlined above, we find that plaintiff has failed to show a sufficient likelihood of its success on the merits of its contract claims as to entitle it to preliminary injunctive relief.

For many of the same reasons, we also find that plaintiff has failed to show a likelihood of success on its federal and state securities and business law claims. In order to prevail on a claim of securities fraud under § 10(b) of the Securities Act of 1934 and Rule 10b-5 issued thereunder, the plaintiff must prove, inter alia, that the defendant made a material misstatement or nondisclosure, or engaged in a manipulative and deceptive course of conduct, and that the defendant acted with scienter. The requirements for a claim under § 17(a) of the Securities Act of 1933 with respect to these elements are, for purposes of this motion, the same as those under § 10(b), except that in certain cases the plaintiff may need only prove negligence. We find the evidence in the record insufficient to establish a likelihood of success with respect to both of these requirements.

ADM disclosed the redemption language both in its Prospectus and in the Indenture. It also disclosed that the proceeds of the Debenture issue would be "invested in long-term or short-term marketable securities and used to repay short-term borrowings incurred in part to purchase long-term marketable securities." These disclosures appear perfectly consistent with the purchase of long-term government securities with Debenture proceeds, and would, at first blush, appear to be adequate. To add force to its claims, plaintiff would have to establish that, at the time the securities were issued, plaintiff contemplated redeeming the Debentures at an early date in conjunction with liquidation of its government securities as part of an overall investment scheme. Were this the case, it is arguable that the failure to reveal this information misled investors as to the increased likelihood of early redemption.

Plaintiff's strongest evidence in support of this claim is that the investment of the proceeds of the Debenture issue in United States Treasury Bills that paid an interest rate lower than 16.08% made no economic sense except as part of an overall scheme to engage in short-term speculation. While plaintiff's claim in this regard finds some support in the evidence, it also requires the fact-finder to engage in considerable theorizing from the prospective of hindsight. It appears just as likely, based on our review of the record, that ADM did not contemplate early redemption when the Debentures were issued, and that the proceeds of the Debentures were invested in government securities simply as an interim holding until such time as ADM decided to employ such funds for other corporate purposes. The failure specifically to disclose that the proceeds of the Debentures were to be used to purchase long-term government bonds as a hedge against falling interest rates does not, in and of itself, provide a strong securities claim.

The second basis of Morgan Stanley's securities claim — that ADM failed to reveal its "restrictive" view of the redemption language — also suffers from serious problems, at least with respect to the alleged failure to disclose such view at the time the Debentures were first issued. In order for Morgan Stanley to prevail on this claim, it would have to show that the interpretation of the provision urged by the defendant was contrary to that prevailing in the investment community when the Debentures were issued. Plaintiff's main evidence on this point is the affidavit testimony of a number of Morgan Stanley employees and other bondholders, presumably representing the informed view of the investment community, stating their opinion that redemption is prohibited where a company engages in contemporaneous lower-cost borrowing. An equally plausible interpretation, and indeed the view supported by plaintiff's own affidavits, is that few investors had ever seriously considered the legal ramifications of redemption under the circumstances faced by

ADM. Indeed, the record reveals a clear awareness on the part of institutional professionals that the right to redemption from the proceeds of a stock issue was very much an open question and that therefore there was a likelihood that an aggressive company in a position similar to that of ADM would attempt to call its bonds under just such circumstances. One bond salesman for Morgan Stanley candidly stated:

> Quite frankly . . . the question whether a court would ultimately find that a call was lawful or unlawful was largely irrelevant to my view of the economic risks for bondholders if any corporation announced a call. . . .
>
> No portfolio manager with whom I have dealt has ever expressed to me a view, one way or the other, as to whether a call by [Archer Daniels] of the Debentures would violate the nonrefunding provisions that govern the Debentures. As far as I know, no institution that I deal with has ever considered the question.

Deposition of Frederic W. Levin, Affidavit of Catherine R. Flickinger, Ex. B. *See also* Affidavit of Joseph W. Hill, Flickinger Aff., Ex. C.

Given evidence of these views, Morgan Stanley will have some difficulty maintaining that ADM's interpretation of the redemption provision "drastically changed the plain meaning on which investors relied." Plaintiff's Memorandum in Support, at 17. Moreover, defendant plausibly explains the high price at which Archer Debentures were trading prior to the redemption announcement as reflecting anticipation of a likely tender offer. Even were this not the case, one would presume that 16% Debentures would trade at a price at least somewhat in excess of the call price during times of lower interest rates under the possibility of redemption was near to certain. The market price at which ADM Debentures were trading was no doubt more reflective of the investment community's perception of what ADM might do than it was of what ADM had the legal right to do.

The view more readily supported by the facts in this record is that ADM revealed all the facts that were required with respect to its rights under the redemption provision and that, indeed, the untested downside risk of the redemption provision had been fully taken into account in evaluating the market value of ADM's securities. On these facts we cannot say that plaintiff has shown a likelihood of showing both a material misstatement or omission and the level of intent necessary to constitute a violation of federal and state securities laws.

Plaintiff's strongest claims, and those most readily supported by the evidence, are that ADM failed to make adequate disclosure with respect to the Stars transaction and its most recent issues of common stock. In addition, a relatively strong argument could be made that, at some point subsequent to these transactions, after ADM began seriously considering an early redemption of its Debentures, and in light of its knowledge of the prevailing market price of the Debentures, plaintiff's failure to disclose its interpretation of the redemption provision amounted to a negligent or reckless material omission. Nevertheless, in light of the evidence presented in support of plaintiff's other securities and business law claims, and viewing the complaint in its entirety, we find that the plaintiff has failed to show a likelihood of success on the merits.

We turn, finally, to the second alternative prong of the requirement for preliminary relief. While plaintiff has doubtless presented serious questions going to the merits making a fair ground for litigation, it has made no showing of a balance of hardships tipping decidedly in its favor. Moreover, in this regard, we find quite persuasive the comments of counsel for Morgan Guaranty, the Indenture Trustee. While expressing no position on the merits, counsel urged that the hardships that would result in the event we were to grant preliminary relief at this late date would be incalculable to bondholders other than the plaintiff who already may have made firm business commitments in anticipation of receipt of the redemption funds as of August 1. In this regard, defendant has agreed to treat all bondholders equally after a trial on the merits or other dispositive motions. Defendant has further agreed that it will not contend that there is a waiver of any rights on the part of any of bondholder who cashes checks issued pursuant to this redemption.

For all of the above reasons, and on the record now before us, plaintiff's application for preliminary injunctive relief is hereby denied.

Decision on the parties' cross-motions for summary judgment is reserved.

SO ORDERED.

ON MOTION FOR SUMMARY JUDGMENT

SAND, DISTRICT JUDGE

On July 29, 1983, this Court denied the application of plaintiff Morgan Stanley & Co., Inc. ("Morgan Stanley") for preliminary injunctive relief, reserving decision on the parties' cross-motions for summary judgment. After a thorough review of the record, for the reasons stated in our prior Opinion, and for the reasons stated below, we now grant the motion of defendant Archer Daniels Midland Company ("ADM") for partial summary judgment on the contract claims (Counts VI, X-XII), and deny Morgan Stanley's motion for summary judgment on the federal and state securities and business law claims. We assume familiarity with the facts of this case as set forth in our prior Opinion denying preliminary relief.

Contract Claims

The plaintiff's contract claims arise out of alleged violations of state contract law.[52] Section 113 of the Indenture provides that the Indenture and the Debentures shall be governed by New York law. Under New York law, the terms of the

---

52 [1] Because plaintiff's pendent contract claims are properly before us, see *United Mine Workers v. Gibbs*, 383 U.S. 715, 86 S. Ct. 1130, 16 L. Ed. 2d 218 (1966), we need not decide whether an independent federal cause of action exists under the Trust Indenture Act of 1939 for breach of a nonmandated provision of the Indenture. *Compare Zeffiro v. First Pennsylvania Banking and Trust Co.*, 623 F.2d 290 (3d Cir. 1980), *cert. denied*, 456 U.S. 1005, 102 S. Ct. 2295, 73 L. Ed. 2d 1299 (1982) (private right of action for breach of indenture provisions mandated by the Act). In any event, a finding that the defendant breached § 316(b) of the Act, which guarantees the right to payment of principal and interest, would, in this case, require a precedent finding that the nonmandated redemption provision was violated under applicable state law/the very question we address with respect to plaintiff's pendent contract claims.

Debentures constitute a contract between ADM and the holders of the Debentures, including Morgan Stanley. *See Friedman v. Airlift International, Inc.*, 44 A.D.2d 459, 355 N.Y.S.2d 613 (1st Dept. 1974); *Van Gemert v. Boeing Co.*, 520 F.2d 1373, 1383 (2d Cir.), *cert. denied*, 423 U.S. 947, 96 S. Ct. 364, 46 L. Ed. 2d 282 (1975), appeal after remand, 553 F.2d 812, 813 (2d Cir. 1977) (applying New York law). The relevant contract terms are printed on the Debentures and, by incorporation, in the Indenture.[53]

We note as an initial matter that where, as here, the contract language in dispute is a "boilerplate" provision found in numerous debentures and indenture agreements, the desire to give such language a consistent, uniform interpretation requires that the Court construe the language as a matter of law. *See Sharon Steel Corp. v. Chase Manhattan Bank, N.A.*, 691 F.2d 1039, 1048-49 (2d Cir. 1982) (applying New York law), *cert. denied*, U.S., 103 S. Ct. 1253, 75 L. Ed. 2d 482 (1983); *cf. Broad v. Rockwell International Corp.*, 642 F.2d 929, 946-48 (5th Cir.) (en banc) (applying New York law), (interpretation of unambiguous contract provision is function for the court rather than the jury) *cert. denied*, 454 U.S. 965, 102 S. Ct. 506, 70 L. Ed. 2d 380 (1981).

In *Franklin Life Insurance Co. v. Commonwealth Edison Co.*, 451 F. Supp. 602 (S.D. Ill. 1978), *aff'd, per curiam on the opinion below*, 598 F.2d 1109 (7th Cir.), *rehearing and rehearing en banc denied, id., cert. denied*, 444 U.S. 900, 100 S. Ct. 210, 62 L. Ed. 2d 136 (1979), the district court found, with respect to language nearly identical to that now before us, that an early redemption of preferred stock was lawful where funded directly from the proceeds of a common stock offering.

Morgan Stanley argues, however, that *Franklin* was incorrectly decided and should therefore be limited to its facts. We find any attempt to distinguish *Franklin* on its facts to be wholly unpersuasive. Commonwealth Edison, the defendant in *Franklin*, issued 9.44% Cumulative Preferred Stock in 1970. The stock agreement contained a redemption provision virtually identical to that at issue in this litigation.[54] The prospectus announcing the preferred stock would be used primarily for interim financing of a long-term construction program. The construction

---

[53] [2] ADM argues that, because Morgan Stanley holds less than 25% of the outstanding Debentures, it has no standing under § 507(2) of the Indenture to maintain its contract claims. Section 507(2) provides that no Debenture holder shall have the right to institute suit with respect to the Indenture unless the holders of not less than 25% of the outstanding Debentures first request the Trustee to institute proceedings in its own name. Such limitations on the rights of bondholders to seek legal relief are not enforceable, however, where the face of the bond does not give adequate notice of the restriction. *Friedman v. Airlift International, Inc.*, 44 A.D.2d 459, 355 N.Y.S.2d 613 (1st Dept. 1974). The ADM Debentures do not explicitly mention the restrictions contained in § 507. In any event, we view the intervention in this action by the Indenture Trustee, Morgan Guaranty, as a waiver of § 507 to the extent applicable.

[54] [3] The redemption provision contained in the preferred stock agreement provided that none of the stock:

> . . . may be redeemed through refunding, directly or indirectly, by or in anticipation of the incurring of any debt or the issuance of any shares of the Prior Preferred Stock or any other stock ranking prior to or on a parity with the Prior Preferred Stock, if such debt had an interest cost to the Company (as defined) or such shares have a dividend cost to the Company of the 9.44% Prior Preferred Stock.

Franklin Life Insurance Co. v. Commonwealth Edison Co., supra, 451 F. Supp. at 613.

program required an estimated expenditure of approximately $2,250,000,000 of which $1,150,000,000 would have to be raised through the sale of additional securities of the company. *Franklin, supra*, 451 F. Supp. at 605. In accord with this estimate, Commonwealth Edison's long-term debt increased from $1.849 billion at the end of 1971 to an amount in excess of $3 billion by the time of trial in 1978. All of this debt was issued at interest rates below 9.44%. In January of 1972, Commonwealth Edison announced its intention to redeem the preferred stock with the proceeds of a common stock issue.

The Franklin Life Insurance Company brought suit, contending that the language of the redemption provision barred redemption where Commonwealth Edison had been borrowing at interest rates below 9.44%, and expected to continue borrowing at such rates in the near future. The district court rejected plaintiff's claims, and held that the redemption was lawful because the refunding was accomplished solely from the proceeds of the common stock issue. In adopting a rule that looked to the source of the proceeds for redemption, the court rejected a "new borrower" theory that would have examined the issuer's general corporate borrowing history. Thus, Edison's borrowing projections and the sizable anticipated increase in its long-term, lower-cost debt was irrelevant, given that the undisputed source of the redemption was the common stock issue.

According to Morgan Stanley, the Franklin court was forced to give this "strained" interpretation to the redemption provision "in order to permit Commonwealth Edison to continue its ongoing capital construction program and at the same time give the redemption provision some meaning." Plaintiff's Reply Memorandum, at 5-6. Because ADM has no similar long-term construction program, Morgan Stanley contends that this Court need not accord ADM the same rights as were provided Commonwealth Edison in *Franklin*.

We disagree. There is no indication in *Franklin* that the court's decision was mandated in any sense by Commonwealth Edison's ongoing, large-scale construction program. Had the *Franklin* court found the redemption unlawful, the result would not have forced termination of Edison's construction program, but merely would have barred redemption of its preferred stock — the same result that would occur were we to declare ADM's redemption unlawful. Morgan Stanley points out, however, that ADM has a choice that was unavailable to Commonwealth Edison: "[I]t [ADM] can issue debt at interest rates lower than 16.08% and not redeem the Debentures, or it can redeem the Debentures and not issue other, lower-interest debt. The latter option was not available to Commonwealth Edison." Plaintiff's Reply Memorandum, at 6. Plaintiff is correct that the latter option was not available to Commonwealth Edison; but the former option was available, just as it is in this action. There is simply no factual basis in *Franklin* from which to infer that Commonwealth Edison would have abandoned its construction program had it been forced to carry its preferred stock to maturity.

Morgan Stanley contends nevertheless that Franklin was wrongly decided, as a matter of law, and that a fresh examination of the redemption language in light of the applicable New York cases would lead us to reject the "source" rule. In this regard, Morgan Stanley suggests a number of universal axioms of contract construction intended to guide us in construing the redemption language as a matter of first impression. For example, Morgan counsels that we should construe the contract terms in light of their "plain meaning," and should adopt the interpretation that best accords with all the terms of the contract. *Prescott, Ball & Turben v. LTV Corp.*, 531 F. Supp. 213, 218 (S.D.N.Y. 1981) (applying New York law); *Broad v. Rockwell International Corp., supra*, 642 F.2d at 947 (applying New York law). Words are not to be construed as meaningless if they can be made significant by a reasonable construction of the contract. *67 Wall Street Co. v. Franklin National Bank*, 37 N.Y.2d 245, 371 N.Y.S.2d 915, 333 N.E.2d 184 (1975). Where several constructions are possible, the court may look to the surrounding facts and circumstances to determine the intent of the parties. *Id.* Finally, Morgan Stanley urges that all ambiguities should be resolved against the party that drafted the agreement. *67 Wall Street Co. v. Franklin National Bank, supra; Prescott, Ball & Turben v. LTV Corp., supra*, 531 F. Supp. at 217.

We find these well-accepted and universal principles of contract construction singularly unhelpful in construing the contract language before us. Several factors lead us to this conclusion. First, there is simply no "plain meaning" suggested by the redemption language that would imbue all the contract terms with a significant meaning. Either party's interpretation of the redemption language would dilute the meaning of at least some of the words — either the "indirectly or directly," "in anticipation of" language, were we to adopt defendant's "source" rule, or the "from the proceeds," "as part of a refunding operation" language, were we to adopt the plaintiff's interpretation. Any attempt to divine the "plain meaning" of the redemption language would be disingenuous at best.

Equally fruitless would be an effort to discern the "intent of the parties" under the facts of this case. It may very well be that ADM rejected an absolute no-call provision in its negotiations with the underwriters in favor of language it viewed as providing "greater flexibility." It is also clear, however, that neither the underwriters nor ADM knew whether such "flexibility" encompassed redemption under the facts of this case. The deposition testimony of ADM officials suggesting that they believed at the time they negotiated the Indenture that they could redeem the Debentures at any time except through lower-cost debt merely begs the question. Had ADM management so clearly intended the Indenture to allow refunding under the circumstances of this case, it surely would have considered that option prior to the suggestions of Merrill Lynch, which appears to represent the first time the idea of early redemption funded directly by the proceeds of a stock issue was presented by any of ADM's investment advisers.

Finally, we view this as a most inappropriate case to construe ambiguous contract language against the drafter. The Indenture was negotiated by sophisticated bond counsel on both sides of the bargaining table. There is no suggestion of disparate bargaining power in the drafting of the Indenture, nor could there be. Moreover, even if we were to adopt this rule, it is not at all clear that ADM would be considered the drafter of the Indenture, given the active participation of the managing underwriter. Indeed, it is arguable that the ambiguous language should be construed in favor of ADM. *See Broad v. Rockwell International Corp., supra*, 642 F.2d at 947 n.20 (purchaser of Debentures may stand in the shoes of the underwriters that originally negotiated and drafted the debentures).

Not only do the rules of contract construction provide little aid on the facts before us, but we find the equities in this action to be more or less in equilibrium. Morgan Stanley now argues, no doubt in good faith, that the redemption is unlawful under the Indenture. Nevertheless, as we noted in our prior opinion, Morgan Stanley employees were fully aware of the uncertain legal status of an early call at the time they purchased the ADM Debentures. To speak of upsetting Morgan's "settled expectations" would thus be rather misleading under the circumstances. By the same token, however, it is also clear that ADM had no expectations with respect to the availability of an early redemption call until the idea was first suggested by Merrill Lynch.

Because we find equitable rules of contract construction so unhelpful on the facts of this case, the decision in Franklin takes on added importance. While it is no doubt true that the decision in that case was a difficult one and in no sense compelled under existing law, we find the reasoning of the court thoroughly convincing given the obvious ambiguity of the language it was asked to construe. We also find the result to be a fair one, primarily for the reasons stated in our prior Opinion denying preliminary relief. Moreover, we note that the decision in Franklin preceded the drafting of the ADM Indenture by several years. We must assume, therefore, that the decision was readily available to bond counsel for all parties. That the parties may not in fact have been aware of the decision at the time the Indenture was negotiated is not dispositive, for the law in force at the time a contract is entered into becomes a part of the contract. *Skandia America Reinsurance Corp. v. Schenck*, 441 F. Supp. 715, 724 (S.D.N.Y. 1977) (applying New York law) ("It is presumed that the parties had [the relevant] law in contemplation when the contract was made, and the contract must be construed in that light.") (citing *Dolman v. United States Trust Co.*, 2 N.Y.2d 110, 116, 157 N.Y.S.2d 537, 541-42, 138 N.E.2d 784, 788-89 (1956). While *Franklin* was decided under Illinois law and is therefore not binding on the New York courts, we cannot ignore the fact that it was the single existing authority on the issue, and was decided on the basis of universal contract principles. Under these circumstances, it was predictable that *Franklin* would affect any subsequent decision under New York law. *Franklin* thus adds an unavoidable gloss to any interpretation of the redemption language.

Finally, we note that to cast aside the holding in *Franklin* would, in effect, result in the very situation the Second Circuit sought to avoid in *Sharon Steel, supra.* In that case, the Court warned that allowing juries to construe boilerplate language as they saw fit would likely result in intolerable uncertainty in the capital markets. To avoid such an outcome, the Court found that the interpretation of boilerplate should be left to the Court as a matter of law. *Sharon Steel, supra*, 691 F.2d at 1048. While the Court in *Sharon Steel* was addressing the issue of varying interpretations by juries rather than by the courts, this distinction does not diminish the uncertainty that would result were we to reject the holding in *Franklin.* Given the paramount interest in uniformly construing boilerplate provisions, and for all the other reasons stated above and in our prior Opinion, we chose to follow the holding in *Franklin.*[55]

---

[55] [4] We note in this regard the "source" rule adopted in *Franklin* in no sense constitutes a license to violate the refunding provision. The Court is still required to make a finding of the true source of the proceeds for redemption. Where the facts indicate that the proposed redemption was indirectly funded

Accordingly, we find that the ADM redemption was lawful under the terms of the Debentures and the Indenture, and that therefore defendant's motion for summary judgment on Counts VI and X through XII is hereby granted.

Securities Claims

For the reasons stated in our Opinion denying preliminary relief, we find that the plaintiff has failed to show an absence of genuine issues of material fact entitling it to judgment as a matter of law. Disputed issues of fact remain with respect to ADM's intent to redeem the Debentures prior to the call date, ADM's interpretation of the breadth of the redemption language at the time the Indenture was negotiated, and ADM's purpose in investing the proceeds of the Debenture issue in long-term government bonds. On this record, we cannot say that the plaintiff has conclusively established both omission of material facts and that degree of scienter sufficient to grant summary judgment.

SO ORDERED.

MUTUAL SAV. LIFE INS. CO. v. JAMES RIVER CORP.

Alabama Supreme Court
716 So. 2d 1172 (1998)

Hooper, Chief Justice

. . .

The plaintiffs in this class action invested in 30-year 10.75% debentures issued by James River Corporation of Virginia. Merrill Lynch, Pierce, Fenner & Smith, Inc., was the dealer-manager for a tender offer made by James River to the bondholders. The tender offer is the subject of this dispute. . . .

The plaintiffs alleged that James River, with the knowing assistance and active

---

by the proceeds of anticipated debt borrowed at a prohibited interest rate, such redemption would be barred regardless of the name of the account from which the funds were withdrawn. Thus, a different case would be before us if ADM, contemporaneously with the redemption, issued new, lower-cost debt and used the proceeds of such debt to repurchase the stock issued in the first instance to finance the original redemption. On those facts, the redemption could arguably be said to have been indirectly funded through the proceeds of anticipated lower-cost debt, since ADM would be in virtually the same financial posture after the transaction as it was before the redemption — except that the new debt would be carried at a lower interest rate. Here, by contrast, there is no allegation that ADM intends to repurchase the common stock it issued to fund the redemption. The issuance of stock, with its concomitant effect on the company's debt/equity ratio, is exactly the type of substantive financial transaction the proceeds of which may be used for early redemption.

Moreover, we fail to see how, on the facts of this case, the redemption could be argued to be a refunding from the proceeds of lower-cost debt. The Zeroes transaction occurred over a year before the redemption and appears completely unrelated to it. The proceeds of that transaction were used to purchase government securities that remain in ADM's portfolio. The Stars transaction, while closer in time, similarly is not fairly viewed as the source of the redemption, given that the proceeds of that transaction were applied directly to reducing ADM's short-term debt. To view the redemption as having been funded *indirectly* "from the proceeds" of the Stars transaction would require us to ignore the direct source of the refunding, the two ADM common stock issues.

encouragement of Merrill Lynch, wrongfully, fraudulently, and prematurely called, retired and refunded with lower-rate debt its $250,000,000 issue of 10.75% debentures. The company issued these 30-year bonds in 1988, and the tender took place in 1992. James River bought back the tendered bonds with the proceeds of a sale of $200,000,000 in notes at 6.75%. The bonds that were not tendered were redeemed with the proceeds of an issuance of preferred stock. The investors claim that this retiring of the bonds violated a clause in their contract known in the bond market as a "non-refund covenant."

Introduction

A brief explanation of the financial terminology used in this case will be helpful. The plaintiffs invested in 10.75% debentures, also known as bonds. A contract known as an indenture governs a bond issuance. One of the key provisions of an indenture defines the ability of the issuer to buy back the bond before the latest possible maturity date. The most common way this is done is through a call and redemption. A redemption occurs when the issuer of a bond compels the bondholder to sell back the bond at a specified price. The indenture defines the call price — the price at which the redemption takes place.

However, certain limitations exist. The indenture in this case (as in most all indentures) prohibited the issuer from paying for the redeemed bonds with money borrowed at an interest rate lower than that of the bond — 10.75% in this case. The issuer must pay for the redeemed bonds with qualified funds (also known as "clean cash"). Thus, the money used to redeem the bonds must be from a qualified source. Callable bonds may be called and redeemed at any time as long as they are paid with qualified funds.

An issuer of bonds also is entitled to make a tender offer at any time for the bonds. Unlike a call and redemption, a tender offer is not governed by the indenture. A company may make a tender offer for noncallable bonds. Because a tender offer is not governed by the indenture, there are no restrictions on the type of funds that an issuer may use to buy back tendered bonds. In other words, an issuer can use lower-rate borrowed money to pay for tendered bonds. Also, when a tender offer is made, the issuer must pay a premium to the bondholder that it would not have to pay if it called the bonds. For example, the call price in this case was $1,086.00 per $1,000 par value, and the tender price was $1,093.75 per $1,000 par value. Therefore, a tender offer is different from a call and redemption.

When a tender offer is made, the bondholder may accept or hold. By holding, the bondholder rejects the tender offer. In this case, James River made a tender offer to buy back its 30-year 10.75% bonds. In the letter notifying bondholders of the tender offer, James River expressed its intention to call any bonds that were not tendered. On the day that the tender offer expired, James River called all of the bonds. Ninety-eight percent of the bondholders accepted the tender offer, while the other 2% of the bondholders chose to have their bonds called. James River paid the bondholders who accepted the tender offer with the proceeds from the sale of $200,000,000 worth of 6.75% medium-term notes. Thus, James River bought back the tendered bonds with money that was borrowed at a rate lower than 10.75%. James River then redeemed the remaining 2% of the bonds. It paid for the redeemed bonds with qualified funds — the proceeds of the issuance of preferred stock. The investors claim that the process of retiring these bonds violated the redemption clause in the indenture because James River replaced the debt with lower-rate debt.

This case involves the interpretation of one paragraph in the contract between James River and the investors regarding redemption of the bonds. That paragraph reads:

> Prior to October 1, 1998, no redemption of Debentures due October 1, 2018, may be made directly or indirectly, in whole or in part, from or in anticipation of the proceeds (or any part of the proceeds) of any moneys borrowed by or for the account of the Company which have an effective interest cost to the Company (calculated in accordance with generally accepted financial practice) of less than 10.75% per annum.

(Emphasis added.) We interpret this paragraph to mean that James River cannot redeem the bonds before the date specified by using money borrowed at a rate lower than the rate at which it had issued the bonds — 10.75%.

The plaintiff investors claimed that James River, with the assistance of Merrill Lynch, breached its contract with them by refunding its bonds in violation of the redemption clause. They also made several tort claims based on the defendants' failure to inform them that the company did not have sufficient qualified funds and on James River's failure to fully disclose its plan to retire the bonds. The investors also made a claim under the Trust Indenture Act ("TIA"), which provides a cause of action when an issuer of bonds has defaulted in payments of interest or principal. The investors also made a separate claim against Merrill Lynch alleging tortious interference with a business relation. The trial court certified a class for the breach-of-contract claim. However, the trial court denied class certification on the tort claims because the laws of each investor's home state would control the claims.

The trial court entered a summary judgment for the defendants on the breach-of-contract claim, and it dismissed the tort claims under Rule 12(b)(6), Ala. R. Civ. P. The trial court dismissed the TIA claim because the bondholders had received all of the interest to which they were entitled. Also, the trial court entered a summary judgment for Merrill Lynch on the tortious-interference claim because that claim was dependent on the breach-of-contract claim, which the trial court disposed of by a summary judgment. The plaintiffs appeal all aspects of the trial court's ruling.

We hold that there was not substantial evidence to counter the defendants' summary judgment motion as to the breach-of-contract claim, the tortious-interference claim, and the TIA (Trust Indenture Act) claim. The trial court properly dismissed the tort claims because the investors did not present a cognizable cause of action. Finally, we conclude that the trial court properly denied class certification as to the tort claims. We affirm the judgment of the trial court.

Breach of Contract

The investors claimed that James River breached the contract by buying back the bonds with money borrowed at a lower rate than the rate at which it had issued the bonds. The trial court entered a summary judgment for the defendants on this issue. "In reviewing the disposition of a motion for summary judgment, we utilize the same standard as that of the trial court in determining whether the evidence before the court made out a genuine issue of material fact." *Bussey v. John Deere Co.*, 531 So. 2d 860, 862 (Ala. 1988). When the movant makes a prima facie showing that there is no genuine issue of material fact, the burden shifts to the nonmovant to present substantial evidence creating such an issue. *Bass v. SouthTrust Bank of Baldwin County*, 538 So. 2d 794 (Ala. 1989). "[S]ubstantial evidence is evidence of such weight and quality that fair-minded persons in the exercise of impartial judgment can reasonably infer the existence of the fact sought to be proved." *West v. Founders Life Assurance Co. of Florida*, 547 So. 2d 870, 871 (Ala. 1989). On a motion for summary judgment, this court must review the record in a light most favorable to the nonmovant and must resolve all reasonable doubts against the movant. *Hanners v. Balfour Guthrie, Inc.*, 564 So. 2d 412 (Ala. 1990).

The investors argue that the defendants breached the contract in order to save James River several million dollars per year in interest payments. They argue that the tender offer was, in effect, a redemption. They claim that the sole purpose for making the tender offer was to refund the bonds, i.e., James River wanted to replace higher-rate debt with lower-rate debt. The investors claim that such a refunding violated the indenture because James River bought back the tendered bonds with money borrowed at a rate less than 10.75%.

The investors also claim that the defendants participated in what has become known as a "simultaneous tender and call" (STAC). They claim that James River, in essence, made its tender offer at the same time that it called the bonds. Because it did so, the investors claim, they were coerced into accepting the tender offer. They argue that this would allow James River to obtain a better rate than it would have received had it bought back the bonds at the call price. They argue that James River accomplished the tender/call so that it could retire the bonds without having to comply with the redemption clause. This is the case because tendered bonds can be bought back with money borrowed at a lower rate than the issue rate. The investors claim that they were faced with the "threat" of accepting the tender offer (with only a slightly higher premium than the call price) or being forced to sell back their bonds at the call price. The investors' major objection to the STAC process is that it is coercive. In a simultaneous tender and call situation, they argue, the investor, knowing the bonds will be redeemed in the call anyway, effectively has no choice but to accept the tender offer.

The trial court determined that the tender offer made by James River must be considered separately from the call. Therefore, the trial court found that the tender and call were not simultaneous. We agree with the trial court. It is first necessary to determine whether the tender offer was distinguishable from a call. The trial court set out a three-part test for making this determination:

> [W]hen a tender offer is made, the issuer must include a premium over the redemption price or market price which is handsome enough to attract

> debenture holders to the offer. Second, in a tender offer the issuer must aggressively solicit acceptances of the offer, often with the assistance of an outside manager. In contrast, the indenture trustee is neither permitted nor required to solicit acceptances, but merely to give notice of the call for redemption. Most importantly, a call for redemption is not an "offer' to redeem, but is a contractually binding demand upon the debenture holders, who have no choice in the matter. On the other hand, a tender offer is not binding and may be voluntarily rejected or accepted in the holders' discretion.

The trial court determined that the offer made by James River was a tender offer rather than a call. We agree. There was a premium over the call price for tendering the bonds. Also, James River employed Merrill Lynch to assist it in soliciting acceptances of the offer. Finally, the tender offer was not binding and the bondholders did not have to accept it. In its letter announcing the offer, James River stated:

> Neither the Company nor Merrill Lynch is recommending that you or any other Bondholder tender or refrain from tendering any or all Bonds owned. Each Bondholder must make an individual decision whether to tender Bonds, and if so, how many Bonds to tender based on personal financial needs and objectives.

Thus, the decision to accept the offer was voluntary. We find no error in the trial judge's holding that the offer was a tender offer. Thus, we conclude that James River did not violate the terms of the contract, because the tender offer was not subject to the indenture and, therefore, was not subject to the limitation regarding the use of money borrowed at a lower rate. The trial judge correctly stated: "Since the non-refund covenant does not apply to tender offers, James River's use of lower interest cost debt proceeds to purchase the debentures is an immaterial fact." The restrictions in the indenture regarding the lower-rate borrowed money apply only to redemptions. The trial judge correctly referred to the fact that the indenture did not broadly define "redeem" to encompass a tender offer or other mode of acquisition. The indenture also failed to mention any limitations on the use of a tender offer to buy back the bonds. The trial judge stated, "Tender offers for nonrefundable debentures clearly appear repugnant to the broad purpose underlying the non-refund covenant. Nonetheless, the Court must give meaning to the express terms set forth in the redemption provisions of the contract documents." If the investors had intended to restrict the use of tender offers to retire the bonds, then they should have included in the indenture a provision that would do that.

The next question we must address is whether the tender and the call were simultaneously made in order to coerce the investors to accept the tender offer. We hold that the trial court correctly determined that the tender and the call should be considered separately. First, we note that the investors took the risk that their bonds would be called at any time, by buying callable bonds. They could have purchased noncallable bonds (at a lower interest rate) if they wanted long-term certainty in their investment. Coercion is a contracted-for element (inherent in the indenture) of a redemption of callable bonds. The issuer has the right to call the bonds at any time. Also, in this case, the tender was a separate voluntary transaction that the investors did not have to accept. The investors could have exercised their right to hold the bonds. In fact, one of the plaintiffs, Larry Wasserman, did not accept the tender offer. He chose to wait for the call and redemption.

At worst, the combined tender offer/redemption notice was designed to exert legitimate economic pressure on most of the debenture holders, who would logically choose to receive the higher tender price instead of the lower redemption price. James River could have called all the bonds without making a tender offer. The tender offer, which resulted in a slightly higher rate of return than the redemption, offered a benefit to the bondholders above that offered in the redemption. The exertion of such economic pressure did not violate the express terms of the indenture. James River's exercise of its ability to effect a mandatory redemption with the proceeds of a preferred stock issuance did not violate the indenture. Thus, James River could, pursuant to the indenture, make a tender offer with borrowed funds followed by a mandatory redemption with the preferred stock proceeds. To the extent debenture holders are dissatisfied with such an arrangement, they should require issuers to prohibit such arrangements in future indentures.

Because we conclude that the tender offer was separate from the call, the only remaining question is whether James River used qualified funds to buy back the redeemed bonds (2% of the bonds). It is undisputed that James River paid for the redeemed bonds with the proceeds of the issuance of preferred stock — a qualified source for the money. The plaintiffs argue that the practical effect of the proffered tender (with an announced future call) produced the same result that would have occurred if James River had simply called all the bonds by using the lower rate debt. However, that result-focused argument ignores the fundamental difference between a tender and a call. The language of the indenture clearly indicates that the non-refund covenant refers to an involuntary call and redemption. The tender offer was a separate transaction that 98% of the investors voluntarily accepted.

The investors contend that the language of the indenture stating that no redemption could be made "directly or indirectly, in whole or in part," with unqualified funds requires the Court to apply an "underlying economic reality" test. The investors cite *Shenandoah Life Ins. Co. v. Valero Energy Corp.*, (No. 9032, June 21, 1988) 14 Del. J. Corp. L. 396 (Del. Ch. 1988) (not published in Atlantic Reporter), in which similar language was at issue, and they ask this Court to focus on the final result of the complete transaction. The investors urge that, under Shenandoah, if it is found that the redemption of the bonds, albeit lawfully made with qualified funds, would not have occurred but for a tender for other bonds using unqualified funds, then an indirect redemption with unqualified funds has occurred. James River responds by pointing out that the courts in *Shenandoah* and *Morgan Stanley & Co. v. Archer Daniels Midland Co.*, 570 F. Supp. 1529 (S.D.N.Y. 1983), also dealing with refund limitation language, confined their scrutiny to analyses of the funds actually used to redeem. We would add that both courts in those cases ruled that the defendants had not violated the subject indentures. We also note that those courts did not restrict their analyses to the result alone, but studied the economic realities underlying the subject transactions. However, those courts used the "source of funds" rule, a rule that we consider more appropriate for deciding whether James River violated the indenture.

In *Shenandoah*, using the "source of funds" rule, the court illustrated the potential sweep of the language condemning direct or indirect use of unqualified funds to redeem by hypothesizing that an issuer might buy an asset with lower-rate borrowed money and sell the asset to generate "qualified" funds for a redemption. *Shenandoah*, 14 Del. J. Corp. L. at 409. Under such a scenario, the actual source of the funds would not be the asset but the borrowed money that was used to acquire the asset that was then liquidated to cash. We hold that the refunding limitation, couched in terms that prohibit direct and indirect activity in whole or in part, should be applied with focus on the funds used for the redemption rather than on the entire transaction involving the successful tender for some bonds and redemption of other bonds. James River did not use lower-rate borrowed money to pay for the redeemed bonds. James River complied with the restrictions in the contract regarding the redemption of the bonds. A broader interpretation of the transaction would effectively rewrite the contract to give the investors more than they bargained for in an arm's-length transaction between sophisticated parties. The trial judge correctly entered the summary judgment for the defendants on the breach-of-contract claim.

§ 3.06 "NO ACTION" CLAUSES AND THE INDENTURE TRUSTEE

Most trust indentures contain provisions restricting the right of a holder of the bonds or debentures issued pursuant thereto to bring suit for a breach by the issuer of the indenture. Such clauses generally do not affect the right of the holder to sue for principal or interest when due.

Set forth below is a fairly standard "no action" clause:

> SECTION 5.04. *Limitations on Suits by Debentureholders.* Except as otherwise expressly provided in this Section, no holder of any Debenture shall have any right by virtue of or by availing of any provision of this Indenture or otherwise to institute any action, suit or proceeding in equity or at law *upon or under or with respect to* this Indenture or for the appointment of a receiver or trustee, or for any other remedy hereunder, *unless* such holder *previously* shall have given to the Trustee written notice of default, as hereinbefore provided, and of the continuance thereof, and unless also the holders of *not less than 25%* in aggregate principal amount of the Debentures then outstanding shall have made *written request* upon the Trustee either to proceed to exercise the powers hereinbefore granted or to institute such action, suit or proceeding in its own name as Trustee hereunder *and* shall have offered to the Trustee such *reasonable indemnity* as it may require against the costs, expenses and liabilities to be incurred therein or thereby, and the Trustee within a reasonable time (which in no event shall be less than 60 days) after its receipt of such notice, request and offer of indemnity shall have failed to institute any such action, suit or proceeding and no direction inconsistent with such written request shall have been given to the Trustee pursuant to Section 5.06; it being understood and intended, and being expressly covenanted by the taker and holder of every Debenture with every other taker and holder and the

Trustee, that no one or more holders of Debentures shall have any right in any manner whatever by virtue of any provision of this Indenture to affect, disturb or prejudice the rights of the holders of any other such Debentures, or to obtain or seek to obtain priority over or preference to any other such holder, or to enforce any right under this Indenture, except in the manner herein provided and for the equal, ratable and common benefit of all holders of Debentures. For the protection and enforcement of the provisions of this Section, each and every Debentureholder and the Trustee shall be entitled to such relief as can be given either at law or in equity.

Nothing herein contained shall, however, affect or impair the right, which is absolute and unconditional, of any Debentureholder to receive, and to institute suit to enforce, the payment of the principal of and premium, if any, and interest on each of such Debentures *at and after the respective due dates of such principal or premium*, if any, or interest, or the obligation of the Company, *which is also absolute and unconditional*, to pay the principal of and premium, if any, and interest on each of the Debentures to the respective holders thereof at the times and places and at the rate and in the coin and currency in the Debentures expressed.

BIRN v. CHILDS CO.

New York Supreme Court, New York County
37 N.Y.S.2d 689 (1942)

WALTER, JUSTICE

Under a trust indenture dated April 1, 1928, and entered into by it with Empire Trust Company, as trustee, defendant Childs Company duly issued for value $6,000,000 principal amount of its Fifteen-Year Five Per Cent. Gold Debentures due April 1, 1943. The indenture provided that an additional $1,400,000 principal amount of such debentures might be issued for the refunding and retirement of a like amount of four-year notes of a named subsidiary. It further provided that an additional $4,600,000 principal amount might be issued (1) to refund, redeem, retire, or pay certain mortgage bonds of another named subsidiary, (2) to provide for the purchase of the preferred stock of another named corporation, or (3) "for the general purposes of the corporation" if its consolidated net earnings for a specified period shall have been at least three times certain specified interest charges.

No collateral was pledged under the indenture, but it provided for a sinking fund to be created in either of two ways: 1. Payments to the trustee on first days of April and October in each year of a sum in cash equal to one per cent of the principal amount of debentures outstanding thereunder on the date of such payment. 2. Delivery to the trustee of debentures "theretofore authenticated and delivered by the Trustee hereunder and remaining uncancelled . . . in lieu of cash in an amount equal to the principal amount of the debentures so delivered." Cash paid in was to be used to purchase outstanding debentures, and all debentures delivered and all debentures so purchased were to be cancelled and cremated.

On March 25, 1931, Childs Company requested the trustee to authenticate debentures of the total principal amount of $4,600,000 (the request being specifically based upon that provision of the indenture which authorized the issue of that amount "for the general purposes of the corporation") and the trustee did so authenticate them. It then placed those debentures in a custody account for Childs Company, and in that sense may be said to have delivered them to Childs Company, but Childs Company never issued any of them to any holder or obligee and never received any consideration therefor. Nevertheless, on various occasions thereafter Childs Company tendered and the trustee accepted, as payments into the sinking fund, debentures from that lot of $4,600,000 instead of either cash or debentures from the lot of $6,000,000; and it is that act which presents the first contention pressed in this action brought by and on behalf of the holders of the unretired or unredeemed portion of said lot of $6,000,000.

Defendants contend that what was done constitutes compliance with the sinking fund provision. Plaintiff contends that the only debentures usable as payments into the sinking fund are those so delivered as to be valid and enforceable obligations of Childs Company.

Plaintiff's contention must prevail. Defendant's contention is based solely upon the view that debentures which it has authenticated and placed in the custody of Childs Company have been "delivered" within the meaning of the phrase "debentures theretofore authenticated and delivered by the trustee hereunder and remaining uncancelled," and that view is not consistent with either the language of the indenture or the promotion of its primary and dominant purpose.

The words "remaining uncancelled" seem to import that the word "delivered" as used in that phrase means such a delivery as effectuates a legal inception, and thus excludes a mere transfer of possession of the paper to the company, for it seems rather strange to speak of "cancelling" a piece of paper which has had no inception as a legally effective instrument. So, too, the sinking fund is expressly provided to be for "the purchase and redemption of the debentures," and that likewise seems to refer only to debentures actually issued, for until actually issued as a legally binding instrument the mere engraved paper is not subject to either purchase or redemption. It also is to be noted that the indenture provides that the $6,000,000 of debentures "shall be authenticated and delivered by the trustee to or upon the order of the corporation," while as to the $4,600,000 it provides that they "may be authenticated and delivered upon the order of the corporation for any one or more of the following purposes," the only relevant one of which is "for the general purposes of the corporation." As to the $4,600,000 there thus literally was no authority to deliver them to the corporation, but only upon its order; and while the difference between "to" and "upon the order of" ordinarily might not be regarded as significant, that difference takes on significance when conjoined with "for the general purposes of the corporation," for I can conceive of no "general purpose" for which the debentures lawfully could be ordered delivered except the borrowing of money or the acquisition of property. The expression "upon the order of the corporation," as distinguished from "to" the corporation, seems to have been carefully chosen to express the idea that the trustee was to "deliver" debentures only when for a general purpose of the corporation they were to go into the hands of a holder for value, and to exclude the idea that it could deliver them to the corporation merely in order to enable the corporation to use them for sinking fund purposes. The provision that in lieu of paying cash into the sinking fund the corporation may deliver to the trustee "debentures theretofore authenticated and delivered by the trustee hereunder" thus plainly means either debentures from the regularly issued $6,000,000 lot or debentures which the trustee has delivered, not to the corporation, but upon the order of the corporation for money borrowed or property acquired by it, i.e., so delivered as to cause them to have had a valid legal inception as binding corporate obligations to pay.

Certainly the usual, normal, and customary object of a sinking fund is to either diminish the debt or create a fund for its payment, and the term itself conveys that idea to the mind of the ordinary investor. To yield to defendants' contention thus would disappoint the reasonable expectations of any purchaser of the $6,000,000 of debentures which were actually issued. And it is not without significance in this connection that the debentures themselves — the instrument which the investor actually sees — state upon their face that Childs Company agrees to pay into the sinking fund semi-annually "an amount equal to one per cent of the principal of the debentures then outstanding thereunder (i.e., under the indenture) to be used for the purchase of debentures for cancellation at a price not greater than the principal amount thereof." Nothing is there said about putting into the sinking fund unissued debentures for which no consideration has been received. Similarly, in the circular upon which the $6,000,000 debentures were sold to the public the reference to the sinking fund is confined to the part which requires semi-annual payments to the trustee, nothing there being said about using unissued debentures. I must assume that the draftsmen of the debentures and of the circular intended to summarize the indenture provisions honestly and fairly, and on that assumption it is clear that they did not construe the indenture as defendants now say it should be construed.

Finally, the very first recital of this indenture — the fundamental declaration of what the parties were about, an appropriate "key to open the minds of the makers of the act," *Bank for Savings v. Grace*, 102 N.Y. 313, 319, 7 N.E. 162, 164 — is that the corporation has duly authorized the "issue" of the debentures therein described, and the word "issue" clearly imports, not only execution by the company and authentication by the trustee, and not only delivery by the trustee to the company, but, also, such delivery to a holder or obligee as will cause, the debenture to be a valid and binding obligation of the company to pay for money borrowed or property acquired. It thus would be merely trifling with the entire undertaking to say that the indenture in any part or by any phrase authorized unissued papers having merely the form and label of debentures to be used for any purpose whatever.

Any contention that the holders of such of the original $6,000,000 of debentures as are now outstanding were not injured by the use of the $4,600,000 of debentures as payments into the sinking fund is effectually disposed of by careful computations submitted by both sides, from which it appears that if the indenture had been complied with as I hold it must be construed there would now be in the sinking fund, in cash or issued debentures, $423,000 more than is actually there.

Plaintiff makes the further contention that there in fact was no authority for the issuance, or even for the execution or authentication, of the $4,600,000 lot of debentures because the prerequisite of net earnings being three times interest charges did not exist, and while that is academic under my construction of the indenture I feel that I should yield to the request that I pass upon the point.

In requesting authentication of $4,600,000 of debentures, Childs Company certified to the trustee that for the twelve months ending December 31, 1930, the net earnings of the company, as defined in the indenture, were $1,944,509.01. That figure concededly was arrived at by eliminating two items of depreciation, one of $812,873.11 and the other of $23,972.61, and if those items be not eliminated the net earnings were far less than three times the aggregate of the specified interest charges. The question presented thus is whether or not the elimination of the items of depreciation was justified, and under the evidence in this case I find that it was not. Childs Company's own report to its stockholders for the year ending December 31, 1930, contains an income statement prepared and certified by certified public accountants employed by Childs Company, and in that income statement the sum of $812,873.11 as "depreciation written off" is deducted in order to show the net profit for the year, and I find nothing in the indenture's definition of "net earnings" which justifies different treatment. It is true that the income statement appended to the report to the stockholders is setup in the form of arriving at "net income" and then deducting depreciation in order to arrive at "net profit," but that is a mere difference of typography. The result is the same as if the depreciation had been put above the line designated as "net income" instead of below it. Defendants' own expert admitted that there is no difference between net income and net profit.

While I thus find for the plaintiff upon the two points urged in her behalf, two further questions must be solved before judgment can be rendered. One relates to the effect of a rather peculiar situation respecting the lot of $1,400,000 principal amount of debentures authorized by the indenture. The other relates to the effect of a provision in the indenture restricting the right of debenture holders to sue. I will discuss those questions in that order.

When the indenture was executed there were outstanding $1,400,000 principal amount of four-year notes of Childs Dining Hall Company, a subsidiary of Childs Company, and $1,400,000 of debentures were reserved "for the refunding and retirement" of those notes. In February, 1931, Childs Company requested the trustee to authenticate $1,400,000 of debentures and the trustee did so, but instead of delivering them "upon the order of" Childs Company the trustee merely held them subject to its further instructions. In the same month the notes of Childs Dining Hall Company were paid and cancelled, and the $1,400,000 of debentures remained in the custody of the trustee for a period of more than ten years until September, 1941, which was some months after this suit was commenced. On September 25, 1941, those debentures were sent by the trustee to Chase National Bank for the account of Childs Company, and on the following day they were returned to the trustee with a request from Childs Company that they be "cancelled and cremated." The letter making that request refers to the debentures as "authenticated but not sold." They were then cremated on October 1, 1941.

What I understand defendants seek to have me hold upon the basis of those facts is that as Childs Company had the right to use the $1,400,000 of debentures to refund and retire the notes of Childs Dining Hall Company it should be treated as having done so, and as having then acquired them by purchase and delivered them into the sinking fund, and that such assumed delivery thereof into the sinking fund in effect cures the default arising from the prior misuse of the $4,600,000 as payments into the sinking fund. Reflection convinces me that such holding cannot be made.

No significance can be attached to the sending of the $1,400,000 of debentures to Chase National Bank. Such sending hardly was anything more than a very temporary change of place of physical custody, but even if treated as a delivery from the trustee to Childs Company, the essential fact remains that those debentures never passed beyond what was at most the possession of Childs Company. The original purpose of using them to refund and retire the notes of Childs Dining Hall Company was abandoned, for what must be assumed to have been good and sufficient reasons, and those notes were simply paid off without using the debentures originally reserved for such refunding and retirement. When they were so paid off the debt evidenced by them was extinguished, and where a debt has been extinguished the mere fact that it might have been refunded affords no reason why ten years later it should be in effect revived, especially where the only reason for the revival is to allow some one to secure absolution for past breaches of his contractual engagements with his other creditors. The $1,400,000 of debentures hence must be here and now treated exactly as Childs Company itself treated them until after this suit was brought, i.e., as unissued and not capable of being used for sinking fund purposes.

I now come to the question of plaintiff's right to maintain the action in view of Section 6 of Article Five of the indenture, the text of which is quoted in the footnote.[56]

The debentures refer to the indenture "for a statement of the terms and conditions upon which the debentures are issued," and as Section 6 of Article Five is one of those terms and conditions the debentures gave holders thereof adequate notice of its existence. This suit is one for the enforcement of a covenant of the indenture, the sinking fund provision, and is not one to enforce payment of the debentures or their coupons, and it thus falls within the scope of Section 6 of Article Five. Plaintiff gave the trustee written notice of what she claimed and I have found

---

[56] [1] "No holder of any debenture or coupon issued hereunder shall have any right to institute any suit, action or proceeding in equity or at law or otherwise for the enforcement of any covenant or remedy under this indenture or for the collection of any sum due from the Corporation under this Indenture, or for the appointment of a receiver, unless such holder previously shall have given to the Trustee written notice of a completed event of default as hereinbefore provided; nor unless, also, the holders of at least twenty-five percent in principal amount of the debentures issued hereunder and then outstanding, shall have made written request upon the Trustee, and shall have afforded to it a reasonable opportunity to institute a suitable action, suit or proceeding in its own name: nor unless, also, they shall have offered to the Trustee security and indemnity satisfactory to it against the costs, expenses and liabilities to be incurred therein or thereby and the Trustee shall have refused or neglected to comply with such request within a reasonable time thereafter, and such notification, request and offer of indemnity are hereby declared, in every case, at the option of the Trustee, to be conditions precedent to the execution of the powers and trusts of this indenture for the benefit of the debenture holders, and to any action or cause of action or any other remedy hereunder. Provided, however, that nothing contained in this Article or elsewhere in this indenture or in the debentures or coupons shall affect or impair the obligation of the Corporation, which is unconditional and absolute, to pay the principal of the debentures to their respective holders or registered owners at the time and place in the debentures expressed or affect or impair the right of action, which is absolute and unconditional, of such holders or registered owners to enforce such payment."

to be a completed event of default, viz., failure to comply with the sinking fund provision. Plaintiff also made written request upon the trustee to institute a suitable action and afforded it a reasonable opportunity to do so, and the trustee refused to comply with the request. It took the position that the sinking fund provision had been complied with, and made no request for any indemnity. All that is lacking, therefore, is that the request to the trustee to sue was not made by the holders of at least twenty-five per cent of the debentures outstanding, and the question presented is whether or not because of that lack the suit must fail.

Restrictive or no-action clauses have been inserted in corporate mortgages and trust indentures for years. In so far as they prevent individual holders from getting special advantages for themselves and protect the rights and security of all holders as a class, and also in so far as they afford the trustee notice and an opportunity for examination, they serve a highly useful purpose and have been uniformly sustained, even though sometimes said to be not favored and to be strictly construed (2 Jones, Bonds and Bond Securities, 4 Ed., § 811; 1 Quindry, Bonds and Bondholders, § 270), but no case has been cited or found which holds that such a clause prevents such a suit as is here brought under such circumstances as are here disclosed.

We are here confronted with what I have found to be a breach of an express covenant to make specified payments or deliveries into a sinking fund created for the benefit of all holders of the outstanding debentures. Under the facts and the law as I find them to be the trustee should have brought the suit. It refused after notice and request to do so. Plaintiff has produced evidence which shows that, because the debentures are payable to bearer, it is difficult if not impossible for her even to locate other holders to the extent of twenty-five per cent of the total debentures outstanding, and she has framed her suit, not as one at law for damages payable to her for her own benefit, but as one in equity for the benefit of all holders. That the restrictive or no-action clause does not operate, under such circumstances, to prevent a court of equity from granting relief at the suit of a single holder was in effect held in *Ettlinger v. Persian Rug & Carpet Co.*, 142 N.Y. 189, 36 N.E. 1055, 40 Am. St. Rep. 587, and *O'Beirne v. Allegheny & Kinzua R. R. Co.*, 151 N.Y. 372, 383, 45 N.E. 873. The mortgage involved in the latter of those cases required that the request to the trustee to sue be made by a majority of the bondholders (see Case on Appeal, pp. 81, 82), and that provision was pressed upon the court in the briefs (151 N.Y. 374, 45 N.E. 873), and yet a suit by one bondholder was upheld.

Even if the indenture be regarded as going so far as by its terms to vest in the trustee alone the sole and exclusive right to enforce the sinking fund provision — the sole and exclusive title to any cause of action arising out of a breach thereof — the situation still is no different from the hosts of incidents in which beneficiaries of a trust are allowed to sue upon causes of action vested in the trustee upon a showing that the trustee unreasonably refuses to sue. Suits by stockholders in the right of their corporation upon causes of action vested in the corporation are the creatures and inventions of courts of equity. Equity also allows other beneficiaries to sue upon causes of action vested in their trustees when the trustee unreasonably refuses to sue. It sometimes is stressed that these restrictive or no-action clauses are matters of contract and that security holders must be held to their contract, but the contract, in its entirety, is one which gives rise to a trust, and upon the question of allowing a beneficiary to sue upon a showing of an unreasonable refusal of the trustee to sue I can perceive no difference between a trust based upon contract and one based on status or one arising by operation of law. In each instance the principle is the same, that equity will not permit a wrong to go unredressed because the trustee unreasonably refuses to sue.

Stating the same result in the terminology of contract rather than the terminology of equity and trusts, such limitation as the clause imposes upon the individual holder's right to sue is subject to the implied condition or covenant that the trustee will not unreasonably refuse to enforce any covenant of the indenture when a breach thereof is brought to its attention, whether it is brought to its attention by one holder or many, and when that implied condition or covenant is broken the limitation disappears.

Plaintiff is entitled to judgment directing Childs Company to pay to the trustee the sum of $423,000, in cash or outstanding debentures, to be held and disposed of by the trustee in accordance with the sinking fund provisions of the indenture. Plaintiff is also awarded one bill of costs against Childs Company only.

The foregoing constitutes the decision required by the Civil Practice Act and judgment is to be entered thereon accordingly.

Settle judgment in conformity herewith.

FELDBAUM v. McCRORY CORP.

Delaware Court of Chancery
1992 Del. Ch. LEXIS 113 (June 1, 1992)

ALLEN, CHANCELLOR

. . . . I turn first to the question of the effect on these actions of clauses in the indentures limiting the ability of bondholders to prosecute claims that they purportedly hold in their capacities as bondholders. For the reasons that follow, I conclude that the "no-action" clauses in the indentures constitute waivers by plaintiffs of any right to bring the following claims against any defendants, without first satisfying the procedural requirements of those clauses: (1) the fraudulent conveyance claims; (2) the claims for breaches of implied covenants of good faith and fair dealing; and (3) those common law fraud claims that are based on injuries allegedly arising from a missed opportunity for plaintiffs' to enjoin the December 1990 transactions. . . .

The no-action clause in the E-II indentures is representative. It reads as follows: A Securityholder may not pursue any remedy with respect to this Indenture or the Securities unless: (1) the Holder gives to the Trustee written notice of a continuing event of default; (2) the Holders of at least a majority in principal amount of outstanding Securities make a written request to the Trustee to pursue the remedy; (3) such Holder or Holders offer to the Trustee indemnity satisfactory to the Trustee against any loss, liability or expense; (4) the Trustee does not comply with the request within 60 days after receipt of the request and the offer of indemnity; and (5) during the 60-day period the Holders of a majority in principal amount of the outstanding Securities do not give the Trustee a direction which is inconsistent with the request. (E-II Indenture § 6.06).

Absent an allegation of fraud in the inducement of the purchase, clauses of this sort are generally applied to foreclose bondholder suits under the indenture, where plaintiff has not complied. *See Elliott Associates, L.P. v. Bio-Response, Inc.*, Del. Ch., C.A. No. 10,624, Berger, V.C. (May 23, 1989); *Friedman v. Chesapeake & Ohio Ry.*, 395 F.2d 663 (2d Cir. 1968); *Ernst v. Film Production Co.*, N.Y. Supr., 264 N.Y.S. 227 (1933). Such clauses are bargained-for contractual provisions which inure, not only to the benefit of issuers, but also to the benefit of the investors in bonds. Such clauses need not prevent the prosecution of meritorious suits.[57] They do, however, make it difficult for individual bondholders to bring suits that are unpopular with their fellow bondholders. This, in fact, is their primary purpose. As the American Bar Foundation's Commentaries on Indentures, § 5.7, at 232 (1971), notes, regarding the Foundation's proposed model no-action clause, the major purpose of this Section is to deter individual debentureholders from bringing independent law suits for unworthy or unjustifiable reasons, causing expense to the Company and diminishing its assets. The theory is that if the suit is worthwhile, [a significant percent][58] of the debentureholders would be willing to join in sponsoring it. . . . An additional purpose is the expression of the principle of law that would otherwise be implied that all rights and remedies of the indenture are for the equal and ratable benefit of all holders. The primary purpose of a no-action clause is thus to protect issuers from the expense involved in defending lawsuits that are either frivolous or otherwise not in the economic interest of the corporation and its creditors. In protecting the issuer such clauses protect bondholders. They protect against the exercise of poor judgment by a single bondholder or a small group of bondholders, who might otherwise bring a suit against the issuer that most bondholders would consider not to be in their collective economic interest. In addition to providing protection against improvident litigation decisions, a no-action clause also protects against the risk of strike suits. Obviously the class features of any such suits make that prospect somewhat more likely and somewhat more risky to the issuer than it would otherwise be. No-action clauses address these twin problems by delegating the right to bring a suit enforcing rights of bondholders to the trustee, or to the holders of a substantial amount of bonds, and by delegating to the trustee the right to prosecute such a suit in the first instance. These clauses also ensure that the proceeds of any litigation actually prosecuted will be shared ratably

---

[57] [9] This, as a practical matter, is especially true of bonds of failing or bankrupt companies whose bonds tend to move into the hands of specialists, so-called vulture funds, for whom, given their small numbers and significant holdings, collective action problems do not present the obstacle to collective action that frequently accompanies wide-spread distribution of financial interests. *See, e.g.*, Marcel Kahan & Bruce Tuckman, *Do Bondholders Lose from Junk Bond Covenant Changes* (Feb. 1992) (unpublished study on file with authors) (exit consent solicitation of bondholders of failing companies appear not to have a "coercive" effect).

[58] [10] The no-action clause proposed by the American Bar Foundation requires that an investor seeking to bring a suit get at least 25% of securityholders (including itself) to ask the Trustee to bring suit before the bondholders — upon the Trustee's refusal to take up the action — may bring suit individually. The no-action clauses at issue in the present case require a would-be plaintiff to join, not 25%, but a majority of debentureholders in asking the trustee to bring suit. I attach no legal importance to this higher threshold.

by all bondholders.[59] In this case, plaintiffs argue that no-action clauses apply only to claims for breaches of express indenture provisions. They assert that their claims, predicated upon breaches of implied obligations of fair dealing, for fraudulent conveyance and for fraud, are not affected by the no-action clauses. Given the purposes for which no-action clauses are designed, I cannot accept plaintiffs' position. No principled reason or factual particularity of this case is advanced that would justify this view. In my opinion, no matter what legal theory a plaintiff advances, if the trustee is capable of satisfying its obligations, then any claim that can be enforced by the trustee on behalf of all bonds, other than a claim for the recovery of past due interest or principle, is subject to the terms of a no-action clause of this type. *See, e.g.*, N.Y. Supr., *Ernst v. Film Production Corp.*, 264 N.Y.S. 227, 228 (1933) (fraudulent conveyance claim); *Elliott Associates, supra* p. 13 (receivership claim and claim for breach of implied covenant of good faith and fair dealing); *Friedman*, 395 F.2d at 664 (contract claim for breach of indenture provisions requiring sinking fund payments, payment of back interest upon any distribution of dividends and payment of principal upon breach of indenture); *Feder v. Union Carbide Corp.*, N.Y. App. Div., 530 N.Y.S.2d 165 (1988) (contract claim for breach of indenture provision requiring the adjustment of terms for conversion to common stock); *Sutter v. Hudson Coal Co.*, N.Y. App. Div., 21 N.Y.S.2d 40 (1940) (contract claim for breach of sinking fund obligations created by indenture); *Relmar Holding Co. v. Paramount Publix Corp.*, N.Y. Supr., 263 N.Y.S. 776 (1932), *aff'd, mem.*, N.Y. App. Div., 237 A.D. 870 (1933) (contract claim for breach of indenture provision prohibiting the creation of liens not shared ratably by the bondholders).

I do not mean to imply that courts will apply no-action clauses to bar claims where misconduct by the trustee is alleged. For the same reason that equity has long recognized that, in some circumstances, corporate shareholders will be excused from making a demand to sue upon corporate directors, but will be permitted to sue in the corporation's name themselves, bondholders will be excused from compliance with a no-action provision where they allege specific facts which if true establish that the trustee itself has breached its duty under the indenture or is incapable of disinterestedly performing that duty. *See Cruden v. Bank of New York* [1990 Transfer Binder] Fed. Sec. L. Rep. (CCH) P. 95, 466 at 97,413 (S.D.N.Y. Sept. 4, 1990).[60] I rather conclude only that, absent circumstances making

---

[59] [11] "No-action" clauses are thus consistent with, if not central to, the indentures in which they are found, for the primary purpose of such indentures is to centralize enforcement powers by vesting legal title to the securities in one trustee. *See* George G. Bogert & George T. Bogert, The Law of Trusts and Trustees, § 250, at 280 (rev. 2d ed. 1992) ("In the case of debenture bonds, . . . the issue is often made payable to a trustee in order that the powers of enforcement may be centralized.").

[60] [12] In *Victor v. Riklis*, No. 91 Civ. 2897 (S.D.N.Y. May 15, 1992), discussed *infra* pp. 18-19, the federal district court for the Southern District of New York addressed *Cruden, supra*, an earlier case in which that court had permitted fraud and RICO claims brought by individual bondholders to proceed in the face of a no-action clause. It concluded that the facts with which it was then presented (which I conclude below are substantively identical to those alleged here) differed from those of the *Cruden* case in that the clause with which it was then presented was broader than that addressed by the court in *Cruden*. It accordingly declared that the *Cruden* holding did not control its determination and declared that the no-action clause with which it was presented barred plaintiffs' claims. I note that, even if there had been no difference between the no-action clauses addressed in the two cases, *i.e.*, the no-action clause interpreted in *Cruden* had been as broad as that considered in *Victor*, the cases likely would still have come out differently. Application of the no-action clause in *Cruden* still may well have not been

application of a no-action clause inappropriate, such as those described above, courts systematically conclude that, in consenting to no-action clauses by purchasing bonds, plaintiffs waive their rights to bring claims that are common to all bondholders, and thus can be prosecuted by the trustee, unless they first comply with the procedures set forth in the clause or their claims are for the payment of past-due amounts. Courts have implicitly concluded that this waiver by a bondholder applies equally to claims against non-issuer defendants as to claims against issuers. *See Norte & Co. v. Manor Healthcare Corp.*, Del. Ch., C.A. Nos. 6827, 6831, Berger, V.C. (Nov. 21, 1985) (dismissing for failure to comply with a no-action clause breach of indenture claims against issuer and codefendants); *Levy v. Paramount Publix Corp.*, N.Y. Supr., 266 N.Y.S. 271, *aff'd*, N.Y. App. Div., 269 N.Y.S.2d 997 (1934) (dismissing for failure to comply with no-action clause breach of fiduciary duty claims against issuer's directors in connection with issuer's alleged fraudulent conveyance); *Relmar Holding*, 262 N.Y.S. 776 (dismissing for failure to comply with no-action clause fraudulent conveyance claim against recipient of transferred assets). The policy favoring the channeling of bondholder suits through trustees mandates the dismissal of individual-bondholder actions no matter whom the bondholders sue. So long as the suits to be dismissed seek to enforce rights shared ratably by all bondholders, they should be prosecuted by the trustee. Moreover, like other no-action clauses, the clauses at issue here explicitly make their scope depend on the nature of the claims brought, not on the identity of the defendant. For example, the E-II clauses quoted earlier begin: "A Securityholder may not pursue any remedy with respect to this Indenture or the Securities unless. . . ."

RABINOWITZ v. KAISER-FRAZER CORP.

New York Supreme Court, Kings County
111 N.Y.S.2d 539 (1952)

Hart, Justice

Defendant Kaiser-Frazer Corporation (hereinafter referred to as Kaiser-Frazer) moves to dismiss the complaint on the grounds that: (1) there is a nonjoinder of indispensable parties, and (2) the plaintiff has not legal capacity to sue.

This action was instituted against the three named defendants, KaiserFrazer, Bank of America National Trust and Savings Association (hereinafter referred to as Bank of America) and Graham-Paige Motors Corporation (hereinafter referred to as Graham-Paige) by the service of summons and verified complaint upon each of them. Graham-Paige joined issue by interposing its answer. Kaiser-Frazer unsuccessfully moved to set aside the service of process upon it. Bank of America, appearing specially, successfully moved to vacate the service of process against it upon jurisdictional grounds. A notice of appeal from the order on that motion was served in April 1950 but up to the present time no further action has been taken to prosecute the appeal.

The plaintiff is the original owner and holder of $10,000 in principal amount of 4%

---

appropriate because the trustee in Cruden was accused of impropriety. In *Victor*, as here, no such conflict was alleged.

Convertible Debentures of Graham-Paige which were issued under an indenture with the Bank of America as trustee and has brought this action in behalf of himself and all other owners of such debentures similarly situated.

The material facts, as alleged in the complaint, may be summarized as follows: Prior to World War II Graham-Paige was engaged primarily in the production, distribution and sale of automobiles and replacement parts therefor. During the war Graham-Paige was engaged almost entirely in the production of war materials. On August 9, 1945, Joseph W. Frazer, then Chairman of the Board of Directors and President of Graham-Paige, and one Henry J. Kaiser were instrumental in the formation of Kaiser-Frazer. On September 20, 1945, Graham-Paige purchased 250,000 shares of common stock of Kaiser-Frazer. On that same date Graham-Paige and Kaiser-Frazer entered into an agreement for joint use of the former bomber plant at Willow Run in Ypsilanti, Michigan, for the manufacture of automobiles and farm equipment. Under this agreement Graham-Paige was entitled to use one-third of Willow Run's automotive production facilities; Kaiser-Frazer the other two-thirds.

In order to obtain its share of the needed capital to convert the Willow Run plant to automobile production and to obtain other working capital, Graham-Paige issued $11,500,000 of 4% Convertible Debentures due April 1, 1956, under an Indenture with Bank of America as trustee. Behind these debentures were pledged the Graham-Paige plant in Detroit, Michigan and the aforesaid 250,000 shares of Kaiser-Frazer common stock.

Graham-Paige covenanted in said Indenture (Article "Third" relating to "Sinking Fund and Redemption of Debentures") that on or before April 1 of each year to and including April 1, 1956, so long as any of the debentures are outstanding, it would pay to the trustee, as and for a Sinking Fund for the retirement of the debentures, an amount in cash equal to 25% of its net earnings for the preceding calendar year.

Article Thirteenth of the Indenture, in so far as applicable herein, also provided:

> § 13.01. Nothing in this Indenture shall prevent . . . any sale or conveyance, subject to the lien of this Indenture on the mortgaged and pledged property, of all or substantially all of the property of the corporation (Graham-Paige) to any other corporation . . . ; provided, however, and the corporation covenants and agrees, that
>
> > (1) Any such . . . sale or conveyance shall be upon such terms as fully to preserve and in no respect to impair the lien of security of this Indenture . . . , and
> >
> > (2) Upon any such . . . sale or conveyance, . . . the corporation to which all or substantially all the property of the Corporation shall be sold or conveyed shall execute with the trustee and record an indenture, satisfactory to the trustee, whereby the successor corporation shall expressly agree to pay duly and punctually the principal of and the interest and premium, if any, on the Debentures according to their tenure, and shall expressly assume the due and punctual performance and observance of all the covenants and conditions of this Indenture to be performed or observed by the Corporation.

> § 13.02. Upon any such . . . sale or conveyance . . . such successor corporation shall succeed to and be substituted for the Corporation with the same effect as if it had been named as the party of the first part (Graham-Paige). . . .

By a contract dated December 12, 1946, effective February 1, 1947, Graham-Paige agreed to sell to Kaiser-Frazer all of its automotive assets (excluding only such assets as had been acquired for use in the manufacture of farm equipment) in consideration, among other things, of the issue to Graham-Paige of 750,000 shares of common stock of Kaiser-Frazer, of an agreement by Graham-Paige to pay Kaiser-Frazer $3,000,000 and by a debenture payment agreement (subsequently executed on February 10, 1947) between Graham-Paige and Kaiser-Frazer whereunder the latter undertook to pay the interest on and the principal of the debentures of Graham-Paige then outstanding ($8,524,000).

The agreement of December 12, 1946 (Article XI), specifically provides that Kaiser-Frazer shall not be required to pay the principal of any or all said 4% Convertible Debentures of Graham-Paige prior to the maturity date thereof (except for default in the payment of interest) and the debenture payment agreement of February 10, 1947, specifically provided (Article V) that except as therein provided Kaiser-Frazer does not "assume or agree to perform any of the promises, covenants, terms or conditions of the Indenture to be performed by" Graham-Paige and that neither the trustee under the indenture nor any debenture holder shall have any rights by virtue of such agreement and that the undertakings of Kaiser-Frazer are solely for the benefit of Graham-Paige and that they are limited to the making to Graham-Paige of the payments Kaiser-Frazer therein agreed to make.

At this point it is significant to note that by virtue of the foregoing provisions Kaiser-Fraser specifically avoided any undertaking on its part to apply 25% of its annual net profits to the sinking fund of the debentures in accordance with the provisions of Article Third of the Debenture. It is this failure of Kaiser-Frazer to have assumed the obligations of the sinking fund and to have paid 25% of its annual profits into such fund which presents the crux of this case and which forms the basis for the recovery sought herein against Kaiser-Frazer.

The complaint then proceeds to allege that the sale in question to the knowledge of Bank of America and Kaiser-Frazer constituted a conveyance of "all or substantially all" of the property of Graham-Paige and thereby terminated Graham-Paige's manufacturing and other activities in the automotive field; that Bank of America and Kaiser-Frazer knew or should have known that the sale as consummated would have the effect of depriving Graham-Paige of an opportunity to earn any moneys in the immediate or foreseeable future and would result in rendering nugatory the provisions in the indenture requiring Graham-Paige to make deposits in the sinking fund.

It is further alleged that by reason of the said sale Bank of America was under a duty, as trustee, and within its powers under the terms of the indenture, to obtain from Kaiser-Frazer a supplemental indenture satisfactory in form to itself, whereby Kaiser-Frazer would expressly assume the performance of all the covenants and conditions of the indenture to be performed by Graham-Paige, particularly those provisions of the indenture (Article Third) relating to the "Sinking Fund and Redemption of Debentures;" that Bank of America failed or refused to perform its duties as trustee in this respect and thereby breached the trust indenture; that by reason of the negligent and wilful misconduct on the part of Bank of America, plaintiff and all other debenture holders similarly situated were deprived, and unless this Court interferes, will be deprived of the benefits of the Sinking Fund provisions of the Indenture to the extent of the automotive assets of Graham-Paige and the earnings of Kaiser-Frazer, to the damage of the debenture holders in the amounts hereinafter set forth, "for which Bank of America is liable." (Complaint paragraph Twenty-sixth.)

It is also alleged that Kaiser-Frazer is bound by the terms of the trust indenture despite its failure to execute a supplemental indenture to assume expressly the provisions relating to the "Sinking Fund;" that Kaiser-Frazer should have deposited with the trustee each year an amount in cash equal to 25% of its net earnings for the next preceding year; to wit, for the year 1947 the sum of $4,753,889.25 and for the year 1948 the sum of $2,590,524.50, making a total of $7,344,413.75, no part of which has been paid, and that Kaiser-Frazer is further obligated to the trustee for future sinking fund payments as provided in Article "Third" of the Indenture.

As of the date of this complaint there was outstanding $8,524,000 principal amount of the said 4% Convertible Debentures of Graham-Paige.

It is also alleged that Graham-Paige made no deposit with the trustee of any part of its net earnings for the years 1947 and 1948; that there was a net income for the calendar year 1947 of $123,766.73 but for the calendar year 1948 Graham-Paige had a net loss of $3,391,113.36, and that Graham-Paige's manufacturing operations of the farm equipment business were closed early in 1949.

The complaint contains the following allegation: "Thirty-Third: This action and the relief herein sought are not for the remedies provided by the Indenture, this being an action invoking the inherent powers of this Court as a court of equity to declare, protect and preserve the rights of the debenture holders. No demand upon the Trustee to institute or prosecute this action is necessary, nor has such demand been made for the reason that the Trustee is a defendant herein and is liable to the plaintiff and other debenture holders similarly situated, for its own negligent and wilful misconduct with respect to the acts herein complained of, and would be demanding that the Trustee sue itself, and such demand would be entirely useless and futile."

After alleging that he has no adequate remedy at law the plaintiff demands judgment as follows:

1. Declaring and decreeing that Kaiser-Frazer has assumed the due and punctual performance and observance of all of the covenants and conditions of the Indenture, dated as of April 1, 1946, between Graham-Paige and Bank of America, with the same effect as if Kaiser-Frazer had been named in the Indenture in place and stead of Graham-Paige.

2. Adjudging and decreeing that Kaiser-Frazer is liable to Bank of America, as Trustee, and shall pay over to Bank of America, as Trustee, or any Successor Trustee, for the benefit of the plaintiff and all other debenture holders similarly

situated, the sum of $7,344,413.75, to be held and disposed of by the Trustee, in accordance with Article "Third" of said Indenture relating to "Sinking Fund and Redemption of Debentures."

3. Declaring and decreeing that so long as any of the said debentures are outstanding, 25% of the net earnings of Kaiser-Frazer, as defined in said Indenture, for each of the calendar years 1949 through 1954 be paid by Kaiser-Frazer to Bank of America, as Trustee, or any Successor Trustee in accordance with said Article "Third" of said Indenture.

4. Adjudging and decreeing that Bank of America be directed to account to the plaintiff and all other debenture holders similarly situated for its acts and for its failure to act as Trustee under said Indenture and that it be surcharged and directed to pay to itself as Trustee or to any Successor Trustee any and all damages sustained by the Trust Estate by reason of such acts or failure to act.

5. Granting such other and further relief as to the Court may seem just and proper together with the costs and disbursements of this action, and reasonable and proper counsel fees to plaintiff's attorneys.

As stated above, plaintiff has instituted this action on behalf of himself and all other bondholders similarly situated. The plaintiff alleges ownership of less than one-eighth of 1% of the outstanding debentures. The objection that plaintiff lacks the legal capacity to sue is predicated on the language of § 8.08 of the Indenture which provides in substance that

> no holder of any Debenture . . . shall have any right to institute any suit . . . unless such holder previously shall have given to the Trustee written notice of default . . . and unless also the holders of not less than 25% in aggregate principal amount of the Debentures then outstanding shall have made written request upon the Trustee to institute such action and the Trustee . . . shall have neglected or refused to institute any such action. . . .

The opposing parties to this motion are in virtual accord as to the general proposition that ordinarily a request upon a trustee to take action must be made by the holders of the prescribed percentage of bonds before a class action may be instituted by a bondholder.

The plaintiff, however, urges that notwithstanding the presence of a "no action" clause, an individual bondholder has the right to bring a class action to protect his interests and the interests of all other bondholders of the same issue whenever the Indenture Trustee has acted in such a manner as to put itself in a position where it cannot faithfully and competently discharge its duty as a fiduciary. It seems to me that plaintiff's position is sound. In the *Ettlinger* case, *supra*, the incompetency of the trustee to act for the bondholders was predicated upon the trustee's absence from this country and his probable insanity. In the *Birn* case the trustee's incompetency was based on its unreasonable refusal to sue. In the *Buel* case the incompetency of the trustee was predicated upon its inconsistent position as trustee of conflicting trusts. In the *Campbell* case, 277 App. Div. 731, 102 N.Y.S.2d 878, where the trustee "renounced" or "abdicated" its function to sue, the Court made the following apposite statement 277 App. Div. at pages 734737, 102 N.Y.S.2d at page 881: "All of those cases, and others like them, presuppose a trustee competent to act, and exercising its judgment in good faith respecting what is best for the bondholders as a whole concerning the matter in issue. If a trustee under such an indenture acts in bad faith, or, abdicating its function with respect to the point in question, declines to act at all, bondholders for themselves and others similarly situated may bring a derivative action in the right of the trustee, rather than in their own individual rights as bondholders. In that event they are not subject to the limitations of Article Seventh of the Indenture, which are not imposed on the trustee or on bondholders acting in the status of the trustee. This subject was considered lucidly, and the same result reached, by Justice Walter in *Birn v. Childs Co.*, Sup., 37 N.Y.S.2d 689, 696. He said: "That the restrictive or no-action-clause does not operate, under such circumstances, to prevent a court of equity from granting relief at the suit of a single holder was in effect held in *Ettlinger v. Persian Rug & Carpet Co.*, 142 N.Y. 189, 36 N.E. 1055, 40 Am. St. Rep. 587, and *O'Beirne v. Allegheny & Kinzua R. Co.*, 151 N.Y. 372, 383, 45 N.E. 873.' "

Plaintiff's affidavit in opposition to the instant motion sets forth that subsequent to the date of the Indenture, Bank of America made several loans to both Kaiser-Frazer and Graham-Paige which were enmeshed with the sale of the automotive assets of the latter to Kaiser-Frazer. The nature of these transactions was such as to create a conflict in the interests of Bank of America as trustee and Bank of America as a creditor of both Graham-Paige and Kaiser-Frazer. As trustee it was bound to protect the interests of the debenture holders and was charged with the duty of requiring Kaiser-Frazer to assume the sinking fund provisions when the latter company acquired the automotive assets of Graham-Paige. On the other hand, as a bank creditor and in its self-interest Bank of America gave its express written consent to the terms of the Sales Agreement whereby Kaiser-Frazer delimited its undertakings with respect to the debentures so that it did not assume the obligations of the Sinking Fund provision of the Indenture. At the same time, in order to protect its own interests, in making a loan of $12,000,000 to Kaiser-Frazer, Bank of America required Kaiser-Frazer to amortize that loan to the extent of 25% of its annual net profits in addition to securing a mortgage on all of Kaiser-Frazer's property as well as on the property of Graham-Paige, the sale of which to Kaiser-Frazer was being contemplated and in the course of negotiation.

It seems to me that when Bank of America consented to Kaiser-Frazer's declination of assuming any of the provisions of the Indenture, including the sinking fund provisions, it placed itself in a position which was antagonistic to and in conflict with the interests of the debenture holders.

As was stated in *Farmer's Loan & Trust Co. v. Northern Pacific R. Co.*, C.C., 66 F. 169, 176: "A trustee cannot be permitted to assume a position inconsistent with or in opposition to his trust. His duty is single, and he cannot serve two masters with antagonistic interests."

The movant urges that under the circumstances of this case plaintiff's proper remedy is to have a new or substitute trustee appointed but such argument is untenable for the same reasons that the Court in the *Ettlinger* case rejected a similar contention. There the Court stated at page 193 of 143 N.Y., at page 1056 of 36 N.E:

> But the special term say that in such event a new trustee should have been appointed. That simply reproduces the same difficulty in another form, for a court would hardly remove a trustee without notice to him, and giving him an opportunity to be heard; and why should a new appointment be made, when any one of the bondholders can equally do the duty of pursuing the foreclosure The court, in such an action, takes hold of the trust, dictates and controls its performance, distributes the assets as it deems just, and it is not vitally important which of the two possible plaintiffs sets the court in motion. The bondholders are the real parties in interest. It is their right which is to be redressed, and their loss which is to be prevented; and any emergency which makes a demand upon the trustee futile or impossible, and leaves the right of the bondholder without other reasonable means of redress, should justify his appearance as plaintiff in a court of equity for the purpose of a foreclosure.

In view of the foregoing it is my view that the "no action" clause involved in the case at bar is inoperative and inapplicable.

NOTE

No-action clauses also found their way into the Pooling and Servicing Agreements utilized in the administration of mortgage-backed securities, and have been held to be enforceable in that context as well. *See Greenwich Financial Services Distressed Mortgage Fund 3, LLC v. Countrywide Financial Corp.*, No. 650474/08, NYLJ 1202473454174 (NY Sup. Ct., Oct. 13, 2010).

§ 3.07 THE MEANING OF THE TERM "ALL OR SUBSTANTIALLY ALL" OF THE ASSETS OF A BUSINESS CORPORATION IN THE CONTEXTS OF TRUST INDENTURES AND OTHER ASPECTS OF CORPORATE FINANCE

Although the *Rabinowitz* court did not undertake to fashion a definition of the phrase "all or substantially all" of the Graham-Paige assets, it clearly implied that a sale of the profitable automotive assets and a retention of the unprofitable farm equipment assets constituted a sale to Kaiser-Frazer of all or substantially all of the Graham-Paige assets.

Corporation lawyers are called upon to make determinations with regard to whether a particular transaction constitutes a sale of all or substantially all of a corporation's assets in contexts other than the construction of a trust indenture. For example, certain states (New York among them — see § 909 of the New York Business Corporation Law, *supra*) require that a sale of "all or substantially all" of the assets of a corporation be authorized by a vote of the shareholders. Many of those same states provide that a stockholder who dissents from such a transaction may exercise a statutory right of appraisal and receive the fair cash value of his shares. Also, contracts often provide that a consent by one or more parties may or may not be required in the event of a sale of "all or substantially all" of the assets of one of the parties to the agreement. For that reason, a purchaser of corporate assets usually insists upon an opinion of counsel for the seller of such assets to the effect that no authorization, consent or approval of any governmental authority or any other person is required in connection with the consummation by the seller of the transaction. This issue also arises in a case of a statutory merger which is deemed to be an assignment of contract rights and the transfer of property interests by operation of law. Deciding whether a particular transaction constitutes a sale of all or substantially all of a corporation's assets is not simply an application of a percentage or statistical test. As the following cases demonstrate, it is sometimes necessary to consider the economic and business realities of the proposed transaction and their effect upon the selling corporation.

STORY v. KENNECOTT COPPER CORP.

New York Supreme Court, New York County
90 Misc. 2d 333, 394 N.Y.S.2d 353 (1977)

Abraham J. Gellinoff, Justice

. . . .

This is an action brought by plaintiff, a shareholder in defendant Kennecott Copper Corporation, against Kennecott and its Board of Directors, assertedly on her own behalf and on behalf of all other shareholders. She seeks to compel defendants to distribute the proceeds of a sale of a subsidiary directly to the shareholders, and demands compensatory and punitive damages, costs and counsel fees. Defendants move for summary judgment dismissing the complaint.

Kennecott is a major copper mining and smelting company. In 1968, it purchased Peabody Coal Company. It paid some six hundred million dollars for Peabody's assets, and has since made capital investments in Peabody totalling approximately five hundred thirty million dollars. Almost from the time of the acquisition, the Federal Trade Commission conducted an investigation that ultimately resulted in an order directing Kennecott to divest itself of its interests in Peabody. That order was confirmed by the United States Court of Appeals, and the Supreme Court has denied certiorari.

Even before the order of divestiture became final, Kennecott management began a program to determine the most economically feasible form of divestiture. The choices appear to have been to either "spin-off" the shares of Peabody by issuing them to Kennecott shareholders, or to sell Peabody. Management has determined to sell the shares of Peabody to a consortium headed by the Newmont Mining Corporation, with certain of Peabody's assets being sold directly to Dampier Mining Company, for a total purchase price of approximately one billion two hundred million dollars. Management has neither sought nor received shareholder approval of this proposed sale. It may not complete the sale without the approval of the Federal Trade Commission, before which an application for approval is now pending.

In her complaint, and in her papers submitted on this motion, plaintiff contends that management has acted improperly in that, pursuant to Section 909 of the

Business Corporation Law, the contemplated transaction is invalid without prior shareholder approval. Moreover, she contends that any use of the proceeds of the contemplated sale other than a distribution to Kennecott's shareholders constitutes corporate waste, and is motivated solely by management's desire to maintain a high level of assets in Kennecott for its own benefit and prestige.

Section 909 of the Business Corporation Law provides, in pertinent part, that:

> (a) A sale, lease, exchange or other disposition of all or substantially all the assets of a corporation, if not made in the usual or regular course of the business actually conducted by such corporation, shall be authorized only in accordance with the following procedure:
>
> > (1) The board shall authorize the proposed sale, lease, exchange or other disposition and direct its submission to a vote of shareholders.
> >
> > (2) Notice of meeting shall be given to each shareholder of record, whether or not entitled to vote.
> >
> > (3) The shareholders shall approve such sale, lease, exchange or other disposition and may fix, or may authorize the board to fix, any of the terms and conditions thereof and the consideration to be received by the corporation therefor, which may consist in whole or in part of cash or other property, real or personal, including shares, bonds or other securities of any other domestic or foreign corporation or corporations, by a vote at a meeting of shareholders of the holders of two-thirds of all outstanding shares entitled to vote thereon.

Defendants assert that Section 909 is inapplicable to the facts of this case, since its interest in Peabody does not constitute "all or substantially all" of Kennecott's assets.

Plaintiff attempts to support her position that Peabody constitutes "all or substantially all" of Kennecott's assets principally with the novel theory that because the Peabody operations were Kennecott's only profitable operations during the past two years, the Peabody assets constitute Kennecott's sole income producing assets, and that only income producing assets may truly be deemed assets. The problem with this construction is twofold. First, no judicial determination and no authority other than plaintiff's own retained expert have subscribed to the theory that only income producing assets may be deemed assets. Kennecott's total assets, excluding Peabody, equal more than a billion dollars. This Court is not prepared to hold that those assets have no value simply because they have not produced a net profit during the past two years. Moreover, the conclusion that the remaining assets of Kennecott are not income producing is not accurate, for during the nine years that Kennecott has owned Peabody, Peabody profits have accounted for but one-third of Kennecott's total net revenues.

Finally, plaintiff contends that Section 909 applies so long as the asset to be sold constitutes an "integral part" of the total business. But the decisions relied upon by plaintiff for that proposition were based on an interpretation of the predecessor statute to Section 909. That statute specifically required shareholder approval as a condition for the sale of "an integral part" of a corporation "essential to the conduct of the business of the corporation" (Stock Corporation Law § 20). No such requirement exists in Section 909; the "integral part" formulation has been expressly deleted.

From the undisputable documentary evidence produced, the Court finds that Peabody does not constitute "all or substantially all" of Kennecott's assets. Shareholder approval of the sale of Peabody pursuant to Section 909 is therefore not necessary.

Defendants have acted properly in determining the sale of Peabody without resort to shareholder approval, the remainder of the allegations of the complaint are inadequate to sustain a claim for relief. First, the wholly conclusory allegations of managerial motives are insufficient. Plaintiff does not assert that defendants are directly profiting from the sale of Peabody. Indeed, the complaint does not challenge the sale itself, but, rather, the use to which the proceeds shall be put. The speculation that defendant Board's prestige and remuneration will be higher the higher Kennecott's total assets, without evidentiary support, is insufficient to survive this motion as is the unsupported claim that reinvestment of the proceeds of the sale into the corporation constitutes corporate waste. Moreover, any complaint with respect to the use of the proceeds of sale is premature. The sale has not been consummated; indeed, it has not been approved by the Federal Trade Commission. And, according to defendants, no determination has as yet been made as to the use of the proceeds.

Accordingly, the Court concludes that defendants are entitled to summary judgment dismissing the complaint. In light of this determination, the motions consolidated herewith to declare this a class action and to stay or limit discovery are rendered academic and denied as moot.

NOTE

The Government's antitrust challenge to Kennecott Copper Corporation's 1968 acquisition of Peabody Coal Company was based on the strict scrutiny of business acquisitions espoused in such cases as *United States v. Von's Grocery*, 384 U.S. 270 (1966). *See generally* G. Edward White, Earl Warren: A Public Life 294–301 (1982). That doctrine in effect required acquiring companies to purchase business segments unrelated to their "core" businesses and thus become "conglomerate" corporations owning a variety of businesses. That structure also theoretically provides some immunity from the vicissitudes of the business cycle. The existence of these diversified corporations gave rise to the leveraged buyouts of the 1980s because certain business segments of an acquired corporation could thereafter be sold to repay some of the acquisition indebtedness without disrupting its other operations. This is what Felix Royaton was referring to when he complained about corporations being torn apart like artichokes. *See* § 3.04, Note (1), *supra.* Since the 1960s, there have been various cycles in antitrust enforcement. Indeed, at one point, enforcement was relaxed to the point where in 2006 Whirlpool and Maytag were allowed to combine their washing machine and dryer businesses, a far cry from disallowing the combination in the *Story* Case.

KATZ v. BREGMAN

Delaware Court of Chancery
431 A.2d 1274 (1981)

Marvel, Chancellor

The complaint herein seeks the entry of an order preliminarily enjoining the proposed sale of the Canadian assets of Plant Industries, Inc. to Vulcan Industrial Packaging, Ltd., the plaintiff Hyman Katz allegedly being the owner of approximately 170,000 shares of common stock of the defendant Plant Industries, Inc., on whose behalf he has brought this action, suing not only for his own benefit as a stockholder but for the alleged benefit of all other record owners of common stock of the defendant Plant Industries, Inc. However, it is contended by defendants that Mr. Katz having been a former chief executive officer of Plant Industries, Inc. and allegedly involved in litigation with present management of the corporate defendant is accordingly disqualified to sue derivatively or for a class. Nonetheless, he would appear to be qualified to sue individually as stockholder of Plant Industries, Inc. for the relief sought. Significantly, at common law, a sale of all or substantially all of the assets of a corporation required the unanimous vote of the stockholders. Folk, The Delaware General Corporation Law, p. 400.

The complaint alleges that during the last six months of 1980 the board of directors of Plant Industries, Inc., under the guidance of the individual defendant Robert B. Bregman, the present chief executive officer of such corporation, embarked on a course of action which resulted in the disposal of several unprofitable subsidiaries of the corporate defendant located in the United States, namely Louisiana Foliage Inc., a horticultural business, Sunaid Food Products, Inc., a Florida packaging business, and Plant Industries (Texas), Inc., a business concerned with the manufacture of woven synthetic cloth. As a result of these sales Plant Industries, Inc. by the end of 1980 had disposed of a significant part of its unprofitable assets.

According to the complaint, Mr. Bregman thereupon proceeded on a course of action designed to dispose of a subsidiary of the corporate defendant known as Plant National (Quebec) Ltd., a business which constitutes Plant Industries, Inc.'s entire business operation in Canada and has allegedly constituted Plant's only income producing facility during the past four years. The professed principal purpose of such proposed sale is to raise needed cash and thus improve Plant's balance sheets. And while interest in purchasing the corporate defendant's Canadian plant was thereafter evinced not only by Vulcan Industrial Packaging, Ltd. but also by Universal Drum Reconditioning Co., which latter corporation originally undertook to match or approximate and recently to top Vulcan's bid, a formal contract was entered into between Plant Industries, Inc. and Vulcan on April 2, 1981 for the purchase and sale of Plant National (Quebec) despite the constantly increasing bids for the same property being made by Universal. One reason advanced by Plant's management for declining to negotiate with Universal is that a firm undertaking having been entered into with Vulcan that the board of directors of Plant may not legally or ethically negotiate with Universal.

In seeking injunctive relief, as prayed for, plaintiff relies on two principles, one that found in 8 Del. C. § 271 to the effect that a decision of a Delaware corporation to sell ". . . all or substantially all of its property and assets . . ." requires not only the approval of such corporation's board of directors but also a resolution adopted by a majority of the outstanding stockholders of the corporation entitled to vote thereon at a meeting duly called upon at least twenty days' notice.

Support for the other principle relied on by plaintiff for the relief sought, namely an alleged breach of fiduciary duty on the part of the board of directors of Plant Industries, Inc. is allegedly found in such board's studied refusal to consider a potentially higher bid for the assets in question which is being advanced by Universal, *Thomas v. Kempner, supra.*

Turning to the possible application of 8 Del. C. § 271 to the proposed sale of substantial corporate assets of National to Vulcan, it is stated in Gimbel v. Signal Companies, Inc., Del. Ch., 316 A.2d 599 (1974) as follows:

> If the sale is of assets quantitatively vital to the operation of the corporation and is out of the ordinary and substantially affects the existence and purpose of the corporation then it is beyond the power of the Board of Directors.

According to Plant's 1980 10K form, it appears that at the end of 1980, Plant's Canadian operations represented 51% of Plant's remaining assets. Defendants also concede that National represents 44.9% of Plant's sales' revenues and 52.4% of its pretax net operating income. Furthermore, such report by Plant discloses, in rough figures, that while National made a profit in 1978 of $2,900,000, the profit from the United States businesses in that year was only $770,000. In 1979, the Canadian business profit was $3,500,000 while the loss of the United States businesses was $344,000. Furthermore, in 1980, while the Canadian business profit was $5,300,000, the corporate loss in the United States was $4,500,000. And while these figures may be somewhat distorted by the allocation of overhead expenses and taxes, they are significant. In any event, defendants concede that ". . . National accounted for 34.9% of Plant's pretax income in 1976, 36.9% in 1977, 42% in 1978, 51% in 1979 and 52.4% in 1980."

While in the case of *Philadelphia National Bank v. B.S.F. Co.*, Del. Ch., 199 A.2d 557 (1969), *rev'd, on other grounds*, Del. Supr., 204 A.2d 746 (1964), the question of whether or not there had been a proposed sale of substantially all corporate assets was tested by provisions of an indenture agreement covering subordinated debentures, the result was the same as if the provisions of 8 Del. C. § 271 had been applicable, the trial Court stating:

> While no pertinent Pennsylvania case is cited, the critical factor in determining the character of a sale of assets is generally considered not the amount of property sold but whether the sale is in fact an unusual transaction or one made in the regular course of business of the seller.

Furthermore, in the case of *Wingate v. Bercut* (C.A.9) 146 F.2d 725 (1945), in which the Court declined to apply the provisions of 8 Del. C. § 271, it was noted that the transfer of shares of stock there involved, being a dealing in securities, constituted an ordinary business transaction.

In the case at bar, I am first of all satisfied that historically the principal business of Plant Industries, Inc. has not been to buy and sell industrial facilities but rather to manufacture steel drums for use in bulk shipping as well as for the storage of petroleum products, chemicals, food, paint, adhesives and cleaning agents, a business which has been profitably performed by National of Quebec. Furthermore, the proposal, after the sale of National, to embark on the manufacture of plastic drums represents a radical departure from Plant's historically successful line of business, namely steel drums. I therefore conclude that the proposed sale of Plant's Canadian operations, which constitute over 51% of Plant's total assets and in which are generated approximately 45% of Plant's 1980 net sales, would, if consummated, constitute a sale of substantially all of Plant's assets. By way of contrast, the proposed sale of Signal Oil in *Gimbel v. Signal Companies, Inc., supra*, represented only about 26% of the total assets of Signal Companies, Inc. And while Signal Oil represented 41% of Signal Companies, Inc. total net worth, it generated only about 15% of Signal Companies, Inc. revenue and earnings.

I conclude that because the proposed sale of Plant National (Quebec) Ltd. would, if consummated, constitute a sale of substantially all of the assets of Plant Industries, Inc., as presently constituted, that an injunction should issue preventing the consummation of such sale at least until it has been approved by a majority of the outstanding stockholders of Plant Industries, Inc., entitled to vote at a meeting duly called on at least twenty days' notice.

NOTES

(1) In *Hollinger Inc. v. Hollinger International, Inc.*, 858 A.2d 342 (Del. Ch. 2004), the Delaware Court of Chancery found that the sale by Hollinger International, Inc. ("International") of Telegraph Group, Ltd. ("Telegraph"), the publisher of two highly prestigious UK publications, did not constitute a sale of all or substantially all of International's assets. The court first stated that "Section 271 [of the Delaware Corporation Law] does not require a vote when a major asset or trophy is sold; it requires a vote only when the assets to be sold, when considered quantitatively and qualitatively, amount to 'substantially all' of the corporation's assets." 858 A.2d at 349. The court then reviewed Telegraph's economic contributions to International's balance sheet, using revenue, book value, and EBITDA to determine Telegraph's quantitative value to International. The court found that in the years 2000 to 2003 Telegraph's percentage contribution to International's revenue increased from 26.8% in 2000 to 49.0% in 2003; over the same time span, Telegraph's book value increased from 19.8% to 35.7% of International's total book value and its percentage contribution to EBITDA increased from 30.3% to 57.4%.[61] The court held, however, that because International would retain other substantial assets, including the publisher of the Chicago Sun-Times, the sale of Telegraph was not "quantitatively vital" to the operations of International. *Id.* at 379. In making this determination the court stated that *Katz v. Bregman* represented a "striking" deviation from statutory language in finding that a sale of a similar proportion of a company's assets could indeed qualify under Section 271. *Id.* at 378 n.53. In

[61] 858 A.2d at 381–82 (footnotes omitted). Figures from 2003 are unaudited.

concluding its analysis, the court stated that "[a]lthough by no means wholly consistent . . . case law has, by and large, refused to find that a disposition involved substantially all the assets of a corporation when the assets that would remain after the sale were, in themselves, substantial and profitable." *Id.* at 385.

EBITDA, an important method of measuring the value of a business enterprise, refers to: earnings before interest, taxes, depreciation and amortization. The difference between it and another valuation measurement, earnings per share, has been described as follows:

> The issue then becomes what benchmark to use in examining changes in the results of business operations post-signing of the merger agreement — EBITDA or earnings per share. In the context of a cash acquisition, the use of earnings per share is problematic. Earnings per share is very much a function of the capital structure of a company, reflecting the effects of leverage. An acquirer for cash is replacing the capital structure of the target company with one of its own choosing. While possible capital structures will be constrained by the nature of the acquired business, where, as here, both the debt and equity of the target company must be acquired, the capital structure of the target prior to the merger is largely irrelevant. What matters is the results of operation of the business. Because EBITDA is independent of capital structure, it is a better measure of the operational results of the business. . . .

Hexion Specialty Chems., Inc. v. Huntsman Corp., 965 A.2d 715, 749 (Del. Ch. 2008). EBITDA is to be distinguished from such business valuation measurements as gross profit (receipts from all sources less cost of goods sold, *i.e.*, materials, labor and allocated overhead) or gross revenue (receipts generated less cost of goods sold). An EBITDA calculation produces a *smaller* figure than does gross profit or gross revenue because the "earnings" component takes into account *all* of the direct operating costs of business, such as research and development, legal and accounting costs and general administrative expenses. EBITDA is not without its critics. Because assets wear out and EBITDA nevertheless excludes depreciation of capital expenses, Warren Buffet has reportedly asked, "Does management think the tooth fairy pays for capital expenditures?"

(2) In construing the term "all or substantially all" of the assets of a business corporation in the context of a *contractual* provision, as distinguished from a *statutory* one, a New York court applied a qualitative test in determining that an asset sale "substantially changed the nature of" the seller's business and "had the effect of materially changing the character" of an investment in the selling corporation, and thus constituted a sale of all or substantially all of that corporation's assets. *HFTP Inv. L.L.C. v. Grupo TMM, S.A.*, 2004 WL 5641710 (N.Y. Sup. Ct. 2004), *aff'd*, 18 A.D.3d 369 (N.Y. App. Div. 2005).

§ 3.08 THE TRUST INDENTURE ACT OF 1939

[A] Historical Data

After the enactment of the Securities Act of 1933 and the Securities Exchange Act of 1934, Congress continued to be concerned about the reasons for the failure of the nation's capital market systems to generate the investor confidence necessary to render that system capable of fulfilling its capital formation functions. It was also determined that, because of the manner in which the bankruptcies and receiverships that followed the 1929 stock market crash were being conducted, the interest of the holders of debt securities, which had been issued by corporations then involved in such procedures, were not adequately protected.

In Section 28 of the Securities Act of 1933, Congress directed the Securities and Exchange Commission to make a study of these matters. A series of hearings were held by the Securities and Exchange Commission and were conducted on behalf of the Commission by William O. Douglas in 1934 and 1935. Douglas was at that time a professor of corporate finance and related subjects at the Yale Law School. He became Commissioner of the SEC in 1936 and chairman in 1937. In 1939 he became a Justice of the Supreme Court. Justice Douglas authored a number of important opinions involving business reorganizations and corporate finance, including *Consolidated Rock Prods. v. Du Bois*, 312 U.S. 510 (1941); and *Pepper v. Litton*, 308 U.S. 295 (1939). The SEC hearings concentrated on the plight of holders of debt securities and the lack of protection afforded that type of investor. As a result of the findings, it was determined that the trust indenture and the indenture trustee afforded little, if any, meaningful protection to those investors. Of particular concern was the fact that the provisions of indentures were negotiated by persons acting on behalf of the issuer and the indenture trustee, and it was concluded that the interests of the bond holder investors were not addressed. Douglas described the work as follows:

> The hours of investigation were endless and the days long. We subpoenaed hundreds of witnesses, holding most of our hearings in Washington. We would start at 9:a.m. and run until 5:00 or later. One of my first witnesses was my old boss, Robert T. Swaine, of the Cravath firm. He had engineered many reorganizations in Wall Street, and we got the anatomy of them from his lips. He told me later, "You stood me on my head and shook all the fillings out of my teeth."
>
> There was, however, no bitterness between us in this regard. The investigations were not conducted as publicity stunts. They were calm and detached and they helped unravel many complex situations.

William O. Douglas, Go East Young Man 260 (1983).

The legislative solution to those problems was the Trust Indenture Act of 1939, which thereafter regulated the terms of indentures relating to publicly offered and certain other debt securities.

The Act provides in effect that a public offering of debt securities in an amount in excess of that established from time to time by the Commission (presently $10 million as provided in Rule 4a-3 of the General Rules and Regulations of the Securities and Exchange Commission under the Trust Indenture Act of 1939) cannot be made unless the debt securities are issued pursuant to an indenture that complies with the requirements of the Act and has been "qualified." An indenture complying with the Act becomes "qualified" at the time the registration statement relating to the debt securities becomes effective.

ZEFFIRO v. FIRST PENNSYLVANIA BANKING & TRUST CO.

United States Court of Appeals, Third Circuit
623 F.2d 290 (1980)

OPINION OF THE COURT

Rosenn, Circuit Judge

The Trust Indenture Act of 1939, 15 U.S.C. § 77aaa *et seq.*, regulates the terms of the agreement between debenture holders and the indenture trustee. This appeal presents to a United States Court of Appeals for the first time the question of whether the Act provides an injured investor with a cause of action in federal court against a trustee for breach of the agreement. We conclude, as did the district court, that a cause of action exists under the Act, allowing injured investors to bring suit in federal court.

. . .

II.

Before proceeding to a discussion of the merits, it may be useful to briefly outline the structure and background of the Trust Indenture Act. A study was conducted by the Securities Exchange Commission (SEC) in 1936 which revealed widespread abuses in the issuance of corporate bonds under indentures.[62] The main problems identified by the study were that the indenture trustee was frequently aligned with the issuer of the debentures and that the debenture holders were widely dispersed, thereby hampering their ability to enforce their rights. Furthermore, courts frequently enforced broad exculpatory terms of the indenture inserted by the issuer, which offered the investors less protection than the traditional standards of fiduciary duty.

Rather than allow the SEC direct supervision of trustee behavior and thereby provide for a more overt intrusion into capital markets, the Act establishes a standard of behavior indirectly by refashioning the form of the indenture itself. The Act is structured so that before a debt Security non-exempted from the Act may be

[62] [2] See Securities and Exchange Commission Report on the Study and Investigation of the Work, Activities, Personnel and Functions of Protective and Reorganization Committees, Part IV, Trustees Under Indentures (1937); *See also* Hearings on H.R. 10292 Before a Subcommittee of the Committee on Interstate and Foreign Commerce, 75th Cong., 3d Sess. 20 (1938).

offered to the public, the indenture under which it is issued must be "qualified" by the SEC. The indenture is deemed "qualified" when registration becomes effective.[63] Before registration of the debenture is declared effective it must be qualified under the following conditions: (1) the security has been issued under an indenture; (2) the person designated as trustee is eligible to serve; and (3) the indenture conforms to the requirements of §§ 310-318, 15 U.S.C. §§ 77jjj-77rrr. Judge Bechtle aptly described the operative provisions of the Act, §§ 310-318, as follows.

> Sections 310 through 318 form the core of the Act in that they outline the substantive duties that the indenture must impose on the trustee. These sections are of three types. The first type is proscriptive in nature, prohibiting certain terms. For example, § 315, 15 U.S.C. § 77ooo(d), prohibits provisions in the indenture which would relieve or exculpate the trustee from liability for negligence. The second type of section is merely permissive in nature. An example of this type of section is § 315(a), 15 U.S.C. § 77ooo(a)(1), which states that the indenture may contain a provision relieving the trustee of liability except for the performance of such duties as are specifically set out in such indenture.
>
> The third type of section, and the most important for our purposes, is mandatory and prescriptive in nature. These sections begin with the phrase "indenture to be qualified shall provide" or "shall require." An example of this type of section is § 311, 15 U.S.C. § 77kkk, which states that the indenture shall require the trustee to establish certain accounts for the benefit of bond holders in the event the trustee also becomes a creditor of the issuer and the issuer defaults on the bonds.

473 F. Supp. at 206.

The SEC has no enforcement authority over the terms of the indenture once the registration statement becomes effective, and it cannot issue a stop order for violation of indenture provisions by the indenture trustee. After the effective date of the indenture the SEC's role is limited to general rulemaking and investigation. 15 U.S.C. §§ 77ddd(c), (d), (e); 77eee(a), (c); 77ggg; 77sss; 77ttt. The Act contains criminal liability for certain willful violations and misrepresentations[64] and express civil liability for any omission or misstatement in the filing documents.[65]

---

[63] [3] § 309, 15 U.S.C. § 77iii. Securities not required to be registered under the 1933 Act are deemed "qualified" when the SEC permits the "application for qualification" to become effective. § 309(a)(2), 15 U.S.C. § 7iii(a)(2). The indenture must still conform to the requirements of §§ 310-318.

[64] [4] Section 325 provides:

> Any person who willfully violates any provision of this subchapter or any rule, regulation, or order thereunder, or any person who willfully, in any application, report, or document filed or required to be filed under the provisions of this subchapter or any rule, regulation, or order thereunder, makes any untrue statement of a material fact or omits to state any material fact required to be stated therein or necessary to make the statements therein not misleading, shall upon conviction be fined not more than $5,000 or imprisoned not more than five years, or both.

15 U.S.C. § 77yyy.

[65] [5] Section 323 provides in pertinent part:

> (a) Any person who shall make . . . any statement in any application, report, or document filed with the Commission . . . which statement was at the time . . . false or misleading with

Enforcement of the terms of the indenture is left to the parties. The plaintiffs in this case contend that the Act necessarily allows for enforcement of the indenture in federal court to insure compliance with the Act. First Pennsylvania argues that, because the Act only mandates certain terms of the indenture in order for it to be qualified by the SEC, the remedy is contractual under state law and not one for federal jurisdiction.

. . .

We hold that the Trust Indenture Act provides injured debenture holders with a federal cause of action for the breach of terms mandated by the Act. The judgment of the district court will be affirmed.

Costs taxed against appellant.

[B] Excerpts from Regulation S-K of the Securities and Exchange Commission

In order to provide a "checklist" for the examiner reviewing a public debt offering, Regulation S-K of the Securities and Exchange Commission under the Securities Act of 1933, as amended, requires in § 229.601(b)(4)(iv) that:

> If any of the securities being registered are, or will be, issued under an indenture to be qualified under the Trust Indenture Act, the copy of such indenture which is filed as an exhibit shall include or be accompanied by:
>
> (A) A reasonably itemized and informative table of contents; and
>
> (B) A cross-reference sheet showing the location in the indenture of the provisions inserted pursuant to Sections 310 through 318(a) inclusive of the Trust Indenture Act of 1939.
>
> Set forth below is an example of the cross-reference sheet referred to in the Regulation:

---

respect to any material fact, or who shall omit to state any material fact required to be stated therein or necessary to make the statements therein not misleading, shall be liable to any person (not knowing that such statement was false or misleading or of such omission) who, in reliance upon such statement or omission, shall have purchased or sold a security issued under the indenture to which such application, report, or document relates, for damages caused by such reliance, unless the person sued shall prove that he acted in good faith and had no knowledge that such statement was false or misleading or of such omission.

15 U.S.C. § 77www.

FSC CORPORATION

15% Senior Sinking Fund Debentures Due 1995

Cross Reference Sheet to Trust Indenture Act of 1939[66]

Trust Indenture Act of 1939 Section Number	Indenture Section Number
310(a)	6.09
310(b)	6.08,6.10(b)
310(c)	Inapplicable
311(a)	6.13(a)
311(b)	6.13(b)
311(c)	Inapplicable
312(a)	7.01, 7.02(a)
312(b)	7.02(b)
312(c)	7.02(c)
313(a)	7.03(a)
313(b)	7.03(b)
313(c)	7.03(c)
313(d)	7.03(d)
314(a)	7.04
314(b)	Inapplicable
314(c)	14.06
314(d)	Inapplicable
314(e)	14.06
314(f)	Inapplicable
315(a)	6.01(a)
315(b)	5.07
315(c)	6.01
315(d)	6.01
315(e)	5.08
316(a)	5.06, 8.04
316(b)	5.04
317(a)	5.02
317(b)	4.05
318(a)	14.09(a)

[66] This Cross Reference Sheet is not a part of the Indenture.

[C] Requirements of, and Form of Compliance with, Section 315 of the Trust Indenture Act

Amendments to the '39 Act

In November 1990, the first amendments to the Trust Indenture Act of 1939 became effective. As a result of the amendments, trust indentures are now deemed to contain certain statutorily permitted provisions unless those provisions are specifically excluded in the document. Moreover, it is no longer necessary to include statutorily mandated provisions in a trust indenture, as they are now part of the Act itself.

TRUST INDENTURE ACT OF 1939

SEC. 315. (a) The indenture to be qualified shall automatically be deemed (unless it is expressly provided therein that any such provision is excluded) to provide that, prior to default (as such term is defined in such indenture) —

(1) the indenture trustee *shall not be liable* except for the performance of such duties as are specifically set out in such indenture; and

(2) the indenture trustee *may conclusively rely*, as to the truth of the statements and the correctness of the opinions expressed therein, in the absence of bad faith on the part of such trustee, upon certificates or opinions conforming to the requirements of the indenture;

but the indenture trustee shall examine the evidence furnished to it pursuant to section 314 to determine whether or not such evidence conforms to the requirements of the indenture.

Notice of Defaults

(b) The indenture trustee shall give to the indenture security holders, in the manner and to the extent provided in subsection (c) of section 313, notice of all defaults known to the trustee, within ninety days after the occurrence thereof; *Provided*, That such indenture shall automatically be deemed (unless it is expressly provided therein that such provision is excluded) to provide that, except in the case of default in the payment of the principal of or interest on any indenture security, or in the payment of any sinking or purchase fund installment, the trustee shall be protected in withholding such notice if and so long as the board of directors, the executive committee, or a trust committee of directors and/or responsible officers, of the trustee in good faith determine that the withholding of such notice is in the interests of the indenture security holders.

Duties of the Trustee in Case of Default

(c) The indenture trustee shall exercise in case of default (as such term is defined in such indenture) such of the rights and powers vested in it by such indenture, and to use the same degree of care and skill in their exercise, as a prudent man would exercise or use under the circumstances in the conduct of his own affairs.

Responsibility of the Trustee

(d) The indenture to be qualified shall not contain any provisions relieving the indenture trustee from liability for its own negligent action, its own negligent failure to act, or its own willful misconduct, except that —

(1) such indenture shall automatically be deemed (unless it is expressly provided therein that any such provision is excluded) to contain the provisions authorized by paragraphs (1) and (2) of subsection (a) of this section;

(2) such indenture shall automatically be deemed (unless it is expressly provided therein that any such provision is excluded) to contain provisions protecting the indenture trustee from liability for any error of judgment made in good faith by a responsible officer or officers of such trustee, unless it shall be proved that such trustee was negligent in ascertaining the pertinent facts; and

(3) such indenture shall automatically be deemed (unless it is expressly provided therein that any such provision is excluded) to contain provisions protecting the indenture trustee with respect to any action taken or omitted to be taken by it in good faith in accordance with the direction of the holders of not less than a majority in principal amount of the indenture securities at the time outstanding (determined as provided in subsection (a) of section 316) relating to the time, method, and place of conducting any proceeding for any remedy available to such trustee, or exercising any trust or power conferred upon such trustee, under such indenture.

Undertaking for Costs

(e) The indenture to be qualified shall automatically be deemed (unless it is expressly provided therein that any such provision is excluded) to contain provisions to the effect that all parties thereto, including the indenture security holders, agree that the court may in its discretion require, in any suit for the enforcement of any right or remedy under such indenture, or in any suit against the trustee for any action taken or omitted by it as trustee, the filing by any party litigant in such suit of an undertaking to pay the costs of such suit, and that such court may in its discretion assess reasonable costs, including reasonable attorneys' fees, against any party litigant in such suit, having due regard to the merits and good faith of the claims or defenses made by such party litigant: *Provided*, That the provisions of this subsection shall not apply to any suit instituted by such trustee, to any suit instituted by any indenture security holder, or group of indenture security holders, holding in the aggregate more than 10 per centum in principal amount of the indenture securities outstanding, or to any suit instituted by any indenture security holder for the enforcement of the payment of the principal of or interest on any indenture security, on or after the respective due dates expressed in such indenture security.

ELLIOTT ASSOC. v. J. HENRY SCHRODER BANK & TRUST CO.

United States Court of Appeals, Second Circuit
838 F.2d 66 (1988)

ALTIMARI, CIRCUIT JUDGE:

This appeal involves an examination of the obligations and duties of a trustee during the performance of its pre-default duties under a trust indenture, qualified under the Trust Indenture Act of 1939, 15 U.S.C. § 77aaa *et seq.* (the "Act"). The instant action was brought by a debenture holder who sought to represent a class of all debenture holders under the trust indenture. The debenture holder alleged in its complaint that the trustee waived a 50-day notice period prior to the redemption of the debentures and did not consider the impact of the waiver on the financial interests of the debenture holders. The debenture holder alleged further that, had the trustee not waived the full 50-day notice period, the debenture holders would have been entitled to receive an additional $1.2 million in interest from the issuer of the debentures. The debenture holder therefore concludes that the trustee's waiver was improper and constituted a breach of the trustee's duties owed to the debenture holders under the indenture, the Act and state law.

The district court dismissed the debenture holder's action after conducting a bench trial and entered judgment in favor of the defendants. The district court held that the trustee's waiver did not constitute a breach of any duty owed to the debenture holders — under the indenture or otherwise — because, as the court found, a trustee's pre-default duties are limited to those duties expressly provided in the indenture. See 655 F. Supp. 1281, 1288-89 (S.D.N.Y. 1987). We agree with the district court that no breach of duty was stated here. Accordingly, we affirm the district court's decision dismissing the action.

FACTS and BACKGROUND

Appellant Elliott Associates ("Elliott") was the holder of $525,000 principal amount of 10% Convertible Subordinated Debentures due June 1, 1990 (the "debentures") which were issued by Centronics Data Computer Corporation ("Centronics") pursuant to an indenture between Centronics and J. Henry Schroder Bank and Trust Company ("Schroder"), as trustee. Elliott's debentures were part of an aggregate debenture offering by Centronics of $40,000,000 under the indenture which was qualified by the Securities Exchange Commission ("SEC") pursuant to the Act.

The indenture and debentures provided, inter alia, that Centronics had the right to redeem the debentures "at any time" at a specified price, plus accrued interest, but the indenture also provided that, during the first two years following the issuance of the debentures, Centronics' right to redeem was subject to certain conditions involving the market price of Centronics' common stock. To facilitate its right to redeem the debentures, Centronics was required to provide written notice of a proposed redemption to the trustee and to the debenture holders. Section 3.01 of the indenture required that Centronics give the trustee 50-day notice of its intention to call its debentures for redemption, "unless a shorter notice shall be satisfactory to the [t]rustee." Section 3.03 of the indenture required Centronics to provide the debenture holders with "[a]t least 15 days but not more than 60 days' notice of a proposed redemption.

At the option of the debenture holders, the debentures were convertible into shares of Centronics' common stock. In the event Centronics called the debentures for redemption, debenture holders could convert their debentures "at any time before the close of business on the last Business Day prior to the redemption date." Subject to certain adjustments, the conversion price was $3.25 per share. The number of shares issuable upon conversion could be determined by dividing the principal amount converted by the conversion price. Upon conversion, however, the debentures provided that "no adjustment for interest or dividends [would] be made."

Debenture holders were to receive interest payments from Centronics semi-annually on June 1 and December 1 of each year. Describing the method of interest payment, each debenture provided that [t]he Company will pay interest on the Debentures (except defaulted interest) to the persons who are registered Holders of Debentures at the close of business on the November 15 or May 15 next preceding the interest payment date. Holders must surrender Debentures to a Paying Agent to collect principal payments. To insure the primacy of the debenture holders' right to receive interest, the indenture provided that "[n]otwithstanding any other provision of this Indenture, the right of the Holder of a Security to receive payment of . . . interest on the Security . . . shall not be impaired."

In early 1986, Centronics was considering whether to call its outstanding debentures for redemption. On March 12, 1986, Centronics' Treasury Services Manager, Neil R. Gordon, telephoned Schroder's Senior Vice President in charge of the Corporate Trust Department, George R. Sievers, and informed him of Centronics' interest in redeeming the debentures. Gordon told Sievers that Centronics "was contemplating redemption" of all of its outstanding debentures, subject to SEC approval and fluctuations in the market for Centronics' common stock. Specifically addressing the 50-day notice to the trustee requirement in section 3.01 of the indenture, Gordon asked Sievers how much time "Schroder would need once the SEC had Centronics' registration materials and an actual redemption date could therefore be set." Sievers responded that "Schroder would only need [one] week" notice of the redemption. Sievers explained that this shorter notice would satisfy section 3.01 because Centronics was proposing a complete rather than a partial redemption, and because there were relatively few debenture holders. Sievers explained that the shorter notice therefore would provide it with sufficient time to perform its various administrative tasks in connection with the proposed redemption.

Shortly thereafter, on March 20, 1986, Centronics' Board of Directors met and approved a complete redemption of all of its outstanding debentures and designated May 16, 1986 as the redemption date. On April 4, 1986 — 42 days prior to the redemption — Centronics' President, Robert Stein, wrote Schroder and informed the trustee that "pursuant to the terms of the Indenture, notice is hereby given that the Company will redeem all of its outstanding 10% Convertible Subordinated

Debentures due June 1, 1990, on May 16, 1986." Centronics then proceeded to file registration materials with the SEC in order to receive clearance for the redemption. Schroder was furnished with copies of all the materials Centronics had filed with the SEC.

On May 1, 1986, the SEC cleared the proposed redemption. On that same day, pursuant to section 3.03 of the indenture, Centronics gave formal notice of the May 16, 1986 redemption to the debenture holders. In a letter accompanying the Notice of Redemption, Centronics' President explained that, as long as the price of Centronics' common stock exceeded $3.75 per share, debenture holders would receive more value in conversion than in redemption. In the Notice of Redemption, debenture holders were advised, inter alia, that the conversion price of $3.25 per share, when divided into each $1,000 principal amount being converted, would yield 307.69 shares of Centronics common stock. Based upon the April 30, 1986 New York Stock Exchange closing price of $5 3/8 per share of Centronics' common stock, each $1,000 principal amount of debenture was convertible into Centronics common stock having an approximate value of $1,653.83. Debenture holders were advised further that failure to elect conversion by May 15, 1986 would result in each $1,000 principal amount debenture being redeemed on May 16 for $1,146.11, which consisted of $1,000 in principal, $100 for the 10% redemption premium, and $46.11 in interest accrued from December 1, 1985 (the last interest payment date) to May 16, 1986 (the redemption date). Finally, the notice of redemption explained that accrued interest was not payable upon conversion: No adjustments for Interest or Dividends upon Conversion. No payment or adjustment will be made by or on behalf of the Company (i) on account of any interest accrued on any Debentures surrendered for conversion or (ii) on account of dividends, if any, on shares of Common Stock issued upon such conversion. Holders converting Debentures will not be entitled to receive the interest thereon from December 1, 1985 to May 16, 1986, the date of redemption.

On May 15, 1986, the last day available for conversion prior to the May 16, 1986 redemption, Centronics' common stock traded at $6 5/8 per share. At that price, each $1,000 principal amount of debentures was convertible into Centronics' common stock worth approximately $2,038. Thus, it was clear that conversion at $2,038 was economically more profitable than redemption at $1,146.11. Debenture holders apparently recognized this fact because all the debenture holders converted their debentures into Centronics' common stock prior to the May 16, 1986 redemption.

Elliott filed the instant action on May 12, 1986 and sought an order from the district court enjoining the May 16, 1986 redemption. Elliott alleged in its complaint that Schroder and Centronics conspired to time the redemption in such a manner so as to avoid Centronics' obligation to pay interest on the next interest payment date, *i.e.*, June 1, 1986. This conspiracy allegedly was accomplished by forcing debenture holders to convert prior to the close of business on May 15, 1986. Elliott contended that, as part of this conspiracy, Schroder improperly waived the 50-day notice in section 3.01 of the indenture and thus allowed Centronics to proceed with the redemption as planned. Elliott claimed that Schroder waived the 50-day notice without considering the impact of that waiver on the financial interests of the debenture holders and that the trustee's action in this regard constituted, inter alia, a breach of the trustee's fiduciary duties. Finally, Elliott alleged that, had it not been for the trustee's improper waiver, debenture holders would have been entitled to an additional payment of $1.2 million in interest from Centronics.

After filing the instant action, Elliott filed a motion pursuant to Fed. R. Civ. P. 23 to have itself certified as representative of a class comprised of "all persons who held, as of May 1, 1986, the 10% convertible subordinated debentures due June 1, 1990 of Centronics Data Computer Corp." Schroder and Centronics filed motions to dismiss the action, or, in the alternative, for summary judgment, on the ground that Elliott's complaint failed to state a claim. Centronics and Schroder also filed counterclaims against Elliott and sought an award of costs and attorneys' fees pursuant to an indenture provision, section 315 of the Act, 15 U.S.C. § 77ooo(e), and Fed. R. Civ. P. 11.

DISCUSSION

The central issue on this appeal is whether the district court properly held that the trustee was not obligated to weigh the financial interests of the debenture holders when it decided on March 12, 1986 to waive Centronics' compliance with section 3.01's 50-day notice requirement. We agree with the district court's conclusion that the trustee was under no such duty. *See* 655 F. Supp. at 1288-89.

At the outset, it is important to sort out those matters not at issue here. First, Elliott does not dispute that Centronics complied in all respects with the indenture's requirement to provide notice of redemption to the debenture holders. Elliott's claim only challenges the sufficiency of the notice to the trustee and the manner in which the trustee decided to waive that notice. Moreover, Elliott does not dispute that Schroder's actions were expressly authorized by section 3.01, which specifically allows the trustee discretion to accept shorter notice of redemption from Centronics if that notice was deemed satisfactory. Finally, except for bald assertions of conflict of interest, Elliott presents no serious claim that Schroder personally benefitted in any way from the waiver, or that, by waiving the notice period, it was taking a position that would harm the interests of the debenture holders and correspondingly inure to the trustee's benefit. Rather, Elliott's claim essentially is that the trustee was under a duty — implied from the indenture, the Act or state law — to secure greater benefits for debenture holders over and above the duties and obligations it undertook in the indenture.

No such implied duty can be found from the provisions of the Act or from its legislative history. Indeed, section 315(a)(1) of the Act allows a provision to be included in indentures (which was incorporated into the indenture at issue here) providing that the indenture trustee shall not be liable except for the performance of such duties [prior to an event of default] as are specifically set out in [the] indenture. *See* 15 U.S.C. § 77ooo(a)(1). Moreover, when the Act was originally introduced in the Senate by Senator Barkley, it provided for the mandatory inclusion of a provision requiring the trustee to perform its pre-default duties and obligations in a manner consistent with that which a "prudent man would assume and perform." See S. 2065, 76th Cong., 1st Sess. s 315(a) (1939) (the "Barkley Bill"); S. Rep. No. 248, 76th Cong., 1st Sess. 25 (1939). However, the version of the Act introduced in the House of Representatives by Representative Cole excluded the imposition of a pre-default "prudent man" duty on the trustee. *See* H.R. 5220, 76th Cong., 1st Sess. § 315 (1939). After extensive hearings on the House and Senate versions of the Act, during which representatives of several financial institutions expressed concern over the imposition of pre-default duties in excess of those duties set forth expressly in the indenture, see Hearings on H.R. 2191 and 5220 Before the Subcomm. of the House on Interstate and Foreign Commerce, 76th Cong., 1st Sess. (1939), Congress enacted the present version of section 315 of the Act. Thus, it is clear from the express terms of the Act and its legislative history that no implicit duties, such as those suggested by Elliott, are imposed on the trustee to limit its pre-default conduct.

It is equally well-established under state common law that the duties of an indenture trustee are strictly defined and limited to the terms of the indenture, *see, e.g., Green v. Title Guarantee & Trust Co.*, 223 A.D. 12, 227 N.Y.S. 252 (1st Dept.), *aff'd*, 248 N.Y. 627, 162 N.E. 552 (1928); *Hazzard v. Chase National Bank*, 159 Misc. 57, 287 N.Y.S. 541 (Sup. Ct. N.Y. County 1936), *aff'd*, 257 A.D. 950, 14 N.Y.S.2d 147 (1st Dept.), *aff'd*, 282 N.Y. 652, 26 N.E.2d 801, *cert. denied*, 311 U.S. 708, 61 S. Ct. 319, 85 L. Ed. 460 (1940), although the trustee must nevertheless refrain from engaging in conflicts of interest. *See United States Trust Co. v. First National City Bank*, 57 A.D. 285, 394 N.Y.S.2d 653 (1st Dept. 1977), *aff'd*, 45 N.Y.2d 869, 410 N.Y.S.2d 580, 382 N.E.2d 1355 (1978).

In view of the foregoing, it is no surprise that we have consistently rejected the imposition of additional duties on the trustee in light of the special relationship that the trustee already has with both the issuer and the debenture holders under the indenture. *See Meckel v. Continental Resources Co.*, 758 F.2d 811, 816 (2d Cir. 1985); *In re W.T. Grant Co.*, 699 F.2d 599, 612 (2d Cir.), *cert. denied*, 464 U.S. 822, 104 S. Ct. 89, 78 L. Ed. 2d 97 (1983); *Browning Debenture Holders' Comm. v. DASA Corp.*, 560 F.2d 1078, 1083 (2d Cir. 1977). As we recognized in *Meckel*, [a]n indenture trustee is not subject to the ordinary trustee's duty of undivided loyalty. Unlike the ordinary trustee, who has historic common-law duties imposed beyond those in the trust agreement, an indenture trustee is more like a stakeholder whose duties and obligations are exclusively defined by the terms of the indenture agreement. 758 F.2d at 816 (citing *Hazzard v. Chase National Bank, supra*). We therefore conclude that, so long as the trustee fulfills its obligations under the express terms of the indenture, it owes the debenture holders no additional, implicit pre-default duties or obligations except to avoid conflicts of interest.

Our analysis here is therefore limited to determining whether the trustee fulfilled its duties under the indenture. As set forth above, section 3.01 requires that, when the company intends to call its debentures for redemption, it must provide the trustee with 50-day notice of the redemption, "unless a shorter notice shall be satisfactory to the [t]rustee." Section 3.02 of the indenture sets forth the manner in which the trustee selects which debentures are to be redeemed when the company calls for a partial redemption. The American Bar Foundation's Commentaries on Model Debenture Indenture Provisions (1971) (the "Commentaries") explains that "[n]otice of the Company's election to redeem all the debentures need not be given to the Trustee since such a redemption may be effected by the Company without any action on the part of the Trustee. . . ." *Id.* at § 11-3, p. 493. Thus, it appears that section 3.01's notice requirement is intended for the trustee's benefit to allow it sufficient time to perform the various administrative tasks in preparation for redemption. While compliance with a full notice period may be necessary in the event of partial redemption, the full notice may not be required in the event of a complete redemption. We find that, although the trustee may reasonably insist on the full 50-day notice in the event of a complete redemption, it nevertheless has the discretion to accept shorter notice when it deems such shorter notice satisfactory.

In his affidavit filed on behalf of Schroder's motion to dismiss, Sievers explained the reasoning behind his decision on behalf of Schroder to waive the notice: On March 12, 1986, I received a phone call from Neil R. Gordon of Centronics Computer Corp. (the "Company") regarding the possibility of the Company effecting a redemption of all of its 10% Convertible Subordinated Debentures Due June 2, 1990 (the "Debentures"). Mr. Gordon specifically inquired about the Trustee's needs under the 50 day notice requirement specified in Section 3.01 of the Indenture dated as of June 1, 1985 (the "Indenture") between Schroder and the Company pursuant to which the Debentures were issued. I told Mr. Gordon that Schroder would need only a week to prepare the notices for a redemption since there were less than two dozen holders to be notified.

. . . .

I know [from] personal knowledge . . . that the notice periods are meant to coordinate with the Trustee's own obligation to give notice to debentureholders in a partial redemption. The Trustee must be informed of a partial optional redemption sufficiently in advance of the time for giving such notice to permit it to make the selection of debentures to be redeemed. . . . If less time is required than the full number of days allowed by the particular indenture, then the trustee can and should waive the unnecessary and unneeded days. This pragmatic consideration is the reason that virtually all indentures modeled after the ABA instrument explicitly provide "unless a shorter notice shall be satisfactory to the Trustee." In view of the fact that only 23 debentureholders held all of the Company's Debentures, the determination to proceed with a redemption of all the Debentures with a notice of less than 50 days would have been within Schroder's discretion and waiver of the 50 day period would have been consistent with the intent of Section 3.01 of the Indenture. I know it to be the case that other corporate trustees under comparable indentures have been asked to waive equivalent notice provisions, *i.e.*, finding that a shorter period of time is satisfactory to the trustee to effect the selection required for a partial redemption. Waiver is most frequently employed where there is a small number of debentureholders relative to the principal amount outstanding. Schroder and other trustees regularly waive the full time of notice on numerous occasions when less time is needed to carry out the functions for which the time period was created. When Schroder received Centronics' May 1, 1986, formal letter, it had more than sufficient time to give the required notice to the 23 debentureholders. Accordingly, Schroder did not object because, in the language of the indenture and according to uniform custom, the "shorter notice shall be (and was indeed) satisfactory to the Trustee."

From Siever's affidavit, it is clear that Schroder complied with the letter and spirit of the indenture when it waived compliance with the full 50-day notice. Schroder was given the discretion to waive full notice under appropriate circumstances, and we find that it reasonably exercised that discretion.

To support its argument that Schroder was obligated to consider the impact of the waiver on the interests of the debenture holders, Elliott relies on our decision in *Dabney v. Chase National Bank*, 196 F.2d 668 (2d Cir. 1952), as suppl'd, 201 F.2d 635 (2d Cir.), *cert. dismissed per stipulation*, 346 U.S. 863, 74 S. Ct. 102, 98 L. Ed. 374 (1953). *Dabney* provided that the duty of a trustee, not to profit at the possible expense of his beneficiary, is the most fundamental of the duties which he accepts when he becomes a trustee. It is a part of his obligation to give his beneficiary his undivided loyalty, free from any conflicting personal interest; an obligation that has been nowhere more jealously and rigidly enforced than in New York where these indentures were executed. "The most fundamental duty owed by the trustee to the beneficiaries of the trust is the duty of loyalty. . . . In some relations the fiduciary element is more intense than in others; it is peculiarly intense in the case of a trust." We should be even disposed to say that without this duty there could be no trust at all. 196 F.2d at 670 (footnotes omitted) (citations omitted); *see United States Trust Co. v. First National City Bank*, 57 A.D.2d 285, 394 N.Y.S.2d 653, 660-61 (1st Dept. 1977), *aff'd*, 45 N.Y.2d 869, 410 N.Y.S.2d 580, 382 N.E.2d 1355 (1978) (adopting *Dabney*). *Dabney* arose, however, in an entirely different factual context than the instant case.

The *Dabney* court examined the conduct of a trustee who knew or should have known that the company for whose bonds it served as trustee was insolvent. While possessing knowledge of the company's insolvency, the trustee proceeded to collect loan obligations from the company. The court held that the trustee's conduct in this regard constituted a breach of its obligation not to take an action which might disadvantage the debenture holders while providing itself with a financial advantage, *i.e.*, the trustee engaged in a conflict of interest. *See* 196 F.2d at 673. Thus, while *Dabney* stands for the proposition that a trustee must refrain from engaging in conflicts of interest, it simply does not support the broader proposition that an implied fiduciary duty is imposed on a trustee to advance the financial interests of the debenture holders during the period prior to default. Because no evidence was offered in the instant case to suggest that Schroder benefitted, directly or indirectly, from its decision to waive the 50-day notice, and thus did not engage in a conflict of interest, it is clear that *Dabney* is inapposite to the instant appeal.

Schroder also contends that, even if we were to find that the trustee owed the debenture holders a duty to consider the impact of the waiver, we would nevertheless be compelled to dismiss this action because the debenture holders were not entitled to payment of accrued interest upon conversion. However, since we agree with the district court that the trustee had no duty to consider the impact of the waiver, we do not decide this question.

CONCLUSION

In view of the foregoing, we affirm the judgment of the district court which dismissed Elliott's action. . . .

Affirmed.

NOTES

(1) An Indenture Trustee can be held liable for the negligent performance of its Section 315 pre-default duties. *See AG Capital Funding Partners v. State Street Bank & Trust Co.*, 11 N.Y.3d 146, 866 N.Y.S.2d 578, 896 N.E.2d 61 (2008).

(2) Set forth below is an example of Indenture provisions implementing Section 315:

ARTICLE VI
THE TRUSTEE

(1) Except during the continuance of an Event of Default,

(i) the Trustee undertakes to perform such duties and only such duties as are specifically set forth in this Indenture, and no implied covenants or obligations shall be read into this Indenture against the Trustee; and

(ii) in the absence of bad faith on its part, the Trustee may conclusively rely, as to the truth of the statements and the correctness of the opinions expressed therein, upon certificates or opinions furnished to the Trustee and conforming to the requirements of this Indenture, but in the case of any such certificates or opinions which by any provision hereof are specifically required to be furnished to the Trustee, the Trustee shall be under a duty to examine the same to determine whether or not they conform on their face to the requirements of this Indenture, but not to verify the contents thereof.

(2) In case an Event of Default has occurred and is continuing, the Trustee shall exercise such of the rights and powers vested in it by this Indenture, and use the same degree of care and skill in their exercise, as a prudent man would exercise or use under the circumstances in the conduct of his own affairs.

(3) No provision of this Indenture shall be construed to relieve the Trustee from liability for its own negligent action, its own negligent failure to act, or its own willful misconduct, except that

(i) this paragraph (3) shall not be construed to limit the effect of paragraph (1) of this Section;

(ii) the Trustee shall not be liable for any error of judgment made in good faith by a Responsible Officer, unless it shall be proved that the Trustee was negligent in ascertaining the pertinent facts;

(iii) the Trustee shall not be liable with respect to any action taken or omitted to be taken by it in good faith in accordance with the direction of the Holders of a majority in aggregate principal amount of the Outstanding Securities relating to the time, method and place of conducting any proceeding for any remedy available to the Trustee, or exercising any trust or power conferred upon the Trustee, under this Indenture;

(iv) no provision of this Indenture shall require the Trustee to expend or risk its own funds or otherwise incur any financial liability in the performance of any of its duties hereunder, or in the exercise of any of its rights or powers, if it shall have reasonable grounds for believing that repayment of such funds or adequate indemnity against such risk or liability is not reasonably assured to it; and

(v) the Trustee shall not be liable for interest on any money received by it acting in its capacity as Trustee hereunder except as the Trustee may agree in writing with the Company.

(4) In the absence of negligence or willful misconduct on the part of the Trustee, the Trustee shall not be responsible for the application of any money by any Paying Agent other than the Trustee.

(5) Whether or not therein expressly so provided, every provision of this Indenture relating to the conduct or affecting the liability of or affording protection to the Trustee shall be subject to the provisions of this Section and the Trust Indenture Act.

[D] Acceleration Provisions and Section 316 of the Trust Indenture Act

The Baltimore & Ohio Railway Company emerged from bankruptcy in 1946 and in connection therewith issued debt securities called income bonds, the interest on which was payable only if the railroad had "Available Income" as defined in the bond indenture. The following observation explains why investors would purchase such a security issued by a recently bankrupt corporation:

> During the Great Depression, a number of railroads had filed for bankruptcy, leaving the prices of their shares and bonds badly depressed. During the war years, however, the railroads had been operating at full capacity and, as a result, were flush with cash. Coming through bankruptcy court, they were . . . reorganized in ways that would unlock their real value.

Robert E. Rubin, In an Uncertain World 41 (2003). (The B&O continued to be viable more than 40 years after the conclusion of the bankruptcy proceedings until its 1987 merger into the C&O described in Note 1 below.)

On May 1, 1968, the unpaid interest on the income bonds, which gave rise to the *Friedman* case, was paid in full. Brief for Appellee at 13, *Friedman v. Chesapeake & O. R. Co.*, 395 F.2d 663 (2d Cir. 1968) (affirming the decision of the District Court set forth below).

FRIEDMAN v. CHESAPEAKE & O. R.R. CO.

United States District Court, Southern District of New York
261 F. Supp. 728 (1966)

OPINION

MacMahon, District Judge.

Plaintiffs move to strike a defense that they lack standing and for leave to serve an amended complaint. Defendant Baltimore and Ohio Railroad Company ("B&O") cross-moves for summary judgment.

The complaint purports to assert a class action on behalf of plaintiffs and all other holders of defendant B&O's convertible 4 1/2% income bonds, due February 1, 2010, and seeks to recover principal and interest on the bonds. The bonds were issued under an indenture which, inter alia, defines and conditions the rights of holders to sue.

The answers of both defendants assert an affirmative defense that plaintiffs lack standing to bring this action because they have failed to perform certain conditions precedent as required by the bonds and the indenture on which plaintiffs' claims are based.

Plaintiffs move under Rule 12(b) of the Federal Rules of Civil Procedure to strike the defense as insufficient in law, and defendant B&O cross-moves under Rule 56(b) of the Federal Rules of Civil Procedure for summary judgment dismissing the complaint. There is no issue as to any material fact relating to the defense. The motions, thus, squarely raise the question of whether the defense is sufficient as a matter of law.

We note at the outset that the bonds are not due until February 1, 2010. Necessarily, therefore, an action to recover the principal does not lie unless the maturity date of the bonds has been accelerated by a completed event of default. The bonds, on their face, clearly refer to the indenture and expressly notify plaintiffs and all holders that "in case an event of default, as defined in the Indenture, shall occur, the principal of the Bonds may be declared, or may become, due and payable, in the manner and with the effect provided in the Indenture." Plaintiffs are thus forced to rely on the indenture in order to accelerate the time of payment.

That plaintiffs have in fact based their claims on the indenture is abundantly clear on the face of the complaint which plainly invokes the aid of certain provisions of the trust indenture in order to accelerate the maturity of the bonds by the alleged occurrence of events of default. Thus, the complaint alleges four claims against both defendants, and the relief sought in all of them is based upon plaintiffs' allegation that there has been a "merger in fact" of the B&O and the Chesapeake and Ohio Railway Company ("C&O").

Coupling their alleged merger in fact with alleged events of default specified in the indenture, plaintiffs claim that the maturity date of the bonds has been accelerated and that both railroads are now obligated to make payment on them. The alleged events of default upon which plaintiffs rely are the payment of dividends by C&O while there was nonpayment of interest on the B&O income bonds for the years 1961 through 1965, failure to make sinking fund payments, and payments into B&O's retirement annuity plans. The foregoing acts, according to the complaint, constitute "a subversion of plaintiffs' rights under the Indenture and their bonds," causing arrears of interest to become immediately due and an acceleration of maturity on the principal of the B&O income bonds.

Assuming, *arguendo*, that the alleged events of default have in fact occurred, Article Eight of the indenture, nonetheless, invests the trustee under the indenture with all rights of action and provides that no action growing out of any provision of the B&O indenture may be instituted upon the bonds unless the trustee fails to act upon the request of [the holders of] 25% in principal amount of the outstanding bonds and the offer of adequate indemnity to the trustee.

As we have shown, plaintiffs must, and do, invoke the aid of certain provisions of the trust indenture to validate their claim. They must, therefore, plead and prove compliance with the requirements and performance of the conditions defined in the indenture as conditions precedent to the maintenance of this action.

The complaint does not allege that the conditions precedent to suit, required by the trust indenture, have been met, and the fact that they have not been complied with is alleged in the challenged affirmative defense and is shown by undisputed affidavits supporting the motion for summary judgment. The complaint, therefore, fails to state a claim upon which relief can be granted, and there being no genuine issue of any material fact respecting the challenged affirmative defense, the motion for summary judgment must be granted, unless there is merit to plaintiffs' remaining contentions which we will now discuss.

Plaintiffs argue that summary judgment is precluded because [§ 316(b) of] the Trust Indenture Act of 1939, 15 U.S.C.A. § 77ppp(b), specifically prohibits any limitation on the right of a bondholder to institute suit for either principal or interest without the bondholders' consent. The short answer to this contention is that the bonds which are the subject of this suit were issued pursuant to the authority of the Interstate Commerce Commission, in accordance with § 20a of the Interstate Commerce Act, 49 U.S.C.A. § 20a, and are expressly exempted from the provisions of the Trust Indenture Act, [§ 304(a)(4)]. Section 3(a)(6) of the Securities Act of 1933, exempts "any security issued by a common or contract carrier, the issuance of which is subject to the provisions of section 20a of Title 49 [Interstate Commerce Act]."

Finally, plaintiffs contend that the challenged defense should not prevail because the trustee has unreasonably refused to sue. This is premised on plaintiffs' demand that the trustee take appropriate action on their claims that there has been a merger in fact and that the declaration and payment of a dividend by C&O constitutes an event of default.

There is no dispute that C&O has paid a dividend, but defendants vigorously deny that there has been a merger in fact or that such payment was a payment by B&O or in any way an event of default under the indenture. Plaintiffs assert that the trustee's failure to sue is so unreasonable that individual bondholders may sue despite the "no action" clause. Plaintiffs cannot so easily escape from the consequences of failing to perform the conditions precedent. The indenture requirement that bondholders may sue where the trustee fails to act, only if requested by the holders of 25% of the principal amount of the outstanding bonds and an offer of adequate indemnity to the trustee, is plainly reasonable.

Plaintiffs' whole case is built upon the claim of a "merger in fact," predicated essentially on C&O's ownership of 90% of B&O's stock, the pooling of equipment, and the coordinated use of facilities and personnel. In approving C&O's acquisition of control of the B&O, the I.C.C. expressly recognized that the transaction was not a merger, and, noting that B&O's very existence was threatened unless its operating expenses were reduced and its earnings increased, found that:

> Under affiliation C&O is willing and can provide the financial assistance needed to restore the B&O's properties to essential standards. This is not a temporary palliative but an effort of the railroads themselves to work out their long-range problems. Through the use of joint facilities and personnel and the pooling of equipment, substantial cost reductions and savings can be effected. Further, the legitimate interests of B&O's creditors and equity holders will be served by C&O control. As a result of the affiliation, B&O will eventually become a stronger railroad and the efficiency and economy of its operations will be increased. Strengthened as a result of the control, B&O's ability to meet adequately the needs of commerce and of the national defense will be enhanced. These take on added significance when we view the large industrial and population centers served by the B&O in 13 States and the District of Columbia.

Chesapeake & 0. Ry. Co. Control, 317 I.C.C. 261, 291(1962).

Plaintiffs' claim of a "merger in fact" borders on the frivolous for it is predicated on semantics. Mere labels, however, cannot alter the fact that the I.C.C. has approved the very transaction and acts which form the basis of plaintiffs' claim. Moreover, railroads may not merge, nor may one railroad assume the obligations of another without I.C.C. approval. Surely, under the circumstances, the trustee's insistence on a request by the prescribed proportion of the bondholders and adequate indemnity before undertaking litigation of the complexity, magnitude, expense, and uncertainty inherent in plaintiffs' tenuous claim is clearly reasonable.

We hold, therefore, that the challenged affirmative defense is sufficient to bar the action as a matter of law.

NOTES AND QUESTIONS

(1) The *Friedman* court found that there was no *de facto* merger of the B&O and the C&O in the 1960s; however, on April 30, 1987 there was a *de jure* merger between the two corporations pursuant to which the public B&O shareholders received $124 per common share and $100 for each preferred share. *See Sornberger v. Chesapeake & O. R. Co.*, 566 A.2d 503 (Md. Ct. Spec. App. 1989).

(2) The *Friedman* court also found that the B&O bonds were not subject to the Trust Indenture Act and thus did not have to consider the bondholders' claim that Section 316(b) of the Act prohibits the enforcement of a "no action" clause when it is interposted as a defense to a suit seeking to accelerate the maturity date of debt instruments.

Section 316 provides as follows:

DIRECTIONS AND WAIVERS BY BONDHOLDERS; PROHIBITION OF IMPAIRMENT OF HOLDER'S RIGHT TO PAYMENT

SEC. 316.

(a) The indenture to be qualified

(1) shall automatically be deemed (unless it is expressly provided therein that any such provision is excluded) to contain provisions authorizing the holders of not less than a majority in principal amount of the indenture securities or if expressly specified in such indenture, of any series of securities at the time outstanding (A) to direct the time, method, and place of conducting any proceeding for any remedy available to such trustee, or exercising any trust or power conferred upon such trustee, under such indenture, or (B) on behalf of the holders of all such indenture securities, to consent to the waiver of any past default and its consequences; or

(2) may contain provisions authorizing the holders of not less than 75 per centum in principal amount of the indenture securities or if expressly specified in such indenture, of any series of securities at the time outstanding to consent on behalf of the holders of all such indenture securities to the postponement of any interest payment for a period not exceeding three years from its due date.

For the purposes of this subsection and paragraph (3) of subsection (d) of section 315, in determining whether the holders of the required principal amount of indenture securities have concurred in any such direction or consent, indenture securities owned by any obligor upon the indenture securities, or by any person directly or indirectly controlling or controlled by or under direct or indirect common control with any such obligor, shall be disregarded, except that for the purposes of determining whether the indenture trustee shall be protected in relying on any such direction or consent, only indenture securities which such trustee knows are so owned shall be so disregarded.

(b) Notwithstanding any other provision of the indenture to be qualified, the right of any holder of any indenture security to receive payment of the principal of and interest on such indenture security, on or after the respective due dates *expressed* in such indenture security, or to institute suit for the enforcement of any such payment on or after such respective dates, shall not be impaired or affected without the consent of such holder, except as to a postponement of an interest payment consented to as provided in paragraph (2) of subsection (a), and except that such indenture may contain provisions limiting or denying the right of any such holder to institute any such suit, if and to the extent that the institution or prosecution thereof or the entry of judgment therein would, under applicable law, result in the surrender, impairment, waiver, or loss of the lien of such indenture upon any property subject to such lien.

(c) The obligor upon any indenture qualified under this title may set a record date for purposes of determining the identity of indenture security holders entitled to vote or consent to any action by vote or consent authorized or permitted by subsection (a) of this section. Unless the indenture provides otherwise, such record date shall be the later of 30 days prior to the first solicitation of such consent or the date of the most recent list of holders furnished to the trustee pursuant to section 312 of this title prior to such solicitation.

It will be observed that § 316(b) requires in effect that the indenture must provide that, without the bondholder's consent, the right of such holder to receive payment of principal on and after the due date "expressed in such indenture security" shall not be impaired.

The question can thus be posed whether the enforcement of a "no action" clause in a suit seeking to accelerate the due date for the payment of principal impairs the right of the holder to receive payment of principal on the date *expressed* in the indenture.

[E] Filing Requirements of the Trust Indenture Act

AFFILIATED COMPUTER SERVS. v. WILMINGTON TRUST CO.

United States District Court, Northern District of Texas
2008 U.S. Dist. LEXIS 10190 (Feb. 12, 2008)

SIDNEY A. FITZWATER, CHIEF JUDGE

* * *

Wilmington contends that even if § 4.03(a) [of the Indenture] does not obligate ACS to make timely SEC filings, § 314(a) of the [Trust Indenture Act the "TIA"] does. Because the Notes are registered, the Indenture is "qualified" within the meaning of 15 U.S.C. § 77ccc(9). Accordingly, § 314 of the TIA must form a part of the Indenture. *See* 15 U.S.C. § 77rrr(c). Moreover, the parties agree that § 4.03 explicitly incorporates § 314(a) of the TIA. Section 314(a) provides, in pertinent part:

Each person who, as set forth in the registration statement or application, is or is to be an obligor upon the indenture securities covered thereby shall —

(1) file with the indenture trustee copies of the annual reports and of the information, documents, and other reports (or copies of such portions of

> any of the foregoing as the [SEC] may by rules and regulations prescribe) which such obligor is required to file with the [SEC][.]

15 U.S.C. § 77nnn(a).

As in § 4.03 of the Indenture, the phrase "is required to file with the [SEC]" modifies the types of reports and documents that are included in the universe of those that ACS must file with the Trustee. Thus § 314 of the TIA obligates ACS to file with Wilmington copies of the reports and documents that ACS files with the SEC, but § 314 does not require that ACS file anything with the SEC. In *Cyberonics* the court concluded that § 314(a) of the TIA "is actually less stringent than the ["Reports" covenant] because it does not specify the time by which Cyberonics must provide [the indenture trustee] with copies of information filed with the SEC." *Cyberonics*, 2007 WL 1729977, at 4[, 2007 U.S. Dist. LEXIS 42779].

Wilmington argues that SEC Rule 19a-1 reflects the agency's interpretation of § 314(a)(1) to require that "eligible indenture obligors" such as ACS file timely reports with the SEC:

> An "eligible indenture obligor" that files with the indenture trustee those Exchange Act reports filed with the Commission . . . has met its duty under Section 314(a)(1) of the Act (15 U.S.C. 77nn[n] (a)(1)) to "file with the indenture trustee all reports required to be filed with the Commission pursuant to Section 13 or Section 15(d) of the Securities Exchange Act of 1934."

17 C.F.R. § 260.19a-1(c). Under Rule 19a-1, ACS satisfies its obligations under § 314(a)(1) by filing with the Trustee "those Exchange Act reports *filed* with the Commission." *Id.* (emphasis added). This SEC rule is completely consistent with the court's construction of § 314(a): the indenture obligor need only file with the Trustee the reports and documents that it has in fact filed with the SEC. SEC Rule 19a-1 does not affirmatively require the indenture obligor to file original documents and reports with the SEC.

Wilmington also contends that the policies of the TIA support its interpretation of § 314(a). Section 302 of the TIA enumerates some practices that adversely affect the public.

> [I]t is hereby declared that the national public interest and the interest of investors in notes, bonds, debentures, evidences of indebtedness, and certificates of interest or participation therein, which are offered to the public, are adversely affected —
>
> . . .
>
> (4) when the obligor is not obligated to furnish to the trustee under the indenture and to such investors adequate current information as to its financial condition, and as to the performance of its obligations with respect to the securities outstanding under such indenture[.]

15 U.S.C. § 77bbb(a). The Indenture's requirement that ACS deliver to the Trustee a copy of all of ACS's required SEC filings within 15 days of filing them with the SEC meets this policy concern. It ensures that the note holders through the Trustee

possess the same financial information concerning the issuing company that the rest of the investment public has. Moreover, Wilmington cannot argue that it was without any current financial information on ACS from September 13, 2006, the day ACS's Form 10-K was due, until January 25, 2006, the day Wilmington received ACS's 10-K and 10-Q reports. During this four-month period, ACS did apprise the Trustee and investors of the company's financial situation and developments in its internal investigation through SEC Form 8-Ks and other public announcements.[67] Thus Wilmington's contention that its note holders were deprived of material financial information necessary to make informed judgments has little merit. Although Wilmington would have been better protected had the Indenture affirmatively obligated ACS to timely file its Exchange Act reports directly with the SEC, the court will not rewrite the clear language of § 4.03(a) of the Indenture and § 314(a)(1) of the TIA on this basis. The court notes that, while urging the court to adopt a policy-based interpretation of the Indenture, when it suits Wilmington's purposes concerning other issues in dispute, it maintains that "Public bondholders must have assurance that indentures will be enforced *according to their terms.*" D. Reply 20 (emphasis added).

C

Wilmington's attempt to distinguish *Cyberonics* on the basis that the indenture in that case was not a qualified indenture is misplaced. Although the indenture in *Cyberonics* was not qualified and thus did not statutorily incorporate § 314 of the TIA, the *Cyberonics* court assumed that the indenture agreement incorporated § 314(a). *Cyberonics*, 2007 WL 1729977, at 4[, 2007 U.S. Dist. LEXIS 42779]. But even if *Cyberonics* could be distinguished on the basis of the applicability of § 314(a) of the TIA, based on the above discussion, the court holds that § 314(a) does not provide an independent obligation for the indenture obligor to timely file reports with the SEC according to §§ 13 and 15(d) of the Exchange Act.

Wilmington argues that reducing § 4.03(a) to a delivery obligation ensuring simultaneous access of information between shareholders and bondholders renders this provision surplusage in an age of electronic filing of SEC reports. Because all public SEC filings are accessible to the public via the Internet on the EDGAR system, Wilmington urges that it would make little sense to have a specific provision in the Indenture solely dealing with the delivery of these SEC filings to the Trustee.

The court acknowledges that the value of a pure delivery obligation in the post-EDGAR world is considerably less than before it. But when the TIA was enacted in 1939, a delivery requirement would have been important, because quick

[67] [3] ACS filed a Form 8-K on November 1, 2006 that included its preliminary financial information for the first quarter of the new fiscal year ending September 30, 2006, a notice that it would not timely file a Form 10-Q for that quarter on account of its ongoing internal investigation, as well as updates on the progress of the internal investigation. Later that month, in a Form 12b-25, ACS stated that it would not timely file a Form 10-Q for the first quarter ending September 30, 2006 and that it expected to complete its internal investigation before the end of the year. A few weeks later in a press release, ACS announced the completion of its internal investigation and estimated that the company's backdating practices would cost it approximately $51 million, plus tax-related expenses. ACS's Form 10-K for the fiscal year ending June 30, 2006 confirmed the accuracy of the press release's estimates.

access to SEC filings was not possible through other means. Thus Wilmington's argument does not apply to the court's interpretation of § 314(a) of the TIA. Moreover, because § 4.03(a) of the Indenture largely mirrors the language of § 314(a), there is no reason to believe that the parties intended it to require anything more than what § 314(a) requires, except for the addition of a 15-day delivery limit. While the parties negotiated the Indenture in 2005, the fact that § 4.03(a) largely restates § 314(a)(1) helps explain why the parties might have included a pure delivery requirement in an era of publicly-available Internet filings. But even with electronic access, a delivery requirement is not meaningless. With a delivery requirement the Trustee knows when the Indenture obligor has filed something with the SEC and is spared the time and expense of printing the documents and reports. Nevertheless, the court's construction of § 4.03(a) does not depend on speculation as to why the parties might have written § 4.03(a) as they did, but rather on § 4.03(a)'s clear language and the context of the Indenture as whole.[68]

§ 3.09 THE SUPPLEMENTAL INDENTURE

BANK OF N.Y. v. TYCO INT'L GROUP, S.A.

United States District Court, Southern District of New York
545 F. Supp. 2d 312 (2008)

SHIRA A. SCHEINDLIN, DISTRICT JUDGE.

[In 1998, and 2003, respectively, a wholly owned subsidiary ("TIGSA") of the publicly traded Tyco International, LTD. ("Tyco") issued several series of Notes pursuant to Indentures under which Bank of New York ("BNY") was the Trustee. Tyco was the guarantor of the Notes. TIGSA was the owner of four business segments which constituted substantially all of TIGSA's (and thus Tyco's) assets. The Indentures permitted the transfer by TIGSA of substantially all of its assets, only if the transferee expressly assumed, in a Supplemental Indenture between it and the Trustee, the obligations of TIGSA under the Notes. In 2007, two of the business segments, medical devices and electronics, were transferred to Tyco and then spun off to the public stockholders of Tyco; the two other businesses, security systems and engineered products and services, were transferred to and retained by Tyco, through TIFSA, a holding company. A proposed Supplemental Indenture

[68] [4] As the *Cyberonics* court noted:

> [The indenture trustee] contends that because it can already obtain documents and reports filed with the SEC from the EDGAR system, [the "Reports" covenant] is meaningless if read as only requiring copies of documents already filed with the SEC and not as an obligation to actually file with the SEC. Again, [the indenture trustee's] argument overlooks the plain language of the provision. It also overlooks another crucial fact that had the parties intended to require filing of the documents, [the "Reports" covenant] could easily have been written to do just that. If, as [the indenture trustee] contends, the objective of the ["Reports" covenant] was to insure filings consistent with SEC requirements and guidelines, the parties could have simply declared so. Instead, the parties agreed that Cyberonics would deliver to [the indenture trustee] copies of reports after it had filed them with the SEC. The agreement should be enforced as it is clearly and unambiguously written, and not read as [the indenture trustee] now asserts that it should be.

Cyberonics, 2007 WL 1729977, at 4 (citations omitted).

provided that Tyco and TIFSA assumed primary liability for the Notes, as distinguished from Tyco's former contingent liability as guarantor thereof. The Trustee refused to sign the Supplemental Indenture because of its contention that Tyco did not become the continuing owner of substantially all the assets of TIGSA and thus was not a permissible transferee under the Indenture.]

III. APPLICABLE LAW

B. *SHARON STEEL*

1. FACTS

In *Sharon Steel*, the Second Circuit held that the validity of a transfer of assets in the course of a liquidation must be evaluated in the context of the overall plan of liquidation.[69] During 1977 and 1978, the obligor on certain notes, UV Industries, Inc. ("UV"), maintained three lines of business: electrical equipment, operated through Federal Pacific Electric Company ("Federal"); metal fabrication, operated through Mueller Brass; and metals mining.[70] Federal provided sixty percent of UV's operating revenue and constituted forty-four percent of the book value of UV's assets.[71]

As part of a plan of liquidation, UV first sold Federal and certain other assets to unrelated purchasers.[72] UV then sold its remaining assets to Sharon Steel Corp. ("Sharon Steel"), which agreed to assume UV's outstanding notes.[73] UV did not obtain noteholder approval before transferring the notes to Sharon Steel, relying instead on the terms of the successor obligor clause. The assets transferred to Sharon Steel represented fifty-one percent of the assets that UV held before it began the liquidation.[74] To formalize its position as obligor, Sharon Steel delivered supplemental indentures to the indenture trustees, who refused to execute them and instead issued notices of default.[75] The indenture trustees then sued claiming that the transfer of assets to Sharon Steel was a breach of the indentures.

2. PROCEEDINGS

After a jury trial, the district court directed a verdict for the indenture trustees.[76] On appeal, the Second Circuit first noted that successor obligor clauses are boilerplate and "'[s]ince there is seldom any difference in the intended meaning

---

[69] [47] *See* 691 F.2d at 1042, 1044.

[70] [48] *See id.* at 1045.

[71] [49] *See id.*

[72] [50] *See id.*

[73] [51] *See id.* at 1046.

[74] [52] *See id.* at 1051.

[75] [53] *See id.* at 1046–47.

[76] [54] *See id.* at 1047.

[boilerplate] provisions are susceptible of standardized expression. . . .' "[77] Because of the importance of uniformity to the efficient functioning of capital markets, the Second Circuit held that the interpretation of boilerplate provisions is a matter of law and should not be submitted to a jury.[78]

The Circuit then turned its attention to the application of the successor obligor clauses. Sharon Steel argued that because it purchased all of the assets UV had at the time of the purchase, the transfer fell within the literal language and terms of the successor obligor clauses. The Circuit rejected this mechanical interpretation of the clauses, instead analyzing them in terms of the interests they were intended to protect.[79]

The Circuit found that successor obligor clauses protect both the borrower, by permitting it to merge, liquidate, or sell its assets, and the lender, by assuring some degree of continuity of assets.[80] In light of these interests, the Circuit held that "boilerplate successor obligor clauses do not permit assignment of the public debt to another party in the course of a liquidation unless 'all or substantially all' of the assets of the company *at the time the plan of liquidation is determined upon* are transferred to a single purchaser."[81] Thus, the court looked to UV's assets when the company first decided to liquidate — *i.e.*, prior to the sale of Federal. Because the assets purchased by Sharon Steel, not including proceeds from the intermediate sales, constituted only fifty-one percent of UV's pre-transaction assets — and fifty-one percent was "[i]n no sense" substantially all — the court held that the transfer of the notes to Sharon Steel was not effective under the successor obligor clauses and UV remained liable on the Notes.[82]

IV. DISCUSSION

A. VALIDITY OF THE TYCO TRANSACTION

The Transaction comprised two transfers of assets. *First*, TIGSA transferred all of its assets to Tyco and used the successor obligor clauses to make Tyco the obligor on the Notes. *Second*, Tyco transferred Tyco Electronics and Covidien to its shareholders. Tyco maintains that the second transfer did not violate the successor obligor clauses because it was not a transfer of substantially all of Tyco's assets. BNY disagrees, arguing that substantially all of Tyco's assets were transferred. BNY further contends that the Transaction as a whole violates the rule of *Sharon Steel.* These two arguments are addressed separately.

---

[77] [55] *Id.* at 1048 (quoting American Bar Foundation, *Commentaries on Indentures* (1971)) (hereinafter *Commentaries*).

[78] [56] *See id.* The Circuit also held that the district court did not err in rejecting evidence of custom, usage, and practical construction in interpreting the clauses. *See id.* at 1048–49.

[79] [57] *See id.* at 1049–50.

[80] [58] *See id.* at 1050 ("We hold, therefore, that protection for borrowers as well as for lenders may be fairly inferred from the nature of successor obligor clauses.").

[81] [59] *Id.* at 1051 (emphasis added).

[82] [60] *Id.* at 1051–52.

1. DISTRIBUTION OF TYCO ELECTRONICS AND COVIDIEN

The successor obligor clauses prohibit Tyco from transferring substantially all of its assets unless the transferee assumes liability for the Notes. Therefore, if Tyco's transfer of Tyco Electronics and Covidien to its shareholders was in fact a transfer of substantially all of Tyco's assets, the Transaction breached the Indentures.

I cannot determine on this record whether Tyco Electronics and Covidien constituted substantially all of Tyco's assets. However, while BNY contends that factual disputes will require a trial on issues of valuation,[83] the parties may be able to stipulate to a sufficiently narrow valuation range to permit the Court to resolve the issue on summary judgment. At this time, however, defendants' motion is denied without prejudice.

2. APPLICABILITY OF *SHARON STEEL*

Even if the spin-off of Tyco Electronics and Covidien did not constitute a transfer of substantially all of Tyco's assets, the Transaction would still violate the successor obligor clauses if *Sharon Steel* applies. In *Sharon Steel*, the Second Circuit held that a transfer of assets pursuant to a plan of liquidation had to be evaluated "at the time the plan of liquidation is determined. . . ."[84] If *Sharon Steel* applies here, the transfer is invalid because Tyco clearly does not hold substantially all of the assets originally held by TIGSA.

Before the Transaction, Tyco was a public corporation that maintained four lines of business through a single holding company, TIGSA. TIGSA was the only obligor on the Notes, and Tyco was a guarantor. After the Transaction, Tyco is a public corporation that maintains two lines of business through a single holding company, TIFSA. Tyco and TIFSA are co-obligors on the Notes. The noteholders remain lenders to Tyco, but Tyco divested itself of two lines of business. In essence, Tyco spun off two of its businesses.

Sharon Steel does not apply to these facts. The transaction in *Sharon Steel* resulted in Sharon Steel, a company unrelated to UV, holding only one of UV's three lines of business and all of UV's debt. The transactions were consummated in the course of the liquidation of UV. Here, Tyco spun off two of its businesses and retained the remainder. Neither the debt nor the engineered products and fire systems businesses left the conglomerate. Tyco was restructured, not liquidated, with TIFSA replacing TIGSA as the holding company and Tyco changing from a guarantor on the Notes to an obligor.[85] There is no indication that successor obligor

---

[83] [61] *See* 10/2/07 Transcript at 27:15–22 ("Gerard E. Harper, Attorney for Intervener Plaintiffs: [I]f your Honor were to decide that *Sharon Steel* [does not apply], then I have the right to assert . . . that the spin-off of Covidien and Tyco Electronics was itself a transfer of all or substantially all of Tyco's assets and, therefore, trigger[ed] the successor obligor clause-a different analytical argument and one that would require an analysis and a trial on the valuation of what was spun off and what was left behind."). Harper entered an appearance as co-counsel for BNY on the same day that certain noteholders, who had intervened as plaintiffs, voluntarily dismissed their claims. *See* 10/17/07 Notice of Appearance.

[84] [62] *Sharon Steel*, 691 F.2d at 1051.

[85] [63] Defendants correctly observe that "[t]he real party backing the Notes was always Tyco," and

clauses were intended to require consent from the noteholders for such internal restructuring, even when coupled with a spin-off of some of the obligor's assets.

In *Sharon Steel*, the Circuit distinguished a "decision to sell off some properties . . . made in the regular course of business" from a "plan of piecemeal liquidation. . . ."[86] In the former situation, the sale is "undertaken because the directors expect the sale to strengthen the corporation as a going concern."[87] In the latter, the sale "may be undertaken solely because of the financial needs and opportunities or the tax status of the major shareholders."[88] Tyco divided its businesses into three entities after its directors determined that separating into three independent companies is the best approach to enable these businesses to achieve their full potential. [Covidien], [Tyco] Electronics and [TIFSA] will be able to move faster and more aggressively — and ultimately create more value for our shareholders — by pursuing their own growth strategies as independent companies.[89]

The Transaction clearly resulted from a decision to sell off some properties made in the regular course of business. The only liquidation involved in the Transaction was that of TIGSA, a holding company with minimal assets other than Tyco's operating businesses, and TIGSA was replaced by TIFSA, also a holding company with minimal assets other than Tyco's operating businesses.

BNY argues that *Sharon Steel* applies because of the liquidation of TIGSA. But the operative entity with respect to the Notes is Tyco, not TIGSA. TIGSA was simply a holding company, and it has been replaced by another holding company. While UV's noteholders found themselves expecting repayment from an entirely new entity, here the noteholders still look to Tyco for repayment.

BNY does not argue that *Sharon Steel* would apply if TIGSA had spun off Tyco Electronics and Covidien but retained the remaining businesses.[90] Similarly, BNY does not dispute that TIGSA could have transferred the Notes to Tyco without violating the successor obligor clauses at the time that TIGSA distributed its assets to Tyco, had Tyco not then spun off Tyco Electronics and Covidien. Thus, the crux of BNY's position is that the combination of spin-off and transfer violated *Sharon Steel*. But the transfer of TIGSA's assets to Tyco was essentially a nullity because it merely substituted Tyco as obligor for Tyco as guarantor. Notwithstanding the

---

that TIGSA was at all relevant times merely a holding company. Defendants' Reply Memorandum of Law in Further Support of Their Cross-Motion for Summary Judgment at 2. In support of this assertion, Tyco indicates that the offering documents for the Notes included "substantial information" about Tyco but "only the barest information concerning TIGSA," and that the Indentures required TIGSA to provide the Indenture Trustee with Tyco's annual reports and SEC filings. *Id.*

[86] [64] *Sharon Steel*, 691 F.2d at 1050.

[87] [65] *Id.*

[88] [66] *Id.*

[89] [67] 1/13/06 Press Release.

[90] [68] Apparently TIGSA did not simply spin off these two businesses because it would have incurred substantial tax liability in Luxembourg. *See* Def. 56.1 ¶¶ 62, 64 (noting that dividends of a Luxembourg company are subject to a fifteen percent withholding tax, while liquidating distributions are not); 12/4/07 Declaration of Marc Seimetz, Attorney at Court ("Avocat à la Cour") and Member of the Luxembourg Bar Association, Ex. M to Gordon Decl. (same).

transfer from TIGSA to Tyco, the Transaction is a spin-off, rather than a liquidation, and *Sharon Steel* does not apply.

3. SUCCESSOR OBLIGOR CLAUSES AND SPIN-OFF TRANSACTIONS

BNY's complaint is essentially that the Notes have lost the protection of Tyco's healthcare and electronics businesses.[91] BNY is correct. However, successor obligor clauses are not intended to protect this interest. Successor obligor provisions have two purposes: "to leave the borrower free to merge, liquidate or to sell its assets in order to enter a wholly new business free of public debt" and to assure the lender "a degree of continuity of assets."[92] Assuming that Tyco Electronics and Covidien did not represent substantially all of TIGSA's assets, the lenders have maintained the requisite degree of continuity of assets. The successor obligor clauses require nothing more.

The Indentures could provide for protection for the noteholders in the event that the obligor disposed of less than substantially all of its assets, but they do not.[93] In the absence of such a provision, the Court will not impose one.[94]

B. BNY'S FAILURE TO EXECUTE THE SUPPLEMENTAL INDENTURES

BNY also argues that Tyco could not substitute itself or TIFSA for TIGSA as obligors on the Notes without BNY's consent. BNY refused to execute the Supplemental Indentures that would have permitted such a substitution on the ground that it was unsure whether the Transaction violated the successor obligor clauses. If the Transaction did violate the clauses, BNY was within its rights in refusing to execute the Supplemental Indentures.

BNY further maintains that it had the authority to refuse to execute the Supplemental Indentures whether or not the Transaction was permitted by the

---

[91] [69] *See* Memorandum of Law in Support of Plaintiff's Motion for Summary Judgment ("Pl. Mem.") at 4–5 ("Noteholders that made loans (some of which, here, for thirty years) to a $60 billion conglomerate boasting of how its diversity could allocate risk over this decades long period now find themselves the unwilling creditors of a new company concededly confined to limited business valued, at best, at a third of the Company to which the Noteholders lent their money."). *See also* Memorandum of Law in Further Support of Plaintiff's Motion for Summary Judgment and in Opposition to Defendants' Cross-Motion for Summary Judgment ("Pl. Rep.") at 8 ("What troubled the Second Circuit in *Sharon Steel* was the notion that a company could, in effect, cheat its public creditors by taking their money and then liquidating its assets. . . .").

[92] [70] *Sharon Steel*, 691 F.2d at 1050.

[93] [71] *See* F. John Stark, III, *et al*, *"Marriot Risk": A New Model Covenant to Restrict Transfers of Wealth from Bondholders to Stockholders*, 1994 Colum. Bus. L. Rev. 503, 546 ("An expanded or separate covenant limiting dispositions of less than substantially all of the borrower's assets or specified assets outside of the ordinary course of business would address issues raised by transactions such as a spin-off.") (citation omitted); *Commentaries* 423 (discussing covenants that limit the issuer's ability to sell less than substantially all of its assets).

[94] [72] *See Lui v. Park Ridge at Terryville Assn.*, 196 A.D.2d 579, 601 N.Y.S.2d 496, 498 (2d Dep't 1993) ("A court should not, under the guise of contract interpretation, 'imply a term which the parties themselves failed to insert' or otherwise rewrite the contract.") (quoting *Mitchell v. Mitchell*, 82 A.D.2d 849, 440 N.Y.S.2d 54, 55 (2d Dep't 1981)).

successor obligor clauses. BNY suggests that regardless of why it chose not to execute the Supplemental Indentures, its decision not to do so prevented Tyco from consummating the Transaction.

The Indentures have different language, but they evince the same intent. Article Seven of the 1998 Indenture provides that

> [TIGSA], Tyco, . . . and the Trustee may from time to time and at any time enter into an indenture or indentures supplemental hereto for one or more of the following purposes . . . (b) to evidence the succession of another corporation . . . and the assumption by the successor Person of the covenants, agreements and obligations of the Issuer pursuant to Article Eight. . . . The Trustee is hereby authorized to join with [TIGSA and] Tyco . . . in the execution of any such supplemental indenture . . . but the Trustee shall not be obligated to enter into any such supplemental indenture which affects the Trustee's own rights, duties or immunities under this Indenture or otherwise.

Article Eight provides that TIGSA can convey substantially all of its assets to an entity only if "the successor entity . . . shall expressly assume the due and punctual payment of the principal of and interest on all the [Notes] . . . by supplemental indenture satisfactory to the Trustee, executed and delivered to the Trustee by such corporation. . . . ."

Because Article Seven states that the trustee is not obligated to execute a supplemental indenture that affects its "rights, duties or immunities" under the Indenture, it implies that the trustee is otherwise obligated to execute supplemental indentures that comply with the Indenture. The requirement in Article Eight that the supplemental indenture be "satisfactory to the Trustee" in the event of a transfer of assets is no different. BNY argues that the Indentures give the trustee discretionary authority to halt an otherwise valid transfer of TIGSA's assets pursuant to the successor obligor clauses. This is implausible. One of the purposes of a successor obligor clause is to give the borrower freedom to transfer substantially all of its assets without the consent of the lenders, provided that the borrower also transfers the obligation on the notes. Requiring the consent of the noteholders' representative would be directly contrary to that purpose.[95]

The Indentures are best read to permit the Indenture Trustee to decline to execute supplemental indentures only if it has a good-faith basis to conclude that the proposed transfers violate the successor obligor clauses. The trustee's role under the Indentures is simply to review the supplemental indentures to ensure that they and the transfer in question comply with the Indentures. If they do so, and if the supplemental indentures do not alter the "rights, duties or immunities" of the trustee, then the trustee must execute them.[96]

---

[95] [78] In *Sharon Steel*, the trustee declined to execute the supplemental indentures. *See* 691 F.2d at 1046–47. The Second Circuit only addressed the successor obligor clause, and did not address whether the transaction would have been invalid even had it complied with the clause because of the trustee's failure to execute the supplemental indentures.

[96] [79] *Cf.* Restatement (Third) of the Law of Trusts § 76(1) ("The trustee has a duty to administer the trust, diligently and in good faith, in accordance with the terms of the trust and applicable law."); *id.*

If a trustee has a good-faith basis for declining to execute a supplemental indenture (because the trustee reasonably believes that it violates a successor obligor clause), but the transfer is ultimately determined not to violate the clause, the fact that the trustee did not approve is insufficient to prevent the transaction from proceeding.[97] If the Supplemental Indentures did not otherwise breach the Indentures, BNY cannot argue that they are invalid for want of BNY's execution.[98]

V. CONCLUSION

For the reasons stated above, the parties' motions are denied. The Clerk of the Court is directed to close these motions (documents no. 34 and 49 on the docket sheet). A status conference is scheduled for March 25, 2008, at 4:30.

§ 3.10 SUBORDINATED DEBT SECURITIES

The following are provisions relating to subordinated debentures. Because of the breadth of the definition of senior indebtedness, the holders thereof rank as priority just above the equity holders. To compensate the holders for the absence of a priority position upon liquidation or dissolution of the issuer, subordinated debentures generally bear a higher rate of interest than "straight" debt and are generally convertible into shares of common stock of the issuer.

CERTAIN SUBORDINATED DEBENTURE PROVISIONS

Senior Indebtedness:

> "Senior Indebtedness" shall mean the principal of and premium, if any, and interest on the following, whether outstanding at the date hereof or hereafter incurred or created unless by the terms of the instrument creating or evidencing such obligations it is provided that such obligations are not superior in right of payment to the Debentures: all obligations of the Company and its Subsidiaries (*other than obligations to make pay-*

---

cmt. b ("[A] trustee may commit a breach of trust by improperly failing to act, as well [as] by improperly exercising the powers of the trusteeship."). I note that "[u]nlike the ordinary trustee, who has historic common-law duties imposed beyond those in the trust agreement, an indenture trustee is more like a stakeholder whose duties and obligations are exclusively defined by the terms of the indenture agreement." *Meckel v. Continental Res. Co.*, 758 F.2d 811, 816 (2d Cir.1985) (citing *Hazzard v. Chase Nat'l Bank*, 159 Misc. 57, 287 N.Y.S. 541 (Sup.Ct.N.Y.Co.1936), *aff'd*, 257 A.D. 950, 14 N.Y.S.2d 147 (1st Dep't 1939), *aff'd*, 282 N.Y. 652, 26 N.E.2d 801 (1940)).

[97] [80] A trustee that refused to execute the supplemental indenture without a good-faith basis for doing so might face liability for this refusal, and certainly would not be able to delay the transaction.

[98] [81] BNY argues that "the issue is not whether the Trustee was obligated to sign, but whether defendants breached the Indentures by going ahead with their transaction without obtaining the Trustee's signature." Pl. Rep. at 16 n. 4. But "it has been established for over a century that 'a party may not insist upon performance of a condition precedent when its non-performance has been caused by the party [if]self.' " *Lomaglio Assocs. v. LBK Marketing Corp.*, 892 F. Supp. 89, 93 (S.D.N.Y.1995) (quoting *Ellenberger Morgan Corp. v. Hard Rock Cafe*, 116 A.D.2d 266, 500 N.Y.S.2d 696, 699 (1st Dep't 1986)). BNY cannot assert that Tyco should have obtained an executed supplemental indenture before performing the Transaction while demurring on whether it had an obligation to execute the Supplemental Indentures.

ments to holders of equity securities of the Company and its Subsidiaries arising out of their ownership of such equity securities), or obligations of others assumed or guaranteed by the Company or its Subsidiaries, for the payment of money, other than the Debentures; and renewals, extensions, refundings, amendments, and modifications of any such obligations.

ARTICLE THREE

Subordination of Debentures

Section 3.01. *Agreement to Subordinate.* The Company covenants and agrees, and each holder of a Debenture, *by his acceptance thereof, likewise covenants and agrees*, that the payment of the principal of, and premium and interest on, each and all of the Debentures is hereby expressly subordinated, to the extent and the manner hereinafter set forth, in right of payment to the prior payment in full of all Senior Indebtedness.

Section 3.02. *Distribution on Dissolution or Reorganization; Subrogation of Debentures.* Upon any distribution of assets of the Company upon dissolution, winding up, liquidation, or reorganization of the Company in any bankruptcy, insolvency, or receivership proceeding or upon an assignment for the benefit of creditors or any other marshalling of the assets and liabilities of the Company or otherwise,

(a) the holders of all Senior Indebtedness shall first be entitled to receive payment in full of the principal thereof and the premium, if any, and interest due thereon before the holders of the Debentures are entitled to receive any payment upon the principal of or premium, if any, or interest on the Debentures;

(b) *any payment or distribution of assets of the Company of any kind or character, whether in cash, property, or securities (other than shares of the Company as reorganized or readjusted or securities of the Company or any other corporation provided for by a plan of reorganization or readjustment the payment of which is subordinate, at least to the extent provided in this Article Three with respect to the Debentures, to the payment of Senior Indebtedness*, to which the holders of the Debentures or the Trustee would be entitled except for the provisions of this Article Three, *shall be paid* by the person making such payment or distribution, whether a trustee in bankruptcy, a receiver or liquidating trustee or otherwise, *directly to the holders of Senior Indebtedness* or their representative or representatives or to the trustee or trustees under any indenture under which any instruments evidencing any of such Senior Indebtedness may have been issued, ratably according to the aggregate amounts remaining unpaid on account of the principal of and the premium, if any, and interest on the Senior Indebtedness held or represented by each, to the extent necessary to make payment in full of all Senior Indebtedness remaining unpaid, after giving effect to any concurrent payment or distribution to the holders of such Senior Indebtedness; and

(c) in the event that, notwithstanding the foregoing, any payment or distribution of assets of the Company of any kind or character, whether in cash, property or securities (other than shares of the Company as reorganized or readjusted or securities of the Company or any other corporation provided for by a plan of reorganization or readjustment the payment on which is subordinate, at least to the extent provided in this Article Three with respect to the Debentures, to the payment of Senior Indebtedness, provided that the rights of the holders of Senior Indebtedness are not altered by such reorganization or readjustment), shall be received by the Trustee or the holders of the Debentures before all Senior Indebtedness is paid in full, such payment or distribution shall be paid over to the holders of such Senior Indebtedness or their representative or representatives or to the trustee or trustees under any indenture under which any instruments evidencing any of such Senior Indebtedness may have been issued, ratably as aforesaid, for application to the payment of all Senior Indebtedness remaining unpaid until all such Senior Indebtedness shall have been paid in full, after giving effect to any concurrent payment or distribution to the holders of such Senior Indebtedness.

Subject to the payment in full of all Senior Indebtedness, the holders of the Debentures shall be subrogated to the rights of the holders of Senior Indebtedness to receive payments or distributions of cash, property or securities of the Company applicable to the Senior Indebtedness until all amounts owing on the Debentures shall be paid in full, and, as between the Company, its creditors other than holders of Senior Indebtedness, and the holders of the Debentures, no payment or distribution of cash, property or securities made to the holders of Senior Indebtedness by virtue of this Article Three which otherwise would have been made to the holders of the Debentures shall be deemed to be a payment by the Company on account of the Senior Indebtedness, and no payment or distribution of cash, property or securities made to holders of Debentures by virtue of the subrogation provided for in this Article Three which otherwise would have been made to the holders of Senior Indebtedness shall be deemed to be a payment on account of the Debentures; it being understood that the provisions of this Article Three are and are intended solely for the purpose of defining the relative rights of the holders of the Debentures, on the one hand, and the holders of the Senior Indebtedness, on the other hand. Nothing contained in this Article Three or elsewhere in this Indenture or in the Debentures is intended to or shall impair, as between the Company, its creditors other than the holders of Senior Indebtedness, and the holders of the Debentures, the obligation of the Company, which is absolute and unconditional, to pay to the holders of the Debentures the principal of and premium, if any, and the interest and Participation Rights on the Debentures as and when the same shall become due and payable in accordance with their terms, or to affect the relative rights of the holders of the Debentures and creditors of the Company other than the holders of Senior Indebtedness, nor shall anything herein or therein prevent the Trustee or the holder of any Debenture from exercising all remedies otherwise permitted by applicable law upon default under this Indenture, subject to the rights, if any, under this Article Three of the holders of Senior Indebtedness in respect of cash, property or securities of the Company received upon the exercise of any such remedy. Upon any distribution of assets of the Company referred to in this Article Three, the Trustee, subject to the provisions of Section 11.01, and the holders of the Debentures shall be entitled to rely upon any order or decree made by any court of competent jurisdiction in which such dissolution, winding up, liquidation or reorganization proceedings are pending or upon a certificate of the liquidating trustee or agent or other person making any distribution to the Trustee or to the holders of the Debentures for the purpose of ascertaining the persons entitled to participate in such distribution, the holders of the Senior Indebtedness and other indebtedness of the Company, the amount thereof or payable thereon, the amount or amounts paid or distributed thereon and all other facts pertinent thereto or to this Article Three.

Section 3.03. *No Payment to Debentureholders if Senior Indebtedness is in Default.* (a) Upon the maturity of any Senior Indebtedness by lapse of time, acceleration or otherwise, all principal thereof and premium, if any, and interest due thereon shall first be paid in full, or such payment duly provided for in cash or in a manner satisfactory to the holder or holders of such Senior Indebtedness, before any payment is made on account of the principal of or premium, if any, or interest or Participation Rights on the Debentures or to acquire any of the Debentures or as a sinking fund for the Debentures (except sinking fund payments made for Debentures acquired before the maturity of such Senior Indebtedness).

(b) Upon the happening of an event of default with respect to any Senior Indebtedness, as defined therein or in the instrument under which it is outstanding, permitting the holders to accelerate the maturity thereof, and, if the default is other than default in payment of the principal of or premium, if any, or interest on such Senior Indebtedness, and written notice thereof shall have been given to the Company and the Trustee by the holder or holders of such Senior Indebtedness or their representative or representatives, then, unless and until such event of default shall have been cured or waived or shall have ceased to exist, no payment shall be made by the Company (and neither the Trustee nor any holder of Debentures shall receive or accept any payment) with respect to the principal of or premium, if any, or interest or Participation Rights on the Debentures or to acquire any of the Debentures or as a sinking fund for the Debentures (except sinking fund payments made for Debentures acquired before such default and notice, if required, thereof).

(c) In the event that the Debentures are declared due and payable before the expressed maturity thereof because of the happening of an

Event of Default under this Indenture, (1) the Company will give prompt notice in writing thereof to the holders of Senior Indebtedness or their representative or representatives, and (2) the holders of Senior Indebtedness shall have the right, so far as concerns the Company, the holders of Debentures and the Trustee, to declare such Senior Indebtedness due and payable upon demand regardless of the expressed maturity thereof, and upon any such declaration in respect of Senior Indebtedness the holders of the Debentures shall not be entitled to receive any payment thereon until all Senior Indebtedness outstanding at the time the Debentures are so declared due and payable shall have been paid in full, or such payment shall have been duly provided for in cash or in a manner satisfactory to the holder or holders of such Senior Indebtedness.

(d) Nothing in this Section 3.03 shall prevent any payment in connection with a redemption of Debentures if the first mailing of notice of such redemption has been made pursuant to Article Five or Article Seven prior to the happening of such event of default and such notice, if any, thereof as provided in clause (b) of this Section 3.03. Nothing in this Section 3.03 shall prevent the application by the Trustee or any paying agent (other than the Company) of any moneys deposited with it under this Indenture to the payment of or on account of the principal of or premium, if any, or interest or Participation Rights on any Debenture if both the date of such deposit and the due date of such payment shall be on or prior to the date of the happening of any default in payment of principal, premium, if any, or interest on Senior Indebtedness or prior to the date on which the notice referred to in clause (b) of this Section 3.03 of the happening of any other event of default with respect to Senior Indebtedness shall be delivered.

(e) Any deposit of moneys by the Company with the Trustee or any paying agent (whether or not stated to be in trust) for the payment of interest or Participation Rights on any Debentures or for the payment of the principal of or premium, if any, on any Debentures at maturity or upon call for redemption (whether for a sinking fund or otherwise) shall be subject to the provisions of this Article Three, and the Trustee will not receive or accept any deposit from the Company for any such payment upon the happening of any of the events specified in clauses (a) or (c) of this Section 3.03 or during the continuance of any default specified in clause (b) of this Section 3.03, and in the event that the Trustee shall receive any such deposit which the Company is not entitled to make, the Trustee will hold such amount in trust for the holders of the Senior Indebtedness remaining unpaid.

Section 3.04. *Payment on Debentures Permitted.* Nothing contained in this Article Three or elsewhere in this Indenture, or in any of the Debentures, shall (a) prevent the application by the Trustee or any paying agent (other than the Company) of any moneys deposited with it hereunder to the payment of or on account of the principal of or premium, if any, or interest or Participation Rights on the Debentures, or (b) affect the obligation of the Company to make, or prevent the Company from making, payment of the principal of or premium, if any, or interest or Participation Rights on the Debentures, except in either case, as otherwise provided in Section 3.03 or Section 7.05 or during the pendency of any dissolution, winding up, liquidation or reorganization of the Company.

Section 3.05. *Authorization of Debentureholders to Trustee to Effect Subordination.* Each holder of Debentures by his acceptance thereof authorizes and directs the Trustee in his behalf to take such actions as may be necessary or appropriate to effectuate the subordination thereof as provided in this Article Three and appoints the Trustee his attorney-in-fact for any and all such purposes.

Section 3.06. *Knowledge of Trustee.* Notwithstanding the provisions of this Article Three or any other provisions of this Indenture, the Trustee shall not be charged with knowledge of the existence of any facts which would prohibit the making of any payment of moneys to or by the Trustee, or the taking of any other action by the Trustee, unless and until the Trustee shall have received written notice thereof from the Company, any Debentureholder, any paying or conversion agent or the holder or representative of any class of Senior Indebtedness, and, prior to the receipt of any such written notice, the Trustee, subject to the provisions of Section 11.01, shall be entitled to assume that no such facts exist.

Section 3.07. *Trustee May Hold Senior Indebtedness.* The Trustee shall be entitled to all the rights set forth in this Article Three with respect to any Senior Indebtedness at the time held by it, to the same extent as any other holder of Senior Indebtedness, and nothing in Section 11.13 or elsewhere in this Indenture shall deprive the Trustee of any of its rights as such holder.

Section 3.08. *Rights of Holders of Senior Indebtedness Not Impaired.* No right of any present or future holder of any Senior Indebtedness to enforce the subordination herein provided shall at any time or in any way be prejudiced or impaired by any act or failure to act on the part of the Company or by any non-compliance by the Company with the terms, provisions and covenants of this Indenture, regardless of any knowledge thereof any such holder may have or be otherwise charged with.

Prior to the enactment of the Bankruptcy Code of 1978, there was a question as to whether a subordination agreement was enforceable in a bankruptcy case. Section 510(a) of the Bankruptcy Code makes it clear that such provisions are enforceable in a bankruptcy case: "A subordination agreement is enforceable in a case under this title to the same extent that such agreement is enforceable under applicable nonbankruptcy law."

The definition of Senior Indebtedness, which is extremely broad, nevertheless contains an exception for obligations to make payments to equity holders arising out of their ownership of such securities. The reason for that exception is that, when a dividend is declared, a debtor-creditor relationship is established between the corporation and the holder of the security with respect to which the dividend is payable. *See Costa Brava P'ship III, L.P. v. Telos Corp.*, 2006 Md. Cir. Ct. LEXIS 21, at *5 (Mar. 30, 2006). Accordingly, even a fully subordinated debt instrument ordinarily has priority over a declared dividend indebtedness.

THE "X" CLAUSE

Section 3.02(b) of the subordination provisions set forth above contains an exception to the priority provisions for the purposes of implementing a bankruptcy plan. That exception is known as the X-Clause, of which there are several versions. A version similar to that set forth above is the subject of the *Envirodyne* decision.

IN RE ENVIRODYNE INDUS.

United States Court of Appeals, Seventh Circuit
29 F.3d 301 (1994)

Posner, Chief Judge

This appeal arises out of an objection by creditors to a plan of reorganization filed by Envirodyne Industries, Inc., a Chapter 11 debtor. Envirodyne had three levels ("tranches," as they are called) of unsecured debt. One, the most senior, consisted of Senior Discount Notes. The plan called for the holders of these notes to receive notes of equivalent value in the reorganized firm. The next level consisted of 14% Senior Subordinated Debentures, and was junior to the Senior Discount Notes. The third level consisted of 13.5% Subordinated Notes and was junior to both the 14% notes (as we shall call them) and the Senior Discount Notes. The 13.5% notes had actually been issued before the Senior Discount Notes and the 14% notes (both issued in 1989 as part of a leveraged buyout of the company), but had been made subordinate to them by the indenture pursuant to which the 13.5% notes were issued. That indenture provided that in the event of a default, "all Superior Indebtedness" (defined to include the 14% notes, though issued later as we have said, together with the Senior Discount Notes) "shall first be paid in full before the Noteholders, or the Trustee, shall be entitled to retain any assets (other than shares of stock of the Company, as reorganized or readjusted or securities of the Company or any other corporation provided for by a plan of reorganization or readjustment, the payment of which is subordinated, at least to the same extent as the Notes, to the payment of all Superior Indebtedness which may at the time be outstanding)."

The plan of reorganization called for the distribution to the 14% noteholders of common stock worth $121 million in the reorganized firm in partial payment of their notes, the face amount of which was $200 million. The [13.5%] noteholders, although owed $100 million, received only $20 million worth of stock, on the theory that by virtue of the subordination provision we quoted they were entitled to nothing until the holders of the Senior Discount Notes and the 14% notes received stock or other securities sufficient in value to satisfy their claims in full. The 13.5% noteholders objected to being subordinated in this fashion. They argued that the words "other than shares of stock in the Company" entitled them to be treated the same as the 14% noteholders if the distribution to creditors took the form of stock rather than new notes, as it has done. The bankruptcy judge rejected the objection and confirmed the plan. The 13.5% noteholders appealed to the district court, which affirmed the bankruptcy judge. They tried but failed to get a stay from the district court and from this court pending their appeal. The plan of reorganization was then implemented . . . .

The parties agree that the parenthetical clause that is the focus of dispute is unambiguous. This use of the word "agree" may seem nonsensical, since the parties assign opposite meanings to the clause. But when opposing parties agree that the document whose meaning they dispute is not ambiguous, all they mean is that they are content to have its meaning determined without the help of any "extrinsic" evidence. What is unusual about this case is that the parties disagree about what counts as extrinsic evidence. The appellants argue that extrinsic evidence is everything except the Chicago Manual of Style, which they contend points unerringly to the interpretation that they favor. The 14% noteholders think that extrinsic evidence of the indenture's meaning would be testimony or documents concerning the intentions of the draftsmen of the indenture rather than scholarly literature on the purposes of the class of clause illustrated by the parenthetical clause in the indenture, such as the American Bar Foundation's Commentaries on Model Debenture Indenture Provisions (1971). They are surely right, though it hardly matters in this case, since the meaning of the clause is plain without regard to what the commentators have said about it.

. . . .

The indenture in this case provides that the holders of the superior indebtedness, which includes the 14% noteholders, are entitled to be paid in full before the 13.5% noteholders can receive any distribution other than (1) shares of stock in the reorganized firm, or (2) securities in the reorganized firm or any other firm created by the reorganization, payment of which is subordinated to the claims of the holders of the superior indebtedness. The appellants argue that the payment clause qualifies only (2), so if the distribution is of stock they are entitled to equal treatment with the holders of superior indebtedness. The 14% noteholders argue that the clause qualifies both (1) and (2). The appellants' argument is entirely grammatical and semantic. They say that the punctuation shows that the payment clause qualifies only (2) and that shares of stock unlike dividends for example, are not paid. We understand neither argument. It is commonplace to set off a series with commas and have a phrase at the end qualifying the entire series rather than the last entry in it. So one might say, "The man, or the woman, who is sitting on the bench." And if one doesn't "pay" stock, neither does one "pay" securities. The term "payment of" is used in the parenthetical clause as a synonym for "receipt of" or "entitlement to."

A better argument for the appellants is that if the draftsmen had wanted to subordinate all securities received by the junior creditors to the claims of the senior creditors, they easily could have said so clearly. It was not necessary to specify shares of stock and securities separately. Or they could have said "shares of stock and other securities" if they wanted to emphasis that there was no exception for stock. On balance the appellants have the better of the purely semantic argument.

But their interpretation makes no sense once the context of the terminology being interpreted is restored.

The class of clause to which the parenthetical clause in this indenture belongs goes by the unilluminating name of "X Clause." American Bar Foundation, *supra* at 570-71, (perhaps "equitable mootness" should be renamed the "X Doctrine.") Such clauses are common in bond debentures, although there is no standard wording. Without the clause, the subordination agreement that it qualifies would require the junior creditors to turn over to the senior creditors any securities that they had received as a distribution in the reorganization, unless the senior creditors had been paid in full. Then, presumably, if the senior creditors obtained full payment by liquidating some of the securities that had been over, the remaining securities would be turned back over to the junior creditors. The X Clause shortcuts this cumbersome procedure and enhances the marketability of the securities received by the junior creditors, since their right to possess (as distinct from pocket the proceeds of) the securities is uninterrupted.

The purpose of the clause as we have explained it bears no relation to the interpretation for which the appellants contend, under which the senior creditors' priority would depend entirely on the form of the distribution. The appellants concede that if the distribution took the form of new notes rather than of stock, the junior creditors would be subordinated. But if the distribution took the form of stock, they argue, the junior creditors would be pooled with the senior creditors, destroying the latter's seniority. We cannot understand why the form in which rights in the assets of the reorganized firm are allocated among the creditors should determine the creditors' priority — and specifically why a distribution in the form of stock should erase the priority of a senior class of creditors. To make priority depend on the form of distribution in this way would, moreover, give senior creditors an incentive to press for liquidation, contrary to the purpose of Chapter 11, since then there would be no distribution of stock and hence no chance for the junior creditors to achieve parity with the seniors.

The X Clause in this case was poorly drafted, but we think its meaning is clear: any securities, including stock, that the junior creditors receive in a reorganization are subordinated to the claims of the Senior creditors. The judgment of the district court is therefore.

AFFIRMED.

NOTE

Chief Judge Posner's conclusion that "the term 'payment of' is used in the parenthetical X-Clause as a synonym for 'receipt of' or 'entitlement to'" provides a Rosetta stone for interpreting the provision and a logical basis for concluding that a priority based pro rata distribution of the same class (*e.g.*, common stock) of security to senior and junior creditors, respectively, can achieve the practical result mandated by the X-Clause. This eliminates any need to provide the seniors with a class of security ranking prior to the one distributed to the juniors. As Judge Posner also points out "one doesn't 'pay' stock, neither does one 'pay' securities." *But see* American Bar Foundation, *Commentaries on Ad Hoc Committee for*

Revision of the 1983 Model Simplified Indenture, Revised Model Simplified Indenture, 55 BUS. LAW. 1115, 1221 (2000) ("If Senior Debt were to receive preferred stock and the subordinated debt were to receive common stock, for example, where the preferred stock precluded distributions to common stockholders until the preferred stock was redeemed, the X-Clause would permit that distribution."), quoted with approval in *Deutsche Bank AG, London Branch v. Metromedia Fiber Network, Inc. (In re Metromedia Fiber Network, Inc.)*, 416 F.3d 136 (2d Cir. 2005).

§ 3.11 NEW YORK STOCK EXCHANGE LISTING REQUIREMENTS REGARDING DEBT SECURITIES

The New York Stock Exchange has promulgated various rules and regulations setting forth criteria which must be complied with by the issuers of the various debt and equity securities which are listed and traded on such exchanges. Those rules and regulations, which include minimum earnings and security market value requirements, are set forth in "Listing Agreements" which are entered into between the Exchange and each of the issuers and in the "Company Manual" published by each of the Exchanges. The Listing Agreement and the requirements in the respective Company Manuals are thus binding upon listed companies and must be considered and complied with in the same manner as applicable state law. Set forth below are excerpts from the New York Stock Exchange Company Manual relating to debt securities. Excerpts from the Manual regarding preferred stock, redemptions of senior securities and stock issuances in connection with acquisitions are set forth elsewhere herein.

NEW YORK STOCK EXCHANGE COMPANY MANUAL

703.06 Debt Securities Offerings Listing Process

(A) Listing Policy

The Exchange has set minimum numerical criteria for the listing of debt securities in Section 1. The Exchange has also set certain numerical delisting criteria.

The Exchange will delist a debt security if the aggregate market value or principal amount that is publicly held is less than $1,000,000.

(B) Description of Issue

The description of the issue should indicate the following information:

- The interest rate or if the interest rate varies, *for example*, "floating" rate securities, the basis for the interest variation.
- The seniority of the security in relation to other issues.
- Whether the issue is convertible.
- Whether the issue is one series of a class of debt securities.

(C) Denomination

The standard unit of trading for debt securities listed on the Exchange is $1,000 original principal amount.

Securities in denominations of $500 and in large denominations that are multiples of $1,000 are permissible if they are exchangeable without charge for $1,000 denominations.

Units of trading of other than $1,000 may be designated by the Exchange for specific issues of bonds denominated in U.S. dollars or foreign currencies.

(D) Indenture Provisions

Deposited Funds to be Impressed with a Trust —

Any indenture which permits the deposit of funds with Trustee, Depository or Paying Agent for the purpose of paying the principal amount or redemption price of debt securities, or releasing a lien or collateral, or satisfying the indenture, must contain provisions which clearly establish that such funds are to be impressed with a trust for the holders of debt securities entitled to the benefits of such payment, lien, collateral or indenture.

§ 3.12 CERTAIN RESTRUCTURING AND REORGANIZATION ISSUES

The excessive use of debt often makes it necessary for corporate and securities lawyers to deal with subsequent restructurings and bankruptcy reorganizations of corporations that had issued debt instruments.

KATZ v. OAK INDUSTRIES INC.

Delaware Chancery Court
508 A.2d 873 (1986)

ALLEN, CHANCELLOR

A commonly used word — seemingly specific and concrete when used in everyday speech — may mask troubling ambiguities that upon close examination are seen to derive not simply from casual use but from more fundamental epistemological problems. Few words more perfectly illustrate the deceptive dependability of language than the term "coercion" which is at the heart of the theory advanced by plaintiff as entitling him to a preliminary injunction in this case. Plaintiff is the owner of long-term debt securities issued by Oak Industries, Inc. ("Oak"), a Delaware corporation; in this class action he seeks to enjoin the consummation of an exchange offer and consent solicitation made by Oak to holders of various classes of its long-term debt. As detailed below that offer is an integral part of a series of transactions that together would effect a major reorganization and recapitalization of Oak. The claim asserted is in essence, that the exchange offer is a coercive device and, in the circumstances, constitutes a breach of contract. This is the Court's opinion on plaintiff's pending application for a preliminary injunction.

I.

The background facts are involved even when set forth in the abbreviated form the decision within the time period currently available requires. Through its domestic and foreign subsidiaries and affiliated entities, Oak manufactures and markets component equipments used in consumer, industrial and military products (the "Components Segment"); produces communications equipment for use in cable television systems and satellite television systems (the "Communications Segment") and manufactures and markets laminates and other materials used in printed circuit board applications (the "Materials Segment"). During 1985, the Company has terminated certain other unrelated businesses. As detailed below, it has now entered into an agreement with Allied-Signal, Inc. for the sale of the Materials Segment of its business and is currently seeking a buyer for its Communications Segment. Even a casual review of Oak's financial results over the last several years shows it unmistakably to be a company in deep trouble. During the period from January 1, 1982 through September 30, 1985, the Company has experienced unremitting losses from operations; on net sales of approximately $1.26 billion during that period (F-3)[99] it has lost over $335 million (F-3). As a result its total stockholders' equity has first shriveled (from $260 million on 12/31/81 to $85 million on 12/31/83) and then disappeared completely (as of 9/30/85 there was a $62 million deficit in its stockholders' equity accounts) (F-6). Financial markets, of course, reflected this gloomy history.[100]

Unless Oak can be made profitable within some reasonably short time it will not continue as an operating company. Oak's board of directors, comprised almost entirely of outside directors, has authorized steps to buy the company time. In February, 1985, in order to reduce a burdensome annual cash interest obligation on its $230 million of then outstanding debentures, the Company offered to exchange such debentures for a combination of notes, common stock and warrants. As a result, approximately $180 million principal amount of the then outstanding debentures were exchanged. Since interest on certain of the notes issued in that exchange offer is payable in common stock, the effect of the 1985 exchange offer was to reduce to some extent the cash drain on the Company caused by its significant debt. About the same time that the 1985 exchange offer was made, the Company announced its intention to discontinue certain of its operations and sell certain of its properties. Taking these steps, while effective to stave off a default and to reduce to some extent the immediate cash drain, did not address Oak's longer-range problems. Therefore, also during 1985 representatives of the Company held informal discussions with several interested parties exploring the possibility of an investment from, combination with or acquisition by another company. As a result of these discussions, the Company and Allied-Signal, Inc. entered into two agreements. The first, the Acquisition Agreement, contemplates the sale to Allied-Signal of the Materials Segment for $160 million in cash. The second

---

[99] [1] Parenthetical references are to pages in the Offeror's Circular and Consent Solicitation appended as Exhibit No. 1 to the Monhait Affidavit.

[100] [2] The price of the company's common stock has fallen from over $30 per share on December 31, 1981 to approximately $2 per share recently. (P-38). The debt securities that are the subject of the exchange offer here involved (see n.3 for identification) have traded at substantial discounts.

agreement, the Stock Purchase Agreement, provides for the purchase by Allied-Signal for $15 million cash of 10 million shares of the Company's common stock together with warrants to purchase additional common stock. The Stock Purchase Agreement provides as a condition to Allied-Signal's obligation that at least 85% of the aggregate principal amount of all of the Company's debt securities shall have tendered and accepted the exchange offers that are the subject of this lawsuit. Oak has six classes of such long term debt.[101] If less than 85% of the aggregate principal amount of such debt accepts the offer, Allied-Signal has an option, but no obligation, to purchase the common stock and warrants contemplated by the Stock Purchase Agreement. An additional condition for the closing of the Stock Purchase Agreement is that the sale of the Company's Materials Segment contemplated by the Acquisition Agreement shall have been concluded.

Thus, as part of the restructuring and recapitalization contemplated by the Acquisition Agreement and the Stock Purchase Agreement, the Company has extended an exchange offer to each of the holders of the six classes of its long-term debt securities. These pending exchange offers include a Common Stock Exchange Offer (available only to holders of the 9 5/8% convertible notes) and the Payment Certificate Exchange Offers (available to holders of all six classes of Oak's long-term debt securities). The Common Stock Exchange Offer currently provides for the payment to each tendering noteholder of 407 shares of the Company's common stock in exchange for each $1,000 9 5/8% note accepted. The offer is limited to $38.6 million principal amount of notes (out of approximately $83.9 million outstanding). The Payment Certificate Exchange Offer is an any and all offer. Under its terms, a payment certificate, payable in cash five days after the closing of the sale of the Materials Segment to Allied-Signal, is offered in exchange for debt securities. The cash value of the Payment Certificate will vary depending upon the particular security tendered. In each instance, however, that payment will be less than the face amount of the obligation. The cash payments range in amount, per $1,000 of principal, from $918 to $655. These cash values however appear to represent a premium over the market prices for the Company's debentures as of the time the terms of the transaction were set. The Payment Certificate Exchange Offer is subject to certain important conditions before Oak has an obligation to accept tenders under it. First, it is necessary that a minimum amount ($38.6 million principal amount out of $83.9 total outstanding principal amount) of the 9 5/8% notes be tendered pursuant to the Common Stock Exchange Offer. Secondly, it is necessary that certain minimum amounts of each class of debt securities be tendered, together with consents to amendments to the underlying indentures.[102] Indeed, under the offer one may not tender securities unless at the same time one

---

[101] [3] The three classes of debentures are: 13.65% debentures due April 1, 2001, 10 1/2% convertible subordinated debentures due February 1, 2002, and 11 7/8% subordinated debentures due May 15, 1998. In addition, as a result of the 1985 exchange offer the company has three classes of notes which were issued in exchange for debentures that were tendered in that offer. Those are: 13.5% senior notes due May 15, 1990, 9 5/8% convertible notes due September 15, 1991 and 11 5/8% notes due September 15, 1990.

[102] [4] The holders of more than 50% of the principal amount of each of the 13.5% notes, the 9 5/8% notes and the 11 5/8% notes and at least 66 2/3% of the principal amount of the 13.65% debentures, 10 1/2% debentures, and 11 7/8% debentures, must validly tender such securities and consent to certain proposed amendments to the indentures governing those securities.

consents to the proposed amendments to the relevant indentures.

The condition of the offer that tendering security holders must consent to amendments in the indentures governing the securities gives rise to plaintiff's claim of breach of contract in this case. Those amendments would, if implemented, have the effect of removing significant negotiated protections to holders of the Company's long-term debt including the deletion of all financial covenants. Such modification may have adverse consequences to debt holders who elect not to tender pursuant to either exchange offer. Allied-Signal apparently was unwilling to commit to the $15 million cash infusion contemplated by the Stock Purchase Agreement, unless Oak's long-term debt is reduced by 85% (at least that is a condition of their obligation to close on that contract). Mathematically, such a reduction may not occur without the Company reducing the principal amount of outstanding debentures (that is the three classes outstanding notes constitute less than 85% of all long-term debt). But existing indenture covenants (See Offering Circular, pp. 38-39) prohibit the Company, so long as any of its long-term notes are outstanding, from issuing any obligation (including the Payment Certificates) in exchange for any of the debentures. Thus, in this respect, amendment to the indentures is required in order to close the Stock Purchase Agreement as presently structured. Restrictive covenants in the indentures would appear to interfere with effectuation of the recapitalization in another way. Section 4.07 of the 13.50% Indenture[103] provides that the Company may not "acquire" for value any of the 9 5/8% Notes or 11 5/8% Notes unless it concurrently "redeems" a proportionate amount of the 13.50% Notes. This covenant, if unamended, would prohibit the disproportionate acquisition of the 9 5/8% Notes that may well occur as a result of the Exchange Offers; in addition, it would appear to require the payment of the "redemption" price for the 13.50% Notes rather than the lower, market price offered in the exchange offer.

In sum, the failure to obtain the requisite consents to the proposed amendments would permit Allied-Signal to decline to consummate both the Acquisition Agreement and the Stock Purchase Agreement. As to timing of the proposed transactions, the Exchange Offer requires the Company (subject to the conditions stated therein) to accept any and all tenders received by 5:00 p.m. March 11, 1986. A meeting of stockholders of the Company has been called for March 14, 1986 at which time the Company's stockholders will be asked to approve the Acquisition Agreement and the Stock Purchase Agreement as well as certain deferred compensation arrangements for key employees. Closing of the Acquisition Agreement may occur on March 14, 1986, or as late as June 20, 1986 under the terms of that Agreement. Closing of the Stock Purchase Agreement must await the closing of the Acquisition Agreement and the successful completion of the Exchange Offers. The Exchange Offers are dated February 14, 1986. This suit seeking to enjoin consummation of those offers was filed on February 27. Argument on the current application was held on March 7.

---

[103] [5] *See* Monhait Aff., Exh. 3, p. 27.

II.

Plaintiff's claim that the Exchange Offers and Consent Solicitation constitutes a threatened wrong to him and other holders of Oak's debt securities[104] appear to be summarized in paragraph 16 of his Complaint:

The purpose and effect of the Exchange Offers is (1) to benefit Oak's common stockholders at the expense of the Holders of its debt securities, (2) to force the exchange of its debt instruments at unfair price and at less than face value of the debt instruments (3) pursuant to a rigged vote in which debt Holders who exchange, and who therefore have no interest in the vote, must consent to the elimination of protective covenants for debt Holders who do not wish to exchange. As amplified in briefing on the pending motion, plaintiff's claim is that no free choice is provided to bondholders by the exchange offer and consent solicitation. Under its terms, a rational bondholder is "forced" to tender and consent. Failure to do so would face a bondholder with the risk of owning a security stripped of all financial covenant protections and for which it is likely that there would be no ready market. A reasonable bondholder, it is suggested, cannot possibly accept those risks and thus such a bondholder is coerced to tender and thus to consent to the proposed indenture amendments. It is urged this linking of the offer and the consent solicitation constitutes a breach of a contractual obligation that Oak owes to its bondholders to act in good faith. Specifically, plaintiff points to three contractual provisions from which it can be seen that the structuring of the current offer constitutes a breach of good faith. Those provisions (1) establish a requirement that no modification in the term of the various indentures may be effectuated without the consent of a stated percentage of bondholders; (2) restrict Oak from exercising the power to grant such consent with respect to any securities it may hold in its treasury; and (3) establish the price at which and manner in which Oak may force bondholders to submit their securities for redemption.

III.

In order to demonstrate an entitlement to the provisional remedy of a preliminary injunction it is essential that a plaintiff show that it is probable that his claim will be upheld after final hearing; that he faces a risk of irreparable injury before final judgment will be reached in the regular course; and that in balancing the equities and competing hardships that preliminary judicial action may cause or prevent, the balance favors plaintiff. *See Shields v. Shields*, Del. Ch., 498 A.2d 161 (1985).

I turn first to an evaluation of the probability of plaintiff's ultimate success on the merits of his claim. I begin that analysis with two preliminary points. The first

[104] [6] It is worthy of note that a very high percentage of the principal value of Oak's debt securities are owned in substantial amounts by a handful of large financial institutions. Almost 85% of the value of the 13.50% Notes is owned by four such institutions (one investment banker owns 55% of that issue); 69.1% of the 9 5/8% Notes are owned by four financial institutions (the same investment banker owning 25% of that issue) and 85% of the 11 5/8% Notes are owned by five such institutions. Of the debentures, 89% of the 13.65% debentures are owned by four large banks; and approximately 45% of the two remaining issues is owned by two banks.

concerns what is not involved in this case. To focus briefly on this clears away much of the corporation law case law of this jurisdiction upon which plaintiff in part relies. This case does not involve the measurement of corporate or directorial conduct against that high standard of fidelity required of fiduciaries when they act with respect to the interests of the beneficiaries of their trust. Under our law — and the law generally — the relationship between a corporation and the holders of its debt securities, even convertible debt securities, is contractual in nature. *See Norte & Co. v. Manor Healthcare Corp.*, Del. Ch. Nos. 6827 and 6831, Berger, V.C. (Nov. 21, 1985); *Harff v. Kerkorian*, Del. Ch., 324 A.2d 215 (1974) *rev'd, on other grounds*, Del. Supr., 347 A.2d 133 (1975); American Bar Foundation, Commentaries on Indentures (1971). Arrangements among a corporation, the underwriters of its debt, trustees under its indentures and sometimes ultimate investors are typically thoroughly negotiated and massively documented. The rights and obligations of the various parties are or should be spelled out in that documentation. The terms of the contractual relationship agreed to and not broad concepts such as fairness define the corporation's obligation to its bondholders.[105]

Thus, the first aspect of the pending Exchange Offers about which plaintiff complains — that "the purpose and effect of the Exchange Offers is to benefit Oak's common stockholders at the expense of the Holders of its debt" — does not itself appear to allege a cognizable legal wrong. It is the obligation of directors to attempt, within the law, to maximize the long-run interests of the corporation's stockholders; that they may sometimes do so "at the expense" of others (even assuming that a transaction which one may refuse to enter into can meaningfully be said to be at his expense[106]) does not for that reason constitute a breach of duty. It seems likely that corporate restructurings designed to maximize shareholder values may in some instances have the effect of requiring bondholders to bear greater risk of loss and thus in effect transfer economic value from bondholders to stockholders. *See generally*, Prokesch, *Merger Wave: How Stocks and Bonds Fare*, N.Y. TIMES, Jan. 7, 1986, at A1, col. 1; McDaniel, *Bondholders and Corporate Governance*, 41 BUS. LAW. 413, 418-423 (1986). But if courts are to provide protection against such enhanced risk, they will require either legislative direction to do so or the negotiation of indenture provisions designed to afford such protection.

The second preliminary point concerns the limited analytical utility, at least in this context, of the word "coercive" which is central to plaintiff's own articulation of his theory of recovery. If, *pro arguendo*, we are to extend the meaning of the word coercion beyond its core meaning — dealing with the utilization of physical force to overcome the will of another — to reach instances in which the claimed coercion

---

105 [7] To say that the broad duty of loyalty that a director owes to his corporation and ultimately its shareholders is not implicated in this case is not to say, as the discussion below reflects, that as a matter of contract law a corporation owes no duty to bondholders of good faith and fair dealing. *See* Restatement of Law, Contracts 2d, § 205 (1979). Such a duty, however, is quite different from the congeries of duties that are assumed by a fiduciary. *See generally*, Bratton, *The Economics and Jurisprudence of Convertible Bonds*, 1984 Wis. L. Rev. 667.

106 [8] On the deeper implications of consent in the establishment of legal norms. *Compare*, Posner, *The Ethical and Political Basis of the Efficiency Norm in Common Law Adjudication*, 8 HOFSTRA L. REV. 487 (1980) *with* West, *Authority, Autonomy and Choice: The Rule of Consent in the Moral and Political Vision of Franz Kafka and Richard Posner*, 99 HARV. L. REV. 384 (1985).

arises from an act designed to affect the will of another party by offering inducements to the act sought to be encouraged or by arranging unpleasant consequences for an alternative sought to be discouraged, then — in order to make the term legally meaningful at all — we must acknowledge that some further refinement is essential. Clearly some "coercion" of this kind is legally unproblematic. Parents may "coerce" a child to study with the threat of withholding an allowance; employers may "coerce" regular attendance at work by either docking wages for time absent or by rewarding with a bonus such regular attendance. Other "coercion" so defined clearly would be legally relevant (to encourage regular attendance by corporal punishment, for example). Thus, for purposes of legal analysis, the term "coercion" itself — covering a multitude of situations — is not very meaningful. For the word to have much meaning for purposes of legal analysis, it is necessary in each case that a normative judgment be attached to the concept ("inappropriately coercive" or "wrongfully coercive," etc.). But, it is then readily seen that what is legally relevant is not the conclusory term "coercion" itself but rather the norm that leads to the adverb modifying it. In this instance, assuming that the Exchange Offers and Consent Solicitation can meaningfully be regarded as "coercive" (in the sense that Oak has structured it in a way designed — and I assume effectively so — to "force" rational bondholders to tender), the relevant legal norm that will support the judgment whether such "coercion" is wrongful or not will, for the reasons mentioned above, be derived from the law of contracts. I turn then to that subject to determine the appropriate legal test or rule. Modern contract law has generally recognized an implied covenant to the effect that each party to a contract will act with good faith towards the other with respect to the subject matter of the contract. *See* Restatement of Law, Contracts 2d, § 205 (1981); *Rowe v. Great Atlantic and Pacific Tea Company*, N.Y. Ct. Apps., 46 N.Y.2d 62, 412 N.Y.S.2d 827, 830, 385 N.E.2d 566, 569 (1978). The contractual theory for this implied obligation is well stated in a leading treatise: If the purpose of contract law is to enforce the reasonable expectations of parties induced by promises, then at some point it becomes necessary for courts to look to the substance rather than to the form of the agreement, and to hold that substance controls over form. What courts are doing here, whether calling the process "implication" of promises, or interpreting the requirements of "good faith", as the current fashion may be, is but a recognition that the parties occasionally have understandings or expectations that were so fundamental that they did not need to negotiate about those expectations. When the court "implies a promise" or holds that "good faith" requires a party not to violate those expectations, it is recognizing that sometimes silence says more than words, and it is understanding its duty to the spirit of the bargain is higher than its duty to the technicalities of the language. Corbin on Contracts (Kaufman Supp. 1984), § 570. It is this obligation to act in good faith and to deal fairly that plaintiff claims is breached by the structure of Oak's coercive exchange offer. Because it is an implied contractual obligation that is asserted as the basis for the relief sought, the appropriate legal test is not difficult to deduce. It is this: is it clear from what was expressly agreed upon that the parties who negotiated the express terms of the contract would have agreed to proscribe the act later complained of as a breach of the implied covenant of good faith — had they thought to negotiate with respect to that matter. If the answer to this question is yes, then, in my opinion, a court is justified in concluding that such act constitutes a breach of the implied covenant of good faith. *See Martin v. Star Publishing Co.*, Del. Supr., 126 A.2d 238 (1956); *Danby v. Osteopathic Hospital Ass'n*, Del. Ch., 101 A.2d 308 (1953) *aff'd*, Del. Supr., 104 A.2d 903 (1954); *Broad v. Rockwell International Corp.*, 5th Cir., 642 F.2d 929, 957 (1981). With this test in mind, I turn now to a review of the specific provisions of the various indentures from which one may be best able to infer whether it is apparent that the contracting parties — had they negotiated with the exchange offer and consent solicitation in mind — would have expressly agreed to prohibit contractually the linking of the giving of consent with the purchase and sale of the security.

IV.

Applying the foregoing standard to the exchange offer and consent solicitation, I find first that there is nothing in the indenture provisions granting bondholders power to veto proposed modifications in the relevant indenture that implies that Oak may not offer an inducement to bondholders to consent to such amendments. Such an implication, at least where, as here, the inducement is offered on the same terms to each holder of an affected security, would be wholly inconsistent with the strictly commercial nature of the relationship. Nor does the second pertinent contractual provision supply a ground to conclude that defendant's conduct violates the reasonable expectations of those who negotiated the indentures on behalf of the bondholders. Under that provision Oak may not vote debt securities held in its treasury. Plaintiff urges that Oak's conditioning of its offer to purchase debt on the giving of consents has the effect of subverting the purpose of that provision; it permits Oak to "dictate" the vote on securities which it could not itself vote. The evident purpose of the restriction on the voting of treasury securities is to afford protection against the issuer voting as a bondholder in favor of modifications that would benefit it as issuer, even though such changes would be detrimental to bondholders. But the linking of the exchange offer and the consent solicitation does not involve the risk that bondholder interests will be affected by a vote involving anyone with a financial interest in the subject of the vote other than a bondholder's interest. That the consent is to be given concurrently with the transfer of the bond to the issuer does not in any sense create the kind of conflict of interest that the indenture's prohibition on voting treasury securities contemplates. Not only will the proposed consents be granted or withheld only by those with a financial interest to maximize the return on their investment in Oak's bonds, but the incentive to consent is equally available to all members of each class of bondholders. Thus the "vote" implied by the consent solicitation is not affected in any sense by those with a financial conflict of interest. In these circumstances, while it is clear that Oak has fashioned the exchange offer and consent solicitation in a way designed to encourage consents, I cannot conclude that the offer violates the intendment of any of the express contractual provisions considered or, applying the test set out above, that its structure and timing breaches an implied obligation of good faith and fair dealing. One further set of contractual provisions should be touched upon: Those granting to Oak a power to redeem the securities here treated at a price set by the relevant indentures. Plaintiff asserts that the attempt to force all bondholders to tender their securities at less than the redemption price constitutes, if not a breach of the redemption provision itself, at least a breach of an implied covenant of good faith and fair dealing associated with it. The flaw, or at least one fatal flaw, in this argument is that the present offer is not the functional equivalent of a redemption which is, of course, an act that the issuer may take unilaterally. In this instance it may happen that Oak will get tenders of a large percentage of its outstanding long-term debt securities. If it does, that fact will, in my judgment, be in major part a function of the merits of the offer (i.e., the price offered in light of the Company's financial position and the market value of its debt). To answer plaintiff's contention that the structure of the offer "forces" debt holders to tender, one only has to imagine what response this offer would receive if the price offered did not reflect a premium over market but rather was, for example, ten percent of market value. The exchange offer's success ultimately depends upon the ability and willingness of the issuer to extend an offer that will be a financially attractive alternative to holders. This process is hardly the functional equivalent of the unilateral election of redemption and thus cannot be said in any sense to constitute a subversion by Oak of the negotiated provisions dealing with redemption of its debt. Accordingly, I conclude that plaintiff has failed to demonstrate a probability of ultimate success on the theory of liability asserted.

V.

An independent ground for the decision to deny the pending motion is supplied by the requirement that a court of equity will not issue the extraordinary remedy of preliminary injunction where to do so threatens the party sought to be enjoined with irreparable injury that, in the circumstances, seems greater than the injury that plaintiff seeks to avoid. *Eastern Shore Natural Gas Co. v. Stauffer Chemical Co.*, Del. Supr., 298 A.2d 322 (1972). That principal has application here. Oak is in a weak state financially. Its board, comprised of persons of experience and, in some instances, distinction, have approved the complex and interrelated transactions outlined above. It is not unreasonable to accord weight to the claims of Oak that the reorganization and recapitalization of which the exchange offer is a part may present the last good chance to regain vitality for this enterprise. I have not discussed plaintiff's claim of irreparable injury, although I have considered it. I am satisfied simply to note my conclusion that it is far outweighed by the harm that an improvidently granted injunction would threaten to Oak. For the foregoing reasons plaintiff's application for a preliminary injunction shall be denied.

IN RE CHATEAUGAY CORP.

United States Court of Appeals, Second Circuit
961 F.2d 378 (1992)

OAKES, CHIEF JUDGE:

Valley Fidelity Bank & Trust Co. ("Valley") and intervenors appeal from a judgment of the United States District Court for the Southern District of New York, Shirley Wohl Kram, Judge, affirming a judgment of the United States Bankruptcy Court for the Southern District of New York, Burton R. Lifland, Chief Judge. The bankruptcy court granted partial summary judgment in favor of the debtor, the LTV Corporation ("LTV"), disallowing Valley's claims to the extent they included unamortized original issue discount ("OID"). On this appeal, Valley argues that the bankruptcy court and district court erred by holding (1) that new OID arose on an exchange of debt securities performed as part of LTV's failed attempt to avoid bankruptcy through a consensual workout, and (2) that amortization of OID should be calculated by the constant interest method, rather than by the straight line method. For the reasons set forth below, we reverse in part and affirm in part. We hold first that while claims must be disallowed to the extent of unamortized OID, no new OID arose on LTV's debt-for-debt exchange, and second, that OID amortization should be calculated by the constant interest method.

FACTS

In July 1986, LTV, a steel company that makes defense and industrial products, filed for Chapter 11 reorganization along with sixty-six of its subsidiaries. LTV filed objections in September 1989 to two proofs of claim, numbers 20,069 and 20,067, filed in November 1987 by Valley on behalf of the holders of two securities, the "Old Debentures" and the "New Notes." Valley is the trustee for both the Old Debentures and the New Notes.

The Old Debentures are $13-7/8 Sinking Fund Debentures due December 1, 2002, of which LTV had by December 1, 1982 issued a total face amount of $150,000,000. Of that face amount, $125,000,000 had been issued to the public, for which LTV received $110,835,000 in cash. The remaining $25,000,000 had been issued to subsidiary pension funds, in lieu of cash contributions of $22,167,000. The proceeds received for the Old Debentures thus amounted to 88.67% of their face value.

The New Notes are LTV 15% Senior Notes due January 15, 2000. In May 1986, LTV offered to exchange $1,000 face amount of New Notes and 15 shares of LTV common stock for each $1,000 face amount of Old Debentures. As of June 1, 1986, $116,035,000 face amount of Old Debentures had been exchanged for the same face amount of New Notes and LTV Common Stock.

In its proofs of claim, Valley did not deduct any amount for unamortized OID. LTV objected to the claims and moved for partial summary judgment, seeking an order disallowing unamortized OID. LTV argued that unamortized OID is unmatured interest which is not allowable by virtue of section 502(b)(2) of the Bankruptcy Code, 11 U.S.C. § 502(b)(2) (1988), and that therefore the claims must be reduced by the amount of unamortized OID. A number of other creditors intervened to address questions of law that they believe may affect their own claims against LTV.

The bankruptcy court granted partial summary judgment for LTV. *In re Chateaugay Corp.*, 109 B.R. 51, 58 (Bankr. S.D.N.Y. 1990). The court held that unamortized OID is not allowable under section 502(b)(2), and that the proper method for calculating unamortized OID is the constant interest method. *Id.* The court also held that as indenture trustee, Valley was the proper party in interest to receive notice of LTV's objections. *Id.* Concluding that the amount of unamortized OID on the Old Debentures could be calculated using uncontroverted evidence, but that the amount on the New Notes could not be calculated until a disputed fact — the fair market value of the Old Debentures at the time of the exchange — was resolved, the court granted LTV's motion except as to the amount of unamortized OID on the New Notes. *Id.*

LTV and Valley thereafter stipulated to $3,554,609 and $8,174,134 as the amount of unamortized OID on the Old Debentures and the New Notes, respectively, calculated in accordance with the bankruptcy court's opinion. After that stipulation, Judge Lifland on March 27, 1990 entered a judgment partially disallowing, in the above amounts, Valley's proofs of claim. The district court affirmed the bankruptcy court's decision in its entirety. *In re Chateaugay Corp.*, 130 B.R. 403, 405 (S.D.N.Y. 1991).

DISCUSSION

I. Original Issue Discount and Section 502(b)(2)

A

Original issue discount results when a bond is issued for less than its face value. The discount, which compensates for a stated interest rate that the market deems too low, equals the difference between a bond's face amount (stated principal amount) and the proceeds, prior to issuance expenses, received by the issuer. OID is amortized, for accounting and tax purposes, over the life of the bond, with the face value generally paid back to the bondholders on the maturity date. If the debtor meets with financial trouble and turns to the bankruptcy court for protection, as in the present case, then OID comes into play as one of the factors determining the amount of the bondholder's allowable claim in bankruptcy.

Section 502 of the Bankruptcy Code, the framework for Chapter 11 claim allowance, provides that a claim shall be allowed "except to the extent that . . . such claim is for unmatured interest." 11 U.S.C. § 502(b)(2) (1988). The first question we face is whether unamortized OID is "unmatured interest" within the meaning of section 502(b)(2). We conclude that it is. As a matter of economic definition, OID constitutes interest. *United States v. Midland-Ross Corp.*, 381 U.S. 54, 57, 85 S. Ct. 1308, 1310, 14 L. Ed. 2d 214 (1965) (treating OID for tax purposes as income, not capital); *see also* Frank J. Slagle, *Accounting for Interest: An Analysis of Original Issue Discount in the Sale of Property*, 32 S.D. L. Rev. 1, 21 n. 108 (1987) ("The amount of the discount represents compensation to the Lender for the use and forbearance of money, i.e., interest."). Moreover, the Bankruptcy Code's legislative history makes inescapable the conclusion that OID is interest within the meaning of section 502(b)(2). The House committee report on that section explains:

> Interest disallowed under this paragraph includes postpetition interest that is not yet due and payable, and any portion of prepaid interest that represents an original discounting of the claim, yet that would not have been earned on the date of bankruptcy. For example, a claim on a $1,000 note issued the day before bankruptcy would only be allowed to the extent of the cash actually advanced. If the original issue discount was 10% so that the cash advanced was only $900, then notwithstanding the face amount of [the] note, only $900 would be allowed. If $900 was advanced under the note

> some time before bankruptcy, the interest component of the note would have to be pro-rated and disallowed to the extent it was for interest after the commencement of the case.

H. Rep. No. 595, 95th Cong., 1st Sess. 352-53 (1977), reprinted in 1978 U.S.C.C.A.N. 5787, 5963, 6308-09.

The courts that have considered the issue under section 502(b)(2) have held that unamortized OID is unmatured interest and therefore unallowable as part of a bankruptcy claim. *In re Public Service Co. of New Hampshire*, 114 B.R. 800, 803 (Bankr. D. N.H. 1990); *In re Allegheny Int'l, Inc.*, 100 B.R. 247, 250 (Bankr. W.D. Pa. 1989); *see also In re Pengo Indus., Inc.*, 129 B.R. 104, 108 (N.D. Tex. 1991). *But cf. In re Radio-Keith-Orpheum Corp.*, 106 F.2d 22, 27 (2d Cir. 1939) (under Bankruptcy Act, allowing debentures issued at a discount for full face amount), cert. denied, 308 U.S. 622, 60 S. Ct. 380, 84 L. Ed. 520 (1940). The Public Service court stated it plainly: "The word "interest' in the statute is clearly sufficient to encompass the OID variation in the method of providing for and collecting what in economic fact is interest to be paid to compensate for the delay and risk involved in the ultimate repayment of monies loaned." 114 B.R. at 803.

Applying this reasoning to the case at hand, we conclude, as did the bankruptcy and district courts, that OID on the Old Debentures, to the extent it was unamortized when the bankruptcy petition was filed, should be disallowed. We now turn to the main issue in dispute: the applicability of section 502(b)(2) to the New Notes, which were issued in a debt-for-debt exchange offer as part of a consensual workout.

B

A debtor in financial trouble may seek to avoid bankruptcy through a consensual out-of-court workout. Such a recapitalization, when it involves publicly traded debt, often takes the form of a debt-for-debt exchange, whereby bondholders exchange their old bonds for new bonds. The debtor hopes that the exchange, by changing the terms of the debt, will enable the debtor to avoid default. The bondholders hope that by increasing the likelihood of payment on their bonds, the exchange will benefit them as well. The debtor and its creditors share an interest in achieving a successful restructuring of the debtor's financial obligations in order to avoid the uncertainties and daunting transaction costs of bankruptcy.

An exchange offer made by a financially troubled company can be either a "fair market value exchange" or a "face value exchange." *See* Marc S. Kirschner, et al., *Prepackaged Bankruptcy Plans: The Deleveraging Tool of the '90s in the Wake of OID and Tax Concerns*, 21 SETON HALL L. REV. 643, 645-47 (1991); Allen L. Weingarten, *Consensual Non-Bankruptcy Restructuring of Public Debt Securities*, 23 Rev. of Sec. & Commodities Reg. 159, 161 (1990). In a fair market value exchange, an existing debt instrument is exchanged for a new one with a reduced principal amount, determined by the market value at which the existing instrument is trading. By offering a fair market value exchange, an issuer seeks to reduce its overall debt obligations. Usually, this is sought only by companies in severe financial distress. A face value exchange, by contrast, involves the substitution of new indebtedness for an existing debenture, modifying terms or conditions but not reducing the principal amount of the debt. A relatively healthy company faced with liquidity problems may offer a face value exchange to obtain short-term relief while remaining fully liable for the original funds borrowed.

The question is whether a face value exchange generates new OID. The bankruptcy court, in an opinion endorsed by the district court, held that it does. The court reasoned that, by definition, OID arises whenever a bond is issued for less than its face amount, and that in LTV's debt-for-debt exchange, the issue price of the New Notes was the fair market value of the Old Debentures. The court therefore concluded that the New Notes were issued at a discount equaling the difference between their face value and the fair market value of the Old Debentures. *In re Chateaugay Corp.*, 109 B.R. at 56-57.

The bankruptcy court's reasoning leaves us unpersuaded. While its application of the definition of OID to exchange offers may seem irrefutable at first glance, we believe the bankruptcy court's logic ignores the importance of context, and does not make sense if one takes into account the strong bankruptcy policy in favor of the speedy, inexpensive, negotiated resolution of disputes, that is an out-of-court or common law composition. *See* H.R. Rep. No. 95-595, 95th Cong., 1st Sess. 220 (1977), reprinted in 1978 U.S.S.C.A.N. 5963, 6179-80; *see also In re Colonial Ford, Inc.*, 24 B.R. 1014, 1015-17 (Bankr. D. Utah 1982) ("Congress designed the Code, in large measure, to encourage workouts in the first instance, with refuge in bankruptcy as a last resort."). If unamortized OID is unallowable in bankruptcy, and if exchanging debt increases the amount of OID, then creditors will be disinclined to cooperate in a consensual workout that might otherwise have rescued a borrower from the precipice of bankruptcy. We must consider the ramifications of a rule that places a creditor in the position of choosing whether to cooperate with a struggling debtor, when such cooperation might make the creditor's claims in the event of bankruptcy smaller than they would have been had the creditor refused to cooperate. The bankruptcy court's ruling places creditors in just such a position, and unreversed would likely result in fewer out-of-court debt exchanges and more Chapter 11 filings. Just as that ruling creates a disincentive for creditors to cooperate with a troubled debtor, it grants a corresponding windfall both to holdouts who refuse to cooperate and to an issuer that files for bankruptcy subsequent to a debt exchange. *See* John C. Coffee, Jr. & William A. Klein, *Bondholder Coercion: The Problem of Constrained Choice in Debt Tender Offers and Recapitalizations*, 58 U. Chi. L. Rev. 1207, 1248-49 & n. 121 (1991); Kirschner, et al., *supra*, 21 Seton Hall L. Rev. at 644-60.

The bankruptcy court's decision might make sense in the context of a fair market value exchange, where the corporation's overall debt obligations are reduced. In a face value exchange such as LTV's, however, it is unsupportable. LTV's liability to the holders of the New Notes was no less than its liability to them had been when they held the Old Debentures. The bankruptcy court, by finding that the exchange created new OID, reduced LTV's liabilities based on an exchange which, because it was a face value exchange, caused no such reduction on LTV's balance sheet.

We hold that a face value exchange of debt obligations in a consensual workout does not, for purposes of section 502(b)(2), generate new OID. Such an exchange does not change the character of the underlying debt, but reaffirms and modifies it.

Cf. In re Red Way Cartage Co., 84 B.R. 459, 461 (Bankr. E.D. Mich. 1988) (in context of preferential transfers, settlement agreement did not create new debt, but only reaffirmed the antecedent debt); *In re Magic Circle Energy Corp.*, 64 B.R. 269, 273 (Bankr. W.D. Okla. 1986) (same, explaining, "We do not accept the proposition that the consolidation of [debt] into a long-term promissory note wrought a metamorphosis wherein the nature of the debt was altered."); *In re Busman*, 5 B.R. 332, 336 (Bankr. E.D. N.Y. 1980) ("the rule [of § 502(b)(2)] is clearly not entrenched as an absolute").

In the absence of unambiguous statutory guidance, we will not attribute to Congress an intent to place a stumbling block in front of debtors seeking to avoid bankruptcy with the cooperation of their creditors. Rather, given Congress's intent to encourage consensual workouts and the obvious desirability of minimizing bankruptcy filings, we conclude that for purposes of section 502(b)(2), no new OID is created in a face value debt-for-debt exchange in the context of a consensual workout. Thus, OID on the new debt consists only of the discount carried over from the old debt, that is, the unamortized OID remaining on the old debt at the time of the exchange.

The cases upon which the bankruptcy court relied in reaching a contrary conclusion are distinguishable. The court found support for its conclusion by looking to tax cases, because under the Internal Revenue Code, for purposes of determining taxable income, an exchange offer generates new OID. *See, e.g., Cities Service Co. v. United States*, 522 F.2d 1281, 1288 (2d Cir. 1974) (holding in tax context that OID arose on exchange because the face amount of the issue exceeded the consideration), cert. denied, 423 U.S. 827, 96 S. Ct. 43, 46 L. Ed. 2d 43 (1975). The tax treatment of a transaction, however, need not determine the bankruptcy treatment. *See, e.g., In re PCH Assocs.*, 55 B.R. 273 (Bankr. S.D.N.Y. 1985) (agreement structured as ground lease for tax benefits treated as joint venture under Bankruptcy Code), *aff'd*, 60 B.R. 870 (S.D.N.Y.), *aff'd*, 804 F.2d 193 (2d Cir. 1986). The tax treatment of debt-for-debt exchanges derives from the tax laws' focus on realization events, and suggests that an exchange offer may represent a sensible time to tax the parties. The same reasoning simply does not apply in the bankruptcy context. See Kirschner, *supra*, 21 Seton Hall L. Rev. at 655-56.

Similarly distinguishable is *In re Allegheny Int'l, Inc.*, 100 B.R. 247 (Bankr. W.D. Pa. 1989), upon which the bankruptcy court relied heavily in determining that new OID was created by LTV's debt exchange. In *Allegheny*, the court considered and rejected the argument "that section 502(b)(2) does not apply . . . to debentures created in the context of an exchange offer." *Id.* at 250. That case, however, involved a debt-for-equity exchange, not a debt-for-debt exchange. The debtor in *Allegheny* offered to exchange debt instruments for previously issued preferred stock. *Id.* at 248. Thus, the stockholders had no claim against the debtor prior to the exchange, and the debtor's balance sheet reflected an increase in overall liabilities from the exchange. We need not decide whether Allegheny was correct. Whether or not its reasoning is sound in the context of a debt-for-equity exchange, it is inapplicable to a debt-for-debt exchange such as LTV's.

II. Calculating OID Amortization

We now turn to the methodology for calculating OID amortization. Valley argues that the proper method for calculating unamortized OID under the Bankruptcy Code is the straight line method, by which the amount of the discount is spread equally over the duration of the maturation of the note. Under the straight line method, the same amount of interest accrues during each day of the instrument's term. LTV argues, in contrast, that the constant interest method — which also goes by the names yield-to-maturity, effective interest, or economic accrual — should be used. The constant interest method calculates OID amortization on the assumption that interest is compounded over time. Under the constant interest method, the amount of interest that accrues each day increases over time.

The bankruptcy court and district court opted for the constant interest method, and we agree. The constant interest method comports more closely than the straight line method with economic reality. See Slagle, supra, 32 S.D. L. Rev. at 24 (criticizing straight line method as a distortion on interest accrual).

One bankruptcy court has held that OID should be calculated by the straight line method for purposes of Bankruptcy Code section 502(b)(2), Allegheny, 100 B.R. at 254, but its reasoning is unconvincing. That court simply noted that the legislative history of section 502(b)(2) provides that unmatured interest should be "pro-rated," and assumed without analysis that the pro-rating must be done so that the increases are constant through time, rather than so that the rate of increase is constant through time. To say that interest must be pro-rated is only to restate the question, which is what method should be used for that pro-rating.

One further point must be addressed regarding the calculation of OID amortization. Our holding today that, for purposes of section 502(b)(2), no new OID is created by a face value debt-for-debt exchange in a consensual workout, means that the old OID is carried over to the new debt. In other words, when the Old Debentures were exchanged for the New Notes, the New Notes carried a discount equaling the amount of OID remaining on the Old Debentures after amortization by the constant interest method. The amount of OID remaining must then be amortized, again employing the constant interest method, over the life of the New Notes. Thus, a creditor's claim in bankruptcy may differ depending on whether the creditor participated in a workout; that difference, however, derives not from any new OID created by the exchange, but from the logical necessity of an amortization schedule that concludes on the maturity date. In the present case, because the New Notes carried an earlier maturity date than the Old Debentures, those bondholders who cooperated with the debtor find themselves with a slightly larger claim in bankruptcy, after the disallowance of unamortized OID, than those who did not.

Accordingly, the judgment of the district court is affirmed in part and reversed in part, and the matter remanded to the district court for remand to the bankruptcy court for further proceedings consistent with this opinion.

NOTE

The following example illustrates why the Indenture Trustee, Valley, argued in favor of utilization of the straight line method, which results in higher interest payments during the early stages of the term of a debt obligation.[107]

FIVE-YEAR 10% ZERO COUPON DEBENTURE	
Maturity Date	February 27, 2008
Amount Payable on Maturity	$1,000
Issue Date	February 27, 2003
Amount Invested	$620.9213
Amount of Return over 5 Years	$379.0787
	$1,000.00

INTEREST CALCULATION		
Year	Straight Line Method Amount	Compounded Method Amount
2004	75.81574	62.09213
2005	75.81574	68.30134
2006	75.81574	75.13148
2007	75.81574	82.64463
2008	75.81574	90.90912
	379.0787	379.0787

UNION BANK v. WOLAS

United States Supreme Court
502 U.S. 151 (1991)

JUSTICE STEVENS delivered the opinion of the Court.

Section 547(b) of the Bankruptcy Code, 11 U.S.C. § 547(b), authorizes a trustee to avoid certain property transfers made by a debtor within 90 days before bankruptcy. The Code makes an exception, however, for transfers made in the ordinary course of business, 11 U.S.C. § 547(c)(2). The question presented is whether payments on long-term debt may qualify for that exception. On December 17, 1986, ZZZZ Best Co., Inc. (Debtor) borrowed seven million dollars from petitioner, Union Bank (Bank).[108] On July 8, 1987, the Debtor filed a voluntary

---

[107] The following presentation was prepared with the able assistance of Steve Milankov of Clifford Chance US LLP.

[108] [1] The Bankruptcy Court found that the Bank and Debtor executed a revolving credit agreement on December 16, 1986, in which the Bank agreed to lend the Debtor $7 million in accordance with the terms of a promissory note to be executed and delivered by the Debtor. No. 87-13692 (Bkrtcy. Ct. C.D. Cal., Aug. 22, 1988), App. to Pet. for Cert. 12a. On December 17, 1987, the Debtor executed and delivered to the Bank a promissory note in the principal sum of $7 million. The promissory note provided that interest would be payable on a monthly basis and would accrue on the principal balance at a rate of.65% per annum in excess of the Bank's reference rate. *Id.*

petition under Chapter 7 of the Bankruptcy Code. During the preceding 90-day period, the Debtor had made two interest payments totalling approximately $100,000 and had paid a loan commitment fee of about $2,500 to the Bank. After his appointment as trustee of the Debtor's estate, respondent filed a complaint against the Bank to recover those payments pursuant to § 547(b).

The Bankruptcy Court found that the loans had been made "in the ordinary course of business or financial affairs" of both the Debtor and the Bank, and that both interest payments as well as the payment of the loan commitment fee had been made according to ordinary business terms and in the ordinary course of business.[109] As a matter of law, the Bankruptcy Court concluded that the payments satisfied the requirements of § 547(c)(2) and therefore were not avoidable by the trustee.[110] The District Court affirmed the Bankruptcy Court's summary judgment in favor of the Bank.[111]

Shortly thereafter, in another case, the Court of Appeals held that the ordinary course of business exception to avoidance of preferential transfers was not available to long-term creditors. *In re CHG International, Inc.*, 897 F.2d 1479 (CA9 1990). In reaching that conclusion, the Court of Appeals relied primarily on the policies underlying the voidable preference provisions and the state of the law prior to the enactment of the 1978 Bankruptcy Code and its amendment in 1984. Thus, the Ninth Circuit concluded, its holding in *CHG International, Inc.* dictated a reversal in this case. 921 F.2d 968, 969 (1990).[112] The importance of the question of law decided by the Ninth Circuit, coupled with the fact that the Sixth Circuit had interpreted § 547(c)(2) in a contrary manner, *In re Finn*, 909 F.2d 903 (1990), persuaded us to grant the Bank's petition for certiorari. 500 U.S. 915 (1991).

I

We shall discuss the history and policy of § 547 after examining its text. In subsection (b), Congress broadly authorized bankruptcy trustees to "avoid any transfer of an interest of the debtor in property" if all five conditions are satisfied and unless one of seven exceptions defined in subsection (c) is applicable.[113] In brief, the five characteristics of a voidable preference are that it (1) benefit a creditor; (2)

---

[109] [2] App. to Pet. for Cert. 14a.

[110] [3] *Id.*

[111] [4] *In re ZZZZ Best Co., Inc.*, No. 88-6285, 1989 U.S. Dist. LEXIS 17500, *1 (C.D. Cal., Aug. 4, 1989).

[112] [5] In so holding, the Ninth Circuit rejected the Bank's argument that the revolving line of credit in this case was not "long-term" because it was for less than one year. 921 F.2d 968, 969 (1990). Because we hold that the ordinary course of business exception applies to payments on long-term as well as short-term debt, we need not decide whether the revolving line of credit was a "long-term" debt.

[113] [6] 11 U.S.C. § 547(b) provides: "Except as provided in subsection (c) of this section, the trustee may avoid any transfer of an interest of the debtor in property — (1) to or for the benefit of a creditor; (2) for or on account of an antecedent debt owed by the debtor before such transfer was made; (3) made while the debtor was insolvent; (4) made — (A) on or within 90 days before the date of the filing of the petition; or (B) between ninety days and one year before the date of the filing of the petition, if such creditor at the time of such transfer was an insider; and (5) that enable such creditor to receive more than such creditor would receive if — (A) the case were a case under chapter 7 of this title; (B) the transfer

be on account of antecedent debt; (3) be made while the debtor was insolvent; (4) be within 90 days before bankruptcy; and (5) enable the creditor to receive a larger share of the estate than if the transfer had not been made. Section 547 also provides that the debtor is presumed to have been insolvent during the 90-day period preceding bankruptcy. 11 U.S.C. § 547(f). In this case, it is undisputed that all five of the foregoing conditions were satisfied and that the interest and loan commitment fee payments were voidable preferences unless excepted by subsection (c)(2).

The most significant feature of subsection (c)(2) that is relevant to this case is the absence of any language distinguishing between long-term debt and short-term debt.[114] That subsection provides:

"The trustee may not avoid under this section a transfer —

. . . .

> "(2) to the extent that such transfer was — (A) in payment of a debt incurred by the debtor in the ordinary course of business or financial affairs of the debtor and the transferee; (B) made in the ordinary course of business or financial affairs of the debtor and the transferee; and (C) made according to ordinary business terms."

Instead of focusing on the term of the debt for which the transfer was made, subsection (c)(2) focuses on whether the debt was incurred, and payment made, in the "ordinary course of business or financial affairs" of the debtor and transferee. Thus, the text provides no support for respondent's contention that § 547(c)(2)'s coverage is limited to short-term debt, such as commercial paper or trade debt. Given the clarity of the statutory text, respondent's burden of persuading us that Congress intended to create or to preserve a special rule for long-term debt is exceptionally heavy. *United States v. Ron Pair Enterprises, Inc.*, 489 U.S. 235, 241-242, 109 S. Ct. 1026, 1030-1031, 103 L. Ed. 2d 290 (1989). As did the Ninth Circuit, respondent relies on the history and the policies underlying the preference provision.

II

The relevant history of § 547 contains two chapters, one of which clearly supports, and the second of which is not inconsistent with, the Bank's literal reading of the statute. Section 547 was enacted in 1978 when Congress overhauled the Nation's bankruptcy laws. The section was amended in 1984. For purposes of the question presented in this case, the original version of § 547 differed in one significant respect from the current version: it contained a provision that the ordinary course of business exception did not apply unless the payment was made

had not been made; and (C) such creditor received payment of such debt to the extent provided by the provisions of this title."

[114] [7] Nor does the definitional section of the Bankruptcy Code, which defines the term "debt" broadly as a "liability on a claim," 11 U.S.C. § 101(11), distinguish between short-term debt and long-term debt.

within 45 days of the date the debt was incurred.[115] That provision presumably excluded most payments on long-term debt from the exception.[116] In 1984 Congress repealed the 45-day limitation but did not substitute a comparable limitation. See Bankruptcy Amendments and Federal Judgeship Act of 1984, Pub. L. 98-353, § 462(c), 98 Stat. 333, 378.

Respondent contends that this amendment was intended to satisfy complaints by issuers of commercial paper[117] and by trade creditors[118] that regularly extended credit for periods of more than 45 days. Furthermore, respondent continues, there is no evidence in the legislative history that Congress intended to make the ordinary course of business exception available to conventional long-term lenders. Therefore, respondent argues, we should follow the analysis of the Ninth Circuit and read § 547(c)(2) as protecting only short-term debt payments. *Cf. In re CHG International*, 897 F.2d, at 1484.

We need not dispute the accuracy of respondent's description of the legislative history of the 1984 amendment in order to reject his conclusion. For even if Congress adopted the 1984 amendment to redress particular problems of specific short-term creditors, it remains true that Congress redressed those problems by entirely deleting the time limitation in § 547(c)(2). The fact that Congress may not have foreseen all of the consequences of a statutory enactment is not a sufficient reason for refusing to give effect to its plain meaning. *Toibb v. Radloff*, 501 U.S., 111 S. Ct. 2197, 115 L. Ed. 2d 145 (1991). Respondent also relies on the history of voidable preferences prior to the enactment of the 1978 Bankruptcy Code. The text

---

[115] [8] As enacted in 1978, § 547(c) provided, in relevant part: "The trustee may not avoid under this section a transfer —

. . . .

> "(2) to the extent that such transfer was- (A) in payment of a debt incurred in the ordinary course of business or financial affairs of the debtor and the transferee; (B) made not later than 45 days after such debt was incurred; (C) made in the ordinary course of business or financial affairs of the debtor and the transferee; and (D) made according to ordinary business terms."

92 Stat. 2549, 2598 (1978)

[116] [9] We use the term "presumably" because it is not necessary in this case to decide whether monthly interest payments on long-term debt were protected by the initial version of § 547(c)(2). *Cf. In re Iowa Premium Service Co., Inc.*, 695 F.2d 1109 (CA8 1982) (en banc) (holding that interest obligations are "incurred" when they become due, rather than when the promissory note is signed). We refer to "most" instead of "all" long-term debt payments because of the possibility that a debtor's otherwise avoidable payment was made within 45 days of the date the long-term loan was made.

[117] [10] Because payments to a commercial paper purchaser within 90 days prior to bankruptcy may be preferential transfers under § 547(b), a purchaser could be assured that the payment would not be avoided under the prior version of § 547(c)(2) only if the commercial paper had a maturity of 45 days or less. Commercial issuers thus complained that the 45-day limitation lowered demand for commercial paper with a maturity in excess of 45 days. See Hearings before the Subcommittee on Judicial Machinery of the Senate Committee on the Judiciary, 96th Cong., 2d Sess., 8-27 (1980) (statements of George Van Cleave, partner, Goldman, Sachs & Co., and James Ledinsky, Senior Vice President, A.G. Becker & Co.).

[118] [11] Trade creditors stated that normal payment periods in many industries exceeded 45 days and complained that the arbitrary 45-day limitation in § 547(c)(2) deprived these trade creditors of the protection of the ordinary course of business exception to the trustee's power to avoid preferential transfers. *See, e.g.*, Hearings on Bankruptcy Reform Act of 1978, before the Subcommittee on Courts of the Senate Committee on the Judiciary, 97th Cong., 1st Sess., 259-260 (1981) (statement of Vyto Gestautas on behalf of the National Association of Credit Management).

of the preference provision in the earlier Bankruptcy Act did not specifically include an exception for payments made in the ordinary course of business.[119] The courts had, however, developed what is sometimes described as the "current expense" rule to cover situations in which a debtor's payments on the eve of bankruptcy did not diminish the net estate because tangible assets were obtained in exchange for the payment. *See Marshall v. Florida National Bank of Jacksonville*, 112 F.2d 380, 382 (CA5 1940); 3 Collier on Bankruptcy P. 60.23, p. 873 (14th ed. 1977). Without such an exception, trade creditors and other suppliers of necessary goods and services might have been reluctant to extend even short-term credit and might have required advance payment instead, thus making it difficult for many companies in temporary distress to have remained in business. Respondent argues that Congress enacted § 547(c)(2) in 1978 to codify that exception, and therefore the Court should construe § 547(c)(2) as limited to the confines of the current expense rule.

This argument is not compelling for several reasons. First, it is by no means clear that § 547(c)(2) should be construed as the statutory analogue of the judicially crafted current expense rule because there are other exceptions in § 547(c) that explicitly cover contemporaneous exchanges for new value.[120] Those provisions occupy some (if not all) of the territory previously covered by the current expense rule. Nor has respondent directed our attention to any extrinsic evidence suggesting that Congress intended to codify the current expense rule in § 547(c)(2).[121]

The current expense rule developed when the statutory preference provision was significantly narrower than it is today. To establish a preference under the Bankruptcy Act, the trustee had to prove that the challenged payment was made at a time when the creditor had "reasonable cause to believe that the debtor [was] insolvent." 11 U.S.C. § 96(b) (1976 ed.). When Congress rewrote the preference provision in the 1978 Bankruptcy Code, it substantially enlarged the trustee's power to avoid preferential transfers by eliminating the reasonable cause to believe requirement for transfers made within 90 days of bankruptcy and creating a presumption of insolvency during that period. See 11 U.S.C. §§ 547(b), (c)(2), (f); H.R. Rep. No. 95-595, p. 178 (1977), U.S. Code Cong. & Admin. News 1978, pp. 5787,

---

[119] [12] Section 60 of the 1898 Bankruptcy Act, as amended and codified in 11 U.S.C. § 96 (1976 ed.), provided in relevant part:

> "(a)(1) A preference is a transfer, as defined in this title, of any of the property of a debtor to or for the benefit of a creditor for or on account of an antecedent debt, made or suffered by such debtor while insolvent and within four months before the filing by or against him of the petition initiating a proceeding under this title, the effect of which transfer will be to enable such creditor to obtain a greater percentage of his debt than some other creditor of the same class.
>
> . . . .
>
> "(b) Any such preference may be avoided by the trustee if the creditor receiving it or to be benefited thereby or his agent acting with reference thereto has, at the time when the transfer is made, reasonable cause to believe that the debtor is insolvent. Where the preference is voidable, the trustee may recover the property. . . ."

[120] [13] Thus, for example, § 547(c)(1) exempts a transfer to the extent that it was a "contemporaneous exchange for new value given to the debtor," and § 547(c)(4) exempts a transfer to a creditor "to the extent that, after such transfer, such creditor gave new value to or for the benefit of the debtor. . . ."

[121] [14] In fact, the legislative history apparently does not even mention the current expense rule. *See* Broome, *Payments on Long-Term Debt as Voidable Preferences: The Impact of the 1984 Bankruptcy Amendments*, 1987 DUKE L.J. 78, 97.

6138. At the same time, Congress created a new exception for transfers made in the ordinary course of business, 11 U.S.C. § 547(c)(2). This exception was intended to "leave undisturbed normal financial relations, because it does not detract from the general policy of the preference section to discourage unusual action by either the debtor or his creditors during the debtor's slide into bankruptcy." H.R. Rep. No. 95-595, at 373, U.S. Code Cong. & Admin. News 1978, p. 6329. In light of these substantial changes in the preference provision, there is no reason to assume that the justification for narrowly confining the "current expense" exception to trade creditors before 1978 should apply to the ordinary course of business exception under the 1978 Code. Instead, the fact that Congress carefully reexamined and entirely rewrote the preference provision in 1978 supports the conclusion that the text of § 547(c)(2) as enacted reflects the deliberate choice of Congress.[122]

III

The Bank and the trustee agree that § 547 is intended to serve two basic policies that are fairly described in the House Committee Report. The Committee explained: "A preference is a transfer that enables a creditor to receive payment of a greater percentage of his claim against the debtor than he would have received if the transfer had not been made and he had participated in the distribution of the assets of the bankrupt estate. The purpose of the preference section is two-fold. First, by permitting the trustee to avoid prebankruptcy transfers that occur within a short period before bankruptcy, creditors are discouraged from racing to the courthouse to dismember the debtor during his slide into bankruptcy. The protection thus afforded the debtor often enables him to work his way out of a difficult financial situation through cooperation with all of his creditors. Second, and more important, the preference provisions facilitate the prime bankruptcy policy of equality of distribution among creditors of the debtor. Any creditor that received a greater payment than others of his class is required to disgorge so that all may share equally. The operation of the preference section to deter "the race of diligence' of creditors to dismember the debtor before bankruptcy furthers the second goal of the preference section — that of equality of distribution." *Id.*, at 177-178, U.S. Code Cong. & Admin. News 1978, pp. 6137, 6138. As this comment demonstrates, the two policies are not entirely independent. On the one hand, any exception for a payment on account of an antecedent debt tends to favor the payee over other creditors and therefore may conflict with the policy of equal treatment. On the other hand, the ordinary course of business exception may benefit all creditors by deterring the "race to the courthouse" and enabling the struggling debtor to continue operating its business. Respondent places primary emphasis, as did the Court of Appeals, on the interest in equal distribution. *See In re CHG*

[122] [15] Indeed, the House Committee Report concludes its discussion of the trustee's avoidance powers with the observation that the language in the preference section of the earlier Bankruptcy Act was "hopelessly complex" and had been "subject to varying interpretations. The bill undoes the numerous amendments that have been heaped on section 60 during the past 40 years, and proposes a unified and coherent section to deal with the problems created by prebankruptcy preferential transfers." H.R. Rep. No. 95-595, p. 179 (1977), U.S. Code Cong. & Admin. News 1978, p. 6139. Respondent's assumption that § 547(c)(2) was intended to preserve pre-existing law is at war with this legislative history.

International, 897 F.2d, at 1483-1485. When a debtor is insolvent, a transfer to one creditor necessarily impairs the claims of the debtor's other unsecured and undersecured creditors. By authorizing the avoidance of such preferential transfers, § 547(b) empowers the trustee to restore equal status to all creditors. Respondent thus contends that the ordinary course of business exception should be limited to short-term debt so the trustee may order that preferential long-term debt payments be returned to the estate to be distributed among all of the creditors. But the statutory text — which makes no distinction between short-term debt and long-term debt — precludes an analysis that divorces the policy of favoring equal distribution from the policy of discouraging creditors from racing to the courthouse to dismember the debtor. Long-term creditors, as well as trade creditors, may seek a head start in that race. Thus, even if we accept the Court of Appeals' conclusion that the availability of the ordinary business exception to long-term creditors does not directly further the policy of equal treatment, we must recognize that it does further the policy of deterring the race to the courthouse and, as the House Report recognized, may indirectly further the goal of equal distribution as well. Whether Congress has wisely balanced the sometimes conflicting policies underlying § 547 is not a question that we are authorized to decide.

IV

In sum, we hold that payments on long-term debt, as well as payments on short-term debt, may qualify for the ordinary course of business exception to the trustee's power to avoid preferential transfers. We express no opinion, however, on the question whether the Bankruptcy Court correctly concluded that the Debtor's payments of interest and the loan commitment fee qualify for the ordinary course of business exception, § 547(c)(2). In particular, we do not decide whether the loan involved in this case was incurred in the ordinary course of the Debtor's business and of the Bank's business, whether the payments were made in the ordinary course of business, or whether the payments were made according to ordinary business terms. These questions remain open for the Court of Appeals on remand. The judgment of the Court of Appeals is reversed and the case is remanded for further proceedings consistent with this opinion. It is so ordered.

JUSTICE SCALIA, concurring.

I join the opinion of the Court, including Parts II and III, which respond persuasively to legislative-history and policy arguments made by respondent. It is regrettable that we have a legal culture in which such arguments have to be addressed (and are indeed credited by a Court of Appeals), with respect to a statute utterly devoid of language that could remotely be thought to distinguish between long-term and short-term debt. Since there was here no contention of a "scrivener's error" producing an absurd result, the plain text of the statute should have made this litigation unnecessary and unmaintainable.

For a detailed exposition of Justice Scalia's view of statutory interpretation, see ANTONIN SCALIA & BRYAN A. GARDNER, READING LAW: THE INTERPRETATION OF LEGAL

Texts (2012). For another view, see Stephen Breyer, Active Liberty: Interpreting a Democratic Constitution (2008).

PROBLEM A

Bissell Industries, Inc. ("Bissell") was incorporated under the laws of the State of New York on October 29, 1929. Its principal executive office and all of its business operations are located in Zena, New York. Its equity capitalization presently consists of 20,000,000 shares of Common Stock, $1.00 par value (the "Common Stock"), 2,000,000 of which are issued and outstanding and traded on Ulster Stock Exchange (the "Exchange") and, 600,000 of which are held in the treasury.

There are also outstanding 5,000 of Bissell's 10% Debentures, due March 1, 2007 (the "Debentures"). The Debentures, each of which was publicly issued in the principal amount of $1,000 on March 1, 1987, are redeemable at the option of Bissell at 100 percent of the principal amount thereof ($1,000 each), plus unpaid interest, on or after March 1, 1992. Certain rights of the holders of the Debentures are set forth in an Indenture, dated as of March 1, 1987, between Bissell and The Hobart Trust Company (the "Indenture"). The Indenture requires Bissell to maintain at all times an excess of assets over liabilities of not less than $20,000,000. If Bissell fails to comply with that affirmative covenant, the Indenture provides that such non-compliance shall constitute an "event of default" and, in that event, the aggregate principal amount of the Debentures ($5,000,000) and the accrued interest thereon shall become immediately due and payable. The Indenture also provides that, in the event of a merger of Bissell with any other corporation, or the sale by Bissell of all or substantially all of its assets, the corporation with which Bissell merges or to which Bissell sells all or substantially all of its assets shall assume all of the obligations of Bissell under the Debentures and Indenture. The Indenture states that a holder of Debentures may not commence an action to enforce any term thereof, or to seek damages for any breach thereof, unless the Indenture Trustee has refused to do so, following a written demand therefor by the holders of at least 25 percent in principal amount of the Debentures.

Bissell is presently structured as a holding company; its assets presently consist primarily of all of the issued and outstanding shares (1,000 each) of common stock of its two Delaware wholly owned subsidiaries, Christina Cosmetics Corporation ("Christina") and Henderson Steel Corporation ("Henderson"). Christina is engaged in the production and sale of various cosmetic and related products. Although historically Christina has been responsible for nearly all of the net income of Bissell, it has been adversely affected by foreign competition, and accounts for only approximately 55 percent of Bissell's revenues, but still comprises approximately 35 percent of Bissell's assets. Henderson, which is engaged in the manufacture and sale of various steel products, accounts for 45 percent of Bissell's revenues and comprises approximately 65 percent of the assets of Bissell.

Bissell has received an unexpected proposal from Rossi and Richard, Ltd., a European merchant banking firm, for the purchase of all of the stock of Christina for a price that would represent a premium of $25,000,000 over the value of such shares as set forth on the consolidated balance sheet of Bissell. The cash purchase price would be payable to Bissell. In the negotiations, Rossi and Richard has insisted that it will not assume the obligations of Bissell under the Indenture and the Debentures to pay principal and interest on the Debentures. You are an associate in the law firm of Scanlon & Gallagher, and Augustine F. Scanlon, the partner-in-charge with respect to Bissell, asks you to write a memorandum discussing the rights of the security holders of Bissell with regard to the proposed sale by Bissell of the Christina stock. Mr. Scanlon plans to discuss the conclusions reached in the memorandum with Kenyon & Flanigan, counsel for The Hobart Trust Company, which has expressed concern about both Bissell's financial condition and the proposed sale of the Christina stock. Write that memorandum for Mr. Scanlon.

PROBLEM B

Woodstock Industries, Inc. ("Woodstock") was incorporated under the laws of the State of New York on March 1, 1967. Its equity capitalization presently consists of 8,000,000 shares of Common Stock, $1.00 par value (the "Common Stock"), 6,000,000 of which are presently issued and outstanding and traded on the Ulster Stock Exchange (a national securities exchange).

There are also outstanding 10,000 of Woodstock's eight percent Senior Series A Debentures, due October 23, 1999, each in the principal amount of $1,000, and aggregating $10 million in principal amount (the "Series A Debentures"), which were issued in a 1996 public offering. Certain rights of the holders of the Series A Debentures are set forth in an Indenture, dated as of October 23, 1996, between Woodstock and The Hamilton Trust Company, as Trustee (the "Indenture"). The Series A Debentures are unsecured and rank pari passu (i.e. equally) with any current and future senior indebtedness of Woodstock. As discussed below, Woodstock's Series B Debentures were also issued pursuant to the Indenture.

There are also outstanding 20,000 of Woodstock's 12 percent Senior Series B Debentures, due October 23, 2017, each in the principal amount of $1,000, and aggregating $20 million in principal amount (the "Series B Debentures"). The Series B Debentures, which rank equally in priority with the Series A Debentures, were also publicly issued pursuant to the Indenture in October 1996. The Series B Debentures are redeemable at the option of Woodstock on and after October 23, 2006 at their principal amount, plus accrued interest.

The Indenture requires that at all times Woodstock's net assets be not less than $50 million and that Woodstock's failure to do so would constitute an event of default, rendering the entire principal amount of the Series A Debentures ($10 million) and the Series B Debentures ($20 million) immediately due and payable. The Indenture states that it may be amended with the consent of the holders of at least a majority in aggregate principal amount of the Series A and the Series B Debentures, voting together as one class. Under the Indenture, any Series A Debentures or Series B Debentures reacquired by Woodstock cannot be voted and are to be disregarded for the purpose of calculating a voting majority. The Indenture further provides that following the obtaining of such consent, the Trustee, in its discretion, may execute a supplemental indenture containing the amendment, whereupon the amendment to the Indenture shall become effective. The Indenture further provides:

> Notwithstanding any other provision of this Indenture, the right of any Holder to receive payment of principal of and interest on the Security, on or after the respective due dates expressed in the Security, or to bring suit for the enforcement of any such payment on or after such respective dates, shall not be impaired or affected without the consent of the Holder.

The Indenture also states that neither a holder of a Series A Debenture nor a holder of a Series B Debenture may commence an action to enforce any term of the Indenture, or to seek damages for any breach thereof, unless the Trustee has refused to do so, following a written demand therefor by the holders of at least 25 percent in principal amount of each of the Series A Debentures and the Series B Debentures.

Woodstock is engaged in the manufacture and sale of computer hardware components, but its operations have not been profitable since 1995. For its fiscal year ended December 31, 1998, Woodstock sustained an operating loss of $50 million. Woodstock's net assets now total $14 million. Also alarming is the fact that its cash and cash equivalents aggregate only $13 million.

It is August 24, 1999. Woodstock had retained the investment banking firm of Bissell & Rossi, which has recommended to Woodstock that, because of its severe and continuing business problems, precarious financial position, and its present cash position, it make an Exchange Offer to the holders of the Series A Debentures and the Series B Debentures. Pursuant to the proposed Exchange Offer, each holder of a Series A Debenture would receive a cash payment equal to 10 cents for each dollar of principal amount of old Series A Debentures held by such holder, and 90 cents in principal amount of a new Series A Debenture for each dollar of principal amount of old Series A Debentures held by such holder that would bear interest at the rate of six percent per annum and would be due and payable on October 1, 2005. Each holder of a Series B Debenture would receive a cash amount equal to 10 cents for each dollar of principal amount of Series B Debentures held by such holder, and 90 cents in principal amount of a new Series B Debenture for each dollar of principal amount of old Series B Debentures held by such holder that would bear interest at the rate of 12 percent per annum and would be due and payable on October 1, 2017. Each holder of a Series A Debenture or a Series B Debenture wishing to accept the Exchange Offer would be required, immediately prior to such acceptance, to execute a written consent to an amendment to the Indenture to provide that any original Series A Debentures or Series B Debentures remaining outstanding after the completion of the Exchange Offer would be fully subordinated to all present and future indebtedness of Woodstock, including the indebtedness evidenced by the new Debentures to be issued in connection with the Exchange Offer. You are an associate in the firm of Judson & Roberts and Christina Roberts, the partner in charge of the Woodstock account, is concerned about the validity of the Exchange Offer and asks you to write a memorandum for her, discussing any legal challenge that the holders of the Series A Debentures may have with respect to the proposed Exchange Offer. Write that memorandum.

Chapter 4

PREFERRED STOCK

§ 4.01 INTRODUCTION

As stated in Chapter 1, preferred stock represents an equity ownership interest in the issuing corporation. The principal characteristics of a preferred stock equity interest are that (a) the holder thereof is entitled to priority treatment over the holders of common or other junior stock with regard to payment of dividends and distributions of net assets upon dissolution and liquidation, and (b) the amounts of such dividend and liquidation preferences are limited to those set forth in the governing instruments.

> When properly authorized and implemented, leaving aside tax considerations (which often play a strong role in the debt-versus-equity debate), preferred stock — especially convertible preferred stock [covered in Chapter 5, *infra*] — may be an optimal instrument of corporate finance in certain corporate finance contexts. Both equity-oriented and debt-like terms can be combined in the same instrument — an instrument well grounded in both statutory law and the corporate charter. Issuer and investor interests can be delicately balanced, and seemingly infinite possibilities for combinations of provisions exist.

Joan MacLeod Heminway, *Federal Interventions in Private Enterprise in the United States: Their Genesis in and Effects on Corporate Finance Instruments and Transactions*, 40 Seton Hall L. Rev. 1487, 1499 (2010).

§ 4.02 LEGAL AUTHORITY FOR ISSUANCE

The rights of a holder of preferred stock are essentially contractual in nature. Unlike the holder of a debt instrument, however, the rights of the preferred stock holder are not set forth in a contract such as a trust indenture, but instead are contained in the issuing corporation's certificate of incorporation, the contents of which must be in compliance with applicable state law.

§ 4.03 EXCERPTS FROM A CERTIFICATE OF INCORPORATION AUTHORIZING THE ISSUANCE OF PREFERRED STOCK

The following are typical provisions of a certificate of incorporation authorizing the issuance of preferred stock:

FOURTH: The total number of shares of all classes of stock which the Corporation shall have authority to issue is twenty million (20,000,000), of which ten million (10,000,000) shares are to be Preferred Stock (hereinafter called the "Preferred Stock"), of the par value of one dollar ($1) each, and ten million (10,000,000) shares are to be Common Stock (hereinafter called the "Common Stock"), of the par value of one dollar ($1) each.

1. Authority is hereby *expressly granted* to the Board of Directors from time to time to issue the Preferred Stock as Preferred Stock of one or more series and in connection with the creation of any such series to fix by the resolution or resolutions providing for the issue of shares thereof the designation, powers, preferences, and relative, participating, optional, or other special rights of such series, and the qualifications, limitations, or restrictions thereof. Such authority of the Board of Directors with respect to each such series shall include, but not be limited to, the determination of the following:

(a) the distinctive designation of, and the number of shares comprising, such series, which number may be increased (except where otherwise provided by the Board of Directors in creating such series) or decreased (but not below the number of shares thereof then outstanding) from time to time by like action of the Board of Directors;

(b) the *dividend* rate or amount for such series, the conditions and dates upon which such dividends shall be payable, the relation which such dividends shall bear to the dividends payable on any other class or classes or any other series of any class or classes of stock, and whether such dividends shall be cumulative, and if so, from which date or dates for such series;

(c) whether or not the shares of such series shall be subject to *redemption* by the Corporation and the times, prices, and other terms and conditions of such redemption;

(d) whether or not the shares of such series shall be subject to the operation of a *sinking fund or purchase fund* to be applied to the redemption or purchase of such shares and if such a fund be established, the amount thereof and the terms and provisions relative to the application thereof;

(e) whether or not the shares of such series shall be *convertible into* or *exchangeable* for shares of any other class or classes, or of any other series of any class or classes, of stock of the Corporation or any other corporation or other entity and if provision be made for conversion or exchange, the times, prices, rates, adjustments, and other terms and conditions of such conversion or exchange;

(f) whether or not the shares of such series shall have *voting rights*, in addition to the voting rights provided by law, and if they are to have such additional voting rights, the extent thereof;

(g) the rights of the shares of such series in the event of any *liquidation*, dissolution, or winding up of the Corporation or upon any distribution of its assets; and

(h) any other powers, preferences, and relative, participating, optional, or other special rights of the shares of such series, and the qualifications, limitations, or restrictions thereof, *to the full extent now or hereafter permitted by law and not inconsistent with the provisions hereof.*

2. All shares of any one series of Preferred Stock shall be identical in all respects except as to the dates from which dividends thereon may be cumulative. All series of the Preferred Stock shall rank equally and be identical in all respects except as otherwise provided in the resolution or resolutions providing for the issue of any series of Preferred Stock.

3. Whenever dividends upon the Preferred Stock at the time outstanding, to the extent of the preference to which such stock is entitled, shall have been paid in full or declared and set apart for payment for all past dividend periods, and after the provisions for any sinking or +purchase fund or funds for any series of Preferred Stock shall have been complied with, the Board of Directors may declare and pay dividends on the Common Stock, payable in cash, stock, or otherwise, and the holders of shares of Preferred Stock shall not be entitled to share therein, subject to the provisions of the resolution or resolutions creating any series of Preferred Stock.

4. In the event of any *liquidation*, dissolution, or winding up of the Corporation or upon the distribution of the assets of the Corporation, all assets and funds of the Corporation remaining, after the payment to the holders of the Preferred Stock of the full preferential amounts to which they shall be entitled as provided in the resolution or resolutions creating any series thereof, shall be divided and distributed among the holders of the Common Stock ratably, except as may otherwise be provided in any such resolution or resolutions. *Neither the merger or consolidation of the Corporation with another corporation nor the sale or lease of all or substantially all the assets of the Corporation shall be deemed to be a liquidation, dissolution, or winding up of the Corporation or a distribution of its assets.*

5. Except as otherwise required by law or provided by a resolution or resolutions of the Board of Directors creating any series of Preferred Stock, the holders of Common Stock shall have the exclusive power to vote and shall have four votes in respect of each share of such stock held by them and the holders of Preferred Stock shall have no voting power whatsoever. Except as otherwise provided in such a resolution or resolutions, the number of authorized shares of the Preferred Stock may be increased or decreased by the affirmative vote of the holders of a majority of the outstanding shares of capital stock of the Corporation entitled to vote.

6. A holder of Preferred Stock or Common Stock of the Corporation shall not have any right as such holder (other than such right, if any, as the Board of Directors in its discretion may by resolution determine pursuant to this Article Fourth) to purchase, subscribe for or otherwise acquire any shares of stock of the Corporation of any class now or hereafter authorized, or any securities convertible into or exchangeable for any such shares, or any warrants or any instruments evidencing rights or options to subscribe for, purchase or otherwise acquire any such shares, whether such shares, securities, warrants or other instruments are now, or shall hereafter be, authorized, unissued or issued and thereafter acquired by the Corporation.

NOTES

(1) The delegation of authority to the Board of Directors to create and issue series of preferred stock is permitted by statutory provisions such as §§ 501 and 502 of the New York Business Corporation Law, *supra*, and by § 151 of the General Corporation Law of the State of Delaware, *supra*. The delegation to the Board of Directors of such authority is set forth in the broadest possible terms so as to provide maximum flexibility in this regard. Utilization of the procedure permits a corporation to effect a corporate finance transaction such as the raising of equity capital or an acquisition transaction with preferred stock which can be created without the delay and expense that would be involved in the calling and conducting of a special meeting of the stockholders for that purpose.

(2) It was this type of "blank check" authority that enabled each of the nation's largest banks in October 2008 to create and issue, on very short notice, a series of preferred stock to the United States Department of the Treasury under the Troubled Assets Relief Program (which came to be known as TARP) pursuant to the Emergency Economic Stabilization Act of 2008. *See generally* Andrew Ross Sorkin, Too Big to Fail 519-28 (2009). *See, e.g.*, J.P. Morgan Chase & Co., Rep. on Form 8K, filed Oct. 31, 2008 (reporting the private placement issuance, in exchange for $25,000,000,000, of "2,500,000 shares of the Company's Fixed Rate Cumulative Perpetual Preferred Stock, Series F, par value $1 and liquidation preference $10,000 per share" and common stock purchase warrants). *See Generally* Joan MacLeod Heminway, *Federal Interventions in Private Enterprise in the United States: Their Genesis in and Effects on Corporate Finance Instruments and Transactions*, 40 Seton Hall L. Rev. 1487 (2010).

WAGGONER v. LASTER

Delaware Supreme Court
581 A.2d 1127 (1990)

Moore, Justice

In this case we review issues involving the alleged creation of preferred stock with super-majority voting rights. Thomas R. Waggoner and Patricia L. Waggoner (the "Waggoners") appeal from a judgment of the Court of Chancery determining that the board of directors (the "Board") of STAAR Surgical Company ("STAAR") consists of LaMar F. Laster ("Laster"), John R. Ford ("Ford"), Howard P. Silverman ("Silverman"), Peter J. Utrata ("Utrata"), and Thomas R. Waggoner ("Waggoner").[1] Waggoner had attempted to replace the other members of the Board by executing a written consent purporting to vote the preferred stock in question. The Court of Chancery assumed without deciding that the preferred stock held by Waggoner was validly issued, but nonetheless ruled that the super-majority voting rights were void. Accordingly, Waggoner's attempted removal of the other directors was improper.

We agree and affirm.

I.

In October, 1982, STAAR was organized by Waggoner as a California corporation to develop, produce, and market patented soft intraocular lenses ("IOLs") and related products used primarily in cataract surgery. Later, in April 1986, the company was reincorporated in Delaware. Its common stock has been traded over-the-counter since July 7, 1983. From its inception, Waggoner has served as STAAR's Chief Executive Officer and President. By 1986, several factors threatened STAAR's continued profitability. It thus embarked on a diversification program which ultimately proved unsuccessful. By 1987, STAAR faced mounting financial difficulties. It was overdrawn by approximately $1 million on a line of credit with the Bank of New York ("BONY"); BONY was demanding personal guarantees from Waggoner on $3.5 million in corporate debt; and STAAR was overdue on additional debt of nearly $1.8 million. When certain stockholders became aware of the mounting debt, they demanded Waggoner's resignation. A compromise was reached, and two of the dissenting shareholders were elected to the Board.[2]

At a board meeting on December 13, 1987, it became clear that only Waggoner was willing and able to guarantee the corporate debt in the near future and on such short notice. Although the evidence was conflicting, the Vice Chancellor assumed without deciding that Waggoner agreed to provide personal guarantees and stock pledges for substantially all of STAAR's debt. In return the Board issued convertible preferred stock to Waggoner as compensation for these agreements. Apparently, because of earlier demands for his resignation, Waggoner required that voting control of STAAR be given to him while his personal guarantees were outstanding. He now contends that the preferred stock issued to him contained super-majority voting rights to achieve that end. By contrast, the other directors and shareholder-plaintiffs maintain that the Board never approved the issuance of the preferred stock, much less preferred stock with super-majority voting rights. STAAR's financial difficulties continued through 1989, at which time the Board sought to raise additional capital by merging with or selling some of its assets to another company. Two companies, Vision Technologies, Inc. ("VTI") and Chiron Corporation ("Chiron"), made proposals to merge with STAAR or to acquire certain of its assets. At a meeting held on July 22, 1989, the four directors other than

---

[1] [1] The plaintiffs consist of the four directors other than Waggoner (Laster, Ford, Silverman and Utrata) and two STAAR shareholders (Joseph C. Gathe and Austin P. Murray).

[2] [2] Utrata joined the Board immediately, and David Brown was elected on December 17, 1987.

Waggoner concluded that VTI's proposal was more viable and terminated negotiations with Chiron.[3] Indeed, the Board unanimously approved a resolution "to proceed expeditiously to attempt to complete the proposed VTI transaction." *Laster v. Waggoner*, Del. Ch., C.A. Nos. 11063 & 11067, Jacobs, V.C., slip op. at 22, [1990 Del. LEXIS 347] 1989 WL 126670 (Rev. Oct. 24, 1989). Waggoner, however, continued to hold discussions personally with Chiron without informing the other directors. Notably, under the Chiron proposal Waggoner would continue to be employed by the successor corporation to STAAR, whereas under the VTI proposal he would be terminated.[4] Moreover, Waggoner had apparently decided that, if necessary, he would remove the other directors using his preferred stock voting rights.

On the evening of August 10, 1989, another director discovered Waggoner conferring with Chiron representatives in STAAR's offices. The Board met the following day to consider removing Waggoner from the Board and stripping him of his positions as President and CEO. Before a vote could be taken, however, Waggoner executed a stockholder's written consent purporting to vote his super-majority voting preferred stock to oust the other directors, to reduce the size of the Board to three members, and named himself and his wife to the new board. Thereafter, Waggoner and his wife held a board meeting at which they purported to remove Laster from his corporate offices and to approve the Chiron transaction. After filing actions in California and the United States Bankruptcy Court, the plaintiffs brought civil actions in Delaware to determine the lawful members of STAAR's board under 8 Del. C. § 225 and to enjoin Waggoner from causing STAAR to enter into the Chiron transaction.[5] After expedited discovery and a full trial, the Vice Chancellor concluded that the board lacked authority under STAAR's certificate of incorporation to issue preferred stock to Waggoner with super-majority voting rights. He concluded that Waggoner's attempt to remove the other directors was invalid. In his decision the Vice Chancellor focused on two events which are relevant to this appeal: STAAR's reincorporation in Delaware in 1986, and the alleged approval and issuance of preferred stock with super-majority voting rights to Waggoner in 1987.

---

[3] [3] VTI proposed to merge the two companies and make a public offering to raise approximately $7 to $10 million in new capital. By contrast, Chiron sought to acquire STAAR's IOL business for $6 million plus a promissory note for $10 million payable in five years. The Board apparently favored VTI's proposal because it would leave STAAR's core business, the production of IOLs, intact.

[4] [4] The appellees suggest that the Chiron proposal would effectively gut the company and disenfranchise shareholders, leaving no assets, cash or continuing business for STAAR's shareholders and creditors. Waggoner, on the other hand, denies that shareholders would be adversely affected and contends that Chiron's proposal to exchange STAAR's assets for $6 million in cash and $10 million in promissory notes would leave sufficient resources to satisfy creditors and provide additional money to distribute to shareholders or invest in new ventures.

[5] [5] The Waggoners also filed a civil action to determine whether they were entitled to vote two million shares of common stock they received upon converting one share of convertible preferred stock previously issued to Waggoner. The Court of Chancery determined that the two million common shares had been invalidly issued but that the Waggoners were still entitled to vote them. *Waggoner v. STAAR Surgical Co.*, No. 11185, Jacobs, V.C., [1991 Del. LEXIS 106] 1990 WL 28979 (Mar. 15, 1990). That decision is now currently before this Court on appeal.

STAAR's Reincorporation in Delaware and Proposal 2

STAAR's California certificate of incorporation authorized the board to issue twenty million shares of common stock; it contained no authority to issue preferred stock. By contrast, STAAR's Delaware certificate of incorporation expressly authorized the board to issue both common and preferred stock. Article Fourth of the Delaware certificate provides: (a) The Corporation shall be authorized to issue THIRTY MILLION (30,000,000) shares, consisting of TWENTY MILLION (20,000,000) shares of Common Stock, each of the par value of $.01 ("Common Stock") and TEN MILLION (10,000,000) shares of Preferred Stock, each of the par value of $.01 ("Preferred Stock"); (b) The designations and the powers, preferences and rights, and the qualifications or restrictions thereof are as follows: Except as otherwise required by statute or provided for by resolution or resolutions of the Board of Directors, as hereinafter set forth, the holders of the Common Stock of the Corporation shall possess the exclusive right to vote for the election of directors and for all other corporate purposes. The Preferred Stock shall each be issued from time to time in one or more series, with such distinctive serial designations as shall be stated and expressed in the resolution or resolutions providing for the issue of such shares from time to time adopted by the Board of Directors; and in such resolution or resolutions providing for the issue of shares of each particular series the Board of Directors is expressly authorized to fix the annual rate or rates of dividends for the particular series and the date from which dividends on all shares of such series issued prior to the record date for the first dividend payment date shall be cumulative; the redemption price or prices for the particular series; the rights, if any, of holders of the shares of the particular series to convert the same into shares of any other series or class or other securities of the Corporation or of any other corporation, with any provisions for the subsequent adjustment of such conversion rights; and to classify or reclassify any unissued Preferred Stock by fixing or altering from time to time any of the foregoing rights, privileges and qualifications. Notably absent from the various powers, preferences and rights enumerated in the third paragraph of subsection (b) of the Delaware certificate was any reference to voting rights or super-majority voting rights. The decision to reincorporate in Delaware and to authorize the Board to issue preferred stock stemmed from two proposals presented to shareholders at the annual meeting on March 17, 1986. Proposal 2 is the significant issue here. It purported to amend STAAR's articles of incorporation to authorize ten million shares of preferred stock at $1.00 par value per share. Proposal 3 was to reincorporate STAAR in Delaware. The parties do not dispute that Proposal 3 was adopted. Both recognize that STAAR filed a valid certificate of incorporation in Delaware on April 3, 1986, approximately two weeks after the annual meeting. The parties' disagreement focuses on Proposal 2. The trial court concluded that "[t]he record does not disclose whether [Proposal 2] was adopted." Laster, slip op. at 34. The evidence at trial centered on the testimony of STAAR's corporate counsel, Elliot H. Lutzker ("Lutzker"), who prepared the Delaware certificate. At his deposition, Lutzker testified that he used and relied upon Proposal 2 in preparing the new certificate, but his testimony as to whether Proposal 2 was adopted and meant to apply to the Delaware certificate was equivocal. Before looking at the proxy materials he stated that "there was no action . . . taken vis-a-vis the California certificate of incorporation." After examining the proxy materials, he stated that the proposed amendment (Proposal 2) was approved by the stockholders, although he remained uncertain whether it applied to the California or the then unformed Delaware corporation. Adding to the confusion, Lutzker repeatedly testified that there was no error in the Delaware certificate as originally filed.[6]

The other evidence of record is no clearer than Lutzker's testimony. The proxy statement for the annual meeting did not state whether Proposal 2 related only to the then-existing California certificate or also to a new Delaware certificate (in the event Proposal 3 was adopted). Moreover, aside from Lutzker's testimony, there is no evidence that Proposal 2 was adopted. Although the California certificate authorized the issuance of preferred shares, it did not use the language of the amendment in Proposal 2. Proposal 2 "authorize[d] the Board of Directors to determine, among other things, with respect to each series of Preferred stock which may be issued . . . whether, and to what extent, the holders of the series would have voting rights in addition to those prescribed by law." By contrast, the Delaware certificate made no reference to the Board's authority to determine the voting rights of preferred shareholders. It also contained the paragraph under Article FOURTH, subsection (b) beginning "Except as otherwise required," yet the original Proposal 2 had no such paragraph.

The Board's Alleged Approval and Issuance of Convertible Preferred Stock to Waggoner

We thus return to the December 13 board meeting, at which the arrangements with Waggoner to guarantee certain STAAR debts were first proposed. This was followed by the board meeting on December 17. The trial court described this latter meeting as follows: The December 17 meeting was conducted by telephone with little or no advance notice, and lasted for approximately 25 minutes. Dr. Utrata, a Board member of only four days' standing, participated between performing surgical operations. Mr. Ford, a trial attorney, participated while speaking from his car phone and while traveling between court appearances. According to the minutes, Mr. Silverman was absent for a portion of the discussion, and Mr. Sodero, a fourth director, intended to (and did) resign at the conclusion of that meeting, to be replaced by Dr. Brown. Laster, slip op. at 8. The minutes of the December 17 meeting, prepared by Lutzker, recite that the Board approved the following resolution: RESOLVED, that pursuant to the authority granted to the Board of Directors in the Certificate of Incorporation, as amended, the Board hereby authorizes the creation of a series of Convertible Preferred Stock, all of which shall be held by Tom Waggoner, or his designees, which shall be converted into two million shares of Common Stock after January 16, 1988, unless all of the personal guarantees and stock pledges of Common Stock by Tom Waggoner now or hereafter in effect are removed, or a binding agreement to such effect is in place by January 16, 1988. In the event that all of the Waggoner guarantees are removed by January

[6] [6] After this action commenced, STAAR filed a certificate of correction, pursuant to 8 Del. C. § 103(f). The certificate of correction stated that the phrase "the voting powers for the particular series [of preferred stock] was inadvertently omitted" from the list of preferred stock rights and powers which the Board was authorized to create. In light of its timing, the trial court gave little weight to the document.

16, 1988, all of the shares of Convertible Preferred Stock shall be redeemed by the Company at $.01 per share. In the event that the two million shares of Common Stock are issued to Tom Waggoner, all of the remaining Convertible Preferred Stock shall be redeemed if all of the Waggoner guarantees and stock pledges are removed. Holders of the Convertible Preferred Stock shall be entitled to elect a majority of the Company's directors and to otherwise vote a majority of the Shares of Common Stock outstanding at any time. The shares of Convertible Preferred Stock, in accordance with the provision of the SEC's safe-harbor rule, shall have a liquidation preference however, [sic] not entitle the holder to any dividends. The trial court found that this resolution was never formally approved by the board. Only Waggoner signed the minutes of the December 17 meeting. Nevertheless, on December 18, 1987, Waggoner was issued 100 shares of preferred stock with the following special rights and preferences.[7] First, Waggoner was authorized to convert one share of the preferred stock into two million shares of common stock unless all of his personal guarantees and pledges were cancelled by January 16, 1988.[8] Second, even after converting one share of the preferred stock into two million shares of common stock, Waggoner retained voting control by virtue of the preferred stock's super-majority voting rights so long as any of his personal guarantees remained outstanding. The Certificate of Designations was signed by Waggoner and Lutzker, but subsequently the rights and preferences were detailed in press releases, memoranda, and Securities and Exchange Commission filings sent to, and in some cases signed by, the directors.

II.

The Court of Chancery determined as a matter of law that STAAR's certificate of incorporation did not expressly authorize the Board to issue preferred stock with super-majority voting rights. In the absence of such express authorization, it concluded that Waggoner's written consent purporting to oust the other directors was invalid. The interpretation of language in a certificate is a question of law subject to de novo review by this Court. *Gilbert v. El Paso*, Del. Supr., 575 A.2d 1131, 1141-42 (1990); *Cavalier Oil Corp. v. Harnett*, Del. Supr., 564 A.2d 1137, 1141 (1989); *Klair v. Reese*, Del. Supr., 531 A.2d 219, 222 (1987). The Court of Chancery also ruled that certain extrinsic evidence of the shareholder's intent was insufficient to warrant reformation of the certificate. Such factual determinations will not be disturbed unless the trial court's findings or inferences are not supported by the record or not the product of an orderly and logical deductive reasoning process.

---

[7] [7] Lutzker could not recall whether the directors were given a draft of the Certificate of the Designations, Rights and Preferences of the new series of preferred stock prior to the December 17 meeting. Arguably, the rights and preferences described by the Certificate take a very broad view of the rights and preferences listed in the resolution allegedly approved by the Board. Some of the directors apparently had different interpretations of what rights and preferences would be granted. Laster and Ford believed that Waggoner's voting control was only exercisable in the event dissident shareholders attempted to oust him. Ford and Utrata thought that all of the preferred stock would convert to two million shares of common stock and that this additional common stock, when combined with Waggoner's own shares of STAAR, would secure his voting control.

[8] [8] When the pledges were not rescinded by January 16, 1988, Waggoner converted one share of preferred stock into two million shares of common stock. The estimated value of the common stock he received at the time of the conversion was $499,000.

Levitt v. Bouvier, Del. Supr., 287 A.2d 671, 673 (1972). The Waggoners assert three points of error. First, they contend that the Court of Chancery erred in determining as a matter of law that STAAR's certificate lacks an express grant of authority to the Board to issue preferred stock with super-majority voting rights. Second, they argue that it erred in failing to reform or correct STAAR's certificate in light of the extrinsic evidence of the intention of the shareholders and drafters to include a provision concerning the voting rights of preferred stock. Finally, they maintain in equity that estoppel should prevent the appellees from denying the validity of the preferred stock with super-majority voting rights issued to Waggoner. The appellees dispute each of these contentions.

III.

The primary issue in this case is whether the Court of Chancery correctly concluded that STAAR's board of directors lacked authority under STAAR's certificate of incorporation to issue convertible preferred stock with super-majority voting rights. Without such authority, those voting rights held by Waggoner, which he contends allow him to vote out the other directors, are null and void.

A.

We start with basics. The Delaware General Corporation Law allows corporations to issue preferred stock with special designations. 8 Del. C. §§ 151(a); 102(a)(4). Section 151, which outlines the general corporate power to issue stock and dividends, provides: Every corporation may issue 1 or more classes of stock . . . which classes . . . may have such voting powers, full or limited, or no voting powers, and such designations, preferences and relative, participating, optional or other special rights, and qualifications, limitations or restrictions thereof, as shall be stated and expressed in the certificate of incorporation or of any amendment thereto, or in the resolution or resolutions providing for the issue of such stock adopted by the board of directors pursuant to authority vested in it by the provisions of its certificate of incorporation. 8 Del. C. § 151(a). Section 102(a)(4), which deals specifically with the technical formation of corporations, provides: The certificate of incorporation shall also set forth a statement of the designations and powers, preferences and rights, and the qualifications, limitations, or restrictions thereof, which are permitted by § 151 of this title in respect of any class or classes of stock or any series of any class of stock of the corporation and the fixing of which by the certificate of incorporation is desired, and an express grant of such authority as it may then be desired to grant to the board of directors to fix by resolution or resolutions any thereof that may be desired but which shall not be fixed by the certificate of incorporation. 8 Del. C. § 102(a)(4). Section 151 specifically includes voting rights among the list of stock attributes that directors may be empowered to set. STAAR's Delaware certificate of incorporation authorized the board to issue preferred stock. Indeed, it specifically allowed the board to establish certain stock preferences, including dividends, redemption prices, conversion rights, and reclassification rights. It did not, however, expressly authorize the board to establish special voting rights for preferred stock. In light of that omission, and Delaware's statutory requirement that such powers be enumerated in the certificate of incorporation, the Vice Chancellor found that the record was insufficient to establish that STAAR's board was expressly authorized to grant preferential voting rights to certain classes of stock.

B.

Conceding that the Delaware certificate fails to expressly list voting rights among the preferences the Board is authorized to grant, the Waggoners nonetheless argue that one portion of STAAR's Delaware certificate contains the blanket authority sufficient to meet Delaware's statutory requirements. They point to the second paragraph of subsection (b), Article FOURTH which provides: *Except as otherwise required by statute or provided for by resolutions of the Board of Directors, as hereinafter set forth,* the holders of the Common Stock shall possess the exclusive right to vote for the election of directors and for all other corporate purposes. (Emphasis added).

A certificate of incorporation is viewed as a contract among shareholders, and general rules of contract interpretation apply to its terms. Rothschild Intl Corp. v. c 474 A.2d 133, 136 (1984); *Wood v. Coastal States Gas Corp.*, Del. Supr., 401 A.2d 932, 937 (1979). Courts must give effect to the intent of the parties as revealed by the language of the certificate and the circumstances surrounding its creation and adoption. *Judah v. Delaware Trust Co.*, Del. Supr., 378 A.2d 624, 628 (1977); *Ellingwood v. Wolf's Head Oil Ref. Co.*, Del. Supr., 38 A.2d 743, 747 (1944). Since stock preferences are in derogation of the common law, they must be strictly construed. *Goldman v. Postal Telegraph Inc.*, 52 F. Supp. 763 (D. Del. 1943); *Barron v. Allied Artists Pictures Corp.*, Del. Ch., 337 A.2d 653 (1975), appeal dismissed, Del. Supr., 365 A.2d 136 (1976); *Holland v. National Automotive Fibres, Inc.*, Del. Ch., 194 A. 124 (1937); *Pennington v. Commonwealth Hotel Constr. Co.*, Del. Ch., 151 A. 228 (1930), *rev'd, in part*, 155 A. 514 (1931); *Gaskill v. Gladys Bell Oil Co*, Del. Ch., 146 A. 337 (1929). An express grant of authority to establish stock preferences cannot be conferred by a general reservation clause worded in a non-specific fashion. *Rothschild*, 474 A.2d at 136; *Gaskill*, 146 A. at 339. In one of the earliest cases to address this issue, the Court of Chancery stated: The power to create preferred stock is granted in § 18 [of the certificate], and it is granted upon the terms set forth in that section. To enact that the stock should have such preference as is stated or expressed in the certificate was equivalent to enacting that it should have no other preferences upon the general principle of interpretation that the expression of one thing is the exclusion of another. *Gaskill*, 146 A. at 339. Moreover, in *Gaskill* the court stated: It is elementary that the rights of stockholders are contract rights. The mere word "preferred" unless it is supplemented by a definition of its significance conveys no special meaning. The holder of preferred stock must therefore refer to the appropriate language of the corporate contract for the ascertainment of his rights. The nub of the present contention is — where may such appropriate language be found. The exceptants say in the certificate of incorporation and nowhere else. In this I think they are correct. *Id.* Subsequently, numerous decisions applying Delaware law have followed *Gaskill* and adhered to the rule that stock preferences are to be strictly construed. *Goldman*, 52 F. Supp. at 767; *Barron*, 337 A.2d at 657 ("[P]references attaching to stock are the exception and are to be strictly construed."). *See also Holland*, 194 A. at 126-27 ("[N]othing should be presumed in their favor . . . [I]f those preferences are stated in terms that are irreconcilable in their repugnancy, a case arises where the clearness necessary for the definition of preferences has not been satisfied."); *Pennington*, 151 A. at 234 ("The general rule is that preferred stock enjoys only those preferences which are specifically defined. . . . [B]efore such an exceptional right is recognized it ought to appear clearly that the parties have intended to create it."). *Cf. Penington*, 155 A. at 520 ("[C]laims for special preferences must be clearly provided by the charter contract."). We think those decisions clearly establish the rule that stock preferences are to be strictly construed in Delaware.[9] We adhere to that view.

Applying the rule of strict construction to the language urged by Waggoner, we find that it is merely a general reservation clause which is insufficient to expressly reserve authority in the board to establish preferences. Such general reservation clauses are commonly found in corporate documents, and we need not impose a strained construction to give the phrase different meaning. The clause is phrased in the negative, and is too general and nonspecific to confer the broad authority suggested by Waggoner. Moreover, the sentence contains the limitation "as hereinafter set forth" which appears to refer to the list of designations, powers, preferences and rights the board was authorized to confer. The power to establish voting rights was conspicuously absent from the enumerated rights and powers granted the board. While that omission may have been accidental, given the requirements of Delaware law this Court cannot presume so and thereafter supply the missing provisions. Under the rule of strict construction, any ambiguity must be resolved against granting the challenged preferences, rights or powers.

C.

Waggoner next argues that extrinsic evidence of the intended terms of the certificate was sufficient to warrant its reformation, relying upon *In re Farm Industries, Inc.*, Del. Ch., 196 A.2d 582, 592 (1963). The trial court noted that this argument rested on "the highly dubious proposition that where a statute requires a grant of power to directors to be expressly stated in the certificate of incorporation and where that certificate contains no such express grant, this Court may resort to extrinsic evidence to supply the missing term by way of interpretation." *Laster*, slip op. at 33-34. Nevertheless, the trial court reviewed the extrinsic evidence and found it insufficient to support Waggoner's assertions.

It is a basic principle of equity that the Court of Chancery has jurisdiction to reform a document to make it conform to the original intent of the parties. *Douglas v. Thrasher*, Del. Supr., 489 A.2d 422, 426 (1985); *Hob Tea Room, Inc. v. Miller*, Del.

---

[9] [9] The only suggestion to the contrary is found at 1 R. Balotti & J. Finkelstein, The Delaware Law of Corporations and Business Organizations § 5.3, at 209 (Supp. 1989) (citing *Breech v. Hughes Tool Co.*, Del. Supr., 189 A.2d 428 (1963)); *In re Klingaman's Estate*, Del. Supr., 128 A.2d 311 (1957); and *Warner Co. v. Leedom Constr. Co.*, Del. Supr., 97 A.2d 884 (1953). None of those cases concern corporate statutes. Moreover, they have been superseded by more recent decisions following the rule that statutes in derogation of the common law are to be strictly construed. *See Gibson v. Keith*, Del. Supr., 492 A.2d 241 (1985); *State v. Brown*, Del. Supr., 195 A.2d 379 (1963); *DeJoseph v. Faraone*, Del. Super., 254 A.2d 257 (1969). This is consistent with the rule adopted by a majority of other jurisdictions. *See* 82 C.J.S. Statutes § 393, at 938 n. 43 (1953 & Supp. 1989).

Supr., 89 A.2d 851, 856-57 (1952). That includes a certificate of incorporation. *In re Farm Industries, Inc.*, 196 A.2d at 592. In doing so, however, Chancery must consider the interests of any third parties affected by the reformation. *See Douglas*, 489 A.2d at 426; *In re Farm Industries, Inc.*, 196 A.2d at 592. Generally, [r]eformation is appropriate, when an agreement has been made, or a transaction has been entered into or determined upon, as intended by all parties interested, but in reducing such agreement or transaction to writing, either through the mistake common to both parties, or through the mistake of the plaintiff accompanied by the fraudulent knowledge and procurement of the defendant, the written instrument fails to express the real agreement or transaction. In such a case the instrument may be corrected so that it shall truly represent the agreement or transaction actually made or determined upon according to the real purpose and intention of the parties. *Douglas*, 489 A.2d at 426 (quoting from 3 Pomeroy's Equity Jurisprudence § 870, (5th ed.)). *See also* 1 E. Folk, R. Ward & E. Welch, Folk on the Delaware General Corporation Law § 151.4, at 218 (1988) (suggesting two requirements for reformation in this context: (i) it must be clear that all present and past shareholders intended certain voting provisions to be included within the certificate, and (ii) there must not be any intervening third party interest). Thus, where a lawyer failed to delineate the voting rights of particular classes of stock in a certificate of incorporation was clearly contrary to the intentions of the parties and no third-party interest was involved, the Court of Chancery correctly reformed the certificate to reflect their intent. *In re Farm Industries, Inc.*, 196 A.2d at 590-02. That was not the case here. The extrinsic evidence centered on Proposal 2 presented to stockholders at the annual meeting on March 17, 1986. The testimony was equivocal on the critical question of whether Proposal 2 was actually adopted by the stockholders. Even if it had been approved, however, it is unclear whether it was meant to apply to the California or Delaware certificate. There were substantive differences between Proposal 2 and the actual terms of the Delaware certificate. The "Except" clause discussed above was added to the Delaware certificate and the reference to voting rights in the list of authorized preferences was deleted from that certificate. Again, there was conflicting evidence on whether Lutzker meant to insert voting rights among the list of enumerated rights and powers that could be granted to the preferred stock. Although he originally testified that the new Delaware certificate was correct as originally filed, but he later filed a certificate of correction with the Delaware Secretary of State to cure the problem raised by this litigation. Given its timing, that correction understandably carries little weight. The evidence presented to the trial court was conflicting. The Vice Chancellor had to evaluate its weight and credibility. Based upon our standard of review, it is apparent that trial court's factual findings are supported by the record and reflect an orderly and logical deductive reasoning process. Accordingly, they stand.

IV.

Finally, Waggoner argues that the doctrine of estoppel should prevent the appellees from objecting to the validity of the preferred stock's super-majority voting rights. Waggoner contends that he was induced to provide personal guarantees and stock pledges in exchange for super-majority voting preferred stock, and that until this lawsuit was filed, his super-majority voting power was never challenged. The appellees maintain that Waggoner failed to establish the necessary factual elements for estoppel, and that as a matter of law even if such facts were established, there can be no estoppel to challenge the void act of creating super-majority voting rights.

The doctrine of equitable estoppel may be invoked "when a party by his conduct intentionally or unintentionally leads another, in reliance upon that conduct, to change position to his detriment." *Wilson v. American Ins. Co.*, Del. Supr., 209 A.2d 902, 903-04 (1965). To establish estoppel it must be shown that the party claiming estoppel lacked knowledge or the means of obtaining knowledge of the truth of the facts in question; relied on the conduct of the party against whom estoppel is claimed; and suffered a prejudicial change of position as a result of his reliance. *Id.* In the corporate context, estoppel has often been used to prevent a stockholder from objecting to the validity of stock which he accepted with knowledge of the irregularities or infirmities in issuing it. 11 W. Fletcher, The Law of Professional Corporations § 5169, at 353-54 (Rev. ed. 1986); *Trounstine v. Remington Rand, Inc.*, Del. Ch., 194 A. 95, 99 (1937) (plaintiff who objected to the reclassification of his preferred stock but nevertheless tendered his shares into exchange estopped to deny validity of the reclassification). Estoppel has also been applied in cases where a stockholder, with knowledge of the facts, consents or acquiesces in the acts of directors or other corporate officers. 12A W. Fletcher, The Law of Professional Corporations § 5862 at 295 (Rev. ed. 1986). *See also Gottlieb v. McKee*, Del. Ch., 107 A.2d 240, 244 (1954) (plaintiff who granted general proxy to management was not estopped from objecting to vote on resolution not mentioned in proxy statement and of which she had no knowledge). Estoppel, however, has no application in cases where the corporation lacks the inherent power to issue certain stock or where the corporate contract or action approved by the directors or stockholders is illegal or void. 11 Fletcher, § 5169, at 354-55 (stock); 12A Fletcher, § 5862, at 295 (corporate contract or action). *See also* Annotation, *Purchaser's Right to Set Up Invalidity of Contract Because of Violation of State Securities Regulation as Affected by the Doctrines of Estoppel or Pari Delicto*, 84 A.L.R.2d 479, 483 (1962, 1979, & Supp. 1990) ("As a general proposition, it has been held that the doctrine of estoppel has no application to an agreement or instrument which is illegal because it violates an express mandate of law or the dictates of public policy."). That rule is recognized in Delaware. In *Triplex Shoe Co. v. Rice & Hutchins, Inc.*, Del. Supr., 152 A. 342, 347-48 (1930), this Court considered whether an amendment to the certificate of incorporation authorizing an exchange of shares could validate previously-issued and illegal no par value stock. It stated: We are unable to see how the amendment could have made stock valid that was void because issued without any authority from the State. Such an amendment might cure certain irregularities, imperfections, and defects in a stock issue that is authorized . . . , but it does not seem to us that it can possibly relate back and validate a stock that was issued without any corporate authority. If the stock issue was void, a nullity, there was nothing to validate, nothing upon which the amendment could operate. *Id.* at 347-48. Waggoner argues that *Triplex* should be limited on its facts to cases involving illegal issuances of stock and should not be extended to deny estoppel for other corporate actions such as the granting of super-majority voting rights. We see no logical basis for adopting such a limitation as a matter of law. The Court of Chancery has assumed without deciding in separate actions that the issuance of preferred stock to

Waggoner was valid, *Waggoner v. STAAR Surgical Co.*, Del. Ch., C.A. No. 11185, Jacobs, V.C., at 14 fn. 7 (Mar. 15, 1990), but that the board was not authorized to endow the preferred stock with super-majority voting rights, *Laster*, slip op. at 37. The former determination is now before us in a separate appeal. However, there is no inconsistency as a matter of law to deny the Waggoners an estoppel as to the validity of super-majority voting rights even if the stock to which they were purportedly attached may otherwise have been validly issued. We thus reject Waggoner's claim of estoppel as a matter of law in light of the trial court's legal and factual determination that the preferred stock's super-majority voting rights were void.[10]

V.

In this action, the Court of Chancery assumed that Waggoner had been issued preferred stock with super-majority voting rights, but it nevertheless concluded that such voting rights were void because the Board lacked authority under STAAR's certificate of incorporation to authorize preferred stock with such special rights. We uphold that determination because the power to establish special voting rights is conspicuously absent from the list of preferences the Board was authorized to confer. No other provision of STAAR's certificate clearly grants the Board such authority. Moreover, the trial court's determination that the extrinsic evidence presented by Waggoner was insufficient to reform the certificate is a logical conclusion supported by the record. Under these circumstances, there is no estoppel to challenge the validity of a void act. The judgment of the Court of Chancery is AFFIRMED.

STAAR SURGICAL COMPANY v. WAGGONER

Delaware Supreme Court
588 A.2d 1130 (1991)

Moore, Justice.

In this latest dispute between the parties we determine the validity of two million shares of STAAR Surgical Company ("STAAR") common stock issued to STAAR's former President and CEO, Thomas R. Waggoner and his wife, Patricia Waggoner ("Waggoner" or "Waggoners"). This is a continuation of the controversy between Waggoner and STAAR. We have already ruled that a provision of the preferred stock STAAR issued to Waggoner, purportedly giving him super-majority voting control of the company, was invalid. See Waggoner v. Laster, Del. Supr. [page 314 supra] ("Waggoner I"). In Waggoner I, we did not otherwise decide the validity of the Waggoners' preferred and common shares.

In this action, the Court of Chancery assumed that the Waggoners' preferred shares were technically invalid because STAAR failed to issue them in conformity

---

[10] [10] This legal conclusion makes it unnecessary for us to reach the factual question of whether the elements of estoppel have been met, but we note that the record suggests substantial questions concerning the Waggoners' lack of knowledge and reliance.

with 8 *Del. C.* § 151. *See Waggoner v. STAAR Surgical Co.*, Del.Ch., C.A. No. 11185, Jacobs, V.C., slip op. at 14 n. 7, 1990 WL 28979[, 1990 Del. LEXIS 33] (March 15, 1990) ("*Waggoner II*"). The trial court nonetheless determined that the Waggoners were equitably entitled to ownership and voting control of their common shares. *Id.* at 15-16.

We find that the Court of Chancery erroneously granted equitable relief. The Waggoners received their common stock through the exercise of their conversion options attached to the preferred shares. Since the preferred shares were invalid, the trial court had no basis to ignore established principles of Delaware corporate law and should not have invoked equitable remedies to resuscitate plainly void stock. Accordingly, we reverse.

* * *

II.

The Court of Chancery specifically assumed that the *preferred shares* "were invalidly issued" because the board failed to formally adopt both the December 17 resolution and the certificate of designation as required by 8 *Del. C.* § 151. *See Waggoner II*, slip op. at 14 n. 7. Nonetheless, the trial court found that the Waggoners were entitled to an order "akin to specific performance" authorizing the issuance of the *common shares* and declaring them eligible to vote. *Id.* at 9. The court reasoned that Waggoner was equitably entitled to receive the two million shares of common stock as consideration for his personal guarantee of STAAR's debts. *Id.* at 9-10.

A.

The question of the validity of the Waggoners' common shares presents a mixed issue of law and fact. This Court, however, exercises plenary review of the trial court's determination of purely legal conclusions including the proper legal standard to judge the validity of shares in a 8 *Del. C.* § 227 action. *See Triplex Shoe Co. v. Rice & Hutchins, Inc.*, Del. Supr., 152 A. 342, 346 (1930).

* * *

[W]e find that it was error to award any type of equitable relief after the trial court essentially concluded that the preferred shares were invalid. Waggoner obtained his common shares only after converting one share of his preferred stock into the common. If the preferred shares were void, it follows *a fortiori* that the common shares, which purportedly derived from the preferred, also were invalid.

B.

We start with basic and clearly applicable provisions of the Delaware General Corporation Law. A corporation can issue more than one class of stock, including preferred shares with a conversion feature. *See, e.g.*, 8 *Del. C.* §§ 151(a), (e) & (g). The powers, preferences, rights and other characteristics of such shares must be fixed in either the certificate of incorporation or through a board resolution adopted pursuant to an explicit grant of authority in the certificate of incorporation. *See* 8 *Del. C.* §§ 102(a)(4), 151(a). There is no dispute that the STAAR certificate of incorporation authorized the board to issue, by resolution, "blank check" preferred stock with such terms and conditions, including:

> [T]he rights, if any, of holders of the shares of the particular series to convert the same into shares of any other series or class or other securities of the corporation. . . .

The Delaware General Corporation Law mandates adoption of a board resolution, when such new shares of so-called "blank check" preferred, are issued. Section 151(a) of the General Corporation Law requires, in part, that all new stock voting powers, designations, preferences and other special rights must either be in the certificate of incorporation or:

> [I]n the resolution or resolutions providing for the issue of such stock *adopted by* the board of directors pursuant to authority expressly vested in it by the provisions of its certificate of incorporation. 8 *Del. C.* § 151(a) (emphasis added).

Section 151(e), which specifically authorizes a company to issue convertible securities, requires, in part, that the corporation issue the new shares:

> [A]t such price or prices or at such rate or rates of exchange and with such adjustments as shall be stated in the certificate of incorporation or in the resolution or resolutions providing for the issue of such stock *adopted by the board of directors as hereinabove provided.* 8 *Del. C.* § 151(e) (emphasis added).

Finally, Section 151(g) requires a corporation to file a certificate of designation when the certificate of incorporation permits the board to issue new securities through a resolution "adopted by the board." The statute provides:

> When any corporation desires to issue any shares of stock of any class or of any series of any class of which the powers, designations, preferences and relative, participating, optional or other rights, if any, or the qualifications, limitations or restrictions thereof, if any, shall not have been set forth in the certificate of incorporation or in any amendment thereto but shall be provided for in *a resolution or resolutions adopted by the board* of directors pursuant to authority expressly vested in it by the certificate of incorporation or any amendment thereto, a *certificate of designations setting forth a copy of such resolution* or resolutions and the number of shares of stock of such class or series as to which the resolution or resolutions apply shall be executed, acknowledged, filed, recorded and shall become effective, in accordance with § 103 of this title. . . . 8 *Del. C.* § 151(g) (emphasis added).

Waggoner concedes that the STAAR board never formally adopted either the board resolution on December 17, 1987, or the certificate of designation. Finally, the trial court found in *Laster* that the certificate of designation did not "set forth" a copy of the December 17, 1987 resolution. Slip op. at 11-12. Indeed, the court ruled that the certificate of designation contained materially different language from that in the resolution. *Id.* at 11 n. 5.

C.

The parties' arguments seem to pass like two ships in the night. STAAR contends that the board's failure to adopt the resolution or the certificate of designation rendered the preferred shares void, thus invalidating the common stock. STAAR relies on *Triplex Shoe Co. v. Rice Hutchins, Inc.*, Del. Supr., 152 A. 342 (1930), for the proposition that illegally issued stock is void and, regardless of the equities, cannot be transferred or voted. The Waggoners, in contrast, focus on the common stock and not the preferred shares. They assert that even if the board failed to technically conform to the clear corporate law, the STAAR directors all agreed at the December 17, 1987 board meeting to issue Waggoner two million shares of common stock as compensation for his guarantee of the BONY loans. Therefore, Waggoner claims, it was clear to all of the parties that he would eventually receive the two million shares if STAAR could not find alternate financing for the loan.

The Waggoners also contest STAAR's interpretation of *Triplex*, claiming that it is distinguishable on its facts. The Waggoners argue that the certificate of incorporation in *Triplex*, and the then current corporate law, did not authorize the board to issue new shares of a certain type of stock. Therefore, they contend, the stock in *Triplex* was void and subsequent board action could not have validated those shares. In contrast, the Waggoners argue that the STAAR certificate of incorporation at all times authorized the board to issue new shares of common stock and thus *Triplex* is not dispositive.

D.

We must reject the Waggoners' attempt to separate the common shares from the preferred stock. We also reject their very limited interpretation of *Triplex*. Stock issued without authority of law is void and a nullity.

It is undisputed that Waggoner could not receive his common stock without exercising the conversion option of at least one preferred share. The December 17, 1987 resolution and the certificate of designation purportedly authorized the issuance of the preferred shares. Without validly issued preferred stock, there was simply no other legal mechanism by which the common shares could be issued. Simply stated, if the preferred shares were void, as the Court of Chancery assumed, then the common stock could not be created out of whole cloth.

Based on the trial court's findings, it is clear that the preferred convertible shares originally issued to the Waggoners were invalid and void under Delaware law. There was no compliance with the terms of 8 *Del. C.* § 151. The directors never formally adopted either the December 17, 1987 resolution or the certificate of designation.

The Waggoners' attempt to trivialize the unassailable facts of this case as mere "technicalities" is wholly unpersuasive. The issuance of corporate stock is an act of fundamental legal significance having a direct bearing upon questions of corporate governance, control and the capital structure of the enterprise. The law properly requires certainty in such matters.

There are many interacting principles of established law at play here. First, it is a basic concept that the General Corporation Law is a part of the certificate of incorporation of every Delaware company. *See* 8 *Del. C.* § 394. Second, a corporate charter is both a contract between the State and the corporation, and the corporation and its shareholders. *See Lawson v. Household Finance Corp.*, Del. Supr., 152 A. 723, 727 (1930). The charter is also a contract among the shareholders themselves. *See Morris v. American Public Utilities Co.*, Del.Ch., 122 A. 696, 700 (1923). When a corporation files a certificate of designation under § 151(g), it amends the certificate of incorporation and fundamentally alters the contract between all of the parties. *See* 8 *Del. C.* §§ 104, 151(g). A party affecting these interrelated, fundamental interests, through an amendment to the corporate charter, must scrupulously observe the law.[11]

Finally, it is a basic concept of our corporation law that in the absence of a clear agreement to the contrary, preferred stock rights are in derogation of the common law and must be strictly construed. *See generally Goldman v. Postal Telegraph, Inc.*, 52 F. Supp. 763, 767 (D. Del. 1943). . . .

This principle of "strict construction" applies with equal force to the creation of preferred stock and its attendant rights, powers, designations and preferences. Accordingly, a board's failure to adopt a resolution and certificate of designation, amending the fundamental document which imbues a corporation with its life and powers, and defines the contract with its shareholders, cannot be deemed a mere "technical" error.

Thus, we must reject the trial court's authorization of the two million shares of common stock on equitable grounds. Stock issued in violation of 8 *Del. C.* § 151 is void and not merely voidable. *See Triplex*, 152 A. at 347. . . . A court cannot imbue void stock with the attributes of valid shares.

E.

The Waggoners argue that the board's failure to ratify its resolution to issue the convertible preferred shares merely rendered the common stock voidable, not void. The Waggoners claim that, unlike *Triplex*, where this Court found that the corporation did not have the power or authority to issue no par stock, STAAR's charter specifically authorized the issuance of their two million shares of common stock. Therefore, the Waggoners conclude that the issuance of the two million shares of common stock was merely a voidable act.

The Court of Chancery has correctly recognized that the available form of equitable relief depends on the facts of each case. If the stock is indeed void, then "cancellation is the proper remedy." However, if the stock is voidable then a court may grant " 'that form of relief [that] is to be most in accord with all of the equities of the case.' " *See Diamond State Brewery, Inc. v. De La Rigaudiere*, Del. Ch., 17 A.2d 313, 318 (1941) (quoting *Blair v. F.H. Smith Co.*, Del. Ch., 156 A. 207, 213 (1931)).

---

[11] [1] We put aside the wholly inapplicable circumstances of correcting mistakes under § 103(f), or the reformation of corporate instruments to reflect the actual intention of the parties. . . . However, the failure of STAAR's Board to approve the December 17 resolution and subsequent certificate of designation was not a mere mistake but reflected a total failure to conform with the corporation law.

We have already rejected the Waggoners' narrow reading of *Triplex* in *Waggoner I* . . . . We cited to *Triplex* in *Waggoner I* for the proposition that the equitable doctrine of estoppel is inapplicable to agreements or instruments that violate either express law or public policy. . . . We also rejected the Waggoners' argument that *Triplex* was limited only to instances where a corporation illegally issued stock. . . . Accordingly, we ruled that the Waggoners could not invoke the equitable doctrine of estoppel to validate the super-majority voting rights associated with their preferred shares after the court had already declared those rights void under the corporation law. . . .

Parity of reason compels us to reach a similar result here. Under the present circumstances, the Court of Chancery had no basis to grant equitable relief "akin" to specific performance after it concluded that the Waggoners' preferred shares were invalid. Neither logic nor equity compel the validation of a legally void act.[12]

The judgment of the Court of Chancery is REVERSED.

§ 4.04 CORPORATE RESOLUTIONS CREATING A SERIES OF PREFERRED STOCK

The following Board of Director's resolutions creating a series of preferred stock are an example of the exercise of the authority granted by charter provisions such as those set forth in Article IV, *supra.* Upon the proper filing of those resolutions with the appropriate state authorities, they become a part of the corporation's certificate of incorporation.

[FORM OF CORPORATE RESOLUTIONS]

RESOLVED that, pursuant to the authority expressly granted to and vested in the Board of Directors of [the] Corporation (the "Corporation") by the provisions of the Certificate of Incorporation of the Corporation, as amended, this Board of Directors hereby creates a series of the Preferred Stock, of the par value of one dollar ($1) each, of the Corporation (the "Preferred Stock") to consist of not more than *4,370,154* shares of the Preferred Stock, and this Board of Directors hereby fixes the designation and the powers, preferences and rights, and the qualifications, limitations or restrictions thereof, of the shares of such series (in addition to the powers, preferences and rights, and the qualifications, limitations or restrictions thereof, set forth in the Certificate of Incorporation of the Corporation, as amended, which are applicable to the Preferred Stock of all series) as follows:

(a) Designation of Series

1. The designation of the series of Preferred Stock created by this resolution shall be "$2.25 Cumulative Series A Preferred Stock" (the "Series A Preferred Stock").

---

[12] [2] Again, we emphasize that our courts must act with caution and restraint when granting equitable relief in derogation of established principles of corporate law. *See Alabama By-Products Corp. v. Neal*, Del. Supr., 588 A.2d 255, 258 (1991).

(b) Cash Dividends on Series A Preferred Stock and Limitations on Dividends on Common Stock of the Corporation ("Common Stock") and any Class or Series of Stock Ranking Junior to the Series A Preferred Stock.

1. Out of the *surplus or net profits* of the Corporation legally available for dividends, the holders of the Series A Preferred Stock shall be entitled to receive, *when and as declared by the Board of Directors*, dividends at the per annum rate of $2.25 per share, *and no more*, payable quarterly on the first business day of April, July, October and January in each year (each such day being hereinafter called a dividend date and each quarterly period ending with a dividend date being hereinafter called a dividend period) to the holders of record on such respective dates as may be determined by the Board of Directors in advance of the payments of each particular dividend for the dividend periods, from the date of cumulation, as hereinafter in subdivision 4 of this paragraph (b) defined (provided, however, that, if the date of cumulation shall be a date less than thirty (30) days prior to a dividend date, the dividend that would otherwise be payable on such dividend date will be payable on the next succeeding dividend date), *before* any sum or sums shall be set aside pursuant to subdivision 2 of this paragraph (b) or paragraph (c) or otherwise for the purchase or redemption of Series A Preferred Stock or any class or series of stock ranking on a parity with the Series A Preferred Stock as to dividends or distribution of assets and before any dividend shall be declared or paid upon or set apart for, or any other distribution shall be ordered or made in respect of, or any payment shall be made on account of the purchase of, the Common Stock or of any class or series of stock ranking junior to the Series A Preferred Stock as to dividends or distribution of assets; *and such dividends upon the Series A Preferred Stock shall be cumulative* (whether or not in any dividend period or periods there shall be *surplus or net profits* of the Corporation legally available for the payment of such dividends), so that, if at any time dividends upon the outstanding Series A Preferred Stock at the per annum rate hereinabove specified from the date of cumulation to the end of the then current dividend period shall not have been paid or declared and a sum sufficient for the payment thereof set apart for such payment, the amount of the deficiency shall be fully paid, but without interest, or dividends in such amount declared and a sum sufficient for the payment thereof set apart for such payment, before any sum or sums shall be paid or set aside pursuant to subdivision 2 of this paragraph (b) or paragraph (c) or otherwise for the purchase or redemption of Series A Preferred Stock or any class or series of stock ranking on a parity with the Series A Preferred Stock as to dividends or distribution of assets and *before* any dividend shall be declared or paid upon or set apart for, any other distribution shall be ordered or made in respect of, or any payment shall be made on account of the purchase of, the Common Stock or of any class or series of stock ranking *junior* to the Series A Preferred Stock as to dividends or distribution of assets.

All dividends declared on the Series A Preferred Stock for any dividend period and on any class or series of stock ranking on parity with the Series A Preferred Stock as to dividends shall be declared pro rata so that the amounts of dividends per share declared for such period on the Series A Preferred Stock and on any class or series of stock ranking on a parity with the Series A Preferred Stock as to dividends that were outstanding during such period shall in all cases bear to each other the same proportions that the respective dividend rates of such stock for such period bear to each other.

2. Out of any surplus or net profits of the Corporation legally available for dividends remaining *after full cumulative dividends* upon the Series A Preferred Stock then outstanding shall have been paid for all past dividend periods, and after or concurrently with making payment of, or declaring and setting apart for payment, full dividends on the Series A Preferred Stock then outstanding to the end of the then current dividend period and *before* any dividends shall be declared or paid upon or set apart for, or any other distribution shall be ordered or made in respect of, or any payment shall be made on account of the purchase of, the Common Stock or of any class of stock ranking *junior* to the Series A Preferred Stock as to dividends or distribution of assets, the Corporation shall set apart for payment on its books (or have paid), in respect of the sinking or purchase fund for the redemption or purchase of the Series A Preferred Stock provided for in paragraph (e) of these resolutions, the sum or sums required for all past periods by the terms of these resolutions as a sinking or purchase fund.

3. Out of any surplus or net profits of the Corporation legally available for dividends *remaining after* full cumulative dividends upon the Series A Preferred Stock then outstanding shall have been paid for all past dividend periods, and *after or concurrently with* making payment of, or declaring and setting apart for payment, full dividends on the Series A Preferred Stock then outstanding to the end of the then current dividend period and *after* the Corporation shall have complied with the provisions of the foregoing subdivision 2 of this paragraph (b) in respect of any and all amounts theretofore required to be set aside or applied in respect of the sinking or purchase fund mentioned in said subdivision 2 then and not otherwise, the holders of the Common Stock or of any class or series of stock ranking junior to the Series A Preferred Stock as to dividends or the distribution of assets, subject to the provisions hereof, shall be entitled to receive such dividends as may from time to time be declared by the Board of Directors; provided that the Corporation will not declare or pay any dividend or make any distribution on, or purchase or retire any Common Stock unless, after giving effect to the proposed dividend or distribution on, or purchase or retirement of, Common Stock, the aggregate of the amount of all dividends paid and distributions made on, and purchases and retirements of, Common Stock subsequent to December 31, 2005 shall not exceed the Consolidated Net Income of the Corporation earned after such date to the date of calculation less the aggregate amount of all dividends paid and distributions made on, after December 31, 2005, the capital stock of the Corporation (other than the Common Stock) to the date of calculation and less the aggregate amounts expended after December 31, 2005, to purchase or retire any such capital stock (other than Common Stock) to the date of calculation. For the purposes of this paragraph (b) dividends or distributions by the Corporation shall include all outstanding investments in and/or loans and advances (whether made by the Corporation or any of its subsidiaries) to any holder, affiliate thereof, or member of an affiliated group of holders of capital stock of the Corporation with voting power sufficient to exercise control of the Corporation, but shall not include (i) investments in and/or loans and advances to any direct or indirect subsidiary of the Corporation or any corporation in which such holder's or group of holders' interest is an indirect

interest solely through the Corporation and its subsidiaries, (ii) any payments made, pursuant to any tax sharing agreement, to any entity with which the Corporation is included in a consolidated income tax return or (iii) dividends payable solely in shares of Common Stock of the Corporation or warrants or rights to subscribe for or purchase any security of the Corporation. Also for the purposes of this subdivision 3 of this paragraph (b) the term "Consolidated Net Income of the Corporation" shall mean the aggregate of the net income of the Corporation and its subsidiaries after eliminating all offsetting debits and credits between the Corporation and its subsidiaries and portions of earnings properly attributable to minority interests, if any, in common stocks of subsidiaries, after making provision for dividends accrued on preferred stock, if any, of subsidiaries not owned by the Corporation or by another subsidiary, and after eliminating: any gains in excess of losses resulting from the sale or other disposition of capital assets (i.e., assets other than current assets), any gains resulting from the write-up of assets, any earnings or losses of any corporation acquired by the Corporation or any subsidiary in a pooling of interests for any year prior to the year of acquisition, any reversal of any contingency reserve, except to the extent that provision for such contingency reserve shall have been made during the period, any reversal of any reserve for tax, except to the extent of any excess of any such reserve over the amount ultimately determined to be due and payable, any portion of the net earnings of any subsidiary which is unavailable, under applicable law or under the terms of any agreement or instrument to which the Corporation or any of its subsidiaries is a party or bound or to which any of the assets of the Corporation or any of its subsidiaries are subject, for payment of dividends to the Corporation, any undistributed earnings from any other person (other than a subsidiary), any tax sharing payments retained by the Corporation pursuant to any tax sharing agreement between the Corporation and any corporation controlling the Corporation, all determined in accordance with generally accepted accounting principles.

4. The term "date of cumulation" as used in this resolution with reference to the Series A Preferred Stock shall be deemed to mean the date on which shares of the Series A Preferred Stock are first issued. In the event of the issue of additional shares of the Series A Preferred Stock, the "date of cumulation" with respect to such additional shares of Series A Preferred Stock shall be deemed to mean the date on which such additional shares of the Series A Preferred Stock are first issued. For the purposes of this resolution the phrase "set apart for payment" in respect of the payment of dividends or sinking funds shall not be construed as requiring deposit of any funds in trust or in any special account, but shall merely mean that out of the funds available for the payment of dividends or sinking or purchase funds, a sum sufficient for the payment of dividends or sinking or purchase funds on the Series A Preferred Stock shall be reserved by appropriate notation on the books of the Corporation.

(c) Redemption of Series A Preferred Stock

All the Series A Preferred Stock, or any part thereof, at any time outstanding *may be redeemed* by the Corporation on or after April 1, 2003, at its election expressed by resolution of the Board of Directors, upon not less than thirty (30) days *previous notice* to the holders of record of the Series A Preferred Stock to be redeemed, given by mail and by publication in such manner as may be prescribed by resolution of the Board of Directors, upon payment of $22 per share *together with the amount of any dividends accrued and unpaid thereon* to the date fixed for redemption (the "redemption price"); provided, however, that Series A Preferred Stock may be redeemed *only after* full cumulative dividends upon the Series A Preferred Stock then outstanding shall have been paid or declared and a sum sufficient for payment thereof set apart for such payment for all past dividend periods and after or currently with making payment of, or declaring and setting apart for payment, full dividends on the Series A Preferred Stock then outstanding (except the shares of Series A Preferred Stock to be redeemed) to the end of the current dividend period. In order to facilitate the redemption of any shares of Series A Preferred Stock that may be chosen for redemption as provided in this paragraph (c) the Board of Directors shall be authorized to exercise its discretion to cause the transfer books of the Corporation to be closed as to such shares not more than 60 days prior to the designated redemption date. Any notice mailed in the manner prescribed by the Board of Directors to the holder at his address as the same shall appear on the books of the Corporation, shall be conclusively presumed to have been given whether or not the holder receives the notice. If less than all the outstanding Series A Preferred Stock is to be redeemed, the redemption may be made either pro rata or by lot in such fair and equitable manner as may be prescribed by resolution of the Board of Directors. The Corporation shall provide moneys for the payment of the redemption price of the shares called for redemption by depositing the amount thereof on or before the redemption date for account of the holders of the Series A Preferred Stock entitled thereto with a bank or trust company having capital and surplus of at least fifty million dollars ($50,000,000). From and after the date fixed in any such notice as the date of redemption (unless default shall be made by the Corporation in providing moneys sufficient for the payment of the redemption price pursuant to such notice) all dividends on the Series A Preferred Stock called for redemption shall cease to accrue and all rights of the holders thereof as stockholders of the corporation, except the right to receive the redemption price as hereinafter provided, shall cease and terminate. After the deposit of such amount with such bank or trust company, the respective holders of record of the Series A Preferred Stock to be redeemed shall be entitled to receive the redemption price at any time upon actual delivery to such bank or trust company of certificates for the number of shares to be redeemed, duly endorsed in blank or accompanied by proper instruments of assignment and transfer thereof duly endorsed in blank. Any interest accrued on funds so deposited shall be paid to the Corporation from time to time and the holders of shares of Series A Preferred Stock to be redeemed shall have no claim to any such interest. Any moneys so deposited which shall remain unclaimed by the holders of such Preferred Stock at the end of five (5) years after the redemption date, shall be paid by such bank or trust company to the Corporation. Series A Preferred Stock redeemed pursuant to the provisions of this paragraph shall have the status of authorized but unissued Preferred Stock, but such shares shall not be reissued as Series A Preferred Stock.

(d) Priority of the Series A Preferred Stock in the Event of Dissolution (i.e., Liquidation Preference)

The Series A Preferred Stock shall be preferred over the Common Stock and any class or series of stock ranking junior to the Series A Preferred Stock as to assets in the event of *any liquidation* or dissolution or winding up of the Corporation, and in that event the holders of the Series A Preferred Stock shall be entitled to receive, out of the assets of the Corporation available for distribution to its stockholders, *$22 per share, together with the amount equal to all dividends accrued and unpaid thereon* to the date of final distribution, for every share of the Series A Preferred Stock held by them before any distribution of the assets shall be made to the holders of the Common Stock or any other class or series of stock ranking junior to the Series A Preferred Stock as to distribution of assets. Upon any liquidation, dissolution or winding up of the Corporation, after payment shall have been made in full on the Series A Preferred Stock as provided in the preceding sentence, but not prior thereto, the Common Stock or any other series or class of stock ranking junior to the Series A Preferred Stock as to distribution of assets shall, subject to the respective terms and provisions, if any, applying thereto, be entitled to receive any and all assets remaining to be paid or distributed and the Series A Preferred Stock shall not be entitled to share therein. If upon any liquidation or dissolution or winding up of the Corporation the amounts payable on or with respect to the Series A Preferred Stock are not paid in full, the holders of shares of the Series A Preferred Stock together with all classes or series of stock ranking on a parity with the Series A Preferred Stock as to distribution of assets shall share ratably in any distribution of assets according to the respective amounts which would be payable in respect of the shares held by them upon such distribution if all amounts payable on or with respect to the Series A Preferred Stock and any other class or series of stock that so ranks on a parity with the Series A Preferred Stock were paid in full. *Neither the merger or consolidation of the Corporation with another corporation nor the sale or lease of all or substantially all the assets of the Corporation shall be deemed to be a liquidation or dissolution or winding up of the Corporation.*

(e) The Sinking or Purchase Fund for the Series A Preferred Stock

The Corporation (unless prevented from doing so by law or by applicable restrictive provisions in these resolutions, in the Certificate of Incorporation or in any mortgage, deed of trust, indenture or loan agreement or arrangement of the Corporation, as in effect from time to time, or for any other reason) shall establish a sinking or purchase fund out of assets legally available therefor and set aside in cash for payment on the first business day of each year commencing with the year 2004 (each such date being herein called the "sinking fund payment date") *such sum as may be required to redeem 6 % of the Series A Preferred Stock originally issued until all the Series A Preferred Stock shall be redeemed or otherwise acquired by the Corporation.* Shares of Series A Preferred Stock acquired or redeemed by the Corporation otherwise than through operation of the sinking or purchase fund may, at the option of the Corporation, be *credited*, at the redemption price per share of the Series A Preferred Stock, against one or more sinking fund requirements which the Corporation may designate and shall reduce the sum required on the sinking fund payment date. If on any sinking fund payment date the funds of the

Corporation legally available therefor, or for any reason herein stated, shall be insufficient (together with any shares voluntarily redeemed or acquired and credited against the sinking or purchase fund requirement) to discharge the sinking or purchase fund requirement in full, such amount of the funds as is legally available and not restricted from such application by the terms of this paragraph (e) shall be set aside for the sinking or purchase fund. Such sinking or purchase fund requirement shall *be cumulative* so that if, for any year or years, such requirement shall not be fully discharged for any reason as it accrues, funds legally available therefor and not restricted from such application by the terms of this paragraph (e) shall be applied thereto until all such requirements are discharged. On each sinking fund payment date the amount set aside on such date shall be used to redeem Series A Preferred Stock in the manner provided in paragraph (c) of this resolution, at the redemption price for the Series A Preferred Stock.

Shares of Series A Preferred Stock redeemed or otherwise acquired by the Corporation may be held in the treasury of the Corporation or cancelled and given the status of authorized and unissued shares, but such shares shall not be reissued as shares of the Series A Preferred Stock.

(f) Voting Rights

1. *Except* as may be otherwise herein or in the Certificate of Incorporation, as amended, of the Corporation or by law otherwise specifically provided, each holder of shares of the Series A Preferred Stock shall at every meeting of stockholders of the Corporation be entitled to *one* vote for each share of the Series A Preferred Stock held by such stockholder and the holders of the Series A Preferred Stock *shall vote together with the holders of the Common Stock* and together with the holders of any class or series of stock, entitled to vote in the manner provided in this sentence, as one class (and not each as a separate class) on any matter that may be brought before any such meeting.

2. If at the time of any annual meeting of the stockholders of the Corporation for the election of directors (A) either (or both) a "default in preference dividends, in the *first* instance," or a "*default in sinking fund payments, in the first* instance," as such terms are hereinafter defined, shall exist, the holders of the Series A Preferred Stock *voting separately as a class* (subject, however, to the provisions of subdivision 5 of this paragraph (f)) shall have the right to elect *two members* of the Board of Directors of the Corporation, and no more, and (B) either (or both) a "*default in preference dividends, in the second* instance," or a "default in sinking fund payments in the *second* instance," as such terms are hereinafter defined, shall exist, the holders of the Series A Preferred Stock *voting separately as a class* (subject, however, to the provisions of subdivision 5 of this paragraph (f)) shall have the right to elect such additional number of directors as shall constitute *a majority* of the Board of Directors of the Corporation, and no more.

Notwithstanding the foregoing whenever any of the above enumerated defaults shall commence to exist and the holders of Series A Preferred Stock shall be entitled to elect directors in accordance with the terms of this subdivision 2 of this paragraph (f), the Secretary of the Corporation (or if at the time the Corporation has no Secretary, then the President of the Corporation) shall call a special meeting of the holders of the outstanding shares of Series A Preferred Stock and any other series of Preferred Stock entitled to vote in the event of such defaults in accordance with subdivision 5 of this paragraph (f) (hereinafter sometimes collectively referred to as the Special Voting Preferred Stock), such special meeting to be held within 120 days after the date of any of such enumerated defaults for the purpose of enabling the holders of the Special Voting Preferred Stock to elect such members of the Board of Directors as herein provided; provided, however, that such special meeting need not be called if an annual meeting of stockholders of the Corporation for the election of directors shall be scheduled to be held within such 120 days.

At any meeting held for the purpose of electing directors at which the holders of the Special Voting Preferred Stock voting as a single class shall have the right to elect directors as provided in this subdivision 2 of this paragraph (f), the presence, in person or by proxy, of a majority of the voting interest of the Special Voting Preferred Stock at the time outstanding shall be required and be sufficient to constitute a quorum of such class for the election of any director by the holders of the Special Voting Preferred Stock as a single class and the majority vote of the Special Voting Preferred Stock so present at such meeting shall be sufficient to elect any such director. For the purposes of the preceding sentence only, so long as RT Corporation, a Delaware corporation ("RT") or any of its affiliates shall own any Common Stock of the Corporation, any Special Voting Preferred Stock owned by RT or any of its affiliates shall not be entitled to cast a vote at such meeting of the Special Voting Preferred Stock and such shares not entitled to vote shall not be counted for quorum purposes. At any such meeting or adjournment thereof, (A) the absence of a quorum of the holders of the Special Voting Preferred Stock shall not prevent the election of directors, if any, to be elected by the holders of stock other than the Special Voting Preferred Stock and the absence of the quorum of stock other than the Special Voting Preferred Stock shall not prevent the election of the directors to be elected by the holders of the Special Voting Preferred Stock, and (B) in the absence of such quorum, either of the holders of the Special Voting Preferred Stock or of the holders of stock other than the Special Voting Preferred Stock (if the meeting shall not be a special meeting solely of the holders of the Special Voting Preferred Stock), or both, a majority of the voting interest, present in person or by proxy, of the class or classes of stock which lack a quorum shall have power to adjourn the meeting for the election of directors which they are entitled to elect, from time to time, without notice other than announcement at the meeting, until a quorum shall be present.

Prior to any such special meeting, *the number of directors of the Corporation shall be increased* to the extent necessary to provide as additional places on the Board of Directors the directorships to be filled by the directors to be elected thereat. Any director elected as aforesaid by the holders of shares of the Special Voting Preferred Stock *shall cease to serve as such director whenever the default or defaults that provided the basis for such election shall cease to exist.* If, prior to the end of the term of any director elected as aforesaid by the holders of shares of the Special Voting Preferred Stock, a vacancy in the office of such director shall occur by reason of death, resignation, removal or disability, or for any other cause, such vacancy shall be filled for the unexpired term by the remaining director or directors elected by the Special Voting Preferred Stock. Any director elected by the holders of shares of the Special Voting Preferred Stock may be removed without cause only by vote of the holders of majority of the votes of the Special Voting Preferred Stock entitled to be cast at an election of directors. For the purposes of this subdivision 2 of this paragraph *(f), a "default in preference dividends, in the first instance"* shall be deemed to have occurred whenever the amount of dividends in arrears upon the Series A Preferred Stock shall be equivalent to *six* full quarter-yearly dividends or more, *and "default in preference dividends, in the second instance"* shall be deemed to have occurred whenever the amount of dividends in arrears upon the Series A Preferred Stock shall be equivalent *to ten* full quarter-yearly dividends or more, and, having so occurred, either of such defaults in preference dividends shall be deemed to exist thereafter until, but only until, *all* dividends in arrears on *all* shares of the Series A Preferred Stock then outstanding, shall have been paid or declared and set apart in trust for payment. For the purposes of this subdivision 2 of this paragraph (f), *a "default in sinking fund payments, in the first instance"* shall be deemed to have occurred whenever the amount of sinking or purchase fund payments in arrears upon the Series A Preferred Stock shall be equivalent to *two* full annual sinking or purchase fund payments or more, and *a "default in sinking fund payments, in the second instance"* shall be deemed to have occurred whenever the amount of sinking or purchase fund payments in arrears upon the Series A Preferred Stock shall be equivalent to *five* full annual sinking or purchase fund payments or more, and, having so occurred either of such defaults shall be deemed to exist thereafter until, but only until, all sinking or purchase fund payments in arrears on all shares of the Series A Preferred Stock then outstanding shall have been paid or declared and set apart in trust for payment. The terms "dividends in arrears" or "sinking funds in arrears" whenever used in this subdivision 2 of this paragraph (f) with reference to the Series A Preferred Stock shall be deemed to mean *(whether or not in any period in respect of any such arrearages there shall have been surplus or net profits of the Corporation legally available for the payment of dividends or sinking funds or whether such dividends or sinking funds are not made for any other reason)* that amount which shall be equal, in the case of dividends, to cumulative dividends at the rate expressed in this resolution for the Series A Preferred Stock for all past quarterly dividend periods less the amount of all dividends paid, or deemed paid, for all such periods upon such Series A Preferred Stock or, in the case of sinking or purchase funds, the cumulative sinking or purchase fund payments at the amount expressed in this resolution for the Series A Preferred Stock for all past sinking fund periods less the amount of all sinking or purchase funds paid, or deemed paid (including credits in lieu of payments), for all such periods upon the Series A Preferred Stock. *Nothing herein contained shall be deemed to prevent an increase in the number of directors of the Corporation pursuant to its By-laws as from time to time in effect so as to provide as additional places on the Board of Directors the directorships to be filled by the directors so to be elected by the holders of shares of the Special Voting Preferred Stock, or to prevent any other change in the number of the directors of the Corporation.*

In the event directors elected by the holders of shares of the Special Voting Preferred Stock constitute *a majority* of the directors of the Corporation and the Corporation has assets legally available for the payment of dividends and/or sinking or purchase funds, *but the Board does not apply* the assets to the payment of dividends and/or sinking or purchase funds in arrears, *the directors elected in an election in which the holders of the Common Stock participated (excluding any directors elected by the Preferred Stock pursuant to any special voting rights, in the event of defaults, granted to such Preferred Stock) (or any director who shall have filled the vacancy of the office of any such director, elected in an election in which the holders of the Common Stock participated, in the manner provided in the By-laws of the Corporation) are hereby authorized as a permanent Committee of the Board of Directors of the Corporation to declare and pay dividends on,* or make sinking or purchase fund payments in respect of, any series of Preferred Stock of the Corporation entitled by its terms to any such declarations, payments or purchases for the purpose of eliminating any arrearages, *provided* that there are assets legally available for any such payments or purchases. *The membership of such Committee may not be changed by the Board of Directors.*

3. So long as any shares of the Series A Preferred Stock shall be outstanding, the Corporation shall not, without the affirmative vote or written consent of the holders of *two-thirds* of the aggregate number of shares of the Series A Preferred Stock at the time outstanding voting separately as a class, (A) *alter or change* the powers, preferences or rights given to the Series A Preferred Stock by this resolution, or (B) *authorize or create* any *class or series* of stock *ranking*, either as to payment of dividends or distribution of assets, *prior* to the Series A Preferred Stock. *In addition to* any requirement imposed by subdivision 4 below, so long as any shares of the Series A Preferred Stock shall be outstanding, the Corporation shall not, without the affirmative vote or written consent of the holders of a *majority* of the aggregate number of the Series A Preferred Stock at the time outstanding (subject, however, to the provisions of subdivision 5 of this paragraph (f)), authorize or create any *class* of stock ranking either as to payment of dividends or distribution of assets, on a *parity* with the Series A Preferred Stock or *increase* the authorized number of the shares of Preferred Stock.

4. So long as any shares of the Series A Preferred Stock shall be outstanding the Corporation shall not, without the affirmative vote or written consent of the holders of a *majority* of the outstanding shares of the Series A Preferred Stock, voting separately as a class,

(A) increase the number of *outstanding* shares of the Series A Preferred Stock or authorize, create or issue any *series or class* of stock ranking, either as to payment of dividends or distribution of assets, on a *parity* with the Series A Preferred Stock outstanding *unless*, after giving effect to the issuance of such stock ranking on such a parity with the Series A Preferred Stock, the Consolidated Net Tangible Assets (including the proceeds from such issuance, whether or not such proceeds are from an Acquisition Transaction as defined in clause (B) below) of the Corporation are equal to at least *two and one-half times* the aggregate liquidation preference of the shares of the Series A Preferred Stock and any class or series of stock ranking on a parity with the Series A Preferred Stock either as to the payment of dividends or the distribution of assets outstanding after such issuance;

(B) *sell* substantially all the assets of the Corporation or consolidate or *merge* the Corporation with or into any other corporation (an "Acquisition

Transaction") for securities *unless* (a) any securities exchanged for Series A Preferred Stock shall be preferred stock the terms of which are *substantially similar* in all material respects to the Series A Preferred Stock exchanged *and* (b) the Consolidated Net Tangible Assets of the surviving corporation available to the Series A Preferred Stock (or to the preferred stock the terms of which are substantially similar to the Series A Preferred Stock in all material respects) immediately after giving effect to the Acquisition Transaction shall be equal to at least *two and one-half times* the aggregate liquidation preference of the Series A Preferred Stock and any class or series of stock ranking on a parity with the Series A Preferred Stock as to the payment of dividends or the distribution of assets outstanding after the Acquisition Transaction; provided that, except for the requirements of subclause (a) of this clause (B), nothing in clause (A) or in this clause (B) shall prevent (or require the vote or consent of the holders of shares of the Series A Preferred Stock with respect to) the issuance of Preferred Stock ranking on a parity as to dividends or distribution of assets with the Series A Preferred Stock issued to acquire a minority interest through a merger or consolidation of any consolidated subsidiary of ABC Corporation, a New York corporation ("ABC"), as any such entity existed on the date of the business combination of ABC and XYZ Inc. (XYZ) with or into the Corporation or any subsidiary thereof, or through a sale of assets between any of the above, unless the minority interests in any such corporation to be so merged or consolidated, or whose assets are so to be so sold, shall have increased (other than through the exercise of employee stock options or existing rights to acquire such corporation's capital stock) through the issuance of equity securities as compared to the minority interests in such corporation on the date of such business combination, in which event this proviso shall not be applicable to such corporation;

(C) issue any shares of any class or series of stock ranking on a parity with the Series A Preferred Stock as to the distribution of assets if after giving effect to such issuance the aggregate liquidation preference of such issue *shall exceed 115% of* the amount or value of the aggregate *proceeds* (whether cash or property) received or to be received by the Corporation in respect of such issuance; or

(D) enter into any Acquisition Transaction in which the holders of Series A Preferred Stock would be required to accept cash *before* the date, in accordance with paragraph (c) of this resolution, on which the Series A Preferred Stock may be redeemed *or* accept cash in an amount *less than the redemption price per share.*

For the purposes of this subdivision 4 of this paragraph (f), "Net Tangible Assets" of a corporation shall mean the sum of all assets (less depreciation and valuation reserves and items deductible under generally accepted accounting principles) which, under generally accepted accounting principles, would appear on the asset side of the balance sheet of such corporation (excluding any shares of stock or any indebtedness of such corporation held in its treasury, any franchises, licenses, permits, patents, patent applications, copyrights, trademarks, trade names, goodwill, experimental or organizational expenses, unamortized debt discount and expense, research and development costs, deferred charges, unamortized excess cost over book value of assets acquired and all other items treated, in accordance with generally accepted accounting principles, as intangibles), less the sum of all items which, in accordance with generally accepted accounting principles, would be included in determining total liabilities as shown on the liability side of the balance sheet and "Consolidated Net Tangible Assets" shall mean the Net Tangible Assets of the Corporation and its subsidiaries on a consolidated basis determined in accordance with generally accepted accounting principles.

5. Notwithstanding anything to the contrary in these resolutions, the Board of Directors of the Corporation may provide, in connection with the issuance of *additional series* of Preferred Stock pursuant to the terms of Article Fourth of the Certificate of Incorporation of the Corporation, as amended, voting rights to the holders of any such series which permit such holders to vote together as a class with the holders of the shares of the Series A Preferred Stock with respect to any of the matters set forth in subdivisions 1, 2 and 3 (second sentence only) of this paragraph (f) if the Board determines that the terms of such series of Preferred Stock warrants such voting rights and, in such event, the holders of shares of the Series A Preferred Stock and the holders of shares of any such other series of Preferred Stock shall vote together as a class and without regard to series and the granting of such rights or any other voting rights with respect to any such other series of Preferred Stock shall not be deemed to alter or change in any respect the powers, preferences, or rights given to the Series A Preferred Stock; provided that each share of such Preferred Stock given voting rights shall not have voting rights in excess of the quotient determined by dividing the liquidation preference of such Preferred Stock, in the event of liquidation or dissolution or winding up of the Corporation, by 22, and if any right accruing to any series of the Preferred Stock to vote for the election of directors in the event of any default in a dividend, sinking or purchase fund payment shall accrue, at a time when the Series A Preferred Stock shall not also be entitled to vote, the Series A Preferred Stock shall be entitled to vote with such series of Preferred Stock, and any other series of Preferred Stock also entitled to so vote, as a single class to elect such number of directors as are to be elected whether or not there has been a default with respect to the rights of the Series A Preferred Stock enumerated in subdivision 2 of this paragraph (f). For the purpose of the proviso to the preceding sentence the liquidation preference of any series of Preferred Stock ranking junior to the Series A Preferred Stock as to distribution of assets shall be determined in accordance with the requirements of clause (C) of subdivision 4 of this paragraph (f) if the liquidation preference to which such series of Preferred Stock is entitled does not meet such requirements.

6. Nothing contained in this paragraph (f) or in these resolutions shall require any vote or consent of the holders of the shares of the Series A Preferred Stock in connection with the authorization or issuance of any one or more additional series of Preferred Stock ranking junior to the Series A Preferred Stock as to dividends and distribution of assets.

(g) Valuation of assets

For the purposes of these resolutions any questions of valuations of assets for any purpose, including, without limitation, determining the amount or value of proceeds from the issuance of any class or series of capital stock or determining the carrying value of assets or liabilities on the books of the Corporation or determining the value of any distribution of assets, shall be conclusively decided by the Board of Directors of the Corporation.

(h) Certain definitions

Notwithstanding anything to the contrary in these resolutions, the term "affiliate" shall have the meaning which the term affiliate has under the Securities Act of 1933 as amended, except that for the purposes of determining affiliation, the reasonable determination of the Board of Directors of the Corporation shall be conclusive; the term "control" shall mean holding the voting interest of 25% or more of the capital stock of a corporation. So long as RT or any of its affiliates shall hold any shares of Common Stock of the Corporation, for the purposes of determining a majority vote of the Series A Preferred Stock outstanding, and of determining a two-thirds vote of the Series A Preferred Stock outstanding under subdivisions 3 and 4 of paragraph (f)(i) in those cases in which the Series A Preferred Stock shall be entitled to vote separately as a single class, then a majority vote shall mean (x) a majority vote of the Series A Preferred Stock outstanding, including the Series A Preferred Stock held by RT and any of its affiliates, and (y) a majority vote of the Series A Preferred Stock outstanding, excluding the shares of Series A Preferred Stock held by RT and any of its affiliates, (ii) in those cases in which more than one series of Preferred Stock shall be entitled to vote together as a single class, then a majority vote shall mean (x) a majority of such shares of Preferred Stock outstanding voting together as a class, including the shares of Preferred Stock held by RT and any of its affiliates, and (y) a majority vote of such outstanding shares of Preferred Stock voting together as a class, excluding any shares of Preferred Stock held by RT and any of its affiliates, and (iii) in those cases in which the Series A Preferred Stock shall be entitled to vote separately as a single class then a two-thirds vote shall mean (x) a two-thirds vote of the Series A Preferred Stock outstanding, including the Series A Preferred Stock held by RT and any of its affiliates, and (y) a majority vote of the Series A Preferred Stock outstanding, excluding the Series A Preferred Stock held by RT and any of its affiliates. RT and its affiliates shall include RT, its affiliates and each successor to any such person (other than a successor which was not an affiliate thereof immediately prior to such succession).

(i) Reports

So long as any Series A Preferred Stock shall be outstanding, the Corporation shall file with the Securities and Exchange Commission such supplementary and periodic information, documents and reports as may be required pursuant to section 13 of the Securities Exchange Act of 1934, as amended, in respect of a security registered pursuant to section 12 of the Securities Exchange Act of 1934, as amended, *to the extent said Commission will accept such filings* and submit annual reports to the holders of the Series A Preferred Stock.

IN RE SUNSTATES CORPORATION SHAREHOLDER LITIGATION

Court of Chancery of Delaware
788 A.2d 530 (2001)

OPINION

LAMB, VICE CHANCELLOR.

I.

Count II of the Amended Complaint is brought as a class action on behalf of the owner of shares of Sunstates Corporation $3.75 Preferred Stock. The complaint alleges that, between 1991 and 1993, and in violation of its certificate of incorporation, Sunstates purchased shares of its common and Preferred Stock when it was in arrears on the Preferred Stock dividend.

The defendants have moved for summary judgment on this claim. They concede the existence of the special limitation in the charter. But they deny its applicability because, as a matter of fact, Sunstates, itself, made no share repurchases. Rather, all reacquired shares were purchased by one or more of Sunstates's subsidiary corporations. Because the Sunstates certificate does not prohibit (although it might have) share repurchases by subsidiaries when the parent is in arrears on its Preferred Stock dividend, defendants argue that they are entitled to judgment in their favor as a matter of law.

Plaintiffs respond that it would render the protective provision of the charter nugatory and illusory if I interpreted it literally to apply only to share repurchases by the corporation itself, since the limitation could so easily be avoided. In a similar vein, they argue that the doctrine of good faith and fair dealing in contracts requires that I interpret the special limitation more broadly to reach the activity of Sunstates's subsidiaries. Finally, they suggest that I should ignore the separate corporate existence of the subsidiaries and treat them as mere agents of the parent corporation for this purpose.

The clause at issue clearly and unambiguously applies the special limitation against share repurchases only to Sunstates and not to its subsidiary entities. Construing that clause strictly, as I must, and recognizing that "nothing should be presumed in [its] favor,"[13] it would be impermissible for me to find that the limitation also governs actions by Sunstates's subsidiaries. The result may be, as plaintiffs argue, that Sunstates was able to avoid the restriction by the simple means of channeling the repurchases through its subsidiaries. Nevertheless, no one who studied the certificate of incorporation should ever have had any other expectation. If the special limitation had been meant to apply to the actions of

---

[13] [1] *Waggoner v. Laster*, Del. Supr., 581 A.2d 1127, 1134 (1990) (quoting *Holland v. Nat'l Auto. Fibres, Inc.*, Del. Ch., 194 A. 124, 126 (1937)).

Sunstates's subsidiaries, the certificate of incorporation could easily have said so.[14]

II.

The pertinent facts are easily stated. Sunstates Corporation is a Delaware corporation having a number of subsidiaries incorporated in various jurisdictions. Article IV, Section 4.3 of the Sunstates certificate of incorporation creates the $3.75 Preferred Stock. Paragraph 3 thereof specifies the dividend rights of that stock and provides that, unless Sunstates is current in its payment of dividends on the Preferred Stock:

> [t]he Corporation shall not (i) declare or pay or set apart for payment any dividends or distributions on any stock ranking as to dividends junior to the $3.75 Preferred Stock (other than dividends paid in shares of such junior stock) or (ii) *make any purchase . . . of . . . any stock ranking as to dividends junior or* pari passu *to the $3.75 Preferred Stock. . . .*

(emphasis added). Paragraph 4(e) of section 4.3 similarly proscribes all non-pro rata purchases of shares of Preferred Stock when dividends are in arrears, as follows:

> [I]n the event that any semiannual dividend payable on the $3.75 Preferred Stock shall be in arrears and until all such dividends in arrears shall have been paid or declared and set apart for payment, the Corporation shall not . . . purchase or otherwise acquire any shares of $3.75 Preferred Stock except in accordance with a purchase offer made by the Corporation on the same terms to all holders of record of $3.75 Preferred Stock for the purchase of all outstanding shares thereof.

Article I, section 1.1 of the certificate defines the "Corporation" to mean Sunstates Corporation. Nothing in the certificate expressly provides that the "Corporation" includes anything but Sunstates Corporation.

In 1991, Sunstates fell into arrears in the payment of the Preferred Stock dividend. Over the next two years, subsidiary corporations controlled, directly or indirectly, by Sunstates bought shares of both common stock and Preferred Stock. The Preferred Shares were not acquired in compliance with the "any and all" tender offer requirement of paragraph 4(e). According to plaintiffs' brief, the repurchases of common stock amounted, over a three year period, to nearly 70 percent of the total outstanding common stock. The Preferred Stock repurchased equaled nearly 30 percent of the total number outstanding.

Plaintiffs point to evidence from which it may be inferred that the decisions to make all these purchases were made by a single person, Clyde Engle. Engle is Sunstates's Chairman and also served as the Investment Officer for Coronet Insurance Company, one of Sunstates's indirect, wholly-owned subsidiaries. Engle

---

[14] [2] Fifty years ago, the fallacy of plaintiffs' argument was recognized in the seminal law review article by Richard M. Buxbaum, Preferred Stock — Law and Draftsmanship, 42 Cal. L. Rev. 243, 257 (1954). In discussing problems in drafting financial restriction clauses in preferred stock contract, Professor Buxbaum stated as follows: "As to all these clauses, *it is vital that all payments, distributions, acquisitions, etc. include those of the subsidiaries; otherwise the provisions can be totally avoided.*" (emphasis added).

controls Sunstates through his ownership control over Telco Capital Corporation, the owner, directly or indirectly, of a majority of Sunstates's common stock. Engle conducted the share repurchase program through Crown Casualty Company and Sunstates Equities, Inc., wholly-owned subsidiaries of Coronet Insurance Company, and through Sew Simple Systems, Inc. and National Assurance Indemnitee Corp., indirect, wholly-owned subsidiaries of Sunstates.

III.

A. Standard of Review

Summary judgment is appropriate where "the pleadings, depositions, answers to interrogatories and admissions on file, together with the affidavits, if any, show that there is no genuine issue as to any material fact and that the moving party is entitled to a judgment as a matter of law."[15] In making this assessment, "the facts of record, including any reasonable hypotheses or inferences to be drawn therefrom, must be viewed in the light most favorable to the non-moving party. . . ."[16] Of course, unsupported allegations and inferences cannot defeat a summary judgment motion.[17]

B. Analysis

Section 151(a) of the Delaware General Corporation Law allows Delaware corporations to issue stock having such "special rights, and qualifications, limitations or restrictions" relating thereto "as shall be stated and expressed in the certificate of incorporation or of any amendment thereto. . . ." Thus, the law recognizes that the existence and extent of rights of preferred stock must be determined by reference to the certificate of incorporation, those rights being essentially contractual in nature.[18] As was said by this court more than 70 years ago:

> It is elementary that the rights of stockholders are contract rights. The mere word "preferred" unless it is supplemented by a definition of its significance conveys no special meaning. The holder of preferred stock must, therefore, refer to the appropriate language of the corporate contract for the ascertainment of his rights. The nub of the present controversy is — where may such appropriate language be found. The exceptants say in the certificate of incorporation and nowhere else. In this I think they are right.[19]

Moreover, the law is settled that, while courts "will employ principles of contract

---

[15] [3] Ct. Ch. R. 56(c).

[16] [4] *Williams v. Geier*, Del. Supr., 671 A.2d 1368, 1375 (1996).

[17] [5] *Id.* at 1385.

[18] [6] *Warner Communications, Inc. v. Chris-Craft Industries, Inc.*, Del. Ch., 583 A.2d 962, 966 (1989).

[19] [7] *Gaskill v. Gladys Belle Oil Co.*, Del. Ch., 146 A. 337, 339 (1929).

interpretation, and read the Certificate in its entirety to arrive at the intended meaning of the words employed in any specific provision,"[20] stock preferences are to be strictly construed and nothing is to be presumed in their favor.[21]

"[A]ny ambiguity must be resolved against granting the challenged preferences, rights or powers."[22]

Plaintiffs advance no construction of the certificate of incorporation that would permit me to read the word "Corporation" to refer to any corporation other than Sunstates. This is hardly surprising since the language at issue is clear in its meaning and there is nothing within the four corners of the certificate suggesting a broader or different interpretation. Thus, as a matter of simple contract interpretation, there is no basis on which to apply the special limitation against share repurchases to any entity other than Sunstates.

As earlier mentioned, plaintiffs do make several other arguments that require discussion. First, they argue that the subsidiary corporations making the share purchases were acting as mere agents for Sunstates and, for that reason, the court should treat their acts as those of Sunstates. Second, they argue that the repurchases violated the implied covenant of good faith and fair dealing. I will address these now.

Plaintiffs' agency theory is both factually and legally flawed. Factually, the record suggests that the repurchases were made to further the interests of Engle, the person who (through several layers of intermediary corporations) controlled Sunstates, and not Sunstates's own interests. Plaintiffs' brief states at page 6, as follows:

> In committing so much money to these repurchases, Engle had two overriding purposes: to prop up the price of Sunstates' common stock, which was the sole asset of Sunstates' parent companies . . . and which was the collateral those companies had used for their loans; and to assemble a large enough block of preferred stock to assure that, in the event that the preferred stockholders ever forced an annual meeting and attempted to exercise their rights to elect half the directors, those shares could be used to block any effort by the class members to secure representation on the Sunstates board [and] assure that [Engle's] hand-picked cronies were re-elected.

Thus, the factual predicate necessary to argue that the purchasing subsidiaries were acting as Sunstates's agents is weak or missing.

The legal flaw in the agency argument is more fundamental. For the purposes of the corporation law, the act of one corporation is not regarded as the act of another merely because the first corporation is a subsidiary of the other, or because the two may be treated as part of a single economic enterprise for some other purpose. Rather, to pierce the corporate veil based on an agency or "alter ego" theory, "the

---

[20] [8] *Sullivan Money Management, Inc. v. FLS Holdings, Inc.*, Del. Ch., C.A. No. 12731, mem. op. at 5, [1993 Del. LEXIS 251] 1992 WL 345453 (Nov. 20, 1992).

[21] [9] See *Waggoner*, 581 A.2d at 1134-35 and cases collected therein.

[22] [10] *Sullivan Money Management*, mem. op. at 6 (quoting *Waggoner*, 581 A.2d at 1135).

corporation must be a sham and exist for no other purpose than as a vehicle for fraud."[23]

Plaintiffs' brief simply ignores this more difficult standard — offering no record evidence from which I might infer that any of the four corporations making the share repurchases was a sham or existed merely to perpetrate a fraud. On the contrary, the record shows that each of those entities was engaged in substantial business operations and was formed or acquired by Sunstates for purposes relating to the pursuit of normal business operations. In the circumstances, it is clear to me that there is no basis in the record or the law of corporate veil-piercing from which I might infer that the program of share repurchases by those subsidiaries should be treated as though Sunstates, itself, was the buyer.

Plaintiffs fare no better in arguing that Sunstates violated the implied covenant of good faith and fair dealing by its subsidiaries' share repurchases. It is true, that, as a general matter, the implied covenant of good faith and fair dealing exists in all contracts. Nevertheless, the circumstances in which it is relied on to find a breach of contract are narrow. As this court has said before:

> . . . the duty [arising from the implied covenant] arises *only* where it is clear from what the parties expressly agreed, that they would have proscribed the challenged conduct as a breach of contract . . . had they thought to negotiate with respect to the matter.[24]

In this case, the only evidence of what the parties "expressly agreed" is found in the prohibition against certain conduct by the "Corporation." That does not provide a reasonable basis to infer that "the parties would have proscribed" share purchases by Sunstates's subsidiaries "had they thought to negotiate with respect to the matter."

On the contrary, the law of this State has clearly stated for many decades that special rights or preferences of preferred stock must be expressed clearly and that nothing will be presumed in their favor.[25] Thus, there is no basis to infer that any person negotiating the terms of the Sunstates certificate of incorporation could have reasonably believed that the limitation of share repurchases found in Article IV, section 4.3, paragraphs 3 and 4, would preclude repurchase activity by any party other than Sunstates. Indeed, it is more readily inferred that whoever negotiated the Sunstates certificate of incorporation knew and understood the scope of the limitations contained therein.[26]

For similar reasons, I am unable to accept plaintiffs' related argument that the

---

[23] [11] *Wallace v. Wood*, Del. Ch., 752 A.2d 1175, 1184 (1999).

[24] [12] *Greytak Enters., Inc. v. Mazda Motors of America, Inc.*, Del. Ch., 622 A.2d 14, 22-23 (1992), *aff'd*, Del. Supr., 609 A.2d 668 (1992) (emphasis added).

[25] [13] *See supra* notes 7-8.

[26] [14] *See supra* note 2. Moreover, "the implied duty to perform in good faith does not come into play" where the topic is either expressly covered in the contract or intentionally omitted therefrom. *Greytak Enters., Inc.*, 622 A.2d at 23. Here, the subject of the scope of the special limitation sued upon is expressly covered in the written contract by the prohibition against the Corporation (defined elsewhere as Sunstates) from making certain share purchases when the Preferred Stock dividend is in arrears.

duty of good faith and fair dealing precluded Sunstates from doing indirectly through its subsidiaries that which it was prevented from doing directly itself. It is true that this court has recognized the possibility of applying such a theory to the enforcement of both corporate duties and contract terms governing corporate securities.[27] It has been careful, however, to limit the scope of such application to situations where the subsidiary was newly created for the purpose of evading the duty or the restriction.[28] In *Shenandoah*, for example, Chancellor Allen nowhere suggests that, in the case of a transaction effected by an existing subsidiary, the court would ignore the separate legal existences of the entities involved.[29] Moreover, he focused his analysis on the ultimate economic reality of the actions taken, viewed at the parent company level alone.

In the final analysis, plaintiffs' arguments run counter to both the doctrine of strict construction of special rights, preferences and limitations relating to stock and the doctrine of independent legal significance. The situation is not unlike that confronted in *Rothschild Int'l Corp. v. Liggett Group, Inc.*[30] There, the plaintiffs owned preferred shares that were entitled to a liquidation preference. To avoid paying this preference, the defendant companies structured a combined tender offer and reverse cash-out merger that eliminated the preferred shares for a price substantially lower than the liquidation preference. Construing the charter provision strictly, the Supreme Court concluded that the charter provision only operated in the case of a liquidation and that there had been no liquidation.[31] Applying the doctrine of independent legal significance, the Supreme Court reiterated "that 'action taken under one section of [the DGCL] is legally independent, and its validity is not dependent upon, nor to be tested by the requirements of other unrelated sections under which the same final result might be attained by different means.'"[32]

IV.

For these reasons, the defendants' motion for partial summary judgment as to Count II of the Amended Complaint will be granted. An order implementing this

---

[27] [15] *Barbieri v. Swing-N-Slide Corp.*, Del. Ch., C.A. No. 14239, Steele, V.C., [1997 Del. Ch. LEXIS 9] 1997 WL 55956 (Jan. 29, 1997) (fiduciary duties of officers or directors); *Shenandoah Life Ins. Co. v. Valero Energy Corp.*, Del. Ch., C.A. No. 9032, Allen, C., 1988 WL 63491[, 1988 Del. Ch. LEXIS 84] (June 21, 1988) (indenture restriction).

[28] [16] *See, e.g.*, *Shenandoah*, mem. op. at 18.

[29] [17] Chancellor Allen was there concerned with the restriction in an indenture prohibiting the redemption of an issuance of debentures by the application, directly or indirectly, of funds borrowed at a lower rate than the debentures. He opined that "[w]hile it is impossible to generalize perfectly concerning all of the situations in which the 'indirectly' language . . . might find application, it does appear that the inclusion of that phrase is intended to reach situations in which the underlying economic reality of the completed transaction is the functional equivalent of a direct loan for purposes of effectuating a redemption and nothing more." *Shenandoah*, mem. op. at 19. Of course, the provision at issue here does not contain the language "directly or indirectly" and, thus, is more narrow in scope that [sic] that addressed in *Shenandoah*.

[30] [18] Del. Supr., 474 A.2d 133 (1984).

[31] [19] *Id.* at 135-36.

[32] [20] *Id.* at 136 (quoting *Orzeck v. Englehart*, Del. Supr. 195 A.2d 375, 378 (1963)).

decision is enclosed.

ORDER

For the reasons set forth in the Memorandum Opinion dated May 2, 2001, defendants' motion for partial summary judgment as to Count II of the Amended Complaint is GRANTED.

IT IS SO ORDERED.

§ 4.05 PREFERRED STOCK DIVIDEND PROVISIONS

State corporation statutes generally provide that dividends can be paid only out of funds legally available for that purpose. It is for that reason that paragraph (b)(1) of the above resolutions creating the Series A Preferred Stock states that cash dividends are to be paid "out of the surplus or net profits of Corporation legally available for dividends." Moreover, the resolutions provide that such dividends are to be paid only "when and as declared by the board of directors." Another formulation of that discretionary concept is that dividends are payable "if, as and when declared" by the board. There is thus no obligation on the part of the board to declare a dividend on the Series A Preferred Stock, and no corresponding right of a holder thereof to receive the same. Instead, the dividend decision is to be made by the directors exercising their business judgment. If, on the other hand, the Series A Preferred Stock terms were to require that the board pay dividends in the event that there were funds legally available therefor, a court would nevertheless be hesitant to enforce those terms. Although dictum in a Delaware Chancery Court opinion, *Leibert v. Grinnell Corp.*, 194 A.2d 846, 851 (Del. Ch. 1963), suggests that such a provision might be valid, it can be expected that a court would require the "clearest expression of intent" for the declaration and dividends to be mandatory. *Crocker v. Waltham Watch Co.*, 53 N.E.2d 230, 237 (Mass. 1944). Courts require this clarity because of strong policy considerations, best stated by Justice Holmes when he wrote that "even if there are net earnings, the holder of stock, preferred as well as common, is entitled to have a dividend declared only out of such part of them as can be applied to dividends consistently with a wise administration of a going concern." *Wabash R. Co. v. Barclay*, 280 U.S. 197, 203 (1930), quoted in *Baron v. Allied Artists Pictures Corp.*, 337 A.2d 653, 658–59 (Del. Ch. 1975), in which the Delaware Chancery Court stated "[t]he determination as to when and in what amounts a corporation may prudently distribute its assets by way of dividends rests in the honest discretion of the directors in the performance of [their] fiduciary duty."

Paragraph (b)(1) of the Series A Preferred Stock terms set forth above also provides that dividends thereon shall be cumulative; and articulates what is meant thereby, namely that the "right" of the holders thereof to unpaid dividends adds up or, accumulates. This is supplemented by a provision that prohibits dividend payments on, or repurchases of, junior stock while there are unpaid cumulative dividends. Although such provisions can benefit the holders of the preferred shares, the existence of a significant amount of unpaid cumulative dividends adversely affects the junior stock. (It was for this reason that in March 2009 the US Treasury exchanged shares of cumulative preferred stock, which it had received from

American International Group Inc. ("AIG") in a 2008 TARP transaction, for shares of a non-cumulative preferred which the Treasury intended subsequently to exchange for shares of common stock of AIG.) The *Guttman* case below explains the legal effect of non-cumulative preferred stock dividend provisions, which are in stark contrast with the Series A cumulative provisions.

GUTTMANN v. ILLINOIS CENTRAL R. CO.

United States Court of Appeals, Second Circuit
189 F.2d 927 (1951)

FRANK, CIRCUIT JUDGE

The trial court's findings of facts — which are amply supported by the evidence and unquestionably are not "clearly erroneous" — establish that the directors acted well within their discretion in withholding declarations of dividends on the non-cumulative preferred stock up to the year 1948. In so holding, we assume, arguendo, that, as plaintiff insists, the standard of discretion in weighing the propriety of the non-declaration of dividends on such preferred stock is far stricter than in the case of non-declaration of dividends on common stock. For, on the facts as found and on the evidence, we think the directors, in not declaring dividends on the preferred in the years 1937-1947, adopted a reasonable attitude of reluctant but contingent pessimism about the future, an attitude proper, in the circumstances, for persons charged, on behalf of all interests, with the management of this enterprise.[33]

The issue, then, is whether the directors could validly declare a dividend on the common stock in 1950 without directing that there should be paid (in addition to preferred dividends on the preferred for that year) alleged arrears of preferred dividends, the amount of which had been earned in 1942-1947 but remained undeclared and unpaid. To put it differently, we must decide whether (a) the directors had the power to declare such alleged arrears of dividends on the preferred and (b) whether they "abused" their discretion in declaring any dividend on the common without ordering the payment of those alleged arrears.

Our lode-star is *Wabash Railway Co. v. Barclay*, 280 U.S. 197, 50 S. Ct. 106, 74 L. Ed. 368, which dealt with the non-cumulative preferred stock of an Indiana railroad corporation. There were no controlling Indiana decisions or statutes on that subject. The United States Supreme Court was therefore obliged to interpret the contract according to its own notions of what the contract meant. We have a similar problem here, since there are no Illinois decisions or statutory provisions which control or guide us. Absent such decisions and statutes, we must take the

---

[33] [2] That the directors were not acting in the interest of the common stockholders in disregard of the interest of the preferred appears from the following: The Union Pacific Railroad holds about 25% of the outstanding common stock (i.e., 348,700 shares out of a total of 1,357,994) and was therefore pretty obviously in control of the Board of Directors. Yet, that same Railroad holds about 52% of the outstanding preferred shares (i.e., 98,270 out of a total of 1 86,457). Union Pacific would plainly be better off if the plaintiff were successful in this suit.

The interest of the public was involved in the reduction of funded debt. For railroads with excessive fixed charges, in periods of stress tend to skimp maintenance and not to improve service.

Wabash opinion as expressing the correct interpretation of the rights of non-cumulative preferred stockholders of this Illinois company. For the difference between the language of the preferred stock here and that in Wabash seems to us to be of no moment.

In the *Wabash* case, plaintiffs, holders of non-cumulative preferred stock, sought an injunction preventing the defendant railroad company from paying dividends on the common stock[34] unless it first paid dividends on the non-cumulative preferred to the extent that the company, in previous years, had had net earnings available for that payment and that such dividends remained unpaid. The Court decided against the plaintiffs. It spoke of the fact that, in earlier years, "net earnings that could have been used for the payment were expended upon improvements and additions to the property and equipment of the road;" it held that the contract with the preferred meant that "if those profits are justifiably applied by the directors to capital improvements and no dividend is declared within the year, the claim for that year is gone and cannot be asserted at a later date." We take that as a ruling that the directors were left with no discretion ever to pay any such dividend. For if they had had that discretion, it would surely have been an "abuse" to pay dividends on the common while disregarding the asserted claim of the non-cumulative preferred to back dividends. Indeed, the plaintiff in the instant case contends that a payment of common dividends, whenever there is such a discretion, constitutes an unlawful "diversion;" and such a "diversion" would be an "abuse" of discretion.[35]

Plaintiff, however, seeks to limit the effect of the *Wabash* ruling to instances where the net earnings, for a given year, which could have been paid to the non-cumulative preferred, have once been expended justifiably for "capital improvements" or "additions to the property or equipment." He would have us treat the words "non-cumulative" as if they read "cumulative if earned except only when the earnings are paid out for capital additions." He argues that the *Wabash* ruling has no application when net earnings for a given year are legitimately retained for any one of a variety of other corporate purposes, and when in a subsequent year it develops that such retention was not necessary. We think the attempted distinction untenable. It ascribes to the Supreme Court a naive over-estimation of the importance of tangibles (because they can be touched and seen) as contrasted with intangibles. Suppose the directors of a corporation justifiably invested the retained earnings for the year 1945 in land which, at the time, seemed essential or highly desirable for the company's future welfare. Suppose that, in 1948, it turned out that the land so purchased was not necessary or useful, and that the directors thereupon caused it to be sold. Plaintiff's position compels the implied concession that the proceeds of such a sale would never be available for payment of so-called arrears of unpaid non-cumulative preferred dividends, and that the directors would forever lack all discretion to pay them.[36] We fail to see any intelligible difference between

[34] [5] And on a class of preferred stock having rights junior to those of the preferred stock held by the plaintiffs.

[35] [6] This becomes the more evident when it is noted that the plaintiff asserts that "non-cumulative" means in effect, "cumulative if earned." For directors have no discretion to pay common dividends without paying arrears of cumulative preferred dividends.

[36] [7] Were plaintiff to contend that the proceeds of such a sale are available for preferred dividends

(1) such a situation[37] and (2) one where annual earnings are properly retained for any appropriate corporate purpose, and where in a later year the retention proves wholly unnecessary.[38] There is no sensible ground for singling out legitimate capital outlays, once made, as the sole cause of the irrevocable destruction of the claims of the preferred. We do not believe that the Supreme Court gave the contract with the preferred such an irrational interpretation. It simply happened that in the *Wabash* case the earnings had been used for capital additions, and that, accordingly, the court happened to mention that particular purpose. Consequently, we think that the Court, in referring to that fact, did not intend it to have any significance. We disregard the decisions of the New Jersey courts, and the decision of the Ninth Circuit, since we think they are at odds with the rationale of the *Wabash* decision.

Here we are interpreting a contract into which uncoerced men entered. Nothing in the wording of that contract would suggest to an ordinary wayfaring person the existence of a contingent or inchoate right to arrears of dividends.[39] The notion that such a right was promised is, rather, the invention of lawyers or other experts, a notion stemming from considerations of fairness, from a policy of protecting investors in those securities. But the preferred stockholders are not — like sailors or idiots or infants — wards of the judiciary. As courts on occasions have quoted or paraphrased ancient poets, it may not be inappropriate to paraphrase a modern poet, and to say that "a contract is a contract is a contract." To be sure, it is an overstatement that the courts never do more than carry out the intentions of the parties: In the interest of fairness and justice, many a judge-made legal rule does impose, on one of the parties to a contract, obligations which neither party actually contemplated and as to which the language of the contract is silent. But there are limits to the extent to which a court may go in so interpolating rights and obligations which were never in the parties' contemplation. In this case we consider those limits clear.

In sum, we hold that, since the directors did not "abuse" their discretion in withholding dividends on the non-cumulative preferred for any past years, (a) no right survived to have those dividends declared, and (b) the directors had no discretion whatever to declare those dividends subsequently.

---

he would logically be required to contend that reserves for depreciation of capital assets are similarly available. For such reserves constitute, in effect, a repayment of investment in capital.

[37] [8] Or one where, in our supposititious case, the corporation, no longer needing the land, could easily sell it at a handsome figure.

[38] [9] The attempted distinction would also come to this: (a) The noncumulative preferred irrevocably loses all rights to a dividend as of a given year, if the earnings for that year are invested in fixed capital, but (b) has an inchoate right in the form of a sort of contingent credit if those earnings are reasonably retained for future investments which are never made and which thereafter show up as wholly unnecessary. This is to say that the preferred take the risk of loss of a dividend as of a year in which it is earned when there is a reasonable need for a present capital investment, but no such risk if there is a present reasonable likelihood of a need for such an investment in the future, which later appears undesirable. We see no rational basis for such a distinction.

[39] [13] Berle, a most brilliant legal commentator on corporate finance, who may be credited with the authorship of plaintiff's basic contention, admitted that "popular interpretation," including that of "investors and businessmen," holds "non-cumulative" to mean "that dividends on non-cumulative preferred stock, once passed or omitted, are 'dead'; can never be made up." *See* Berle, Non-Cumulative Preferred Stock, 23 Columbia Law Review (1923) 358, 36-365.

From the point of view of the preferred stockholders, the bargain they made may well be of a most undesirable kind. Perhaps the making of such bargains should be prevented. But, if so, the way to prevent them is by legislation, or by prophylactic administrative action authorized by legislation, as in the case of the S.E.C. in respect of securities, including preferred stocks, whether cumulative or non-cumulative, issued by public utility holding companies or their subsidiaries. The courts are not empowered to practice such preventive legal medicine, and must not try to revise, extensively, contracts already outstanding and freely made by adults who are not incompetents.

Affirmed.

NOTES

(1) The following language is appropriate for resolutions creating a non cumulative preferred stock:

> Dividends on the Series B Preferred Stock shall not be cumulative. Holders of Series B Preferred Stock shall not be entitled to receive any dividends not declared by the Board of Directors or any duly authorized committee of the Board of Directors, and no interest, or sum of money in lieu of interest, shall be payable in respect of any dividend not so declared. If the Board of Directors does not declare a dividend on the Series B Preferred Stock to be payable in respect of any Dividend Period before the related Dividend Payment Date, such dividend will not accrue and the Company will have no obligation to pay a dividend for that Dividend Period on the Dividend Payment Date or at any future time, whether or not dividends on the Series B Preferred Stock are declared for any future Dividend Period. Holders of the Series B Preferred Stock shall not be entitled to any dividends, whether payable in cash, securities or other property, other than dividends (if any) declared and payable on the Series B Preferred Stock as specified in this Section.

(2) The existence of unpaid cumulative preferred stock dividends can be a significant impediment to a corporation's ability to obtain common stock equity at the very time additional capital is needed; however, the Board of Governors of the Federal Reserve System considers *non cumulative* preferred stock an appropriate level of regulatory capital for bank holding companies. The Board has stated that "by allowing the noncumulative waiver of dividends, noncumulative perpetual preferred securities avoid the accumulation of deferred dividends, which could possibly impede an issuer's ability to raise additional equity in times of stress" (letter dated January 23, 2006 to Wachovia Corporation).

§ 4.06 ADJUSTABLE DIVIDEND RATE PREFERRED STOCK

One result of the volatility of interest rates in the United States during the early 1980s was the use of adjustable rate preferred stock. The dividend rate on adjustable note stock is often tied to a U.S. Treasury Index and is adjustable quarterly between a minimum and maximum range. These securities are particularly attractive to corporate investors, because, irrespective of whether the stock has an adjustable rate, a corporation is generally entitled, based upon its ownership interest in the distributing corporation, to exclude from its taxable income a significant percentage of the dividends it receives.

§ 4.07 THE LIQUIDATION PREFERENCE

The provisions of the Series A Preferred Stock *supra,* which stock was distributed in a merger and held by the public, relating to its liquidation preference contain the following: "Neither the merger or consolidation of the corporation with another corporation nor the sale or lease of all or substantially all the assets of the Corporation shall be deemed to be a liquidation or dissolution or winding-up of the Corporation." The reason for the inclusion of that sentence or similar language in preferred stock provisions is that, in its absence, a substantial question can arise as to whether holders of preferred stock are entitled to their liquidation preference in the event of a merger or similar transaction.

ANDERSON v. CLEVELAND-CLIFFS IRON CO.

Ohio Court of Common Pleas
87 N.E.2d 384 (1948)

McNamee, Judge

Plaintiffs are the owners of 4,327 shares of the preferred stock of the old Cleveland-Cliffs Iron Company, defendant herein. The intervening petitioners seeking the same relief as plaintiffs, and upon identical grounds, are the owners of 1,270 shares of the preferred stock of defendant corporation. The individual defendants are directors of said corporation. On April 24, 1947, the directors of The Cleveland-Cliffs Iron Company approved an "Agreement of Consolidation" by the terms of which it was proposed to consolidate the assets and liabilities of the defendant corporation with the assets and liabilities of the Cliffs corporation in a new corporation also to be known as The Cleveland-Cliffs Iron Company.

The "Agreement of Consolidation" was submitted to and voted upon by the stockholders at a special meeting called for that purpose, on June 16, 1947. More than two-thirds of the voting power of the corporation approved the Agreement. The proposal also was approved by more than two-thirds of the voting power of the Cliffs Corporation. On June 9, 1947, the Agreement of Consolidation was declared effective by the respective Boards of Directors of the constituent corporations and filed in the office of the Secretary of State.

In their petition filed on July 7, 1947, plaintiffs seek an order restraining defendant from consummating the consolidation agreement and other equitable relief, but no application for a temporary restraining order was made prior to the filing of the Agreement of Consolidation with the Secretary of State.

Plaintiffs attack the Consolidation Agreement on two principal grounds:

1. That it is illegal as constituting a perversion of the purposes of the

consolidation statute (G.C. § 8623-67).

2. That the Consolidation Agreement was unfairly presented to the stockholders by the Board of Directors and officers of the corporation. It is claimed also that in the event the Court finds the Consolidation Agreement to be valid plaintiffs are entitled to receive the liquidation value of their stock including the dividend arrearages thereon in accordance with the provisions of their preferred share contracts.

. . . .

8. Plaintiffs assert they are entitled to specific performance of their preferred share contracts and ought to receive payment of the voluntary liquidation price of $128.66 per share because the consolidation effected a dissolution of the Iron Company within the meaning of the following provision of the shareholders' contract:

> Upon the dissolution, liquidation or winding up of the Corporation the holders of record of preferred shares shall be entitled to receive out of the assets of the Corporation, if such dissolution, liquidation or winding up be voluntary, an amount equal to $102.50 per share and no more, or if such dissolution, liquidation or winding up be involuntary, an amount equal to $100 per share and no more, in either case with all dividends accrued or in arrears, for each of their preferred shares, before any distribution of the assets shall be made to the holders of common shares.

It is held generally that upon a consolidation becoming effective, the constituent corporations are dissolved in the sense that the separate existence of each constituent terminates.

. . . .

In *Petry v. Harwood Electric Co.*, 280 Pa. 142, 124 A. 302, 303, 33 A.L.R. 1249, preferred shareholders of a constituent corporation sued for specific performance of their preferred share contracts which provided: "In case of the dissolution of the company, the preferred stock shall be first paid and redeemed at its par value, in preference to the common stock, out of the property or assets of the company."

The court held that the merger there under review worked a dissolution "so far as the preferred stockholders are concerned, and they, therefore, are entitled to receive payment according to the terms of their contract and out of the assets of the defendant."

The *Petry* case was followed in two Federal tax cases which applied the law of Pennsylvania. See *Pennsylvania Co. for Insurance v. Commissioner Internal Revenue*, 3 Cir., 75 F.2d 719; *J. M. Smucker Co. v. Keystone Stores Corporation*, D.C., 12 F. Supp. 286.

Except for the last two cited cases, the *Petry* case stands alone.

In *Windhurst v. Central Leather Co.*, 105 N.J. Eq. 621, 149 A. 36, affirmed, 107 N.J. Eq. 528, 153 A. 402, the opposite conclusion was reached.

In denying the preferred shareholders' request for specific performance in that case the court said: "It may appear, when superficially examined, as if the results and consequences of a merger are similar in some respects to a dissolution. For example, the name of one or both of the merging companies may be lost. The relation between the various stockholders of one of the corporations may be materially changed, as in the case here. But, on the other hand, the language of those sections which deal with mergers show that these changes are incident to the uniting of the two corporations. The members of the board are not continued as trustees, and the act does not provide that either of the corporations shall be dissolved; it is not provided that the board of either shall proceed to wind up its business and affairs. There is no provision for liquidation and distribution. On the contrary, the act says that the stock shall be delivered up for conversion into shares of the capital stock for the new creation. The very provision for appraisal proves that dissolution does not result. The plain meaning of the act is that the corporations are to be continued as a joint or consolidated whole."

In *Adams v. United States Distributing Corp.*, 184 Va. 134, 34 S.E.2d 244, 162 A.L.R. 1227, the Supreme Court of Virginia held that, upon a merger of their corporation with several others, preferred shareholders were not entitled to specific performance of their contracts. The court expressly stated its preference for the reasoning of the *Windhurst* case, *supra*, to that of the *Petry* case, *supra*.

In *Otis & Company v. Securities Exchange Commission*, 1945, 323 U.S. 624, 65 S. Ct. 483, 89 L. Ed. 511, the Supreme Court of the United States had before it a plan of simplification of capital structure of the United Light and Power Company of Maryland, which provided for the dissolution of the corporation and the distribution of its assets in a manner that failed to recognize the preferential rights of preferred shareholders upon statutory dissolution of the corporation. Preferred shareholders sought to enjoin the plan and demanded the liquidation preferences set forth in their contracts. In denying the relief sought the Supreme Court held that the results accomplished by the proposed liquidation could have been secured by merger or consolidation in which event the effects of statutory liquidation would have been avoided. In this connection the Court said:

> The Commission's order of March 20, 1941, for the liquidation and dissolution of Power was a step in the simplification of the holding company system which simplification was enjoined by section 11(b) (2) of the Act [15 U.S.C.A. § 79K (b) (2)]. Satisfaction of the great-grandfather clause might have been obtained in this or other holding company systems by an order for merger, consolidation or recapitalization between top holding companies or between associate companies in the lower tiers of the corporate hierarchy. Such procedure would avoid the liquidation of Power. *Cf. Windhurst v. Central Leather Co.*, 105 N.J. Eq. 621, 149 A. 36; *Porges v. Vadsco Sales Corporation*, Del. Ch., 32 A.2d 148, 151. The selection by the Commission of one method of system adjustment to accomplish simplification rather than another is an incident which ought not to affect rights. The exercise of legislative power by Congress through section 11(b)(2) to accomplish simplification as a matter of public policy and the Commission's administration of the Act by dissolution of this particular company results in a type of liquidation which is entirely distinct from the liquidation of the corporation, whether voluntary or involuntary' envisaged by the charter

provisions of Power for preferences to the senior stock.

323 U.S. at page 631, 65 S. Ct. at page 487, 89 L. Ed. 511.

While the last cited case is not precisely in point the Supreme Court's apparent approval of the doctrine of the *Windhurst* case is significant.

Wholly apart from precedential considerations it is clear that the term "dissolution" as used in the preferred shareholders contract means statutory dissolution. The phrase "holders of record of preferred shares" and the words "holders of common shares" refer to all of the shareholders. Likewise the designation of amounts to be distributed to the preferred shareholders "*before* any distribution of the assets shall be made to the holders of common shares" (emphasis supplied) contemplates a contingency requiring complete distribution of assets to all of the shareholders. Upon consolidation of a corporation there is no complete distribution of assets to all of the shareholders of the constituent companies. The shares of those approving the agreement are transmuted into shares or other considerations of the new company and dissenting shareholders are entitled to the fair cash value of their shares, which may be collected as a debt.

Section 8623-68 provides, in part:

> When the agreement of consolidation is signed, acknowledged and filed as required in the preceding section the separate existence of the constituent corporations shall cease, and the constituent corporation shall become a single corporation in accordance with the said agreement, possessing all the rights, privileges, powers, franchises and immunities as well of a public as of a private nature, and being subject to all the liabilities and duties of each of such corporations so consolidated; and all property, real, personal and mixed, and all debts and liabilities due on whatever account, and all other things in action of or belonging to each of such corporations shall be vested in the consolidated corporation, and all property, rights, privileges, powers, franchises, and immunities and all and every other interest shall thereafter be as effectually the property of the consolidated corporation as fully as they were the property of the several and respective constituent corporations.

The foregoing section provides that upon consolidation the separate existence of the constituent corporations shall cease but it also provides that the constituent corporations shall become a single corporation. The constituent corporations continue to function as components of a consolidated whole. The properties of the constituents retain their character as corporate property. The privileges, immunities, rights, powers and franchises of each constituent continue as corporate attributes. The duties and liabilities of the constituent corporations continue to exist as corporate duties and liabilities. A distribution of corporate assets to all of the individual owners thereof would defeat the purpose of the consolidation statute. The necessity for such distribution arises where there is a complete cessation of the business and economic functions of the corporation concomitant with its legal demise. Until this occurs there is no occasion for a division of the corporate net assets among the shareholders. But when this contingency arises the preferred shareholders are entitled to their preferential rights in such distribution by virtue of the terms of the contract hereinabove set forth. In the opinion of the Court the consolidation did not effect "dissolution" of the defendant corporation within the meaning of that term as used in the liquidating clause of the shareholders contracts.

Both reason and the weight of authority require a denial of the plaintiffs prayer for specific performance.

. . . .

ROBINSON v. T.I.M.E.-DC, INC.

United States District Court, Northern District of Texas
566 F. Supp. 1077 (1983)

WOODWARD, CHIEF JUDGE

The above case came on for trial on March 29, 1983 with all attorneys and parties present. The case was tried before the court without a jury on March 29, 30, 31, and April 1, 1983, and after hearing and considering the pleadings, the evidence, and the briefs and arguments of the parties, the court files this memorandum opinion which shall constitute the court's findings of fact and conclusions of law.

The court has jurisdiction under 28 U.S.C. § 1331. The case was originally filed in the Eastern District of Tennessee and transferred by that Court to this Court for all proceedings.

The plaintiff, Jack Robinson, was at one time the owner of approximately 29,000 shares of preferred stock in T.I.M.E.-DC as well as some common stock in T.I.M.E.-DC. T.I.M.E.-DC was at one time one of the largest trucking firms in the industry in the United States and operated on a nationwide basis.

Plaintiff brings this suit in the form of a derivative stockholder's action and in addition to T.I.M.E.-DC, has named as defendants herein the members of the board of directors of T.I.M.E.-DC, and certain other corporations, to-wit: NLI; National City Lines; Contran Corporation; and Contran Holding Company. Mr. Harold Simmons became affiliated with T.I.M.E.-D.C. in November of 1980 and at about that time became chairman of its board of directors. The other individual defendants are the other members of the board of T.I.M.E.-DC.

Mr. Simmons is the trustee, for the benefit of his children, of the Simmons Trust, which owns 99% of Contran Corporation, which has now been merged with Contran Holding Company. The Simmons Trust is deemed to have control of Contran Corporation as well as National City Lines, Inc. National City Lines, Inc. owns 82% of the stock in NLI, a corporation, as well as various percentages of shares in other affiliated corporations which are not parties to this case. National City Lines, Inc. acquired control of T.I.M.E.-D.C. in 1980, at or about the time that Mr. Simmons became the chairman of the board of T.I.M.E.-DC.

In addition to its nation-wide trucking activities, T.I.M.E.- D.C. also had a retail tire outlet and engaged in the special commodities trucking activities, which involved an independent trucker hauling on behalf of T.I.M.E.-DC a full truck load of commodities that T.I.M.E. was unable to handle.

After the new board of directors was formed for T.I.M.E.-DC in late 1980, the corporation known as NLI was incorporated as a wholly owned subsidiary of T.I.M.E.-DC and T.I.M.E.-DC conveyed its real estate holdings to NLI on or about December 31, 1980.

On January 16, 1981, at a meeting of the board of directors of T.I.M.E.-DC, approval was given to the transfer of the corporate real estate holdings to NLI. On January 19th, a press release was issued by T.I.M.E.-DC informing the public of this transaction and indicating that T.I.M.E.-DC, which owned all of the stock in NLI, would "spin-off" its stock ownership in NLI to T.I.M.E.-DC's common stockholders. The plaintiff was aware of the information contained in this press release. He testified that he received a copy of it soon thereafter. (Tr. 427).

Shortly after the board meeting on January 16, 1981, the management of T.I.M.E.-DC entered into negotiations with East Texas Motor Freight (E.T.M.F.) in which the parties contemplated a merger of the two corporations. These negotiations continued until sometime in early May of 1981, when the parties were unable to reach a final agreement and the negotiations were canceled.

On May 21, 1981, a meeting of the shareholders of T.I.M.E.-DC was held. At that time, the stockholders were made aware of the cessation of negotiations between T.I.M.E.-DC and E.T.M.F. and although there were discussions concerning the transfer of the real estate interests from T.I.M.E.-DC to NLI and the prospective spin-off, no further corporate action was taken at that time, as shown by the minutes of this meeting (Defendants' Ex. 10).

On June 15, 1981 a meeting was held with the board of directors of T.I.M.E.-DC and at that time the board ratified the conveyance of all of the real estate interests of T.I.M.E.-DC to NLI in return for the receipt by T.I.M.E.-DC of all of the common stock of NLI. The board further approved a plan to spin-off this NLI stock on a share-to-share basis to T.I.M.E.-DC's common stockholders. The meeting was continued to June 19, 1981, and on that date a press release was issued to the public setting forth these actions. (Defendants' Ex. 13). Notice was also sent to the stockholders of T.I.M.E.-DC informing these stockholders of the action of the board pertaining to the stock dividend and spin-off. (Defendants' Exs. 14 and 15).

The evidence indicates that the real estate transferred to NLI had a book value (cost less depreciation) of approximately $20 million dollars, but possibly an actual market value of approximately $40 million dollars.

The plaintiff, Mr. Robinson, had visited with one of the officers of T.I.M.E.-DC just prior to the stockholders' meeting on May 21, 1981, seeking information concerning the above proposed actions, and voiced the complaint that it was his feeling the plan was inequitable and illegal. His principal complaint was that, although he would receive the arrearage on the accrued cumulative dividends on his 29,000 shares of preferred stock in T.I.M.E.-DC, which at that time constituted 90¢; per share, he would not be allowed to convert his preferred stock to common stock in T.I.M.E.-DC and participate in the dividend of NLI common stock unless he forfeited his right to the preferred cumulative dividend. He also made this protest at the meeting of the stockholders on May 21st, as appears in the minutes of that meeting. (Defendants' Ex. 10).

Mr. Robinson's complaint and disagreement with the plan was made known to Mr. Harold Simmons, chairman of the board of T.I.M.E.- DC, and upon his direction the plans and record dates were changed so as to permit T.I.M.E.-DC's preferred stockholders to both receive their 90¢; per share cumulative preferred dividends and, if they so desired, also convert their preferred shares into common stock of T.I.M.E.-DC and thereby receive the stock dividend of NLI common stock in the spin-off. The Certificate of Incorporation of T.I.M.E.-DC relating to the preferred stock in T.I.M.E.-DC not only provided that preferred shares would be guaranteed a 72¢; per share dividend each year before any common stock dividend could be declared, but also provided that upon the liquidation of T.I.M.E.-DC each preferred stockholder would receive $10 in cash. (Defendants' Ex. 1). Each preferred share was also redeemable by T.I.M.E.-DC at a price of $20 per share. (Defendants' Ex. 1).

Mr. Robinson elected to both take his accrued cumulative preferred dividends at a rate of 90¢; per share on his preferred stock and then convert his preferred stock to common stock in T.I.M.E.-DC, and thereby receive the common stock dividend in NLI pursuant to the spin-off arrangements.

. . . .

. . . [P]laintiff alleges that there has been a liquidation of T.I.M.E.-DC as a viable corporation. Admittedly, when T.I.M.E.- DC's real estate was transferred to NLI, a wholly-owned corporation, this may have technically reduced materially the assets of T.I.M.E.- D.C. by at least $20 million dollars if book value is used and perhaps by as much as $40 million dollars if actual market value is used. Solely the transfer to NLI of T.I.M.E.-DC's real estate did not in fact reduce T.I.M.E.-DC's assets, as at that point in time, all NLI stock was still held by T.I.M.E.-DC. The contract between T.I.M.E.-DC and its preferred stockholders, which consisted of the Certificate of Incorporation of T.I.M.E.-DC, Inc., expressly states and provides on page 5, in paragraph (e), as follows:

> Neither the merger nor consolidation of the Corporation into or with any other corporation, nor the merger or consolidation of any other corporation into or with any other corporation into or with the Corporation, *nor a sale, transfer or lease of all or any part of the assets of the Corporation, shall be deemed to be a liquidation, dissolution, or winding up of the Corporation within the meaning of this paragraph (e).* (emphasis added).

Under Delaware law, the rights of shareholders are contract rights and to determine those rights the court must interpret the certificate of incorporation in accordance with the law of contracts. Preferred shareholders possess only those rights which are granted to them by the provisions embodied in the certificate of incorporation. *Id.*

When viewed in the context of the specific provision of the certificate of incorporation quoted above, it is clear that neither separately nor in conjunction did the transfer of T.I.M.E.-DC's real estate to NLI and the subsequent spin-off constitute a "liquidation" of T.I.M.E.-DC which would have entitled T.I.M.E.-DC's preferred shareholders to receive their $10 per share liquidation preference.

Further, the facts establish that after the transfer and spin-off, T.I.M.E.-DC continued as an operating corporation in the trucking industry, and it had assets remaining of more than $45 million. (Defendants' Ex. 31). There is no evidence that in their completion of the spin-off T.I.M.E.-DC's board of directors intended in any way to dissolve or wind up its corporate affairs. But on the contrary, it appears that all parties intended to continue to operate it as a viable corporation. Therefore, the transactions involving the spin-off of NLI stock do not constitute a basis for affording any relief to the plaintiff on the theory that such transactions constituted a liquidation of T.I.M.E.-DC which, had such liquidation occurred, would have entitled the preferred stockholders to receive their $10 per share liquidation preference.

Later, on April 1, 1982, the Teamsters Union struck T.I.M.E.-D.C. and effectively shut down its nation-wide operations. T.I.M.E.-D.C. did continue some of its minor operations, such as the retail tire business and the special commodities trucking operations, but otherwise it ceased doing business because of the strike. Realizing that the strike would be of a long duration, the board of directors and officers made a public decision to sell other assets of the corporation. As a matter of fact, approximately 90% of the entire rolling stock of T.I.M.E.-DC was sold. The court finds that this was a valid business transaction made within the sound judgment of the management of T.I.M.E.-DC in order to prevent the deterioration of its assets, to raise cash to provide security, and to take care of immediate corporate obligations.[40] The decision to sell this portion of the rolling stock, although it shut down the major trucking operations at the time, was caused not by the spin-off arrangement with NLI, but rather was the result of the strike, wholly divorced, separate, and apart from the spin-off. Even after these sales, there was not a liquidation or dissolution of the affairs of the corporation that would entitle recovery by plaintiff under his liquidation preference theory. Late in 1982, the strike was settled on terms acceptable to the management of T.I.M.E.-DC and beginning in the earlier part of this year, T.I.M.E.-DC again commenced trucking operations between Los Angeles and Seattle, and is gradually trying to regain its position as a major carrier in the industry. The assets of T.I.M.E.-DC were never distributed to its stockholders. Although income was practically nil, as compared to what it formerly had been, the management and board of directors of T.I.M.E.-DC took every reasonable action to preserve the assets of the corporation in order to permit it to be in a favorable position to commence operations when the strike ended, as now has occurred.

These sales of assets did not add up to a liquidation or dissolution of the corporate affairs of T.I.M.E.-DC and nothing in the provisions of the certificate of incorporation concerning preferred stock gave plaintiff the right to receive a $10 per share payment at the time of the spin-off, the sale of T.I.M.E.-DC's rolling stock, or at any other time to date.

---

[40] [1] The court does not have before it and hence expresses no view with regard to the question of whether the sales of T.I.M.E.-DC's rolling stock and the sales by NLI of real estate interests formerly belonging to T.I.M.E.-DC, both of which occurred following the Teamsters' strike, satisfied the requirements of § 271 of the Delaware Corporation Law. Sec. 271 requires that the majority of all outstanding stock of the corporation must vote to authorize the corporation's board to "sell, lease, or exchange all or substantially all of its property and assets" before any such action may be undertaken.

Plaintiff's complaint herein is with the transactions surrounding the spin-off.

. . . .

Therefore, all relief prayed for by plaintiff is hereby denied. A judgment will be entered accordingly.

LC CAPITAL MASTER FUND v. JAMES

Delaware Chancery Court
990 A.2d 435 (2010)

STRINE, VICE CHANCELLOR.

I. Introduction

Plaintiff LC Capital Master Fund, Ltd. ("LC Capital"), a preferred stockholder of QuadraMed Corporation ("QuadraMed"), seeks to enjoin the acquisition by defendant Francisco Partners II, L.P. ("Francisco Partners") of QuadraMed (the "Merger") because the consideration to be received by the preferred stockholders of QuadraMed does not exceed the "as if converted" value the preferred were contractually entitled to demand in the event of a merger. That "as if converted" value was based on a formula in the certificate of designation (the "Certificate") governing the preferred stock, and gave the preferred the bottom line right to convert into common at a specified ratio (the "Conversion Formula") and then receive the same consideration as the common in the Merger. The plaintiff purports to have the support of 95% of the preferred stockholders in seeking injunctive relief and I therefore refer to the plaintiff as the preferred stockholders.

Based on certain contractual rights that the preferred had in the event that a merger did not take place, the preferred stockholders argue that the QuadraMed board of directors (the "Board") had a fiduciary duty to allocate more of the merger consideration to the preferred. Notably, the preferred stockholders do not argue that the Board breached any fiduciary duty owed to all stockholders; in particular, they do not claim that the board did not fulfill its fiduciary duty to obtain the highest value reasonably attainable, a duty commonly associated with *Revlon.*[41] Rather, the preferred stockholders contend that the preferred stock has a strong liquidation preference and certain non-mandatory rights to dividends that the Board failed to accord adequate value, and that as a result of these *contractual* rights, the QuadraMed Board owed the preferred a *fiduciary* duty to accord it more than it was contractually entitled to receive by right in a merger. The preferred stockholders seek to enjoin the Merger because of this supposed breach of duty.

In this decision, I find that the preferred stockholders have not proven a reasonable probability of success on the merits of their fiduciary duty claim. Under Delaware law, a board of directors may have a gap-filling duty in the event that there is no objective basis to allocate consideration between the common and preferred stockholders in a merger. But, when a certificate of designations does not provide the preferred with any right to vote upon a merger, does not afford the preferred a right to claim a liquidation preference in a merger, but does provide the

---

[41] [2] Revlon, Inc. v. MacAndrews & Forbes Holdings, Inc., 506 A.2d 173 (Del.1986).

preferred with a contractual right to certain treatment in a merger, I conclude that a board of directors that allocates consideration in a manner fully consistent with the bottom-line contractual rights of the preferred need not, as an ordinary matter, do more. Consistent with decisions like . . . *In re Trados Incorporated Shareholder Litigation*,[42] once the QuadraMed Board honored the special contractual rights of the preferred, it was entitled to favor the interests of the common stockholders. By exercising its discretion to treat the preferred entirely consistently with the Conversion Formula the preferred bargained for in the Certificate, the QuadraMed Board acted equitably toward the preferred.

For that reason alone, I would deny the preliminary injunction. But, given that plaintiff LC Capital purports to represent 95% of the preferred stockholders, has an appraisal right, and an appraisal action is therefore easily maintainable, I would be reluctant to enjoin the transaction and thereby deprive the QuadraMed common stockholders, who under any reasonable measure are entitled to the bulk of the Merger consideration, from determining for themselves whether to accept the Merger. The balance of the equities in this unique context would seem to weigh in favor of requiring the preferred stockholders, who I have no doubt are unwilling to post a full injunction bond, to seek relief through appraisal or through an equitable action for damages.

In the pages that follow, I explain these reasons for denying the preliminary injunction motion in more detail.

II. Factual Background

* * *

Under the terms of the challenged merger agreement (the "Merger Agreement"), Francisco Partners will acquire QuadraMed at a price of $8.50 per share of common stock. The preferred stockholders will receive $13.7097 in cash in exchange for each share of preferred stock. The price for the preferred stock set forth in the Merger Agreement was pegged to the conversion right the Certificate granted to the preferred stockholders in the event of a merger. That conversion right allowed the preferred stockholders to convert their preferred shares into common shares and then to receive the same consideration as the common stock received in the merger. The conversion was determined by using the Conversion Formula of 1.6129 shares of preferred stock to one share of common stock. That is, in order to value the preferred stock, the merging parties agreed to simply cash out the preferred stock at the price the preferred stockholders would receive if they exercise their right to convert to common stock.

The preferred stockholders seek to enjoin the Merger on the grounds that the defendants breached their fiduciary duties of care and loyalty. But, the preferred stockholders do not allege that the defendants breached their *Revlon* duties as to *all* shareholders by approving a transaction that does not fully value QuadraMed as an entity. Instead, the preferred stockholders argue that the Merger consideration was unfairly allocated between the common and preferred stock. That is, the

[42] [4] [2009 Del. Ch. LEXIS 128 (July 24, 2009)].

preferred stockholders do not challenge the overall adequacy of the Merger consideration. Rather, the preferred stockholders claim that they simply did not receive a big enough slice of the pie because the Board allocated the Merger consideration to the preferred stock on an "as-if converted" basis, which the preferred stockholders believe understates the value of their shares.

1. The Rights of the Preferred Stockholders

Requesting a preliminary injunction is the only means the preferred stockholders have to block the transaction because, per the Certificate, the preferred stock does not have the right to vote on a merger. The circumstances in which the preferred stock has voting rights are limited to: (1) if the Certificate were to be amended in a way "that materially adversely affects the voting powers, rights or preferences" of the preferred stockholders; (2) if any class of shares with ranking before or in parity with the preferred stock were to be created; and (3) if the company were to incur "any long term, senior indebtedness of the Corporation in an aggregate principal amount exceeding $8,000,000. Relatedly, if four quarterly dividends are in arrears, the preferred stockholders can elect two substitute directors.

The Certificate includes a number of other rights for the preferred stock that are arguably relevant to the current dispute. As mentioned, the preferred stock has a dividend right. This provides for the payment of a dividend of $1.375 per year, but it is to be paid only "when, as and if authorized and declared" by the Board.

The Certificate also provides a liquidation preference of $25 (plus accrued dividends) for each share of preferred stock. But, the Certificate does not afford the preferred stock a right to force a liquidation. Most relevantly, the Certificate expressly provides that a merger does not trigger the preferred stock's liquidation preference.

The preferred stockholders also point out that the Certificate includes a mandatory conversion right that allows QuadraMed to force the preferred stockholders to convert into common shares. The preferred stockholders stress that this provision of the Certificate may only be used by QuadraMed to force conversion when the company's common stock hits a price of $25 per share, far above the $8.50 per common share Merger value. But, like the liquidation preference, the mandatory conversion provision does not have bite in a merger. That is, the Certificate does not provide that, in the event of a merger, the preferred stockholders must be converted at a formula that affords the preferred stockholders an implied common stock value of $25 per share.

To the contrary, in a merger, the preferred stockholders will receive either: 1) the consideration determined by the Board in a merger agreement; or 2) if the preferred choose, the right to convert their shares using the Conversion Formula into common shares and re[ceive] the same consideration as the common stockholders. The bottom line right of the preferred stockholders in a merger, therefore, is not tied to its healthy liquidation preference or the company's mandatory conversion strike price-it is simply the right to convert the shares into common stock at the Conversion Formula and then be treated pari passu with the common.

2. The Board's Decision To Accept Francisco Partners' Bid for QuadraMed

Over the years, QuadraMed received expressions of interest from a number of potential acquirors. From 2008 to date, QuadraMed has been seriously considering a sale. From early on in this strategic process, the preferred stockholders demanded a high price, even $25, for their stock, apparently under the mistaken view that they had a right to their liquidation preference in the event of a merger. Initially, some bidders indicated an interest in either meeting the preferred stockholders' asking price-which would mean paying much more for the preferred stock than the common-or at least allowing the preferred stock to remain outstanding after the consummation of a merger. For example, Francisco Partner's first bid for QuadraMed, made in October 2008, offered to acquire the company at $11 per share of common stock and to allow the preferred stock to remain outstanding. And, a later bid, received August 31, 2009 from a bidder referred to as "Bidder D" in the proxy materials, proposed acquiring QuadraMed for $10.00 per share of common stock, and $25.00 par value for each share of preferred stock. By "par value," Bidder D seems not to have meant to offer the preferred stockholders $25 per share in current value but a security with the future potential of reaching that value. But this was perhaps not as clearly expressed as it could have been.

As the negotiations continued, moreover, both Francisco Partners and Bidder D revised their offers downward. After several months of negotiating, Francisco Partners submitted a revised offer of $9.50 per share of common stock, with the requirement that the preferred stock be cashed-out. In March 2009, the Board rejected this offer, and negotiations with Francisco Partners were suspended. And, after its initial approach, Bidder D made very plain its earlier position and explained that it "never intended to offer face value" for the preferred stock and was instead interested in paying $10 per share of common stock and reaching agreement with the holders of preferred stock on the terms of a debt instrument with a $25 face value, but a present value equal to $10 per share on an as-if converted basis. Therefore, the treatment of the preferred stock and common stock under Bidder D's initial proposal and under the Merger is not as different as at first appears.

In light of the various bids being made for the company, QuadraMed's outside counsel, Crowell & Moring, LLP ("Crowell & Moring"), sent the QuadraMed Board a memorandum on September 1, 2009 addressing the legal issues relating to apportioning merger consideration between the common stock and preferred stock (the "September 2009 Memorandum"). In substance, the September 2009 Memorandum was Crowell & Moring's distillation of and update to a memorandum that Richards, Layton & Finger, P.A. ("Richards Layton"), QuadraMed's Delaware counsel, had prepared in June 2006. In 2006, while QuadraMed was in negotiations over a possible acquisition by a private equity firm, referred to as "Bidder B" in QuadraMed's proxy materials, Richards Layton authored a memorandum, dated June 22, 2006, that provided a general overview of the legal authority relevant to allocating merger consideration between common stock and preferred stock in a merger. The memorandum was addressed to counsel, Crowell & Moring, not the QuadraMed Board Crowell & Moring's September 2009 Memorandum summarized Richards Layton's 2006 advice and discussed this court's April 2009 decision *In re*

Appraisal of Metromedia Int'l Group, Inc.,[43] which addressed the allocation of merger consideration between common and preferred stock in the context of an appraisal action.

The QuadraMed Board formed a special committee of independent directors (the "Special Committee") to evaluate the various bids. QuadraMed's Board is comprised of six individuals: Duncan James, William Jurika, Lawrence English, James Peebles, Robert Miller, and Robert Pevenstein (collectively, the "Special Committee members"). The Special Committee was comprised of Jurika, English, Peebles, Miller, and Pevenstein-that is, all of the Special Committee members except James, who was also QuadraMed's Chief Executive Officer. With the exception of Jurika, who owns over 650,000 shares of QuadraMed common stock, the Special Committee members hold a nominal amount of QuadraMed shares and in the money stock options. The preferred stockholders have not presented any evidence that these members' holdings of QuadraMed shares and options constitute a material portion of their personal wealth.

In early autumn 2009, after Bidder D's approach in August, QuadraMed's investment bankers shopped the deal. At this time, Francisco Partners made a second bid, offering $8.50 per share of common stock and requiring the cash-out of the preferred stock on an as-if converted basis, which yielded a value of $13.7097 per preferred share. Francisco Partners insisted on cashing out the preferred stock because it did not want to bear the risk of a voluntary conversion of the preferred stock into common stock after the Merger. The evidence also indicates that Francisco Partners wanted to increase QuadraMed's borrowing after the Merger, and therefore wanted to eliminate the preferred stock because the Certificate gives the preferred stock a right to vote on any incurrence of debt in excess of $8,000,000.

Because the preferred stockholders were demanding more consideration than the common stock, one of the questions before the Special Committee was what fiduciary duties it owed to the common stock and preferred stock when allocating the proposed Merger's consideration. The evidence indicates that the Special Committee carefully considered the duties it owed to both the preferred and common stockholders, and was concerned about any perception that it was favoring one class over the other. In a series of meetings, the Special Committee reviewed the bids, and at those meetings, QuadraMed's counsel informed the Special Committee that the Board could adopt a merger agreement that cashed out the preferred stockholders, and that, if the Board respected the bottom line contractual rights of the preferred stockholders in a merger, it did not have to allocate additional value to the preferred stockholders. Indeed, Crowell & Moring said that the Board had to be careful about giving the preferred stockholders more unless there were special reasons to do so. Crowell & Moring also reported that Francisco Partner's counsel, Shearman & Sterling, LLP, had also reached the conclusion that a cash out of the preferred stock at closing was permissible under Delaware law, and that Francisco Partners would not insist on an "appraisal out" provision in the Merger Agreement so as to satisfy any concerns the Special Committee might have regarding the treatment of the preferred stock.

[43] [24] 971 A.2d 893 (Del.Ch.2009).

Meanwhile, Bidder D had been attempting to persuade the preferred stockholders to take a new debt security with a current value equal to what the common would receive but with a future upside. But, Bidder D found it "extremely difficult" to convince the holders of preferred stock to exchange their stock for a new debt security, and its bid foundered. Once Bidder D withdrew its offer on November 22, 2009, Francisco Partners became the only remaining bidder for QuadraMed. Although the Special Committee resisted cashing out the preferred stock for some time, the Committee eventually relented once it became clear that Francisco Partners would not do a deal that allowed QuadraMed's preferred stock to survive the Merger.

On December 7, 2009, a Special Committee meeting was held to consider approval of the Merger with Francisco Partners. At that meeting, Piper Jaffray, QuadraMed's financial advisor, presented an opinion that $8.50 per common share was fair to the common stockholders from a financial point of view. There was no separate opinion addressing the fairness of the Merger to the preferred stockholders. After deliberation, the Special Committee unanimously approved the Merger with Francisco Partners. From the meeting minutes, it appears that the Special Committee was wary of doing a deal that allocated more consideration to the preferred stock than to the common stock for two reasons: (1) shifting additional merger consideration to the preferred stock would cause the holders of common stock, who were the only stockholders who had a right to vote on the Merger, to vote against the transaction; and (2) there was no special reason to deviate from the Conversion Formula provided in the Certificate for allocating consideration to the preferred stock.

In the latter regard, it is fair to say that the Special Committee's equitable heartstrings were not moved to bestow upon the preferred stockholders anything better than receipt of the same treatment as the common stockholders on an as-if converted basis. Had a particular bidder insisted, after negotiations with the preferred, on doing a deal with differential consideration, the Special Committee would seem to have had an open and receptive mind if the proposal offered a more favorable valuation to all stockholders. But even then, the Special Committee, I infer, would have harbored a concern if the allocation system strayed too far (in either direction) from the Conversion Formula in the Certificate.

III. Legal Analysis

* * *

B. The Preferred Stockholders Have Not Met Their Burden To Justify Enjoining The Merger

1. The Preferred Stockholders Have Not Shown That The QuadraMed Board Likely Breached Its Fiduciary Duties By Allocating To The Preferred Stock The Bottom Line Consideration Contractually Owed To Them

The contending arguments of the parties are starkly divergent. The preferred stockholders, pointing to the decisions of this court in *Jedwab v. MGM Grand*

Hotels, Inc.[44] and *In re FLS Holdings, Inc. Shareholders Litigation*,[45] argue that the QuadraMed board had the duty to make a "fair" allocation of the Merger consideration between the common and preferred stockholders. To do this fairly, the preferred stockholders argue that the board had to set up some form of negotiating agent, with the duty and discretion to exert leverage on behalf of the preferred stockholders in the allocation process. This need, the preferred stockholders say, is heightened because of an unsurprising fact: the directors of QuadraMed own common stock and do not own preferred stock. Indeed, the preferred stockholders say, every member of the Special Committee owned common stock and one member, Jurika, owned over five million dollars worth. How, they say, could such directors fairly balance the interests of the preferred against their own interest in having the common get as much as possible? At the very least, the preferred imply, the QuadraMed Board should have charged certain directors with representing the preferred, and enabled them to retain qualified legal and financial advisors to argue for the preferred and to value the preferred based on its unique contractual rights and their economic value.

By contrast, the defendants say that the QuadraMed Board discharged any fiduciary obligation of fairness it had by: 1) fulfilling its *Revlon* obligations to all equity holders, including the preferred, to seek the highest reasonably available price for the corporation; and 2) allocating to the preferred the percentage of value equal to their bottom line right, in the event of a merger, to convert and receive the same consideration as the common. Given that the preferred stockholders had no contractual right to impede, vote upon, or receive consideration higher than the common stockholders in the Merger, the defendants argue that the Board's decision to accord them the value that the preferred were entitled to contractually demand in the event of a merger cannot be seen as unfair. That is especially so when the preferred bases its claim for a higher value entirely on contractual provisions that do not guarantee them any share of the company's cash flows if the company does not liquidate, and that do not even condition a merger on the payment of any accrued, but undeclared dividends. Indeed, because the QuadraMed Board honored all contractual rights belonging to the preferred, the defendants say it was the duty of the Board not to go further and bestow largesse on the preferred stock at the expense of the common stock.

The defendants cite *In re Trados Inc. Shareholder Litigation*[46]. . . for the proposition that it was the Board's duty, once it had ensured treatment of the preferred in accord with their contractual rights, to act in the best interests of the common. To have added a dollop of crème fraiche on top of the merger consideration to be offered to the preferred would itself, in these circumstances, have amounted to a breach of fiduciary duty. Finally, the defendants argue that even if there is a case where directors might be found to be "interested" in a transaction simply because they own common stock and no preferred stock, this is not that case. For example, a sizable premium to the preferred of 10% to 20% would cause a reduction in the common stock price of approximately $1.30 to $2.60 per share. Because four

---

[44] [38] 509 A.2d 584 (Del.Ch.1986).

[45] [39] [1993 Del.Ch. LEXIS 57 (Apr. 2, 1993)].

[46] [40] [2009 Del.Ch. LEXIS 128 (July 24, 2009)].

of the five Special Committee members own very modest common stock stakes, this would reduce those Special Committee members' Merger take by, at most, several thousand dollars, an amount the preferred stockholders have done nothing to show is material to these directors.

In my view, the defendants have the better of the arguments. After reviewing the evidence, I perceive no basis to find that the directors sought to advantage the common stockholders at the unfair expense of the preferred stockholders. What the preferred stockholders complain about is that the directors did not perceive themselves as having a duty to allocate more Merger consideration to the preferred than the preferred could demand as an entitlement under the Certificate. Had the Board been advised properly and had the right mindset, the preferred stockholders say, they would have given weight to various contractual rights of the preferred, such as their liquidation preference rights, and determined that on the basis of those rights, they should get a higher share than the Certificate guaranteed they could demand. Ideally, in fact, the Board should have employed a bargaining agent on their behalf to vigorously contend for the proposition that the largest part of the roast should be put on the preferred stockholders' plate.

In arguing for this, I admit that the preferred stockholders can point to cases in which broad language supporting something like a duty of this kind to preferred stockholders was articulated. In *FLS Holdings*, for example, Chancellor Allen found that:

> FLS was represented in its negotiations . . . exclusively by directors who . . . owned large amounts of common stock. . . . No independent adviser or independent directors' committee was appointed to represent the interests of the preferred stock who were in a conflict of interest situation with the common. . . . [N]o mechanism employing a truly independent agency on behalf of the preferred was employed before the transaction was formulated. Only the relatively weak procedural protection of an investment banker's ex post opinion was available to support the position that the final allocation was fair.[47]

Likewise, in *Jedwab*, Chancellor Allen said that directors owe preferred stockholders a fiduciary duty to "exercise appropriate care in negotiating [a] proposed merger" in order to ensure that preferred shareholders receive their " 'fair' allocation of the proceeds of [a] merger."[48]

A close look at those cases, however, does not buttress the preferred stockholders' arguments. Notable in both cases was the absence of any contractual provision such as the one that exists in this case. That is, from what one can tell from *FLS Holdings* and *Jedwab*, there was no objective contractual basis-such as the conversion mechanism here-in either of those cases for the board to allocate the merger consideration between the preferred and the common. In the absence of such a basis, the only protection for the preferred is if the directors, as the backstop fiduciaries managing the corporation that sold them their shares, figure out a fair

---

[47] [42] [1993 Del. Ch. LEXIS 57].

[48] [43] 509 A.2d at 594.

way to fill the gap left by incomplete contracting. Otherwise, the preferred would be subject to entirely arbitrary treatment in the context of a merger.

The broad language in *FLS Holdings* and *Jedwab* must, I think, be read against that factual backdrop. I say so for an important reason. Without this factual context, those opinions are otherwise in sharp tension with the great weight of our law's precedent in this area. In his recent decision in *Trados*, Chancellor Chandler summarized the weight of authority very well:

> Generally the rights and preferences of preferred stock are contractual in nature. This Court has held that directors owe fiduciary duties to preferred stockholders as well as common stockholders where the right claimed by the preferred "is not to a preference as against the common stock but rather a right shared equally with the common." Where this is not the case, however, "generally it will be the duty of the board, where discretionary judgment is to be exercised, to prefer the interests of the common stock-as the good faith judgment of the board sees them to be-to the interests created by the special rights, preferences, etc., of preferred stock, where there is a conflict." Thus, in circumstances where the interests of the common stockholders diverge from those of the preferred stockholders, it is *possible* that a director could breach her duty by improperly favoring the interests of the preferred stockholders over those of the common stockholders.[49]

* * *

This, of course, is not to say that the QuadraMed Board did not owe the preferred stockholders fiduciary duties in connection with the Merger. The Board certainly did. But those were the duties it also owed to the common. In the context of a sale of a company, those are the duties articulated in *Revlon* and its progeny; namely, to take reasonable efforts to secure the highest price reasonably available for the corporation. Notably, the preferred stockholders do not argue that the Board fell short of its obligations in this regard. They simply want more of the proceeds than they are guaranteed by the Certificate. But I do not believe that the Board acted wrongly in viewing itself as under no obligation to satisfy that desire.

* * *

Another counterproductive consequence would result from accepting the preferred stockholders' arguments. For its entire history, our corporate law has tried to insulate the good faith decisions of disinterested corporate directors from judicial second-guessing for well-known policy reasons. The business judgment rule embodies that policy judgment. When mergers and acquisitions activity became a more salient and constant feature of corporate life, our law did not cast aside the values of the business judgment rule. Rather, to deal with the different interests manager-directors may have in the context of responding to a hostile acquisition offer or determining which friendly merger partner to seek out, our law has consistently provided an incentive for the formation of boards comprised of a

---

[49] [44] *Trados*, [2009 Del. Ch. LEXIS 128] (quoting *Jedwab*, 509 A.2d at 594, and *Equity-Linked Investors, L.P. v. Adams*, 705 A.2d 1040, 1042 (Del. Ch. 1997)).

majority of independent directors who could act independently of management and pursue the best interests of the corporation and its stockholders This impetus also recognized that managers' incentives and the temptations they face, when combined with fallible human nature, make it advisable to have independent directors to monitor the corporation's approach to law compliance, risk, and executive compensation. Consistent with this viewpoint, it has been thought that having directors who actually owned a meaningful, long-term common stock stake was a useful thing, because that would align the interests of the independent directors with the common stockholders and give them a personal incentive to fulfill their duties effectively.

To hold that independent directors are disabled from the protections of the business judgment rule when addressing a merger because they own common stock, and not the corporation's preferred stock, is not, therefore, something that should be done lightly. Corporate law must work in practice to serve the best interests of society and investors in creating wealth. Director compensation is already a difficult enough issue to address without adding on the need to ponder whether the independent directors need to buy or receive as compensation a share of any preferred stock issuance made by the corporation, for fear that, if they do not have an equally-weighted portfolio of some kind, they will not be able to impartially balance questions that potentially affect the common and preferred stockholders in different ways. Adhering to the rule of . . . *Trados*, and other similar cases, which hold that it is the duty of directors to pursue the best interests of the corporation and its common stockholders, if that can be done faithfully with the contractual promises owed to the preferred, avoids this policy dilemma. Admittedly, it does not solve for certain situations that directors might create themselves by authorizing multiple and sometimes exotic classes of common stock, situations that have led this court to, as a matter of necessity, consider the directors' portfolio balance, but it at least does not exacerbate the already complex challenge of compensating independent directors in a sensible way. And, given the unique nature of preferred stock and the often-fraught circumstances that lead to its issuance, our law should be chary to somehow suggest that otherwise independent directors should be receiving shares of this kind at the risk of facing being called "non-independent" or, worse, being deemed by loose reasoning to be "interested" and therefore somehow personally liable under the entire fairness standard for a merger allocation decision.

Here, the plaintiffs have also failed to impugn the Board's entitlement to the business judgment rule for a more mundane reason. Even if the court must, as I think it does not in this situation, consider whether the otherwise independent directors comprising the Special Committee could, because of their ownership of common stock and no preferred stock, impartially balance the interests at stake, the plaintiffs have not advanced facts that support a reasonable inference that any of the Special Committee members are materially self-interested. I say *any* forthrightly. As to director Jurika, who owns a large common stock stake, a shift in the merger consideration of 10% to the preferred would cost him approximately $500,000. That amount of money, of course, would be material to most Americans. But most Americans are not corporate directors, and do not have a $5.6 million stake of common stock in any company. And, the plaintiffs have not advanced any reason to believe that the hypothetical 10% shift would be important to Jurika. The man could be as rich as Croesus or Jimmy Buffett. The plaintiffs have a burden here and they have not even tried to meet it. As to the other directors on the Special Committee, they have failed even more obviously. Directors English, Miller, Peebles, and Pevenstein own only $61,284 worth of common stock and in the money options collectively. Even a fairly drastic shift of 20% of the merger consideration from the preferred to the common would only reduce those directors' collective take by approximately $28,000, and the plaintiffs do not make any attempt to show that this would be material to these directors' personal economic circumstances. Thus, even under the plaintiffs' theory, the business judgment rule, and not the entire fairness standard, applies to the Special Committee's decision.

Finally, the preferred stockholders have not established a likelihood of success on their claim that the defendants breached their duty of care. The record reveals that the Board complied with its *Revlon* duties by actively seeking the best value and considered whether the preferred should get more than the contractual bottom line. Finding no special reason for better treatment, the Board allocated the preferred stockholders their share of the Merger proceeds in accord with those bottom line rights. The preferred stockholders may not like that decision, but it was made on a thoughtful basis informed by advice of counsel, and there is no hint of any lapse in care.

* * *

IV. Conclusion

For the reasons discussed above, I refuse to enjoin the transaction. The preferred stockholders' motion is therefore denied . . . .

NOTE

In venture capital transactions in which a startup company raises capital in a private placement, the investors often receive convertible preferred stock "in the hopes of realizing returns on their investment by disposing of their shares [acquired upon conversion] in or following an initial public offering [of common stock] by the company *or* pursuant to an acquisition of the company." Timothy J. Harris, *Modeling the Conversion Decisions of Preferred Stock*, 58 Bus. Law. 587 (2003) (emphasis supplied).

In order for the investor to realize a return in the event of an acquisition of the company, the liquidation preference terms of such preferred stock (unlike the publicly held Series A Preferred Stock created by the directors' resolutions set forth above) provide that a merger or sale of all or substantially all of the assets of the corporation *shall* constitute a liquidation of the corporation.

The following is an example of such privately held preferred stock provisions:

> 5. Liquidation Rights.
>
> Upon any voluntary or involuntary liquidation, dissolution or winding-up of the Company, each holder of shares of the Series A Preferred Stock then

outstanding will be entitled to payment out of the assets of the Company available for distribution of an amount equal to Twenty-Five Thousand dollars ($25,000) (the "Liquidation Preference") per share of Series A Preferred Stock held by such holder, plus (a) an amount equal to accrued and unpaid dividends, if any, to the date fixed for liquidation, dissolution or winding-up and (b) an additional amount equal to 8% per annum of the Liquidation Preference per share for the period commencing on the Series A Preferred Stock Issue Date and ending on the Business Day immediately preceding the date fixed for liquidation, dissolution or winding-up, in each case before any distribution is made on any Junior Securities, including, without limitation, the Common Stock. After payment in full of the Liquidation Preference and all other amounts to which holders of Series A Preferred Stock are entitled pursuant to this Section 5, such holders will not be entitled to any further participation in any distribution of assets of the Company. If, upon any voluntary or involuntary liquidation, dissolution or winding-up of the Company, the amounts payable with respect to the Series A Preferred Stock and all other Parity Securities are not paid in full, the holders of the Series A Preferred Stock and the Parity Securities will share equally and ratably in any distribution of assets of the Company in proportion to the full liquidation preference and accumulated and unpaid dividends, if any, to which each is entitled (including, in the case of the Series A Preferred Stock, all amounts payable pursuant to the first sentence of this Section 5. For the purposes of this Section 5, the following shall be deemed to be a voluntary or involuntary liquidation, dissolution or winding-up of the Company:

(i) The voluntary sale, conveyance, exchange or transfer (for cash, shares of stock, securities or other consideration) of all or substantially all of the property or assets of the Company in a single transaction or series of related transactions;

(ii) the merger or consolidation of one or more other entities into or with the Company, the merger or consolidation of the Company into or with one or more other entities, other business combination involving the Company, a sale of stock of the Company, or series or combination of such transactions, if (a) the holders of the Series A Preferred Stock do not receive securities of the surviving corporation with substantially similar rights to the Series A Preferred Stock and (b) the stockholders holding the outstanding shares of voting stock of the Company immediately prior to such transaction or transactions do not, immediately after the consummation of such transaction or transactions hold a majority of the outstanding shares of voting stock of the surviving entity.

No interest shall accrue on any payment upon liquidation after the date thereof.

§ 4.08 INTERPRETATION AND EFFECT OF CLASS VOTING PROVISIONS

[A] Special Directors

The provisions regarding voting rights of the Series A Preferred Stock set forth above state that, whenever the amount of dividends in arrears upon the preferred stock shall be equal to *six* full quarterly dividends, the holders of Series A Preferred Stock shall have the right to elect two members of the board of directors. Those two directors are sometimes referred to as "watchdog" directors. Although they are directors in every sense of the term and are vested with rights and obligations of directors generally, their special purpose on the board is to further the interest and protect the rights of the holders of preferred stock. Although they are a distinct minority (the Preferred Stock provisions specifically provide that the number of directors of the corporation may be increased to provide for their election or otherwise increase the number of directors), their mere presence on the board acts as an inducement to the other directors to declare and pay the dividend arrearages as soon as reasonably and prudently possible.

The closely negotiated Series A Preferred Stock provisions set forth above further provide that in the event that the dividend arrearages are equal to *10* full quarterly-yearly dividends, the holders of the preferred stock are entitled to elect a majority of the board of directors of the corporation. Again, these directors are charged with the duty of managing the corporation and, as a majority of the board, have responsibilities substantially greater in scope than protecting the rights of preferred stockholders. The Series A Preferred Stock provisions further provide that in the event that the preferred stockholders have elected a majority of the board of directors and the corporation acquires legally available funds for the payments of dividends, the minority directors (elected by the holders of the common stock) shall constitute a committee of the board of directors for the purpose of declaring and paying the preferred stock arrearages. The reason for this latter provision is that, as is demonstrated in the next case, there have been instances where the preferred stock directors have declined to declare and pay preferred stock dividends, even though the corporation has legally sufficient funds therefor.

BARON v. ALLIED ARTISTS PICTURES CORP.

Delaware Court of Chancery
337 A.2d 653 (1975)

Brown, Vice Chancellor

Plaintiff originally brought suit as a stockholder of the defendant Allied Artists Pictures Corporation, a Delaware corporation, (hereafter "Allied") to have the 1973 election of directors declared illegal and invalid and to have a master appointed to conduct a new election pursuant to 8 Del. C. §§ 225 and 227. He has since filed a second action seeking the same relief as to the 1974 election of directors, and the two causes have been consolidated for decision based upon the cross-motions of the parties for summary judgment. Both sides to the controversy agree that there is no material dispute of fact and that the matter is a proper one for determination by summary judgment.

Plaintiff charges that the present board of directors of Allied has fraudulently perpetuated itself in office by refusing to pay the accumulated dividend arrearages on preferred stock issued by the corporation which, in turn, permits the preferred stockholders to elect a majority of the board of directors at each annual election so long as the dividend arrearage specified by Allied's certificate of incorporation exists. Defendants contend that the recent financial history and condition of the corporation has justified the nonpayment of the preferred dividend arrearages, at least to the present, and they further ask that the plaintiff's claims be dismissed because they constitute a purchased grievance.

By way of background, Allied was originally started in the mid-1930's as Sterling Pictures Corporation and later changed its name to Monogram Films under which it gained recognition for many B-pictures and western films. In the early 1950's it changed its name to the present one. Around 1953, with the advent of television, it fell upon hard times. Being in need of capital, Allied's certificate of incorporation was amended in 1954 to permit the issuance of 150,000 shares of preferred stock at a par value of $10.00, with the dividends payable quarterly on a cumulative basis. The amended language of the certificate provides that the preferred shareholders are entitled to receive cash dividends "as and when declared by the Board of Directors, out of funds legally available for the purpose. . . ." The amended certificate further provides that

> . . . in case at any time six or more quarterly dividends (whether or not consecutive) on the Preferred Stock shall be in default, in whole or in part, then until all dividends in default on the Preferred Stock shall have been paid or deposited in trust, and the dividend thereon for the current quarterly period shall have been declared and funds for the payment thereof set aside, the holders of the Preferred Stock, voting as a class, shall have the right, at any annual or other meeting for the election of directors, by plurality vote to elect a majority of the Directors of the Corporation.

In addition, the amended certificate requires that a sinking fund be created as to the preferred stock into which an amount equal to ten per cent of the excess of consolidated net earnings over the preferred stock dividend requirements for each fiscal year shall be set aside. From this sinking fund the preferred stock is to be redeemed, by lot, at the rate of $10.50 per share.

Thereafter, as to the preferred stock issued under the 1954 offering, regular quarterly dividends were paid through March 30, 1963. Subsequently, Allied suffered losses which ultimately impaired the capital represented by the preferred stock as a consequence of which the payment of dividends became prohibited by 8 Del. C. § 170. Allied has paid no dividends as to the preferred shares since 1963. By September 1964 the corporation was in default on six quarterly dividends and thus the holders of the preferred stock became entitled to elect a majority of the board of directors. They have done so ever since.

As of December 11, 1973 election of directors, Kalvex, Inc. owned 52 per cent of the outstanding preferred stock while owning only 625 shares of Allied's 1,500,000 shares of common stock. Since the filing of the first action herein Kalvex has taken steps to acquire a substantial number of common shares or securities convertible into the same. Thus unquestionably Kalvex, through its control of the preferred shares, is in control of Allied, although its holdings are said to represent only 7 1/2 per cent of the corporation's equity.

Plaintiff points out that the defendant Emanual Wolf, as director, president and chief executive officer of Allied at an annual salary of $100,000, is also president and chief executive officer of Kalvex. Defendant Robert L. Ingis, a director, vice-president and chief financial officer of Allied, is the executive vice-president of Kalvex. Defendants Strauss and Prager, elected as directors by the preferred shareholders, are also vice-presidents of Allied. Of the four directors nominated by management to represent the common stockholders, and duly elected, two serve Allied at salaried positions and two serve as counsel for Allied receiving either directly or through their firms substantial remuneration for their efforts. Plaintiff asserts that for fiscal 1973, the officers and directors of Allied, as a group, received $402,088 in compensation.

Returning briefly to other fortunes of the corporation, in 1964 Allied was assessed a tax deficiency of some $1,400,000 by the Internal Revenue Service. At the end of fiscal 1963, it had a cumulative deficit of over $5,000,000, a negative net worth of over $1,800,000 and in that year had lost more than $2,700,000. As a consequence Allied entered into an agreement with the Internal Revenue Service to pay off the tax deficiency over a period of years subject to the condition that until the deficiency was satisfied Allied would pay no dividends without the consent of Internal Revenue.

Thereafter Allied's fortunes vacillated with varying degrees of success and failure which, defendants say, is both a hazard and a way of life in the motion picture and theatrical industry. Prior to fiscal 1973 there were only two years, 1969 and 1970, when its preferred capital was not impaired. But plaintiff points out that in 1970 the preferred capital surplus was $1,300,000 at a time when the preferred dividend arrearages were only $146,500. And, while recognizing that Allied suffered net income loss of over $3,000,000 in the following year, 1971, plaintiff further points out that during several years between 1964 and 1973 the corporation had, on occasion, sufficient net income to contribute to the sinking fund or to pay the dividend arrearages. Defendants argue that when viewed overall it was not until the end of the fiscal year terminating June 30, 1973 that Allied had, for the first time, a capital surplus available for preferred dividends, and that this surplus was only $118,000, or less than half of the amount necessary to liquidate the preferred dividend arrearage. (If this constitutes a dispute of fact, I do not consider it to be material for the purpose of this decision.)

Starting with 1972, Allied's financial condition began to improve substantially. It acquired the rights to, produced and distributed the film "Cabaret," which won eight Academy Awards and became the largest grossing film in Allied's history up to that time. It thereafter took a large gamble and committed itself for $7,000,000 for the production and distribution of the film "Papillon." In his initial litigation plaintiff complained vigorously of this, but he has since abandoned his objection since

"Papillon" proved to be even a greater financial success than "Cabaret." For fiscal 1973 Allied had net income in excess of $1,400,000 plus a $2,000,000 tax carry-over remaining from its 1971 losses. Presumably its financial situation did not worsen prior to the December 11, 1974 election of directors although unquestionably it has gone forward with financial commitments as to forth-coming film releases.

Throughout all of the foregoing, however, the Internal Revenue agreement, with its dividend restriction, persisted. Prior to the 1973 election the balance owed was some $249,000 and as of the 1974 election, one final payment was due, which presumably has now been made. Prior to the 1973 election, Allied was in default on forty-three quarterly preferred dividends totalling more than $270,000. By the time of the 1974 election, the arrearages exceeded $280,000.

Without attempting to set forth all of the yearly financial data relied upon by the plaintiff, his position is, quite simply, that for one or more years since the preferred shareholders have been in control of Allied the corporate financial statements show that there was either a net income for the preceding fiscal year or a capital surplus at the end of the preceding fiscal year in an amount larger than the accumulated preferred dividend arrearages, and that consequently the board of directors elected by the preferred shareholders, being only a caretaker board, had a duty to use such funds to pay the dividend arrearage, and also the balance due on the Internal Revenue agreement, if necessary, and to thereupon return control of the corporation to the common stockholders at the next annual election. Specifically, plaintiff charges that the corporation had both the legal and financial capability to pay off the Internal Revenue obligation and the dividend arrearage prior to both the 1973 and 1974 annual election of directors which, had it been done, would have prevented the preferred shareholders, as controlled by Kalvex, from reelecting a majority of the board. Thus, plaintiff seeks the Court to order a new election at which Allied's board of directors will be elected by the common stockholders.

Plaintiff stresses that he is not asking the Court to compel the payment of the dividend arrearages, but only that a new election be held because of the preferred board's allegedly wrongful refusal to do so. Since the certificate of incorporation gives preferred shareholders the contractual right to elect a majority of the directors as long as dividends are six quarters in arrears, plaintiff, in effect, is asking that this contractual right be voided because of the deliberate refusal of the preferred shareholders to see themselves paid as soon as funds became legally available for that purpose.

Plaintiff has cited a wealth of authorities standing for various accepted propositions of corporate law, the most prominent of which hold that incumbent directors cannot issue stock without consideration or otherwise manipulate corporate machinery so as to maintain or perpetuate control in a particular group of stockholders. Although plaintiff contends that in principle this is what the defendants are doing here, he offers no authorities which apply this prohibition to a factual situation such as the present one.

Despite the approach that plaintiff attempts to take, I fail to see how his relief can be granted without reaching the question of whether the dividend arrearages should have been paid. While preferences attaching to stock are the exception and are to be strictly construed, it is well established that the rights of preferred stockholders are contract rights. In *Petroleum Rights Corporation v. Midland Royalty Corp.*, 19 Del. Ch. 334, 167 A. 835 (1933), a somewhat similar provision of the corporate charter extended to preferred shareholders the right to elect a majority of the board when six quarterly dividends became in arrears, which right continued "*so long as the surplus . . . applicable to the payment of dividends shall be insufficient to pay all accrued dividends.*" The Chancellor there held that as long as there was the prescribed default in dividends and the surplus remained insufficient, the preferred stockholders were entitled to elect a majority of the board. It was argued to him that this right of election and control was limited by the language "so long as the surplus . . . shall be insufficient" and that the accumulation of a surplus sufficient to pay all accrued dividends constituted a condition subsequent, the existence of which would forthwith defeat the right to elect control. This view was rejected, on the theory that if accepted it would mean that the sole purpose of such a scheme would be to put the preferred in control to force a payment of passed dividends once a dividend fund became available. The Chancellor concluded that a shift of control should not be made to turn on the personal interests of the preferred shareholders in dividends alone but, in addition, on the consideration that if surplus fell below unpaid dividends the time had arrived to try a new management. 167 A. 837. He also stated as follows at 167 A. 836:

> . . . if the surplus does in fact exceed the six quarterly dividends in arrear and the preference stock should elect a majority of the board and the board should resolve not to pay the dividends, the right of the preference stock to continue to elect a majority of the board would undoubtedly terminate.

I interpret this to mean that the contractual right to elect a majority of the board continues until the dividends can be made current in keeping with proper corporate management, but that it must terminate once a fund becomes clearly available to satisfy the arrearages and the preference board refuses to do so. Plaintiff seeks to limit this requirement to a mere mathematical availability of funds, and indeed the charter language in *Petroleum Rights* may have intended such a result. Here, however, Allied's charter, and thus its contract with its preferred shareholders, does not limit the right merely until such time as a sufficient surplus exists, as it did in *Petroleum Rights*, but rather it entitles the preferred shareholders to their dividends only "as and when declared by the Board of Directors, out of funds legally available for the purpose." This obviously reposes a discretion in Allied's board to declare preferred dividends, whether it be a board elected by the common or by the preferred shareholders.

The general rule applicable to the right to receive corporate dividends was succinctly stated by Justice Holmes in *Wabash Ry. Co. v. Barclay*, 280 U.S. 197, 203, 50 S. Ct. 106, 107, 74 L. Ed. 368 (1930):

> When a man buys stock instead of bonds he takes a greater risk in the business. No one suggests that he has a right to dividends if there are no net earnings. But the investment presupposes that the business is to go on, and therefore even if there are net earnings, the holder of stock, preferred as well as common, is entitled to have a dividend declared only out of such part of them as can be applied to dividends *consistently with a wise administration of a going concern.* (Emphasis added.)

Although one purpose of allowing the preferred to elect a majority of the board may be to bring about a payment of the dividend delinquencies as soon as possible, that should not be the sole justification for the existence of a board of directors so elected. During the time that such a preference board is in control of the policies and business decisions of the corporation, it serves the corporation itself and the common shareholders as well as those by whom it was put in office. Corporate directors stand in a fiduciary relationship to their corporation and its shareholders and their primary duty is to deal fairly and justly with both.

The determination as to when and in what amounts a corporation may prudently distribute its assets by way of dividends rests in the honest discretion of the directors in the performance of this fiduciary duty. Before a court will interfere with the judgment of a board of directors in refusing to declare dividends, fraud or gross abuse of discretion must be shown. And this is true even if a fund does exist from which dividends could legally be paid. As stated by the Chancellor in *Eshleman v. Keenan, supra*, at 194 A. 43:

> That courts have the power in proper cases to compel the directors to declare a dividend, is sustained by respectable authorities. But that they should do so on a mere showing that an asset exists from which a dividend may be declared, has never, I dare say, been asserted anywhere. In such a case a court acts only after a demonstration that the corporation's affairs are in a condition justifying the declaration of the dividend as a matter of prudent business management and that the withholding of it is explicable only on the theory of an oppressive or fraudulent abuse of discretion.

Plaintiff here appears to be asking that an exception be carved from these well established principles where the nonpayment of dividends and arrearages results in continued control by the very board which determines not to pay them. As I understand his argument, he asks for a ruling that a board of directors elected by preferred shareholders whose dividends are in arrears has an absolute duty to pay off all preferred dividends due and to return control to the common shareholders as soon as funds become legally available for that purpose, regardless of anything else. Thus, in effect, he would have the court limit the discretion given the board by the certificate of incorporation, and make the decision to pay arrearages mandatory upon the emergence of a lawful financial source even though the corporate charter does not require it (as perhaps it did in *Petroleum Rights*). He has offered no precedent for such a proposition, and I decline to create one.

Plaintiff's attempt to distinguish his action by asserting that he does not seek to compel the payment of the dividend arrearages, but only to return control to the common stockholders, has a hollow ring. In either case the basic question is whether or not the board has wrongfully refused to pay dividends even if funds did exist which could have been used for such purpose. The established test for this is whether the board engaged in fraud or grossly abused its discretion. The mere existence of a legal source from which payment could be made, standing alone, does not prove either.

When the yearly hit-and-miss financial history of Allied from 1964 through 1974 is considered along with the Internal Revenue obligation during the same time span, I cannot conclude, as a matter of law, that Allied's board has been guilty of perpetuating itself in office by wrongfully refusing to apply corporate funds to the liquidation of the preferred dividend arrearages and the accelerated payment of the Internal Revenue debt. Thus I find no basis on the record before me to set aside the 1974 annual election and to order a new one through a master appointed by the court.

This also applies to plaintiff's argument that Allied has failed to make the required payments into the sinking fund so as to gradually redeem the preferred stock and thus systematically reduce the accumulation of the preferred dividend arrearage. It is not disputed that the legal advice and decision to defer annual contributions to the sinking fund pending rectification of Allied's financial position was given and made prior to the election of the first board of directors by the preferred shareholders, and thereafter merely continued by them.

Moreover, even accepting plaintiff's figures, the sum that could have been contributed to the sinking fund since 1963, under the formula set forth in the corporate charter, would not have been sufficient to redeem all outstanding preferred stock by the time of the elections in question. Thus, even if sinking fund contributions had been religiously made each year without regard to Allied's other obligations and losses, there would still have been preferred stock and preferred dividend arrearages, albeit in a lesser amount.

It is clear, however, that Allied's present board does have a fiduciary duty to see that the preferred dividends are brought up to date as soon as possible in keeping with prudent business management. *Petroleum Rights Corporation v. Midland Royalty Corp., supra; Eshleman v. Keenan, supra.* This is particularly true now that the Internal Revenue debt has been satisfied in full and business is prospering. It cannot be permitted indefinitely to plough back all profits in future commitments so as to avoid full satisfaction of the rights of the preferred to their dividends and the otherwise normal right of the common stockholders to elect corporate management. While previous limitations on net income and capital surplus may offer a justification for the past, continued limitations in a time of greatly increased cash flow could well create new issues in the area of business discretion for the future.

Because of the above conclusions, I find it unnecessary to deal with the contention of defendants' that the complaints should be dismissed because of embodying a purchased grievance by plaintiff.

Plaintiff's motion for summary judgment is denied. Defendants' motion for summary judgment is granted. Order on notice.

The voting provisions of the Series A Preferred Stock set forth above solve the problem presented in the *Baron* case by designating the minority directors elected by the holders of the Common Stock as a Committee of the Board with authority to declare and pay dividends on the Series A Shares.

NOTE

It is also possible to provide for the election of special directors in the event that a corporation fails to pay dividends on *non-cumulative* preferred stock:

VOTING RIGHTS

(a) General. The holders of the Series B Preferred Stock shall not have any voting rights except as set forth below or as otherwise from time to time required by law.

(b) Series B Preferred Stock Directors. Whenever, at any time or times, dividends payable on the shares of the Series B Preferred Stock have not been paid for an aggregate of four quarterly Dividend Periods or more, whether or not consecutive, the authorized number of directors of the Company shall automatically be increased to accommodate the number of the Preferred Directors specified below and the holders of the Series B Preferred Stock shall have the right, voting as a separate class, to elect the greater of two directors and a number of directors (rounded upward) equal to 20% of the total number of directors of the Company after giving effect to such election (hereinafter the "Preferred Directors" and each a "Preferred Director") to fill such newly created directorships at the Company's next annual meeting of stockholders (or at a special meeting called for that purpose prior to such next annual meeting) and at each subsequent annual meeting of stockholders until dividends payable on all outstanding shares of the Series B Preferred Stock have been declared and paid in full for four consecutive quarterly Dividend Periods, at which time such right shall terminate with respect to the Series B Preferred Stock, except as herein or by law expressly provided, subject to revesting in the event of each and every subsequent payment failure of the character above mentioned; *provided* that it shall be a qualification for election for any Preferred Director that the election of such Preferred Director shall not cause the Company to violate any corporate governance requirements of any securities exchange or other trading facility on which securities of the Company may then be listed or traded that listed or traded companies must have a majority of independent directors. Upon any termination of the right of the holders of shares of the Series B Preferred Stock to vote for directors as provided above, the Preferred Directors shall cease to be qualified as directors, the term of office of all Preferred Directors then in office shall terminate immediately and the authorized number of directors shall be reduced by the number of the Preferred Directors elected pursuant hereto. Any Preferred Director may be removed at any time, with or without cause, and any vacancy created thereby may be filled, only by the affirmative vote of the holders of a majority of the shares of the Series B Preferred Stock at the time outstanding voting separately as a class. If the office of any Preferred Director becomes vacant for any reason other than removal from office as aforesaid, the remaining Preferred Directors may choose a successor who shall hold office for the unexpired term in respect of which such vacancy occurred.

[1] Duties of Directors Elected By Holders of Preferred Stock

IN RE TRADOS INCORPORATED SHAREHOLDER LITIGATION

Delaware Court of Chancery
2009 Del. Ch. LEXIS 128 (July 24, 2009)

CHANDLER, CHANCELLOR.

This is a purported class action brought by a former stockholder of Trados Incorporated ("Trados," or the "Company") for breach of fiduciary duty arising out of a transaction whereby Trados became a wholly owned subsidiary of SDL, plc ("SDL"). Of the $60 million [paid] by SDL, Trados' preferred stockholders received approximately $52 million. The remainder was distributed to the Company's executive officers pursuant to a previously approved bonus plan. Trados' common stockholders received nothing for their common shares.

Plaintiff contends that this transaction was undertaken at the behest of certain preferred stockholders that desired a transaction that would trigger their large liquidation preference and allow them to exit their investment in Trados. Plaintiff alleges that the Trados board favored the interests of the preferred stockholders, either at the expense of the common stockholders or without properly considering the effect of the merger on the common stockholders. Specifically, plaintiff alleges that the four directors designated by preferred stockholders had other relationships with preferred stockholders and were incapable of exercising disinterested and independent business judgment. Plaintiff further alleges that the two Trados directors who were also employees of the Company received material personal benefits as a result of the merger and were therefore also incapable of exercising disinterested and independent business judgment. . . .

As explained below, plaintiff has alleged facts sufficient, at this preliminary stage, to demonstrate that at least a majority of the members of Trados' seven member board were unable to exercise independent and disinterested business judgment in deciding whether to approve the merger. Accordingly, I decline to dismiss the breach of fiduciary duty claims arising out of the board's approval of the merger. . . .

I. BACKGROUND

A. The Parties

Before the merger, Trados developed software and services used by businesses to make the translation of text and material into other languages more efficient. Founded in 1984 as a German entity, Trados moved to the United States in the mid-1990s with the hope of going public, and became a Delaware corporation in March 2000. To better position itself for the possibility of going public, Trados accepted investments from venture capital firms and other entities. As a result, preferred stockholders had a total of four designees on Trados' seven member board. Each of the seven members of Trados' board at the time of the board's approval of the merger is named as a defendant in this action.

David Scanlan was the board designee of, and a partner in, Wachovia Capital Partners, LLC ("Wachovia"). At the time of the merger, Wachovia owned 3,640,000 shares of Trados' Series A preferred stock (100% of that series) and 1,007,151 shares of Trados' Series BB preferred stock (approximately 24% of that series).

Lisa Stone was the board designee of Rowan Entities Limited and Rowan Nominees Limited RR (together, the "Rowan Entities"), transferees of Trados' preferred stock held by Hg Investment Managers Limited (collectively, "Hg"). Stone was a director and employee of both Hg Investment Managers Limited and the Rowan Entities. At the time of the merger, Hg owned 1,379,039 shares of Trados' common stock (approximately 4.3%), 2,014,302 shares of Trados' Series BB preferred stock (approximately 48.3% of that series), 5,333,330 shares of Trados' Series C preferred shares (all of that series), and 862,976 shares of Trados' Series D preferred stock (approximately 28.6% of that series).

* * *

Sameer Gandhi was a board designee of, and a partner in, several entities known as Sequoia. Sequoia owned 5,255,913 shares of Trados' Series E preferred stock (approximately 32% of that series).

Joseph Prang was also a board designee of Sequoia. Prang owned Mentor Capital Group LLC ("Mentor Capital"), which owned 263,810 shares of Trados' Series E preferred stock (approximately 1% of that series).

Wachovia, Hg, Sequoia, and Mentor combined owned approximately 51% of Trados' outstanding preferred stock. Plaintiff alleges that these preferred stockholders desired to exit their investment in Trados.[50]

Two of the three remaining director defendants were employees of Trados. Jochen Hummel was acting President of Trados from April 2004 until September or October 2004, and was also the Company's chief technology officer. Joseph Campbell was Trados' CEO from August 23, 2004 until the merger. The remaining Trados director was Klaus-Dieter Laidig.

B. The Negotiations

In April 2004, the Trados board began to discuss a potential sale of the Company, and later formed a mergers and acquisitions committee, consisting of Stone,

---

[50] [2] Compl. ¶¶ 30, 35-37, 44, 51, 79, 84, 101-102. Plaintiff alleges, for example, that in January 2003 Gandhi wrote that Sequoia's "only real opportunity is to capture a fraction of our 13m investment," and that in June 2003 Gandhi acknowledged that Trados' long term prospects were improving, but wrote that Sequoia "d[id] not own enough of the company to make a meaningful return." Id. ¶ 30. Plaintiff further alleges that by mid-2004 Wachovia wanted to exit its investment in Trados because Scanlan felt that the investment was underperforming and consuming too much of his time relative to the size of the investment. Id. ¶ 35. Plaintiff also contends that Hg and Mentor wanted to exit their investments in Trados.

Gandhi, and Scanlan, to explore a sale or merger of Trados. Around the same time, the Company's President and CEO was terminated due to, among other issues, a perception by the rest of the board that Trados was underperforming. The board appointed Hummel as an interim President, but instructed him to consult with Gandhi and Scanlan before taking material action on behalf of the Company. In July 2004, Campbell was hired as the Company's CEO, effective August 23, 2004. Gandhi described Campbell as "a hard-nosed CEO whose task is to grow the company profitably or sell it."[51] At the time Campbell joined Trados, however, the Company was losing money and had little cash to fund continuing operations.[52] At a July 7, 2004 meeting, Trados' board determined that the fair market value of Trados' common stock was $0.10 per share.

In June 2004, Trados engaged JMP Securities, LLC, an investment bank, to assist in identifying potential alternatives for a merger or sale of the Company. By July 2004, JMP Securities had identified twenty seven potential buyers of Trados, and contacted seven of them, including SDL. By August 2004, JMP Securities had conducted discussions with SDL CEO Mark Lancaster, who made an acquisition proposal in the $40 million range. Trados informed Lancaster that it was not interested in a deal at that price, and Campbell formally terminated JMP Securities in September 2004.

* * *

Trados' financial condition improved markedly during the fourth quarter of 2004, in part due to Campbell's efforts to reduce spending and bring in additional cash through debt financing. By the time of the December 2004 board meeting, Trados had arranged to borrow $2.5 million from Western Technology Investment, with the right to borrow an additional $1.5 million.

Despite the Company's improved performance, the board continued to work toward a sale of the Company. In December 2004, Gandhi reported to Sequoia Capital that the Company's performance was improving, but that Campbell's "mission is to architect an M & A event as soon as practicable." At a February 2, 2005 board meeting, Campbell presented positive financial results from the fourth quarter of 2004, including record revenue and profit from operations. As a result of its improved performance and the lack of an immediate need for cash, the board extended by six months the period during which it could obtain additional cash from Western Technology Investment.

* * *

In January 2005, SDL initiated renewed merger discussions with Campbell. Upon learning of SDL's interest, the Trados board expressed that it was not

---

[51] [3] Compl. ¶ 40. In June 2004, Gandhi also reported to Sequoia that a "banker has also been retained to explore the M & A options for the business. I would expect that the company is sold within the next 18 months (perhaps sooner)." Id.

[52] [4] Plaintiff alleges that Campbell believed that his "mission on joining TRADOS was to help the company understand its future path, which in the mind of the outside board members at that time was some type of either merger or acquisition event due to the company's performance that year and prior years." Compl. ¶ 44.

interested in any transaction involving less than a "60-plus" million dollar purchase price. Lancaster first discussed a transaction at $50 million, but later offered $60 million. At the February 2, 2005 meeting, the board instructed Campbell to continue negotiating with Lancaster under the general terms SDL proposed, including the $60 million price. In mid-February 2005, Campbell made inquiries with two other potential acquirers of Trados, but neither expressed any substantive interest.

In a theme that runs throughout his allegations, plaintiff alleges that there was no need to sell Trados at the time because the Company was well financed and experiencing improved performance under Campbell's leadership. For example, plaintiff contends that by February 2005 Trados was beating its revenue budget for the year, a trend that continued as Trados beat its revenue projections for the first quarter of 2005 and through the end of May 2005.

By February 2005, Campbell and Lancaster agreed to the basic terms of a merger at $60 million. Trados then re-engaged JMP securities, which plaintiff alleges acted as little more than a "go-between." In April 2005, SDL and Trados signed the letter of intent for the merger at the $60 million price.

* * *

D. The Merger

The director defendants unanimously approved the merger, and on June 19, 2005 Trados and SDL entered into an Agreement and Plan of Merger. Of the $60 million merger price, approximately $7.8 million would go to management [pursuant to the terms of a bonus plan] and the remainder would go to the preferred stockholders in partial satisfaction of their $57.9 million liquidation preference. Plaintiff alleges that the directors know both of these facts, and thus knew that the common shareholders would receive nothing in the merger. The merger was consummated on July 7, 2005.

* * *

On July 21, 2005, plaintiff filed a petition for appraisal, seeking payment of the fair value of his stock as of the date of the merger. Almost three years later, on July 3, 2008, plaintiff commenced a second action, both individually and purportedly on behalf of a class of former stockholders of Trados, against the director defendants. On December 12, 2008, plaintiff filed the First Amended Verified Complaint (the "Complaint"), which includes new facts allegedly discovered by plaintiff in discovery conducted as part of the appraisal action. Defendants have moved for dismissal of the Complaint for failure to state a claim upon which relief may be granted.

II. ANALYSIS

* * *

C. Fiduciary Duty Claims

Count I of the Complaint asserts a claim that the director defendants breached their fiduciary duty of loyalty to Trados' common stockholders by approving the merger. Plaintiff alleges that there was no need to sell Trados at the time because the Company was well-financed, profitable, and beating revenue projections. Further, plaintiff contends, "in approving the Merger, the Director Defendants never considered the interest of the common stockholders in continuing Trados as a going concern, even though they were obliged to give priority to that interest over the preferred stockholders' interest in exiting their investment."

* * *

Directors of Delaware corporations are protected in their decision-making by the business judgment rule, which "is a presumption that in making a business decision the directors of a corporation acted on an informed basis, in good faith and in the honest belief that the action taken was in the best interests of the company."[53]

The rule reflects and promotes the role of the board of directors as the proper body to manage the business and affairs of the corporation.[54]

The party challenging the directors' decision bears the burden of rebutting the presumption of the rule.[55] If the presumption of the rule is not rebutted, then the Court will not second-guess the business decisions of the board.[56] If the presumption of the rule is rebutted, then the burden of proving entire fairness shifts to the director defendants.[57] A plaintiff can survive a motion to dismiss under Rule 12(b)(6) by pleading facts from which a reasonable inference can be drawn that a majority of the board was interested or lacked independence with respect to the relevant decision.[58]

A director is interested in a transaction if "he or she will receive a personal financial benefit from a transaction that is not equally shared by the stockholders" or if "a corporate decision will have a materially detrimental impact on a director, but not on the corporation and the stockholders."[59] The receipt of any benefit is not sufficient to cause a director to be interested in a transaction. Rather, the benefit received by the director and not shared with stockholders must be "of a sufficiently material importance, in the context of the director's economic circumstances, as to have made it improbable that the director could perform her fiduciary duties . . . without being influenced by her overriding personal interest. . . ."[60]

---

[53] [24] Aronson v. Lewis, 473 A.2d 805, 812 (Del. 1984).

[54] [25] 8 Del. C. § 141(a); In re CompuCom Sys., Inc. Stockholders Litig., 2005 WL 2481325, at 5[, 2005 Del. Ch. LEXIS 145] (Del. Ch. Sept. 29, 2005).

[55] [26] Cede & Co. v. Technicolor, Inc., 634 A.2d 345, 361 (Del.1993).

[56] [27] Id.

[57] [28] Id.

[58] [29] Orman v. Cullman, 794 A.2d 5, 22-23 (Del. Ch. 2002).

[59] [30] Rales v. Blasband, 634 A.2d 927, 936 (Del. 1993).

[60] [31] In re Gen. Motors Class H S'holders Litig., 734 A.2d 611, 617 (Del.Ch.1999); see Orman, 794 A.2d at 23.

"Independence means that a director's decision is based on the corporate merits of the subject before the board rather than extraneous considerations or influences."[61] At this stage, a lack of independence can be shown by pleading facts that support a reasonable inference that the director is beholden to a controlling person or "so under their influence that their discretion would be sterilized."[62]

Plaintiff's theory of the case is based on the proposition that, for purposes of the merger, the preferred stockholders' interests diverged from the interests of the common stockholders. Plaintiff contends that the merger took place at the behest of certain preferred stockholders, who wanted to exit their investment. Defendants contend that plaintiff ignores the "obvious alignment" of the interest of the preferred and common stockholders in obtaining the highest price available for the company. Defendants assert that because the preferred stockholders would not receive their entire liquidation preference in the merger, they would benefit if a higher price were obtained for the Company.[63] Even accepting this proposition as true, however, it is not the case that the interests of the preferred and common stockholders were aligned with respect to the decision of whether to pursue a sale of the company or continue to operate the Company without pursuing a transaction at the time.

* * *

The merger triggered the $57.9 million liquidation preference of the preferred stockholders, and the preferred stockholders received approximately $52 million dollars as a result of the merger. In contrast, the common stockholders received nothing as a result of the merger, and lost the ability to ever receive anything of value in the future for their ownership interest in Trados. It would not stretch reason to say that this is the worst possible outcome for the common stockholders. The common stockholders would certainly be no worse off had the merger not occurred.

Taking, as I must, the well-pleaded facts in the Complaint in the light most favorable to plaintiff, it is reasonable to infer that the common stockholders would have been able to receive some consideration for their Trados shares at some point in the future had the merger not occurred.[64] This inference is supported by

---

[61] [32] Aronson, 473 A.2d at 816.

[62] [33] Rales, 634 A.2d at 936.

[63] [35] Defendants also contend that the preferred stockholders would receive payment on an as converted basis with the common stockholders. Id. at 12-13 ("[T]he preferred would receive the first $57.9 million of any transaction, and would thereafter receive payment on an as converted basis with the common stockholders."); see Compl. ¶ 37 ("[O]nce the Liquidation Preferences of Sequoia Capital and Mentor Capital's preferred stock were satisfied in a sale or acquisition of Trados, those entities would not share in any further consideration, which mostly would go to Trados' common stockholders.") (emphasis added); Pl.'s Answering Br. 22-23.

[64] [36] On a motion to dismiss for failure to state a claim, I am required to draw all reasonable inferences in favor of the non-moving party. As a result, there are sometimes reasonable (even, potentially, more likely) inferences that must be passed over at this stage of the proceedings. For example, it would be reasonable to infer from the allegations in the Complaint that pursing the transaction with SDL was in the best interest of the Company because it secured the best value reasonably available for the Company's stakeholders and did not harm the common shareholders

plaintiff's allegations that the Company's performance had significantly improved and that the Company had secured additional capital through debt financing. Thus, it is reasonable to infer from the factual allegations in the Complaint that the interests of the preferred and common stockholders were not aligned with respect to the decision to pursue a transaction that would trigger the liquidation preference of the preferred and result in no consideration for the common stockholders.[65]

* * *

Generally, the rights and preferences of preferred stock are contractual in nature.[66] This Court has held that directors owe fiduciary duties to preferred stockholders as well as common stockholders where the right claimed by the preferred "is not to a preference as against the common stock but rather a right shared equally with the common."[67] Where this is not the case, however, "generally it will be the duty of the board, where discretionary judgment is to be exercised, to prefer the interests of common stock — as the good faith judgment of the board sees them to be — to the interests created by the special rights, preferences, *etc.*, of preferred stock, where there is a conflict."[68] Thus, in circumstances where the interests of the common stockholders diverge from those of the preferred stockholders, it is *possible* that a director could breach her duty by improperly favoring the interests of the preferred stockholders over those of the common stockholders.[69] As explained above, the factual allegations in the Complaint support a reasonable inference that the interests of the preferred and common stockholders

---

because, in fact, there was no reasonable chance that they would ever obtain any value for their stock even absent the transaction. Nothing in this Opinion is intended to suggest that it would necessarily be a breach of fiduciary duty for a board to approve a transaction that, as a result of liquidation preferences, does not provide any consideration to the common stockholders.

[65] [38] Defendants do not argue that the board had an obligation to the preferred stockholders to pursue a transaction that would trigger the large liquidation preference of the preferred stock. Thus, it is reasonable to infer, at this stage, that one option would be for the Company to continue to operate without paying the large liquidation preference to the preferred, subject of course, to any other contractual rights the preferred stockholders may have had. Indeed, in a situation in which the liquidation preference of the preferred exceeded the consideration that could be achieved in a transaction, it would arguably be in the interest of the common stockholders not to pursue any transaction that would trigger the liquidation preference. It is also reasonable to infer that the preferred stockholders would benefit from a transaction that allowed them to exit the investment while also triggering their liquidation preference, something they did not have a contractual right to force the Company to do. Again, at this stage, I am required to make reasonable inferences in plaintiff's favor, even if there are other reasonable inferences that can be drawn from the alleged facts and that would result in dismissal of the Complaint.

[66] [39] Jedwab v. MGM Grand Hotels, Inc., 509 A.2d 584, 594 (Del.Ch.1986) ("[W]ith respect to matters relating to preferences or limitations that distinguish preferred stock from common, the duty of the corporation and its directors is essentially contractual and the scope of the duty is appropriately defined by reference to the specific words evidencing that contract. . . ."); see Matulich v. Aegis Commc'ns Group, Inc., 942 A.2d 596, 599-600 (Del.2008).

[67] [40] Jedwab, 509 A.2d at 594.

[68] [41] Equity-Linked Investors, L.P. v. Adams, 705 A.2d 1040, 1042 (Del.Ch.1997) (citing Katz v. Oak Indus., Inc., 508 A.2d 873, 879 (Del.Ch.1986)).

[69] [42] See Blackmore Partners, L.P. v. Link Energy LLC, 864 A.2d 80, 85-86 (Del.Ch.2004) ("[T]he allegation that the Defendant Directors approved a sale of substantially all of [the company's] assets and a resultant distribution of proceeds that went exclusively to the company's creditors raises a reasonable inference of disloyalty or intentional misconduct. Of course, it is also possible to infer (and the record at

diverged with respect to the decision of whether to pursue the merger. Given this reasonable inference, plaintiff can avoid dismissal if the Complaint contains well-pleaded facts that demonstrate that the director defendants were interested or lacked independence with respect to this decision.

Defendants may be correct that the facts in *Blackmore Partners* are somewhat more "extreme" than those alleged in the complaint because the Court in *Blackmore Partners* found "a basis in the complaint to infer that the value of [the company's] assets exceeded its liabilities by least $25 million." *Blackmore Partners*, 864 A.2d at 85. The Court in *Blackmore Partners*, however, concluded, even in the absence of factual allegations that supported an inference of interest or lack of independence by the directors, that "the allegation that the Defendant Directors approved a sale of substantially all of [the company's] assets and a resultant distribution of proceeds that went exclusively to the company's creditors raises a reasonable inference of disloyalty or intentional misconduct." *Id.* at 86. Here, in contrast, there is an allegation that a majority of the board was interested in the decision to pursue the transaction; accordingly, the Court need not conclude that the decision to approve the transaction, of itself, raises "a reasonable inference of disloyalty or intentional misconduct."

1. The Director Defendants' Approval of the Merger

Plaintiff has alleged facts that support a reasonable inference that Scanlan, Stone, Gandhi, and Prang, the four board designees of preferred stockholders, were interested in the decision to pursue the merger with SDL, which had the effect of triggering the large liquidation preference of the preferred stockholders and resulted in no consideration to the common stockholders for their common shares. Each of these four directors was designated to the Trados board by a holder of a significant number of preferred shares. While this, alone, may not be enough to rebut the presumption of the business judgment rule, plaintiff has alleged more.

---

a later stage may well show) that the Director Defendants made a good faith judgment, after reasonable investigation, that there was no future for the business and no better alternative for the unit holders. Nevertheless, based only the facts alleged and the reasonable inferences that the court must draw from them, it would appear that no transaction could have been worse for the unit holders and reasonable to infer, as the plaintiff argues, that a properly motivated board of directors would not have agreed to a proposal that wiped out the value of the common equity and surrendered all of that value to the company's creditors."). Defendants contend that Blackmore Partners can be distinguished from this case because "the Court in Blackmore Partners found that defendants favored creditors to whom they did not owe fiduciary duties over unit holders to whom they did owe fiduciary duties" and that plaintiff "does not, and cannot, allege that the Director Defendants favored anyone to whom they did not owe a fiduciary duty." Reply Br. of Director Defendants in Further Support of their Mot. to Dismiss ("Defs. Reply Br.") 23. As explained above, however, preferred stockholders are owed the same fiduciary duties as common stockholders when the right claimed by the preferred is "a right shared equally with the common." Jedwab, 509 A.2d at 594. If and when the interests of the preferred stockholders diverge from those of the common stockholders, the directors generally must "prefer the interests of common stock-as the good faith judgment of the board sees them to be-to the interests created by the special rights, preferences, etc., of preferred stock." Equity-Linked Investors, 705 A.2d at 1042. Based on the allegations in the Complaint, it does not appear that the preferred stockholders had any contractual right to force a transaction that would trigger their liquidation preference. Moreover, the transaction with SDL was, under at least one reasonable inference that can be drawn from the Complaint, not in the best interest of Trados' common stockholders.

Plaintiff has alleged that Scanlan, Stone, Gandhi, and Prang each had an ownership or employment relationship with an entity that owned Trados preferred stock. Scanlan was a partner in Wachovia; Stone was a director, employee and part owner of Hg; Gandhi was a partner in several entities referred to as Sequoia; and Prang owned Mentor Capital. Plaintiff further alleges that each of these directors was dependent on the preferred stockholders for their livelihood. As detailed above, each of these entities owned a significant number of Trados' preferred shares, and together these entities owned approximately 51% of Trados' outstanding preferred stock. The allegations of the ownership and other relationships of each of Scanlan, Stone, Gandhi, and Prang to preferred stockholders, combined with the fact that each was a board designee of one of these entities, is sufficient, under the plaintiff-friendly pleading standard on a motion to dismiss, to rebut the business judgment presumption with respect to the decision to approve the merger with SDL.

* * *

At oral argument, defendants relied on *Dubroff v. Wren Holdings, LLC*[70] for support of the argument that plaintiff had failed to state a claim because he had not alleged that the preferred stockholders were acting in concert or had otherwise formed a controlling group. The discussion of a "control group" in *Wren Holdings* was in connection with the general rule that "equity dilution" claims are derivative, rather than direct. As explained in *Wren Holdings*, there is an exception to this general rule "where a controlling shareholder causes the corporate entity to issue more equity to the controlling shareholder at the expense of the minority shareholders."[71] The emphasis on a control group in *Wren Holdings* arose from the plaintiffs' attempt to establish that certain of the defendants had collectively formed a controlling shareholder group so that plaintiffs would be able to bring a direct claim for the alleged equity dilution.[72] Here, in contrast, there is no need for plaintiff to allege that there was a controlling shareholder or control group in order to establish that individual director defendants were interested.[73]

* * *

Plaintiff has alleged facts that support a reasonable inference that a majority of the board was interested or lacked independence with respect to the decision to approve the merger. Accordingly, plaintiff has alleged sufficient facts to survive defendants' motion to dismiss the fiduciary duty claims based on the board's decision to approve the merger.[74]

---

[70] [46] [2009 Del. Ch. LEXIS 89] (Del. Ch. May 22, 2009).

[71] [47] [2009 Del. Ch. LEXIS 89].

[72] [48] [2009 Del. Ch. LEXIS 89].

[73] [49] While it is true that an individual stockholder that is not a controlling stockholder can generally vote in its individual interest, the same cannot be said of directors designated to the board by such a stockholder.

[74] [57] Because, at this stage, plaintiff has rebutted the business judgment presumption for a majority of the board, I need not reach plaintiff's allegations as to the remaining director defendants.

III. CONCLUSION

For the reasons set forth above, defendants' motion to dismiss is granted in part and denied in part. The motion to dismiss is denied with respect to the claim in Count I for breach of fiduciary duty arising out of the board's approval of the merger . . .

NOTE

In *Morgan v. Cash*, 2010 Del. Ch. LEXIS 148 (July 16, 2010), the court, in rejecting a claim that a third-party bidder had aided and abetted a breach of fiduciary duty owed to common stock holders by directors elected by the holders of preferred stock of the target, stated:

> To hold that a claim for aiding and abetting against a bidder is stated simply because a bidder knows that the target board owns a material amount of preferred stock, knows that the target's value is in a range where a deal might result in no consideration to the common stockholder, and that the bidder nonetheless insists on a price below the level that yields a payment to the common stockholders would set a dangerous and irresponsible precedent. The reality is that there are entities whose value is less than the value to which its preferred stockholders and bondholders are due in a sale. If our law makes it a presumptive wrong for a bidder to deal with a board dominated by preferred stockholder representatives, then value-maximizing transactions will be deterred. It is hardly unusual for corporate boards to be comprised of representatives of preferred stockholders, who often bargain for representational rights when they put their capital up in risky situations. Notably, those capital investments often end up benefiting common stockholders by helping corporations weather tough times. What [plaintiff] asks is that this court hold that the mere fact that a bidder knowingly enters into a merger with a target board dominated by preferred holders at a price that does not yield a return to common stockholders creates an inference that the bidder knowingly assisted in fiduciary misconduct by the target board. That is not and should not be our law, particularly when the plaintiff cannot even plead facts suggesting that the bidder was paying materially less, or in this case even anything at all less than, fair market value.

[B] Judicial Construction of Preferred Stock and Statutory Voting Provisions

FLETCHER INTERNATIONAL, LTD v. ION GEOPHYSICAL CORPORATION

Delaware Chancery Court
2010 Del. Ch. LEXIS 125 (May 28, 2010)

Parsons, Vice Chancellor.

In a letter opinion issued on March 24, 2010, I examined part of Fletcher International, Ltd.'s ("Fletcher") motion for partial summary judgment relating to the issuance of a convertible promissory note (the "ION S.àr.l. Note") by ION Geophysical Corporation ("ION") through its wholly-owned subsidiary ION International S.àr.l. ("ION S.àr.l.").[75] In that opinion, I denied Fletcher's motion "insofar as it could be construed as a request for a preliminary injunction effectively invalidating ION's issuance of the ION S.àr.l. Note or requiring that ION repay funds borrowed under that Note," but reserved judgment on certain other issues raised by Fletcher's motion.[76] This Memorandum Opinion addresses those issues.

Specifically, this Court now must determine (1) whether Fletcher has a contractual right to consent to the issuance of any security by a subsidiary of ION, (2) whether the ION S.àr.l. Note is such a security and, if it is, whether ION violated Fletcher's rights by issuing it without first seeking Fletcher's consent, and (3) whether ION's board of directors breached their fiduciary duty to Fletcher by failing to seek Fletcher's timely consent to issuance of the ION S.àr.l. Note or disclose material facts to Fletcher in connection with that Note.

Having examined the language of the relevant documents and finding no ambiguity, I hold that Fletcher does have a contractual right to consent to the issuance of any security-as that term is defined under Delaware and federal law-by a subsidiary of ION. Additionally, after examining the features of the ION S.àr.l. Note, particularly its convertibility feature, I conclude that it is a security of ION S.àr.l. that was issued by ION S.àr.l. Therefore, I hold that ION violated the terms of Section 5(B)(ii) of the Certificates of Rights and Preferences governing Fletcher's preferred stock by issuing the Note without Fletcher's consent. Finally, because Fletcher's claims against ION's board of directors for breach of fiduciary duty in connection with the issuance of the ION S.àr.l. Note seek to remedy the same conduct complained of in Fletcher's claim for breach of contract, I grant summary judgment for Defendants on that claim.

---

[75] [1] See Fletcher Int'l, Ltd. v. ION Geophysical Corp., [2010 Del. Ch. LEXIS 61 (Mar.24, 2010)].

[76] [2] *Id.*

I. BACKGROUND

A. The Parties

Plaintiff, Fletcher, is a Bermuda corporation and the beneficial owner of all outstanding Series D Preferred Stock of ION.

Defendant ION is a technology-focused seismic solutions company organized in Delaware. Defendant ION S.àr.l. is a Luxembourg private company. Defendants also include members of ION's board of directors . . . the "Director Defendants").

B. Facts

Beginning on February 15, 2005, and pursuant to the terms of an agreement between Fletcher and ION on that date, Fletcher purchased 30,000 shares of Series D-1, 5,000 shares of Series D-2, and 35,000 shares of Series D-3 Cumulative Convertible Preferred Stock of ION. Fletcher completed its last purchase in February 2008 and remains the sole holder of all outstanding Series D Preferred Stock.

The Certificates of Rights and Preferences for the Series D-1, D-2, and D-3 Preferred Stock (the "Certificates") establish the rights, preferences, privileges, and restrictions of holders of that stock. Section 5(B)(ii) of the Certificates provides, in pertinent part, that:

> The Holders shall have the following voting rights . . . The consent of Holders of at least a Majority of the Series [D-1, D-2, and D-3] Preferred Stock [respectively], voting separately as a single class with one vote per share, in person or by proxy, either in writing without a meeting or at an annual or a special meeting of such Holders called for the purpose, shall be necessary to: . . . permit any Subsidiary of [ION] to issue or sell, or obligate itself to issue or sell, except to [ION] or any wholly owned Subsidiary, any security of such Subsidiaries.

On October 23, 2009, ION issued a press release announcing, among other things, that ION had caused the issuance of two convertible promissory notes to BGP, Inc. ("BGP"), including the ION S.àr.l. Note, under its amended credit facility as one of several transactions intended to lead to the formation of a joint venture between ION and BGP (the "BGP Transactions"). Before the BGP Transactions closed on March 25, 2010, the amount of money drawn down under the ION S.àr.l. Note was convertible into shares of ION common stock at the discretion of the holder of the Note. After closing, however, the then-outstanding principal amounts due under the Note were to be converted automatically into shares of ION common stock unless the holder elected otherwise

* * *

D. Parties' Contentions

The Complaint asserts eight counts against ION, ION S.àr.l., and the Director Defendants, including claims for breaches of contract and fiduciary duty. The pending motion, however, deals only with the first two of those counts.

In Count I, Fletcher avers that, under Section 5(B)(ii) of the Certificates, ION cannot issue securities of its subsidiaries through any of those subsidiaries without Fletcher's consent and that ION violated that provision by unilaterally permitting ION S.àr.l. to issue the Note. In Count II, Fletcher argues that the Director Defendants breached their fiduciary duties of loyalty by failing to (1) provide Fletcher with a timely and meaningful vote on the issuance of the Note and (2) disclose all material facts concerning the ION S.àr.l. Note.

Defendants contend that Fletcher's motion must be denied as to Count I because the ION S.àr.l. Note is not a security as that term is used in Section 5(B)(ii) of the Certificates. In this regard, Defendants first argue that the parties intended "security" to include only equity securities. Second, they claim that, when analyzed under the *Reves* "family resemblance" test and viewed in the context in which it was issued, the Note represents nothing more than a commercial loan. Third, Defendants suggest the motion for summary judgment should be denied because Fletcher did not provide the only reasonable interpretation of "security." Defendants also urge denial of summary judgment on Count II because there is no difference between Fletcher's breach of contract and breach of fiduciary duty claims.

II. ANALYSIS

* * *

. . . I first analyze Fletcher's claim as it relates to Count I by examining Section 5(B)(ii) of the Certificates to determine if the meaning of "any security" in that provision is ambiguous and, if it is not, whether the ION S.àr.l. Note fits within the meaning of that term.

B. Did ION Violate Fletcher's Rights by Issuing the ION S.àr.l. Note Without Seeking Fletcher's Consent (Count I)?

Fletcher contends that, under Section 5(B)(ii) of the Certificates, ION must obtain Fletcher's consent before an ION subsidiary may issue "any security" of that subsidiary. There is no dispute that ION S.àr.l. is a subsidiary of ION. The parties do contest, however, whether the ION S.àr.l. Note fits within the ambit of a "security" as that term is used in the Certificates. A preferred stockholder's rights are primarily contractual in nature, and the construction of preferred stock provisions are matters of contract interpretation for the courts. Thus, before determining what "any security" means, I review briefly some pertinent principles of contract interpretation.

While the ultimate goal of contract interpretation is to give effect to the parties' shared intent, Delaware adheres to the "objective" theory of contracts and its courts interpret the language of a contract as it "would be understood by an objective, reasonable third party." As such, I must endeavor to determine not only what "the parties to the contract intended it to mean, but what a reasonable person in the position of the parties would have thought it meant."[77]

Because "[l]anguage in a vacuum may take on any number of meanings,"[78] the Court examines contractual language in the context of the document "as a whole" and "give[s] each provision and term effect, so as not to render any part of the contract mere surplusage."[79] Indeed, a court will "more readily assign contract language its intended meaning if it reads the language at issue within the context of the agreement in which it is located."[80]

This Court ordinarily allows the plain meaning of a contract to control, unless it is ambiguous. Importantly, "the language of an agreement . . . is not rendered ambiguous simply because the parties in litigation differ concerning its meaning."[81] The Court need only find ambiguity where the contested provisions are "reasonably or fairly susceptible of different interpretations or may have two or more different meanings."[82] Thus, unambiguous words in a contract, though undefined, typically are given their ordinary meaning unless multiple, reasonable interpretations exist. With these principles in mind, I turn to the language of the Certificates at issue here.

1. Is the phrase "any security" in Section 5(B)(ii) ambiguous?

The Certificates do not define "any security," as that phrase is used in Section 5(B)(ii), nor did the parties discuss the meaning of that phrase during negotiations. Nevertheless, Fletcher argues that the term is unambiguous and must be viewed as co-extensive with the statutory definition of security under Delaware and federal law. To support this interpretation of "any security," Fletcher notes that, in their respective definition sections, the Certificates define "Other Securities" as "any *stock . . . and other securities* of" ION. While not directly applicable to Section 5(B)(ii), that definition, according to Fletcher, reflects an understanding that "the term 'securities' [as used in that Section, encompasses] something beyond stock because the definition includes the phrase 'and other securities' in addition to any stock." I find Fletcher's interpretation reasonable because the disputed term "security" is used in the context of a contract prescribing the rights of holders of preferred stock in a publicly-traded corporation, over which the securities laws cast a long shadow.

---

[77] [21] Rhone — Poulenc Basic Chem. Co. v. Am Motorists Ins. Co., 616 A.2d 1192, 1196 (Del. 1992).
. . .

[78] [22] *USA Cable v. World Wrestling Fed'n Entm't, Inc.*, [2000 Del. Ch. LEXIS 87 (June 27, 2000)].

[79] [23] *Kuhn Constr., Inc. v. Diamond State Port Corp.*, 990 A.2d 393 (Del. Mar.8, 2010).

[80] [24] *USA Cable*, [2000 Del. Ch. LEXIS 87] ("Accordingly, while the canons of contract interpretation instruct an examination of the explicit contract language in order to determine the clause's meaning, one must simultaneously read that language within the context of the contract surrounding that language in order to best elicit the most appropriate meaning.").

[81] [26] *City Investing Co. Liquid. Trust v. Cont'l Cas. Co.*, 624 A.2d 1191, 1198 (Del. 1993).

[82] [27] *Rhone-Poulenc*, 616 A.2d at 1196; *see also E.I. du Pont de Nemours & Co., Inc. v. Allstate Ins. Co.*, 693 A.2d 1059, 1061 (Del. 1997) ("Contract language is not ambiguous simply because the parties disagree on its meaning."); *Chambers*, [2005 Del. Ch. LEXIS 118].

Defendants initially countered Fletcher's argument by asserting that, based on the parties' course of conduct and the business context in which the Certificates were drafted, "any security" must be interpreted to mean only "equity securities." Specifically, Defendants argued that Section 5(B)(ii) was intended to address only the sale of equity of an ION subsidiary (which could dilute the value of Fletcher's investment), not debt (which would not). Defendants did not, however, point to any cases or evidence indicating that their narrow, idiosyncratic interpretation is reasonable, consistent with the plain meaning of the phrase "any security," or in line with Fletcher's understanding of that phrase at the time the parties entered into the Certificates. Moreover, the definition of "Other Securities" in the Certificates contradicts even Defendants' subjective interpretation by indicating that the parties understood that term to encompass more than simply equity securities when they drafted those documents.

But, even if I accepted Defendants' unsupported claim that they subjectively understood Section 5(B)(ii) to include only equity securities, it would be immaterial because I must interpret "any security" objectively. In that regard, the evidence suggests that a reasonable person in the position of the parties likely would have understood the term "any security" to include instruments generally recognized to be securities under federal and state securities statutes and regulations. Defendants did not present any reasonable, alternative definition. Therefore, I hold that "security" is not ambiguous and must be afforded its ordinary meaning as it has developed under federal and state law.

2. Is the ION S.àr.l. Note a "security"?

Even under this definition, however, the question remains whether a convertible promissory note, like the ION S.àr.l. Note, is indeed a security. Fletcher acknowledges that certain classes of notes are not securities, but contends that notes that are convertible into stock unquestionably meet the definition of a "security" under both Delaware and federal law. In response, Defendants claim that, under the *Reves* "family resemblance" test, the ION S.àr.l. Note is not a security because the commercial context in which the Note was issued indicates that it was, in reality, nothing more than a commercial bank loan.[83] In this regard, Defendants minimize the importance of the Note's convertibility feature as "simply a mechanism designed" to allow this "loan" to be more conveniently unwound if the BGP Transactions failed to close. For the reasons addressed below, I find Defendants' argument unpersuasive and hold that, as a debt instrument convertible into equity securities, the ION S.àr.l. Note qualifies as a "security" under Section 5(B)(ii) of the Certificates.

The United States Supreme Court held in *Reves v. Ernst & Young* that all notes presumptively fall within the definition of a "security."[84] This presumption can be rebutted only by showing that a particular note bears a strong resemblance to one

[83] [33] *See Reves v. Ernst & Young*, 494 U.S. 56, 63, 110 S. Ct. 945, 108 L.Ed.2d 47 (1990).

[84] [35] 494 U.S. 56, 65, 110 S. Ct. 945, 108 L. Ed.2d 47 (1990). The *Reves* test was adopted by the Delaware Supreme Court in *Boo'ze v. State*, [846 A.2d 237] (Del. 2004).

of a judicially crafted list of categories of instruments that are not securities.[85] To determine if a strong resemblance exists, a court must examine (1) the motivations that would prompt a reasonable seller and buyer to enter into the transaction, (2) the plan of distribution of the instrument, (3) the reasonable expectations of the investing public, and (4) the existence of some factor that significantly reduces the risk of the instrument, thus rendering application of the securities statutes unnecessary. *Reves* emphasized, however, that when examining these four factors, courts should remember that the "fundamental essence of a 'security' [is] its character as an 'investment.' "

Though *Reves* clearly applies to instruments solely evidencing debt, the convertibility feature of the ION S.àr.l. Note may eliminate the need to examine that instrument under the "family resemblance" test. Indeed, some courts have held convertible notes to be securities without any apparent examination under *Reves.* Other courts have applied the *Reves* factors and, predictably, found a convertible note to be a security.

In this case, the hybrid nature of the ION S.àr.l. Note, which its holder could convert at any time into common stock of ION, strongly supports finding it to be a security under Delaware and federal securities law.[86] Moreover, even considering the ION S.àr.l. Note under the "family resemblance" test, I hold it to be a security because the Note is most naturally understood as an investment in ION, rather than a purely commercial or consumer transaction. The Note is "freely assignable and transferable" by its holder, convertible into common shares of a publicly traded company, and subject to an investment risk, even if that risk is arguably small. These factors all support the conclusion that the ION S.àr.l. Note is an "investment," as that term is used in *Reves*, and, thus, a security. Furthermore, when I compare it to the judicially crafted list of notes that are clearly not securities, I find that the ION S.àr.l. Note "neither fits into . . . nor bears a strong family resemblance to any of those categories." Thus, I hold that the Note is a security as that term is used in Section 5(B)(ii) of the Certificates.[87]

---

[85] [36] The types of notes generally not considered securities include [1] a "note delivered in consumer financing, [2][a] note secured by a mortgage on a home, [3][a] short-term note secured by a lien on a small business or some of its assets, [4][a] note evidencing a 'character' loan to a bank customer, [5] short-term notes secured by an assignment of accounts receivable, or [6] a note which simply formalizes an open-account debt incurred in the ordinary course of business (particularly if, as in the case of the customer of a broker, it is collateralized)." 494 U.S. at 65 (quoting *Exch. Nat'l Bank v. Touche Ross & Co.*, 544 F.2d 1126, 1138 (2d Cir. 1976)).

[86] [41] The investment in the ION S.àr.l. Note apparently was conceived initially as a bridge loan from the Bank of China to ION S.àr.l. in connection with the BGP Transactions. According to the terms of ION's amended credit facility, under which the Note was issued, however, the anticipated repayment of the Note at closing would have triggered certain *pro rata* repayment requirements. *See supra* note 7. Considering that option undesirable, the parties to the BGP Transaction included a convertibility function in the Note to avoid the repayment requirement.

[87] [45] This conclusion is buttressed by the fact that the ION S.àr.l. Note was issued with a legend that begins: "THE SECURITIES REPRESENTED BY THIS CONVERTIBLE PROMISSORY NOTE HAVE NOT BEEN REGISTERED UNDER THE SECURITIES ACT OF 1933. . . .". . . . Such a legend is required whenever a security is sold pursuant to an exception to the registration requirements of the Securities Act of 1933 ("Securities Act"). *See* 17 C.F.R. § 230.144A(d)(2) ("The seller and any person acting on its behalf [must take] reasonable steps to ensure that the purchaser is aware that the seller may rely on the exemption from the provisions of section 5 [of the Act provided by this

> When the Note was issued, it was understood that, as the Note's holder, the Bank of China almost certainly would exercise its right to convert it into ION common stock because the option to convert was issued in the money. *See supra* note 9. As Brian Hanson, CFO of ION, stated in his deposition: "I think absolutely the Chinese . . . will exercise their conversion rights [to convert the Note into shares of ION common stock] . . . prior to having their . . . rights expire." Tr. 68-69. Hanson further declared that "the intent behind the bridge loan . . . was to advance the equity investment" reflected in the BGP Transactions. *Id.* at 69-70.

Defendants add another wrinkle to this analysis, however. Specifically, they argue that issuance of the ION S.àr.l. Note does not violate Section 5(B)(ii) because the Note is convertible into shares of ION, not ION S.àr.l.[88] According to this argument, because the Note is convertible into ION's common stock, it must be considered a security of ION, and because ION did not need Fletcher's consent to issue its own securities under the Certificates, Fletcher's voting rights were not violated. Fletcher responds that, even though the ION S.àr.1 Note contains an option allowing it to be converted into shares of ION stock, the Note is still a security of ION S.àr.l. because it issued the Note. I agree with Fletcher in this regard.

By its terms, the ION S.àr.l. Note closely resembles an option contract whereby ION S.àr.l. grants the holder of the Note an option to voluntarily convert the amount drawn down under that Note into shares of ION common stock. Generally, an option to purchase an equity security-like the ION S.àr.l. Note-is itself a security. Additionally, at least some courts have held that options should be considered securities of the entity issuing them. One basis for treating options as a security of the entity issuing them, as opposed to the entity issuing the underlying securities, is that options and their underlying securities are frequently sold on different markets and constitute separate financial products.

Here, the ION S.àr.l. Note, though convertible into securities of ION, was issued by ION S.àr.l., which received the benefit and bore the burden of issuing that Note. I, therefore, find that the Note is a security of ION S.àr.l. and hold that ION violated Fletcher's consent rights when it allowed its subsidiary to issue such a security without first seeking Fletcher's consent.

---

section" in order for the exemption to apply). The Note also states that "[i]n the event of any proposed transfer . . . the Issuer may require . . . that it receive reasonable transfer documentation that is sufficient to evidence that such proposed transfer complies with the Securities Act and other applicable state and foreign securities laws.". . . . While it may be true, as Defendants suggest, that the legend was added by the lawyers negotiating the terms of the ION S.àr.l. Note simply out of "an abundance of caution," *see* Tr. 54-55, its inclusion nevertheless evidences Defendants' own recognition that the Note could be viewed by investors and regulators as a security subject to the Securities Act.

[88] [46] Defendants base this argument on the facts that, according to the Certificates, ION does not need Fletcher's consent to issue its own securities and need only seek such consent when one of its subsidiaries issues "any security *of such Subsidiaries.*" POB Ex. A § 5(B)(ii) (emphasis added).

C. Did the Director Defendants Breach Their Duty of Disclosure (Count II)?

Having determined that ION violated Fletcher's consent rights by issuing the ION S.àr.l. Note, I next turn to Fletcher's motion for summary judgment on Count II.

Fletcher claims that the Director Defendants breached their fiduciary duties to Fletcher as a preferred stockholder by failing to (1) provide Fletcher with a timely, meaningful, and informed vote in connection with the issuance of the ION S.àr.l. Note or (2) disclose fully and fairly all material information within the board's control in connection with issuance of the ION S.àr.l. Note. Defendants urge the Court to deny summary judgment on Count II, claiming that there is no difference between Fletcher's contractual and fiduciary duty claims, all of which stem from Section 5(B)(ii) of the Certificates and the same alleged wrongdoing. I agree with Defendants' contention.

The Director Defendants' failure to seek Fletcher's consent before issuing the ION S.àr.l. Note implicates rights defined by the Certificates as opposed to those that may be defined by fiduciary duty principles. Also, the Director Defendants premised their decision not to disclose material information in connection with issuance of the ION S.àr.l. Note on their belief that Fletcher was not entitled to vote on that transaction. Whether that decision was right or wrong, the Director Defendants acted on the basis of their interpretation of Section 5(B)(ii) of the Certificates. Therefore, any fiduciary duty claims asserted by Fletcher based on an alleged violation of either the duty of loyalty or the "duty of disclosure" arise out of and are superfluous to the breach of contract claims raised in Count I. As such, I grant summary judgment in favor of Defendants as to Count II.

The rights of preferred stockholders are primarily contractual in nature. Yet, while a board of directors does not owe fiduciary duties to preferred stockholders to the same extent as common stockholders, that is not to say that such duties are nonexistent or that preferred stockholders only may seek to hold directors liable for violation of explicit contractual duties. Indeed, "it has been recognized that directors may owe duties of loyalty and care" to preferred stockholders, particularly in cases where nonexistent contractual rights leave "the holder of preferred stock [in an] exposed and vulnerable position vis-à-vis the board of directors." Thus, if preferred stockholders "share a right equally with the common shareholders the directors owe the preferred shareholders the same fiduciary duties they owe the common shareholders *with respect to those rights.*" For instance, directors owe preferred stockholders a duty to disclose material information in connection with common voting rights. But, rights arising from documents governing a preferred class of stock, such as the Certificates, that are enjoyed solely by that preferred class, do not give rise to fiduciary duties because such rights are purely contractual in nature.

Even when directors do owe fiduciary duties to preferred stockholders, however, if claims for breach of such duties are based on the same facts underlying a breach of contract claim and relate to "rights and obligations expressly provided by contract," then such claims are "superfluous." As a result, unless the fiduciary duty claims are based on duties and rights *not* provided for by contract, a plaintiff cannot maintain both contractual and fiduciary duty claims arising out of the same alleged wrongdoing.

In this case, Fletcher's right to vote on an ION subsidiary's issuance of securities is provided for in Section 5(B)(ii) of the Certificates and, as a result, is "essentially contractual" in nature. Because Fletcher can remedy the violation of that voting right through its breach of contract claim, it has no need to assert a fiduciary duty claim based on the same contractual consent rights. Additionally, the duty to disclose material information to preferred stockholders in connection with the right to vote is premised on there actually being a vote. Here, the Director Defendants determined that Fletcher was not entitled to vote based on their interpretation of the Certificates and, not surprisingly, saw no need to disclose information to Fletcher in connection with the BGP Transactions. But whether or not that decision was correct, it is inextricably intertwined with Fletcher's claim that Defendants breached the Certificates. Any remedy for Defendants' conduct may thus be obtained under Count I, and there is no need for an overlapping breach of fiduciary duty claim. Therefore, I grant summary judgment on Count II in favor of Defendants.

III. CONCLUSION

For the foregoing reasons, I grant Fletcher's motion for summary judgment on Count I to the extent it seeks declaratory judgment that Section 5(B)(ii) of the Certificates is valid and binding on ION and that ION breached its obligations under that section by permitting ION S.àr.l. to issue the ION S.àr.l. Note without first obtaining Fletcher's consent. Additionally, I deny Fletcher's motion on Count II and, instead, grant summary judgment on that claim in favor of Defendants.

TERRY v. PENN CENTRAL CORP.

United States Court of Appeals, Third Circuit
668 F.2d 188 (1981)

ADAMS, CIRCUIT JUDGE

The Penn Central Corporation ("Penn Central"), an appellee in this case, has sought to acquire Colt Industries Inc. ("Colt"), also an appellee, by merging Colt with PCC Holdings, Inc. ("Holdings"), a wholly-owned subsidiary of Penn Central. Howard L. Terry and W. H. Hunt, the appellants, are shareholders of Penn Central who objected to the transaction. In a diversity action before the United States District Court for the Eastern District of Pennsylvania, appellants sought injunctive and declaratory relief to enforce voting and dissenters' rights to which appellants asserted they were entitled. Appellants further sought to enjoin Holdings from proceeding with the proposed merger, and in particular moved to enjoin a vote on the transaction, scheduled for October 29, 1981, by the shareholders of Penn Central. In an opinion issued on October 22, 1981, Judge Pollak denied appellants' requests. Appellants thereupon filed an appeal in this Court, and then petitioned for a temporary injunction against the proposed shareholder vote until the appeal on the merits of the district court order could be heard. On October 27, following oral argument, we entered an order denying the petition for temporary injunction, stating that appellants had failed to demonstrate a sufficient likelihood of prevailing on the merits. C.A. No. 81-3955. The shareholders of Penn Central voted, as scheduled, on October 29. Pursuant to an expedited hearing schedule, the appeal from the district court's denial of injunctive and declaratory relief was submitted to this Court following oral argument on November 5.

After argument on appeal, the shareholders disapproved of the merger, and the corporations thereafter publicly announced their abandonment of this particular merger. Penn Central, however, has not abandoned its proposed series of acquisitions, of which the Colt acquisition was merely one instance.

I.

Penn Central is the successor to the Penn Central Transportation Corporation, which underwent a reorganization under the bankruptcy laws that was completed in 1978. No longer involved in the railroading business, Penn Central, since 1978, has had the advantage, for tax purposes, of a large loss carry-forward. In order to put that loss carry-forward to its best use, Penn Central has embarked on a program of acquiring corporations whose profits could be sheltered. To this end Penn Central created Holdings, a wholly-owned subsidiary which was to acquire the businesses that Penn Central desired. The first acquisition under the plan was Marathon Manufacturing Company ("Marathon"), in 1979. In the Marathon acquisition, a [series] of preferred Penn Central stock was created, [from the 30,000,000 authorized shares of Preferred Stock] and 6,646,182 million shares of "First Series Preference Stock" w[ere] issued to the owners of Marathon stock. Appellants were shareholders of Marathon who thereby obtained shares of this First Series Preference Stock. Terry was promptly elected to the Penn Central board of directors.

In 1981, Penn Central decided upon another acquisition: Colt. The management and directors of Colt and Penn Central agreed upon a merger of Colt into Holdings, compensated for by issuance of a [9,297,163 shares of] second series of Penn Central preference stock to Colt shareholders. Terry opposed the merger at the directors' meeting, and sought to preclude the consummation of the transaction.

Appellants proffered before the district court and reiterate before this Court a number of arguments. First, appellants assert that under the terms of the Penn Central Articles of Incorporation, as amended in 1979, the holders of First Series Preference Stock are entitled to a class vote on a transaction such as the Colt-Holdings merger, in which vote a two-thirds majority of First Series shareholders would be required to authorize the merger.[89]

. . .

[89] [1] Appellants also asserted in the district court that they were entitled to a class vote under New York Law, N.Y. Bus. Corp. Law § 804(a). The district court held that New York law was not applicable, and appellants do not seek review of that ruling in this Court.

II.

Appellants assert that under Section 5(d) of the Penn Central Amended Articles of Incorporation,[90] they are entitled, as holders of First Series Preference Stock, to a class vote on the authorization of the issuance of any later series of preference stock. Specifically, they maintain that Penn Central may not issue the proposed Second Series Preference Stock to the acquired company's shareholders without the approval of two-thirds of the present First Series shareholders. Reviewing the language of Section 5(d), we note that a careful distinction is drawn between the rights of Preference shareholders against other shareholders on the one hand, and of First Series stockholders against other Series stockholders on the other. Because the proposed merger does not create shares that are superior in any way to the Preference shares generally, we conclude that the only language even arguably relevant is the language addressing the rights of First Series stockholders against the issuance of a later series. Section 5(d) provides, in that respect, that First Series shareholders are entitled to a class vote before the corporation may modify the Articles of Incorporation or authorize a merger that would "adversely affect the First Series Preference Stock but would not adversely affect each other series of Preference Stock." No class vote, however, is required for the issuance of "any shares of any class or series of capital stock which is subordinate to shares of First Series Preference Stock. . . ." Appellants construe these sections as requiring a

---

[90] [4] That Section provides:

(d) The Corporation may, in the manner provided by Article Ninth hereof and as permitted by Pennsylvania law, from time to time alter or change the voting rights, preferences, qualifications, privileges, limitations, restrictions, options, conversion rights or other special or relative rights of the First Series Preference Stock; provided, however, that without the affirmative vote of the holders of at least two-thirds of the outstanding shares of all series of Preference Stock, the Corporation shall not amend, alter, change, add or insert any provision in these Articles which, or authorize the merger or consolidation of the Corporation with any other corporation if the plan of such merger or consolidation contains any provision which if contained in these Articles, would (i) make any adverse change in the voting rights, preferences, qualifications, privileges, limitations, restrictions, options, conversion rights or special or relative rights of Preference Stocks, (ii) authorize a new class of stock senior or superior to Preference Stock or (iii) increase the number of authorized shares of a senior or superior class of stock, and, without the affirmative vote of the holders of at least a majority of the outstanding shares of all series of Preference Stock, the Corporation shall not amend, alter, change, add or insert any provision in these Articles which, or authorize the merger or consolidation of the Corporation with any other corporation if the plan of such merger or consolidation contains any provision which if contained in these Articles, would increase the authorized number of shares of Preference Stock. *Without the affirmative vote of the holders of at least two-thirds of the outstanding shares of First Series Preference Stock, the Corporation shall not amend, alter, change, add or insert any provision in these Articles which, or authorize the merger or consolidation of the Corporation with any other corporation if the plan of such merger or consolidation contains any provision which if contained in these Articles, would adversely affect the First Series Preference Stock but would not adversely affect each other series of Preference Stock.* The holders of First Series Preference Stock shall not be entitled to participate in any such class vote if provision is made pursuant to Section 6 for the redemption at or prior to the time when any such alteration or change is to take effect of all shares of First Series Preference Stock at the time outstanding. *Nothing in this Section 5 shall require a class vote or consent in connection with the authorization, designation, increase or issuance of any shares of any class or series of capital stock which is subordinate to shares of First Series Preference Stock as to dividends and liquidation preference*, or in connection with the authorization, designation, increase or issuance of any bonds, mortgages, debentures or other obligations of the Corporation, or because of any adjustment in the provisions of First Series Preference Stock made pursuant to Section 4(c). (Emphasis added)

class vote for the issuance of this Second Series Preference Stock because it is not "subordinate," but rather on a par with, the First Series stock, and because the proposed Second Series stock allegedly has some voting rights superior to those of First Series stock such that its creation "adversely affects" First Series stock but not other series of preference stock.

As the district court held, this argument misconstrues section 5(d). The district court found that, at the time of the creation of the First Series Preference Stock, the persons acquiring that stock specifically sought and were denied the right to a class vote on the issuance of subsequent series of equivalent preference stock-the very right they now claim. Moreover, the district court found, again as a factual matter, that the proposed Second Series shareholders would not have any rights superior to those holding First Series stock. Neither finding is clearly erroneous, and we therefore conclude that nothing in Section 5(d) requires a class vote by the First Series shareholders on the issuance of the proposed Second Series.

. . . .

NOTE

The terms of the Series A Preferred Stock set forth earlier in this chapter (the "Series A Preferred Stock") provide in certain cases for a separate class vote in the event of the issuance of a parity preferred.

WARNER COMMUNICATIONS INC. v. CHRIS-CRAFT INDUSTRIES, INC.

Delaware Court of Chancery
583 A.2d 962 (1989)

ALLEN, CHANCELLOR

Pending is a motion for judgment on the pleadings. Plaintiffs seek a determination that the related holders of Warner Communications Inc.'s Series B Variable Rate Cumulative Convertible Preferred stock ("Series B Preferred") are not entitled to a class vote upon a proposed merger among Warner, its controlling shareholder Time Incorporated (now renamed Time Warner Inc.) and TW Sub Inc., a wholly owned subsidiary of Time Warner. Plaintiffs in this declaratory judgment action are the parties proposing the merger — Warner, Time and TW Sub, all of which are Delaware corporations. Defendants are two corporations, Chris-Craft Industries, Inc. and its controlled subsidiary, BHC, Inc., which together with its wholly owned subsidiary, is the holder of the Series B Preferred stock. For purposes of this opinion, plaintiffs generally will be referred to as Warner; Time Warner, for purposes of clarity, will be referred to as Time and the holders of the Series B Preferred will be referred to as BHC. The merger in question is the proposed "back end" of a transaction, the first stage of which was a public tender offer for 51% of Warner's common stock for cash that closed on July 24, 1989. In that merger, the Series B Preferred stock would be cancelled and BHC as the holder of it would receive a new senior security, Time Series BB Convertible Preferred. For purposes of this motion (but for those purposes only), plaintiffs have stipulated that

that substitution would adversely affect defendants. For the reasons that follow, I conclude that BHC has no right under the Warner certificate of incorporation to a class vote on the proposed merger. In brief, I reach this conclusion upon consideration of the pertinent provisions of the Series B Preferred stock's certificate of designation read in the context of the entire document and in the context of the established corporation law. This consideration compels the conclusion that the drafters of this document did not intend the holder of the Series B Preferred to possess a veto over every merger in which its interest would be adversely affected. Such a right was conferred expressly but only in narrowly defined circumstances concededly not present here. Absent such circumstances, I conclude that there is no right in the holders of the Series B Preferred to a class vote on a merger. The statement of the reasoning that leads to this conclusion entails a separate treatment of each of the two certificate of designation provisions — Section 3.3(i) and Section 3.4(i) — upon which BHC predicates its contrary assertion. The facts are as admitted in the Answer and the Reply to Counterclaim. Neither party contends that there are material facts in dispute at this stage (on the assumption that the Series B Preferred shareholders will be adversely affected by the merger) and both assert that the legal question presented is appropriately addressed on the pleadings as they now exist.

I. The Series B Preferred Stock

The Series B Preferred was issued pursuant to an Exchange Agreement dated as of December 29, 1983 among Warner, Chris-Craft and BHC. Under that Exchange Agreement, Warner obtained BHC preferred stock convertible into 42.5% of BHC's outstanding common stock. BHC obtained the entire issue, 15,200,000 shares, of Warner's Series B Preferred stock. As provided in the certificate of designation creating the Series B Preferred, each share of that stock is entitled to a quarterly dividend equal to the greater of (a) $0.125 or (b) 200% of the regular quarterly dividend, if any, payable on a share of Warner common stock.[91]

Each share is convertible into common stock in accordance with a complex formula, and each carries the same voting rights as the common stock, except in the event that a dividend is in default. In that event, the Series B Preferred stock "voting as a class" elects three directors. Generally, however:

> Except as otherwise by the Certificate of Incorporation or by law provided, the shares of Series B Stock and the shares of Common Stock . . . shall be voted together as one class. Certificate of Designation, Section 3.1. Two provisions do otherwise provide, and it is they that provide the ground upon which the parties' ongoing battle[92] is now fought. Section 3.3 of the certificate of designation creates a right in the holders of the Series

[91] [1] A two-for-one stock split in 1986 resulted in a proportionate adjustment of the original formula, which was the greater of (a) $0.125 or (b) 100% of the regular quarterly dividend, if any, on common stock.

[92] [2] These parties have not had harmonious relations. *See, e.g., Warner Communications Inc., et al. v. Chris-Craft Industries, Inc., et al.*, Del. Ch., C.A. No. 10817, 1989 WL 51662[, 1989 Del. Ch. LEXIS 62] (May 15, 1989).

B Preferred to participate with other holders of Warner preferred in a class vote under certain circumstances. Section 3.4(i) of the certificate creates a right in the holders of Series B Preferred stock alone to a series vote in certain circumstances. Section 3.3 provides in pertinent part as follows:

> So long as any shares of Series B Stock shall be outstanding and unless the consent or approval of a greater number of shares shall then be required by law, (i) the affirmative vote or written consent of the holders of at least two-thirds of the total number of the then outstanding shares of Series B Stock and of any other series of Preferred Stock having the right to vote as a class on such matter, voting as a class, shall be necessary to alter or change any rights, preferences or limitations of the Preferred Stock so as to affect the holders of all of such shares adversely. . . .

In pertinent part, Section 3.4 provides as follows:

> So long as any shares of Series B Stock shall be outstanding and unless the consent or approval of a greater number of shares shall then be required by law, without first obtaining the consent or approval of the holders of at least two-thirds of the number of shares of the Series B Stock at the time outstanding, given in person or by proxy either in writing or at a meeting at which the holders of such shares shall be entitled to vote separately as a class, the Corporation shall not (i) amend, alter or repeal any of the provisions of the Certificate of Incorporation or By-laws of the Corporation so as to affect adversely any of the preferences, rights, powers or privileges of the Series B Stock or the holders thereof. . . .

The Proposed Warner-Time Merger

Time and Warner have executed a merger agreement, which was amended and restated as of June 16, 1989. That agreement contemplates a two-step transaction by which Time would acquire all of the outstanding stock of Warner. The first step was completed on July 24, 1989 when Time accepted for purchase 100 million shares of Warner common stock, representing approximately 50% of Warner's common stock, at $70 per share in cash. Under the amended merger agreement, the tender offer is to be followed by a merger in which TW Sub will be merged into Warner which will survive as a wholly owned subsidiary of Time. The Warner common stock, other than that held by Time, will be converted into securities, cash or other property.[93] The Warner Series B Preferred is to be converted into Time Series BB Preferred stock. The rights and preferences of the Time Series BB Preferred are set forth in a proposed form of certificate of designation.

Since the parties have stipulated for the purposes of this motion that the holders of Warner Series B Preferred will be adversely affected by the back-end merger, it is unnecessary to summarize the terms of the Time BB Preferred. The amended merger agreement provides that shares of Warner common stock and Warner Series B Preferred stock, the holders of which comply with all provisions of the

---

[93] [3] The pleadings do not disclose, nor is it pertinent for present purposes, just what form that consideration will take.

General Corporation Law concerning appraisal rights, will not be converted in the back-end merger.

. . .

III.

BHC contends that it is entitled to a class vote on the proposed merger under two distinct provisions of Warner's certificate of incorporation. First, defendants argue that Section 3.3(i) of the certificate of designation gives BHC the right to a class vote. It contends that Section 3.3(i) protects against any corporate action that alters or changes "any rights or preferences" of the preferred stock so as to adversely affect the preferred shareholders. The proposed merger, it says, will alter the rights of the Series B Preferred (and on this motion presumptively in an adverse way) by substituting a new security — Time BB Preferred — for the Series B Preferred. Thus, it concludes, Section 3.3(i) requires that BHC be afforded the opportunity to vote on that merger separately. Second, defendants argue that Section 3.4(i) of the certificate of designation entitles BHC to a vote on the back-end merger because the Warner certificate of incorporation will admittedly be amended by the merger and necessarily so under Section 243 of the Delaware corporation law. That amendment they say — eliminating the provisions authorizing the Series B Preferred — will adversely affect BHC and will trigger the right to a class vote under Section 3.4(i). Finally, defendants contend that the fact that Section 3.4(iii) (quoted below at pp. 22-23) specifically addresses mergers does not preclude other sections, such as Sections 3.3(i) and 3.4(i), from applying to mergers. Warner answers that it is Section 3.4(iii) of the certificate of designation that is the dispositive provision relating to mergers. That section requires supermajority approval of a merger by the holders of Series B Preferred if in the merger they receive equity securities that are not the highest ranked equity securities of the surviving, resulting or acquiring corporation. Warner points out that under the merger the holders of Series B Preferred stock will receive Time Series BB Preferred stock which will be the senior equity security of Time. Thus, plaintiffs contend that Section 3.4(iii) is the pertinent provision and it grants no right to vote on the back-end merger to the Series B Preferred shareholders. As to BHC's claim that Sections 3.3(i) and 3.4(i) do grant it the right to a class vote in these circumstances, Warner contends first that Section 3.3(i) was intended to protect only rights and preferences of the entire class of preferred stock, not rights and preferences granted to one or more particular series of preferred stock. The only right or preference necessarily shared by every series of preferred stock, plaintiffs continue, is the right granted in Article Fourth (C), clause (2) of Warner's certificate of incorporation to share ratably in dividends and asset distribution in certain circumstances.[94] That right, they say, will not be affected in the merger as the Time

[94] [4] That provision reads as follows:

> The Corporation may issue the Preferred Stock in series. The Board of Directors shall have authority to establish and designate each such series before issuance, to distinguish the shares of each series from shares of all other series, and to fix the number of shares included in each such series and, except as otherwise provided in this Article, the variations in the relative rights, preferences and limitations as between series, provided that when the stated

Series BB Preferred will be protected by an identical provision in Time's charter.

Second, it is argued that Section 3.4(i), which requires supermajority approval by the Series B Preferred shares in order to amend Warner's certificate of incorporation or bylaws "so as to affect adversely" the Series B Preferred, does not grant defendants a vote in the back-end merger because it is the merger, not the amendments to the certificate of incorporation, that will (presumably) adversely affect defendants.

IV.

In evaluating these contending positions, it should first be noted that the existence and extent of special stock rights are determined by reference to the issuer's certificate of incorporation; such rights are essentially contractual in nature. *Rothschild International Corp. v. Liggett Group, Inc.*, Del. Supr., 474 A.2d 133, 136 (1984); *Wood v. Coastal States Gas Corp.*, Del. Supr., 401 A.2d 932, 937 (1979); *Ellingwood v. Wolf's Head Oil Refining Co.*, Del. Supr., 38 A.2d 743, 747 (1944). In determining them, a court should apply the same techniques of contract interpretation generally applied to contractual disputes. Thus, the certificate of designation should be construed in its entirety, and an attempt should be made to reconcile all of the certificate's provisions "in order to determine the meaning intended to be given to any portion of it." *Ellingwood, supra*, at 747. *See Wood, supra*, at 937. While the effort is to arrive at the intended meaning of the words employed, it is generally said that rights or preferences over common stock should be clearly expressed and not presumed. *Rothschild, supra*, at 136; *Ellingwood, supra*, at 747; *Rainbow Navigation, Inc. v. Yonge*, Del. Ch., C.A. No. 9432, [1989 Del. Ch. LEXIS 41] 1989 WL 40805 (April 24, 1989).

V.

For the reasons set forth below, I conclude that defendants' claims are not sound and that plaintiffs are entitled to declaratory judgment to the effect that they seek. This conclusion follows from the following, more detailed conclusions that: 1. Section 3.4(i) does not create a right to a class vote on the proposed merger despite the fact that Warner's certificate of incorporation is being amended in the merger because, in the circumstances, the amendment itself will not "adversely affect" the Series B Preferred. (*See* pp. 967-968, *infra*); 2. Assuming Section 3.3(i) covers "rights" other than those created by the ratability provision of Warner's charter (see n.6 regarding that assumption), then with respect to alteration or change of such rights by charter amendment, the same reasoning that supports the conclusion that the proposed merger does not trigger a class vote under Section 3.4(i) requires an identical conclusion with respect to 3.3(i). (*See* pp. 968-969, *infra*). 3. If the amendment of Warner's certificate does not trigger the class vote provisions of

---

dividends and amounts payable on liquidation are not paid in full, the shares of all series of Preferred Stock shall share ratably in the payment of dividends including accumulations, if any, in accordance with the sums which would be payable on such shares if all dividends were declared and paid in full, and in any distribution of assets other than by way of dividends in accordance with the sums which would be payable on such distribution if all sums payable were discharged in full. . . .

either 3.4(i) or 3.3(i), the dispositive question becomes whether the merger itself may trigger that result under the language of Section 3.3(i). Stated differently, the core issue here may be said to be whether the predicate words of Section 3.3(i), "alter or change," are to be read to include "convert pursuant to a merger." I conclude that Section 3.3(i) does not create a right to a class vote on a merger that will convert the Series B Preferred stock into other securities, other property or cash. (*See* pp. 968-971 *infra*).

A.

As here pertinent, Section 3.4(i) provides a right to a series vote (*i.e.*, the Series B Preferred voting alone) in the event of a charter amendment that amends, alters or repeals any provision of the certificate of incorporation so as to adversely affect the Series B Preferred or its holders. Warner will be the surviving corporation in the proposed merger. Its charter will be amended in the merger. It is assumed that the substitution of the merger consideration for the Series B Preferred stock is damaging to defendants. Nevertheless, Section 3.4(i) does not, in my opinion, grant a right to a series vote in these circumstances because the adverse effect upon defendants is not caused by an amendment, alteration or repeal of any provision of Warner's certificate of incorporation. Rather, it is the conversion of the Warner Series B Preferred into Time Series BB Preferred that creates the adverse effect. But the conversion of the Warner Series B Preferred into the Time BB Preferred does not depend to any extent upon the amendment of the Warner certificate of incorporation under Section 242 of the General Corporation Law. That conversion will occur pursuant to Section 251 of the statute which authorizes mergers and defines the steps necessary to effectuate a merger. Given that the merger itself is duly authorized,[95] the conversion of the Series B Preferred stock could occur without any prior or contemporaneous amendment to the certificate. Since the merger does contemplate the conversion of the Series B Preferred into the securities of another company, it is to be expected that the certificate would be amended to reflect the removal of these securities from the firm's capital structure. Section 243 requires such a step as a housekeeping matter, but that section does not require that amendment to be contemporaneous with the retirement of the stock and it surely does not make conversion of the stock dependent upon the amendment it contemplates. Rather, the amendment contemplated is necessitated by the merger; such an amendment, like the conversion, flows from the merger and is not a necessary condition of it. Stated in terms of the language of Section 3.4(i), given the existence of the merger, the amendments of the certificate of incorporation can in no event themselves be said to "affect" BHC "adversely," even if one assumes, as I do on this motion, that the substitution of the Time BB Preferred stock for Warner Series B Preferred stock does have an adverse affect.

---

[95] [5] There is no claim that Section 242(b)(2), which does create a right to a class vote when a charter amendment alters or changes the rights of the shares of a particular class of stock, itself creates a right to a class vote on the merger.

B.

I turn then to Section 3.3(i). It requires a class vote (the Series B stock voting with any other series of preferred stock that has a vote on the question presented) in order to: "alter or change any rights . . . of the Preferred stock so as to affect the holders of all such shares adversely." The central concern of Section 3.3(i) is action that would "alter or change" rights of the "Preferred Stock."[96]

In addressing Section 3.3(i), it is analytically helpful to break down the universe of acts that might arguably "alter or change . . . rights of Preferred Stock" into two classes: amendments to a certificate of incorporation and other forms of acts, such as mergers, that might affect the holders of preferred stock. At first blush, Section 3.3(i) appears to be principally directed to charter amendments, because under Delaware law, special stock rights and preferences are set forth in a corporate charter. Such rights must be stated in, or derivable in a manner clearly set forth in, the certificate of incorporation (8 Del. C. § 151(a)) or set forth in a certificate of designation which, when effective (8 Del. C. § 103), amends and becomes a part of the certificate of incorporation (8 Del. C. § 151(g)). Insofar as Section 3.3(i) does address charter amendments, the amendments that will follow the Warner-Time merger fail to trigger its provisions for the same reason that those amendments fail to trigger a series vote under Section 3.4(i): the amendments contemplated in the merger will not themselves adversely affect the preferred stock.

The pending motion may thus be seen to come down to the question whether the class vote contemplated by Section 3.3(i) can, in addition to being triggered by an amendment to the certificate of incorporation that "alters . . . rights . . . adversely," be triggered by other forms of transactions in which the interests of holders of the preferred — and arguably "the rights . . . of the Preferred Stock" — are adversely affected. Specifically, does Section 3.3(i) reach mergers? Will the Series B Preferred be altered or changed in the merger within the meaning of Section 3.3(i)? Concededly, the shares of that stock will be converted into a new security by operation of law in the merger. Did the parties that drafted Section 3.3(i) intend conversion of stock in a merger to be contemplated within the phrase "alter or change" I cannot conclude, viewing the certificate of designation in its entirety, that there is even a reasonable likelihood that they did. The draftsmen of this language-the negotiators to the extent it has actually been negotiated[97] — must be deemed to have understood, and no doubt did understand, that under Delaware law (and generally) the securities whose characteristics were being defined in the certificate of designation could be converted by merger into "shares or other

---

[96] [6] For purposes of this motion, I assume but do not decide that defendants are correct that "any rights . . . of Preferred Stock" is not limited to those rights necessarily shared by every series of preferred stock because conferred in a provision of the certificate of incorporation of general applicability (*i.e.*, in this instance, the ratability provision quoted in n.4), but would extend to any rights of holders of preferred stock (and perhaps varying rights with respect to a single "matter"). It is remarkable, in any event, how much overlap exists between Sections 3.3(i) and 3.4(i). The latter section is broader in several respects — it covers all charter amendments, not simply those altering the terms of preferred stock; it covers bylaw amendments; it includes adverse effects upon "holders" as well as upon the stock.

[97] [7] In all events, it is agreed that Section 3.3 was not negotiated by Chris-Craft or BHC, but comes precisely from the terms of prior issues of Warner preferred stock.

securities of the corporation surviving or resulting from [a] merger or consolidation" or into "cash, property, rights or securities of any other corporation." 8 Del. C. § 251(b); *Federal United Corporation v. Havender*, Del. Supr., 11 A.2d 331 (1940). Those shares, for example, could be converted into a right to receive cash or other property in a merger and such a conversion would not entitle a holder of stock with a stated value upon liquidation to that value (*Rothschild, supra*); nor would such a cash out merger constitute a redemption of callable securities. *Dart v. Kohlberg, Kravis, Roberts & Co.*, Del. Ch., C.A. No. 7366, Hartnett, V.C., [1985 Del. Ch. LEXIS 473] 1985 WL 21145 (May 6, 1985), slip op. at 13.

It is thus elementary that the possibility of a merger represents a possibility of the most profound importance to a holder of stock with special rights or preferences. *See generally* Buxbaum, *Preferred Stock — Law and Draftsmanship*, 42 Calif. L. Rev. 243, 298-309 (1954). When one turns to the certificate of designation to ascertain whether the language of Section 3.3(i) was intended to incorporate changes effected through mergers, one is struck by two factors that together compel the conclusion that it was not. The first is the close similarity between the operative language of Section 3.3(i) and Section 242(b)(2) of the General Corporation Law. The second involves a comparison of the language of Section 3.3(i) with other sections of the certificate of designation in which the drafters of that document specifically and expressly treated the possibility of a future merger. The language of Section 3.3(i) is closely similar to the language of Section 242(b)(2) of the corporation law statute governing amendments to a certificate of incorporation. That section creates a right to a class vote under certain circumstances. It provides in pertinent part: The holders of the outstanding shares of a class shall be entitled to vote as a class upon a proposed amendment . . . if the amendment would . . . alter or change the powers, preferences or special rights of the shares of such class so as to affect them adversely. 8 Del. C. § 242(b)(2). The parallel language of Section 3.3(i), as quoted above, provides in pertinent part: . . . the affirmative vote of at least two-thirds of the . . . outstanding shares of Series B Stock . . . shall be necessary to alter or change any rights, preferences or limitations of the Preferred Stock so as to affect the holders of all such stock adversely. Certificate of Designation, Section 3.3. The parallel is plain. It is therefore significant, when called upon to determine whether Section 3.3(i) creates a right to a class vote on a merger, to note that the language of Section 242(b)(2) does not itself create a right to a class vote on a merger. The voting requirements for a merger are generally set forth in Section 251(c) of our corporation law statute.[98] Under Section 251, unless a charter provision creates a right to a class vote, a merger is authorized by the company's shareholders when "a majority of the outstanding stock of the corporation entitled to vote thereon shall be voted for the adoption of the agreement [of merger]." 8 Del. C. § 251(c). Unlike Section 242(b), Section 251 contains no class vote requirement.

Our bedrock doctrine of independent legal significance (*e.g., Orzeck v. Englehart*, Del. Supr., 195 A.2d 375 (1963); *Rothschild, supra*) compels the conclusion that satisfaction of the requirements of Section 251 is all that is required legally to effectuate a merger. It follows, therefore, from rudimentary principles of corporation law, that the language of 242(b)(2), which so closely parallels the language of

[98] [8] *But see* 8 Del. C. § 251(f) (stating narrow exceptions to voting requirement).

3.3(i), does not entitle the holders of a class of preferred stock to a class vote in a merger, even if (as we assume here) the interests of the class will be adversely affected by the merger.[99] *See, e.g., Dart v. Kohlberg, Kravis, Roberts & Co., supra.* Indeed, this is so apparent that Chris-Craft does not argue that it has such rights under Section 242.

Since I take this legal conclusion to be the general understanding among corporation law specialists (*e.g.*, Buxbaum, 42 CALIF. L. REV. at 294, n. 266), I can only conclude that it is extraordinarily unlikely that the drafters of Section 3.3(i), who obviously were familiar with and probably expert in our corporation law, would have chosen language so closely similar to that of Section 242(b)(2) had they intended a merger to trigger the class vote mechanism of that section. This conclusion is further supported by a review of other provisions of the certificate of designation. These provisions demonstrate that the drafters were mindful of the effects a merger might have and shaped some special protections in light of the risks posed. For example, Section 6.7 specifically creates protections for the convertibility feature of the Series B Preferred ". . . in case of any consolidation or merger of the Corporation with or into another corporation. . . ." More pointedly, the drafters did expressly address the possibility of a merger in connection with the very question of a class vote by the preferred and adopted the limited protection afforded by Section 3.4(iii): So long as any shares of Series B Stock shall be outstanding . . . without first obtaining the consent or approval of the holders of at least two-thirds of the number of shares of the Series B Stock at the time outstanding . . . the Corporation shall not . . . (iii) be a party to any transaction involving a merger, consolidation or sale of all or substantially all of the Corporation's assets in which the shares of Series B Stock either remain outstanding or are converted into the right to receive equity securities of the surviving, resulting or acquiring corporation (meaning the corporation whose securities are delivered in exchange for assets or securities of the Corporation) unless such corporation shall have, after such merger, consolidation or sale, no equity securities either authorized or outstanding (except such stock of the Corporation as may have been authorized or outstanding immediately preceding such merger or consolidation or such stock of the surviving, resulting or acquiring corporation as may be issued in exchange therefor) ranking prior, as to dividends or in liquidation, to the Series B Stock or to the stock of the surviving, resulting or acquiring corporation issued in exchange therefor. Certificate of Designation, Section 3.4. Thus, in Section 3.4(iii), the certificate of designation does specifically address the voting requirements of a corporate transaction that would "convert" the Series B Preferred to the securities of another corporation and creates a right to a class vote in a subset of all such cases: when the "surviving, resulting or acquiring corporation" has no equity securities ranking prior to the Series B Preferred except any securities that ranked prior to it before the transaction. The parties agree that Section 3.4(iii) does not

---

[99] [9] In *Dalton v. American Investment Company*, Del. Ch., 490 A.2d 574 (1985), *aff'd*, Del. Supr., 501 A.2d 1238 (1985), this court rejected a claim that because their shares would be adversely affected by a merger, the holders of a class of preferred stock were entitled to a class vote. There the court addressed the matter factually and found no adverse effect. *Dalton* only accepted per arguendo the theory that Section 242(b)(2) created a right to a class vote on a merger that would adversely affect preferred shares; it would be an error, in my opinion, to read that case as an implicit acceptance of that theory.

require a class vote here. This section does not explicitly preclude the possibility of a certificate-created requirement for a class vote upon a merger which does not insert prior equity into the capital structure of the firm. Nevertheless, the only fair inference from Section 3.4(iii) is that it was intended to provide the only certificate-created requirement for a series or class vote upon a merger. Can Section 3.3(i) fairly be read to contradict that obvious inference? Far from contradicting it, the reading of that section implied by the parallel with Section 242(b)(2) supports the conclusion that the certificate of designation creates no right for the Series B Preferred to a class vote with respect to the proposed Warner-Time merger.

I recognize that this interpretation of Section 3.3(i) threatens to render it redundant in light of Section 3.4(i).[100] An interpretation that gives an effect to each term of an agreement, instrument or statute is to be preferred to an interpretation that accounts for some terms as redundant. However, no plausible interpretation of Sections 3.3(i) and 3.4(i) and (iii) has been suggested that would accomplish that task here. Not only do I find implausible any interpretation of Section 3.3(i) that would extend its words to a merger in which the Series B Preferred was converted into another security, but such an interpretation — while giving Section 3.3(i) some room to operate — would render Section 3.4(iii) redundant. Thus, the problem of redundancy seems inescapable.

. . . .

For these reasons, I conclude that the Warner certificate of incorporation does not afford to BHC, as the holder of the Series B Preferred stock, a right to vote upon the proposed Warner-Time merger as a separate class. Plaintiffs may submit a form of implementing order on notice.

ELLIOTT ASSOCIATES v. AVATEX CORPORATION

Delaware Supreme Court
715 A.2d 843 (1998)

VEASEY, CHIEF JUSTICE:

In this case of first impression, we hold that certain preferred stockholders have the right to a class vote in a merger where: (1) the certificate of incorporation expressly provides such a right in the event of any "amendment, alteration or repeal, whether by merger, consolidation or otherwise" of any of the provisions of the certificate of incorporation; (2) the certificate of incorporation that provides protections for the preferred stock is nullified and thereby repealed by the merger; and (3) the result of the transaction would materially and adversely affect the rights, preferences, privileges or voting power of those preferred stockholders. In so holding, we distinguish prior Delaware precedent narrowly because of the inclusion by the drafters of the phrase, "whether by merger, consolidation or otherwise."

---

[100] [10] It does not quite render Section 3.3(i) redundant as this case presents no occasion to consider corporate transactions, other than mergers and charter amendments, that might arguably affect preferred stock under Section 3.3(i). *E.g.*, dissolution.

Facts

Defendant Avatex Corporation ("Avatex") is a Delaware corporation that has outstanding both common and preferred stock. The latter includes two distinct series of outstanding preferred stock: "First Series Preferred" and "Series A Preferred."[101] Plaintiffs in these consolidated cases are all preferred stockholders of defendant Avatex. The individual defendants are all members of the Avatex board of directors.

Avatex created and incorporated Xetava Corporation ("Xetava") as its wholly-owned subsidiary on April 13, 1998, and the following day announced its intention to merge with and into Xetava. Under the terms of the proposed merger, Xetava is to be the surviving corporation. Once the transaction is consummated, Xetava will immediately change its name to Avatex Corporation. The proposed merger would cause a conversion of the preferred stock of Avatex into common stock of Xetava.[102] The merger will effectively eliminate Avatex' certificate of incorporation, which includes the certificate of designations creating the Avatex preferred stock and setting forth its rights and preferences.[103] The terms of the merger do not call for a class vote of these preferred stockholders. Herein lies the heart of the legal issue presented in this case.

Plaintiffs filed suit in the Court of Chancery to enjoin the proposed merger, arguing, among other things, that the transaction required the consent of two-thirds of the holders of the First Series Preferred stock. Defendants responded with a motion for judgment on the pleadings, which the Court of Chancery granted, finding that the provisions governing the rights of the First Series Preferred stockholders do not require such consent.

The plaintiffs allege that, because of Avatex' anemic financial state, "all of the value of Avatex is [currently] in the preferred stock." By forcing the conversion of the preferred shares into common stock of the surviving corporation, however, the merger would place current preferred stockholders of Avatex on an even footing

---

[101] [1] Plaintiffs concede that the rights of the Series A Preferred are not implicated in this appeal.

[102] [2] On June 5, 1998, Avatex announced that it would delay execution of the proposed merger while it examined the conversion ratio originally contemplated. In its representations to this Court, Avatex has stated that it will not conduct a vote of the common stockholders until August 17, 1998, at the earliest, and that it is not likely to move forward with the transaction until this Court rules on plaintiffs' voting-rights claim. In fact, counsel for defendants represented to this Court that "Avatex is continuing to move forward with the merger and we expect to get a prompt decision from [the Supreme Court] that would give us some guidance as to the structuring of this particular transaction, or lead us to reconsider possibly some other transaction, depending on the outcome of this ruling." These representations potentially raise the specter of an advisory opinion. See Stroud v. Milliken Enter., Inc., Del. Supr., 552 A.2d 476 (1989) (issue not yet ripe where operative facts found only in litigant's letter to trial court seeking reaction of opposing counsel and court to proposed transaction). We are comfortable, however, that the issue before us is ripe for adjudication. The Avatex board has publicly stated its intention to pursue the merger, and has filed preliminary proxy materials with the SEC to that effect.

[103] [3] When certificates of designations become effective, they constitute amendments to the certificate of incorporation so that the rights of preferred stockholders become part of the certificate of incorporation. Accordingly, we will use the term "certificate" to refer to the certificate of incorporation. See Kaiser Aluminum Corp. v. Matheson, Del. Supr., 681 A.2d 392, 394 n. 3 (1996) (citing 8 Del. C. §§ 102(a)(4), 151(g)).

with its common stockholders. In fact, the Avatex preferred stockholders will receive in exchange for their preferred stock approximately 73% of Xetava common stock, and the common stockholders of Avatex will receive approximately 27% of the common stock of Xetava.

Under the terms of the Avatex certificate of incorporation, First Series stockholders have no right to vote except on:

> (a) any "amendment, alteration or repeal" of the certificate of incorporation "whether by merger, consolidation or otherwise," that
>
> (b) "materially and adversely" affects the rights of the First Series stockholders.

The text of the terms governing the voting rights of the First Series Preferred Stock is set forth in the certificate of designations as follows:

> Except as expressly provided hereinafter in this Section (6) or as otherwise . . . required by law, the First Series Preferred Stock shall have no voting rights.
>
> . . .
>
> So long as any shares of First Series Preferred Stock remain outstanding, the consent of the holders of at least two-thirds of the shares of the First Series Preferred Stock outstanding at the time (voting separately as a class . . .) . . . shall be necessary to permit, effect or validate any one or more of the following:
>
> . . .
>
> (b) The amendment, alteration or repeal, whether by merger, consolidation or otherwise, of any of the provisions of the Restated Certificate of Incorporation or of [the certificate of designations] which would materially and adversely affect any right, preference, privilege or voting power of the First Series Preferred Stock or of the holders thereof . . . .[104]

---

[104] [6] In addition, Section 4 of the Avatex certificate of incorporation provides, in relevant part:

> So long as any of the preferred stock remains outstanding, the consent of the holders of at least a majority of all outstanding shares of preferred stock shall be necessary for effecting or validating any amendment, alteration or repeal of any of the provisions of this Article [including certain board resolutions] which increase or decrease the par value of the preferred stock or would adversely affect the rights or preferences of the preferred stock, or of the holders thereof.

See also 8 Del. C. § 242(b)(2) (providing by statute a class vote in certain circumstances). When an amendment to a certificate of incorporation is sought to be effected under that section:

> The holders of the outstanding shares of a class shall be entitled to vote as a class upon a proposed amendment, whether or not entitled to vote thereon by the certificate of incorporation, if the amendment would increase or decrease the aggregate number of authorized shares of such class, increase or decrease the par value of the shares of such class, or alter or change the powers, preferences, or special rights of the shares of such class so as to affect them adversely.

Id. Because the merger here implicates a different statute (8 Del. C. § 251, which does not itself require a class vote), the provisions of Section 242 are not implicated, the two statutes being of

These are the operative terms of Section 6 of the certificate of designations (with emphasis supplied) setting forth the rights and preferences of the First Series Preferred stock that became effective March 18, 1983. On September 14, 1983 a new certificate of designations became effective with respect to the Second Series Preferred stock. There is, however, no Second Series Preferred stock outstanding. Unlike the First Series certificate, Section 6 of the Second Series certificate expressly provides the Second Series Preferred stock with a right to vote on any consolidation or merger (with certain exceptions not relevant here) to which Avatex is a party:

> So long as any shares of the Second Series Preferred Stock remain outstanding, the consent of the holders of at least a majority of the shares of the Second Series Preferred Stock outstanding at the time . . . shall be necessary to permit or approve any of the following:
>
> (b) The consolidation or merger of the Corporation with or into any other corporation unless . . . .
>
> We discuss this provision further in our analysis of the legal issue involved.

. . .

Analysis

Delaware law permits corporations to create and issue stock that carries no voting power.[105] Professor Buxbaum, in his seminal article on preferred stock nearly 45 years ago, noted, among many other cogent observations, that: (a) statutes often permit alteration of preferred stock rights and preferences by merger;[106] (b) the merger may be with a "paper subsidiary created for that purpose with no independent business validity";[107] (c) "corporate articles [often] require consent of two-thirds (or a majority) of the preferred shareholders as a class for the consummation of any merger . . . .";[108] and (d) courts have struggled with "controls in the name . . . of 'fairness' and generally abandoned them [, which] is as it should be [since the] issue is one of corporate power."[109]

The Avatex certificate of incorporation provides that Avatex preferred shares have no right to vote except on matters set forth therein or required by law.[110] This

---

independent legal significance. See Warner Communications Inc. v. Chris-Craft Indus., Inc., Del. Ch., 583 A.2d 962, 970, aff'd, Del. Supr., 567 A.2d 419 (1989). Likewise, Section 4 of the Avatex certificate is not applicable. Similarly, the Avatex Series A Preferred stock, which is not implicated in this appeal, has the right to a two-thirds class vote if the corporation seeks to "amend, alter, repeal or waive" any provision of the certificate of incorporation. But the additional language of the First Series Preferred, "whether by merger, consolidation or otherwise," significantly is missing from the rights granted to the Series A Preferred.

105 [10] See 8 Del. C. § 151(a).

106 [11] Richard Buxbaum, Preferred Stock-Law and Draftsmanship, 42 Cal. L. Rev. 243, 303 (1954).

107 [12] Id. at 300, n. 295.

108 [13] Id. at 307.

109 [14] Id. at 309.

110 [15] This last qualification is irrelevant to this case since, as the Court of Chancery correctly noted,

denial of the right to vote is subject to an exception carved out for any "amendment, alteration or repeal" of the certificate "whether by merger, consolidation or otherwise" that "materially and adversely" affects the rights of the preferred stockholders. Such an event requires the consent of two-thirds of the First Series Preferred stockholders voting as a class.

This appeal, then, reduces to a narrow legal question: whether the "amendment, alteration or repeal" of the certificate of incorporation is caused "by merger, consolidation or otherwise" thereby requiring a two-thirds class vote of the First Series Preferred stockholders, it being assumed for purposes of this appeal that their rights would be "materially and adversely" affected. The Court of Chancery answered this question in the negative. Although we respect that Court's craftsmanlike analysis, we are constrained to disagree with its conclusion.

Relying primarily on Warner Communications Inc. v. Chris-Craft Industries Inc.,[111] the Court of Chancery held that it was only the conversion of the stock as a result of the merger, and not the amendment, alteration or repeal of the certificate, that would adversely affect the preferred stockholders.[112] It is important to keep in mind, however, that the terms of the preferred stock in Warner were significantly different from those present here, because in Warner the phrase "whether by merger, consolidation or otherwise" was not included. The issue here, therefore, is whether the presence of this additional phrase in the Avatex certificate is an outcome-determinative distinction from Warner.

In Warner, the question was whether the Series B preferred stock of Warner Communications, Inc. had the right to a class vote on a proposed merger of Warner with Time, Inc. (renamed Time Warner Inc.) and TW Sub, its wholly-owned subsidiary. As the first step in a two-step transaction, Time had acquired approximately 50% of Warners' common stock in a tender offer. The second step was the "back-end" merger in which TW Sub was merged into Warner, which survived as a wholly-owned subsidiary Time. The Warner common stock not held by Time was converted into cash, securities and other property. In the merger, the Warner Series B preferred would be converted into Time Series BB preferred stock. The parties stipulated that the Warner Series B stockholders would thereby be adversely affected.[113]

The Chancellor held that the drafters of the Warner Series B certificate of designations did not intend for two-thirds of the Series B stockholders to have a veto over every merger in which their interest would be adversely affected because the right to vote was conferred expressly (as it must under Delaware law),[114] and

---

there is no requirement in the Delaware General Corporation Law ("DGCL") that preferred stockholders vote to approve a proposed merger. See R. Franklin Balotti & Jesse A. Finkelstein, The Delaware Law of Corporations and Business Organizations § 9.15, at 9-26 (3d ed. 1998) ("Whether or not the holders of shares are entitled to vote on a merger is governed by the provisions of the certificate of incorporation setting forth the voting rights of the shares of stock.").

[111] [16] 583 A.2d 962.

[112] [17] Mem. Op. at 16-18.

[113] [18] Warner, 583 A.2d at 965.

[114] [19] See, e.g., Rothschild Int'l Corp. v. Liggett Group, Inc., Del. Supr., 474 A.2d 133, 136 (1984). This issue is further explicated hereafter. See infra notes 46 and 47 and accompanying text.

"only in narrowly defined circumstances . . . not present here."[115] The two provisions in the certificate of designations involved in Warner were as follows. Section 3.3 provided:

> So long as any shares of Series B Stock shall be outstanding and unless the consent or approval of a greater number of shares shall then be required by law, . . . the affirmative vote or written consent of the holders of at least two-thirds of the total number of the then outstanding shares of Series B Stock . . . voting a class, shall be necessary to alter or change any rights, preferences or limitations of the Preferred Stock so as to affect the holders of all such shares adversely . . . .[116]

Section 3.4 provided:

> So long as any shares of Series B Stock shall be outstanding and unless the consent or approval of a greater number of shares shall then be required by law, without first obtaining the consent or approval of the holders of at least two-thirds of the number of shares of the Series B Stock . . . the Corporation shall not (i) amend, alter or repeal any of the provisions of the Certificate of Incorporation or By-laws of the Corporation so as to affect adversely any of the preferences, rights, powers or privileges of the Series B Stock or the holders thereof . . . .[117]

We note again that nowhere in the Series B certificate of designations was found the phrase "by merger, consolidation or otherwise," which is the key phrase in the present case. Nevertheless, the heart of the Warner rationale, which we must address here, is that it was not the amendment, alteration or repeal of the Warner certificate that adversely affected the Warner Series B stock. The Chancellor held that it was only the conversion of the Warner Series B Preferred to Time Series BB Preferred that caused the adverse effect, and, moreover, that the conversion was permissible under 8 Del. C. § 251, which (unlike 8 Del. C. § 242) does not require a class vote on a merger.[118] Further, the Chancellor held that no contractual protection of the Warner Series B stock provided for a class vote on a merger. The Chancellor summarized his rationale in Warner as follows:

> 1. Section 3.4(i) does not create a right to a class vote on the proposed merger despite the fact that Warner's certificate of incorporation is being amended in the merger because, in the circumstances, the amendment itself will not "adversely affect" the Series B Preferred.
>
> 2. [T]he same reasoning that supports the conclusion that the proposed merger does not trigger a class vote under Section 3.4(i) requires an identical conclusion with respect to 3.3(i).
>
> 3. If the amendment of Warner's certificate does not trigger the class vote provisions of either 3.4(i) or 3.3(i), the dispositive question becomes

[115] [20] Warner, 583 A.2d at 964.

[116] [21] Id. at 964-65 (emphasis supplied).

[117] [22] Id. at 965 (emphasis supplied).

[118] [23] Id. at 969-70.

> whether the merger itself may trigger that result under the language of Section 3.3(i). Stated differently, the core issue here may be said to be whether the predicate words of Section 3.3(i), "alter or change," are to be read to include "convert pursuant to a merger." I conclude that Section 3.3(i) does not create a right to a class vote on a merger that will convert the Series B Preferred stock into other securities, other property or cash.[119]

In more detail, he continued:

> Section 3.4(i) provides a right to a series vote . . . in the event of a charter amendment that amends, alters or repeals any provision of the certificate of incorporation so as to adversely affect the Series B Preferred or its holders. Warner will be the surviving corporation in the proposed merger. Its charter will be amended in the merger . . . . Nevertheless, Section 3.4(i) does not, in my opinion, grant a right to a series vote in these circumstances because the adverse effect upon defendants is not caused by an amendment, alteration or repeal of any provision of Warner's certificate of incorporation. Rather it is the conversion of the Warner Series B Preferred into Time Series BB Preferred that creates the adverse effect.[120]

. . .

This conclusion is further supported by a review of other provisions of the certificate of designation . . . . [T]he drafters did expressly address the possibility of a merger in connection with the very question of a class vote by the preferred and adopted the limited protection afforded by Section 3.4(iii):

> [W]ithout . . . consent . . . of the Series B Stock . . . the Corporation shall not . . . (iii) be a party to any transaction involving a merger, consolidation or sale . . . in which the shares of Series B Stock . . . are converted into the right to receive equity securities of the surviving, resulting or acquiring corporation . . . unless such corporation shall have, after such merger, consolidation or sale, no equity securities either authorized or outstanding . . . ranking prior, as to dividends or in liquidation, to the Series B Stock or to the stock of the surviving, resulting or acquiring corporation issued in exchange therefor.[121]

Plaintiffs here argue that Warner is distinguishable for three reasons: (1) the fact that the words "whether by merger, consolidation or otherwise" were not present in the Warner Series B certificate; (2) in Warner, unlike here, the preferred stockholders did not remain as stockholders of the surviving corporation, whose certificate arguably was amended and on which the preferred stockholders in Warner were relying for a right to a class vote; and (3) in Warner, unlike here, the merger was not an attempt simply to change the rights of the preferred stock, but rather there was economic and business substance to that transaction beyond an effort to do indirectly what could not be done directly.

---

[119] [24] Id. at 967.

[120] [25] Id.

[121] [26] Id. at 970 (emphasis in original).

In our view, only the first reason is valid in this appeal. The third reason cited is not before us because we do not examine the economic quality of the merger for purposes of this appeal.[122] The second reason strikes us as a distinction without a difference.[123] Here the First Series Preferred stock of Avatex is converted to common stock of the surviving corporation, Xetava, a newly formed corporation admittedly a wholly owned subsidiary of Avatex created for the sole purpose of effecting this merger and eliminating the rights of the Avatex First Series Preferred. In Warner, the Warner, Series B Preferred also received a new security-Time Series BB Preferred-a senior security[124] issued by the surviving corporation, Time (renamed Time Warner). This was accomplished by using TW Sub, Time's wholly-owned subsidiary, as the merger partner of Warner. Since we do not reach the question of the economic quality of the transaction,[125] it makes no difference for purposes of this analysis (as plaintiffs argue) that in Warner there were two distinct acts that operated independently-that the substitution of charters was between Warner and TW Sub and the exchange of shares was between Warner and Time. The operative events here are that the proposed downstream merger of Avatex into Xetava results in the conversion of Avatex stock to Xetava stock and the elimination "by merger" of the certificate protections granted to the Avatex First Series Preferred. Thus, it is both the stock conversion and the repeal of the Avatex certificate that causes the adverse effect to the First Series Preferred. In Warner, it was only the stock conversion that caused the adverse effect because the phrase, "whether by merger, consolidation or otherwise" was not present.

The relevant statutory provisions are found in Sections 251(b) and 251(e) of the Delaware General Corporation Law ("DGCL"), which provide, in pertinent part:

> § 251. Merger or consolidation of domestic corporations.
>
> . . .
>
> (b) The board of directors of each corporation which desires to merge or consolidate shall adopt a resolution approving an agreement of merger or consolidation. The agreement shall state: (1) The terms and conditions of the merger or consolidation; (2) the mode of carrying the same into effect; (3) in the case of a merger, such amendment or changes in the certificate of incorporation of the surviving corporation as are desired to be effected by the merger, or, if no such amendments or changes are desired, a statement

---

122 [27] See Weinberger v. UOP, Inc., Del. Supr., 457 A.2d 701, 715 (1983) (abolishing business-purpose requirement theretofore applied to parent-subsidiary mergers and overruling Singer v. Magnavox Co., Del. Supr., 380 A.2d 969 (1977)).

123 [28] Defendants argue that "as a practical matter, plaintiffs' argument makes no sense because it would allow the preferred stock to be converted without a class vote into a less attractive security issued by a third party. Plaintiffs understandably cannot explain why a class vote should be required prior to their receipt of a less advantageous security from the surviving corporation in the merger, but no class vote is required prior to their receipt of an equally unattractive security from a third party." Defendants' Ans. Brief at 27-28.

124 [29] It is to be remembered that in Warner the Series B preferred did have the limited merger protection of Section 3.4(iii) stating that they had the right to receive a comparable senior security of the surviving corporation or else they had a class vote. See supra, text accompanying note 26.

125 [30] Weinberger, 457 A.2d at 701, 715.

> that the certificate of incorporation of the surviving corporation shall be its certificate of incorporation; (4) in the case of a consolidation, that the certificate of incorporation of the resulting corporation shall be as is set forth in an attachment to the agreement; (5) the manner of converting the shares of each of the constituent corporations into shares or other securities of the corporation surviving or resulting from the merger or consolidation and, if any shares of any of the constituent corporations are not to be converted solely into shares or other securities of the surviving or resulting corporation, the cash, property, rights or securities of any other corporation or entity which the holders of such shares are to receive in exchange . . . ; and (6) such other details or provisions as are deemed desirable . . . .
>
> . . .
>
> (e) In the case of a merger, the certificate of incorporation of the surviving corporation shall automatically be amended to the extent, if any, that changes in the certificate of incorporation are set forth in the agreement of merger.[126]

In short, Section 251 of the DGCL describes three ways that a merger or consolidation can affect the certificate of a constituent corporation:

(1) Section 251(b)(3) Amendments. First, the merger agreement may call for amendments to the pre-existing certificate of the surviving corporation.[127]

(2) Displacement and Substitution by Merger. Second, the merger can designate the certificate of one of the constituent corporations as the certificate of the surviving entity, and thereby render the certificate of every other constituent corporation a legal nullity.[128]

(3) Displacement and Substitution via Consolidation. Finally, in the case of a consolidation, the certificate of the resulting corporation displaces and renders a legal nullity the certificate of every disappearing constituent corporation.[129]

In speaking of the "amendment, alteration or repeal" of the Avatex certificate by "merger, consolidation or otherwise," the drafters must have been referring to some or all of the events permitted by Section 251. Therefore, Section 251 provides the relevant backdrop for the interpretation of the First Series Preferred voting rights.

Avatex argued below, and the Court of Chancery appears to have agreed,[130] that

---

[126] [31] 8 Del. C. §§ 251(b), (e).

[127] [32] 8 Del. C. §§ 251(b)(3), (e).

[128] [33] 8 Del. C. § 251(b)(3).

[129] [34] 8 Del. C. § 251(b)(4).

[130] [35] The Court of Chancery observed that its reading

> does not render a nullity the phrase "by merger, consolidation or otherwise," as it is easy to imagine situations where, in connection with a merger or other similar transaction, the holders of First Series Preferred would have a right to a class vote on a proposed "amendment, alteration repeal" of some provision of the Avatex Restated Certificate or the First Series Certificate proposed in connection with that transaction, although not upon the merger itself. See Section 251(b)(3) of the DGCL (resolution approving merger shall specify amendments, if

only a Section 251(b)(3) Amendment to the surviving corporation's charter amounts to an "amendment, alteration or repeal" within the meaning of the provisions defining the voting rights of the preferred stockholders. Accordingly, the argument runs, these provisions would apply only in the circumstance (not present here) where Avatex survives the merger and its certificate is amended thereby. Since the proposed merger with Xetava does not contemplate any such amendments to the disappearing Avatex certificate, the argument goes, the transaction can go forward without a First Series class vote.

The difficulty with this reading is that it fails to account for the word consolidation, which appears in the phrase "by merger, consolidation or otherwise." A consolidation cannot entail a Section 251(b)(3) Amendment because in a consolidation there is no "surviving corporation" whose pre-existing certificate is subject to amendment. The resulting corporation in a consolidation is a completely new entity with a new certificate of incorporation.[131] All the certificates of the constituent corporations simply become legal nullities in a consolidation. In short, Avatex' proposed reading of the relevant provisions would render the word consolidation mere surplusage, and is problematic for that reason.[132]

Although the transaction before us is not a consolidation, the drafters' use of the word consolidation is significant. They must have intended the First Series Preferred stockholders to have the right to vote on at least some mergers or other transactions whereby the Avatex certificate-and indeed, Avatex itself-would simply disappear. Consolidation, by definition, implicates the disappearance of all constituent corporations. Here, Avatex disappears, just as it would in a consolidation. Under the terms of the proposed merger, Xetava will be the surviving entity and, since Avatex will cease its independent existence, its certificate becomes a legal nullity, as defendants concede. In our view, this constitutes a repeal, if not an amendment or alteration. Thus, the proposed merger is potentially within the class of events that trigger First Series Preferred voting rights.

The first question is: What will happen as a result of the merger to the "rights, preferences, privileges or voting power" of the Avatex First Series Preferred stock as set forth in the existing Avatex certificate They disappear when the preferred stockholders of Avatex become common stockholders of Xetava under its certificate that does not contain those protections. We assume, as did the trial court,[133] that their elimination would affect the First Series Preferred stockholders adversely.

The second question is: What act or event will cause this adverse effect if the merger is consummated: The trial court held that, "[a]s in Warner," the adverse effect on the plaintiffs "will not flow from any 'amendment, alteration or repeal' of the First Series Certificate (however accomplished) but from the conversion into

---

any, to the certificate of the surviving corporation).

Mem. Op. at 20 n. 4.

131 [36] See 8 Del. C § 251(b)(4).

132 [37] See Sonitrol Holding Co. v. Marceau Investissements, Del. Supr., 607 A.2d 1177, 1184 (1992) (under "cardinal rule of contract construction," court should give effect to all contract provisions).

133 [38] Mem. Op. at 17.

common stock of the First Series Preferred in the Proposed Merger."[134] The Court so held notwithstanding that it had noted the distinguishing language of the certificate here — not present in Warner — "whether by merger, consolidation or otherwise." But the Court dismissed this distinction by concluding that this "language only modifies the phrase 'amendment, alteration and repeal' and does not independently create a right to a class vote in the case of every merger."[135] But that is not the issue here where there is no contention that the First Series Preferred have a right to a class vote on every merger.[136]

The First Series Preferred holders claims to have the right to a class vote only if (a) a transaction effects the "amendment, alteration or repeal" of the rights provided in the certificate, and (b) "any right, preference, privilege or voting power of the First Series Preferred" would thereby be materially and adversely affected. For example, plaintiffs make clear that the First Series Preferred would not have a class vote on mergers where they receive the same security in a new entity or are cashed out. The attributes of the First Series Preferred would be intact but for the merger or might be continued if the certificate of the corporation surviving the merger — Xetava — provided for separate classes of stock, guaranteeing to these holders those same attributes. In our view, the Court of Chancery misapplied Warner's holding that "the amendment contemplated [as a "housekeeping" measure post-merger] is necessitated by the merger [and the] amendment, like the conversion, flows from the merger and is not a necessary condition of it."[137] This was the case in Warner, but is not here. The error of the trial court here was in its conclusion that the observation in Warner quoted above "is at least equally apposite here, where Avatex is to be merged with and into Xetava and will simply cease to maintain a separate corporate existence as a matter of law, without the necessity of any amendment, alteration or repeal" of the certificate.[138]

In our view, the merger does cause the adverse effect because the merger is the corporate act that renders the Avatex certificate that protects the preferred stockholders a "legal nullity," in defendants' words. That elimination certainly fits within the ambit of one or more of the three terms in the certificate: *amendment* or *alteration* or *repeal*. The word *repeal* is especially fitting in this context because it contemplates a nullification, which is what defendants concede happens to the Avatex certificate.[139]

---

[134] [39] Id. at 17-18.

[135] [40] Id. at 17 (emphasis supplied).

[136] [41] Contrast the rights the Second Series Preferred would have had if there had been any shares outstanding (i.e., the right to vote on every merger, with certain specifically enumerated exceptions not relevant here).

[137] [42] Warner, 583 A.2d at 968.

[138] [43] Mem. Op. at 18.

[139] [44] In modern dictionary usage the term *repeal* has definite meaning:

> repeal 1. to revoke or withdraw formally or officially; 2. to revoke or annul; 3. the act of repealing; revocation abrogation. . . .
>
> — Syn. 2. nullify, abolish, rescind, invalidate.

Random House Unabridged Dictionary 1633 (2d ed. 1993). Similar definitions may be found in law dictionaries of England going back to the very early nineteenth century:

Articulation of the rights of preferred stockholders is fundamentally the function of corporate drafters. Construction of the terms of preferred stock is the function of courts. This Court's function is essentially one of contract interpretation against the background of Delaware precedent. These precedential parameters are simply stated: Any rights, preferences and limitations of preferred stock that distinguish that stock from common stock must be expressly and clearly stated, as provided by statute.[140] Therefore, these rights, preferences and limitations will not be presumed or implied.[141] The other doctrine states that when there is a hopeless ambiguity attributable to the corporate drafter that could mislead a reasonable investor such ambiguity must be construed in favor of the reasonable expectation of the investor and against the drafter.[142] This latter doctrine is not applicable here because there is no ambiguity.

In our view, the rights of the First Series Preferred are expressly and clearly stated in the Avatex certificate. The drafters of this instrument could not reasonably

---

> REPEAL, from the Fr. *rappel*, i.e. *revocatio*. A Revocation; as the *repealing* of a statute is the revoking or disannulling it.

2 The Law-Dictionary (2d ed. 1809). The terms *amendment* and *alteration* incompletely describe the effect of the proposed merger on the Avatex charter. *Repeal* implicates nullification, which is the total (not partial) amendment or alteration. The proposed merger does not call for any changes on the face of the Avatex charter, but rather contemplates that charter will be wholly displaced by an independent document.

[140] [45] See 8 Del. C. § 151(a), which provides, in pertinent part:

> (a) Every corporation may issue 1 or more classes of stock or 1 or more series of stock within any class thereof, any or all of which classes may be of stock with par value or stock without par value and which classes or series may have such voting powers, full or limited, or no voting powers, and such designations, preferences and relative, participating, optional or other special rights, and qualifications, limitations or restrictions thereof, as shall be stated and expressed in the certificate or incorporation or of any amendment thereto, or in the resolution or resolutions providing for the issue of such stock adopted by the board of directors pursuant to authority expressly vested in it by the provisions of its certificate of incorporation. . . .

Id. (emphasis supplied).

[141] [46] Rothschild Int'l Corp. v. Liggett Group Inc., Del. Supr., 474 A.2d 133, 136 (1984). See also Waggoner v. Laster, Del. Supr., 581 A.2d 1127, 1134-35 (1990). In Waggoner, the term "strictly construed" was used when describing the judicial approach to determining stock preferences in a case where the holding was that a general reservation clause in a certificate of incorporation was insufficient to expressly reserve authority in the board to establish preferences. We continue to approve that holding, but we do not approve the continued use of the term "strict construction" as appropriately describing the judicial process of analyzing the existence and scope of the contractual statement of preferences in certificates of incorporation or certificates of designations. We believe that the appropriate articulation of that analysis was set forth in our opinion in Rothschild: "Preferential rights are contractual in nature and therefore are governed by the express provisions of a company's certificate of incorporation. Stock preferences must also be clearly expressed and will not be presumed." 474 A.2d at 136. The term "strict construction" (as contrasted to "liberal construction") is often used to describe the approach to statutes in derogation of common law, see Waggoner, 581 A.2d at 1135 n. 9, or to certain contracts (e.g., forfeitures, penalties and restrictive covenants, see 4 Walter H.E. Jaeger, Williston on Contracts § 602A (3d ed. 1961)). In light of other doctrines, continued use of the term "strict construction" as a substitute for, or gloss on, the Rothschild formulation is problematic. See infra note 47.

[142] [47] This latter doctrine is stated in this Court's decision in Kaiser Aluminum, where there was a hopeless ambiguity-a patent drafting error-that arose, not in the creation of preferred stock rights, but in the statement of the antidilution provision that protected the preferred stock on a recapitalization of the common shares into which the preferred was convertible. See also SI Management L.P. v. Wininger, Del. Supr., 707 A.2d 37, 42 (1998).

have intended any consequence other than granting to the First Series Preferred stock the right to consent by a two-thirds class vote to any merger that would result in the elimination of the protections in the Avatex certificate if the rights of the holders of that stock would thereby be adversely affected. The First Series Preferred stock rights granted by the corporate drafters here are the functional equivalent of a provision that would expressly require such consent if a merger were to eliminate any provision of the Avatex certificate resulting in materially adverse consequences to the holders of that security.

The drafters were navigating around several alternatives. First, all parties agree that pure amendment protection available to the First Series Preferred stockholders as granted by Section 242(b)(2) of the DGCL and Section 4 of the certificate does not-absent the very phrase at issue here-apply to this merger. Although Warner was decided after the Avatex certificate of designations became effective, Warner clearly supports this view and it continues to be valid precedent for that proposition.[143] Second, all parties agree that if Avatex would have been the survivor, and its certificate were amended in the merger as contemplated by 8 Del. C. § 251(c)(3), the First Series Preferred would have the right to consent by two-thirds class vote. Third, all parties agree that the right to consent to any merger that was granted (subject to certain exceptions not relevant here) to the Second Series Preferred Stock (of which none is outstanding) was not intended to be granted to the First Series holders whose rights are more narrowly circumscribed. In their case: (a) the merger must be the cause of an "amendment alteration or repeal" of the certificate (not all mergers do this); and (b) their rights must be adversely affected (which does not inevitably occur in a merger).

If Section 6 of the certificate does not guarantee a class vote to the First Series Preferred in this merger, what could it conceivably be interpreted to mean? Defendants argue that the certificate can be construed to apply only in the second instance noted above — namely, in the case where Avatex is the survivor and its certificate is amended, altered or repealed, as contemplated by Section 251(b)(3). But, as plaintiffs point out, this cannot be the only outcome the drafters intended because the certificate grants the First Series Preferred this protection in a consolidation where Section 251(b)(3) does not apply.[144] Because the word consoli-

---

[143] [48] 583 A.2d at 970 (relying on Orzeck v. Englehart, Del. Supr., 195 A.2d 375 (1963), for the "bedrock doctrine of independent legal significance," which establishes that class voting rights granted under 8 Del. C. § 242(b)(2) and parallel contractual provisions in a certificate do not apply in a merger and that only the provisions of 8 Del. C. § 251 and any express certificate provisions need be satisfied).

[144] [49] We need not wrestle with the words "or otherwise" as the Court of Chancery did in applying a different provision in Sullivan Money Management Inc. v. FLS Holdings Inc., Del. Ch., C.A. No. 12731, 18 Del. J. Corp. L. 1183, 1190, [1993 Del. LEXIS 251] 1992 WL 345453 (Nov. 20, 1992), aff'd, Del. Supr., 628 A.2d 84 (1993) (holding that Warner governs and that certificate providing class vote to preferred in the event of "change, by amendment to the Certificate . . . or otherwise the terms and provisions of the . . . Preferred Stock so as to affect adversely the rights and preferences of the holders . . ." does not require class vote in cash-out merger because the term "or otherwise" did not clearly and expressly apply to mergers).

Defendants also rely on Aaron v. Empresas La Moderna, N. D. Cal. No. C 97-0233 FMS, 1997 U.S. Dist. LEXIS 17194 (1997), a decision of the United States District Court for the Northern District of California, in which the court was called upon to apply Delaware law. The court applied Warner to a certificate provision substantially identical to that presented here (mandating that a vote of preferred

dation is included, it cannot reasonably be argued that the protections of Section 6 of the certificate applicable to the First Series Preferred are confined to a Section 251(b)(3) amendment. Therefore, the term consolidation cannot be ignored or wished away as surplusage, as defendants argue. It is well established that a court interpreting any contractual provision, including preferred stock provisions, must give effect to all terms of the instrument, must read the instrument as a whole, and, if possible, reconcile all the provisions of the instrument.[145]

Conclusion

The Court of Chancery held, and defendants contend on appeal, that Warner compels a different result from that which we reach because Warner held that there it was only the stock conversion, not the amendment that adversely affected the preferred. But the short answer here is that the language of the First Series Preferred stock is materially different from the language in Warner because here we have the phrase, "whether by merger, consolidation or otherwise." This provision entirely changes the analysis and compels the result we hold today. Here, the repeal of the certificate and the stock conversion cause the adverse effect.

It is important to place what we decide today in proper perspective. The outcome here continues a coherent and rational approach to corporate finance.[146] The contrary result, in our view, would create an anomaly and could risk the erosion of uniformity in the corporation law. The Court of Chancery was mindful of this concern in referring to our general observations in Kaiser that the courts should avoid creating enduring uncertainties as to the meaning of boilerplate provisions in financial instruments.[147] To be sure, there are some boilerplate aspects to the preferred stock provisions in the Avatex certificate and those found in other cases.

---

stock is necessary for any "amendment, alteration or repeal whether by merger, consolidation or otherwise"). The court simply held that Warner applied, and compelled the same result because "a stock conversion pursuant to a merger that adversely affects the preferred shareholders is distinct from changes to a certificate of incorporation following a merger." Slip op. at 19. We need not discuss the distinguishing characteristics of that case as argued by plaintiffs. It is sufficient to say, with all due respect to the court in Aaron, that Warner was simply misapplied because the certificate provisions in Aaron-as in this case-are materially different from those in Warner. We pause to note that our certification procedure might have aided the court in Aaron to seek an answer from this Court to the question whether Warner compelled the result there or is distinguishable. Del. Const. art. IV, § 11(a); Supr. Ct. R. 41.

[145] [50] See Kaiser Aluminum, 681 A.2d at 395; Sonitrol Holding Co., 607 A.2d at 1184.

[146] [51] See Buxbaum, supra note 11, at 243:

> PREFERRED STOCK is an anomalous security. It is a debt security when it claims certain absolute rights. . . . It is an equity security when it tries to control the enterprise through a practical voting procedure or to share in excess distributions of corporation profits. Of course, a share of preferred stock is actually a composite of many rights.
>
> . . .
>
> The primary source of a share's legal rights is the share contract. There is no ideal preferred stock but only a collection of attributes which the share contract says makes up a share of preferred stock. The share contract, in turn, is found in the articles of incorporation and the applicable state statutes.

(footnotes omitted).

[147] [52] Mem. Op. at 22 (citing Kaiser, 681 A.2d at 398).

But one is struck by the disuniformity of some crucial provisions, such as the differences that exist when one compares the provisions in Warner and Sullivan with those presented here. That lack of uniformity is no doubt a function of (a) the adaptations by different drafters of some standard provisions; (b) negotiations by preferred stock investors seeking certain protections; (c) poor drafting; or (d) some combination of the above. The difference between the provisions in the Warner certificate and the Avatex provisions are outcome-determinative because we find there is no reasonable interpretation of the Avatex certificate that would deny the First Series Preferred a class vote on an "amendment, alteration or repeal . . . by merger, consolidation or otherwise" of the protective provisions of the Avatex certificate.

The path for future drafters to follow in articulating class vote provisions is clear. When a certificate (like the Warner certificate or the Series A provisions here) grants only the right to vote on an amendment, alteration or repeal, the preferred have no class vote in a merger. When a certificate (like the First Series Preferred certificate here) adds the terms "whether by merger, consolidation or otherwise" and a merger results in an amendment, alteration or repeal that causes an adverse effect on the preferred, there would be a class vote. When a certificate grants the preferred a class vote in any merger or in any merger where the preferred stockholders receive a junior security, such provisions are broader than those involved in the First Series Preferred certificate. We agree with plaintiffs' argument that these results are uniform, predictable and consistent with existing law relating to the unique attributes of preferred stock.

The judgment of the Court of Chancery is reversed and the matter is remanded for further proceedings consistent with this Opinion.

See the merger voting provisions of the Series A Preferred Stock set forth *supra*.

FEDERATED DEPARTMENT STORES, INC.

United States Bankruptcy Court, Southern District of Ohio
1991 Bankr. LEXIS 743 (May 31, 1991) (unreported opinion)

Opinion by: AUG

This case is before the Court pursuant to the Motion of Allied Stores Corporation for order authorizing amendment of Preferred Shares Rights Certificate (doc. 3930). Objections were filed by CSL Investments, the Resolution Trust Corporation (as Receiver for FarWest Savings & Loan Association and as Conservator for FarWest Savings & Loan Association F.A.) and a consortium of certain other Preferred Shareholders. Responses in support of the motion were filed by the Federated Unsecured Creditors Committee, the Federated Pre-Merger Bondholders Committee and Allied Unsecured Creditors Committee. The Court held a hearing on May 7, 1991.

The Court has jurisdiction over this matter pursuant to 28 U.S.C. §§ 157 and 1334 and this is a core proceeding pursuant to 28 U.S.C. § 157(b) (2).

For the reasons stated herein we find that elimination of the voting rights associated with the Preferred Shares is in the best interests of Allied, the other FSI affiliates, their respective estates, creditors and the Preferred Shareholders. We therefore GRANT the motion of Allied Stores Corporation.

The Court makes the following findings of fact and conclusions of law.

FACTS

Allied Stores Corporation seeks an order authorizing Allied through its corporate Secretary to amend the "Certificate of Designations, Preferences and Relative, Participation, Optional and Other Special Rights of Preferred Stock and Qualifications, Limitations and Restrictions Thereof" (the Rights Certificate) which establishes the rights and preferences of Allied's $3.3125 Cumulative Exchange Preferred Stock, Series A (the Preferred Shares). The amendment to the Rights Certificate would eliminate all prospective voting rights associated with the Preferred Shares during the pendency of Allied's Chapter 11 case in order to avoid a potential federal income tax liability for as much as $234 million. These taxes would be incurred by Allied, Federated Department Stores, Inc. and each of the other Chapter 11 debtors that are subsidiaries of Allied or Federated or members of the FSI Group.[148]

On March 13, 1987, in connection with the issuance and sale of the Preferred Shares, Allied's Board of Directors adopted the Rights Certificate. It provides that the Preferred Shareholders shall have the right, voting separately as a class, to elect two additional directors to the Allied Board upon any failure of Allied to pay dividends on the Preferred Shares for six consecutive quarters. There are no voting rights currently associated with the Preferred Shares. Allied has not paid dividends on the Preferred Shares since December 15, 1989; and thus, under the terms of the Rights Certificate voting rights may attach to the Preferred Shares on June 15, 1991. This event could trigger the previously mentioned tax consequences. Allied therefore seeks the entry of an order pursuant to 11 U.S.C. Section 105 which would eliminate any and all prospective voting rights associated with the Preferred Shares during the pendency of Allied's Chapter 11 case and until such time as a confirmed plan of reorganization for Allied becomes effective.

In addition Allied states that it believes that under Section 362 of the Bankruptcy Code, the filing of a Chapter 11 petition may preclude the attachment of new rights to its capital stock during the pendency of its Chapter 11 case, but it is not proceeding under this theory at the present time. (*See* Allied's motion-doc. 3930 at 4, footnote 2).

FSI and its subsidiaries and affiliates own one hundred percent of Allied's issued

---

[148] [1] Allied and its operating subsidiaries became members of the FSI Group after the Campeau Corporation, an Ontario corporation, completed a series of stock purchase transactions through which, in 1986, Campeau obtained an indirect controlling interest in Allied's predecessor. Allied currently is a direct wholly owned subsidiary of Federated Holdings II, Inc., which in turn is a direct wholly owned subsidiary of Federated Holdings III, Inc. Holdings III is a direct wholly owned subsidiary of FSI (formerly known as Campeau Corporation (U.S.), Inc.), which in turn is a direct wholly owned subsidiary of Campeau.

and outstanding common stock, but none of the Preferred Shares. Pursuant to Section 1504 of the Internal Revenue Code, Allied has been included in FSI's affiliated group since 1987 and files consolidated tax returns with FSI. Allied generally may be included in the FSI Group only so long as other members of the FSI Group own stock in Allied representing at least eighty percent of the voting power and eighty percent of the value of Allied's issued and outstanding capital stock. 26 U.S.C. Section 1504(a)(2). In applying this test for the inclusion of a subsidiary corporation in a parent's affiliated group, Section 1504 ignores straight preferred stock which is limited and preferred as to dividends and does not participate in corporate growth to any significant extent. Allied fears that if voting rights were to attach to the Preferred Shares on June 15, 1991 that such shares would cease to be treated as "straight" preferred stock. In addition, it could be asserted that the Preferred Shares represent more than twenty percent of the total value of Allied's issued and outstanding capital stock. Thus, there is a risk that if voting rights attach to the Preferred Shares, Allied could be held ineligible for inclusion in the FSI Group. Each member of the FSI Group (including Allied) could then be held severally liable for as much as $234 million in federal income taxes.

Allied requests that the Court invoke its powers under the "reorganization effectuation" provisions of the governing state statute. Allied is a Delaware corporation and section 303 of the Delaware General Corporation Law, 8 Del. C. Section 303 (1953) provides, in relevant part, as follows:

> § 303 Reorganization under a statute of the United States; effectuation.
>
> (a) Any corporation of this State, a plan of reorganization of which, pursuant to any applicable statute of the United States relating to reorganizations of corporations, has been or shall be confirmed by the decree or order of a court of competent jurisdiction, may put into effect and carry out the plan and the decrees and orders of the court or judge relative thereto and may take any proceeding and do any act provided in the plan or directed by such decrees and orders without further action by its directors or stockholders. Such power and authority may be exercised, and such proceedings and acts may be taken, as may be directed by such decrees or orders . . . , by designated officers of the corporation . . . , with like effect as if exercised and taken by unanimous action of the directors and stockholders of the corporation.
>
> (b) Such corporation may, in the manner provided in subsection (a) of this section, but without limiting the generality or effect of the foregoing . . . , amend its certificate of incorporation, and make any change in its capital or capital stock, or any other amendment, change, or alteration, or provision, authorized by this chapter. . . .

Discussion

Allied argues that the proposed amendment actually benefits the Preferred Shareholders by saving the estate from incurring unanticipated tax liabilities. However, Allied further points out that its plan of reorganization does not provide for payment of any kind to the Allied Preferred Shareholders. Despite this fact, we do not see the motion as merely a device to foreclose the Preferred Shareholders from participating in corporate governance or these reorganization proceedings. We see this motion as a means to prevent a huge tax liability and the possible undoing of this debtor's reorganization. The Preferred Shareholders will be entitled to vote on the plan of reorganization. As we have previously held, the Preferred Shareholders are "parties in interest." (*See* Order Denying Motion to Direct Appointment of Official Committee of Preferred Shareholders of Allied Stores Corporation (June 6, 1990)).

As stated before, the reason for Allied's motion is a fear that adding Preferred Shareholders to the Board of Directors would precipitate a disaffiliation which would result in dire tax consequences. The Resolution Trust Corporation admitted at the hearing that the tax problems were real and not fabricated. The debtors pointed to tax uncertainties which would loom in the case in the event the Preferred Shareholders were added to the Board.

The Preferred Shareholders, on the other hand, describe their position as a negotiating position rather than a legal position. In other words, they seek compensation for a loss of voting rights. We find that this is a last ditch effort on the part of the Preferred Shareholders to be compensated in some manner for what they see as a valuable albeit obscure voting right. The Preferred Shareholders should not be allowed to threaten the whole reorganization by setting off avoidable tax consequences.

This result does not run afoul of Section 303 of Delaware Corporation Law because it is made in connection with an ongoing plan formulation. *See In re Acequia, Inc.*, 787 F.2d 1352 (9th Cir. 1986). In *Acequia* the Court permitted a modification of shareholder rights. The Idaho statute in question was even more restrictive than the one before us, because Idaho law requires prior confirmation of a plan of reorganization before modification of shareholder rights. We note that the Delaware statute is much broader because it provides that a plan of reorganization "has been or shall be confirmed." A proposed plan was filed in this case on April 29, 1991. At this time there is a reasonably good prospect that a plan will be confirmed in this case.

We find that Allied is justified in its request to amend its Rights Certificate. Read in tandem, Section 303 of the Delaware General Corporation Law and section 105(a) of the Bankruptcy Code allow the amendment. *See In re Gaslight Club, Inc.*, 782 F.2d 767, 771-72 (7th Cir. 1986); *In re United Press International, Inc.*, 60 B.R. 266, 272-73 (Bankr. D. D.C. 1986); *In re Johns-Manville Corp.*, 52 B.R. 879, 889 (Bankr. S.D.N.Y. 1985) *aff'd*, 60 B.R. 842 (S.D.N.Y.), *rev'd and remanded for evidentiary hearing on other grounds*, 801 F.2d 60 (2d Cir. 1986).

Accordingly, IT IS HEREBY ORDERED THAT:

1. Allied shall be, and hereby is, authorized and instructed, pursuant to section 105(a) of the Bankruptcy Code, 11 U.S.C. § 105(a), and section 303 of the Delaware General Corporation Law, 8 Del. C. § 303 (1953), to amend paragraph (8) (ii) of the Rights Certificate by adding at the end thereof a new clause (g), such clause (g) to read in its entirety as follows:

(g) Notwithstanding anything to the contrary herein contained, the provisions of clauses (a) through (f), inclusive, of this paragraph (8)(ii) shall be of no force or effect at all times prior to the time at which (i) an order in Case No. 1-90-00131 in the United States Bankruptcy Court for the Southern District of Ohio, Western Division (the "Bankruptcy Court"), confirming a plan of reorganization for the Corporation shall have become final and nonappealable and not subject to any stay, and such plan of reorganization shall have become effective or (ii) an order amending or repealing this clause (g) shall have been entered by a court of competent jurisdiction and shall have become final and nonappealable and not subject to any stay; *provided, however*, that if any plan of reorganization for the Corporation shall provide for the cancellation of the Cumulative Exchangeable Preferred Stock, the provisions of clauses (a) through (f), inclusive, of this paragraph (8)(ii) shall continue to be of no force or effect, notwithstanding the fact that an order confirming such plan of reorganization shall have become final and nonappealable and not subject to any stay.

2. Allied shall be, and hereby is, authorized and instructed to (a) cause a certificate of amendment setting forth the foregoing amendment to paragraph (8)(ii) of the Rights Certificate to be filed with the Secretary of State of the State of Delaware, pursuant to sections 103 and 303 of the Delaware General Corporation Law, 8 Del. C. §§ 103 and 303 (1953), and (b) take or cause to be taken all other actions, including the making of appropriate filings or recordings, that may be required under the Delaware General Corporation Law to effectuate the Rights Certificate Amendment;

3. The President or any Vice President of Allied shall be, and hereby is, authorized and instructed to execute, file and have recorded such certificate of amendment and to take such other actions on behalf of Allied as may be required under the Delaware General Corporation Law to effectuate the Rights Certificate Amendment, and the Secretary or any Assistant Secretary of Allied shall be and hereby is, authorized and instructed to certify or attest to any of the foregoing actions; and

4. The Rights Certificate Amendment shall be and hereby is, deemed effective immediately upon the filing of a certificate of amendment setting for the Rights Certificate Amendment with the Secretary of State of the State of Delaware, pursuant to sections 103 and 303 of the Delaware General Corporation Law, 8 Del. C. §§ 103 and 303 (1953).

IT IS SO ORDERED.

§ 4.09 REDEMPTION PROVISIONS

Set forth below is a notice of redemption of securities similar to the Series A Preferred Stock created pursuant to the resolutions set forth in § 4.04, *supra*.

NOTICE OF REDEMPTION OF ALL OF THE OUTSTANDING SHARES OF $2.25 CUMULATIVE SERIES A PREFERRED STOCK OF XYZ, INC.

Redemption Date: August 31, 2004

NOTICE IS HEREBY GIVEN that, pursuant to the provisions of the Certificate of Incorporation, as amended, of XYZ, Inc. (the "Company") and a resolution duly adopted by its Board of Directors, all of the outstanding shares of $2.25 Cumulative Series A Preferred Stock, par value $1.00 per share and annual cumulative dividend preference of $2.35 per share ("Preferred Stock"), are hereby called for redemption and will be redeemed on August 31, 2004 (the "Redemption Date") at $22 per share (the "Redemption Price) plus dividends of $.38 per share which will accrue from July 1, 2004 to August 31, 2004, for a total redemption payment of $22.38 per share.

Stockholders should present their Preferred Stock with the enclosed Letter of Transmittal, properly executed, to the Hamilton Bank and Trust Company of Clinton, New York. Such presentment will entitle all stockholders to receive payment on the Redemption Date for each share redeemed at the rate of $22 per share plus the accrued dividend of $.38 per share. Payment of the Redemption Price plus the accrued and unpaid dividend will be made on or after the Redemption Date upon delivery and surrender by (i) mail of certificates for Preferred Stock at the offices of Hamilton Bank and Trust Company of Clinton, New York, Corporate Reorganization Department, 234 Main Street, Clinton, New York 13323 or (ii) hand at the Hamilton Bank and Trust Company of Clinton, New York, 234 Main Street, Clinton, New York 13323.

Amounts sufficient to redeem all outstanding shares of Preferred Stock will be deposited by the Company with the redemption agent, Hamilton Bank and Trust Company of Clinton, New York, by the opening of business on August 31, 2004 for payment to the holders of the Preferred Stock upon surrender of their certificates therefor. From the time of such deposit, the holders thereof shall cease to be stockholders with respect to Preferred Stock and shall have no rights in or claim against the Company with respect thereto other than the right to receive payment of the Redemption Price for such shares, plus accrued and unpaid dividends without interest, upon surrender of the certificates as set forth above. If any holder of Preferred Stock fails to claim the amount so deposited within five years after the Redemption Date, the Hamilton Bank and Trust Company of Clinton, New York and the Company shall be relieved of all responsibility in respect thereof to holders of the shares called for redemption.

The Company has mailed a copy of this Notice to the holders of record of Preferred Stock as of July 16, 2004, together with the related Letter of Transmittal. Additional copies of the Letter of Transmittal may be obtained by any holder from the Hamilton Bank and Trust Company of Clinton, New York, Corporate Reorganization Department, 234 Main Street, Clinton, New York 13323.

XYC, Inc.

Christina M. Bissell
Secretary

July 25, 2004

RAUCH v. RCA CORPORATION

United States Court of Appeals, Second Circuit
861 F.2d 29 (1988)

MAHONEY, CIRCUIT JUDGE:

Plaintiff Lillian S. Rauch appeals from a judgment of the United States District Court for the Southern District of New York, John F. Keenan, Judge, dismissing her class action complaint challenging the propriety of a merger effected by defendants for failure to state a claim upon which relief can be granted. The district court held that Rauch's action was barred by Delaware's doctrine of independent legal significance. We affirm.

Background

This case arises from the acquisition of RCA Corporation ("RCA") by General Electric Company ("GE"). On or about December 11, 1985, RCA, GE and Gesub, Inc. ("Gesub"), a wholly owned Delaware subsidiary of GE, entered into an agreement of merger. Pursuant to the terms of the agreement, all common and preferred shares of RCA stock (with one exception) were converted to cash, Gesub was then merged into RCA, and the common stock of Gesub was converted into common stock of RCA. Specifically, the merger agreement provided (subject in each case to the exercise of appraisal rights) that each share of RCA common stock would be converted into $66.50, each share of $3.65 cumulative preference stock would be converted into $42.50, and each share of $3.50 cumulative first preferred stock (the stock held by plaintiff and in issue here, hereinafter the "Preferred Stock") would be converted into $40.00.[149] A series of $4.00 cumulative convertible

[149] [1] Section 1.6 of the Agreement of Merger provides in part: As of the Effective Date, by virtue of the Merger and without any action on the part of the holders thereof . . . (e) Each other outstanding share of $3.50 Cumulative First Preferred Stock, without par value, of the Company (a "$3.50 Preferred Share"), except those held by stockholders who have validly perfected appraisal rights under the Delaware General Corporation Law, shall be converted into the right to receive $40.00 in cash, without interest. Notwithstanding the foregoing, if a class vote of the holders of the $3.50 Preferred Shares is

first preferred stock was called for redemption according to its terms prior to the merger.

On February 27, 1986, plaintiff, a holder of 250 shares of Preferred Stock, commenced this diversity class action on behalf of a class consisting of the holders of Preferred Stock. It is undisputed that this action is governed by the law of Delaware, the state of incorporation of both RCA and Gesub. Plaintiff claimed that the merger constituted a "liquidation or dissolution or winding up of RCA and a redemption of the [Preferred Stock]," as a result of which holders of the Preferred Stock were entitled to $100 per share in accordance with the redemption provisions of RCA's certificate of incorporation,[150] that defendants were in violation of the rights of the holders of Preferred Stock as thus stated; and that defendants thereby wrongfully converted substantial sums of money to their own use. Plaintiff sought damages and injunctive relief.

Defendants moved to dismiss the complaint pursuant to Fed. R. Civ. P. 12(b)(6), and plaintiff cross-moved for summary judgment. The district court concluded that the transaction at issue was a bona fide merger carried out in accordance with the relevant provisions of the Delaware General Corporation Law. Accordingly, the district court held that plaintiff's action was precluded by Delaware's doctrine of independent legal significance, and dismissed the complaint.

Discussion

. . .

According to RCA's Restated Certificate of Incorporation, the owners of the Preferred Stock were entitled to $100 per share, plus accrued dividends, upon the redemption of such stock at the election of the corporation. Plaintiff contends that the merger agreement, which compelled the holders of Preferred Stock to sell their shares to RCA for $40.00, effected a redemption whose nature is not changed by referring to it as a conversion of stock to cash pursuant to a merger. Plaintiff's argument, however, is not in accord with Delaware law.

It is clear that under the Delaware General Corporation Law, a conversion of shares to cash that is carried out in order to accomplish a merger is legally distinct from a redemption of shares by a corporation. Section 251 of the Delaware General Corporation Law allows two corporations to merge into a single corporation by adoption of an agreement that complies with that section. Del. Code Ann. tit. viii, § 251(c) (1983). The merger agreement in issue called for the conversion of the shares of the constituent corporations into cash. The statute specifically authorizes

---

required to effect the foregoing and such vote is not obtained, then each outstanding $3.50 Preferred Share shall remain outstanding and represent one validly issued, fully paid and nonassessable $3.50 Preferred Share of the Surviving Corporation [RCA].

[150] [2] RCA's Restated Certificate of Incorporation, paragraph Fourth, Part I, provides in relevant part: (c) The First Preferred Stock at any time outstanding may be redeemed by the Corporation, in whole or in part, at its election, expressed by resolution of the Board of Directors, at any time or times upon not less than sixty (60) days' previous notice to the holders of record of the First Preferred Stock to be redeemed, given as hereinafter provided, at the price of one hundred dollars ($100) per share and all dividends accrued or in arrears. . . .

such a transaction: The agreement shall state . . . the manner of converting the shares of each of the constituent corporations into shares or other securities of the corporation surviving or resulting from the merger or consolidation and, if any shares of any of the constituent corporations are not to be converted solely into shares or other securities of the surviving or resulting corporations, the cash . . . which the holders of such shares are to receive in exchange for, or upon conversion of such shares . . . , which cash . . . may be in addition to or in lieu of shares or other securities of the surviving or resulting corporation. . . . *Id.* § 251(b). Thus, the RCA-GE merger agreement complied fully with the merger provision in question, and plaintiff does not argue to the contrary.

Redemption, on the other hand, is governed by sections 151(b) and 160(a) of the Delaware General Corporation Law. Section 151(b) provides that a corporation may subject its preferred stock to redemption "by the corporation at its option or at the option of the holders of such stock or upon the happening of a specified event." DEL. CODE ANN. tit. viii, § 151(b) (1983). In this instance, the Preferred Stock was subject to redemption by RCA at its election. *See supra* note 2. Nothing in RCA's certificate of incorporation indicated that the holders of Preferred Stock could initiate a redemption, nor was there provision for any specified event, such as the Gesub-RCA merger, to trigger a redemption.[151]

Plaintiff's contention that the transaction was essentially a redemption rather than a merger must therefore fail. RCA chose to convert its stock to cash to accomplish the desired merger, and in the process chose not to redeem the Preferred Stock. It had every right to do so in accordance with Delaware law. As the district court aptly noted, to accept plaintiff's argument "would render nugatory the conversion provisions within Section 251 of the Delaware Code."

Delaware courts have long held that such a result is unacceptable. Indeed, it is well settled under Delaware law that "action taken under one section of [the Delaware General Corporation Law] is legally independent, and its validity is not dependent upon, nor to be tested by the requirements of other unrelated sections under which the same final result might be attained by different means." *Rothschild Int'l Corp. v. Liggett Group*, 474 A.2d 133, 136 (Del. 1984) (quoting *Orzeck v. Englehart*, 41 Del. Ch. 361, 365, 195 A.2d 375, 378 (Del. 1963)). The rationale of the doctrine is that the various provisions of the Delaware General Corporation Law are of equal dignity, and a corporation may resort to one section thereof without having to answer for the consequences that would have arisen from invocation of a different section. *See Hariton v. Arco Electronics, Inc.*, 41 Del. Ch. 74, 77, 188 A.2d 123, 125 (Del. 1963) (" 'the general theory of the Delaware Corporation Law [is] that action taken pursuant to the authority of the various sections of that law constitute acts of independent legal significance and their validity is not dependent on other sections

[151] [3] Plaintiff points, however, to DEL. CODE ANN. tit. viii, § 251(e) (1983), which provides that "[i]n the case of a merger, the certificate of incorporation of the surviving corporation shall automatically be amended to the extent, if any, that changes in the amendment are set forth in the agreement of merger." Plaintiff contends that the agreement of merger "purports to alter or impair existing preferential rights," Brief for Plaintiff-Appellant at 14, thus requiring a class vote under other provisions of Delaware law. There are a number of problems with this contention, but the decisive threshold difficulty is that no "existing preferential rights" are altered or impaired in any way, since the holders of Preferred Stock never had any right to initiate a redemption.

of the Act'") (quoting *Langfelder v. Universal Laboratories, Inc.*, 68 F. Supp. 209, 211 n. 5 (D. Del. 1946), *aff'd*, 163 F.2d 804 (3d Cir. 1947)).

Rothschild Int'l Corp. v. Liggett Group is particularly instructive. In that case, certain preferred shareholders of Liggett were entitled to a $100 per share liquidation preference under Liggett's certificate of incorporation. Liggett, however, undertook a combined tender offer and reverse cash-out merger (similar to the instant transaction) whereby Liggett became a wholly owned subsidiary of Grand Metropolitan Ltd., and the preferred shareholders in question received $70 per share. *Id.*, 474 A.2d at 135-36. A preferred shareholder then brought a class action in which it claimed breach of contract and breach of fiduciary duty, asserting that the transaction was the equivalent of a liquidation of Liggett which entitled preferred shareholders to the $100 per share liquidation preference. The Delaware Supreme Court concluded, however, that "there was no "liquidation' of Liggett within the well-defined meaning of that term" because "the reverse cash-out merger of Liggett did not accomplish a "liquidation' of Liggett's assets." *Id.* at 136. Accordingly, the Court held that the doctrine of independent legal significance barred plaintiff's claim. *Id.*

In so holding, the Court stated that "[i]t is equally settled under Delaware law that minority stock interests may be eliminated by merger. And, where a merger of corporations is permitted by law, a shareholder's preferential rights are subject to defeasance. Stockholders are charged with knowledge of this possibility at the time they acquire their shares." *Id.* at 136-37 (citing *Federal United Corp. v. Havender*, 24 Del. Ch. 318, 332-34, 11 A.2d 331, 338 (Del. 1940)). Thus, the defendants were entitled to choose the most effective means to achieve the desired reorganization, "subject only to their duty to deal fairly with the minority interest." *Id.* at 136.

The instant action presents a most analogous situation. Plaintiff claims that the Gesub-RCA merger was, in effect, a redemption. However, there was no redemption within the well-defined meaning of that term under Delaware law, just as there had been no liquidation in *Liggett*. Thus, because the merger here was permitted by law, defendants legitimately chose to structure their transaction in the most effective way to achieve the desired corporate reorganization, and were subject only to a similar duty to deal fairly.

We note in this regard that plaintiff's complaint nowhere alleges that the $40.00 per share conversion rate for the Preferred Stock was unfair. Rather, "[p]laintiff is complaining of a breach of contractual rights, entirely divorced from the purported 'fairness' of the transaction." Brief for Plaintiff-Appellant at 23.[152] Moreover, as the district court stated: "Delaware provides specific protection to shareholders who believe that they have received insufficient value for their stock as the result of a merger: they may obtain an appraisal under § 262 of the General Corporation Law." Plaintiff, however, explicitly disavows any appraisal theory or remedy, consistent with her position that fairness is not the issue.

---

[152] [4] In view of this statement, we deem it irrelevant that the merger agreement provides for redemption of a series of $4.00 cumulative convertible first preferred stock, but not for redemption of plaintiff's Preferred Stock. Since the holders of Preferred Stock had no right to initiate a redemption, the only conceivable relevance of the redemption of another class of preferred stock would be to a fairness claim, which plaintiff has forsworn.

The doctrine of independent legal significance has been upheld by the Delaware courts in related corporate contexts, as well. *See, e.g., Field v. Allyn*, 457 A.2d 1089 (Del. Ch.), *aff'd, mem.*, 467 A.2d 1274 (Del. 1983) (tender offer followed by cash-out merger does not constitute "sale of assets" to which shareholder meeting provisions of Del. Gen. Corp. Law § 271 are applicable); *Orzeck v. Englehart*, 41 Del. Ch. 361, 195 A.2d 375 (Del. 1963) (purchase by corporation with its stock of stock of seven other corporations, as a result of which selling stockholders acquire control of purchasing corporation, does not constitute de facto merger to which statutory appraisal rights apply); *Hariton v. Arco Electronics, Inc.*, 41 Del. Ch. 74, 188 A.2d 123 (Del. 1963) (sale of corporate assets for shares of stock of purchasing corporation, followed by distribution of those shares to shareholders of, and dissolution of, selling corporation, does not constitute de facto merger to which statutory appraisal rights apply). Plaintiff's attempt to distinguish these cases on their facts is unavailing. While the details of the transactions may vary from case to case, the principle of the rule is clear and its application here cannot be seriously questioned.

Plaintiff invokes *Sharon Steel Corp. v. Chase Manhattan Bank*, 691 F.2d 1039 (2d Cir. 1982), *cert. denied*, 460 U.S. 1012, 103 S. Ct. 1253, 75 L. Ed. 2d 482 (1983), in which case we said: Where contractual language seems designed to protect the interests of both parties and where conflicting interpretations are argued, the contract should be construed to sacrifice the principal interests of each party as little as possible. An interpretation which sacrifices a major interest of one of the parties while furthering only a marginal interest of the other should be rejected in favor of an interpretation which sacrifices marginal interests of both parties in order to protect their major concerns. *Id.* at 1051.

Plaintiff contends that this general principle should lead us to override the Delaware doctrine of independent legal significance and rule that the holders of Preferred Stock had a "major interest" in its redemption, whereas it was a matter of relatively less importance to defendants whether they redeemed or converted the Preferred Stock.

It is an adequate response to say that this contention has no basis in Delaware law, which we are bound to apply in this diversity litigation. The protection afforded by Delaware law is the "imperative duty to accord to the minority fair and equitable terms of conversion." *Sterling v. Mayflower Hotel Corp.*, 33 Del. Ch. 293, 303, 93 A.2d 107, 113 (Del. 1952). Plaintiff makes no claim of unfairness, and no plausible argument that Sharon Steel's general statement concerning contract interpretation should prompt us to disregard a settled and controlling principle of Delaware corporate law.

Conclusion

The judgment of the district court dismissing the complaint is affirmed.

In applying the doctrine of independent legal significance, the *Rauch* court noted that there was no claim that the cash merger price was unfair to the preferred stock holders. See generally C. Stephen Bigler & Blake Rohrbacher, *Form or Substance? The Past, Present and Future of the Doctrine of Independent Legal Significance*, 63

BUS. LAW. 1 (2007), for a discussion of the effect of alleged unfairness on the application of the doctrine.

§ 4.10 NEW YORK STOCK EXCHANGE LISTING REQUIREMENTS REGARDING PREFERRED STOCK

NYSE LISTING REQUIREMENTS

703.05 Preferred Stock Offerings Listing Process

(A) Listing Policy

The Exchange has not set any minimum numerical criteria for the listing of preferred stock. The issue must be of sufficient size and distribution, however, to warrant trading in the Exchange market system. The Exchange has set certain numerical delisting criteria for preferred stock. The Exchange will normally give consideration to suspending or removing a preferred stock if the aggregate market value of publicly-held shares is less than $2,000,000 and the number of publicly-held shares is less than 100,000.

. . . .

(D) Redemption Rights

The following describes the redemption rights of preferred shareholders.

Redemption —

- Redemption provisions should provide for a redemption date which is no less than 30 days nor more than 90 days following notification to holders.
- Rights of preferred shareholders may be terminated in advance of the redemption date provided that adequate notice has been published that sufficient funds will be made available to shareholders within 90 days. No rights should be terminated, even if the redemption date has passed, if there is a default in funds available for redemption.
- If an issue is convertible, conversion privileges should continue for a reasonable period after the redemption notice is published.
- Partial redemption should be pro rata or by lot.

(E) Exceptions to Minimum Voting Rights

In the application of the policy relating to the [below]-stated minimum voting provisions for preferred stock, the Exchange may make exception in a case where the laws of the state of incorporation preclude, or make virtually impossible, the conferring of exclusive voting rights upon any particular class of stock.

Exception may also be made in cases where the preferred stock has provisions which, while not conforming exactly to the above-stated minimum provisions, give the stock the practical equivalent of those minimum provisions.

Exception may also be made in a case where the company agrees to submit to its stockholders at a reasonably early date, a proposal to amend the voting provisions of the preferred stock to conform, at the least, to the minimum provisions stated above, along with the management's recommendation to stockholders that the proposal be adopted.

However, such exceptions are made only after consideration of the circumstances of the particular case, and it should not be assumed, in any case, that they will be made. Any company contemplating issuance of a preferred stock which it desires to list on the Exchange, and which, for any reason, does not have, at the least, the voting provisions described above, is urged to discuss the matter with the company's Exchange representative at an early date and, if at all possible, before definitive steps are taken to fix the provisions of the class.

. . . .

313.00 Voting Rights

(A) Voting Rights Policy

On May 5, 1994, the Exchange's Board of Directors voted to modify the Exchange's Voting Rights Policy, which had been based on former SEC Rule 19c-4. The Policy is more flexible than Rule 19c-4. Accordingly, the Exchange will continue to permit corporate actions or issuances by listed companies that would have been permitted under Rule 19c-4, as well as other actions or issuances that are not inconsistent with the new Policy. In evaluating such other actions or issuances, the Exchange will consider, among other things, the economics of such actions or issuances and the voting rights being granted. The Exchange's interpretations under the Policy will be flexible, recognizing that both the capital markets and the circumstances and needs of listed companies change over time. The text of the Exchange's Voting Rights Policy is as follows:

Voting rights of existing shareholders of publicly traded common stock registered under Section 12 of the Exchange Act cannot be disparately reduced or restricted through any corporate action or issuance. Examples of such corporate action or issuance include, but are not limited to, the adoption of time phased voting plans, the adoption of capped voting rights plans, the issuance of super voting stock, or the issuance of stock with voting rights less than the per share voting rights of the existing common stock through an exchange offer.

. . . .

(C) Preferred Stock, Minimum Voting Rights Required

Preferred stock, voting as a class, should have the right to elect a minimum of two directors upon default of the equivalent of six quarterly dividends. The right to elect directors should accrue regardless of whether defaulted dividends occurred in consecutive periods.

The right to elect directors should remain in effect until cumulative dividends have been paid in full or until non-cumulative dividends have been paid regularly for at least a year. The preferred stock quorum should be low enough to ensure that the right to elect directors can be exercised as soon as it accrues. In no event should the quorum exceed the percentage required for a quorum of the common stock required for the election of directors. The Exchange prefers that no quorum requirement be fixed in respect of the right of a preferred stock, voting as a class, to elect directors when dividends are in default.

The Exchange recommends that preferred stock should have minimum voting rights even if the preferred stock is not listed.

Increase in Authorized Amount or Creation of a Pari Passu Issue. —

- An increase in the authorized amount of a class of preferred stock or the creation of a pari passu issue should be approved by a majority of the holders of the outstanding shares of the class or classes to be affected. The Board of Directors may increase the authorized amount of a series or create an additional series ranking pari passu without a vote by the existing series if shareholders authorized such action by the Board of Directors at the time the class of preferred stock was created.

Creation of a Senior Issue —

- Creation of a senior equity security should require approval of at least two-thirds of the outstanding preferred shares. The Board of Directors may create a senior series without a vote by the existing series if shareholders authorized such action by the Board of Directors at the time of the existing series of preferred stock was created.

- A vote by an existing class of preferred stock is not required for the creation of a senior issue if the existing class has previously received adequate notice of redemption to occur within 90 days. However, the vote of the existing class should not be denied if all or part of the existing issue is being retired with proceeds from the sale of the new stock.

Alteration of Existing Provisions —

- Approval by the holders of at least two-thirds of the outstanding shares of a preferred stock should be required for adoption of any charter or by-law amendment that would materially affect existing terms of the preferred stock.

- If all series of a class of preferred stock are not equally affected by the proposed changes, there should be a two-thirds approval of the class and a two-thirds approval of the series that will have a diminished status.

- The charter should not hinder the shareholders' right to alter the terms of a preferred stock by limiting modification to specific items, e.g., interest rate, redemption price.

§ 4.11 MODIFICATIONS OF PREFERRED STOCK PROVISIONS

BOVE v. COMMUNITY HOTEL CORP.

Rhode Island Supreme Court
249 A.2d 89 (1969)

JOSLIN, JUSTICE

This civil action was brought in the superior court to enjoin a proposed merger of The Community Hotel Corporation of Newport, Rhode Island, a defendant herein, into Newport Hotel Corp. Both corporations were organized under the general corporation law of this state and are hereinafter referred to respectively as "Community Hotel" and "Newport." No oral testimony was presented and a trial justice sitting without a jury decided the case on the facts appearing in the exhibits and as assented to by the parties in the pretrial order. The case is here on the plaintiffs' appeal from a judgment denying injunctive relief and dismissing the action.

Community Hotel was incorporated on October 21, 1924, for the stated purpose of erecting, maintaining, operating, managing and leasing hotels; and it commenced operations in 1927 with the opening of the Viking Hotel in Newport. Its authorized capital stock consists of 6,000 shares of $100 par value six per cent prior preference cumulative preferred stock, and 6,000 shares of no par common stock of which 2,106 shares are issued and outstanding. The plaintiffs as well as the individual defendants are holders and owners of preferred stock, plaintiffs having acquired their holdings of approximately 900 shares not later than 1930. At the time this suit was commenced, dividends on the 4,335 then-issued and outstanding preferred shares had accrued, but had not been declared, for approximately 24 years, and totalled about $645,000 or $148.75 per share.

Newport was organized at the instance and request of the board of directors of Community Hotel solely for the purpose of effectuating the merger which is the subject matter of this action. Its authorized capital stock consists of 80,000 shares of common stock, par value $1.00, of which only one share has been issued, and that to Community Hotel for a consideration of $10.

The essentials of the merger plan call for Community Hotel to merge into Newport, which will then become the surviving corporation. Although previously without assets, Newport will, if the contemplated merger is effectuated, acquire the sole ownership of all the property and assets now owned by Community Hotel. The plan also calls for the outstanding shares of Community Hotel's capital stock to be converted into shares of the capital stock of Newport upon the following basis: Each outstanding share of the constituent corporation's preferred stock, together with all accrued dividends thereon, will be changed and converted into five shares of the $1.00 par value common stock of the surviving corporation; and each share of the constituent corporation's no par common stock will be changed and converted into one share of the common stock, $1.00 par value, of the surviving corporation.

Consistent with the requirements of G.L. 1956, § 7-5-3,[153] the merger will become effective only if the plan receives the affirmative votes of the stockholders of each of the corporations representing at least two-thirds of the shares of each class of its capital stock. For the purpose of obtaining the required approval, notice was given to both common and preferred stockholders of Community Hotel that a special meeting would be held for the purpose of considering and voting upon the proposed merger. Before the scheduled meeting date arrived, this action was commenced and the meeting was postponed to a future time and place. So far as the record before us indicates, it has not yet been held.

The plaintiffs argue that the primary, and indeed, the only purpose of the proposed merger is to eliminate the priorities of the preferred stock with less than the unanimous consent of its holders. Assuming that premise, a preliminary matter for our consideration concerns the merger of a parent corporation into a wholly-owned subsidiary created for the sole purpose of achieving a recapitalization which will eliminate the parent's preferred stock and the dividends accumulated thereon, and whether such a merger qualifies within the contemplation of the statute permitting any two or more corporations to merge into a single corporation.

It is true, of course, that to accomplish the proposed recapitalization by amending Community Hotel's articles of association under relevant provisions of the general corporation law[154] would require the unanimous vote of the preferred shareholders, whereas under the merger statute, only a two-third vote of those stockholders will be needed. Concededly, unanimity of the preferred stockholders is unobtainable in this case, and plaintiffs argue, therefore, that to permit the less restrictive provisions of the merger statute to be used to accomplish indirectly what otherwise would be incapable of being accomplished directly by the more stringent amendment procedures of the general corporation law is tantamount to sanctioning a circumvention or perversion of that law.

The question, however, is not whether recapitalization by the merger route is a subterfuge, but whether a merger which is designed for the sole purpose of

---

[153] [1] Section 7-5-3 in pertinent part provides:

> Said agreement shall be submitted to the stockholders of each constituent corporation at a meeting thereof called separately for the purpose of taking the same into consideration. . . . At said meeting said agreement shall be considered and the stockholders of said corporation shall vote by ballot, in person or by proxy, for the adoption of rejection of the said agreement, each share entitling the holder thereof to one (1) vote, and if the votes of the stockholders of each such corporation representing at least two-thirds of the shares of each class of its capital stock shall be for the adoption of said agreement . . . the agreement so adopted and certified . . . shall thence be taken and deemed to be the agreement and act of consolidation or merger of said corporation

. . . .

[154] [2] Section 7-2-18, as amended, provides that a corporation may ". . . from time to time when and as desired amend its articles of association . . ." and § 7-2-19, as amended, provides that "Unless otherwise provided in the articles of association, every such amendment shall require the affirmative vote of the following proportion of the stockholders, passed at a meeting duly called for the purpose:

. . . .

(b) Where the amendment diminishes the stipulated rate of dividends on any class of stock or the stipulated amount to be paid thereon in case of call or liquidation, the unanimous vote of the stockholders of such class and the vote of a majority in interest of all other stockholders entitled to vote.

cancelling the rights of preferred stockholders with the consent of less than all has been authorized by the legislature. The controlling statute is § 7-5-2. Its language is clear, all-embracing and unqualified. It authorizes any two or more business corporations *which were or might have been organized* under the general corporation law to merge into a single corporation; and it provides that the merger agreement shall prescribe ". . . the terms and conditions of consolidation or merger, the mode of carrying the same into effect . . . *as well as the manner of converting the shares of each of the constituent corporations into shares or other securities of the corporation resulting from or surviving such consolidation or merger*, with such other details and provisions as are deemed necessary."[155] (italics ours) Nothing in that language even suggests that the legislature intended to make *underlying purpose* a standard for determining permissibility. Indeed, the contrary is apparent since the very breadth of the language selected presupposes a complete lack of concern with whether the merger is designed to further the mutual interests of two existing and nonaffiliated corporations or whether alternatively it is purposed solely upon effecting a substantial change in an existing corporation's capital structure.

Moreover, that a possible effect of corporate action under the merger statute is not possible, or is even forbidden, under another section of the general corporation law is of no import, it being settled that the several sections of that law may have independent legal significance, and that the validity of corporate action taken pursuant to one section is not necessarily dependent upon its being valid under another. *Hariton v. Arco Electronics, Inc.*, 40 Del. Ch. 326, 182 A.2d 22, affd, 41 Del. Ch. 74, 188 A.2d 123; *Langfelder v. Universal Laboratories Inc., D.C.*, 68 F. Supp. 209, affd, 3 Cir., 163 F.2d 804.

We hold, therefore, that nothing within the purview of our statute forbids a merger between a parent and a subsidiary corporation even under circumstances where the merger device has been resorted to solely for the purpose of obviating the necessity for the unanimous vote which would otherwise be required in order to cancel the priorities of preferred shareholders. *Federal United Corp. v. Havender, supra*; *Hottenstein v. York Ice Machinery Corp.*, 3 Cir., 136 F.2d 944; 7 Fletcher, Cyclopedia of Corporations, chap. 43, § 3696.1, page 892.

A more basic problem, narrowed so as to bring it within the factual context of this case, is whether the right of a holder of cumulative preferred stock to dividend arrearages and other preferences may be cancelled by a statutory merger. That precise problem has not heretofore been before this court, but elsewhere there is a considerable body of law on the subject. There is no need to discuss all of the authorities. For illustrative purposes it is sufficient that we refer principally to cases involving Delaware corporations. That state is important as a state of incorporation, and the decisions of its courts on the precise problem are not only referred to and relied on by the parties, but are generally considered to be the leading ones in the field.

---

155 [3] The quoted provision is substantially identical to the Delaware merger statute (Del. Rev. Code (1935) C. 65, § 2091) construed in *Federal United Corp. v. Havender*, 24 Del. Ch. 318, 11 A.2d 331, *infra* pp. 93-94.

The earliest case in point of time is *Keller v. Wilson & Co.*, 21 Del. Ch. 391, 190 A. 115 (1936). Wilson & Company was formed and its stock was issued in 1925 and the law then in effect protected against charter amendments which might destroy a preferred shareholder's right to accumulated dividends. In 1927 that law was amended so as to permit such destruction, and thereafter the stockholders of Wilson & Company, by the required majorities, voted to cancel the dividends which had by then accrued on its preferred stock. In invalidating that action the rationale of the Delaware court was that the right of a holder of a corporation's cumulative preferred stock to eventual payment of dividend arrearages was a fixed contractual right, that it was a property right in the nature of a debt, that it was vested, and that it could not be destroyed by corporate action taken under legislative authority subsequently conferred, without the consent of all of the shareholders.

Consolidated Film Industries, Inc. v. Johnson, 22 Del. Ch. 407, 197 A. 489 (1937), decided a year later, was an almost precisely similar case. The only difference was that Consolidated Film Industries, Inc. was not created until after the adoption of the 1927 amendment, whereas in the earlier case the statutory amendment upon which Wilson & Company purported to act postdated both its creation and the issuance of its stock. Notwithstanding the *Keller* rationale that an investor should be entitled to rely upon the law in existence at the time the preferred stock was issued, the court in this case was . . . unable to discover a difference in principle between the two cases." In refusing to allow the proposed reclassification, it reasoned that a shareholder's fixed contractual right to unpaid dividends is of such dignity that it cannot be diminished or eliminated retrospectively even if the authorizing legislation precedes the issuance of its stock.

Two years elapsed before *Federal United Corp. v. Havender, supra*, was decided. The issue was substantially the same as that in the two cases which preceded. The dissenting stockholders had argued, as might have been expected, that the proposed corporate action, even though styled a "merger," was in effect a *Keller* type recapitalization and was entitled to no different treatment. Notwithstanding that argument, the court did not refer to the preferred stockholder's right as "vested" or as "a property right in the nature of a debt." Neither did it reject the use of *Keller*-type nomenclature as creating "confusion" or as "substitutes for reason and analysis" which are the characterizations used respectively in *Davison v. Parke, Austin & Lipscomb, Inc.*, 285 N.Y. 500, 509, 35 N.E.2d 618, 622; Meck, *Accrued Dividends on Cumulative Preferred Stocks; The Legal Doctrine*, 55 Harv. L. Rev. 7, 76. Instead, it talked about the extent of the corporate power under the merger statute; and it held that the statute in existence when Federal United Corp. was organized had in effect been written into its charter, and that its preferred shareholders had thereby been advised and informed that their rights to accrued dividends might be extinguished by corporate action taken pursuant thereto.

Faced with a question of corporate action adjusting preferred stock dividends, and required to apply Delaware law under *Erie R.R. v. Tompkins*, 304 U.S. 64, 58 Sup. Ct. 817, 82 L. Ed. 1188, it is understandable that a federal court in *Hottenstein v. York Ice Machinery Corp.*, 3 Cir., 136 F.2d 944, 950, found *Keller, Johnson* and *Havender* irreconcilable and said,

> If it is fair to say that the decision of the Supreme Court of Delaware in the *Keller* case astonished the corporate world, it is just to state that the decision of the Supreme Court in *Havender* astounded it, for shorn of rationalization the decision constitutes a repudiation of principles enunciated in the Keller case and in *Consolidated Film Industries v. Johnson, supra.*

With *Keller's* back thus broken, *Hottenstein* went on to say that under Delaware law a parent corporation may merge with a wholly owned inactive subsidiary pursuant to a plan cancelling preferred stock and the rights of holders thereof to unpaid accumulated dividends and substituting in lieu thereof stock of the surviving corporation.

Only four years intervened between *Keller* and *Havender*, but that was long enough for Delaware to have discarded "vested rights" as the test for determining the power of a corporation to eliminate a shareholder's right to preferred stock dividend accumulation, and to have adopted in its stead a standard calling for judicial inquiry into whether the proposed interference with a preferred stockholder's contract has been authorized by the legislature. The *Havender* approach is the one to which we subscribe as being the sounder, and it has support in the authorities.

The plaintiffs do not suggest, other than as they may have argued that this particular merger is a subterfuge, that our merger statute will not permit in any circumstances a merger for the sole reason that it affects accrued, but undeclared, preferred stock dividends. Rather do they argue that what should control is the date of the enactment of the enabling legislation, and they point out that in *Havender*, Federal United Corp. was organized and its stock was issued subsequent to the adoption of the statute authorizing mergers, whereas in this case the corporate creation and the stock issue preceded adoption of such a statute. That distinguishing feature brings into question what limitations, if any, exist to a state's authority under the reserved power to permit by subsequent legislation corporate acts which affect the preferential rights of a stockholder. More specifically, it raises the problem of whether subsequent legislation is repugnant to the federal and state constitutional prohibitions against the passage of laws impairing the obligations of contracts, because it permits elimination of accumulated preferred dividends by a lesser vote than was required under the law in existence at the time of the incorporation and when the stock was issued.

The mere mention of the constitutional prohibitions against such laws calls to mind *Trustees of Dartmouth College v. Woodward*, 17 U.S. 518, 4 Wheaton 518, 4 L. Ed. 629, where the decision was that a private corporation charter granted by the state is a contract protected under the constitution against repeal, amendment or alteration by subsequent legislation. Of equal significance in the field of corporation law is Mr. Justice Story's concurring opinion wherein he suggested that application of the impairment clause upon acts of incorporation might be avoided if a state legislature, coincident with granting a corporate charter, reserved as a part of that contract the right of amendment or repeal. With such a reservation, he said, any subsequent amendment or repeal would be pursuant, rather than repugnant, to the terms of the contract and would not therefore impair its obligation.

Our own legislature was quick to heed Story's advice, and in the early part of the 19th century, when corporations were customarily created by special act, the power to alter, amend, or revoke was written directly into each charter. Later, when the practice changed and corporations, instead of being created by special enactment, were incorporated under the general corporation law, the power to amend and repeal was reserved in an act of general application, and since at least as far back as 1844 the corporation law has read in substance as it does today viz., ". . . The charter or articles of association of every corporation hereafter created may be amended or repealed at the will of the general assembly." Section 7-1-13.

The language in which the reserved power is customarily stated is not, however, self-explaining, and the extent of the legislative authority under it has frequently been a source of difficulty. Recognizing that problem, but not answering it, the United States Supreme Court said in a frequently quoted passage:

> The authority of a state under the so-called reserve power is wide; but it is not unlimited. The corporate charter may be repealed or amended, and, within limits not now necessary to define, the inter-relations of state, corporation and stockholders may be changed; but neither vested property rights nor the obligation of contracts of third persons may be destroyed or impaired.

Coombes v. Getz, 285 U.S. 434, 441-442, 52 S. Ct. 435, 436, 76 L. Ed. 866, 871.

The problem is not novel in this court. In *State v. Brown & Sharpe Mfg. Co., supra*, n.5, we said that the reservation of the power to alter or amend does not confer upon the state arbitrary control over the rights and property belonging to a body of corporators. Additionally, relying on *Shields v. Ohio*, 95 U.S. 319, 24 L. Ed. 357, we adopted as a "just and proper" rule that amendments or alterations proposed under the power, if they are to satisfy the constitutional requirement, must be reasonable, must be in good faith, and must not be inconsistent with the scope and object of the act of incorporation.

The plaintiffs go further than *Brown & Sharpe Mfg. Co., supra*. They judge the legislation, not by the "just and proper" rule, but by the date when it came into existence; and they insist that any legislation, if enacted subsequent to the creation of a corporation and the issuance of its preferred stock, may not be a source of authority for corporate action which deprives a holder of his stock or of its preferential rights or of the dividends accrued thereon. An attempt to do so, they say, constitutes an unconstitutional exercise of the reserved power. On this issue, as on most others in this case, the authorities are not in accord.

On the one side, there is a body of law which speaks of the three-fold nature of the stockholder's contract and, while agreeable to an exercise of the reserved power affecting only the contractual relationship between the state and the corporation, rejects as unconstitutional any exercise which affects the relationship between the stockholder and the corporation or between the stockholders inter sese. Under this view, subsequent legislation purporting to permit a corporate act to cancel accrued preferred dividends would obviously be an improper exercise of the power inasmuch as the essence of a preferred stockholder's contract is its definition of his relationship with the corporation and with the other stockholders vis-a-vis such matters as the distribution of the profits of the enterprise or the division of its capital and surplus account in the event of liquidation.

The other side of the argument considers that the question is primarily one of statutory construction and that so long as the statute authorizes the corporate action, it should make no difference whether its enactment preceded or postdated the birth of the corporation or the issuance of its stock. The basis for this viewpoint is that the terms of the preferred stockholder's contractual relationship are not restricted to the specifics inscribed on the stock certificate, but include also the stipulations contained in the charter or articles of association as well as the pertinent provisions of the general corporation law. One of those provisions is, of course, the reserved power; and so long as it is a part of the preferred shareholder's contract, any subsequent legislation enacted pursuant to it, even though it may amend the contract's original terms, will not impair its obligation in the constitutional sense. It is as if the stock certificate were inscribed with the legend "All of the terms and conditions hereof may be changed by the legislature acting pursuant to the power it has reserved in G.L.1956, § 7-1-13."

Speaking to this question, it has been said that

> It is no more unconstitutional to permit the Legislature, under the reserved power, to authorize a corporation to abolish dividends which have accrued in the past, than it is to authorize a corporation to abolish dividends which may accrue in the future. There is a difference in degree, but not one of kind. In both cases there is interference with a contractual relationship between the stockholders and the corporation or between the stockholders inter sese. But this the Legislature is permitted to do, certainly under the reserved power in the Constitution and in the General Corporation Law, to alter or amend the charters of corporations. . . .

McNulty v. W. & J. Sloane, 184 Misc. 835, 845, 54 N.Y.S.2d 253, 263.

It remains to be ascertained how the diverse views jibe with our own precedents. While we have no direct authority, two early cases discuss in some detail the extent to which a shareholder's rights may be affected by corporate action taken under authority of legislation enacted pursuant to the reserved power. The first is *Bailey v. Trustees of Power Street Methodist Episcopal Church*, 6 R.I. 491. There a pewholder held title under deeds which expressly subjected his pews to such rates and taxes as his grantor, an unincorporated church society, might impose for its general expenses and repairs. When the church society subsequently incorporated, its charter specified that the assent of the majority of the pewholders was prerequisite to the imposition of a pew tax. Thereafter a charter amendment enacted pursuant to the reserved power restored to the society ". . . the untrammelled power to tax the pews according to the tenor of the deeds of the pewholders. . . ." The validity of a tax assessed pursuant to that amendment was upheld, the court saying that the immunity from taxation conferred by the original charter, rather than being permanent, existed only during the pleasure of the general assembly; and that the assembly in amending the charter" . . . certainly impaired the obligation of no contract contained either in the deeds or the charter, and derogated from no right or interest of the pewholders of a fixed or permanent character."

Bailey, while to a considerable degree apposite, does not directly assist on whether in matters of this kind the controlling law should be that in effect when the corporation is organized and the stock issued. This is so because in Bailey the pews, when acquired, were taxable by the society without necessity of shareholder acquiescence and all that was accomplished by the charter amendment permitting assessment was to restore that status as it had originally existed. The same accommodation, however, will not serve to explain *Gardner v. Hope Ins. Co.*, 9 R.I. 194. There, when the defendant insurance company was chartered and when the plaintiff's stock was issued, the law in existence did not permit fully paid stock to be assessed. By subsequent amendment enacted pursuant to the reserved power, Hope Insurance Co. was empowered to assess stock previously issued notwithstanding that it may have been fully paid, in order ". . . to fill up the capital stock to its original amount." An assessment made pursuant to that authorization was upheld, the court saying at 199-200:

> The legislature have reserved the power, at any time to alter or repeal the charter, or any of its provisions. The corporators accepted it upon this condition, and agreed that its provisions might be changed, and every purchaser of stock in this company has assented to these terms, and has agreed to hold his shares subject to this liability to change. There is no limit to the power expressed in the act. In terms it is unlimited.

While we do not, particularly in the light of what has been written since, necessarily subscribe to the reasoning of *Gardner* in its entirety, it is a precedent. And if in that case subsequent legislation enacted pursuant to the reserved power may with propriety be a source of authority for an insurance company to revoke a stockholder's freedom from assessment on his fully paid stock, then certainly in the instant case such legislation may also with equal propriety be the basis for a corporation to employ the merger device as a means of cancelling preferred stock and the dividends accumulated thereon. In each instance, to be sure, the stockholder's contractual rights have been altered, but in each instance the alterations are permitted by the stockholder's contract into which the law reads the reserved power to amend or repeal. That power is a part of the charter or articles of association of every Rhode Island corporation. *Gardner v. Hope Insurance Co., supra.*

One other case, although perhaps distinguishable because it involves a public utility, merits mention. It is the case of *Narragansett Electric Lighting Co. v. Sabre*, 50 R.I. 288, 146 A. 777, 66 A.L.R. 1553, where the special legislative act incorporating the Narragansett Electric Company authorized the Narragansett Electric Lighting Company upon the approval of at least two-thirds of its shareholders to transfer and convey all of its assets to the newly incorporated company. Notwithstanding that the vendor company as originally chartered lacked power to transfer all of its assets, the sale was sustained as against the complaint of a dissenting shareholder that the obligation of his contract had been impaired by the subsequent legislation. *See also East Providence Water Co. v. Public Utilities Comm'n*, 46 R.I. 458, 128 A. 556.

On the basis of our own precedents we conclude that the merger legislation, notwithstanding its effect on the rights of its stockholders, did not necessarily constitute an improper exercise of the right of amendment reserved merely because it was subsequent.

. . . .

NOTE

The *Bove* court referred to Justice Story's suggestion in his concurring opinion in *Dartmouth College* that a state may avoid an impairment of contract issue by reserving the authority to amend a state corporation law and a corporate charter. Section 110 of the New York Business Corporation Law is an example of such a reservation of authority:

> The legislature reserves the right, at pleasure, to alter, amend, suspend or repeal in whole or in part this chapter, or any certificate of incorporation or any authority to do business in this state, of any domestic or foreign corporation, whether or not existing or authorized on the effective date of this chapter.

It is to be observed that § 110 reserves the right to alter not only a corporation statute, but also a certificate of incorporation. *See Lord v. Equitable Life Assurance Soc.*, 194 N.Y. 212, 87 N.E. 443 (1909).

Class voting requirements (which are statutory or are set forth in a certificate of incorporation) for amendments to a certificate of incorporation that would adversely affect preferred stockholders cannot, under the New York statutory structure, be entirely circumvented through utilization of the merger device, as was done in the *Bove* case. Although the protection formerly afforded such stockholders by Section 903 of the New York Business Corporation Law would appear to have been lessened to some extent by the 1998 amendments to the BCL, it would still provide for a separate class vote under certain circumstances. Section 903 formerly provided that if a proposed merger "contains any provision which, if contained in an amendment to the certificate of incorporation, would entitle the holders of shares of such class or series to vote and to vote as a class thereon," the merger must "be authorized by vote of the holders of a majority of all outstanding shares of each such class or series." Section 903, as amended in 1998 and set forth in Chapter 1, *supra*, now provides that separate class voting is available only if (i) the affected shares remain outstanding after the proposed merger or will be converted into the right to receive shares of the surviving corporation *and* (ii) the certificate of incorporation of the surviving corporation contains a provision which is not presently applicable to the shares and would entitle the holders to a separate class vote if an amendment containing the same were proposed. The Delaware General Corporation Law does not contain a comparable provision.

Accordingly, it would appear that the Delaware law would still permit the Bove type transaction, especially since Delaware has abandoned the "valid business purpose" requirement at least for acquisition mergers. *See* Chapter 7, *infra*.

PROBLEM A

Woodstock Industries, Inc. ("Woodstock") was incorporated under the laws of the State of New York on March 1, 1967. Its equity capitalization presently consists of 8,000,000 shares of Common Stock, $1.00 par value (the "Common Stock"), 6,000,000 of which are presently issued and outstanding and traded on the Ulster Stock Exchange (a national securities exchange). The Certificate of Incorporation of Woodstock also authorizes Woodstock to issue 1,000,000 shares of Preferred Stock, $1.00 par value (the "Preferred Stock"), and specifically provides that, with respect to any Preferred Stock that Woodstock may issue, the Board of Directors of Woodstock may fix the terms thereof with respect to dividend rates as well as liquidation and conversion rights. No shares of Preferred Stock of Woodstock have ever been issued.

Woodstock is engaged in the manufacture and sale of computer hardware components, and its operations have not been profitable since 1996. For its fiscal year ended December 31, 1998, Woodstock sustained an operating loss of $50 million. Woodstock's net assets now total $37 million. Also alarming is the fact that its cash and cash equivalents aggregate only $13 million. The market price of the shares of Common Stock of Woodstock has dropped from $20.00 per share in July 1993 to its present level of $7.00 per share.

Woodstock has retained the investment banking firm of Hutch & Maisic to devise a plan that would result in an increase in the market price of the Common Stock of Woodstock, which is presently $7.00 per share. That firm has suggested that Woodstock offer to exchange a new class of stock, to be designated the Series A Redeemable Preferred Stock, for up to 25 percent of the 6,000,000 outstanding shares of Common Stock of Woodstock, or 1,500,000 shares. The proposed exchange would be on a share-for-share basis. The new proposed Preferred Stock would have full voting rights with the Common Stock, an annual cumulative dividend rate of $2.50 per share, and a liquidation preference of $24.00 per share (or an aggregate of $37,500,000 for the proposed 1,500,000 shares). The proposed Preferred Stock would be redeemable at the option of Woodstock at a redemption price of $24.00 per share, payable either in cash or notes of Woodstock at the option of the holder of the new proposed Preferred Stock. The purpose of the redemption price would be to insure that, to the extent legally possible, holders of the proposed Preferred Stock who hold their shares until they are redeemed would receive $24.00 per share, without regard to future fluctuations in the market price of the Common Stock. You are an associate in the firm of Judson & Roberts and Christina Roberts, the partner in charge of the Woodstock Account, has asked you to write a Memorandum to her (a) commenting generally upon the legal procedures that would be involved in the creation of the proposed Preferred Stock, with particular reference to her question as to whether a special meeting of the shareholders of Woodstock would be required, (b) discussing the validity of the terms of the proposed Preferred Stock, (c) explaining what is meant by cumulative dividends, and (d) explaining whether or not the $24.00 per share liquidation preference of the proposed Preferred Stock (aggregating $37,500,000) would become payable in the event that Woodstock should merge with, or sell more than one-half of its assets to, another corporation. Write that Memorandum to Ms. Roberts.

PROBLEM B

Woodstock Industries, Inc. ("Woodstock") was incorporated under the laws of the State of New York on October 29, 1929. Its principal executive office and all of its business operations are located in Zena, New York. Its equity capitalization presently consists of (a) 20,000,000 shares of Common Stock, $1.00 par value (the "Common Stock"), 2,000,000 of which are issued and outstanding and traded on Ulster Stock Exchange (the "Exchange") and, 600,000 of which are held in the treasury of Woodstock and (b) 5,000,000 shares of Cumulative Convertible Preferred Stock, par value $1.00 per share (the "Preferred Stock"), of which 1,000,000 are issued and outstanding and also traded on the Exchange. The Preferred Stock, which was issued on April 2, 1974, has a cumulative annual dividend rate of $2.80 per share, payable quarterly; is redeemable at the option of Woodstock at any time after April 2, 1979 at $25 per share, plus accrued dividends, has a liquidation preference of $25 per share; and is presently convertible into two shares of Woodstock's Common Stock. The terms of the Certificate of Incorporation of Woodstock relating to the Preferred Stock also provide that, in the event Woodstock merges with or into another corporation, the holders of the Preferred Stock thereafter remaining outstanding shall, upon conversion thereof, be entitled to receive the securities and property receivable by the holders of the Common Stock upon the effectiveness of any such merger. The Preferred Stock has no voting rights whatsoever, except as may otherwise be provided by law.

Woodstock is presently structured as a holding company; its assets presently consist primarily of all of the issued and outstanding shares (1,000 each) of common stock of its two Delaware wholly-owned subsidiaries, Christina Cosmetics Corporation ("Christina") and Henderson Steel Corporation ("Henderson"). Christina is engaged in the production and sale of various cosmetic and related products. Although historically Christina has been responsible for nearly all of the net income of Woodstock, it has been adversely affected by foreign competition, and accounts for only approximately 55 percent of Woodstock's revenues, but still comprises approximately 35 percent of Woodstock's assets. Henderson, which is engaged in the manufacture and sale of various steel products, accounts for 45 percent of Woodstock's revenues and comprises approximately 65 percent of the assets of Woodstock.

Ten percent of the issued and outstanding shares of Common Stock of Woodstock (200,000 shares) is owned by Bissell Associates, Inc. of Princeton, New Jersey ("Bissell"), which acquired such shares in a series of open market and private purchases in early 1995, in what was to have been the first step of a subsequently abandoned attempt by Bissell to acquire control of Woodstock.

Woodstock has not been profitable in recent years. For its fiscal year ended December 31, 1998, Woodstock sustained operating losses of three million dollars; because of that loss, and operating losses sustained during the four fiscal years ended December 31, 1993 through December 31, 1997, respectively, the assets of Woodstock exceeded its liabilities by $15,000,000 at December 31, 1998. The market price of the shares of Common Stock of Woodstock has dropped to its present level of only $5.00 per share. As a result of these developments, the Board of Directors of Woodstock has not declared or paid a dividend on the Preferred

Stock since 1994. Preferred Stock arrearages now aggregate $11.20 per share, or $11,200,000.

As a result of the non-payment of dividends, the market price per share of the Preferred Stock is now $12.00 per share.

Notwithstanding the Corporation's past and present difficulties, Woodstock's management remains optimistic about its future prospects. Woodstock's investment banking firm, Derm & Judd, is in general agreement with that view, and has suggested that Woodstock seek to raise additional capital by making a private offering of 500,000 shares of Common Stock, and that the corporation be recapitalized to eliminate the $11,200,000 of accrued cumulative dividends on the Preferred Stock without reduction of the net assets of Woodstock. It has been suggested that the recapitalization be effected by a merger of Woodstock into a new corporation ("New Woodstock") and that as a result of the merger each share of Preferred Stock would be converted into a senior debenture of New Woodstock, which would bear interest at prevailing market rates and would be redeemable at the option of Woodstock at a redemption price payable either in cash or shares of Common Stock, also at the option of Woodstock.

Woodstock's management asks you to advise them as to (1) whether it is legally possible to effect such recapitalization in the manner suggested, and (2) what voting and other rights the holders of the Preferred Stock would have in the event that the recapitalization is proposed and carried out. Woodstock's management also wants to know if a legal challenge is made to the suggested recapitalization what claims could be expected to be made, and if there would be any defenses to any such claims.

Chapter 5

CONVERTIBLE SECURITIES

§ 5.01 INTRODUCTION

PITTSBURGH TERMINAL CORP. v. BALTIMORE & O. R.R. CO.

United States Court of Appeals, Third Circuit
680 F.2d 933 (1982)

ADAMS, CIRCUIT JUDGE, DISSENTING. . . .

I.

Convertible debentures frequently are characterized as "hybrids," embodying the attributes of both debt and equity securities. As such, they have proven to be an attractive and effective means of corporate financing. Like most debt securities, convertible debentures provide a fixed rate of return and assure the investor priority, over common shareholders, in claims on the issuer's assets. Should the market price of the common stock rise, however, the debenture holder may exercise an option to convert the debt security into shares of common stock. "Thus there is the opportunity to benefit from a rise in stock prices from the comparative safety of a debt . . . position." Katzin, *Financial and Legal Problems in the Use of Convertible Securities*, 24 BUS. LAW. 359, 361(1969).

From the corporation's standpoint, the issuance of convertible debentures can be similarly advantageous. Primarily, the convertible securities provide a way to raise new capital indirectly — by permitting management " 'to raise funds today at tomorrow's higher common stock prices.' " Fleischer & Cary, *The Taxation of Convertible Bonds and Stock*, 74 HARV. L. REV. 473, 474 (1961) (quoting Pilcher, Raising Capital with Convertible Securities 61, 138 (1955)). In addition,

> the new funds will be contributing to income by the time the debentures are converted. In the interim, while the company is putting the new money effectively to work, the charge takes the form of interest — deductible for tax purposes — rather than a reduction in income per share. Thus the dilution of earnings which traditionally accompanies an equity issue is deferred until the firm is making more money.

Id. (footnote omitted). Finally, because the conversion feature is so attractive to investors, the issuer can often offer the debentures at an interest rate lower than that required on other debt securities. Katzin, *supra*, at 362. *But see* Klein, *The*

Convertible Bond: A Peculiar Package, 123 U. PA. L. REV. 547, 55859 (1975) (referring to this rationale as "flimflam").

Whatever financial advantages attach to the issuance or purchase of convertible debentures, the legal status of these hybrid securities remains inherently complex. As debt securities, the debentures impose a specific set of obligations on the corporation — namely, the regular payment of interest and the repayment of principal upon maturity. As equity securities, in contrast, the debentures may require a broader range of duties from the issuer. The difficulty lies not in the characterization of the debenture as either debt or equity — for it is both — but in determining, in each case, the extent to which the investor is owed rights and remedies beyond those commonly accorded debt holders.[1]

The traditional view is that the convertible debenture holder is a mere creditor until conversion, whose relationship with the issuing corporation is governed by contract and statute. In an early Massachusetts decision, for example, the court rejected a convertible note holder's claim that he had an equitable interest in newly-issued shares of stock. *Pratt v. American Bell Telephone Co.*, 141 Mass. 225, 5 N.E. 307 (1886). The plaintiff was "in no sense a stockholder," declared the court; his "right and interest as a stockholder of the corporation were postponed to the time when he made his option and demand his stock. Pending this time, the contract gave him the right to payment of the coupons attached to the notes, and nothing more." 5 N.E. at 311.

Several years later, Justice Holmes expanded upon this principle, holding for the Supreme Court of Massachusetts that the debenture holder had no right, apart from contract, to object to corporate actions that dilute or destroy the value of the conversion option:

> [the option] imposes no restriction upon the obligor in regard to the issue of new stock, although the issue may be upon such terms as to diminish the value of the right. It leaves the management of the company in accordance with its other interests unhampered. It is simply an option to take stock as it may turn out to be when the time for choice arrives. The bondholder does not become a stockholder by his contract, in equity any more than at law. . . .
>
> . . . [T]he contract does not prevent the corporation from consolidating with another in such a way as to make performance impossible, any more than it prevents the issue of new stock in such a way as to make performance valueless.

Parkinson v. West End St. Ry. Co., 173 Mass. 446, 53 N.E. 891, 892 (1899). *See also Gay v. Burgess Mills*, 30 R.I. 231, 74 A. 714 (1909). And in *Lisman v. Milwaukee, L.S. & W. Ry. Co.*, 161 F. 472 (E.D. Wis. 1908), *aff'd.* 170 F. 1020 (7th Cir. 1909), the

---

[1] [1] *See Green v. Hamilton Int'l Corp*, No. 76 Civ. 5433 (S.D.N.Y. July 14, 1981) ("If the wrongs alleged in this case impacted upon the securities so as to undermine the debtor-creditor relationship, a contract analysis is appropriate, and plaintiffs . . . were owed no special duty outside the bounds of the contract. If the wrongs alleged impinged upon the equity aspects, then the analysis would more properly treat plaintiffs like shareholders to whom the majority shareholders and directors of a corporation owe a duty of 'honesty, loyalty, good faith and fairness.' ").

court held that convertible debenture holders could not complain when the railroad company in which they had invested merged with another railroad. The fact that the parties "were bound to" have anticipated such a consolidation when they entered into the option contract was dispositive.

The rights and remedies of convertible debenture holders have expanded since the turn of the century. Most notably, the Securities Exchange Act of 1934 accords convertible debenture holders the federal statutory rights of "equity security holders,"[2] able, for example, to employ section 10(b) of the Act to protect against fraud or manipulative devices. 15 U.S.C. § 78j. Congress's explicit recognition of convertibles as equity, as well as debt, securities has had significant consequences. In *Kusner v. First Pennsylvania Corp.*, 531 F.2d 1234 (3d Cir. 1976), for instance, this Court held that a convertible debenture holder, who alleged that he had purchased the securities in reliance on a false and misleading prospectus, had standing to sue under section 10(b). *Kusner* depicts the precise sort of situation in which a section 10(b) remedy is appropriate to debenture holders in their role as equity investors. As the Court explained, in such a case, the debenture holder's need for accurate information about the corporation was as pressing as any shareholder's:

> If during the conversion period the value of the common stock (a function of its market price and dividend position) greatly exceeds the value of the fixed payment and interest obligation, a holder probably will exercise the conversion privilege. The possibility that the value of common stock will increase to a point where it exceeds the value of the bond is the sales feature with which the issuer obtained a lower-than-market interest rate on the bond. Thus . . . a misrepresentation in the prospectus that would be material to a stock purchaser would be material to a convertible bond purchaser. The convertible bond purchaser may well have been defrauded of the interest differential.

531 F.2d at 1238 (footnote omitted)

§ 5.02 LEGAL AUTHORITY FOR ISSUANCE

As is the case with respect to corporate finance transactions generally, it is imperative that the law of the state of incorporation of the issuing corporation authorize the issuance of the type of security to be utilized in connection with a particular transaction. In the case of convertible securities, for example, the issuance thereof is specifically authorized by Section 519 of the New York Business Corporation Law and by Section 151(e) of the Delaware General Corporation Law, *supra* § 1.08.

---

[2] [2] The Act defines the term "equity security" broadly to include "any stock or similar security; or any security convertible, with or without consideration, into such a security 15 U.S.C. § 78c(11). *See Chemical Fund, Inc. v. Xerox Corp.*, 377 F.2d 107, 110 (2d Cir. 1967); *In re Will of Migel*, 71 Misc. 2d 640, 336 N.Y. S.2d 376, 379 (1972).

§ 5.03 CONSIDERATION FOR SHARES ISSUED UPON CONVERSION OF SENIOR SECURITIES

It is also imperative that, as in the case of all stock issues, shares of stock issued upon conversion of senior securities, such as preferred stock or debentures, be legally issued and fully paid shares. Section 504(g) of the New York Business Corporation Law provides, in effect, that the consideration received by the corporation for shares issued upon conversion shall be, in the case of convertible debt instruments, the principal sum of and accrued interest on the debt instruments surrendered for conversion and, in the case of convertible preferred stock, the stated capital represented by the shares converted; in each case, the consideration received for the issuance of such shares also includes any additional consideration paid by the holder thereof for the new shares or any amounts of stated capital or surplus that are allocated to the new shares. In the latter case, the corporation itself provides consideration for the issuance of shares and it is "paid for" by the holders of the common stock who "own" the residual equity interest of the corporation, including the legal surplus.

Delaware takes a different approach. Under Section 151(e) of the Delaware General Corporation Law, stock of any class (or any series thereof) may be made convertible into, or exchangeable for, at the option of either the holder thereof or the corporation, or upon the occurrence of a specified event, shares of any other class or classes of stock of the corporation, at such price or at such rate or rates of exchange and with such adjustments as shall be stated in the certificate of incorporation (or certificate of designations, if applicable). Under Sections 152 and 153, at the time of issuance of preferred stock, the board of directors must determine that the corporation is receiving sufficient consideration for the issuance of such shares. With respect to stock having a par value (as is usually the case), the board must determine that the corporation is receiving consideration with a value at least equal to the aggregate par value of the shares so issued. The statute presumes that the shares of convertible preferred stock will be fully paid upon the receipt of the consideration. The certificate of incorporation (or designations) establishes the formula (i.e., the price or rate) by which those shares may be converted. The corporation does not receive additional consideration upon the conversion of convertible preferred stock (other than, in one sense, the reacquisition or cancellation of the outstanding shares). All of the consideration for the issuance of shares of convertible preferred stock is received up-front, at the time of issuance of such shares. The "consideration," as it were, for the underlying shares of common stock, is included in the determination for the issuance of the convertible preferred stock.

§ 5.04 PROVISIONS RELATING TO CONVERTIBLE SECURITIES

[A] Introduction

Conversion is the act of exchanging one security for another and usually involves the acquisition of shares of common stock upon surrender of the senior security, such as preferred stock or a debenture. The number of shares of common or junior stock acquirable upon exercise of the conversion privilege is determined by the conversion "rate" or conversion "price." A conversion rate expresses the number of shares of common stock acquirable upon conversion; a conversion price expresses a dollar amount that is the per share "price" which the holder of the convertible security must "pay" for each share of common stock. The "funds" that the holders of the convertible security "pay" for the junior stock is represented by the principal amount of the debt security if that is the type of senior convertible security involved or by a dollar amount assigned to each share of convertible preferred stock for that purpose. Prior to the mid 1960s, nearly all convertible securities were expressed as a conversion rate. More recently, convertible debt securities have been expressed in terms of conversion price and so have some issues of convertible preferred stock. Examples of both conversion "rate" and conversion "price" provisions are set forth below.

[B] Example of Preferred Stock Conversion Rate Provisions

(f)(i) The shares of the Series A Preferred Stock shall be convertible at the option of the holders thereof at any time at the office or agency maintained by the Corporation in the Borough of Manhattan, The City of New York, for that purpose and at such other place or places, if any, as the Board of Directors may determine, into fully paid and non-assessable shares (calculated to the nearest 1/100 of a share) of the Common Stock *at the rate of 1.33 shares* of the Common Stock for each share of the Series A Preferred Stock; provided, however, that in case of the redemption of any shares of the Series A Preferred Stock, such right of conversion shall cease and terminate, as to the shares duly called for redemption, at the close of business on the date fixed for redemption, unless default shall be made in the payment of the redemption price. Upon conversion the Corporation shall make no payment or adjustment on account of dividends accrued or in arrears on the Series A Preferred Stock surrendered for conversion.

(ii) The number of shares of the Common Stock and the number of shares of other classes of the Corporation, if any, into which each share of the Series A Preferred Stock is convertible *shall be subject to adjustment from time to time only as follows*:

(A) In case the Corporation shall (1) take a record of the holders of the Common Stock for the purpose of entitling them to receive a dividend declared payable in shares of the Common Stock, (2) subdivide the outstanding shares of the Common Stock, (3) combine the outstanding shares of the Common Stock into a smaller number of shares, or (4) issue by reclassification of the Common Stock any shares of the Corporation, each holder of the Series A Preferred Stock and shall thereafter be entitled upon the conversion of each share thereof held by him to receive for each such share the number of shares of the Corporation which he would have owned or have been entitled to receive after the happening of that one of the events described above which shall have happened had such share of the Series A Preferred Stock been converted immediately prior to the happening of such event, the adjustment to become effective immediately after the opening of business on the day next following (x) the record date or (y) the day upon which such subdivision, combination or reclassification shall become effective.

(B) In case of any consolidation or merger of the Corporation with or into another corporation, or in case of any sale or conveyance to another corporation of all or substantially all the property of the Corporation, each holder of the Series A Preferred Stock then outstanding and thereafter remaining outstanding shall have the right thereafter to convert each share held by him *into the kind and amount of shares of stock, other securities, cash and property receivable upon such consolidation, merger, sale, or conveyance* by a holder of the number of shares of Common Stock into which such share might have been converted immediately prior to such consolidation, merger, sale or conveyance, *and shall have no other conversion rights*; in any such event, effective provision shall be made, in the certificate of incorporation of the resulting or surviving corporation or otherwise, so that the provisions set forth herein for the protection of the conversion rights of the shares of the Series A Preferred Stock shall thereafter be applicable, as nearly as reasonably may be, to any such other shares of stock, other securities, cash and property deliverable upon conversion of the shares of the Series A Preferred Stock remaining outstanding or other convertible stock or securities received by the holders in place thereof, and any such resulting or surviving corporation shall expressly assume the obligation to deliver, upon the exercise of the conversion privilege, such shares, other securities, cash or property as the holders of the shares of the Series A Preferred Stock remaining outstanding, or other convertible stock or securities received by the holders in place thereof, shall be entitled to receive pursuant to the provisions hereof, and to make provision for the protection of the conversion right as above provided. In case securities other than Common Stock, cash or property shall be issuable, payable, or deliverable by the Corporation upon conversion as aforesaid, then all reference in this paragraph (f) shall be deemed to apply, so far as appropriate and as nearly as may be, to such other securities, cash or property.

(C) In case the Corporation shall issue rights to all holders of the Common Stock entitling them (for a period expiring within 60 days after the record date for determination of stockholders entitled to receive such rights) to subscribe for or purchase shares of the Common Stock *at a price per share less than the current market price per share of the Common Stock* (as defined in Subsection (D) below) at such record date, the number of shares of the Common Stock into which each share of the Series A Preferred Stock shall thereafter be convertible shall be determined by multiplying the number of shares of the Common Stock into which such share of the Series A Preferred Stock was theretofore convertible by a fraction, of which the numerator shall be the number of shares of the Common Stock outstanding on the date of issuance of such rights plus the number of additional shares of the Common Stock offered for subscription or purchase, and of which the denominator shall be the number of shares of the Common Stock outstanding on the date of issuance of such rights plus the number of shares of the Common Stock which the aggregate offering price of the total number of shares so offered would purchase at such current market price. Such adjustment shall be made whenever such rights are issued and shall become effective retroactively immediately after the record date for the determination of stockholders entitled to receive such rights.

(D) For the purpose of any computation under Subsection (C) above, the current market price per share of the Common Stock at any date shall be deemed to be the average of the daily closing prices for the thirty consecutive business days commencing forty-five business days before the day in question. The closing price for each day shall be the last reported sales price regular way or, in case no such reported sale takes place on such day, the average of the reported closing bid and asked prices regular way, in either case on the New York Stock Exchange. The term "business day" as used in this Subsection (D) means any day on which said Exchange shall be open for trading.

(E) No fractional share of the Common Stock shall be issued upon any conversion but, in lieu thereof, there shall be paid to each holder of shares of the Series A Preferred Stock surrendered for conversion who but for the provisions of this Subsection (E) would be entitled to receive a fraction of a share on such conversion, as soon as practicable after the date such shares are surrendered for conversion, an amount in cash equal to the same fraction of the market value of a full share of the Common Stock, unless the Board of Directors shall determine to adjust fractional shares by the issue of fractional scrip certificates or in some other manner. For such purpose, the market value of a share of the Common Stock shall be the last reported sales price regular way on the day immediately preceding the date upon which shares are surrendered for conversion, or, in case no such sale takes place on such day, the average of the reported closing bid and asked prices regular way on such day, in either case on the New York Stock Exchange.

(F) No adjustment in the number of shares of the Common Stock into which each share of the Series A Preferred Stock is convertible shall be required unless such adjustment would require an increase or decrease of at least 1100th of a share in the number of shares of the Common Stock into which such share is then convertible; provided, however, that any adjustments which by reason of this Subsection (F) are not required to be made shall be carried forward and taken into account in any subsequent adjustment.

(G) Whenever any adjustment is required in the shares into which each share of the Series A Preferred Stock is convertible, the Corporation shall forthwith (I) keep available at each of its offices and agencies at which the Series A Preferred Stock is convertible a statement describing in reasonable detail the adjustment and the method of calculation used and (II) cause a copy of such statement to be mailed to the holders of record of the shares of the Series A Preferred Stock.

(iii) The Corporation shall at all times reserve and keep available out of the authorized but unissued shares of the Common Stock the full number of shares of the Common Stock into which all shares of the Series A Preferred Stock from time to time outstanding are convertible, but shares of the Common Stock held in the treasury of the Corporation may in its discretion be delivered upon any conversion of shares of the Series A Preferred Stock.

(iv) The Corporation will pay any and all issue and other taxes that may be payable in respect of any issue or delivery of shares of the Common Stock on conversion of shares of the Series A Preferred Stock pursuant hereto. The Corporation shall not, however, be required to pay any tax which may be payable in respect of any transfer involved in the issue and delivery of any shares of the Common Stock in a name other than that in which the shares of the Series A Preferred Stock so converted were registered and no such issue or delivery shall be made unless and until the person requesting such issue or delivery has paid to the Corporation the amount of any such tax or has established, to the satisfaction of the Corporation, that such tax has been paid.

(v) Shares of the Series A Preferred Stock converted into Common Stock shall have the status of authorized but unissued shares of Preferred Stock, but such shares shall not be reissued as shares of the Series A Preferred Stock.

(g) Except as may be otherwise herein or in the Certificate of Incorporation of the Corporation or by statute otherwise specifically provided, each holder of shares of the Series A Preferred Stock shall at every meeting of stockholders of the Corporation be entitled to one vote for each of the Series A Preferred Stock held by such stockholder, and the holders of the Series A Preferred Stock and of the Common Stock shall vote together as one class on any matter that may be brought before any such meeting.

(h) So long as shares of the Series A Preferred Stock shall be outstanding, the Corporation shall not, without the affirmative vote or written consent of the holders of two-thirds of the aggregate number of shares of the Series A Preferred Stock at the time outstanding, alter or change the powers, preferences or rights of the Series A Preferred Stock as set forth in this resolution so as to affect the Series A Preferred Stock adversely.

[C] Example of Preferred Stock Conversion Price Provisions

(f) *Conversion Rights.* The holders of shares of this Series shall have the right, at their option, to convert each shares of this Series into 0.8403 shares of Common Stock of the Corporation at any time on and subject to the following terms and conditions:

(1) The shares of this Series shall be convertible at the office of any transfer agent for this Series, and at such other office or offices, if any, as the Board of Directors may designate, into fully paid and non-assessable shares (calculated as to each conversion to the nearest 1100th of a share) of Common Stock of the Corporation, *at the conversion price, determined as hereinafter provided,* in effect at the time of conversion, *each share of this Series being taken at $25.00 for the purpose of such conversion.* The price at which shares of Common Stock shall be delivered upon conversion (herein called the "conversion price") *shall be initially $29.75 per share* of Common Stock. The conversion price shall be adjusted as provided in paragraph (4) below.

(2) In order to convert shares of this Series into Common Stock the holder thereof shall surrender at any office hereinabove mentioned the certificate or certificates therefor, duly endorsed in blank or accompanied by proper instruments of assignment and transfer thereof duly endorsed in blank, together with any payment required by this paragraph (2) and transfer tax stamps or funds therefor, if required pursuant to paragraph (8) below, and give written notice to the Corporation at said office that he elects to convert such shares. Shares of this Series surrendered for conversion during the period from the close of business on any record date for the payment of a dividend on such shares to the opening of business on the date for payment of such dividend shall (except in the case of shares which have been called for redemption on a redemption date within such period) be accompanied by payment of an amount equal to the dividend payable on such dividend payment date on the shares of this

Series being surrendered for conversion. Except as provided in the preceding sentence, no payment or adjustment shall be made upon any conversion on account of any dividends accrued on the shares of this Series surrendered for conversion or on account of any dividends on the Common Stock issued upon such conversion.

Shares of this Series shall be deemed to have been converted immediately prior to the close of business on the day of the surrender of such shares of conversion in accordance with the foregoing provisions, and the person or persons entitled to receive the Common Stock issuable upon such conversion shall be treated for all purposes as the record holder or holders of such Common Stock at such time; provided, however, that any such surrender on any date when the stock transfer books of the Corporation shall be closed shall constitute the person or persons in whose name or names the certificates for such shares of Common Stock are to be issued as the record holder or holders thereof for all purposes immediately prior to the close of business on the next succeeding day on which such stock transfer books are opened and such conversion shall be at the conversion price in effect at such time on such succeeding day. As promptly as practicable on or after the conversion date, the Corporation shall issue and shall deliver at said office a certificate or certificates for the number of full shares of Common Stock issuable upon such conversion, together with a cash payment in lieu of any fraction of a share, as hereinafter provided, to the person or persons entitled to receive the same. In case shares of this Series are called for redemption, the right to convert such shares shall cease and terminate at the close of business on the redemption date, unless default shall be made in payment of the redemption price.

(3) No fractional shares of Common Stock shall be issued upon conversion of shares of this Series, but, instead of any fraction of a share of Common Stock which would otherwise be issuable in respect of the aggregate number of shares of this Series surrendered for conversion at one time by the same holder, the Corporation shall pay a cash adjustment of such fraction in an amount equal to the same fraction of the Closing Price of a share of Common Stock on the date on which such shares of this series were duly surrendered for conversion, or, if such date is not a Trading Day, on the next Trading Day.

(4) The conversion price shall be adjusted from time to time as follows:

(A) In case the Corporation shall (i) pay a dividend or make a distribution on its outstanding shares of Common Stock in Common Stock, (ii) subdivide its outstanding shares of Common Stock, (iii) combine its outstanding shares of Common Stock into a smaller number of shares, or (iv) issue any shares by reclassification of its shares of Common Stock, the conversion price in effect at the time of the record date for such dividend or distribution or the effective date of such subdivision, combination or reclassification shall be adjusted, effective at the opening of business on the business day next following such record date or effective date, so that the holder of any shares of this Series surrendered for conversion after such record date or effective date shall be entitled to receive the number of shares of capital stock of the Corporation which he would have owned or been entitled to receive had such shares of this Series been converted immediately prior to such time. If, as a result of an adjustment made pursuant to this clause (A), the holder of any share thereafter surrendered for conversion shall become entitled to receive shares of two or more classes of capital stock of the Corporation, the Board of Directors (whose determination shall be conclusive) shall determine the allocation of the adjusted conversion price between or among shares of such classes of capital stock.

(B) In case the Corporation shall hereafter issue rights or warrants to all holders of its Common Stock entitling them (for a period expiring within forty-five days after the record date mentioned below) to subscribe for or purchase shares of Common Stock *at a price per share less than the current market price per share* (as determined pursuant to clause (D) below) on the record date mentioned below, the conversion price shall be adjusted so that the same shall equal the price determined by multiplying the conversion price in effect immediately prior to such record date by a fraction, of which the numerator shall be the number of shares of Common Stock outstanding on such record date plus the number of shares of Common Stock which the aggregate offering price of the total number of shares of Common Stock so offered would purchase at such current market price and of which the denominator shall be the number of shares of Common Stock outstanding on such record date plus the number of additional shares of Common Stock offered for subscription or purchase. Such adjustment shall become effective at the opening of business on the business day next following the record date for the determination of stockholders entitled to receive such rights or warrants; and to the extent that shares of Common Stock are not delivered after the expiration of such rights or warrants, the conversion price shall be readjusted (but only with respect to shares of this Series converted after such expiration) to the conversion price which would then be in effect had the adjustments made upon the distribution of such rights or warrants been made upon the basis of delivery of only the number of shares of Common Stock actually delivered. The right to acquire shares of Common Stock pursuant to the Corporation's Dividend Reinvestment Plan as in effect on September 1, 1983, as the same may be amended from time to time, or pursuant to any successor dividend reinvestment plan, shall not be deemed to be a right giving rise to any adjustment to the conversion price. For the purposes of this clause (B), the number of shares of Common Stock at any time outstanding shall not include shares held in the treasury of the Corporation. The Corporation shall not issue any rights or warrants in respect of shares of Common Stock held in the treasury of the Corporation.

(C) In case the Corporation shall distribute to all holders of its Common Stock evidences of its indebtedness or assets (including securities, but excluding any cash dividend or distributions out of surplus or net profits legally available therefor and dividends referred to in clause (A) above) or subscription rights or warrants (excluding those referred to in clause (B) above), then in each such case the conversion price shall be adjusted so that the same shall equal the price determined by multiplying the conversion price in effect immediately prior to the record date mentioned below by a fraction of which the numerator shall be the current market price per share (determined as provided in clause (D) below) of the Common Stock on such record date less the then fair market value (as determined by the Board of Directors of the Corporation, whose determination shall be conclusive) of the portion of the assets or evidences of indebtedness so distributed or of such subscription rights or warrants applicable to one share of Common Stock, and the denominator shall be such current market price per share of the Common Stock. Such adjustment shall become effective on the opening of business on the business day next following the record date for the determination of stockholders entitled to receive such distribution.

(D) For the purpose of any computation under clause (B) or above, the current market price per share of Common Stock on any date shall be deemed to be the average of the daily Closing Price for the thirty consecutive Trading Days selected by the Corporation commencing not more than forty-five Trading Days before the day in question.

(E) In any case in which this paragraph (4) shall require that an adjustment as a result of any event become effective at the opening of business on the business day next following a record date, the Corporation may elect to defer until after the occurrence of such event (i) issuing to the holder of any shares of this Series converted after such record date and before the occurrence of such event the additional shares of Common Stock issuable upon such conversion over and above the shares of Common Stock issuable upon such conversion on the basis of the conversion price prior to adjustment and (ii) paying to such holder any amount in cash in lieu of a fractional share of Common Stock pursuant to paragraph (3) above; and, in lieu of the shares the issuance of which is so deferred, the Corporation shall issue or cause its transfer agents to issue due bills or other appropriate evidence of the right to receive such shares should such event occur.

(F) Any adjustment in the conversion price otherwise required by this paragraph (4) to be made may be postponed up to, but not beyond, three years from the date on which it would otherwise be required to be made provided that such adjustment (plus any other adjustments postponed pursuant to this clause (F) and not theretofore made) would not require an increase or decrease of more than $0.50 in such price and would not, if made, entitle the holders of all then outstanding shares of this Series upon conversion to receive additional shares of Common Stock equal in the aggregate to 3% or more of the then issued and outstanding shares of Common Stock. All calculations under this Section (f) shall be made to the nearest cent or to the nearest 1/100 of a share, as the case may be.

(G) The Corporation may (but shall not be obligated to) make such reductions in the conversion price, in addition to those required by clauses (A), (B) and (C) above, as it considers to be advisable in order that any event treated for Federal income tax purposes as a dividend of stock or stock rights shall not be taxable to the recipients.

(5) Whenever the conversion price is adjusted as herein provided:

(A) The Corporation shall compute the adjusted conversion price in accordance with this Section (f) and shall prepare a certificate signed by the Treasurer of the Corporation setting forth the adjusted conversion price, and such certificate shall forthwith be filed with the transfer agent or agents for this Series; and

(B) a notice stating that the conversion price has been adjusted and setting forth the adjusted conversion price shall, as soon as practicable, be mailed to the holders of record of the outstanding shares of this Series.

(6) In case:

(A) the Corporation shall declare a dividend (or any other distribution) on its Common Stock payable otherwise than in cash out of its retained earnings; or

(B) the Corporation shall authorize the granting to the holders of its Common Stock of rights to subscribe for or purchase any shares of capital stock of any class or of any other rights; or

(C) of any reclassification of the capital stock of the Corporation (other than a subdivision or combination of its outstanding shares of Common Stock), or of any consolidation or merger to which the Corporation is a party and for which approval of any stockholders of the Corporation is required, or of the sale or transfer of all or substantially all the assets of the Corporation; or

(D) of the voluntary or involuntary dissolution, liquidation or winding up of the Corporation;

then the Corporation shall cause to be mailed to the transfer agent or agents for this Series and to the holders of the outstanding shares of the Series, at least 20 days (or 10 days in any case specified in clause (A) or (B) above prior to the applicable record date hereinafter specified, a notice stating (x) the date on which a record is to be taken for the purpose of such dividend, distribution or rights, or, if a record is not to be taken, the date as of which the holders of Common Stock of record to be entitled to such dividend, distribution or rights are to be determined, or (y) the date on which such reclassification, consolidation, merger, sale, transfer, dissolution, liquidation or winding up is expected to become effective, and the date as of which it is expected that holders of Common Stock of record shall be entitled to exchange their shares of Common Stock for securities or other property deliverable upon such reclassification, consolidation, merger, sale, transfer, dissolution, liquidation or winding up.

(7) The Corporation shall at all *times reserve and keep available, free* from pre-emptive rights, out of its authorized but unissued Common Stock, for the purpose of effecting the conversion of the shares of this Series, the full number of shares of Common Stock then deliverable upon the conversion of all shares of this Series then outstanding, provided, that nothing contained herein shall be construed to preclude the Corporation from satisfying its obligations in respect to the conversion of the shares by delivery of purchased shares of Common Stock which are held in the treasury of the Corporation.

(8) The Corporation *shall pay any and all taxes* that may be payable in respect of the issuance or delivery of shares of Common Stock on conversion of shares of this Series pursuant hereto. The Corporation shall not, however, be required to pay any tax which may be payable in respect of any transfer involved in the issue and delivery of shares of Common Stock in a name other than that in which the shares of this Series so converted were registered, and no such issue or delivery shall be made unless and until the person requesting such issue shall have paid to the Corporation the amount of any such tax, or shall have established, to the satisfaction of the Corporation, that such tax shall have been paid.

(9) For the purpose of this Section (f) the term "Common Stock" shall include any stock of any class of the Corporation which has no

preference in respect of dividends or of amounts in the event of any voluntary or involuntary liquidation, dissolution or winding up of the Corporation, and which is not subject to redemption by the Corporation. However, except as otherwise provided in paragraph (11), shares issuable on conversion of shares of this Series shall include only shares of the class designated as Common Stock of the Corporation as of the original date of issue of this Series or shares of any class or classes resulting from any reclassification or reclassifications thereof and which have no preference in respect of dividends or of amounts payable in the event of any voluntary or involuntary liquidation, dissolution or winding up of the Corporation and which are not subject to redemption by the Corporation, provided that if at any time there shall be more than one such resulting class, the shares of each such class, then so issuable shall be substantially in the proportion which the total number of shares of such class resulting from all such reclassifications bears to the total number of shares of all such classes resulting from all such reclassifications.

(10) As used in this Section (f), the term "Closing Price" on any day shall mean the reported last sales price regular way on such day on the New York Stock Exchange, or, if not reported for such Exchange, on the Composite Tape, or, in case no such reported sale takes place on such day, the average of the reported closing bid and asked prices regular way on the New York Stock Exchange, or, if the Common Stock is not listed or admitted to trading on such Exchange, on the principal national securities exchange on which the Common Stock is listed or admitted to trading, or, if not listed or admitted to trading on any national securities exchange, the average of the closing bid and asked prices in the over-the-counter market as furnished by any New York Stock Exchange member firm selected from time to time by the Corporation for that purpose, or, if no such quotations are available, the fair market price as determined by the Corporation (whose determination shall be conclusive); and the term "Trading Day" shall mean, so long as the Common Stock is listed or admitted to trading on the New York Stock Exchange (or any successor to such Exchange), a date on which the New York Stock Exchange (or such successor) is open for the transaction of business, or, if the Common Stock is not listed or admitted on such Exchange, a date on which the principal national securities exchange on which the Common Stock is listed is open for the transaction of business, or, if the Common Stock is not listed or admitted to trading on any national securities exchange, a date on which any New York Stock Exchange member firm is open for the transaction of business.

(11) If either of the following shall occur, namely: (a) any consolidation or merger to which the Corporation is a party, *other than* a consolidation or a merger in which consolidation or merger the Corporation is a continuing corporation *and which* does not result in any reclassification of, or change (other than a change in par value or

from par value to no par value or from no par value to par value, or as a result of a subdivision or combination) in, outstanding shares of the Common Stock, or (b) any sale or conveyance to another corporation of the property of the Corporation as an entirety or substantially as an entirety, then the holder of each share then outstanding shall have the right to convert such share *only into the kind and amount of shares of stock and other securities and property receivable upon such consolidation, merger, sale or conveyance by a holder of the number of shares of Common Stock issuable upon conversion of such share immediately prior to such consolidation, merger, sale or conveyance, subject to adjustments* which shall be as nearly equivalent as may be practicable to the adjustments provided for in paragraph (4) above. *The provisions of this paragraph (11) shall similarly apply to successive consolidations, mergers, sales or conveyances.*

(12) Notwithstanding anything elsewhere contained in this Certificate, any funds which at any time shall have been deposited by the Corporation or on its behalf with any paying agent for the purpose of paying dividends on or the redemption price of any of the shares of this Series and which shall not be required for such purposes because of the conversion of such shares, as provided in this Section (f), shall, upon delivery to the paying agent of evidence satisfactory to it of such conversion, after such conversion be repaid to the Corporation by the paying agent.

(13) Any shares of this Series which shall at any time have been converted into shares of Common Stock shall, after such conversion, have the status of authorized but unissued shares of Preferred Stock, without designation as to series until such shares are once more designated as part of a particular series by the Board of Directors.

[D] Convertible Debentures

CONVERSION PRICE PROVISIONS

Subject to the provisions of the Indenture, the registered holder of this Debenture is entitled, as his option, to convert this Debenture, or any portion hereof which is $1,000 or an integral multiple thereof, at the office or agency to be maintained by the Company in accordance with the Indenture into shares of Common Stock of the Company (as said shares shall be constituted at the conversion date) *at the conversion price equal to $3.00 of this debenture for each share* of Common Stock, or at the adjusted conversion price in effect at the conversion date determined as provided in the Indenture, at any time prior to maturity but not earlier than October 15, 2007 or such earlier date as may be established as provided in the Indenture except (a) when this Debenture or any portion hereof has been called for redemption, whether for the sinking fund or otherwise, in which case this Debenture is not so convertible after the close of business on the date fixed for redemption, and (b) during the period between the close of business on any interest payment record date and the close of business on the next following interest payment date unless (i) payment of an amount equal to six months' interest payable on the principal amount of this Debenture to be converted is made to the Company or (ii) this Debenture, or the portion hereof to be so converted, shall have been called for redemption and the date fixed for such redemption shall be prior to such interest payment date; however, any amounts so paid to the Company shall be repaid on the next following interest payment date to the holder hereof who shall be registered on the registry books of the Company on the interest payment record date next preceding such conversion. As provided in the Indenture, the conversion price is subject to adjustment in certain cases as set forth therein. The Company is not required to issue fractional shares upon any such conversion but shall make adjustment therefor in cash on the basis of the current market value of such fractional interest as provided in the Indenture. Upon any partial conversion of this Debenture, the holder shall receive a new Debenture or Debentures in principal amount equal to the unconverted portion of this Debenture.

[E] Duties of Convertible Debenture Indenture Trustee

Set forth below are exculpatory provisions found in trust indentures relating to convertible debt securities. The references to Section 7.1 of the Indenture in question relate to provisions elsewhere in the Indenture which are permitted to be included therein by Section 315 of The Trust Indenture Act of 1939, as amended, which is set forth in § 3.08, *supra*.

RESPONSIBILITY OF TRUSTEE FOR CONVERSION PROVISIONS

The Trustee, subject to the provisions of Section 7.1, and any Conversion Agent shall not at any time be under any duty or responsibility to any Holder of Securities to determine whether any facts exist which may require any adjustment of the Conversion Rate, or with respect to the nature or extent of any such adjustment when made, or with respect to the method employed, herein or in any supplemental indenture provided to be employed, in making the same, or whether a supplemental indenture need be entered into or to recalculate or verify the content of any certificate filed with it by the Company pursuant to the terms of this Article. Neither the Trustee, subject to the provisions of Section 7.1, nor any Conversion Agent shall be accountable with respect to the validity or value (or the kind or amount) of any Common Stock, or of any other securities or property or cash, which may at any time be issued or delivered upon the conversion of any Security; and it or they do not make any representation with respect thereto. Neither the Trustee, subject to the provisions of Section 7.1, nor any Conversion Agent shall be responsible for any failure of the Company to make or calculate any cash payment or to issue, transfer or deliver any shares of Common Stock or share certificates or other securities or property or cash upon the surrender of any Security for the purpose of conversion; and the Trustee, subject to the provisions of Section 7.1, and any Conversion Agent shall not be responsible for any failure of the Company to comply with any of the covenants of the Company contained in this Article.

§ 5.05 THE CONVERSION PREMIUM

The difference between the market price of the issuer's common stock at the time of the issuance of a convertible debenture and the conversion price is often called the conversion premium. The market price of the common stock is generally lesser than the conversion price of the convertible security. For example, in *Broad v. Rockwell International Corp., infra*, the market price of the Collins common stock at the time the convertible debentures were issued was $60.00 per share, and the conversion price was $72.50, thus representing a conversion premium of 20 percent.

Because of the urgent need of many financial firms for increased capital in the lead-up to the 2008 Credit Crises and the resulting negotiating leverage of investors, the use of a conversion premium was abandoned in certain cases. For example, in August 2007, Bank of America purchased for $2 billion shares of a non-voting convertible preferred stock of Countrywide Financial Corporation. The dividend rate was 7.25 percent, and the shares were convertible into shares of common stock of Countrywide at a price of $18 per share at the same time the market price was $21.82. In July 2008, presumably to its later regret, Bank of America acquired all of the outstanding shares of common stock of Countrywide for $4.25 per share.

§ 5.06 COVENANTS GENERALLY MADE BY THE ISSUER OF CONVERTIBLE SECURITIES

Taxes and Conversion. — The issue of Stock Certificates on conversions of Debentures shall be without charge to the converting Debentureholder for any tax in respect of the issue thereof. The Company shall not, however, be required to pay any tax which may be payable in respect of any transfer involved in the issue and delivery of shares in any name other than that of the holder of the Debenture converted, and the Company shall not be required to issue or deliver any such stock certificate unless and until the person or persons requesting the issue thereof shall have paid to the Company the amount of such tax or shall have established to the satisfaction of the Company that such tax has been paid.

Company to Reserve Common Stock. — The Company shall at all times reserve and keep available, free from preemptive rights, out of its authorized and unissued Common Stock, for the purpose of effecting the conversion of the Debentures, such number of its duly authorized shares of Common Stock as shall from time to time be sufficient to effect the conversion of all outstanding Debentures.

If any shares of Common Stock require registration with or approval of any governmental authority under any Federal or State law, before such shares may be validly issued upon conversion of Debentures, the Company covenants that it will in good faith and as expeditiously as possible endeavor to secure such registration or approval, as the case may be.

The Company covenants that all shares of Common Stock issued upon conversion of Debentures will upon issue be fully paid and non-assessable by the Company and free from all taxes, liens, and charges with respect to the issue thereof.

Before taking any action that should cause an adjustment reducing the Conversion Price below the then par value, if any, of the shares of Common Stock issuable upon conversion of the Debentures, the Company will take any corporate action which may, in the opinion of its counsel, be necessary in order that the Company may validly and legally issue fully paid and non-assessable shares of such Common Stock at such adjusted Conversion Price.

§ 5.07 INTERPRETATION AND EFFECT OF ANTI-DILUTION PROVISIONS

For the right of conversion to be meaningful, the investor must be assured either that the amount and character of the security received upon conversion will remain stable or that adjustments will be made to protect his investment should the attributes of this underlying security be changed. To protect the convertible shareholder's interest against such changes in the underlying securities, "anti-dilution" clauses are generally included as a matter of course in modem convertible securities or in the charter or indenture creating them. In the absence of specific provisions to protect against dilution, there is a great probability that narrow and literal interpretation of the contractual right to convert would limit the right to precisely what was specified, without adjustment for subsequent substantial changes in the attributes of the underlying security.

Stanley A. Kaplan, *Piercing the Corporate Boilerplate: Anti-Dilution Clauses in Convertible Securities*, 33 U. Chi. L. Rev. 1, 2–3 (1965).

CONVERSION ADJUSTMENT EXAMPLES

The adjustment provisions in paragraph (C) of the Preferred Stock Conversion Rate Provisions, *supra*, provide for an adjustment in the conversion rate, which, initially, was 1.33 shares. The following is a simple example of how the provisions of paragraph (C) would work. Assume that the issuer has 10 shares of common stock outstanding with a current market value of $10.00 per share and that the issuer offers to its common stockholders the right to purchase an aggregate of 10 additional shares of common stock at a price of $5.00 per share. The new conversion rate is calculated as follows:

10 + 10	=	20				
10 + 5	=	15				
1.33	X	20	=	26.6	=	1.77
1	15	15				

The new conversion rate would be 1.77.

An example of an application of the Preferred Stock Conversion Price provisions contained in Paragraph (B) *supra*, relating to the $29.75 conversion price follows. (The following example assumes the same facts as set forth immediately above.)

10 + 5	=	15				
10 + 10	=	20				
$29.75	X	15	=	446.25	=	$22.31
1		20		20		

The new conversion price would be $22.31.

BROAD v. ROCKWELL INTERNATIONAL CORP.

United States Court of Appeals, Fifth Circuit

642 F.2d 929 (1981)

This case, which is before us for rehearing en banc, turns on the construction of an indenture dated as of January 1, 1967 (the "Indenture"). The original parties to the Indenture were Collins Radio Company, an Iowa corporation ("Collins"), and The Chase Manhattan Bank (National Association), a national banking association ("Chase"). The Indenture governed the terms of $40,000,000 principal amount of 4 7/8% Convertible Subordinated Debentures due January 1, 1987 (the "Debentures"), which were issued by Collins in January 1967. By means of a supplemental indenture executed in May 1970, United States Trust Company of New York, a New York corporation (the "Trust Company"), succeeded Chase as Trustee under the Indenture.

The events that triggered this lawsuit occurred in the fall of 1973, when Rockwell International Corporation, a Delaware corporation ("Rockwell"), acquired Collins in a cash merger. The central question in the case is this: In what form did the conversion rights of the holders of the Debentures survive the merger under the terms of the Indenture?

David Broad brought this class action on behalf of himself and all others who at the time of the merger were holders of the Debentures. He sued Rockwell, Collins, the controlling persons of both,[3] and the Trust Company, alleging that the defendants breached the terms of the Indenture, breached their respective fiduciary duties, and violated various provisions of the federal securities laws. The

---

[3] [1] The liability Broad would seek to impose on each of these controlling persons appears to be purely derivative in nature. We therefore refer to only the corporate defendants throughout the remainder of the opinion, and our disposition of the claims against the corporate defendants necessarily includes within its scope the claims against the individual defendants.

district court granted a directed verdict in favor of the defendants at the close of *Broad*'s case-in-chief, holding that (1) the defendants' interpretation of the Indenture and their actions in accord with that interpretation were correct and nonactionable as a matter of state law, and (2) for a number of reasons, no reasonable jury could have found violations of the federal securities laws based on the evidence Broad had adduced at trial. A panel of this court affirmed as to the directed verdict on the federal securities counts, but reversed and remanded on the pendent state-law claims; a majority of the full court, however, vacated the panel's decision under Fifth Circuit Local Rule 17 and ordered that the appeal be reheard en banc. *Broad v. Rockwell International Corp.*, 614 F.2d 418, vacated and rehearing en banc granted, 618 F.2d 396 (5th Cir. 1980).

On rehearing en banc, we agree with the panel that the district court acted properly in directing a verdict on the federal securities claims, although we reach that conclusion on narrower grounds than those relied upon by the panel. We disagree, however, with the panel's construction of the Indenture, and hold instead that the district court properly construed that document's provisions. Accordingly, for the reasons set out herein, we affirm the judgment of the district court.

I. EVENTS LEADING TO THIS APPEAL

A. The Factual Background to This Litigation

In reviewing the trial court's grant of a directed verdict at the close of Broad's case-in-chief, we use the familiar standard articulated in *Boeing Co. v. Shipman*, 411 F.2d 365 (5th Cir. 1969) (en banc).[4] Viewed in the light most favorable to Broad, the following is a general outline of the relevant facts adduced prior to the directed verdict; more detail is provided as necessary throughout the opinion.[5]

---

[4] [2] We held in Boeing as follows:

> On motions for directed verdict and for judgment notwithstanding the verdict the Court should consider all of the evidence — not just that evidence which supports the non-mover's case — but in the light and with all reasonable inferences most favorable to the party opposed to the motion. If the facts and inferences point so strongly and overwhelmingly in favor of one party that the Court believes that reasonable men could not arrive at a contrary verdict, granting of the motions is proper. On the other hand, if there is substantial evidence opposed to the motions, that is, evidence of such quality and weight that reasonable and fair-minded men in the exercise of impartial judgment might reach different conclusions, the motions should be denied, and the case submitted to the jury. A mere scintilla of evidence is insufficient to present a question for the jury. The motions for directed verdict and judgment n.o.v. should not be decided by which side has the better of the case, nor should they be granted only when there is a complete absence of probative facts to support a jury verdict. There must be a conflict in substantial evidence to create a jury question. However, it is the function of the jury as the traditional finder of the facts, and not the Court, to weigh conflicting evidence and inferences, and determine the credibility of witnesses.

411 F.2d at 374-75 (footnote omitted). Accord, *Dwoskin v. Rollins, Inc.*, 634 F.2d 285, 289 (5th Cir. 1981) (employing this standard in reviewing directed verdict granted on ground that plaintiff had failed to raise a jury question on scienter in suit based on Rule 10b-5). Almost all of the material facts in this case are undisputed, although the parties differ considerably in the legal characterization they would have us place on those facts.

[5] [3] In our discussion of the facts, we draw to some extent on the language of the panel opinion, 614 F.2d at 422-24.

In January 1967, Collins issued and sold to the public $40,000,000 aggregate principal amount of Debentures. The Debentures bore interest at the rate of 4 7/8% per year and matured on January 1, 1987, unless sooner redeemed by Collins. They were convertible, at the option of the holders thereof, into the common stock of Collins ("Collins Common Stock"), which had a par value of $1 per share. The Debentures were offered to the public through an underwriting syndicate managed by two New York investment banking firms-Kidder, Peabody & Co. Incorporated and White, Weld & Co.

At the time the Debentures were marketed in 1967, Collins was a prosperous enterprise chiefly engaged in the development and production of radio communications and aircraft navigation equipment. The proceeds of the public offering, like the proceeds of previous offerings of debentures by Collins in the 1960s, were to be used to finance capital additions and to increase working capital for the expansion of Collins' business. During the period immediately before the offering of the Debentures, Collins Common Stock had traded on the New York Stock Exchange for approximately $60 per share. If a holder of Debentures were to choose to exercise his conversion privilege, Collins would issue to him, in exchange for his Debentures, one share of Collins Common Stock for every $72.50 principal amount of Debentures. This meant that conversion might become economically attractive if the market price of Collins Common Stock rose more than $12.50 over its market price of $60 per share at the time of the offering of the Debentures.

Beginning in its 1969 fiscal year, however, Collins suffered a series of economic reversals, manifested by declining sales and reduced income. In the midst of a generally declining stock market, Collins' fading fortunes did not go unnoticed: during the 1971 calendar year, Collins Common Stock never traded on the New York Stock Exchange at more than $21 per share, and in the fourth quarter of that year it was selling for as little as $9.75 per share. Collins was on the verge of bankruptcy. It was at that point, however, that Collins became affiliated with Rockwell.

In August 1971, Collins shareholders overwhelmingly approved the terms of an agreement by which Rockwell invested $35,000,000 in Collins, receiving in return two new series of Collins securities: preferred stock that was convertible into Collins class A common stock, and warrants to purchase additional class A common stock. As sole holder of the new issue of preferred stock, Rockwell also received, and soon exercised, the right to elect a majority of Collins' board of directors. In addition to the $35,000,000 investment, Rockwell provided some managerial assistance to Collins and guaranteed up to $20,000,000 in borrowings by MCI Leasing, Inc., a customer of Collins, so that MCI could order up to $33,000,000 worth of equipment from Collins. Rockwell indicated that while it did not, as of July 1971, purpose that there be a merger between the two companies, it would not rule out the possibility that future events might make such a proposal attractive to it.

By 1973 such a proposal had evidently become attractive. In August of that year, Rockwell made a tender offer for Collins Common Stock, offering the shareholders $25 cash per share tendered. As part of the offer, Rockwell disclosed that if the offer were successful, it intended to propose a merger of Collins into Rockwell at that same figure of $25 per share. The tender offer was successful, and by October 1,

1973, Rockwell had acquired approximately 75% of the outstanding Collins Common Stock.

In accordance with the intentions it had stated prior to the tender offer, Rockwell duly entered into an Agreement and Plan of Merger with Collins dated as of October 8, 1973 (the "Merger Plan"), which provided that on the effective date of the merger, each holder of Collins Common Stock (other than Rockwell itself, of course) would receive $25 per share in cash upon surrender of the certificates evidencing such stock. Under Iowa law (which was applicable because Collins was an Iowa corporation), the approval of a majority of the Collins board of directors and of the holders of two-thirds of the outstanding shares of each class of Collins stock was required for a merger. As a result of the tender offer, Rockwell itself controlled more than two-thirds of the outstanding Collins Common Stock; but it did not hold the 90% needed under Iowa law to effect a "short-form" merger in which no vote of the shareholders would be necessary. As a result, a vote of the Collins shareholders was taken on November 2, 1973, and the Merger Plan was approved by the vote of the holders of approximately 84.5% of the Collins Common Stock. The merger was effected on November 14, 1973, and from that date until the present Collins has operated only as an internal division of Rockwell.

These events, of course, were not without effect upon the Debentures. After they were first offered to the public in 1967, Debentures in the principal amount of $1000 at times traded at almost $60 above face value. Later, however, as Collins' business fortunes diminished and the price of Collins Common Stock slumped dramatically, the market price of the Debentures fell as well. The only class member to testify at trial, William E. Barnes, testified that from 1969 through August 1973 he invested $194,000 in Debentures with an aggregate principal amount of $320,000; though the first Debentures he purchased were selling at well above their principal amount, the Debentures he later purchased were discounted to well below $600 per $1000 principal amount, and his average purchase price for all of his Debentures was about $606 for each $1000 principal amount of Debentures.[6]

The first significant activities of the Trust Company, other than its performance of routine administrative duties as substitute Trustee under the Indenture, came in the fall of 1973 when the Trust Company was called upon to consider whether the terms of a proposed supplemental indenture to be executed by Rockwell, as successor by merger to the obligations of Collins under the Indenture, complied with the terms of the Indenture. Under that supplemental indenture, Rockwell would assume in full all of the obligations of Collins under the Indenture, including the obligation to pay interest, and eventually to repay the principal, on the outstanding Debentures until they either were redeemed or matured in 1987. With regard to the conversion feature of the Debentures, the proposed supplemental indenture provided that each holder of a Debenture would have the right to convert

---

[6] [4] Mr. Barnes, a rural mail carrier from Welder, Texas, admitted that in saving Collins from bankruptcy, Rockwell had performed a "verified miracle." He also conceded that as of July 1977, his Debentures were trading at about $775 per $1000 in principal amount, providing him with a net paper profit of more than $50,000 in addition to the roughly $15,000 in interest from the Debentures that he had received. The interest, of course, was paid on the face value of the Debentures rather than on their discounted market value.

his Debenture into the amount of cash that would have been payable to him under the Merger Plan had he converted his Debenture into Collins Common Stock immediately prior to the merger. In other words, a holder of Debentures could, at any time while his Debentures were outstanding, choose to convert them into exactly that which he would have received had he converted immediately before the merger and participated therein as a holder of Collins Common Stock. Because the holders of Collins Common Stock received no common stock in the merger, the holder of Debentures would have no right to convert into common stock — either of Collins (who would have no more common stock) or of Rockwell — after the merger. Rockwell's view of its post-merger obligations under the Indenture was shared by its counsel (the New York firm of Chadbourne, Parke, Whiteside & Wolff), and by Collins and Collins' counsel (the Los Angeles firm of Gibson, Dunn & Crutcher).

In order to determine whether the proposed terms of the supplemental indenture complied with the terms of the Indenture, the Trust Company engaged the New York law firm of Curtis, Mallet-Prevost, Colt & Mosle. Two partners in that firm — John P. Campbell and John N. Marden undertook a review of the Indenture and the applicable law. Campbell and Marden took the position in September 1973 that a court might in the future find that the intent of the parties at the time the Indenture was executed was that the right to convert into common stock would survive a merger of Collins into another company, and that every holder of Debentures would have the right to convert his Debentures into common stock of the surviving company as long as the Debentures remained outstanding. Since the Indenture required that Rockwell assume all of Collins' obligations under the Indenture in the event of a merger, Campbell and Marden contended that Rockwell would be bound to agree in a supplemental indenture with terms providing for a conversion right of the Debentures into the common stock of Rockwell ("Rockwell Common Stock"), unless Rockwell could obtain the consent of each holder of Debentures that such a right could be extinguished. Furthermore, they contended, Rockwell's voting control of Collins prior to the merger imposed upon Rockwell and the directors of Collins a fiduciary obligation to the holders of Debentures.

The record indicates that discussions and exchanges of memoranda and drafts of opinions between counsel for Rockwell and Collins on the one hand, and counsel for the Trust Company on the other hand, continued for several weeks, and their disagreement was heated. There is also evidence in the record indicating that Rockwell exerted considerable pressure on the Trust Company to change its position, threatening the withdrawal of certain other business from the Trust Company and possible litigation if the Trust Company blocked the merger by refusing to execute a supplemental indenture. At something of an impasse with counsel for Rockwell, Campbell advised the Trust Company on September 18, 1973, that it could follow any of four alternative courses of action: (1) the Trust Company could decline to execute a supplemental indenture (thus blocking the Collins-Rockwell merger) unless the supplemental indenture provided for a right to convert into Rockwell Common Stock; (2) the Trust Company, as a policy decision, could refuse to take a position as to the rights of the holders of the Debentures after the merger, relying on the provisions in the Indenture and in the supplemental indenture by which Rockwell would indemnify the Trust Company from liability in any lawsuits that might later be brought; (3) the Trust Company could resign as

Trustee under the Indenture; or (4) the Trust Company could seek a declaratory judgment with respect to the conversion rights of the holders of Debentures after the merger. Campbell recommended alternative (2), and the Trust Company ultimately followed that recommendation.

Thus, on October 11, 1973, Rockwell sent a letter to the holders of the Debentures to notify them of the proposed merger between Rockwell and Collins. The text of the letter read as follows:

> Rockwell International Corporation ("Rockwell") has proposed the merger of Collins Radio Company ("Collins") into Rockwell. Pursuant to the terms of the proposed merger Rockwell would assume all of Collins obligations, including Collins obligations under the Indenture, dated as of January 1, 1967, relating to Collins 4 7/8% Convertible Subordinated Debentures due January 1, 1987 (respectively the "Indenture" and the "Debentures").
>
> Rockwell and United States Trust Company of New York, the Successor Trustee under the Indenture (the "Trustee"), intend to execute a Supplemental Indenture to the Indenture on or about November 1, 1973. This Supplemental Indenture is to be effective on the effective date of the merger of Collins into Rockwell and will provide for the assumption by Rockwell of the due and punctual payment of the principal of and interest on the Debentures and the due and punctual performance and observance by Rockwell of all the terms, covenants and conditions of the Indenture. The Supplemental Indenture does not alter or impair the rights accorded under the Indenture to holders of the Debentures and does not change the provisions of the Indenture.
>
> With regard to the conversion rights of holders of the Debentures, counsel for Rockwell and counsel for Collins have each advised that under Section 4.11 of the Indenture, the Section that provides for the adjustment of conversion rights upon a merger or similar event, a holder of a Debenture, upon effectiveness of the proposed merger, would have the right, until the expiration of the conversion right of such Debenture, to convert the Debenture into the amount of cash that would have been payable with respect to the number of shares of Collins Common Stock into which the Debenture could have been converted immediately prior to effectiveness of the proposed merger. The current conversion price of $72.50 entitles the holder of a $1,000 Debenture to convert it into 13.79 shares of Collins Common Stock. Pursuant to the merger each share of Collins Common Stock outstanding immediately prior to the merger (other than those held by Rockwell) is to be converted into $25. Thus, after the merger, a $1,000 Debenture will be convertible into $344.75 in cash.
>
> The Trustee has advised that it does not take a position with regard to this letter or the statements herein, and that it has consulted with its counsel who confirmed that as Trustee it should not take a position with regard thereto.

> Neither the proposed merger nor the proposed Supplemental Indenture requires action by the Debentureholders. Upon effectiveness of the merger, the Debentures will represent indebtedness of Rockwell. You will not need to surrender or exchange your Debentures for new debentures.

The letter was signed by both the president and the chairman of the board of Rockwell.[7]

According to Campbell's testimony by deposition, at some point prior to the merger he abandoned his interpretation of the Indenture in favor of the interpretation advanced by counsel for Rockwell and Collins. When asked to explain why he had abandoned his earlier position, Campbell answered as follows:

> It started out with a premise that we must find law to support the position which [Broad] now assert[s]. I made, I thought, a very good try and had almost convinced myself by starting with the conclusion and working back to get the authority. It was a good dog, but it wouldn't hunt. I fell down.

Other evidence in the record, however, indicates that as late as January 1974, Campbell continued to see some validity in his earlier view.

Nonetheless, on November 14, 1973, the merger was effected, and a supplemental indenture between Rockwell and the Trust Company was executed, effective as of November 1, 1973. The supplemental indenture provided that Rockwell would assume Collins' obligations on the Debentures. Specifically, it provided that after the merger, the holders of the Debentures had the right to convert the debentures into that which they would have received in the Merger Plan had they converted immediately before the merger's effective date. In accordance with the October 11 letter, Rockwell has consistently interpreted this to mean that the Debentures could be converted into cash, but not into the common stock of either Rockwell or Collins; the conversion rate was $344.75 in cash for each $1000 in principal amount of Debentures surrendered.

B. Action in the District Court

Plaintiff David Broad, a holder of Debentures at the time of the merger, filed this class action in federal court against Rockwell, Collins, the controlling persons of

---

[7] [5] This letter touched off a wave of inquiries by holders of Debentures about the status of their conversion rights. Some apparently were of the impression that Rockwell's October 11 letter did not foreclose the possibility that the Debentures would be convertible at the holder's option into either cash or Rockwell Common Stock. Others contended that Rockwell could not "eliminate" their right to convert into Collins Common Stock without paying them new consideration or providing a conversion right into Rockwell Common Stock. Many holders of Debentures requested copies of the Indenture, which were provided. Some requested copies of the opinions from the respective counsel for Rockwell, Collins, and the Trust Company, but those requests were refused. The Trust Company did, however, initially indicate to a number of holders of Debentures that it disagreed with Rockwell's interpretation of the Indenture without indicating to Rockwell that it was doing so. When Rockwell accused the Trust Company of "fomenting litigation," Campbell replied that the Trust Company had withheld from Rockwell its answers to the letters on the basis of his advice as to the Trust Company's fiduciary obligation to represent the holders of debentures.

both, and the Trust Company. Broad alleged two claims under the federal securities laws — specifically, under section 10(b) of the Securities Exchange Act of 1934, 15 U.S.C. § 78j(b) (1976), and under Rule 10b-5 promulgated by the Securities and Exchange Commission thereunder, 17 C.F. R. § 240.10b-5 (1980).[8] His two federal claims were, as a logical matter, urged essentially in the alternative. His main claim was that the defendants had collectively engaged in a fraudulent scheme to deny the holders of debentures their rights under the Indenture to convert into common stock at any time until the Debentures matured in 1987 or were sooner redeemed. In the alternative, he claimed that at the time the debentures were issued in 1967, the defendants had omitted to disclose a material fact with regard to the terms of the Debentures — specifically, that under the terms of the Indenture, the right to convert into Collins Common Stock could, in the event of a merger, be replaced with the right to convert into only that which the holders of Collins Common Stock received in the merger.[9]

Broad also alleged a number of pendent state-law claims.[10] Essentially, these claims were that all the defendants had breached the Indenture; that all the defendants had breached the covenant of good faith and fair dealing implied into the Indenture by law; that Rockwell had breached a fiduciary duty which it owed the holders of the Debentures by virtue of its control of both parties to the 1973 merger; and that the Trust Company had breached its fiduciary duty as Trustee for the holders of the debentures. The argument that the defendants had breached the Indenture was also urged in the alternative: Broad first contended that the Indenture unambiguously provided for a right to convert into common stock that would survive any merger. But if not unambiguously susceptible to the interpretation he urged in his first argument, Broad contended that the Indenture was at the least ambiguous, and that the intent of the parties at the time the Indenture was executed was that the right to convert into common stock would survive any merger.

Broad sought three alternative forms of relief for the class: (1) "restoration" of the option to convert into Rockwell Common Stock (since no Collins Common Stock existed after the merger); (2) a judgment for the difference between the redemption price (10 3/14% of principal amount) and the market value of the Debentures as of the date of judgment, with interest from the date of the merger; or (3) redemption at 10 3/14% of the principal amount of the Debentures.

At the close of Broad's case-in-chief on the third day of trial, the district court granted the defendants' motions for a directed verdict on all of these claims. With regard to the claim that the defendants omitted to disclose a material fact in connection with the issuance of the Debentures in 1967 and subsequent to that time, the court held that the record was devoid of evidence from which reasonable persons could find that any defendant acted with scienter, even if recklessness were

---

[8] [6] These claims were within the district court's subject-matter jurisdiction under § 27 of the Securities Exchange Act of 1934, 15 U.S.C. § 78aa (1976), and under 28 U.S.C. §§ 1331 and 1337(1976).

[9] [7] Broad has from time to time resisted the characterization of his Rule 10b-5 claims as being in the alternative, but we see no way in which they can logically be reconciled.

[10] [8] These claims were within the district court's subject-matter jurisdiction under the pendent jurisdiction doctrine of *United Mine Workers v. Gibbs*, 383 U.S. 715, 86 S. Ct. 1130, 16 L. Ed. 2d 218 (1966).

sufficient to satisfy the scienter requirement under Rule 10b-5. Additionally, the court held that the Trust Company had no duty to disclose this allegedly omitted fact since it had no connection with the Debentures until 1970. With regard to the claim that the defendants had schemed to deprive the holders of the Debentures of their conversion rights, the court held that any of three grounds justified the directed verdict: first, there was no evidence from which reasonable men could find that the defendants acted with scienter, even if reckless conduct were sufficient to satisfy the scienter requirement; second, Rockwell correctly construed the Indenture in 1973 and fully respected the rights of the holders of the Debentures in the merger; and last, the wrongs alleged in this claim did not occur in connection with a purchase or sale of a security, since the holders of the Debentures still held their Debentures after the merger.

With regard to the state-law claims, the court held that even if Broad's claim that the Indenture was ambiguous had been timely made,[11] that argument was unfounded: the Indenture was unambiguous, and its terms were as Rockwell contended. The court held that its ruling on this question of law foreclosed Broad's breach of contract claim, since it was undisputed that Rockwell's conduct was in full compliance with the court's interpretation of the Indenture. The court further held that Rockwell's compliance with the Indenture also foreclosed any breach of fiduciary duty claims, and that the record was devoid of evidence from which reasonable persons could conclude that Rockwell acted with bad motives. As to the Trust Company, the court held that it had only those duties specified in the Indenture and in the Trust Indenture Act of 1939 (the "Trust Indenture Act"), 15 U.S.C. §§ 77aaa-77bbbb (1976), and that it had not breached any of those duties.

As an alternate ground for the directed verdict on all counts, the court held that the record was devoid of evidence from which reasonable persons could find actual damages, and that none of the equitable remedies requested by Broad would have been appropriate even if he had prevailed on one or more of his theories of liability.

C. The Panel Opinion

On appeal, a panel of this court affirmed the directed verdict on the federal securities claims, but reversed and remanded on the state-law claims. With regard to the Rule 10b-5 claim that the defendants had omitted to disclose in 1967 and thereafter until the merger the possibility that the right to convert into common stock would be altered in the event of a merger, the panel agreed with the district court that there was no evidence in the record from which reasonable persons could find that any of the defendants had acted with scienter. 614 F.2d at 439-41. With regard to the Rule 10b-5 claim that in 1973 the defendants had engaged in a fraudulent scheme to deprive the holders of the Debentures of their rights to convert into Collins Common Stock, the panel agreed with the district court that as regards the holders of the Debentures there had been no "purchase or sale" of a

[11] [9] The claim that the Indenture was ambiguous was actually not included in Broad's complaint, and neither did it appear in the summary of the parties' contentions that was filed in lieu of a pretrial order. Nonetheless, since the district court did not specifically hold that such an argument had been waived, but instead reached the merits of the ambiguity argument, and since the panel opinion has reviewed the district court's ruling on that argument, we too will include it in our discussion of the case.

security, rejecting Broad's argument that the loss of the conversion right was analogous to a constructive or forced sale. *Id.* at 435-39. Having agreed with the district court that there could be no liability on the federal securities claims, the panel declined to discuss the district court's alternative ground for the directed verdict on those claims-that the record was devoid of evidence from which reasonable persons could find actual damages. *Id.* at 439 n.24.

The panel parted ways with the district court on the question of the Indenture's ambiguity, however, holding that the Indenture was ambiguous as a matter of law because it did not speak "with the requisite clarity" to the post-merger conversion rights of the holders of the Debentures. That being the case, the panel held that the jury should have been allowed to determine whether Rockwell and the Trust Company had acted in accord with the intent of the parties at the time the Indenture was executed. *Id.* at 426-29. Further, since under New York law every contract contains an implied covenant of fair dealing, the panel held that the jury should have been allowed to determine whether' the defendants had dealt fairly with the holders of the Debentures. *Id.* at 429-30.

With regard to the fiduciary duty claims, the panel held that Rockwell's duties to the holders of the Debentures should be considered to have been met if on remand the jury were to find either (1) that Rockwell complied with the intent of the parties at the time of the execution of the Indenture, or (2) that despite its breach of the Indenture, Rockwell acted in good faith based on a reasonable understanding of the Indenture. *Id.* at 430-31. As to the Trust Company's fiduciary duty, the panel held that the Trust Indenture Act imposed no fiduciary obligations in addition to those imposed by applicable state law. *Id.* at 431-32. Returning to state law, the panel held that the Trust Company was cloaked with a fiduciary duty to the holders of the Debentures under New York law, and that it was for the jury to decide whether the Trust Company had violated that duty. *Id.* at 432.

On the question of the measure of damages applicable to the state-law claims, the panel agreed with the district court that equitable relief such as redemption of the Debentures or restoration of the common stock conversion privileges would be inappropriate. But the panel held that if on remand the jury found that the defendants had breached the Indenture, the district court could apply the default provisions set out in the Indenture, which provided that the principal and accrued interest on the Debentures would be accelerated to be due and payable immediately as of the time of the default. *Id.* at 433.

[For Part II.A, see § 3.04, *supra.*]

. . . .

B. Conversion Rights at Common Law and the Need for Contractual Antidilution Provisions

In the case at bar, there are specific portions of the Indenture that set out the rights of the holders of the Debentures, and the obligations of the Trustee and issuer, in the event that the issuer is merged into another company. Nonetheless, the common law's treatment of conversion rights upon merger is important in this case in two different respects. First, it must be determined whether the common law provides the holders of the Debentures with rights in addition to the rights that are set out in the Indenture. Second, an understanding of the common law's treatment of conversion rights upon merger explains the historical development of boilerplate contractual antidilution provisions of the sort found in the Indenture.

The Commentaries explain in brief the possible dangers to the conversion rights of the holders of debentures that might attend certain actions by the issuer of the debentures:

> The anti-dilution provisions are designed to preserve the value of the conversion privilege against diminution by certain voluntary corporate acts. For example, if the conversion price is $25 a share at a time when the common stock has a market value of $30 a share, the conversion right is clearly valuable. If the Company should then split its stock 3 for 1, the market price of its shares would be reduced to approximately $10 per share. Thus the value of the right to convert at $25 per share would have been virtually destroyed, by that voluntary corporate action, in the absence of appropriate protective provisions.
>
> Inasmuch as ownership of a convertible debenture does not give the holder the rights of a shareholder, the holder of a convertible debenture would have almost no protection against acts by the Company which would adversely affect the value of the common stock issuable on conversion, such as a split-up of shares, stock dividends, distribution of assets, issuance or sale of other convertible securities, issuance of options, issuance or sale of common stock at prices below the current conversion or market price, merger, sale of assets or dissolution and liquidation of the Company. Events of this type are customarily described as "diluting" the value of the conversion privilege, and if protection is desired against such dilution, appropriate provisions must be included in the indenture.

Commentaries at 527 (1971) (emphasis added; footnote omitted). As justification for the phrase we have italicized above, the Commentaries cite Parkinson v. West End Street Railway Co., 173 Mass. 446, 53 N.E. 891 (1899) (per Holmes, J.).

Justice Holmes' decision in Parkinson was aptly cited by the authors of the Commentaries for the proposition that antidilution protection must be provided by contract if it is to be provided at all, for Parkinson holds that there is no such protection at common law. The plaintiff in Parkinson held Highland Street Railway bonds that were convertible into Highland's preferred stock. When West End Street Railway acquired Highland "subject to all [of Highland's] duties, restrictions, and liabilities," *Id.* at 447, 53 N.E. at 891, the existing holders of Highland's preferred stock received West End preferred stock or preemptive rights thereto in exchange for their Highland stock. West End refused, however, to convert the Highland bonds into West End preferred stock. The Massachusetts Supreme Court denied relief:

> [T]he contract does not prevent the corporation from consolidating with another in such a way as to make performance impossible, any more than it prevents the issue of new stock in such a way as to make performance valueless. . . . A consolidation which makes no arrangement for furnishing stock in the new company, and which ends the existence of the old ones, as

> a general rule may be presumed to put an end to the right of bondholders to call for stock, not because the law has not machinery for keeping such a right alive, but because, not being bound to do so, it has made dispositions which manifestly take no account of it.

Id. at 448-49, 53 N.E. at 892. Thus, according to Parkinson, mergers may extinguish all conversion rights, absent explicit contractual provisions to the contrary. The same idea is expressed in Lisman v. Milwaukee, Lake Shore & Western Railway Co., 161 F. 472 (C.C.E.D. Wis. 1908), *aff'd, mem.*, 170 F. 1020 (7th Cir.), *cert. denied*, 214 U.S. 520, 29 S. Ct. 700, 53 L. Ed. 1065 (1909):

> [I]t would appear that the [issuer] might, in the interest of its stockholders, go out of existence without giving the holder of a convertible bond any just cause of complaint.
>
> . . . In the sale and purchase both railway companies were acting within their strict legal rights to promote the interests of their respective stockholders. This change of ownership was only one of several vicissitudes liable to happen during 20 years in the life of the corporation, which might render the outstanding option valueless, and still afford no cause of action to the debenture holder. Nothing has taken place which the debenture holders were not bound to anticipate . . . If [as a result of the consolidation] the hope of speculative venture on the stock market was extinguished, it is damnum absque injuria.

Id. at 477-78.

Broad has cited no persuasive authority which would indicate that the common law of New York or of any other jurisdiction would provide any additional protection for his conversion rights upon merger, other than that protection which might be included in the Indenture.[12] But the common law cases cited by the parties do shed light on the origin of and need for boilerplate antidilution provisions of the sort at issue here.

As the Lisman case points out, holders of debentures were charged at common law with the knowledge that various voluntary corporate actions might dilute — or even render nugatory — the value of their debentures' conversion feature; because dilution was (at least constructively) within their contemplation when they purchased the security, there was no unfairness in denying the holders of debentures any compensation in the event of such dilution. But of course, even before the occurrence of a diluting event, this risk of dilution itself significantly diminished the value of the conversion feature. As Justice Holmes noted in Parkinson, however, the law does have machinery through which, if the parties so choose, the value of the conversion right may be protected. The draftsmen of indentures may guard against dilution through the insertion of any of three types of special contractual provisions.

The first and most drastic type of provision is the outright prohibition of certain types of voluntary corporate conduct. Such prohibitory covenants are more

---

[12] [16] We leave aside for the moment the question of whether Broad can claim such protection from an implied covenant of fair dealing, as suggested by the panel opinion, 614 F.2d at 429-30. We deal with this issue in part III-A of this opinion, *infra*.

typically used to protect the value of the debt obligation represented by the debenture.[13] But prohibitory covenants may also be used to protect the value of the conversion feature . . . *e.g.*, by means of an absolute ban on mergers. The efficacy of this means of antidilution protection must be balanced against the loss of business flexibility it means for the issuer. Some sorts of corporate conduct can be limited with little loss of flexibility, but other restrictions may so hamstring the company that they threaten its continued existence.

Happily, there are two less restrictive means of antidilution protection that do not bear such high costs in terms of business flexibility, as the following excerpt from the Commentaries indicates:

> In modern convertible debenture indentures it is virtually universal to provide some anti-dilution protection [that provides for the adjustment of the conversion price upon the taking of specific actions by the issuer that would cause the value of the conversion right to be diluted], usually in combination with provisions [requiring advance notice to the debenture-holders of such acts], plus a provision for equitable adjustment in the event of a merger or other reorganization [in which the issuer is the surviving company]. However, adjustment of the conversion price by itself cannot provide the debentureholder with protection against all events which might substantially affect the conversion privilege. For example, when the Company is to be merged into another corporation and the Company's common stock is to be replaced by convertible preferred stock or debentures of the surviving corporation, adjustment of the conversion price would not provide adequate protection. Thus it is now customary to provide that the debenture-holder will be given the right to convert his debentures into whatever securities are to replace the common stock of the Company.

Commentaries at 528 (emphasis added).[14] Professor and former SEC Chairman Cary makes the same point:

> As a consequence of cases such as Parkinson, it has been found necessary in the conversion contract to provide for protection in the event of consolidations, mergers, conveyance of substantially all assets, capital reorganizations and reclassifications. If any of these occur the instrument frequently provides that the holder of the convertible security shall have the right thereafter to convert it "into the kind and amount of shares of stock and other securities and property receivable . . . by a holder of the number of shares of capital stock into which such [convertible security] might have been converted immediately prior to such reclassification, change, consolidation, merger, sale, or conveyance."

[13] [17] For example, the issuer may be prohibited from exceeding negotiated limits on the funded (long-term) debt it incurs. This preserves a margin of safety for the holders of debentures by "preventing a dilution of the debentureholder's position and a weakening of the Company's financial structure through the creation of what is considered in the particular case to be an excessive amount of additional debt." *Commentaries* at 370.

[14] [18] Although the quoted text refers only to providing a right to convert into the *securities* of the surviving company, the actual antidilution provision suggested in the *Commentaries* is of broader scope. *See* n.19, *infra*.

W. Cary & M. Eisenberg, *Cases and Materials on Corporations* 1155 (5th ed. unabr. 1980) (ellipsis and bracketed portion in original). The *Commentaries* contain a suggested antidilution provision with strikingly similar language to that set out in the above passage.[15]

While the common law's treatment of conversion rights in the event of merger provides a useful background, and while various antidilution provisions promulgated by the American Bar Foundation and the commentators are useful for purposes of comparison, the resolution of this case ultimately turns upon our construction of the specific language in the Indenture under which the Debentures were issued in 1967.

C. The Applicable Rules of Construction

Though the parties are residents of many different states, and though the events with which we are concerned are national in scope, there is no dispute over which state's law governs in construing the contract. Section 17.12 of the Indenture provides in pertinent part as follows:

> This Indenture and each and every provision hereof and of the Debentures shall be deemed to be a contract made under the laws of the State of New York, and for all purposes shall be construed in accordance with the laws of said State.

Thus, we will apply settled principles of New York law in construing the Indenture — although those principles of contract construction are very nearly universal throughout the United States.

The process of contract interpretation is the means through which the scope of the parties' agreement and their respective rights thereunder are determined. Under New York law, a written contract is to be interpreted so as to give effect to the intention of the parties as expressed in the unequivocal language they have employed. Due consideration must be given to the purpose of the parties in making the contract, and a fair and reasonable interpretation consistent with that purpose must guide the courts in enforcing the agreement.

The interpretation of an unambiguous contract provision is a function for the

---

[15] [19] The sample provision in the *Commentaries* reads as follows:

> If any capital reorganization or reclassification of the capital stock of the Company, or consolidation or merger of the Company with another corporation, or the sale of all or substantially all of its assets to another corporation, shall be effected in such a way that holders of Common Stock shall be entitled to receive stock, securities or assets with respect to or in exchange for Common Stock, then, as a condition of such reorganization, reclassification, consolidation, merger or sale, the Company or such successor or purchasing corporation, as the case may be, shall execute with the Trustee a supplemental indenture providing that the Holder of each Debenture then outstanding shall have the right thereafter and until the expiration of the period of convertibility to convert such Debenture into the kind and amount of stock, securities or assets receivable upon such reorganization, reclassification, consolidation, merger or sale by a holder of the number of shares of Common Stock into which such Debenture might have been converted immediately prior to such reorganization, reclassification, consolidation, merger or sale, subject to adjustments which shall be as nearly equivalent as may be practicable to the adjustments provided for in this Article Thirteen.

Commentaries at 549-50.

court rather than for a jury, and matters extrinsic to the agreement may not be considered when the intent of the parties can be gleaned from the face of the instrument.

A court may not rewrite a term of a contract by "interpretation" when that term is clear and unambiguous on its face. In interpreting the contract, a court must be concerned with what the parties intended, but only to the extent that they evidenced what they intended by what they wrote. Neither may a court rewrite a contract to accord with its instinct for the dispensation of equity under the facts of a case.

Finally, under New York law, the entire contract must be considered, and, as between possible interpretations of an allegedly ambiguous term, that will be chosen which best accords with the sense of the remainder of the contract, and that interpretation is favored which will make every part of the contract effective. All parts of the agreement are to be reconciled, if possible, in order to avoid an inconsistency. A specific provision will not be set aside in favor of a catch-all clause. And the normal rule of construction that any fair doubt as to the meaning of the words chosen by the drafting party should be resolved against that party is inapplicable when there are not two possible and reasonable interpretations.[16] Because courts are to adjudicate the rights of the parties according to the unambiguous terms of the contract, they therefore must give the words and phrases employed in the contract their plain meaning.

---

[16] [20] Broad has argued in the district court and on appeal that any ambiguities in the Indenture should be construed against Rockwell, since its predecessor company, Collins, drafted the Indenture. Given our holding *infra* in parts II-D and 11-E of this opinion that the Indenture is unambiguous, we need not reach this issue.

We note, however, that the record in this case does not necessarily support Broad's logic. An equally plausible argument could be made that any ambiguities in the Indenture should be construed against Broad rather than against Rockwell, for the *underwriters' counsel* drafted the provisions at issue in this litigation. See part IV-A of this opinion, *infra*. Broad, as a purchaser from an underwriter (at least indirectly), succeeded to the contractual rights and stands in the shoes of the underwriter who originally purchased those Debentures.

That such arguments, pro and con, can be made at all is itself instructive. While as a matter of abstract contract law it is proper to construe ambiguities against the drafter of a contract, that tenet of contract law has only limited practical significance in the context of construing an indenture. To the extent the rule is practicable at all, it can only be readily applied to those terms that were actually discussed and thought about by the parties — which is almost never the case with boilerplate provisions such as the ones at issue here. On these facts, it is difficult to fathom how even the most diligent, attentive, and intelligent jury could reach a rational conclusion as to the intent of the parties at the time the contract was executed, even were they instructed to construe any ambiguities in the Indenture (the written embodiment of the parties' intent) against the drafter of that document. They would have little on which to base their decision other than the language of the Indenture itself.

Further, given that many other indentures contain language identical to that found in the Indenture at issue here, there is a significant likelihood that other courts would feel bound by a finding by this court that as a matter of law this language is ambiguous. Thus, there is a significant likelihood as well that different juries, construing identical indentures in an attempt to divine "the intent of the parties," would reach different conclusions. This would indeed be anomalous, since the principal goal of using boilerplate language in such contracts is that there be uniform construction of those provisions.

In a different case, construing an indenture with different terms, we might be compelled to direct that a jury attempt such a difficult feat if we found the indenture to be ambiguous as a matter of law. In the case at bar, however, our holding *infra* that the Indenture is unambiguous spares any jury the obligation of undertaking that unenviable task.

As a matter of law, be it the law of New York or any other jurisdiction with which we are acquainted, the Indenture either is or is not ambiguous. It either does or does not adequately demonstrate the intent of the parties from its own four corners.[17] We cannot emphasize too strongly that the resolution of this issue is for the district court in the first instance, rather than for a jury; and because it is a question of law, we review the district court's decision with the full freedom to substitute our own judgment for that of the court below. The opinions of the many lawyers who have reviewed the Indenture before this litigation reached this court may be quite relevant for some other purposes — *e.g.*, for determining the defendants' good faith or the lack thereof. We may, but certainly need not, find the force of their legal reasoning compelling, and adopt it as our own. But on the initial and often determinative question of whether the contract sufficiently demonstrates the intent of the parties so as to be enforceable only by reference to the four corners of the document, it does not matter at all how many lawyers have in the past pronounced this contract to be ambiguous or unambiguous. Neither does it matter in whose behalf, or with what motives, or when, they made such arguments. We note that virtually every case involving the interpretation of a contract comes to us with two sets of lawyers and two sets of clients with sharply differing views of the meaning of the contract. But interpreting contracts is ultimately the business of the courts.

D. The Meaning of Section 4.11 of the Indenture

The structure of the Indenture is fairly typical of convertible debenture indentures generally.[18] As might be expected, there is an article of the Indenture

---

[17] [21] Broad has argued from time to time in this litigation that we should look to various documents other than the Indenture — *e.g.*, the face of the Debentures, the prospectus under which the Debentures were marketed, and various advertisements and press releases published by the defendants — as alternate sources of contractual rights. With regard to the Debentures and the prospectus, those documents specifically and repeatedly incorporate the Indenture by reference, and warn the investor that the contractual obligations and rights that attend the Debentures are governed solely by the Indenture. The suggestion that the press releases and advertisements constitute enforceable contract provisions in this situation is patently absurd. Those documents may be highly relevant, of course, to Broad's federal securities claims; but they are not a source of contractual rights.

[18] [22] The negotiated "business" portions of the indenture are largely interspersed through the first six articles. Article One contains defined terms. Article Two provides for the form of the Debentures and for certain ministerial processes connected with their issue, registration, and exchange. Article Three sets out the extent to which the debt represented by the Debentures is subordinated to senior indebtedness of Collins. Article Four sets out the conversion privileges. Article Five provides for the redemption of Debentures, and Article Six for the sinking fund mechanism used to redeem a portion of the issue each year. Article Seven contains formal covenants of the issuer (*e.g.*, duty to pay principal, premium, and interest on the Debentures, to maintain corporate offices and a corporate existence) as well as certain special provisions that were negotiated by the issuer and the lead underwriter (*e.g.*, restrictions on incurring funded debt and on paying especially large dividends).

The remainder of the Indenture is largely boilerplate. Article Eight provides certain bookkeeping details. Article Nine defines events of default and the remedies therefor. Article Ten provides for the duties of the Trustee, which are largely governed by the Trust Indenture Act of 1939, 15 U.S.C. §§ 77aaa-77bbbb (1976). Article Eleven contains rules for determining the ownership of Debentures and for determining what constitutes collective action by the holders of Debentures. Article Twelve provides for meetings of the holders of Debentures. Article Thirteen authorizes the execution in certain

devoted wholly to the conversion rights of the holders of the Debentures, and a section within that article which addresses the possibility of a merger of Collins with another company: Article Four of the Indenture is entitled "Conversion of Debentures," and the next-to-last section of that Article, Section 4.11, is described in the Indenture's table of contents as governing the "[c]ontinuation of the conversion privilege in case of a consolidation, merger or sale of assets." We note that there is no provision in the Indenture which explicitly mandates that the holders of the Debentures should have a continuing right to convert into common stock after a merger. Aside from his few arguments based on the language of Section 4.11, Broad basically argues his case by implication from more general language that is not specifically addressed to the merger context. But because Section 4.11 is more specifically addressed to the merger context than any other provision of the Indenture, we begin our discussion with that particular provision, to see if the language thereof clearly and unambiguously conveys the intent of the parties.

Section 4.11 provides, in pertinent part, as follows:

> In case of any consolidation of [Collins] with, or merger of [Collins] into, any other corporation . . . , the corporation formed by such consolidation or the corporation into which [Collins] shall have been merged . . . shall execute and deliver to the [Trust Company] a supplemental indenture . . . providing that the holder of each Debenture then outstanding shall have the right (until the expiration of the conversion right of such Debenture) to convert such Debenture into the kind and amount of shares of stock and other securities and property receivable upon such consolidation [or] merger . . . by a holder of the number of shares of Common Stock of [Collins] into which such Debenture might have been converted immediately prior to such consolidation [or] merger. . . .

Parsing this section into logical units, we note that it serves two purposes. First, it specifies what the Trust Company and Collins' successor must do in the event of a merger in which Collins is not the surviving company: they must execute a supplemental indenture that will formally provide for the conversion rights of the holders of Debentures after the merger. There is no question in this case but that Rockwell and the Trust Company complied with this directive, for they did execute a supplemental indenture detailing the post-merger conversion rights of the holders of Debentures. Rather, the question is whether the interpretation they have placed on the language of the Indenture and the supplemental indenture — that after the merger, the holder of a Debenture would have the right to convert a Debenture in the principal amount of $1000 only into $344.75 in cash — fairly and adequately accords to the holders of Debentures their valid rights under the Indenture.

---

circumstances of supplemental indentures. Article Fourteen comprises provisions intended to apply in the event of a consolidation, merger, or sale of assets of Collins. Article Fifteen contains the procedures for satisfaction and discharge of the Indenture. Article Sixteen limits the personal liability of certain of the company's controlling persons. Article Seventeen, the final article, contains miscellaneous provisions, including a choice of law provision specifying that the Indenture shall be governed by the laws of New York State.

Many of the provisions of the Indenture that are pertinent to this lawsuit are set out in an appendix to the panel opinion, 614 F.2d at 441-47.

The second part of Section 4.11 provides by its terms that after the merger, the holder of each Debenture shall have the right to convert that Debenture into something — but what? It cannot be Collins Common Stock, for there will be no more of that after the merger. It therefore must be something else other than Collins Common Stock. The nature of the "something else" into which the holder of a Debenture can convert his Debenture is specified by reference to what the holders of the Collins Common Stock received in the merger: he can convert into the kind of "shares of stock and other securities and property" that the holders of Collins Common Stock received as part of the Merger Plan. Thus, if the holders of Collins Common Stock had received Rockwell Common Stock in the merger in exchange for giving up their shares of Collins Common Stock, the holders of Debentures would have been entitled, at any time after the merger for so long as their Debentures were outstanding, to convert into Rockwell Common Stock. Alternately, if the holders of Collins Common Stock had received Rockwell debentures in exchange for their Collins Common Stock, the holders of the Debentures would have been entitled to convert into Rockwell debentures.

Broad suggests that the use of the conjunctive "and" in Section 4.11 ("shares of stock and other securities and property") means that in every instance of a merger, the holders of the Debentures would be entitled to receive all three types of property specified above. This might be a plausible construction, but for the fact that it would make meaningless the qualification to that phrase that follows immediately thereafter — "receivable upon such consolidation [or] merger . . . by a holder of . . . shares of Common Stock of [Collins]." We decline to read Section 4.11 as a mandatory directive that any plan of merger between Collins and another company had to include provisions for the receipt by the holders of Collins Common Stock of both stock on the one hand, and other securities and property on the other. Had the parties to the contract wished to fashion such a bizarre provision, they certainly would have done so in a more explicit fashion.

Thus, the plain meaning of Section 4.11 is that after a merger, the nature of that "something else" into which the holders of Debentures are entitled to convert in lieu of Collins Common Stock is exactly equivalent to the nature of the "something" that the holders of Collins Common Stock received in the merger. No substantive limit or mandatory specification is provided in Section 4.11 as to what the holders of Collins Common Stock may receive in the merger; but whatever types of compensation the shareholders may receive in exchange for their Collins Common Stock, the holders of the Debentures are entitled to convert into each and all of those types.

In the case at bar, it is undisputed that the holders of Collins Common Stock received only cash in exchange for their shares; under the terms of the Merger Plan, they did not receive stock or any other type of property. Thus, the nature of the "something else" into which the holders of Debentures are entitled to convert in lieu of Collins Common Stock is cash — not Rockwell Common Stock, not other securities, and not other types of property besides cash.

But Section 4.11 also specifies the quantity of the "something else" into which the holders of the Debentures are entitled to convert after the merger. Like the nature of the "something else," the quantity of the "something else" is defined by reference to what the holders of Collins Common Stock received in the merger. Under Section 4,11, each holder of Debentures is entitled to convert each of his Debentures into that amount of the "something else" which was receivable under the terms of the Merger Plan "by a holder of the number of shares of Common Stock of [Collins] into which such Debenture might have been converted immediately prior to such . . . merger."

Thus, Section 4.11 gives us a formula for computing the quantity of the "something else." There are two variables in the formula: the conversion price of the Debentures immediately prior to the merger, and the quantity of the "something" received by the holders of Collins Common Stock in exchange for each share they surrendered as part of the Merger Plan. Section 4.11 directs that we first determine the number of shares of Collins Common Stock that a holder of Debentures would have been entitled to receive had he converted his Debentures immediately prior to the merger. As of the date of the merger, nothing had happened to trigger any of the conversion price adjustment provisions set out elsewhere in Article Four of the Indenture. Therefore, the conversion price originally specified when the Debentures were issued — $72.50 — was still in effect at the time of the merger. At this conversion price, the Debentures were convertible immediately prior to the merger at the rate of 13.79 shares of Collins Common Stock per $1000 in principal amount of the Debentures surrendered.

The formula next provides that we take the quantity of the "something" that was received by the holders of Collins Common Stock in the merger in exchange for each share of Common Stock they surrendered ($25 cash), and multiply that "something" by the number of shares of Collins Common Stock into which the Debentures would have been convertible (13.79 shares per $1000 Debenture). The result is that each $1000 principal amount of Debenture is convertible into $344.75 cash (13.79 x $25).

Under the plain language of Section 4.11, then, we are compelled to the conclusion that Rockwell and the Trust Company correctly fulfilled their duties to execute a supplemental indenture providing for the post-merger conversion rights of the holders of Debentures; further, they correctly calculated those rights as specified by the terms of Section 4.11. Unless there is some compelling reason that we should not give the language of this Section its plain meaning, Broad's breach of contract claim must fail.

E. Reconciling Section 4.11 with the Remainder of the Indenture

1. The "Iowa law" argument. — Broad's first argument against giving the language of Section 4.11 its plain meaning is based indirectly on the "and other securities and property" clauses. Broad concedes that under New York law, the term "property" includes cash within its scope. But, he argues, the parties could not have intended at the time of the Indenture's execution that the right to convert into cash could be substituted for the right to convert into Collins Common Stock. As support for this argument, he notes that Collins was incorporated under the laws of Iowa, and that as of 1967, when the Indenture was executed, Iowa law did not permit a merger in which the shareholders of the merged company received only cash in exchange for their shares. Rockwell and the Trust Company concede that

such a merger was not possible under Iowa law until 1970.

The actual language of Section 4.11, however, is entirely inconsistent with Broad's argument. If the intent of the parties was that the right to convert into Collins Common Stock would be replaced in the event of a merger with a right to convert into only common stock of another company, then the phrase "and other securities and property" would be meaningless surplusage with no effect. Under the New York rules of contract construction discussed above, contracts should be construed so as to give meaning to all provisions. The phrase "and other securities and property" can only have meaning if the contract is interpreted to mean that the parties intended that the holders of Debentures should be entitled to convert into whatever types of compensation the holders of Collins Common Stock could receive under the state law governing mergers at any given point in time.

We note as well that it would be entirely inconsistent with the tone and purpose of the remainder of the Indenture — which was drafted to provide, insofar as humanly possible, for every imaginable contingency — to impute to the parties an intent to freeze as of the year 1967 the nature of the property into which the Debentures were convertible. If that were in fact their intent, it would have ill served the holders of the Debentures. As our discussion above in Part II-B of this opinion indicates, the conversion rights of the holders of Debentures are purely contractual in nature. Absent a contractual provision specifying that the conversion right would be replaced with the right to convert into something other than Collins Common Stock, post-merger holders of Debentures have no right to convert into anything. Thus, if the intent of the parties was that the right of the holders of the Debentures to convert into Collins Common Stock would be replaced with the right to convert into only whatever common stock the holders of Collins Common Stock received under the Merger Plan, the holders of Debentures would be entitled to convert into nothing, since the holders of Collins Common Stock received no common stock. The construction of the Indenture that we instead adopt is by far more flexible and equitable to all concerned.

2. Other arguments based on Article Four. — Broad next argues that the Indenture elsewhere provides an absolute, unabridgeable right to convert into Collins Common Stock at any time while the Debentures are outstanding. He first points to Section 4.01, which provides in pertinent part as follows:

> Subject to and upon compliance with the provisions of this Article Four, at the option of the holder thereof, any Debenture . . . may, at any time [while the Debentures are outstanding] be converted . . . into fully paid and non-assessable shares . . . of Common Stock of [Collins]. . . .

Broad would have us read the "at any time" language as precluding the effect we would otherwise give to the language of Section 4.11.

In the first place, if there were any conflict between the above-quoted language of Section 4.01 and Section 4.11, the latter would control under principles of New York contract law, since of the two sections, Section 4.11 is more specifically addressed to the merger context. But in fact there is no conflict. Broad's suggested construction would make sense only if we were to ignore the introductory phrase of Section 4.01 — "[subject] to and upon compliance with the provisions of this Article

Four." Section 4.11 is part of Article Four, and Section 4.01, by its very terms, is explicitly made subject to that article. Thus, the "at any time" language of Section 4.01 is implicitly qualified by reference to Section 4.11 to mean "at any time except in the merger context, at which point Section 4.11 becomes applicable."

Broad makes a similar argument based on the language of Section 4.07, which provides in pertinent part as follows:

> [Collins] shall at all times reserve and keep available, free from pre-emptive rights, out of its authorized but unissued Common Stock, for the purpose of effecting the conversion of the debentures, the full number of shares of Common Stock then issuable upon the conversion of all outstanding Debentures.

Again, were there a conflict between this Section and Section 4.11, the latter would control because it is more specifically addressed to the merger context. Nonetheless, we find no conflict. Even though not prefaced by the "subject to . . . the provisions of this Article Four" language, Section 4.07 by its terms only applies in those circumstances when the conversion right, if exercised, would result in the issuance of Collins Common Stock. The obligation to maintain sufficient shares of Collins Common Stock can have no meaning when there is no longer a conversion right into that stock. There is no such right after a merger in which Collins is not the surviving company. Under this interpretation, Sections 4.11 and 4.07 mesh perfectly.

It is also noteworthy that Article Four contains lengthy and complex provisions which mandate the adjustment of the conversion price upon specified conditions that would otherwise dilute the value of conversion feature. Nowhere in Article Four, nor elsewhere within the four corners of the Indenture, is there any formula by which one could determine the ratio at which the Debentures would be converted into the surviving corporation's common stock. It would seem likely that such a formula would have been provided along with all the other conversion price adjustments, had the intent of the parties to the Indenture been that there should be an absolute right to convert into common stock of some sort, even in the event of a merger in which Collins and the Collins Common Stock would disappear.[19]

3. Arguments based on Article Fourteen. — Section 14.01 provides in pertinent part as follows:

> Nothing in this Indenture shall prevent any consolidation or merger of [Collins] with or into any other corporation or corporations (whether or not affiliated with [Collins]) . . . ; provided, however, and [Collins] hereby covenants and agrees, that upon any such . . . merger, . . . the due and punctual payment of the principal of (and premium, if any) and interest on

[19] [23] Such a formula could have been drafted with little difficulty, had the parties intended that there be an absolute right to convert into the surviving company's common stock. For example, the drafters could have provided that a post-merger holder of Debentures would have the right to convert into that number of shares of the surviving company's common stock which had an aggregate market value immediately prior to the merger that was equal to the aggregate market value of the number of shares of Collins Common Stock into which the holder of Debentures could have converted immediately prior to the merger.

> all of the Debentures, according to their tenor, and the due and punctual performance and observance of all the terms, covenants and conditions of this Indenture to be performed or observed by [Collins], shall be expressly assumed, by indenture supplemental hereto, satisfactory in form to the [Trust Company], executed and delivered to the [Trust Company] by the corporation formed by such consolidation, or by the corporation into which [Collins] shall have been merged.

We begin by noting that the first phrase of this Section strongly supports the construction of the Indenture proffered by Rockwell and the Trust Company and accepted by the district court: if the Indenture provided an absolute right to convert into Collins Common Stock, there could be no completed merger of Collins into another company. The fact that Section 14.01 qualifies the entire Indenture evidences a strong and compelling intent of the parties that Collins should not be prevented from merging into another company by its obligations to the holders of the Debentures under the Indenture.

Broad's argument is based on the second clause of Section 14.01, which requires that the surviving corporation in a merger expressly assume "the due and punctual performance and observance of all the terms, covenants and conditions of this Indenture." He argues that this requires the surviving company to observe the covenants made by the issuer in Sections 4.01 and 4.07 — the "at all times" covenants discussed above in part II-E-2 of this opinion. Unfortunately for Broad, however, we have determined that those sections are not at all inconsistent with the interpretation we have placed on Section 4.11: in effect, Section 4.11 overrides those Sections. It is undisputed that Rockwell and the Trust Company did execute a supplemental indenture providing that Rockwell would observe all of those covenants applicable after the merger; likewise, it is undisputed that Rockwell has abided by those covenants, including the honoring of the debt obligation on the Debentures. Rockwell also stands ready to honor the conversion rights set out in the supplemental indenture, which have been adjusted pursuant to Section 4.11.

Section 14.02 provides in pertinent part as follows:

> In case of any such . . . merger, . . . and upon the execution by the successor corporation of an indenture supplemental hereto, as provided in Section 14.01, and upon compliance by such successor corporation with all applicable provisions of Section 4.11, such successor corporation shall succeed to and be substituted for [Collins]. . . .
>
> In case of any such . . . merger, . . . such changes in phraseology and form (but not in substance) may be made in the Debentures thereafter to be issued as may be appropriate.

As stated above, Rockwell and the Trust Company did execute a proper supplemental indenture as provided for in Section 14.01, and they did comply with the applicable provisions of Section 4.11 in executing that supplemental indenture. Rockwell has properly succeeded to Collins' rights and obligations under the Indenture. Broad's arguments under Sections 14.01 and 14.02 must fail.

4. Arguments based on Article Thirteen. — Article Thirteen of the Indenture governs the circumstances in which the issuer and the Trustee can execute a

supplemental indenture. Section 13.01, which is described in the Indenture's table of contents as specifying the "[purposes for which supplemental indentures may be entered into without consent of the Debentureholders," provides in pertinent part as follows:

> [Collins], when authorized by a resolution of its Board of Directors, and the [Trust Company], subject to the conditions and restrictions in this Indenture contained, may from time to time and at any time enter into an indenture or indentures supplemental hereto . . . for one or more of the following purposes:
>
> > (a) to make provision with respect to the conversion rights of holders of the Debentures pursuant to the requirements of Section 4.11;
> >
> > (b) to evidence the succession of another corporation to [Collins], or successive successions, and the assumption by the successor corporation of the covenants, agreements and obligations of [Collins] pursuant to Article Fourteen;
> >
> > (c) to add to the covenants and agreements of [Collins] in this Indenture contained such further covenants and agreements thereafter to be observed, and . . . to surrender any right or power herein reserved to or conferred upon [Collins];
> >
> > (d) to cure any ambiguity or to correct or supplement any defective or inconsistent provision contained in this Indenture or in any supplemental indenture; and
> >
> > (e) to make such provisions with respect to matters or questions arising under this Indenture as may be necessary or desirable and not inconsistent with this Indenture; provided that such action shall not adversely affect the interests of the holders of any of the Debentures.
>
> The [Trust Company] is hereby authorized to join in the execution of any supplemental indenture authorized or permitted by the terms of this Indenture. . . .
>
> Any supplemental indenture authorized by the provisions of this Section 13.01 may be executed by [Collins] and the [Trust Company] without the consent of the holders of any of the Debentures at the time outstanding, notwithstanding any of the provisions of Section 13.02.

We begin by noting that the first clause of this section reinforces our conclusions in part II-D of this opinion, supra, that Section 4.11 of the Indenture is intended to "make provision with respect to the conversion rights of holders of the Debentures" in the event of merger. Section 4.11, it will be recalled, requires in part that the surviving company in a merger execute a supplemental indenture in which is detailed the precise nature of the post-merger conversion rights of the holders of the Debentures, as calculated by the formula set out in Section 4.11.

Broad and the defendants have argued vigorously the question whether the last phrase in clause (e) of Section 13.01 modifies the entire section, or only clause (e). We agree with the defendants that under the most logical reading of Section 13.01, the phrase "provided that such action shall not adversely affect the interests of the holders of any of the Debentures" logically modifies only clause (e).[20] Next, as we have noted before, Section 4.11 is the most specific recitation of the rights of the holders of the Debentures in the event of a merger; clause (a) of Section 13.01 ties in directly, and with equal specificity, to Section 4.11. Were there a conflict between those two provisions and the catch-all last phrase of clause (e) of Section 13.01, the former provisions would govern.

But more fundamentally, the execution of a supplemental indenture that complies with the directives of Section 4.11 does not "adversely affect the interest of the holders of any of the Debentures." The holders of Debentures have a legitimate interest only in those rights that are accorded them under the Indenture. Section 4.11 specifies what those rights are in the event of a merger; therefore, the execution of a supplemental indenture that complies with the requirements of Section 4.11 cannot be adverse to the legitimate interests of the holders of Debentures.

Broad also argues from the language of Section 13.02, despite the specific statement in Section 13.01 that a supplemental indenture required by Section 4.11 and clause (a) of Section 13.01 may be executed notwithstanding anything in Section 13.02. This statement in Section 13.01 should, and does, foreclose any arguments under Section 13.02.

But even under Section 13.02, which is described in the Indenture's table of contents as providing for the "[m]odification of Indenture with consent of holders of 66 2/3% in principal amount of Debentures," there is no help for Broad. Section 13.02 requires the permission of the holders of two-thirds of the Debentures before the issuer and the Trustee may execute a supplemental indenture that in any manner changes the rights and obligations of the parties to the Indenture or of the holders of the Debentures; certain types of alterations, including alterations of "the right to convert the [Debentures] into [Collins] Common Stock at the prices and upon the terms provided in this Indenture," are prohibited outright unless the Trustee and the issuer can obtain "the consent of the holder of each Debenture so affected." (Emphasis added.) Even were Section 13.02 applicable to those supplemental indentures that are required by Section 4.11 and clause (a) of Section 13.01, Section 13.02 would not prohibit that type of supplemental indenture, and neither would it require the consent of the holders of two-thirds or all of the Debentures: it is indisputable that one of the "terms provided in [the] Indenture" is Section 4.11 itself, and thus such a supplemental indenture does not alter the conversion rights of the holders of the Debentures. Rather, the supplemental indenture required

[20] [24] Clause (e) is as close to being an "openended" provision as anything in the Indenture; it would only make sense to limit the broad grant of the power to "make such provisions . . . as may be necessary or desirable" to those situations in which the interests of the holders of Debentures would not be adversely affected, lest the issuer's and Trustee's rights become so vague and unlimited as to render the entire contract unenforceable. The fact that this phrase is appended to the end of clause (e), rather than being set out after clauses (a) through (e) on a separate line beginning at the left margin, is also indicative of an intent that the phrase modify only clause (e). Further, elsewhere in the document, where the context clearly indicates that modifying phrases are intended to apply to several sequentially numbered clauses, those phrases are set out on separate line which begins at the left margin, or in introductory segments that precede all of the numbered clauses.

under Section 4.11 merely evidences that all the requisite formalities for the clarification and protection of those rights have been complied with — *i.e.*, that the formula set out in Section 4.11 has become applicable, and that the surviving company of the merger has formally accepted all the other obligations of, and been fully substituted for, the original issuer.

F. Our Conclusions With Respect to the Indenture

We conclude, after examining the entire Indenture in addition to those portions discussed specifically above, that the district court was correct in its conclusion that the Indenture is unambiguous. The intent of the parties is clearly evident from the four corners of the document. Section 4.11 fully and unambiguously sets out the conversion rights of the holders of the Debentures in the event of a merger in which Collins is not the surviving corporation: the holder of any outstanding Debenture is entitled to convert his Debenture into only that which he would have received had he converted it into Collins Common Stock immediately prior to the merger. On the facts of this case, that means a converting holder of a Debenture is entitled to receive $344.75 in cash for each $1000 in principal amount of the Debenture. Accord, *Brucker v. Thyssen-Bornemisza Europe N. V.*, 424 F. Supp. 679, 688-90 (S.D.N.Y. 1976) (construing virtually identical indenture provisions against similar claims in similar context, and finding no abridgement of the rights of the holders of debentures because "the debenture holders have never had an absolute right [under the indenture] to convert into [the issuer's] stock in a merger"), aff'd, mem. sub non. *Brucker v. Indian Head, Inc.*, 559 F.2d 1202 (2d Cir.), *cert. denied*, 434 U.S. 897, 98 S. Ct. 277, 54 L. Ed. 2d 183 (1977). *Cf. Broenen v. Beaunit Corp.*, 440 F.2d 1244, 1248-49 (7th Cir. 1970) (under New York law, provision virtually identical to Section 4.11 of the Indenture mandated that holders of convertible debentures receive conversion right into that which holders of common stock received in a three-cornered merger, which was common stock of surviving company's parent company); *Wood v. Coastal States Gas Corp.*, 401 A.2d 932, 939 (Del. 1979) (holder of convertible preferred stock after recapitalization is to receive "not what he would have received before recapitalization; that was the common stock. . . . Certainly [clause similar to Section 4.11 of the Indenture] is meaningless if the common share remains issuable after recapitalization" (emphasis in original)); *B.S.F. Corp. v. Philadelphia National Bank*, 204 A.2d 746, 750-51 (Del. 1964) (construing virtually identical provisions in the context of a sale of "substantially all" of the issuer's assets).

It is not the function of a court to rewrite a contract's terms in the process of "interpretation" to make them accord with the court's sense of equity. And yet, even were we inclined to do so, we are by no means certain that the outcome would be any different in this case.

Broad's persistent complaint has been that the Debentures' conversion feature was suddenly and arbitrarily liquidated, without permission or compensation. While the conversion feature has not technically been eliminated, since the holders of the Debentures retain the right to convert into $344.75 in cash for each $1000 principal amount of Debentures, it is true that the merger did eliminate the possibility that the holders of the Debentures would benefit as a result of the future profitability of the Collins business, just as the merger eliminated that possibility for the holders of Collins Common Stock. A purchaser of Debentures, however, takes the risks inherent in the equity feature of the security, risks that are shared with the holders of Collins Common Stock. One of those risks is that Collins might merge with another company — which is effectively the risk that any individual investor's assessment of the value of Collins Common Stock, based on Collins' prospects for the future, will be replaced by the collective judgment of the marketplace and the other investors in Collins who might vote in favor of the merger. This — like the risk that Collins' future operations might be lackluster, with the result that conversion might never be economically attractive — is simply a risk inherent in this type of investment.

The terms of the merger necessarily reflected the business prospects of Collins as of 1973. The fact that the initial high hopes that the holders of Debentures had for the equity securities of Collins — hopes that were identical to those of the equity shareholders — were defeated by the economic setbacks Collins suffered between 1967 and 1973 is not alleged in this lawsuit to be anyone's fault, least of all Rockwell's or the Trust Company's. When the market set the price of Collins Common Stock at less than $20, that price reflected the current aggregate judgment of the marketplace as to Collins' prospects for the future. The tendering shareholders, and those who gave up their shares in the merger, actually received a premium of roughly $5 per share over the market price — a bonus of some 25%. The post-merger conversion terms mandated by Section 4.11 accorded the holders of the Debentures the benefit of that premium. They were accorded, as a result of the equity feature of the Debentures, the same treatment that the holders of Collins Common Stock received, and they received value based, in part, on Collins' prospects for the future. Insofar as the debt feature of the Debentures is concerned, they benefited by the merger in that the Debentures are now backed by a financially more secure corporation.

Based upon our interpretation of the Indenture, and without hesitation given the nature of convertible debentures, we affirm the judgment of the district court with regard to Broad's breach of contract claims. We turn next to the other associated state-law claims that were within the pendent jurisdiction of the district court.

III. ASSOCIATED STATE-LAW CLAIMS

A. The Implied Covenant of Fair Dealing

As we understand New York law, every contract governed by the laws of that State necessarily contains an implied-by-law covenant to act fairly and in good faith in the course of performing the contract. The panel that first heard this case thought the Indenture to be ambiguous on the question of the conversion rights remaining with the holders of Debentures after a merger, and held that the evidence produced by Broad prior to the directed verdict raised a jury question as to whether Broad and the Trust Company had dealt fairly and in good faith with the holders of Debentures in the light of that ambiguity. 614 F.2d at 429-30. Having reached a different conclusion than the panel did on the ambiguity issue, we are compelled to a different result on the good faith and fair dealing issue as well.

We note first that this implied covenant of good faith and fair dealing cannot give the holders of Debentures any rights inconsistent with those explicitly set out in the Indenture. "[W]here the instrument contains an express covenant in regard to any subject, no covenants are to be implied with respect to the same subject *Burr v. Stenton*, 43 N.Y. 462, 464 (1871). "It is . . . well established in New York that, where the expressed intention of contracting parties is clear, a contrary intent will not be created by implication." *Neuman v. Pike*, 591 F.2d 191, 194 (2d Cir. 1979) (citing and applying New York law). The covenant is breached only when one party to a contract seeks to prevent its performance by, or to withhold its benefits from, the other. The mere exercise of one's contractual rights, without more, cannot constitute such a breach.

. . . .

B. The Breach of Fiduciary Duty Claims

In part IV-C-I of its opinion, 614 F.2d at 430-31, the panel held that Rockwell owed the holders of Debentures a fiduciary duty of good faith and fair dealing because it controlled both parties to the 1973 merger. But the panel also held that if, on remand, the jury were to find that Rockwell had fully complied with its obligations under the Indenture, its fiduciary obligations also would have been discharged as a matter of law.

We may assume, without deciding, that the panel was correct in its conclusion that Rockwell was charged with a fiduciary duty to the holders of Debentures. But since we have determined in part II of this opinion that Rockwell fully complied with its obligations under the Indenture, there is no need for a jury to hear this claim, even if the panel's analysis is correct: under that analysis, as applied in the light of our holding with respect to the Indenture, Rockwell can have no liability for breach of fiduciary duty. Accordingly, we affirm the judgment of the district court with respect to the breach of fiduciary duty claim against Rockwell.

In part IV-C-2 of its opinion, 614 F.2d at 431-32, the panel held that the Trust Indenture Act did not create any fiduciary obligations in addition to those imposed on the Trust Company under state law. For the reasons stated by the panel, we agree, and so hold. Accord, *Browning Debenture Holders' Committee v. DASA Corp.*, 560 F.2d 1078, 1083 (2d Cir. 1977) (finding such a claim frivolous). There remains the question of the Trust Company's liability for breach of fiduciary duty under applicable state law.

The panel relied on *Dabney v. Chase National Bank*, 196 F.2d 668 (2d Cir. 1952), and *United States Trust Co. v. First National City Bank*, 57 A.D.2d 285, 394 N.Y.S.2d 653 (1st Dept. 1977), *aff'd, mem.*, 45 N.Y.2d 869, 410 N.Y.S.2d 580, 382 N.E.2d 1355 (1978), for its conclusion that even in the absence of a default, an indenture trustee is cloaked under New York law with a fiduciary duty to the holders of debentures that may extend beyond its strict obligations under the indenture. Both *Dabney* and *City Bank* involved conflicts of interest in which the trustee put itself in a position of advantage over the beneficiaries of the trust. Arguably, the Trust Company faced a similar conflict of interest in the case at bar when Rockwell threatened to bring a lawsuit, to withdraw other business it had with the Trust Company, and to force the Trust Company's resignation as Trustee if it refused to execute the supplemental indenture necessary for the merger.

Be that as it may, however, there is no actionable wrong in this case. We assume, without deciding, that the panel was correct in concluding that under New York law, the Trust Company's obligations "exceeded the narrow definitions of its duties in the indenture and encompassed fiduciary duties as well." 614 F.2d at 432. And had we agreed with the panel that the Indenture was ambiguous, there would be a real question whether the holders of Debentures had received in the supplemental indenture all that was contractually due them under the Indenture. Were that question answered in the negative, there would have been the further question whether the Trust Company had adequately discharged its duties to the holders of Debentures with the "absolute singleness of purpose" required by New York law. *Dabney*, 196 F.2d at 671. The evidence in the record regarding the advice given the Trust Company by its counsel prior to the execution of the supplemental indenture undoubtedly would have been relevant to the Trust Company's defensive claim that it had acted in good faith and on advice of counsel.

But the question of whether the holders of Debentures received in the supplemental indenture all that was contractually due to them is conclusively answered by our holding in part II of this opinion, supra. Regardless of the Trust Company's motives, or its prior opinion as to the meaning of the Indenture, there is no question but that the Trust Company's ultimate execution — executing the supplemental indenture — fully protected what we have determined to be the legitimate rights of the holders of Debentures under the Indenture. Broad has cited no New York authority for the proposition that an indenture trustee has a duty, fiduciary or otherwise, to seek for the holders of debentures any benefits that are greater than those contractually due them; indeed, there is support in the New York cases for the opposite conclusion. *See Hazzard v. Chase National Bank*, 159 Misc. 57, 287 N.Y.S. 541 (Sup. Ct. 1936), *aff'd, mem.*, 257 A.D. 950, 14 N.Y.S.2d 147 (1st Dept. 1939), *aff'd, mem.*, 282 N.Y. 652, 26 N.E.2d 801, *cert. denied*, 311 U.S. 708, 61 S. Ct. 319, 85 L. Ed. 460 (1940). We hold that the Trust Company had no duty, as a matter of law, to do anything other than that which it in fact did. Thus, there is no question for a jury as to whether there has been a breach of fiduciary duty. Accordingly, we affirm the judgment of the district court with respect to both the state and federal breach of fiduciary duty claims against the Trust Company.[21]

IV. THE FEDERAL SECURITIES CLAIMS

We reach at last Broad's federal securities claims, which provided the jurisdictional predicate for the pendent state-law claims we have heretofore discussed. Broad alleges two separate claims under section 10(b) of the Securities Exchange Act of 1934, 15 U.S.C. § 78j(b) (1976), and Rule 10b-5 promulgated thereunder, 17 C.F.R. § 240.10b-5 (1980). We deal with those claims in turn, and though we reach

---

[21] [27] Given our holdings on the liability issues under each of Broad's state-law claims, we find it unnecessary to reach the district court's alternate ground for the directed verdict — *i.e.*, that no damages had been sustained as a matter of state law. We also find it unnecessary to reach Rockwell's argument that the panel erred in holding that the filing of a class action by Broad was adequate notice of default under the terms of the Indenture, 614 F.2d at 433.

the same ultimate conclusion as did the district court and the panel, we emphasize that we do so on far narrower grounds. We make no new law under Rule 10b-5 today, but merely apply well-settled principles to the facts of this case.

A. The Failure to Disclose the Post-Merger Conversion Terms Set Out in the Indenture

In his first federal claim, Broad essentially alleges that at the time the Debentures were issued in 1967, and thereafter up until the time of the merger in the fall of 1973, the defendants omitted to disclose a material fact with regard to the contractual terms under which the Debentures operated — specifically, that under the terms of the Indenture, the right to convert into Collins Common Stock could, in the event of a merger, be replaced with the right to convert into only that which the holders of Collins Common Stock received in the merger. Broad argues that this constituted a knowing, intentional, and reckless failure to disclose a material fact. The language of Section 4.11, of course, was available to anyone who cared to look at the Indenture, so Broad's claim can only be that the defendants should have made specific reference in the prospectus and other materials to that provision of the Indenture. His claim can alternately be read as a misrepresentation claim — *i.e.*, that various statements on the face of the Debentures, in the press releases and advertisements, and in the prospectus (all to the effect that the Debentures were convertible into Collins Common Stock at any time up until 1987) were misleading.

It is a familiar proposition since the Supreme Court's decision in *Ernst & Ernst v. Hochfelder*, 425 U.S. 185, 96 S. Ct. 1375, 47 L. Ed. 2d 668 (1976), that as part of his case a plaintiff must allege and prove that the defendants acted with "scienter" — "a mental state embracing an intent to deceive, manipulate, or defraud." *Id.* at 193-94 n.12, 96 S. Ct. at 1381 n.12. The holding of that case was that mere negligence is insufficient to support liability in a private suit for damages under Rule 10b-5. The Court specifically left open, however, the question of whether recklessness could satisfy the scienter requirement. *Id. See also Aaron v. SEC*, 446 U.S. 680, 686 n.5, 100 S. Ct. 1945, 1950 n.5, 64 L. Ed. 2d 611(1980) (adopting definition of scienter as "a mental state embracing intent to deceive, manipulate, defraud" in the context of SEC enforcement proceedings, but leaving open the question of whether scienter may also include reckless behavior).

. . . .

The panel opinion in this case agreed with our sister circuits that recklessness, properly defined and adequately distinguished from mere negligence, could satisfy the scienter requirement. The panel adopted the definition of recklessness that was articulated by the Seventh Circuit in *Sundstrand* and *Sanders*. 614 F.2d at 43940. During the period that this case was pending before the en banc court, several other panels also addressed the topic in varying degrees. In particular, while noting that the en banc court had not yet spoken on this question, a panel of this court explicitly held in *G. A. Thompson & Co. v. Partridge*, 636 F.2d 945, 961-62 & nn. 32-34 (5th Cir. 1981), that "severe recklessness" was sufficient to satisfy the scienter requirement. Accordingly, we hold that in the context of a private action for money damages brought under section 10(b) and Rule 10b-5, the requirement that the plaintiff prove scienter — i.e., a mental state embracing intent to deceive, manipulate, or defraud

— is satisfied by proof that the defendants acted with severe recklessness. Severe recklessness is limited to those highly unreasonable omissions or misrepresentations that involve not merely simple or even inexcusable negligence, but an extreme departure from the standards of ordinary care, and that present a danger of misleading buyers or sellers which is either known to the defendant or is so obvious that the defendant must have been aware of it.

Applying this standard to the case at bar, we note that there is precious little testimony in the record concerning the events at the time the Debentures were issued. The creators of and original parties to the Indenture were Collins on the one hand, and a team of underwriters on the other. The underwriters were managed by Kidder, Peabody & Co. Incorporated and White, Weld & Co. Both sides were represented by counsel: Collins by Lynch, Dallas, Smith & Harman of Cedar Rapids, Iowa, and the underwriters by Sullivan & Cromwell of New York. C. J. Lynch of the Lynch, Dallas firm testified by deposition that the basic form of the Indenture was lifted from indentures that Collins and these underwriters had used in prior convertible debenture offerings by Collins; those indentures from the prior offerings had been drafted in the first instance by Kidder, Peabody's counsel, Sullivan & Cromwell.

The Indenture that emerged for the 1967 offering was only partially the result of actual negotiation between the parties. In the normal course of events, the issuer and the lead underwriter actively negotiate the business portions of an indenture, which deal with such provisions as the aggregate principal amount of the debentures, their maturity date, the interest rate they bear, the subordination of the debt they represent to any senior indebtedness, the rate at which they may be converted into common stock, the redemption prices and dates, and so forth. The remainder of the indenture is invariably made up of boilerplate provisions that typically are not discussed at all by either the representatives of the issuer or those of the lead underwriter; indeed, most of those provisions are not even discussed by counsel for the respective parties, and many of them are required by federal law to be inserted into the indenture verbatim. Mr. Lynch's testimony in this case indicates that the drafting of the Indenture for the 1967 Collins Debenture issue was absolutely typical of industry practice: the boilerplate provisions, including those upon which this lawsuit turns, were never specifically discussed.

Such testimony as there is indicates that no party specifically considered at that time the possibility that Section 4.11 of the Indenture would be called into play at some future date, although Mr. Lynch testified that he had at some point "reviewed" the language of that section on Collins' behalf and found it satisfactory. There is no indication in the record that anyone acting for either Collins or the underwriters considered the inclusion in the prospectus and other sales materials of a detailed description of the operation of Section 4.11. Indeed, the testimony in the record overwhelmingly indicates that the parties thought themselves to be under no legal duty to disclose in detailed fashion in the prospectus and other sales materials any of the Indenture's provisions for more remote future contingencies. Neither is there evidence to raise a jury question on whether the defendants engaged in a continuing course of conduct to deceive subsequent purchasers after the Debentures were issued. Counsel for Broad even conceded, in arguing against the defendants' motions for a directed verdict in the trial court, that there was insufficient evidence to raise a jury question of scienter on this count.

Given all of this, we conclude that Broad's evidence on this count could support no more than a finding of simple negligence by the defendants in failing to disclose the workings of Section 4.11 in the prospectus and other sales materials. Accordingly, we affirm the judgment of the district court with regard to this claim under Rule 10b-5.

B. The Scheme to Deprive the Holders of Debentures of Their Right to Convert into Common Stock

In his second claim under Rule 10b-5, Broad alleges that the defendants collectively schemed to defraud the holders of Debentures of their right to convert the Debentures into common stock, substituting therefor a right to convert into cash. The panel opinion affirmed the district court's directed verdict on this claim on the ground that there had been no purchase or sale of the Debentures at the time of the merger because the supplemental indenture did not so substantially change the underlying security as to fall within the forced or constructive sale doctrine. 614 F.2d at 435-39.

We agree that the directed verdict on this count was proper as a matter of law, but we base our decision on a different ground. We have concluded in part II of this opinion, supra, that as a matter of law, the holders of Debentures received in the supplemental indenture all to which they were contractually entitled under the Indenture. There is no doubt but that there was concerted, intentional conduct by the defendants to bring about that result. But as a matter of law, there was no violation of section 10(b) or Rule 10b-5 because there was no fraud. "Section 10(b) is aptly described as a catch-all provision, but what it catches must be fraud." *Chiarella v. United States*, 445 U.S. 222, 23435, 100 S. Ct. 1108, 1118, 63 L. Ed. 2d 348 (1980) (criminal prosecution under section 10(b) and Rule 10b-5). It is elementary that section 10(b) and Rule 10b-5 reach only conduct involving manipulation or deception. The defendants' conduct involved neither; they merely carried out their contractual obligations. As a conceptual matter, they could not have fraudulently schemed to deprive the holders of Debentures of a right that those holders did not in fact have. Accordingly, we affirm the judgment of the district court with regard to this claim under Rule 10b-5.

V. CONCLUSION

The district court correctly interpreted the Indenture to provide unambiguously that upon a merger between Collins and another corporation in which Collins was not the surviving company, the sole conversion right of the holders of Debentures was to convert into the kind and amount of property (be it stock, other securities, cash, or other property) that would have been received by a holder of Debentures had he exercised his conversion right immediately prior to the merger. Because there was no question but that the defendants have properly recognized this right, the district court correctly directed a verdict for the defendants on the state-law breach of contract, breach of implied covenant of fair dealing, and breach of fiduciary duty claims. The district court also properly directed a verdict on the first federal securities claim — that the defendants omitted to disclose the workings of Section 4.11 at the time the Debentures were marketed — because Broad's evidence failed to raise a jury question on scienter. Finally, the court properly directed a verdict on the second federal securities claim — that the defendants had schemed to defraud the holders of Debentures of their right to convert into common stock — because as a matter of law, given the correct interpretation of the Indenture, there was no fraudulent conduct and hence no violation of section 10(b) and Rule 10b-5. Accordingly, the judgment of the district court is Affirmed.

NOTES

(1) The *Broad* three-judge panel took a different view of the interplay between Section 4.11 and Article 13 of the Collins Indenture than that of the en banc panel:

> We do not think that on its face the Collins debenture agreement speaks with the requisite clarity to the issue before us. To be sure, § 4.11 does deal in the most detail with the conversion rights in the event of a merger, but § 4.11 does not specify a limitation on the reach of the provisions of Article Thirteen, which protects the debenture holders against any supplemental indenture which would adversely affect the interests of the debenture holders.

614 F.2d at 428.

(2) Section 913 of the New York Business Corporation Law (reproduced in Chapter 1, § 1.07), provides for an acquisition technique known as a mandatory share exchange, which produces the same result as a reverse triangular merger without the necessity of merging a subsidiary of the acquirer into the target corporation. Because few, if any, anti-dilution clauses refer to a mandatory share exchange, there is the possibility that under the *Parkinson* rule conversion rights might be lost in such a transaction. For this reason, Section 913(i)(2) provides: "With respect to convertible securities and other securities evidencing a right to acquire shares of a subject corporation, a binding share exchange pursuant to this section shall have the same effect on the rights of the holders of such securities as a merger of the subject corporation."

(3) The acquisition transaction that forms the setting for the issues presented and decided in *Broad* involves a classic multi-step "going private" transaction of the type considered in Chapter 7, *infra*, which deals with the rights of the holders of *target company* securities in mergers and acquisitions.

As in the case with regard to the rights of preferred stockholders generally, questions pertaining to the meaning and effect of anti-dilution clauses are determined by application of principles of contract construction. As the following cases demonstrate, the rights of the parties turn on the meaning the court ascribes to such phrases as "reorganization" and "recapitalization."

STEPHENSON v. PLASTICS CORP. OF AM.

Minnesota Supreme Court
150 N.W.2d 668 (1967)

SHERAN, JUSTICE

Appeal from a district court judgment.

Action was instituted by plaintiffs against defendants on the theory that defendant Plastics Corporation of America, Inc., (hereafter called Plastics) breached contract obligations springing from stock purchase warrants issued by it, and that defendant United Fabricators and Electronics, Inc. (hereafter called United) participated in the resulting wrong to the plaintiffs by conduct constituting willful and malicious inference with the contract relationship. Defendant Plastics denied the claimed breach of contract and cross-claimed for indemnity as against United in the event plaintiffs should prevail. United denied the alleged breach of contract and the asserted unlawful interference. Each defendant moved for judgment on the pleadings. United's motion was granted; Plastics' was denied.

In deciding whether the order of the trial judge in United's favor can be sustained, we are limited to the facts asserted in the pleadings interpreted in the light most favorable to the plaintiffs.

THE WARRANTS

The stock subscription warrants are dated December 16, 1960. It will be helpful, at the outset, to place their provisions in these compartments:

(A) The principal object of the agreements.

(B) Corporate changes conceived as affecting the principal object of the agreements.

(C) Mechaninisms provided for preserving the principal object of the agreements in the event of such changes.

(D) Provisions for notice of such corporate changes.

A. PRINCIPAL OBJECT

The principal object to the agreements was to afford the holders or their assigns (such as these plaintiffs) the option for a period of 5 years to obtain 30,000 shares of the "capital" stock of the company at the price of $1 per share. It is specifically provided that the warrants were not to entitle the holders to any voting rights or other rights as a stockholder of the company.

B. ANTICIPATED CORPORATE CHANGES

In an apparent effort to prevent a defeat of the basic purpose of the warrants by a change in corporate circumstances, 12 different possible situations are anticipated in paragraph 3 of the agreements:

(1) A distribution upon capital stock payable in capital stock, *i.e.*, a "stock dividend."[22]

(2) A division ("split") of the outstanding capital stock.

(3) A combining ("reverse split") of outstanding capital stock.

(4) A cash dividend upon stock not payable from net earnings or earned surplus.[23]

(5) Such a dividend upon stock but not payable in cash.

(6) A capital "reorganization."[24]

(7) A reclassification of stock.

(8) A consolidation with another corporation.

(9) A merger with another corporation.

---

[22] [2] 3(a). "In case the company shall declare any dividend or other distribution upon its outstanding capital stock payable in capital stock or shall subdivide its outstanding shares of capital stock into a greater number of shares, then the number of shares of capital stock which may thereafter be purchased upon the exercise of the rights represented hereby shall be increased in proportion to the increase through such dividend or subdivision and the purchase price per share shall be decreased in such proportion. In case the Company shall at any time combine the outstanding shares of its capital stock into a smaller number of shares, the number of shares of capital stock which may thereafter be purchased upon the exercise of the rights represented hereby shall be decreased in proportion to the decrease through such combination and the purchase price per share shall be increased in such proportion."

[23] [3] 3(b). "In case the Company shall declare a dividend upon the capital stock payable otherwise than out of earnings or surplus (other than paid-in surplus) or otherwise than in capital stock, the purchase price per share in effect immediately prior to the declaration of such dividend shall be reduced by an amount equal, in the case of a dividend in cash, to the amount thereof, payable per share of the capital stock or, in the case of any other dividend, to the fair value thereof per share of the capital stock as determined by the Board of Directors of the Company. For the purposes of the foregoing a dividend other than in cash shall be considered payable out of earnings or surplus (other than paid-in surplus) only to the extent that such earnings or surplus are charged an amount equal to the fair value of such dividend as determined by the Board of Directors of the Company. Such reductions shall take effect as of the date on which a record is taken for the purpose of such dividend, or, if a record is not taken, the date as of which the holders of capital stock of record entitled to such dividend are to be determined."

[24] [4] 3(c). "If any capital reorganization or reclassification of the capital stock of the Company, or consolidation or merger of the Company with another corporation, or the sale of all or substantially all of its assets to another corporation shall be effected, then, as a condition of such reorganization, reclassification, consolidation, merger or sale, lawful and adequate provision shall be made whereby the holder hereof shall thereafter have the right to purchase and receive upon the basis and *upon the terms and conditions specified in this Warrant* and in lieu of the shares of the capital stock of the Company immediately theretofore purchasable and receivable upon the exercise of the rights represented hereby, such shares of stock, securities or assets as may be issued or payable with respect to or in exchange for a number of outstanding shares of such capital stock equal to the number of shares of such capital stock immediately theretofore purchasable and receivable upon the exercise of the rights represented hereby had such reorganization, reclassification, consolidation, merger or sale not taken place, and in any such case appropriate provision shall be made with respect to the rights and interests of the holder of this Warrant to the end that the provisions hereof (including without limitation provisions for adjustment of the purchase price per share and of the number of shares purchasable upon the exercise of this Warrant) shall thereafter be applicable, as nearly as may be in relation to any shares of stock, securities or assets thereafter deliverable upon the exercise hereof." (Italics supplied.)

(10) *The sale of all or substantially all of the assets of the corporation to another corporation.*

(11) An offer to holders of capital stock for pro rata subscription for additional shares of stock or any other rights.[25]

(12) A voluntary or involuntary dissolution.

C. CONTEMPLATED ADJUSTMENT

In the event of the occurrence of situations 1 to 3 (stock dividends; splits; reverse splits) the warrants provide for adjustment by decrease or increase in the number of shares purchasable and the price per share to be paid.[26]

In situations 4 and 5 (depleting dividend) the adjustment is to be accomplished by reducing the purchase price per share (*i.e.*, $1 per share) by (a) the amount of the dividend, if paid in cash, and (b) the fair value of distributed assets other than cash.[27]

In situations 6 to 10 (reorganization; stock reclassification; consolidation; merger; sale of all or substantially all assets) it is required by paragraph 3(c) of the agreement that "appropriate provision" be made for the protection of the rights and interests of the warrant holders.[28]

Paragraph 3(c) Which deals with situations 6 to 10 concludes with this sentence:

> . . . Any such shares of stock, securities or assets which the holder hereof may be entitled to purchase pursuant to this paragraph (c) shall be included within the term "capital stock" as used herein.

This sentence becomes significant when considered in conjunction with paragraph 2 of the agreements which concludes with this sentence:

> . . . The Company further covenants and agrees that *during the period within which the rights represented by this Warrant may be exercised*, the Company will at all times have authorized, and reserved, a sufficient number of shares of capital stock to provide for the exercise of the rights represented by this Warrant . . . [Italics supplied.]

We interpret these provisions, considered together, to impose on Plastics an obligation to have reserved a sufficient number of shares of United stock to provide for the exercise of the rights represented by the warrants if the arrangement planned and executed by the seven directors of the two corporations, described hereinafter, amounted to a *reorganization*; stock reclassification; consolidation; merger; or *a sale of all as substantially all of Plastics' assets to United.*

Paragraph 3(c) provided with respect to situations 8 to 10 (consolidation; merger; sale of all or substantially all of assets) that the successor corporation should be

---

[25] [5] Reference to situations 11 and 12 is to be found in the notice provision set out in footnote 11.

[26] [6] *See* footnote 2, *supra.*

[27] [7] *See* footnote 3, *supra.*

[28] [8] *See* footnote 4, *supra.*

required to assume "the obligation to deliver to such [warrant] holder such shares of stock, securities or assets as, in accordance with the foregoing provisions, such holder may be entitled to purchase."[29]

D. NOTICE PROVISIONS

In situations 1 to 3 (stock dividends; splits; reverse splits) set out above, the company obligates itself to give notice to the warrant holder stating "the purchase price per share resulting from such adjustment and the increase or decrease, if any, in the number of shares purchasable at such price upon the exercise of this Warrant."[30]

In situations 1 (stock dividend) and 4 to 12 (dividends; reorganization, reclassification; consolidation; merger; sale of all or substantially all of assets; subscription offer; dissolution) a 20-day notice to the warrant holder is required by paragraph 3(e) which notice in situations 4 and 5 (dividends), 11 (subscription offer), and 12 (dissolution) at least, must specify "the date on which the holders of capital stock shall be entitled thereto," and in situations 6 (reorganization), 7 (reclassification), 8 (consolidation), 9 (merger), 10 (sale) and 12 (dissolution) must specify "the date on which the holders of capital stock shall be entitled to exchange their capital stock for securities or other property."[31]

---

[29] [9] 3(c). ". . . The Company shall not effect any such consolidation, merger or sale, unless prior to or simultaneously with the consummation thereof the successor corporation (if other than the Company) resulting from such consolidation or merger or the corporation purchasing such assets shall assume by writing instrument executed and mailed or delivered to the holder hereof at the last address of such holder appearing on the books of the Company, the obligation to deliver to such holder such shares of stock, securities or assets as, in accordance with the foregoing provisions, such holder may be entitled to purchase."

[30] [10] 3(d) "Upon any adjustment of the number of shares of capital stock which may be purchased upon the exercise of the rights represented hereby and/or of the purchase price per share, then and in each such case the Company shall give written notice thereof, by first class mail, postage prepaid, addressed to the holder of this Warrant at the address of such holder as shown on the books of the Company, which notice shall state the purchase price per share resulting from such adjustment and the increase or decrease, if any, in the number of shares purchasable at such price upon the exercise of this Warrant, setting forth in reasonable detail the method of calculation and the facts upon which such calculation is based."

[31] [11] "In case at any time:

(1) the Company shall pay any dividend payable in stock upon its capital stock or make any distribution (other than regular cash dividends paid at an established annual rate) to the holders of its capital stock;

(2) the Company shall offer for subscription pro rata to the holders of its capital stock any additional shares of stock of any class or other rights;

(3) there shall be any capital reorganization, or reclassification of the capital stock of the Company, or consolidation or merger of the Company with, or sale of all or substantially all of its assets to, another corporation; or

(4) there shall be a voluntary or involuntary dissolution, liquidation or winding up of the Company; then, in any one or more of such cases, the Company shall give to the holder of this Warrant (aa) at least twenty days' prior written notice of the date on which the books of the Company shall close or a record shall be taken for such dividend, distribution of subscription rights or for determining rights to vote in respect of any such reorganization, reclassification, consolidation, merger, sale, dissolution, liquidation or winding up, and (bb) in the case of any such reorganization, reclassification, consolidation, merger, sale, dissolution, liquidation or

THE CORPORATE CHANGE

In the latter part of 1964 and at a time when the warrants analyzed above were outstanding, Plastics was controlled and governed by a board of seven directors who agreed among themselves:

(1) A part of the assets of Plastics then devoted to the production of thermoplastic products by one of the divisions of Plastics should be transferred to a newly created corporation; the newly created corporation should, in exchange, transfer *all* of its stock to Plastics. (The new corporation, United Fabricators and Electronics, Inc., which we refer to as "United," was incorporated March 11, 1965.)

(2) *All* of the stock of the newly created corporation to be transferred to Plastics should be distributed to Plastics shareholders of record on February 22, 1965, and warrant holders exercising their stock options by March 16, 1965. (This agreement to distribute all of the stock of the newly created corporation to Plastics shareholders of necessity made it impossible for Plastics to reserve a sufficient number of shares of United's stock to provide for the exercise of an option with respect to such stock after March 16, 1965, but before expiration of the 5-year option period.)

(3) Three of the seven directors then in control of Plastics should resign and become the directors of United. The four remaining should continue in control of Plastics.

(4) The United stock to be acquired by the four directors of Plastics as a result of the distribution contemplated by step (2) above should be exchanged for the Plastics stock held by the three departing directors so that the one group would be in control of United and the other in control of Plastics when the transaction was completed.

Agreements were made intending to bind the seven directors and the corporations (Plastics and United) to this plan, and these agreements have been fully executed.

On February 24, 1965, Plastics gave notice to holders of stock purchase warrants, including plaintiffs, reading as follows:

> You are hereby notified that the Directors of Plastics Corporation of America, Inc. have authorized a distribution on March 31, 1965 to the common shareholders of said corporation of one (1) share of United Fabricators & Electronics, Inc. for each two (2) shares of Plastics Corporation of America, Inc. held of record on February 22, 1965.

---

winding up, at least twenty days' prior written notice of the date when the same shall take place. Such notice in accordance with the foregoing clause (aa) shall also specify, in the case of any such dividend, distribution or subscription rights, the date on which the holders of capital stock shall be entitled thereto, and such notice in accordance with the foregoing clause (bb) shall also specify the date on which the holders of capital stock shall be entitled to exchange their capital stock for securities or other property deliverable upon such reorganization, reclassification, consolidation, merger, sale, dissolution, liquidation or winding up, as the case may be. Each such written notice shall be given by first class mail, postage prepaid, addressed to the holder of this Warrant at the address of such holder as shown on the books of the Company.

> Inasmuch as the holders of Stock Purchase Warrants of Plastics Corporation of America, Inc. are entitled to twenty days' notice of such distribution, the Directors have established March 16, 1965 as the record date for such distribution for the holders of Stock Purchase Warrants who shall hereafter become a shareholder by reason of the exercise of such Warrants.

Plaintiffs did not undertake to exercise their option to purchase Plastics stock until December 1965. We assume for present purposes (but do not decide) that they made an effective exercise of the option embodied in the warrants before the expiration of the 5-year period specified in it.

The theory of plaintiffs' pleading is that they are entitled upon exercise of their option before the expiration of the 5-year period to have the shares of Plastics stock specified in the warrants and in addition that number of the shares of United stock which would have been distributed to plaintiffs had they been stockholders when the distribution of United stock was in fact made; and that if specific performance is impossible, damages should be awarded.

1. In our opinion, the order of the trial court granting judgment for United against plaintiffs on the pleadings can be sustained if, but only if, any one of these legal conclusions follow from the facts summarized:

> (a) The warrants created no right in plaintiffs to share in the distribution of United stock in any event.
>
> (b) Any right to share in the distribution of United stock was extinguished by plaintiffs' failure to exercise their option within the time specified by the notice.
>
> (c) The right of plaintiffs to share in the distribution of United stock springs from the contracts between plaintiffs and Plastics; and United did nothing to interfere with or obstruct the performance of these contracts.

2a. If the distribution of United stock was a dividend not charged to net earnings or earned surplus, plaintiffs would have no right as against United because in such event, by the terms of the warrants, plaintiffs' position was to be protected by reducing the purchase price per share of Plastics stock by the fair value of the United stock determined as of the date of distribution. In our opinion, it cannot be held on the present record that the parties to the warrants included a transaction of this kind to be treated as a dividend.

Minn. St. 302.22, subd. 2, provides:

A corporation may declare dividends in cash or property only as follows:

(1) Out of earned surplus;

(2) Out of paid-in surplus . . .

(3) Out of its net earnings for its current or for the preceding fiscal year . . .

There is a difference between the transactions involved in the present case and a "dividend" in the usual sense of that word. In *Hoberg v. John Hoberg Co.*, 170 Wis. 50, 173 N.W. 639, 173 N.W. 952, it was held that a corporation's pro rata distribution to its stockholders of recently acquired stock of another corporation was not a dividend, emphasizing that no attempt was made to meet a dividend obligation by the transfer. *See* 13 Words and Phrases, pp. 94, 104. In determining whether a transaction constitutes a "dividend," consideration must be given to the context in which the term "dividend" is used; the consequences that turn upon the answer to the question; and the facts of the particular case. *See* 13 Words and Phrases, p. 94. We believe that it would be premature to rule as a matter of law upon the limited record now before us that the present transaction was intended to be a "dividend" within the meaning of the warrants.

Ordinarily the object of a dividend is to enable the shareholders to enjoy the fruits of a corporate operation. It is at least inferable that the purpose of the distribution of United's stock to Plastics shareholders was intended primarily (a) to enable the directors who remained with Plastics to acquire the stock of that corporation distributed to the three directors who were taking over the management of United and (b) to give the three departing directors control of the newly created corporation through exchange of their Plastics stock for the distributed shares of United coming into the hands of the four Plastics directors who remained. In fact it is reasonable to infer that this exchange of United's stock for Plastics after the distribution was an essential part of the agreement between the seven directors and that but for this understanding the "spin-off" would never have taken place. So considered, we cannot say that the warrants declare clearly and unambiguously that a transaction of this character was intended to be treated as a "dividend" within the meaning of the language of the warrants.

We do not disagree with United's contention that a "spin-off" can involve or be executed by a means of a dividend of a new company's stock to the old company's shareholders. We hold only that the question cannot be resolved in the present situation without the aid of extrinsic evidence.

2b. If the transaction does not represent a "dividend" within the meaning of the warrants, then what was it? Plaintiffs contend that it was a capital reorganization (situation 6 above) or a sale of all or substantially all of the assets of the corporation to another corporation (situation 10 above). If so (unless the notice set out above served to accelerate the time within which plaintiffs' opinion was exercisable with respect to the distribution), the corporation was obligated by the terms of the warrants to reserve a sufficient number of shares of United stock to permit the exercise of the right of the warrant holders to acquire it for the full 5-year term of the warrants. This is so because paragraph 3(c) of the agreement provides that, in the event of any capital reorganization or the sale of all or substantially all of the corporate assets to another corporation, "lawful and adequate provision shall be made whereby the holder hereof shall thereafter have the right to purchase and receive . . . such shares of stock, securities or assets as may be issued or payable with respect to or in exchange for a number of outstanding shares of such capital stock equal to the number of shares of such capital stock immediately theretofore purchasable and receivable upon the exercise of the rights represented hereby had such reorganization, . . . or sale not taken place." The obligation to hold the required number of shares of United in reserve follows from the concluding sentence of paragraph 3(c)[32] requiring that any such shares of stock or assets be included within the term "capital stock" as used in the warrants.

2c. Although not free from ambiguity, we believe it would be possible for the plaintiffs to establish that the transaction here involved was a "capital reorganization" within the meaning of the warrants. The net result was that each Plastics shareholder held an interest represented by stock in exactly the same assets after the transaction as before. Before the transaction this interest was represented by stock in one corporation only; after the transaction the interest was represented by stock held in two corporations. All that was changed was the "organization."

The pertinent Federal and Minnesota income tax provisions declare transactions of this kind to be "reorganizations."[33]

United cites Minn. St. 301.55, dealing with compromise arrangements and reorganizations of corporations in proceedings for dissolution, for the proposition that the Minnesota Business Corporation Law views a reorganization in the common business sense that at no time two or more going business corporations will be in existence. Even if § 301.55 were to state that the "reorganization" for the purposes of said statute involved the going out of existence of one corporation and the coming into existence of another,[34]

United points out that the warrant contracts provide that upon reorganization a warrant holder is entitled to receive "*in lieu* of the shares of the capital stock of the Company immediately theretofore purchasable and receivable" certain stock or other assets of the transferee corporation. (Italics supplied.) It asserts that this shows that the parties to the warrant contracts contemplated that upon the

---

[32] [12] The sentence, to which reference has been made, reads: "Any such shares of stock, securities or assets which the holder hereof may be entitled to purchase pursuant to this paragraph (c) shall be included within the term 'capital stock' as used herein."

[33] [13] Section 308(a) of the 1954 Internal Revenue Code, 68A Stat. 120, 26 U.S.C.A. § 368(a), provides in part:

(a) REORGANIZATION. —

(1) IN GENERAL. — For purposes of parts I and II and this part, the term "reorganization" means —

. . . .

(D) a transfer by a corporation of *all or a part* of its assets to another corporation if immediately after the transfer the transferor, or one or more of its shareholders (including persons who were shareholders immediately before the transfer), or any combination thereof, is in control of the corporation to which the assets are transferred; but only if, in pursuance of the plan, stock or securities of the corporation to which the assets are transferred are distributed in a transaction which qualifies under section 354, 355, or 356.

Section 355 covers, inter alia, a corporation's distributions to its shareholders of stock of a corporation which it controlled immediately before the distribution.

Minn. St. 290.136, subd. 9(a) (1) (D), is identical to the Federal provision.

United asserts that the present transaction was taxed as an ordinary dividend rather than as a reorganization, but this fact does not establish that it was a dividend as the term is used in the warrant.

[34] [14] The term is sometimes used in this sense. Sec. 15 Fletcher, Cyc. of Corporations (1961 Rev. ed.) § 7205; 30A Words and Phrases, p. 712. which it does not, still this would not necessarily delineate the outer boundaries of the meanings of the term in question.

reorganization a new corporation would take over and completely supersede the old one.

However, this provision does not compel the interpretation defendant would give it. It may simply mean that the warrant holder is entitled to a certain amount of stock of the old corporation, and in addition thereto (and in lieu merely of *more* stock of the old corporation), a certain amount of stock of the new corporation. Especially is this interpretation justifiable in light of the fact that the words in question also control where there has been a sale of "all or substantially all" of Plastics' assets. In the event of a sale of only substantially all of Plastics' assets, the agreement probably contemplates the warrant holding receiving both Plastics stock and stock of the vendee.

Defendant points out that the stock warrants' reference to Plastics' duty to require the "successor corporation" to assume the duty to honor the stock warrants covers *only* situations of consolidation, merger, or sale of all or substantially all of Plastics' assets and urges that this must mean that "capital reorganization" comprehends only situations involving a structural change *within* Plastics. But a change in Plastics' structure resulting in the birth of a new corporation is not necessarily excluded from the term "capital reorganization" by this language. The same may be said of the fact that the warrants referred to the giving of 20-day notice of the date that the books would close and a record would be taken "for determining rights to vote in respect of any such reorganization." Defendant insists this means that only "reorganizations" upon which shareholders vote in accordance with § 301.55 are included. Again, the argument is persuasive, but not so clear that plaintiffs should not be allowed to present evidence on the matter.

2d. In the alternative, plaintiffs urge that the evidence may establish that the transaction was a sale of "all or substantially all" of Plastics' assets. The complaint does not allege any particular proportion of Plastics' assets as having been transferred, merely stating that "the assets of its United Fabricators and Electronics Division, and certain other assets" were transferred.[35] Thus, at this stage of the proceedings, no proper evidence has been adduced on such matters as the proportion of Plastics' assets which were transferred; the nature of those assets (as compared to that of the assets retained); the relationship of the assets transferred and of those retained in Plastics' past and present objects and purposes; or the degree to which the transfer was unusual and out of the ordinary course of Plastics' business.

THE NOTICE

3. We cannot say as a matter of law that plaintiffs' right to share in the distribution of United stock was extinguished by plaintiffs' failure to exercise their option within the time specified in the notice of February 24, 1965, there being no

[35] [15] Defendant asserts that the claim that transfer was of substantially all of Plastics' assets "is clearly refuted by facts contained in the pleadings which make it clear that the spin-off involved something less than one-half of PCA's net worth," citing a portion of the complaint and certain documents made part of Plastics' pleadings. Plastics' pleadings are not to be considered as admitted on this motion on the pleadings; moreover, the portions cited do not clearly support defendant's assertion.

express language in the warrants entitling the corporation to accelerate the time within which the option could be fully exercised.

Merritt-Chapman & Scott Corp. v. New York Trust Co., (2 Cir.) 184 F.2d 954, is a decision in which Circuit Judge Thomas W. Swann discusses the problem in an opinion with which Judge Learned Hand concurred and from which Judge Charles E. Clark dissented. The issue in that case was whether a notice strikingly similar to the one here involved served to accelerate the time limitation of an opinion in its application to a stock dividend. In holding that the option rights of the warrant holder embraced the stock dividend, even though the option was not exercised before the time specified in the notice, the majority opinion states (184 F.2d 958):

> . . . The appellate must, and does, contend that the notice provision is for the purpose of giving the warrant holders notice that unless they exercise their warrants by the record date, they will forfeit those promised rights. Certainly the language of [the provision] is not aptly chosen to express such a forfeiture. . . .

Circuit Judge Clark, in dissenting, reasoned that the provisions for notice appearing in the warrant there involved must have been intended to limit the power of the warrant holder to assert rights with respect to the stock dividend because no other purposes for the time limitation in the notice could be conceived. Why, he wrote, "should the draftsmen have painted the lily further unless the sixty days was intended as a definite period for the taking of some action?" 184 F.2d 960. The answer to this question may be found, we feel, in the circumstance that the warrant holders are not entitled to any voting rights or other rights as stockholders of the company before effective exercise of the option to purchase. A function of the notice required by the terms of this warrant could be to notify the warrant holder of a corporate change which might make early acquisition of voting rights or other stockholders' prerogatives desirable and enable the warrant holders to improve their position by acquiring a stockholder status.

. . .

CONCLUSION

The difficulty we have had with this case comes from the fact that the provisions of the warrants do not seem to deal specifically with a situation such as that described in the pleadings where, in an apparent effort to resolve a conflict in business judgment as between the directors, the assets of the original corporation are divided with one group given operating control of one phase of the corporate activity and the other assuming control of the elaborate effort to anticipate all possible changes that might affect the rights of warrant holders, to attribute to Plastics a general intent that the option rights of persons in the position of these plaintiffs should not be diminished by an arrangement which seems to have been particularly responsive to the needs of those in control of the corporation. But the language of the warrants is not so clear and unequivocal as to give a solution to the present problem without affording the parties an opportunity to present such evidence as may be available to clarify the ambiguities which have been discussed.

We do not decide that a case of unlawful interference with contract has been made by plaintiffs. Whether it has or not must depend on the interpretation ultimately given to the warrants; upon whether the agreements and acts done pursuant thereto by United disabled and prevented Plastics from performing its obligations under the warrants; and whether, if so, United's participation in the transaction was justified.

We decide only that United was not entitled to judgment on the pleadings.

Reversed and remanded.

WOOD v. COASTAL STATES GAS CORP.

Delaware Supreme Court
401 A.2d 932 (1979)

DUFFY, JUSTICE

This appeal is from an order of the Court of Chancery dismissing the complaints in a consolidated class action filed by the owners of two series of preferred stock[36] in Coastal State Gas Corporation (Coastal), a Delaware corporation. The suit is against Coastal, two of its subsidiaries and its chief executive officer. While this litigation is part of a complex controversy in a mosaic of many persons and disputes, it is entirely between the owners of Coastal's preferred stock and the owners of its common stock.

I

The facts out of which the dispute arises involve the sale and delivery of natural gas to many cities and corporate users in the State of Texas and, although our involvement is limited, we must recite some of them to put the appeal into context. For that purpose, the relevant facts are these:

A significant part of Coastal's business is the gathering, transporting and marketing of natural gas, all of which is conducted by a subsidiary, Coastal States Gas Producing Co. (Producing), also a defendant in this action. Producing, in turn, has a subsidiary, Lo-Vaca Gathering Co. (Lo-Vaca), another defendant, which supplies the gas to intrastate customers in Texas, including the Cities of Austin, Brownsville, Corpus Christi and San Antonio.

As a result of several factors associated with the "energy crisis" in the early 1970s, the wellhead price of natural gas increased significantly (from about 20¢; per 1000 cubic feet to about $2.00 for the same quantity) and LoVaca was unable to honour its obligations to deliver gas to its customers at contract prices. In 1973, Lo-Vaca sought and obtained interim permission from the Railroad Commission of Texas (the agency vested with jurisdiction over intrastate utilities in Texas) to increase its rates; that authorization permitted Lo-Vaca to pass to its customers

---

[36] [1] One series is designated, "$1.83 Cumulative Convertible Preferred Stock, Series B," and the other, "$1.19 Cumulative Convertible Preferred Stock, Series A." The certificate of rights and preferences for each series is identical and thus what is said herein of one is applicable to both. We will refer to the stock in the regular as "Series A," or "Series B," or the "preferred stock."

certain of its own cost increases. After the higher rates went into effect, a large number of Lo-Vaca industrial and municipal customers filed suits against Lo-Vaca, Producing, Coastal and Oscar Wyatt (Coastal's chief executive officer, the owner of the single largest block of its common stock and a defendant in this suit) for breach of contract.

In December 1977, the Commission entered a final order denying LoVaca's original petition for the rate relief and, in effect, rescinding the interim order which had authorized the increase. The Commission then directed Lo-Vaca to comply with the contract rates and ordered Coastal, Producing and Lo-Vaca to refund the rate increment which had been charged to customers under the 1973 interim order. It is estimated that the refundable amounts exceeds $1.6 billion — which is about three times Coastal's net worth.

Given this state of affairs, with its obvious and enormous implications for a large section of Texas, settlement negotiations were undertaken and, eventually, a complex plan evolved. It is unnecessary for us to detail the plan, but the following summary states its substance:

(1) The substantial litigation and disputes between the natural gas sales customers of Lo-Vaca and Coastal, Producing, Lo-Vaca and Wyatt, which developed as a result of the "Lo-Vaca problem," will be settled;

(2) Producing will be renamed "Valero Energy Corporation," restructured into a corporate enterprise and spun off from Coastal; it will consist principally of Producing's present gas utility pipe-line and extraction plant operations, including Lo-Vaca, and a Texas retail gas distribution division of Coastal;

(3) There will be transfers to a trust for the benefit of the customers who adopt the settlement plan ("Settling Customers") of: (a) approximately 1,196,218 shares (or about 5.3%) of the voting securities of Coastal; (b) a one-year interest-bearing promissory note of Valero in the principal amount of $8,000,000; (c) 13.4% of the outstanding shares of the common stock of Valero; and (d) 1,150,000 shares ($115,000,000 aggregate liquidation value) of Valero Preferred Stock, $8.50 Cumulative Series A;

(4) Coastal will issue to Valero approximately 805,130 shares (with approximately $80,513,000 aggregate liquidation value) of Coastal's $8.50 Cumulative Preferred Stock, Series D, $3313 par value (which is a new class of stock);

(5) A long-term program will be established providing for the expenditure of $180,000,000 to $230,000,000 (subject to certain increases or decreases, with a maximum commitment estimated at $495,000,000), by Coastal to find and develop gas reserves to be made available to the Lo-Vaca System and to be offered for sale by Coastal to Valero at discounted prices and, in turn, resold to Lo-Vaca (or, in some instances, to third parties) at higher prices, with the net proceeds (in excess of the cost of gas) received by Valero on such resale to be paid to the trust for the benefits of certain Settling Customers;

(6) There will be a new gas sales rate structure for Lo-Vaca designed to stabilize it as a viable public utility.

In addition, there will be a distribution by Coastal, in the form of an extraordinary dividend chargeable to earned surplus, to its common stockholders (except Wyatt) of the balance (86.6%) of the Valero common stock not transferred to the trust referred to in (3)(c) above.[37] Shareholders will receive one share of Valero for each share of Coastal common held at the time of the spin-off. It is this distribution which is at the center of this litigation between the preferred and common stockholders of Coastal. And Coastal's dividend history of annual payments to the preferred but none (with one exception) to the common suggests a reason for this. Coastal has paid regular quarterly dividends of $.2975 per share on the $1.19 Series A and $.4575 per share on the $1.83 Series B since each was issued. Only one dividend of $.075 per share has been paid on the common in the last twenty years.

Coastal's Board of Directors unanimously approved the settlement[38] and, in August 1978, the Commission gave its approval. The Coastal management then submitted the plan for approval at a special meeting of its stockholders called for November 10.

. . .

Holders of the Series A and Series B preferred stock, (plaintiffs), filed an action in the Court of Chancery to enjoin the special shareholders meeting. They alleged that the settlement plan breaches the "Certificate of the Designations, Preferences and Relative, Participating Optional or other Special Rights" (Certificate) of the Series A and Series B preferred stock. In essence, plaintiffs say that the plan violates their Certificate rights because the preferred will not receive any of the Valero shares, that is, the 86.6% to be distributed entirely to the Coastal common.

After a trial on the merits, the Vice Chancellor entered judgment for defendants and ordered plaintiffs to pay the costs of giving notice to the members of the class of the pendency of the action. *See* Court of Chancery Rule 23. The Court determined that the settlement plan and, more specifically, the spin-off of Producing and the distribution of Valero stock to the common stockholders of Coastal, is not a "recapitalization" within the meaning of the Certificate. (If it is, all parties concede that the preferred is entitled to participate in the distribution of the Valero shares.) The Vice Chancellor reasoned that a key phrase, "in lieu of," in the Certificate implies that the existing shares of Coastal common must be exchanged for something else before there is a "recapitalization" which creates rights in the preferred. And he found support for that conclusion in another Certificate provision which permits Coastal to pay a dividend to holders of common stock, in other than its own common, without affecting the rights of the preferred.

The Court also ruled that the holders of the preferred stock were not entitled to vote as a class on the settlement plan, because the requirements of the Certificate for such a vote had not been met.

---

[37] [2] The Valero shares trade on a "when issued" basis at $6.50 to $7.00 per share (against an assumed market value of $6.50 per share).

[38] [3] Fletcher Yarbough, who had been nominated by the Securities and Exchange Commission to serve as a director on the Coastal Board, testified at trial that the:

> ". . . complex of problems relating to Lo-Vaca, both before the Railroad Commission and in the litigation, simply had to be settled, that there was a truly unacceptably high risk that this problem could destroy the corporation and the value of the shares of the corporation . . ."

Finally, the Court considered plaintiffs' claims that the settlement plan is unfair to the preferred, unjustly enriched the common and did not have a proper business purpose, and concluded that the rights of the preferred are found, under the circumstances of this case, solely in the Certificate, not in concepts of fairness or fiduciary duty.

On appeal, plaintiffs challenge each of these rulings, as well as the order requiring them to pay the costs of giving notice to the class.

II

Before discussing the merits of the controversy, we emphasize that this lawsuit is not a general attack upon the settlement plan. On the contrary, plaintiffs say that they approve the plan and hope to see it executed. As we have observed, the case involves a dispute between the preferred vis-a-vis the common over participation rights in the Valero stock to be distributed as part of the spin-off. As we understand it, that is the extent of plaintiffs' attack upon the plan.

The preferred has a conversion right to exchange for the common on a one-to-one basis. Briefly stated, the preferred argues that a distribution of Valero stock to the common only, and without provision for permitting the preferred to share therein now or at the time of conversion, violates its Certificate rights. We now examine those rights in some detail.

A.

In pertinent part, the Certificate states:

> CONVERSION OF . . . PREFERRED STOCKS
> INTO COMMON STOCK
>
> (a) Subject to the provisions of this Article . . . , the holder of record of any . . . Preferred Stock shall have the right, at his option, at any time after the issuance of such share(s) to convert each share of . . . Preferred Stock into one fully-paid and non-assessable share of Common Stock of the Corporation.
>
> . . . .
>
> (c) Conversion of . . . Preferred Stock shall be subject to the following additional terms and provisions:
>
> . . . .
>
> > (4) In the event that the Corporation shall at any time subdivide or combine in a greater or lesser number of shares the outstanding shares of Common Stock, the number of shares of Common Stock issuable upon conversion of the . . . Preferred Stock shall be proportionately increased in the case of subdivision or decreased in the case of a combination effective in either case at the close of business on the date when such subdivision or combination shall become effective.

> (5) In the event that the Corporation shall be recapitalized, consolidated with or merged into any other corporation, or shall sell or convey to any other corporation all or substantially all of its property as an entirety, provision shall be made as part of the terms of such recapitalization, consolidation, merger, sale or conveyance so that any holder of . . . Preferred Stock may thereafter receive in lieu of the Common Stock otherwise issuable to him upon conversion of his . . . Preferred Stock, but at the conversion ratio stated in this Article . . . which would otherwise be applicable at the time of conversion, the same kind and amount of securities or assets as may be distributable upon such recapitalization, consolidation, merger, sale or conveyance with respect to the Common Stock of the Corporation.
>
> (6) In the event that the Corporation shall at any time pay to the holders of Common Stock a dividend in Common Stock, the number of shares of Common Stock issuable upon conversion of the . . . Preferred Stock shall be proportionately increased, effective at the close of business on the record date for determination of the holders of Common Stock entitled to such dividend.
>
> (7) No adjustment of the conversion ratio shall be made by reason of any declaration or payment to the holders of the Common Stock of the Corporation of a dividend or distribution payable in any property or securities other than Common Stock, any redemption of the Common Stock, any issuance of any securities convertible into Common Stock, or for any other reason, except as expressly provided herein.
>
> (8) The Corporation shall at all times reserve and keep available solely for purpose of issuance upon conversion of . . . Preferred Stock, as herein provided, such number of shares of Common Stock as shall be issuable upon the conversion of all outstanding . . . Preferred Stock.

B.

For most purposes, the rights of the preferred shareholders as against the common shareholders are fixed by the contractual terms agreed upon when the class of preferred stock is created. And, as to the conversion privilege, it has been said that the rights of a preferred shareholder are "least affected by rules of law and most dependent on the share contract." Buxbaum, *Preferred Stock-Law and Draftsmanship*, 42 CAL. L. REV. 243, 279 (1954).

Our duty, then, is to construe the contract governing the preferred shares. In so doing, we employ the methods used to interpret contracts generally; that is, we consider the entire instrument and attempt to reconcile all of its provisions "in order to determine the meaning intended to be given to any portion of it." *Ellingwood v. Wolfs Head Oil Refining Co., supra* at 747. More to the point, we must construe the several qualifications of the conversion privilege which are stated in Sections (c)(4)-(7) of the Certificate.

C.

The basic conversion privilege is stated in Section (a) of the Certificate: at the option of the holder, each share of preferred is convertible into one share of common. That is the governing norm, fixing the ratio between the classes. It is the benchmark from which the holder of a preferred share may, at a time of his choice, elect to move from that status to that of a common shareholder. The right of the preferred to make the choice is absolute-at least, in contract terms. And the *time* at which the choice may be made is likewise absolute. The circumstances under which the choice is made, or may be made, is another matter. The price which the market places upon the respective shares may well be a significant circumstance influencing a decision, to convert or to not convert at any given time. In this case, for example, Coastal had not, for some twenty years prior to 1977, paid a dividend on the common stock while the preferred had regularly received the specified dividend. Obviously, the market value of the respective shares reflected that experience. But, assuming silence on the subject in the conversion contract (as here), the preferred has no right to any particular market price ratio between the shares. However, the preferred is ordinarily given (as here) anti-dilution or anti-destruction rights in the conversion contract.

Section (c)(4) in the Coastal Certificate is such an "anti-dilution" clause. It provides for a proportionate change in the conversion ratio in the event of a stock split or a stock combination (that is, a reverse split). In each of those events, the number of outstanding shares of Coastal common would change so, in order to preserve the parity relationship, a proportionate adjustment to the conversion ratio is essential.[39] In brief, (c)(4) prohibits the common from diluting the conversion right by requiring a proportionate adjustment if the number of outstanding shares is increased (and a similar adjustment if there is a decrease resulting from a reverse split).

Section (c)(6) is directed to the same anti-dilution purpose. While (c)(4) applies to subdivisions and combinations (which enlarge or decrease the number of outstanding shares), (c)(6) is directed to a stock dividend, that is, the issuance of Coastal shares to its stockholders as a dividend. That, too, is a circumstance which, by definition, would dilute the prior parity relationship and, to prevent that, the conversion ratio is "proportionately increased" by (c)(6).

Since Coastal is neither splitting nor reverse-splitting its shares, nor distributing them as a dividend, (c)(4) and (6) do not directly apply to this case.

D.

This brings us to (c)(5) which plaintiffs contend is the heart of the matter. The short of it is that unless the plaintiffs can find something in this paragraph which, directly or by implication, prohibits Coastal from distributing the Valero stock to the holders of its common, without giving its preferred a right to participate therein

[39] [4] For example: if the Coastal common were split three for one, the number of outstanding shares would be tripled and, upon conversion thereafter, a preferred stockholder would be entitled to receive three shares of common for each share of preferred surrendered.

(now or at the time of conversion), then, under our settled law . . . the preferred has no such right. The Vice Chancellor found none. Nor do we.

Given the significance of (c)(5) in the dispute, we quote it again, this time omitting the references to consolidations, mergers, sales, and so on, which are not directly germane here. Thus:

> In the event that the Corporation shall be recapitalized, . . . provision shall be made as part of the terms of such recapitalization, . . . so that any holder of . . . Preferred Stock may thereafter receive in lieu of the Common Stock otherwise issuable to him upon conversion of his . . . Preferred Stock, but at the conversion ratio stated in this Article . . . which would otherwise be applicable at the time of conversion, the same kind and amount of securities or assets as may be distributable upon such recapitalization . . . with respect to the Common Stock of the Corporation.

After noting that the "recapitalization" has no generally accepted meaning in law or accounting, the Vice Chancellor focused on the phrase, "in lieu of," as it appears in (c)(5) and concluded that, before the Section becomes applicable, the "Common Shares of Coastal must cease to exist and something [must] be given in lieu of them." Since the Coastal shares will continue in being after the spin-off, he concluded that the plan is not a capitalization within the meaning of the Certificate.

Plaintiffs contend that Section (c)(5) is the key to analysis of the Certificate. They say that the settlement plan constitutes a "recapitalization" of the Coastal, which triggers the adjustment called for in that section.

Relying on the significant changes which the plan will effect in Coastal's capital structure, plaintiffs argue that there will be a recapitalization in fact and law.

Section (c)(5) contains what is typically considered to be "anti-destruction" language. *See Buxbaum, supra* at 287. Transactions listed therein — a merger of consolidation, for example — are the kind of events that will not merely dilute the conversion privilege by altering the number of shares of common but, rather, may destroy the conversion privilege by eliminating the stock into which a preferred share is convertible. We focus, however, on the preferred's claim of right if Coastal "shall be recapitalized."

At trial, both sides offered the testimony of experts as to what "recapitalization" means. Professor Sametz noted that there is not a precise or specific definition, but the term implies a "fundamental realignment of relationships amongst a company's securities" or a "reshuffling of the capital structure."

The parties have also cited cases[40] from other jurisdictions, but we are not persuaded that such cases considered language reasonably comparable to that at issue here; so they are of little help. And the same is true of general financial terminology. The point is that we must decide the controversy under the facts in this case and, for present purposes, that means the Certificate language.

---

[40] [7] *See for example, Stephenson v. Plastics Corporation of America*, Minn. Supr., 276 Minn. 400, 150 N.W.2d 668 (1967); *United Gas Improvement Co. v. Commissioner of Internal Revenue*, 3 Cir., 142 F.2d 216, 218 (1944); *Commissioner of Internal Revenue v. Neustadt's Trust*, 2 Cir., 131 F.2d 528 (1942).

We agree with plaintiffs that the changes which the plan will bring to Coastal's financial structure are enormous. And it may be concluded that, collectively, these amount to a "reshuffling of the capital structure" under the general definition to which Professor Sametz testified. But that is not the test. The critical question concerns what is said in the contract.

Section (c)(5) provides that in the event of "recapitalization" one of the provisions shall be that a holder of preferred may "thereafter" receive — something. *When* he may receive it is clear: he may receive it "upon conversion" after the recapitalization has taken place. After that event, he may receive, not what he would have received *before* recapitalization; that was the common stock which was "otherwise issuable to him upon conversion." Certainly this clause is meaningless if the common share remains issuable to him *after* recapitalization. And so is the remainder of the paragraph which requires that the same conversion ratio be retained by distributing to the preferred, upon conversion, the "same kind and amount of securities or assets as may be distributable upon said recapitalization . . . with respect to the Common." The "same kind and amount" would be distributable to the common only if the common had been exchanged for something else. This was the situation the draftsman contemplated by the provision that the preferred "may receive" the "same kind and amount" of property "in lieu of the Common Stock."

Since the settlement plan does not include an exchange of the common and, given the added circumstances that the dividend or liquidated preference of the preferred is not threatened and that earned surplus is ample to support the distribution of the Valero shares to the common, the settlement plan does not include a recapitalization within the meaning of Section (c)(5).

E.

We turn now to (c)(7) which, we think, is related to what is said in (c)(5) and our construction of it; (c)(7) states:

> No adjustment of the conversion ratio shall be made by reason of any declaration or payment to the holders of the Common Stock of the Corporation of a dividend or distribution payable in any property or securities other than Common Stock, any redemption of the Common Stock, any issuance of any securities convertible into Common Stock, or for any other reason, except as expressly provided herein.

This section, plainly and clearly, lists transactions which do not call for an adjustment to the conversion ratio. Thus an adjustment is not made for:

(1) a dividend payable to holders of the common in property other than Coastal common,

(2) a redemption of the common,

(3) an issuance of securities convertible into common,

(4) "any other reason."

Section (c)(7) concludes with the phrase, "except as expressly provided herein," which creates an ambiguity that must be resolved.

Plaintiffs contend that the phrase relates to all of Section (c), including (c)(5), and thus if a property dividend (the Valero stock) is regarded as a recapitalization," the latter section controls. It is somewhat difficult to follow that argument but, as we understand it, plaintiffs contend that (c)(7) does not apply here.

In our opinion, the phrase, "except as expressly provided herein," refers to those paragraphs of Section (c) which "expressly . . . [provide]" for a change in the conversion ratio. In so doing, the phrase does modify the preceding phrase, "any other reason' (which is all-encompassing). But the transactions referred to are those in (c)(4) and (c)(6), and thus they are the exceptions "expressly provided" for. There are no exceptions provided for in (c)(7) and, therefore, the phrase would be meaningless if it were construed as applying to (c)(7).

Section (c)(7) states flatly that an adjustment shall not be made in the conversion ratio in the event any of the three specified events occurs: a dividend in property other than Coastal common, a redemption of the common or the issue of securities convertible into common. And the three specifics are enlarged by the general reference to "any other reason." Given what we believe to be mandatory language ("[n]o adjustment . . . shall be made") prohibiting a change in the conversion ratio, we conclude that such a change may be made only if it is "expressly provided" in Section (c), and, as we have said, that means by the anti-dilution provisions of (c)(4) and (c)(6), i.e., by a stock split, reverse split or a stock dividend. It is only in those paragraphs that provisions are found for an *adjustment* in the conversion ratio.[41] Section (c)(5), on the other hand, is not directed merely to an adjustment in the exchange ratio; it is directed toward maintaining parity between the common and the preferred after a specified event has occurred: thus a conversion after recapitalization, merger or consolidation shall be "at the conversion ratio stated in this Article." The "conversion ratio" referred to here is the parity to throughout the Article (i.e., the Certificate).[42]

But even if one were to find some inconsistency or contradiction between (c)(5) and (c)(7), then, under familiar and well-settled rules of construction, the specific language of (c)(7) (as applied to the Valero stock) controls over any general language in (c)(5) regarding recapitalization.

F.

We have reviewed Sections (c)(4) through (c)(7) independently but failed to find therein any merit to the contentions which plaintiffs argue. And considering the paragraphs together confirms our conclusion. So viewed, the basic scheme is that parity between the common and preferred is maintained through any changes in the number of outstanding shares which are unaccompanied by other balance sheet changes: thus a stock split, reverse split or stock dividend changes only the number of shares outstanding without any change in corporation assets. Sections (c)(4) and

---

[41] [8] The adjustment called for is an increase or decrease, as the case may be, of the number of shares of common to be received for each share of preferred which is converted.

[42] [9] Assuming Section (c)(5) could possibly be interpreted to contemplate an adjustment of the conversion ratio, none would be appropriate under our view of these facts since we have concluded that the settlement plan here does not include a recapitalization within the meaning of Section (c)(5).

(c)(6) provide for continuing parity by making the appropriate adjustment to the conversion ratio (that is, what will be given for one share of preferred) in such instance. But it appears that a reduction in assets by distribution to the common may be made without adjustment to that exchange basis. Thus a cash dividend is permissible under (c)(7),[43] or other corporate assets (stock in a listed company, for example) may be distributed under that paragraph. And if the distribution of assets is in the form of a redemption of the common, that, too, is permissible. In short, dividends and other distribution of corporate assets are permissible without change in the exchange basis. Speaking generally, such distributions are the ordinary and permissible way in which the holders of common stock share in the earnings of the enterprise. In saying this, we emphasize once more that there is not a charge here that the liquidation preference or the dividend of the preferred is in any way threatened. Nor is fraud involved.

In summary, we conclude that a distribution of the Valero stock to the holders of Coastal common is permissible under Section (c)(7) and may be made without adjustment to the conversion ratio; such distribution is not a recapitalization under Section (c) (5).

III

Next, plaintiffs contend that the settlement plan should have been put to a special (two-thirds) vote of the preferred shareholders as a class, as provided for in Section VII of the Certificate.[44] That section states in part:

> So long as any shares of . . . Preferred Stock are outstanding, the Corporation shall not, without the affirmative vote or the written consent as provided by law, of the holders of at least two-thirds (23) of the outstanding shares of . . . Preferred Stock, voting as a class.
>
> (a) create, authorize or issue any class or series of stock ranking either as to payment of dividends or distribution of assets prior to the . . . Preferred Stock; or
>
> (b) change the preferences, rights or powers with respect to the Preferred Stock so as to affect such stock adversely[.]

For most purposes, the voting rights of the preferred shareholders are found in Section IV of the Certificate and, for most purposes, their rights are the same as the holders of the common. In our opinion, the special voting provisions for which plaintiffs argue are triggered only by the two events stated above. And neither of those has occurred.

Thus, shares are not to be issued under the settlement plan which would rank superior to plaintiffs' shares, either as to payment of dividends or distribution of assets. And the settlement plan will not change the preferences, rights or powers of

---

[43] [10] Mr. Katzin testified that Coastal has a substantial earned surplus to which the Valero distribution is to be charged.

[44] [11] Plaintiffs rely upon their Certificate rights, not upon any Delaware statute. *Cf.* 8 Del. C. § 242(c).

the preferred. As we have said, the special features of the preferred stock are those fixed by the share contract and the settlement plan comports with that contract, as we have construed it. It follows that Coastal has not "change[d] the preferences, rights or powers" of the preferred shareholders and, so, the latter are not entitled to vote on the plan as a class.

Affirmed.

LOHNES v. LEVEL 3 COMMUNS., INC.

United States Court of Appeals, First Circuit
272 F.3d 49 (2001)

Selya, Circuit Judge

The primary issue raised in this appeal is whether the terms "capital reorganization" and/or "reclassification of stock," as used in a stock warrant, encompass a stock split. Asserting the affirmative of this proposition, a warrantholder, plaintiff-appellant Paul R. Lohnes, claims that a stock split effectuated by defendant-appellee Level 3 Communications, Inc. (Level 3) triggered an antidilution provision in the warrant that automatically increased the number of shares of stock to which he was entitled. Level 3 resists this claim. The district court concluded that the language of the warrant could not reasonably be construed to encompass a stock split and, accordingly, granted Level 3's motion for summary judgment. *Lohnes v. Level 3 Communications, Inc.*, 135 F. Supp. 2d 105, 106 (D. Mass. 2001). We affirm.

I. BACKGROUND

. . .

The appellant is both a trustee and a beneficiary of C.E.M. Realty Trust (the Trust). In February of 1998, the Trust leased 40,000 square feet of commercial space to XCOM Technologies, Inc. (XCOM). The details of the lease transaction need not concern us, save for the fact that, as part of the consideration, XCOM issued a stock warrant to the appellant. The parties negotiated the principal terms of the warrant — the number of shares, the exercise price, and the expiration date — and XCOM's lawyer then drafted the document. The warrant specified that its exercise would be governed by Massachusetts law. It empowered the holder to purchase, at his discretion but within a fixed period, 100,000 shares of XCOM common stock at $0.30 per share.

Unbeknownst to the appellant, XCOM's days as an independent entity were numbered. Shortly after the appellant executed the lease and accepted the warrant, Level 3 acquired XCOM in a stock-for-stock transaction and converted XCOM into a wholly-owned subsidiary. As part of this transaction, Level 3 agreed to assume XCOM's warrant obligations and satisfy them with shares of Level 3's common stock (using a designated share exchange formula). Following this paradigm, the appellant's unexercised warrant for XCOM shares was duly converted into a warrant to purchase 8,541 shares of Level 3's common stock. The appellant does not challenge this conversion (which took effect in April of 1998).

The next significant development occurred on July 14, 1998. On that date, Level 3's board of directors authorized a two-for-one stock split, to be effectuated in the form of a stock dividend granting common shareholders one new share of stock for each share held.[45] The board set the record date as July 30, 1998. On July 20, Level 3 issued a press release announcing the stock split, but it did not provide the appellant with personalized notice.

The split occurred as scheduled. Adhering to generally accepted accounting practices, Level 3 adjusted its balance sheet to account for the split by increasing its common stock account in the amount of $1,000,000 and reducing paid-in-capital by a like amount. These accounting entries had no net effect on either the retained earnings or the net equity of the company.

Despite the sharp reduction in the share price that accompanied the stock split, the appellant paid no heed until approximately three months after the record date. When his belated inquiry revealed what had transpired, the appellant contacted Level 3 to confirm that the stock split had triggered a share adjustment provision, thus entitling him to 17,082 shares (twice the number of shares specified in the warrant). Level 3 demurred on the ground that the warrant did not provide for any share adjustment based upon the occurrence of a stock split effected as a stock dividend.

Dissatisfied by Level 3's response, the appellant exercised the warrant and received 8,541 shares of Level 3's common stock. He then sued Level 3 in a Massachusetts state court alleging breach of both the warrant and the implied duty of good faith and fair dealing. Citing diversity of citizenship and the existence of a controversy in the requisite amount, Level 3 removed the action to the federal district court. . . .

. . .

In due course, the district court ruled that, as a matter of law, a stock split, effected as a stock dividend, did not constitute a "capital reorganization" as that term was used in the warrant and, accordingly, granted the motion for summary judgment. . . .

II. METHODOLOGY OF REVIEW

We begin our analysis by outlining the legal framework that governs our review. Next, we apply well-worn principles of contract interpretation to resolve the appellant's contention that the terms "capital reorganization" and "reclassification of stock" encompass a stock split implemented as a stock dividend. In this endeavor,

---

[45] [10] A corporation effects a "stock split" by increasing the number of shares outstanding without changing the proportional ownership interests of each shareholder. Companies typically execute a stock split by issuing a "stock dividend" to current shareholders, *i.e.*, "paid in stock expressed as a percentage of the number of shares already held by a shareholder." *Black's Law Dict.* 493 (7th ed. 1999) (cross-referencing definition of "dividend"). Stock splits lower the price per share, thereby fostering increased marketability and wider distribution of shares.

Technically, not all stock dividends are stock splits, and the two may, in limited instances, receive different accounting treatment. In the instant matter, however, "stock split" and "stock dividend" are two sides of the same coin, and we use the terms interchangeably.

our principal task is to determine the ambiguity *vel non* [or the absence thereof] of the disputed terms. Thus, we investigate whether either term is reasonably susceptible to the interpretation urged by the appellant. As part of this exercise, we consider (and reject) the appellant's belated attempt to introduce expert testimony bearing on this question. We conclude by addressing the appellant's claim that Level 3 breached the implied duty of good faith and fair dealing inherent in the warrant.

. . .

III. THE CONTRACT INTERPRETATION CLAIMS

A stock warrant is an instrument that grants the warrantholder an option to purchase shares of stock at a fixed price. *See Black's Law Dict.* 1441 (7th ed. 1999); II James Cox et al., *Corporations* § 18.15 (1995 & 1999 Supp.); 6A William Meade Fletcher, *Fletcher Cyclopedia of the Law of Private Corps.* § 2641 (perm. ed. 1997); *see also Tribble v. J.W. Greer Co.*, 83 F. Supp. 1015, 1022 (D. Mass. 1949) (holding, under Massachusetts law, that a stock warrant is "a contract by which the corporation gives an irrevocable option to the holder to purchase authorized corporate stock within a period of time at a price and upon terms specified in the contract"). Against the backdrop of this well-established definition, we turn to the appellant's contract interpretation claims. We divide our discussion into seven segments.

A. Applicable Legal Principles.

Time-honored principles of contract law govern our analysis. We begin with bedrock: the determination of whether a contract is ambiguous is a question of law within the province of the judge. *Fashion House, Inc. v. K Mart Corp.*, 892 F.2d 1076, 1083 (1st Cir. 1989); *RCI N.E. Servs. Div. v. Boston Edison Co.*, 822 F.2d 199, 202 (1st Cir. 1987). Contract language ordinarily is considered ambiguous "where an agreement's terms are inconsistent on their face or where the phraseology can support reasonable differences of opinion as to the meaning of the words employed and obligations undertaken." *Fashion House*, 892 F.2d at 1083.

A court's determination that a contract is or is not ambiguous has important implications. If a court holds that a contract is unambiguously worded, it typically will construe the document based upon the plain and natural meaning of the language contained therein. *Smart v. Gillette Co. Long-Term Disability Plan*, 70 F.3d 173, 178 (1st Cir. 1995); *Hiller v. Submarine Signal Co.*, 325 Mass. 546, 91 N.E.2d 667, 669 (1950). For the most part, a court interpreting an unambiguous agreement need not consult extrinsic evidence to impart meaning to its terms. *Smart*, 70 F.3d at 179. A court may, however, consider extrinsic evidence for the limited purpose of evaluating whether a term is ambiguous in the first place, but only if the extrinsic evidence "suggests a meaning to which the challenged language is reasonably susceptible." *Id.* at 180.

If, however, ambiguity looms — that is, if "the plain meaning of a contract phrase does not spring unambiguously from the page or from the context" — then the interpretive function involves a question of fact. *RCI N.E.*, 822 F.2d at 202. In such cases, a court may consider extrinsic evidence insofar as it sheds light on what the parties intended. *Robert Indus., Inc. v. Spence*, 362 Mass. 751, 291 N.E.2d 407, 409 (1973).

B. Parsing the Warrant.

The warrant at issue here contained a two-paragraph antidilution provision which, upon the occurrence of certain described events, automatically adjusted the number of shares to which the warrantholder would be entitled upon exercise of the warrant. In all, share adjustments were engendered by five separate contingencies: capital reorganization, reclassification of common stock, merger, consolidation, and sale of all (or substantially all) the capital stock or assets. However, the warrant did not explicitly provide for an adjustment of shares in the event of a stock split. The appellant attempts to plug this lacuna [gap] by equating a stock split with a capital reorganization and/or a reclassification of stock. This argument brings the following paragraph of the antidilution provision into play:"

Reorganizations and Reclassifications. If there shall occur any capital reorganization or reclassification of the Common Stock, then, as part of any such reorganization or reclassification, lawful provision shall be made so that the Holder shall have the right thereafter to receive upon the exercise hereof the kind and amount of shares of stock or other securities or property which such Holder would have been entitled to receive if, immediately prior to any such reorganization or reclassification, such Holder had held the number of shares of Common Stock which were then purchasable upon the exercise of this Warrant."

Building upon the premise that either "capital reorganization" or "reclassification of stock" encompasses a stock split, the appellant concludes that Level 3's stock split activated the share adjustment mechanism set forth in the quoted paragraph.

As said, the appellant bears the burden of establishing the existence of a genuine issue of material fact. Given the circumstances of this case, the only way for him to succeed in this endeavor is by showing that one of the disputed terms ("capital reorganization" or "reclassification of stock") is shrouded in ambiguity, that is, that reasonable minds plausibly could reach opposite conclusions as to whether either term extended to stock splits. To appraise the success of the appellant's efforts, we ponder each term separately.

C. Capital Reorganization.

Since the warrant does not elaborate upon the meaning of "capital reorganization," we turn to other sources. Massachusetts law offers no discernible guidance. Outside of Massachusetts, the closest case is *Prescott, Ball & Turben v. LTV Corp.*, 531 F. Supp. 213 (S.D. N.Y. 1981). There, the plaintiffs owned debentures, issued pursuant to a trust indenture, which were convertible into common stock of LTV Corp. (LTV). LTV's board ratified a spin-off proposal calling for the distribution of all the shares of a wholly-owned LTV subsidiary to LTV's common stockholders on a pro rata basis. The distribution stood to reduce LTV's stated capital and retained earnings by $62.4 million and $30.3 million, respectively. *Id.* at 215. The plaintiffs argued that the proposed distribution of the subsidiary's stock entailed a capital reorganization that triggered an antidilution provision contained in the trust indenture.[46] The defendants countered that the spin-off was merely a dividend, and, therefore, did not trigger the share adjustment machinery established in the antidilution provision.

The *Prescott* court sided with the defendants. It noted that the "only way" the defendants could prevail was if the terms of the trust indenture made it unambiguously clear that the parties did not intend to treat the spin-off as a capital reorganization. *Id.* at 217. Finding the terms of the trust indenture to be unambiguous, the court ruled that:

> The plain language of the Trust Indenture contemplates an exchange or alteration in the existing ownership form of the interest held by LTV common shareholders before a particular transaction can be classified as a capital reorganization for purposes of the Trust Indenture. No such exchange or alteration is involved in the proposed distribution of the [LTV subsidiary's] stock. The proposed distribution therefore does not activate the [antidilution adjustment provision in] the Trust Indenture.

Id. at 219-20.

The district court deemed *Prescott* dispositive, *see Lohnes*, 135 F. Supp. 2d at 106, and indeed, *Prescott* bears several similarities to the case at bar. In neither instance was the term "capital reorganization" defined in the controlling document or in the applicable state law. Moreover, the *Prescott* court was required to apply principles of contract law to construe the letter of the controlling document and determine whether a share adjustment provision designed to prevent dilution was triggered by a stock dividend. Finally, neither case involved an exchange of existing shares; rather, the stock split orchestrated by Level 3 was effected by distributing additional shares to its existing shareholders in much the same manner that shares in the wholly-owned subsidiary were distributed to LTV's stockholders.

Despite these similarities, we stop short of endorsing the district court's declaration that *Prescott* should be given controlling effect. The *Prescott* court, finding cases from other jurisdictions and general financial terminology to be of "little help," ultimately restricted its analysis to the four corners of the trust indenture there at issue. 531 F. Supp. at 218. In contrast, we consider ourselves bound to grapple with the intricacies of Massachusetts law and, in performing that task, to search for guidance in case law from other courts, the statutes of foreign jurisdictions, and common financial usage — all of which are appropriate benchmarks for gauging the reasonableness vel non of the appellant's sweeping definition of "capital reorganization." Thus, we treat *Prescott* as suggestive evidence that stock splits do not constitute capital reorganizations, but refrain from according it decretory significance.

---

[46] [11] This provision read in pertinent part:

> Each Debenture shall after such capital reorganization . . . be convertible into the kind and amount of shares of stock or other securities or property of the Guarantor . . . to which the holder of the number of shares of Common Stock deliverable (immediately prior to the time of such capital reorganization . . .) upon conversion of such Debenture would have been entitled upon such capital reorganization.

Prescott, 531 F. Supp. at 215.

Also of interest is *Wood v. Coastal States Gas Corp.*, 401 A.2d 932 (Del. 1979). There, a corporation's preferred shareholders challenged a settlement that required the parent corporation, inter alia, to spin off a subsidiary and distribute a portion of the subsidiary's stock to the parent company's common shareholders. *Id.* at 935-36. The preferred shareholders argued that the spin-off constituted a recapitalization, thereby triggering an antidilution adjustment in their stock certificates. The court rejected this argument, holding that the settlement plan did not constitute a recapitalization. *Id.* at 941. Like *Prescott*, this case suggests that the term "capital reorganization" is not so elastic as the appellant claims, but it does not fully answer the question that we must decide.

Moving beyond the case law,[47] the meaning of the term "capital reorganization" in common legal parlance seemingly belies the appellant's ambitious definition. The preeminent legal lexicon defines "reorganization," in pertinent part, as a "[g]eneral term describing corporate amalgamations or readjustments occurring, for example, when one corporation acquires another in a merger or acquisition, a single corporation divides into two or more entities, or a corporation makes a substantial change in its capital structure." *Black's Law Dict.* 1298 (6th ed. 1990). The first two prongs of this definition are clearly inapposite here. That leaves only the question of whether a stock split entails a "substantial change in [a corporation's] capital structure." We think not.

First and foremost, the accounting mechanics that accompany a stock split are mere window dressing. *See generally* Robert S. Anthony & James S. Reece, *Accounting Principles* 37-39 (7th ed. 1995). To be sure, a stock split effected through the distribution of shares in the form of a stock dividend results in an increase in the common stock at par account and an offsetting decrease in additional paid-in capital, *id.*, but this subtle set of entries has no effect on total shareholder equity or on any other substantive aspect of the balance sheet. *See* FASB, Accounting Research Bulletin No. 43; *see also* III Cox, *supra* § 20.20 ("A share split-up does not, however, make any representations as to any accumulation of earnings or surplus or involve any increase of the legal capital."). Because a stock split does not entail a substantial change in a corporation's capital structure, the unelaborated term "capital reorganization" cannot plausibly include a stock split effected as a stock dividend.

D. Reclassification of Stock.

We turn next to the phrase "reclassification of stock." Two Massachusetts cases seem worthy of mention. In the first, a corporation took advantage of a new statute authorizing the issuance of preferred stock and amended its charter to divide its previously undifferentiated stock into common and preferred shares. *Page v. Whittenton Mfg. Co.*, 211 Mass. 424, 97 N.E. 1006, 1007-08 (1912). The Massachu-

[47] [12] The appellant attempts to leverage a solitary dictum from *Commissioner of Internal Revenue v. Marshman*, 279 F.2d 27 (6th Cir. 1960), into a broad proposition that stock splits are the functional equivalent of capital reorganizations. The reference, contained not in the *Marshman* court's analysis but in its factual overview, *id.* at 29, had no bearing on the merits of the case (which dealt with the tax liabilities stemming from a husband's surrender of a stock-purchase option, pursuant to a divorce and property settlement). Accordingly, *Marshman* does not advance the appellant's cause.

setts Supreme Judicial Court approved the corporation's actions. It held that a corporation could classify stock into common and preferred shares (providing preferred shareholders with cumulative dividends and a liquidation preference) so long as that classification was effected through a charter amendment. *Id.* at 1007. Although Page uses the verb "classify," we view what transpired as a reclassification. *See* XIII *Oxford English Dict.* 339 (2d ed. 1989) (defining "reclassify" as "[t]o classify again; to alter the classification of").

In *Boston Safe Deposit & Trust Co. v. State Tax Comm'n*, 340 Mass. 250, 163 N.E.2d 637 (Mass. 1960), the court considered the tax implications of a reclassification of stock. The reclassification in question involved the partial substitution of redeemable, convertible, cumulative, nonvoting shares for nonredeemable, nonconvertible, noncumulative, voting shares. *Id.* at 642. The court held that the reclassification constituted a taxable event under Massachusetts law. *Id.* at 643.

Our reading of the Massachusetts cases leads us to conclude that the sine qua non of a reclassification of stock is the modification of existing shares into something fundamentally different. At the end of the day, the stockholders in *Page* held a different class of shares, while the stockholders in *Boston Safe* gained some privileges while losing the right to vote. Thus, *Page* and *Boston Safe*, respectively, illustrate two ways in which a security can be altered fundamentally: (a) by changing the class of stock, or (b) by modifying important rights or preferences linked to stock.

Stock splits effected as stock dividends do not entail any such fundamental alteration of the character of an existing security. For example, Level 3's stock split in no way altered its shareholders' proportionate ownership interests, varied the class of securities held, or revised any of the attributes associated with the stock. What is more, the stock split did not have a meaningful impact on either the corporation's balance sheet or capital structure. For those reasons, we perceive no principled basis on which to stretch the definition of "reclassification of stock" to encompass a stock split.

A rule promulgated by the Securities and Exchange Commission confirms our intuition. This rule extends the protections of the Securities Act of 1933 to shareholders who are offered securities in a business combination and are required to decide "whether to accept a new or different security in exchange for their existing security." SEC Rule 145, 17 C.F.R. § 230.145 (preliminary note). While the rule extends to reclassifications of stock, it explicitly exempts stock splits from the reclassification rubric. *See* SEC Rule 145, 17 C.F.R. § 230.145. The upshot of this carve-out is unmistakable: the SEC does not consider shares received in conjunction with a stock split to constitute a "new or different security."

To cinch matters, while no Massachusetts statute defines the term "reclassification of stock," two states have enacted pertinent statutes. Under Louisiana law, a reclassification of stock is defined as

> amendment of the articles to change the authorized number of shares of an existing class or series; to authorize shares of a new class or series; to change the designation, par value (including change of par-value shares to shares without par value or vice versa), preferences, limitations or relative

> rights, including cancellation or modification of the right to receive accumulated dividends which have not been declared, or variations in relative rights, of the issued, and authorized but unissued, shares of any existing class or series; or to change the issued shares of any existing class or series into a greater or smaller number of shares of the same class or series (subject to such changes as the reclassification may make in the designation, par value, preferences, limitations or relative rights or variations in relative rights, thereof) or of another class or series, and to cancel any issued shares in connection with a reduction in the number thereof.

La. Rev. Stat. Ann. § 12:1 (West 2000).

The stock split effected by Level 3 implicates none of the categories established by the Louisiana legislature.[48]

Pennsylvania's statutory definition goes one step further; it expressly provides that the term "reclassification" excludes "a stock dividend or split effected by distribution of [the company's] own previously authorized shares pro rata to the holders of shares of the same or any other class or series pursuant to action solely of the board of directors." 15 Pa. Con. Stat. Ann. § 1103 (West 2001).

Although this case must be decided under Massachusetts law, we regard these statutes and rules as relevant and informative. *Cf. Ambrose v. New Engl. Ass'n of Schs. & Colls., Inc.*, 252 F.3d 488, 497-98 (1st Cir. 2001) (noting that, in exercising diversity jurisdiction, a federal court should consult case law from other jurisdictions when the forum state's highest court has not yet spoken). Moreover, they afford enlightenment as to common usage and as to what a reasonable person would (or would not) consider to be encompassed within the ambit of a particular term. So viewed, these statutes and rules reinforce our intuition that the term "reclassification of stock" does not encompass a stock split.[49]

To say more on this point would be supererogatory. Since Level 3's declaration of a stock split did not authorize a new class of stock, change the shareholders' proportionate ownership, alter the par value of the shares, or otherwise modify shareholders' voting rights or preferences, that action did not constitute a reclassification of stock.

---

[48] [13] While Louisiana's definition of "reclassification of stock" encompasses a "change in the issued shares of any existing class or series into a greater or smaller number of shares of the same class or series," we believe that a stock split effected as a stock dividend does not trigger this contingency. The stock split at issue did not involve a change in the "issued" Level 3 shares, but, rather, the issuance of new Level 3 shares. The distinction is subtle, but it is real: the Louisiana reclassification rubric is designed to have effect when changes in the voting rights, proportional ownership, and dividend entitlement of *previously issued shares* are on the agenda. That was not the case here.

[49] [14] We note that the corporate codes of two other states likewise contain references to stock reclassifications that fortify our reading of Massachusetts law. *See* Cal. Corp. Code App. § 1902 (West 2000) (listing accounting requirements for "reclassification of outstanding shares into shares of another class"); Md. Code Ann., Corps. & Ass'n s § 2-208 (West 2000) (requiring filing of supplemental articles if "board of directors classifies or reclassifies any unissued stock by setting or changing the preferences").

E. The Overall Plan of Reorganization.

The appellant also makes a conclusory claim that the July 1998 stock split was part and parcel of a comprehensive corporate reorganization (and, thus, animated the warrant's antidilution provision). He did very little to develop this claim below, and he has not remedied that shortfall on appeal. For that reason, we deem the claim abandoned. *See United States v. Zannino*, 895 F.2d 1, 17 (1st Cir. 1990) (explaining that, to preserve a point for appellate review, "[i]t is not enough merely to mention a possible argument in the most skeletal way, leaving the court to do counsel's work").

In any event, the claim lacks merit. As best we can understand it, the appellant hypothesizes that the stock split was an offshoot of a corporate reorganization launched by Level 3 in 1997. In that year, Level 3 shifted direction away from construction and mining activities in order to pursue its interests in communications and business services. Between August 1997 and May 1998, the company dramatically modified its capital structure by splitting off its construction business and eliminating two series of stock. Although none of these transactions involved XCOM or otherwise impacted the appellant, he implies that the July 1998 stock split, effected to increase the marketability of the company's shares as a prelude to raising capital in the public markets, should be viewed as an essential component of the company's overall capital reorganization and stock reclassification, thereby triggering the warrant's antidilution provision.

We reject the appellant's intimation that the stock split is magically transformed into a capital reorganization or reclassification of stock based upon its inclusion in a long-term business plan that also contains a number of more complex financial maneuvers. Taken to its logical extreme, the appellant' s argument invites us to deem *any* corporate activity engaged in by Level 3 while in the midst of reorganizing its capital structure as a capital reorganization and reclassification of stock. We are unable to perceive any principled basis on which we could accept this invitation.

. . .

G. The Denouement.

. . .

We have found no legal usage of the terms "capital reorganization" or "reclassification of stock" that supports the proposition that a reasonable person plausibly could have believed that either term encompassed a stock split. This is made crystal clear when one contrasts the warrant received by the appellant with a warrant issued by XCOM approximately ten months earlier to a different party — a warrant that contained more than six full pages of antidilution protections (including explicitly-worded share adjustments for stock splits and stock dividends). Moreover, the appellant has failed to adduce any credible evidence that the parties here somehow intended to adopt such an unusually expansive interpretation of the terms "capital reorganization" and/or "reclassification of stock."

If more were needed — and we doubt that it is — the maxim *expressio unius est exclusio alterius* instructs that, "when parties list specific items in a document, any item not so listed is typically thought to be excluded." *Smart*, 70 F.3d at 179. Here, the warrant's antidilution protection extended expressly to five designated contingencies: capital reorganizations, reclassification of the common stock, merger, consolidation, or sale of all (or substantially all) the capital stock or assets. Since nothing within the four corners of the warrant hints at additional contingencies, we apply this maxim and conclude that the parties intended stock splits to be excluded from the list of events capable of triggering the share adjustment machinery.

The appellant is left, then, with his reliance on the principle of *contra proferentum* the hoary aphorism that ambiguities must be construed against the drafter of an instrument. *E.g., Merrimack Valley Nat'l Bk. v. Baird*, 372 Mass. 721, 363 N.E.2d 688, 690 (1977). This reliance is mislaid. In order to invoke this principle, the proponent first must demonstrate that there is an ambiguity. *Shea v. Bay State Gas Co.*, 383 Mass. 218, 418 N.E.2d 597, 602 (1981). Here, the appellant has failed to show that the interpretation which he urges is, "under all the circumstances, a reasonable and practical one." *Id.* Accordingly, we have no occasion to apply the principle of *contra proferentum.*

IV. THE IMPLIED COVENANT OF GOOD FAITH AND FAIR DEALING

Although the terms "capital reorganization" and "reclassification of stock," as they appear in the warrant, are inherently unambiguous and do not encompass stock splits, the appellant mounts one further attack. He posits that Level 3 had a legal obligation, under the implied contractual covenant of good faith and fair dealing, to provide him with personalized, advance warning of the stock split. The appellant further argues that Level 3 breached this obligation by failing to advise him specifically about the adverse impact that the stock split would have on the warrant if the appellant did not exercise it before the record date. This argument lacks force.

Under Massachusetts law, every contract includes an implied duty of good faith and fair dealing. *Anthony's Pier Four, Inc. v. HBC Assocs.*, 411 Mass. 451, 583 N.E.2d 806, 820 (1991). This implied covenant forbids a party from doing "anything which will have the effect of destroying or injuring the rights of the other party to receive the fruits of the contract." *Druker v. Roland Wm. Jutras Assocs.*, 370 Mass. 383, 348 N.E.2d 763, 765 (1976) (quoting *Uproar Co. v. Nat'l Broadcasting Co.*, 81 F.2d 373, 377 (1st Cir. 1936)).

The most prominent flaw in the appellant's attempt to wield this club is that he misperceives the fruits of the bargain that he struck. After all, a warrantholder does not become a shareholder unless and until he exercises his purchase option. *See Gandal v. Telemundo Group, Inc.*, 23 F.3d 539, 546 (D.C. Cir. 1994); *see also* Fletcher, *supra* at § 2641 ("A warrant holder becomes a shareholder on the date that he or she attempts to exercise his or her warrant."). Consequently, a warrantholder's right to insist that the corporation maintain the integrity of the shares described in the warrant, if it exists at all, must be found in the text of the warrant itself. *Helvering v. S.W. Consol. Corp.*, 315 U.S. 194, 200-01, 62 S. Ct. 546,

86 L. Ed. 789 (1942). Put another way, the fruits of the contract were limited to those enumerated in the warrant.

An examination of the warrant reveals quite clearly that Level 3 was not contractually bound to provide the appellant with individualized notice of the stock split. The warrant contained language stating that "[u]ntil the exercise of this Warrant, the Holder shall not have or exercise any rights by virtue hereof as a stockholder of the Company." This disclaimer hardly could have been written more plainly.

Furthermore, the warrant contained a notice provision which, by its terms, pertained to "notices, requests and other communications hereunder." Applying the settled definition of "hereunder," Level 3 was only obligated to provide notice for events contemplated in the warrant agreement. *See* VII *Oxford English Dict.* 165 (2d ed. 1989) (defining "hereunder"). Because the warrant contained no provision that even arguably required Level 3 to furnish individualized notice of the stock split to the appellant, the failure to give such notice could not constitute a breach of the implied duty of good faith and fair dealing.[50]

An illustrative case is *FDIC v. LeBlanc*, 85 F.3d 815 (1st Cir. 1996). There, the defendant acquired a parcel of property with borrowed funds, securing the loan with a mortgage and personal guaranty. *Id.* at 817. The FDIC, as receiver, succeeded to the lender's interests. *Id.* at 818. When it sought to collect on the guaranty, the defendant asserted that it had breached the implied duty of good faith and fair dealing under Massachusetts law by refusing to take steps desired by the defendant but not required by the loan documents. *Id.* at 821-22. Discerning no evidence that the FDIC had deprived the defendant of the benefits of the loan agreement, we upheld an order for summary judgment in favor of the FDIC. *Id.* at 822. We emphasized that, in the absence of an agreement to do particular acts, Massachusetts law imposed no obligation on the FDIC to take the "affirmative steps" that would have benefitted the borrower. *Id.* While we readily acknowledged that the FDIC had taken a "hard-nosed" approach, we pointed out that it had "no duty at all" under the loan documents to act in the borrower's interest. *Id.* So it is here: Level 3 was under no obligation to act affirmatively by providing the appellant with individualized notice in the absence of a provision to that end in the warrant itself.

V. CONCLUSION

We need go no further. In light of the appellant's inability to show that a reasonable person plausibly could construe either "capital reorganization" or "reclassification of stock" to include stock splits, we conclude that these terms, as they appear in the warrant, were unambiguous and did not cover the contingency of a stock split effected as a stock dividend. It follows that the stock split in question here did not trip the warrant's antidilution provision. By like token, Level 3 did not

---

[50] [7] We note in passing that Level 3's general press release announced the stock split ten days in advance of the record date and provided the appellant with constructive notice of the stock split. Thus, the appellant had ample opportunity to exercise the warrant and avoid the dilutive effects of which he now complains.

breach the implied covenant of good faith and fair dealing by neglecting to give special notice beyond what the warrant itself required. The bottom line, then, is that the district court was correct in granting Level 3's motion for summary judgment.

Affirmed.

REISS v. FIN. PERFORMANCE CORP.

New York Court of Appeals
764 N.E.2d 958 (2001)

Smith, J.

The issue here is whether warrants to purchase shares of stock of defendant corporation must be adjusted in light of a reverse stock split authorized by defendant corporation after plaintiffs received warrants. We answer that question in the negative.

Shortly after September 30, 1993, in partial repayment of a loan, defendant authorized the issuance of warrants enabling plaintiff Rebot Corporation to purchase up to 1,198,904 shares of defendant's common stock for 10 cents per share until September 30, 1998. Defendant also issued warrants to plaintiff Marvin Reiss, in recognition of his services to defendant as a director of the corporation, entitling him to purchase 500,000 shares of common stock at 10 cents per share until August 31, 1998. Although a warrant issued earlier, on September 1, 1993, to Robert S. Trump was accompanied by a warrant agreement providing for a reverse stock split, no other agreement accompanied the authorization of the plaintiffs' warrants. Thus, the warrants given to Rebot and Reiss, unlike the warrants given to Trump, did not incorporate the warrant agreement provisions requiring adjustment in the event of a reverse stock split.

In 1996, defendant's shareholders approved a one-for-five reverse split of its common stock, and, as a consequence, each stockholder owned one-fifth of the original number of shares with the value of each share increased fivefold. In 1998, Rebot and Reiss sought to exercise a portion of their warrants, claiming that in accordance with the terms of the agreement, they were entitled to buy all of the stock specified in the warrants at 10 cents per share, without adjustment to reflect the reverse stock split. Defendant rejected the request. Plaintiffs thereafter initiated this action, seeking a declaratory judgment permitting the exercise of their warrants to purchase the full number of shares stated in the warrants at 10 cents a share. Plaintiffs also sought extension of the expiration dates of the warrants.

Supreme Court denied injunctive relief and dismissed the action. A divided Appellate Division modified by declaring judgment in defendant's favor. Relying on *Cofman v. Acton Corp.*, 958 F.2d 494 [1st Cir. 1992], the Appellate Division held that an essential term of the contract was missing and, according to its determination of the intent of the parties, supplied a term providing for adjustment of the number of shares stated in the warrants. . . . We now modify to reinstate the first cause of action for declaratory relief.

Duly executed stock warrants are contracts entitling the holder to purchase a specified number of shares of stock for a specific price during a designated time period. Here, the warrants are enforceable according to their terms. They have all the material provisions necessary to make them enforceable contracts, including number of shares, price, and expiration date, and were drafted by sophisticated and counseled business persons. As this Court stated in *W.W.W. Assocs. v. Giancontieri*, "when parties set down their agreement in a clear, complete document, their writing should as a rule be enforced according to its terms" (77 N.Y.2d 157, 162, 565 N.Y.S.2d 440, 566 N.E.2d 639 [1990]; *see also, Breed v. Insurance Co.*, 46 N.Y.2d 351, 355, 413 N.Y.S.2d 352, 385 N.E.2d 1280 [1978]).

Haines v. City of New York, 41 N.Y.2d 769, 396 N.Y.S.2d 155, 364 N.E.2d 820 [1977] is instructive. *Haines* involved an agreement between the City, the Town of Hunter and the Village of Tannersville under which the City assumed "all costs of construction and subsequent operation, maintenance and repair" of a sewage system and agreed to extend the sewer lines to accommodate the growth of the respective communities (*id.*, at 770, 396 N.Y.S.2d 155, 364 N.E.2d 820). From time to time, the City fulfilled its obligations under the contract. Fifty years after the contract agreement, the system reached full capacity and the City refused to grant the plaintiff permits for connections to its sewer lines on the ground that it had no obligation to further expand the plant or build a new one to accommodate additional development.

The agreement was silent as to the City's obligations in the event that the municipalities' usage exceeded the capacity of the plant which the City agreed to build. The municipalities, which had intervened in the plaintiff's action against the City, requested that the Court imply a term to the agreement to address this uncovered contingency by requiring the City to expand the sewage plant or construct new facilities to accommodate the new property development. The Court, however, declined to imply such a term where the contingency was clearly foreseeable by the municipalities, holding that "the contract does not obligate the [C]ity to provide sewage disposal services for properties in areas of the municipalities not presently served or even to new properties in areas which are presently served where to do so could reasonably be expected to significantly increase the demand on present plant facilities" (*id.*, at 773, 396 N.Y.S.2d 155, 364 N.E.2d 820). At the very least, *Haines* stands for the proposition that this Court will not imply a term where the circumstances surrounding the formation of the contract indicate that the parties, when the contract was made, must have foreseen the contingency at issue and the agreement can be enforced according to its terms (*see also, Rowe v. Great Atl. & Pac. Tea Co.*, 46 N.Y.2d 62, 72, 412 N.Y.S.2d 827, 385 N.E.2d 566 [1978]).

That the warrants do not address the contingency of a reverse stock split does not, of itself, create an ambiguity. "An omission or mistake in a contract does not constitute an ambiguity [and] * * * the question of whether an ambiguity exists must be ascertained from the face of an agreement without regard to extrinsic evidence" (*Schmidt v. Magnetic Head Corp.*, 97 A.D.2d 151, 157, 468 N.Y.S.2d 649 [1983]). "[E]xtrinsic and parol evidence is not admissible to create an ambiguity in a written agreement which is complete and clear and unambiguous on its face" (*W.W.W. Assocs., supra*, at 163, 565 N.Y.S.2d 440, 566 N.E.2d 639, quoting *Intercontinental Planning v. Daystrom, Inc.*, 24 N.Y.2d 372, 379, 300 N.Y.S.2d 817,

248 N.E.2d 576 [1969]). Even where a contingency has been omitted, we will not necessarily imply a term since "courts may not by construction add or excise terms, nor distort the meaning of those used and thereby 'make a new contract for the parties under the guise of interpreting the writing' " (*Schmidt, supra*, 97 A.D.2d, at 157, 468 N.Y.S.2d 649, quoting *Morlee Sales Corp. v. Manufacturers Trust Co.*, 9 N.Y.2d 16, 19, 210 N.Y.S.2d 516, 172 N.E.2d 280 [1961]).

Although defendant claims that to enforce the terms of the warrants creates a windfall for plaintiffs, the record evidences that the parties may have intentionally omitted incorporation of a warrant agreement containing a provision for adjustment for a reverse stock split. For example, one month earlier defendant issued warrant agreements to other investors that did contain specific reference to a reverse split adjustment provision. The Trump warrant agreement is one such agreement, providing that "if at any time or from time to time, the number of outstanding shares of Common Stock of the Corporation is decreased by a reverse split, consolidation or reclassification of shares of Common Stock, or otherwise, then, after the effective date * * * each Warrant shall be decreased in proportion to the decrease in outstanding shares and the then applicable Warrant Price shall be appropriately increased."

Further, *Cofman v. Acton Corp. (supra)*, the decision relied upon by the Appellate Division majority, is inapposite here. In *Cofman*, as part of a settlement agreement, a corporation allowed 12 partnerships (Partnerships) to make a one-time demand on the corporation for payment of a sum equal to the price of a share of common stock minus $7 multiplied by 7,500. This provision was a "sweetener," added to the settlement of $120,000, in case the price of a share of stock increased. Later, the corporation executed a reverse stock split, decreasing the number of shares and increasing the price of a share of common stock by a multiple of five. Partnerships sued the corporation for enforcement of the agreement, seeking to use the price of the stock after the reverse split to calculate the settlement. Partnerships argued that the plain language required that the warrants be valued as of the time of their exercise and the defendant corporation assumed the risk of a reverse stock split by not negotiating a different provision. The corporation also relied on the plain language of the warrants, contending that it was entitled to the value of the stock existing when the agreement was signed. The Massachusetts District Court found for the corporation.

Applying Massachusetts law, the First Circuit affirmed the District Court, concluding that Partnerships would not have agreed to a forward stock split because it could have eviscerated the value of the stock. The First Circuit held that the parties had not given any thought to dilution and that an essential term of the contract was missing. Just as Partnerships should not suffer by dilution of the value of the stock, so Acton should not suffer by reverse dilution.

The Appellate Division, applying the Cofman analysis, reasoned that, in the event of a forward stock split, supplying a term providing for the proportionate adjustment of the number of shares that could be purchased, and the exercise price, would be necessary to save the warrant holders from having the value of their warrants "eviscerated" (279 A.D.2d 13, at 18, 715 N.Y.S.2d 29). The Appellate Division then followed *Cofman* in taking a second step, reasoning that "just as plaintiffs should not suffer from the possibility of dilution of their warrants resulting from a stock split, so too Financial should not suffer from the consolidation of its shares resulting from a declaration of a reverse stock split" (*id.*, at 19, 715 N.Y.S.2d 29). The second step, however, does not necessarily follow from the first, particularly on these facts, where there is evidence that the parties contemplated including an adjustment provision but did not do so.

It may be that Reiss would be entitled to a remedy if Financial performed a forward stock split, on the theory that he "did not intend to acquire nothing" (*Cofman, supra*, 958 F.2d, at 497). We should not assume that one party intended to be placed at the mercy of the other (*Wood v. Duff-Gordon*, 222 N.Y. 88, 91, 118 N.E. 214 [1917]). It does not follow, however, that Financial should be given a comparable remedy to save it from the consequences of its own agreements and its own decision to perform a reverse stock split.

. . .

Accordingly, the order of the Appellate Division should be modified, with costs to plaintiffs, by remitting the case to Supreme Court for further proceedings in accordance with this opinion and, as so modified, affirmed. The certified question should be answered in the negative.

BERNSTEIN v. CANET

Delaware Chancery Court
1996 Del. Ch. LEXIS 63 (June 11, 1996)

CHANDLER, VICE CHANCELLOR

Plaintiff Brian Bernstein ("Plaintiff") owns 11,000 shares of Series A Cumulative Convertible Preferred Stock (the "Preferred Stock") of the defendant corporation, IVF America, Inc. ("IVF"), a publicly held Delaware corporation. Plaintiff brings this action on behalf of himself and on behalf of the remaining holders of Preferred Stock against IVF and IVF's directors (the "Director Defendants" and collectively with IVF, the "Defendants") in connection with IVF's offer to convert the Preferred Stock into common stock. Count I seeks a declaration that the offer to convert triggered the preferred shareholders' anti-dilution rights and IVF's duty to provide notice thereof. In Count II, Plaintiff asks the Court to require Defendants to adjust the conversion rate of the Preferred Stock and to give notice thereof to the holders of the Preferred Stock. . . .

Before me now are cross motions for judgment on the pleadings. Defendants ask this Court to grant judgment on the pleadings in their favor . . . and to dismiss the action . . . Plaintiff opposes Defendants' motion to dismiss and seeks partial judgment on the pleadings in his favor. All parties contend that the issue, whether the offer to convert triggered the preferred shareholders' anti-dilution rights, is ripe for decision. I heard oral argument on the cross motions on June 4, 1996.

. . .

I. BACKGROUND

IVF, a publicly traded Delaware company, provides services to clinical facilities and physicians practices that deliver assisted reproductive technology throughout the United States. In May of 1993, IVF issued two million shares of Preferred Stock to the public. In connection with the public offering, IVF filed a Certificate of Designation ("COD") with the State of Delaware which, in conjunction with Delaware law, governs the preferred shareholder's rights and preferences, as well as the limitations on those rights. *Staar Surgical Co.* v. *Waggoner*, Del. Supr., 588 A.2d 1130, 1135 (1991).

The COD provides that the preferred shareholders may convert their Preferred Stock into common stock at any time and from time to time (the "Conversion Right") and establishes a formula for determining the conversion rate. COD § 5(i), (ii). The COD also provides that if IVF takes certain specified actions which dilute the financial value of the Preferred Stock, then these actions trigger the COD's anti-dilution provisions. In those situations, the COD requires IVF to adjust the conversion rate (the "Anti-dilution Right") to maintain the parity relationship of the common and preferred shares. COD § 5. For example, if IVF sells or issues its common stock for a price less than $8.00 per share, then IVF must adjust the conversion rate following a specified formula COD § 5(ii)(E). Additionally, the COD also provides that within ten days of taking an action which triggers a conversion rate adjustment. IVF must notify the preferred shareholders in writing that it will adjust the conversion rate (the "Notification Right"). COD § (ii)(M).

The COD also limits the preferred shareholders' Anti-dilution Right by designating certain actions which IVF may take which are exempted from triggering the Anti-dilution right. For example, the Anti-dilution Right is not triggered "upon *conversion* of the Series A Preferred Stock." COD ¶ 5(ii)(L) (emphasis added) the "Exemption Provision").

In October of 1994, IVF initiated a change in its capital structure by offering its preferred shareholders the opportunity to convert each share of Preferred Stock into three shares of common stock plus a cash payment of $.20 (the "Offer"). At the time of the Offer, the COD provided preferred shareholders with the benchmark conversion rate of 1.1222 shares of common per one share of Preferred Stock. Since the Offer's conversion rate provided a greater number of shares than the benchmark rate provided under the COD, the Offer provided the Preferred Shareholders with an incentive to convert their shares before the Offer expired on November 10, 1994. Consequently, holders of over half of the outstanding two million shares of Preferred Stock accepted the offer and converted their shares into common stock. Following the Offer, IVF retired and cancelled approximately 1.149 million preferred shares and converted these shares into 3.449 million shares of common stock. The parties disagree as to the exact number of preferred shares that IVF retired and cancelled, but acknowledge that this dispute is immaterial.

The preferred shareholders who did not participate in the Offer retained their preferred shares and the rights and preferences associated with those shares. These preferences included (1) the right to cumulative dividends at the rate of $.80 per share; (2) the right, upon conversion, to receive for each share converted, 1.1222 shares of common stock, subject to adjustment; (3) the liquidation preference of

$10.00 per share plus accumulated and unpaid dividends. *See* IVF Prospectus at 20.

On December 13, 1994, Plaintiff filed a complaint alleging that the Offer triggered the preferred shareholders' Anti-dilution Rights as designated in the COD. Plaintiff contends that IVF breached its contract duty under the COD by failing to adjust the conversion rate following the Offer and by failing to provide notice of the adjustment to the preferred shareholders. . . . If the Court finds that the Offer triggered the preferred shareholders' Anti-dilution Rights, Plaintiff estimates that the COD's formula would adjust the conversion rate to three shares of common stock plus $1.60 per share of Preferred Stock.

. . .

II. ARGUMENT AND ANALYSIS

A. Principles Governing Preferred Shareholder's Rights

The parties agree that the preference and rights associated with the preferred stock are contractual in nature. *Wood v. Coastal States Gas Corp.*, Del. Supr., 401 A.2d 932, 937 (1979). Thus, the COD, as well as Delaware contract law, govern the Conversion Right in question. *Id.* Accordingly, I must apply principles of contract interpretation, reading the COD in its entirety, to determine the meaning of the provision in question. *Id., see also Sullivan Money Management, Inc. v. FLS Holdings, Inc.*, Del. Ch., C.A. No. 12731, Jacobs, V.C. (Nov. 20, 1992), Mem. Op. at 5, *aff'd.* Del. Supr., 628 A.2d 84 (1993).

Moreover, the parties do not dispute that Delaware law requires me to strictly construe the preferred shareholders' stock preferences. *See generally Rothschild Int'l Corp. v. Ligget Group Inc.*, Del. Supr., 747 A.2d 133 (1984). Under this rule of strict construction, preferred shareholders possess rights and preferences over common stock only if the COD clearly expresses the right. *Id.* at 136; *See also Sullivan Money*, Del. Ch., C.A. No. 12731 at 5. Thus, the Court may not presume that the COD grants a right, and instead must resolve any ambiguity against granting the alleged preference or right. *Rothschild.* 747 A.2d at 136.

Accordingly, unless Plaintiff can point to an anti-dilution provision which directly requires Defendants to adjust the conversion rate, then the preferred shareholders have no such right. *Hood v. Coastal States Gas Corp.*, Del. Supr., 401 A.2d 932, 938 (1979). However, even assuming that Plaintiff can point to an anti-dilution provision which applies to the Offer, the Defendants are not required to adjust the conversion rate if an Exemption Provision applies to the Offer. *Id., see also Wood*, Del. Supr., 401 A.2d at 942. If an inconsistency between these key sections exists, then specific language in the Exemption Provision section governing conversions controls over general language in Section Five regarding anti-dilution. *Cf. Wood*, Del. Supr., 401 A.2d at 941 (stating that specific language which exempts certain events from causing an adjustment to the conversion ratios controls over general language contained in the anti-dilution provision.)

B. Contentions of the Parties

Interestingly, all parties believe that if the Offer involved a "conversion," then the COD's Exemption Provision controls so that the Offer did not trigger the preferred shareholders' Anti-dilution Rights. Further, all parties presume that if the Court construes the Offer as an "exchange," then the Offer activated the preferred shareholders' Anti-dilution Rights.

In Defendants' view, Plaintiff has no right to the relief he seeks. Defendants argue that the COD's Exemption Provision expressly excludes any adjustment to the Preferred Stock's conversion rate where the holders of Preferred Stock convert their shares into common stock. Since in its prospectus, IVF offered to convert shares, rather than sell or issue shares, Defendants argue that the Offer did not trigger the preferred shareholders' Anti-dilution Rights.

Defendants also insist that Plaintiff may not re-characterize IVF's offer as an "exchange" offer. Defendants rely on the COD § 5(ii)(A) which establishes the procedure IVF will follow in converting the Preferred Stock into common stock. That section provides that, upon conversion, IVF will retire and cancel the Preferred Stock. IVF did, in fact, retire and cancel the Preferred Stock after the Offer. Thus, in Defendants' view, the Offer involved a conversion of stock by the plain terms of the COD. Defendants contend that the Court should follow the plain language of the COD and construe the transaction as a conversion rather than an exchange of stock.

Defendants cite *Shields v. Shields*, Del. Ch. 498 A.2d 161 (1985) in support of their position that IVF's Offer falls within the "conversion" category of the Exemption provision. In *Shields*, a shareholder sought specific performance of a shareholder's agreement, claiming that a stock for stock merger was, in effect, an "exchange" of stock which triggered his right of first refusal. The Court held that the merger involved a conversion of stock rather than a sale, transfer or exchange under the shareholder agreement, because the shares ceased to exist after the merger. Based upon *Shields*, Defendants here argue that, because the Preferred Stock ceased to exist after the exchange, the Offer involved a conversion.

Plaintiff, however, argues that the Offer did not involve a "conversion" of the Preferred Stock, but rather an "exchange" of that Preferred Stock for common stock valued at less than $8.00. Such an exchange, Plaintiff argues, triggers the COD's Anti-dilution rights. Plaintiff reasons that, at the time of the Offer, the market valued one share of Preferred Stock at $3.125 while one share of common stock was worth $1.00. Under the terms of the Offer, IVF provided to shareholders who accepted the Offer, three shares of common stock and $.20 per one preferred share. Thus, in Plaintiff's view, IVF sold or issued common stock in exchange for less than $8.00. Plaintiff argues that such an exchange triggered IVF's contractual duty to adjust the conversion rate pursuant to section 5(ii)(E) of the COD which provides that sales or issuances of stock for a value of less than $8.00 activates the Anti-dilution Rights provision. Notably, however, section 5(ii)(E) by its express terms does not purport to govern "exchanges." In addition, because the Offer triggered IVF's contractual duty to adjust the conversion rate, Plaintiff asserts the Offer simultaneously triggered the Defendants' contractual and fiduciary obligation to notify the preferred shareholders of the forthcoming adjustment.

Moreover, Plaintiff contends the Offer did not involve a "conversion." Thus, Plaintiff believes the COD's Exemption Provision does not exempt the transaction from triggering an adjustment to the COD's conversion rate. Plaintiff argues that the COD establishes the "definition" of "conversion" in Section 5(ii), entitled "Procedure for Conversion." That alleged "definition" establishes a benchmark conversion rate which, at the time of the Offer, entitled a preferred shareholder to receive 1.1222 shares of common and $.20 per one share of preferred. Plaintiff believes that the COD provides that a conversion only occurs if it occurs at the benchmark conversion rate. In other words, an offer with any conversion rate other than one to 1.1222, in Plaintiff's view, is not, in fact, a "conversion" pursuant to the COD. Since IVF extended the Offer with a different, albeit better, exchange rate (*i.e.*, one to three) Plaintiff contends that the Court should not construe the Offer as a "conversion" within the meaning of the COD.

In addition, Plaintiff cites *Coastal* for the proposition that the Court may not consider the generally accepted meaning of the term "conversion" in determining how to characterize the Offer. Instead, Plaintiff asserts that the Court must only consider the "definition" provided by the COD.

C. Analysis

While the COD provides a procedure in the event that a preferred shareholder exercises his Conversion Right, in my view, this procedure does not "define" conversion. The COD does not purport to provide a definition of conversion, nor does it capitalize the term for reference purposes. Furthermore, the COD does not prohibit IVF from offering to convert Preferred Stock at a higher rate. Instead, the COD merely guarantees preferred shareholders a benchmark rate of conversion. In fact, reading the COD as the Plaintiff suggests would provide the preferred shareholders with greater Anti-dilution Rights than the COD expressly contains. Such an interpretation is inconsistent with the rule of strict construction which provides that the Court must resolve any ambiguity against granting the preferred shareholder expanded rights. *Rothschild*, Del. Supr., 747 A.2d at 136; *Sullivan Money*, Del. Ch., C.A. No. 12731 at 5. Thus, I reject Plaintiff's contention that the COD provides that a "conversion" occurs only if the procedure in the COD is followed.

Moreover, quite opposite to Plaintiff's suggestion, I do not understand the *Coastal* Court to have prohibited this Court from using generally accepted financial terminology to decide the objective meaning of terms contained in a document. Instead, the *Coastal* Court merely noted that no precise definition for the term "recapitalization" exists, yet the Court accepted the general proposition that a "recapitalization" involved a shuffling of the capital structure. In spite of this general understanding of the term "recapitalization," the Court found the general meaning unhelpful in interpreting the document at issue in that case, and also found that case law from other jurisdictions did not use language comparable to the language used in that document. Thus, the *Coastal* Court determined whether a "recapitalization" had occurred by using only the language of the document itself.

In other situations, however, the Court has relied upon generally accepted financial definitions to determine the rights of preferred shareholders. For example, the *Rothschild* Court accepted Fletcher Cyclopedia's definition of the term "liquidation" in determining whether a transaction triggered the preferred shareholders' liquidation rights. *Rothschild,* Del. Supr., 474 A.2d at 136.

In the present case, while the COD provides a *procedure* for a preferred shareholder to follow to exercise his Conversion Right, this procedure does not "*define*" conversion. Thus, I reject Plaintiff's contention that a conversion occurs only if the procedure in the COD is followed. Since the COD does not, in fact, define the term "conversion," I use both the generally accepted definition of that term, as well as the language within the COD, to determine the issue. *Rothschild,* Del. Supr., 474 A.2d at 136.

In a second line of argument, Plaintiff suggests that, pursuant to *Sterling v. Mayflower Hotel Corp.*, Del. Supr., 93 A.2d 107 (1952), the offer constitutes an "exchange" because it was "voluntary" rather than compulsory. I, however, do not find this distinction helpful. Even the *Sterling* Court noted that the distinction between an exchange and a conversion for purposes of determining fair value in a merger transaction was "wholly unsubstantial." Fletcher Cyclopedia's definition of "conversion right" supports the *Sterling* Court's characterization of the distinction as unsubstantial, since Fletcher uses the term "exchange" within the definition of the term "conversion right:"

A conversion right is the right to exchange one's shares for a specified number of another class of shares.

Fletcher Cyc Corp § 5306 (Perm Ed). Furthermore, the section of the Delaware Code which grants corporations the authority to issue convertible stock uses the term "exchange" interchangeably with the term "conversion:" "Any stock of any class . . . may be made convertible into, or exchangeable for . . . the same or any other class . . . of stock of the corporation . . . ." 8 Del. C. § 151(e).

Since a "conversion" involves an exchange of shares, the parties' suggested approach to the present case of differentiating a "conversion" from an "exchange" is not helpful in determining whether the Offer is exempted from triggering a preferred shareholders' Anti-dilution Rights. Clearly, the Offer involved an exchange of preferred shares for a specified number of common shares. Thus, the transaction was a "conversion" according to the generally accepted meaning of that term. Moreover, since IVF followed the COD's conversion procedure by retiring the Preferred Stock it received, the Offer was a "conversion" under the terms contained within the COD, albeit at a higher conversion rate than the COD's benchmark conversion rate.

Having determined that one may properly consider the Offer as involving a conversion, I turn to the issue whether the conversion triggered the COD's Anti-dilution Right. As previously noted, the COD's Conversion Rights section lists certain events which trigger the Anti-Dilution rights. For instance, IVF's "sale or issuance" of common stock for less than $8.00 triggers the Anti-dilution Right. Also as noted above, Plaintiff must demonstrate that the Offer falls within one of these categories to invoke the preferred shareholders' Anti-dilution Rights. As explained above, Plaintiff's attempt to add the term "exchange" in this triggering section is ineffective first because the COD does not include "exchange" in its list of triggering events and, secondly, because the Offer involved a "conversion" rather than merely an exchange. Perhaps the Plaintiff would argue that the Offer involved an "issuance" of stock for less than $8.00 because IVF must have "issued" common stock to replace the Preferred Stock as part of the conversion procedure. Although this argument is plausible, it is important to note that, in the event of a conversion, the COD does not require IVF to adjust the conversion rate. Hence, reading the COD in its entirety, the terms "issuance or sale" which trigger the Anti-dilution Rights necessarily must involve situations *other than* conversions. Reading the entire COD, I conclude that the terms "conversion" and "sale or issuance" are mutually exclusive. I conclude that the Offer did not involve an "issuance or sale" of stock for less than $8.00 and, therefore, the Offer did not trigger the Anti-dilution Right provided in this section. Accordingly, Plaintiff has failed to point to any specific provision which affords Anti-dilution Rights to the remaining holders of the Preferred Stock. Since I may not presume that the COD grants a right, and instead must resolve any ambiguity against granting the alleged preference or right, and since Plaintiff has failed to point to an Anti-dilution Provision which directly required Defendants to change the conversion rate, I find that the preferred holder has no such right in this instance. *Wood v. Coastal States Gas Corp.*, Del. Supr., 401 A.2d 932, 938 (1979).

In the alternative, I may approach the issue of whether the Offer effects the preferred shareholders' Anti-dilution Rights by considering whether the Offer is exempted from triggering those rights by the COD's Exemption Provision. Again, the relevant language of the Exemption Provision is as follows: "No adjustment shall be made upon conversion of the Series A Preferred Stock." COD § 5(ii)(L). One could argue that the term "conversion" within the Exemption Provision means *any and all conversions* or one could argue that the exemption is limited to conversions at the 1.2222 to one rate specified within the procedure for conversions as established in the Conversion Rights section of the COD. The Exemption Provision does not define the term conversion; nor does it cross reference the term here with the previous sections. Further, the subsection does not attempt to limit this exemption in any manner, leaving the term "conversion" to be construed as broad and unrestricted. Moreover, considering the COD in its entirety, it [i]s clear that the drafters provided Anti-dilution Rights only in limited circumstances. Thus, a more narrow interpretation of the preferred shareholders' Anti-dilution Rights, coupled with a broad reading of the term "conversion" within the Exemption Provision, seems more consistent with the entirety of the COD. Therefore, I conclude as a matter of law that the Exemption Provision applies to the Offer since the offer involved a "conversion." Hence, the Exemption Provision prevented the Offer from triggering the preferred shareholders' Anti-dilution Rights.

BROENEN v. BEAUNIT CORP.

United States Court of Appeals, Seventh Circuit
440 F.2d 1244 (1970)

Swygert, Chief Judge

This is an action for damages and equitable relief brought by a holder of one $2,000 face value certificate representing two shares of 4 1/4 per cent convertible subordinated debentures due August 1, 1990 of Beaunit Corporation (hereinafter called "Old Beaunit"), a nonsurviving party to the corporate merger which gave rise to this action. Jurisdiction is based upon diversity of citizenship in that the plaintiff, who seeks to represent all such debenture holders for purposes of this action, is a resident of Wisconsin and none of the corporate defendants are residents of that state. The jurisdictional amount requirement of 28 U.S.C. § 1332 is satisfied by reason of the class nature of the claims asserted as noted and explained by the district court below.[51]

Plaintiff's claim is predicated on the theory that defendants each violated or caused the violation of the covenants of a certain indenture executed in August of 1965 between Old Beaunit and Manufacturers Hanover Trust Company ("Manufacturers Hanover") pursuant to which Manufacturers Hanover became trustee for purposes of the issuance and subsequent conversions, if any, of $25,000,000 principal amount of the above described 4 1/4 per cent convertible debentures of Old Beaunit. Plaintiff alleges that she purchased her two shares of the debentures on September 3, 1968 and has owned them continuously since that time without exercise of the convertible privilege.

On February 23, 1967, El Paso Natural Gas Company ("El Paso"), EPNG Corp. (a wholly-owned subsidiary of El Paso which was a mere corporate shell) and Old Beaunit executed an agreement of merger by which Old Beaunit was to be merged into EPNG in a three-cornered merger. The merger was effected on October 11, 1967, so that Old Beaunit merged into EPNG which simultaneously changed its corporate name to Beaunit Corporation ("New Beaunit"). On the same date, a supplemental indenture was executed by New Beaunit, El Paso and Manufacturers Hanover pursuant to the merger agreement and in compliance with the requirements of § 5.10 of the original indenture. The supplemental indenture provided, inter alia, that the conversion privilege inherent in the convertible debentures was to be exercisable so as to allow conversion of the debentures into common stock of El Paso, the parent corporation of EPNG (and, hence, of New Beaunit). It is undisputed that under the merger agreement and supplemental indenture a debenture holder who exercised the conversion privilege would receive the same number of shares of El Paso common stock upon conversion whether he converted immediately prior to or after the effective date of the merger.

Plaintiff's claim of injury derives from the fact that, as the parties all agree, the federal income tax effect of the post-merger relationship of the parties to the merger is such as to render the conversion of the debentures into El Paso common

---

[51] [1] *Broenen v. Beaunit Corp.*, 305 F. Supp. 688, 691-92 (E.D. Wis. 1969).

stock, should such occur, an exchange of property which requires recognition for purposes of taxation. The parties herein also agree that conversion would not have been an event requiring income tax recognition but for the three-cornered form of this particular merger. As Fleischer and Cary have noted:

> The so-called "convertible-bond rule" has been in existence since 1920. It was promulgated in Article 1563, Regulations 45, pursuant to the Revenue Act of 1918, and made applicable to subsequent revenue acts by a series of revenue rulings. The rule may be stated as follows: Where the owner of a bond exercises the right provided in the instrument to convert it into another security of the *obligor corporation*, the conversion is not considered a closed transaction for tax purposes and therefore does not result in the realization of gain or loss.[52]

Plaintiff asserts that the nonrecognition of gain or loss upon the exercise of the conversion privilege is a major inducement to purchase convertible bonds and that the loss of this attractive feature of Beaunit convertibles has caused a permanent reduction in the market value of the debentures. Plaintiff further avers that the cause of this reduction, the undesirable tax treatment of a postmerger conversion, derives from defendants having breached or having caused the breach of the original indenture.

The plaintiff and all defendants filed the briefed cross motions for summary judgment in the district court, and each defendant moved to dismiss the cause for failure to state claim upon which relief could be granted. El Paso also moved that service of process upon it be quashed and that the action against it be dismissed for lack of personal jurisdiction. The district court granted the motions of all defendants for summary judgment, denied all other motions and dismissed the cause. We agree that the defendants were entitled to summary judgment as a matter of law, and we affirm that finding of the district court for the reasons which follow. Since we affirm dismissal of the action against all defendants on the ground stated above, we find it unnecessary to pass on the other issues raised by defendants on this appeal.

Plaintiff argues that the form of the merger of October 11, 1967 violates certain covenants contained in §§ 13.01 and 13.02 of the original indenture between Old Beaunit and Manufacturers Hanover of which the debenture holders are, of course, third party beneficiaries. She urges that New Beaunit breached and that El Paso procured, precipitated and participated in breaches of the indenture. She further contends that Manufacturers Hanover violated its fiduciary duties or violated its specific obligations under the indenture, or both, by failing to object to such breaches, by failing to notify debenture holders of the breaches and by participating in the execution of the supplemental indenture which she contends violates the original indenture because of an allegedly unauthorized division of Old Beaunit's obligations thereunder.

Section 13.01 of the indenture provides in pertinent part:

---

[52] [2] Fleischer & Cary, The Taxation of Convertible Bonds and Stock, 74 HARV. L. REV. 473, 477-78 (1961) (footnote omitted and emphasis added).

> *Consolidation, Merger or Sale of Assets Permitted.*
>
> The Company covenants that it will not merge or consolidate with any other corporation or sell or convey all or substantially all of its assets to any person, firm or corporation, (i) unless . . . *the successor corporation* (if other than the Company) shall be a corporation organized and existing under the laws of the United States of America or a State thereof and such corporation [sic] *shall expressly assume* the due and punctual payment of the principal of (and premium, if any) and interest on all the Debentures, according to their tenor, and the *due and punctual performance and observance of all of the covenants and conditions of this Indenture to be performed by the Company* by supplemental indenture satisfactory to the Trustee, executed and delivered to the Trustee by such corporation, and (ii) unless the Company or such successor corporation, as the case may be, shall not, immediately after such merger or consolidation, or such sale or conveyance, be in default in the performance of any such covenant or condition. (Emphasis added.)

Plaintiff's argument is that the italicized language of the foregoing section of the indenture was breached by the substitution of El Paso common stock as the security into which the Old Beaunit debentures became convertible after the merger. She contends that as a result of the substitution, EPNG/New Beaunit did not assume the performance of "all of the covenants and conditions of this Indenture to be performed by [Old Beaunit]" after the merger, as required by § 13.01, but rather EPNG/New Beaunit assumed some of those obligations and El Paso assumed others, most notably the performance of many of the covenants relating to the post-merger exercise of the conversion privilege.

We find that no breach of § 13.01 of the original trust indenture occurred as a result of the form of the merger of October 11, 1967.

The effect and obvious intent of § 13.01 is that, for a merger to be permissible thereunder, any successor corporation to Old Beaunit must be legally responsible after the merger for the performance of the obligations of Old Beaunit vis-a-vis debenture holders. It is very clear from the supplemental indenture of October 11, 1967 that precisely such a state of affairs existed after the instant merger. The agreement of merger of February 23, 1967 provided in paragraph 3(f) that the conversion privilege of the Old Beaunit debentures would be exercisable in favor of El Paso common stock and required that:

> [A]n appropriate supplemental indenture shall be entered into between [Manufacturers Hanover] and [EPNG/New Beaunit], and El Paso if it is deemed advisable to include El Paso as a party, providing for the assumption of [the 4 1/4 per cent convertible subordinated] Debentures by [EPNG/New Beaunit]. . . .

The supplemental indenture as executed pursuant thereto contained three "articles." Article I, which was entitled "Amendments," contained amendatory language required by the merger to be substituted for that of the original indenture because of the changed identities and relationships of the parties, none of which was in derogation of any of the obligations of EPNG/New Beaunit to the debenture holders. Article II, which was entitled "Additional Provisions and Covenants," contained what its title Suggests, including a section 1 which provided:

> [EPNG/New Beaunit] hereby expressly assumes the due and punctual payment of the principal of (and premium, if any) and interest on all the Debentures, according to their tenor, and the due and punctual performance and observance of all of the covenants and conditions of the Indenture to be performed by [Old Beaunit].

The express and unambiguous language of section 1 of the supplemental indenture thus clearly rebuts plaintiff's contention which is the essence of her theory of this action, *i.e.*, that El Paso and EPNG/New Beaunit had wrongfully divided the legal responsibility of performing the obligations of Old Beaunit to the debenture holders as established by the original indenture. The foregoing language leaves no doubt that after the merger the primary and undivided responsibility for the performance of all obligations with regard to the debentures lay with EPNG/New Beaunit. Article III (entitled "Miscellaneous") of the agreement of merger similarly contained no provision in derogation of EPNG/New Beaunit's primary responsibility to the debenture holders. The relationship of the parties after the merger thus amounted to a substitution of EPNG/New Beaunit in all material respects with regard to the debenture obligations plus the addition of El Paso as a guarantor that its subsidiary would faithfully perform its duties to debenture holders.

Moreover, plaintiff's contention that the language of the original indenture must be construed as prohibiting a three-cornered merger as in the instant case is unpersuasive. Section 5.10 of the indenture provided as follows:

> *Provision in Case of Consolidation or Merger.*
>
> In case of any . . . merger of [Old Beaunit], the corporation into which [Old Beaunit] shall have been merged . . . shall execute and deliver to the Trustee a supplemental indenture providing that the holder of each Debenture then outstanding shall have the right thereafter . . . to convert such Debenture into the kind and amount of shares of stock and *other securities and property* receivable upon . . . such merger . . . by a holder of the number of shares of Common Stock of [Old Beaunit] into which such Debenture might have been converted immediately prior to such . . . merger . . . (Emphasis added.)

We find, as did the district court, that the language of § 5.10 expressly contemplated and authorized the substitution of "other securities and property" for common stock of the successor corporation as that into which the debentures are to be convertible after a merger. Plaintiff contends that this cannot be, because the language of § 5.10 was standard boilerplate in such indentures before such three-cornered mergers were permitted by New York law. While it is true that not until a year after the adoption of the Business Corporation Law in 1961 did the New York statutes authorize the exchange of "cash or other consideration" in a statutory merger such as took place here, it does not follow that § 5.10 must be construed so as to render it consistent with antecedent statutory law. It is an ancient principle of contract law that parties are presumed to have contracted with knowledge of and consistent with the law in effect at the time of execution of a contract. It must be presumed, therefore, that the parties to the indenture knew that at the time of execution of the indenture the applicable statute authorized the use of "other securities and property" as consideration in statutory mergers and that they understood and intended the obvious purport of the language of § 5.10 of the indenture to authorize such exchange.

Plaintiff also contends that each of the defendants breached § 13.02 of the indenture, caused such breach to occur, or failed to protest such breach or report its occurrence to debenture holders. She asserts substantially identical reasons for her position with regard to § 13.02 as those asserted regarding § 13.01. The pertinent part of § 13.02 provided:

> *Succession by Successor Corporation.*
>
> In case of any such merger, consolidation, sale or conveyance and upon any such assumption by the successor corporation, such successor corporation shall succeed to and be substituted for the Company, with the same effect as if it had been named herein as the party of the first part.

Defendants have asserted on oral argument that § 13.02 of the indenture is not a covenant at all, but merely represents a formal clause to insure continuity of interest for the benefit of the successor corporation upon the occurrence of any substantial change in corporate form or identity. However, we need not reach this point because we find that plaintiff's argument with regard to the alleged breach of § 13.02 is identical to that advanced regarding the alleged breach of § 13.01, i.e., that an impermissible division of assumption of duties occurred because of the form of the merger. Plaintiff's contention that § 13.02 was breached is thus bottomed on the same theory as her § 13.01 argument and must fail for the reasons we have stated above.

Moreover, plaintiff's claim would not succeed even were we to construe §§ 13.01 and 13.02 in the manner she asserts we must. Such a construction would generate some degree of conflict between §§ 13.01 and 13.02 on the one hand and § 5.10 on the other, it is true. However, as the district court aptly noted:

> . . . [Section] 5.10 is specifically addressed to the question as to what items may be used for conversions following a merger, whereas [§§ 13.01 and 13.02 deal] only with the obligations of a successor to a merger generally. Specific provisions must control general ones.[53]

Plaintiff has also asserted that El Paso, rather than EPNG/New Beaunit, should be treated as the real successor corporation following the merger. We find no validity in that assertion. We note that section 1 of the agreement of merger and section 1(b) of the supplemental indenture identity EPNG/New Beaunit as the "surviving corporation." "Surviving corporation" is defined by the New York Business Corporation Law as:

---

[53] [7] *Broenen v. Beaunit Corp.*, 305 F. Supp. 688, 694 (E.D. Wis. 1909) (citations omitted).

> The [existing corporation that is participating in a merger with one or more other corporations] into which one or more other [such] corporations have merged.[54]

"Surviving corporation" and "successor corporation" are thus obviously synonymous, and, in this instance, both refer to EPNG/New Beaunit. The gist of this contention of plaintiff appears to be an alternative theory that the indenture was breached because El Paso, rather than EPNG/New Beaunit was the successor corporation, and it did not assume all of the obligations of Old Beaunit to the debenture holders. For plaintiff to succeed on this theory, we would have to hold, in effect, that the presence of EPNG/New Beaunit in the merger was a mere sham to be disregarded. That we are not prepared to do. As the district judge said below, "While [EPNG/New] Beaunit has no separate shareholders of its own, it is a corporation separate from El Paso."[55]

Finally, we must comment on the overriding theory of plaintiff's cause of action which is that, because the nonrecognition of gain or loss for income tax purposes upon conversion of the debentures was a major attraction to potential purchasers, an unalterable commitment that nonrecognition would always obtain must somehow be implicit in the indenture. We do not believe that any such obligation was contemplated by the parties to the indenture or understood and relied upon by the purchasers of the convertible debentures. A chief reason for our belief that such was not contemplated is the fact that the favorable nonrecognition rule to which plaintiff adverts is derived from periodic revenue rulings which from time to time have reincorporated an expired treasury regulation into the mysteries of our burgeoning body of federal income tax law.[56] Such a precarious source for the nonrecognition rule would not lead a reasonable man to count heavily on its continuation, no matter how long it had been around. Revenue rulings are, of course, ephemeral, and anyone sufficiently sophisticated to understand the nonrecognition rule should certainly be capable of inquiring as to whether one could depend on continuity of its benefits.

In addition, it is clear that, even under the more restrictive New York Stock Corporation Law which the Business Corporation Law replaced, the surviving corporation either of a simple two-party merger or a three-cornered merger as took place here could have provided for exercise of the conversion privilege for stock warrants rather than for common stock of the surviving corporation consistent with § 5.10 of the indenture herein.[57] It is clear that a conversion subsequent to a merger where warrants were substituted for common stock for purposes of conversion would have been a taxable event.[58] The parties to the indenture thus clearly did not contemplate any warranty of nonrecognition on conversion.

The summary judgment entered for defendants by the district court is affirmed.

---

[54] [8] N.Y. Bus. Corp. Law § 901(a) (4) (McKinney 1963).

[55] [9] *Broenen v. Beaunit Corp.*, 305 F. Supp. 688, 694 (E.D. Wis. 1969) (citations omitted).

[56] [10] Fleischer & Cary, *The Taxation of Convertible Bonds and Stock*, 74 Harv. L. Rev. 473, 477-78 (1961).

[57] [11] *See* N.Y. Stock Corp. Law § 86 (McKinney 1951) (superseded in 1961).

[58] [12] Int. Rev. Code of 1954, § 354; Treas. Reg. § 1.354-1(e) (1956).

NOTE

It will be observed that Section 913(i)(2) of the New York Business Corporation Law, set forth in Section 1.07, *supra*, provides that a binding share exchange shall have the same effect as a merger upon the rights of holders of convertible securities issued by the corporation that is the subject of the binding share exchange. Presumably this subsection was added to the New York mandatory share exchange provisions because it is most unlikely that anti-dilution provisions make specific reference to mandatory share exchanges and, in the absence of such a specific reference, the holder of a convertible security may have no protection at all. *See, e.g., Broad v. Rockwell International, supra.*

§ 5.08 EFFECT OF REDEMPTION UPON THE CONVERSION RIGHT

VAN GEMERT v. BOEING CO.

United States Court of Appeals, Second Circuit
520 F.2d 1373 (1975)

Oakes, Circuit Judge

This appeal is from a judgment dismissing the amended complaint in a consolidation class action brought by non-converting holders of The Boeing Company's "412% Convertible Subordinated Debentures, due July 1, 1980." The complaint was jurisdictionally based on the Securities Exchange Act of 1934 as amended, the Securities Act of 1933 as amended, the Trust Indenture Act of 1939 as amended and the principles of pendent jurisdiction. The gist of the complaint was that the appellants and their class had inadequate and unreasonable notice of Boeing's intention to redeem or call the convertible debentures in question and were hence unable to exercise their conversion rights before the deadline in the call of midnight, March 29, 1966. Their damage lay in the fact that the redemption price for each $100 of principal amount of debentures was only $103.25, while under the conversion rate of, at a minimum, two shares of common stock for each $100 of principal amount of debentures, the stock was worth $316.25 on March 29, 1966, the cut-off date for the exercise of conversion privileges, or within 30 days thereafter, $364.00. The named appellants number 56, and the total loss alleged is over $2 million.

The United States District Court for the Southern District of New York, Sylvester J. Ryan, Judge, held that Boeing complied with the notice provisions spelled out in the debentures and in the Indenture of Trust Dated July 1, 1958 (the Indenture), between Boeing and The Chase Manhattan Bank (Chase), Trustee, and that it was required to do no more, that the Trust Indenture Act of 1939 was not violated; that if Boeing's Listing Agreement with the New York Stock Exchange (NYSE) were violated, it gave appellants no claim for relief; and that even if, as appellants claim, an adjustment in the conversion rate were required, and that failure to make the adjustment gave rise to a cause of action, appellants had no standing to raise the claim since they did not exercise their conversion rights. We reverse and remand on the ground that there was an obligation on Boeing's part to give reasonably adequate notice of the redemption to the debenture holders, which obligation was not fulfilled in this instance.

Most of the facts are not in dispute; indeed, we commend the parties, and the court below, for agreeing to a 59-page statement as to facts, incorporating some 55 exhibits, and to what certain witnesses would testify if called at trial.

THE ISSUE OF DEBENTURES

On July 15, 1958, each Boeing shareholder was given the right to purchase $100 of convertible debentures for each 23 shares of stock then held. The debentures were to pay interest of 4 1/2 per cent per annum and were to be convertible by the debenture-holder into common stock at a rate (subject to adjustment) of two shares per $100 principal amount of debentures. Chase was appointed trustee under the Indenture Agreement, and the debentures, as well as the stock reserved for issuance upon conversion of the debentures, were listed on the NYSE. Application for such listing had been made pursuant to a Listing Agreement between Boeing and the Exchange.

Subscriptions for a total of $29,578,500 of debentures were received and the balance of $1,019,100 was purchased by the underwriters. Chase as trustee then authenticated and the subscription agent delivered by registered mail the entire $30,597,600 aggregate amount of debentures in coupon form to the persons designated in the warrants surrendered or their agents, but no list of these was kept by Boeing or Chase.

A number of provisions in the debenture, the Indenture Agreement, the prospectus, the registration statement for the debentures and the Listing Agreement with the NYSE dealt with the possible redemption of the debentures by Boeing and the notice debenture-holders were to receive of a redemption call so that they might timely exercise their right to convert the debentures into common stock rather than have their debentures redeemed at face value. The debentures themselves provided:

> The holder of this Debenture is entitled, at his option, at any time on or before July 1, 1980, or in case this Debenture shall be called for redemption prior to such date, *up to and including but not after the tenth day prior to the redemption date, to convert this Debenture* . . . at the principal amount hereof, or such portion hereof, into shares of Capital Stock of the Company. . . .
>
> . . .
>
> > The Debentures are *subject to redemption* as a whole or in part, at any time or times, at the option of the Company, *on not less than 30 nor more than 90 days' prior notice, as provided in the Indenture*, at the following redemption prices (expressed in percentages of the principal amount) . . .
>
> . . .

> This Debenture may be registered as to principal upon presentation at the office or agency of the Company, in the Borough of Manhattan, The City of New York, New York . . .

(Emphasis added.)

The Indenture itself, a 113-page printed booklet, provides in Art. V, § 5.02, as follows:

> In case the Company shall desire to exercise the right to redeem all or any part of the debentures, as the case may be, pursuant to Section 5.01, it shall publish prior to the date fixed for redemption a notice of such redemption at least twice in an Authorized Newspaper, the first such publication to be not less than 30 days and not more than 90 days before the date fixed for redemption. Such publication shall be in successive weeks but on any day of the week . . .[59]

The Indenture also provided that debenture-holders who registered their bonds would receive notice by mail of any redemption call by the Boeing directors.

While the prospectus for the debenture issue did not refer to any registration rights, it did state that redemption could occur "on not less than 30 days' and not more than 90 days' published notice."

The NYSE Listing Agreement dated November 5, 1957, incorporated by reference into the listing application filed by Boeing in respect to the debenture issue, provided in Part III, Paragraph 4, as follows:

> 4. The Corporation will *publish immediately to the holders* of any of its securities listed on the Exchange *any action taken* by the Corporation *with respect* to dividends or to the allotment of rights to subscribe or *to any rights or benefits pertaining to the ownership of its securities listed on the Exchange;* and will give prompt notice to the Exchange of any such action; and *will afford the holders of its securities listed on the Exchange a proper period within which* to record their interests and *to exercise their rights*. . . .

(Emphasis added.)

Section A10 of the NYSE "Company Manual" specifically defines what is meant by publicity in the Listing Agreement:

> Publicity: The term "publicity," as used . . . below, and as used in the listing agreement in respect of redemption action, refers to a general news release, and not to the formal notice or advertisement of redemption sometimes required by provisions of an indenture or charter.
>
> Such news release shall be made as soon as possible after corporate action which will lead to, or which looks toward, redemption is taken . . . and shall be made by the fastest available means, i.e., telephone, telegraph or hand-delivery.

---

[59] [6] An "Authorized Newspaper" is defined as one published at least five days a week and of general circulation in the borough of Manhattan, N.Y. *See* Indenture, Art. 1, § 1.01.

> To insure coverage which will adequately inform the public, the news should be released to at least one or more newspapers of general circulation in New York City which regularly publish financial news, or to one or more of the national news-wire services (Associated Press, United Press International), in addition to such other release as the company may elect to make.

Section A10 of the Company Manual also provides specifically that when a convertible security is to be redeemed, the news release must include the rate of conversion and the date and time when the conversion privilege expires. It further provides that in addition to the immediate news release the company must give notice immediately to the NYSE itself, so as to enable the NYSE to take any necessary action with respect to further trading in the security.

THE CALL AND ITS CIRCUMSTANCES — HEREIN OF THE NOTICE ACTUALLY GIVEN

On February 28, 1966, the Boeing board of directors inter alia authorized the president, vice president-finance or treasurer to call for redemption on a date to be selected by them or any one of them, all of the convertible debentures outstanding under the indenture of July 1, 1958. That same day a news release, headlining 1965 sales and net earnings, and referring to a contemplated stock increase, stock split and post-split dividends, mentioned that "[t]he company's management was also authorized to call for redemption at a future date all of the company's outstanding 4 1/2 percent convertible subordinated debentures." This statement, which did not mention even the tentative dates for redemption and expiration of the conversion rights of debenture holders that had been settled upon, was released by the Boeing "News Bureau" nationally to the financial editors of the New York Times, the New York Herald- Tribune, the Wall Street Journal and other major national newspapers, in addition to the major wire services (Associated Press, United Press International and Dow Jones & Co.).

A short time after the February 28 board meeting, Boeing firmed up the key dates, complied with the indenture notice requirements and communicated to some extent with the Exchange proper. On March 2, 1966, at the home office in Seattle, at a meeting of Boeing officers, bankers and lawyers, it was decided to fix March 8 as the date for the first publication of the formal notice of redemption, April 8 as the redemption date and March 29 as the date for expiration of the conversion privilege. The second date for publication of the formal notice, March 18, was also fixed upon at this March 2 meeting, and Chase was notified to publish the redemption notice on those dates in all editions of the Wall Street Journal. All editions of the Journal carried the formal notices on March 8 and 18; the notices were in due form if not of extensive size.[60] It is conceded by the appellants that the formal requirements of the Indenture were met by the Company and Trustee.

It was not until March 7, the day before the publication of the first formal notice of redemption, that the NYSE was itself notified of the firmed-up dates for

[60] [7] We estimate their size as 5" x 5 1/2".

redemption,[61] conversion and notice. This was done by a telephone call from Company counsel in Seattle to the Exchange. While the court below found in part that "Boeing did comply with the publicity requirements of the Exchange" and while Company counsel "felt" on the basis of his telephone call "that we had complied with the recommended procedures [of the Stock Exchange Manual]," this finding and feeling are in the face of Boeing's response *admitting* appellants' demand for admission.

That Boeing did not issue any general publicity release, as that term is defined in Section A-10 of the New York Stock Exchange Company manual, concerning the call of the debentures during the period from March 1, through March 24, 1966.

This admission was reconfirmed by counsel for Boeing below and on appeal in the course of an "opening" statement to the court. The original news release of February 28 did not qualify since the dates of conversion and redemption had not been fixed and the Manual requires in the case of convertible securities that the publicity set forth "the rate of conversion and the date and time when the conversion privilege will finally expire" and that if such data are not known at the time publicity is given initially, "similar publicity shall be given immediately it becomes known or determined." The formal notices did not qualify since the Manual refers to a "general news release," and not to the formal notice or advertisement of redemption. In this regard it is interesting to note that a letter dated March 9 from the stock list department of the Exchange to Boeing indicates that "We have noted the recent advertisement advising of the call for redemption" and also asks for a copy of the authorizing resolution.

There was, in short, no general news release as called for by the Listing Agreement as amplified in the Company Manual until on the eve of expiration of the conversion rights, March 25, 1966, it appeared that $10,849,300 face amount of debentures — over one-half of those outstanding at that time — remained unconverted. At that point Boeing issued a press release[62] and then on March 28 the Company republished its earlier advertisement in all editions of the Wall Street Journal (Eastern, Mid-Western, Pacific Coast and South-West) and the New York

---

[61] [8] The Exchange had been sent a communication concerning the redemption on March 1, 1966, but at that time no redemption date had been established.

[62] [9] DEBENTURE CONVERSION DATE MARCH 29

Final date for conversion of The Boeing Company's 4 1/2 per convertible subordinated debentures to Boeing common stock is Tuesday, March 29, as announced in advertising by the company on March 8, 9 and 10.

The conversion rights provide for issuance of two shares of common stock in the company for each $100 bond. The company's notice of redemption announced that all outstanding debentures would be redeemed on or after April 8 at the redemption price of 103.25 per cent of their principal amount, together with accrued interest to that date.

Closing price of the stock as of March 25 was $154.5, representing a substantial advantage to holders of the bonds if the conversion is elected.

From January 1, 1965 through March 25, 1966, the sales price for the common stock of The Boeing Company ranged from a high of $175.25 to a low of $60.375 per share. As was pointed out in the notice of redemption, so long as the market price of the common stock is $52.24 or more per share, a debenture holder would receive upon conversion before the March 29 deadline, common stock having a greater value than the cash he would receive if he surrendered the debenture for redemption.

Times, and additional advertisements were placed. This later action had what the court below termed a "dramatic and widespread rippling effect." Some $9,305,000 of debentures were converted on March 28 and 29. The ripples, however, had not spread to the appellants' class by the midnight deadline on the 29th; they literally went to sleep with $1.5 million of debentures that were worth $4 million if only converted.

It is true, however, and the court did properly find, that in addition to the publication of the two formal indenture notices, notices of the dates of the call and the expiration of the conversion privilege on March 29, 1966, were carried on the following services: NYSE ticker on March 8, 23, 24, 25, 26 and 28, 1966; NYSE Bulletin on March 11, 18 and 25, 1966; The Commercial and Financial Chronicle on March 14, 21 and 28, 1966; Standard & Poor's Bond Outlook on March 19, 1966; Standard & Poor's Called Bond Record on March 9, 11, 18 and 25, 1966; Moody's Industrials on March 11, 1966. Articles about these dates were also carried in the Seattle Post Intelligencer on March 25, 1966; the Seattle Times on March 27, 1966; and the Financial World on March 23, 1966; and the notice was also carried in the Associated Press Bond Tables published on one or more days in at least 30 newspapers published in major cities across the United States. But almost all of these notices or items were in fine print, buried in the multitude of information and data published about the financial markets and scarcely of a kind to attract the eye of the average lay investor or debenture holder. On March 9, 1966, the listing in the New York Times for the convertible debentures read, for example: "Boeing cv 4 1/2 s 80." The change on March 10 was to "Boeing 4 1/2 s 80 cld," giving the investor in Dubuque or Little Rock or Lampasas only 19 days to pick up this change and figure that "cld" meant "called." Proof of the inadequacy of these notices lies in the fact that, despite the dramatic disparity between the value of the debentures unconverted and the conversion stock, over one-half of the debentures outstanding on the date of the first notice remained unconverted until the general publicity release on the eve of expiration of the conversion privilege.

Because the appellants place some emphasis on the fact, although we do not reach their contention of unreasonable notice based on it, we should mention that Boeing made no attempt to mail notice to the original subscribers (which could have been done at concededly nominal expense), and neither Boeing nor Chase inquired of or gave notice to collecting banks which had tendered for collection coupons bearing the payment dates of July 15, 1965, or January 15, 1966, the last two coupons before the redemption, either of which might have had some beneficial effect.

THE CONTENTIONS OF THE PARTIES

Boeing rests its defense primarily upon the notice specified in the debentures and Indenture, pointing out that in 1958 when the debentures were issued, "the risk that actual notice might not be received by subsequent holders of the debentures was clearly accepted by all even remotely familiar with the nature of such debentures." (Brief at 20-21.) It was "just such a risk" that led Boeing to extend to its stockholders and others who were investing $30 million in these securities the opportunity to register, an opportunity availed of by only 7 per cent of the debenture holders.[63] For the proposition that notice by publication provided for here was "standard and conformed with the custom and practice prevailing in the trade in 1958," we are referred by Boeing to *Gampel v. Burlington Industries, Inc.*, 43 Misc. 2d 846, 252 N.Y.S.2d 500 (Sup. Ct. 1964), where Justice Korn did not discuss the custom and practice in the trade but did hold that publication in the Wall Street Journal even during a newspaper delivery strike conformed to a provision in the Burlington Industries debentures similar to the one in the case at bar.[64]

There are four main strings to the appellants' bow. The first is that Boeing is civilly liable under federal law for violation of the NYSE Listing Agreement and Section A10 of the NYSE Company Manual since their requirements are an extension of the Securities Exchange Act of 1934 and an integral part of the statutory scheme under which exchanges are required to adopt rules, 15 U.S.C. § 78f, which may be ordered by the Commission to be altered, 15 U.S.C. § 78s, and the violation of which may give rise to a civil action under federal law. The second is that appellants are third party beneficiaries under state law of the Boeing-NYSE Listing Agreement, as amplified by the Company Manual. The third claim of appellants is that the Indenture is in the nature of a contract of adhesion, a standardized contract between parties of disparate bargaining power, unconscionable features of which are unenforceable as a matter of policy, a concept perhaps first advanced as to indentures of trust covering convertible debentures in a student note, *Convertible Securities: Holder Who Fails to Convert Before Expiration of the Conversion Period*, 54 Cornell L. Rev. 271(1969). The fourth ground is that the call was illegal and therefore void because it was based upon a conversion rate of 2.00 shares per $100 face amount of debentures when as a result of two stock dividends and an acquisition it should have been on a 2.05 or a 2.08 ratio.

THE FEDERAL LAW CLAIM

The claim that Boeing is civilly liable under federal law for violation of the NYSE Listing Agreement and Section A10 of the Company Manual is a colorable one. The Listing Agreement and Company Manual are "instruments corresponding" to rules of the Exchange within Section 6(a)(3) of the Securities Exchange Act of 1934. For the debentures here in question to be listed on the Exchange, application under the Listing Agreement had to be made. Boeing did not comply with the publicity requirements of the Exchange. In *O'Neill v. Maytag*, 339 F.2d 764, 770 (2d Cir. 1964), we did say, however, in the context of a stockholder's derivative suit arising out of an air carrier's purchase of its own stock, that a transaction which violated an Exchange rule did not give rise to a cause of action under federal law, at least against a listed company or its officers.

But as the Supreme Court held in *J. L. Case Co. v. Borak*, 377 U.S. 426, 84 S. Ct. 1555, 12 L. Ed. 2d 423 (1964), private parties have both derivative and direct rights of action to bring suit for violations of the Securities Exchange Act of 1934 and SEC

[63] [12] Through April 8, 1966, $1,838,000 in face amount of the debentures were registered as to principal and interest and $337,700 as to principal only; thus, approximately 7 per cent of the debentures were in fact registered so that their holders thereby automatically received notice from the trustee.

[64] [13] *See generally* Miller, *How to Call Your Convertibles*, Harv. Bus. Rev. 66 (May/June 1971).

rules and regulations issued thereunder, rights the explication of which take up a fair amount of Second Circuit judicial time. We extended this at least by dictum to include violation of stock exchange and securities dealers' association rules designed for the direct protection of investors, at least in a suit against an Exchange member, in *Colonial Realty Corp. v. Bache & Co.*, 358 F.2d 178 (2d Cir.), *cert. denied*, 385 U.S. 817, 87 S. Ct. 40, 17 L. Ed. 2d 56 (1966). There, Judge Friendly, speaking for a unanimous court, pointed out that "the concept of supervised self-regulation is broad enough to encompass a rule which provides what amounts to a substitute for a regulation by the SEC itself." 358 F.2d at 182. Again, "[a] particular stock exchange rule could thus play an integral part in SEC regulation notwithstanding the Commission's decision to take a backseat role in its promulgation and enforcement . . ." *id.*, giving as an example NYSE Rule 452 which prohibits a member from voting stock held in a street name without specific instructions from the beneficial owner. *Id.* at n. 4. Judge Friendly then went on to say that what emerges is that whether the courts are to imply federal civil liability for violation of exchange or dealer association rules by a member cannot be determined on the simplistic all-or-nothing basis urged by the two parties; rather, the court must look to the nature of the particular rule and its place in the regulatory scheme, with the party urging the implication of a federal liability carrying a considerably heavier burden of persuasion than when the violation is of the statute or an SEC regulation. The case for implication would be strongest when the rule imposes an explicit duty unknown to the common law.

. . .

Nevertheless, we do not now take the position that appellees advance and the court below apparently accepted, that violation of an exchange rule cannot under any circumstances give rise to civil liability under the federal acts. Such a position would be in conflict with our own most recent statements on this subject as well as some of the developing ease law.

It would also run contrary to a position we find inviting, that to the American investing public listing on the New York Stock Exchange carries with it implicit guarantees of trustworthiness. The public generally understands that a company must meet certain qualifications of financial stability, prestige, and fair disclosure, in order to be accepted for that listing, which is in turn so helpful to the sale of the company's securities. Similarly it is held out to the investing public that by dealing in securities listed on the New York Stock Exchange the investor will be dealt with fairly and pursuant to law. This would be particularly true as to the convertible securities market which differs from the market for other corporate debt in that it is composed primarily of individuals. Some investors miss the notices of redemption and of expiration of conversion rights, while others "do not know that they should look for them." Note, 54 CORNELL L. REV. at 274 n. 16.

Appellees argue, however, that the self-regulation system of the 1934 Act applies in its terms only to Exchange *members*, as opposed to *issuers*, and that the legislative history indicated congressional intention not to extend coverage of the Exchange rules and regulations to issuers. In this connection appellees maintain that Congress did consider such an extension as evidenced by a proposed § 12(b)(1) to the Securities Exchange Act quoted in Cong. Rec. 8584 (1934), which was never adopted. *Id.* at 85-86. The provision, however, was to require listed companies to agree with the Exchange to comply with the Exchange Act and the Commission's rules and regulations, and much of the debate related to whether the provision was necessary at all since such companies would have to comply with the law regardless of any such agreement.[65] Omitting the section in question would apparently indicate merely a recognition that the provision was unnecessary. The legislative history is thus at most equivocal on the question whether Congress intended to insulate issuers from liability in the event that they violated an Exchange rule.[66]

THE INADEQUACY OF THE BOEING NOTICE

The notice Boeing gave, we hold, had two deficiencies. First, Boeing did not adequately apprise the debenture holders what notice would be given of a redemption call. Investors were not informed by the prospectus or by the debentures that they could receive mail notice by registering their debentures, and that otherwise they would have to rely primarily on finding one of the scheduled advertisements in the newspaper or on keeping a constant eye on the bond tables. Second, the newspaper notice given by Boeing was itself inadequate.

The first factor we think highly significant. Many of the debenture holders might well have decided to register their bonds, had the significance of registration, or of the failure to register, been brought home in the materials generally available to the purchasers of the debentures. No detailed information as to notice was given on the face of the debentures, even in the fine print. The debentures stated simply:

> The debentures are subject to redemption, as a whole or in part, at any time or times, at the option of the Company, in not less than 30 nor more than 90 days' prior notice, as provided in the Indenture . . .

There was no indication that registration would mean that a debenture holder would receive mail notice. Nor was there any indication of the extent of newspaper notice to be provided — either as to the papers that would be used or how often the notice would be published. Debenture holders were simply referred by the debenture, as well as by the prospectus, to the 113-page Indenture Agreement, which, to be sure, was available to debenture holders or prospective purchasers

---

[65] [17] Senator Hastings made the following statement in connection with the legislation:

> I do not quite understand why they want to get the issuer of the security on record, in the form of an agreement, not to violate a particular law, because it must be admitted that, if the law itself is valid, and if the rules and regulations made by the commission are valid, and the person entering into the agreement has brought himself within the law by offering his securities for sale, then certainly, it seems to me, the point of compelling him to sign a paper that he will abide by the laws and rules made by the commission must have back of it something which those of us who studied the bill do not quite understand.

78 Cong. Rec. at 8585 (1934). While Senator Hastings' amendment was defeated, the language he objected to was deleted in conference.

[66] [18] Provisions of the Listing Agreement requiring the corporation to, e.g., "promptly notify the Exchange of any changes of officers or directors," Part 1, 2, would not seem to give rise in any event to a liability to a securities holder. The provisions of the Listing Agreement here in question, however, were to "afford the holders of its securities listed on the Exchange a proper period within which . . . to exercise their rights. . . ."

upon request, but which was not circulated generally with the warrants or debentures.

We have dwelt at length in the facts on the newspaper notice actually given. While it may have conformed to the requirements of the Indenture it was simply insufficient to give fair and reasonable notice to the debenture holders.

The duty of reasonable notice arises out of the contract between Boeing and the debenture holders, pursuant to which Boeing was exercising its right to redeem the debentures. An issuer of debentures has a duty to give adequate notice either on the face of the debentures, *Abramson v. Burroughs Corp.*, CCH Fed. Sec. L. Rep. [1971-72 transfer binder] ¶ 93,456 (S.D.N.Y. 1972) (Lumbard, C. J., sitting by designation), or in some other way, of the notice to be provided in the event the company decides to redeem the debentures. Absent such advice as to the specific notice agreed upon by the issuer and the trustee for the debenture holders, the debenture holders' reasonable expectations as to notice should be protected.

For less sophisticated investors (it will be recalled that warrants for the purchase of debentures were issued to all Boeing shareholders), putting the notice provisions only in the 113-page Indenture Agreement was effectively no notice at all. It was not reasonable for Boeing to expect these investors to send off for, and then to read understandingly, the 113-page Indenture Agreement referred to in both the prospectus and the debentures themselves in order to find out what notice would be provided in the event of redemption.

Boeing could very easily have run more than two advertisements in a single paper prior to the eleventh hour (March 28), at which time it issued its belated news release and advertised for the third time in the Wall Street Journal and for the first time in the New York Times. Moreover, in the same period that the debentures were in the process of being redeemed, Boeing was preparing for its annual meeting (to be held April 24). Proxy materials were being prepared throughout March and were finally mailed sometime between March 24 and March 30. Management could readily have arranged the redemption dates and the proxy mailing so that notice of the redemption dates could have been included in the envelope with the proxy materials. Thus at no extra cost except that of printing brief notices, at least all Boeing shareholders would have received mail notice, and presumably a significant number of the plaintiff class owned Boeing common stock, as well as debentures, in 1966. Had Boeing attempted such mail notice, or mail notice to original subscribers, and also given further newspaper publicity either by appropriate news releases or advertising earlier in the redemption period, we would have a different case and reasonable and sufficient notice might well be found.

. . . .

What one buys when purchasing a convertible debenture in addition to the debt obligation of the company incurred thereby is principally the expectation that the stock will increase sufficiently in value that the conversion right will make the debenture worth more than the debt. The debenture holder relies on the opportunity to make a proper conversion on due notice. Any loss occurring to him from failure to convert, as here, is not from a risk inherent in his investment but rather from unsatisfactory notification procedures. . . .

Of course, it may be suggested that the appellee corporation itself was not the beneficiary of the appellants' loss; rather, the corporate stockholders benefitted by not having their stock watered down by the number of shares necessary to convert appellants' debentures. But an award against Boeing will in effect tend to reduce pro tanto the equity of shareholders in the corporation and thus to a large extent those who were benefitted, one might almost say unjustly enriched, will be the ones who pay appellants' loss.

On the foregoing basis it is unnecessary for us to determine whether there is any cause of action under the Trust Indenture Act, as appellants contend. Nor, because appellants would not have standing to assert it, do we ground liability upon or make reference in the context of liability to appellants' argument that the call was illegal in the first instance because it was based upon an improper conversion rate.

DAMAGES AND THE "CONVERSION RATE"

We must, however, in remanding to the district court for a determination of damages, take note of the conversion rate argument which was rejected by the court below. That argument was essentially that the 4 per cent stock dividend declared in November, 1958, the 2 per cent stock dividend declared in November, 1959, and the acquisition by Boeing on March 31, 1960, of substantially all the assets of Vertol Aircraft Corp. necessitated an adjustment in the conversion rate of two shares of Boeing stock for each $100 of debentures in accordance with Section 4.05 of the Indenture.[67] At all times after these three transactions, Boeing treated the conversion rate as 2.0448. Because that rate was under 2.045, no adjustment was required under the Indenture § 4.05(f), which provided in part that

Whenever the amount by which the conversion rate would be changed in accordance with the foregoing provisions of this Section 4.05 is less than one-twentieth of a share of Capital Stock the Company at its option need not make such adjustment at that time.

Appellants on the other hand contend that the proper conversion rate was at least 2.045 or as high as 2.08.

On November 4, 1958, Boeing declared a 4 per cent stock dividend and issued 281,537 shares therefor. Section 4.05(b)iv states that in the case of shares so issued the consideration therefor shall be "deemed to be the number of shares so issued multiplied by the market value thereof."[68] Boeing initially calculated the market value by including the stock dividend shares in the number of shares outstanding to obtain the market value of the post dividend stock, i.e., by dividing the closing price

---

[67] [24] The section is four printed pages long and therefore will not be reprinted here in its entirety.

[68] [25] Market value in connection with a limited stock dividend is defined in Section 1.01 as follows:

> For the purposes of this definition market value shall mean the last reported sale price of the Capital Stock of the New York Stock Exchange (or if not listed on the New York Stock Exchange, then on any national securities exchange where listed) on the date of declaration of each stock dividend involved or, if there shall not have been a sale on such date, on the basis of the average of the bid and asked quotations therefor on said exchange on such date, or if the Capital Stock shall not then be listed on any national Securities exchange, on the basis of the average of the bid and asked quotations in the over-the-counter market on such date.

of the stock on November 4 of $56.875 by 1.04 since there were 104 shares where there had been 100. This resulted in a market value figure rounded off to $54.75 which, multiplied by the number of stock dividend shares issued, gave a total consideration therefor of $15,414,151.[69] On this basis the calculated rate was 1.9927 but since the indenture required that the conversion rate not be below 2.00, n.26 *supra*, the rate remained at 2.00. Appellants agree that the rate should be 2.00 but contend that the consideration for the stock dividend shares should be treated as at $14,076,850, the figure which would result from a flat 2.00 or $50 per share rate (above which stock dividend shares could not be valued under the limitations of Section 4.05(a), n.26 *supra*).

Initially the 2 per cent stock dividend of 147,489 shares on November 2, 1959, was treated by Boeing in the same way as the previous year's dividend. The November 2, 1959, closing price of $30.375 per share was divided by 1.02 to obtain a quotient of $29.77 which, multiplied by the number of shares (147,489), gave additional consideration of $4,390,748 to be added to the aggregate consideration (under Section 4.05(b)) after the prior stock dividend.

The gist of appellants' complaint about the conversion rate is that in connection with the acquisition of Vertol Aircraft assets in 1960 for 472,736 shares of Boeing, not only were the Vertol assets overevaluated and evaluated at the wrong time so as to obtain the highest evaluation, but the prior stock dividend adjustments were recomputed to the debenture holders' disadvantage. The argument is that all this was done having the conversion rate precisely in mind and with the purpose of keeping it at 2.044999 or below so as to avoid adjustment. (*See* Exhibit 28.)

The recomputation of the stock dividend adjustments was as follows. The full share price of $56.875 at the close of the 1958 dividend day was taken, that is, the stock dividend shares were not included in the number of shares outstanding. Thus the consideration received was calculated at $16,012,417 (281,537 x 56.875) rather than the $15,414,151 previously used. The same was done in connection with the 1959 2 per cent stock dividend, resulting in increased consideration of $4,479,979 rather than the $4,390,748 previously used. Appellants urge that Boeing thereby "added" consideration received of $1,935,567 from the 1958 dividend (because appellants would treat that as $14,075,850) and $87,843 from the 1959 dividend, thus leaving at the end of this recomputation a conversion rate of 2.0052 rather than one of 2.0161. But the lower court found, and we agree, that while appellants' computations, or at least Boeing's original ones, better represent the economic realities and more accurately follow general accounting practice, there was discretion in the Board under Section 1.01, n.25 *supra*, not to include the dividend shares in computing the market value.

In connection with the Vertol acquisition, the value placed on it for purposes of

---

[69] [26] That consideration and the number of shares issued were to be added to the initial consideration of $351,872,350 and 7,037,447 (valued at $50 per share) shares. Under the basic conversion rate formula the product of $100 and the number of resulting shares is divided by the aggregate consideration. The resulting quotient, adjusted to the nearest one-hundredth, shall thereafter be the conversion rate (until further adjusted) if it is greater than the basic conversion rate [of 2.00 shares for each $100 debenture]." Sec. 4.05(a). But if the adjusted rate is less than 2.00 the basic conversion rate of 2.00 governs.

determination of the conversion rate was the market value of the Boeing stock on November 13, 1959, at 3358, for a total of $15,895,748. Appellants argue that three different valuations would have been more accurate and fairer: the valuation on March 31, 1960, of the Vertol assets as recorded on the Boeing books at $12,435,138.47; that on January 18, 1960, when the contract of acquisition was signed and the Boeing stock worth 3058; or that on March 30, 1960, when the contract was closed and the Boeing stock worth 2418. Any one of these valuation measures would have increased the conversion ratio to over 2.045. But Section 4.05(b)(2) of the Indenture provided that "in the case of the issuance of shares for consideration in whole or in part other than cash, the consideration other than cash shall be deemed to be the fair value thereof as determined by the board of directors." The district court's finding was that there was not evidence that Boeing "had any purpose of deliberately hurting its debenture holders" and that while it was true that on November 13, 1959, the acquisition was still tentative, the board of directors had a colorable right to fix the fair value of the consideration as of November 13, 1959. That decision was one made, the court below found, in good faith and with the approval of accountants, auditors, investment bankers and counsel. Consequently, the court found that the decision was not subject to attack. See *Morris v. Standard Gas & Electric Co.*, 31 Del. Ch. 20, 63 A.2d 577 (1949). We do not believe the trial court's findings clearly erroneous. On those findings the conclusion of law was correct. In short, we affirm so much of the trial court's opinion as relates to the conversion rate.

Judgment affirmed in part; reversed and remanded in part.

MECKEL v. CONTINENTAL RESOURCES CO.

United States Court of Appeals, Second Circuit
758 F.2d 811 (1985)

Cardamone, Circuit Judge.

The issue on this appeal is whether there was a genuine issue of disputed fact as to whether notice of redemption was mailed to debenture holders advising them of their option to convert their debentures into common stock by a certain date. Appellants, agents for several debenture holders, instituted an action alleging that the holders failed to take advantage of the favorable conversion option because the redemption notice was inadequate. The substance of their argument below was, in effect, that "a word to the wise is sufficient," and since some holders did not act timely in their own best interests, the "word" obviously must not have been sent. The district court found that the notice given fully satisfied the legal obligations of those whose duty it was to give notice and granted summary judgment dismissing the complaint. We affirm.

I

Plaintiffs-appellants are the nine general partners of J & W Seligman & Co. (Seligman or Seligman partners), a New York brokerage firm, who brought suit in the United States District Court for the Southern District of New York (Stewart, J.)

against Florida Gas Company (Florida Gas) and its successor Continental Resources Company and Florida Exploration Company (jointly referred to as Continental) and against Citibank, N.A., defendants-appellees. The undisputed facts reveal that on April 1, 1969 Florida Gas issued $15,000,000 of 5 3/4% convertible, subordinated debentures, redeemable at any time, due 20 years later in 1989. The conversion price was $23.41 per share of common stock. Citibank agreed to act as trustee for the debenture holders and entered into an indenture agreement with Florida Gas dated April 1, 1969. Both the indenture agreement and the debentures themselves provided for notice to be given by a mailing. The debenture called for "notice by mail." Section 1105 of the indenture stated.

Notice of redemption shall be given by first-class mail, postage prepaid, mailed not less than 30 nor more than 60 days prior to the Redemption Date, to each Holder of Debentures to be redeemed at his last address appearing in the Debentures Register.

In June 1979 Continental Resources Company and Florida Gas agreed to merge. Incident to the merger, Florida Gas voted to redeem all outstanding 1969 debentures. It thereupon instructed Citibank to prepare and mail a redemption notice to debenture holders. The notice gave debenture holders until August 20, 1979, to convert their debentures into common stock.

Citibank claims that on July 16, 1979 it sent the redemption notice by first-class mail to the approximately 190 debenture holders. The market price of Florida Gas common stock on the New York Stock Exchange at the end of July 1979 was $48 per share, more than double the $23.41 per share conversion price available for debenture holders. As of August 20, 1979 slightly over one-half million dollars in debentures remained unconverted and 54 holders of these instruments had not exercised their conversion option. The Seligman partners sought to recover for the failure of three of their customers, for whom they were acting as agents, to convert their $42,000 worth of debentures into common stock. Seligman's damages arose from its voluntarily crediting these three customers' accounts for any losses they may have sustained, and not from any direct loss Seligman incurred as a debenture holder.[70]

The gravamen of the complaint is that defendants failed to provide adequate notice of redemption. The Seligman partners allege breach of fiduciary duty, unjust enrichment, breach of the indenture agreement and various violations of securities laws, including violation of Rule 10b-5. The partners also claim that the indenture, which provided that notice of a redemption need only be sent by first-class mail, is an unenforceable contract of adhesion. The complaint further asserts that Florida Gas breached certain rules of the New York Stock Exchange (NYSE or Exchange) by failing to issue a press release and provide general publicity concerning the redemption. Finally, the partners sought class certification on behalf of all those debenture holders who did not timely convert.

---

[70] [1] Seligman, as the registered holder of the debentures holding them in its own name on behalf of its customers, had standing to sue as the signatory agent of the holders. Fed. R. Civ. P. 17(a); *Bache & Co. v. International Controls Corp.*, 324 F. Supp. 998, 1004-05 (S.D.N.Y.1971), *aff'd* 469 F.2d 696 (2d Cir.1972). . . .

II

The record before us demonstrates that on July 16, 1979 Florida Gas directed Citibank to call the entire outstanding series of debentures, and that August 20, 1979 was set as the Redemption Date. In response to this request, a Citibank employee sent a notice of redemption to each holder by first-class mail, postage prepaid. Seligman was included in the mailing. Proof of mailing of the notice is established by the affidavit of a Citibank employee who "caused" the notice to be mailed, and by the affidavit and deposition of a Citibank manager who testified about the regular procedures Citibank used to mail notices to debenture holders.

The manager's affidavit and deposition testimony described the procedures Citibank used to assure proper mailing. After obtaining a mailing list from a computer registry, Citibank used four methods to verify that the number of labels, envelopes, stuffed envelopes and stamped envelopes conformed to the count of holders as of the record date. First, under the regular office procedure a computer generates a complete set of mailing labels based upon Citibank's registry of debenture owners and nominees. These labels are reviewed and matched against a separate printout. Second, after the employees of the mail room label the envelopes by machine, the machine counts the number of envelopes labeled and that number is checked against the number of labels delivered to the mail room. Third, a different machine encloses a notice of redemption in each envelope, which is sealed and metered. The number of envelopes sealed and metered is then compared with the number generated by the labeling machine, the computer printout, and the number of labels generated. The final check is when the postage meter is read to verify the number of envelopes to be mailed. The notices are then delivered to the Post Office. Seligman does not contend that its name and address were not accurately reflected in the computer registry. Nor is there evidence that any of the notices were returned to Citibank from the Post Office. Out of approximately 190 debenture holders, 54, or almost 30%, failed to convert prior to the redemption date.

Appellants' counsel conducted an informal survey of the 53 other debenture holders (in addition to Seligman) who failed to convert. A copy of a class action complaint accompanied each questionnaire. The purpose of the survey was to determine how many, if any, holders failed to convert because they had not received the notice. Accepting the district court's characterization of the results of the survey, we find that Seligman presented "an unsigned list of fourteen individual debenture holders, half of whom are described as stating that they never received notice and half of whom are described as stating that they have no recollection of receiving notice." *Meckel v. Continental Resources Co.*, 586 F. Supp. 407, 409 (S.D.N.Y.1984).

On April 16, 1984 Judge Stewart issued a decision granting summary judgment to Continental and Citibank. *Id.* at 411. He held that the indenture only required that the notice be sent by first-class mail, that there was no genuine dispute of the fact that Citibank had made a proper mailing, that there was no basis for imposing a duty higher than that imposed by the indenture, and that neither Florida Gas nor Citibank was required to give actual notice. Accordingly, the district judge dismissed all of plaintiffs' claims that were based on inadequate notice. Judge Stewart also dismissed the claims relating to alleged violations of the Rules of the

NYSE. He found that the Rules did not apply to these debentures because they were neither listed for trading on the Exchange, nor the subject of a listing application, and held it unnecessary to consider whether a private right of action exists under the Exchange rules. . . . Seligman's appeal challenges. the grant of summary judgment in favor of appellees Continental and Citibank and the resulting dismissal of Seligman's complaint.

III

Six of the eight claims contained in Seligman's complaint are based on its argument that defendants failed to give adequate notice of the redemption. First, appellants argue that the notice was inadequate as a matter of law under the Trust Indenture Act. Seligman urges that Citibank's failure to go beyond the terms of the Indenture — for example, by sending a follow-up mailing or using registered mail — violated its obligation of reasonable care and skill under the Trust Indenture Act . . . . The indenture provided that notice be given by first-class, postage prepaid mail. That is all the law required Citibank to do.

Trust indentures are important mechanisms for servicing corporate debt and banks play an essential role in the process that brings corporate financings to the public market. It is important that a bank's obligations with respect to notice be limited to those agreed upon, subject only to the requirement that the provision for notice be reasonable. That Congress recognized these significant economic considerations is reflected in [Section 15](a)(1) of the Trust Indenture Act. This governing statute specifically states that an "indenture . . . may provide that . . . the indenture trustee shall not be liable except for the performance of such duties as are specifically set out in such indenture." Paragraph 6.01(a) of the indenture states that "(1) the Trustee undertakes to perform such duties and only such duties as are specifically set forth in this Indenture, and no implied covenant or obligation shall be read into this Indenture against the Trustee. . . ." An indenture trustee is not subject to the ordinary trustee's duty of undivided loyalty. Unlike the ordinary trustee, who has historic common-law duties imposed beyond those in the trust agreement, an indenture trustee is more like a stakeholder whose duties and obligations are exclusively defined by the terms of the indenture agreement. *See Hazzard v. Chase National Bank*, 159 Misc. 57, 287 N.Y.S. 541 (Sup. Ct. N.Y. Cty.1936), *aff'd*, 257 A.D. 950, 14 N.Y.S.2d 14 (1st Dep't 1939), *aff'd*, 282 N.Y. 652, 26 N.E.2d 801 (1940), *cert. denied*, 311 U.S. 708, 61 S. Ct. 319, 85 L. Ed. 460 (1940).

Second, Seligman claims that the indenture provision is an adhesion contract because it only provides for notice by first-class mail, which, Seligman argues, is contrary to what a debenture holder might reasonably expect. In our view the provision in the debentures that notice would be given "by mail" was not inherently unfair or unreasonable and it satisfied the debenture holders' reasonable expectations as to the notice that they would receive. The debentures provide that they "are subject to redemption upon not less than 30 days notice by mail . . . at any time . . . at the election of [Florida Gas]" Appellants argue that this provision is ambiguous and that, properly construed, the debentures require more than a single first-class mailing of notice. They urge as authority *Van Gemert v. Boeing Co.*, 520 F.2d 1373 (2d Cir.), *cert. denied*, 423 U.S. 947, 96 S. Ct. 364, 46 L. Ed.2d 282 (1975), which held that the defendants were required to give notice which conformed to "the debenture holders' reasonable expectations as to notice," *id.* at 1383. Such "reasonable expectations," appellants contend, required defendants to mail notice by certified or registered mail, to make follow-up efforts to reach debenture holders who did not convert, or to supplement mailed notice with published notice. This argument is unpersuasive.

To begin, the debentures here were not ambiguous. They stated explicitly that notice would be given "by mail." The contrast with the debentures at issue in *Van Gemert* is striking. Those debentures contained no indication as to the type of notice of redemption that was to be provided. It was the total lack of a notice provision in the debentures that we held necessary as a condition precedent to an imposition of a duty to provide "reasonable" notice. Nor was the notice given here unreasonable. In *Van Gemert* the notice actually given and found by us not conform to the debenture holders' reasonable expectations was not notice sent by first-class mail, but rather notice given by publication in the Wall Street Journal. In fact, we strongly implied that notice by mail would have been adequate. *Id.* at 1384 (suggesting that including notice in mailing of proxy materials would have been reasonable). Moreover, appellants' argument that notice by mail is unconscionable because of the inequality of bargaining power and the probability that notice will not be received is contradicted by the very source upon which it relies. Note, *Convertible Securities: Holder Who Fails to Convert Before Expiration of the Conversion Period*, 54 Cornell L. Rev. 271, 279, 281 (1969) (recommending notice by mail). Therefore, even if the debentures had not been explicit as the form of notice to be given, we would remain unconvinced that notice given by first-class mail was unreasonable.

Third, Seligman attacks the legal sufficiency of Citibank's affidavits describing its regular office procedures, which served as its sole proof of compliance with the mailing requirements. Appellants contend that since Citibank did not submit an affidavit by a person with actual knowledge of the mailing or the routine office procedure, defendants' proof was insufficient and did not entitle them to the presumption of mailing and receipt. Appellants further argue that the employee's affidavit regarding her "causing" the mailing and the manager's affidavit describing standard office procedures were deficient as proof because neither affiant had personal knowledge, as Fed. R. Civ. P. 56(e) requires. They point out that the manager admitted in his deposition that he was not familiar with the transaction at issue because he "wasn't doing that work at the time." Similarly, the employee admitted that she had no recollection of anything pertaining to Florida Gas. Moreover, appellants continue, this employee did not work in the mailroom, go to the post office, state the procedures that were followed, and did not personally do the mailing. While this argument has superficial appeal, it is contrary to New York law. In *Bossuk v. Steinberg*, 58 N.Y.2d 916, 460 N.Y.S.2d 509, 447 N.E.2d 56 (1983), the Court of Appeals rejected the argument that there was insufficient proof of mailing "because the . . . employee who actually did so was not produced[,]" finding that "[t]he proof of the . . . regular course of business in this regard sufficed." *Id.* at 919, 460 N.Y.S.2d 509, 447 N.E.2d 56. Thus, under New York law personal knowledge is required only to establish regular office procedure, not the particular mailing. Here, the presence of such proof establishes prima facie evidence of the mailing and creates a rebuttable presumption as to receipt.

Fourth, appellants deny that they received the notice and allege that other debenture holders' non-receipt could be inferred from either their failure to convert or from their responses to the survey. New York law holds that when, as here, there is proof of the office procedure followed in a regular course of business, and these procedures establish that the required notice has been properly addressed and mailed, a presumption arises that notice was received. The mere denial of receipt does not rebut that presumption. There must be-in addition to denial of receipt-some proof that the regular office practice was not followed or was carelessly executed so the presumption that notice was mailed becomes unreasonable. *See Nassau Insurance Co. v. Murray*, 46 N.Y.2d 828, 829-30, 414 N.Y.S.2d 117, 386 N.E.2d 1085 (1978). Whether the sender's duty is to sound the drum-beat, send up the smoke signal, or mail the notice, proof that he performed suffices, regardless of what the receiver heard, saw, or read. Under *Nassau*, the controlling inquiry is only whether Citibank fulfilled its duty to send the notice, not whether the holders received it.

But there remains the question whether proof that notice was not received is evidence that it was not mailed. One recent New York case rejected this obverse of the presumption of receipt upon proof of mailing, and held that mere denial of receipt does not raise a question of fact as to mailing. *See Engel v. Lichterman*, 95 A.D.2d 536, 544, 467 N.Y.S.2d 642 (2d Dep't 1983) (rejecting position advanced by Gibbons, J., concurring and dissenting, that "if a letter were not received, then it should be presumed not to have been properly mailed," *id.* at 551, 467 N.Y.S.2d 642). Thus, Seligman's mere denial of receipt is not enough. Although appellants do not contest the adequacy of Citibank's regular office procedures, we do not read the memorandum decision in *Nassau* or the majority's opinion in *Engel* to hold that direct proof of divergence from routine procedure is the sole or exclusive means to rebut proof that notice was mailed. We think that in the context of a mass mailing there may be circumstantial evidence rebutting proof of mailing, without direct proof that the routine office procedure was either not followed or carelessly carried out.

The district court found that the only grounds to find disputed issues of fact were the inferences that might be drawn from the relatively small percentage of holders who converted and from the fact that seven of those who did not convert stated that they had never received notice and seven stated that they did not recall receiving notice. We agree with Judge Stewart that this evidence of lack of receipt is insufficient to create an issue of fact regarding mailing. The burden to produce such proof, after defendants demonstrated that they mailed the notice, fell to Seligman. *See* Fed. R. Civ. P. 56(e). In the circumstances of the present case, few inferences can be drawn from the percentage who did not convert. Many reasons-running the gamut from neglect to a belief that conversion will not be economically advantageous at that time-may exist for a failure to convert. In fact, a number of the non-converting debenture holders contacted in appellants' survey affirmatively stated that they had not converted even though they had received the notice mailed by Citibank. Moreover, the evidence of some holders who merely could not recall receipt is not the kind of proof that will defeat a presumption of mailing. Thus, it would take more substantial proof than that present in this record to create a genuine issue of fact warranting jury resolution of whether notice was properly sent.

IV

It is unnecessary for us to consider whether a private right of action exists under Section A2 of the Rules of the NYSE because the district court properly held that as the Florida Gas debentures were not listed for trading on the Exchange, Section A2 did not apply. *See* New York Stock Exchange Company Manual, § A2 (Aug. 1, 1977) (NYSE Rules applicable only to securities listed on the NYSE and subject to a listing agreement). Nor is there merit to appellants' argument that the debenture holders, as third party beneficiaries of the NYSE Company Manual and the Florida Gas Listing Agreement, had a right to published notice of the redemption. No suggestion that the contracting parties intended to benefit Seligman can be gleaned from the NYSE Company Manual or the Florida Gas Listing Agreement. *See Port Chester Electrical Constr. Corp. v. Atlas*, 40 N.Y.2d 652, 655, 389 N.Y.S.2d 327, 357 N.E.2d 983 (1976).

Finally, in view of our conclusion that appellants' claims are without merit, we find it unnecessary to address Citibank's claims that Seligman's own office procedure for handling mail was the proximate cause of its damages and that in any event Seligman would not have relied on the notice. . . .

Accordingly, the grant of summary judgment below is affirmed.

§ 5.09 STAND-BY PURCHASE ARRANGEMENTS

If the aggregate market value of the shares of common stock issuable upon conversion of an outstanding redeemable senior security is in excess of the aggregate redemption price of such senior security, the issuer can in effect cause a conversion of the entire senior security issue by calling the same for redemption. After the redemption date, the redeemable senior security is no longer outstanding and, therefore, if the senior security is a debt instrument, it no longer represents a liability of the corporation on its balance sheet; if it is a preferred stock, it no longer represents an impediment to the payment of common stock dividends. In order to obtain the cash that the corporation must pay to the holders of any such senior security, which may be redeemed without the holder exercising the conversion privilege, notwithstanding the value of the common stock, the issuing corporation may enter into an agreement with a "stand-by purchaser," usually an investment banking firm. The stand-by purchaser agrees to purchase from the corporation that number of shares of common stock of the corporation that would have been issuable upon conversion of the senior securities which have not been submitted for redemption on the redemption date. The purchase price payable by the stand-by purchaser for such shares of common stock is an amount equal to the aggregate conversion price of the senior securities that are actually redeemed. The stand-by purchaser is thus able to purchase the shares of common stock at a discount from the market price of such shares representing the difference between the aggregated current market price and the aggregate conversion price. The purchaser usually obtains an undertaking by the issuer to register such shares under The

Securities Act of 1933, and makes a public offering of the shares, realizing a profit thereon. In another form of the transaction the stand-by purchaser also accepts tenders of the security to be redeemed at a price in excess of the redemption price and then itself converts the security into common stock.

§ 5.10 EXCHANGEABLE SECURITIES

Exchangeable securities are senior securities that, upon surrender to the issuer corporation in accordance with the terms thereof, may be exchanged for securities other than common stock of the issuer. Set forth below are provisions generally found in a prospectus relating to a public offering of exchangeable debentures that may be exchanged for shares of common stock of another corporation. The shares of that other corporation are deposited by the issuer with an escrow agent that agrees with the issuer to deliver shares of such common stock upon surrender of the debentures for exchange. The issuer of the shares of common stock to be so acquired upon such exchange often has been a subsidiary of the issuer of the debentures.

Debentures

General. The Debentures are to be issued under an Indenture dated as of July 2, 2012 (the "Indenture") between the Company and Hobart National Bank and Trust Company of Chicago ("Hobart"), as Trustee ("Trustee"). The Debentures will be obligations of the Company, subordinate in right of payment to Senior Indebtedness of the Company as described in *Subordination* and secured to a limited extent as described in *Pledge of Securities.* The Debentures will be exchangeable prior to maturity, unless previously redeemed, at the exchange rate set forth on the cover of this Prospectus for shares of Subsidiary Common Stock, subject to modification, as described in *Exchange Modifications*, plus accrued interest. The shares of Common Stock for which all the Debentures are to be exchangeable (collectively, the "Subsidiary Shares") are to be deposited pursuant to an Escrow Agreement to be dated as of the date of the Indenture (the "Escrow Agreement") between the Company and Hobart as Escrow Agent ("Escrow Agent").

The Debentures will mature on July 2, 2027 and will bear interest from July 2, 2012 at the annual rate set forth on the cover of this Prospectus, payable semi-annually on January 2 and July 2 to holders of record at the close of business on the preceding December 15 or June 15. Interest will be paid by checks mailed to such holders. The Debentures will be issued in fully registered form only in denominations of $1,000 and multiples thereof. The Debentures may be presented for payment, registration, transfer or exchange at locations maintained by the Company pursuant to the Indenture.

Statements in this Section of the Prospectus are brief summaries of certain provisions of the Indenture and Escrow Agreement, do not purport to be complete and are qualified in their entirety by reference to the

Indenture and Escrow Agreement, copies of which are filed as Exhibits to the Registration Statement. The section references in this Section are to the Indenture, unless specified otherwise.

Exchange for Subsidiary Shares. The Debentures will be exchangeable, from the date of issue, for Subsidiary Shares, subject to modification, at an exchange rate of 22 Subsidiary Shares per $1,000 principal amount of Debentures (subject to modification), plus accrued interest, in accordance with procedures set forth in the Indenture. Only multiples of $1,000 principal amount of Debentures will be exchangeable. The right to exchange a Debenture will expire on the earlier of (a) the business day preceding the date fixed for its redemption or (b) its final maturity. *(Section 5.01).* In certain limited circumstances, the right to exchange may be terminated as described in *Termination of Exchange Right.*

Generally, accrued unpaid interest at the stated rate will be paid at the time exchange occurs. If any Debenture not called for redemption is exchanged between a record date for the payment of interest and the next succeeding interest payment date, the interest for the full six month period will be paid only to the registered holder of such Debenture as of such record date, but the exchanging Debentureholder will be required to pay an amount equal to any unearned interest so paid. The Escrow Agent will hold the proceeds of the exchange as collateral for the return of any such unearned interest. *(Section 5.03(e)).*

The Company will agree to use its best efforts to cause registration statements under the Securities Act of 1933 (the "1933 Act") with respect to Subsidiary Shares and any other securities to be deliverable upon exchange of Debentures to become and remain effective and prospectuses for such securities to be updated and other reasonable actions under federal and state securities laws to be taken to the extent necessary to permit exchanges. The Company has entered into a registration rights agreement with Subsidiary covering the registration of the Subsidiary Shares under the 1933 Act.

If the Company's counsel should determine that an exchange would be unlawful under the 1933 Act or otherwise, the Company would have the right to suspend its obligations to exchange until the Company's counsel determines such an exchange would be lawful. *(Section 5.04).*

The Escrow Agent shall not have the authority to exchange on a voluntary basis (for example, in the context of a cash tender offer) any of the securities held by it for cash, securities or other property. In certain situations this could be detrimental to the interests of the holders of the Debentures and might require such holders to exchange their Debentures in order to participate in any such voluntary exchange.

The Company will retain the right to vote the securities held by the Escrow Agent and may vote such securities in its own interest, which may be contrary to the interests of Debentureholders.

Pledge of Securities. The Company will pledge the Subsidiary Shares and other property from time to time deposited with the Escrow Agent as collateral security for the Company's obligations under the Debentures and the Indenture. *(Section 16.01).* The Escrow Agent will hold the collateral for the Trustee and Debentureholders. *(Section 16.06; Escrow Agreement, Section 25).* Debentureholders will have only limited rights in the collateral. Upon acceleration of indebtedness evidenced by a Debenture, its holder may elect to take from the collateral only the securities and cash allocated thereto deliverable upon such Debenture's exchange as if an exchange had occurred at the time of acceleration. If a Debentureholder elects to take collateral, such holder will have no further rights against the Company for principal or exchange, both of which will be deemed satisfied. *(Section 16.03).* Debentureholders could claim the status of secured creditors in the event of bankruptcy or similar proceedings against the Company, but if they do so, they will have waived their right to claims for deficiencies, except with respect to claims for interest past due at, or unpaid interest accrued through, the time of acceleration. The exercise of rights of the Debentureholders, like those of other secured creditors, may be subject to delay in bankruptcy or similar proceedings, and the Debentureholders' rights may be affected in such proceedings.

Federal Tax Consequences of Exchange. Under presently applicable law, gain or loss will be recognized by a holder of Debentures upon exchange of such Debentures to the extent of the difference between the fair market value of the SBS Shares or other proceeds of such exchange at the time of the exchange and the tax basis of such holder in the Debentures. If a Debenture is a capital asset in the hands of a holder, such gain or loss shall constitute a capital gain or loss, except that if the Debentures are found to have been issued with the intention that they be called before their stated maturity date as described under *Original Issue Discount on Debentures*, such gain would constitute ordinary income to the extent of the original issue discount not theretofore includible in gross income.

Cash Dividends. The Company will be entitled to receive and retain all cash dividends on the Subsidiary Shares and on any other securities deliverable upon exchange, to the extent paid out of retained earnings, consolidated earnings or earned surplus ("Cash Dividends"). *(Section 5.07(a)).* Any cash that is deliverable upon exchange of Debentures may be invested at the direction of the Company in certain qualifying securities. Any interest or gain on such investments shall be for the benefit of the Company. The Company shall be responsible for any losses on such investments. *(Section 5.06(b); Escrow Agreement, Section 12).*

Exchange Modifications. Various transactions relating to Subsidiary, such as mergers, recapitalizations or distributions other than Cash Dividends, could result in a modification ("Exchange Modification") of the property deliverable upon exchange. Generally, the property resulting from such modification will be held available for exchange, except that a sufficient amount will be sold to pay taxes of the Company attributable to the transaction. Except as set forth in the Indenture, no payment or adjustment will be made upon an exchange of a Debenture for any Cash Dividends.

Upon the occurrence of an Exchange Modification, the Company will order the Escrow Agent to sell all proceeds received in such Exchange Modification other than Equity Securities as defined below and to pay to the Company the amount necessary to pay the Company's taxes arising from the Exchange Modification and the subsequent sale. The taxes will be based on the Company's estimate of its marginal rate of taxation for the then current year. If necessary in certain circumstances, Equity Securities may be sold to obtain cash to pay the amount of such taxes to the Company. *(Section 5.07).* The net proceeds of any Exchange Modification with respect to the Subsidiary Shares or other securities deliverable upon exchange will then be allocated among all Debentures outstanding at the opening of business on the record date for payment or distribution or, if there is none, the effective date of such Exchange Modification. *(Section 5.07).* An "Equity Security" is an Subsidiary Share or any other investment security of a corporation which has the right without limitation as to amount either to all or a share of the current and liquidating dividends of such corporation, subject to the prior payments of dividends on securities of such corporation, if any, entitled to a preference. *(Section 5.02(b)).*

From time to time, the Company may segregate such property as it determines may be necessary to pay taxes, subject to calculations of taxes or determination of taxability, and such amounts shall be delivered to Debentureholders only upon determination that such amounts are not so necessary. If the Company contests or litigates the taxability of an Exchange Modification, the reasonable estimated costs of such contest will be paid out of the proceeds of the Exchange Modification. *(Sections 5.07(g), 5.13).*

Termination of Exchange Right. The right of Debentureholders to exchange Debentures may be terminated at the Company's election only if at any time the securities deliverable upon exchange do not include any Equity Securities. Such termination shall occur 30 days after the Company gives written notice thereof to the Debentureholders, noting which period Debentureholders will have the right to exchange Debentures, subject to the other provisions respecting exchange. *(Section 5.12).*

Redemption. The Debentures may be redeemed at the option of the Company after July 2, 2013 as a whole at any time or from time to time in part on not less than 30 nor more than 60 days' prior notice at a redemption price of 105% of their principal amount through July 1, 2019, and at 100% thereafter, in each case, together with accrued interest to the date fixed for redemption. *(Section 4.01(a)).* The Debentures will also be redeemable on like notice through the operation of the sinking fund described below.

Sinking Fund. The Indenture will require the Company to provide for the retirement prior to maturity, by redemption through operation of a sinking fund, of an annual amount equal to 10% of the maximum principal amount of Debentures that will have been outstanding at any one time at

100% of principal amount, together with interest accrued to the redemption date, commencing on July 2, 2020, and in each of the years thereafter to and including 2026. The Company may, at its option, receive credit against sinking fund payments for the principal amount of (a) Debentures acquired by the Company, and surrendered for cancellation, and (b) Debentures redeemed or called for redemption otherwise than through the operation of the sinking fund. Debentures not selected for sinking fund redemption and exchanged for SBS Shares or any other securities and cash deliverable upon such exchange will be credited against the remaining sinking fund payments pro rata; Debentures so selected and so exchanged will reduce the applicable sinking fund payment. *(Section 4.03).*

§ 5.11 NEW YORK STOCK EXCHANGE LISTING REQUIREMENTS REGARDING CONVERTIBLE SECURITIES RESERVES FOR CONVERTIBLE SECURITIES LISTING PROCESS

NEW YORK STOCK EXCHANGE COMPANY MANUAL

§ 703.07

(A) Policy

If a company intends to list a senior debt, warrant or equity security that is convertible into common stock, it should apply for the listing of the common stock reserved for conversion in the listing application for the senior debt, warrant or equity security.

If the company does not plan to list the convertible senior debt, warrant or equity security, it still must file a listing application in connection with the shares to be reserved for conversion of those securities. The application should be filed prior to the issuance of the senior debt or equity security regardless of when that security is convertible into the underlying common stock.

An adjustment of previously listed conversion reserves may be necessary if certain anti-dilution provisions of convertible securities are triggered. Since this normally occurs when the company is issuing additional common stock for some purpose, the adjustment of reserves should be included in the listing application filed in connection with that issuance, e.g., a stock split.

(B) Filing a Listing Application Relative to Reserves for Convertible Securities

The general instructions for preparation and filing of a listing application are described in Para. 703.01. The listing application format is presented in Para. 903.02.

(C) Supporting Documents

The following documents must be filed in support of the listing application. (If the company is listing a convertible security and the securities for the conversion reserve, it must file the documents required for listing the convertible security in addition to those outlined below.)

- Opinion of counsel.
- Prospectus — 4 copies, both preliminary and final.
- Current Form of Listing Fee Agreement (if not previously filed). (See Para. 902.01.)
- Current Form of Listing Agreement (if not previously filed). (See Para. 901.00.)

§ 5.12 POISON PILL PROVISIONS

[A] Introduction

A poison pill security is an instrument which, through utilization of an ingenious anti-dilution provision, effectively requires a potential acquirer to negotiate directly with the board of directors of a public target company instead of commencing an unsolicited tender offer or acquiring a significant amount of the target corporation's stock, as it would otherwise do. A poison pill security involves the utilization of the following corporate finance elements: (i) a distribution to common stockholders of rights to purchase securities of the distributing corporation; (ii) redemption for a minimal amount of such rights; and (iii) utilization of an anti-dilution clause. The provisions of a poison pill security (which in effect constitutes an agreement between a target corporation and its stockholders) are set forth in a Rights Agreement between the corporation and a banking institution that acts as Rights Agent for the stockholders. The role of the Rights Agent in a poison pill security is in some respects analogous to that of an indenture trustee, and the Rights Agreement is in some respects similar to a trust indenture.

As originally issued and distributed, a poison pill security is a right to purchase stock (usually preferred stock) of the issuing corporation at a price substantially in excess of the then and presumably future market price; by virtue of the operation of an anti-dilution provision, however, the right is changed into a right to purchase either shares of common stock of the issuing (target) corporation or of the acquiring corporation (if the target merges into it). In each case the purchase price is an amount equal to one half of the then market value of such securities, terms which would of course result in substantial dilution to an acquiring party or its security holders, and thus constitutes the "poison." Poison pill securities do not, however, constitute an insurmountable obstacle to an acquisition transaction. Instead, by virtue of the redemption feature of the poison pill security, the board of directors of a target company may, assuming a satisfactory agreement with an acquiring party is reached, either (a) redeem (and thus cancel) the poison pill security or (b) amend the terms of the poison pill security to make it inapplicable to the contemplated transaction. Were it not for the redemption feature, the implementation of a poison pill would in all likelihood constitute a breach of the fiduciary duties that the board of directors of a target company owes to its stockholders in a takeover context.

MORAN v. HOUSEHOLD INTERNATIONAL, INC.

Delaware Supreme Court
500 A.2d 1346 (1985)

McNeilly, Justice:

This case presents to this Court for review the most recent defensive mechanism in the arsenal of corporate takeover weaponry — the Preferred Share Purchase Rights Plan ("Rights Plan" or "Plan"). The validity of this mechanism has attracted national attention. Amici curiae briefs have been filed in support of appellants by the Securities and Exchange Commission ("SEC")[71] and the Investment Company Institute. An amicus curiae brief has been filed in support of appellees ("Household") by the United Food and Commercial Workers International Union.

In a detailed opinion, the Court of Chancery upheld the Rights Plan as a legitimate exercise of business judgment by Household. *Moran v. Household International, Inc.*, Del. Ch., 490 A.2d 1059 (1985). We agree, and therefore, affirm the judgment below.

I

The facts giving rise to this case have been carefully delineated in the Court of Chancery's opinion. *Id.* at 1064-69. A review of the basic facts is necessary for a complete understanding of the issues. On August 14, 1984, the Board of Directors of Household International, Inc. adopted the Rights Plan by a fourteen to two vote.[72] The intricacies of the Rights Plan are contained in a 48-page document entitled "Rights Agreement." Basically, the Plan provides that Household common stock-holders are entitled to the issuance of one Right per common share under certain triggering conditions. There are two triggering events that can activate the Rights. The first is the announcement of a tender offer for 30 percent of Household's shares ("30% trigger") and the second is the acquisition of 20 percent of Household's shares by any single entity or group ("20% trigger").

If an announcement of a tender offer for 30 percent of Household's shares is made, the Rights are issued and are immediately exercisable to purchase 1100 share of new preferred stock for $100 and are redeemable by the Board for $.50 per Right. If 20 percent of Household's shares are acquired by anyone, the Rights are issued and become non-redeemable and are exercisable to purchase 1100 of a share of preferred. If a Right is not exercised for preferred, and thereafter, a merger or consolidation occurs, the Rights holder can exercise each Right to purchase $200 of the common stock of the tender offeror for $100. This "flip-over" provision of the

---

[71] [1] The SEC split 3-2 on whether to interview in this case. The two dissenting Commissioners have publicly disagreed with the other three as to the merits of the Rights Plan. 17 Securities Regulation & Law Report 400; The Wall Street Journal, March 20, 1985, at 6.

[72] [2] Household's Board has ten outside directors and six who are members of management. Messrs. Moran (appellant) and Whitehead voted against the Plan. The record reflects that Whitehead voted against the Plan not on its substance but because he thought it was novel and would bring unwanted publicity to Household.

Rights Plan is at the heart of this controversy. Household is a diversified holding company with its principal subsidiaries engaged in financial services, transportation and merchandising. HFC, National Car Rental and Vons Grocery are three of its wholly-owned entities. Household did not adopt its Rights Plan during a battle with a corporate raider, but as a preventive mechanism to ward off future advances. The Vice-Chancellor found that as early as February 1984, Household's management became concerned about the company's vulnerability as a takeover target and began considering amending its charter to render a takeover more difficult. After considering the matter, Household decided not to pursue a fair price amendment.[73]

In the meantime, appellant Moran, one of Household's own Directors and also Chairman of the Dyson-Kissner-Moran Corporation, ("D-K-M") which is the largest single stockholder of Household, began discussions concerning a possible leveraged buy-out of Household by D-K-M. D-K-M's financial studies showed that Household's stock was significantly undervalued in relation to the company's break-up value. It is uncontradicted that Moran's suggestion of a leveraged buy-out never progressed beyond the discussion stage. Concerned about Household's vulnerability to a raider in light of the current takeover climate, Household secured the services of Wachtell, Lipton, Rosen and Katz ("Wachtell, Lipton") and Goldman, Sachs & Co. ("Goldman, Sachs") to formulate a takeover policy for recommendation to the Household Board at its August 14 meeting. After a July 31 meeting with a Household Board member and a pre-meeting distribution of material on the potential takeover problem and the proposed Rights Plan, the Board met on August 14, 1984. Representatives of Wachtell, Lipton and Goldman, Sachs attended the August 14, 1984 meeting. The minutes reflect that Mr. Lipton explained to the Board that his recommendation of the Plan was based on his understanding that the Board was concerned about the increasing frequency of "bust-up"[74] takeovers, the increasing takeover activity in the financial service industry, such as Leucadia's attempt to take over Arco, and the possible adverse effect this type of activity could have on employees and others concerned with and vital to the continuing successful operation of Household even in the absence of any actual bust-up takeover attempt. Against this factual background, the Plan was approved.

Thereafter, Moran and the company of which he is Chairman, D-K-M, filed this suit. On the eve of trial, Gretl Golter, the holder of 500 shares of Household, was permitted to intervene as an additional plaintiff. The trial was held, and the Court of Chancery ruled in favor of Household.[75] Appellants now appeal from that ruling to this Court.

---

[73] [3] A fair price amendment to a corporate charter generally requires supermajority approval for certain business combinations and sets minimum price criteria for mergers. *Moran*, 490 A.2d at 1064, n.1.

[74] [4] "Bust-up" takeover generally refers to a situation in which one seeks to finance an acquisition by selling off pieces of the acquired company.

[75] [5] The Vice-Chancellor did rule in favor of appellants on Household's counterclaim, but the ruling is not at issue in this appeal.

II

The primary issue here is the applicability of the business judgment rules as the standard by which the adoption of the Rights Plan should be reviewed. Much of this issue has been decided by our recent decision in *Unocal Corp. v. Mesa Petroleum Co.*, Del. Supr., 493 A.2d 946 (1985). In *Unocal*, we applied the business judgment rule to analyze Unocal's discriminatory self-tender. We explained: When a board addresses a pending takeover bid it has an obligation to determine whether the offer is in the best interest of the corporation and its shareholders. In that respect a board's duty is no different from any other responsibility it shoulders, and its decisions should be no less entitled to the respect they otherwise would be accorded in the realm of business judgment. *Id.* at 954 (citation and footnote omitted). Other jurisdictions have also applied the business judgment rule to actions by which target companies have sought to forestall takeover activity they considered undesirable. *See Gearhart Industries, Inc. v. Smith International*, 5th Cir., 741 F.2d 707 (1984) (sale of discounted subordinate debentures containing springing warrants); *Treco, Inc. v. Land of Lincoln Savings and Loan*, 7th Cir., 749 F.2d 374 (1984) (amendment to by-laws); *Panter v. Marshall Field*, 7th Cir., 646 F.2d 271 (1981) (acquisitions to create antitrust problems); *Johnson v. Trueblood*, 3rd Cir., 629 F.2d 287 (1980), *cert. denied*, 450 U.S. 999, 101 S. Ct. 1704, 68 L. Ed. 2d 200 (1981) (refused to tender); *Crouse-Hinds Co. v. InterNorth, Inc.*, 2d Cir., 634 F.2d 690 (1980) (sale of stock to favored party); *Treadway v. Cane Corp.*, 2d Cir., 638 F.2d 357 (1980) (sale to White Knight), *Enterra Corp. v. SGS Associates*, E.D. Pa., 600 F. Supp. 678 (1985) (standstill agreement); *Buffalo Forge Co. v. Ogden Corp.*, W.D.N.Y., 555 F. Supp. 892, *aff'd*, (2d Cir.) 717 F.2d 757, *cert. denied*, 464 U.S. 1018, 104 S. Ct. 550, 78 L. Ed. 2d 724 (1983) (sale of treasury shares and grant of stock option to White Knight); *Whittaker Corp. v. Edgar*, N.D. Ill., 535 F. Supp. 933 (1982) (disposal of valuable assets); *Martin Marietta Corp. v. Bendix Corp.*, D. MD., 549 F. Supp. 623 (1982) (Pac-Man defense).[76]

This case is distinguished from the ones cited, since here we have a defensive mechanism adopted to ward off possible future advances and not a mechanism adopted in reaction to a specific threat. This distinguishing factor does not result in the Directors losing the protection of the business judgment rule. To the contrary, pre-planning for the contingency of a hostile takeover might reduce the risk that, under the pressure of a takeover bid, management will fail to exercise reasonable judgment. Therefore, in reviewing a pre-planned defensive mechanism it seems even more appropriate to apply the business judgment rule. *See Warner Communications v. Murdoch*, D. Del., 581 F. Supp. 1482, 1491 (1984).

Of course, the business judgment rule can only sustain corporate decision making or transactions that are within the power or authority of the Board. Therefore, before the business judgment rule can be applied it must be determined whether the Directors were authorized to adopt the Rights Plan.

---

[76] [6] The "Pac-Man" defense is generally a target company countering an unwanted tender offer by making its own tender offer for stock of the would-be acquirer. Block & Miller, *The Responsibilities and Obligations of Corporate Directors in Takeover Contests*, 11 Sec. Reg. L.J. 44, 64 (1983).

III

Appellants vehemently contend that the Board of Directors was unauthorized to adopt the Rights Plan. First, appellants contend that no provision of the Delaware General Corporation Law authorizes the issuance of such Rights. Secondly, appellants, along with the SEC, contend that the Board is unauthorized to usurp stockholders' rights to receive hostile tender offers. Third, appellants and the SEC also contend that the Board is unauthorized to fundamentally restrict stockholders' rights to conduct a proxy contest. We address each of these contentions in turn.

A.

While appellants contend that no provision of the Delaware General Corporation Law authorizes the Rights Plan, Household contends that the Rights Plan was issued pursuant to 8 Del. C. §§ 151(g) and 157. It explains that the Rights are authorized by § 157[77] and the issue of preferred stock underlying the Rights is authorized by § 151.[78] Appellants respond by making several attacks upon the authority to issue the Rights pursuant to § 157.

Appellants begin by contending that § 157 cannot authorize the Rights Plan since § 157 has never served the purpose of authorizing a takeover defense. Appellants contend that § 157 is a corporate financing statute, and that nothing in its legislative history suggests a purpose that has anything to do with corporate control or a takeover defense. Appellants are unable to demonstrate that the legislature, in its adoption of § 157, meant to limit the applicability of § 157 to only the issuance of Rights for the purposes of corporate financing. Without such affirmative evidence, we decline to impose such a limitation upon the section that the legislature has not. *Compare Providence & Worchester Co. v. Baker*, Del. Supr., 378 A.2d 121, 124 (1977) (refused to read a bar to protective voting provisions into 8 Del. C. § 212(a)). As we noted in *Unocal:* [O]ur corporate law is not static. It must grow and develop in response to, indeed in anticipation of, evolving concepts and needs. Merely because the General Corporation Law is silent as to a specific matter does not mean that it is prohibited. 493 A.2d at 957. *See also Cheff v. Mathes* Del. Supr., 199 A.2d 548 (1964). Secondly, appellants contend that § 157 does not authorize the issuance of sham rights such as the Rights Plan. They contend that the Rights were designed

---

[77] [7] The power to issue rights to purchase shares is conferred by 8 Del. C. § 157 which provides in relevant part: Subject to any provisions in the certificate of incorporation, every corporation may create and issue, whether or not in connection with the issue and sale of any shares of stock or other securities of the corporation, rights or options entitling the holders thereof to purchase from the corporation any shares of its capital stock of any class or classes, such rights or options to be evidenced by or in such instrument or instruments as shall be approved by the board of directors.

[78] [8] Del. C. § 151(g) provides in relevant part: When any corporation desires to issue any shares of stock of any class or of any series of any class of which the voting powers, designations, preferences and relative, participating, optional or other rights, if any, or the qualifications, limitations or restrictions thereof, if any, shall not have been set forth in the certificate of incorporation or in any amendment thereto but shall be provided for in a resolution or resolutions adopted by the board of directors pursuant to authority expressly vested in it by the provisions of the certificate of incorporation or any amendment thereto, a certificate setting forth a copy of such resolution or resolutions and the number of shares of stock of such class or series shall be executed, acknowledged, filed, recorded, and shall become effective, in accordance with § 103 of this title.

never to be exercised, and that the plan has no economic value. In addition, they contend the preferred stock made subject to the Rights is also illusory, citing *Telvest, Inc. v. Olson*, Del. Ch., C.A. No 5798, Brown, V.C. (March 8, 1979). Appellants' sham contention fails in both regards. As to the Rights, they can and will be exercised upon the happening of a triggering mechanism, as we have observed during the current struggle of Sir James Goldsmith to take control of Crown Zellerbach. See Wall Street Journal, July 26, 1985, at 3, 12. As to the preferred shares, we agree with the Court of Chancery that they are distinguishable from sham securities invalidated in *Telvest, supra.* The Household preferred, issuable upon the happening of a triggering event, have superior dividend and liquidation rights. Third, appellants contend that § 157 authorizes the issuance of Rights "entitling holders thereof to purchase from the corporation any shares of its capital stock of any class. . . ." Therefore, their contention continues, the plain language of the statute does not authorize Household to issue rights to purchase another's capital stock upon a merger or consolidation. Household contends, inter alia, that the Rights Plan is analogous to "anti-destruction" or "anti-dilution" provisions which are customary features of a wide variety of corporate securities. While appellants seem to concede that "anti-destruction" provisions are valid under Delaware corporate law, they seek to distinguish the Rights Plan as not being incidental, as are most "anti-destruction" provisions, to a corporation's statutory power to finance itself. We find no merit to such a distinction. We have already rejected appellants' similar contention that § 157 could only be used for financing purposes. We also reject that distinction here. "Anti-destruction" clauses generally ensure holders of certain securities of the protection of their right of conversion in the event of a merger by giving them the right to convert their securities into whatever securities are to replace the stock of their company. *See Broad v. Rockwell International Corp.*, 5th Cir., 642 F.2d 929, 946, *cert. denied*, 454 U.S. 965, 102 S. Ct. 506, 70 L. Ed. 2d 380 (1981); *Wood v. Coastal States Gas Corp.*, Del. Supr., 401 A.2d 932, 937-39 (1979); *B.S.F. Co. v. Philadelphia National Bank*, Del. Supr., 204 A.2d 746, 750-51 (1964). The fact that the rights here have as their purpose the prevention of coercive two-tier tender offers does not invalidate them. Fourth, appellants contend that Household's reliance upon § 157 is contradictory to 8 Del. C. § 203.[79] Section 203 is a "notice" statute which generally requires that timely

[79] [9] Del. C. § 203 provides in relevant part: (a) No offeror shall make a tender offer unless: (1) Not less than 20 nor more than 60 days before the date the tender offer is to be made, the offeror shall deliver personally or by registered or certified mail to the corporation whose equity securities are to be subject to the tender offer, at its registered office in this State or at its principal place of business, a written statement of the offeror's intention to make the tender offer. . . . (2) The tender offer shall remain open for a period of at least 20 days after it is first made to the holders of the equity securities, during which period any stockholder may withdraw any of the equity securities tendered to the offeror, and any revised or amended tender offer which changes the amount or type of consideration offered or the number of equity securities for which the offer is made shall remain open at least 10 days following the amendment; and (3) The offeror and any associate of the offeror will not purchase or pay for any tendered equity security for a period of at least 20 days after the tender offer is first made to the holders of the equity securities, and no such purchase or payment shall be made within 10 days after an amended or revised tender offer if the amendment or revision changes the amount or type of consideration offered or the number of equity securities for which the offer is made. If during the period the tender offer must remain open pursuant to this section, a greater number of equity securities is tendered than the offeror is bound or willing to purchase, the equity securities shall be purchased pro rata, as nearly as may be, according to the number of shares tendered during such period by each equity security holder.

notice be given to a target of an offeror's intention to make a tender offer. Appellants contend that the lack of stronger regulation by the State indicates a legislative intent to reject anything which would impose an impediment to the tender offer process. Such a contention is a non sequitur. The desire to have little state regulation of tender offers cannot be said to also indicate a desire to also have little private regulation. Furthermore, as we explain infra, we do not view the Rights Plan as much of an impediment on the tender offer process.

Fifth, appellants contend that if § 157 authorizes the Rights Plan it would be unconstitutional pursuant to the Commerce Clause and Supremacy Clause of the United States Constitution. Household counters that appellants have failed to properly raise the issues in the Court of Chancery and are, therefore, precluded from raising them. Moreover, Household counters that appellants' contentions are without merit since the conduct complained of here is private conduct of corporate directors and not state regulation.

It is commonly known that issues not properly raised in the trial court will not be considered in the first instance by this Court. Supreme Court Rule 8. We cannot conclude here that appellants have failed to adequately raise their constitutional issues in the Court of Chancery. Appellants raised the Commerce Clause and Supremacy Clause contentions in their "pre-trial memo of points and authorities" and in their opening argument at trial. The fact that they did not again raise the issues in their post-trial briefing will not preclude them from raising the issues before this Court.

Appellants contend that § 157 authorization for the Rights Plan violates the Commerce Clause and is void under the Supremacy Clause, since it is an obstacle to the accomplishment of the policies underlying the Williams Act. Appellants put heavy emphasis upon the case of *Edgar v. MITE Corp.*, 457 U.S. 624, 102 S. Ct. 2629, 73 L. Ed. 2d 269 (1982), in which the United States Supreme Court held that the Illinois Business Takeover Act was unconstitutional, in that it unduly burdened interstate commerce in violation of the Commerce Clause.[80] We do not read the analysis in Edgar as applicable to the actions of private parties. The fact that directors of a corporation act pursuant to a state statute provides an insufficient nexus to the state for there to be state action which may violate the Commerce Clause or Supremacy Clause. *See Data Probe Acquisition Corp. v. Datatab, Inc.*, 2d. Cir., 722 F.2d 1, 5 (1983).

Having concluded that sufficient authority for the Rights Plan exists in 8 Del. C. § 157, we note the inherent powers of the Board conferred by 8 Del. C. § 141(a),[81] concerning the management of the corporation's "business and affairs", also

[80] [10] Justice White, joined by Chief Justice Burger and Justice Blackman also concluded that the Illinois Business Takeover Act was pre-empted by the Williams Act. *Edgar*, 457 U.S. at 630, 102 S. Ct. at 2634.

[81] [11] 8 Del. C. § 141(a) provides: (a) The business and affairs of every corporation organized under this chapter shall be managed by or under the direction of a board of directors, except as may be otherwise provided in this chapter or in its certificate of incorporation. If any such provision is made in the certificate of incorporation, the powers and duties conferred or imposed upon the board of directors by this chapter shall be exercised or performed to such extent and by such person or persons as shall be provided in the certificate of incorporation.

provides the Board additional authority upon which to enact the Rights Plan. *Unocal*, 493 A.2d at 953.

B.

Appellants contend that the Board is unauthorized to usurp stockholders' rights to receive tender offers by changing Household's fundamental structure. We conclude that the Rights Plan does not prevent stockholders from receiving tender offers, and that the change of Household's structure was less than that which results from the implementation of other defensive mechanisms upheld by various courts. Appellants' contention that stockholders will lose their right to receive and accept tender offers seems to be premised upon an understanding of the Rights Plan which is illustrated by the SEC amicus brief which states: "The Chancery Court's decision seriously understates the impact of this plan. In fact, as we discuss below, the Rights Plan will deter not only two-tier offers, but virtually all hostile tender offers." The fallacy of that contention is apparent when we look at the recent takeover of Crown Zellerbach, which has a similar Rights Plan, by Sir James Goldsmith. WALL STREET JOURNAL, July 26, 1985, at 3, 12. The evidence at trial also evidenced many methods around the Plan ranging from tendering with a condition that the Board redeem the Rights, tendering with a high minimum condition of shares and Rights, tendering and soliciting consents to remove the Board and redeem the Rights, to acquiring 50% of the shares and causing Household to self-tender for the Rights. One could also form a group of up to 19.9% and solicit proxies for consents to remove the Board and redeem the Rights. These are but a few of the methods by which Household can still be acquired by a hostile tender offer.

In addition, the Rights Plan is not absolute. When the Household Board of Directors is faced with a tender offer and a request to redeem the Rights, they will not be able to arbitrarily reject the offer. They will be held to the same fiduciary standards any other board of directors would be held to in deciding to adopt a defensive mechanism, the same standard as they were held to in originally approving the Rights Plan. *See Unocol*, 493 A.2d at 954-55, 958. In addition, appellants contend that the deterrence of tender offers will be accomplished by what they label "a fundamental transfer of power from the stockholders to the directors." They contend that this transfer of power, in itself, is unauthorized. The Rights Plan will result in no more of a structural change than any other defensive mechanism adopted by a board of directors. The Rights Plan does not destroy the assets of the corporation. The implementation of the Plan neither results in any outflow of money from the corporation nor impairs its financial flexibility. It does not dilute earnings per share and does not have any adverse tax consequences for the corporation or its stockholders. The Plan has not adversely affected the market price of Household's stock. Comparing the Rights Plan with other defensive mechanisms, it does less harm to the value structure of the corporation than do the other mechanisms. Other mechanisms result in increased debt of the corporation. *See Whittaker Corp v. Edgar, supra* (sale of "prize asset"), *Cheff v. Mathes, supra*, (paying greenmail to eliminate a threat), *Unocal Corp. v. Mesa Petroleum Co., supra*, (discriminatory self-tender). There is little change in the governance structure as a result of the adoption of the Rights Plan. The Board does not now have unfettered discretion in refusing to redeem the Rights. The Board has no more discretion in refusing to redeem the Rights than it does in enacting any defensive mechanism. The contention that the Rights Plan alters the structure more than do other defensive mechanisms because it is so effective as to make the corporation completely safe from hostile tender offers is likewise without merit. As explained above, there are numerous methods to successfully launch a hostile tender offer.

C.

Appellants' third contention is that the Board was unauthorized to fundamentally restrict stockholders' rights to conduct a proxy contest. Appellants contend that the "20% trigger" effectively prevents any stockholder from first acquiring 20% or more shares before conducting a proxy contest and further, it prevents stockholders from banding together into a group to solicit proxies if, collectively, they own 20% or more of the stock.[82] In addition, at trial, appellants contended that read literally, the Rights Agreement triggers the Rights upon the mere acquisition of the right to vote 20% or more of the shares through a proxy solicitation, and thereby precludes any proxy contest from being waged.[83]

Appellants seem to have conceded this last contention in light of Household's response that the receipt of a proxy does not make the recipient the "beneficial owner" of the shares involved which would trigger the Rights. In essence, the Rights Agreement provides that the Rights are triggered when someone becomes the "beneficial owner" of 20% or more of Household stock. Although a literal reading of the Rights Agreement definition of "beneficial owner" would seem to include those shares which one has the right to vote, it has long been recognized that the relationship between grantor and recipient of a proxy is one of agency, and the agency is revocable by the grantor at any time. Henn, *Corporations* § 196, at 518. Therefore, the holder of a proxy is not the "beneficial owner" of the stock. As a result, the mere acquisition of the right to vote 20% of the shares does not trigger the Rights. The issue, then, is whether the restriction upon individuals or groups from first acquiring 20% of shares before waging a proxy contest fundamentally restricts stockholders' right to conduct a proxy contest. Regarding this issue the Court of Chancery found: Thus, while the Rights Plan does deter the formation of proxy efforts of a certain magnitude, it does not limit the voting power of individual shares. On the evidence presented it is highly conjectural to assume that a particular effort to assert shareholder views in the election of directors or revisions of corporate policy will be frustrated by the proxy feature of the Plan. Household's witnesses, Troubh and Higgins described recent corporate takeover battles in which insurgents holding less than 10% stock ownership were able to secure corporate control through a proxy contest or the threat of one. *Moran*, 490 A.2d at 1080. We conclude that there was sufficient evidence at trial to support the Vice-Chancellor's finding that the effect upon proxy contests will be minimal. Evidence at trial established that many proxy contests are won with an insurgent

---

[82] [12] Appellants explain that the acquisition of 20% of the shares trigger the Rights, making them non-redeemable, and thereby would prevent even a future friendly offer for the ten-year life of the Rights.

[83] [13] The SEC still contends that the mere acquisition of the right to vote 20% of the shares through a proxy solicitation triggers the rights. We do not interpret the Rights Agreement in that manner.

ownership of less than 20%, and that very large holdings are no guarantee of success. There was also testimony that the key variable in proxy contest success is the merit of an insurgent's issues, not the size of his holdings.

IV

Having concluded that the adoption of the Rights Plan was within the authority of the Directors, we now look to whether the Directors have met their burden under the business judgment rule.

The business judgment rule is a "presumption that in making a business decision the directors of a corporation acted on an informed basis, in good faith and in the honest belief that the action taken was in the best interests of the company." *Aronson v. Lewis*, Del. Supr., 473 A.2d 805, 812 (1984) (citations omitted). Notwithstanding, in *Unocal* we held that when the business judgment rule applies to adoption of a defensive mechanism, the initial burden will lie with the directors. The "directors must show that they had reasonable grounds for believing that a danger to corporate policy and effectiveness existed. . . . [T]hey satisfy that burden by showing good faith and reasonable investigation. . . ." *Unocal*, 493 A.2d at 955 (citing *Cheff v. Mathes*, 199 A.2d at 554-55). In addition, the directors must show that the defensive mechanism was "reasonable in relation to the threat posed." *Unocal*, 493 A.2d at 955. Moreover, that proof is materially enhanced, as we noted in *Unocal*, where, as here, a majority of the board favoring the proposal consisted of outside independent directors who have acted in accordance with the foregoing standards. *Unocal*, 493 A.2d at 955; *Aronson*, 473 A.2d at 815. Then, the burden shifts back to the plaintiffs who have the ultimate burden of persuasion to show a breach of the directors' fiduciary duties. *Unocal*, 493 A.2d at 958. There are no allegations here of any bad faith on the part of the Directors' action in the adoption of the Rights Plan. There is no allegation that the Directors' action was taken for entrenchment purposes. Household has adequately demonstrated, as explained above, that the adoption of the Rights Plan was in reaction to what it perceived to be the threat in the market place of coercive two-tier tender offers. Appellants do contend, however, that the Board did not exercise informed business judgment in its adoption of the Plan. Appellants contend that the Household board was uninformed since they were, inter alia, told the plan would not inhibit a proxy contest, were not told the plan would preclude all hostile acquisitions of Household, and were told that Delaware counsel opined that the plan was within the business judgment of the Board. As to the first two contentions, as we explained above, the Rights Plan will not have a severe impact upon proxy contests and it will not preclude all hostile acquisitions of Household. Therefore, the Directors were not misinformed or uninformed on these facts. Appellants contend the Delaware counsel did not express an opinion on the flip-over provision of the Rights, rather only that the Rights would constitute validly issued and outstanding rights to subscribe to the preferred stock of the company.

To determine whether a business judgment reached by a board of directors was an informed one, we determine whether the directors were grossly negligent. *Smith v. Van Gorkom*, Del. Supr., 488 A.2d 858, 873 (1985). Upon a review of this record, we conclude the Directors were not grossly negligent. The information supplied to the Board on August 14 provided the essentials of the Plan. The Directors were given beforehand a notebook which included a three-page summary of the Plan along with articles on the current takeover environment. The extended discussion between the Board and representatives of Wachtell, Lipton and Goldman, Sachs before approval of the Plan reflected a full and candid evaluation of the Plan. Moran's expression of his views at the meeting served to place before the Board a knowledgeable critique of the Plan. The factual happenings here are clearly distinguishable from the actions of the directors of Trans Union Corporation who displayed gross negligence in approving a cash-out merger, *Id.* In addition, to meet their burden, the Directors must show that the defensive mechanism was "reasonable in relation to the threat posed." The record reflects a concern on the part of the Directors over the increasing frequency in the financial services industry of "boot-strap" and "bust-up" takeovers. The Directors were also concerned that such takeovers may take the form of two-tier offers.[84] In addition, on August 14, the Household Board was aware of Moran's overture on behalf of D-K-M. In sum, the Directors reasonably believed Household was vulnerable to coercive acquisition techniques and adopted a reasonable defensive mechanism to protect itself.

In conclusion, the Household Directors receive the benefit of the business judgment rule in their adoption of the Rights Plan. The Directors adopted the Plan pursuant to statutory authority in 8 Del. C. §§ 141, 151, 157. We reject appellants' contentions that the Rights Plan strips stockholders of their rights to receive tender offers, and that the Rights Plan fundamentally restricts proxy contests. The Directors adopted the Plan in the good faith belief that it was necessary to protect Household from coercive acquisition techniques. The Board was informed as to the details of the Plan. In addition, Household has demonstrated that the Plan is reasonable in relation to the threat posed. Appellants, on the other hand, have failed to convince us that the Directors breached any fiduciary duty in their adoption of the Rights Plan. While we conclude for present purposes that the Household Directors are protected by the business judgment rule, that does not end the matter. The ultimate response to an actual takeover bid must be judged by the Directors' actions at that time, and nothing we say here relieves them of their basic fundamental duties to the corporation and its stockholders. *Unocal*, 493 A.2d at 954-55, 958; *Smith v. Van Gorkom*, 488 A.2d at 872-73; *Aronson*, 473 A.2d at 812-13; *Pogostin v. Rice*, Del. Supr., 480 A.2d 619, 627 (1984). Their use of the Plan will be evaluated when and if the issue arises. . . .

. . . .

[84] [14] We have discussed the coercive nature of two-tier tender offers in *Unocal*, 493 A.2d at 956, n.12. We explained in *Unocal* that a discriminatory self-tender was reasonably related to the threat of two-tier tender offers and possible greenmail.

ACCOUNT v. HILTON HOTELS CORP.

Supreme Court of Delaware
780 A.2d 245 (2001)

WALSH, JUSTICE.

In this appeal from the Court of Chancery, we revisit the question of whether the board of directors of a Delaware corporation may unilaterally adopt a poison pill rights plan. The appellant challenged the authority of the defendant, Hilton Hotels Corporation ("Hilton"), to adopt such a plan and require its common shareholders' adherence to its terms. The plaintiff shareholders rejected participation in the plan and thereafter commenced an action in the Court of Chancery seeking to invalidate its issuance. The Court of Chancery rejected that effort, ruling that under the principle of *stare decisis*, Hilton's entitlement to implement the rights plan was not subject to challenge. We agree and affirm.

I

Hilton is a Delaware corporation that owns, manages and franchises hotels worldwide. Appellant/plaintiff-below, Leonard Loventhal Account (the "Trust") claims to be, and is assumed to have been at all relevant times, a holder of Hilton common stock. In 1988, the Hilton Board adopted a rights plan and upon its expiration ten years later adopted a second rights plan (the "Rights Plan"). On November 29, 1999, in connection with a merger with Promos Hotel Corporation, Hilton adopted the plan now under attack. The plan was implemented through a written agreement (the "Rights Agreement") between Hilton and Chase Mellon Shareholder Services L.L.C., as the Rights Agent. The Agreement provides for one right, in the form of a dividend of one preferred share purchase right, to be attached to each share of Hilton common stock. Each right entitles the holder to purchase for $80 one one-hundredth of a share of Series A Junior Participating Preferred Stock. Upon the occurrence of a triggering event, the rights entitle the holder to purchase two shares of Hilton common stock at half-price.

Hilton informed its shareholders of the new Rights Agreement by letter dated November 30, 1999, which also included a summary of the Rights Agreement. The letter stated that:

> [n]o action on your part is required at this time, and no money should be sent to Hilton. The rights will automatically attach to the shares of Common Stock you hold and will trade with them. There is no need to send in your certificates to have this reference added. You will be notified if the Rights are ever triggered and become exercisable.

The Trust responded by letter dated January 18, 2000, informing Hilton that the Trust refused to accept the rights Hilton was attempting to attach to the Trust's shares. The Trust further wrote that it did not agree "to being deemed or treated as an owner of rights and does not agree that the rights may be attached to or trade with the shares of Hilton common stock that the Trust owns." Nor did the Trust agree to have a legend evidencing the rights attached to its stock certificates.

Finally, the Trust separately requested that 100 shares of Hilton common stock that it owned be registered of record in the name of the Trust.

On February 26, 2000, the Trust received a stock certificate with a legend incorporating the terms of the Rights Plan. The certificate also indicated that it evidenced rights that are attached to the shares of common stock. On February 20, 2000, the Trust filed an individual and class action suit challenging certain provisions of the Rights Agreement.

II

In the Court of Chancery, the Trust advanced five Counts or claims challenging the Hilton Rights Plan. The first four Counts are directed to the basic, operative terms of the Rights Plan. In Count I, the Trust claims, in effect, that the Rights Plan is not a valid and enforceable agreement as to any shareholder who rejects its terms. Counts II, III, and IV are an attack on various implementing provisions of the Plan. In Count II, the Trust asserts that the issuance of legend-bearing restrictions violates Delaware law and Hilton's by-laws. In Count III, the Trust claims that requiring that the rights be traded in tandem with the underlying common stock violates § 202 of the Delaware General Corporation Law ("DGCL"). In Count IV, the Trust contends that the implementing provisions have altered Hilton's common stock contrary to its certificate of incorporation and provisions of the DGCL. Finally, in Count V, the Trust attacks a feature of the Rights Plan contained in section 31 that purports to relieve directors of "any liability" for implementing the Rights Plan. Hilton moved to dismiss the complaint for failure to state a claim upon which relief can be granted, arguing, in effect, that settled Delaware law rendered the Trust's claims unsupportable.

The Chancellor considered each of the claims advanced by the Trust and concluded that they were without merit and dismissible as a matter of law. *See Leonard Loventhal Account v. Hilton Hotels Corp.*, Del. Ch., No. 17803, 2000 WL 1528909[, 2000 Del. Ch. LEXIS 149], Chandler, C. (Oct. 10, 2000). The Chancellor ruled that the Trust's attack on the mechanism and format of the Rights Plan was foreclosed by a consistent body of law beginning with the seminal decision in *Moran v. Household Int'l., Inc.*, Del. Ch., 490 A.2d 1059, *aff'd*, Del. Supr., 500 A.2d 1346 (1985), upholding so called "poison pill" defenses bottomed on rights plans. Under the doctrine of *stare decisis*, the Chancellor ruled that the Trust's challenges to the Hilton Rights Plan were barred. With respect to Count V, directed to section 31 of the Hilton Rights Plan, the Chancellor ruled that in view of Hilton's concession that the exculpatory provision was not intended to relieve the directors of their continuing fiduciary duties under the Rights Plan, the challenge to section 31 was moot.

On appeal, the Trust contends that the Court of Chancery erred in dismissing the complaint by misinterpreting the doctrine of *stare decisis* and employing an incorrect legal standard on a motion to dismiss. This Court reviews *de novo* a lower court's decision to grant a motion to dismiss. *See Malone v. Brincat*, Del. Supr., 722 A.2d 5, 9 (1998). Dismissal is appropriate under Court of Chancery Rule 12(b)(6) only where it appears "with a reasonable certainty that a plaintiff would not be entitled to the relief sought under any set of facts which could be proven to support the action." *Rabkin v. Philip A. Hunt Chem. Corp.*, Del. Supr., 498 A.2d 1099, 1104 (1985). In addition, whether claims are barred from consideration under the doctrine of *stare decisis* presents a question of law that is subject to *de novo* review. *See Fiduciary Trust Co. v. Fiduciary Trust Co.*, Del. Supr., 445 A.2d 927, 930 (1982).

The Chancellor concluded that *Moran* and its progeny created a series of precedents that could not be challenged in like litigation, *i.e.*, a shareholder could not seek to invalidate a rights plan adopted on the *Household* pattern. Although this Court has not had occasion in the recent past to elaborate on the doctrine of *stare decisis*, it is well established in Delaware jurisprudence. Once a point of law has been settled by decision of this Court, "it forms a precedent which is not afterwards to be departed from or lightly overruled or set aside . . . and [it] should be followed except for urgent reasons and upon clear manifestation of error." *Oscar George, Inc. v. Potts*, Del. Supr., 115 A.2d 479, 481 (1955). The need for stability and continuity in the law and respect for court precedent are the principles upon which the doctrine of *stare decisis* is founded. *See Gannett Co., Inc. v. Kanaga*, Del. Supr., 750 A.2d 1174, 1181 (2000). In determining whether *stare decisis* applies, this Court should examine whether there is: "a judicial opinion by the [C]ourt, on a point of law, expressed in a final decision." *State v. Phillips*, Del. Ch., 400 A.2d 299, 308 (1979). The doctrine of *stare decisis* operates to fix a specific legal result to facts in a pending case based on a judicial precedent directed to identical or similar facts in a previous case in the same court or one higher in the judicial hierarchy. *See Allegheny Gen. Hosp. v. N.L.R.B.*, 3rd Cir., 608 F.2d 965, 969-70 (1979), *abrogated on other grounds by St. Margaret Mem'l Hosp. v. N.L.R.B.*, 3rd Cir., 991 F.2d 1146 (1993).

The doctrine of *stare decisis* finds ready application in Delaware corporate law. It is settled Delaware law that a corporation chartered under the laws of this State may adopt shareholder rights plans. *See Moran v. Household Int'l, Inc.*, Del. Supr., 500 A.2d 1346 (1985). In *Moran*, this Court determined that the adoption of a rights plan was a valid exercise of the board's authority.[85] Preliminarily, we concluded that 8 Del. C. §§ 157 and 141(a) provided the board sufficient authority upon which to enact the rights plan. *See Moran*, 500 A.2d at 1353. This Court also determined that the rights plan did not "usurp stockholders' rights to receive tender offers." *Id.* at 1354. Finally, we held that the rights plan would not have the unauthorized effect of restricting stockholders' rights to conduct a proxy contest. *See id.* at 1355-56.

In Count I of its complaint, the Trust seeks to invalidate the enforceability of the Rights Plan as to any shareholder who does not "accept" its terms. It posits its argument on section 16 of the Rights Plan which recites "AGREEMENT OF RIGHTS HOLDERS. Every holder of a Right by *accepting the same consents and agrees* with [Hilton] and the Rights Agent and with every holder of a Right that. . . ." (emphasis supplied). In essence, the Trust argues that a rights plan agreement is a multi-party instrument requiring consent of all contracting parties, including affected shareholders, for its enforceability.

---

[85] [1] The plaintiff in *Moran* argued that the DGCL did not authorize the issuance of a rights plan, the board impermissibly usurped the stockholders' rights to receive hostile tender offers through adoption of the rights plan, and the board was unauthorized to restrict stockholders' rights to conduct a proxy contest. *See Moran*, 500 A.2d at 1351.

It is indisputable that *Moran* established a board's authority to adopt a rights plan. As the Chancellor pointed out below, "There is simply no legal requirement that the Hilton shareholder must be a party to the Rights Plan or formally vote to accept the Rights Plan to ensure that the Plan is enforceable." *Loventhal*, 2000 WL 1528909 at *5[, 2000 Del. Ch. LEXIS 149]. While it is technically correct to argue that *Moran* did not explicitly pass upon the question of whether a rights plan required express consent of all parties affected by it, there is little doubt that *Moran, inter alia*, denied objecting shareholders the right to oppose implementation of a rights plan. *Moran* addressed a fundamental question of corporate law in the context of takeovers: whether a board of directors had the power to adopt unilaterally a rights plan the effect of which was to interpose the board between the shareholders and the proponents of a tender offer. The power recognized in *Moran* would have been meaningless if the rights plan required shareholder approval. Indeed it is difficult to harmonize *Moran's* basic holding with a contention that questions a Board's prerogative to unilaterally establish a rights plan.

Moran, of course, did not address whether every provision that might be includable in a rights plan would be sustainable under all circumstances, although later decisions of the Court of Chancery and this Court did consider such permutations. *See, e.g., Quickturn Design Sys. v. Shapiro*, Del. Supr., 721 A.2d 1281 (1998); *Carmody v. Toll Bros., Inc.*, Del. Ch., 723 A.2d 1180 (1998). The Trust seeks to hold its shares free of the restrictions of the Rights Plan. If that claim is legally sustainable as to the Trust, it is equally available to every Hilton shareholder. Indeed, the Trust seeks class status to assert that argument broadly. To recognize viability of the contractual claim would emasculate the basic holding of *Moran*, both as to this case and *in futuro*, that directors of a Delaware corporation may adopt a rights plan unilaterally. The Chancellor determined that the doctrine of *stare decisis* precluded that result and we agree.

III

In Count II, the Trust contends that the Rights Agreement violates 6 *Del. C.* § 8-401 and 8 Del. C. § 158, and sections 24 and 25 of Hilton's by-laws, by altering and legending the certificates for Hilton common stock and restricting the registration or transfer of Hilton common stock. The Trust argues that the Court of Chancery improperly invoked the doctrine of *stare decisis* because the Household rights plan did not contain a legending provision and the validity of the rights plan in *Moran* was not contested under 6 Del. C. § 8-401 and 8 *Del. C.* § 158.

The Chancellor, however, did not rely on *stare decisis* in dismissing this claim. He first determined that § 157 permitted the placing of the legend on the stock certificate and then concluded that the legend placed on the certificate "was validly approved by the Hilton Board in accordance with the Delaware Supreme Court's ruling in *Moran*." Loventhal, 2000 WL 1528909 at *8[, 2000 Del. Ch. LEXIS 149]. The Chancellor further noted that while § 158 gives shareholders the right to receive a certificate that does not contain inappropriate legends, the legend in this case is authorized by § 157 and therefore not inappropriate. *See id.* (citing *Bender v. Memory Metals, Inc.*, Del. Ch., 514 A.2d 1109 (1986)). *Moran's* approval of the substance of the legend as appropriate is a sufficient basis for rejecting this claim even if not precisely controlled by *stare decisis.*

IV

The Trust alleges in Count III that the adoption of the Rights Plan imposed an impermissible transfer restriction on the Hilton common stock it owns. It contends that the Court of Chancery erred in dismissing this claim on *stare decisis* grounds because the transfer, certificate and legending provisions on which the Trust's § 202 claim is based were not wholly present in Household's plan and there are important factual differences between the Household and Hilton plans. Specifically, the Trust points to sections 3.1, 3.2, and 3.3 of the Rights Agreement, which it contends were not contained in the Household rights plan and which mandate that the transfer of common stock include the transfer of rights. In addition, the Trust contends that the court erred because it is challenging Hilton' s use of the rights, an issue *Moran* expressly left open.

The Chancellor determined that there were no significant operational differences between the relevant provisions of the Household rights plan and the Hilton Rights Plan, noting that "[t]he plaintiff in *Moran* directly challenged the Household rights plan as imposing an impermissible transfer restriction on Household common stock under § 202(b), just as this plaintiff attempts to do before this Court." *See id.* at *7. In *Moran*, the Court of Chancery, ruled that "the Rights Plan does not affect the trading of Household shares or the registration of shares once traded. The negotiability of shares is not conditioned and shares remain freely transferable as provided by § 159 of the DGCL." *Moran*, 490 A.2d at 1079. The Trust's restriction on transferability claim is clearly precluded on *stare decisis* grounds.

V

Count IV of the Trust's complaint alleges that the Rights Plan impermissibly altered Hilton's common stock in violation of §§ 151 and 242 of the DGCL and Hilton's certificate of incorporation. The Trust contends that this alteration was effected by the placement of a legend explicitly incorporating all the terms of the Rights Agreement on the certificates for common stock. The Court of Chancery held that this claim was directly raised and rejected by the trial court in *Moran* and concluded that, in *Moran*, no amendment was necessary and correspondingly no amendment to Hilton's certificate of incorporation was necessary here either. Although the Trust contends that the present circumstances are distinguishable from *Moran* because Hilton has placed on its common stock certificates a legend that explicitly incorporates all the terms of the Rights Agreement as previously noted, the legend does little more than make explicit what the board has enacted substantively under the authority granted in *Moran*.

VI

In Count V of the complaint, the Trust seeks declaratory relief to the effect that section 31 of the Rights Agreement violates 8 Del. C. § 102(b)(7) because it purports to relieve the Hilton directors from non-monetary liability for breaches of fiduciary duty. Although section 31 contains broad exculpatory language, Hilton conceded before the Chancellor that it was not intended to foreclose shareholder rights to assert fiduciary-based claims.[86] At argument in the Court of Chancery, counsel for Hilton stated that "[t]he provision only applies to the Company, the Rights Agent, 'the holders of the rights, as such' and other 'parties' to the agreement. Section 31 thus is not an attempt to limit liability to stockholders generally but rather only addresses claims brought under the [Rights Plan]." Hilton rejected that concession in argument before this Court. In light of this statement, the Chancellor held that Count V was rendered moot. The court did, however, require the order accompanying dismissal to include language stating that section 31 does not affect the rights of the shareholders with respect to the Hilton board nor the duties owed by the members of the board to the shareholders. The order, however, did not state this count was dismissed as moot.

The Trust contends that the effect of the Chancellor's ruling was not to render moot its attack on the power purportedly granted by section 31. Rather, the Trust argues that this was a decision in the Trust's favor and judgment should be so entered. Therefore, the claim is not moot and judgment should have been rendered for the plaintiff.

The practical effect of Hilton's concession that section 31 is simply a "non-recourse" provision directed to claims by rights holders and is not intended to relieve the directors of their fiduciary duty of loyalty owed to Hilton shareholders is to justify the denial of relief under Count V. But the Chancellor did condition the dismissal of Count V on the insertion of language in the court's order of October 10, 2000 reflecting the limitation on the scope of section 31. Moreover, the Chancellor deferred consideration of plaintiff's entitlement to an award of counsel fees until disposition of this appeal. Thus, while we affirm the dismissal of Count V, we decline to characterize the effect of that dismissal on any further award of counsel fees.[87] That matter is not before us at this time and must await determination by the Chancellor.

The judgment of the Court of Chancery is affirmed.

---

[86] [2] Section 31, after imparting broad authority to the directors to interpret and administer the Rights Agreement, provides that:

> All such actions, calculations, interpretations and determinations (including for purposes of clause (y) below, all omissions with respect to the foregoing) that are done or made by the Board of directors of the Company in good faith shall (x) be final, conclusive and binding on the Company, the Rights Agent, the holders of the Rights, as such, and all other parties, and (y) not subject the Board of Directors to any liability to the holders of the Rights.

[87] [3] The Court of Chancery entered judgment in Hilton's favor pursuant to Court of Chancery Rule 54(b), permitting an appeal to this Court with respect to the matters adjudicated. That ruling did not conclude the litigation, however, since the Court specifically reserved jurisdiction presumably to consider an application for an award of counsel fees. *Lipson v. Lipson*, Del. Supr., ___A.2d ___, 2001 WL 710207, [2001 Del. LEXIS 283,] No. 108, 2001, Holland, J. (June 21, 2001).

BANK OF NEW YORK CO. v. IRVING BANK CORP.

New York Supreme Court, New York County
536 N.Y.S.2d 923 (1988)

Herman Cahn, Justice

The Bank of New York ("BNY") brings this motion seeking a preliminary injunction enjoining Irving Bank Corporation ("IBC") from enforcing the "flip-in" provision of its rights agreement adopted by the Board of IBC on May 19, 1988. BNY seeks a determination that the flip-in amendment is ultra vires as a matter of New York law.

In September, 1987, BNY announced its intention of acquiring all of the outstanding shares of IBC. The Court notes that an offer to purchase shares of IBC has also been received from Banca Commerciale Italiana (BCI). By news release dated July 5, 1988, IBC announced that its board determined that the latest BCI "transaction" — offer was superior to BNY's "best and final bid." The Court also notes that BNY's approval from the Federal Reserve Board expires on July 9, 1988; although an application for a further extension may be made, there is no assurance that one will be granted. Further, it should be noted that the Court by this decision does not arrive at any decision as to which offer — that of BNY or of IBC is superior, the Court does not have a sufficient record on which to make such a decision, insofar as such decision is a "business judgment," it is properly one for the IBC Board of Directors to make. Only under certain limited conditions will the Court consider whether that business judgment should be overruled. Those issues are not now before the Court. This decision concerns itself with the legality of the rights amendment of May 19, 1988. On October 9, 1987, the IBC Board adopted a "rights agreement" as one method by which it could resist the acquisition, unless an offer which it deemed more acceptable was received. This Court previously invalidated an amendment to the rights agreement which restricted the powers of a future board of directors of IBC unless elected in a specified manner.

(a) The May 19th amendment.

At issue on this motion is an amendment to the rights agreement adopted by the IBC Board on May 19, 1988. The amendment has the effect of making acquisition of twenty percent or more of IBC shares prohibitively expensive and unprofitable unless the IBC Board approves such acquisition, at which time the IBC Board can have IBC redeem the rights. Commonly referred to as a flip-in amendment it works as follows: if any person or entity acquires control of twenty percent or more of the shares of IBC, each right will entitle the holder with the exception of the twenty percent or more shareholders, to purchase $400 of IBC common shares for $200. The amendment expires upon the earlier of all regulatory approval sought by IBC or on April 19, 1989. This amendment of the rights agreement greatly dilutes the twenty percent shareholder's equity and voting rights and thus makes acquisition of all or a majority of the shares extremely expensive for the twenty percent acquirers. For example, if the flip-in is triggered when the common share of IBC is trading at $72 per share, each IBC right holder, with the exception of the twenty percent or more holder, will be entitled to purchase from IBC approximately 5 4/7 shares of IBC for $200, while the twenty percent holder could buy none from IBC. Thus, all rights holders, except the acquiring shareholder would be able to have more than six shares and votes for each common share previously owned, ... The acquiring shareholder, through purchases in the open market, could obtain less than three shares per $200 expenditure and thus obtain less than four shares and votes per shares previously owned, ... (If the acquiring shareholder is able to purchase the applicable number of shares in the open market.) BNY seeks to enjoin enforcement of this provision. This Court notes that the flip-in amendment is the only provision of the rights agreement herein contested.

The Law

Business Corporation Law, Section 501 authorizes the creation and issuance of shares by a corporation. It directs that "subject to the designations, relative rights, preferences and limitations applicable to separate series, each share shall be equal to every other share of the same class." (BCL 501(c).) BNY argues that the flip-in provision violates BCL, Section 501(c) in that it discriminates among shares of the same class by entitling all common shareholders, except the twenty percent shareholder, to exercise the flip-in right to obtain more IBC shares at a bargain price from IBC. IBC argues (a) that there is no issue of discrimination among shares, but rather the issue relates to rights issued pursuant to BCL, Section 505 and not BCL, 501. Said statute (BCL, 505) does not contain prohibition against discrimination among rights; (b) that in fact there is no discrimination at all, that is, that all stockholders receive equal rights, that all are subject to their benefits and burdens on equal terms; and (c) that BCL, Section 622 authorizes a corporation to discriminate in the issuance of its shares and/or rights by providing that the preemptive rights of shareholders to preserve their position in a corporation regarding voting and dividend rights allows a provision in the certificate of incorporation which does away with such preemptive rights. (IBC's certificate of incorporation provides that its shareholders do not have preemptive rights.) Recently the Court of Appeals has interpreted BCL, 501(c) and its mandate that every share shall be equal to every other share in the same class. *FeBland v. Two Trees Management Co.*, 66 N.Y.2d 556, 498 N.Y.S.2d 336, 489 N.E.2d 223 (1985), involved a contested transfer fee on the transfer of shares in a cooperative corporation. The transfer fee varied from $50 to $200 per share according to whom the shares had been purchased from and how long they had been owned. The Court rejected the argument that BCL, 501(c) was intended "not to proscribe a distinction between shareholders." 66 N.Y.2d at 567, 498 N.Y.S.2d 336, 489 N.E.2d 223. The flip-in amendment herein works a similar impermissible discrimination among shareholders of the same class. It favors certain shareholders over others. IBC argues that such discrimination is permissible in the distribution of rights. (BCL, 505.) The same argument was made and rejected in *Amalgamated Sugar Co. v. NL Industries*, 644 F. Supp. 1229 (1986), where the Court applying substantially similar provisions of New Jersey law stated as follows: Defendant "assert that Section 14A:7-7 of the New Jersey Business Corporation Act and not 14A:7-1 is applicable to the NLI plan. Section 14A:7-7 authorizes corporations to issue rights to purchase shares of stock from the corporation 'for such consideration, and upon such terms and conditions as may be fixed by the board.' " The defendants assert that there is nothing in that section, 14A:7-7 that prohibits the terms and conditions fixed by the board from being discriminatory. "I do not accept that broad reading of 14A:7-7. Such a reading would allow the boards of directors of corporations to circumvent the provisions of 14A:7-1. It is axiomatic that one cannot read one section of a statute to accomplish an end that is impermissible under another section of the statute." And that's 644 F. Supp. at 1235 and 1236.

IBC cites *Harvard Industries, Inc. v. Tyson*, (1986-87 Transfer Binder), Federal Securities Law Reporter (CCH), Paragraph 93, 064 at 95, 293 (Eastern District of Michigan, 1986), for the proposition that cases upholding flip-in provisions are "better reasoned." The Court in that case stated: "The Court agrees with the defendant, however, and, adopts the position of the better reasoned cases that such a rights plan does not discriminate among shares but, rather, among shareholders, which is not forbidden." And that's at page 95, 294.

However, such discrimination among shareholders is specifically prohibited in New York by *FeBland, supra.* Furthermore, to the extent that BCL, 501(c) has since been amended to remove cooperative corporations from the *FeBland* reading of 501(c), the legislature has expressed its approval of the FeBland reasoning as it affects non-cooperative corporations. IBC cites *Moran v. Household International*, 500 A.2d 1346 (Delaware, 1985) for the proposition that a flip-over rights plan upheld in that case is similar to a flip-in rights provision with which we are concerned here. It is claimed that thus, the flip-in provision should also be upheld. However, a flip-over rights provision entitled all shareholders to purchase shares in an acquiring corporation at a discounted rate. Thus, the evil sought to be addressed herein, that of discrimination among shareholders of the same class of stock, is absent in a flip-over provision. IBC's argument that BCL, 622 authorizes the discriminatory treatment herein is also without merit. BNY correctly argues that the preemptive rights section relates to the potential dilution that existing holders of equity shares "would suffer as a group as a result of the issuance of shares or the granting of rights to purchase shares to non-holders." See number 3 White, New York Corporations, Section 622.01 at page 6-528 (preemptive right is shareholder's "right to purchase or subscribe for newly issued shares before such shares are purchased or subscribed for by non-shareholders"). In addition, the Court will not read BCL, Section 622 to contradict the express mandate of BCL, Section 501(c), a provision which may not be avoided by provision in the certificate of incorporation. As to the application herein relating to Section 912, BCL, the legislature has adopted BCL, 912 as a comprehensive defensive mechanism. Through the utilization of Section 912, a board of directors can successfully inhibit a hostile or unfriendly takeover for some time, as specifically set forth therein. That an agreeable offer is made under which the shareholders receive the highest value for their corporation is a goal to which the board should subscribe. The Court will not, on the record now before it, direct the IBC Board to give approval or waive rights under Section 912, BCL. Such direction could only be made after a complete factual hearing on the issue of the Board's exercise of its business judgment. In conclusion, BNY's motion for a preliminary injunction enjoining enforcement of the flip-in provision of the rights plan adopted on May 19, 1988, is granted. The plaintiffs have demonstrated a likelihood of success on the merits on this issue. Irreparable injury without the requested relief is likely in that without such relief the tender offer, economically, could not be completed within the time limits imposed by regulatory agencies. Accordingly, the equities tip in plaintiff's favor.

NOTES

(1) The holding in *Bank of New York* was statutorily overruled by the passage, shortly after the decision, of amendments to the New York Business Corporation Law. Those amendments are set forth in the italicized portions of Sections 501(c) and 505(a)(2)(ii) as provided in Section 1.08 herein.

(2) Since the legality of the poison pill was established in *Moran* and other decisions, more than 1,500 publicly traded corporations have adopted pills.

VERSATA ENTERS. v. SELECTICA, INC.

Delaware Supreme Court
5 A.3d 586 (2010)

Holland, Justice

This is an appeal from a final judgment entered by the Court of Chancery. On November 16, 2008 the Board of Directors of Selectica, Inc. ("Selectica") reduced the trigger of its "poison pill" Shareholder Rights Plan from 15% to 4.99% of Selectica's outstanding shares and capped existing shareholders who held a 5% or more interest to a further increase of only 0.5% (the "NOL Poison Pill"). Selectica's reason for taking such action was to protect the company's net operating loss carryforwards ("NOLs"). When Trilogy, Inc. ("Trilogy") subsequently purchased shares above this cap, Selectica filed suit in the Court of Chancery on December 21, 2008, seeking a declaration that the NOL Poison Pill was valid and enforceable. On January 2, 2009, Selectica implemented the dilutive exchange provision (the "Exchange") of the NOL Poison Pill, which reduced Trilogy's interest from 6.7% to 3.3%, and adopted another Rights Plan with a 4.99% trigger (the "Reloaded NOL Poison Pill"). Selectica then amended its complaint to seek a declaration that the Exchange and the Reloaded NOL Poison Pill were valid.

Trilogy and its subsidiary Versata Enterprises, Inc. ("Versata") counterclaimed that the NOL Poison Pill, the Reloaded NOL Poison Pill, and the Exchange were unlawful on the grounds that, before acting, the Board failed to consider that its NOLs were unusable or that the two NOL poison pills were unnecessary given Selectica's unbroken history of losses and doubtful prospects of annual profits. Trilogy and Versata also asserted that the NOL Poison Pill and the Reloaded NOL Poison Pill were impermissibly preclusive of a successful proxy contest for Board control, particularly when combined with Selectica's staggered director terms. After trial, the Court of Chancery held that the NOL Poison Pill, the Reloaded NOL Poison Pill, and the Exchange were all valid under Delaware law.

Trilogy and Versata now appeal and assert two claims of error. First, they contend that the Court of Chancery erred in applying the Unocal test for enhanced judicial scrutiny when confronting what they frame as a question of first impression.

The issue (as framed by them) is: "what are the minimum requirements for a reasonable investigation before the board of a never-profitable company may adopt a [Rights Plan with a 4.99% trigger] for the ostensible purpose of protecting NOLs from an 'ownership change' under Section 382 of the Internal Revenue Code?" Second, they submit that the Court of Chancery erred in holding that the two NOL poison pills, either individually or in combination with a charter-based classified Board, did not have a preclusive effect on the shareholders' ability to pursue a successful proxy contest for control of the Company's board. We conclude that both arguments are without merit.

* * *

Facts[88]

The Court of Chancery described this as a case about the value of net operating loss carryforwards ("NOLs") to a currently profitless corporation, and the extent to which such a corporation may fight to preserve those NOLs. The Court of Chancery also provided a helpful overview of the concepts surrounding NOLs, their calculation, and possible impairment.

NOLs are tax losses, realized and accumulated by a corporation, that can be used to shelter future (or immediate past) income from taxation.[89] If taxable profit has been realized, the NOLs operate either to provide a refund of prior taxes paid or to reduce the amount of future income tax owed. Thus, NOLs can be a valuable asset, as a means of lowering tax payments and producing positive cash flow. NOLs are considered a contingent asset, their value being contingent upon the firm's reporting a future profit or having an immediate past profit.

Should the firm fail to realize a profit during the lifetime of the NOL (twenty years), the NOL expires. The precise value of a given NOL is usually impossible to determine since its ultimate use is subject to the timing and amount of recognized profit at the firm. If the firm never realizes taxable income, at dissolution it's NOLs, regardless of their amount, would have zero value.

In order to prevent corporate taxpayers from benefiting from NOLs generated by other entities, Internal Revenue Code Section 382 establishes limitations on the use of NOLs in periods following an "ownership change." If Section 382 is triggered, the law restricts the amount of prior NOLs that can be used in subsequent years to reduce the firm's tax obligations.[90] Once NOLs are so impaired, a substantial portion of their value is lost.

The precise definition of an "ownership change" under Section 382 is rather complex. At its most basic, an ownership change occurs when more than 50% of a firm's stock ownership changes over a three-year period. Specific provisions in

---

88 [1] The facts are taken from the Court of Chancery's opinion.

89 [2] NOLs may be carried backward two years and carried forward twenty years.

90 [3] The annual limitation on the use of past period NOLs following a change-in-control is calculated as the value of the firm's equity at the time of the ownership change, multiplied by a published rate of return, the federal long term exemption rate.

Section 382 define the precise manner by which this determination is made. Most importantly for purposes of this case, the only shareholders considered when calculating an ownership change under Section 382 are those who hold, or have obtained during the testing period, a 5% or greater block of the corporation's shares outstanding.

The Parties

Selectica, Inc. ("Selectica" or the "Company") is a Delaware corporation, headquartered in California and listed on the NASDAQ Global Market. It provides enterprise software solutions for contract management and sales configuration systems. Selectica is a micro-cap company with a concentrated shareholder base: the Company's seven largest investors own a majority of the stock, while fewer than twenty-five investors hold nearly two-thirds of the stock.[91]

Trilogy, Inc. ("Trilogy") is a Delaware corporation also specializing in enterprise software solutions. Trilogy stock is not publicly traded, and its founder, Joseph Liemandt, holds over 85% of the stock. Versata Enterprises, Inc. ("Versata"), a Delaware corporation and a subsidiary of Trilogy, provides technology powered business services to clients.

Before the events giving rise to this action, Versata and Trilogy beneficially owned 6.7% of Selectica's common stock. After they intentionally triggered Selectica's Shareholder Rights Plan through the purchase of additional shares, Versata's and Trilogy's joint beneficial ownership was diluted from 6.7% to approximately 3.3%.

James Arnold, Alan B. Howe, Lloyd Sems, Jim Thanos, and Brenda Zawatski are members of the Selectica Board of Directors (the "Board").[92] Zawatski and Thanos also served as Co-Chairs of the Board during the events at issue in the case.[93] In this role, they handled the day-to-day operations of the Company, as Selectica had been without a Chief Executive Officer since June 30, 2008.

Selectica's Historical Operating Difficulties

Since it became a public company in March 2000, Selectica has lost a substantial amount of money and failed to turn an annual profit, despite routinely projecting near-term profitability. Its IPO price of $30 per share has steadily fallen and now languishes below $1 per share, placing Selectica's market capitalization at roughly $23 million as of the end of March 2009. By Selectica's own admission, its value today "consists primarily in its cash reserves, its intellectual property portfolio, its customer and revenue base, and its accumulated NOLs." By consistently failing to

---

[91] [4] However, because of the Shareholder Rights Plan first instituted in 2003, no stockholder holds more than 15% of the outstanding shares.

[92] [5] Alan Howe was elected to the Board on January 12, 2009, after the events at issue in this case. He has not been charged with any breach of fiduciary duty and has not been served with process. Trilogy purports to name Howe as a Counterclaim-Defendant solely "in order to afford [Trilogy] complete relief."

[93] [6] On August 19, 2009, Thanos stepped down as Co-Chair and Zawatski became sole Chair of the Board and continued to handle the Company's daily operations.

achieve positive net income, Selectica has generated an estimated $160 million in NOLs for federal tax purposes over the past several years.

Selectica's Relationship with Trilogy

Selectica has had a complicated and often adversarial relationship with Trilogy, stretching back at least five years. Both companies compete in the relatively narrow market space of contract management and sales configuration. In April 2004, a Trilogy affiliate sued Selectica for patent infringement and secured a judgment that required Selectica, among other things, to pay Trilogy $7.5 million. While their suit was pending, in January 2005 Trilogy made an offer to buy Selectica for $4 per share in cash — a 20% premium above the then-trading price — which Selectica's Board rejected. Nevertheless, during March and April of that year, a Trilogy affiliate acquired nearly 7% of Selectica's common stock through open market trades. In early fall 2005, Trilogy made another offer for Selectica's shares at a 16%-23% premium, which was also rejected.

In September 2006, a Trilogy-affiliated holder of Selectica stock sent a letter to the Board questioning whether certain stock option grants had been backdated.[94] The following month, Trilogy filed another patent infringement lawsuit against Selectica. That action was settled in October 2007, when Selectica agreed to a one-time payment of $10 million, plus an additional amount of not more than $7.5 million in subsequent payments to be made quarterly. In late fall 2006, Trilogy sold down its holdings in Selectica.

Steel Partners

Steel Partners is a private equity fund that has been a Selectica shareholder since at least 2006 and is currently its largest shareholder. One of Steel Partners' apparent investment strategies is to invest in small companies with large NOLs with the intent to pair the failing company with a profitable business in order to reap the tax benefits of the NOLs. Steel Partners has actively worked with Selectica to calculate and monitor the Company's NOLs since the time of its original investment.

By early 2008, Steel Partners was advocating a quick sale of Selectica's assets, leaving a NOL shell that could be merged with a profitable operating company in order to shelter the profits of the operating company. In October 2008, Steel Partners informed members of Selectica's Board that it planned to increase its ownership position to 14.9% just below the 15% trigger of the 2003 Rights Plan, which it later did. Jack Howard, President of Steel Partners, lobbied for a Board seat twice in 2008, citing his experience dealing with NOLs, but was rebuffed.

---

[94] [7] A special committee empanelled by the Board ultimately concluded that certain options had, in fact, been backdated. Consequently, Selectica was required to restate its financial statements to record additional stock-based compensation and related tax effects for past option grants and incurred fees associated with the investigation in excess of $6.2 million. This episode also led to the resignation of Selectica's then-Chairmen and Chief Executive Officer Stephen Bannion (who had been the Company's Chief Financial Officer at the time of the grants of question) and the appointment of then-Director Robert Jurkowski to the Chief Executive and Chair position.

Selectica Investigates Its NOLs

In 2006, at the urging of Steel Partners, Selectica directed Alan Chinn, its outside tax adviser, to perform a high-level analysis into whether its NOLs were subject to any limitations under Section 382 of the Internal Revenue Code. Chinn concluded that five prior changes in ownership had caused the forfeiture of approximately $24.6 million in NOLs. Selectica provided the results of this study to Steel Partners, although not to any other Selectica shareholder.

In March 2007, again at Steel Partner's recommendation, Selectica retained a second accountant who specialized in NOL calculations, John Brogan of Burr Pilger & Mayer, LLP, to analyze the Company's NOLs more carefully and report on Chinn's Section 382 analysis. Brogan had previously analyzed the NOLs at other Steel Partners ventures. Brogan ultimately determined that Chinn's conclusions were erroneous.

The Company engaged Brogan to perform additional work on the topic of NOLs in June 2007. One of Steel Partners' employees, Avi Goodman, worked closely with Brogan on the matter, although Brogan was working for and being paid by Selectica and received no compensation from Steel Partners. Brogan's draft letter opinion, concluding that the Company had not undergone an "ownership change" for Section 382 purposes since 1999, was shared with Steel Partners, although again not with any other outside investors.

In the fall of 2007, Brogan proposed a third, more detailed, Section 382 study, which Selectica's then-CEO, Robert Jurkowski, opposed. In February 2008, the Board voted against spending $40,000-$50,000 to fund this Section 382 study. By July, however, the Board asked Brogan to update his study. Brogan delivered the draft opinion that, as of March 31, 2008, the Company had approximately $165 million in NOLs. Brogan was later asked to advise the Board in the fall of 2008 on the updated status of its NOLs when the Board moved to amend its Rights Plan.

Lloyd Sems Elected Director

In April 2008, the Board began interviewing candidates for an open board seat, giving preference to the Company's large stockholders. Selectica investor Lloyd Sems had previously expressed interest in joining the Board and had sought support from certain shareholders, including Steel Partners, through Howard, and Lloyd Miller, another large Selectica shareholder not affiliated with Steel Partners. Both Miller and Howard wrote to the Board in support of Sems' appointment, although Sems was already favored by the Board by that time. In June 2008, Sems was appointed to the Board.

As large shareholders, Sems, Howard, and Miller had periodically discussed Selectica as early as October 2007. At that time, Sems had e-mailed Howard, stating, "I wanted to get your opinion of how or if you would like me to proceed with [Selectica]." Howard replied, "Lloyd [Miller] said he would call you about [Selectica]." Both before and after his appointment to the Board, Sems discussed with Howard and Miller a number of the proposals that Sems ultimately advocated as a director, including that Selectica should buy back its stock, that Selectica should consider selling its businesses, that the NOLs were important and should be preserved through the adoption of a Rights Plan with a 5% trigger, and that Jurkowski should be removed as CEO.

Selectica Restructures and Explores Alternatives

In early July 2008, after determining that the Company needed to change course, the Board terminated Jurkowski as CEO and eliminated several management positions in the sales configuration business. Later that month, prompted by the receipt of five unsolicited acquisition offers over the span of a few weeks, the Board announced that it was in the process of selecting an investment banker (ultimately, Jim Reilly of Needham & Company) to evaluate strategic alternatives for the Company and to assist with a process that ultimately might result in the Company's sale. In view of the potential sale, the Board decided to forgo the expense of replacing Jurkowski and, instead, asked Zawatski and Thanos jointly to assume the title of Co-Chair and to perform operational oversight roles on an interim basis.

The Needham Process

Needham has actively carried outs its task of evaluating Selectica's strategic options since its selection by the Board. Needham first discussed with the Board the various strategic choices that the Company could take. These included a merger of equals with a public company, a reverse IPO or other going-private transaction, the sale of certain assets, and the use of cash to acquire another company, as well as stock repurchases or the issuance of dividends if Selectica decided to continue as an independent public company in the absence of sufficient market interest for an acquisition.

In October 2008, Needham prepared an Executive Summary of the assets and operations of Selectica and subsequently reached out to potential buyers, keeping in touch with various interested parties throughout the remainder of the year and into the first part of 2009. By February 2009, at least half a dozen parties had come forward with letters of intent and were in the process of meeting with Selectica management and conducting due diligence in the Company, with Needham evaluating their various proposals for the purchase of all or part of Selectica's operations. As of April 2009, Selectica, through Needham, had signed a letter of intent and entered into exclusive negotiations with a potential buyer.

Trilogy's Offers Rejected

On July 15, 2008, Trilogy's President, Joseph Liemandt, called Zawatski to inquire generally about the possibility of an acquisition of Selectica by Trilogy. On July 29, Trilogy Chief Financial Officer Sean Fallon, Trilogy Director of Finance Andrew Price, and Versata Chief Executive Officer Randy Jacobs participated in a conference call with Selectica Co-Chairs Zawatski and Thanos on the same topic. During the call, Thanos inquired as to how Trilogy would calculate a value for the Company's NOLs. Fallon replied that Trilogy, "really [did not] pursue them with as much vigor as other[s] might since that is not our core strategy."[95]

The following evening, Fallon contacted Zawatski and outlined two proposals for Trilogy to acquire Selectica's business: (1) Trilogy's purchase of all of the assets of Selectica's sales configuration business in exchange for the cancellation of the $7.1 million in debt Selectica still owed under the October 2007 settlement with Trilogy; or (2) Trilogy's purchase of Selectica's entire operations for the cancellation of the debt plus an additional $6 million in cash. Fallon subsequently followed up with an email reiterating both proposals and suggesting that either proposal would allow Selectica to still make use of its NOLs through the later sale of its corporate entity.

Shortly thereafter, the Board rejected both proposals, made no counterproposal, and there were no follow-up discussions. On October 9, 2008, Trilogy made a second bid to acquire all of the Selectica's assets for $10 million in cash plus the cancellation of the debt, which the Board also rejected. Although Trilogy was invited to participate in the sale process being overseen by Needham, Trilogy was apparently unwilling to sign a non-disclosure agreement, which was a prerequisite for participation. Around this same time, Trilogy had begun making open-market purchases for Selectica stock, although the Board apparently was not aware of this fact at the time.

Trilogy Buys Selectica Stock

On the evening of November 10, Fallon contacted Zawatski and informed her that Trilogy had purchased more than 5% of Selectica's outstanding stock and would be filing a Schedule 13D shortly, which it did on November 13.[96] On a subsequent call with Zawatski and Reilly, Fallon explained that Trilogy had begun buying because it believed that "the company should work quickly to preserve whatever shareholder value remained and that we were interested in seeing this process that they announced with Needham, that we were interested in seeing that accelerate. . . ." Within four days of its 13D filing, Trilogy had acquired more than 320,000 additional shares, representing an additional 1% of the Company's outstanding shares.

NOL Poison Pill Adopted

In the wake of Trilogy's decision to begin acquiring Selectica shares, the Board took actions to gauge the impact of these acquisitions, if any, on the Company's NOLs, and to determine whether anything needed to be done to mitigate their effects. Sems immediately asked Brogan to revise his Section 382 analysis — which had not been formally updated since July — to take into account the recent purchases. The revised analysis was delivered to Sems and the Company's new CFO, Richard Heaps, on November 15. It showed that the cumulative acquisition of

---

[95] [8] However, as part of its 2005 effort to acquire Selectica, Trilogy had performed "a pretty detailed analysis" of Selectica's NOLs. Johnston testified that this analysis was occasionally updated and that similar analyses had been performed on a dozen or so other acquisition targets.

[96] [9] The November 13, 2008, Schedule 13D reported that Versata and affiliates had purchased 1,437,891 shares of Selectica stock, increasing its ownership to 5.1%.

stock by shareholders over the past three years stood at 40%, which was roughly unchanged from the previous calculation, due to some double counting that occurred in the July analysis.[97]

The Board met on November 16 to discuss the situation and to consider amending Selectica's Shareholder Rights Plan, which had been in place since February 2003. As with many Rights Plans employed as protection devices against hostile takeovers, Selectica's Rights Plan had a 15% trigger. The Board considered an amendment that would reduce that threshold trigger to 4.99% in order to prevent additional 5% owners from emerging and potentially causing a change-in-control event, thereby devaluing Selectica's NOLs. Also present at the meeting were Heaps, Brogan, and Reilly, along with Delaware counsel.

Heaps gave an overview of the Company's existing Shareholder Rights Plan and reviewed the stock price activity since Trilogy had filed its Schedule 13D, noting that shares totaling approximately 2.3% of the Company had changed hands in the two days following the filing. Brogan reviewed the Section 382 ownership analysis that his firm had undertaken on behalf of the Company, noting that additional acquisitions of roughly 10% of the float by new or existing 5% holders would "result in a permanent limitation on use of the Company's net operating loss carryforwards and that, once an ownership change occurred, there would be no way to cure the use limitation on the net operating loss carryforwards." He further advised the Board that "net operating loss carryforwards were a significant asset" and that he generally advises companies to consider steps to protect their NOLs when they experience a 30% or greater change in beneficial ownership. Lastly, Brogan noted that, while he believed that the cumulative ownership change calculations would decline significantly over the next twelve months, "it would decline only modestly, if at all, over the next three to four months," meaning that "the Company would continue to be at risk of an ownership change over the near term."

Reilly discussed the Company's strategic alternatives and noted that Steel Partners and other parties had expressed interest in pursuing a transaction that would realize the value of Selectica's NOLs. He also reviewed potential transaction structures in which the Company might be able to utilize its NOLs. Responding to questions from the Board, Reilly noted that "it is difficult to value the Company's net operating loss carryforwards with greater precision, because their value depends, among other things, on the ability of the Company to generate profits." He confirmed that "existing stockholders may realize significant potential value" from the utilization of the Company's NOLs, which would be "significantly impaired" if a Section 382 ownership change occurred.

At the request of the Board, Delaware counsel reviewed the Delaware law standards that apply for adopting and implementing measures that have an anti-takeover effect. The Board then discussed amending the existing Shareholder Rights Plan, and the possible terms of such an amendment. These included: the pros and cons of providing a cushion for preexisting 5% holders, the appropriate effective date of the new Shareholder Rights Plan, whether the Board should have

---

[97] [10] A more formal analysis was provided on November 26, finding a 38.8% change in ownership over the relevant period.

authority to exclude purchases by specific stockholders from triggering the Rights Plan, and whether a review process should be implemented to determine periodically whether the Rights Plan should remain in effect.

The Board then unanimously passed a resolution amending Selectica's Shareholder Rights Plan, by decreasing the beneficial ownership trigger from 15% to 4.99%, while grandfathering in existing 5% shareholders and permitting them to acquire up to an additional 0.5% (subject to the original 15% cap) without triggering the NOL Poison Pill.

The Board resolution also established an Independent Director Evaluation Committee (the "Committee") as a standing committee of the Board to review periodically the rights agreement at the behest of the Board and to "determine whether the Rights [Plan] continues to be in the best interest of the Corporation and its stockholders." The Committee was also directed to review "the appropriate trigger percentage" of the Rights Plan based on corporate and shareholder developments, any broader developments relating to rights plans generally — including academic studies of rights plans and contests for corporate control — and any other factors it deems relevant. The Board set April 30, 2009, as the first date that the Committee should report its findings.

Trilogy Triggers NOL Poison Pill

The Board publicly announced the amendment of Selectica's Rights Plan on Monday, November 17. Early the following morning, Fallon e-mailed Trilogy's broker, saying "[W]e need to stop buying SLTC. They announced a new pill and we need to understand it." Fallon also sent Liemandt a copy of Selectica's 8-K containing the amended language of the NOL Poison Pill. Trilogy immediately sought legal advice about the NOL Poison Pill. The following morning, Liemandt e-mailed Price, with a copy to Fallon, asking, "What percentage of [Selectica] would we need to buy to ruin the tax attributes that [S]teel [P]artners is looking for?"[98] They concluded that they would need to acquire 23% to trigger a change-in-control event.

Later that week, Trilogy sent Selectica a letter asserting that a Selectica contract with Sun Microsystems constituted a breach of the October 2007 settlement and seeking an immediate meeting with Selectica purportedly to discuss the breach, even though members of Trilogy's management had been on notice of the contract as early as July. Fallon, Liemandt, and Jacobs from Trilogy, along with Zawatski, Thanos, and Heaps from Selectica met on December 17. The parties' discussions at this meeting are protected by a confidentiality agreement that had been circulated in advance. However, Selectica contends that "based solely on statements and conduct outside that meeting, it is evident that Trilogy threatened to trigger the NOL Poison Pill deliberately unless Selectica agreed to Trilogy's renewed efforts to extract money from the Company."

---

[98] [11] Liemandt testified that his question meant, "what is the amount that we can buy without hurting it, which is the other way of asking, what's the amount you can buy to ruin it." Price testified, however, that he understood the question as being more straightforward, specifically, "what percentage would we have to buy to trigger a change of control as per Section 382."

On December 18, Trilogy purchased an additional 30,000 Selectica shares, and Trilogy management verified with Liemandt his intention to proceed with "buying through" the NOL Poison Pill. The following morning, Trilogy purchased an additional 124,061 shares of Selectica, bringing its ownership share to 6.7% and thereby becoming an "Acquiring Person" under the NOL Poison Pill. Liemandt testified that the rationale behind triggering the pill was to "bring accountability" to the Board and "expose" what Liemandt characterized as "illegal behavior" by the Board in adopting a pill with such a low trigger. Fallon asserted that the reason for triggering the NOL Poison Pill was to "bring some clarity and urgency" to their discussions with Selectica about the two parties' somewhat complicated relationship by "setting a time frame that might help accelerate discussions" on the direction of the business.

Fallon placed a telephone call to Zawatski on December 19 to advise her that Trilogy had bought through the NOL Poison Pill. During a return call by Zawatski later that evening, Fallon indicated that Trilogy felt, based on the conversations from December 17, that Selectica no longer wanted Trilogy as a shareholder or creditor. He then proposed that Selectica repurchase Trilogy's shares, accelerate the payment of its debt, terminate its license with Sun, and make a payment to Trilogy of $5 million "for settlement of basically all outstanding issues between our companies." Zawatski recalled that Fallon told her that Trilogy had triggered the pill "to get our attention and create a sense of urgency;" that, since the Board would have ten days to determine how to react to the pill trigger, "it would force the board to make a decision."

Board Considers Options and Requests a Standstill

The Selectica Board had a telephonic meeting on Saturday, December 20, to discuss Trilogy's demands and an appropriate response. The Board discussed "the desirability of taking steps to ensure the validity of the Shareholder Rights Plan," and ultimately passed a resolution authorizing the filing of this lawsuit, which occurred the following day. On December 22, Trilogy filed an amended Schedule 13D disclosing its ownership percentage and again the Selectica Board met telephonically to discuss the litigation. It eventually agreed to have a representative contact Trilogy to seek a standstill on any additional open market purchases while the Board used the ten-day clock under the NOL Poison Pill to determine whether to consider Trilogy's purchases "exempt" under the Rights Plan, and if not, how Selectica would go about implementing the pill.

The amended Rights Plan allowed the Board to declare Trilogy an "Exempt Person" during the ten-day period following the trigger, if the Board determined that Trilogy would not "jeopardize or endanger the availability to the Company of the NOLs. . . ." The Board could also decide during this window to exchange the rights (other than those held by Trilogy) for shares of common stock. If the Board did nothing, then after ten days the rights would "flip in" automatically, becoming exercisable for $36 worth of newly-issued common stock at a price of $18 per right.

The Board met again by telephone the following day, December 23, to discuss the progress of the litigation and to consider the potential impact of the various alternatives under the NOL Poison Pill. The Board agreed to meet in person the following Monday, December 29, along with the Company's financial, legal, and accounting advisors, to evaluate further the available options. The Board also voted to reduce the number of authorized directors from seven to five.

On Wednesday, December 24, the Board met once again by telephone upon learning that the Company's counsel had not succeeded in convincing Trilogy to agree to a standstill. The Board resolved that Zawatski should call Fallon to determine whether Trilogy was willing "to negotiate a standstill agreement that might make triggering the remedies available under the Shareholder Rights Plan, as amended, unnecessary at this time." Zawatski spoke with Fallon on the morning of December 26. Fallon stated that Trilogy did not want to agree to a standstill, that relief from the NOL Poison Pill was not Trilogy's goal, and that Trilogy expected that the NOL Poison Pill would apply to it. Fallon reiterated that the ten-day window would help "speed [the] course" towards a resolution of their claims.

The Board and its advisors met again on December 29. Thanos provided an update on recent developments at the Company, including financial results, management changes, and the Needham Process, as well as an overview of the make-up of the Company's shareholder base. Reilly then provided a more detailed report on the status of the Needham Process. Thereafter, Brogan presented his firm's updated analysis of Selectica's NOLs, which found that the Company had at least $160 million in NOLs and that there had been a roughly 40% ownership change by 5% holders over the three-year testing period. Since those were not expected to "roll off" in the near term, there was "a significant risk of a Section 382 ownership change."

Brogan subsequently discussed the possible consequences of the two principal mechanisms for implementing the triggered NOL Poison Pill to the change-in-control analysis. He stated that employing a share exchange would not likely have a materially negative impact on the Section 382 analysis. He expressed concern, however, about the uncertain effect of a flip-in pill on subsequent ownership levels (specifically, the possibility that a flip-in pill would, itself, trigger a Section 382 ownership change). Reilly once again addressed the Board to explain the ways he believed the NOLs would be valuable to the Company in its ongoing exploration of strategic alternatives, and reiterated his opinion that an ownership change would "reduce the value of the Company."

The Board also discussed Trilogy's settlement demands. It found them "highly unreasonable" and "lack[ing] any reasonable basis in fact," and that "it [was] not in the best interests of the Company and its stockholders to accept Trilogy/Versata's settlement demands relating to entirely separate intellectual property disputes as a precondition to negotiating a standstill agreement to resolve this dispute." The Board discussed Trilogy's actions at some length, ultimately concluding that they "were very harmful to the Company in a number of respects," and that "implementing the exchange was reasonable in relation to the threat imposed by Trilogy." In particular, that was because (1) the NOLs were seen as "an important corporate asset that could significantly enhance stockholder value," and (2) Trilogy had intentionally triggered the NOL Poison Pill, publicly suggested it might purchase additional stock, and had refused to negotiate a standstill agreement, even though an additional 10% acquisition by a 5% shareholder would likely trigger an ownership change under Section 382.

The Board then authorized Delaware counsel to contact Trilogy in writing, one final time, to seek a standstill agreement. It also passed resolutions delegating the full power of the Board to the Committee to determine whether or not to treat Trilogy or its acquisition as "exempt," and nominating Alan Howe as a new member of the Board. On the evening of December 29, Selectica's Delaware counsel e-mailed Trilogy's trial counsel at the Board's instruction, seeking a standstill agreement "so that the Board could consider either declaring them an 'Exempt Person' under the Rights Plan . . . or alternatively, settle the litigation altogether in exchange for a long term agreement relating to your clients' ownership of additional shares." The following afternoon, Trilogy's counsel responded that Trilogy was not willing to agree to the proposed standstill.

Two days later, on December 31, the Board met telephonically and was informed of Trilogy's latest rejection of a standstill agreement. The Board discussed its options with its legal advisors and ultimately concluded that the NOL Poison Pill should go into effect and that an exchange was the best alternative and should be implemented as soon as possible in order to protect the NOLs, even at the risk of disrupting common stock trading. The Board directed advisers to prepare a technical amendment to the NOL Poison Pill to clarify the time at which the exchange would become effective.

Board Adopts Reloaded Pill and Dilutes Trilogy Holdings

On January 2, the Board met telephonically once more, reiterating its delegation of authority to the Committee to make recommendations regarding the implementation of the NOL Poison Pill. The Board also passed a resolution expressly confirming that the Board's delegation of authority to the Committee included the power to effect an exchange of the rights under the NOL Poison Pill and to declare a new dividend of rights under an amended Rights Plan (the "Reloaded NOL Poison Pill"). The Board then adjourned and the Committee — comprised of Sems and Arnold — met with legal and financial advisors, who confirmed that there had been no new agreement with representatives from Trilogy, reiterated that the NOLs remained "a valuable corporate asset of the Company in connection with the Company's ongoing exploration of strategic alternatives," and advised the Committee members of their fiduciary obligations under Delaware law.

Reilly presented information to the Committee about the current takeover environment and the use of Rights Plans (specifically, the types of pills commonly employed and their triggering thresholds), and reviewed the Company's then-current anti-takeover defenses compared with those of other public companies. Reilly stated that "a so-called NOL rights plan with a 4.99% trigger threshold is designed to help protect against stock accumulations that would trigger an 'ownership change,' " and that "implementing appropriate protections of the Company's net operating loss carryforwards was especially important at present," given Trilogy's recent share acquisitions superimposed on the Company's existing Section 382 ownership levels. Finally, Reilly reviewed the proposed terms and conditions of the Reloaded NOL Poison Pill, discussed the methodology for determining the exercise price of the new rights, and made recommendations. The Committee sought and obtained reconfirmed assurances by its financial and legal advisors that the NOLs were a valuable corporate asset and that they remained at a significant risk of being impaired.

The Committee concluded that Trilogy should not be deemed an "Exempt Person," that its purchase of additional shares should not be deemed an "Exempt Transaction," that an exchange of rights for common stock (the "Exchange") should occur, and that a new rights dividend on substantially similar terms should be adopted. The Committee passed resolutions implementing those conclusions, thereby adopting the Reloaded NOL Poison Pill and instituting the Exchange.

The Exchange doubled the number of shares of Selectica common stock owned by each shareholder of record, other than Trilogy or Versata, thereby reducing their beneficial holdings from 6.7% to 3.3%. The implementation of the Exchange led to a freeze in the trading of Selectica stock from January 5, 2009 until February 4, 2009, with the stock price frozen at $0.69. The Reloaded NOL Poison Pill will expire on January 2, 2012, unless the expiration date is advanced or extended, or unless these rights are exchanged or redeemed by the Board some time before.

ANALYSIS

Unocal Standard Applies

In *Unocal*, this Court recognized that "our corporate law is not static. It must grow and develop in response to, indeed in anticipation of, evolving concepts and needs."[99] The Court of Chancery concluded that the protection of company NOLs may be an appropriate corporate policy that merits a defensive response when they are threatened. We agree.

The *Unocal* two part test is useful as a judicial analytical tool because of the flexibility of its application in a variety of fact scenarios.[100] Delaware courts have approved the adoption of a Shareholder Rights Plan as an antitakeover device, and have applied the *Unocal* test to analyze a board's response to an actual or potential hostile takeover threat.[101] Any NOL poison pill's principal intent, however, is to prevent the inadvertent forfeiture of potentially valuable assets, not to protect against hostile takeover attempts.[102] Even so, any Shareholder Rights Plan, by its nature, operates as an antitakeover device. Consequently, notwithstanding its primary purpose, a NOL poison pill must also be analyzed under *Unocal* because of its effect and its direct implications for hostile takeovers.

---

[99] [12] Unocal Corp. v. Mesa Petroleum Co., 493 A.2d 946, 957 (Del.1985). [Reproduced on page 650 of the casebook.]

[100] [13] Paramount Communications, Inc. v. Time, Inc., 571 A.2d 1140, 1153 (Del.1990).

[101] [14] Moran v. Household Int'l, Inc., 500 A.2d 1346, 1356 (Del.1985).

[102] [15] The Court of Chancery found that "typically, companies with large NOLs would not be at risk of takeover attempts if the NOLs are the company's principal asset, as the takeover would likely trigger a change in control and impair the asset."

Threat Reasonably Identified

The first part of *Unocal* review requires a board to show that it had reasonable grounds for concluding that a threat to the corporate enterprise existed. The Selectica Board concluded that the NOLs were an asset worth preserving and that their protection was an important corporate objective. Trilogy contends that the Board failed to demonstrate that it conducted a reasonable investigation before determining that the NOLs were an asset worth protecting. We disagree.

The record reflects that the Selectica Board met for more than two and a half hours on November 16. The Court of Chancery heard testimony from all four directors and from Brogan, Reilly, and Heaps, who also attended that meeting and advised the Board. The record shows that the Board first analyzed the NOLs in September 2006, and sought updated Section 382 analyses from Brogan in March 2007, June 2007, and July 2008. At the November 16 meeting, Brogan advised the Board that the NOLs were a "significant asset" based on his recently updated calculations of the NOLs' magnitude. Reilly, an investment banker, similarly advised the Board that the NOLs were worth protecting given the possibility of a sale of Selectica or its assets. Accordingly, the record supports the Court of Chancery's factual finding that the Board acted in good faith reliance on the advice of experts[103] in concluding that "the NOLs were an asset worth protecting and thus, that their preservation was an important corporate objective."

The record also supports the reasonableness of the Board's decision to act promptly by reducing the trigger on Selectica's Rights Plan from 15% to 4.99%. At the November 16 meeting, Brogan advised the Board that the change-of-ownership calculation under Section 382 stood at approximately 40%. Trilogy's ownership had climbed to over 5% in just over a month, and Trilogy intended to continue buying more stock. There was nothing to stop others from acquiring stock up to the 15% trigger in the Company's existing Rights Plan. Once the Section 382 limitation was tripped, the Board was advised it could not be undone.

At the November 16 meeting, the Board voted to amend Selectica's existing Rights Plan to protect the NOLs against a potential Section 382 "change of ownership." It reduced the trigger of its Shareholders Rights Plan from 15% to 4.99% and provided that existing shareholders who held in excess of 4.99% would be subject to dilutive consequences if they increased their holdings by 0.5%. The Board also created the Review Committee (Arnold and Sems) with a mandate to conduct a periodic review of the continuing appropriateness of the NOL Poison Pill.

The Court of Chancery found the record "replete with evidence" that, based upon the expert advice it received, the Board was reasonable in concluding that Selectica's NOLs were worth preserving and that Trilogy's actions presented a

---

[103] [16] The Delaware General Corporation Law Section § 141(e), states:

> A member of the board of directors, or a member of any committee designated by the board of directors, shall, in the performance of such member's duties, be fully protected in relying in good faith . . . upon such information, opinions, reports or statements presented to the corporation . . . by any other person as to matters the member reasonably believes are within such other person's professional or expert competence and who has been selected with reasonable care by or on behalf of the corporation.

Del. Code Ann. tit. 8, § 141(e) (2010).

serious threat of their impairment. The Court of Chancery explained those findings, as follows:

> The threat posed by Trilogy was reasonably viewed as qualitatively different from the normal corporate control dispute that leads to the adoption of a shareholder rights plan. In this instance, Trilogy, a competitor with a contentious history, recognized that harm would befall its rival if it purchased sufficient shares of Selectica stock, and Trilogy proceeded to act accordingly. It was reasonable for the Board to respond, and the timing of Trilogy's campaign required the Board to act promptly. Moreover, the 4.99% threshold for the NOL Poison Pill was driven by our tax laws and regulations; the threshold, low as it is, was measured by reference to an external standard, one created neither by the Board nor by the Court [of Chancery]. Within this context, it is not for the Court [of Chancery] to second-guess the Board's efforts to protect Selectica's NOLs.

Those findings are not clearly erroneous.[104] They are supported by the record and the result of a logical deductive reasoning process.[105] Accordingly, we hold that the Selectica directors satisfied the first part of the *Unocal* test by showing "that they had reasonable grounds for believing that a danger to corporate policy and effectiveness existed because of another person's stock ownership."[106]

Selectica Defenses Not Preclusive

The second part of the *Unocal* test requires an initial evaluation of whether a board's defensive response to the threat was preclusive or coercive and, if neither, whether the response was "reasonable in relation to the threat" identified.[107] Under *Unitrin*, a defensive measure is disproportionate and unreasonable *per se* if it is draconian by being either coercive or preclusive.[108] A coercive response is one that is "aimed at 'cramming down' on its shareholders a management-sponsored alternative."[109]

A defensive measure is preclusive where it "makes a bidder's ability to wage a successful proxy contest and gain control either 'mathematically impossible' or 'realistically unattainable.' "[110] A successful proxy contest that is mathematically impossible is, *ipso facto*, realistically unattainable. Because the "mathematically impossible" formulation in *Unitrin* is subsumed within the category of preclusivity described as "realistically unattainable," there is, analytically speaking, only one

---

[104] [17] *Homestore, Inc. v. Tafeen*, 888 A.2d 204, 217 (Del.2005).

[105] [18] *Levitt v. Bouvier*, 287 A.2d 671, 673 (Del.1972).

[106] [19] *Unocal Corp. v. Mesa Petroleum Co.*, 493 A.2d at 955 (citing *Cheff v. Mathes*, 199 A.2d at 554-55).

[107] [20] Unocal Corp. v. Mesa Petroleum Co., 493 A.2d at 955.

[108] [21] *Unitrin, Inc. v. Am. Gen. Corp.*, 651 A.2d at 1387.

[109] [22] *Id.* at 1387 (citing *Paramount Communications, Inc. v. Time, Inc.*, 571 A.2d at 1154-1155 (Del.1990)). There are no allegations contended that the NOL Poison Pill, the Exchange, and the Reloaded NOL Poison Pill are coercive.

[110] [23] *Carmody v. Toll Bros., Inc.*, 723 A.2d 1180, 1195 (Del.Ch.1998) (quoting *Unitrin, Inc. v. Am. Gen. Corp.*, 651 A.2d at 1389).

test of preclusivity: "realistically unattainable."

Trilogy claims that a Rights Plan with a 4.99% trigger renders the possibility of an effective proxy contest realistically unattainable. In support of that position, Trilogy argues that, because a proxy contest can only be successful where the challenger has sufficient credibility, the 4.99% pill trigger prevents a potential dissident from signaling its financial commitment to the company so as to establish such credibility. In addition, Professor Ferrell, Trilogy's expert witness, testified that the 5% cap on ownership exacerbates the free rider problem already experienced by investors considering fielding an insurgent slate of directors, and makes initiating a proxy fight an economically unattractive proposition.[111]

This Court first examined the validity of a Shareholder Rights Plan in *Moran v. Household International, Inc.*[112] In *Moran* the Rights Plan at issue had a 20% trigger.[113] We recognized that, while a Rights Plan "does deter the formation of proxy efforts of a certain magnitude, it does not limit the voting power of individual shares."[114]

In *Moran*, we concluded that the assertion that a Rights Plan would frustrate proxy fights was "highly conjectural" and pointed to "recent corporate takeover battles in which insurgents holding less than 10% stock ownership were able to secure corporate control through a proxy contest or the threat of one."[115]

The 5% trigger that is necessary for a NOL poison pill to serve its primary objective imposes a lower threshold than the Rights Plan thresholds that have traditionally been adopted and upheld as acceptable anti-takeover defenses by Delaware courts. Selectica submits that the distinguishing feature of the NOL Poison Pill and Reloaded NOL Poison Pill — the 5% trigger — is not enough to differentiate them from other Rights Plans previously upheld by Delaware courts, and that there is no evidence that a challenger starting below 5% could not realistically hope to prevail in a proxy contest at Selectica. In support of those arguments Selectica presented expert testimony from Professor John C. Coates IV and Peter C. Harkins.

Professor Coates identified more than fifty publicly held companies that have implemented NOL poison pills with triggers at roughly 5%, including several large, well-known corporations, some among the Fortune 1000. Professor Coates noted that 5% Rights Plans are customarily adopted where issuers have "ownership

---

[111] [24] According to Professor Ferrell, the free rider problem is that, even if an investor believes that replacing the board would result in a material benefit to shareholders, the investor has to bear the full cost of a proxy fight while only receiving her proportionate fraction of the benefit bestowed upon shareholders. Professor Ferrell testified that, along with the reduced likelihood of success at a 5% position, the capped position would mean that the challenger would be unable to internalize more of the benefits by increasing her share ownership.

[112] [25] *Moran v. Household Int'l, Inc.*, 500 A.2d 1346, 1356 (Del.1985).

[113] [26] *Id.* at 1355.

[114] [27] *Id.*

[115] [28] *Id.* This Court additionally noted that "many proxy contests are won with an insurgent ownership of less than 20%," and that "the key variable in proxy contest success is the merit of an insurgent's issues, not the size of his holding." *Id.*

controlled" assets, such as the NOLs at issue in this case. Professor Coates also testified that Selectica's 5% Rights Plan trigger was narrowly tailored to protect the NOLs because the relevant tax law, Section 382, measures ownership changes based on shareholders who own 5% or more of the outstanding stock.

Moreover, and as the Court of Chancery noted, shareholder advisory firm RiskMetrics Group now supports Rights Plans with a trigger below 5% on a case-by-case basis if adopted for the stated purpose of preserving a company's net operating losses.[116] The factors RiskMetrics will consider in determining whether to support a management proposal to adopt a NOL poison pill are the pill's trigger, the value of the NOLs, the term of the pill, and any corresponding shareholder protection mechanisms in place, such as a sunset provision causing the pill to expire upon exhaustion or expiration of the NOLs.[117]

Selectica expert witness Harkins of the D.F. King & Co. proxy solicitation firm analyzed proxy contests over the three-year period ending December 31, 2008. He found that of the fifteen proxy contests that occurred in micro-cap companies where the challenger controlled less than 5.49% of the outstanding shares, the challenger successfully obtained board seats in ten contests, five of which involved companies with classified boards.[118] Harkins opined that Selectica's unique shareholder profile would considerably reduce the costs associated with a proxy fight, since seven shareholders controlled 55% of Selectica's shares, and twenty-two shareholders controlled 62%. Harkins testified that "if you have a compelling platform, which is critical, it would be easy from a logistical perspective; and from a cost perspective, it would be *de minimis* expense to communicate with those investors, among others." Harkins noted that to win a proxy contest at Selectica, one would need to gain only the support of owners of 43.2% plus one share.[119]

The Court of Chancery concluded that the NOL Poison Pill and Reloaded NOL Poison Pill were not preclusive. For a measure to be preclusive, it must render a successful proxy contest realistically unattainable given the specific factual context. The record supports the Court of Chancery's factual determination and legal

---

[116] [29] Coates' Report at 11 (citing Simpson Thacher & Bartlett, LLP, Client Memo: Rights Plans Offer Special Benefits for Companies Whose Market Capitalization Has Declined to $500 Million or Below (2009), available at www.stblaw.com/content/Publications/pub795.pdf and RiskMetrics Group, U.S. Proxy Guidelines Concise Summary (Digest of Selected Key Guidelines) (2009), www.riskmetrics.com/sites/default/files/2009RMGUSPolicyConciseSummaryGuideline.pdf).

[117] [30] *Id.*

[118] [31] There were eight such contests at micro-cap companies in which the challenging shareholder held less than 4.99% of the outstanding shares. Challengers prevailed in six of these contests, including at three companies that had classified boards.

[119] [32] Trilogy rejects Selectica's position that due to the concentrated shareholder base, one could simply pick up the phone and call the shareholders, because Steel Partners, Director Sems, and Lloyd Miller owned 23.5% of Selectica's stock at the time. Thus, their opposition would result in having to conduct a traditional proxy contest. However, twenty-two shareholders own a combined 62% of the stock. If the 23.5% owned by Steel Partners, Sems, and Miller are subtracted from 62%, that leaves 38.5% of Selectica owned by nineteen shareholders. Those nineteen shareholders plus the 4.99% amount allowed before triggering the pill would equal 43.49% of Selectica's shares, an amount slightly in excess of what Harkins testified would be needed to win a proxy contest.

conclusion that Selectica's NOL Poison Pill and Reloaded NOL Poison Pill do not meet that preclusivity standard.

Our observation in *Unitrin* is also applicable here: "[I]t is hard to imagine a company more readily susceptible to a proxy contest concerning a pure issue of dollars."[120] The key variable in a proxy contest would be the merit of the bidder's proposal and not the magnitude of its stockholdings.[121] The record reflects that Selectica's adoption of a 4.99% trigger for its Rights Plan would not preclude a hostile bidder's ability to marshal enough shareholder votes to win a proxy contest.

Trilogy argues that, even if a 4.99% shareholder could realistically win a proxy contest "the preclusiveness question focuses on whether a challenger could realistically attain sufficient board control to remove the pill." Here, Trilogy contends, Selectica's charter-based classified board effectively forecloses a bid conditioned upon a redemption of the NOL Poison Pill, because it requires a proxy challenger to launch and complete two successful proxy contests in order to change control. Therefore, Trilogy argues that even if a less than 5% shareholder could win a proxy contest, Selectica's Rights Plan with a 4.99% trigger in combination with Selectica's charter-based classified board, makes a successful proxy contest for control of the board "realistically unattainable."

Trilogy's preclusivity argument conflates two distinct questions: first, is a successful proxy contest realistically attainable; and second, will a successful proxy contest result in gaining control of the board at the next election? Trilogy argues that unless both questions can be answered affirmatively, a Rights Plan and a classified board, viewed collectively, are preclusive. If that preclusivity argument is correct, then it would apply whenever a corporation has both a classified board and a Rights Plan, irrespective whether the trigger is 4.99%, 20%, or anywhere in between those thresholds.

Classified boards are authorized by statute[122] and are adopted for a variety of business purposes. Any classified board also operates as an antitakeover defense by preventing an insurgent from obtaining control of the board in one election.[123] More than a decade ago, in *Carmody*, the Court of Chancery noted "because only one third of a classified board would stand for election each year, a classified board would *delay — but not prevent — a hostile acquiror from obtaining control of the board*, since a determined acquiror could wage a proxy contest and obtain control of two thirds of the target board over a two year period, as opposed to seizing control in a single election."[124] The fact that a combination of defensive measures makes it more difficult for an acquirer to obtain control of a board does not make

---

[120] [33] Unitrin, Inc. v. Am. Gen. Corp., 651 A.2d at 1383.

[121] [34] *Id.*

[122] [35] Del. Code Ann. tit. 8, § 141(d) (2010).

[123] [36] *MM Companies, Inc. v. Liquid Audio, Inc.*, 813 A.2d 1118, 1122 (Del.2003) (citing Lucian Arye Bebchuk, John C. Coates, IV & Guhan Subramanian, *The Powerful Antitakeover Force of Staggered Boards: Theory, Evidence, and Policy*, 54 Stanford L. Rev. 887 (2002)). *See also* Martin Lipton, *Pills, Polls and Professors Redux*, 69 U. Chi. L. Rev. 1037, 1059 (2002), & John C. Coates IV, *Takeover Defenses in the Shadow of the Pill: A Critique of the Scientific Evidence*, 79 Tex. L.Rev. 271, 328-29 (2000).

[124] [37] *Carmody v. Toll Bros., Inc.*, 723 A.2d at 1186 n. 17 (emphasis added).

such measures realistically unattainable, i.e., preclusive.[125]

In *Moran*, we rejected the contention "that the Rights Plan strips stockholders of their rights to receive tender offers, and that the Rights Plan fundamentally restricts proxy contests."[126] We explained that "the Rights Plan will not have a severe impact upon proxy contests and it will not *preclude* all hostile acquisitions of Household."[127] In this case, we hold that the combination of a classified board and a Rights Plan do not constitute a preclusive defense.[128]

Range of Reasonableness

If a defensive measure is neither coercive nor preclusive, the *Unocal* proportionality test "requires the focus of enhanced judicial scrutiny to shift to 'the range of reasonableness.' "[129] Where all of the defenses "are inextricably related, the principles of *Unocal* require that such actions be scrutinized collectively as a unitary response to the perceived threat."[130] Trilogy asserts that the NOL Poison Pill, the Exchange, and the Reloaded NOL Poison Pill were not a reasonable collective response to the threat of the impairment of Selectica's NOLs.

The critical facts do not support that assertion. On November 20, within days of learning of the NOL Poison Pill, Trilogy sent Selectica a letter, demanding a conference to discuss an alleged breach of a patent settlement agreement between the parties. The parties met on December 17, and the following day, Trilogy resumed its purchases of Selectica stock.

Fallon testified that he and Liemandt had a discussion wherein Fallon advised Liemandt that Trilogy had purchased additional shares, but not enough to trigger the NOL Poison Pill. Fallon then asked if Liemandt really wanted to trigger the pill, and Liemandt expressly directed Fallon to proceed. On December 19, 2008, Trilogy bought a sufficient number of shares to become an "Acquiring Person" under the NOL Poison Pill. According to Fallon, this was done to " 'bring some clarity and urgency' to Trilogy's discussions with Selectica about the two parties' somewhat complicated relationship by 'setting a time frame that might help accelerate discussions' on the direction of the business."

Fallon described Trilogy's relationship with Selectica as a "three-legged stool," referring to Trilogy's status as a competitor, a creditor, and a stockholder of Selectica. The two companies had settled prior patent disputes in 2007 under terms

---

[125] [38] *In re Gaylord Container Corp. Shareholders Litig.*, 753 A.2d 462, 482 (Del.Ch.2000).

[126] [39] Moran v. Household Int'l, Inc., 500 A.2d at 1357.

[127] [40] Id. at 1356 (emphasis added).

[128] [41] We note that Selectica no longer has a classified Board. After trial, the Selectica Board amended its charter to eliminate its staggered board structure. On October 15, 2009 the Court of Chancery granted Trilogy's Second Motion for Judicial Notice, which requested the court to take judicial notice of the Selectica proxy statement that referenced the foregoing charter amendment eliminating the staggered board terms.

[129] [42] Unitrin, Inc. v. Am. Gen. Corp., 651 A.2d at 1388 (quoting Paramount Communications, Inc. v. QVC Network, Inc., 637 A.2d 34, 45-46 (Del.1994)).

[130] [43] Unitrin, Inc. v. Am. Gen. Corp., 651 A.2d at 1387 (citing Gilbert v. El Paso Co., 575 A.2d 1131, 1145 (Del.1990)).

that included a cross-license of intellectual property and quarterly payments from Selectica to Trilogy based on Selectica's revenues from certain products. Selectica argues that Trilogy took the unprecedented step of deliberately triggering the NOL Poison Pill — exposing its equity investment of under $2 million to dilution — primarily to extract substantially more value for the other two "legs" of the stool.

Trilogy's deliberate trigger started a ten business day clock under the terms of the NOL Poison Pill. If the Board took no action during that time, then the rights (other than those belonging to Trilogy) would "flip-in" and become exercisable for deeply discounted common stock. Alternatively, the Board had the power to exchange the rights (other than those belonging to Trilogy) for newly-issued common stock, or to grant Trilogy an exemption. Three times in the two weeks following the triggering, Selectica offered Trilogy an exemption in exchange for an agreement to stand still and to withdraw its threat to impair the value and usability of Selectica's NOLs. Three times Trilogy refused and insisted instead that Selectica repurchase its stock, terminate a license agreement with an important client, sign over intellectual property, and pay Trilogy millions of dollars. After three failed attempts to negotiate with Trilogy, it was reasonable for the Board to determine that they had no other option than to implement the NOL Poison Pill.

The Exchange employed by the Board was a more proportionate response than the "flip-in" mechanism traditionally envisioned for a Rights Plan. Because the Board opted to use the Exchange instead of the traditional "flip-in" mechanism, Trilogy experienced less dilution of its position than a Rights Plan is traditionally designed to achieve.

The implementation of the Reloaded NOL Poison Pill was also a reasonable response. The Reloaded NOL Poison Pill was considered a necessary defensive measure because, although the NOL Poison Pill and the Exchange effectively thwarted Trilogy's immediate threat to Selectica's NOLs, they did not eliminate the general threat of a Section 382 change-in-control. Following implementation of the Exchange, Selectica still had a roughly 40% ownership change for Section 382 purposes and there was no longer a Rights Plan in place to discourage additional acquisitions by 5% holders. Selectica argues that the decision to adopt the Reloaded NOL Poison Pill was reasonable under those circumstances. We agree.

The record indicates that the Board was presented with expert advice that supported its ultimate findings that the NOLs were a corporate asset worth protecting, that the NOLs were at risk as a result of Trilogy's actions, and that the steps that the Board ultimately took were reasonable in relation to that threat.[131] Outside experts were present and advised the Board on these matters at both the November 16 meeting at which the NOL Poison Pill was adopted and at the Board's December 29 meeting. The Committee also heard from expert advisers a third time at the January 2 meeting prior to instituting the Exchange and adopting the Reloaded NOL Poison Pill.

Under part two of the *Unocal* test, the Court of Chancery found that the combination of the NOL Poison Pill, the Exchange, and the Reloaded NOL Poison Pill was a proportionate response to the threatened loss of Selectica's NOLs. Those

[131] [44] Del. Code Ann. tit. 8, § 141(e) (2010).

findings are not clearly erroneous.[132] They are supported by the record and the result of a logical deductive reasoning process.[133] Accordingly, we hold that the Selectica directors satisfied the second part of the *Unocal* test by showing that their defensive response was proportionate by being "reasonable in relation to the threat" identified.[134]

Context Determines Reasonableness

Under a *Unocal* analysis, the reasonableness of a board's response is determined in relation to the "specific threat," at the time it was identified.[135] Thus, it is the specific nature of the threat that "sets the parameters for the range of permissible defensive tactics" at any given time.[136] The record demonstrates that a longtime competitor sought to increase the percentage of its stock ownership, not for the purpose of conducting a hostile takeover but, to intentionally impair corporate assets, or else coerce Selectica into meeting certain business demands under the threat of such impairment. Only in relation to that specific threat have the Court of Chancery and this Court considered the reasonableness of Selectica's response.

The Selectica Board carried its burden of proof under both parts of the *Unocal* test. Therefore, at this time, the Selectica Board has withstood the enhanced judicial scrutiny required by the two part *Unocal* test. That does not, however, end the matter.[137]

As we held in *Moran*, the adoption of a Rights Plan is not absolute.[138] In other cases, we have upheld the adoption of Rights Plans in specific defensive circumstances while simultaneously holding that it may be inappropriate for a Rights Plan to remain in place when those specific circumstances change dramatically. The fact that the NOL Poison Pill was reasonable under the specific facts and circumstances of this case, should not be construed as generally approving the reasonableness of a 4.99% trigger in the Rights Plan of a corporation with or without NOLs.[139]

To reiterate *Moran*, "the ultimate response to an actual takeover bid must be judged by the Directors' actions at that time."[140] If and when the Selectica Board "is faced with a tender offer and a request to redeem the [Reloaded NOL Poison Pill], they will not be able to arbitrarily reject the offer. They will be held to the same fiduciary standards any other board of directors would be held to in deciding to adopt a defensive mechanism."[141] The Selectica Board has no more discretion in

---

[132] [45] *Homestore, Inc. v. Tafeen*, 888 A.2d at 217.

[133] [46] *Levitt v. Bouvier*, 287 A.2d at 673.

[134] [47] Unocal Corp. v. Mesa Petroleum Co., 493 A.2d at 955.

[135] [48] See, e.g., Moran v. Household Int'l, Inc., 500 A.2d at 1354.

[136] [49] Unitrin, Inc. v. Am. Gen. Corp., 651 A.2d at 1384.

[137] [50] Moran v. Household Int'l, Inc., 500 A.2d at 1357.

[138] [51] Id. at 1354.

[139] [52] Unitrin, Inc. v. Am. Gen. Corp., 651 A.2d at 1378 (citing Moran v. Household Int'l, Inc., 500 A.2d at 1355 and Revlon, Inc. v. MacAndrews & Forbes Holdings, Inc., 506 A.2d 173, 179 (Del.1986)).

[140] [53] Moran v. Household Int'l, Inc., 500 A.2d at 1357.

[141] [54] Id. at 1354.

refusing to redeem the Rights Plan "than it does in enacting any defensive mechanism."[142] Therefore, the Selectica Board's future use of the Reloaded NOL Poison Pill must be evaluated if and when that issue arises.[143]

* * *

Conclusion

The judgment of the Court of Chancery [is] affirmed.

PROBLEM A

Woodstock Industries, Inc. ("Woodstock") was incorporated under the laws of the State of New York on January 30, 1940. Its equity capitalization presently includes 20,000,000 shares of Common Stock, $1 par value (the "Common Stock of Woodstock"), 7,000,000 of which are presently issued and outstanding and traded on the Ulster Stock Exchange (a national securities exchange). Woodstock has never paid a dividend on the Common Stock of Woodstock. The Certificate of Incorporation of Woodstock also authorizes Woodstock to issue 10,000,000 shares of Preferred Stock, $1.00 par value (the "Preferred Stock"), and specifically provides that, with respect to any Preferred Stock which Woodstock may issue, the Board of Directors of Woodstock may create one or more separate series thereof and fix the terms thereof with respect to dividends, as well as liquidation and conversion rights. Two thousand shares of the Preferred Stock were issued in a hastily arranged private placement on March 1, 2000 as the Series A Preferred Stock. Each share of the Series A Preferred Stock has cumulative annual dividend rate of $2.25 per share, payable quarterly on the first business day of April, July, October and January in each year; is redeemable at the option of Woodstock at any time after March 1, 2005 at $100 per share, plus accrued dividends; has a liquidation preference of $100 per share; and is convertible into the Common Stock of Woodstock at a conversion price of $20 per share. The resolutions of the Board of Directors of Woodstock creating the Series A Preferred Stock also provide that Woodstock may not be a party to any merger unless it is approved by the holders of at least a majority of the outstanding shares of Series A Preferred Stock, voting separately as a class; the resolutions are silent, however, as to whether a merger of Woodstock shall constitute a liquidation of Woodstock.

There are also outstanding $20,000 of Woodstock's eight percent Senior Debentures, due February 1, 2016 each in the principal amount of $1,000, and aggregating $20 million in principal amount (the "Senior Debentures") which were issued in a February 1, 2001 public offering. The Senior Debentures are also traded on the Ulster Stock Exchange and are redeemable at the option of Woodstock at 100 percent of the principal amount thereof ($1,000 each), plus unpaid interest, on or after February 1, 2007. Certain rights of the holders of the Senior Debentures are set forth in an Indenture, dated as of February 1, 2001, between Woodstock and The Hobart Trust Company, as Trustee (the "Indenture").

---

142 [55] Id.

143 [56] Id. at 1357.

Each of the $1,000 Senior Debentures is convertible (until it is redeemed) into shares of Common Stock of Woodstock at a conversion price of $10 per share. The Indenture provides that in the event that Woodstock merges with or into another corporation, the holder of each Senior Debenture then outstanding shall have the right thereafter to convert such Senior Debenture into the kind and amount of shares of stock and other securities and property receivable upon such merger by a holder of the number of shares of Common Stock of Woodstock into which such Senior Debenture might have been converted immediately prior to such merger. The Senior Debentures are publicly traded, unsecured and rank pari passu (*i.e.*, equally) with any current and future senior indebtedness of Woodstock.

The Indenture, which provides that it is to be governed by and construed in accordance with New York law, requires that at all times Woodstock's assets exceed its liabilities by not less than $30 million and that Woodstock's failure to comply with that Indenture requirement would constitute an event of default, rendering the entire aggregate principal amount of the Senior Debentures ($20 million) immediately due and payable.

The Indenture also states that a holder of a senior Debenture may not commence an action to enforce any term of the Indenture, or to seek damages for any breach thereof, unless the Trustee has refused to do so, following a written demand therefor by the holders of at least 25 percent in principal amount of the Senior Debentures.

Woodstock is engaged in the manufacture and sale of camping and hiking equipment and apparel.

Owing to a resurgence in sales of camping and hiking equipment to the ever increasing number of retirement age baby-boomers who are leaving the job market, Woodstock has become profitable and the market price of the Common Stock of Woodstock has increased to $30 per share, and the assets of Woodstock now exceed its liabilities by $35,000,000. Dividends on the Series A Preferred Stock continue to be paid. Interest rates in the United States have dropped substantially since February 1, 2001, and a corporation of Woodstock's financial condition can now issue debentures at an interest rate of not more than five percent. Woodstock has been advised by Derm & Jud, its investment banking firm, to eliminate the $20,000,000 indebtedness on its balance sheet represented by the Senior Debentures. Derm & Jud has suggested that Woodstock redeem the Senior Debentures at the redemption price. That firm has expressed its opinion, as investment bankers, that, if the Senior Debentures are called for redemption, it is highly unlikely that Woodstock would be required to pay any significant portion of the approximately $20,000,000 aggregate redemption price.

You are an associate in the firm of Palen & Carmel, and Maisie Henderson, the partner in charge of the Woodstock account, has asked you to write her a memorandum discussing the questions as to whether (i) the proposed redemption is legally possible, (ii) from a legal point of view, it is highly unlikely that Woodstock will be required to pay any significant portion of the approximately $20,000,000 aggregate redemption price, and (iii) whether there are any steps that Woodstock can take to eliminate the possibility that it would have to pay any portion of the redemption price. Write that Memorandum.

PROBLEM B

Woodstock Widget Corporation ("Woodstock") was incorporated under the laws of the State of New York on March 1, 1967. Its principal executive office and all of its business operations are located in Geneva, New York. Its equity capitalization presently consists of (a) 10,000,000 shares of Common Stock, $1.00 par value (the "Common Stock"), of which 2,000,000 shares are issued and outstanding and traded on the Hobart Stock Exchange (a national securities exchange) (the "Exchange") and (b) 10,000,000 shares of Preferred Stock, par value $1.00 per share, of which 1,000,000 shares were publicly issued on February 1, 1990 as the Series A Preferred Stock, pursuant to authority expressly granted to the Board of Directors of Woodstock in the Certificate of Incorporation of Woodstock. The 1,000,000 outstanding shares of Series A Preferred Stock are also traded on the Exchange. Each share of the Series A Preferred Stock has a cumulative annual dividend rate of $2.25 per share, payable quarterly on the first business day of April, July, October and January in each year; is redeemable at the option of Woodstock at any time after February 1, 1995 at $100 per share, plus accrued dividends; and has a liquidation preference of $100 per share. The terms of the Series A Preferred Stock are silent as to whether a merger, consolidation or sale of all or substantially all of the assets of Woodstock shall be deemed to be a liquidation of Woodstock. The terms of the Series A Preferred Stock provide that the Series A Preferred Stock has no voting rights whatsoever, except as may otherwise be provided by law.

There are also outstanding 5,000 of Woodstock's seven percent Senior Convertible Debentures, due April 2, 2016 (the "Senior Debentures"). The Senior Debentures were publicly issued in the principal amount of $1,000 each on April 2, 1996; are also traded on the Exchange and are convertible into Common Stock of Woodstock at a conversion price of $75 per share. Certain rights of the holders of the Senior Debentures are set forth in an Indenture, dated as of April 2, 1996, between Woodstock and The Novack Trust Company (the "Indenture"). The Indenture provides that the Senior Debentures are redeemable at the option of Woodstock at 100 percent of the principal amount thereof ($1000 each), plus accrued interest on or after April 2, 2001. The Indenture also provides that, in the event that Woodstock merges into any other corporation, the corporation into which Woodstock merges shall assume all of the obligations of Woodstock under the Senior Debentures and the Indenture. The Indenture further provides that, in the event of any merger to which Woodstock is a party, the Senior Debentures shall, after any such merger, be convertible into the securities and property received by the holders of Common Stock of Woodstock in connection with any such merger; however, no provision is made in the Indenture for an adjustment to the conversion price in the event of a stock split or stock dividend by Woodstock. The Indenture further states that a holder of Senior Debentures may not commence an action to enforce any term thereof, or to seek damages for any breach thereof, unless the Indenture Trustee has refused to do so, following a written demand therefor by the holders of at least 25 percent in principal amount of the Senior Debentures.

Woodstock's wholly-owned New York subsidiary, Bissell Enterprises, Inc. ("Bissell"), is engaged in the business of manufacturing outdoor swimming pools.

Despite the current economic uncertainty, the markets for Woodstock's widget products and Bissell's swimming pools have remained steady over the past two years; and Woodstock has remained profitable for each of the last two fiscal years. Dividends have been paid regularly on the Series A Preferred Stock; however, no dividends have ever been paid on the Common Stock of Woodstock.

By virtue of a breakthrough in widget technology, and extremely warm summer weather, Woodstock has continued to be profitable. Woodstock has been approached by Henderson Industries, Inc., a New York corporation ("Henderson"), the shares of Common Stock of which are listed on the Exchange. In preliminary discussions with Woodstock, Henderson has proposed that Henderson acquire Woodstock in a transaction which would be structured as follows. Henderson would form under the laws of the State of New York a new wholly owned subsidiary to be called Henderson Sub, Inc. ("Henderson Sub"). Henderson Sub would be merged with and into Woodstock in a reverse triangular merger. At the effective time of the merger, each outstanding share of Henderson Sub owned by Henderson would be converted into and exchanged for one share of Common Stock of Woodstock, which would be the surviving corporation in the merger. Also at the effective time of the merger, each outstanding share of Common Stock of Woodstock would be converted into and exchanged for one share of Common Stock of Henderson, and each outstanding share of Series A Preferred Stock of Woodstock would be converted into the right to receive a cash payment equal to $60 per share, which would be in excess of the present market value of the Series A Preferred Stock, which is $50 per share.

You are an associate in the firm of Bissell & Rossi, and Carmel Palen, the partner in charge of the Woodstock account, has asked you to prepare a Memorandum to her discussing the effect of the proposed merger upon the rights of the holders of Woodstock's outstanding securities, as well as any rights or claims which any such holder might assert in connection with the proposed merger. Write that Memorandum.

Chapter 6

DISTRIBUTIONS IN RESPECT OF EQUITY SECURITIES

§ 6.01 LEGAL AND BUSINESS ASPECTS OF DIVIDENDS

The primary reason for an investor's purchase of common stock is the potential for capital appreciation, which is generally expected to consist of an increase in the market value of the security, as well as dividends received with respect thereto. Indeed, dividends have contributed approximately 40 percent of the returns historically realized by equity investors. A well-known stock valuation technique, known as the Dividend Discount Model, assigns "a present value to future payouts, including an assumed liquidating dividend when the company was sold or liquidated." Erin E. Arvedlund, *Show Us the Money*, BARRON'S, Apr. 1, 2002, at 29. Professor Jeremy Siegel of the Wharton School has observed that:

> In the 19th century and first half of the 20th century the average dividend yield on stocks was 5.8%. It was not until 1958 that the dividend yield on stocks fell below the interest rate on long-term government bonds and even through the 1980s the dividend yield averaged 4.3%.

Jeremy J. Siegel, *The Dividend Deficit*, WALL ST. J., Feb. 13, 2002, at A20.

By the end of the twentieth century, however, common stock "dividends fell out of favor" and dividend paying companies actually became less attractive to many investors. For example, in 1999 only one of the 15 best performing stocks in the Standard and Poor's 500 Index paid a dividend. There were several reasons for this development. As a result of the bull market of the 1990s (or, as it is often referred to in hindsight, the stock market bubble), dividends became a much smaller part of the total return on common stocks. Many established corporations, particularly large technology companies, chose to invest their surplus cash in their businesses. Stockholders in so-called growth companies (*i.e.*, corporations which at least appeared to increase their profits year over year) actually preferred that such companies refrain from paying dividends all together, and instead use their cash to make investments intended to result in increased profits. Consequently, "the dividend yield sunk to 1.2% at the market peak in March 2000." *Id.*

The U.S. tax laws also contributed to the decline in common stock dividends. Historically dividends received by individual investors were generally taxed at ordinary income rates. Moreover, unlike interest payments on debt securities, dividend payments are not deductible for corporate income tax purposes. Because capital gains have been generally taxed at a lower rate than dividends, it became more "tax efficient" for corporations to repurchase shares from stockholders than to pay dividends. Stock repurchases reduce the number of shares outstanding and thus increase a corporation's earnings per share as well as the market price of the remaining outstanding shares. Higher share prices are attractive not only to actual investors, but also to corporate insiders who have been granted stock options which increase in value as prices on their corporation's shares rise.

As the full extent of the 1990s numerous financial frauds, distortions of accounting principles and customer abuses by financial institutions began to be uncovered at the beginning of the twenty-first century, many in the financial community began to reconsider the virtues of common stock dividend payments.

In commenting on the effects of the Enron scandal, Professor Siegel, again placing the matter in historical context, stated that:

> In the 19th century there was no Securities and Exchange Commission, [Financial Accounting Standards Board], or any of the other numerous agencies that oversee our securities markets today . . . . Given the total lack of standards back then, how did a firm signal that its earnings were real? The old-fashioned way, by paying dividends, an action that gave tangible evidence of the firm's profitability and proof that the firms' earnings were authentic. . . .

Id.

Lawyers and law students should find Professor Siegel's historical emphasis persuasive. "Today we study the day before yesterday, in order that yesterday may not paralyze today, and today may not paralyze tomorrow." BENJAMIN N. CARDOZO, THE NATURE OF THE JUDICIAL PROCESS 54 (Yale Univ. Press 1921) (quoting the noted English Common Law Historian F.W. Maitland).

The realization that dividends on common stock often are an indication of *genuine* (as distinguished from reported) earnings and thus should be attractive to investors converged with two other significant developments.

First, the notion that corporate profits are necessarily enhanced by company management's investing in the business rather than distributing them to shareholders began to be called into question:

> "In the 1980s, everybody decided they were growth companies," and many stopped paying dividends . . . . "But really, the economy might have been more productive had more dividends been paid to shareholders, had Corporate America let them decide what to do with excess capital, and let the marketplace allocate that money."

Arvedlund, *supra* (quoting institutional advisor Marc Gerstein).

Second, a 2003 change in the tax law reduced the individual income tax rate on dividends to 15 percent from as high as 39 percent. As a result, U.S. corporations started paying common stock dividends in unprecedented amounts.

Although dividend payments are not necessarily a sign of strong earnings or even financial health, by 2005 many publicly traded corporations were increasing the amount of dividends paid in respect of their common stock or commencing such payments, thus calling to mind the maxim, "the more things change, the more they stay the same."

Set forth below are several cases which arose in a mergers and acquisitions context and involve the application of basic legal principles applicable to the declaration and payment of dividends on shares of common stock.

BRITISH PRINTING & COMMUNICATION CORP. PLC v. HARCOURT BRACE JOVANOVICH, INC.

United States District Court, Southern District of New York
664 F. Supp. 1519 (1987)

KEENAN, DISTRICT JUDGE

Introduction

Before the Court is a motion for an order pursuant to Fed. R. Civ. P. 65 enjoining the implementation of a recapitalization planned by a major publicly-owned corporation. Finding that the movant has failed to demonstrate irreparable injury and either a likelihood of success on the merits or a balance of hardships tipping decidedly in favor of the movant, the Court denies the motion. Having heard testimony at a hearing over three days, and on the basis of numerous submissions, the Court makes the following findings of fact and conclusions of law:

Findings of Fact

Plaintiff British Printing & Communication Corporation plc ("BPCC") is a British corporation with its headquarters in Oxford, England. Its chairman and chief executive officer is Robert Maxwell. BPCC is owned by Pergamon Holding Foundation ("Pergamon"), an entity organized under Lichtensteinian law. The identity of the owners of Pergamon, and thus ultimately of BPCC, is a closely-guarded secret. BPCC is one of the world's largest publishing communications and information companies, earning in 1986 more than 120 million dollars. It holds the majority of the outstanding 638% convertible subordinated debentures of defendant Harcourt Brace Jovanovich, Inc. ("HBJ"), with a principal amount of $9,490,000.

HBJ is a New York corporation with its principal place of business in Orlando, Florida. It pursues three main lines of business: publishing, life and health insurance and theme parks. Publishing, the original field in which HBJ began operations in 1919, remains the core of its business. Within the publishing field, HBJ concentrates on educational publishing, from pre-kindergarten through graduate and professional schools. Transcript ("Tr.") 266-67. The chairman of the board of directors of HBJ is William Jovanovich ("Jovanovich"). He and the fourteen other members of HBJ's board are named individually as defendants herein. HBJ's common stock has been traded publicly since 1960 and is listed on the New York Stock Exchange.

The First Boston Corporation ("First Boston") is an investment banking corporation organized under the laws of Massachusetts and having its principal place of business in New York, New York. First Boston has for several years acted as HBJ's principal financial advisor and has participated in two public securities offerings by that company. Tr. 273-74. First Boston Securities Corporation ("FBSC") is a wholly-owned subsidiary of First Boston. Incorporated under the laws of Delaware, FBSC has been used by First Boston as a vehicle for the extension of financing in major corporate transactions on several prior occasions.

On Monday, May 18, 1987, Jovanovich received at HBJ's offices in Orlando a letter sent via telecopier from Maxwell, proposing a merger of BPCC with HBJ in exchange for payment to HBJ shareholders of $44.00 per share of common stock. The letter, PX 2, stated that Maxwell and the other directors of BPCC were prepared to meet with HBJ "to review all aspects of such a transaction, including price." It further stated that BPCC had reason to believe that financing was available to it for such transaction. The proposed merger would be conditioned on HBJ's cancellation of a public offering then being contemplated. The letter stated that BPCC had no plans to change the headquarters or replace the management of HBJ were a merger to be consummated.

The Maxwell letter of May 18 had been preceded minutes before by a telephone call placed by Maxwell to Jovanovich's office. Jovanovich's secretary had informed Maxwell that Jovanovich was not in. Tr. 269. Shortly after the letter was sent, BPCC issued a release to the press, advising that it had made the proposal to HBJ and including a copy of the Maxwell letter. DX F.

Several hours later, Jovanovich issued a press release in response to the proposal, describing it as "preposterous as to intent and value." Jovanovich Deposition ("Dep.") 76-77. Jovanovich based this opinion on his own estimate of the value of HBJ, the manner in which the proposal was made (and publicized) and his opinion of Maxwell as a businessman. Jovanovich Dep. 67-73. HBJ contacted its senior management personnel, its outside directors and representatives of First Boston. A meeting of the board of directors was scheduled for May 21, 1987. Jovanovich requested that First Boston advise the board with respect to the Maxwell proposal and the alternatives it might consider. Tr. 112-14. First Boston had previously studied HBJ and the publishing business in general for several years in its investment banking capacity and was, in its own view, very familiar with the value of the company. Tr. 445. In connection with the planned public offering by HBJ, First Boston had reviewed financial reports and earnings projections for the forthcoming years. Tr. 274.

Among those contacted in connection with the Maxwell proposal was J. William Brandner ("Brandner"), a director of HBJ who serves as executive vice-president of the company and as chairman of HBJ Insurance. Tr. 265. Brandner is also a member of the "office of the president" of HBJ, a senior management group. Brandner, a certified public accountant who had been chief financial officer of HBJ, believed that the Maxwell proposal was inadequate as to price, based in part on his experience in the potential acquisition by HBJ of several other publishing houses and in the actual acquisition by HBJ of CBS Publishing. Tr. 269. He also doubted the sincerity of the offer because it was immediately made public, rather than becoming the subject of private negotiation. *Id.*

Brandner was then in California, participating in a public presentation to potential investors in HBJ's planned securities offering. *Id.* 270. Jovanovich asked Brandner to return to Orlando, which he did. There, he met with Jovanovich and others to discuss the proposal. It was decided that Brandner would be primarily responsible for the negotiations with First Boston concerning its role in responding to the proposal and its informational needs. *Id.* at 271. Brandner was also charged with presenting to the other members of management the relevant information and options raised by the proposal. He and others met with representatives of First Boston on the following day, Tuesday the 19th of May, in Orlando in order to inform First Boston of the situation and provide it with the necessary information.

Brandner and John Berardi, the senior vice president and treasurer of HBJ, met on Wednesday, May 20, with representatives of Morgan Guaranty Trust in New York, New York to seek financing for possible transactions in response to the Maxwell proposal. Morgan had served as HBJ's primary bank for several decades. Over Wednesday and Thursday, May 21, Brandner and Berardi spent at least seven hours with representatives of Morgan in attempt to secure a line of credit. HBJ had not, however, made any commitments to Morgan at that time. Tr. 274-78.

On Thursday morning, prior to that day's meeting between the HBJ representatives and those of Morgan, First Boston first suggested to Brandner and Berardi the possible implementation of a "public leveraged buyout," whereby shareholders would receive a large cash dividend and still retain ownership in HBJ, which would then be a highly-leveraged company. *Id.* at 278-79. This suggested alternative was passed on to Jovanovich and other members of management by telephone that day. *Id.* at 279.

Since Tuesday afternoon, May 19, First Boston had been working in Orlando to arrive at an opinion as to the adequacy of the Maxwell proposal. A formal agreement retaining First Boston ("the engagement letter") was signed by Ralph Caulo, a member of the board, on behalf of HBJ on Thursday, May 21. *Id.* at 282. The engagement letter provided that First Boston would undertake "a comprehensive study and analysis of the business, operations, financial conditions and prospects" of HBJ. DX G. This analysis was to be based entirely on information available to the public or provided by HBJ to First Boston, rather than upon an independent appraisal of HBJ. *Id.* First Boston also agreed to render an opinion with respect to the adequacy of the Maxwell proposal ("the adequacy opinion") and to render, if requested, an opinion regarding the fairness to HBJ and its shareholders of whatever consideration might be paid to them in the event that an alternative to the Maxwell proposal were to be implemented. *Id.*

In exchange for receiving the foregoing services, HBJ agreed to pay First Boston $500,000 immediately plus an additional $500,000 upon the rendering to the board of HBJ of the adequacy opinion. PX 7. If HBJ were to undertake some form of recapitalization, First Boston would receive under the terms of the engagement letter $7.5 million. If half of HBJ's stock or all of its assets were to be acquired, First Boston would be paid a fee equal to 0.4% of the consideration paid in the transaction by which the acquisition was made. In the event that neither a recapitalization nor a change of control were to occur at HBJ, First Boston would receive under the engagement letter a $1 million independence fee. Under these terms, First Boston would receive $9 million if the adequacy opinion were rendered and if HBJ were acquired by BPCC at the $44 per share price, but would receive only $8.5 million if it rendered the adequacy opinion and if HBJ did recapitalize itself.

At 8:00 p.m. on Thursday, May 21, the Board assembled to consider the Maxwell proposal and HBJ's possible responses. Present were all of HBJ's directors but for Trammell Crow, who was then in the Orient. Of the directors present, six are officers of HBJ: Jovanovich, Brandner, Ralph D. Caulo, Robert L. Edgell, Peter Jovanovich (the son of William Jovanovich) and Jack O. Snyder. Five other directors have business relationships with the company of varying significance: Marta Casals Istomin, Walter Johnson and former Senator Eugene J. McCarthy each receive consulting fees in exchange for rendering services to HBJ; Paul Gitlin performs pre-publication review of manuscripts to be published by the tradebook division (to protect against libel suits); and Peter J. Ryan was formerly a partner in the law firm of Fried, Frank, Harris, Shriver and Jacobson, HBJ's outside counsel. The largest payment to a non-management director of HBJ (other than Trammell Crow) was $75,000, received by Walter Johnson in return for his services as an editorial and marketing consultant for Johnson Reprint Corporation, a subsidiary of HBJ. PX 38. The economic significance to Johnson of this payment is probably negligible in comparison to the value of his holdings of HBJ stock, approximately $90 million. Lesser amounts were paid to the other directors who receive consulting fees. These amounts are generally of the same order of magnitude as those received for being a director of HBJ. Tr. 401-05. The remaining directors present, Theodore M. Black, Virginia B. Smith, and Dr. Michael B. Winston, have no business relationship with HBJ apart from their directorships.

In addition to the directors, several others were present at the 8:00 p.m. meeting on Thursday: Berardi, Charles Harris of the law firm of Smith MacKinnon, Mathews & Harris (a firm that has represented HBJ in corporate matters); Bruce Starling, a senior vice president of HBJ, and two secretaries, a Miss McQuillan and a Mrs. de Carlo. Tr. 284-85.

The initial discussion took place over dinner and concerned the general background of events beginning with the Maxwell proposal. Copies of the Maxwell letter were given to the directors as well as other materials. The circumstances of the proposal were discussed, including Maxwell's immediate release of his letter to the press. The directors considered the advisability of holding the shareholders' meeting scheduled the following day and having received advice of counsel, resolved that it be cancelled. Tr. 285-86.

At this time, representatives of First Boston were invited into the meeting, in order to make a presentation concerning the adequacy of the Maxwell proposal. First Boston presented a slide show consisting of various charts reflecting the results of different valuation analyses they had performed. The slide show was accompanied by the distribution of hard copy of the charts to the directors. Tr. 286-87. First Boston employed three primary methodologies in arriving at a valuation of HBJ, which would then reveal whether the Maxwell proposal was adequate. These consisted of a comparable acquisition analysis for the various segments of HBJ, a comparable company analysis and a discounted cash flow analysis. Tr. 287-88, 439. Each analysis assumed that the business segments of HBJ would continue as going concerns. Tr. 439.

In its comparable acquisition analysis, First Boston examined the amounts paid in recent years for the acquisitions of companies comparable to the various segments of HBJ. Tr. 441. The comparable company analysis performed by First Boston consisted of a comparison of the aggregate market value of companies in the lines of business of the HBJ segments, analyzed in relation to the net earnings of the company. As part of this analysis, First Boston also studied the relationship of revenues and of operating income to the total market value of those companies considered comparable to HBJ segments. Tr. 440-41. First Boston's discounted cash flow analysis was based on projections of the future cash flow of the business segments for the next ten years discounted to present value. Tr. 440; DX QQ. In its projections of future operating income, First Boston used more conservative estimates than did HBJ in making its own projections. The First Boston figures ranged from 3 percent to 50 percent lower than HBJ's projections. Tr. 447-49. These projections were arrived at in part from a "normalization" of present financial data, a process by which gains or losses attributable to discreet events not likely to recur are factored out of the projections. On such event, for example, was HBJ's acquisition of CBS Publishing. Tr. 449-51.

In arriving at the valuations of individual segments of HBJ, First Boston took into account the taxes normally expected to be incurred by those segments. This primarily meant income taxes. The taxes accounted for did not, however, include any capital gains tax to which the sale of the segments would be subject. This was a reflection of the fundamental assumption that the segments were to be valued as going concerns of which the value to HBJ would be realized through income rather than through a sale of the segments. Tr. 452; Jovanovich Dep. 259. First Boston did perform a "break-up valuation" in order to predict what price an acquirer might be willing to pay for the stock of HBJ in order to then sell off HBJ's assets. This method of valuation was employed in assessing the adequacy of the Maxwell proposal and did take into account capital gains taxes on the hypothetical sale of the assets of HBJ upon acquisition. The break-up valuation was not used in First Boston's subsequent valuation opinion used by the board to determine HBJ's surplus. Tr. 453-54.

By aggregating the valuation figures for each segment of HBJ and comparing the results of the three methodologies employed, First Boston arrived at a range of figures that it believed best reflected the value of HBJ. Comparing this range of values to the total represented by the Maxwell proposal, First Boston concluded that the Maxwell proposal was inadequate, and so advised the board of HBJ. Tr. 287, 298; Winston Dep. 78-79. The board did not, however, decide then to reject the Maxwell proposal. Tr. 305.

At this point, representatives of First Boston outlined for the directors the recapitalization that it had previously suggested to management. Tr. 298; PX 10; Jovanovich Dep. 127. The basic elements described were a payment of a special dividend to the shareholders of HBJ consisting of cash and additional securities, increased ownership of HBJ stock by the employee stock ownership plan ("ESOP") and financing for these transactions from First Boston and Morgan. Tr. 298; PX 10. This recapitalization would allow HBJ to give its shareholders immediate value while allowing them to retain the benefit of potential growth of the company. Smith Dep. 34. With the understanding that a more definite recapitalization proposal would be developed over the coming weekend, the board adjourned until the next morning, Friday, May 22, 1987. PX 10.

Friday morning's meeting was short. It had been scheduled to coincide with the now-cancelled public offering and, before addressing the Maxwell proposal and the possible alternatives, the board dealt with more routine matters concerning, among other things, the retirement of officers and bank resolutions. Tr. 307. The board then reviewed the discussions of the previous meeting and reached a consensus that the Maxwell proposal was inadequate with respect to price and of too little seriousness to merit further consideration. Smith Dep. 38-39. First Boston's adequacy opinion, PX 9, had not yet been formally distributed to the board. PX 10.

Alvin Shoemaker, the chairman of First Boston was next invited to address the board. Tr. 115, 307, PX 10. Shoemaker expressed concern that Maxwell might attempt a "street sweep" immediately after the up-coming Memorial Day weekend. Tr. 116. In a street sweep, a potential acquirer abandons his attempt to acquire a company by bidding and instead purchases as many shares as possible on the open market, particularly from arbitrageurs. Tr. 117, 307-08. This possibility created a need for expedition in responding to the Maxwell proposal, as those who were not confident of the long-term value of HBJ's stock might be convinced to sell their shares for a less than adequate price. Tr. 117. Thus, it would be necessary to assure the shareholders that they would receive greater value than that offered by Maxwell, through a swift response by the board. *Id.*; Jovanovich Dep. 239-40. Shoemaker discussed with the directors their responsibilities to shareholders in such a situation, answering questions by former Senator McCarthy, Virginia Smith, and other directors. Questions came from both those holding management positions at HBJ and those who did not. Tr. 118-120. Finally, Shoemaker discussed the recapitalization plan briefly. Tr. 309. The board then adjourned until Monday evening, May 25. Over the weekend, members of HBJ's management worked with representatives of First Boston, Morgan and legal advisers to prepare a detailed recapitalization plan and make the necessary financial arrangements. Tr. 310-12.

On Monday the 25th, Memorial Day, the board met at approximately 8:00 p.m. PX 10. It was at this meeting that the details of the proposed recapitalization plan were presented to the board. Tr. 313; Jovanovich Dep. 253-54; PX 10.

The plan called for a distribution of a special dividend to holders of HBJ common stock, consisting of $40 in cash and a single share of preferred stock to be valued at approximately $10. Shareholders would retain their existing shares. Tr. 122, 312, 314. These shares would be referred to as "stub" shares, and their value would be diminished because of the cost of making the special dividend. Tr. 122. The total paid to the shareholders would then be somewhere in the range of $55 to $57, as a result of the recapitalization. Tr. 125, 312. The retention of the stub shares would allow shareholders to participate in the future economic growth of HBJ after the implementation of the recapitalization plan.

A second part of the plan, as described to the directors at the Memorial Day board meeting, was to be the contribution of a new issue of convertible preferred stock to the pre-existing ESOP, PX 10; Jovanovich Dep. 229-30, and an offer to the ESOP of HBJ common shares repurchased on the open market. PX 10; Tr. 320, 322-23. This would provide an incentive for employees to work more productively, which would be essential to the ultimate success of the recapitalization plan. Tr. 126; Jovanovich Dep. 229-31; Smith Dep. 105. This was particularly important because the cost of the special dividend would require HBJ to restrict its spending in the near future, thus impinging on its ability to offer other financial incentives to its employees. Tr. 126. The trustees of the ESOP, who were members of HBJ's management, had obtained independent legal and financial advisers to scrutinize the role of the ESOP in this aspect of the recapitalization plan. Those advisers had worked throughout the previous weekend in order to be able to carry out that task. Tr. 311. The ESOP plan contained a "pass-through" provision under which shares allocated to individual participants' accounts would be voted by the participants. The trustees of the ESOP have agreed with the New York Stock Exchange that they will vote the unallocated shares for and against proposals to shareholders in the same proportion as the allocated shares are voted. Tr. 352, 371-72.

These elements of the recapitalization plan were presented to the directors in an oral presentation accompanied by a slide show and hard copy of the materials shown in the slide show. Tr. 313; DX M.

The discussion next focused on the financing arrangements that would allow HBJ to accomplish this recapitalization. Temporary, or "bridge," financing was to be provided by First Boston (through FBSC), which was prepared to commit $985 million in order to provide immediate cash for share purchases and for the payment of the special dividend. As a condition of making this commitment, First Boston required that it be allowed to purchase sufficient shares of HBJ stock to give it some voice in the running of the company. Tr. 147-50. Accordingly, the plan provided for HBJ to sell to First Boston 40,000 shares of a new issue of Exchangeable Redeemable Preferred Stock ("ERPS"), at a total price in excess of $80 million. Tr. 316; DX M. These shares would carry a total of 8,160,000 votes, representing a cost of approximately $10 per vote, an amount equivalent to the expected price at which HBJ's shares would be trading "ex dividend," i.e., without the right to receive the special dividend because purchased after the record date for payment of the dividend. There are no agreements or tacit understandings between HBJ and First Boston concerning how First Boston will exercise its votes from these shares. Jovanovich Dep. 211-12; Tr. 146, 321-22. It was expected that First Boston would vote its shares as would any other investor. In fact, part of the reason First Boston wanted a share of the equity of HBJ was to allow it to benefit from the future economic growth of HBJ, as would other shareholders. Tr. 147.

This bridge financing by First Boston is expected to be retired through the sale of high-risk, high-yield, subordinated securities, known as "junk bonds." PX 10; Winston Dep. 139; Tr. 374-75. In addition, permanent financing is to be provided by Morgan, as the leader of a lending syndicate which would lend $1.9 billion to HBJ. Tr. 325-26; PX 10. The bank loan must, under the terms of the loan agreement, be used to retire existing debt, so that the Morgan syndicate and First Boston will be the only remaining creditors of HBJ. *Id.* Despite the size of the bank loan, the bridge financing is necessary because the retirement of existing debt and the allocation of working capital out of the bank loan leaves too little available for the payment of the special dividend. Tr. 326.

Following the description of the recapitalization plan in detail and questions addressed to that by board members, discussion turned to the likely effects of the transaction on the future of HBJ. Management described to the rest of the directors the restrictions on spending and cost reductions that would be required in order to meet interest payments. The directors each were presented with documents depicting the cash flow requirements necessary to make those payments and detailing the anticipated source and application of those funds. Tr. 328-29; PX 10; Winston Dep. 154-55. The directors discussed the possible sale of certain assets (primarily undeveloped land), the reduction of HBJ's work force through attrition, and the forgoing of planned new projects. PX 10. These steps were compared to the likely results of an acquisition of HBJ by BPCC, which was expected to result in the merger of HBJ's overseas operations with those of BPCC and a concomitant loss of one-half to two-thirds of employees' jobs, the withdrawal of HBJ from the trade publishing business, and the sale of its elementary and secondary school publishing business and of its magazine publishing division. PX 10; Jovanovich Dep. 272-78; Tr. 330. At the conclusion of this discussion, the board adjourned its meeting until the following morning, Tuesday, May 26. PX 10.

On Tuesday morning, the board reviewed the discussions of the previous night, including the cash flow projections and the cost-reduction measures required by the proposed recapitalization. PX 10; Smith Dep. 135-37; Tr. 327-30. The directors questioned the officers of HBJ extensively on their ability to meet the requirements of the recapitalization plan. Tr. 330; Winston Dep. 160-61; PX 10. Representatives of First Boston and Morgan again reviewed with the directors the terms of the financing, referring them to documents earlier provided to each director. PX 10; Tr. 328. It was pointed out that First Boston required the right to purchase the new issue of HBJ stock as a condition of its loan to HBJ and that the loan agreement contained default provisions and allowed First Boston to call in the loan if a change in control were to occur at HBJ. PX 10; Tr. 328; Winston Dep. 134; Smith Dep. 82. This latter provision was required by First Boston to ensure that it would not be faced with a lengthy commitment to new management which might not be as reliable in running HBJ as First Boston believed HBJ's present management to be. Tr. 145-46.

The next item reviewed by the board was the costs of the proposed recapitalization, which were agreed to be high, but comparable to the costs of similar transactions performed by other companies in the past. PX 10; Tr. 330-31. Among these fees were those to be paid to First Boston in connection with its extension of the bridge loan and its possible underwriting of the junk bond issue. First Boston would receive a $29 million fee for extending the bridge financing and a 312 percent underwriting discount upon the issuance of the junk bonds. Tr. 154. The latter fee should amount to approximately $35 million, which amount must be paid to First Boston even if the bonds are not issued. Tr. 159; PX 49. The total transactional costs of the recapitalization, including Morgan's fee of $46 million for arranging the $1.9 billion loan, would amount, it was explained to the board, to approximately $125-130 Million. PX 10; PX 49.

Following additional review of the proposed recapitalization plan, the meeting was adjourned until 3:00 p.m. that afternoon, May 26, 1987.

When the board resumed its meeting that afternoon, the non-management directors decided to meet separately to discuss the issues raised in the previous meetings, apparently at the suggestion of Shoemaker and Jovanovich. Tr. 128, 335;

Winston Dep. 161-64; PX 10. Dr. Winston led the meeting, during which the non-management directors formulated additional questions that they wished to ask management and others. Smith Dep. 120-22; Winston Dep. 166. They then questioned separately Harris, certain members of management and representatives of First Boston. Winston Dep. 169-71. Having received answers to their questions, the non-management directors then concluded their separate meeting and invited in the remainder of the board. The separate meeting had lasted between 20 and 90 minutes. PX 10; Tr. 335, 408; Smith Dep. 120; Winston Dep. 164. Its probable true length was 45 minutes to an hour.

When the management directors returned, the board reviewed a press release describing the proposed recapitalization and revised it at the suggestion of Virginia Smith. PX 10. The directors then considered an opinion letter furnished by First Boston on its valuation of HBJ. DX J. That letter expressed a valuation of HBJ at the low end of the range calculated by First Boston, which was nevertheless sufficiently high to support the payment of the special dividend. As well as the First Boston valuation letter, the directors received and reviewed copies of a letter from Arthur Anderson & Co. (the accounting firm) regarding the liabilities of the company, DX O; a memorandum from Berardi concluding that the recapitalization plan would not render HBJ unable to pay its debts and other obligations as they became due, DX P; a memorandum from the officers of HBJ certifying that the financial projections employed by First Boston and others in designing the recapitalization had been reasonably prepared on the basis of the best available information, DX Q; and two letters from Richard Udell (the administrative vice president and general counsel to HBJ) concerning the likelihood of HBJ's incurring liability as the result of various litigation pending or expected to be brought against HBJ; DX R. The directors reviewed each of these documents and discussed them among themselves and with officers of the company and counsel. Tr. 337. Jovanovich indicated that he had spoken to Trammell Crow about the proposed recapitalization and that Crow had expressed his support for it. PX 10.

The board of directors, having concluded its review of the proposed recapitalization and the supporting documents, thereupon voted unanimously to reject the Maxwell proposal and to approve the recapitalization. A press release announcing their decision was approved and disseminated. Tr. 337-39.

This litigation ensued.

Conclusions of Law

To obtain a preliminary injunction, the moving party must demonstrate that it will suffer irreparable harm absent the granting of such relief and either a likelihood of success on the merits, or sufficiently serious questions going to the merits of the litigation and a balance of hardships tipping decidedly in favor of equitable relief. *Norlin Corp. v. Rooney, Pace Inc.*, 744 F.2d 255, 260 (2d Cir. 1984); *see Hanson Trust PLC v. ML SCM Acquisition Inc.*, 781 F.2d 264, 272-73 (2d Cir. 1986) ("Hanson II"). The preliminary injunction is "one of the most drastic tools in the arsenal of judicial remedies [and] must be used with great care, lest the forces of the free market, which in the end should determine the merits of takeover disputes, [be] nullified." *Hanson Trust PLC v. SCM Corp.*, 774 F.2d 47, 60 (2d Cir.

1985) ("Hanson I"). The Court will consider these factors in turn.

Irreparable Harm

BPCC contends that it will be irreparably harmed absent some form of preliminary relief because the implementation of the recapitalization plan by HBJ will prevent any future takeover of HBJ. This, BPCC contends, effectively deprives shareholders of the opportunity to obtain the maximum possible value for their investment, which they might otherwise obtain in a contest for control of HBJ. BPCC premises this contention on the sale of the preferred stock to First Boston, the contribution and sale of stock to the ESOP and the provision in HBJ's loan agreements with First Boston and Morgan which allow for the debt to be called in immediately upon a change of control at HBJ.

These transactions do not, however, foreclose a successful bid for control of HBJ. While First Boston may be favorably disposed to the present management of HBJ, there is no agreement or implied understanding which would compel First Boston to favor them if an attractive offer were made for First Boston's stock or to vote against a proposed merger with BPCC or any other entity. This is also true of the ESOP. BPCC has offered nothing but speculation to support its contention that the ESOP trustees would vote as a block with management or First Boston on future transactions. The "pass-through" provision of the ESOP ensures that all allocated shares held by the ESOP will be voted by HBJ's employees, not by management. The trustees have agreed with the New York Stock Exchange that they will vote those shares not yet allocated for and against any proposal to the shareholders in the same proportion as the allocated shares are voted. Thus, the contribution and sale of stock to the ESOP does not "lock up" voting control over those shares with the management of HBJ. Even if that were the case, moreover, the trustees would be bound by law to act in the best interests of the ESOP beneficiaries and to tender its shares if that were in the beneficiaries' best interests. *See* 29 U.S.C. § 1104; *Donovan v. Bierwirth*, 680 F.2d 263 (2d Cir.), *cert. denied*, 459 U.S. 1069, 103 S. Ct. 488, 74 L. Ed. 2d 631 (1982).

Nor do the change of control provisions in HBJ's loan agreements preclude a takeover of the company. The would-be acquirer need only obtain sufficient financing of its own with which to replace the loans in order to render those provisions nugatory. Even absent such alternative financing, the acquirer would quite possibly be able to assure First Boston and Morgan that it is capable of running HBJ as efficiently as does present management and thereby dissuade them from calling in the loans.

In sum, none of these aspects of the recapitalization plan prohibit an acquisition of HBJ by an entity with sufficient capital and determination. That they might discourage less well-equipped suitors, while providing immediate value to HBJ's shareholders, does not constitute the sort of irreparable harm that the Court ought to protect through injunctive relief. To do so would interfere with the forces of the free market on which shareholders depend to increase their investment.

Nor does the payment of the special dividend itself create irreparable harm to BPCC as a shareholder. The debt incurred in order to provide that dividend will be offset by the payment of the dividend (plus cost-reductions implemented because of the recapitalization). The net result of the recapitalization is therefore to neither decrease nor increase the value of HBJ to its shareholders but to allow them to realize that value, in part immediately, more fully than they might otherwise.

The true risk of harm arising from the declaration of the special dividend is to the creditors of HBJ, who might be left without adequate recourse should HBJ fail to meet its financial obligations. The only significant creditors remaining after the recapitalization, however, will be First Boston and the Morgan syndicate. Because they favor the recapitalization, the Court need not enjoin it to protect their interests. BPCC surely should not be heard to argue that it understands the true interests of creditors better than do the creditors themselves.

Finally, the possibility that HBJ stock will be delisted from the New York Stock Exchange because of the Exchange's net worth rules is speculative and insufficient to warrant the granting of relief. In contrast, the threat of delisting in *Norlin v. Rooney, Pace Inc.*, 744 F.2d at 260, was much more concrete — the Exchange had already expressed its intent to delist the stock there. No such event has occurred in this case.

Likelihood of Success on the Merits

As stated above, BPCC must show that it is likely to succeed on the merits in order to satisfy the first alternative ground for granting injunctive relief, assuming the Court were to agree that it had demonstrated irreparable harm. The Court concludes that BPCC has failed to make that showing.

The parties agree that the propriety of the action taken by HBJ's directors must be determined according to the law of New York, the state in which HBJ is incorporated. New York law imposes two principal duties on corporate directors: a duty of due care in the execution of directoral responsibilities and a duty of loyalty to the best interests of the corporation and its shareholders. *Hanson II*, 781 F.2d at 273-74; *Norlin v. Rooney, Pace Inc.*, 744 F.2d at 264. *Cf.* Plato, *The Republic Part Four [Book Three]* at 180 (Penguin Classics 2d ed. 1974) (". . . we must look for the Guardians who will stick most firmly to the principle that they must always do what they think best for the community."). In assessing the conduct of directors under New York law, the Court is barred by the "business judgment rule" from second-guessing actions taken by the directors "in good faith and in the exercise of honest judgment in the lawful and legitimate furtherance of corporate purposes." *Auerbach v. Bennett*, 47 N.Y.2d 619, 629, 419 N.Y.S.2d 920, 926, 393 N.E.2d 994, 1000 (1979). This business judgment rule applies in the contexts of bids for corporate control as in other contexts and "affords directors wide latitude in devising strategies to resist unfriendly advances." *Norlin v. Rooney, Pace Inc.*, 744 F.2d at 264; *see Hanson II*, 781 F.2d at 273. The latitude afforded directors in such circumstances is not, of course, unlimited. *Hanson II*, 781 F.2d at 273.

The initial burden of proving that corporate directors have breached a fiduciary duty rests with the plaintiff. *Id.; Crouse-Hinds Co. v. Internorth, Inc.*, 634 F.2d 690, 701-04 (2d Cir. 1980). Where a plaintiff is able to make a prima facie showing of self-interest on the part of the directors, the burden shifts to the directors to demonstrate that the transaction is fair and in the best interests of the corporation and its shareholders. *Norlin v. Rooney, Pace Inc.*, 744 F.2d at 264. The interest of directors in retaining their positions as directors is not by itself sufficient to cause the burden to shift to them. *Crouse-Hinds Co. v. Internorth, Inc.*, 634 F.2d at 702. BPCC argues that the consulting relationships between certain non-management directors and HBJ renders them self-interested. These relationships are not of substantial economic significance, however, and do not result in payment to the directors involved substantially in excess of normal directors' fees. Because the receipt of directors' fees is not sufficient to show self-interest by a board member, *see, e.g., In re E.F. Hutton Banking Practices Litigation*, 634 F. Supp. 265, 271 (S.D.N.Y. 1986), the Court does not believe that the directors were truly self-interested in the recapitalization. (Nor do Walter Johnson's substantial stock holdings in HBJ provide him with any interest conflicting with those of other shareholders.) Nevertheless, the Court concludes that the better course is to apply the more stringent rule and examine the transaction as if the directors were self-interested, because of the importance of the recapitalization to HBJ and its shareholders and because of the preliminary nature of the fact finding process on this application for injunctive relief. Accordingly, the Court concludes that the burden of demonstrating the fairness of the transaction to the corporation and its shareholders must rest with the directors.

The Court believes that no lengthy analysis is necessary before concluding that the directors satisfied their duty of due care in examining the Maxwell proposal and in responding to it. The primary requirement of the duty of due care is that the directors make an informed decision, having availed themselves of the advice of experts and using the available time to consider their options carefully. *See Hanson II*, 781 F.2d at 274-77.

The directors met five separate times over six days to consider the Maxwell proposal and the alternatives available to them. They consulted financial advisers who had been familiar with HBJ from past association and who engaged in a near-Herculean effort to provide the board with advice soundly based on thorough analysis and to structure the alternative transaction that appeared best to all concerned. The board did not rely on conclusory statements of their advisers, but reviewed carefully and questioned the support for the advice they received. Those advisers had been provided with the best information then available to HBJ in order to perform their tasks. The directors appropriately considered the effects of the recapitalization on HBJ and its shareholders and the effects of a failure to act swiftly. They availed themselves of the time they reasonably believed they had in which to act. In sum, it is difficult to see how the directors could have been more diligent or better informed under the circumstances.

That the board declined to approach BPCC for negotiations does not indicate that the directors did not fully investigate the relevant facts. It was reasonable to conclude from the terms of the Maxwell proposal and the manner in which it was made and publicized that BPCC did not intend to negotiate in good faith towards a purchase of HBJ at a fair price.

That management played an important role in providing information to the board's advisers and in working with them to plan the recapitalization was proper and detracts in no way from the conclusion that the directors exercised due care. Management was to receive no greater benefits from the recapitalization than would HBJ's employees and shareholders. Moreover, it possessed the information and expertise vital to the development of an effective response to the Maxwell proposal.

Concluding then that the directors of HBJ did not breach their duty of due care, the Court must address the question of their loyalty to HBJ and its shareholders, of the fairness of the recapitalization.

BPCC does not contend that the shareholders received no value from the recapitalization, arguing instead that they received less than otherwise might be available because the board acted to entrench the incumbent management rather than to further the interests of the shareholders. The evidence adduced by BPCC is insufficient to support this conclusion.

BPCC urges that the sale of exchangeable redeemable preferred stock to First Boston was designed solely to place votes in friendly hands in order to entrench management. The record reveals, however, that it was First Boston that insisted on the right to purchase the stock as a condition of providing the bridge financing, as a way of ensuring that it had a voice in HBJ's management (so as to protect its loan to HBJ) and as an investment. BPCC adduced no evidence of a secret or open agreement between First Boston and any other entity concerning how it would vote or dispose of its shares. In addition, First Boston paid a price for that stock equivalent to the market price for the comparable common stock being traded on the market ex dividend.

Similarly, BPCC's reliance on the stock transactions involving the HBJ ESOP is of no avail to it. The evidence was uncontradicted in showing that the ESOP was created for a valid purpose long before the Maxwell proposal. The sale and contribution of HBJ stock to the ESOP as part of the recapitalization plan was intended to serve as an incentive for increased employee productivity, an essential element of the plan's success. No credible evidence to the contrary was adduced. The possibility of an entrenchment motive underlying this transaction is belied by the fact that neither management as a whole nor the ESOP trustees control how the stock held by the ESOP is voted. Whether to tender the stock to a potential acquirer of HBJ would be decided by the trustees under the constraints of their legal obligation to act in the best interests of the ESOP beneficiaries.

The Court concludes that BPCC has failed to demonstrate that the recapitalization plan of HBJ is unfair to HBJ or its shareholders or that it was improperly motivated by a desire to entrench the present management of HBJ.

BPCC's final argument against the recapitalization is that HBJ does not have adequate surplus as defined under New York law to allow it to declare and pay the special dividend. BPCC's attack on this aspect of the recapitalization is two-pronged. New York law permits the declaration or payment of dividends out of surplus only. N.Y. Bus. Corp. Law § 510(b). BPCC urges that the surplus must be based on the valuation of assets reflected on the books of the corporation. No direct support is cited for that proposition. The leading case on revaluing assets for the determination of surplus makes no mention of the requirement. *Randall v. Bailey*,

23 N.Y.S.2d 173 (Sup. Ct. 1940), *aff'd*, 262 App. Div. 844, 29 N.Y.S.2d 512 (Sup. Ct. 1941), *aff'd*, 288 N.Y. 280, 43 N.E. 43 (1942). It thus appears that New York law imposes no such requirement and that BPCC's attack on this ground must fail.

The second prong of BPCC's argument is addressed to the amount at which HBJ's assets were valued by the board. BPCC contends that the assets were valued too aggressively and that future earnings were wrongly considered in arriving at the valuation. *Randall v. Bailey* supports the use of the "going concern" value of a business in determining surplus under New York law. 23 N.Y.S.2d at 177-78; *see also Hayman v. Morris*, 36 N.Y.S.2d 756, 767-68 (Sup. Ct. N.Y. Co. 1942); *Morris v. Standard Gas & Electric Co.*, 63 A.2d 577 (Del. Ch. 1949) (Delaware law). In addition, the evidence adduced at the hearing revealed that the directors had reasonably relied on expert advice offered by First Boston and that First Boston had been conservative in its valuation of HBJ, reducing the financial forecasts supplied by HBJ's management and adhering to the lower end of the calculated range of values. BPCC has not shown that that valuation was unreasonably high.

Thus, the Court concludes that BPCC has not demonstrated a likelihood of success on the merits.

Balance of Hardships

The balance of hardships tips decidedly in favor of denying the preliminary relief requested. As stated above, BPCC and the other shareholders of HBJ will suffer no significant injury under the recapitalization plan. Were the Court to enjoin its implementation, however, HBJ would incur substantial interest charges without receiving the attendant benefits of recapitalization. First Boston would be unable to exercise its voice in the affairs of HBJ as required to protect its investment. Most important, to grant the injunctive relief requested would deprive HBJ's shareholders of the value to which they are entitled under the plan. Because of the intricacies of financing, the opportunity to receive this dividend, once delayed, may be lost permanently. Moreover, the expectations of the marketplace upon which investors have bought and sold HBJ stock would be defeated. To do so on the basis of the evidence adduced on this motion would be unfair to all those investors who have acted upon their expectations.

Conclusion

For the foregoing reasons, the motion for a preliminary injunction is denied. SO ORDERED.

NOTE

The revaluation of corporate assets approved by the District Court in reliance on *Randall v. Bailey* is often referred to as unrealized appreciation. A noted commentator has observed that:

> Modern accounting does not favor unrealized appreciation of assets. In the quest for orderly computation of periodic profits and losses, earnings are assigned to the accounting period in which revenue is "realized," *i.e.*,

> converted into cash or equivalent. A recognition of unrealized appreciation as "revenue" or "earnings" upsets this orderly arrangement because it is premature as a matter of timing. . . . Accounting practice therefore tends to recognize unrealized appreciation only in unusual situations, such as quasi-reorganizations. . . .
>
> I rather suspect that the affection with which *Randall v. Bailey* is held in the hearts of many corporation lawyers is due . . . to its ringing declaration of judicial independence from accountants, economists, investment analysts, business and other laymen in the interpretation of a statute.

Miguel A. de Capriles, *New York Business Corporation Law: Article 5-Corporate Finance*, 11 Buffalo L. Rev. 461, 469 (1962).

In the light of the recent accounting and auditing scandals, that independence is perhaps not misplaced; however, certain state insurance corporation statutes prohibit the utilization of unrealized appreciation for determining whether a corporation has assets legally available for the payment of dividends; *e.g.*, § 215 Ill. Comp. Stat. Ann. 5/27(1)(b) (LexisNexis 2005); N.D. Cent. Code § 26.1-10-05.1(b) (2005); S.C. Code Ann. § 38-21-170(C) (2004).

IVANHOE PARTNERS v. NEWMONT MINING CORP.

Delaware Court of Chancery
533 A.2d 585 (1987)

Jacobs, Vice Chancellor

. . . .

The proposed restructuring program involved Newmont declaring a nondiscriminatory $33 per share dividend and selling its nongold assets to finance the dividend, thereby leaving Newmont with its core gold business. Management believed that in the near term, the dividend would provide shareholders with greater value than the face value of the Ivanhoe offer, while in the long term it would permit stockholders to participate in the company's future growth. The dividend would also put money into Gold Fields' hands that could be used to make open market purchases at an overall relatively low cost.

. . . .

The class plaintiffs seek preliminarily to enjoin the dividend on the ground that it was enacted in furtherance of the defendants' scheme to entrench the Newmont Board, and on the additional ground that the dividend constitutes waste.

When briefing and oral argument were scheduled, all parties agreed that the only transaction in issue on the preliminary injunction motion was the street sweep. Although the class plaintiffs had filed an amended complaint which included a claim for relief against the dividend, those plaintiffs' opening brief was addressed solely to the street sweep and did not mention the dividend. Two days later, only hours before the defendants' briefs were to be filed and one day before the oral argument, the class plaintiffs gave notice for the first time that they intended to challenge the dividend. Their supplemental brief on that issue was filed the next day, i.e., the day of the argument. The defendants objected, insisting that they could not (and should not be compelled to) prepare a response in the short time remaining. Without prejudice to that objection, the Court permitted the class plaintiffs to address the dividend issue at oral argument.

The foregoing indicates that the challenge to the dividend was an afterthought. As a procedural matter, it comes too late. But, as a substantive matter, the argument falls as well.

The class plaintiffs concede that the dividend does not violate either the Delaware General Corporation Law or Newmont's certificate of incorporation or by-laws. That being the case, this Court can interfere with the Board's decision to pay the dividend only if (a) the dividend was the product of self-dealing and the directors fail to prove that the dividend is entirely fair, or if (b) no self-dealing is present and the plaintiff is able to prove that the dividend ". . . cannot be grounded on any reasonable business objective." *Sinclair Oil Corporation v. Levien*, Del. Supr., 280 A.2d 717, 721 (1971). Where the business judgment rule applies (that is, where no self-dealing is shown), the motives for declaring a dividend are immaterial unless the plaintiff can show that the dividend payments resulted from improper motives and amounted to waste. *Id.* As stated by the Delaware Supreme Court in *Gabelli & Co., Inc.*, Del. Supr., 479 A.2d 276, 280 (1984), ". . . before the courts will interfere with the [business] judgment of the board of directors in such matter, fraud or gross abuse of discretion must be shown." *See also Burton v. Exxon Corporation*, 583 F. Supp. 405, 415 (S.D.N.Y. 1984) (applying Delaware law).

In determining the proprietary of the $33 dividend, the business judgment rule is applicable because no self-dealing is shown. The dividend is to be paid to all Newmont shareholders in proportion to their stock interest, and the defendants will receive no greater proportionate share than would the minority stockholders. *Sinclair Oil Corporation v. Levien*, 280 A.2d at 721-722. The record discloses no fraud or gross abuse of discretion by Newmont directors, nor has it been shown that the dividend cannot be grounded on any reasonable business objective. To the contrary, the dividend would appear to further several legitimate business objectives of the Newmont Board: (i) it permits shareholders to realize immediately a portion of the corporation's value, (ii) it defeats an unsolicited partial tender offer reasonably regarded by the Board as coercive and not in the shareholder's best interests, and (iii) it induced Gold Fields to restrict voluntarily its stock ownership to 49.9% of Newmont's outstanding shares and its right to exercise its voting power to take control of Newmont, possibly to the detriment of public stockholders.

Nor is there merit to the claim that the dividend amounts to waste. The class plaintiffs argue that the dividend will leave Newmont with a net deficit in shareholder's equity. But where, as here, a dividend complies with 8 Del. C. § 170, the alleged excessiveness of the amount alone does not state a cause of action. *Sinclair Oil Corporation v. Levien*, 280 A.2d at 721. Moreover, the argument ignores the fact that Newmont's nongold assets will be sold in the restructuring and the proceeds will be used to eliminate any temporary deficit.

. . . .

GABELLI & CO. v. LIGGETT GROUP, INC.

Delaware Supreme Court
479 A.2d 276 (1984)

HERRMANN, CHIEF JUSTICE:

This appeal from the Court of Chancery involves a class action brought by a minority stockholder to compel the payment of a dividend on the theory that the majority stockholder breached its fiduciary duty to the minority stockholders by causing the corporation to refrain from declaring the dividend solely for the purpose of enabling the majority stockholder to obtain the dividend funds for itself after a merger of the corporation with a wholly-owned subsidiary of the majority stockholder and a cash-out of the minority stockholders. The Court of Chancery granted summary judgment in favor of the defendants. We affirm.

I.

The following facts are undisputed:

In April 1980, the defendant GM Sub Corporation ("GM Sub"), a wholly-owned subsidiary of defendant Grand Metropolitan Limited ("Grand Met") formed to acquire the defendant Liggett Group, Inc. ("Liggett"), commenced a tender offer for "any and all" of Liggett's approximately 8.4 million common shares at the price of $50 per share. In the first quarter of 1980, Liggett common stock traded on the New York Stock Exchange in the range of $3418 to $4134 per share.

The Liggett Board of Directors resisted GM Sub's tender offer and recommended to its shareholders that the offer be rejected as inadequate.

On May 12,[1] Standard Brands Incorporated ("Standard Brands") commenced a rival tender offer for up to 4,000,000 shares of Liggett's common stock at $65 per share. The Standard Brands offer was endorsed by the Board of Directors of Liggett as being fair. On May 14, GM Sub amended the terms of its tender offer to increase the price to $69 per share. On the same day, shortly after GM Sub announced its increased offer, Standard Brands publicly announced the withdrawal of its offer. On May 15, Liggett's Board of Directors resolved to approve GM Sub's amended offer of $69 and to recommend that it be accepted by Liggett's shareholders as a fair price.

The Offer to Purchase sent to Liggett stockholders in connection with the tender offer stated that Grand Met and GM Sub intended "as promptly as possible [after the conclusion of the tender offer] to seek to have [Liggett] consummate a merger with [GM Sub] or an affiliate of [GM Sub]." Further, it was stated in the Offer that GM Sub intended to pay the tender offer price of $69 per share in connection with the merger cash-out of shares not tendered.

As a result of the tender offer, GM Sub acquired 87.4% of Liggett's outstanding

---

[1] [1] The sequence of dates is set forth in detail in order to relate them to the plaintiffs claim of entitlement to a third-quarter dividend.

common stock. The plaintiff Gabelli & Co., Inc. Profit Sharing Plan ("Gabelli") did not tender its 800 shares in response to the offer.

Immediately following consummation of the tender offer, preparations for the merger were commenced. During the month of June 1980, an Agreement and Plan of Merger (the "Merger Agreement") and a preliminary Information Statement, as required by the Securities and Exchange Commission, were prepared and submitted to the Liggett Board of Directors for approval. On June 30, the Liggett Board approved the Merger Agreement.

Upon the approval of the Merger Agreement, preliminary copies of the Information Statement were filed with the SEC pursuant to its Rule that this be done at least 10 days prior to mailing the final Statement to the shareholders. After receiving the comments of the SEC on July 15, the finalized Information Statement was duly prepared and sent to Liggett shareholders on July 18.

The stockholders' meeting approving the merger was held 20 days later on August 7, and the merger became effective on that date. The minority shareholders who were merged out in August received the same $69 per share price paid to the shareholders who tendered their shares in June. Gabelli surrendered its shares in the merger cash-out and accepted the $69 price. Neither Gabelli nor any other shareholder attempted to block the merger. The only stock appraisal proceeding arising from the merger was voluntarily dismissed.

Historically, Liggett had paid quarterly dividends to its common shareholders in an amount of $.625 per share in March, June, September and December of each year. On June 2, 1980, prior to the consummation of the merger and during the pendency of the tender offer, a quarterly dividend of $.625 per share was paid to the holders of Liggett common stock as of a record date of May 15, 1980. The dividend at issue in this case is a third-quarter dividend, which in prior years had been declared in late July, with a mid-August record date and payment in September. No such dividend was declared or paid to Liggett stockholders for the third quarter of 1980. The merger transaction involved approximately 300 million dollars; the dividends claimed on behalf of the minority stockholders involved approximately $677,000.

II.

By its original complaint filed prior to the consummation of the merger, Gabelli brought this action to compel Liggett's Board to declare a third-quarterly dividend for 1980. Gabelli there alleged that "Grand Met, by reason of its majority and controlling position in Liggett, owes a fiduciary duty to Liggett's minority shareholders," and that "Grand Met is breaching its fiduciary duty to Liggett's minority shareholders by causing Liggett to eliminate its regular dividend to enable Grand Met to obtain the Liggett dividend money for itself upon the merger of Liggett and Grand Met." The prayer of the complaint was for judgment "[R]equiring that Liggett pay the omitted quarterly dividend of $.625 per share." The complaint did not seek to enjoin the consummation of the merger or attack the fairness of the price offered.

The Court of Chancery granted the defendants' motion to dismiss the complaint with leave to amend [*Gabelli & Co., Inc. Profit Sharing Plan v. Liggett Group, Inc., et al.*, Del. Ch., 444 A.2d 261 (1982)], on the ground that the complaint failed to state a claim upon which relief could be granted, stating:

> In order for the plaintiff to state a cause of action, therefore, it must allege the existence of two mutually dependent factors. The first is the plaintiff's right to the dividend in question. If such a cognizable right or entitlement exists, however, plaintiff must also necessarily claim, if a cause of action is to be stated, that the impending merger and the consideration being offered did not account for the value of the dividend which would have been forthcoming if the merger had not taken place.

(444 A.2d at 265.) The Trial Court further held that in order to show that it was entitled to the dividend in question, Gabelli was obliged to plead and prove that the dividend was withheld as a result of an oppressive abuse of discretion in the context of an unfair merger. *Id.* at 266.

In April 1982, Gabelli amended its complaint to allege that Grand Met breached its fiduciary duty to Liggett's minority shareholders at the time of the merger ". . . by setting the merger at $69 to be in parity with the tender, but without consideration for the dividend which was being omitted." Otherwise, the amended complaint was substantially the same as the original complaint. Again, the prayer of the amended complaint was for judgment, requiring Liggett to pay a 1980 third-quarterly dividend of $.625 per share.

The defendants moved for summary judgment, supported by an affidavit addressed primarily to the fairness of the merger price. Gabelli took no discovery; it rested its position solely upon the allegations of its complaint.

In granting summary judgment in favor of the defendants, the Trial Court stated that Gabelli's position, based as it was solely on its unsupported complaint, was "merely a restatement of its position" on the motion to dismiss the complaint and was without merit for the reasons stated in the Court's prior opinion. Gabelli appeals.

III.

In our view, this case commenced as, and continues to be, no more nor less than an action to compel the declaration and payment of a dividend by the Board of Directors of Liggett for the benefit of about 13% of its stockholders who were then in the final stages of being cashed-out in a merger transaction for a price conceded to be fair for the acquisition of all of the assets of Liggett.

As so simplified, it is abundantly clear upon the undisputed facts that summary judgment for the defendants was correctly granted.

There is no showing by the plaintiff anywhere in this case that, given the extraordinary circumstances existing in Liggett's affairs in late July 1980, the Board of Liggett abused its discretion in the exercise of its business judgment by not declaring a third-quarter dividend in accord with the corporation's dividend history of prior years. In the absence of such showing, the plaintiff may not prevail in this action to compel the dividend.

It is settled law in this State that the declaration and payment of a dividend rests in the discretion of the corporation's board of directors in the exercise of its business judgment; that, before the courts will interfere with the judgment of the board of directors in such matter, fraud or gross abuse of discretion must be shown, *Moskowitz v. Bantrell*, Del. Supr., 190 A.2d 749 (1963). There, this Court quoted with approval the time-honored statement of Chancellor Wolcott in *Eshleman v. Keenan*, Del. Ch., 194 A. 40, 43 (1937) that courts act to compel the declaration of a dividend only upon a demonstration "that the withholding of it is explicable only on the theory of an oppressive or fraudulent abuse of discretion." *See also Baron v. Allied Artists Pictures Corp.*, Del. Ch., 337 A.2d 653, 659 (1975).

Gabelli has not alleged fraud; and it has made no showing that the failure of Liggett's Board to declare a third-quarter dividend, under the undisputed facts and circumstances of this case, is explicable only on the theory of a gross or oppressive abuse of discretion. As has been noted, Gabelli took no discovery in this case. It made no effort by interrogatory, affidavit, deposition, or otherwise, to raise any genuine issue of material fact as to whether, in the final stages of the cash-out merger, the Liggett Board abused its discretion in electing not to declare a final dividend in addition to the cash-out merger price which the Board itself had approved and recommended as fair. On the other hand, in support of their motion for summary judgment, the defendants presented the affidavit of the Secretary of Liggett containing explanation and justification for the merger time-table which resulted in the non-payment of the dividend. Gabelli produced no affidavit or other evidence in response.

On the record before us, the non-payment of a final dividend by the Liggett Board in the final stages of the cash-out merger, is reasonably "explicable" (in the language of *Eshleman*) for at least 2 reasons: (1) It would have been unfair to the holders of 87% of the stock, who accepted the tender offer upon the recommendation of the Board, to reward by a "farewell" or "bonus" dividend the holders of the remaining 13% who, for some unannounced reason, declined to accept the tender-offer and held out for the merger cash-out with the risk-free assurance of receiving the same price per share; and (2) It would have been unreasonable to supplement the $69 per share, which had been approved by the Board as a fair price for Liggett and all of its assets, by a last minute dividend declared in the final stages of the merger cash-out process.

Gabelli has summarized the crux of its case as follows:

> Simply put, plaintiff does not urge that the Liggett board of directors was necessarily required to pay the July 1980 dividend. Instead, plaintiff claims that Grand Met, for its own gain, wrongfully prevented Liggett from declaring a dividend it would otherwise have declared.

The plaintiff has placed nothing on this record to raise a genuine issue of material fact as to whether (1) Grand Met[2] actually "prevented" the Liggett Board from declaring the dividend; or (2) the Liggett Board actually would have "otherwise" declared the dividend. The undisputed facts before us, and the reasonable infer-

---

[2] [1] For convenience in this connection, we follow the plaintiffs naming of Grand Met rather than its subsidiary GM Sub. as the majority stockholder.

ences to be drawn therefrom, are to the contrary.

IV.

Gabelli has attempted to avoid the force and effect of the law governing the declaration of dividends, and to overcome its failure to show any material issue of fact suggesting an abuse of discretion by the Liggett Board, by the claim that Grand Met, in its position as dominant majority stockholder, engaged in self-dealing such as to require that its conduct be subjected to the "intrinsic fairness" test discussed by this Court in *Sinclair Oil Corp. v. Levien*, Del. Supr., 280 A.2d 717 (1971).

The plaintiff rests its entire case upon the statement in Sinclair (280 A.2d at 720) that self-dealing

> . . . occurs when the parent, by virtue of its domination of the subsidiary, causes the subsidiary to act in such a way that the parent receives something from the subsidiary to the exclusion of, and detriment to, the minority stockholders of the subsidiary.

Upon that basis, Gabelli builds the contention that the conduct of the defendants is not to be tested by the business judgment rule under which a court will not interfere with the judgment of a board of directors unless there is a showing of gross and palpable overreaching, and as to which the plaintiff has the burden of proof; that, by reason of the applicability of the intrinsic fairness test, the burden of proof shifts in this case to the defendants to prove, subject to judicial scrutiny, that the conduct under attack was objectively fair. See *Sinclair*, 280 A.2d at 719-720. Gabelli's position is manifestly untenable.

In support of its position, and in an effort to show its "detriment" under the *Sinclair* language, Gabelli argues that Grand Met "usurped the minority's share of the dividend;" that it "retained the minority's share" of the dividend funds; that it "misappropriated the Liggett dividend for itself." All such contentions are based upon the assumption that, under the law and the facts of this case, Gabelli had a right or entitlement to a third-quarter dividend which Grand Met "usurped," "retained," or "misappropriated."

The record does not justify any such assumption for the following reasons: (1) Gabelli had no right or entitlement to a third-quarter dividend in the absence of a declaration thereof, especially under the extraordinary circumstances of this case; (2) Gabelli was not prevented from tendering its shares and receiving full payment therefor promptly, the tender offer being for "any and all" shares; (3) Gabelli had no valid reason in July to expect extra compensation for its stock, by dividend or otherwise, over and above that paid to the great majority of its fellow stockholders in June; (4) The merger price of $69 per share, conceded here to have been a fair price for all assets of Liggett including cash on hand, fully compensated Gabelli for its shares, including any right to receive any additional dividends.

In view of the foregoing undisputed facts and law, Gabelli has demonstrated no such "self-dealing" or "detriment" as to warrant the application of the *Sinclair* intrinsic fairness test upon which Gabelli has based its entire case.

The foregoing makes manifest the ineffectiveness of Gabelli's amendment to its complaint to allege that the $69 merger price was established "without consideration for the dividend which was being omitted." This allegation also presupposes that Gabelli had some right or entitlement to an undeclared third-quarter dividend which the defendants took from it wrongfully and to its "detriment." For the reasons stated, the fallacy of the assumption is clear. The amendment to the complaint was of no assistance to Gabelli in its effort to invoke the intrinsic fairness test.

. . . .

We conclude that there is no error in the Trial Court's grant of summary judgment in favor of the defendants.

IN RE C-T OF VIRGINIA, INC.

United States Court of Appeals, Fourth Circuit
958 F.2d 606 (1992)

WILKINSON, CIRCUIT JUDGE:

This case presents the question of whether the leveraged acquisition of a corporation, structured in the form of a cash-out merger and consummated at arm's length, is subject to restrictions on distributions to shareholders under Virginia law. The case involves an action brought by an official committee of unsecured creditors of a corporation now in bankruptcy against the former directors of that corporation. The creditors, suing on behalf of the corporation, claimed that the leveraged acquisition created an illegal distribution to shareholders under the Virginia Stock Corporation Act, VA. CODE ANN. § 13.1-601 *et seq.* (Michie 1989). We agree with the district court that the merger did not create a distribution under Virginia law and therefore affirm its judgment.

I.

The facts underlying this case are not in dispute. C-T of Virginia, Inc., formerly Craddock-Terry Shoe Corp., is a Virginia corporation engaged in the manufacture, wholesale, and mail-order sale of shoes. Prior to the purchase that is the subject of this action, C-T was a publicly owned corporation whose stock was traded on the over-the-counter market. In April 1985, C-T hired a financial adviser, Prudential-Bache Securities, Inc., to study the strategic alternatives available to the company. Prudential recommended that C-T's management pursue a leveraged buyout ("LBO") of the company. Prudential indicated that an LBO would both realize maximum value for C-T's shareholders and maintain the viability of the post-LBO enterprise.

On May 20, 1985, C-T's board of directors accepted Prudential's recommendation and authorized management to explore the possibility of a management-sponsored LBO at $15 per share. (C-T common stock was trading for $14.25 per share when this authorization was announced.) The board retained the right to consider other proposals made to the corporation. On June 12, 1985, Southwestern General Corp. made such an unsolicited offer, which proposed a merger at $17.50 per share.

Southwestern withdrew this offer on August 26, 1985, however, after President Reagan refused to impose limitations on shoe imports.

C-T received a second unsolicited offer on November 11, 1985, from HH Holdings, Inc. Holdings is a Delaware holding company owned by Sidney Kimmel and Alan Salke. Neither Holdings, Kimmel, nor Salke had any prior relationship or contact with C-T or the members of its board of directors. Holdings proposed a cash merger in which C-T shareholders would receive $19 per share of common stock. After the directors announced this offer, several owners of substantial amounts of C-T common stock urged that the directors reject the offer and demand $20 per share instead. Holdings agreed to the merger at $20 per share, and an Agreement in Principle was signed on December 11, 1985.

The parties formalized the transaction in an Agreement and Plan of Merger executed on January 24, 1986. The merger agreement structured the purchase in the form of a reverse triangular merger. For purposes of the merger, Holdings formed HH Acquisition, Inc., a wholly owned subsidiary. The merger agreement provided that on April 30, 1986, Acquisition would merge into C-T, leaving C-T as the surviving corporation wholly owned by Holdings. The funds necessary to purchase all outstanding shares of C-T, about $30 million, would be deposited with the exchange agent, Sovran Bank, before or at the closing of the transaction. At the moment that the merger was effected, the outstanding shares of C-T common stock would be automatically canceled, and the former shareholders would receive the right to submit their canceled stock certificates to Sovran for payment of $20 per canceled share. Also at that time, the directors of C-T would resign and be replaced by Salke, John W. Baker, and Roland K. Peters.

The financing for the merger was arranged solely by Holdings. Holdings provided about $4 million of its own money. It obtained the balance, approximately $26 million, in the form of bank loans secured by C-T's assets. The pre-merger directors did not solicit proposed financing, negotiate the terms of the financing or of the security, or participate in or authorize the encumbering of C-T's assets. The merger agreement did obligate C-T to provide Holdings, Acquisition, and the financing banks access to C-T's properties, personnel, and books and records and to cooperate with Holdings' efforts to secure financing. Further, the pre-merger directors approved the repurchase of C-T's preferred stock, which was a prerequisite to effectuation of the merger.

C-T's board of directors approved the merger agreement and unanimously voted to recommend that the shareholders approve the merger, which they did on April 17, 1986. The transaction was consummated as planned on April 30. The surviving corporation struggled along for about eighteen months, and it filed for bankruptcy under Chapter 11 on October 21, 1987.

In October 1989, the Official Committee of Unsecured Creditors of C-T filed this action in federal court against the pre-merger directors and officers of the corporation. The complaint alleged that the directors and officers breached their fiduciary duties owed to the corporation and that the directors had approved a distribution in violation of Va. Code Ann. §§ 13.1-653 and 13.1-692 (Michie 1989). The district court granted the defendants' motion to dismiss the former claim. 124 B.R. 689, 692-93 (W.D. Va. 1990). It denied the directors' motion to dismiss the unlawful distribution claim, however, finding that under some factual circumstances the merger might have been a distribution. *Id.* at 693-94.

Subsequently, the district court granted the directors' motion for summary judgment on the illegal distribution claim. 124 B.R. 694 (W.D. Va. 1990). The court found application of the restriction on distributions "inconsistent with Virginia's statutory scheme," because the merger provisions of the Virginia Stock Corporation Act — unlike the sale of corporate assets provisions, see Va. Code Ann. § 13.1-724 (Michie 1989) — "make[ ] no mention of distributions." 124 B.R. at 696-97. The court also concluded that the transaction was not "a distribution clothed in the garb of a merger" to evade the distribution restrictions. *Id.* at 697. The court concluded, finally, that, even if the merger involved a distribution, the directors did not "vote[ ] for or assent[ ] to" it, a prerequisite to liability under Va. Code Ann. § 13.1-692 (A) (Michie 1989). For the latter holding, the court relied on the fact that the directors did not authorize the encumbering of C-T's assets, which occurred after they had resigned their offices. 124 B.R. at 699.

C-T appeals the summary judgment against it on the distribution claim.

II.

Modern distribution statutes derive from eighteenth century restrictions on when a corporation could pay dividends to its shareholders. *See* Revised Model Business Corporation Act § 6.40 historical n.1 (1986) (hereinafter RMBCA). Restrictions on a corporation's purchase of its own shares, and on other forms of distributions, were enacted later. *See* J. Choper, J. Coffee, & C. Morris, Cases and Materials on Corporations 1007 (3d ed. 1989). All states now impose limitations on the power of a corporation to make various distributions to its shareholders, see RMBCA § 6.40 statutory comparison 1, and federal courts must, of course, pay strict attention to the language of the relevant state statute. Virginia's corporate law statute, including the distribution provisions, was substantially revised in 1985. *See* 1985 Va. Acts 868 (codified at VA. CODE ANN. §§ 13.1-601 to -800 (Michie 1989)). The Virginia statute defines "distribution" as follows: "Distribution" means a direct or indirect transfer of money or other property, except its own shares, or incurrence of indebtedness by a corporation to or for the benefit of its shareholders in respect of any of its shares. A distribution may be in the form of a declaration or payment of a dividend; a purchase, redemption, or other acquisition of shares; a distribution of indebtedness of the corporation; or otherwise. VA. CODE ANN. § 13.1-603 (Michie 1989). Not all distributions are unlawful. Rather, a distribution is prohibited only if, after it is made, the corporation fails either of two insolvency tests: No distribution may be made if, after giving it effect: 1. The corporation would not be able to pay its debts as they become due in the usual course of business; or 2. The corporation's total assets would be less than the sum of its total liabilities plus (unless the articles of incorporation permit otherwise) the amount that would be needed, if the corporation were to be dissolved at the time of the distribution, to satisfy the preferential rights upon dissolution of shareholders whose preferential rights are superior to those receiving the distribution. *Id.* § 13.1-653(C). Directors face potential personal liability when the corporation makes an unlawful distribution:

Unless he complies with the applicable standards of conduct described in § 13.1-690,[3]

> a director who votes for or assents to a distribution made in violation of this chapter or the articles of incorporation is personally liable to the corporation and its creditors for the amount of the distribution that exceeds what could have been distributed without violating this chapter or the articles of incorporation.

Id. § 13.1-692(A). There is, however, no provision in the Virginia Stock Corporation Act by which creditors can recover a distribution from the shareholders directly. Rather, a creditor's only remedy is against the directors, who then may seek contribution from shareholders who received the distribution. *Id.* § 13.1-692(B)(2).

III.

We now address the central question in this case: whether the merger involved a distribution to shareholders within the meaning of § 13.1-603. For the reasons set forth below, we conclude that the transaction does not fall within the statutory definition of distribution and, therefore, that the directors cannot be subjected to potential liability under § 13.1-692.[4]

A.

Appellant argues that the plain meaning of the statute contradicts the district court's conclusion that the merger did not create a distribution under Virginia law. It claims that the purchase of the premerger shareholders' shares in C-T entailed a distribution because the payment of the purchase price of $20 per share was a "transfer of money . . . by a corporation to . . . its shareholders." Since this purchase was funded primarily through loans secured by the assets of C-T, the argument runs, the value of the corporation — and hence the financial position of its creditors — was diminished. According to appellant, it is irrelevant whether the funds that are transferred to shareholders derive from the corporation's capital surplus, retained earnings, or new loans secured by corporate assets, and it is likewise immaterial that the payment resulted from a cash-out merger; appellant claims that the legislature intended the statute to have "the broadest range of inclusion" and thereby "pick up all forms of transfer of the assets of a corporation to its shareholders."

---

[3] [1] Section 13.1-690 establishes, inter alia, the following standard of conduct for directors: "A director shall discharge his duties as a director, including his duties as a member of a committee, in accordance with his good faith business judgment of the best interests of the corporation." VA. CODE ANN. § 13.1-690(A) (Michie 1989). Because we hold that the merger in this case was not a distribution, we need not consider whether the actions of C-T's pre-merger directors satisfied § 13.1-690.

[4] [2] Our resolution of this case makes it unnecessary to consider whether, if the merger did involve a distribution, the former directors of C-T "vote[d] for or assent[ed] to" it. VA. CODE ANN. § 13.1-692(A) (Michie 1989). In addition, appellant has not argued before this court, as it did before the district court, see 124 B.R. at 697, that the transaction was "a distribution clothed in the garb of a merger." *Id.* (citing *Wieboldt Stores, Inc. v. Schottenstein*, 94 B.R. 488 (N.D. Ill. 1988)). Accordingly, we need not address whether ss 13.1-653 and 13.1-692 apply when a transfer of money or property to shareholders is disguised as a merger in an attempt to avoid the statutory restrictions on distributions.

We do not share appellant's view of the statute. The Virginia Stock Corporation Act provides a precise definition of the word "distribution:" "[A] direct or indirect transfer of money or other property, except its own shares, or incurrence of indebtedness by a corporation to or for the benefit of its shareholders in respect of any of its shares." VA. CODE ANN. § 13.1-603 (Michie 1989). Payment of the merger consideration to C-T's former shareholders simply does not fit within the plain language of this definition. The key language, for our purposes here, is the requirement that the transfer of money or property be "by a corporation to . . . its shareholders." When post-merger C-T transferred $20 per canceled share to C-T's pre-merger shareholders, they were no longer the corporation's — "its" — shareholders, for their ownership interest had been lawfully canceled as of the effective time of the merger.

Similarly, we must reject appellant's argument that the encumbering of C-T's assets to raise sufficient funds to pay for the merger was a distribution because it represented the "incurrence of indebtedness by a corporation . . . for the benefit of its shareholders." *Id.* The financing for the merger was negotiated not by C-T's pre-merger directors for the benefit of C-T's pre-merger shareholders, but by the new owners and directors of the corporation. Moreover, the financing closed simultaneously with the closing of the merger. Accordingly, at the time the encumbering was undertaken, the pre-merger shareholders' ownership interests were canceled and, therefore, C-T did not incur debt "for the benefit of its shareholders."

Appellant's attempt to shoehorn the payment of merger consideration into the statutory definition of distribution must thus prove unsuccessful, for its argument fails to appreciate the significance of the fact that the transaction at issue represented the arm's-length purchase of C-T by Holdings. The distribution statute is aimed by its terms at actions taken by a corporation to enrich unjustly its own shareholders at the expense of creditors and to the detriment of the continuing viability of the company. It does not cover third-party payments to acquire the stock of a corporation or the encumbering of assets after a change in corporate ownership, and it is not intended to obstruct an arm's-length acquisition of an enterprise by new owners who have their own plans for commercial success. The reason for this distinction is simple: A corporate acquisition, structured as a merger, is simply a different animal from a distribution. Distribution statutes, as noted above, derive from the regulation of corporate dividends and traditionally apply to situations in which shareholders, after receiving the transfer from the corporation, retain their status as owners of the corporation. Distribution statutes have not been applied to wholesale changes in corporate ownership, as is the case here, and C-T has presented no evidence that the Virginia legislature intended the statutory definition to expand the applicability of distribution restrictions beyond their traditional scope. Appellant insists, however, that the text of the statute does not exclude from the definition of distribution transfers incident to changes in corporate control. Appellant relies on the fact that § 13.1-603 states that "[a] distribution may be in the form of . . . a purchase, redemption, or other acquisition of shares." This language, however, is not nearly as broad as C-T suggests. To begin with, it is subject to the general requirement that the corporation act for the benefit of its shareholders. Further, the language functions in this context to prevent a corporation from disguising a distribution in the form of a partial acquisition of shares — e.g., by "purchasing" twenty-five percent of each shareholder's shares, which would have the effect of transferring corporate assets to the shareholders without the corporation receiving any consideration in exchange and without changing the ownership structure in the slightest. The inclusion of purchases, redemptions, and other acquisitions within the ambit of distributions, therefore, is not an indication that the statutory definition applies when all outstanding shares of the corporation are purchased at a market rate in the course of an arm's-length purchase of the corporation.

None of this discussion should suggest that the transaction in this case was not subject to extensive regulation. Article 12 of the Virginia Stock Corporation Act provides detailed procedures that govern mergers, see Va. Code Ann. §§ 13.1-716, -718 (Michie 1989), and mandates review of the articles of merger by the Virginia State Corporation Commission, see *id.* § 13.1-720(B). As the district court observed, Article 12 "makes no mention of distributions," and the Virginia legislature could easily have provided a cross-reference to the distribution statutes had it intended the latter to apply to mergers. 124 B.R. at 696-97. Further, Virginia law prohibits transfers of money or corporate shares that are made "with intent to delay, hinder or defraud creditors," Va. Code Ann. § 55-80 (Michie 1986), or that are "not upon consideration deemed valuable in law," *id.* § 55-81 (Michie Supp. 1991). Finally, federal bankruptcy law provides that a trustee in bankruptcy may avoid any transfer made within one year before bankruptcy, if the debtor "received less than a reasonably equivalent value in exchange" and was insolvent at the time of, or became insolvent as a result of, the transfer. 11 U.S.C.A. § 548(a)(2)(A) and (B)(i) (West Supp. 1991). The existence of other state and federal enactments that potentially address this kind of transaction suggests the inadvisability of importing the distribution statutes into a context that the legislature did not intend.

B.

Other reasons impel us to hold that the leveraged acquisition of C-T was not a distribution under Virginia law. In this case appellant asks a federal court to apply a state distribution statute in a wholly novel way. It has not directed our attention to any decision by any court, state or federal, that has applied distribution restrictions to an arm's-length merger. "Federal judges are disinclined to make bold departures in areas of law that we have no responsibility for developing." *Afram Export Corp. v. Metallurgiki Halyps, S.A.*, 772 F.2d 1358, 1370 (7th Cir. 1985). Moreover, the reach of the rule of law appellant seeks is extremely broad: appellant conceded to the district court that, under its interpretation of the statutory definition, every merger would henceforth be a distribution. See 124 B.R. at 696. Accepting appellant's argument, therefore, would expose the defendants and directors of other Virginia corporations to a wholly unanticipated form of personal liability and would place a cloud over all corporate acquisitions that have closed within the past two years, see Va. Code Ann § 13.1-692(C) (Michie 1989) (two-year statute of limitations for actions alleging personal liability for illegal distributions).

More fundamentally, application of distribution restrictions in the context of changes in corporate control would place directors under conflicting legal duties. In this case, for example, the district court found that, after the announcement that the directors had authorized a management-sponsored LBO, the company was for sale. 124 B.R. at 692 (relying on *In re Time, Inc., Shareholder Litig.*, 571 A.2d 1140 (Del. 1989.)) Thus, under *Revlon, Inc. v. MacAndrews & Forbes Holdings, Inc.*, 506 A.2d 173 (Del. 1986), the fiduciary duties owed by the pre-merger directors to C-T's shareholders required that the directors "sell [the company] to the highest bidder," *id.* at 182, and seek the highest price possible from that bidder. By negotiating with Holdings and getting Holdings to increase its offer price from $19 to $20, C-T's pre-merger directors were simply fulfilling these well-recognized fiduciary duties. Indeed, had the directors refused to consummate the transaction because Holdings planned to acquire the bulk of the merger consideration by leveraging the company's assets, C-T's shareholders would likely have sued them for breach of fiduciary duty. If we accepted appellant's proffered interpretation of the definition of distribution, however, C-T's pre-merger directors would have been required not only to maximize the sale price, but also to ensure the solvency of the post-sale corporation. How directors could successfully navigate these narrow waters — subject to the possibility of massive personal liability should they falter on either side — is left unexplained.

Moreover, it is difficult for us to conceive how distribution restrictions would effectively function in the corporate acquisitions context. In determining whether a proposed distribution is legal, directors must apply two sophisticated insolvency tests. *See* VA. CODE ANN § 13.1-653(C) (Michie 1989). In applying these tests, directors must assess the future business prospects and decisions of the company. *See* RMBCA § 6.40 comment 2. When, after a distribution, directors continue to operate the company and set its business policy, such a task is manageable and within their competence. In cases involving corporate acquisitions, however, the pre-acquisition directors typically depart their positions in the corporation after the transaction. Not only do they therefore lack any control over the future course of the company's business, but they also may be fully unaware of new management's plans and strategies. Indeed, the primary rationale for a change in corporate ownership and control is the new owners' belief that, by altering the company's business strategy and structure, they can make the company more profitable than it was under old management. In this situation, it seems both unrealistic and perverse to charge the old directors under the distribution statute with knowledge and responsibility for the actions of the new owners. We cannot believe that the legislature intended such a result.

We also do not share appellant's view that non-application of the distribution statute would be unfair to creditors. In this case, it is possible that the leveraged acquisition of C-T hastened or caused the company's downfall. On the other hand, C-T's creditors may have actually benefitted from the acquisition. *See* Baird & Jackson, *Fraudulent Conveyance Law and Its Proper Domain*, 38 VAND. L. REV. 829, 853 (1985). The infusion of $4 million in new capital and the presence of a more effective management team may have permitted C-T to survive longer than it otherwise would have and may also have increased the chances that the company would survive over the long-term. In other words, it is impossible to conclude a priori whether a leveraged transaction such as that here on balance benefits or harms creditors of the target corporation. It is possible to say, however, that a creditor cannot avoid bearing the risk that his debtor will make a bad business decision:

> A creditor who lends a debtor money is taking advantage of the debtor's comparative advantage in using that money productively. A creditor necessarily defers to the debtor's skills in converting the money into other assets. The risk that both the creditor and debtor take is that the use the debtor makes of the money will benefit both parties. The creditor provides the capital, the debtor provides the know-how. The creditor is relying on the debtor's skill and judgment when it makes the loan. Only by giving the debtor discretion can the creditor hope to profit. Giving a debtor discretion, however, necessarily gives him the ability not only to make good decisions, but bad ones as well.

Id. at 838. Finally, it is important to recognize that, since LBOs are a well-known element in contemporary business life, creditors are well-positioned to protect themselves. "[T]he debtor-creditor relationship is essentially contractual." *Id.* at 835. If a creditor fears the prospect of a future leveraged acquisition of its debtor, it can protect itself by bargaining for security interests or protective provisions in its loan agreements that restrict the ability of its debtor to subject itself to a leveraged acquisition without the creditor's approval. *See id.* at 834-36; *see also* Kummert, *State Statutory Restrictions on Financial Distributions by Corporations to Shareholders: Part I*, 55 Wash. L. Rev. 359, 374 n. 63, 395 (1980) (noting "the extensive use by large or long term creditors of contract provisions that supersede the statutory provisions with far more rigorous restrictions on financial distributions by the corporate debtor").

In addition, we note that even if corporate acquisitions are not subject to state distribution restrictions, protection is accorded creditors by the law of creditors' rights, particularly fraudulent conveyance statutes. *See generally* Sherwin, *Creditors' Rights Against Participants in a Leveraged Buyout*, 72 Minn. L. Rev. 449, 464-505 (1988) (discussing the application of fraudulent conveyance law to leveraged buyouts); Note, *Fraudulent Conveyance Law and Leveraged Buyouts*, 87 Colum. L. Rev. 1491 (1987) (same). In contrast to state corporate law, the law of creditors' rights is designed and better equipped to protect creditors in situations such as that presented here. For example, state fraudulent conveyance statutes, see, *e.g.*, Va. Code Ann. §§ 55-80, 55-81 (Michie 1986 & Supp. 1991), and federal bankruptcy law, see 11 U.S.C.A. § 548(a) (West 1979 & Supp. 1991), enable creditors to recapture transferred funds by attacking the transaction directly. In contrast, distribution restrictions merely impose personal liability on directors, without any provision for a direct recoupment of the distributed assets from the shareholders who received them. *See* Va. Code Ann § 13.1-692(A) and (B) (Michie 1989).

In attacking the transaction here, appellant fails to acknowledge all the risks inherent in it. Holdings' acquisition of C-T was an uncertain financial proposition for C-T's shareholders as well as its creditors. Although the post-merger corporation failed in this case some eighteen months after the leveraged acquisition, it was anything but clear at the time of the transaction that the corporation would enter bankruptcy. Indeed, C-T's new owners were so confident of its future success that they invested $4 million of their own money in it. Thus, had the domestic shoe market rebounded after the acquisition, the market price of a share in C-T may have risen substantially above the $20 that the pre-merger shareholders received. In that situation, the shareholders — not C-T's creditors — would be complaining today. Both this corporate acquisition and the lending of money to pre-merger C-T involved risk — the same risk that inheres in all legitimate business activity. State distribution statutes simply do not authorize courts to rearrange the losses that inevitably result from risks taken in the hope of gains.

IV.

In sum, we conclude that Holdings' leveraged acquisition of C-T, accomplished in the form of an arm's-length merger between Holdings' subsidiary Acquisition and C-T, did not create a distribution under Virginia law. The judgment of the district court is therefore AFFIRMED.

MUNFORD v. VALUATION RESEARCH CORP. (IN RE MUNFORD, INC.)

United States Court of Appeals, Eleventh Circuit
97 F.3d 456 (1996)

HATCHETT, CHIEF JUDGE

In this corporate leveraged-buy-out merger case, we affirm the district court's ruling that Georgia's stock distribution and repurchase statutes apply.

FACTS

In May 1988, the Panfida Group offered to purchase Munford, Inc., a public company on the New York Stock Exchange, through a leverage buy out (LBO) structured as a reverse triangle merger for $18 per share. Under the terms of the proposed merger agreement, the Panfida Group agreed to create Alabama Acquisition Corporation (AAC) and a subsidiary, Alabama Merger Corporation (AMC), and through AAC or AMC deposit the funds necessary to purchase Munford, Inc.'s outstanding stock with Citizens & Southern Trust Company. As evidence of its commitment to purchase Munford, Inc., the Panfida Group bought 291,100 of Munford, Inc.'s stock. In June 1988, the Panfida Group also told Munford, Inc.'s board of directors that it, upon the sale of Munford, Inc., intended to put additional capital into Munford, Inc. but would only invest as much as Citibank required to finance the proposed merger.

After consulting its lawyers and financial experts at Shearson Lehman Brothers (Shearson), the board of directors accepted the Panfida Group's offer pending shareholder approval of the purchase agreement. Prior to the directors seeking shareholder approval, the Panfida Group learned that Munford, Inc. had potential environmental liability. Consequently, the Panfida Group reduced the purchase price from $18.50 a share to $17 a share. On October 18, 1988, the shareholders approved the merger plan. On November 29, 1988, the sale of Munford, Inc. to the Panfida Group closed. Pursuant to the purchase agreement, the LBO transaction converted each share of common stock into the right to receive the merger price of $17 per share and extinguished the shareholders' ownership in Munford, Inc. On January 2, 1990, thirteen months after the merger, Munford, Inc. filed for Chapter 11 proceedings in bankruptcy court.

PROCEDURAL HISTORY

On June 17, 1991, Munford, Inc. brought an adversary proceeding in bankruptcy court in the Northern District of Georgia on behalf of itself and unsecured creditors pursuant to 11 U.S.C. §§ 544(b) and 1107(a) (1988), seeking to avoid transfers of property, disallow claims and recover damages against former shareholders, officers, directors, and Shearson. In Count III of its complaint, Munford, Inc. asserted that the directors violated legal restrictions under Georgia's distribution and share repurchase statutes in approving the LBO merger. Specifically, Munford, Inc. asserts that the LBO transaction constituted a distribution of corporate assets that rendered Munford, Inc. insolvent. The directors moved for summary judgment contenting that the Georgia distribution and repurchase statutes did not apply to LBO mergers. On August 10, 1994, the district court, adopting the bankruptcy court's report and recommendation in part, denied the directors' motion for summary judgment on Munford, Inc.'s stock repurchase and distribution claim, ruling that Georgia's stock distributions and repurchase restrictions applied to LBO transactions. The district court also found that a genuine issue of material fact existed as to whether the LBO merger rendered Munford, Inc. insolvent in violation of Georgia law. On August 26, 1994, the district court amended its order and entered final judgment pursuant to Federal Rules of Civil Procedure 54(b) to permit this appeal Fed. R. Civ. P. 54(b).

CONTENTIONS

The directors contend that the district court erred in concluding that the LBO merger constituted a distribution of assets within the meaning of Georgia's distribution and repurchase statutes. They contend that these statutes do not apply to an arm's-length sale of a company to a third party through an LBO merger. In the alternative, the directors contend that they should not face personal liability for alleged violations of Georgia's distribution and repurchase statutes because they approved the LBO merger in good faith with the advice of legal counsel.

Munford, Inc. contends that the district court properly denied the directors' motion for summary judgment on this claim.

ISSUE

The sole issue on appeal is whether the district court erred in ruling that Georgia's stock distribution and repurchase statutes apply to a leverage acquisition of a corporation.

DISCUSSION

We review the denial of summary judgment *de novo* applying the same legal standard that controlled the district court in rendering its decision. *Brown v. Crawford*, 906 F.2d 667, 669 (11th Cir. 1990), *cert. denied*, 500 U.S. 933, 111 S. Ct. 2056, 114 L. Ed. 2d 461 (1991).

Georgia's capital surplus distribution statute provides, in pertinent part:

> (a) The board of directors of a corporation may from time to time distribute to shareholders out of capital surplus of the corporation a portion of its assets in cash or property subject to the following [provision]:
>
> > (1) No such distribution shall be made at a time when the corporation is insolvent or when such distribution would render the corporation insolvent[.]

O.C.G.A. § 14-2-91 (1988). Similarly, Georgia's stock repurchasing statute prohibits directors of a corporation from repurchasing the corporation's shares when such purchase would render the corporation insolvent. O.C.G.A. § 14-2-92(e) (1982).[5] Under both statutes, directors who vote for or assent to a corporate distribution or stock repurchase in violation of these statutes are jointly and severally liable for the amount distributed or paid to the extent the payments violated the restrictions. O.C.G.A. § 14-2-154(a)(1), (2) (1982).

The directors appeal the district court's denial of summary judgment contenting that Georgia's distribution and share repurchase statutes do not apply to LBO mergers. The directors argue that Georgia's distribution and repurchase statutes only apply in circumstances where the directors take assets of the corporation and either distribute them to shareholders or use them to repurchase shares. In both cases, the directors assert, control of the company does not change hands and the directors determine the source of the assets used. The directors note that in this case the Panfida Group owned Munford, Inc. at the completion of the LBO merger and thereafter ran the company. The directors therefore argue that only Georgia's merger statutes apply to this transaction.

The district court denied the directors' motion for summary judgment adopting the reasoning of the bankruptcy court. The bankruptcy court, in analyzing the LBO merger, considered the substance of the transaction and equated the LBO merger to a stock distribution or repurchase, disregarding the fact that Munford, Inc. had new owners and stock holders as a result of the merger at the time the shareholders received the LBO payments. The bankruptcy court specifically found that: (1) the directors "approved or assented to the underlying [m]erger [a]greement which structured and required payment to the shareholders"; (2) the merger agreement contemplated the Panfida Group's pledging of "virtually all of Munford[, Inc.]'s assets as collateral" for the loan that funded the LBO payments made to the shareholders; and (3) the directors knew or should have known "the source, purpose, or use of" Munford, Inc.'s assets prior to or at the time the directors approved the merger plan. Based on these findings, the bankruptcy court concluded

---

[5] [1] On July 1, 1989, O.C.G.A. § 14-2-640 superseded O.C.G.A. §§ 14-2-91 and 14-2-92(e).

that a reasonable jury could conclude that the merger rendered Munford, Inc. insolvent in violation of Georgia's distribution and stock repurchase statutes.

In reaching its conclusion, the bankruptcy court rejected a Fourth Circuit case that refused to apply Virginia's corporate distribution statute to recapture payments made to shareholders pursuant to an LBO merger. *See C-T of Virginia, Inc. v. Barrett*, 958 F.2d 606 (4th Cir. 1992).

In *C-T of Virginia*, the Fourth Circuit held that the LBO merger did not constitute a distribution within the meaning of Virginia's share repurchase and distribution statutes reasoning that Virginia's distribution statute

> [was] not intended to obstruct an arm's-length acquisition of an enterprise by new owners who have their own plans for commercial success. The reason for this distinction is simple: a corporate acquisition, structured as a merger, is simply a different animal from a distribution.

C-T of Virginia, 958 F.2d at 611. The court in *C-T of Virginia* further reasoned that because such distribution statutes derive from the regulation of corporate dividends courts should limit their restriction to situations in which shareholders after receiving the transfer from the corporation retain their status as owners of the corporation.

The bankruptcy court, in this case, rejected this line of reasoning, reasoning that the legislature enacted the distribution and share repurchase statutes of the Georgia Code to protect creditors "by prohibiting transfers at a time when a corporation is insolvent or would be rendered insolvent." Such intent, the bankruptcy court noted, "furthers the longstanding principle that creditors are to be paid before shareholders." We agree with the district court and the reasoning of the bankruptcy court and decline to join the Fourth Circuit in holding that "[a] corporate acquisition, structured as a merger, is simply a different animal from a distribution." *C-T of Virginia, Inc.*, 958 F.2d at 611.

We note that the LBO transaction in this case did not merge two separate operating companies into one combined entity. Instead, the LBO transaction represented a 'paper merger' of Munford, Inc. and AMC, a shell corporation with very little assets of its own. To hold that Georgia's distribution and repurchase statutes did not apply to LBO mergers such as this, while nothing in these statutes precludes such a result, would frustrate the restrictions imposed upon directors who authorize a corporation to distribute its assets or to repurchase shares from stockholders when such transactions would render the corporation insolvent. We therefore affirm the district court's ruling that Georgia's restrictions on distribution and stock repurchase apply to LBO.

[3] In the alternative, the directors argue that their approval of the LBO merger should not subject them to liability under the distribution and repurchase statutes because they approved the merger in good faith and with the advice of legal counsel. Because we are not aware of any Georgia courts that recognize good faith or reasonable reliance on legal counsel's advice as an affirmative defense to liability under Georgia's distribution and repurchase statutes, we reject this argument.

CONCLUSION

For the reasons stated above, we affirm the district court's denial of the directors' motion for summary judgment on Munford, Inc.'s stock distribution and repurchase claim.

AFFIRMED.

One way to deal with the problem presented in Valuation Research is to condition the completion of a cash merger on the receipt of an opinion from a recognized financial advisor to the effect that, after the merger, and after giving effect to any related borrowing, the acquired, surviving corporation is solvent. *See, e.g.*, Maytag Corporation Proxy Statement dated July 18, 2005, at 63 (relating to its then proposed acquisition by Triton Acquisition Holding Co.).

IN RE ENVIRODYNE INDUS.

United States Court of Appeals, Seventh Circuit
79 F.3d 579 (1996)

CUMMINGS, CIRCUIT JUDGE:

Defendants in this case failed to tender shares of stock in a corporation entering a shortform merger under Delaware law. Their equity interest was thus converted into debt and they retained the right to redeem their canceled shares for a specified amount without interest. They failed to do so, however, before the newly formed corporation filed for Chapter 11 bankruptcy, and Defendants now complain that the Bankruptcy Court improperly subordinated their claims to those of other general unsecured creditors. We affirm the decision to subordinate Defendants' claims under 11 U.S.C. § 510(c).

In 1989, organizers formed Emerald Acquisition Corporation ("Emerald") and Emerald Sub One, Inc. ("Emerald Sub"), a wholly owned subsidiary of Emerald, for the purpose of acquiring Envirodyne Industries, Inc. ("Former Envirodyne"). Emerald Sub was organized specifically to purchase the outstanding shares of common stock of Former Envirodyne. These entities entered into a merger agreement whereby Emerald Sub purchased tendered shares of Former Envirodyne at $40 per share. Emerald Sub purchased 13,104,980 shares tendered and not withdrawn out of approximately 18,382,324 shares issued and outstanding. On June 1, 1989, Emerald Sub and Former Envirodyne were merged under Delaware General Corporation Law, section 253, with current Envirodyne as the surviving entity.

Shareholders had a right to redeem their stock at $40 per share or dissent from the merger and obtain an appraisal under Delaware law. As of the effective date of the merger, however, Former Envirodyne's stock was canceled, and non-tendering shareholders ceased to be equity holders and instead became creditors current Envirodyne. In essence, non-tendering shareholders were "cashed-out." The merger agreement provided that these cashed-out shareholders were entitled to receive $40 per share of Former Envirodyne stock upon demand, but without interest. Each of the Defendants before this Court is a non-tendering stockholder of Former Envirodyne or a representative or successor in interest thereof. It is unclear from the record why Defendants failed to redeem their non-interest-bearing shares of Former Envirodyne for over three years after the merger.

On January 7, 1993, Envirodyne filed voluntary petitions for Chapter 11 bankruptcy. Its balance sheet reflected liabilities of $2,175,520 due to non-tendering, cashed-out shareholders of Former Envirodyne. Under the reorganization plan, general unsecured creditors received 32.28 shares of common stock in reorganized Envirodyne for each $500 of allowed claims (which was estimated to be approximately two-thirds of the allowed amount of the claims), and Envirodyne agreed to seek to subordinate the claims of non-tendering shareholders of Former Envirodyne. Pursuant to the plan and on September 23, 1993, Envirodyne commenced an adversary proceeding in Bankruptcy Court seeking equitable subordination of the non-tendering shareholders' claims to those of other general unsecured creditors. Subordination was granted by the Bankruptcy Court on cross-motions for summary judgment. *In re Envirodyne Indus., Inc.*, 176 B.R. 825 (Bankr. N.D. Ill. 1995), and the district court later affirmed. Thereafter, Envirodyne's stock declined in value and, as a result, the general unsecured creditors received distributions amounting only to about one-third of the allowed amount of their claims; the Defendants received no distribution.

The sole issue on appeal is whether the Bankruptcy Court properly subordinated Defendants' claims to those of other general unsecured creditors under Section 510(c) of the Bankruptcy Code, 11 U.S.C. § 510(c), without requiring proof of wrongful conduct on the part of Defendants. The Bankruptcy Code provides as follows:

> Notwithstanding subsections (a) and (b) of this section, after notice and a hearing, the court may:
>
> (1) under principles of equitable subordination, subordinate for purposes of distribution all of part of another allowed claim to all or part of another allowed claim or all or part of an allowed interest to all or part of another allowed interest; or
>
> (2) order that any lien securing such a subordinated claim be transferred to the estate.

11 U.S.C. § 510(c). Exactly what "principles of equitable subordination" Congress had in mind is not clear from the Bankruptcy Code, but we have previously held based on the legislative history that Congress intended courts to develop the appropriate principles, which might be broader than the principles existing prior to Section 510(c)'s enactment. *In re Virtual Network Servs. Corp.*, 902 F.2d 1246, 1249-1250 (7th Cir. 1990); *Kham & Nate's Shoes No. 2, Inc. v. First Bank of Whiting*, 908 F.2d 1351, 1356 (7th Cir. 1990). Defendants' primary contention is that, at a minimum, equitable subordination requires inequitable conduct on the part of the creditor. But *Virtual Network* has disposed of that issue as well:

> In sum, we conclude that § 510(c)(1) authorizes courts to equitably subordinate claims to other claims on a case-by-case basis without requiring in

> every instance inequitable conduct on the part of the creditor claiming parity among other unsecured general creditors.

902 F.2d at 1250; see also *In re Vitreous Steel Prods. Co.*, 911 F.2d 1223, 1237 (7th Cir. 1990) (the Section 510(c) inquiry is to be made on a case-by-case basis focusing on fairness to other creditors). Accord *In re CF & I Fabricators of Utah, Inc.*, 53 F.3d 1155 (10th Cir. 1995); certiorari granted, _ U.S. _, 116 S. Ct. 558, 133 L. Ed. 2d 458 (1995); *In re First Track Lines, Inc.*, 48 F.3d 210 (6th Cir. 1995); certiorari granted, _ U.S. _, 116 S. Ct. 558, 133 L. Ed. 2d 458 (1995); *Burden v. United States*, 917 F.2d 115 (3d Cir. 1990); *Schultz Broadway Inn v. United States*, 912 F.2d 230 (8th Cir. 1990).

Defendants argue that *Virtual Network* carved out only a limited no-fault subordination rule for non-pecuniary loss claims, such as tax penalties and punitive damage awards. We find no language in the opinion limiting out review of congressional intent to non-pecuniary loss claims. Rather, we concluded in *Virtual Network* that Congress intended to give courts authority for developing principles of equitable subordination — principles that may or may not include a requirement of inequitable conduct. We ultimately held that inequitable conduct is not required for subordination of non-pecuniary loss tax penalty claims, but that limited holding takes nothing away from our general interpretation of Section 510(c). The flexible approach of *Virtual Network* makes sense in light of the Bankruptcy Code's primary goal of equality of distribution and the fluid concept of equity at the heart of Section 510(c) subordination.

In support of their argument, Defendants also rely on *In re Mansfield Tire & Rubber Co.*, 942 F.2d 1055 (6th Cir. 1991), certiorari denied, 502 U.S. 1092, 112 S. Ct. 1165, 117 L. Ed. 2d 412, which found that *Virtual Network* was inapplicable to an excise tax payable to the government under 26 U.S.C. § 4971. The Sixth Circuit there stated that "whatever persuasive value [*Virtual Network* and its progeny] may have had for a case concerning nonpecuniary loss penalties, they are inapposite here." *Id.* at 1061 (emphasis in original). But *Mansfield* was premised on the fact that Section 507 of the Bankruptcy Code establishes that priority of an "excise tax," 11 U.S.C. § 507(a)(7)(E), precluding such taxes from being otherwise "susceptible to subordination" within the meaning of Section 510(c), 942 F.2d at 1062. As such, *Mansfield* does not support Defendants' argument that *Virtual Network* carved out a limited no-fault exception. In fact, the Sixth Circuit has since confirmed our understanding of *Mansfield*; see *First Track Lines*, 48 F.3d at 213, and further stated that Section 510(c) allows for nofault equitable subordination under developing principles in the courts. *Id.* at 218.

We thus adopt the flexible approach of *Virtual Network* in which a court must look to the origin and nature of the unsecured claim and decide whether equity requires that it be subordinated to claims of other general unsecured creditors. In this regard, Defendants make their alternative argument: that the nature of their unsecured claims is such that the Bankruptcy Court should not have exercised its power (which we hold above that it has) to subordinate Defendants' claims to those of other unsecured creditors absent inequitable conduct. They analogize to cases dealing with debt arising from an asset purchase of an existing company by the debtor in which courts have required inequitable conduct for subordination. *See, e.g.*, *In re EDC, Inc.*, 930 F.2d 1275 (7th Cir. 1991). But the asset purchase cases are easily distinguished, both because the debtor in such cases receives assets in exchange for incurring debt, unlike Defendants here, and because they involve subordination of secured claims to unsecured claims.

More persuasive are cases involving the claims of former shareholders in stock redemptions. In such cases, courts generally use equitable subordination to subordinate the claims of former shareholders who redeemed their stock to the issuing corporation in exchange for debt. *See, e.g., Robinson v. Wangemann*, 75 F.2d 756 (5th Cir. 1935). The former shareholders, considered creditors rather than equity holders, are in form equivalent to other general unsecured creditors. Nonetheless, courts look to the substance of the transaction. Because the stock redemption is a transaction by which a corporation acquires its own stock from stockholders, it is simply a method of distributing a proportion of the assets to stockholders. *See id.* at 757. In substance, the former stockholders become equity holders rather than creditors on par with the corporation's other creditors. Thus subordination of claims in bankruptcy is equitable: "The assets of the corporation are the common pledge of its creditors, and stockholders are not entitled to receive any part of them unless creditors are paid in full." *Id.*

Defendants are legally creditors of Envirodyne, no doubt, just as the former shareholders in *Robinson* were legally creditors of the corporation to which they redeemed their stock. But Defendants' claims are, in substance, based on equity interests. When they invested in Former Envirodyne, they positioned themselves to benefit if the company performed well, but they also accepted the risk that the company might perform poorly. Thus Defendants accepted risks and benefits that Former Envirodyne's unsecured creditors did not, and as such their equity interests were legally subordinate to possible claims of unsecured creditors. Their current status as creditors arose from their failure to tender shares in the Emerald Sub short-form merger under Delaware law, as well as their failure to redeem their non-interest-bearing shares of Former Envirodyne in the three years subsequent to the merger. No amount of maneuvering can obscure the true nature of Defendants' interest. We further agree with the district judge's analysis that subordination is even more compelling here than in a stock redemption case. In a stock redemption, the shareholders make a conscious decision to relinquish their equity for debt. In this case, however, Defendants became creditors because they failed to redeem their shares, and their dilatory behavior is inexplicable given that they merely held non-interest-bearing canceled shares of Former Envirodyne. Thus their claims in bankruptcy are far weaker than other general unsecured creditors.

Defendants' proffered distinction of the stock redemption cases places form over substance and is thus contrary to the very rationale of those cases. Defendants argue that any risk or benefit they accepted as shareholders of Former Envirodyne came to an end after the merger, taking away any equity interest they had; left only with debt of the company, they assumed no more risk after the merger than any other unsecured creditor. We are not persuaded. Defendants' argument ignores the crux of the stock redemption cases: that the proper focus is on the nature and origin of the claim. Their claims indisputably arose out of an equity interest in Former Envirodyne, and the essential nature of the claims did not change after the merger. As in a stock redemption, where the stockholder accepting debt as payment for the stock assumes the risk of future insolvency, Defendants assumed the risk of Envirodyne's insolvency when they failed to tender their shares during the merger or anytime thereafter. Though in both cases the claims are legally those of creditors, they are in origin and nature claims based on equity interests. Nothing in the denomination "creditor" exempts a claimant from Section 510(c) equitable subordination.

Further, the fact that Delaware law converted Defendants' surviving interest into debt rather than equity does not change our analysis. The form of the transaction does not alter the origin and nature of Defendants' claims as essentially equity interests. We find no precedent for the proposition that where state law deems a claimant a creditor, a Bankruptcy Court may not subordinate his claims to those of other unsecured creditors under Section 510(c). That provision gives Bankruptcy Courts broad power to subordinate claims based on "principles of equitable subordination." Such power naturally affords discretion to consider the substance of unsecured claims in order to implement the primary bankruptcy goal of achieving a fair distribution of the estate among all creditors. In this case, Delaware law affected the form of Defendants' claims, not their substance. In any event, we do not see a conflict between federal and state law in this case: state law determined the validity of the claims and federal bankruptcy law determined their priority among other valid claims.

Finally, Defendants argue that even if inequitable conduct is not a prerequisite to subordination, harm to the other unsecured creditors absent subordination is. We need not reach the legal question involved because we reject Defendants' premise — that the bankruptcy result for the other unsecured creditors is the same regardless of whether the court subordinates Defendants' claims. They correctly note that all of Envirodyne's general unsecured creditors received 32.28 shares of common stock in reorganized Envirodyne, an amount which will not change regardless of the subordination issue. However, Defendants ignore the fact that any distribution to them will affect the value of the shares and therefore the distribution to the other creditors. The effect on other unsecured creditors might be even more substantial in light of the unexpected decline in Envirodyne's stock since confirmation of the reorganization plan.

In conclusion, we hold that Section 510(c) of the Bankruptcy Code authorizes courts to subordinate the unsecured claims of non-tendering, cashed-out shareholders of a short-form merger under Delaware law to those of other general unsecured creditors, and we further hold that equitable subordination was appropriate on the facts of this case. We also deny Envirodyne's petition to strike portions of Defendants' reply brief to this Court.

ISQUITH v. CAREMARK INT'L

United States Court of Appeals, Seventh Circuit
136 F.3d 531 (1998)

Posner, Chief Judge.

This is a class action suit under Rule 10b-5 of the SEC and other antifraud provisions of federal securities law, with supplemental claims under state corporation law. The suit, against Baxter International (the pharmaceutical manufacturer) and a spun-off former wholly owned subsidiary of Baxter called Caremark, charges that Baxter submitted a fraudulent statement to the Securities and Exchange Commission in connection with the spinoff. The district judge granted a motion to dismiss, holding that there was no purchase or sale of securities; relinquished jurisdiction over the supplemental claims, pursuant to 28 U.S.C. § 1367(c)(3); and so dismissed the entire case.

The complaint alleges that in 1991, when Caremark was still part of Baxter, the government began investigating Caremark for suspected Medicare and Medicaid fraud. While publicly denying any wrongdoing, Baxter feared the worst. Why is unclear, since a parent ordinarily is not liable for its subsidiary's torts; and if it is, a spinoff will not insulate it. We need not unravel these mysteries; all that is important is that, according to the complaint (the only source of factual allegations in the case), Baxter decided to try to insulate itself from any potential liability by spinning off Caremark, that is, by transferring the ownership of the subsidiary from Baxter to Baxter's shareholders, each to receive shares of Caremark proportional to their shares in Baxter, with the result that Caremark would no longer be a subsidiary of Baxter but an independent company. In order to avoid having to register the new security created to effectuate the spinoff — for the shares of Caremark, as of Baxter, were to be publicly traded — Baxter needed a "no action" letter from the SEC. The Commission issued the letter upon Baxter's agreeing to file an "information statement," see 17 C.F.R. § 240.14c-2, that would among other things disclose the purpose of the spinoff. The statement said that the purpose of the spinoff was to avoid a looming competitive conflict between Caremark and other lines of Baxter's business. That, according to the complaint, was a lie; the purpose of the spinoff was to minimize the liability of Baxter's shareholders for Caremark's fraud. But because the SEC issued the requested "no action" letter, the spinoff — which did not require the consent of the shareholders — went through, and Baxter shareholders found themselves holding Baxter plus Caremark shares (one of the latter for every four of the former) rather than just Baxter shares.

The immediate effect of the transaction was to reduce the market value of Baxter stock because the spinoff had diminished Baxter's assets. But the market value of Baxter and Caremark stock — the only thing investors would care about — exceeded the value of Baxter stock before the spinoff. Eventually, however, the investing public got wind of Caremark's troubles, and the market value of its shares headed south. In 1995 Caremark pleaded guilty to criminal charges of fraud based on conduct going back to 1986 and paid the government $160 million.

The plaintiff class consists of the owners of Baxter shares at the time of the spinoff. The claim is that the spinoff constituted a forced "sale" of Caremark shares to them and that the sale was effected by fraud because, had the true purpose of the spinoff been revealed, owners of Baxter shares could have gotten the courts to block it; Baxter would then have been kept intact and Baxter stock would, they claim, today be worth more than the current combined value of Baxter and Caremark stock. It is difficult to see why, since Baxter's Caremark subsidiary, as it would have remained, would still have had to pony up the $160 million to the government. But the plaintiff argues, and in the posture of the case we must, though skeptical, accept, that the spinoff destroyed valuable synergies between Baxter and its Caremark subsidiary. If, however, whether on this or some other basis, the plaintiff could have gotten the spinoff enjoined, this implies that she can still sue for damages — as she has done, in the supplemental state law claim now pending in state court. So it is very difficult to see how Baxter's coyness about the purpose of the suit hurt her or the other members of the class. She says she may have a statute of limitations problem with her state law claim. But if that problem is due to Baxter's fraud in concealing Caremark's troubles, she can set up that fraud as a defense to the statute of limitations — the defense of fraudulent concealment. *See, e.g., Cada v. Baxter Healthcare Corp.*, 920 F.2d 446, 451 (7th Cir. 1990).

The plaintiff hints that the SEC, too, would have blocked, or at least delayed, the spinoff had it learned of Caremark's illegalities. Yet she points to nothing in the laws administered by the SEC that would have authorized the Commission to impede the transaction had Baxter confessed that its motivation was to lighten its liabilities. That is not an improper motivation, and anyway the Commission's concern is with the completeness and accuracy of information provided to investors rather than with what the information reveals about the soundness or even morality of the investment. *Santa Fe Industries, Inc. v. Green*, 430 U.S. 462, 477-78 (1977); 1 Louis Loss & Joel Seligman, Securities Regulation 391 (3d ed. 1989). So if Baxter had come clean, the SEC would still have had no grounds for refusing to issue a no-action letter. And, at worst, Baxter would then have had to register the Caremark stock.

There is a lot more that is wrong with this suit. Suppose Baxter had been candid with the SEC — and hence the public, because both the information statement and the noaction letter were public documents, and the statement, at least, was mailed to the shareholders — about Caremark's liability. Then the market value of Baxter's shares would have fallen immediately, discounting any anticipated losses resulting from that liability, and the plaintiff class would have taken its hit then — before they could do anything about it — rather than later. Although investors who bought stock in Baxter or Caremark after the spinoff and in reliance on the stated purpose might have been hurt by Baxter's lack of candor, they are not members of the class. They have their own suit. The class in the present suit is limited to owners of Baxter shares at the time of the spinoff. If we assume with the plaintiff that Baxter would have been liable for its subsidiary's fraud, the spinoff shifted that liability to Caremark. Without the spinoff, it would have remained with Baxter. Since the members of the class owned both companies, the spinoff merely shifted liability from one pocket of their trousers to another. As for the loss of synergy, that has nothing to do with fraud. It is not a loss resulting from a misrepresentation or a misleading omission; it is a compounding of the poor business judgment that resulted in Caremark's getting into trouble with the government. The federal securities laws are not a remedy for poor business judgment. *Searls v. Glasser*, 64 F.3d 1061, 1069 (7th Cir. 1995); *DiLeo v. Ernst & Young*, 901 F.2d 624, 627 (7th Cir. 1990); *Acito v. IMCERA Group, Inc.*, 47 F.3d 47, 53 (2d Cir. 1995).

The biggest problem with the suit is not the difficulty we're having figuring out how the members of the class could have been hurt by the alleged fraud in concealing the true purpose of the spinoff; for it is too early in the litigation to decide that this puzzle cannot be solved. Rather, it is the absence of other elements of federal securities fraud, such as that there have been a sale (or purchase — but for every purchase there is a sale). *Blue Chip Stamps v. Manor Drug Stores*, 421 U.S. 723 (1975); *Davidson v. Belcor, Inc.*, 933 F.2d 603, 605-06 (7th Cir. 1991); *Cohen v. Stratosphere Corp.*, 115 F.3d 695, 700-02 (9th Cir. 1997). The members of the class did not buy or sell shares in Baxter. They did not buy or sell shares in Caremark. They simply received one share of Caremark stock for every four shares they owned of Baxter. They no more "bought" Caremark stock than the recipient of a stock dividend — which the plaintiff concedes the distribution of the Caremark stock was — buys the stock that he receives as a dividend. *See Rathborne v. Rathborne*, 683 F.2d 914 (5th Cir. 1982); *cf. Gelles v. TDA Industries, Inc.*, 44 F.3d 102 (2d Cir. 1994).

Words are protean in the hands of lawyers, so it can be argued that the Baxter shareholders were forced in effect to "buy" Caremark shares, "paying" for them by the reduction in the value of their Baxter shares as a result of the diminution in Baxter's assets that was brought about by the spinoff. But to accept this argument we would have to have a reason for wanting to play with words in this way, and we cannot think of any that advances the purposes of the securities laws. Those laws create a remedy, so far as bears on this case, for someone who is induced by ("relied on," the courts usually say) a misrepresentation or a misleading omission to buy or sell a stock. *O'Brien v. Continental Illinois National Bank & Trust Co.*, 593 F.2d 54, 60 (7th Cir. 1979); *In re NationsMart Corp. Securities Litigation*, 130 F.3d 309, 321 (8th Cir. 1997); *Rubinstein v. Collins*, 20 F.3d 160, 166 (5th Cir. 1994). This presupposes that the someone had a choice, a choice distorted by the fraud. The members of the class in this case had no choice. They made no investment decision. They therefore cannot have been induced by the alleged fraud to buy or sell any securities even if the spinoff can somehow be thought of as effecting a sale of their shares in Baxter.

"The members of the class in this case had no choice. . . ." No investment choice, that is. They could have sued to try to stop the spinoff. *Goldberg v. Meridor*, 567 F.2d 209, 218-21 (2d Cir. 1977) (Friendly, J.), holds that this option is enough to establish the materiality of a misleading statement to investors. *See also Field v. Trump*, 850 F.2d 938, 946-48 (2d Cir. 1988). But we rejected the doctrine of the *Goldberg* case in *LHLC Corp. v. Cluett, Peabody & Co.*, 842 F.2d 928, 931-32 (7th Cir. 1988), and *Harris Trust & Savings Bank v. Ellis*, 810 F.2d 700, 704 (7th Cir. 1987); it is not good law in this circuit. *Goldberg* would allow every complaint about the mismanagement of a corporation that issues securities subject to federal securities law to be shoehorned into federal court on the theory that management had defrauded the shareholders by concealing the mismanagement. This would carry the securities laws far outside their intended domain. And it would violate the principle that the only loss of which complaint is possible under the antifraud provisions of those laws is a loss that candor would have averted. *Caremark, Inc. v. Coram Healthcare Corp.*, 113 F.3d 645, 648-49 (7th Cir. 1997); *Bastian v. Petren Resources Corp.*, 892 F.2d 680 (7th Cir. 1990); *Robbins v. Koger Properties, Inc.*, 116 F.3d 1441, 1447-49 (11th Cir. 1997). Candor would not have averted the consequences of whatever mismanagement or misfortune resulted in Caremark's scrape with the federal government. Even a successful suit to block the spinoff would not have eliminated the liability to the government that is the ultimate cause of the harm for which the plaintiff seeks redress, and anyway so far as appears the plaintiff can still bring such a suit, albeit now for damages rather than for injunctive relief. Even if she cannot, and even if, had it not been for the alleged fraud, the plaintiff would have succeeded in getting the spinoff enjoined, the cases that we have just cited show that she cannot maintain this suit, because the fraud did not cause the loss of investment value of which she complains — the scrape over Medicare and Medicaid did that.

This is a bit overstated; that scrape was the major cause of the loss in value, but there are also those synergies allegedly lost because the spinoff was not enjoined. If we assume that a damages suit is somehow blocked, or that the value of those lost synergies could somehow not be quantified (in which event the damages remedy would be inadequate) — and if we ignore the fact that if this is so, the plaintiff cannot obtain damages, the only relief sought, in the present suit either — then it would be the case that the fraud in the information statement filed with the SEC had caused a loss to the plaintiff. But as the cases we have cited (Bastian and the others) make clear, it would not be a loss that a suit under the antifraud provisions of the securities laws can be based on. For it would not be a loss of the kind that these laws are concerned with, namely a loss of investment value as a consequence of the concealment or distortion of the truth. In the lingo of securities law, the plaintiff would have shown "transaction causation" (the transaction, here the spinoff and resulting change in the form of the plaintiff's holdings, would not have occurred but for the fraud) but not "loss causation" (a loss produced by a discrepancy between the actual market value of a stock and what that value would have been had there been no misrepresentation). Had Baxter claimed that the spinoff would not sacrifice any synergies between Caremark and Baxter's remaining units, and the claim was a deliberate falsehood, the resulting drop in the value of Baxter's or Caremark's stock when the truth emerged would be a proper basis for suit. No such false claim is alleged. Not a lie about synergies, but a corporate reorganization, caused the loss of investment value consequent upon their destruction.

The plaintiff directs us to another esoteric and dubious judge-made doctrine, called the "fundamental change" doctrine. 8 Loss & Seligman, supra, at 3707-11. It began life as the "forced seller" doctrine of *Vine v. Beneficial Finance Co.*, 374 F.2d 627, 634-35 (2d Cir. 1967). Vine, a minority shareholder squeezed out by the majority, was allowed to characterize the transaction as a sale. Which in a sense it was, as he was forced to exchange stock for cash; that is what a squeeze-out does. But precisely because it was a forced sale, the plaintiff had not been induced to make it by a misrepresentation or misleading omission. There was no inducing; there was compulsion. And exactly the same thing is true here. The members of the class were not given a choice about whether to receive Caremark shares.

The doctrine of the Vine decision was limited in *Rathborne v. Rathborne, supra.*

That case involved a spinoff, just like the present one, and the court held that the spinoff was not a sale of securities, since it did not effect a "fundamental change" in the plaintiff's holding. To the same effect, see *Gelles v. TDA Industries, Inc., supra*, 44 F.3d at 104-05. When *Vine* is read in light of these and other cases, such as *Sargent v. Genesco, Inc.*, 492 F.2d 750, 764-65 (5th Cir. 1974), and also in light of the Supreme Court's decision in *Blue Chip Stamps*, which made clear that the relevant provisions of the securities laws are limited to purchases and sales, the "forced seller" doctrine is seen to be limited to situations in which the nature of the investor's holding is so far altered as to allow the alteration to be characterized as a sale, as in the exchange of stock for cash in Vine itself. A change in form will not count as a sale and so will not be actionable; the change must be in some sense "fundamental" rather than nominal; hence the renaming of the doctrine. *See* 8 Loss & Seligman, *supra*, at 3710-11. The distinction is critical in this case. In a squeeze-out, stock is exchanged for cash; the person squeezed out no longer has any interest in the corporation; that is unquestionably a change in his bundle of property rights. In a spinoff there is no exchange, no forced exit from the corporation, but merely the receipt by the corporation's shareholders of additional stock. Only the form in which the members of the class owned Baxter's assets was changed; it was changed from stock in one corporation to stock in two corporations. After the change the class members owned the same proportion, carrying the same rights, of the same pool of assets. Before, their ownership interest was denominated in shares of Baxter; after, in shares of Baxter and Caremark; the interest itself — the amount of assets owned by the members of the class — was unchanged.

So the fundamental-change doctrine, successor to the defunct forced-seller doctrine, is inapplicable to this case. And anyway we very much doubt that the doctrine retains any validity in any class of case, even in squeeze-out cases. In *Santa Fe Industries, Inc. v. Green, supra*, 430 U.S. at 473-77, decided after *Vine*, the Supreme Court made clear for the first time that securities fraud does not include the oppression of minority shareholders, which is what the plaintiff in *Vine* was complaining about. No more does securities fraud include unsound or oppressive corporate reorganizations, which is the essential complaint of the plaintiff class in this case. The fraud in concealing the purpose of the spinoff is merely the lever by which the class hopes to force into federal court a lawsuit over the wisdom of the spinoff. No doubt there should be legal remedies against fundamental changes in a corporation's structure that are undertaken in bad faith and hurt the shareholders; in fact there are; but a suit for securities fraud is not one of them. The office of securities fraud is to protect investors from being induced to make unsound sales or purchases by misrepresentations or misleading omissions.

This is implicit in the requirement that the plaintiff, to maintain his suit, have relied on the fraud, *e.g., Basic Inc. v. Levinson*, 485 U.S. 224, 243 (1988), meaning that he changed his position because of it. It is implicit in the decisions that hold that there can be no suit under the securities laws by someone who has not made an investment decision, that is, who has not made a choice, a voluntary decision albeit one induced by the fraud, to buy or sell securities. *Davidson v. Belcor, Inc., supra*, 933 F.2d at 608; *Norris v. Wirtz*, 719 F.2d 256, 259-60 (7th Cir. 1983); *O'Brien v. Continental Illinois National Bank & Trust Co., supra*, 593 F.2d at 59-60. There was no investment decision in *Vine*. Our plaintiff relies on *SEC v. Datronics*

Engineers, Inc., 490 F.2d 250 (4th Cir. 1973), but that case is inapposite because while the SEC indeed obtained an injunction against spinoffs, their only purpose had been to evade the registration requirements of the securities laws. There is no claim here that the failure to register the Caremark shares violated any such requirement.

It is true that *Vine*, like this case, had a fraud "handle," and that might seem to take it out from under the rule of the Santa Fe case. The plaintiff claimed that the defendant had by means of fraud obtained the shares of enough other shareholders to be in a position to squeeze him out, to his injury. But that injury strikes us as too remote from the fraud to be actionable in a suit under the securities laws. It is one thing to say, as the Supreme Court did in *Basic Inc. v. Levinson, supra*, in adopting the "fraud on the market" theory of liability under the securities laws, that a misrepresentation directed at a group of investors may become impounded in the price of the stock (when members of the group buy or sell under the inducement of the misrepresentation) and so may induce a purchase or sale by other investors. The misrepresentation induces action by those other investors, albeit indirectly. The misrepresentations in *Vine* were not directed at Vine and did not induce him to do anything; it made him vulnerable to a completely different kind of fraud — the abuse of minority shareholders by means of squeeze-outs, a form of fraud that the federal securities laws do not reach. And similarly in this case, the fraud by which Baxter allegedly obtained swift approval of the spinoff did not induce the members of the plaintiff class to buy or sell Baxter shares. It just made them vulnerable to what was neither a misrepresentation nor a purchase or sale of securities, but merely an involuntary change in the form of their holdings. Our *O'Brien* case featured the same fraud handle, see *O'Brien v. Continental Illinois National Bank & Trust Co., supra*, 593 F.2d at 60, yet we held that there was no purchase or sale of securities. We adhere to that decision, and note its inconsistency with the fundamental-change doctrine. But even if, as we greatly doubt, the doctrine is good law, it is, as we have explained, inapplicable to this case. To recapitulate: there was no forced sale, because only the form of the plaintiff's investment was changed; and anyway there was no reliance, no investment decision, because the plaintiff did not have a choice whether or not to accept the new stock.

Affirmed.

NOTES

(1) Chief Judge Posner noted that the parent of the spun off subsidiary had obtained a "no action" letter from the Division of Corporation Finance of the SEC to the effect that the distribution of the shares of the subsidiary did not require registration under the Securities Act of 1933. A "no action" letter is a written confirmation to the effect that if a proposed course of action is taken as described in the "no action" request, (*e.g.*, a spin off without '33 Act registration) the Division will not recommend to the SEC that it take enforcement action with respect thereto. In 1997, the Division published Legal Bulletin No. 4 which sets forth the conditions which must be met if the spinoff is to be effected without '33 Act registration; one of those conditions is that, in order to provide "adequate information to its shareholders and the trading markets" the parent of a non '34 Act

reporting company to be spun off must provide its shareholders with an Information Statement that substantially complies with Regulations 14a and 14c under the '34 Act. In the Bulletin, the Division stated that, absent unusual circumstances, it will no longer issue "no action" letters with respect to spinoffs and that persons should instead rely on Legal Bulletin 4. As it does in the case of "no action" letters, the Bulletin contains the following disclaimer: "The statements in this legal bulletin represent the views of the staff of the Division of Corporation Finance. This bulletin is not a rule, regulation or statement of the [SEC]. Further the [SEC] has neither approved nor disapproved its content."

(2) For an example of a spin off Information Statement, see that of Discovery Holding Company dated July 11, 2005 relating to a spinoff of that corporation from Liberty Media Corporation.

§ 6.02 STOCK DIVIDENDS AND STOCK SPLITS

A stock dividend is a dividend payable in the paying corporation's equity securities, usually common stock. (A dividend, such as a spin off, which is payable in stock of another corporation, is a property dividend, not a stock dividend.) A stock split generally results in an increase or decrease in the number of outstanding shares of common stock. A reclassification of stock effects a change of the equity security into other property, such as a different class or type of security, or cash.

NEW YORK STOCK EXCHANGE COMPANY MANUAL

703.02 Stock Split/Stock Rights Listing Process

(A) Introduction

Stock Splits —

There are many factors which a company must consider in evaluating the merits of splitting its stock. Studies by the Exchange indicate that a properly timed stock split can contribute to an increase in and broadening of the shareholder base and can also be an important means of improving market liquidity. Generally speaking, a properly timed stock split, when effected under appropriate circumstances, serves as an excellent means of generating greater investor interest. Postsplit price is also an important consideration, especially when a company is competing in the financial marketplace for investor attention with other high quality securities.

. . . .

Stock Dividends —

Many listed companies find it preferable at times to pay dividends in stock rather than cash, particularly in those cases in which a substantial part of earnings is retained by the company for use in its business. In order to guard against possible misconception by the shareowners of the effect of stock dividends on their equity in the company, and of their relation to current earnings, the Exchange has adopted certain standards of disclosure and accounting treatment.

Distinction between a Stock Dividend, a Partial Stock Split, and a Stock Split in Exchange Policy:

Stock Dividend — A distribution of less than 25 % of the outstanding shares (as calculated prior to the distribution).

Partial Stock Split — A distribution of 25 % or more but less than 100 % of the outstanding shares (as calculated prior to the distribution).

Stock Split — A distribution of 100% or more of the outstanding shares (as calculated prior to the distribution).

Accounting Treatment. —

In accordance with generally accepted accounting principles, the following accounting treatment is required for the various distributions:

Stock Dividend — Capitalize retained earnings for the fair market value of the additional shares to be issued. Fair market value should closely approximate the current share market price adjusted to give effect to the distribution.

Partial Stock Split — Requires capitalization of paid-in capital (surplus) for the par or stated value of the shares issued only where there is to be no change in the par or stated value. In those circumstances where the distributions of small stock splits assume the character of stock dividends through repetition of issuance under circumstances not consistent with the intent and purpose of stock splits, the Exchange may require that such distributions be accounted for as stock dividends, i.e., capitalization of retained earnings.

Stock Split — Requires transfer from paid-in capital (surplus) for the par or stated value of the shares issued unless there is to be a change in the par or stated value.

Stock splits can be effected in one of two ways. The more traditional, or historical method of carrying out a stock split is to amend the certificate of incorporation to reduce appropriately the par value of the outstanding shares and, if necessary or desirable, to increase the number of authorized shares of common stock. Because an amendment to the certificate of incorporation is involved, the traditional stock split requires a stockholders' meeting, proxy statement, and related items. The 1964 Cerro Corporation stock split documentation set forth immediately below is an example of the historical or traditional stock split.

Another way of effecting a stock split is to have the board of directors of the corporation declare a 100 percent stock dividend. Assuming that the corporation has a sufficient number of authorized but unissued shares, the modern type of stock split can be carried out simply by having the board of directors authorize the declaration and payment of the stock dividend. The documentation relating to the Winns Stores, set forth below following the Cerro Corporation materials, is an example of the modern type of stock split.

CERRO CORPORATION
300 PARK AVENUE
NEW YORK, N.Y. 10022

October 14, 1964

To the Stockholders:

The Notice and Proxy Statement which follow relate to a proposed amendment to the Certificate of Incorporation of the corporation to effect a split of the Corporation's Common Stock, a reduction in the par value of each share of such stock and an increase in the number of shares of such stock which the Corporation is authorized to issue. The amendment is proposed and recommended by your Board of Directors and will be acted upon at a special meeting of stockholders to be held at the Corporation's offices in New York on November 10, 1964.

The manner in which the stock split would be effected, if the proposal to be voted upon is approved, is essentially as follows:

The stock will be split on a three-shares-for-two basis. The split will become effective at the close of business on November 13, 1964.

Stockholders will keep their existing stock certificates. Therefore, existing certificates should not be sent to the Corporation.

On or about December 4, a certificate representing one additional share for each two held will be mailed to holders of record at the close of business on November 13. One third of the shares you will then hold will be represented by a new certificate and the remaining two thirds by the certificate(s) you held before. After the stock split all the shares will have a par value of $3.33 per share, even though the old certificates will not state the new par value but the prior par value of $5.00 per share.

Stockholders entitled to receive a fractional share interest, as a result of the stock split, will be given an opportunity to purchase an additional fraction required to make up a full share or sell the fraction to which they are entitled.

The Corporation is now authorized to issue 250,000 shares of Preferred Stock, par value $100 each, and 6,000,000 shares of Common Stock, par value $5.00 each. No change is being requested in the authorized Preferred Stock, none of which is issued or outstanding. Stockholder approval is being sought to change the presently authorized Common Stock into 9,000,000 shares with a par value of $3.33, in order to be able to effect the stock split, and further to increase the number of shares of authorized Common Stock, par value $3.33 per share, to a total of 15,000,000 shares. The reasons for the increase in the authorized Common Stock are stated in the annexed Proxy Statement.

Affirmative vote by holders of a majority of the total number of shares of Common Stock outstanding is needed for approval of the proposed amendment of the Certificate of Incorporation. Whether or not you plan to attend the meeting, you are requested to mark, sign and return promptly the accompanying proxy form. If you do attend the meeting, you may vote in person should you so desire.

Very truly yours,

President

CERRO CORPORATION
300 PARK AVENUE
NEW YORK, N.Y. 10022

NOTICE OF SPECIAL MEETING OF STOCKHOLDERS
To Be Held November 10, 1964

TO THE STOCKHOLDERS:

A special meeting of the stockholders of Cerro Corporation (a New York corporation) will be held at the office of the Corporation, 300 Park Avenue, New York, N.Y. (15th Floor), on Tuesday, November 10, 1964, at 10:30 A. M., Eastern Standard Time, for the purpose of:

Considering and acting upon a proposed resolution authorizing amendment of the Certificate of Incorporation of the Corporation to increase the Corporation's capital stock from $55,000,000 to $75,000,000; to change the 6,000,000 shares of presently authorized Common Stock, par value $5.00 each, into 9,000,000 shares, par value $3.3313 each; to authorize 6,000,000 additional shares of Common Stock, par value $3.3313 each; and to change each share of Common Stock, par value $5.00 each, issued and outstanding, including treasury shares, into 1 1/2 shares with a par value of $3.3313 each.

The proposed resolution authorizing the amendment of the Certificate of Incorporation is attached as Exhibit A to the annexed Proxy Statement.

The Transfer Books will not be closed for the special meeting. Only stockholders of record at the close of business on October 9, 1964 will be entitled to vote at the meeting.

By order of the Board of Directors: Michael D. David, Secretary, New York, N.Y.
October 14, 1964

IT IS IMPORTANT THAT YOUR STOCK BE REPRESENTED AT THIS MEETING. IF YOU ARE NOT ABLE TO BE PRESENT AT THE MEETING. PLEASE SIGN THE ENCLOSED PROXY (blue form) AND MAIL IN ENCLOSED ENVELOPE. BECAUSE OF THE AMOUNT OF DETAIL WORK NECESSARY TO PREPARE FOR THE MEETING, THE IMMEDIATE RETURN OF YOUR PROXY WILL BE APPRECIATED.

CERRO CORPORATION
INCORPORATED IN NEW YORK
PROXY STATEMENT

Special Meeting of Stockholders to be held November 10, 1964

Solicitation and Revocability of Proxy

The accompanying proxy is solicited by the management of Cerro Corporation for use at the special meeting of stockholders of the Corporation to be held on November 10, 1964. Execution of the proxy will not in any way affect the stockholder's right to attend the meeting and vote in person, and the stockholder giving the proxy has the power to revoke it at any time before it is exercised.

The Corporation will bear the cost of solicitation of proxies and will reimburse persons holding stock in their names or those of their nominees for their expenses in sending soliciting material to their principals. In addition to the solicitation of proxies by the use of the mails, proxies may also be solicited by regularly engaged employees of the Corporation by telephone, telegraph, cable, and personal interview. It is not expected that any solicitation will be made by specially engaged employees of the Corporation or other paid solicitors.

Voting Securities

Only stockholders of record at the close of business on October 9, 1964 will be entitled to vote at the special meeting. The Corporation has only one class of voting securities currently outstanding, its Common Stock, of which 3,788,438 shares were outstanding on the record date, exclusive of shares held in treasury. Each stockholder is entitled to one vote for each share of stock held by him.

Proposed Increase in Authorized Capital, Reduction of Par Value of Common Stock, Increase in Authorized Common Stock and Stock Split

On September 17, 1964, the Board of Directors of the Corporation adopted a resolution declaring it advisable and recommending that the stockholders of the Corporation adopt a resolution authorizing amendment of the Certificate of Incorporation of the Corporation to:

(a) increase the authorized capital stock from $55,000,000 to $75,000,000;

(b) change 6,000,000 shares of the authorized Common Stock with a par value of $5.00 per share (including shares issued and outstanding and in treasury) into 9,000,000 shares with a par value of $3.3313 per share;

(c) authorize 6,000,000 additional shares of Common Stock with a par value of $3.3313 per share; and

(d) change each share of Common Stock with a par value of $5.00 per share issued and outstanding (including shares held in treasury) on November 13, 1964 into one and one-half shares with a par value of $3.3313 per share.

The resolution proposed for adoption by the stockholders is set forth in *Exhibit A* which is a part of this Proxy Statement.

An affirmative vote of holders of a majority of the shares of the Corporation's Common Stock issued and outstanding at the close of business on October 9, 1964, is required for adoption of the proposed resolution.

The Board of Directors believes the proposed stock split, by increasing the number of shares outstanding and proportionately reducing the market value of each share, will tend to broaden investor interest in Cerro shares and improve their marketability. This should redound to the benefit of Cerro shareholders and the Corporation.

If authorized by the stockholders, the amendment of the Certificate of Incorporation will become effective as of the close of business on November 13, 1964, at which time the determination of stockholders entitled to receive additional shares of Common Stock, distributable in accordance with the stock split, will be made. It will *not* be necessary for stockholders to send their existing stock certificates to the Corporation or its Transfer Agent. Stock certificates in the hands of stockholders representing issued shares of $5.00 par value will be deemed, after November 13, 1964, to represent the same number of shares of Common Stock with a par value of $3.3313 per share. Stock certificates representing the additional shares that stockholders will be entitled to receive will be mailed on or about December 4, 1964. No fractional share certificates will be issued. In lieu thereof, each stockholder otherwise entitled to a one-half share interest will be issued an Order Form which he may use on or before January 5, 1965, to direct Irving Trust Company, as Agent, either to purchase an additional one-half share interest required to entitle him to one full share or to sell his one-half share interest and remit the proceeds to him.

As stated above, on October 9, 1964, there were issued and outstanding 3,788,438 shares of the Corporation's Common Stock (exclusive of shares held in treasury) of $5.00 par value each. The number of such shares that will be outstanding on the effective date of the amendment, in the event the above-mentioned resolution is adopted by the stockholders, may be increased to the extent that the Corporation's 512 % Subordinated Debentures Due 1979 (the "Debentures") are converted into Common Stock and to the extent that options under the Corporation's stock option plans and an option granted to Mr. I.J. Furst are exercised between October 9, 1964 and the effective date of the amendment.

On October 9, 1964, Debentures in the principal amount of $26,158,400 were outstanding and were then convertible into 661,809 shares of the Corporation's present Common Stock at the ratio of 2.531 shares for each $100 principal amount of Debentures. On the same date, 143,273 shares of Common Stock were subject to options granted under stock option plans and to Mr. Furst, and 17,000 shares were reserved but not yet optioned under the Cerro Corporation Stock Option Plan of 1964.

If the proposed resolution with respect to amendment of the Certificate of Incorporation is adopted by the stockholders, the number of shares of Common Stock reserved for issuance upon conversion of the Debentures and the number of shares reserved for issuance under the stock option plans and under the option held by Mr. Furst will be correspondingly adjusted for the three-for-two split on the effective date of the amendment.

On October 9, 1964, a total of 44,000 shares of Common Stock were held in the Corporation's treasury. Such shares were reacquired by the Corporation after they had been issued and were outstanding, and such shares will also be split three-for-two on the effective date of the amendment. Under New York law, such treasury stock does not participate in dividends and is not voting stock. The treasury shares may be used to acquire property or for other corporate purposes or such shares may be cancelled.

Except for issuance of reserved shares, as may be necessary, the Board has no present intention to issue any of the authorized but unissued Common Stock that will result from the amendment to the Certificate of Incorporation, and knows of no plans, arrangements or undertakings in that regard. Any of the authorized but unissued shares not reserved for the purposes stated above will be available for issuance by the Board from time to time for any proper corporate purpose not requiring further action by the stockholders.

The proposed stock split will neither affect a stockholder's proportionate interest in the Corporation nor result in any change in the Corporation's capital stock or surplus accounts. Financial statements are not furnished herewith since they are not deemed material for the exercise of prudent judgment by the stockholders in regard to the proposed amendment to the Certificate of Incorporation.

The Corporation has been advised by counsel that, under existing Federal tax laws, the split would result in no taxable gain or loss to the stockholders.

The split would have the effect, however, of increasing brokerage commissions and New York State stock transfer taxes applicable to certain stock transactions. For example, the brokerage commission and New York State stock transfer tax on the sale of 100 shares of the present $5.00 par value Common Stock, assuming a price of $57.00 per share, would be $48.70, while the same costs (including the so-called "odd-lot differential") for the sale of 150 shares of the proposed new $3.3313 par value Common Stock at an assumed price of $38.00 would be $80.95.

Dividends

If the proposed stock split is authorized and becomes effective, it is the present intention of the Corporation's Board of Directors to declare, at its meeting to be held in December 1964, a quarterly cash dividend of 35 cents per full share of Common Stock of the new par value of $3.3313 per share to holders of record of such full shares on the record date set for the payment of such dividend. This is equivalent to 5212 cents per share on the present $5.00 par value shares.

On September 1, 1964 the Board declared a quarterly dividend of 45 cents per Common share payable September 29 to holders of record September 14. Earlier payments per share have been made as follows: 40 cents in June of the current year, 35 cents in March, 3212 cents in December, 1963 and 2712 cents in September, 1963. A five percent stock dividend was also distributed on April 30, 1964.

Other Matters

The Management of the Corporation is not aware of any matters, other than those referred to above, that may come before the meeting. If any other matters are properly presented to the meeting for action, it is intended that the persons named in the proxies will have discretionary authority to vote on such matters.

By Order of the Board of Directors:

MICHAEL D. DAVID
Secretary

New York, N.Y. October 14, 1964

EXHIBIT A

Text of Proposed Resolution Authorizing Amendment of the Certificate of Incorporation of Cerro Corporation

"RESOLVED, That the President or any Vice President, and the Secretary or Assistant Secretary of the Corporation, are hereby authorized to sign, verify, and deliver to the Department of State of the State of New York on November 13, 1964, to become effective at the close of business on that day, a Certificate of Amendment of the Certificate of Incorporation of the Corporation under Section 805 of the Business Corporation Law of the State of New York to:

(1) increase the authorized capital stock of the Corporation from $55,000,000 to $75,000,000, to consist of 250,000 shares of Preferred Stock with a par value of $100 per share (as presently authorized) and 15,000,000 shares of Common Stock with a par value of $3.3313 per share, the increase as it pertains to the Common Stock representing (a) change of the 6,000,000 shares of the Common Stock with a par value of $5.00 a share presently authorized (including shares issued and outstanding and held in treasury) into 9,000,000 shares of Common Stock with a par value of $3.3313 per share, and (b) increase of 6,000,000 shares in the number of shares of Common Stock with a par value of $3.3313 per share authorized to be issued;

(2) amend Section THIRD and paragraph (A) of Section FOURTH of the Certificate of Incorporation to read as follows:

THIRD: The amount of the capital stock of the Corporation is SEVENTY-FIVE MILLION DOLLARS ($75,000,000).

FOURTH: (A) The total number of shares which the Corporation may issue is Fifteen Million Two Hundred and Fifty Thousand (15,250,000), of which Two Hundred Fifty Thousand (250,000) are designated Preferred Stock with a par value of One Hundred Dollars ($100) per share and Fifteen Million (15,000,000) are designated Common Stock with a par value of Three Dollars and Thirty-Three and One-Third Cents ($3.3313) per share; and

(3) change each share of Common Stock with a par value of $5.00 per share issued and outstanding at the close of business on November 13, 1964, including shares held in treasury on that date, to one and one-half (112) shares with the par value of $3.3313 per share, certificates for the additional shares thereby created to be distributed on or about December 4, 1964 to stockholders of record at the close of business on November 13, 1964, said Certificate of Amendment to contain such other provisions as General Counsel to the Corporation may deem necessary or appropriate to carry out the intent of the foregoing."

WINN'S STORES, INCORPORATED
1235 GEMBLER RD.
POST OFFICE DRAWER 20007
SAN ANTONIO, TEXAS 78286
(512) 333-4224

May 25, 1979

Dear Shareholder:

On April 27, 1979, the Board of Directors of Winn's Stores, Incorporated (the "Company") declared a two-for-one stock split, to be effected in the form of a stock dividend, payable on May 25, 1979 to shareholders of record on May 11, 1979. Enclosed is a certificate representing the number of shares of the Company's Common Stock, par value $1.25 per share, issuable to you as a result of the stock split.

The Company's tax advisors are of the opinion that the issuance of shares of the Company's Common Stock by reason of the stock split does not result in taxable income to shareholders for Federal income tax purposes.

Yours very truly,

LYNN H. SPEARS
Chairman of the Board

CERTIFICATE

The undersigned, C.W. Carroll, Secretary of Winn's Stores, Incorporated, a Texas corporation (the "Company"), hereby certifies that the following resolutions were duly adopted by the Board of Directors of the Company on April 26, 1979 and that such resolutions have not been altered, amended, modified or rescinded and remain in full force and effect:

RESOLVED: That, in order to effect a two-for-one stock split-up, there is hereby declared a stock dividend upon the 1,265,000 shares of Common Stock, par value $1.25 per share, of the Company presently issued and outstanding, which stock dividend shall be a one hundred percent (100%) stock dividend consisting of 1,265,000 shares of the Common Stock of the

Company and which shall be issued by the Company from its authorized but unissued shares and shall be payable on May 25, 1979 to shareholders of record at the close of business on May 11, 1979 so that each shareholder will receive one additional share for each share held of record by such shareholder at the close of business on such record date; and further

RESOLVED: That upon the issuance of 1,265,000 shares of Common Stock in effecting such split-up through such stock dividend, there shall be transferred from and charged against the Company's retained earnings account, and transferred and credited to the common stock account, the sum of $1,581,250, the aggregate par value of such shares; and further

RESOLVED: That upon the issuance and delivery of the certificates representing such shares, the same shall constitute and evidence the validly issued, fully paid and non-accessible shares of Common Stock of the Company; and further

RESOLVED: That the appropriate officers of the Company are hereby authorized and directed to do all such acts and things as may be necessary and proper to effect such stock split-up in the form of a stock dividend and to cause certificates representing such shares to be duly issued and delivered and otherwise to carry out and give effect to the foregoing resolutions.

IN WITNESS WHEREOF, I have set my hand this day of May, 1979.

C.W. Carroll
Secretary

In addition to the type of stock dividend discussed above, there is the form of stock dividend utilized in connection with PIK (i.e., payment in kind) capital stock, usually preferred stock. Set forth below are provisions relating to a PIK preferred stock.

B. Preferred Stock.

. . . .

(C) Dividends.

. . . .

Any dividend payments made with respect to Cumulative Exchangeable Preferred Stock shall be made in cash; provided that, during the period ending on and including the first dividend payment date after the fifth anniversary of the original issuance of the Cumulative Exchangeable Preferred Stock or ending on such earlier dividend payment date as the Corporation may elect by written notice to the holders of the Cumulative Exchangeable Preferred Stock (the "Pay in Kind Period"), such dividends may be made, in the sole discretion of the Corporation, in cash or by issuing additional fully paid and nonassessable shares of Cumulative Exchangeable

Preferred Stock at the rate of 0.175 of one share of Cumulative Exchangeable Preferred Stock for each $9.3328 of such dividend not paid in cash, and the issuance of such additional shares shall constitute full payment of such dividend.

APPLEBAUM v. AVAYA, INC.

Delaware Supreme Court
812 A.2d 880 (2002)

Veasey, Chief Justice

In this appeal, we affirm the judgment of the Court of Chancery holding that a corporation could validly initiate a reverse stock split and selectively dispose of the fractional interests held by stockholders who no longer hold whole shares. The Vice Chancellor interpreted Section 155 of the Delaware General Corporation Law to permit the corporation, as part of a reverse/forward stock split, to treat its stockholders unequally by cashing out the stockholders who own only fractional interests while opting not to dispose of fractional interests of stockholders who will end up holding whole shares of stock as well as fractional interests. In the latter instance the fractional shares would be reconverted to whole shares in an accompanying forward stock split.

We hold that neither the language of Section 155 nor the principles guiding our interpretation of statutes dictate a prohibition against the disparate treatment of stockholders, for this purpose. We also hold that the corporation may dispose of those fractional interests pursuant to Section 155(1) by aggregating the fractional interests and selling them on behalf of the cashed-out stockholders where this method of disposition has a rational business purpose of saving needless transaction costs.

A further issue we address is whether, as an alternative method of compensation, the corporation may satisfy the "fair price" requirement of Section 155(2) by paying the stockholders an amount based on the average trading price of the corporation's stock. Here, the Vice Chancellor properly held that the trading price of actively-traded stock of a corporation, the stock of which is widely-held, will provide an adequate measure of fair value for the stockholders' fractional interests for purposes of a reverse stock split under Section 155.

FACTS

Avaya, Inc. is a Delaware corporation that designs and manages communications networks for business organizations and large non-profit agencies. The enterprise is a descendant of the industry standard-bearer, AT&T. Avaya was established as an independent company in October of 2000 when it was spun off from Lucent Technologies. Lucent itself is a spin-off of AT&T. Because its capital structure is the product of two spin-off transactions, the outstanding stock of Avaya is one of the most widely-held on the New York Stock Exchange. Over 3.3 million common stockholders own fewer than 90 shares of Avaya stock each.

Although a large number of stockholders hold a small stake in the corporation, Avaya incurs heavy expenses to maintain their accounts. Avaya spends almost $4 million per year to print and mail proxy statements and annual reports to each stockholder as well as to pay transfer agents and other miscellaneous fees. Stockholders who own their stock in street names cost Avaya an additional $3.4 million in similar administrative fees.

Since the cost of maintaining a stockholder's account is the same regardless of the number of shares held, Avaya could reduce its administrative burden, and thereby save money for its stockholders, by decreasing its stockholder base. In February of 2001, at the corporation's annual meeting, the Avaya board of directors presented the stockholders with a transaction designed to accomplish this result. The Avaya board asked the stockholders to grant the directors authorization to engage in one of three alternative transactions:

(1) a reverse l-for-30 stock split followed immediately by a forward 30-for-1 stock split of the Common stock.

(2) a reverse 1-for-40 stock split followed immediately by a forward 40-for-l stock split of the Common stock.

(3) a reverse 1-for-50 stock split followed immediately by a forward 50-for-l stock split of the Common stock.

We refer in this opinion to all three of these alternative transactions as the "Proposed Transaction" or the "Reverse/Forward Split." Regardless of the particular ratio the board chooses, at some future date the Reverse Split will occur at 6:00 p.m., followed by a Forward Split one minute later. Once selected, the effective date of the Split will be posted on Avaya's website.

The transaction will cash out stockholders who own stock below the minimum number ultimately selected by the directors for the Reverse/Forward Split pursuant to those three alternative options. Stockholders who do not hold the minimum number of shares necessary to survive the initial Reverse Split will be cashed out and receive payment for their resulting fractional interests (the "cashed-out stockholders" or "targeted stockholders"). Stockholders who own a sufficient amount of stock to survive the Reverse Split will not have their fractional interests cashed out. Once the Forward Split occurs, their fractional holdings will be converted back into whole shares of stock.

Avaya will compensate the cashed-out stockholders through one of two possible methods. Avaya may combine the fractional interests and sell them as whole shares on the open market. In the alternative, the corporation will pay the stockholders the value of their fractional interests based on the trading price of the stock averaged over a ten-day period preceding the Reverse Split. Stockholders who hold their Avaya stock in street names have been advised to contact their nominees to see that they receive the same consideration as stockholders who have their interests registered in their own names.[6]

---

[6] [1] In the Proxy Statement the Board explains that "Avaya intends for the Reverse/Forward Split to treat shareholders holding Common Stock in street name through a nominee . . . in the same manner as shareholders whose shares are registered in their names. Nominees will be instructed to effect the

To illustrate the Proposed Transaction through a hypothetical, assume Stockholder A owns fifteen shares of stock and Stockholder B owns forty-five shares of stock. If Avaya chooses to initiate a Reverse 1-for-30 Stock Split, Stockholder A will possess a fractional interest equivalent to one-half a share of stock. Stockholder B will hold one whole share of Avaya stock and a fractional interest equivalent to one-half a share. Using the provisions of Section 155(1) or (2) of the Delaware General Corporation Law,[7] Avaya would cash out Stockholder A since he no longer possesses a whole share of stock. Stockholder A would no longer be an Avaya stockholder. Stockholder B will remain a stockholder because Avaya will not cash out the fractional interest held by her. Stockholder B's fractional interest remains attached to a whole share of stock. When Avaya executes the accompanying Forward 30-for-1 Stock Split, Stockholder B's interest in one and one-half shares will be converted into forty-five shares of stock, the same amount that she held prior to the Transaction.

At the annual meeting, Avaya stockholders voted to authorize the board to proceed with any one of the three alternative transactions. Applebaum, a holder of twenty-seven shares of Avaya stock, filed an action in the Court of Chancery to enjoin the Reverse/Forward Split. Under any one of the three alternatives Applebaum would be cashed out because he holds less than thirty shares.

PROCEEDINGS IN THE COURT OF CHANCERY

Applebaum asked the Court of Chancery to enjoin the Proposed Transaction, alleging that Avaya's treatment of fractional interests will not comport with the requirements set forward in Title 8, Section 155 of the Delaware Code. Applebaum argued that Section 155 does not permit Avaya to issue fractional shares to some stockholders but not to others in the same transaction. Even if Avaya could issue fractional shares selectively, Applebaum contended that the methods by which Avaya plans to cash-out the smaller stockholders do not comply with subsections (1) and (2) of Section 155.

After considering cross-motions for summary judgment, the Court of Chancery

---

Reverse/Forward Split for their beneficial holders. However, nominees may have different procedures and shareholders holding shares in street name should contact their nominees."

[7] [2] 8 Del. C. § 155 provides:

> Fractions of shares. A corporation may, but shall not be required to, issue fractions of a share. If it does not issue fractions of a share, it shall (1) arrange for the disposition of fractional interests by those entitled thereto, (2) pay in cash the fair value of fractions of a share as of the time when those entitled to receive such fractions are determined or (3) issue scrip or warrants in registered form (either represented by a certificate or uncertificated) or in bearer form (represented by a certificate) which shall entitle the holder to receive a full share upon the surrender of such scrip or warrants aggregating a full share. A certificate for a fractional share or an uncertificated fractional share shall, but scrip or warrants shall not unless otherwise provided therein, entitle the holder to exercise voting rights, to receive dividends thereon and to participate in any of the assets of the corporation in the event of liquidation. The board of directors may cause scrip or warrants to be issued subject to the conditions that they shall become void if not exchanged for certificates representing the full shares or uncertificated full shares before a specified date, or subject to the conditions that the shares for which scrip or warrants are exchangeable may be sold by the corporation and the proceeds thereof distributed to the holders of scrip or warrants, or subject to any other conditions which the board of directors may impose.

denied Applebaum's request for an injunction and held that the Reverse/Forward Split would comply with Section 155 and dispose of the cashed-out stockholders' interests in a fair and efficient manner.[8] Applebaum appeals the final judgment entered for the defendants. We affirm.

ISSUES ON APPEAL

Applebaum claims the Court of Chancery erred by: (1) holding that Title 8, Section 155 permits Avaya to issue fractional shares to the surviving stockholders but not issue fractional shares to the cashed-out stockholders; (2) holding that Avaya can combine the fractional interests and sell them on the open market; (3) holding that Avaya can instruct nominees to participate in the Split even if a particular nominee holds a sufficient amount of stock on behalf of all of its beneficial holders to survive the Split; (4) granting summary judgment and holding that the payment of cash for fractional interests based on a ten-day average of the trading price of Avaya stock constitutes "fair value" under Section 155; and (5) holding that the meaning of "fair value" in Sections 155(2) is different from Section 262 and thus failing to value the fractional shares as proportionate interests in a going concern.

SECTION 155 DOES NOT PREVENT AVAYA FROM DISPOSING OF FRACTIONAL INTERESTS SELECTIVELY

Applebaum questions the board's authority to treat stockholders differently by disposing of the fractional interests of some stockholders but not others. Applebaum contends that Avaya will issue fractional shares in violation of Section 155. According to this view of the transaction, during the one minute interval between the two stock splits the corporation will not issue fractional shares to stockholders who possess holdings below the minimum amount. Those stockholders will be cashed out. Stockholders who hold stock above the minimum amount, by contrast, will be issued fractional shares that will be reconverted in the Forward Split into the same number of whole shares owned by those stockholders before the Reverse Split.

Applebaum argues that Section 155 prevents Avaya from achieving this disparate result by providing that:

> A corporation may, but shall not be required to, issue fractions of a share. If it does not issue fractions of a share, it shall (1) arrange for the disposition of fractional interests by those entitled thereto, (2) pay in cash the fair value of fractions of a share as of the time when those entitled to receive such fractions are determined. . . .[9]

Applebaum reads Section 155 to mean that Avaya can employ the cash-out methods provided in Section 155 only if the corporation "does not issue fractions of a share."[10]

---

[8] [3] *Applebaum v. Avaya, Inc.*, 805 A.2d 209 (Del. Ch. 2002).

[9] [4] (4) 8 Del. C. § 155.

[10] [5] *Id.*

This Court reviews de novo the Court of Chancery's decision to grant Avaya's motion for summary judgment.[11] We need not reach the merits of Applebaum's interpretation of Section 155 because he has based his argument on the flawed assumption that Avaya will issue fractional shares. Since the Reverse/Forward Split is an integrated transaction, Avaya need not issue any fractional shares. The initial Reverse Split creates a combination of whole *shares* and fractional *interests*. Avaya will use either Section 155(1) or (2) to cash out the fractional interests of stockholders who no longer possess a whole share of stock. Fractional *interests* that are attached to whole *shares* will not be disposed of. Nor will they be represented by fractions of a share. Fractional shares are unnecessary because the surviving fractional interests will be reconverted into whole shares in the Forward Split.[12]

Applebaum correctly notes that Avaya stockholders are not treated equally in the Proposed Transaction. The disparate treatment, however, does not arise by issuing fractional shares selectively. It occurs through the selective disposition of some fractional interests but not others. The provisions of Section 155 do not forbid this disparate treatment. While principles of equity permit this Court to intervene when technical compliance with a statute produces an unfair result,[13] equity and equality are not synonymous concepts in the Delaware General Corporation Law.[14] Moreover, this Court should not create a safeguard against stockholder inequality that does not appear in the statute.[15] Here there is no showing that Applebaum was treated inequitably. From all that appears on this record, the proposed transaction was designed in good faith to accomplish a rational business purpose-saving transaction costs.[16]

Our jurisprudence does not prevent Avaya from properly using Section 155 in a creative fashion that is designed to meet its needs as an on-going enterprise.[17] The

---

[11] [6] *Telxon Corp. v. Meyerson*, 802 A.2d 257, 261 (Del. 2002).

[12] [7] Shares of stock are issued to provide a verifiable property interest for the residual claimants of the corporation. See *Kalageorgi v. Victor Kainkin. Inc.*, 750 A.2d 531, 538 (Del. Ch. 1999) (stating that "Corporate securities are a species of property right"), *aff'd*, 748 A.2d 913 (Del. 2000). We do not believe Avaya must issue fractional shares to recognize a property interest that, by the terms of the transaction, will last only sixty seconds.

[13] [8] *See, e.g., Schnell v. Chris-Craft Indus.*, 285 A.2d 437, 439 (Del. 1971).

[14] [9] *See Nixon v. Blackwell*, 626 A.2d 1366, 1376 (Del. 1993) ("It is well established in our jurisprudence that stockholders need not always be treated equally for all purposes."); *see also Unocal Corp. v. Mesa Petroleum Co.*, 493 A.2d 946, 957 (Del. 1985); *Cheff v. Mathes*, 199 A.2d 548, 554-56 (Del. 1964).

[15] [10] *See, e.g., Williams v. Geier*, 671 A.2d 1368, 1385 n.36 (Del. 1996) (noting "Directors and investors must be able to rely on the stability and absence of judicial interference with the State's statutory prescriptions"); *Nixon*, 626 A.2d at 1379-81 (absent legislation there should be no "special, judicially-created rules for minority investors"); *American Hardware Corp. v. Savage Arms. Corp.*, 136 A.2d 690, 693 (Del. 1957) (rejecting argument based on an interpretation that would "import serious confusion and uncertainty into corporate procedure").

[16] [11] See *Sinclair v. Levien*, 280 A.2d 717, 720 (Del. 1971) (board action presumed valid if it "can be attributed to any rational business purpose"); *see also Williams*, 671 A.2d at 1377-78 (board action in recommending charter amendment for stockholder action covered by business judgment rule in the absence of rebuttal demonstrating violation of fiduciary duty).

[17] [12] *See Grimes v. Alteon Inc.*, 804 A.2d 256, 266 (Del. 2002) (noting that corporations "should have the freedom to enter into new and different forms of transactions") (citations omitted).

subsections listed in Section 155 merely require the corporation to compensate its stockholders when it chooses not to recognize their fractional interests in the form of fractional shares.[18] Based upon this record, we conclude that Avaya is free to recognize the fractional interests of some stockholders but not others so long as the corporation follows the procedures set forth in Section 155.

AVAYA MAY PROCEED WITH ANY OF ITS ALTERNATIVE PLANS TO DISPOSE OF THE FRACTIONAL INTERESTS

The balance of Applebaum's appeal challenges the alternative methods by which Avaya proposes to dispose of the fractional interests. The Court of Chancery concluded that Avaya could proceed under Section 155(1) by aggregating the fractional interests and selling them on behalf of the cashed-out stockholders. The Court also held that Avaya could employ Section 155(2), which requires payment of the "fair value" of the fractional interests, by paying the cashed-out stockholders an amount based on the avenge trading price of Avaya stock. We agree with the decision of the Court of Chancery and address separately the issues based on each subsection of the statute.

SECTION 155(1) PERMITS AVAYA TO SELL THE FACTIONAL INTEREST ON BEHALF OF THE STOCKHOLDERS

The stockholders have authorized Avaya to compensate the cashed-out stockholders by combining their fractional interests into whole shares and then selling them on the stockholders' behalf. Section 155(1) permits Avaya to "arrange for the disposition of fractional interests by those entitled thereto."[19]

Applebaum claims that Avaya cannot use Section 155(1) because the corporation will sell whole shares rather than "fractional interests." According to this rendition of the transaction, the fractional interests held by the targeted stockholders must be reconverted into whole shares in the Forward Split. Otherwise, their fractional interests will be diluted.[20] Avaya must reconvert the interests back to their initial value as whole shares in order to sell the combined fractional interests. Thus, Avaya would be selling whole shares rather than fractional interests.

Applebaum's argument incorrectly assumes that Avaya must issue fractions of a share in the Proposed Transaction. After the Reverse Split takes place, the stockholders holding shares below the minimum amount will be cashed out. The fractional interests will not be represented as shares and are therefore not involved in the Forward Split. Avaya will then aggregate the fractional interests and

---

[18] [13] *See* Ward, Welch & Turezyn, Folk On The Delaware General Corporation Law § 155.1 (4th ed. 2002) (stating "a corporation may refuse to issue share fractions . . . [but] if the corporation chooses to ignore share fractions, it must elect one of the three alternatives authorized by Section 155 . . .").

[19] [14] 8 Del C. § 155(1).

[20] [15] Applebaum provides the following example: "[I]f the Minimum Number is 30, a holder of 10 pre-split shares will have a fractional interest of 1/3 of a share upon consummation of the Reverse Split. One minute later, the whole shares with their attendant fractional shares are multiplied by 30 in the Forward Split. If the 1/3 share fractional interest is not also multiplied by 30 in the Forward Split, it would be reduced to 1/90th of a post-Forward Split share." Appellant's Br. at 23 n.10.

repackage them as whole shares which the corporation will sell on the open market. The statute does not mandate any set procedure by which the fractional interests must be disposed of so long as those interests are sold in a manner that secures the proportionate value of the cashed-out holdings.

Applebaum also contends that Avaya cannot sell the fractional interests on behalf of the cashed-out stockholders. If Avaya sells the interests for the stockholders, Applebaum argues that the corporation will not comply with Section 155(1) because the interests are not disposed of by "those entitled thereto." As the Vice Chancellor noted, Applebaum presents a strained reading of Section 155(1).[21] The Court of Chancery correctly reasoned that "In the eyes of equity, such sales would be 'by' " the stockholders.[22]

Applebaum's interpretation also ignores the corporation's responsibility under Section 155(1) to "arrange" for the disposition of fractional interests. Since fractional shares cannot be listed on the major stock exchanges,[23] the corporation must arrange for their aggregation in order to sell them.[24] Aggregation is normally performed by

> affording to the stockholder an election to sell the fractional share or to purchase an additional fraction sufficient to make up a whole share. The elections are forwarded to a trust company or other agent of the corporation who matches up the purchases and sales and issues certificates for the whole shares or checks for payment of the fractional shares. . . .[25]

The general practice requires the corporation to act as an intermediary to package the fractional interests into marketable shares. If the corporation were not permitted to do so, the fractional interests of the cashed-out stockholders would be dissipated through the transaction costs of finding other fractional holders with whom to combine and sell fractional interests in the market.[26]

AVAYA MAY INSTRUCT NOMINEES TO EXECUTE THE PROPOSED TRANSACTION ON BEHALF OF THE BENEFICIAL OWNERS

To execute the Reverse/Forward Split, Avaya stated in its proxy statement that "Nominees will be instructed to effect the Reverse/Forward Split for their beneficial holders." Applebaum argues that nominees cannot be forced to elect to receive cash in exchange for the fractional interests held by their beneficial holders if the nominee's combined holdings for all of its beneficial holders exceeds the minimum amount of stock necessary to survive the Reverse Split.

Applebaum misstates the responsibility of a corporation to stockholders who

---

[21] [16] *Applebaum*, 805 A.2d at 218.

[22] [17] *Id.*

[23] [18] *See* Drexler, Black & Sparks, Delaware Corporation Law and Practice, § 17.04 (2001).

[24] [19] Balotti & Finkelstein, Delaware Law of Corporations and Business Organizations, § 5.15 (2002).

[25] [20] *Id.*

[26] [21] *See Applebaum*, 805 A.2d at 218.

hold their interests through nominees and brokers. Nominees, as agents of the beneficial owners,[27] owe a duty to take the necessary steps to afford the true owners the opportunity to realize the benefits of the Proposed Transaction. The Court of Chancery properly held that the Reverse/Forward Split could operate at the level of the corporate ledger.[28] Avaya is not required to take any additional actions to effect the transaction for stockholders who own their stock through a nominee.[29] The beneficial stockholders are responsible for making proper arrangements with their agents.[30]

Applebaum also raises a disclosure issue related to the instructions for beneficial owners. The proxy statement informs stockholders that nominees "will be instructed to effect" the transaction. Applebaum argues that this statement is misleading because, as explained above, he contends that a nominee has the option either to effect the split or refrain from doing so it the aggregate amount of the beneficial holders' stock is sufficient to survive the Reverse Split. The proxy statement places the beneficial owners on notice that they must make arrangements with their nominees to receive payment from the transaction.[31] The proxy statement is not misleading because it accurately states that the nominees must execute the transaction on behalf of the beneficial holders.

THE TEN-DAY TRADING AVERAGE BY WHICH AVAYA PROPOSES TO COMPENSATE THE CASHED-OUT STOCKHOLDERS CONSTITUTES "FAIR VALUE" UNDER SECTION 155(2)

As an alternative to selling the fractional interests on behalf of the stockholders, Avaya may opt to pay the stockholders cash in an amount based on the trading price of Avaya stock averaged over a ten-day period preceding the Proposed Transaction. To do so, Avaya relies on Section 155(2), which provides that a corporation may "pay in cash the fair value of fractions of a share as of the time when those entitled to receive such fractions are determined."[32]

The corporation owes its cashed-out stockholders payment representing the "fair value" of their fractional interests. The cashed-out stockholders will receive fair value if Avaya compensates them with payment based on the price of Avaya stock averaged over a ten-day period preceding the Proposed Transaction. While market price is not employed in all valuation contexts,[33] our jurisprudence recognizes that

---

[27] [22] *See O'Malley v. Boris*, 742 A.2d 845, 849 (Del. 1999).

[28] [23] *Applebaum*, 805 A.2d at 220.

[29] [24] *See Enstar Corp. v. Senouf*, 535 A.2d 1351, 1354 (Del. 1987) ("The legal and practical effects of having one's stock registered in street name cannot be visited upon the issuer. The attendant risks are those of the stockholder . . . .").

[30] [25] *See, e.g., Enstar*, 535 A.2d at 1354 (stating that the holder of record must demand appraisal rights); *see also* 8 *Del C.* § 219(c) ("The stock ledger shall be the only evidence as to who are the stockholders entitled to examine the stock ledger, the list required by this section or the books of the corporation, or to vote in person or by proxy at any meeting of stockholders.").

[31] [26] *Applebaum*, 805 A.2d at 220-21.

[32] [27] 8 Del. C. § 155(2).

[33] [28] *See e.g.*, 8 Del C. § 262(h) ("In determining . . . fair value," in an appraisal proceeding, "the

in many circumstances a property interest is best valued by the amount a buyer will pay for it.[34]

The Vice Chancellor correctly concluded that a well-informed, liquid trading market will provide a measure of fair value superior to any estimate the court could impose.[35]

Applebaum relies on two instances where the Court of Chancery intimated that a Section 155(2) valuation may be similar to a going concern valuation employed in an appraisal proceeding. In *Chalfin v. Hart Holdings Co.*,[36] the Court of Chancery rejected a market price offered by a majority stockholder because the stock was not traded in an active market. In *Metropolitan Life Ins. Co. v. Aramark Corp.*,[37] the Court of Chancery declined to apply a private company discount presented by a controlling stockholder seeking to squeeze out the minority stockholders. Neither case applies here.

The court cannot defer to market price as a measure of fair value if the stock has not been traded actively in a liquid market.[38] In *Chalfin*, for example, the Court of Chancery held that the controlling stockholder could not offer as "fair value" in a reverse stock split the same amount alleged to be the past trading value because the stock had not been publicly traded for "some time."[39] The "market price" offered by the controlling stockholder was based on stale information.[40] An active trading market did not exist to monitor the corporation's performance. Thus, a more thorough valuation would have been necessary.

Avaya stock, by contrast, is actively traded on the NYSE. The concerns noted in *Chalfin* are not pertinent to the Proposed Transaction because the market continues to digest information currently known about the company. The value of Avaya's stock is tested daily through the purchase and sale of the stock on the open market.

Court shall take into account all relevant factors."); *Smith v. Van Gorkom*, 488 A.2d 858, 876 (Del. 1985) (holding that a decision by the board of directors to approve a merger did not fall within the proper exercise of business judgment because the directors failed to consider the intrinsic worth of the corporation where the stock traded at a depressed market value).

[34] [29] *Cf.* 8 Del. C. § 262(b)(1) (denying appraisal rights for stock listed on a national securities exchange, interdealer quotation system by the National Association of Securities Dealers, Inc. or held of record by more than 2,000 holders); *Revlon, Inc. v. MacAndrews & Forbes Holdings*, 506 A.2d 173, 182 (Del. 1986) (noting that an auction for the sale of a corporation is an appropriate method by which to secure the best price for the stockholders); *Baron v. Pressed Metals of America, Inc.*, 123 A.2d 848, 854 (Del. 1956) (noting that the "best price" a corporation could hope to obtain for the sale of a corporate asset "was what someone would be willing to pay" for it).

[35] [30] *Applebaum*, 805 A.2d at 215-16.

[36] [31] *Chalfin v. Hart Holdings Co.*, 1990 WL 181958[, 1990 Del. Ch. LEXIS 188] (Del. Ch.).

[37] [32] *Metropolitan Life Ins. Co. v. Aramark Corp.*, 1998 Del. Ch. LEXIS 70 (Del. Ch.).

[38] [33] *Chalfin*, 1990 WL 181958 at *4-5[, 1990 Del. Ch. LEXIS 188] (Del. Ch.).

[39] [34] *Id.* at *1.

[40] [35] *See Seagraves v. Urstadt Prop. Co.*, 1996 WL 159626 (Del. Ch.) at *7[, 1996 Del. Ch. LEXIS 36] ("To be reliable, market price must be established in an active market."); *Cf. Gimbel v. Signal Companies, Inc.*, 316 A.2d 599, 615, (Del. Ch. 1974) (holding that an expert valuation of oil and gas properties should have been updated to account for market fluctuations), *aff'd* 316 A.2d 619 (Del. 1974).

In a related argument, Applebaum contends that the trading price cannot represent fair value because the stock price is volatile, trading at a range of prices from $13.70 per share to $1.12 per share over the past year.[41] The volatility in trading does not necessarily mean that the market price is not an accurate indicator of fair value. Avaya stock is widely-held and actively traded in the market. The ten-day average has been recognized as a fair compromise that will hedge against the risk of fluctuation. Corporations often cash out fractional interests in an amount based on the average price over a given trading period.[42]

Applebaum also misunderstands the appropriate context for which a going-concern valuation may be necessary under Section 155(2). In both *Chalfin* and *Aramark*, the Court of Chancery recognized that a transaction employing Section 155 may warrant a searching inquiry of fair value if a controlling stockholder initiates the transaction.[43] When a controlling stockholder presents a transaction that will free it from future dealings with the minority stockholders, opportunism becomes a concern.[44] Any shortfall imposed on the minority stockholders will result in a transfer of value to the controlling stockholder. The discount in value could be imposed deliberately[45] or could be the result of an information asymmetry where the controlling stockholder possesses material facts that are not known in the market.[46] Thus, a Section 155(2) inquiry may resemble a Section 262 valuation if the controlling stockholder will benefit from presenting a suspect measure of valuation, such as an out-dated trading price,[47] or a wrongfully imposed private company

---

[41] [36] Appellant's Br. at 13.

[42] [37] *See* DREXLER ET AL. *supra* n.18 § 17.04 (2001) (stating "Merger agreements frequently provide for the payment of cash based on trading prices during an agreed period. While this technically may not key to an exact time when the persons entitled to fractions are determined . . . it is thought to better reflect fair values.").

[43] [38] *Chalfin*, 1990 WL 181958 at *3 n.3[, 1990 Del. Ch. LEXIS 188] (noting that market price might satisfy the fair value requirement under Section 155(2) but not "where the market price was set by the issuer company, acting as the primary (if not the sole) buyer"); *Aramark*, 1998 Del. Ch. LEXIS 70 at *8 (going concern valuation is necessary when the controlling stockholder is performing the "functional equivalent" of a squeeze-out merger).

[44] [39] *Weinberger v. UOP, Inc.*, 457 A.2d 701, 710 (Del. 1983), ("Given the absence of any attempt to structure this transaction on an arm's length basis, [the controlling stockholder] . . . cannot escape the effects of the conflicts it faced . . .").

[45] [40] *Chalfin*, 1999 WL 181958 at *3 n.3[, 1990 Del. Ch. LEXIS 188]. *Cf. Van Gorkom*, 488 A.2d at 877 (holding that merger price offered by CEO in a leveraged buyout could not be accepted as adequate without further investigation since the offer only calculated the amount that would allow the CEO to perform the transaction); Weinberger 457 A.2d at 711 (holding that outside directors for subsidiary company could not rely solely on fairness report prepared by individuals associated with the parent corporation to determine a fair price for the subsidiary's stock in a squeeze-out merger).

[46] [41] *See, e.g., Glassman v. Unocal Exploration Corp.*, 777 A.2d 242, 248 (Del. 2001) (a fair value determination must be based on "all relevant factors" in a short-form merger because the transaction presented by the controlling stockholder may be "timed to take advantage of a depressed market, or a low point in the company's cyclical earnings, or to precede an anticipated positive development . . . ."). *See also* Robert B. Thompson, *Exit, Liquidity, and Majority Rule: Appraisal's Role in Corporate Law*, 84 Geo. L.J. 1, 36 (1995) (arguing that an appraisal valuation may be necessary in a squeeze-out context if "the minority does not have a choice and is being forced out, perhaps because of an anticipated increase in value that will only become visible after the transaction, [in which case] exclusion [of the minority stockholders] can easily become a basis for oppression of the minority").

[47] [42] *Chalfin*, 1990 WL 181958 at *3[, 1990 Del. Ch. LEXIS 188].

discount.[48]

Although the Reverse/Forward Split will cash out smaller stockholders, the transaction will not allow the corporation to realize a gain at their expense. Unlike the more typical "freeze-out" context, the cashed-out Avaya stockholders may continue to share in the value of the enterprise. Avaya stockholders can avoid the effects of the proposed transaction either by purchasing a sufficient amount of stock to survive the initial Reverse Split or by simply using the payment provided under Section 155(2) to repurchase the same amount of Avaya stock that they held before the transaction.

The Reverse/Forward Split merely forces the stockholders to choose affirmatively to remain in the corporation. Avaya will succeed in saving administrative costs only if the board has assumed correctly that the stockholders who received a small interest in the corporation through the Lucent spin off would prefer to receive payment, free of transaction costs, rather than continue with the corporation. The Transaction is not structured to prevent the cashed-out stockholders from maintaining their stakes in the company. A payment based on market price is appropriate because it will permit the stockholders to reinvest in Avaya, should they wish to do so.

THE MEANING OF "FAIR VALUE" UNDER SECTION 155(2) IS NOT IDENTICAL TO THE CONCEPT OF "FAIR VALUE" IN SECTION 262

The Court of Chancery correctly interpreted "fair value" in Section 155 to have a meaning independent of the definition of "fair value" in Section 262 of the Delaware General Corporation Law.[49] Relying on the maxim that the same words used in different sections must be construed to have the same meaning,[50] Applebaum argues that "fair value" under Section 155(2) requires the court to perform a valuation similar to an appraisal proceeding. Borrowing from appraisal concepts that require that shares of stock be valued as proportionate interests in a going concern, Applebaum contends that the average trading price would be inadequate because the market price possesses an inherent discount that accounts for the holder's minority stake in the company.[51]

The Delaware General Assembly could not have intended Section 155(2) to have the same meaning as the fair value concept employed in Section 262.[52] The

---

[48] [43] *Aramark*, 1998 Del. Ch. LEXIS at *8.

[49] [44] 8 Del. C. § 262(a) (providing that "Any stockholder of a corporation of this State who holds shares of stock on the date of the making of a demand pursuant to subsection (d) . . . who continuously holds such shares through the effective date of the merger or consolidation . . . who has neither voted in favor of the merger or consolidation nor consented thereto . . . shall be entitled to an appraisal by the Court of Chancery of the fair value of the stockholder's shares of stock . . .").

[50] [45] *See* 2B Singer, Statutes and Statutory Construction, § 51.02 (6th ed. 2000).

[51] [46] *See Cavalier Oil, Corp. v. Harnett*, 564 A.2d 1137, 1145 (Del. 1989).

[52] [47] *Hariton v. Arco Electronics, Inc.*, 188 A.2d 123, 124 (Del. 1963) ("[t]he general theory of the Delaware Corporation Law that action taken pursuant to the authority of the various sections of that law constitute acts of independent legal significance and their validity is not dependent on other sections of the Act.") (quoting *Langfelder v. Universal Laboratories*, 68 F. Supp. 209, 211 (D. Del. 1946)).

reference to fair value in Section 155 first appeared in 1967.[53] The General Assembly did not place the term fair value in Section 262 until 1976.[54] Furthermore, the case law developing the concept of fair value under the appraisal statute did not acquire its present form until this Court discarded the Delaware block method and underscored the necessity of valuing a corporation as a going concern.[55] This Court has not suggested similar valuation guidelines for the right to receive "fair value" under Section 155(2). Finally, Section 262(b)(2)(c) expressly excludes fractional interests from the appraisal remedy when the stock is traded on a national exchange. When applied in the context of a merger or consolidation, Applebaum's interpretation of "fair value" under Section 155(2) would accord the stockholder of a constituent corporation an appraisal of fractional interests to which the stockholder is not entitled under the "market out" exception provided in Section 262.[56]

As this Court noted in *Alabama By-Products v. Cede & Co.*, the right to an appraisal is a narrow statutory right that seeks to redress the loss of the stockholder's ability under the common law to stop a merger.[57] The Reverse/Forward Split permitted under Section 155 does not present the same problem and is ill-suited for the same solution provided for in Section 262.

The valuation of a stockholder's interest as a "going concern" is necessary only when the board's proposal will alter the nature of the corporation through a merger. When a corporation merges with another corporation, the dissenting stockholder is entitled to the value of the company as a going concern because the nature of the corporation's future "concern" will be vastly different.[58] In a merger requiring an appraisal, the dissenting stockholder's share must be measured as a proportionate interest in a going concern because the proponents of the merger will realize the full intrinsic worth of the company rather than simply the market price of the stock. Thus, when a minority stockholder is confronted with a freeze-out merger, the Section 262 appraisal process will prevent the proponents of the merger from "reaping a windfall" by placing the full value of the company as a going concern into the merged entity while compensating the dissenting stockholder with discounted consideration.[59]

---

[53] [48] 56 Del. Laws, ch. 50.

[54] [49] 60 Del. Laws, ch. 371.

[55] [50] *See Weinberger*, 457 A.2d at 703.

[56] [51] Section 262(b)(1) denies appraisal rights to stockholders of a merging corporation if their stock is listed on a national securities exchange, interdealer quotation system, or held of record by more than 2,000 holders. 8 Del. C. § 262(b)(1). Similarly, under Section 262(b)(2)(c), those same stockholders are not afforded an appraisal right for cash they receive "in lieu of fractional shares" of the stock. 8 Del. C. § 262(b)(2)(c).

[57] [52] 657 A.2d 254, 258 (Del. 1995); *see also* WARD et al. *supra* n.13 § 262.1 ("Delaware recognizes the stockholders' appraisal right only in the case of a merger or consolidation."); *see also Glassman*, 777 A.2d at 247 (discussing short-form mergers authorized by Title 8, Section 253 of the Delaware Code and noting that appraisal is the appropriate remedy for the inability to block the transaction).

[58] [53] *See Paskill Corp. v. Alcoma Corp.*, 747 A.2d 549, 553 (Del. 2000) (discussing a recent analysis that justifies appraisal rights as a method by which proponents of a merger are forced to internalize the net benefits and costs of engaging in a "risk altering transaction") (quoting Peter V. Letsou, *The Role of Appraisal in Corporate Law*, 39 B.C. L. REV. 1121, 1123-24 (1998)).

[59] [54] *See Cavalier Oil*, 564 A.2d at 1145 ("[T]o fail to accord to a minority shareholder the full

Avaya will not capture its full going-concern value in the Reverse/Forward Split. As the Vice Chancellor noted, if the cashed-out stockholders were awarded the value of the company as a going concern, they, rather than the corporation, would receive a windfall. The cashed-out stockholders could capture the full proportionate value of the fractional interest, return to the market and buy the reissued stock at the market price, and realize the going concern value a second time should Avaya ever merge or otherwise become subject to a change of control transaction.[60]

CONCLUSION

The judgment of the Court of Chancery is affirmed.

In the aftermath of the 2008 Credit Crisis, the reverse stock split technique was utilized by financial institutions whose share prices had dropped precipitously. For example, Citigroup Inc. split each of its 10 outstanding shares of common stock into one share, and American International Group, Inc. effected a one-for-twenty reverse split, thus causing the market price of the remaining outstanding shares to increase substantially.

§ 6.03 PURCHASE BY A CORPORATION OF ITS OWN SHARES

[A] State Statutory Provisions

The leading case of *Trevor v. Whitworth*[61] established as the law of England the rule that a corporation could not properly go into the market and purchase its own shares. If it bought them for resale it would be "trafficking in shares" rather than engaging in the business for which it was chartered. If it bought them for retirement it would be unlawfully reducing capital without the court approval required by the Companies Act.

Trevor was not long followed in the United States. American statutes and decisions today generally sanction a corporate purchase of its own shares if made "out of surplus" or "out of earned surplus," or forbid it only if capital is impaired or the purchase will impair the capital. Where shares are by their terms redeemable (as are most preferred issues) their purchase if generally permitted not only out of surplus but out of capital as well, unless at the time of purchase the corporation is insolvent (i.e., unable to meet its debts as they mature in the ordinary course of business), or the purchase will render it insolvent.[62]

---

proportionate value of his shares imposes a penalty for lack of control, and unfairly enriches the majority shareholder who may reap a windfall from the appraisal process by cashing out a dissenting shareholder, a clearly undesirable result.").

60 [55] *Applebaum*, 805 A.2d at 217.

61 [1] 12 App. Cas. 400 (1887).

62 [2] Typical of the modern statutory approach are § 513 of the N.Y. Bus. Corp. Law and § 5 of the

Israels, *Corporate Purchase of its Own Share — Are There New Overtones?*, 50 CORNELL L. REV. 620 (1965)

A purchase by a corporation of its own shares results in a distribution to a holder of its equity securities; accordingly, such a transaction is generally subject to the statutory restrictions on the payment of dividends. Those restrictions are designed to offer some protection to the creditors of the corporation.

An example of statutory authorization of and restrictions on the acquisition by a corporation of its own shares is Section 513 of the New York Business Corporation Law, Section 1.07, *supra*.

[B] Other State Law Issues

HECKMANN v. AHMANSON
California Court of Appeal
214 Cal. Rptr. 177 (1985)

JOHNSON, J.

Plaintiffs, stockholders in Walt Disney Productions, are suing to recover the payoff in the greenmailing[63] of Disney. Defendants are the Disney directors who paid the greenmail and the "Steinberg Group"[64] to whom the money, approximately $325 million, was paid.

Plaintiffs obtained a preliminary injunction which, in effect, imposes a trust on the profit from the Disney-Steinberg transaction, approximately $60 million, and requires the Steinberg Group to render periodic accountings of the disposition of the entire proceeds. The Steinberg Group appeals from this preliminary injunction. We affirm.

As will be discussed more fully below, if plaintiffs prove the Steinberg Group

---

ABA-ALI Model Bus. Corp. Act (1960). These statutes cover both of the aspects mentioned and also permit purchases for the purpose of eliminating fractional shares, collecting or compromising indebtedness due the corporation or in satisfaction of the appraisal rights of shareholders dissenting from a merger, consolidation or material amendment to the certificate of incorporation. Older New York cases cast doubt upon the enforceability of the corporation's contractual obligation to purchase its own shares for possible lack of "mutuality" because there might be no available surplus when the obligation matured. N.Y. Bus. Corp. Law § 514 specifically overrules these cases, stating the rule in precisely opposite terms: the obligation is specifically enforceable to the extent that "at the time for performance" the purchase would be proper under § 513.

63 [1] A greenmailer creates the threat of a corporate takeover by purchasing a significant amount of the company's stock. He then sells the shares back to the company at a premium when its executives, in fear of their jobs, agree to buy him out. For further discussion of greenmail see, Lowenstein, *Pruning Deadwood in Hostile Takeovers: A Proposal for Legislation*, (1983) 83 COLUM. L. REV. 249, 311 & fn. 249; Greene & Junewicz, *A Reappraisal of Current Regulation of Mergers and Acquisitions*, (1984) 132 U. OF PA. L. REV. 647, 706-707.

64 [2] The "Steinberg Group" consists of defendants, Saul P. Steinberg, Reliance Financial Services Corporation, Reliance Group, Inc., Reliance Group Holdings, Inc., Reliance Insurance Company, Reliance Insurance Company of New York, United Pacific Insurance Company, United Pacific Life Insurance Company, and United Pacific Insurance Company of New York.

breached a fiduciary duty to the corporation and its shareholders in the sale of stock to the corporation the plaintiffs would be entitled to a constructive trust upon the profits of that sale. Plaintiffs have established a reasonable probability of proving breach of fiduciary duties by the Steinberg Group. The trial court could reasonably conclude from the evidence a preliminary injunction was necessary to prevent the dissipation or disappearance of the profit during the pendency of the action and the balance of hardships involved in granting or denying the injunction incline in plaintiffs' favor.

FACTS AND PROCEEDINGS BELOW

In March 1984 the Steinberg Group purchased more than two million shares of Disney stock. Probably interpreting this as the opening shot in a takeover war, the Disney directors countered with an announcement Disney would acquire Arvida Corporation for $200 million in newly-issued Disney stock and assume Arvida's $190 million debt.[65] The Steinberg Group countered this move with a stockholders' derivative action in federal court to block the Arvida transaction. Nonetheless, on June 6, 1984, the Arvida transaction was consummated.

Undeterred by its failure to halt Disney's purchase of Arvida, the Steinberg Group proceeded to acquire some two million additional shares of Disney stock, increasing its ownership position to approximately 12 percent of the outstanding Disney shares. On June 8, 1984, the Steinberg Group advised Disney's directors of its intention to make a tender offer for 49 percent of the outstanding shares at $67.50 a share and its intention to later tender for the balance at $72.50 a share. The director's response was swift. On the evening of the same day, the directors proposed Disney repurchase all the stock held by the Steinberg Group. Agreement was reached on June 11.

Under the agreement with the Steinberg Group, Disney purchased all the stock held by the group for $297.4 million and reimbursed the estimated costs incurred in preparing the tender offer, $28 million, for a total of $325.4 million, or about $77 per share. The Steinberg Group garnered a profit of about $60 million. In return, the Steinberg Group agreed not to purchase Disney stock and to dismiss its individual causes of action in the Arvida litigation. It did not dismiss the derivative claims.

Disney borrowed the entire sum necessary to repurchase its shares. This transaction, coupled with the debt assumed in the Arvida purchase, increased Disney's total indebtedness to $866 million, two-thirds of Disney's entire share-holder equity. Upon the announcement of its agreement with the Steinberg Group, the price of Disney stock dropped below $50 per share. Thus, the Steinberg Group received a price 50 percent above the market price following the transaction.

The gravamen of the action against the Steinberg Group is that it used its tender

---

[65] [3] Like the puff fish, a corporate delicacy will often attempt to avoid being swallowed up by making itself appear less attractive to a potential predator. *See* Lowenstein, *supra*, at p. 313; Nathan & Sobel, *Corporate Stock Repurchases in the Context of Unsolicited Takeover Bids*, (1980) 35 Bus. Lawyer 1545, 1547 & fn. 2; Rosenzweig, *The Legality of "Lock-Ups" [etc.]*, (1983) 10 Sec. Reg. Law J. 291, 299; Prentice, *Target Board Abuse of Defensive Tactics [etc.]*, (1983) J. of Corp. Law 337, 341, 343; Greene & Junewicz, *supra*, 132 U. Pa. L. Rev. at p. 702.

offer and the Arvida litigation to obtain a premium price for its shares in violation of its fiduciary duties to Disney and the other shareholders. The complaint seeks, among other things, rescission of Disney's repurchase agreement with the Steinberg Group, an accounting and a constructive trust upon all funds the Steinberg Group received from Disney.

After due notice and hearing, the trial court issued a preliminary injunction enjoining the Steinberg Group from transferring, investing or disposing of the profit[66] from its sale of Disney stock except in accordance with the standards applicable to a prudent trustee under Civil Code section 2261. The injunction also requires the Steinberg Group to notify plaintiffs and the court of every change in the form or vehicle of investment of the entire proceeds of the repurchase agreement. The injunction became effective upon plaintiffs' posting an undertaking in the sum of $1 million.

DISCUSSION

. . .

II. Plaintiffs Demonstrated a Reasonable Probability of Success on the Merits Entitling Them to a Constructive Trust upon the Profits the Steinberg Group Received from Its Sale of Disney Stock.

A. Liability of the Steinberg Group as an Aider and Abettor of the Disney Directors' Breach of Fiduciary Duty.

Although we have found no case in which a greenmailer was ordered to return his ill-gotten gains, precedent for such a judgment exists in California law.

In *Jones v. H. F. Ahmanson & Co.* (1969)1 Cal. 3d 93, 108-109 [81 Cal. Rptr. 592, 460 P.2d 464], our Supreme Court adopted the shareholders' Magna Carta set forth in *Pepper v. Litton* (1939) 308 U.S. 295 [84 L. Ed. 28, 60 S. Ct. 238]: "A director is a fiduciary. . . . So is a dominant or controlling stockholder or group of stockholders. . . . Their powers are powers of trust. . . . 'He who is in such a fiduciary position cannot serve himself first and his cestuis second. He cannot manipulate the affairs of his corporation to their detriment and in disregard of the standards of common decency and honesty. . . . He cannot use his power for his personal advantage and to the detriment of the stockholders. . . . For that power is at all times subject to the equitable limitation that it may not be exercised for the aggrandizement, preference, or advantage of the fiduciary to the exclusion or detriment of the cestuis. Where there is a violation of these principles, equity will undo the wrong or intervene to prevent its consummation.' " (*Id.*, at pp. 306-311 [84 L. Ed. at pp. 289-292].) The ultimate question "is whether or not under all the

---

66 [4] The profit, for purposes of the preliminary injunction, was defined as the difference paid by defendants for the stock, approximately $63.25 per share, and the total amount received under the repurchase agreement, approximately $77.50 per share, together with income earned on that amount from the date of receipt. This totals approximately $60 million.

circumstances the transaction carries the earmarks of an arm's length bargain." (*Id.*, at pp. 306307 [84 L. Ed. at p. 289].)

Ahmanson involved a scheme in which the majority stockholders set up a holding company in a manner which made the minority shares unmarketable. (1 Cal. 3d at p. 114.) The court held the facts alleged in the complaint stated a cause of action for breach of fiduciary duty. "[D]efendants chose a course of action in which they used their control of the Association to obtain an advantage not made available to all stockholders. They did so without regard to the resulting detriment to the minority stockholders and in the absence of any compelling business purpose." (1 Cal. 3d at p. 114.)

While there may be many valid reasons why corporate directors would purchase another company or repurchase the corporation's shares, the naked desire to retain their positions of power and control over the corporation is not one of them.[67] (*See Anderson v. Albert & J. M. Anderson Mfg. Co.* (1950) 325 Mass. 343 [90 N.E.2d 541, 544]; *Bennett v. Propp* (1962) 41 Del. Ch. 14 [187 A.2d 405, 408]; *Schilling v. Belcher* (5th Cir. 1978) 582 F.2d 995, 1003-1005 [Florida law]; 1 Ballantine & Sterling, Cal Corporation Laws (4th ed. 1984) § 143.02, subd. (d), pp. 8-58-59; Lynch & Steinberg, *The Legitimacy of Defensive Tactics In Tender Offers* (1979) 64 CORNELL L. REV. 901, 914-915.)

If the Disney directors breached their fiduciary duty to the stockholders, the Steinberg Group could be held jointly liable as an aider and abettor. The Steinberg Group knew it was reselling its stock at a price considerably above market value to enable the Disney directors to retain control of the corporation. It knew or should have known Disney was borrowing the $325 million purchase price. From its previous dealings with Disney, including the Arvida transaction, it knew the increased debt load would adversely affect Disney's credit rating and the price of its stock. If it were an active participant in the breach of duty and reaped the benefit, it cannot disclaim the burden. (*Gray v. Sutherland* (1954) 124 Cal. App. 2d 280, 290 [268 Cal. Rptr. 754]; *Bancroft-Whitney Co. v. Glen* (1966) 64 Cal. 2d 327, 353 [49 Cal. Rptr. 825, 411 P.2d 921, 24 A.L.R.3d 795].) "Where there is a common plan or design to commit a tort, all who participate are jointly liable whether or not they do the wrongful 2cts." (*Certified Grocers of California, Ltd. v. San Gabriel Valley Bank* (1983) 150 Cal. App. 3d 281, 289 [197 Cal. Rptr. 710.)

The Steinberg Group contends there was no evidence presented to the trial court that the repurchase agreement was motivated by the Disney directors' desire to perpetuate their own control instead of a good faith belief the corporate interest would be served thereby. (*See Fairchild v. Bank of America* (1961) 192 Cal. App. 2d 252, 256 [13 Cal. Rptr. 491]; *cf. Klaus v. Hi-Shear Corporation* (9th Cir. 1975) 528 F.2d 225, 233 with *Kors v. Carey* (1960) 39 Del. Ch. 47 [158 A.2d 136] and *Cheff v. Mathes* (1964) 41 Del. Ch. 494 [199 A.2d 548].)

At this point in the litigation, it is not necessary the court be presented with a "smoking gun." We believe the evidence presented to the court was sufficient to demonstrate a probability of success on the merits. The acts of the Disney directors

[67] [5] We recognize the Disney directors were not parties to the proceedings on the preliminary injunction nor this appeal and have not had the opportunity to tell their side of the story.

— and particularly their timing — are difficult to understand except as defensive strategies against a hostile takeover. The Steinberg Group began acquiring Disney stock in March 1984. In May 1984 the Disney directors announced Disney would acquire Arvida and its $190 million debt. Trying to make the target company appear less attractive is a well-recognized defensive tactic by a board seeking to retain control. (*See* fn. 3, *supra.*) Furthermore, the Steinberg Group announced its tender offer for 49 percent of the outstanding Disney shares on June 8,1984. Immediately following this announcement, the Disney directors began negotiations to repurchase two days later. (*Cf. Joseph E. Seagram & Sons, Inc. v. Abrams* (S.D.N.Y. 1981) 510 F. Supp. 860, 861-862.)

Once it is shown a director received a personal benefit from the transaction, which appears to be the case here, the burden shifts to the director to demonstrate not only the transaction was entered in good faith, but also to show its inherent fairness from the viewpoint of the corporation and those interested therein. (*Lynch v. Cook* (1983) 148 Cal. App. 3d 1072, 1082 [196 Cal. Rptr. 544]; and see, Rosenzweig, *supra*, at p. 294.) The only evidence presented by the Disney directors was the conclusory statement of one of its attorneys that "[t]he Disney objective in purchasing [the] stock was to avoid the damage to Disney and its shareholders which would have been the result of [the] announced tender offer." This vague assertion falls short of evidence of good faith and inherent fairness. (*Cf. Schilling v. Belcher, supra*, 582 A.2d at p. 1004; *Klaus v. Hi-Shear Corporation, supra*, 528 F.2d at p. 233.)

B. Liability of the Steinberg Group for Breach of Fiduciary Duty to the Disney Shareholders.

When the Steinberg Group filed suit against Disney to block Disney's purchase of Arvida it assumed a fiduciary duty to the other shareholders with respect to the derivative claims.

"A stockholder who institutes [a derivative suit] sues purely as a trustee to redress corporate injuries. He has the unquestioned right to sue, but it is in no sense his duty to sue. . . . He is a trustee pure and simple, seeking in the name of another a recovery for wrongs that have been committed against that other. His position in the litigation is in every legal sense the precise equivalent of that of the guardian ad litem." (*Whitten v. Dabney* (1915) 171 Cal. 621, 629, 630-631 [154 p. 312].) The United States Supreme Court set forth in strong terms the strict obligations of a plaintiff in a derivative suit: "[A] stockholder who brings suit on a cause of action derived from the corporation assumes a position, not technically as a trustee perhaps, but one of a fiduciary character. He sues, not for himself alone, but as representative of a class comprising all who are similarly situated. The interests of all in the redress of the wrongs are taken into his hands, dependent upon his diligence, wisdom and integrity. And while the stockholders have chosen the corporate director or manager, they have no such election as to a plaintiff who steps forward to represent them. He is a self-chosen representative and a volunteer champion." (*Cohen v. Beneficial Loan Corp.* (1949) 337 U.S. 541, 549 [69 S. Ct. 1221, 93 L. Ed. 1528,1538].)

One who assumes such a fiduciary role cannot abandon it for personal aggrandizement. (*Young v. Higbee Co.* (1945) 324 U.S. 204, 213 [65 S. Ct. 594, 89 L. Ed. 890, 898]; *Lemer v. Boise Cascade, Inc.* (1980) 107 Cal. App. 3d 1, 7 [165 Cal. Rptr. 555].) In the case before us plaintiffs have demonstrated a reasonable probability the Steinberg Group breached its fiduciary duty to the other shareholders by abandoning the Arvida litigation.

In its verified complaint in federal district court, Reliance Insurance Company, part of the Steinberg Group, alleged, among other things, that Disney's purchase of Arvida was contrary to sound business judgment and a waste of corporate assets since the purchase price was excessive, the purchase would erode Disney's profitability, substantially increase its debt load and make it more difficult and expensive for Disney to acquire the capital necessary to complete its current projects. It also claimed the Arvida purchase would depress the value of Disney common stock. In bringing the action, Reliance alleged it would fairly and adequately represent the interests of Disney and all other stockholder lots were similarly situated.

While distinguishable on narrow grounds, *Young v. Higbee Co.* is a useful precedent in the case before us. In *Young*, two preferred shareholders of the Higbee Company filed objections to the company's reorganization plan which favored junior creditors over preferred stockholders. Plaintiffs lost in the district court and filed an appeal. While the appeal was pending in the circuit court, plaintiffs sold their appeal rights to the junior creditors for about six times the value of their preferred stock. The junior creditors proceeded to dismiss the appeal. Young, a preferred shareholder, sued the turn-coat plaintiffs for an accounting. The plaintiffs, now defendants, argued they had appealed only in their own names, not on behalf of the class of preferred stockholders and, therefore, they owed no duty to anyone but themselves. (324 U.S. at pp. 206-209 [89 L. Ed. at pp. 894-96].)

The Supreme Court rejected this argument and held a trust would be imposed on the proceeds from the sale of the appeal rights for the benefit of the remaining preferred shareholders. (*Id.*, at p. 212 [89 L. Ed. at p. 897].) The court reasoned, "[E]ven though their objection to confirmation [of the reorganization plan] contained no formal class suit allegations, the success or failure of the appeal was bound to have a substantial effect on the interests of all other preferred stockholders. The liability of one who assumes a determining position over the rights of others must turn on something more substantial than mere formal allegations in a complaint." (*Id.*, at p. 209 [89 L. Ed. at pp. 895-96].) Although these "plaintiffs" could not be compelled to appeal nor to prosecute an appeal already taken contrary to their own interests (*id.*, at p. 212 [89 L. Ed. at p. 897]), "[t]hey cannot avail themselves of the statutory privilege of litigation for the interest of a class and then shake off their self-assumed responsibilities to others by a simple announcement that henceforth they will trade in the rights of others for their own aggrandizement." (*id.*, at p. 213.)

The Steinberg Group stresses that in Young the claims of the plaintiffs were inseparable from those of the other preferred stockholders who, upon dismissal of the appeal, were bound, under the doctrine of res judicata, to the judgment of the lower court. Here, the Steinberg Group sued on its individual claims as well as derivative claims and the sale of its standing as derivative plaintiff does not bar other shareholders from litigating those same derivative claims.

We do not believe the result in Young stemmed from its unusual facts. Rather, it was consistent with a long-established rule of equity, the rule of individual loyalty, which prevents a fiduciary from profiting at the expense of his beneficiary. (324 U.S. at pp. 213, 214 [89 L. Ed. at p. 898]; and see *Meinhard v. Salmon* (1928) 249 N.Y. 458 [164 N.E. 545, 546] [Cardozo, J.].) Furthermore, there are more similarities than dissimilarities between Young and the case before us. In both cases the ersatz class representatives sold their standing to pursue the class claims in exchange for a substantial profit to persons with adverse interests. In both cases the plaintiffs did not actually dismiss their actions. Instead, they sold their rights to persons with adverse interests knowing those persons would move to dismiss and with the clear intention of aiding them to do so. In both cases the plaintiffs not only profited but, as we explain below, the other shareholders were damaged by the plaintiffs self-dealing.

Despite its dire warnings about the Arvida acquisition and its promise to fairly and adequately represent the interests of Disney and its shareholders, the Steinberg Group abandoned the federal litigation just two weeks after it was filed. The Steinberg Group sold all of its Disney shares to Disney at a $60 million profit, dismissed its individual claims in the Arvida litigation and promised not to oppose any motion to dismiss the derivative claims.

A trier of fact could reasonably find the Steinberg Group did not fairly and adequately represent the Disney shareholders but, instead, used its position as class representative for its own financial advantage.

The Steinberg Group abandoned its derivative claims when it sold its stock back to the corporation. Once a derivative plaintiff sells its stock, it no longer has standing to prosecute the derivative claims on behalf of the remaining shareholders. (*See Lewis v. Knutson* (5th Cir. 1983) 699 F.2d 230, 238 and cases cited therein; 7A Wright & Miller, Federal Practice and Procedure (1972) § 1839, p. 437.)

It is argued the Steinberg Group breached no fiduciary duty in merely dismissing its individual claims and selling its stock. It did not dismiss the derivative claims; and the sale of stock, even though to the defendants in the action, is not a "compromise" within the meaning of rule 23.1 of the Federal Rules of Civil Procedure. (*See Malcolm v. Cities Service Co.* (D. Del. 1942) 2 F.R.D. 405, 407.)[68] A current shareholder would appear to have the right to intervene in the derivative claims under rule 24 subdivision (a)(2). (*Malcolm, ibid.*)

The foregoing argument avoids the issue. The Steinberg Group could not have unilaterally dismissed or compromised the derivative claims even if it wanted to. (*See* rule 23.1, *supra.*) Therefore, the fact it did not do so is not dispositive of plaintiffs' claim of breach of fiduciary duty. In *Shelton v. Pargo, Inc.* (4th Cir. 1978) 582 F.2d 1298, the court recognized settlement of the class representative's individual claims may indeed affect the fulfillment of the fiduciary duty owed the class.

"The parties, who are settling their individual claims, are not merely members of

---

[68] [6] The court, in Malcolm, did not address the question whether, in selling her standing as a class representative to the defendants, plaintiff breached a fiduciary duty to the other shareholders.

a putative class; they are the representative parties, without whose presence as plaintiffs the case could not proceed as a class action. Had the appellees been other than the representative parties, there would be no objection to a voluntary settlement of their claim. But, by asserting a representative role on behalf of the alleged class, these appellees voluntarily accepted a fiduciary obligation towards the members of the putative class they thus have undertaken to represent. They may not abandon the fiduciary role they assumed at will or by agreement with the [defendant], if prejudice to the members of the class they claimed to represent would result or it they have improperly used the class action procedure for their personal aggrandizement." (*Id.*, at p. 1305; fns. omitted.) The court cited as authority, among other cases, *Cohen v. Beneficial Loan Corp., supra*, and *Young v. Higbee Co., supra*, 324 U.S. 204. (*See also Rothenberg v. Security Management Co., Inc.* (11th Cir. 1982) 667 F.2d 958, 961; *Blum v. Morgan Guaranty Trust Co. of New York* (5th Cir. 1976) 539 F.2d 1388, 1390; and *G.A. Enterprises, Inc. v. Leisure Living Commun., Inc.* (1st Cir. 1975) 517 F.2d 24, 27.) These cases hold a plaintiff breaches the duty to fairly and adequately represent the other shareholders when he uses the derivative action as leverage to achieve his own personal objectives.

In *Young*, the shareholders were damaged by loss of the right to appeal from an unfavorable judgment. In the case at bench, the Steinberg Group not only sold its right to pursue the derivative claims, it affirmatively promised not to oppose dismissal of those claims. This agreement not only undercuts the merits of the suit, it could be interpreted to mean the Steinberg Group will refuse to cooperate with a potential substitute plaintiff by sharing informal discovery, legal research and the like. Thus, even assuming another shareholder picks up the gauntlet, the cause has become sidetracked and possibly more difficult and expensive due to the action of the Steinberg Group. Furthermore, as shown below, the stockholders and Disney are in a worse position financially than before the Steinberg Group intervened into their corporate affairs.

The duty of the plaintiff in a derivative suit is analogous to the duty of care owed by a volunteer rescuer to the rescuee. It is significant that both the California and United States Supreme Court focused on the volunteer status of a plaintiff in a derivative action, a "volunteer champion" in the words of Justice Jackson. (*Cohen v. Beneficial Loan Corp., supra*, 337 U.S. at p. 549 [93 L. Ed. at p. 1538]; and *see Whitten v. Dabney, supra*, 171 Cal. at p. 629.) Under tort law principles one who, having no initial duty to do so, undertakes to come to the aid of another is under a duty to exercise due care in performance and is liable if failure to exercise such care increases the risk of harm or the harm is suffered because of the other's reliance upon the undertaking. (*Williams v. State of California* (1983) 34 Cal. 3d 18, 23 [192 Cal. Rptr. 233, 664 P.2d 137]; Rest. 2d Torts, § 323, p. 135.) Although we are not concerned here with physical harm, we believe the analogy apt.

In filing its derivative suit, the Steinberg Group volunteered to prevent Disney from acquiring the large debt associated with Arvida "which," it alleged, "could materially diminish Disney earnings and . . . threaten its long-term profitability." Instead of preventing the Arvida acquisitions, the Steinberg Group bailed out of the lawsuit, and out of Disney, with $325 million of Disney's money. According to plaintiffs, Disney borrowed the entire amount used to buy off the Steinberg Group. This loan together with the $190 million Arvida debt increased Disney's total indebtedness to about $830 million compared to about $585 million before the Steinberg Group came on the scene. This increased debt load resulted in a lowering of Disney's credit rating and a plunge of 16 points in the price of Disney stock from 65 1/8, the trading day before the repurchase agreement, to 49 1/2 a week later.

Thus, it can be argued, with a reasonable probability of success, the Disney shareholders are worse off after the intervention of their "volunteer champion" then they were before. They are like the citizens of a town whose volunteer fire department quits fighting the fire and sells its equipment to the arsonist who set it (who obtains the purchase price by setting fire to the building next door).

We conclude, therefore, plaintiffs have established a reasonable probability of success on the claim the Steinberg Group breached its fiduciary duty as a plaintiff in the stockholders' derivative action.[69]

Having already found adequate grounds to support the preliminary injunction, we need not address the novel question whether greenmailing is an unfair business practice within the meaning of section 17200.

The record is inadequate at this time on the question whether the Steinberg Group was a controlling shareholder when it sold its stock to Disney. Although it never owned more than about 12 percent of the outstanding Disney stock this is not determinative of control. The question, a factual one, is what amount of influence it could exert on the corporation by reason of its holdings. (*See* Berle, *supra*, at p. 630; Brudney, *supra*, at p. 1073, fn. 2.)

DISPOSITION

The array of law and facts advanced by plaintiffs evaluated against defendants' countercontentions demonstrates a reasonable probability that plaintiffs will be successful although, we stress, the final decision must await trial and a trial might well produce a different result. As to hardship, we believe the trial court reasonably concluded detriment to the plaintiffs if the proceeds and profits are dissipated or untraceable exceeds any hardship to the Steinberg Group in complying with the investment and accounting provisions of the preliminary injunction.

The order granting a preliminary injunction is affirmed.

NOTE

For an example of a state "anti-greenmail" statute, see section 513(c) of the New York Business Corporation Law in § 1.08, *supra*.

---

[69] [7] Plaintiffs also contend the Steinberg Group violated the fiduciary duty owed by controlling shareholders to the other shareholders, (*see, e.g., Jones v. H. F. Ahmanson & Co., supra*, 1 Cal. 3d at pp. 109-111; Brudney, *Equal Treatment of Shareholders in Corporate Distributions and Reorganizations* (1983) 71 Cal. L. Rev. 1072, 1106-1114; Berle, *The Price of Power: Sale of Corporate Control* (1965) 50 Cornell L.Q. 628) and that it engaged in unfair business practices in violation of Business & Professions Code section 17200.

IN RE SPM MFG. CORP.

United States Bankruptcy Court, District of Massachusetts
163 B.R. 411 (1994)

Opinion

This case raises the following question: If a corporation in sound financial condition delivers a promissory note for the purchase of its own stock, should the balance due on the note be equitably subordinated to other unsecured debt when the corporation later becomes insolvent and goes into bankruptcy years later? The question has particular significance for close corporations because they frequently make such stock purchases at the death or retirement of a principal stockholder. It also involves a conflict between the Bankruptcy Code and Massachusetts corporate law. I answer the question in the affirmative.

I. Facts

The Shaine Foundation (the "Claimant") has filed an unsecured claim in the sum of $542,246.96. The Official Unsecured Creditors' Committee (the "Committee") objects to the claim, contending it should be subordinated under principles of equitable subordination. Although subordination should be litigated in an adversary proceeding, Fed. R. Bankr. P. 7001, the Claimant does not raise this point of procedure. I elide it for this reason and also because there is no factual dispute suitable to resolution in an adversary proceeding.

The claim is for the balance due under a note dated May 27, 1982 for $662,925, which SPM Manufacturing Corporation (the "Debtor") delivered in connection with redemption of its stock owned by the Claimant. The Claimant is a charitable trust controlled by members of the Shaine family, who are also the Debtor's stockholders, directors and officers. In 1978, a member of the Shaine family bequeathed the Claimant shares of the Debtor's capital stock. In May of 1982, the Claimant sold to the Debtor 3,240 shares of the Debtor's preferred stock, at $30 per share, and 1,500 shares of the Debtor's Class B Common stock, at $377.15 per share, delivering the note in question for the full purchase price. The Debtor retained the purchased shares as treasury stock. The note, which bears interest at the rate of 12% per year, is payable over 15 years in equal monthly installments of $7,956.26. It contains no subordination provisions, and as a result of payment default is now payable in full.

The Debtor, a Massachusetts corporation, was in the business of manufacturing items such as calendars and wedding albums, with a main office in Holyoke, Massachusetts. The Debtor's certified financial statements of December 31, 1982 disclose a net worth of $2,988,916 after deduction of $1,679,682 for redeemed shares including the shares purchased through delivery of the note. During 1982, the Debtor earned $433,957, net of taxes, and in 1983 it earned $267,037, net of taxes, after having recently changed to a LIFO (last-in, first-out) system of accounting. If the Debtor has continued to report its income on a FIFO (first-in, first-out) basis, its 1992 net income would have been $583,855. At the end of 1982, the Debtor's current assets exceeded its current liabilities by $3,144,294. It is now in liquidation under chapter 7. It is without surplus and unable to pay its debts in full even if this claim is subordinated.

II. Principles of Equitable Subordination

The Committee requests subordination of the claim under principles of equitable subordination. Those principles, applicable only in bankruptcy, are traditionally based upon inequitable conduct of a claimant who is an insider of the debtor.[70] Subordination is not warranted by the mere fact the claimant is a stockholder; the claimant must have been guilty of some type of wrongful action.[71]

The Committee asserts no inequitable conduct on the part of the Claimant or members of the Shaine family who control the Claimant. I assume for purposes of this opinion that the purchase transaction is not voidable under fraudulent transfer law and complied with Massachusetts corporate law. Based upon the circumstances existing in 1982, the redemption does not appear to have jeopardized the Debtor's existence.

A corporation's redemption of its own stock is in essence a dividend for which the corporation received no consideration.[72] When the transaction is so viewed, an argument could perhaps be mounted that the act of creating redemption debt is itself inequitable. But this would prove too much in light of the important role played by stock redemptions in the world of close corporations. And we are dealing with a transaction which was presumptively valid under fraudulent transfer law and corporate law.

The Committee relies solely on the fact the claim arises from redemption of the Debtor's stock. Whether this is sufficient to equitably subordinate the claim requires a close examination of section 510(c) of the Bankruptcy Code and its legislative history.

Section 510(c) provides that "the court may . . . under principles of equitable subordination, subordinate for purposes of distribution all or part of an allowed claim to all or part of another allowed claim. . . ."[73] The House report states: "This section is intended to codify case law, such as *Pepper v. Litton* . . . and *Taylor v. Standard Gas and Electric Co.* . . . and is not intended to limit the court's power in any way. The bankruptcy court will remain a court of equity."[74] This legislative history could be read to indicate a court is authorized to subordinate a claim only by reason of the claimant's misconduct under facts such as those present in *Pepper* and *Taylor*. On the other hand, the report's disavowal of any intent to limit the

---

[70] [1] *Pepper v. Litton*, 308 U.S. 295 (1939); *Taylor v. Standard Gas & Electric Co.*, 306 U.S. 307 (1939); *Benjamin v. Diamond (In re Mobile Steel Co.)*, 563 F.2d 692 (5th Cir. 1977).

[71] [2] *Comstock v. Group of Institutional Investors*, 335 U.S. 211 (1948).

[72] [3] *E.g., Consove v. Cohen (In re Roco Corp.)*, 701 F.2d 978, 982 (1st Cir. 1983); *Gold v. Lippman (In re Flying Mailmen Serv., Inc.)*, 539 F.2d 866, 870 (2d Cir. 1976); *Robinson v. Wangemann*, 75 F.2d 756, 757 (5th Cir. 1935).

[73] [4] 11 U.S.C. § 510(c) (1988).

[74] [5] H.R. Rep. No. 595, 95th Cong., 1st Sess. 359 (1977) reprinted in, 1978 U.S.C.C.A.N. 5963, 6315.

court's equitable powers might indicate Congress did not intend to restrict the grounds for equitable subordination.

The Senate report is equally ambiguous on this point. It says: "These principles [of equitable subordination] are defined by case law, and have generally indicated that a claim may normally be subordinated only if its holder is guilty of misconduct."[75] Statements made on the floor of the House and Senate go much further. They say:

> It is intended that the term "principles of equitable subordination" follow existing case law and leave to the courts the development of that principle. To date, under existing case law, a claim is generally subordinated only if [the] holder of such claim is guilty of inequitable conduct, or the claim itself is of a status susceptible to subordination, such as a penalty or a claim for damages arising from the purchase or sale of a security of the debt.[76]

Here we have an express indication of Congressional intent that courts have the power to subordinate a claim because of its nature or origin. Floor statements made by individual members of Congress are of course less authoritative than committee reports. But the committee reports here are ambiguous. And there was no conference report. Statements made on the floor were a substitute for a conference report. Taking all this into consideration, I conclude from these references to penalty claims and security claims that Congress intended courts to have the power to equitable subordinate claims because of their nature or origin. Decisions equitably subordinating penalties or punitive damage claims in chapter 11 have come to this conclusion based on the same legislative history.[77] They reject the need for creditor misconduct and subordinate such claims because to allow them parity with other claims would penalize creditors for the debtor's misconduct.[78]

Several decisions rendered under the prior Bankruptcy Act subordinated redemption debt by reason of its source and without reliance on state statues regulating stock redemptions, which are discussed later. *Robinson v. Wangemann*[79] is perhaps the best known of this genre. The court stressed that redemption is merely a method for a corporation to make a distribution to a stockholder, and the corporation acquires nothing of value in return. In subordinating the claim because of its source, the court said:

The assets of a corporation are the common pledge of its creditors, and stockholders are not entitled to receive any part of them unless creditors are paid in full. When such a transaction is had regardless of the good faith of the parties, it

---

[75] [6] S. Rep. No. 989, 95th Cong. 2d Sess. 74 (1978), reprinted in, 1978 U.S.C.C.A.N. 5787, 5860.

[76] [7] 124 Cong Rec. H11,095 (daily ed. Sept. 20, 1978); S17,412 (daily ed. Oct. 6, 1978), reprinted in, 1978 U.S.C.C.A.N. 5787, 5963, 6315, 6436.

[77] [8] *E.g., In re Virtual Network Services Corp.*, 902 F.2d 1246 (7th Cir. 1990).

[78] [9] *Id. See also Burden v. United States (In re Burden)*, 917 F.2d 115 (3d Cir. 1990) (court persuaded by floor statements that Congress intended courts to be able to equitably subordinate tax penalty claim in chapter 13 by reason of the nature of the claim; case remanded for trial court to consider equities, which need not include claimant misconduct).

[79] [10] 75 F.2d 756 (5th Cir. 1935).

is essential to its validity that there be sufficient surplus to retire the stock, without prejudice to creditors, at the time payment is made out of assets. . . . It is necessary to a recovery that the corporation should be solvent and have sufficient surplus to prevent injury to creditors when the payment is actually made. The was an implied condition in the original note and the renewals.[80]

Robinson v. Wangemann is a policy statement that redemption debt must come behind general creditors on bankruptcy because of the priority creditors enjoy in bankruptcy over stockholders. Other courts, including the court of appeals of this circuit, also adopted this position under the Act.[81]

Decision under the Code have taken the same view. In *Liebowitz v. Columbia Packing Co.*,[82] the court believed it immaterial that the corporation was solvent or had sufficient surplus at the time the obligation to pay for the redeemed stock was incurred. The court equated a redemption claim with stockholder status, stating: "The underlying nature of the transaction survives, and the note remains and equity obligation."[83] Finding the debtor insolvent both when the redemption note became payable an d when the trustee's subordination claim was asserted, the court subordinated the note to all unsecured claims. The court made no mention of any applicable corporate redemption statute. It relied upon its powers under principles of equitable subordination, but without discussion of why wrongful conduct by the claimant was unnecessary. Some courts agree with *Liebowitz* that the origin of stock redemption debt justifies its equitable subordination.[84] Others decline to subordinate the debt on the ground equitable subordination requires misconduct on the part of the claimant.[85]

Subordination of redemption debt raises policy considerations which are similar to those present in the subordination of damage claims arising from the purchase or sale of the debtor's stock, such as a claim for violation of the securities laws in issuance of the stock. Section 510(b) of the Code expressly subordinates such security claims to the claims of other creditors.[86] In a case decided under the Prior Act, the Second Circuit subordinated claims for security law violation under principles of equitable subordination.[87] This reflects the thinking that only shareholders should bear the risk of fraud or other illegality in the issuance of shares.[88]

---

[80] [11] *Id.* at 757-58.

[81] [12] *E.g., In re Hawaii Corp.*, 694 F.2d 179 (9th Cir. 1982) (court stated it was following 9th circuit *McConnell* decision, but subordinated debt without reference to state statute, in reliance on *Robinson*); *Matthews Bros. v. Pullen*, 268 F.827, 828 (1st Cir. 1920) (court stating, without reference to any corporate statute, stockholder cannot through executory contract "cease to be a stockholder, and become a creditor, to share in competition with other creditors in the assets of the corporation when bankrupt.")

[82] [13] 56 B.R. 222 (D. Mass. 1985), *aff'd, per curiam*, 802 F.2d 439 (1st Cir. 1986).

[83] [14] *Id.* at 224.

[84] [15] *E.g., In re Dino & Artie's Automatic Transmission Co., Inc.*, 68 B.R. 264 (Bankr. S.D.N.Y. 1986).

[85] [16] *In re Stern-Slegman-Prins Co.*, 86 B.R. 994, 1000 (Bankr. W.D. Mo. 1988).

[86] [17] 11 U.S.C. § 510(b) (1988).

[87] [18] *Jezarian v. Raichle (In re Stirling Homex Corp.)*, 579 F.2d 206 (2d Cir. 1978), *cert. denied*, 439 U.S.1074 (1979).

[88] [19] H.R. Rep. No. 595, 95th Cong. 1st Sess. 194-96 (1977), reprinted in, 1978 U.S.C.C.A.N. 5787,

Assigning the risk to shareholders is justified on the ground that only shareholders have the ability to participate in profits.[89] Subordination of claims arising from purchase or sale of the debtor's stock is likened to subordination of stock to debt under the absolute priority rule.[90]

Much the same considerations justify subordination of redemption debt. Indeed, there is more reason for subordination of redemption debt than subordination of damage claims arising from stock purchase. A stock purchase claimant is attempting to recover only the cost of his investment, whereas a stock redemption claimant is usually seeking profit in the sale of the stock. A redemption claimant is usually seeking profit in the sale of the stock. A redemption claimant, moreover, is trying to recover what is essentially a liquidating dividend on his stock. And because of the absence of consideration, prior payments on the claim will have contributed to the debtor's financial collapse. I conclude that this claim must be equitably subordinated for these reasons.

The argument against subordination of redemption debt analogizes redemption on credit to redemption for cash coupled with a loan back to the corporation. If the case redemption and loan back would have been valid under corporate law and fraudulent transfer law, the argument runs, why should redemption debt be different?[91] The answer is two-fold. First, a redemption with an immediate loan back should be integrated into one transaction consisting of a redemption on credit, because the parties presumably contemplated both transactions from the beginning. Second, likening redemption on credit to a cash redemption and loan back misses the point. Loan debt is not priority which redemption debt and other debt should enjoy under principles of equitable subordination based upon their respective natures.

III. Massachusetts Corporate Law

Many courts look, at least initially, to state corporate law in passing upon the validity and priority of stock redemption claims in bankruptcy. Corporation statutes typically restrict the price of the redemption to the corporation's surplus, prohibiting redemption out of capital. In a redemption on credit, the courts examine the applicable statute to see if it prohibits payment, as well as purchase, out of capital. If the statute does prohibit payment out of capital, these courts subordinate the claim to all other claims.[92] In so interpreting the statute, the courts construe the

---

6154-6157. *See* John J. Slain & Homer Kripe, *The Interface Between Securities Regulation and Bankruptcy — Allocating the Risk of Illegal Securities Issuance Between Security Holders and the Issuer's Creditors*, 48 N.Y.U.L. Rev. 261 (1973).

[89] [20] *Id.*

[90] [21] *Id.*

[91] [22] *See* David R. Herwitz, *Installment Repurchase of Stock: Surplus Limitations*, 79 Harv. L. Rev. 303 (1965). *See also Wolff v. Heidritter Lumber Co.*, 12 N.J. Eq. 34, 163A. 140 (Ch. 1932) (upholding validity of redemption debt in corporation's liquidation because transaction equivalent in substance to permissible cash purchase with loan back to corporation).

[92] [23] *E.g., LaGrand Steel Products Co. v. Goldberg (In re Poole, McGonigle & Dick, Inc.)*, 796 F.2d 318 (9th Cir. 1986), *opinion amended*, 804 F.2d 576 (9th Cir. 1986) (statute prohibited purchase "or payment for" corporation's own shares when purchase "or payment" would make it insolvent); *Gold v.*

debtor's promise of payment to be conditional upon the debtor having sufficient surplus at the time of payment.[93] Other state statutes expressly look only to the corporation's condition at the time the obligation is incurred.[94]

The decisions reading state statutes to require surplus to be sufficient at the time payment is due can be misinterpreted. They do not necessarily mean the court would grant the claimant parity with general creditors if the statute required surplus to be sufficient only at the time of the purchase. The courts may have intended to apply the state surplus test merely as a preliminary step. In some of these decisions, the courts imply they would subordinate the redemption claim even if the state surplus test governed only the original purchase.[95]

Some decisions construe the applicable corporate statute to require only sufficient surplus at the time the obligation is incurred. In *In re Stern-Slegman-Prins Co.*,[96] for example, the statute permitted the "purchase" of a corporation's own shares, provided capital would not be impaired. The court concluded the statute applied only to the initial purchase, and declined to subordinate the debt in the corporation's subsequent bankruptcy.

Massachusetts has no statute requiring that the price of a stock redemption not exceed the corporation's surplus. Indeed, there is no Massachusetts statute expressly authorizing stock redemption. Massachusetts does, however, have statutes imposing liability upon stockholders and directors for redemptions made when the corporation is insolvent or which render the corporation insolvent.

The statute imposing liability upon stockholders impliedly grants a defense

---

Lippman (In re Flying Mailmen Service, Inc.), 539 F.2d 866 (2d Cir. 1976) (statute permitted purchase of own shares "except when currently the corporation is insolvent or would thereby be made insolvent"); *McConnell v. Butler*, 402 F.2d 362 (9th Cir. 1968) (statute permitted "payment" to extent of current earned surplus) (; *In re Trimble Co.*, 339 F.2d 838 (3d Cir. 1964) *appeal after remand*, 479 F.2d 103 (3d Cir. 1973) (statute unspecific on time purchase is measured against surplus; court construed it to apply to time of payment). *See also Mountain State Steel Foundries, Inc. v. C.I.R.*, 284 F.2d 737 (4th Cir. 1960) (statute permitted corporation to "use its funds" for purchase of own shares when this would not cause impairment of capital; court held interest deductions permissible so long as capital not impaired).

[93] [24] *Id.*

[94] [25] The Model Business Corp. Act, and the many state statutes patterned after it, prohibits a "distribution" (defined to include delivery of a promissory note) if after the distribution the corporation would be insolvent in either the bankruptcy or equity sense. Redemption debt is expressly placed on a parity with other debt. *See* Model Business Corp. Act § 6.40 (1984), 1 Model Business Corp. Act 474-75 (1988 & Supp. 1991). The Delaware statute validates a redemption obligation if at the time the obligation was incurred the corporation's capital "was not then impaired or did not thereby become impaired." DEL. CODE ANN. tit. 8, § 160 (1986 & Supp. 1994).

[95] [26] For example, in *LaGrand Steel Products Co. v. Goldberg (In re Poole, McGonigle & Dick, Inc.)*, 796 F.2d 318, 322-23 (9th Cir. 1986), the Ninth Circuit spoke of principles of equitable subordination and approved the line of decisions discussed earlier which subordinate redemption debt by reason of the debt's nature without regard to any state surplus test. In another case, in remanding for findings on the state surplus test, the court reserved decision on the "troublesome question whether equitable subordination of a former shareholder is appropriate even though local law permits the transaction and even thought there was not fraud or overreaching." *Reiner v. Washington Plate Glass Co., Inc.*, 711 F.2d 414, 417 (D.C. Cir. 1983).

[96] [27] 86 B.R. 994 (Bankr. W.D. Mo. 1988).

against payment of redemption debt if the statute's insolvency test is not met. It reads in pertinent part:

> Stockholders to whom a corporation makes any distribution, whether by way of dividend, repurchase or redemption of stock, or otherwise, except a distribution of stock of the corporation, if the corporation is, or is thereby rendered insolvent, shall be liable to the corporation for the amount of such distribution made, or for the amount of such distribution which exceeds that which could have been made without rendering the corporation insolvent, but in either event, only to the extent of the amount paid or distributed to them respectively. . . .

Mass. Gen. L. Ch. 156B, § 45.

The statute imposing liability upon directors is similar. It provides:

> If the corporation is insolvent or is rendered insolvent by any such distribution [whether by way of a dividend, repurchase or redemption of stock, or otherwise, except a distribution of stock of the corporation] . . . the directors who voted to authorize such distribution shall be jointly and severally liable to the corporation for the amount of such distribution made when the corporation is insolvent, or for the amount of such distribution which exceeds that which could have been made without rendering the corporation insolvent, but in either event only to the extent such distribution, or such excess, is not repaid to the corporation. In no event shall the directors who authorized any such distribution be liable under this section if such distribution could have been made without . . . rendering the corporation insolvent at the time when such distribution was authorized, although subsequent payment of such distribution or any part thereof causes such . . . insolvency.

Mass. Gen. L. Ch. 156B, § 61.

The stockholders statute is opaque on whether in a redemption for a promissory note the "distribution" is the note or the payments under it. The statute imposing liability on directors, on the other hand, distinguishes between (i) a "distribution" which "could have been made" without insolvency when it was "authorized," and (ii) subsequent "payment of such distribution" causing insolvency. In this context, the phrase "subsequent payment of such distribution" would seem to include payment under a promissory note. This second sentence was added in 1980.[97] Legislative history is lacking.

It is possible to conclude from the distinction section 61 makes between "payment" and "distribution" that "distribution" in section 45 on stockholder liability refers only to delivery of the promissory note, so that the corporation's insolvency at the time payment is due is immaterial to enforcement of the note. But consideration concerning director liability are different from those relevant to stockholder liability. There is obvious unfairness in imposing liability upon directors who authorized a redemption that posed no threat to the corporation's financial health at the time of authorization. There is fairness, in contrast, in subordinating

---

[97] [28] 1980 Mass. Acts 265.

what is essentially a claim to a dividend when the corporation becomes insolvent. The Massachusetts legislature was apparently only concerned with the plight of directors. Its failure to make an equivalent amendment protecting the note payment rights of former stockholders could even be taken as an indication that the legislature intended to impose liability upon them if they are paid after the corporation's insolvency, so that an insolvent corporation would have defense to the claim prior to payment. But these are speculations. In the final analysis, the statute is ambiguous.

No reported decision has resolved this ambiguity. In *Brigham v. M.J. Corp.*,[98] the Supreme Judicial Court of Massachusetts did nothing more than recognize the uncertainty of when insolvency was relevant under the former version of section 61.

There are, however, Massachusetts redemption cases decided before the present statutory framework. Section 45 was enacted in 1964.[99] Prior to then, the Massachusetts corporation statutes contained no section imposing liability upon stockholders for distributions made to them. They prohibited amendment of a corporation's charter to reduce its authorized capital stock during insolvency and imposed liability upon stockholders for debts existing at the time of any prohibited reduction.[100] Directors were made liable for declaring a "dividend" if the corporation was insolvent or was thereby rendered insolvent, but there was no mention of stock redemptions.[101]

Barrett v. W.A. Webster Lumber Co.[102] was decided in that year. The plaintiff, a preferred stockholder, sought to restrain the defendant from enforcing the corporation's note given to the defendant in redemption of the defendant's stock. The corporation was solvent at the time of the redemption. It then had assets whose value exceeded all its liabilities (including the defendant's note) plus the stated capital of preferred stock, but the asset values did not exceed liabilities plus stated capital of preferred and common stock taken together. The corporation's assets was less than its liabilities, and it was attempting to settle with its creditors at 75 cents on the dollar.

The court in *Barrett* said it regarded the question to be whether the initial redemption was invalid because the company's liabilities plus its capital exceeded the value of its assets, even though asset values then exceeded all liabilities. Continuing to focus only on the company's financial condition at the time of the redemption, the court emphasized the company could then pay all its debts plus all preferred stockholders, including the plaintiff, and that the decline in its asset values could not have been reasonably anticipated. The latter observation seems questionable in view of the company's inability to pay its current liabilities at the time of the redemption. Rejecting the contention that a corporation can purchase it stock only out of surplus, the court ruled the redemption had violated no rights of the plaintiff as a preferred stockholder. The court affirmed the lower court's denial

---

[98] [29] 352 Mass. 674, 679-80, 227 N.E.2d 915, 919-20 (1967).

[99] [30] 1964 Mass. Acts. 723 § 1.

[100] [31] *See* Mass. Gen. L. ch. 156 §§ 35, 45 (repealed 1964 Mass. Acts. of 723, § 1).

[101] [32] *See* Mass. Gen. L. ch. 156 § 37 (repealed 1964 Mass. Acts. of 723, § 1).

[102] [33] 275 Mass. 302, 175 N.E. 765 (1931).

of the requested injunction against payment of the defendant's redemption notes.

Barrett was concerned with the rights of a preferred stockholder, not a creditor. The court seemed to acknowledge the rights of creditors to complain about a redemption. It said: "[T]he great weight of authority holds that a corporation may buy its own stock if the purchase is made in good faith and does not prejudice the rights of creditors."[103]

The rights of creditor were present in *Scriggins v. Thomas Dalby Co.*,[104] decided a few years later. A creditor brought suit to enjoin the defendant from enforcing payment of notes given to the defendant in redemption of his stock. The corporation was solvent at the time of the redemption, but it was not shown that its surplus then exceeded the redemption price. The corporation was also solvent when the payee brought two actions on the notes. But it had become insolvent by the time of trial of those actions, which were consolidated with the creditor's suit for the injunction.

The *Scriggins* court affirmed the propriety of redemption for a price in excess of surplus, as well as the ability of a corporation to purchase its own stock "if creditors would not be prejudices."[105] The creditor argued than an implied term of the redemption contract was that the contract would not be carried out if at the time fixed for performance the corporation was insolvent or performance would render the corporation insolvent. Stating it did not decide this point, the court ruled that even assuming the proposition to be so, it had no application to the case because the corporation was solvent when the notes in question matured and when suit on them was brought. The court then said, "Changes thereafter in the financial condition of the corporation did not affect the enforceability as a matter of law of the matured obligations upon which these actions were brought."[106] From what the court had said previously, one would interpret this sentence to mean merely that the rights of parties are fixed as of the time of commencement of suit. But as authority for the statement, the court cites the *Barrett* decision, which had focused entirely on the corporation's condition at the time it incurred the redemption debt.

In summary, Massachusetts cases decided prior to the passage of section 45 are as ambiguous as section 45 is on the question of whether the corporation must be solvent at the time the payment in question is due. There are intimations in *Scriggins* that solvency is required at the time of payment, but the court's meaning is uncertain, due in no small measure to its citation of *Barrett*. All that can be said with certainty is that in *Scriggins* the court declined to rule on the question, just as it later declined to do in *Brigham*.

It is nevertheless my obligation to attempt to predict how the Supreme Judicial Court of Massachusetts would rule.[107] I conclude from *Barrett* and *Scriggins* the court would interpret section 45 not to impose liability upon a stockholder for having received, when the corporation is insolvent, payment under a redemption

---

[103] [34] 275 Mass. at 307, 175 N.E. 765 (1931).

[104] [35] 290 Mass. 414, 195 N.E. at 768.

[105] [36] 290 Mass. 420, 195 N.E. 752.

[106] [37] 290 Mass. at 421, 195 N.E. at 753.

[107] [38] *In re Miller*, 113 B.R. 98, 101 (Bankr. D. Mass. 1990).

note delivered when the corporation was solvent. It follows that the court would not require current solvency for enforcement of the obligation. The claim would therefore stand in parity with other debt outside of bankruptcy.

IV. Supremacy of Section 510(c) of Bankruptcy Code

Section 510(c) of the Bankruptcy Code must nevertheless control. Congress enacted it in the exercise of its constitutional authority "[t]o establish . . . uniform laws on the subject of bankruptcies throughout the United States."[108]

Under the Supremacy Clause, the "Constitution, and the laws of the United States which shall be made in Pursuance thereof . . . shall be the Supreme Law of the land . . . anything in the Constitution or laws of any state to the contrary notwithstanding."[109]

Application of the Supremacy Clause requires suspension of a state insolvency law so long as federal bankruptcy legislation is in effect.[110] The Supreme Judicial Court of Massachusetts has accordingly declared the Massachusetts insolvency law to be suspended.[111]

The Supremacy Clause requires more than denial of a state's ability to enact comprehensive insolvency legislation. Ever since *Gibbons v. Ogden*,[112] the Supremacy Clause has rendered invalid state laws that "interfere with, or are contrary to the laws of Congress, made in pursuance of the Constitution."[113] The question is whether the state statute in question "stands as an obstacle to the accomplishment and execution of the full purposes of Congress."[114] In *Perez v. Campbell*,[115] the Supreme Court interpreted the Supremacy Clause to require invalidation of a state statute which suspended an individual's driver's license and car registration for nonpayment of a judgment arising from a motor vehicle accident, even thought the judgment liability had been discharged in bankruptcy. The Court struck the statute down because of its conflict with the debtor's discharge in bankruptcy, the embodiment of the fresh start policy of bankruptcy law. In response to the argument that the purpose of the law was to promote highway safety, the Court ruled the effect of the law and not its purpose is relevant.

Section 45 of chapter 156B of the Massachusetts General Laws, as I believe it would be interpreted by the Supreme Judicial Court of Massachusetts, is in direct conflict with section 510(c) of the Bankruptcy Code. Section 510(c) requires subordination of this claim to all unsecured claims. Application of section 45 would give the claim parity with all unsecured claims. Section 510(c) is based upon the

---

[108] [39] U.S. Const. art. I, § 8.

[109] [40] U.S. Const. art. VI.

[110] [41] *International Shoe Co. v. Pinkus*, 278 U.S. 261 (1929).

[111] [42] *Goldstein v. Columbia Diamond Ring Co.*, 366 Mass. 835, 323 N.E.2d 344 (1975).

[112] [43] 22 U.S. 1 (Wheat) (1824).

[113] [44] *Id.* at 211.

[114] [45] *Perez v. Campbell*, 402 U.S. 637, 649 (1979); *Hines v. Davidowitz*, 312 U.S. 52, 67 (1941).

[115] [46] 402 U.S. 637 (1979).

bankruptcy policy favoring a fair distribution to creditors, a policy as basic as the fresh start policy before the court in Perez. The conflict is similar to that present when a state statute requires payment of state taxes as a condition to issuance of a liquor license. Bankruptcy court decisions in this district have invalidated application of such statutes to Code debtors because of their conflict with the priority scheme of the Bankruptcy Code.[116]

Under the teaching of *Perez*, it makes no difference that the purpose of section 45 may be to promote certainty in the enforcement of a contract reflecting a significant business transaction. It is enough that the effect of the statute's application is to conflict with federal law.

A separate order has issued subordinating the claim.

UNOCAL CORP. v. MESA PETROLEUM CO.

Delaware Supreme Court
493 A.2d 946 (1985)

MOORE, JUSTICE

We confront an issue of first impression in Delaware — the validity of a corporation's self-tender for its own shares which excludes from participation a stockholder making a hostile tender offer for the company's stock.

The Court of Chancery granted a preliminary injunction to the plaintiffs, Mesa Petroleum Co., Mesa Asset Co., Mesa Partners II, and Mesa Eastern, Inc. (collectively "Mesa")[117] enjoining an exchange offer of the defendant, Unocal Corporation (Unocal) for its own stock. The trial court concluded that a selective exchange offer, excluding Mesa, was legally impermissible. We cannot agree with such a blanket rule. The factual findings of the Vice Chancellor, fully supported by the record, establish that Unocal's board, consisting of a majority of independent directors, acted in good faith, and after reasonable investigation found that Mesa's tender offer was both inadequate and coercive. Under the circumstances the board had both the power and duty to oppose a bid it perceived to be harmful to the corporate enterprise. On this record we are satisfied that the device Unocal adopted is reasonable in relation to the threat posed, and that the board acted in the proper exercise of sound business judgment. We will not substitute our views for those of the board if the latter's decision can be "attributed to a rational business purpose." *Sinclair Oil Corp. v. Levy* Del. Supr., 280 A.2d 717, 720 (1971). Accordingly, we reverse the decision of the Court of Chancery and order the preliminary injunction vacated.[118]

---

[116] [47] *In re Kick-Off, Inc.*, 82 B.R. 648 (Bankr. D. Mass. 1987), *aff'd*, 19888 WL 123927 (D. Mass. 1988); *Aegean Fare, Inc. v. Licensing Board for City of Boston (In re Aegan Fare, Inc.)*, 35 B.R. 923 (Bankr. D. Mass. 1983).

[117] [1] T. Boone Pickens, Jr., is President and Chairman of the Board of Mesa Petroleum and President of Mesa Asset and controls the related Mesa entities.

[118] [2] This appeal was heard on an expedited basis in light of the pending Mesa tender offer and Unocal exchange offer. We announced our decision to reverse in an oral ruling in open court on May 17, 1985 with the further statement that this opinion would follow shortly thereafter. *See infra* n.5.

I.

The factual background of this matter bears a significant relationship to its ultimate outcome.

On April 8, 1985, Mesa, the owner of approximately 15% of Unocal's stock, commenced a two-tier "front loaded" cash tender offer for 64 million shares, or approximately 37% of Unocal's outstanding stock at a price of $54 per share. The "back-end" was designed to eliminate the remaining publicly held shares by an exchange of securities purportedly worth $54 per share. However, pursuant to an order entered by the United States District Court for the Central District of California on April 26, 1985, Mesa issued a supplemental proxy statement to Unocal's stockholders disclosing that the securities offered in the second-step merger would be highly subordinated, and that Unocal's capitalization would differ significantly from its present structure. Unocal has rather aptly termed such securities "junk bonds."[119]

Unocal's board consists of eight independent outside directors and six insiders. It met on April 13, 1985, to consider the Mesa tender offer. Thirteen directors were present, and the meeting lasted nine and one-half hours. The directors were given no agenda or written materials prior to the session. However, detailed presentations were made by legal counsel regarding the board's obligations under both Delaware corporate law and the federal securities laws. The board then received a presentation from Peter Sachs on behalf of Goldman Sachs & Co. (Goldman Sachs) and Dillon, Read & Co. (Dillon Read) discussing the bases for their opinions that the Mesa proposal was wholly inadequate. Mr. Sachs opined that the minimum cash value that could be expected from a sale or orderly liquidation for 100% of Unocal's stock was in excess of $60 per share. In making his presentation, Mr. Sachs showed slides outlining the valuation techniques used by the financial advisors, and others, depicting recent business combinations in the oil and gas industry. The Court of Chancery found that the Sachs presentation was designed to apprise the directors of the scope of the analyses performed rather than the facts and numbers used in reaching the conclusion that Mesa's tender offer price was inadequate.

Mr. Sachs also presented various defensive strategies available to the board if it

---

[119] [3] Mesa's May 3, 1985 supplement to its proxy statement states: (i) following the Offer, the Purchasers would seek to effect a merger of Unocal and Mesa Eastern or an affiliate of Mesa Eastern (the "Merger") in which the remaining Shares would be acquired for a combination of subordinated debt securities and preferred stock; (ii) the securities to be received by Unocal shareholders in the Merger would be subordinated to $2,400 million of debt securities of Mesa Eastern, indebtedness incurred to refinance up to $1,000 million of bank debt which was incurred by affiliates of Mesa Partners II to purchase Shares and to pay related interest and expenses and all then-existing debt of Unocal; (iii) the corporation surviving the Merger would be responsible for the payment of all securities of Mesa Eastern (including any such securities issued pursuant to the Merger) and the indebtedness referred to in item (ii) above, and such securities and indebtedness would be repaid out of funds generated by the operations of Unocal; (iv) the indebtedness incurred in the Offer and the Merger would result in Unocal being much more highly leveraged, and the capitalization of the corporation surviving the Merger would differ significantly from that of Unocal at present; and (v) in their analyses of cash flows provided by operations of Unocal which would be available to service and repay securities and other obligations of the corporation surviving the Merger, the Purchasers assumed that the capital expenditures and expenditures for exploration of such corporation would be significantly reduced.

concluded that Mesa's two-step tender offer was inadequate and should be opposed. One of the devices outlined was a self-tender by Unocal for its own stock with a reasonable price range of $70 to $75 per share. The cost of such a proposal would cause the company to incur $6.1-6.5 billion of additional debt, and a presentation was made informing the board of Unocal's ability to handle it. The directors were told that the primary effect of this obligation would be to reduce exploratory drilling, but that the company would nonetheless remain a viable entity.

The eight outside directors, comprising a clear majority of the thirteen members present, then met separately with Unocal's financial advisors and attorneys. Thereafter, they unanimously agreed to advise the board that it should reject Mesa's tender offer as inadequate, and that Unocal should pursue a self-tender to provide the stockholders with a fairly priced alternative to the Mesa proposal. The board then reconvened and unanimously adopted a resolution rejecting as grossly inadequate Mesa's tender offer. Despite the nine and one-half hour length of the meeting, no formal decision was made on the proposed defensive self-tender.

On April 15, the Board met again with four of the directors present by telephone and one member still absent.[120] This session lasted two hours. Unocal's Vice President of Finance and its Assistant General Counsel made a detailed presentation of the proposed terms of the exchange offer. A price range between $70 and $80 per share was considered, and ultimately the directors agreed upon $72. The board was also advised about the debt securities that would be issued, and the necessity of placing restrictive covenants upon certain corporate activities until the obligations were paid. The board's decisions were made in reliance on the advice of its investment bankers, including the terms and conditions upon which the securities were to be issued. Based upon this advice, and the board's own deliberations, the directors unanimously approved the exchange offer. Their resolution provided that if Mesa acquired 64 million shares of Unocal stock through its own offer (the Mesa Purchase Condition), Unocal would buy the remaining 49% outstanding for an exchange of debt securities having an aggregate par value of $72 per share. The board resolution also stated that the offer would be subject to other conditions that had been described to the board at the meeting, or which were deemed necessary by Unocal's officers, including the exclusion of Mesa from the proposal (the Mesa exclusion). Any such conditions were required to be in accordance with the "purport and intent" of the offer.

Unocal's exchange offer was commenced on April 17, 1985, and Mesa promptly challenged it by filing this suit in the Court of Chancery. On April 22, the Unocal board met again and was advised by Goldman Sachs and Dillon Read to waive the Mesa Purchase Condition as to 50 million shares. This recommendation was in response to a perceived concern of the shareholders that, if shares were tendered

---

[120] [4] Under Delaware law directors may participate in a board meeting by telephone. Thus, 8 Del. C. § 141(i) provides:

Unless otherwise restricted by the certificate of incorporation or by-laws, members of the board of directors of any corporation, or any committee designated by the board, may participate in a meeting of such board or committee by means of conference telephone or similar communications equipment by means of which all persons participating in the meeting can hear each other, and participation in a meeting pursuant to this subsection shall constitute presence in person at such meeting.

to Unocal, no shares would be purchased by either offeror. The directors were also advised that they should tender their own Unocal stock into the exchange offer as a mark of their confidence in it.

Another focus of the board was the Mesa exclusion. Legal counsel advised that under Delaware law Mesa could only be excluded for what the directors reasonably believed to be a valid corporate purpose. The directors' discussion centered on the objective of adequately compensating shareholders at the "back-end" of Mesa's proposal, which the latter would finance with "junk bonds." To include Mesa would defeat that goal, because under the proration aspect of the exchange offer (49%) every Mesa share accepted by Unocal would displace one held by another stockholder. Further, if Mesa were permitted to tender to Unocal, the latter would in effect be financing Mesa's own inadequate proposal.

On April 24, 1985 Unocal issued a supplement to the exchange offer describing the partial waiver of the Mesa Purchase Condition. On May 1, 1985, in another supplement, Unocal extended the withdrawal, proration and expiration dates of its exchange offer to May 17, 1985.

Meanwhile, on April 22, 1985, Mesa amended its complaint in this action to challenge the Mesa exclusion. A preliminary injunction hearing was scheduled for May 8, 1985. However, on April 23, 1985, Mesa moved for a temporary restraining order in response to Unocal's announcement that it was partially waiving the Mesa Purchase Condition. After expedited briefing, the Court of Chancery heard Mesa's motion on April 26.

On April 29, 1985, the Vice Chancellor temporarily restrained Unocal from proceeding with the exchange offer unless it included Mesa. The trial court recognized that directors could oppose, and attempt to defeat, a hostile takeover which they considered adverse to the best interests of the corporation. However, the Vice Chancellor decided that in a selective purchase of the company's stock, the corporation bears the burden of showing: (1) a valid corporate purpose, and (2) that the transaction was fair to all of the stockholders, including those excluded.

Unocal immediately sought certification of an interlocutory appeal to this Court pursuant to Supreme Court Rule 42(b). On May 1, 1985, the Vice Chancellor declined to certify the appeal on the grounds that the decision granting a temporary restraining order did not decide a legal issue of first impression, and was not a matter to which the decisions of the Court of Chancery were in conflict.

However, in an Order dated May 2, 1985, this Court ruled that the Chancery decision was clearly determinative of substantive rights of the parties, and in fact decided the main question of law before the Vice Chancellor, which was indeed a question of first impression. We therefore concluded that the temporary restraining order was an appealable decision. However, because the Court of Chancery was scheduled to hold a preliminary injunction hearing on May 8 at which there would be an enlarged record on the various issues, action on the interlocutory appeal was deferred pending an outcome of those proceedings.

In deferring action on the interlocutory appeal, we noted that on the record before us we could not determine whether the parties had articulated certain issues which the Vice Chancellor should have an opportunity to consider in the first instance. These included the following:

> a) Does the directors' duty of care to the corporation extend to protecting the corporate enterprise in good faith from perceived depredations of others, including persons who may own stock in the company?
>
> b) Have one or more of the plaintiffs, their affiliates, or persons acting in concert with them, either in dealing with Unocal or others, demonstrated a pattern of conduct sufficient to justify a reasonable inference by defendants that a principle objective of the plaintiffs is to achieve selective treatment for themselves by the repurchase of their Unocal shares at a substantial premium?
>
> c) If so, may the directors of Unocal in the proper exercise of business judgment employ the exchange offer to protect the corporation and its shareholders from such tactics? *See Pogostin v. Rice*, Del. Supr., 480 A.2d 619 (1984).
>
> d) If it is determined that the purpose of the exchange offer was not illegal as a matter of law, have the directors of Unocal carried their burden of showing that they acted in good faith?

See Martin v. American Potash & Chemical Corp., 92 A.2d at 302.

After the May 8 hearing the Vice Chancellor issued an unreported opinion on May 13, 1985 granting Mesa a preliminary injunction. Specifically, the trial court noted that "[t]he parties basically agree that the directors' duty of care extends to protecting the corporation from perceived harm whether it be from third parties or shareholders." The trial court also concluded in response to the second inquiry in the Supreme Court's May 2 order, that "[a]lthough the facts, . . . do not appear to be sufficient to prove that Mesa's principle objective is to be bought off at a substantial premium, they do justify a reasonable inference to the same effect."

As to the third and fourth questions posed by this Court, the Vice Chancellor stated that they "appear to raise the more fundamental issue of whether directors owe fiduciary duties to shareholders who they perceive to be acting contrary to the best interests of the corporation as a whole." While determining that the directors' decision to oppose Mesa's tender offer was made in a good faith belief that the Mesa proposal was inadequate, the court stated that the business judgment rule does not apply to a selective exchange offer such as this.

On May 13, 1985 the Court of Chancery certified this interlocutory appeal to us as a question of first impression, and we accepted it on May 14. The entire matter was scheduled on an expedited basis.[121]

---

[121] [5] Such expedition was required by the fact that if Unocal's exchange offer was permitted to proceed, the proration date for the shares entitled to be exchanged was May 17, 1985, while Mesa's tender offer expired on May 23. After acceptance of this appeal on May 14, we received excellent briefs from the parties, heard argument on May 16 and announced our oral ruling in open court at 9:00 a.m. on May 17. *See supra* n.2.

II.

The issues we address involve these fundamental questions: Did the Unocal board have the power and duty to oppose a takeover threat it reasonably perceived to be harmful to the corporate enterprise, and if so, is its action here entitled to the protection of the business judgment rule?

Mesa contends that the discriminatory exchange offer violates the fiduciary duties Unocal owes it. Mesa argues that because of the Mesa exclusion the business judgment rule is inapplicable, because the directors by tendering their own shares will derive a financial benefit that is not available to all Unocal stockholders. Thus, it is Mesa's ultimate contention that Unocal cannot establish that the exchange offer is fair to all shareholders, and argues that the Court of Chancery was correct in concluding that Unocal was unable to meet this burden.

Unocal answers that it does not owe a duty of "fairness" to Mesa, given the facts here. Specifically Unocal contends that its board of directors reasonably and in good faith concluded that Mesa's $54 two-tier tender offer was coercive and inadequate, and that Mesa sought selective treatment for itself. Furthermore, Unocal argues that the board's approval of the exchange offer was made in good faith, on an informed basis, and in the exercise of due care. Under these circumstances, Unocal contends that its directors properly employed this device to protect the company and its stockholders from Mesa's harmful tactics.

III.

We begin with the basic issue of the power of a board of directors of a Delaware corporation to adopt a defensive measure of this type. Absent such authority, all other questions are moot. Neither issues of fairness nor business judgment are pertinent without the basic underpinning of a board's legal power to act.

The board has a large reservoir of authority upon which to draw. Its duties and responsibilities proceed from the inherent powers conferred by 8 Del. C. § 141(a), respecting management of the corporation's "business and affairs."[122] Additionally, the powers here being exercised derive from 8 Del. C. § 160(a), conferring broad authority upon a corporation to deal in its own stock.[123] From this it is now well established that in the acquisition of its shares a Delaware corporation may deal selectively with its stockholders, provided the directors have not acted out of a sole or primary purpose to entrench themselves in office.

---

[122] [6] The general grant of power to a board of directors is conferred by 8 Del. C: § 141(a), which provides:

> (a) The business *and affairs* of every corporation organized under this chapter shall be managed by or under the direction of a board of directors, except as may be otherwise provided in this chapter or in its certificate of incorporation. If any such provision is made in the certificate of incorporation, the powers and duties conferred or imposed upon the board of directors by this chapter shall be exercised or performed to such extent and by such person or persons as shall be provided in the certificate of incorporation. (Emphasis added.)

[123] [7] This power under 8 Del. C. § 160(a), with certain exceptions not pertinent here, is as follows:

> (a) Every corporation may purchase, redeem, receive, take or otherwise acquire, own and hold, sell, lend, exchange, transfer or otherwise dispose of, pledge, use and otherwise deal in and with its own shares; . . .

Finally, the board's power to act derives from its fundamental duty and obligation to protect the corporate enterprise, which includes stockholders, from harm reasonably perceived, irrespective of its source. Thus, we are satisfied that in the broad context of corporate governance, including issues of fundamental corporate change, a board of directors is not a passive instrumentality.[124]

Given the foregoing principles, we turn to the standards by which director action is to be measured. In *Pogostin v. Rice*, Del. Supr., 480 A.2d 619 (1984), we held that the business judgment rule, including the standards by which director conduct is judged, is applicable in the context of a takeover. *Id.* at 627. The business judgment rule is a "presumption that in making a business decision the directors of a corporation acted on an informed basis, in good faith and in the honest belief that the action taken was in the best interests of the company." *Aronson v. Lewis*, Del. Supr., 473 A.2d 805, 812 (1984) (citations omitted). A hallmark of the business judgment rule in that a court will not substitute its judgment for that of the board if the latter's decision can be "attributed to any rational business purpose." *Sinclair Oil Corp. v. Levien*, Del. Supr., 280 A.2d 717, 720 (1971).

When a board addresses a pending takeover bid it has an obligation to determine whether the offer is in the best interests of the corporation and its shareholders. In that respect a board's duty is no different from any other responsibility it shoulders, and its decisions should be no less entitled to the respect they otherwise would be accorded in the realm of business judgment.[125] *See also Johnson v. Trueblood*, 629 F.2d 287, 292-293 (3d Cir. 1980). There are, however, certain caveats to a proper exercise of this function. Because of the omnipresent specter that a board may be acting primarily in its own interests, rather than those of the corporation and its shareholders, there is an enhanced duty which calls for judicial examination at the threshold before the protections of the business judgment rule may be conferred.

This Court has long recognized that:

> We must bear in mind the inherent danger in the purchase of shares with corporate funds to remove a threat to corporate policy when a threat to control is involved. The directors are of necessity confronted with a conflict of interest, and an objective decision is difficult.

Bennett v. Propp, Del. Supr., 187 A.2d 405, 409 (1962). In the face of this inherent conflict directors must show that they had reasonable grounds for believing that a danger to corporate policy and effectiveness existed because of another person's stock ownership. *Cheff v. Mathes*, 199 A.2d at 554-55. However, they satisfy that

---

[124] [8] Even in the traditional areas of fundamental corporate change, i.e., charter amendments [8 Del. C. § 242(b)], mergers [8 Del. C. §§ 251(b), 252(c), 253(a), and 254(d)], sale of assets [8 Del. C. § 271(a)], and dissolution [8 Del. C. § 275(a)], director action is a prerequisite to the ultimate disposition of such matters. *See also Smith v. Van Gorkom*, Del. Supr., 488 A.2d 858, 888 (1985).

[125] [9] This is a subject of intense debate among practicing members of the bar and legal scholars. Excellent examples of these contending views are: Block & Miller, *The Responsibilities and Obligations of Corporate Directors in Takeover Contests*, 11 Sec. Reg. L.J. 44 (1983); Easterbrook & Fischel, *Takeover Bids, Defensive Tactics, and Shareholders' Welfare*, 36 Bus. Law. 1733 (1981); Easterbrook & Fischel, *The Proper Role of a Target's Management in Responding to a Tender Offer*, 94 Harv. L. Rev. 1161 (1981); Herzei, Schmidt & Davis, *Why Corporate Directors Have a Right To Resist Tender Offers*, 3 Corp. L. Rev. 107 (1980); Lipton, *Takeover Bids in the Targets Boardroom*, 35 Bus. Law. 101 (1979).

burden "by showing good faith and reasonable investigation . . . ." *Id.* at 555. Furthermore, such proof is materially enhanced, as here, by the approval of a board comprised of a majority of outside independent directors who have acted in accordance with the foregoing standards.

IV.

A.

In the board's exercise of corporate power to forestall a takeover bid our analysis begins with the basic principle that corporate directors have a fiduciary duty to act in the best interests of the corporation's stockholders. *Guth v. Loft, Inc.*, Del. Supr., 5 A.2d 503, 510 (1939). As we have noted, their duty of care extends to protecting the corporation and its owners from perceived harm whether a threat originates from third parties or other shareholders.[126] But such powers are not absolute. A corporation does not have unbridled discretion to defeat any perceived threat by any Draconian means available.

The restriction placed upon a selective stock repurchase is that the directors may not have acted solely or primarily out of a desire to perpetuate themselves in office. *See Cheff v. Mathes*, 199 A.2d at 556; *Kors v. Carey*, 158 A.2d at 140. Of course, to this is added the further caveat that inequitable action may not be taken under the guise of law. *Schnell v. Chris-Craft Industries, Inc.*, Del. Supr., 285 A.2d 437, 439 (1971). The standard of proof established in *Cheff v. Mathes* and discussed *supra* at page 16, is designed to ensure that a defensive measure to thwart or impede a takeover is indeed motivated by a good faith concern for the welfare of the corporation and its stockholders, which in all circumstances must be free of any fraud or other misconduct. *Cheff v. Mathes*, 199 A.2d at 554-55. However, this does not end the inquiry.

B.

A further aspect is the element of balance. If a defensive measure is to come within the ambit of the business judgment rule, it must be reasonable in relation to the threat posed. This entails an analysis by the directors of the nature of the takeover bid and its effect on the corporate enterprise. Examples of such concerns may include: inadequacy of the price offered, nature and timing of the offer, questions of illegality, the impact on "constituencies" other than shareholders (i.e., creditors, customers, employees, and perhaps even the community generally), the risk of nonconsummation, and the quality of securities being offered in the exchange. *See* Lipton and Brownstein, *Takeover Responses and Directors' Responsibilities: An Update*, p. 7, ABA National Institute on the Dynamics of Corporate Control (December 8, 1983). While not a controlling factor, it also seems to us that

[126] [10] It has been suggested that a board's response to a takeover threat should be a passive one. Easterbrook & Fischel, *supra*, 36 Bus. Law. at 1750. However, that clearly is not the law of Delaware, and as the proponents of this rule of passivity readily concede, it has not been adopted either by courts or state legislatures. Easterbrook & Fischel, *supra*, 94 Harv. L. Rev. at 1194.

a board may reasonably consider the basic stockholder interests as stake, including those of short term speculators, whose actions may have fueled the coercive aspect of the offer at the expense of the long term investor.[127] Here, the threat posed was viewed by the Unocal board as a grossly inadequate two-tier coercive tender offer coupled with the threat of greenmail.

Specifically, the Unocal directors had concluded that the value of Unocal was substantially above the $54 per share offered in cash at the front end. Furthermore, they determined that the subordinated securities to be exchanged in Mesa's announced squeeze out of the remaining shareholders in the "back-end" merger were "junk bonds" worth far less than $54. It is now well recognized that such offers are a classic coercive measure designed to stampede shareholders into tendering at the first tier, even if the price is inadequate, out of fear of what they will receive at the back end of the transaction.[128] Wholly beyond the coercive aspect of an inadequate two-tier tender offer, the threat was posed by a corporate raider with a national reputation as a "greenmailer."[129]

In adopting the selective exchange offer, the board stated that its objective was either to defeat the inadequate Mesa offer or, should the offer still succeed, provide the 49% of its stockholders, who would otherwise be forced to accept "junk bonds," with $72 worth of senior debt. We find that both purposes are valid.

However, such efforts would have been thwarted by Mesa's participation in the exchange offer. First, if Mesa could tender its shares, Unocal would effectively be subsidizing the former's continuing effort to buy Unocal stock at $54 per share. Second, Mesa could not, by definition, fit within the class of shareholders being protected from its own coercive and inadequate tender offer.

---

[127] [11] There has been much debate respecting such stockholder interests. One rather impressive study indicates that the stock of over 50 percent of target companies, who resisted hostile takeovers, later traded at higher market prices than the rejected offer price, or were acquired after the tender offer was defeated by another company at a price higher than the offer price. *See* Lipton, *supra* 35 Bus. Law. at 106-109, 132-133. Moreover, an update by Kidder Peabody & Company of this study, involving the stock prices of target companies that have defeated hostile tender offers during the period from 1973 to 1982 demonstrates that in a majority of cases the target's shareholders benefited from the defeat. The stock of 81% of the targets studied has, since the tender offer, sold at prices higher than the tender offer price. When adjusted for the time value of money, the figure is 64%. *See* Lipton & Brownstein, *supra* ABA Institute at 10. The thesis being that this strongly supports application of the business judgment rule in response to takeover threats. There is, however, a rather vehement contrary view. *See* Easterbrook & Fischel, *supra* 36 Bus. Law at 1739-1745.

[128] [12] For a discussion of the coercive nature of a two-tier tender offer see e.g., Brudney & Chirelstein, *Fair Shares in Corporate Mergers and Takeovers*, 88 Harv. L. Rev. 297, 337 (1974); Finkelstein, *Antitakeover Protection Against Two-Tier and Partial Tender Offers: The Validity of Fair Price, Mandatory Bid, and Flip-Over Provisions Under Delaware Law*, 11 Sec. Reg. L.J. 291, 323 (1984); Lipton, *supra;* 35 Bus. Law. at 113-14; Note, *Protecting Shareholders Against Partial and Two-Tiered Takeovers: The Poison Pill Preferred*, 97 Harv. L. Rev. 1964, 1966 (1984).

[129] [13] The term "greenmail" refers to the practice of buying out a takeover bidder's stock at a premium that is not available to other shareholders in order to prevent the takeover. The Chancery Court noted that "Mesa has made tremendous profits from its takeover activities although in the past few years it has not been successful in acquiring any of the target companies on an unfriendly basis." Moreover, the trial court specifically found that the actions of the Unocal board were taken in good faith to eliminate both the inadequacies of the tender offer and to forestall the payment of "greenmail."

Thus, we are satisfied that the selective exchange offer is reasonably related to the threats posed. It is consistent with the principle that "the minority stockholder shall receive the substantial equivalent in value of what he had before." *Sterling v. Mayflower Hotel Corp.*, Del. Supr., 93 A.2d 107, 114 (1952). *See also Rosenblatt v. Getty Oil Co.*, ___ A.2d ___, ___ (1985). This concept of fairness, while stated in the merger context, is also relevant in the area of tender offer law. Thus, the board's decision to offer what it determined to be the fair value of the corporation to the 49% of its shareholders, who would otherwise be forced to accept highly subordinated "junk bonds," is reasonable and consistent with the directors' duty to ensure that the minority stockholders receive equal value for their shares.

V.

Mesa contends that it is unlawful, and the trial court agreed, for a corporation to discriminate in this fashion against one shareholder. It argues correctly that no case has ever sanctioned a device that precludes a raider from sharing in a benefit available to all other stockholders. However, as we have noted earlier, the principle of selective stock repurchases by a Delaware corporation is neither unknown nor unauthorized. *Cheff v. Mathes*, 199 A.2d at 554; *Bennett v. Propp*, 187 A.2d at 408; *Martin v. American Potash & Chemical Corporation*, 92 A.2d at 302; *Kaplan v. Goldsamt*, 380 A.2d 568-569; *Kors v. Carey*, 158 A.2d at 140-141; 8 Del. C. § 160. The only difference is that heretofore the approved transaction was the payment of "greenmail" to a raider or dissident posing a threat to the corporate enterprise. All other stockholders were denied much favored treatment, and given Mesa's past history of greenmail, its claims here are rather ironic.

However, our corporate law is not static. It must grow and develop in response to, indeed in anticipation of, evolving concepts and needs. Merely because the General Corporation Law is silent as to a specific matter does not mean that it is prohibited. *See Providence and Worcester Co. v. Baker*, Del. Supr., 378 A.2d 121, 123-124(1977). In the days when *Cheff Bennett, Margin* and *Kors* were decided, the tender offer, while not an unknown device, was virtually unused, and little was known of such methods as two-tier "front-end" loaded offers with their coercive effects. Then, the favored attack of a raider was stock acquisition followed by a proxy contest. Various defensive tactics, which provided no benefit whatever to the raider, evolved. Thus, the use of corporate funds by management to counter a proxy battle was approved. *Hall v. Trans-Lux Daylight Picture Screen Corp.*, Del. Supr., 171 A. 226 (1934); *Hibbert v. Hollywood Park, Inc.*, Del. Supr., 457 A.2d 339 (1983). Litigation, supported by corporate funds, aimed at the raider has long been a popular device.

More recently, as the sophistication of both raiders and targets has developed, a host of other defensive measures to counter such ever mounting threats has evolved and received judicial sanction. These include defensive charter amendments and other devices bearing some rather exotic, but apt, names: Crown Jewel, White Knight, Pac Man, and Golden Parachute. Each has highly selective features, the object of which is to deter or defeat the raider.

Thus, while the exchange offer is a form of selective treatment, given the nature of the threat posed here the response is neither unlawful nor unreasonable. If the board of directors is disinterested, has acted in good faith and with due care, its decision in the absence of an abuse of discretion will be upheld as a proper exercise of business judgment.

To this Mesa responds that the board is not disinterested, because the directors are receiving a benefit from the tender of their own shares, which because of the Mesa exclusion, does not devolve upon all stockholders equally. *See Aronson v. Lewis*, Del. Supr., 473 A.2d 805, 812 (1984). However, Mesa concedes that if the exclusion is valid, then the directors and all other stockholders share the same benefit. The answer of course is that the exclusion is valid, and the directors' participation in the exchange offer does not rise to the level of a disqualifying interest. The excellent discussion in *Johnson v. Trueblood*, 629 F.2d at 292-293, of the use of the business judgment rule in takeover contests also seems pertinent here.

Nor does this become an "interested" director transaction merely because certain board members are large stockholders. As this Court has previously noted, that fact alone does not create a disqualifying "personal pecuniary interest" to defeat the operation of the business judgment rule. *Cheff v. Mathes*, 119 A.2d at 554.

Mesa also argues that the exclusion permits the directors to abdicate the fiduciary duties they owe it. However, that is not so. The board continues to owe Mesa the duties of due care and loyalty. But in the face of the destructive threat Mesa's tender offer was perceived to pose, the board has a supervening duty to protect the corporate enterprise, which includes the other shareholders, from threatened harm.

Mesa contends that the basis of this action is punitive, and solely in response to the exercise of its rights of corporate democracy.[130] Nothing precludes Mesa, as a stockholder, from acting in its own self-interest. *But see, Allied Chemical & Dye Corp. v. Steel & Tube Co. of America*, Del. Ch., 120 A. 486, 491(1923) (majority shareholder owes a fiduciary duty to the minority shareholders). However, Mesa, while pursuing its own interests, has acted in a manner which a board consisting of a majority of independent directors has reasonably determined to be contrary to the best interests of Unocal and its other shareholders. In this situation, there is no support in Delaware law for the proposition that, when responding to a perceived harm, a corporation must guarantee a benefit to a stockholder who is deliberately provoking the danger being addressed. There is no obligation of self-sacrifice by a corporation and its shareholders in the face of such a challenge.

Here, the Court of Chancery specifically found that the "directors' decision [to oppose the Mesa tender offer] was made in the good faith belief that the Mesa tender offer is inadequate." Given our standard of review under *Levitt v. Bouvier*, Del. Supr., 287 A.2d 671, 673 (1972), and *Application of Delaware Racing*

---

[130] [14] This seems to be the underlying basis of the trial court's principal reliance on the unreported Chancery decision of *Fisher v. Moltz*, Del. Ch. No. 6068 (1979), published in 5 Del. J. Corp. L. 530 (1980). However, the facts in *Fisher* are thoroughly distinguishable. There, a corporation offered to repurchase the shares of its former employees, except those of the plaintiffs, merely because the latter were then engaged in lawful competition with the company. No threat to the enterprise was posed, and at best it can be said that the exclusion was motivated by pique instead of a rational corporate purpose.

Association, Del. Supr., 213 A.2d 203, 207 (1965), we are satisfied that Unocal's board has met its burden of proof. *Cheff v. Mathes*, 199 A.2d at 555.

VI.

In conclusion, there was directorial power to oppose the Mesa tender offer, and to undertake a selective stock exchange made in good faith and upon a reasonable investigation pursuant to a clear duty to protect the corporate enterprise. Further, the selective stock repurchase plan chosen by Unocal is reasonable in relation to the threat that the board rationally and reasonably believed was posed by Mesa's inadequate and coercive two-tier tender offer. Under those circumstances the board's action is entitled to be measured by the standards of the business judgment rule. Thus, unless it is shown by a preponderance of the evidence that the directors' decisions were primarily based on perpetuating themselves in office, or some other breach of fiduciary duty such as fraud, overreaching, lack of good faith, or being uninformed, a Court will not substitute its judgment for that of the board.

In this case that protection is not lost merely because Unocal's directors have tendered their shares in the exchange offer. Given the validity of the Mesa exclusion, they are receiving a benefit shared generally by all other stockholders except Mesa. In this circumstance the test of *Aronson v. Lewis*, 473 A.2d at 812, is satisfied. *See also Cheff v. Mathes*, 199 A.2d at 554. If the stockholders are displeased with the action of their elected representatives, the powers of corporate democracy are at their disposal to turn the board out. *Aronson v. Lewis*, Del. Supr., 473 A.2d 805, 811 (1984). *See also* 8 Del. C. §§ 141(k) and 211(b).

With the Court of Chancery's findings that the exchange offer was based on the board's good faith belief that the Mesa offer was inadequate, that the board's action was informed and taken with due care, that Mesa's prior activities justify a reasonable inference that its principle objective is greenmail, and implicitly, that the substance of the offer itself was reasonable and fair to the corporation and its stockholders if Mesa were included, we cannot say that the Unocal directors have acted in such a manner as to have passed an "unintelligent and unadvised judgment." *Mitchell v. Highland-Western Glass Co.*, Del. Ch., 167 A. 831, 833 (1933). The decision of the Court of Chancery is therefore REVERSED, and the preliminary injunction is VACATED.

NOTE

The holding in *Unocal* was in effect administratively *overruled* by the Securities and Exchange Commission when it adopted Rule 13e-4(f)(8) under the Securities Exchange Act of 1934, as amended.

That Rule provides, in pertinent part, as follows:

(f) *Manner of Making Tender Offer.*

. . .

(8) No issuer or affiliate shall make a tender offer unless:

(i) The tender offer is open to all security holders of the class of securities subject to the tender offer; and

(ii) The consideration paid to any security holder for securities tendered in the tender offer is the highest consideration paid to any other security holder for securities tendered in the tender offer.

The "all-holders" Rule applies to both issuer and third party tender offers and was adopted in 1986 by a 3-2 vote of the Commission.

[C] Certain Sections of the Securities Exchange Act of 1934 and Certain Rules Promulgated by the Securities and Exchange Commission Thereunder

SECURITIES EXCHANGE ACT

Sec. 10. It shall be unlawful for any person, directly or indirectly, by the use of any means or instrumentality of interstate commerce or of the mails, or of any facility of any national securities exchange —

. . .

(b) To use or employ, in connection with the purchase or sale of any security registered on a national securities exchange or any security not so registered, . . . any manipulative or deceptive device or contrivance in contravention of such rules and regulations as the Commission may prescribe as necessary or appropriate in the public interest or for the protection of investors.

SEC RULES

Rule 10b-5. Employment of Manipulative and Deceptive Devices.

It shall be unlawful for any person, directly or indirectly, by the use of any means or instrumentality of interstate commerce, or of the mails, or of any facility of any national securities exchange

(1) To employ any device, scheme, or artifice to defraud,

(2) To make any untrue statement of a material fact or to omit to state a material fact necessary in order to make the statements made, in the light of the circumstances under which they were made, not misleading, or

(3) To engage in any act, practice, or course of business which operates or would operate as a fraud or deceit upon any person, in connection with the purchase or sale of any security.

Rule 10b5-1. Trading "on the basis of" material nonpublic information in insider trading cases.

> *Preliminary Note to Rule 10b5-1*: This provision defines when a purchase or sale constitutes trading "on the basis of" material nonpublic information in insider trading cases brought under Section 10(b) of the Act and Rule 10b-5 thereunder. The law of insider trading is otherwise defined by judicial opinions construing Rule 10b-5, and Rule 10b5-1 does not modify the scope of insider trading law in any other respect.

(a) *General.* The "manipulative and deceptive devices" prohibited by Section 10(b) of the Act (15 U.S.C. 78j) and Rule 10b-5 thereunder include, among other things, the purchase or sale of a security of any issuer, on the basis of material nonpublic information about that security or issuer, in breach of a duty of trust or confidence that is owed directly, indirectly, or derivatively, to the issuer of that security or the shareholders of that issucr, or to any other person who is the source of the material nonpublic information.

(b) *Definition of "on the basis of."* Subject to the affirmative defenses in paragraph (c) of this section, a purchase or sale of a security of an issuer is "on the basis of" material nonpublic information about that security or issuer if the person making the purchase or sale was aware of the material nonpublic information when the person made the purchase or sale.

(c) *Affirmative defenses.*

(1)(i) Subject to paragraph (c)(1)(ii) of this section, a person's purchase or sale is not "on the basis of" material nonpublic information if the person making the purchase or sale demonstrates that:

(A) before becoming aware of the information, the person had:

(1) entered into a binding contract to purchase or sell the security,

(2) instructed another person to purchase or sell the security for the instructing person's account, or

(3) adopted a written plan for trading securities;

(B) the contract, instruction, or plan described in paragraph (c)(1)(i)(A) of this Section:

(1) specified the amount of securities to be purchased or sold and the price at which and the date on which the securities were to be purchased or sold;

(2) included a written formula or algorithm, or computer program, for determining the amount of securities to be purchased or sold and the price at which and the date on which the securities were to be purchased or sold; or

(3) did not permit the person to exercise any subsequent influence over how, when, or whether to effect purchases or sales; provided, in addition, that any other person who, pursuant to the

contract, instruction, or plan, did exercise such influence must not have been aware of the material nonpublic information when doing so; and

(C) the purchase or sale that occurred was pursuant to the contract, instruction, or plan. A purchase or sale is not "pursuant to a contract, instruction, or plan" if, among other things, the person who entered into the contract, instruction, or plan altered or deviated from the contract, instruction, or plan to purchase or sell securities (whether by changing the amount, price, or timing of the purchase or sale), or entered into or altered a corresponding or hedging transaction or position with respect to those securities.

(ii) Paragraph (c)(1)(i) of this section is applicable only when the contract, instruction, or plan to purchase or sell securities was given or entered into in good faith and not as part of a plan or scheme to evade the prohibitions of Rule 10b5-1.

(iii) This subparagraph (c)(1)(iii) defines certain terms as used in paragraph (c).

(A) *Amount.* "Amount" means either a specified number of shares or other securities or a specified dollar value of securities.

(B) *Price.* "Price" means the market price on a particular date or a limit price, or a particular dollar price.

(C) *Date.* "Date" means, in the case of a market order, the specific day of the year on which the order is to be executed (or as soon thereafter as is practicable under ordinary principles of best execution). "Date" means, in the case of a limit order, a day of the year on which the limit order is in force.

(2) A person other than a natural person also may demonstrate that a purchase or sale of securities is not "on the basis of" material nonpublic information if the person demonstrates that:

(i) The individual making the investment decision on behalf of the person to purchase or sell the securities was not aware of the information; and

(ii) The person had implemented reasonable policies and procedures, taking into consideration the nature of the person's business, to ensure that individuals making investment decisions would not violate the laws prohibiting trading on the basis of material nonpublic information. These policies and procedures may include those that restrict any purchase, sale, and causing any purchase or sale of any security as to which the person has material nonpublic information, or those that prevent such individuals from becoming aware of such information.

Rule 10b5-2. Duties of trust or confidence in misappropriation insider trading cases.

Preliminary Note to Rule 10b5-2: This section provides a non-exclusive definition of circumstances in which a person has a duty of trust or confidence for purposes of the "misappropriation" theory of insider trading under Section 10(b) of the Act and Rule 10b-5. The law of insider trading is otherwise defined by judicial opinions construing Rule 10b-5, and Rule 10b5-2 does not modify the scope of insider trading law in any other respect.

(a) *Scope of Rule.* This section shall apply to any violation of Section 10(b) of the Act (15 U.S.C. 78j(b)) and § 240.10b-5 thereunder that is based on the purchase or sale of securities on the basis of, or the communication of, material nonpublic information misappropriated in breach of a duty of trust or confidence.

(b) *Enumerated "duties of trust or confidence."* For purposes of this section, a "duty of trust or confidence" exists in the following circumstances, among others:

(1) Whenever a person agrees to maintain information in confidence;

(2) Whenever the person communicating the material nonpublic information and the person to whom it is communicated have a history, pattern, or practice of sharing confidences, such that the recipient of the information knows or reasonably should know that the person communicating the material nonpublic information expects that the recipient will maintain its confidentiality; or

(3) Whenever a person receives or obtains material nonpublic information from his or her spouse, parent, child, or sibling; *provided*, however, that the person receiving or obtaining the information may demonstrate that no duty of trust or confidence existed with respect to the information, by establishing that he or she neither knew nor reasonably should have known that the person who was the source of the information expected that the person would keep the information confidential, because of the parties' history, pattern, or practice of sharing and maintaining confidences, and because there was no agreement or understanding to maintain the confidentiality of the information.

Rule 10b-18. Purchases of certain equity securities by the issuer and others.

Preliminary Notes to Rule 10b-18

1. Rule 10b-18 provides an issuer (and its affiliated purchasers) with a "safe harbor" from liability for manipulation under sections 9(a)(2) of the Act and Rule 10b-5 under the Act *solely* by reason of the manner, timing, price, and volume of their repurchases when they repurchase the issuer's common stock in the market in accordance with the section's manner, timing, price, and volume conditions. As a safe harbor, compliance with Rule 10b-18 is voluntary. To come within the safe harbor, however, an issuer's repurchases must satisfy (on a daily basis) each of the section's four conditions. Failure to meet any one of the four conditions will remove all of the issuer's

repurchases from the safe harbor for that day. The safe harbor, moreover, is not available for repurchases that, although made in technical compliance with the section, are part of a plan or scheme to evade the federal securities laws.

2. Regardless of whether the repurchases are effected in accordance with Rule 10b-18, reporting issuers must report their repurchasing activity as required by Item 703 of Regulations S-K and S-B (17 CFR 229.703 and 228.703) and Item 15(e) of Form 20-F (17 CFR 249.220f) (regarding foreign private issuers), and closed-end management investment companies that are registered under the Investment Company Act of 1940 must report their repurchasing activity as required by Item 8 of Form N-CSR (17 CFR 249.331; 17 CFR 274.128).

(a) *Definitions.* Unless otherwise provided, all terms used in this section shall have the same meaning as in the Act. In addition, the following definitions shall apply:

(1) *ADTV* means the average daily trading volume reported for the security during the four calendar weeks preceding the week in which the Rule 10b-18 purchase is to be effected.

(2) *Affiliate* means any person that directly or indirectly controls, is controlled by, or is under common control with, the issuer.

(3) *Affiliated purchaser* means:

(i) A person acting, directly or indirectly, in concert with the issuer for the purpose of acquiring the issuer's securities; or

(ii) An affiliate who, directly or indirectly, controls the issuer's purchases of such securities, whose purchases are controlled by the issuer, or whose purchases are under common control with those of the issuer; *provided, however,* that "affiliated purchaser" shall not include a broker, dealer, or other person solely by reason of such broker, dealer, or other person effecting Rule 10b-18 purchases on behalf of the issuer or for its account, and shall not include an officer or director of the issuer solely by reason of that officer or director's participation in the decision to authorize Rule 10b-18 purchases by or on behalf of the issuer.

(4) *Agent independent of the issuer* has the meaning contained in § 242.100 of this chapter.

(5) *Block* means a quantity of stock that either:

(i) Has a purchase price of $200,000 or more; or

(ii) Is at least 5,000 shares and has a purchase price of at least $50,000; or

(iii) Is at least 20 round lots of the security and totals 150 percent or more of the trading volume for that security or, in the event that trading volume data are unavailable, is at least 20 round lots of the security and totals at least one-tenth of one percent (.001) of the outstanding shares of the security, exclusive of any shares owned by any affiliate;

Provided, however, That a block under paragraph (a)(5)(i), (ii), and (iii) shall not include any amount a broker or dealer, acting as principal, has accumulated for the purpose of sale or resale to the issuer or to any affiliated purchaser of the issuer if the issuer or such affiliated purchaser knows or has reason to know that such amount was accumulated for such purpose, nor shall it include any amount that a broker or dealer has sold short to the issuer or to any affiliated purchaser of the issuer if the issuer or such affiliated purchaser knows or has reason to know that the sale was a short sale.

(6) *Consolidated system* means a consolidated transaction or quotation reporting system that collects and publicly disseminates on a current and continuous basis transaction or quotation information in common equity securities pursuant to an effective transaction reporting plan or an effective national market system plan (as those terms are defined in § 242.11600 of this chapter).

(7) *Market-wide trading suspension* means a market-wide trading halt of 30 minutes or more that is:

(i) Imposed pursuant to the rules of a national securities exchange or a national securities association in response to a market-wide decline during a single trading session; or

(ii) Declared by the Commission pursuant to its authority under section 12(k) of the Act (15 U.S.C. 78 *l* (k)).

(8) *Plan* has the meaning contained in § 242.100 of this chapter.

(9) *Principal market* for a security means the single securities market with the largest reported trading volume for the security during the six full calendar months preceding the week in which the Rule 10b-18 purchase is to be effected.

(10) *Public float value* has the meaning contained in § 242.100 of this chapter.

(11) *Purchase price* means the price paid per share as reported, exclusive of any commission paid to a broker acting as agent, or commission equivalent, mark-up, or differential paid to a dealer.

(12) *Riskless principal transaction* means a transaction in which a broker or dealer after having received an order from an issuer to buy its security, buys the security as principal in the market at the same price to satisfy the issuer's buy order. The issuer's buy order must be effected at the same price per-share at which the broker or dealer bought the shares to satisfy the issuer's buy order, exclusive of any explicitly disclosed markup or markdown, commission equivalent, or other fee. In addition, only the first leg of the transaction, when the broker or dealer buys the security in

the market as principal, is reported under the rules of a self-regulatory organization or under the Act. For purposes of this section, the broker or dealer must have written policies and procedures in place to assure that, at a minimum, the issuer's buy order was received prior to the offsetting transaction; the offsetting transaction is allocated to a riskless principal account or the issuer's account within 60 seconds of the execution; and the broker or dealer has supervisory systems in place to produce records that enable the broker or dealer to accurately and readily reconstruct, in a time-sequenced manner, all orders effected on a riskless principal basis.

(13) *Rule 10b-18 purchase* means a purchase (or any bid or limit order that would effect such purchase) of an issuer's common stock (or an equivalent interest, including a unit of beneficial interest in a trust or limited partnership or a depository share) by or for the issuer or any affiliated purchaser (including riskless principal transactions). However, it does *not* include any purchase of such security:

(i) Effected during the applicable restricted period of a distribution that is subject to § 242.102 of this chapter;

(ii) Effected by or for an issuer plan by an agent independent of the issuer;

(iii) Effected as a fractional share purchase (a fractional interest in a security) evidenced by a script certificate, order form, or similar document;

(iv) Effected during the period from the time of public announcement (as defined in § 230.165(f)) of a merger, acquisition, or similar transaction involving a recapitalization, until the earlier of the completion of such transaction or the completion of the vote by target shareholders. This exclusion does *not* apply to Rule 10b-18 purchases:

(A) Effected during such transaction in which the consideration is solely cash and there is no valuation period; or

(B) Where:

(1) The total volume of Rule 10b-18 purchases effected on any single day does not exceed the lesser of 25% of the security's four-week ADTV or the issuer's average daily Rule 10b-18 purchases during the three full calendar months preceding the date of the announcement of such transaction;

(2) The issuer's block purchases effected pursuant to paragraph (b)(4) of this section do not exceed the average size and frequency of the issuer's block purchases effected pursuant to paragraph (b)(4) of this section during the three full calendar months preceding the date of the announcement of such transaction; and

(3) Such purchases are not otherwise restricted or prohibited;

(v) Effected pursuant to § 240.13e-1;

(vi) Effected pursuant to a tender offer that is subject to § 240.13e-4 or specifically excepted from § 240.13e-4; or

(vii) Effected pursuant to a tender offer that is subject to section 14(d) of the Act (15 U.S.C. 78n(d)) and the rules and regulations thereunder.

(b) *Conditions to be met.* Rule 10b-18 purchases shall not be deemed to have violated the anti-manipulation provisions of sections 9(a)(2) or 10(b) of the Act (15 U.S.C. 78i(a)(2) or 78j(b)), or Rule 10b-5 under the Act, solely by reason of the time, price, or amount of the Rule 10b-18 purchases, or the number of brokers or dealers used in connection with such purchases, if the issuer or affiliated purchaser of the issuer effects the Rule 10b-18 purchases according to each of the following conditions:

(1) *One broker or dealer.* Rule 10b-18 purchases must be effected from or through only one broker or dealer on any single day; *Provided, however,* that:

(i) The "one broker or dealer" condition shall not apply to Rule 10b-18 purchases that are not solicited by or on behalf of the issuer or its affiliated purchaser(s);

(ii) Where Rule 10b-18 purchases are effected by or on behalf of more than one affiliated purchaser of the issuer (or the issuer and one or more of its affiliated purchasers) on a single day, the issuer and all affiliated purchasers must use the same broker or dealer; and

(iii) Where Rule 10b-18 purchases are effected on behalf of the issuer by a broker-dealer that is not an electronic communication network (ECN) or other alternative trading system (ATS), that broker-dealer can access ECN or other ATS liquidity in order to execute repurchases on behalf of the issuer (or any affiliated purchaser of the issuer) on that day.

(2) *Time of purchases.* Rule 10b-18 purchases must not be:

(i) The opening (regular way) purchase reported in the consolidated system;

(ii) Effected during the 10 minutes before the scheduled close of the primary trading session in the principal market for the security, and the 10 minutes before the scheduled close of the primary trading session in the market where the purchase is effected, for a security that has an ADTV value of $1 million or more and a public float value of $150 million or more; and

(iii) Effected during the 30 minutes before the scheduled close of the primary trading session in the principal market for the security, and the 30 minutes before the scheduled close of the primary trading session in the market where the purchase is effected, for all other securities;

(iv) However, for purposes of this section, Rule 10b-18 purchases may be effected following the close of the primary trading session until the termination of the period in which last sale prices are reported in the consolidated system so long as such purchases are effected at prices that do not exceed the lower of the closing price of the primary trading session in the principal market for the security and any lower bids or sale prices subsequently reported in the consolidated system, and all of this section's conditions are met. However, for purposes of this section, the issuer may use one broker or dealer to effect Rule 10b-18 purchases during this period that may be different from the broker or dealer that it used during the primary trading session. However, the issuer's Rule 10b-18 purchase may not be the opening transaction of the session following the close of the primary trading session.

(3) *Price of purchases.* Rule 10b-18 purchases must be effected at a purchase price that:

(i) Does not exceed the highest independent bid or the last independent transaction price, whichever is higher, quoted or reported in the consolidated system at the time the Rule 10b-18 purchase is effected;

(ii) For securities for which bids and transaction prices are not quoted or reported in the consolidated system, Rule 10b-18 purchases must be effected at a purchase price that does not exceed the highest independent bid or the last independent transaction price, whichever is higher, displayed and disseminated on any national securities exchange or on any inter-dealer quotation system (as defined in § 240.15c2-11) that displays at least two priced quotations for the security, at the time the Rule 10b-18 purchase is effected; and

(iii) For all other securities, Rule 10b-18 purchases must be effected at a price no higher than the highest independent bid obtained from three independent dealers.

(4) *Volume of purchases.* The total volume of Rule 10b-18 purchases effected by or for the issuer and any affiliated purchasers effected on any single day must not exceed 25 percent of the ADTV for that security; *However*, once each week, in lieu of purchasing under the 25 percent of ADTV limit for that day, the issuer or an affiliated purchaser of the issuer may effect one block purchase if:

(i) No other Rule 10b-18 purchases are effected that day, and

(ii) The block purchase is *not* included when calculating a security's four week ADTV under this section.

(c) *Alternative conditions.* The conditions of paragraph (b) of this section shall apply in connection with Rule 10b-18 purchases effected during a trading session following the imposition of a market-wide trading suspension, except:

(1) That the time of purchases condition in paragraph (b)(2) of this section shall not apply, either:

(i) From the reopening of trading until the scheduled close of trading on the day that the market-wide trading suspension is imposed; or

(ii) At the opening of trading on the next trading day until the scheduled close of trading that day, if a market-wide trading suspension was in effect at the close of trading on the preceding day; and

(2) The volume of purchases condition in paragraph (b)(4) of this section is modified so that the amount of Rule 10b-18 purchases must not exceed 100 percent of the ADTV for that security.

(d) *Other purchases.* No presumption shall arise that an issuer or an affiliated purchaser has violated the anti-manipulation provisions of Section 9(a)(2) or 10(b) of the Act (15 U.S.C. 78i(a)(2) or 78j(b)), or Rule 10b-5 under the Act, if the Rule 10b-18 purchases of such issuer or affiliated purchaser do not meet the conditions specified in paragraph (b) or (c) of this section.

McCORMICK v. FUND AM. COS.

United States Court of Appeals, Ninth Circuit
26 F.3d 869 (1994)

OPINION OF THE COURT

FLETCHER, CIRCUIT JUDGE

Plaintiff William M. McCormick appeals the dismissal of his claims on summary judgment. Between 1983 and 1989, McCormick was CEO of the Fireman's Fund Insurance Company (FFIC), a wholly-owned subsidiary of defendant Fund American Companies (FAC). When McCormick resigned from FFIC, he owned approximately 500,000 performance shares and option shares in FAC. The vesting period for these securities ran through the end of 1991. McCormick sold all of his securities back to FAC in May 1990. At that time, FAC was involved in negotiations for the sale of FFIC to a large foreign insurer. Those discussions were ultimately fruitful, and as a result of the sale of FFIC, the market value of FAC shares nearly doubled.

Before the buyout of McCormick's securities was completed, company officials told McCormick about the pending discussions with the foreign insurer, and about the likely increase in the value of FAC stock if the sale were made. After the sale, McCormick claimed that the officials had misrepresented or omitted many material facts. He brought suit against FAC under § 10(b) of the Securities Exchange Act of 1934, and also alleged various related state statutory and common-law claims. The district court granted summary judgment in favor of FAC on all claims. We affirm.

FACTS

1. FAC's initial discussion with investment banker

On January 4, 1990, John J. Byrne, CEO and chairman of the board of FAC, and Robert Marto, FAC's executive vice president and chief financial officer, met in New York with Robert Lusardi, a senior vice president at Lehman Brothers, investment bankers for FFIC. The three men discussed a possible sale of a minority interest in FFIC. Lusardi told the FAC executives that he thought the sale of a minority interest was not a good idea. McCormick contends that Lusardi also told Byrne and Marto that the best strategy would be to sell FFIC outright, but Marto denied in his deposition that Lusardi had made such a statement, and nothing in the testimony cited by McCormick indicates otherwise.

The parties disagree about whether, later in January 1990, Lusardi was retained to find a buyer for FFIC. Byrne and Marto both denied in their depositions that any retainer arrangement was entered into until July 1990. McCormick, however, cites to FAC's November 1990 proxy statement, in which it is stated that "FAC engaged Lehman Brothers as of January 15, 1990, to act as FAC's agent for the purpose of identifying opportunities for the sale of FAC and/or FFIC and its subsidiaries." Proxy Statement at 23.

2. Lusardi's February meeting and subsequent activity

On February 8, 1990, Lusardi went to Germany and met with representatives of Allianz, a large German insurance company, to inquire whether Allianz was interested in purchasing either a minority stake in FFIC or the whole company. Lusardi testified that he had not been "authorized per se" to do this, but that it is in the nature of investment banking to test the waters without such specific authorization. Lusardi also testified that he had missed a similar opportunity for FAC on an earlier occasion, and that he was anxious not to repeat his mistake.

On February 21, 1990, Lusardi wrote a letter to Alexander Hoyos of Allianz, stating in pertinent part that

> To demonstrate that the transaction [discussed on February 8] would indeed be completed by the company, and that we were "authorized" to discuss it, the company's senior management has agreed to be available for a preliminary meeting at our offices in New York. Depending on whom Allianz sends to the meeting, the Chief Financial Officer and/or the Chairman and Chief Executive Officer would attend. Their schedules are such that they are available to meet during March 13 to 16th. Lusardi testified that he had learned that the FAC executives would be available on those days through a conversation with Marto. No meeting took place in March. Apparently Lusardi continued to provide Allianz with information about FFIC through April of 1990.

3. May 4 meeting between Allianz and FAC and subsequent events

On April 26, 1990, Lusardi scheduled a meeting for May 4 between Allianz representatives and Marto and Jay Brown, president and CEO of FFIC. At some point before Marto and Brown attended the meeting, which was held at Allianz's offices in Munich, they asked Byrne for permission to attend. It is unclear when this occurred. Brown remembered Byrne asking him in March when it would be convenient for him, Brown, to meet with Allianz. Brown, however, said that the conversation took place "on or about May 1." Byrne also testified that at the time he believed that all Allianz was interested in buying was a 20% share in FFIC.

At the May 4 meeting, Brown gave an overview of FFIC and its insurance business; Marto talked about FAC's other assets. Marto also discussed various ways in which to structure a possible sale: Allianz might buy either FAC or FFIC; if FFIC were purchased, FAC would be willing to reinsure up to half of FFIC's reserves, and/or to buy back any non-insurance assets at book value. Marto also mentioned a firm selling price — $3.4 or $3.5 billion.

Brown testified that he was unable to determine whether or not Allianz had any interest at all in the transaction. Byrne testified that both Brown and Marto reported back to him that the Allianz representatives had sat poker-faced during FAC's presentation. Subsequently, after Allianz had expressed an interest in further negotiations, Brown told Lusardi that the Allianz representatives showed more respect for FFIC at the May 4 meeting than they had shown five years earlier, when they had offered a very low bid. Brown also told Lusardi that the meeting had gone "fairly well."

On May 9, Marto sent Allianz confidential information, along with a confidentiality agreement which Allianz was to execute. Marto had previously disclosed some nonpublic information at the May 4 meeting. Also on May 9, Marto wrote a letter to Allianz confirming that FAC was willing to buy back at book value any of FFIC's non-insurance assets, and to reinsure up to 50% of FFIC's reserves. On May 14, Lusardi told Byrne and Marto that Allianz was interested in further discussions in early June. Around this time, Byrne began to realize that "more had been going on than [he] had realized," and he planned to get to the bottom of it with Marto and Lusardi after finishing his work for the shareholders' and directors' meeting scheduled for May 16.

4. The buyout of McCormick's securities

On April 27, Byrne proposed to McCormick that FAC repurchase his securities for $6 million. On May 14, Byrne raised the offer to $8 million; this amounted to a per-share price of $38 at a time when the shares were trading for $31 per share.[131] Byrne stated that this was the last offer FAC would make to McCormick that year. McCormick signed a buyout agreement and release on May 15 so that Byrne could present it for approval at the directors' meeting scheduled for May 16. At the time he signed the agreement, McCormick had been told nothing about FAC's discussions with Allianz.

---

[131] [1] The $8 million figure also included $1.3 million for McCormick's nonstock benefits.

On the morning of May 16, however, Byrne was approached by George Gillespie, a member of FAC's board of directors and a partner at the law firm of Cravath, Swain & Moore, general counsel for FAC. Gillespie had learned about the Allianz developments from another Cravath partner, who had drafted the May 9 confidentiality agreement at Marto's request. Gillespie told Byrne that he was very concerned about allowing McCormick to go through with the buyout without first being told about the Allianz developments. Byrne agreed that disclosure should be made, and told Marto to brief McCormick on the Allianz discussions.

That briefing was memorialized in the following acknowledgment, dated May 16, 1990 and signed by McCormick and Marto (the Acknowledgment):

> On this date, while the Human Resources Committee of the Board of Directors of Fund American was meeting, among other things to consider the proposed buy-out of William McCormick's employment contract interests, including his almost 500,000 shares of Fund American stock, in various forms, Mr. McCormick and Robert Marto met. Mr. Marto advised Mr. McCormick that the preliminary discussions were about to commence with a possible foreign buyer of Fireman's Fund Insurance Company (FFIC) and that a confidentiality letter had been sent to such possible foreign buyer. If a transaction were to eventuate, after presumably extensive due diligence, the price might well exceed $50 per Fund American share-a price well above the approximately $38 per Fund American share/option called for by Mr. McCormick's buy-out proposal before the Human Resources Committee. The Committee is concerned that Mr. McCormick understand the foregoing and, if the buyout goes forward in the terms discussed, that Mr. McCormick acknowledge that he has been fully and adequately informed of the foregoing facts and circumstances.

McCormick's briefing was largely confined to the items specified in the Acknowledgment. McCormick asked Marto for the name of the foreign buyer, but was told that this was confidential. McCormick also asked Byrne about the transaction. In particular, McCormick asked Byrne if he had known about the possible sale when he first approached McCormick with the buyout proposal on April 27. Byrne said that he did not. Byrne did tell McCormick that as of May 16, there had been a preliminary meeting with the potential buyer. The parties then went through with the buyout of McCormick's shares.[132]

5. Post-Buyout events

Two days after the buyout, FAC and Allianz scheduled a meeting for early June 1990; in June, Allianz representatives came to San Francisco for several days of discussions with FAC representatives. As late as mid-July 1990, however, both Byrne and Lusardi were doubtful that the sale would go through, since the parties disagreed about price. But on August 1, 1990, Allianz and FAC agreed that Allianz

---

[132] [2] Counsel for McCormick conceded at oral argument that while McCormick may technically have been bound to go through with the buyout on the basis of the agreement he signed on May 15, 1990, the parties' understanding at the time was that he could have backed out of the bargain after the May 16 disclosure.

would buy FFIC for $3.315 billion. FAC agreed to buy back the non-insurance assets. The price of FAC stock eventually rose to about $50 per share.

6. Litigation

After McCormick had been successful in getting FAC to invest in his new insurance venture, PennCorp, he demanded an additional $5 million in connection with the May 16 buyout. When FAC refused, McCormick sued, alleging violation of federal and state securities laws, common law breach of fiduciary duty, fraud, negligent misrepresentation, and rescission. At the heart of all of the claims are eight alleged omissions and seven alleged misrepresentations in the Acknowledgment and the briefing which accompanied it.

DISCUSSION

We review the district court's summary judgment ruling de novo. *In re Apple Computer Secs. Litig.*, 886 F.2d 1109, 1112 (9th Cir. 1989), *cert denied*, 496 U.S. 943, 110 S. Ct. 3229, 110 L. Ed. 2d 676 (1990). Summary judgment is appropriate if there is no genuine dispute of material fact and the moving party is entitled to judgment as a matter of law. Id. Although materiality, the dispositive issue here, is a "fact-specific issue which should ordinarily be left to the trier of fact," summary judgment may nevertheless be justified "in appropriate cases." Id. at 1113. Summary judgment is only appropriate if no rational finder of fact could find that the alleged misrepresentations and omissions were material. Id. at 1115.

I. Violation of Federal Securities Laws

To make out a claim under § 10(b) of the Securities and Exchange Act, 15 U.S.C. § 78j(b), and Rule 10b-5, 17 C.F.R. § 240.10b-5, plaintiff must show that there has been a misstatement or omission of material fact, made with scienter, which proximately caused his or her injury. *McGonigle v. Combs*, 968 F.2d 810, 817 (9th Cir.), *cert. dismissed*, ___ U.S. ___, 113 S. Ct. 399, 121 L. Ed. 2d 325 (1992). In addition, the misstatement or omission complained of must be misleading; in the case of an omission, "[s]ilence, absent a duty to disclose, is not misleading under Rule 10b-5." *Basic Inc. v. Levinson*, 485 U.S. 224, 239 n. 17, 108 S. Ct. 978, 987 n. 17, 99 L. Ed. 2d 194 (1988).

A. Duty to Disclose

FAC's conduct on May 16, 1990 indicated that at that time it recognized a duty either to disclose to McCormick material nonpublic information relating to the transaction it was about to engage in with him, or to refrain from repurchasing his securities. FAC's brief, however, together with counsel's comments at oral argument, suggests that in the course of litigation FAC has distanced itself from that position.

The original position was the correct one. Numerous authorities have held or otherwise stated that the corporate issuer in possession of material nonpublic information, must, like other insiders in the same situation, disclose that information to its shareholders or refrain from trading with them. *Smith v. Duff & Phelps, Inc.*, 891 F.2d 1567, 1572-75 (11th Cir. 1990) (duty to disclose merger negotiations to an employee who departs voluntarily and cashes in his shares as a condition of termination); *Jordan v. Duff & Phelps, Inc.*, 815 F.2d 429, 435-39 (7th Cir. 1987) (same), *cert. dismissed*, 485 U.S. 901, 108 S. Ct. 1067, 99 L. Ed. 2d 229 (1988); *Kohler v. Kohler Co.*, 319 F.2d 634, 638 (7th Cir. 1963) ("underlying principles [mandating disclosure of material nonpublic information] apply not only to majority stockholders of corporations and corporate insiders, but equally to corporations themselves"); *Green v. Hamilton Internat'l Corp.*, 437 F. Supp. 723, 728 (S.D.N.Y. 1977) ("there can be no doubt that the prohibition against insider' trading extends to a corporation"); VII Louis Loss & Joel Seligman, Securities Regulation 1505 (3d ed. 1991) ("When the issuer itself wants to buy or sell its own securities, it has a choice; desist or disclose"); Richard Jennings & Harold Marsh, Securities Regulation 1044 n. 12 (6th ed. 1987) ("the issuer itself is, of course, also covered [by insider trading laws]"); Daniel J. Winnike, *Rule 10b-5's Effect on Employer Stock Repurchases and Option Cancellations on Termination of Employment*, 19 Sec. Reg. L.J. 227, 237-38 (1991) ("there is little doubt that the relationship between a corporation and its shareholders engenders the type of trust and confidence" necessary to trigger the duty to disclose or abstain); *see also Levinson v. Basic, Inc.*, 786 F.2d 741, 746 (6th Cir. 1986) ("courts have held that a duty to disclose [merger] negotiations arises in situations such as where the corporation is trading in its own stock"), *vacated on other grounds*, 485 U.S. 224, 108 S. Ct. 978, 99 L. Ed. 2d 194 (1988); *Arber v. Essex Wire Corp.*, 490 F.2d 414, 418 (6th Cir.), *cert. denied*, 419 U.S. 830, 95 S. Ct. 53, 42 L. Ed. 2d 56 (1974); *Grigsby v. CMI Corp.*, 590 F. Supp. 826, 830 (N.D. Cal. 1984), *aff'd*, 765 F.2d 1369 (9th Cir. 1985).[133] *Cf. Glazer v. Formica Corp.*, 964 F.2d 149, 157 (2d Cir. 1992) (publicly-held corporation had no duty to disclose because there was no suggestion that corporation was trading in its own stock); *Backman v. Polaroid Corp.*, 910 F.2d 10, 13 (1st Cir. 1990) (same).

This hardly resolves the issues presented by this lawsuit, however. FAC was required to disclose only material information, and to avoid material misrepresentations. *McGonigle*, 968 F.2d at 817. Materiality is a separate inquiry, and the crux of this case.

B. Material Omissions and Misrepresentations

In *Basic v. Levinson*, the Supreme Court applied in a § 10(b) case involving undisclosed merger negotiations the standard for materiality it had previously announced in the proxy solicitation context: an omitted fact is material if there is "a substantial likelihood that the disclosure of the omitted fact would have been viewed by the reasonable investor as having significantly altered the "total mix" of

---

[133] [3] The particular difficulties posed when the nonpublic information in question concerns negotiations for a merger or sale were aptly summarized by one court over 30 years ago: [W]hat is a company to do in circumstances such as these when delicate preliminary but serious negotiations are being conducted at a time when it is desirable to try to buy out a disaffected stockholder? The options seem to us to be: (1) to refuse to disclose and refrain from buying during negotiations; (2) to disclose and attempt to buy during negotiations; and (3) if it clearly appears that the selling stockholder is in no way relying on nondisclosure, to take a chance on litigation. . . . *Rogen v. Ilikon Corp.*, 361 F.2d 260, 268 (1st Cir. 1966) (footnote omitted).

information made available." 485 U.S. at 231-32, 108 S. Ct. at 983 (quoting *TSC Industries, Inc. v. Northway, Inc.*, 426 U.S. 438, 449, 96 S. Ct. 2126, 2132, 48 L. Ed. 2d 757 (1976)). The Court also endorsed the method for assessing materiality discussed in *SEC v. Texas Gulf Sulphur*, 401 F.2d 833 (2d Cir. 1968), *cert. denied*, 394 U.S. 976, 89 S. Ct. 1454, 22 L. Ed. 2d 756 (1969): materiality depends upon a balancing of the magnitude of the corporate event in question and the likelihood that the event will occur. 485 U.S. at 238-39, 108 S. Ct. at 987.

This case involves a somewhat different application of the concepts of magnitude and probability. We need not determine whether, given the likelihood that FFIC would be sold (indisputably an event of great magnitude), disclosure of the potential sale was required: FAC did disclose that a sale was possible. McCormick's argument is that he was not adequately informed about the likelihood itself. He argues that while FAC told him about the possible sale, it omitted or misrepresented those facts which would have shown him just how likely it was that the deal would go through. Had he known those facts, he argues, he would never have sold his securities.

We do not find the authorities cited by either side to be particularly helpful to our task of applying the general principles announced in *Basic* to the facts of this case. Defendant contends that the reasoning in *Taylor v. First Union Corp.*, 857 F.2d 240 (4th Cir. 1988), *cert. denied*, 489 U.S. 1080, 109 S. Ct. 1532, 103 L. Ed. 2d 837 (1989), is "dispositive" of this case, but it is not. In *Taylor*, shareholders in Bank A sold their stock to Bank B, which was at the time involved in preliminary merger negotiations with Bank A. These negotiations were not disclosed to the shareholders. The Fourth Circuit reversed a jury verdict in favor of the shareholders and against the banks. The court concluded, first, that the banks' failure to disclose the merger discussions was not actionable because, according to *Basic*, "[s]ilence, absent a duty to disclose, is not misleading under Rule 10b-5," and the banks had no such duty. *Taylor*, 857 F.2d at 243 (quoting *Basic*, 485 U.S. at 239 n. 17, 108 S. Ct. at 987 n. 17). In the present case, however, as noted above, FAC, as a repurchaser of its own stock did have a duty to disclose material information to the selling shareholder.[134]

The *Taylor* court also held that it did not matter whether or not a duty to disclose existed, because the omission complained of was not material. But the circumstances in *Taylor* were very different from the circumstances here: in Taylor, at the time plaintiffs' stock was purchased, a merger between the two banks would have been illegal; it was only after a subsequent Supreme Court decision that it became feasible. 857 F.2d at 244. Moreover, in *Taylor* there had been no actual negotiations or instructions to investment bankers. *Id.* The situation is otherwise here.

Defendant also relies on *Glazer v. Formica*, where the corporate defendant did not tell investors of discussions in which it was engaged with a group which subsequently acquired it in a leveraged buyout. The Second Circuit affirmed summary judgment for the defendant. It did so, however, not because the undisclosed negotiations were immaterial, but rather because the company had no

[134] [4] That duty did not obtain in *Taylor* because Bank A, in which plaintiffs were shareholders, did not purchase plaintiffs' shares; while Bank B, which did buy their shares, did not owe any special duty to them because they were not Bank B shareholders. *See Taylor*, 857 F.2d at 246-47. The situation in *Taylor* was similar to what the situation would have been here if Allianz, rather than FAC, had bought McCormick's stock. But that is not what happened.

duty to disclose those negotiations. 964 F.2d at 156-57. But again, that argument is unavailable to FAC, because FAC was trading with one of its own shareholders.

The *Glazer* court also held that the first in the series of interactions between the company and the group which led the leveraged buyout was not in itself material activity. *Id.* at 155. This initial contact consisted of a single phone call from the potential buyer, requesting further discussions with the defendant company. *Id.* at 152. This was far less substantial, and far less extended, than the series of interactions which FAC had had with Allianz by May 16. The fact that the phone call in *Glazer* was not material therefore says little about whether or not the contacts between FAC and Allianz were.

Finally, defendant relies on *Starkman v. Marathon Oil Co.*, 772 F.2d 231 (6th Cir. 1985), *cert. denied*, 475 U.S. 1015, 106 S. Ct. 1195, 89 L. Ed. 2d 310 (1986). Defendant does so in error; *Starkman* was decided before *Basic*, and it cited as authoritative a bright-line test for determining the materiality of merger negotiations which the Basic Court rejected. Compare 772 F.2d at 243 (citing the "agreement-in principle" test) with 485 U.S. at 232-36, 108 S. Ct. at 993-86 (rejecting that test). Defendant's reliance on *Starkman* is misplaced.

The precedent plaintiff cites does not afford much more assistance. McCormick is certainly correct that claims such as his — based on the theory that the investor was not adequately informed of the likelihood of some major corporate event — have been recognized under the federal securities laws. *E.g., American General Ins. Co. v. Equitable General Corp.*, 493 F. Supp. 721 (E.D. Va. 1980) (defendant makes some disclosure about pending merger negotiations, but misrepresents the likelihood of success by mischaracterizing the negotiations as "preliminary"). The facts of *American General*, however, are not, as plaintiff puts it, "hauntingly similar" to the facts of this case. In *American General*, the defendant flat-out lied to the plaintiff, providing a warranty which stated that defendant was not attempting to negotiate any merger agreement, when in fact it was doing so. *Id.* at 737. No such blatant misrepresentations were made here.

Nor does plaintiff derive much benefit from *Holmes v. Bateson*, 583 F.2d 542 (1st Cir. 1978). In *Holmes*, defendants did not tell plaintiff of pending merger negotiations even after they had been advised by their lawyer that the securities laws required disclosure. *Id.* at 556. Eventually, plaintiff's attorney did find out that a merger was planned (whether from defendants or from some other source the opinion does not explain). Even then, however, plaintiff failed to appreciate the favorable consequences of a merger because defendants consistently misrepresented the worth of their own company, and then told plaintiff's attorney that there was not much money to be made out of the merger. *Id.* at 551. Here, by contrast, when FAC disclosed the fact that negotiations with a possible buyer were ongoing, it also made consequences of the projected deal very clear: the market value of McCormick's securities would rise dramatically. Thus unlike the investor in Holmes, McCormick knew that he risked losing greater profits by selling while negotiations were pending.

Plaintiff's other cases are also unhelpful, since they involve defendants who made no disclosure whatsoever. *SEC v. Sharpiro*, 494 F.2d 1301 (2d Cir. 1974); *Dungan v. Colt Industries*, 532 F. Supp. 832 (N.D. Ill. 1982). In short, the case law does not provide us with any easy answers at the level of generality the parties suggest. Rather, we, like the district court, must examine the alleged omissions and misrepresentations one by one and cumulatively, in order to determine whether singly or together they were both misleading and material.

C. The Eight Omissions

1. FAC retained Lehman Bros., as of January 15, to sell FFIC

A preliminary question is whether this statement, which plaintiff argues should have been made to him, is true. Marto testified that a sale of FFIC as a whole was not discussed at the January 4 meeting, and the testimony of the three persons who attended the meeting indicates that even their discussion about the sale of a minority interest in FFIC was informal (and pessimistic). Moreover, Lusardi testified that when he met with Allianz in February, he was acting on his own initiative. And the FAC executives testified that no formal retainer agreement was drawn up until July.

To contradict these assertions, McCormick points to FAC's November 1990 proxy statement, in which it is stated that Lehman Brothers was "engaged as of January 15, 1990, to act as FAC's agent for the purpose of identifying opportunities for sale of FAC and/or FFIC and its subsidiaries." This language is picked up from the retainer agreement, which is dated "as of January 15, 1990." The retainer agreement itself, however, clearly was not drafted until long after January 1990.

While it appears to us that the back-dating of the contract was intended to govern rights between Lehman Brothers and FAC rather than to serve as an accurate account of events as they actually occurred, we are nevertheless disturbed by defendant's refusal to address the references to January 15 in the proxy statement and the retainer agreement itself. We acknowledge that it is possible that the dating of the contract was meant to reflect a recognition that Lusardi was authorized to represent FAC in the months following January 4. Thus it is not entirely clear that the statement plaintiff says should have been included was untrue.

But even if Lusardi was retained on January 15, this was not a material fact. As the district court pointed out, some involvement of investment bankers should have been apparent to McCormick. The time of involvement would not have signaled much about whether negotiations had gone beyond preliminary exploration, and McCormick knew that preliminary discussions had begun. The only fact that McCormick could not have gleaned from the Acknowledgment was that the investment banker had been looking for a possible buyer for several months, and that at some point along the way FAC had given him the green light. But the fact that the banker had been searching is subsumed into the fact that he found a possible buyer. The details of FAC's arrangements with Lehman Brothers were not material.

2. In February, FAC committed in writing to entertain the sale of FFIC

Again, a preliminary question is whether this statement is true. We see nothing in the record to support it. On February 21, Lusardi wrote to Allianz, and stated that the CFO and CEO would be available for a meeting in late March. Lusardi testified that he learned about the executives' schedules from Marto. But this does not mean that Marto (or anyone else at FAC) committed to anything in writing. FAC can hardly be faulted for omitting to say something that was not true.

3. FAC pursued Allianz and conducted face-to-face negotiations in Germany

Once again, we must be concerned with the accuracy of the information plaintiff argues should have been disclosed. If anyone "pursued" Allianz, it was Lusardi. Lusardi told Marto about this "pursuit," and Marto put his stamp of approval on it, as reflected in Lusardi's February 21 letter.

Here again, the result of the pursuit is the critical fact, not the pursuit itself. McCormick was told the result: that there had been a preliminary meeting. Arguably, who pursued whom in setting up the meeting was a material fact in establishing FAC's level of interest in the deal, but it is simply not true that FAC was the pursuer. Lusardi was.

A fact clearly omitted from the Acknowledgment was that the foreign buyer was Allianz. Plaintiff says that this piece of information alone would have made him decide not to sell his securities: Allianz is a very large insurance company, and plaintiff believed that it had "more money than God."

What McCormick knew was that there had already been discussions and that further discussions had been scheduled. Presumably no buyer would waste its time with such activity if it didn't have the money to buy the target company. However, there may have been something about the size and wealth of Allianz which would have indicated to sophisticated investors that it was more likely to consummate the deal than other potential buyers, serious though they might be. If that were true, then knowing that the buyer was Allianz would at least arguably have altered the total mix of information.

In this case, FAC neither disclosed nor failed to disclose; instead, it told plaintiff that it had certain information (the name of the buyer), but that the information was confidential.

McCormick decided to proceed despite FAC's refusal to identify the potential buyer. We conclude, particularly in light of McCormick's considerable sophistication, that this quasi-disclosure was sufficient. We are persuaded by the reasoning of *Jensen v. Kimble*, 1 F.3d 1073 (10th Cir. 1993). In that case, as here, a sophisticated investor was offered a favorable deal on his securities; meanwhile, negotiations concerning a crucial event in the life of the corporation (there, a merger) were pending. In *Jensen*, much as in this case, plaintiff knew that the merger was contemplated, and asked defendant to identify the players. Defendant declined to do so. The Tenth Circuit held that this omission was not actionable under Rule 10b-5 because defendant had "specifically advised" plaintiff of the nondisclosures complained of. 1 F.3d at 1077. In other words, since plaintiff "knew what he didn't know," there was nothing misleading in the omission — and Rule 10b-5 penalizes only those who are responsible for misleading omissions or misrepresentations. *Id.* at 1078.

In this case, similarly, McCormick knew that he didn't know the name of the buyer. Hence, while that information may have been material, defendant's failure to disclose it was not misleading, and hence not actionable.

4. Nonpublic information had already been furnished to Allianz

Once again, the disclosures which were made cured this omission. McCormick knew that a confidentiality letter had been sent; he should have been able to infer from this fact that confidential information would be sent too.

5. After review of nonpublic information, Allianz asked for further discussions

McCormick also argues that the timing of FAC's disclosure to Allianz of nonpublic information was important: McCormick's argument is that a company which expresses interest in buying another company after having reviewed confidential information — which may well be unfavorable — is more likely to consummate a transaction than is a company which has asked for further talks without yet having seen the information.

We reject this argument. First, we do not think it pertains to McCormick's situation. Confidential information is often dispatched along with the confidentiality letter. McCormick was told that such a letter had been sent, and as a sophisticated business executive, he should have known that there was at least a possibility that the information itself had been sent along with it.

Second, even assuming that this possibility was not apparent to McCormick, the undisclosed fact — the timing of the dispatch of confidential information — was not material in light of the disclosure which was made. McCormick knew that negotiations had begun and indeed had reached a point where FAC was able to estimate the likely rise in the value of its stock. McCormick was on notice that sale was being contemplated, and contemplated fairly seriously. Details about precisely who knew how much at what stage of the negotiations were just that: details. They did not significantly after the total mix of information.

. . . .

7. FAC had agreed to reinsure up to 50% of FFIC's reserves

In both instances, it would be more accurate to say that FAC had offered to do these things than that it had "agreed" to do them. As defendant points out repeatedly, while FAC made these offers in the May 4 meeting and the May 9 letter, Allianz did not respond to them in any specific way.

McCormick appears to suggest that even the fact that offers had been made was material. First, he suggests that the fact that details concerning the structure of the deal had been discussed suggests that the negotiations between the parties had reached a relatively advanced stage. However, the very magnitude of the offers which had been made and not yet accepted (the buy-back of assets would reduce the net price of FFIC by 67%) reveals that major issues still remained to be decided, and that discussions were still in an early stage. In addition, as the district court pointed out, McCormick should have inferred that the transaction had been discussed in at least some detail: otherwise, FAC would not have been able to estimate, even in round numbers, the likely rise in stock price.

Second, McCormick suggests that the fact that FAC was willing to be so flexible showed how eager it was for the sale to go through. Willingness, however, if not eagerness, could have been inferred from the fact that there already had been and would be more discussions with the foreign buyer. Moreover, while flexibility as to structure and reinsurance may have shown eagerness to sell, FAC appears to have been quite inflexible with respect to price; in fact, it appears that the whole deal nearly broke down in the middle of July because of the parties' inability to agree about price. Thus McCormick would have learned little new about the likelihood that a sale would take place if he had been told FAC was willing to consider various options in structuring the deal.

8. FAC and Lusardi had planned meetings with a tax expert to discuss post-sale holding company issues

On May 14, apparently at the request of Marto or Byrne, Lusardi scheduled a meeting between FAC executives and a tax expert at Lehman Brothers; the purpose of the meeting was to discuss tax consequences of the potential transaction, including the consequences if FAC were to come under the 1940 Holding Company Act.

As with many of the omissions above, this was not material in light of the disclosure that was made: McCormick knew that FAC was engaged in discussions with a foreign buyer, and could have inferred that some investigation into the tax consequences of the deal would have been concomitant with those discussions.

The Seven Misrepresentations[135]

1. A confidentiality letter was sent to Allianz

McCormick's argument is that this was a misrepresentation because it implied that only a letter had been sent, and not that confidential information had been sent too.

Assuming this inference could be drawn, the statement was not materially misleading. McCormick should have inferred that confidential information would soon be sent, or indeed had already been sent along with the letter. See supra, discussion of Omissions #4 and #5. McCormick was not materially misled about the level of FAC's interest in the deal.

---

[135] [5] The first three alleged misrepresentations are contained in the Acknowledgment. The last four were made when McCormick spoke with Byrne after having been briefed by Marto on the substance of the Acknowledgment.

2. Preliminary discussions were about to start

McCormick argues that this statement was misleading insofar as it suggested that discussions had not already begun. As noted above, however, McCormick admitted that Byrne told him that some discussions had already taken place.

McCormick also takes issue with the word "preliminary," arguing that it is misleading because Lusardi had been talking to Allianz for three months, and "substantive negotiations" were under way. Yet "preliminary" was not a misnomer: FAC itself had only met with Allianz for two hours (the May 4 meetings), and its various suggestions about how the deal might be structured had been neither accepted nor rejected. This statement does not amount to a misrepresentation.

3. The buyer's due diligence had not yet begun

McCormick derives this alleged misrepresentation from the statement in the Acknowledgment that a transaction might take place "after presumably extensive due diligence."

There is no misrepresentation here. First, the statement does not indicate that due diligence had not yet begun, but rather that a transaction might go through after due diligence had been completed. Second, even if the statement did imply that due diligence had not begun, McCormick has not pointed to anything showing that it had begun. He appears to argue that he knows now that due diligence had already begun because the "agreement" between the parties that FAC would buy back FFIC's non-insurance assets and reinsure FFIC's reserves must have been the result of Allianz's due diligence investigation. But as explained above, there is no evidence of any such agreement; only of an offer by FAC to structure the deal in these ways if desirable.

4. Byrne did not know about the Allianz developments when he proposed the buyout on April 27

Whether or not this statement is true is a matter of conflict within the testimony of the FAC executives. Byrne testified that between the January 4 meeting with Lusardi, and May 1, when Marto and Brown asked him if they could go to Germany to talk with Allianz, he knew nothing of any discussions about selling FFIC. On the other hand, Brown said he believed Byrne had asked him in March to name a date when it would be convenient for Brown to meet with Allianz.[136]

McCormick does not explain in any detail why it was material that Byrne may have known about Allianz's interest[137] before he approached McCormick with the

[136] [6] In addition, Lusardi wrote in a notation on an April 5 letter to Allianz that "The issue we discussed should be resolved. I believe it comes from the chairman" — that is, Byrne. Although Lusardi testified that he hadn't had any discussions with Byrne at the time, and didn't know what the notation referred to, the notation itself provides contrary evidence.

[137] [7] FAC argues at one point that it is simply untrue that Allianz demonstrated an interest before April 27-regardless of what Byrne knew or did not know by that date. FAC suggests that the first expression of interest came on May 14, when Allianz told Lusardi that it was planning a trip to San Francisco to meet with FAC. But FAC defines the term "interest" to narrowly. It could at least be argued

buyout offer. But McCormick's theory seems to be that if Byrne had the possible sale of FFIC in mind when he made the offer to repurchase McCormick's securities, then possibly his decision to make that offer was motivated by self-interest: if the corporation could recapture the securities before the sale to Allianz, all of the shareholders (including Byrne) could reap some part of profits which McCormick would have gotten if he had held onto his stock.

The relevance of Byrne's motives to the probability that the Allianz deal would go through is not obvious at first glance. The fact that one person is trying to cheat another out of profits by doing x does not necessarily mean that y (on which the scheme also depends) will come about. McCormick may be suggesting, however, that if he knew Byrne was trying to buy him out — at some loss to the company — in the hope that later he and other shareholders would profit from this, then he, McCormick, might have concluded that Byrne actually thought the deal was going to go through (otherwise why accept the short-term loss). And if Byrne was willing to take this risk, then McCormick might have concluded that in fact the deal probably would go through.

The problem with this theory is that the facts don't support it. Byrne's uncontradicted testimony is that far from scheming to enrich himself by buying McCormick's shares, he did not, until he was cautioned by Gillespie, even put the buyout and the possible sale of FFIC together in his mind. More importantly, at the time that Byrne authorized Brown and Marto to attend a meeting with Allianz — whether that was in March or on May 1 — he still thought that the deal Lusardi was contemplating involved a sale of a 20% interest in FFIC. Byrne's testimony defeats both the theory that his motive for buying out McCormick was self-dealing, and the theory that from that motive, McCormick could have discerned an increased likelihood that the Allianz sale would go through. Hence any misrepresentation was immaterial as a matter of law.

5. Byrne did not want to sell FFIC

McCormick has not shown that this was a misrepresentation. He has shown only that FFIC eventually was sold, not that Byrne wanted to sell it despite his protestations.

But even if Byrne lied, and really did want to sell FFIC, that misrepresentation must be evaluated in light of other statements which were made. McCormick was told, and acknowledged that he was told, that FAC was involved in ongoing discussions regarding the sale of FFIC. In light of this disclosure, it would not have been reasonable for him to infer that because Byrne did not want to sell the insurance company, it was unlikely that it would be sold. The fact that FAC was involved in discussions with a possible buyer meant that it was considering selling its subsidiary despite whatever reservations Byrne may have had. *See Glazer*, 964 F.2d at 152, 155 (no misrepresentation where company said both that the best thing would be for it to remain independent, and that it would consider any legitimate

---

that Allianz showed interest simply by meeting with Marto and Brown on May 4. Accordingly, it could also be argued that if Byrne knew before April 27 that the May 4 meeting was planned, he also knew about Allianz's interest on April 27, and was untruthful when he told McCormick that he didn't.

proposal to acquire the company). Any misrepresentation that was made was immaterial as a matter of law.

6. The potential buyer could not meet Byrne's price

FAC says that this is not a misrepresentation because Allianz would not and in fact never did meet FAC's asking price. FAC wanted $3.5 billion, and Allianz ended up paying just over $3.3 billion.

McCormick appears to argue that the statement was misleading because it indicated not only that Allianz would not meet FAC's asking price, but also that it could not do so — whereas in fact Allianz had "more money than God." Even such wealth, however, does not necessarily mean that Allianz "could have" met the asking price. A company might be very rich, but still in the minds of — and according to the representations of — its officers, might be unable to meet a given price, within the constraints of the budget available for acquisitions.

In any event, McCormick has not produced any evidence showing that Allianz "could" have paid $3.5 billion; and the fact is that Allianz never did. Without knowing in some detail about the finances of Allianz (and we don't), it is a mistake to think we (or McCormick) can make meaningful distinctions between "would not" and "could not." The statement that Allianz could not meet the asking price is not, on the record before us, a misrepresentation.

7. The Allianz development was a sudden one, and was unlikely to materialize

McCormick testified that the impression he was left with after he had been briefed by Marto and had spoken with Byrne was that Allianz representatives had first called that day or the day before. McCormick also states that Byrne told him that the chances the deal would go through were not greater than 50-50.

Taking the second point first, there is nothing in the record that shows that on May 16, the chances that the deal would come off were any greater than 50%; indeed, nearly two months later the deal nearly broke down.

As for the impression that the Allianz development was very recent, this was in large part correct. Allianz had announced that it was interested in further talks only two days before Marto and Byrne briefed McCormick; before that, the only face-to-face discussions between the two parties had occurred at the May 4 meeting, during which Allianz was noticeably unresponsive. Moreover, McCormick was told that there had already been preliminary discussions; whether those had taken place one day ago or twelve days ago is not material.

CONCLUSION

In *Basic v. Levinson*, the Supreme Court listed several factors indicating that a merger or acquisition is likely to materialize: "board resolutions, instructions to investment bankers, and actual negotiations between principals or their intermediaries." 485 U.S. at 239, 108 S. Ct. at 987. In this case, while there had not yet been any board resolution, the principals had begun to negotiate, and were about to engage in a round of much more intensive discussions. For nearly three months, FAC's investment banker had been authorized by FAC's CFO to discuss the sale of FFIC. Under these circumstances, there is at the very least a question of fact as to whether or not the Allianz development was material. Because FAC disclosed some information to McCormick, we must decide whether or not that disclosure was sufficient.

There is no question but that there were many details about which McCormick was not told: for example, he was not told about the involvement of the investment bankers, the disclosure of confidential information to the buyer, or the substance of the May 4 meeting and the meetings and correspondence between Lusardi and Allianz which had preceded it. McCormick was told that there had been meetings and that there would be further meetings, and he was told this by FAC's top command. He was also told that in the event of a sale, his stock could rise in value to $50/share. In light of these disclosures, details pertaining to the activity which had led up to FAC's meetings, and to what had transpired in those meetings, diminished greatly in importance. It was self-evident that activity not described in detail had occurred.

In sum, although the disclosure which was made was both general and succinct, the details McCormick claims he was deprived of would not have added useful information. McCormick was a sophisticated businessman, and he was the former CEO of FFIC and a director of FAC at the time of the events in question. His reading of the Acknowledgment must be seen against that background. The disclosures which the Acknowledgment reflects told him enough. More details would not have significantly altered the total mix of information. After all there was no deal with Allianz, and no assurance whatsoever that there would be one. McCormick was advised, in effect, that if there were an offer, FAC would not sell without achieving about $50/share. The disclosures were accurate, and the information was adequate for McCormick to act upon. Nor was anything which was set forth in the Acknowledgment or said by Marto or Byrne both material and misleading. McCormick's Rule 10b-5 claim therefore fails.[138]

. . .

SEC v. CARTER HAWLEY HALE STORES, INC.

United States Court of Appeals, Ninth Circuit
760 F.2d 945 (1985)

Skopil, Circuit Judge

The issue in this case arises out of an attempt by The Limited ("Limited"), an Ohio corporation, to take over Carter Hawley Hale Stores, Inc. ("CHH"), a publicly-held Los Angeles corporation. The SEC commenced the present action for injunctive relief to restrain CHH from repurchasing its own stock in an attempt to

---

[138] [8] Since plaintiff's failure to establish the materiality of the omissions and alleged misrepresentations is dispositive of his claim, we do not reach defendant's other arguments for summary judgment in its favor; lack of scienter, and the preclusive effect of a general waiver signed by McCormick.

defeat the Limited takeover attempt without complying with the tender offer regulations. The district court concluded CHH's repurchase program was not a tender offer. The SEC appeals from the district court's denial of its motion for a preliminary injunction. We affirm.

FACTS AND PROCEEDINGS BELOW

On April 4, 1984 Limited commenced a cash tender offer for 20.3 million shares of CHH common stock, representing approximately 55% of the total shares outstanding, at $30 per share. Prior to the announced offer, CHH stock was trading at approximately $23.78 per share (pre-tender offer price). Limited disclosed that if its offer succeeded, it would exchange the remaining CHH shares for a fixed amount of Limited shares in a second-step merger.

In compliance with section 14(d) of the Securities Exchange Act of 1934 ("Exchange Act"), 5 U.S.C. § 78n(d) (1982), Limited filed a schedule 14D-l disclosing all pertinent information about its offer. The schedule stated that (l) the offer would remain open for 20-days, (2) the tendered shares could be withdrawn until April 19, 1984, and (3) in the event the offer was oversubscribed, shares would be subject to purchase on a pro rata basis.

While CHH initially took no public position on the offer, it filed an action to enjoin Limited's attempted takeover. *Carter Hawley Hale Stores, Inc. v. The Limited, Inc.*, 587 F. Supp. 246 (C.D. Cal. 1984). CHH's motion for an injunction was denied. *Id.* From April 4, 1984 until April 16, 1984, CHH's incumbent management discussed a response to Limited's offer. During that time 14 million shares, about 40% of CHH's common stock, were traded. The price of CHH stock increased to approximately $29.25 per share. CHH shares became concentrated in the hands of risk arbitrageurs.

On April 16, 1984 CHH responded to Limited's offer. CHH issued a press release announcing its opposition to the offer because it was "inadequate and not in the best interests of CHH or its shareholders." CHH also publicly announced an agreement with General Cinema Corporation ("General Cinema"). CHH sold one million shares of convertible preferred stock to General Cinema for $300 million. The preferred shares possessed a vote equivalent to 22% of voting shares outstanding. General Cinema's shares were to be voted pursuant to CHH's Board of Directors recommendations. General Cinema was also granted an option to purchase Walden Book Company, Inc., a profitable CHH subsidiary, for approximately $285 million. Finally, CHH announced a plan to repurchase up to 15 million shares of its own common stock for an amount not to exceed $500 million. If all 15 million shares were purchased, General Cinema's shares would represent 33% of CHH's outstanding voting shares.

CHH's public announcement stated the actions taken were "to defeat the attempt by Limited to gain voting control of the company and to afford shareholders who wished to sell shares at this time an opportunity to do so." CHH's actions were revealed by press release, a letter from CHH's Chairman to shareholders, and by documents filed with the Securities and Exchange Commission ("SEC") — a Schedule 14D-9 and Rule 13e-l transaction statement. These disclosures were reported by wire services, national financial newspapers, and newspapers of general circulation. Limited sought a temporary restraining order against CHH's repurchase of its shares. The application was denied. Limited withdrew its motion for a preliminary injunction.

CHH began to repurchase its shares on April 16, 1984. In a one-hour period CHH purchased approximately 244,000 shares at an average price of $25.25 per share. On April 17, 1984 CHH purchased approximately 6.5 million shares in a two-hour trading period at an average price of $25.88 per share. By April 22, 1984 CHH had purchased a total of 15 million shares. It then announced an increase in the number of shares authorized for purchase to 18.5 million.

On April 24, 1984, the same day Limited was permitted to close its offer and start purchasing, CHH terminated its repurchase program, having purchased approximately 17.5 million shares, over 50% of the common shares outstanding. On April 25, 1984 Limited revised its offer, increasing the offering price to $35.00 per share and eliminating the second-step merger. The market price for CHH then reached a high of $32.00 per share. On May 21, 1984 Limited withdrew its offer. The market price of CHH promptly fell to $20.62 per share, a price below the pre-tender offer price.

On May 2, 1984, two and one-half weeks after the repurchase program was announced and one week after its apparent completion, the SEC filed this action for injunctive relief. The SEC alleged that CHH's repurchase program constituted a tender offer conducted in violation of section 13(e) of the Exchange Act, 15 U.S.C. § 78m(e) and Rule 13e-4, 17 C.F.R. § 240.13e-4. On May 5, 1984 a temporary restraining order was granted. CHH was temporarily enjoined from further stock repurchases. The district court denied SEC's motion for a preliminary injunction, finding the SEC failed to carry its burden of establishing "the reasonable likelihood of future violations . . . [or] . . . a 'fair chance of success on the merits' " . . . *SEC v. Carter Hawley Hale Stores, Inc.*, 587 F. Supp. 1248, 1257 (C.D. Cal. 1984) (citations omitted). The court found CHH's repurchase program was not a tender offer, because the eight-factor test proposed by the SEC and adopted in *Wellman v. Dickinson*, 475 F. Supp. 783 (S.D.N.Y. 1979), *aff'd, on other grounds*, 682 F.2d 355 (2d Cir. 1982), *cert. denied*, 460 U.S. 1069 (1983), had not been satisfied. *SEC v. Carter Hawley Hale Stores, Inc.*, 587 F. Supp. at 1255. The court also refused to adopt, at the urging of the SEC, the alternative test of what constitutes a tender offer as enunciated in *S-G Securities, Inc. v. Fuqua Investment Co.*, 466 F. Supp. 1114 (D. Mass. 1978). 587 F. Supp. at 1256-57. On May 9, 1984 the SEC filed an emergency application for an injunction pending appeal to this court. That application was denied.

DISCUSSION

. . .

The SEC urges two principal arguments on appeal: (1) the district court erred in concluding that CHH's repurchase program was not a tender offer under the eight-factor Wellman test, and (2) the district court erred in declining to apply the definition of a tender offer enunciated in S-G Securities, 466 F. Supp. at 1126-27.

Resolution of these issues on appeal presents the difficult task of determining whether CHH's repurchase of shares during a third-party tender offer itself constituted a tender offer.

1. The Williams Act

A. Congressional Purposes

The Williams Act amendments to the Exchange Act were enacted in response to the growing use of tender offers to achieve corporate control. *Edgar v. Mite Corp.*, 457 U.S. 624, 632 (1982) (citing *Piper v. Chris-Craft Industries*, 430 U.S. 1, 22 (1977)). Prior to the passage of the Act, shareholders of target companies were often forced to act hastily on offers without the benefit of full disclosure. *See* H.R. Rep. No. 1711, 90th Cong., 2d Sess. (1968), reprinted in 1968 U.S. Code, Cong. & Admin. News 2811 ("House Report 1711"). The Williams Act was intended to ensure that investors responding to tender offers received full and fair disclosure, analogous to that received in proxy contests. The Act was also designed to provide shareholders an opportunity to examine all relevant facts in an effort to reach a decision without being subject to unwarranted pressure. House Report 1711.

This policy is reflected in section 14(d), which governs third-party tender offers, and which prohibits a tender offer unless shareholders are provided with certain procedural and substantive protections, including: full disclosure; time in which to make an investment decision; withdrawal rights; and pro rata purchase of shares accepted in the event the offer is oversubscribed. 15 U.S.C. § 78m(d) (1981); 17 C.F.R. § 240.14d-6 (1984); 17 C.F.R. § 240.14d-7(a)(l)-14d-7(a)(2) (1984).

There are additional congressional concerns underlying the Williams Act. In its effort to protect investors, Congress recognized the need to "avoid favoring either management or the takeover bidder." *Edgar*, 456 U.S. at 633; *See also Financial General Bank Shares, Inc. v. Lance*, [19781 Fed. Sec. L. Rptr. (CCH) ¶ 95.403 at 93.424-25 (D. D.C 1978) (quoting *Rondeau v. Mosin Paper Corp.*, 422 U.S. 49, 58 (1975)). The Supreme Court has recognized that to serve this policy it is necessary to withhold "from management or the bidder any undue advantage that could frustrate the exercise of informed choice." *Edgar*, 456 U.S. at 634. Congress was also concerned about avoiding undue interference with the free and open market in securities. *City Investing Co. v. Simcox*, 633 F.2d 56, 62 n.14 (7th Cir. 1980) (noting less burdensome regulations in cases involving certain open market purchases); see also 113 Cong. Rec. 856 (1968). Each of these congressional concerns is implicated in the determination of whether CHH's issuer repurchase program constituted a tender offer.

B. Issuer Repurchases Under Section 13(e)

Issuer repurchases and tender offers are governed in relevant part by section 13(e) of the Williams Act and Rules 13e-1 and 13e-4 promulgated thereunder. 15 U.S.C. § 78m(e) (1981); 17 C.F.R. § 240.13e-l (1984); 17 C.F.R. § 240.13e-4 (1984).

The SEC argues that the district court erred in concluding that issuer repurchases, which had the intent and effect of defeating a third-party tender offer, are authorized by the tender offer rules and regulations. The legislative history of these provisions is unclear. Congress apparently was aware of an intent by the SEC to regulate issuer tender offers to the same extent as third-party offers. Senate Hearings 214-16, 248; Exchange Act Release No. 16,112 [1979] Fed. Sec. L. Rptr. (CCH) ¶ 82.182 at 82.205 (Aug. 16, 1979) (proposed amendments to tender offer rules). At the same time, Congress recognized issuers might engage in substantial repurchase programs . . . inevitably affect[ing] market performance and price levels." House Hearings at 14-15; *see also* House Report 1711 at 2814-15. Such repurchase programs might be undertaken for any number of legitimate purposes, including with the intent "to preserve or strengthen . . . control by counteracting tender offer or other takeover attempts. . . ." House Report 1711 at 2814; House Hearings at 15. Congress neither explicitly banned nor authorized such a practice. Congress did grant the SEC authority to adopt appropriate regulations to carry out congressional intent with respect to issuer repurchases. The legislative history of section 13(e) is not helpful in resolving the issues.

There is also little guidance in the SEC Rules promulgated in response to the legislative grant of authority. Rule 13e-l prohibits an issuer from repurchasing its own stock during a third-party tender offer unless it discloses certain minimal information. 17 C.F.R. § 240.13e-l (1984). The language of Rule 13e-l is prohibitory rather than permissive. It nonetheless evidences a recognition that not all issuer repurchases during a third-party tender offer are tender offers. *Id.* In contrast, Rule 13e-4 recognizes that issuers, like third parties, may engage in repurchase activity amounting to a tender offer and subject to the same procedural and substantive safeguards as a third-party tender offer. 17 C.F.R. § 240.13e-4 (1984). The regulations do not specify when a repurchase by an issuer amounts to a tender offer governed by Rule 13e-4 rather than 13e-l.

We decline to adopt either the broadest construction of Rule 13e-4, to define issuer tender offers as virtually all substantial repurchases during a third-party tender offer, or the broadest construction of Rule 13e-l, to create an exception from the tender offer requirements for issuer repurchases made during a third-party tender offer. Like the district court, we resolve the question of whether CHH's repurchase program was a tender offer by considering the eight-factor test established in *Wellman*, 587 F. Supp. at 1256-57.

To serve the purposes of the Williams Act, there is a need for flexibility in fashioning a definition of a tender offer. *See Smallwood v. Pearl Brewing Co.*, 489 F.2d 579 (5th Cir.), *cert. denied*, 419 U.S. 873 (1974). The *Wellman* factors seem particularly well suited in determining when an issuer repurchase program during a third-party tender offer will itself constitute a tender offer. *Wellman* focuses, inter alia, on the manner in which the offer is conducted and whether the offer has the overall effect of pressuring shareholders into selling their stock. *Wellman*, 475 F. Supp. at 823-24. Application of the *Wellman* factors to the unique facts and circumstances surrounding issuer repurchases should serve to effect congressional concern for the needs of the shareholder, the need to avoid giving either the target or the offeror any advantage, and the need to maintain a free and open market for securities.

2. Application of the *Wellman* Factors.

Under the *Wellman* test, the existence of a tender offer is determined by examining the following factors:

> (1) Active and widespread solicitation of public shareholders for the shares of an issuer; (2) solicitation made for a substantial percentage of the issuer's stock; (3) offer to purchase made at a premium over the prevailing market price; (4) terms of the offer are firm rather than negotiable; (5) offer contingent on the tender of a fixed number of shares, often subject to a fixed maximum number to be purchased; (6) offer open only for a limited period of time; (7) offeree subjected to pressure to sell his stock; [and (8)] public announcements of a purchasing program concerning the target company precede or accompany rapid accumulation of a large amount of target company's securities.

475 F. Supp. at 823-24.

Not all factors need be present to find a tender offer; rather, they provide some guidance as to the traditional indicia of a tender offer. *Id.* at 824; *See also Zuckerman v. Franz*, 573 F. Supp. 351, 358 (S.D. Fla. 1983).

The district court concluded CHH's repurchase program was not a tender offer under *Wellman* because only "two of the eight indicia" were present. 587 F. Supp. at 1255. The SEC claims the district court erred in applying *Wellman*, because it gave insufficient weight to the pressure exerted on shareholders; it ignored the existence of a competitive tender offer; and it failed to consider that CHH's offer at the market price was in essence a premium, because the price had already risen above pre-tender offer levels.

A. Active and Widespread Solicitation

The evidence was uncontroverted that there was "no direct solicitation of shareholders." 587 F. Supp. 1253. No active and widespread solicitation occurred. *See Brascan Ltd. v. Edper Equities Ltd.*, 477 F. Supp. 773, 789 (S.D.N.Y. 1979) (no tender offer where defendant "scrupulously avoided any solicitation upon the advice of his lawyers"). Nor did the publicity surrounding CHH's repurchase program result in a solicitation. 587 F. Supp. 1253-54. The only public announcements by CHH were those mandated by SEC or Exchange rules. *See Ludlow Corp. v. Tyco Laboratories*, 529 F. Supp. 62, 68-69 (D. Mass. 1981) (schedule 13d filed by purchaser could not be characterized as forbidden publicity); *Crane Co. v. Harsco Corp.*, 511 F. Supp. 294, 303 (D. Dela. 1981) (Rule 13e-l transaction statement and required press releases do not constitute a solicitation); but *cf. S-G Securities, Inc.*, 466 F. Supp. at 1119-21 (tender offer present where numerous press releases publicized terms of offer).

B. Solicitation for a Substantial Percentage of Issuer's Shares

Because there was no active and widespread solicitation, the district court found the repurchase could not have involved a solicitation for a substantial percentage of CHH's shares. 587 F. Supp. 1253-54. It is unclear whether the proper focus of this factor is the solicitation or the percentage of stock solicited. The district court probably erred in concluding that, absent a solicitation under the first *Wellman* factor, the second factor cannot be satisfied, see *Hoover Co. v. Fuqua Industries*, [1979-80] Fed. Sec. L. Rprt. (CCH) ¶ 97,107 at 96,148 n.4 (N.D. Ohio 1979) (second *Wellman* factor did not incorporate the type of solicitation described in factor one), but we need not decide that here. The solicitation and percentage of stock elements of the second factor often will be addressed adequately in an evaluation of the first Wellman factor, which is concerned with solicitation, and the eighth *Wellman* factor, which focuses on the amount of securities accumulated. In this case CHH did not engage in a solicitation under the first *Wellman* factor but did accumulate a large percentage of stock as defined under the eighth *Wellman* factor. An evaluation of the second Wellman factor does not alter the probability of finding a tender offer.

C. Premium Over Prevailing Market Price

The SEC contends the open market purchases made by CHH at market prices were in fact made at a premium not over market price but over the pre-tender offer price. At the time of CHH's repurchases, the market price for CHH's shares (ranging from $24.00 to $26.00 per share) had risen above the pre-tender offer price (approximately $22.00 per share). Given ordinary market dynamics, the price of a target company's stock will rise following an announced tender offer. Under the SEC's definition of a premium as a price greater than the pre-tender offer price, a premium will always exist when a target company makes open market purchases in response to a tender offer even though the increase in market price is attributable to the action of the third-party offeror and not the target company. See *LTV Corp. v. Grumman Corp.*, 526 F. Supp. 106, 109 & n.7 (E.D.N.Y. 1981) (an increase in price due to increased demand during a tender offer does not represent a premium). The SEC definition not only eliminates consideration of this Wellman factor in the context of issuer repurchases during a tender offer, but also underestimates congressional concern for preserving the free and open market. The district court did not err in concluding a premium is determined not by reference to pre-tender offer price, but rather by reference to market price. This is the definition previously urged by the SEC, Exchange Act Release No. 16,385 [1979-80] Fed. Sec. L. Rptr. (CCH) ¶ 82,374 at 82,605 (Nov. 29, 1979) (footnotes omitted) (proposed amendments to tender offer rules) (premium defined as price "in excess of . . . the current market price. . . ."), and is the definition we now apply. See *LTV Corp.*, 526 F. Supp. at 109 & n.7.

D. Terms of Offer Not Firm

There is no dispute that CHH engaged in a number of transactions or purchases at many different market prices. 587 F. Supp. at 1254.

E. Offer Not Contingent on Tender of Fixed Minimum Number of Shares

Similarly, while CHH indicated it would purchase up to 15 million shares, CHH's purchases were not contingent on the tender of a fixed minimum number of shares. 587 F. Supp. at 1254.

F. Not Open For Only a Limited Time

CHH's offer to repurchase was not open for only a limited period of time but rather was open "during the pendency of the tender offer of The Limited." 587 F. Supp. at 1255. The SEC argues that the offer was in fact open for only a limited time, because CHH would only repurchase stock until 15 million shares were acquired. The fact that 15 million shares were acquired in a short period of time does not translate into an issuer-imposed time limitation. The time within which the repurchases were made was a product of ordinary market forces, not the terms of CHH's repurchase program.

G-H. Shareholder Pressure and Public Announcements Accompanying a Large Accumulation of Stock

With regard to the seventh *Wellman* factor, following a public announcement, CHH repurchased over the period of seven trading days more than 50% of its outstanding shares. 587 F. Supp. at 1255. The eighth *Wellman* factor was met.

The district court found that while many shareholders may have felt pressured or compelled to sell their shares, CHH itself did not exert on shareholders the kind of pressure the Williams Act proscribes. *Id.*

While there certainly was shareholder pressure in this case, it was largely the pressure of the marketplace and not the type of untoward pressure the tender offer regulations were designed to prohibit. *See Panter v. Marshall Field & Co.*, 646 F.2d 271, 286 (7th Cir.) (where no deadline and no premium, shareholders "were simply not subjected to the proscribed pressures the Williams Act was designed to alleviate"), *cert. denied*, 554 U.S. 1092 (1981); *Brascan Ltd. v. Edper Equities*, 477 F. Supp. at 789-92 (without high premium and threat that the offer will disappear, large purchases in a short time do not represent the kind of pressure the Williams Act was designed to prevent); *Kennecott Copper Corp. v. Curtis-Wright Corp.*, 449 F. Supp. 951, 961 (S.D.N.Y.), *aff'd, in relevant part, rev'd, in part*, 584 F.2d 1195, 1207 (2d Cir. 1978) (where no deadline and no premium, no pressure, other than normal pressure of the marketplace exerted on shareholders).

CHH's purchases were made in the open market, at market and not premium prices, without fixed terms and were not contingent upon the tender of a fixed minimum number of shares. CHH's repurchase program had none of the traditional indicia of a tender offer. *See, e.g., Energy Ventures, Inc. v. Appalachian Co.*, 587 F. Supp. 734, 735 (D. Del. 1984) (major acquisition program involving open market purchases not subject to tender offer regulation); *Ludlow Corp. v. Tyco Laboratories, Inc.*, 529 F. Supp. at 68 (no tender offer where shareholders not pressured into making hasty ill-advised decision due to premium, fixed terms, or active solicitation); *LTV Corp. v. Grumman*, 526 F. Supp. at 109 (massive buying program, with attendant publicity, made with intent to defeat third-party tender offer, not itself a tender offer); *Brascan Ltd. v. Edper Equities*, 477 F. Supp. at 792 (the pressure the Williams Act attempts to eliminate is that caused by "a high premium with a threat that the offer will disappear within a certain time").

The shareholder pressure in this case did not result from any untoward action on the part of CHH. Rather, it resulted from market forces, the third-party offer, and the fear that at the expiration of the offer the price of CHH shares would decrease.

The district court did not abuse its discretion in concluding that under the *Wellman* eight factor test, CHH's repurchase program did not constitute a tender offer.

3. Alternative *S-G Securities* Test.

The SEC finally urges that even if the CHH repurchase program did not constitute a tender offer under the *Wellman* test, the district court erred in refusing to apply the test in *S-G Securities*, 466 F. Supp. at 1114. Under the more liberal *S-G Securities* test, a tender offer is present if there are

> (1) A publicly announced intention by the purchaser to acquire a block of the stock of the target company for purposes of acquiring control thereof, and (2) a subsequent rapid acquisition by the purchaser of large blocks of stock through open market and privately negotiated purchases.

Id. at 1126-27.

There are a number of sound reasons for rejecting the *S-G Securities* test. The test is vague and difficult to apply. It offers little guidance to the issuer as to when his conduct will come within the ambit of Rule 13e-4 as opposed to Rule 13e-1. *SEC v. Carter Hawley Hale Stores*, 587 F. Supp. at 1256-57. A determination of the existence of a tender offer under *S-G Securities* is largely subjective and made in hindsight based on an ex post facto evaluation of the response in the marketplace to the repurchase program. *Id.* at 1257. The SEC's contention that these concerns are irrelevant when the issuer's repurchases are made with the intent to defeat a third-party offer is without merit. *See, e.g., LTV Corp. v. Grumman Corp.*, 526 F. Supp. at 109-10 (Rule 13e-l may apply to open market purchases even when made to thwart a tender offer); *Crane Co. v. Harsco Corp.*, 511 F. Supp. 294, 300-301 (D. Dela. 1981) (same).

The SEC finds further support for its application of the two-pronged *S-G Securities* test in the overriding legislative intent "to ensure that shareholders . . . are adequately protected from pressure tactics . . . [forcing them to make] . . . ill-considered investment decisions." The *S-G Securities* test does reflect congressional concern for shareholders; however, the same can be said of the *Wellman* test. The legislative intent in the context of open market repurchases during third-party tender offers is, at best, unclear. 587 F. Supp. 1256; see pages 8-11, *supra*. The *S-G Securities* test, unlike the *Wellman* test, does little to reflect objectively the multiple congressional concerns underlying the Williams Act, including due regard for the free and open market in securities. See pages 7-8, *supra*.

We decline to abandon the Wellman test in favor of the vague standard enunciated in *S-G Securities*. The district court did not err in declining to apply the *S-G Securities* test or in finding CHH's repurchases were not a tender offer under *Wellman*.

AFFIRMED.

PROBLEM A

Woodstock Widget Corporation ("Woodstock") was incorporated under the laws of the State of New York on October 29, 1929. Its capitalization presently consists of 2,000,000 shares of Common Stock, $1.00 par value (the "Common Stock"), 1,000,000 of which are issued and outstanding and traded on the Ulster Stock Exchange (a national securities exchange), and 158,000 of which are held in the treasury of Woodstock, and 500,000 shares of Cumulative Convertible Preferred Stock, par value $1.00 per share (the "Preferred Stock"), of which 250,000 are issued and outstanding and traded in the over-the-counter market. The Preferred Stock, which was issued on May 17, 1988, has a cumulative annual dividend rate of $2.80 per share, payable quarterly (in aggregate amounts of $175,000) is redeemable at the option of Woodstock at $50.00 per share, plus accrued dividends, at any time after May 17, 1993, has a liquidation preference of $50.00 per share, and is presently convertible into two shares of Woodstock's Common Stock. The terms of the Certificate of Incorporation of Woodstock relating to the Preferred Stock also provides that, in the event Woodstock merges with or into another corporation, the holders of the Preferred Stock shall, upon conversion thereof, be entitled to receive the securities or property receivable by the holders of the Common Stock upon the effectiveness of any such merger. The Preferred Stock has full voting rights with the Common Stock, and, in addition, the holders of the Preferred Stock are entitled to elect two additional members of the Board of Directors of Woodstock (presently consisting of seven members) in the event that the cumulative dividends are not declared and paid for six consecutive quarterly dividend payment periods. Dividends on the Preferred Stock have been paid regularly since the shares were issued.

There are also outstanding 100,000 of Woodstock's 10 percent Subordinated Convertible Debentures, due February 1, 2021. These Debentures, which were publicly issued in the aggregate principal amount of $5,000,000 in July 1986, and also are traded in the over-the-counter market, are fully subordinated to any other present and future indebtedness of Woodstock, and are presently convertible into four shares of Common Stock. The Debentures are redeemable at 100 percent of the principal amount ($50.00 each), plus unpaid interest, on or after July 13, 1981. Certain rights of the holders of the Debentures are set forth in an Indenture, dated as of July 13, 1986, between Woodstock and the Saugerties Trust Company (the "Indenture"). The Indenture requires Woodstock to maintain at all times an excess of assets over liabilities of not less than $4,500,000, and retained earnings of at least $1,250,000. The Indenture also provides that, in the event of a merger of Woodstock with any other corporation, the Debentures shall be convertible into the securities received by the holders of the Common Stock of Woodstock in connection with any such merger. The Indenture states that a holder of Debentures may not commence an action to enforce any term thereof, or to seek damages for any breach thereof, unless the Indenture Trustee has refused to do so following a written demand therefor by the holders of at least 25 percent in principal amount of the Debentures.

For its fiscal year ending December 31, 1994, Woodstock sustained operating losses of three million dollars; because of the loss and operating losses sustained during the four previous fiscal years, Woodstock retained earnings account presently stands at $212,000. The assets of Woodstock exceeded its liabilities by $600,000 at December 31, 1994.

You are an associate in the law firm that acts as counsel to Woodstock. While Alfred T. Palen, a partner in charge of the Woodstock account, is vacationing in St. Maarten, you receive a telephone call from the President of Woodstock, who says that the chief internal accounting officer of Woodstock has advised him that there will not be sufficient legally available funds to pay the forthcoming quarterly dividend in the Preferred Stock. The president of Woodstock says, "We are having cash flow problems, but with all the other troubles we are having around here, I don't want the company defaulting on its contractual obligations." He further advises you that, in his opinion, Woodstock's widget manufacturing facilities, located in Bearsville, N.Y., have a present value at least five times greater than their $1,500,000 book value, which appears on Woodstock's certified balance sheet at December 31, 1998. The President says, "I understand that we can jack up the value of the Bearsville plant and create earnings sufficient to pay the Preferred Stock dividend — what do you think? Can you take a shot at this, or do we have to wait for Palen?"

You advise Woodstock's president that the firm will respond to his question by letter. Write a draft of that letter to him.

PROBLEM B

Bissell Enterprise, Inc. ("Bissell") was incorporated under the laws of the State of New York on March 1, 1967. Its capitalization presently consists of 2,000,000 shares of Common Stock, par value $1.00 per share (the "Common Stock"), 1,000,000 shares of which are issued and outstanding and traded on the Ulster Stock Exchange (a national securities exchange) and 158,000 shares of which are held in the treasury of Bissell.

Bissell is structured as a holding company; its assets consist primarily of all of the issued and outstanding shares (1,000 each) of common stock of its two Delaware wholly owned subsidiaries, Christina Cosmetics Corporation ("Christina") and M P. Associates, Inc. Christina is engaged in the production and sale of various cosmetic and related products. Although for many years Christina has been responsible for nearly all of the net income of Bissell, it has been adversely affected by foreign competition, and presently accounts for only approximately 55 percent of Bissell's revenues, but still comprises approximately 75 percent of Bissell's assets. M P. Associates, Inc., which renders executive consulting services, presently accounts for 45 percent of Bissell's revenues and comprises approximately 25 percent of the assets of Bissell.

Rossi Industries, Inc. ("Rossi"), has begun a program of open market purchases of Bissell's Common Stock and has acquired 25 percent of Bissell's outstanding Common Stock, or 250,000 shares. For business reasons unrelated to the fortunes of Bissell (which are improving as a result of the enactment of legislation restricting foreign imports of cosmetics), Rossi has decided to dispose of its equity interest in Bissell. Rossi has advised Bissell that Rossi has been approached by Raider Incorporated ("Raider") with a proposal whereby Raider would purchase the Bissell Common Stock held by Rossi at a 50 percent premium over the $5.00

per share market price of Bissell's Common Stock or a total consideration of $1,875,000, representing a per share price of $7.50. It has been Raider's practice to acquire the entire equity interest in a target corporation through a series of so-called going private transactions. It is also Raider's practice to summarily and ungracefully discharge the entire incumbent management of such acquired corporation. Raider's acquisition activities have been marked by a series of stockholder's suits, claiming that the terms of such other going private transactions have been grossly unfair to the stockholders of the target corporation. The Board of Directors of Bissell has decided that it would be a good idea for Bissell to purchase from Rossi the shares of Bissell's Common Stock held by Rossi and to match the price therefore that has been offered to Rossi by Raider. Bissell would have to borrow funds necessary to make such a purchase. You have been asked to prepare an opinion letter for Bissell's Board of Directors, discussing the question of whether Bissell's proposed purchase from Rossi is legally possible, and what challenges, if any, could be made to the transaction by any of the security holders of Bissell; write the opinion.

Chapter 7

INVESTMENT BY THE ISSUER OF SECURITIES — ACQUISITIONS

§ 7.01 TYPES OF ACQUISITION TRANSACTIONS

[A] Corporate Acquisitions — Various Structures

An acquisition transaction is an investment by a corporation in another business enterprise. An acquisition is a unique form of investment, however, in that it involves the purchase of a business enterprise, or at least a major portion thereof. Investments usually involve the purchase of securities (usually equity) representing substantially less than a controlling interest of a business corporation.

An acquisition can be effected through the utilization of one of three basic structures: (i) a merger or consolidation, (ii) a purchase of shares, or (iii) a purchase of assets. A merger is a transaction in which one corporation merges into another and disappears; a consolidation is a transaction in which two corporations combine into a new third corporation.

A purchase of assets in this context involves the acquisition of all or substantially all of the revenue producing assets of a business corporation or a segment thereof, consisting of real and personal property, as well as patents, know-how, other intellectual property and contract rights. As a general proposition, the liabilities of the transferor corporation are not assumed by the buyer unless it expressly does so by contract. There are instances, however, where liabilities of the transferor corporation are assumed by operation of law. One example of this is the "successor liability" doctrine, under which certain contingent liabilities of the transferor, such as those for product liability, are deemed to have been assumed by the purchaser of the assets.

A merger or consolidation and a purchase of assets are transactions in which the affected corporation is a party and the completion of such a transaction is therefore a corporate act which must be authorized by the directors and possibly the shareholders of the corporation in accordance with applicable state law.

An acquisition of shares involves individual purchase transactions with each of the shareholders of the acquired corporation. As a practical matter, therefore, an acquisition of the entire equity interest of a publicly held corporation cannot be effected through an acquisition of shares. Although a substantial number of shares of a publicly held corporation's outstanding shares may be acquired either in a purchase from a single investor or a small group thereof (a so-called "block purchase") or in a series of individual purchase transactions comprising part of an overall solicitation by the acquiring party to the shareholders pursuant to a tender offer (which is an invitation to the shareholders of the target corporation by the acquiring party to submit, or "tender" their shares for purchase), the acquisition of the shares not so acquired must be effected through a corporate transaction, such as a merger unless unanimity can be obtained.

[B] Certain Legal Consequences of Acquisitions

DELAWARE GENERAL CORPORATION LAW

§ 259(a) Status, rights, liabilities, etc. of constituent and surviving or resulting corporations following merger or consolidation

(a) When any merger or consolidation shall have become effective under this chapter, for all purposes of the laws of this State the separate existence of all the constituent corporations, or of all such constituent corporations except the one into which the other or others of such constituent corporations have been merged, as the case may be, shall cease and the constituent corporations shall become a new corporation, or be merged into one of such corporations, as the case may be, possessing all the rights, privileges, powers and franchises as well of a public as of a private nature, and being subject to all the restrictions, disabilities and duties of each of such corporations so merged or consolidated; and all and singular, the rights, privileges, powers and franchises of each of said corporations, and all property, real, personal and mixed, and all debts due to any of said constituent corporations on whatever account, as well for stock subscriptions as all other things in action or belonging to each of such corporations shall be vested in the corporation surviving or resulting from such merger or consolidation; and all property, rights, privileges, powers and franchises, and all and every other interest shall be thereafter as effectually the property of the surviving or resulting corporation as they were of the several and respective constituent corporations, and the title to any real estate vested by deed or otherwise, under the laws of this State, in any of such constituent corporations, shall not revert or be in any way impaired by reason of this chapter; but all rights of creditors and all liens upon any property of any of said constituent corporations shall be preserved unimpaired, and all debts, liabilities and duties of the respective constituent corporations shall thenceforth attach to said surviving or resulting corporation, and may be enforced against it to the same extent as if said debts, liabilities and duties had been incurred or contracted by it.

EXAMPLE OF CONTRACTUAL LIMITATIONS UPON THE ASSUMPTION OF LIABILITIES BY A CORPORATE PURCHASER OF ASSETS

. . . .

Excluded Obligations. Without in any manner affecting the limitations on the obligations to be assumed by Buyer contained herein, but rather to identify more particularly certain obligations of Seller which are not to be assumed by Buyer, it is agreed that Buyer shall not assume nor be liable for, and Seller expressly agrees to remain liable for, all of its obligations not being assumed by Buyer hereunder, including, without limitation, the following described liabilities, obligations, contracts and commitments of Seller as of the Closing Date (hereinafter sometimes collectively referred to as the "Excluded Obligations"):

(a) intra and inter company (among Seller and its consolidated subsidiaries or affiliates) payables;

(b) all current and long-term liabilities of Seller, whether or not relating to [the Division being acquired], which are not set forth on (i) the Balance Sheet of [the Division being acquired] as of January 31, 2005 or (ii) on the Closing Balance Sheet; nothing herein shall be deemed to require Buyer to pay or perform any liabilities of Seller;

(c) all liabilities relating or pertaining to any "Employee Welfare Benefit Plan" or "Employee Pension Benefit Plan," as such terms are defined by Sections 3(l) and 3(2), respectively, of the Employee Retirement Income Security Act of 1974, as amended ("ERISA"), whether or not any of such plans are funded, and whether or not any of such plans are qualified under Section 401(a) of the Internal Revenue Code of 1954, as amended (the "Code"), including but not limited to any liability to the Pension Benefit Guaranty Corporation (the "PBGC") arising out of or relating to Seller's maintenance of any such plans, or other employee benefits provided by Seller, and Buyer shall have no liability whatsoever to employees of Seller with respect to accrued benefits under any such plans for such employees' service with Seller, whether or not any of such employees are offered employment by, or become employees of, Buyer. Seller will not take any action with respect to the terms of any of its employee benefit pension plans which would adversely affect such accrued pension benefits of such employees;

(d) all federal, state and local sales, transfer, franchise, gross receipts, excise and income taxes arising out of the conduct of business by Seller prior to the Closing Date, including, but not limited to, the conduct of the business and operations of (the Division being acquired) prior to the Closing Date;

(e) all liabilities or claims for personal injury or other similar or dissimilar damage to person, property or business based upon or arising from occurrences, sales or other transactions prior to the Closing Date, whether or not such occurrences relate or pertain in any way to [the Division being acquired], and whether or not Seller has received notice of such claims prior to the Closing Date;

(f) all liabilities or obligations to employees of Seller who do not become employees of Buyer on the Closing Date whether or not reflected on the Closing Balance Sheet including obligations, if any, for severance pay, accrued vacation pay or other benefits of or for such employees which, if included on the Closing Balance Sheet, shall not be included in the determination of the Closing Net Worth, or in the accrued expenses being assumed by Buyer; and

(g) all other liabilities, obligations, contracts and commitments (whether known or unknown, contingent or fixed), whether arising out of the ownership and operation of the business of Seller (including [the Division being acquired] prior to the Closing Date or otherwise, to the extent not expressly agreed to be assumed by Buyer under this Agreement.

SCHMIDT v. FINANCIAL RESOURCES CORP.

Arizona Court of Appeals
680 P.2d 845 (1984)

BIRDSALL, CHIEF JUDGE

This appeal challenges the entry of a summary judgment requiring a successor corporation to pay a judgment debt of its predecessor following a merger. The appellant is Financial Resources Corporation, an Arizona corporation resulting from a merger between that entity and American Leasco, another Arizona corporation. Appellee and plaintiff in the action below is Walter H. Schmidt (Schmidt). In August 1980 Schmidt sued American Leasco for damages arising out of an agency agreement. On November 4, 1982, after a trial in Pima County Superior Court in cause number 189953, a jury returned a verdict in favor of Schmidt and against American Leasco. Our court affirmed the judgment on appeal. *See Walter H. Schmidt v. American Leasco*, ___ Ariz. ___, ___ P.2d ___ (No. 2 CA-CIV 4825, filed December 15, 1983).

On March 29, 1982, American Leasco had formally merged into Financial Resources Corporation. Upon learning of this merger, Schmidt sought to collect his judgment from Financial Resources Corporation. The appellant denied liability for the judgment against American Leasco. Schmidt then filed a complaint against Financial Resources Corporation on February 10, 1983, seeking payment of the $30,000 judgment rendered in his favor against American Leasco. Thereafter, the superior court granted Schmidt's motion for summary judgment which was entered on June 21, 1983. This appeal followed.

The only issue presented is whether the superior court correctly held that Financial Resources Corporation is responsible for the judgment against American Leasco following the merger. The appellant urges two reasons for reversal. It contends the trial court erred in granting judgment against the appellant for the full amount of the judgment against American Leasco because 1) American Leasco's assets at the time of the merger were less than the judgment against it, and 2) because the judgment against American Leasco contained $25,000 in punitive damages. We affirm.

The law in Arizona provides that any surviving or new corporation resulting from a merger is responsible for all the debts and liabilities of any corporation so merged. A.R.S. § 10-076(B)(5) states:

> 5. Such surviving or new corporation shall thenceforth be responsible and liable for all the liabilities and obligations of each of the corporations so merged or consolidated; and any claim existing or action or proceeding pending by or against such corporation may be prosecuted as if such merger or consolidation had not taken place, or such surviving or new corporation may be substituted in its place. Neither the rights of creditors nor any liens upon the property of any such corporation shall be impaired by such merger or consolidation.

Appellant nevertheless contends that Financial Resources Corporation is liable for the American Leasco debt only to the extent of assets transferred by American Leasco to Financial Resources Corporation in the merger. Appellant cites *Valley Bank v. Malcolm*, 23 Ariz. 395, 204 P. 207 (1922), as a basis for this argument. The *Malcolm* decision, however, simply does not support this proposition. First, *Malcolm* was decided long before Arizona's enactment in 1976 of A.R.S. § 10-076 as part of the Arizona Business Corporation Act. This more recent legislative pronouncement accordingly governs this action.

In addition, the *Malcolm* decision is inapplicable to the facts of this case, because *Malcolm* involved a corporate sale of assets as opposed to a merger situation. In *Malcolm*, an insolvent bank sold assets to a separate purchasing corporation. The question faced by the court in that case was whether the purchasing corporation could be held liable for the general debts of the insolvent bank. The case before this court, however, is radically different. Here, American Leasco, the debtor corporation, has merged and become a part of a continuing corporate business entity. In such a merger situation, the Arizona statute must govern with respect to the surviving corporate entity. Further, the law in other jurisdictions is consistent with A.R.S. § 10-076 and its application to the merger in issue in this case. *See, e.g., Ladjevardian v. Laidlaw-Coggeshall, Inc.*, 431 F. Supp. 834 (S.D.N.Y. 1977); *Beals v. Washington International, Inc.*, 386 A.2d 1156 (Del. 1978); *Johnson v. Marshall & Huschart Machinery Co.*, 384 N.E.2d 141 (Ill. App. Ct. 1978); *Gaswint v. Case*, 509 P.2d 19 (Or. 1973).

Moreover, there is also no support for appellant's contention that a successor corporation may not be liable for the punitive damage portion of the judgment owed Schmidt. A.R.S. § 10-076 plainly provides that "all" liabilities and obligations of a merged corporation become the responsibility of any successor corporation. This includes punitive damages. *Western Resources Life Insurance Company v. Gerhardt*, 553 S.W.2d 783 (Tex. Civ. App. 1977). Appellant's argument on this point, as well as its argument with respect to the points discussed earlier, fails to recognize that the merged corporation does not cease functioning. Rather, following merger, the merged corporation and its assets continue to function as a part of the successor corporation in its business and income-producing activities. *Cf. Arizona Corporation Commission v. California Insurance Company*, 28 Ariz. 128, 236 P. 460 (1925). "A business cannot shrug off personal liability to its creditors simply by merging, consolidating, switching from partnership to corporate form or vice versa, or changing its name." *Nelson v. Pampered Beef-Midwest, Inc.*, 298 N.W.2d 281, 288 (Iowa 1980). The superior court correctly determined that Financial Resources Corporation is liable for the entire $30,000 judgment owed Schmidt by American Leasco.

Appellee is awarded reasonable attorney fees on appeal pursuant to A.R.S. § 12-341.01(A).

SCHUMACHER v. RICHARDS SHEAR CO.

New York Court of Appeals
451 N.E.2d 195 (1983)

SIMMONS, J.

Plaintiff Otto F. Schumacher was blinded in one eye when he was struck by a scrap of flying metal ejected by a model 300-ton shearing machine he was operating at work. He and his wife sue defendant Richards Shear Company, Inc., who manufactured and sold the machine to his employer, and defendant Logemann Brothers Company, Inc., who subsequently purchased substantially all of Richards' assets. They seek to recover compensatory and derivative damages for the injury on theories of strict products liability and negligence. Richards Shear has interposed a cross claim against Logemann. The issue on this appeal is whether defendant Logemann is liable to plaintiff for the tortious conduct of Richards Shear or for its own conduct subsequent to acquiring Richards Shear's assets.

Defendant Logemann maintains that it is not liable in an action in strict products liability as a successor of Richards Shear under the rule of *Hartford Acc. & Ind. Co. v. Canron, Inc.* (43 N.Y.2d 823) or under extensions of that rule recognized in other jurisdictions, and that it cannot be held liable for its own nonfeasance because it had no common-law duty to warn plaintiff of any defect in the machine. It moved for summary judgment dismissing the complaint and the cross claim. Special Term granted the motion and the Appellate Division affirmed with two Judges dissenting. The dissenters found factual issues warranting a trial on whether defendant Logemann's failure to warn plaintiff's employer of danger from the machine constituted negligence.

. . . .

There should be a modification. Defendant Logemann's motion for summary judgment should be granted dismissing the first cause of action in strict products liability and denied insofar as it seeks dismissal of the cause of action alleging a negligent failure to warn. We hold that the rule in *Hartford Acc. & Ind. Co. v. Canron, Inc. (supra)* applies to personal injury cases and bars recovery from defendant Logemann for any fault of Richards Shear. Moreover, there are no facts alleged which warrant our consideration or application of the "product line" or "continuity of enterprise" theories extending liability to a successor corporation. The court is also unanimous in its recognition that a negligence cause of action for failure to warn may exist on behalf of an employee injured by an unsafe machine against a manufacturing corporation which subsequently acquires all or part of the assets of the manufacturer of the machine. The duty arises because of the relationship between the acquiring corporation and the purchaser of the machinery, plaintiff's employer in this case, and because of the knowledge which the acquiring corporation possesses or has reason to possess concerning the risk of personal injury created by operation of the machine without a safety guard. We disagree only on whether evidence submitted by plaintiff in response to defendant's motion for summary judgment is sufficient to create an issue of fact. A majority of the court believes it is. Accordingly, Logemann's motion for summary judgment should have been denied as to the failure to warn cause of action.

Plaintiff, an employee of Wallace Steel and Supply Company, was injured on April 17, 1978 when he was struck by a piece of metal thrown from a hydraulic shearing machine while he was operating it. The machine was purchased by plaintiff's employer from Richards Shear in January, 1964. It is plaintiff's contention that the machine was defective in design and manufacture, because it did not have a guard to deflect metal ejected from the machine, and that Richards Shear and Logemann should have taken measures to correct the existing dangerous condition or have alerted users of it.

Logemann's status as a "successor" arises principally from a "License and Sales Agreement" dated January, 1968 in which Richards Shear granted to Logemann, among other things, the exclusive right to manufacture and sell Richards Shear products, improvements, and inventory, and to use the trade name "Richards." In substance, the transaction was a sale of all assets because thereafter Richards Shear discontinued its business of selling, manufacturing and servicing shears. Currently, it has no liability insurance, employees, or business volume and it has few assets.

In February, 1968, approximately four years after plaintiff's employer purchased the machine from Richards Shear, Logemann contacted plaintiff's employer, Wallace Steel, and notified it of the acquisition of the Richards Shear product line along with the inventories and blueprints for new shears. In July, 1968, a former Richards Shear serviceman was sent by Logemann to service and check Wallace Steel's machine. Thereafter, in April, 1976, Logemann again contacted Wallace Steel and solicited business with respect to the shear machine, made assurances concerning service, and notified Wallace Steel of its acquisition of another former Richards Shear serviceman. Logemann also supplied Wallace Steel with replacement parts for the machine.

It is the general rule that a corporation which acquires the assets of another is not liable for the torts of its predecessor. There are exceptions and we stated those generally recognized in *Hartford Acc. & Ind. Co. v. Canron, Inc.* (43 N.Y.2d 823, 825, *supra*). A corporation may be held liable for the torts of its predecessor if (1) it expressly or impliedly assumed the predecessor's tort liability, (2) there was a consolidation or merger of seller and purchaser, (3) the purchasing corporation was a mere continuation of the selling corporation, or (4) the transaction is entered into fraudulently to escape such obligations. Nothing in the record suggests liability under any of these theories. The only arguable basis upon which plaintiffs can predicate a finding of successor liability is to characterize Logemann as a "mere continuation" of Richards Shear Company. The exception refers to corporate reorganization, however, where only one corporation survives the transaction; the predecessor corporation must be extinguished. Since Richards Shear survived the instant purchase agreement as a distinct, albeit meager, entity, the Appellate Division properly concluded that Logemann cannot be considered a mere continuation of Richards Shear.

Plaintiffs also contend that liability may be imposed on defendant Logemann for strict products liability based upon recent decisions in other jurisdictions which have extended successor liability. The courts that have addressed the issue impose strict products liability on a successor corporation, based upon a balancing approach, where there has been a basic "continuity of the enterprise" of the seller corporation (*Turner v. Bituminous Cas. Co.*, 397 Mich. 406, *supra*), an expansion of the traditional merger or consolidation exceptions, or where the successor corporation continues to produce the predecessor's product in the same plant (*Ray v. Alad Corp.*, 19 Cal. 3d 22, *supra* ["product line" exception]). We do not adopt the rule of either case but note that both are factually distinguishable in any event. Applying the test adopted by the Michigan Supreme Court in *Turner* to the instant facts, plaintiffs would have no claim against defendant Logemann as a matter of law because the factors manifesting continuity of corporate responsibility, such as continuity of management, key personnel, and physical location are not present in this case. Logemann did not purchase the manufacturing plant or equipment of Richards Shear and except for the hiring of two servicemen, no employees of Richards Shear became employees of Logemann. A stronger claim may be based upon the "product line" theory developed by the California Supreme Court in *Ray v. Alad Corp. (supra).* In *Ray*, the court, noting its rule on successor liability (which is the same as New York's), stated that where none of the four exceptions for imposing liability were present, it would consider the policies underlying strict tort liability for defective products to determine whether an exception to the general rules insulating the defendant therein from liability were warranted. These policies included the availability of remedies for the injured plaintiff as well as the fairness of requiring the successor to assume a responsibility for defective products. However, the *Ray* case presented unique facts which are clearly distinguishable from the present case and the California court's policy decision was obviously influenced by them. Those circumstances, the dissolution of the prior corporation shortly after the purchase of its equipment and the use by the successor corporation of essentially the same factory, name and office personnel after the transactions to produce the same product, are not present in this case.

The order of the Appellate Division should be modified by denying defendant's motion to grant summary judgment as to plaintiff's second cause of action sounding in negligence and as so modified, affirmed.

LOVING & ASSOCS. v. CAROTHERS

Minnesota Court of Appeals
619 N.W.2d 782 (2000)

OPINION

LANSING, JUDGE.

Loving & Associates, Inc., sued Gibson Carothers to enforce a personal guaranty he issued to Loving to secure a line of credit to Lake Street Shirts, Inc. The district court granted Carothers summary judgment on Loving's claims, reasoning that the 1992 merger of Lake Street Shirts, Inc., and Stafford Blaine Designs, Ltd., discharged Carothers's obligations under the guaranty by operation of law. Because we conclude that a merger does not necessarily discharge a guaranty by operation of law and that genuine issues of material fact remain to be decided, we reverse and remand.

FACTS

Lake Street Shirts, Inc. (LSS), is a Minnesota corporation in the business of screen-printing t-shirts and sweatshirts for sale to card and gift shops nationwide. Gibson Carothers and Herbert Fick incorporated LSS in 1989. Carothers owned 26% of the company's stock and was its chairman and a director. But he was not involved in the company's day-to-day operations.

In April 1989, LSS sought a line of credit from Loving & Associates, Inc., a national supplier of athletic apparel. Loving agreed to extend LSS credit, but it insisted on a personal guaranty from Carothers. Carothers thus signed a personal guaranty securing payment of "all sums owed by the Company [identified as 'Lake Street Shirts'] to Loving and the performance by the Company of all terms and conditions of purchase orders * * * whether now existing or hereinafter entered into between the Company and Loving." The guaranty was a continuing guaranty revocable only "by notice in writing to Loving." Carothers did not envision the possibility of a merger when he signed the guaranty.

In 1992, a major distributor of LSS decided it would no longer distribute LSS shirts. In response, Fick proposed a merger between LSS and Stafford Blaine Designs, Ltd. (Stafford I), a company Fick had incorporated in 1988 to distribute high-end, licensed, screen-printed clothing. Carothers was not a shareholder in Stafford I and was not involved in its management or day-to-day operations.

In August 1992, LSS and Stafford I merged into Stafford-Lake, Inc., which later assumed the name Stafford-Blaine Designs, Ltd. (Stafford II). According to Fick, other than as a minority shareholder, "Carothers had essentially no say in whether the companies merged or not." Under the terms of the merger agreement, LSS and Stafford I ceased to exist and Stafford-Lake, the surviving corporation, assumed their liabilities and obligations. The merger agreement also provided that the merger would not affect the rights of the constituent corporations' creditors. Carothers received a 12% ownership share in Stafford II.

The record shows no perceptible change in LSS's operating procedures or management structure after the merger. LSS retained its pre-merger address and continued to operate under the name Lake Street Shirts Co. pursuant to a certificate of assumed name Stafford II filed in 1993. Fick continued to manage LSS and remained Loving's principal contact. In turn, Loving continued to extend credit to LSS on the same terms as before the merger. At Fick's request, Loving maintained separate accounts for LSS, Stafford I, and Aardvark Graphics, Stafford I's predecessor.

The parties disagree on when Fick informed Loving of the merger. Without specifying a time frame, Fick claims he told Loving of the merger and apprised Loving of the financial status of the newly formed corporation from time to time thereafter. Loving, on the other hand, claims it first learned of the merger in

December 1995, when Fick wrote a letter to all creditors informing them that Stafford II was having financial difficulties.

At the time of the merger, LSS was grossing approximately $3 million in annual sales. Stafford I was grossing $3.7 million. Although the merger forced Stafford II to move into a more expensive facility and resulted in increased operating expenses, Stafford II remained profitable and paid Loving's bills through 1994.

In 1995, however, Stafford II began experiencing financial difficulties as a result of rapid expansion, poor management, production difficulties, and industry changes. In response, it sent all creditors several proposals to restructure the debt. Loving was among Stafford II's creditors, and it was also on the committee assigned to review the restructuring proposals and to report to the remaining creditors. Although Stafford II continued to operate under the various plans agreed to by its creditors, in 1998 management decided to sell the company's assets.

Relying on Carothers's guaranty, Loving then brought this action to recover $37,529.98 owing on the LSS account for goods delivered between November and December 1995.[2] Carothers refused payment and moved for summary judgment, claiming the merger had discharged the guaranty by operation of law. Loving opposed Carothers's summary-judgment motion but did not move for summary judgment itself. The district court agreed that the merger had discharged the guaranty by operation of law and granted Carothers summary judgment. This appeal followed.

ISSUE

As a matter of law, did the merger between Lake Street Shirts, Inc., and Stafford-Blaine Designs, Ltd., discharge Carothers from liability under the guaranty for the post-merger performance of Lake Street Shirts?

ANALYSIS

Whether a continuing guaranty extends to debts incurred by a debtor after it merges with another organization is a question of first impression in Minnesota. Relying on Minn. Stat. § 302A.641 (1998), the district court held that the merger of LSS and Stafford I discharged Carothers's obligations under the guaranty by operation of law because LSS ceased to exist upon the merger. Alternatively, the district court held that the guaranty unambiguously extended only to the debts of the company originally existing as Lake Street Shirts. We disagree that Carothers has established a basis for summary judgment on either ground.

---

[2] [1] Stafford I owed Loving more than $100,000 for goods delivered between October 1995 and March 1998. Loving brought a separate action against Fick, seeking to enforce Fick's personal guaranty for Stafford I's debts. The district court denied Fick summary judgment on Loving's claims, reasoning that issues of material fact remained on whether Fick's post-merger conduct evidenced an intent to honor the guaranty as a continuing guaranty.

I. The Effect of the Merger Statute

MINN. STAT. § 302A.641 governs the effect of mergers. It provides that upon a merger, "[t]he separate existence of all constituent organizations * * * ceases[.]" MINN. STAT. § 302A.641, subd. 2(b). But it also provides that the surviving organization inherits the rights and privileges of the constituent organizations and becomes responsible for their liabilities and obligations. *Id.*, subd. 2(d), (e). For that reason, a constituent organization ceases to exist upon a merger only in the sense that it has no separate existence.

A corporation is essentially the legal identity of a set of contractual obligations and entitlements. *United States Shoe Corp. v. Hackett*, 793 F.2d 161, 163 (7th Cir. 1986). These obligations and entitlements do not cease to exist when the legal identity that embodies them changes. Instead, they transfer to the surviving organization by operation of law. *Id.* at 163-64. A merger does not, therefore, necessarily extinguish a continuing guaranty as a matter of law. *See CBS, Inc. v. Film Corp. of America*, 545 F. Supp. 1382, 1387 (E.D. Pa. 1982) (concluding "the rights of a company pursuant to a guaranty agreement survive the merger of that company with another, even though the originally guaranteed company is not the survivor corporation of the merger"); *see also Essex Int'l, Inc. v. Clamage*, 440 F.2d 547, 550 (7th Cir. 1971) (stating "a merger or consolidation involving the creditor corporation does not necessarily discharge a guarantor any more than a mere change in corporate name does").

By the same token, a continuing guaranty is not enforceable as a matter of law merely because it survives a merger. Contrary to Loving's argument, a guaranty is not a "right or privilege" of a constituent organization within the meaning of MINN. STAT. § 302A.641, subd. 2(d). Instead, it is an independent contract between a guarantor and a creditor and is collateral to the contractual obligation between the creditor and a debtor. *Schmidt v. McKenzie*, 215 Minn. 1, 6-8, 9 N.W.2d 1, 3-4 (1943). Because guaranties confer a right on the creditor rather than the debtor, a guaranty securing the performance of a constituent organization does not vest in the surviving corporation upon a merger by operation of MINN. STAT. § 302A.641, subd. 2(d). *See Worth Corp. v. Metropolitan Cas. Ins. Co.*, 142 Misc. 734, 255 N.Y.S. 470, 472 (App. Term 1932) (stating surety's post-merger liability does not depend on whether surviving corporation succeeds to constituent corporation's assets).

Through caselaw, courts have developed a rule that combines both contractual and a multi-factor equitable analysis to determine whether a guaranty is enforceable after a debtor undergoes a change in composition or business structure. Virtually all courts agree that whether a guaranty is enforceable to secure post-merger obligations depends in the first instance on the terms of the guaranty. But when a guarantee does not provide for the contingency of a change in the debtor's composition or business structure, the inquiry necessarily broadens to whether the merger alters the debtor's identity significantly and thereby changes without the debtor's consent the obligation the guarantor initially assumed under the guaranty. *See, e.g., United States Shoe Corp.*, 793 F.2d at 162-63; *Essex*, 440 F.2d at 550. Combining a contractual and a multi-factor equitable or commercial-reasonableness analysis prevents a guarantor from circumventing a continuing guaranty simply by changing the name, composition, or legal identity of the organization whose performance the guaranty secures and thereby guards against the elevation of form over substance. This dual approach is consistent with the Restatement of Suretyship and Guaranty. *See* Restatement (Third) of Suretyship and Guaranty § 37 (1996). We adopt this approach in evaluating whether the guaranty at issue in this case extends to LSS's post-merger debts.

II. The Terms of the Guaranty

We first turn to the terms of the guaranty. Because a guaranty is a contract, its terms must be understood in their plain and ordinary sense in light of the parties' intentions and the circumstances under which the guaranty was given. *Marquette Trust Co. v. Doyle*, 176 Minn. 529, 533, 224 N.W. 149, 151 (1929). The terms of a guarantor's obligation may not be unduly restricted by technical interpretation. *Bradshaw v. Barber*, 125 Minn. 479, 481-82, 147 N.W. 650, 650 (1914). Nor, on the other hand, may they be enlarged beyond the fair and natural import of the guaranty's terms. *Id.*

Relying on the terms of the guaranty and on *Borg Warner Acceptance Corp. v. Shakopee Sports Ctr., Inc.*, 431 N.W.2d 539 (Minn. 1988), Loving argues the guaranty unambiguously extends to the post-merger debts of LSS because it is unconditional and revocable only by written notice to Loving. In *Borg Warner*, the court held that stockholders who had withdrawn from the corporation whose debts they had guaranteed remained liable for obligations the corporation incurred after they withdrew because they failed to revoke the guaranty. *Id.* at 541.

We disagree that Carothers's failure to revoke the guaranty renders it enforceable as a matter of law. Because an unrevoked continuing guaranty may be revoked by operation of law, a guarantor's failure to revoke, although relevant, is not dispositive. *Borg Warner* is limited to its facts and applies only in cases in which the principal retains its identity after undergoing a change in composition or structure.

Carothers does not dispute that the guaranty, until terminated, is enforceable to secure LSS's pre-merger debts. But he argues he is not liable for LSS's post-merger obligations because, by its terms, the guaranty unambiguously secures only the pre-merger performance of Lake Street Shirts, not its post-merger performance. Carothers claims that because the parties did not contemplate a merger when they signed the guaranty, to construe the guaranty as extending to LSS's post-merger performance would amount to redrafting the original contract. Carothers relies on *Wheeling Steel Corp. v. Neu*, 90 F.2d 139 (8th Cir. 1937), a case in which the court refused to hold the guarantor liable for the obligations of a company other than the company specifically referred to in the guaranty, even though both companies were substantially identical.

We are not persuaded by Carothers's claim that the guaranty unambiguously extends only to Lake Street Shirts's pre-merger performance. By its terms, the guaranty extends to "the performance by [Lake Street Shirts] of all terms and conditions of purchase orders * * * whether now existing or hereinafter entered into between [Lake Street Shirts] and Loving." The guaranty unconditionally guarantees the present and future performance of "Lake Street Shirts" and is silent on the consequences of a merger. By asking us to read the guaranty as extending only to the pre-merger performance of Lake Street Shirts, Carothers is thus asking us to read a limitation into the guaranty that may have been intended but is neither expressly stated nor reasonably implied. We decline to do so. Instead, we conclude that absent language expressly disclaiming or assuming liability for Lake Street Shirts's performance in the event of a merger, the guaranty's enforceability depends on whether the merger changed the identity of Lake Street Shirts and imposed on Carothers without his consent an obligation that differed materially from the obligation he undertook when he signed the guaranty.

III. New Identity and Increased Risk

Whether changes in the principal are of sufficient magnitude to justify releasing a guarantor is a determination courts must make on a case-by-case basis. *Fehr Bros., Inc. v. Scheinman*, 121 A.D.2d 13, 509 N.Y.S.2d 304, 307-08 (1986). Courts agree that minimal changes do not affect a guarantor's obligation. See Annotation, Change in Name, Location, Composition, or Structure of Obligor Commercial Enterprise Subsequent to Execution of Guaranty or Surety Agreement as Affecting Liability of Guarantor or Surety to the Obligee, 69 A.L.R.3d 567, 572 (1976). The reincorporation and name-change of a principal, for example, have been held to be insufficient to discharge a guarantor's obligations absent a corresponding change in operating procedures or business structure. *See, e.g., Folk v. Continental Can Co.*, 97 F.2d 322, 324 (4th Cir. 1938) (upholding guaranty after change in principal's business structure on finding that "[t]he business of the old company was conducted as usual by the [new company] with substantially the same officers and with the same assets which the new company had absorbed"). This is particularly true when the guarantor himself participates in the change or the change could reasonably have been anticipated. *See, e.g., New York Am., Inc. v. Hub Advertising Agency*, 136 Misc. 596, 240 N.Y.S. 367, 368 (N.Y. City Ct. 1930) (holding guarantor was "estopped from using the cloak of a corporate entity to which he himself was a party to relieve him of any liability under [guaranty issued before incorporation to secure partnership's debts]"); *People v. Backus*, 117 N.Y. 196, 22 N.E. 759, 760 (1889) (upholding guaranty after bank's corporate existence was extended through renewal of its charter pursuant to an amendment to the National Banking Act on finding that guarantors had signed the guaranty knowing that bank was subject to banking laws, which could be amended at any time); *Richardson v. Steuben County*, 226 N.Y. 13, 122 N.E. 449, 451-52 (1919) (holding change in membership of partnership that owned bank did not release surety from liability for bank's obligations because banking houses ordinarily continue their identity for generations and could do so only through a constant succession of partners).

Whether more substantial changes in the principal affect a guarantor's obligation depends primarily on (a) whether the changes result in a new principal in terms of management, control, operating procedures, and business dealings; and (b) whether the changes materially alter the nature of the performance required of the guarantor. Thus, changes that allow the principal to survive as an independent entity and do not affect the guarantor's original undertaking do not discharge a guaranty. *See, e.g., Alton Banking & Trust Co. v. Sweeney*, 135 Ill. App. 3d 96, 89 Ill. Dec. 926, 481 N.E.2d 769, 773-74 (1985) (change in principal's business from used-car lot to new-car dealership did not constitute material change warranting guarantor's release from obligations under continuing guaranty, where guarantor owned both businesses and assented to the change, and amount of dealership's indebtedness did not exceed amount specified in guaranty); New York Am., 240 N.Y.S. at 368 (partnership's decision to incorporate did not release partner-guarantor from liability for new corporation's debts because new corporation continued to conduct same business, at same address, under same name, with same directors and stockholders; business relation between creditor and principal continued unaffected; and partner-guarantor participated in decision to incorporate and became stockholder and director of newly formed corporation); *Caldor, Inc. v. Mattel, Inc.*, 817 F. Supp. 408 (S.D. N.Y. 1993) (finding that merger and subsequent spinoff of subsidiary, with resulting loss of control by parent-guarantor, did not fundamentally alter parent-guarantor's risk under guaranty because subsidiary continued to operate same business under substantially same conditions as before merger and spinoff).

On the other hand, changes that result in a significantly different business organization and increase the guarantor's exposure to liability serve to release the guarantor from obligations under the guaranty. Thus, the merger of a principal into another corporation discharged the guarantor's obligation under a continuing guaranty because the principal did not survive the merger as an independent entity. *Worth Corp.*, 255 N.Y.S. at 474-75. Instead, it assumed the name, character, corporate structure, and organization of the surviving corporation. *Id.* at 473. Similarly, the incorporation of a sole proprietorship and the subsequent acquisition of majority control by new stockholders released the guarantors from liability because they changed "the essential nature of the business enterprise[,]" diluted the guarantors' control over the business, and "greatly expanded" their liability. *Teledyne Mid-Am. Corp. v. HOH Corp.*, 486 F.2d 987, 990 (9th Cir. 1973).

Carothers's post-merger liability under the guaranty thus depends on whether the merger changed Lake Street Shirts's corporate identity significantly and thereby materially increased the risk Carothers assumed when he signed the guaranty. Other relevant factors include whether Carothers participated in effecting the merger or otherwise assented to it, whether he could reasonably have anticipated a material increase in the risk he assumed under the guaranty, whether Loving had notice of the change before performing, and whether Carothers opted to revoke the guaranty. *See United States Shoe Corp.*, 793 F.2d at 163 (stating "guarantor may consent to the increased risk by creating it"); *Fehr Bros.*, 509 N.Y.S.2d at 310 (concluding guarantor, "in making a voluntary business decision which created the conditions causing the risk to increase and in failing to carry out the simple task of relieving himself of his obligations by providing written notice to plaintiff of his intent to terminate the guaranty, implicitly consented to that increased risk"); *Mountain States Tel. & Tel. v. Lee*, 95 Idaho 134, 504 P.2d 807, 808-09 (1972) (guarantor not released after formation of new principal corporation because he participated in change as stockholder and officer, failed to revoke, and did not inform creditor of the change).

A. New Identity

Our review of the undisputed facts in the record shows that the merger did not result in a significantly new entity, the debts of which Carothers never intended to guarantee. LSS continued to operate the same business, under the same name, at the same address, under substantially the same management. Fick continued to oversee the company's day-to-day operations. The record contains no indication that the company's operating procedures changed. And the relationship between LSS and Loving did not change: Loving continued to extend credit to LSS as an entity separate from Stafford II under the same terms as before the merger, continued to deal with Fick as its principal contact, and continued to maintain a separate account for LSS. The record thus conclusively establishes that LSS did not undergo a change of identity after the merger.

B. Increased Risk

The next question then is whether as a matter of law the merger materially increased the risk Carothers undertook when he signed the guaranty. Minnesota courts have used an increased-risk analysis in determining whether a material alteration in the contract between the principal and the creditor discharges a guarantor. *See, e.g., Minnesota Fed. Sav. & Loan Ass'n v. Central Enters. of Superior, Inc.*, 311 Minn. 46, 51, 247 N.W.2d 46, 50 (1976); *Estate of Frantz v. Page*, 426 N.W.2d 894, 898 (Minn. App. 1988), review denied (Minn. Sept. 16, 1988).

Carothers argues that his risk increased as a result of the merger because LSS doubled in size and his control over LSS decreased in direct proportion to his ownership interest in Stafford II. But a bigger business entity does not necessarily create a materially bigger risk. In fact, Stafford II was profitable until 1994 despite the increase in size. Additionally, it is unlikely that Carothers's alleged loss of control over LSS affected his risk under the guaranty because Carothers was not involved in the day-to-day operations of LSS and LSS continued under substantially the same management as before the merger.

Loving argues that because it maintained a separate account for LSS, Carothers's post-merger risk remained limited to LSS's debts and is thus consistent with the risk he assumed when he signed the guaranty. But the record does not establish whether the merger resulted in a significant increase in capital that would have allowed LSS to obtain more credit from Loving than it could have obtained before the merger. Arguably, a significant increase in capital and the resulting increase in LSS's ability to obtain credit may have increased the risk inherent in LSS's separate account when Carothers signed the guaranty. We thus conclude that a question of fact remains on whether the merger increased Carothers's risk under the guaranty. A fact question also remains on whether Loving knew of the merger before it extended additional credit to LSS. Because the record raises issues of material fact, summary judgment is not appropriate. Accordingly, we reverse and remand.

DECISION

The merger of LSS and Stafford I did not release Carothers by operation of law from liability under the guaranty for the post-merger performance of LSS. Because the guaranty is silent on the contingency of a merger and fact questions remain on whether the merger impermissibly increased the risk Carothers assumed under the guaranty initially, we reverse and remand.

Reversed and remanded.

§ 7.02 DUTIES OWED TO AND RIGHTS OF THE SECURITY HOLDERS OF THE ACQUIRED CORPORATION

CLAGETT v. HUTCHISON

United States Court of Appeals, Fourth Circuit
583 F.2d 1259 (1978)

K.K. Hall, Circuit Judge

This appeal arises out of a civil action commenced by C. Thomas Clagett, Jr., and others who were minority shareholders of the Laurel Harness Racing Association, Inc. (Laurel). Jurisdiction was predicated upon diversity of citizenship. The plaintiffs sought recovery of monetary damages from Richard H. Hutchison, Jr. (Hutchison), once the majority controlling common stockholder of Laurel, and the subsequent purchasers of all or a portion of Hutchison's controlling common stock.

In relevant part, plaintiffs alleged that through certain stock transfers, the various defendants had breached two of the fiduciary duties they owed to the plaintiffs as minority shareholders.

First. Plaintiffs charged that, under Maryland law, defendant Hutchison, in the sale of his controlling common stock to defendants, Steven Sobechko, James Sobechko and Joseph Shamy, an attorney, had a duty to investigate the ability of that group to manage Laurel and to make inquiry into their characters and financial stability. (Count I). The same duty was alleged to exist between the Sobechkos and Shamy in the subsequent transfer of a portion of their stock to defendant Mike Brown. (Count II). And finally, the same duty was alleged to exist between the Sobechkos, Shamy and Brown in their transfer of the controlling common stock to defendant Daniel J. Rizk. (Count III).[3]

Second. Plaintiff charged that, under Maryland law, Hutchison, as the majority controlling common shareholder of Laurel, owed a fiduciary duty to the minority shareholders, including plaintiffs, to afford to them an equal opportunity to sell their shares on the same terms and conditions which were offered to him. (Count I). In Count II as against Hutchison's purchasers the same duty was alleged, and the

---

[3] [1] Count IV alleged mismanagement against defendant Rizk. However, the plaintiffs abandoned the claims of mismanagement which were set forth in various parts of the four counts of the Complaint below. No mismanagement claims are urged in this appeal.

Sobechkos and Shamy were charged with aiding and abetting Hutchison's violation of the "equal opportunity" rule.

All six defendants moved to dismiss, arguing that the Complaint failed to state a claim upon which relief could be granted under Maryland law. F.R.C.P. 12(b). The district court held, on the facts of this case, that neither of plaintiffs' theories of recovery stated a claim upon which relief could be granted, and the suit was dismissed. Plaintiffs appeal, and we affirm.

I. FACTS

There is no dispute as to the facts. Laurel, a Maryland corporation, owned a harness racing track and operated harness race meets, pursuant to a license granted to it by the Maryland Racing Commission at Laurel, Maryland.[4] During the relevant time period of this suit, from October 8, 1974, through March 25, 1976, there were 125,000 shares of the common stock of Laurel issued and then outstanding which stock was held by approximately 300 stockholders. The common stock of Laurel was thinly traded on the public market. While defendant Hutchison was president of Laurel, he executed an agreement to sell his common stock to defendants Steven Sobechko, James Sobechko and Joseph Shamy for $43.75 per share. At that time he owned a majority of Laurel's common stock or approximately 67,662 shares. According to the Complaint, the then-prevailing market price for a share of Laurel common stock fluctuated between $7.50 and $10.00 per share. On that same date, Hutchison allegedly caused the trio purchasing his stock to similarly extend the $43.75 per share offer to certain designated minority shareholders. The plaintiffs were not included in the designated group to receive the beneficence of Hutchison.

The actual stock transfer from Hutchison to the Sobechkos and Shamy occurred on May 12, 1975. The plaintiffs discovered the pending stock transfer just before it occurred through a news article on April 27, 1975.

Next, between May 12, 1975, and November 5, 1975, while Laurel was under the control of the Sobechkos and Shamy, some unspecified portion of their common stock was transferred to defendant Mike Brown. The foursome continued in control of Laurel.

Finally, on March 25, 1976, the Sobechkos, Shamy and Brown transferred their stock and the controlling majority of Laurel to defendant Daniel J. Rizk. This was the final stock transfer involved in this litigation.

Summarily, the plaintiffs sought recovery of monetary damages for the loss in value of their common stock in Laurel due to the alleged breaches of the duty to investigate and the breach of the equal opportunity rule.

---

[4] [2] Annotated Code of Maryland, Art. 78 B.

II. THE DUTY TO INVESTIGATE

Plaintiffs contend that a majority shareholder who sells the controlling interest in a corporation owes a fiduciary duty to the minority shareholders to investigate the character, integrity, financial stability and managerial ability of the prospective purchasers where such a seller is in a position to foresee the likelihood that the purchasers will defraud, loot or mismanage the company. And, on appeal, plaintiffs point to four factual circumstances which they argue were of sufficient gravity to place a duty upon Hutchison to investigate the purchasers of his stock.

First, a significant premium was paid to Hutchison for the price of his stock. Second, the actual closing on the Hutchison-Sobechko-Shamy transaction was scheduled to take place at some time from six to twelve months following the execution of the stock purchase agreement. Third, the contract precluded any change in the financial condition of Laurel pending closing on the transaction between Hutchison and the Sobechkos and Shamy. Fourth, Hutchison arranged for certain designated minority shareholders, not including the plaintiffs, to have their shares purchased by the Sobechkos and Shamy. Plaintiffs have cited no Maryland state court decision squarely on point, but rely upon our decision in *Swinney v. Keebler Company*, 480 F.2d 573 (4th Cir. 1973). They argue that the four "suspicious circumstances" set forth above were sufficient to indicate a likelihood of fraud would exist if the transfer was completed from Hutchison to the Sobechkos and Shamy.

The defendants counter by arguing that under Maryland law, minority shareholders have no individual right to recover from former majority stockholders for any alleged breach or breaches of the duty to investigate. They argue that, in reality, the suit is one to recover for mismanagement of Laurel, and such a recovery can be obtained only by a direct suit by the corporation itself, or by having the interests of the corporation advanced in a stockholders' derivative action.[5]

Alternatively, defendants argue that even if there is a duty to investigate under Maryland law, under the facts in this case, the four suspicious circumstances set forth above were neither suspicious nor sufficient to place Hutchison on notice of the likelihood of fraud by the Sobechkos and Shamy.

We adhere to our decision in *Swinney, supra*, and although we likewise have been unable to locate any Maryland state court decision directly on point, we believe the district court reached a correct result through its application of *Swinney* and its legal estimate of what the Maryland state courts would do if presented with this case. This suit was properly dismissed.

Under ordinary circumstances, a director or an officer of a corporation has the same right as any other stockholder to buy or to sell his stock. *See Llewellyn v. Queen City Dairy, Inc.*, 187 Md. 49, 58-9, 48 A.2d 322 (1946); *Swinney v. Keebler Co.*, 480 F.2d at 577. However, if, as this court noted in *Swinney*,

> . . . the sellers of control are in a position to foresee the likelihood of fraud on the corporation, . . . or on the remaining stockholders, at the hands of

[5] [3] As noted previously, the mismanagement claims have been abandoned. We are not presented with claims which would derivatively benefit Laurel, but are presented with personal claims of the plaintiffs for their individual damages.

> the transferee, their fiduciary duty imposes a positive duty to investigate the motives and reputation of the would-be purchaser [or purchasers]; and unless such a reasonable investigation shows that to a reasonable man no fraud is intended or likely to result, the sellers must refrain from the transfer of control.

480 F.2d at 578.

Applying *Swinney* to the four circumstances set forth by plaintiffs which are alleged to be "suspicious," we hold that upon this record, they are insufficient to state a claim upon which relief could be granted.

First. While the price paid for Hutchison's shares was indeed a premium price, it was nevertheless a premium paid for the element of control of the corporation. The premium payment is further justifiable since Laurel was a commercial business subject to further development as an ongoing business. Thus, the premium price paid to Hutchison cannot be said to be so unreasonable as to place him on notice of the likelihood of fraud on the corporation or the remaining stockholders. Finally, as a matter of logic, it seems farfetched to pay a 400% premium for stock simply in order to acquire control of a corporation in order to loot it. Certainly a cheaper corporate enterprise could be acquired for such malevolent purposes.

Second. It is true that the written agreement between Hutchison, the Sobechkos and Shamy provided that closing on the agreement was scheduled for some time from six to twelve months following the execution of the agreement.

Third. It is also true that the agreement precluded any change in the financial condition of Laurel pending closing on that transaction. We hold that these two factors, whether taken alone or in conjunction with the premium price paid to Hutchison, are not sufficiently suspicious in this case to invoke Swinney's duty to investigate. This argument was not entertained by the court below, and we would not ordinarily pass on it. However, it is clear to us that postponing the closing to attempt to obtain financing through a pledge of personal assets for a personal loan,[6] together with a contractual guarantee from the seller to the buyers to preserve the financial condition of Laurel pending closing, constituted prudent business practice rather than "suspicious" circumstances. The agreement essentially preserved the status quo of Laurel while allowing the purchasers to shop for financing favorable to them.

Fourth. It is true that Hutchison arranged for the purchase of some, but not all, of the outstanding minority shares of Laurel, and that the plaintiffs were not included in this group who were given the option to sell at the higher price received by Hutchison. From this, plaintiffs argue that Hutchison had some reason to believe that the future plans of the Sobechkos and Shamy were not in the best interests of Laurel and its minority stockholders. Defendants counter by noting that selling one's own stock and including others in such a sale, is a private act, sanctioned in law, and not alone "suspicious." We agree.

---

[6] [4] The facts presented in this case differ markedly from those presented in *Insuranshares, supra.* There, the assets of the corporation were pledged for a personal loan rather than pledging personal assets for a personal loan. 35 F. Supp. at 25. Other much more "suspicious" circumstances also were present in *Insuranshares.*

Thus, we believe that no duty to investigate should, upon the record now before us, have been placed upon Hutchison in his transfer of control to the Sobechkos and to Shamy, and Count I of the Complaint was properly dismissed. We further hold that the remaining counts of the Complaint were properly dismissed by the district court.

Count II alleged the transfer of "a portion" of stock from the Sobechkos and Shamy to Brown. (Complaint Count II, paragraph 38). No allegation of a transfer of "control" was set forth in this count of the Complaint, and no duty to investigate arose absent a transfer of control.

Count III alleged the transfer of control from the Sobechkos, Shamy and Brown to Rizk through sale of their stock to Rizk. However, as the district court held, there were no allegations of suspicious circumstances to place a duty to investigate upon the trio of the Sobechkos, Shamy and Brown in their sale of control to Rizk. Accordingly, dismissal here was proper also.

Finally, Count IV dealt only with allegations of mismanagement on the part of defendant Rizk. As above-noted, the mismanagement claims have been abandoned, and in any event, no transfer of control was alleged from Rizk to any transferee, nor was a breach of the duty to investigate alleged. Accordingly, dismissal of Court IV was also correct.

III. EQUAL OPPORTUNITY

The plaintiffs further argue that Hutchison, as the seller of the controlling shares of Laurel, owed a fiduciary duty to the minority shareholders of Laurel, including the plaintiffs, to afford them an equal opportunity to sell their minority shares or a pro rata part of their shares to the purchaser of the controlling stock on the same or substantially the same terms and conditions which were offered to Hutchison. If the offer to purchase the minority shares is extended, then the minority shareholders have the option to sell their shares or a pro rata portion of them at that price, or to continue their investment in the corporation, despite the transfer. Further, it is argued that such a rule would bar the controlling shareholder from securing an advantageous business arrangement for himself while abandoning the minority shareholders to the mercy of the new purchasers who would not control the corporation.

Plaintiffs cite no Maryland law precisely on point, but instead argue that the equal opportunity rule should properly follow from the Maryland law which prohibits a controlling stockholder from using his control for some ulterior purpose adverse to the interests of the corporation and its stockholders.

Plaintiffs rely upon three decisions from other jurisdictions in support of the equal opportunity rule: *Jones v. H.F. Ahmanson & Co.*, 1 Cal. 3d 93, 81 Cal. Rptr. 592, 460 P.2d 464 (1969); and *Donahue v. Rodd Electrotype Co. of New England, Inc.*, 367 Mass. 578, 328 N.E.2d 505 (1975); *Perlman v. Feldman*, 219 F.2d 173 (2d Cir. 1955), *cert. denied*, 349 U.S. 952, 75 S. Ct. 880, 99 L. Ed. 1277 (1955). *See also* Andrews, *Stockholder's Right to Equal Opportunity in the Sale of Shares*, 78 Harv. L. Rev. 505, 515 (1965).

Defendants counter that the rule of equal opportunity, while nice theoretically, is simply not the law. Neither the Maryland cases cited, nor the *Jones, Donahue* or *Perlman* cases, *supra*, support such a holding. *See also* Jararas, *Equal Opportunity in the Sale of Controlling Shares: A Reply to Professor Andrews*, 32 U. Chi. L. Rev. 240 (1965).

The district court distinguished *Jones, Donahue* and *Perlman* and held that the Maryland courts would not adopt the equal opportunity rule. We agree.

First, the equal opportunity rule has been rather soundly rejected. Second, the rule, if applied, would likely result in the stifling of many financial transactions due either to a purchaser's inability to purchase the additional shares, or from a lack of inclination to purchase those shares. *See* Andrews, 78 Harv. L. Rev. at 517; Jararas, 32 U. Chi. L. Rev. at 425-6; Letts, *Sale of Control Stock and the Rights of Minority Shareholders*, The Business Lawyer, January, 1971, at 631.

IV. CONCLUSION

At oral argument, plaintiffs' counsel pointed to additional facts not in the record, which indicated that various of the purchasers of Hutchison's stock could have engaged in conduct that would, if proven, constitute serious misconduct, perhaps even conduct which was criminal in nature. These facts are not before us. Accordingly, we confine our result in this case to the facts now before us, and leave the plaintiffs open to pursue any remedies which may yet be available to them.

ZETLIN v. HANSON HOLDINGS, INC.

New York Court of Appeals
397 N.E.2d 387 (1979)

MEMORANDUM

The order of the Appellate Division should be affirmed, with costs.

Plaintiff Zetlin owned approximately 2% of the outstanding shares of Gable Industries, Inc., with defendants Hanson Holdings, Inc., and Sylvestri together with members of the Sylvestri family, owning 44.4% of Gable's shares. The defendants sold their interests to Flintkote Co. for a premium price of $15 per share, at a time when Gable was selling on the open market for $7.38 per share. It is undisputed that the 44.4% acquired by Flintkote represented effective control of Gable.

Recognizing that those who invest the capital necessary to acquire a dominant position in the ownership of a corporation have the right of controlling that corporation, it has long been settled law that, absent looting of corporate assets, conversion of a corporate opportunity, fraud or other acts of bad faith, a controlling stockholder is free to sell, and a purchaser is free to buy, that controlling interest at a premium price (*see Barnes v. Brown*, 80 N.Y. 527; *Levy v. American Beverage Corp.*, 265 A.D. 208, 38 N.Y.S.2d 517; *Essex Universal Corp. v. Yates*, 2nd Cir., 305 F.2d 572).

Certainly, minority shareholders are entitled to protection against such abuse by controlling shareholders. They are not entitled, however, to inhibit the legitimate interests of the other stockholders. It is for this reason that control shares usually command a premium price. The premium is the added amount an investor is willing to pay for the privilege of directly influencing the corporation's affairs.

In this action plaintiff Zetlin contends that minority stockholders are entitled to an opportunity to share equally in any premium paid for a controlling interest in the corporation. This rule would profoundly affect the manner in which controlling stock interests are now transferred. It would require, essentially, that a controlling interest be transferred only by means of an offer to all stockholders, i.e., a tender offer. This would be contrary to existing law and if so radical a change is to be effected it would best be done by the Legislature.

COOKE, C.J., and JANSEN, GABRIELLI, JONES, WACHTLER, FUCHSBERG and MEYER, JJ., concur in memorandum.

Order affirmed.

In addition to the duties owed to the security holders of an acquired corporation as a matter of corporate law, the federal securities laws impose obligations upon a person who acquires what is considered to be a significant amount of stock of a publicly traded corporation. Two statutes that impose such obligations are Sections 13(d) and 16(b) of the Securities Exchange Act of 1934, as amended.

CHROMALLOY AMERICAN CORP. v. SUN CHEMICAL CORP.

United States Court of Appeals, Eighth Circuit
611 F.2d 240 (1979)

HENLEY, CIRCUIT JUDGE.

This case, arising under disclosure provisions of the Securities Exchange Act of 1934, 15 U.S.C. § 78m(d) (1977), requires us to decide whether the district court[7] erred in the partial grant and partial denial of preliminary injunctive relief.

Plaintiff-appellant Chromalloy American Corporation (Chromalloy) appeals the denial of injunctive relief which would compel defendant Sun Chemical Corporation to disclose its proposals for control of Chromalloy, and which would halt the purchase of Chromalloy stock by Sun for ninety days. Defendants-appellees Sun Chemical Corporation (Sun) and Norman E. Alexander cross-appeal from the district court's order that Sun disclose an intention to obtain control of Chromalloy.

We assume jurisdiction on appeal pursuant to 28 U.S.C. § 1292(a). Finding no

---

[7] [1] The Honorable John F. Nangle, United States District Judge for the Eastern District of Missouri.

error of law and no abuse of discretion in the district court's actions, we decline to reverse.

I. Procedural and Factual Background

In January, 1978 Sun Chemical Corporation began purchasing significant amounts of Chromalloy stock on the New York Stock Exchange. Chromalloy is a diversified corporation with revenues in fiscal year 1978 of nearly $1.4 billion and net earnings of $47 million, while Sun is a considerably smaller corporation with 1978 revenues of $394 million and net earnings of $20 million. Norman E. Alexander is Chief Executive Officer and Chairman of Sun's Board of Directors, and has been instrumental in instigating and furthering the purchase of Chromalloy stock by Sun Chemical Corporation.

By February 5, 1979 Sun had acquired 605,620 shares, or 5.2 per cent, of Chromalloy's total outstanding shares.[8] Sun was therefore required to comply with the disclosure provisions of § 13(d) of the Securities Exchange Act, 15 U.S.C. § 78m(d)(1) (1976).[9] Pursuant to the disclosure requirements, Sun on February 5, 1979 filed its first Schedule 13D. Sun stated that its acquisitions were for investment; that it had no present intention of seeking control of Chromalloy; that it presently intended to continue to increase its holdings; that the amount of such increase had not been determined; that Sun had been discussing with certain directors and members of Chromalloy management the possible increase in Sun's holdings; and that Sun might "at any time determine to seek control of Chromalloy." In four subsequent amendments to the Schedule 13D between April, 1979 and late July, 1979 Sun reported its plans to purchase additional stock, its unsuccessful attempt to gain representation on the Chromalloy Board, and its negotiations regarding a "stand-still" agreement whereby Sun would limit its purchases for a period of time as a condition of representation on the Chromalloy Board. In each of the amendments to its Schedule 13D Sun disclaimed any intent to control Chromalloy.

By late July, 1979 Sun's ownership had increased to nearly ten per cent of Chromalloy's outstanding stock. Following a large block purchase of stock by Sun at the end of July, Chromalloy filed the present action for injunctive and declaratory relief, alleging violations of Sections 13(d) and 14(d) of the Securities Exchange Act, the Missouri Take-Over Bid Disclosure Act, and § 203 of the Delaware General Corporation Law. Only the Count requesting injunctive relief pursuant to Section 13(d) of the Securities Exchange Act, 15 U.S.C. § 78m(d), is relevant to this appeal.

. . .

The district court found that Norman Alexander and Sun "have had the intent to control Chromalloy from the beginning," and that "[d]efendants have intended to exert considerable influence over the Board of Directors of Chromalloy, and, through this influence, direct the policies and management of Chromalloy." Pursuant to 15 U.S.C. § 78m(d), the court enjoined further acquisition of Chromalloy

---

8 [2] Percentages assume conversion of the Chromalloy preferred stock held by Sun.

9 [3] Hereinafter "Williams Act" or "Section 13(d)."

stock until Sun's Schedule 13D was amended to reflect this intention.

On August 21, 1979 Chromalloy was granted leave to brief the issue of whether further injunctive relief was required. Chromalloy sought further disclosures by Sun, the mailing of a corrected disclosure statement to Chromalloy stockholders at Sun's expense, and a "cooling off" period of ninety days during which Sun's purchases would be enjoined while information was disseminated to investors and the public. On August 29, 1979 the court denied Chromalloy's request for additional injunctive relief, at the same time approving Sun's version of an amended Schedule 13D.

In the court-approved Schedule 13D, Sun acknowledged its "intention to continue to seek representation on the Board of Directors of [Chromalloy] and to exercise, if possible, considerable influence over the Board of Directors of [Chromalloy] and thereby seek to direct the policies and management of [Chromalloy]." Sun stated its intention to acquire sufficient shares of Chromalloy stock to utilize the equity method of accounting, that is, twenty per cent of the combined voting power of all classes of Chromalloy stock. Sun disclosed that insofar as "a combination of arithmetic and influence constitutes control of [Chromalloy], it is Sun's intention, absent unforeseen contingencies, to attempt to ultimately obtain control of [Chromalloy]."

Upon being advised that this amended Schedule 13D had been filed with the Securities and Exchange Commission, the district court lifted the preliminary injunction then in effect to allow appellees to resume purchasing Chromalloy stock.

. . .

III. Issues on Appeal

Chromalloy's position on appeal is that the district court correctly ordered Sun to disclose a control intention, but abused its discretion in refusing to order further disclosures. The disclosures sought by Chromalloy include Sun's wish to use Chromalloy money to pay for transactions with Sun, as allegedly required by Item 3 of Section 13D;[10] Sun's plans upon obtaining control to cause Chromalloy to acquire the assets of Sun, as allegedly required by Item 4 of Schedule 13D;[11] Sun's

---

[10] [4] Item 3 of Schedule 13D, as amended by the SEC effective May 30, 1978, provides in relevant part:

> *Source and Amount of Funds or Other Consideration.* State the source and the amount of funds or other consideration used or to be used in making the purchases, and if any part of the purchase price is or will be represented by funds or other consideration borrowed or otherwise obtained for the purpose of acquiring, holding, trading or voting the securities, a description of the transaction and the names of the parties hereto.

SEC Exchange Act, Release Nos. 33-5925, 34-14692, IC-10212; 43 F.R. 18484, 18498 (April 28, 1978); [1978 Transfer Binder] Fed. Sec. L. Rep. (CCH) ¶ 81,571.

[11] [5] Item 4, as amended by the SEC effective May 30, 1978, provides in relevant part:

> *Purpose of Transaction.* State the purpose or purposes of the acquisition of securities of the issuer. Describe any plans or proposals which the reporting persons may have which relate to or would result in:
>
> (a) The acquisition by any person of additional securities of the issuer, or the disposition of securities of the issuer;

proposals to sell various divisions of Chromalloy as allegedly required by Item 4 of Schedule 13D;[12] and Sun's offer to "take care of" certain Chromalloy officers in return for support, as allegedly required by Item 6 of Schedule 13D.[13] Chromalloy also argues that a properly amended Schedule 13D should contain the warning that Sun's previous Schedule 13D and amendments were false and should not be relied upon. Moreover, in order to properly disseminate this information, Chromalloy contends that a cooling off period and a stockholder mailing are required. On cross-appeal, Sun contends that the district court erred as a matter of law in finding that Sun has a purpose to acquire control of Chromalloy.

The issues on appeal are governed by recent SEC revisions in Schedule 13D, particularly in Item 4. Under the former terms of Item 4, a securities purchaser was required to state the purpose of his purchase, and if one purpose was to acquire control, to describe any plans or proposals for major corporate changes.[14] In the revised version of Item 4,[15] effective more than six months before Sun's first Schedule 13D filing, the term "control" is not used. Rather, a securities purchaser is required to disclose the purpose of the purchase and, in addition, to disclose certain plans or proposals regardless of whether the underlying purpose is to acquire control of the issuer.[16] The Securities and Exchange Commission has expressly noted that under revised Item 4, "plans or proposals which result in or

---

(b) An extraordinary corporate transaction, such as a merger, reorganization or liquidation, involving the issuer or any of its subsidiaries;

(c) A sale or transfer of a material amount of assets of the issuer or any of its subsidiaries;

. . .

(f) Any other material change in the issuer's business or corporate structure . . . .

SEC Exchange Act Release Nos. 33-5925, 34-14692, IC-10212; 43 F.R. 18484, 18498 (April 28, 1978); [1978 Transfer Binder] Sec. L. Rep. (CCH) ¶ 81,571.

12 [6] *See* n.5, *supra*, for text of Item 4.

13 [7] Item 6, as amended by the SEC effective May 30, 1978, provides in relevant part:

> *Contracts, Arrangements, Understandings or Relationships with Respect to Securities of the Issuer.* Describe any contracts, arrangements, understandings or relationships (legal or otherwise) among the persons named in Item 2 and between such persons and any person with respect to any securities of the issuer, including but not limited to transfer or voting of any of the securities, finder's fees, joint ventures, loan or option arrangements, puts or calls, guarantees of profits, division of profits or loss, or the giving or withholding of proxies, naming the persons with whom such contracts, arrangements, understandings or relationships have been entered into.

SEC Exchange Act Release Nos. 33-5925, 34-14692, IC-10212; 43 F.R. 18484, 18499 (April 28, 1978); [1978 Transfer Binder] Fed. Sec. L. Rep. (CCH) ¶ 81,571.

14 [8] Item 4 of Schedule 13D previously provided:

> *Purpose of Transaction.* State the purpose or purposes of the purchase or proposed purchase of securities of the issuer. *If the purpose or one of the purposes of the purchase or proposed purchase is to acquire control* of the business of the issuer, describe any plans or proposals which the purchasers may have to liquidate the issuer, to sell its assets or to merge it with any other persons, or to make any other major change in its business or corporate structure.

(emphasis added). 17 C.F.R. § 240.13d-101 (1978).

15 [9] 43 F.R. 18498 (April 28, 1978). The text of Item 4 is set forth, *supra*, at n.5.

16 [10] SEC Exchange Act Release Nos. 33-5925, 34-14692, IC-10212; 43 F.R. 18484, 18493 (April 28, 1978); [1978 Transfer Binder] Fed. Sec. L. Rep. (CCH) ¶ 81,571.

relate to extraordinary corporate transactions have been made a separate item of disclosure."[17]

Under the provisions of the revised SEC regulations, we are confronted with two distinct questions: first, whether the district court erred in finding that Sun has a disclosable purpose to acquire control, and second, whether the district court abused its discretion in refusing to order disclosure of Sun's proposals for corporate changes aside from Sun's control intent.

IV. The Disclosure of Control Purpose

In assessing Sun's obligation to disclose a control purpose, we look to the definition of "control" appearing in Rule 12b-2(f), 17 C.F.R. § 240.12b-2 (1979), made applicable to Schedule 13D filings by 17 C.F.R. § 240.12b-1 (1979).[18] Rule 12b-2(f) provides:

> *Control.* The term "control" (including the terms "controlling", "controlled by" and "under common control with") means the possession, directly or indirectly, of the power to direct or cause the direction of the management and policies of a person, whether through the ownership of voting securities, by contract, or otherwise.

Sun argues that the district court erred under this definition in ordering Sun to disclose an intent to acquire control of Chromalloy. First, the district court is said to have improperly equated Sun's intention to influence Chromalloy policies with an intention to seek control. Second, Sun alleges that the district court did not find a "fixed plan" by Sun to acquire control of Chromalloy. Finally, the "reasonable doubt" language of Rule 12b-22, 17 C.F.R. § 240.12b-22 (1979).[19] is said by Sun to limit a purchaser's obligation to disclose control intentions. While these arguments present close questions, we hold that the district court neither erred as a matter of law nor abused its discretion in ordering the disclosure of Sun's control purpose.

Contrary to Sun's first contention, Sun's desire to influence substantially the policies, management and actions of Chromalloy amounts to a purpose to control Chromalloy. There is ample support in the record for the finding of a control purpose. Sun has disclosed its plans to acquire twenty per cent of Chromalloy's stock, its attempts to gain representation on Chromalloy's Board, and its intention to review continually its position with respect to Chromalloy. The district court further found that Sun has prepared an "acquisition model" with Chromalloy as a

---

[17] [11] *Id.*

[18] [12] Although revised Item 4 does not use the term "control", we assume that any control purpose is still measurable against the definition of control appearing in Rule 12b-2(f).

Cases decided before the revision of Item 4 have considered the definition of "control" in Rule 12b-2(f) to be controlling. *TSC Industries, Inc. v. Northway, Inc.*, 426 U.S. 438, 451 n.13, 96 S. Ct. 2126, 48 L. Ed. 2d 757 (1976); *Graphic Sciences, Inc. v. International Mogul Mines Ltd.*, 397 F. Supp. 112, 125 & n.37 (D.D.C. 1974). The Southern District of New York, in a case decided after the effective date of the revised form, considered a number of circumstances in determining control intent without reference to the definition of control in Rule 12b-2(f). *Transcon Lines v. A.G. Becker, Inc.*, 470 F. Supp. 356, 376-78 (S.D.N.Y. 1979).

[19] [13] Made applicable to Schedule 13D filings by 17 C.F.R. § 240.12b-1 (1979).

"target"; that Norman Alexander first learned of the investment opportunities in Chromalloy when a brokerage firm informed him that the thirty-five per cent of common stock held by insiders was not in a solid management block; that Norman Alexander's private memoranda have been concerned from the start with the split on Chromalloy's Board of Directors as a possible avenue to power; and that according to an investment banker, Sun's projected twenty per cent interest in Chromalloy would be a wise business decision only if Sun is attempting to gain control. Taken together, these facts support the finding that Sun proposes to control Chromalloy through a combination of numbers and influence.

As a matter of law, Rule 12b-2(f) contemplates that influence can be an element of control. Control is defined to include "the [*indirect*] power to . . . cause the direction of . . . policies." Disclosure of a control purpose may be required where the securities purchaser has a perceptible desire to influence substantially the issuer's operations. *Gulf & Western Industries, Inc. v. Great Atlantic & Pacific Tea Co.*, 476 F.2d 687, 696-97 (2d Cir. 1973) (tender offer context); *Graphic Sciences, Inc. v. International Mogul Mines Ltd.*, 397 F. Supp. 112, 125-27 (D.D.C. 1974).

Moreover, the Securities Exchange Act is remedial legislation and is to be broadly construed in order to give effect to its intent. *Tcherepnin v. Knight*, 389 U.S. 332, 336, 88 S. Ct. 548, 19 L. Ed. 2d 564 (1967); *Bath Industries v. Blot*, 427 F.2d 97 (7th Cir. 1970). To protect the investing public through full and fair disclosure of Sun's intentions, the district court was justified in defining control to include working control and substantial influence. *Graphic Sciences, Inc. v. International Mogul Mines Ltd., supra*, 397 F. Supp. at 125.[20]

Sun next contends that the district court failed to find a "fixed plan" to acquire control of Chromalloy. This fact is not determinative. Item 4 of Schedule 13D[21] requires disclosure of a purpose to acquire control, even though this intention has not taken shape as a fixed plan. We do not agree with Sun's contention that disclosure of Sun's control purpose will mislead investors by overstating the definiteness of Sun's plans. *Cf. Missouri Portland Cement Co. v. Cargill, Inc.*, 498 F.2d 851, 872 (2d Cir.), *cert. denied*, 419 U.S. 883, 95 S. Ct. 150, 42 L. Ed. 2d 123 (1974) (disclosure of intention to substantially expand target company would be misleading where purchaser's twenty year study included this possibility but where no plan was adopted); *Susquehanna Corp. v. Pan American Sulphur Corp.*, 423 F.2d 1075, 1084-85 (5th Cir. 1970) (disclosure of plan for merger would be misleading where plan subsisted for only two days before repudiation); *Electronic Specialty Co. v. International Controls Corp.*, 409 F.2d 937, 948 (2d Cir. 1969) (disclosure that purchaser "would give consideration" to merger was sufficient disclosure, where merger was proposed as alternative to tender offer). The cited cases stress that disclosure of plans for specific corporate changes can be misleading until these assume definite, non-contingent form. Disclosure of a purchaser's *purpose* in acquiring stock is a different matter. Item 4 specifically requires disclosure of a purpose to acquire control, regardless of the definiteness or even the existence of any plans to implement this purpose.

---

[20] [14] *See also* L. Loss, Securities Regulation 782 (2d ed. 1961) (in the context of other securities regulations, the difference between control and controlling influence is one of degree).

[21] [15] 43 F.R. 18498 (April 28, 1978). The text of Item 4 is set forth, *supra*, at n.5.

Finally, we find no merit in Sun's argument that SEC Rule 12b-22 limits the obligation to disclose a control purpose. Rule 12b-22 allows registrants under Sections 13 and 15(d) of the Securities Exchange Act to disclaim the *existence* of control:

> *Disclaimer of control.* If the existence of control is open to reasonable doubt in any instance, the registrant may disclaim the existence of control and any admission thereof; in such case, however, the registrant shall state the material facts pertinent to the possible existence of control.

17 C.F.R. § 240.12b-22 (1970). This rule on its face is inapposite to Item 4 of Schedule 13D, since Item 4 requires disclosure of "the *purpose* of the acquisition," while Rule 12b-22 is concerned with *existing* control. We have found no relevant authority, nor has Sun offered any, to support the contention that Rule 12b-22 modifies the obligation of a purchaser to disclose a control purpose.

In sum, we find no error of law and abuse of discretion in the district court's order that Sun disclose a purpose to seek control of Chromalloy.

V. Additional Disclosures Sought by Chromalloy

We also perceive no abuse of discretion in the district court's refusal to order disclosures beyond Sun's court-approved Schedule 13D.

Admittedly, the purpose of Section 13(d) is to "alert the market place to every large, rapid aggregation or accumulation of securities, regardless of technique employed, which might represent a potential shift in corporate control." *Financial General Bankshares, Inc. v. Lance*, [1978 Transfer Binder] Fed. Sec. L. Rep. (CCH) ¶ 96,403 at 93,424 (D.D.C. 1978), *quoting from GAF Corp. v. Milstein*, 453 F.2d 709, 717 (2d Cir. 1971), *cert. denied*, 406 U.S. 910, 92 S. Ct. 1610, 31 L. Ed. 2d 821 (1972). The disclosure provisions are intended to protect investors, and to enable them to receive the facts necessary for informed investment decisions. *Graphic Sciences, Inc. v. International Mogul Mines Ltd., supra*, 397 F. Supp. at 124 n.36 (D.D.C. 1974), *quoting from Tcherepnin v. Knight, supra*, 389 U.S. at 336, 88 S. Ct. 548. However, the objective of full and fair disclosure can be endangered as much by overstating the definiteness of plans as by understating them. *Missouri Portland Cement Co. v. Cargill, Inc., supra*, 498 F.2d at 872, *cert. denied*, 419 U.S. 883, 95 S. Ct. 150, 42 L. Ed. 2d 123 (1974); *Susquehanna Corp. v. Pan American Sulphur Co., supra*, 423 F.2d at 1085; *Electronic Specialty Co. v. International Controls Corp., supra*, 409 F.2d at 948; *S-G Securities, Inc. v. Fuqua Investment Co.*, 466 F. Supp. 1114, 1128 (D. Mass. 1978).

In the present case, Sun's long-range hopes for certain corporate changes could prove misleading to investors if disclosed as firm proposals. The district court's findings of fact indicate that Sun has made the following tentative overtures towards corporate changes: Norman Alexander once told Moody's Investors Services that any deal with Chromalloy "would be done with Chromalloy's money or they would get out"; Alexander "hoped" Chromalloy would eventually seek to acquire the assets of Sun; Sun commissioned a study to recommend which divisions of Chromalloy are most feasible to sell off; Alexander expressed the opinion that a profit could be realized if a trim-down of Chromalloy were properly executed; and Alexander offered to "take care of" certain Chromalloy Board members in return for their support. Each of these items involves little more than an unconsummated hope, feasibility study, or opinion, not a firm plan or proposal. We note also that Sun and Alexander have to date been denied a seat of Chromalloy's Board of Directors, and are seemingly not in a position to precipitate any of the hoped-for changes.

The degree of specificity with which future plans must be detailed in Schedule 13D filings presents a difficult question. *S-G Securities, Inc. v. Fuqua Investment Co., supra*, 466 F. Supp. at 1128. Thus, within the scope of its discretion, the district court might have required further disclosures of Sun. However, given the arguable danger of overstatement and the rule that parties are not required to disclose plans which are contingent or indefinite, *Missouri Portland Cement Co. v. H.K. Porter Co.*, 535 F.2d 388, 398 (8th Cir. 1976) (tender offer context), we hold that the district court's order refusing further disclosures involved no abuse of discretion.[22]

VI. Additional Injunctive Relief

The final issue on appeal is whether the district court abused its discretion in refusing Chromalloy's request for a cooling off period, the mailing of a restated Schedule 13D to Chromalloy shareholders at Sun's expense, and the publication of a restated Schedule 13D in the press.[23]

We consider the argument for additional injunctive relief in light of the principles set forth by the Supreme Court in *Rondeau v. Mosinee Paper Corp.*, 422 U.S. 49, 95 S. Ct. 2069, 45 L. Ed. 2d 12 (1975). The Court in *Rondeau* considered the availability of injunctive relief to remedy a § 13(d) violation following compliance with the reporting requirements. Recognizing that the injunctive process is designed to deter, not to punish, *id.*, at 61, the Court held that injunctive relief under the Williams Act was subject to traditional equitable limitations. Relief beyond compliance with the reporting requirements is justified only if the petitioner can show irreparable harm in the absence of such relief. *Id.*[24]

We have concluded that the Schedule 13D approved by the district court adequately discloses Sun's control intention. Given Sun's compliance with § 13(d), we do not perceive such ongoing harm to Chromalloy or its present shareholders[25]

---

[22] [16] The district court properly suggested that additional injunctive relief might be required in the future by "unforeseen contingencies." We express no opinion as to events which would necessitate such relief, noting only that the full and fair disclosure objectives of the Williams Act are to be observed. *Piper v. Chris-Craft Industries, Inc.*, 430 U.S. 1, 26-29, 97 S. Ct. 926, 51 L. Ed. 2d 124 (1975).

[23] [17] Chromalloy has abandoned on appeal its demand for an offer of rescission to shareholders who have sold to Sun.

[24] [18] Because this case involves only the availability of injunctive relief *following compliance* with § 13(d), we are not required to decide what circumstances might justify a decree enjoining a shareholder who is *currently* in violation of § 13(d) from acquiring further shares or exercising voting rights, pending compliance with the reporting requirements. The posture of the case is identical to *Rondeau* in this respect. *Rondeau v. Mosinee Paper Corp., supra*, 422 U.S. at 59 n.9, 97 S. Ct. 926.

[25] [19] We do not reach the issue of harm to former Chromalloy shareholders who may have sold to Sun without attempting to garner a control premium. Chromalloy on appeal has pressed the interests of present shareholders and the public in requesting additional relief, perhaps recognizing that a cooling-off period and additional dissemination of information cannot redress the harm, if any, suffered by past

as would justify a cooling-off period or a stockholder mailing. Shareholders who were misinformed by Sun's original Schedule 13D and amendments have been reapprised by the same form of communication. The present case is distinguishable from *Weeks Dredging & Contracting, Inc. v. American Dredging Co.*, 451 F. Supp. 468 (E.D. Pa. 1978), where the court required that the target company's misleading statements to the press be corrected by a shareholder mailing.

There is also no precedent for a cooling-off period. In the closely analogous context of misleading tender offers, courts have held that a misleading tender offer is adequately cured by an amended offer. *Corenco Corp. v. Schiavone & Sons, Inc.*, 488 F.2d 207, 214-15 (2d Cir. 1973) (specifically rejecting a cooling-off period in tender offer context. *See also Missouri Portland Cement Co. v. H.K. Porter Co., supra*, 535 F.2d 388 (defective tender offer can be cured by an amending offer).

The disclosure requirements established by Congress are not intended to provide a weapon for current management to discourage takeover bids or prevent large accumulations of stock. *Piper v. Chris-Craft Industries, Inc.*, 430 U.S. 1, 26-35, 97 S. Ct. 926, 51 L. Ed. 2d 124 (1977); *Rondeau v. Mosinee Paper Corp., supra*, 422 U.S. at 58, 97 S. Ct. 926; *Universal Container Corp. v. Horowitz*, [1977-78] Fed. Sec. L. Rep. (CCH) ¶ 96,161 (S.D.N.Y. 1977); S. Rep. No. 550, 90th Cong., 1st Sess., 3 (1967); H.R. Rep. No. 1711, 90th Cong., 2d Sess., 4 (1968). Further injunctive relief, particularly a cooling-off period, would in the present case serve largely as a dilatory tool in the hands of current management, and for this reason was properly denied.

In sum, appellant has failed to sustain the burden of demonstrating abuse of discretion in the district court's denial of further disclosures, a cooling-off period, and a stockholder mailing. Appellees likewise fail to convince us that the district court erred as a matter of law in requiring the disclosure of Sun's control purpose.

Affirmed.

EDITEK, INC. v. MORGAN CAPITAL, L.L.C.

United States Court of Appeals, Eighth Circuit
150 F.3d 830 (1998)

FAGG, CIRCUIT JUDGE.

Editek, Inc. brought this lawsuit against Morgan Capital, L.L.C. and its officers, Alex and David Bistricer (collectively Morgan Capital), under § 16(b) of the Securities Exchange Act of 1934 (the 1934 Act), 15 U.S.C. § 78p(b), to recover claimed short-swing profits. Section 16(b) applies only to corporate insiders: directors, officers, and beneficial owners of more than ten percent of a corporation's registered equity securities (ten percent beneficial owners). Only the ten percent beneficial owner category is involved here. Based on a misreading of the applicable rules, the district court concluded Editek's complaint failed to allege facts that, if

shareholders who have already sold to Sun. These shareholders have an adequate remedy at law through an action for damages. *Rondeau v. Mosinee Paper Corp., supra*, 422 U.S. at 60, 97 S. Ct. 926; *Missouri Portland Cement Co. v. H.K. Porter*, 535 F.2d 388, 395, 399 (8th Cir. 1976).

proven, would make Morgan Capital a beneficial owner at the legally required time. On that basis, the district court granted Morgan Capital's motion to dismiss under Federal Rule of Civil Procedure 12(b)(6). Editek appeals. We reverse and remand for further proceedings.

The purpose of § 16(b) is to prevent corporate insiders from exploiting inside information to turn a quick profit trading in their company's stock. *See* 15 U.S.C. § 78p(b) (1994); *Foremost-McKesson, Inc. v. Provident Sec. Co.*, 423 U.S. 232, 234 (1976). To achieve this purpose, Congress enacted a flat rule: any profit realized by an insider "from any purchase and sale, or any sale and purchase, of any equity security of such issuer . . . within any period of less than six months, . . . shall inure to and be recoverable by the issuer." 15 U.S.C. § 78p(b). A further provision of the statute applies only to ten percent beneficial owners. To be liable under § 16(b), a ten percent beneficial owner must have been such "both at the time of the purchase and sale, or the sale and purchase, of the security involved." Id. As the Supreme Court has made clear, to be a ten percent beneficial owner "at the time of the purchase," a person must have already become a ten percent beneficial owner before the purchase. *See Foremost-McKesson*, 423 U.S. at 249-50. Because an owner below the statutory threshold presumptively lacks access to inside information, the acquisition that takes a buyer above ten percent ownership does not count as a "purchase" matchable against a later sale for § 16(b) purposes. *See id.* at 253-54 & n.28; 17 C.F.R. § 240.16a-2(c) (1997).

With these principles in mind, we set forth the relevant background, accepting as true the facts asserted in Editek's complaint and construing the complaint in the light most favorable to Editek. . . . Around February 1, 1996, Editek issued shares of preferred stock, convertible into Editek common stock, and sold some shares to Morgan Capital in a private placement. Editek acknowledges in its brief that the preferred shares were nonvoting. Thus, only the underlying common stock, not the preferred stock, counts for purposes of determining Morgan Capital's ten percent beneficial ownership status. *See* Ownership Reports and Trading By Officers, Directors and Principal Security Holders, Exchange Act Release No. 28,869, [1990-1991 Transfer Binder] Fed. Sec. L. Rep. (CCH) ¶ 84,709, at 81,252 n.36 (Feb. 8, 1991). Morgan Capital had the right to convert its preferred stock into Editek common stock beginning sixty days after issuance of the preferred stock. Despite the complaint's vagueness about the issuance date, the parties now agree March 30 marked the start of the conversion period. The conversion price floated: the number of common shares Morgan Capital would acquire at conversion would be based on the average closing price of Editek common stock for the five trading days just before the conversion date. In other words, as the price of Editek common stock dropped, the number of common shares Morgan Capital's preferred stock would buy increased. Around March 28, 1996, the price of Editek common stock fell low enough that Morgan Capital's preferred stock was worth more than ten percent of the outstanding shares of Editek's common stock. On May 1, 1996, Morgan Capital received more than ten percent of Editek's outstanding common stock when it exercised its conversion right. According to Editek, this conversion was the "purchase" matchable against later sales for § 16(b) purposes. Later that month and the next, Morgan Capital sold part of its newly acquired Editek common stock, realizing a profit of at least $500,000.

. . . [T]he district court concluded Editek could not show that Morgan Capital was a beneficial owner of Editek common stock before the conversion. In the district court's view, Editek's complaint alleged a transaction that made Morgan Capital a ten percent beneficial owner — the conversion itself — followed by profitable sales. Because such conduct is not unlawful, the district court dismissed Editek's complaint. *See Editek, Inc. v. Morgan Capital*, L.L.C., 974 F. Supp. 1229, 1234 (D. Minn. 1997).

The district court's decision turns entirely on the term beneficial owner, which the governing regulations define in two different ways. For purposes other than determining ten percent beneficial ownership, "the term beneficial owner shall mean any person who . . . has or shares a direct or indirect pecuniary interest in the equity securities . . . ." 17 C.F.R. § 240.16a-1(a)(2). For the purpose of determining ten percent beneficial ownership, the meaning of beneficial owner is a bit more complicated. Rule 16a-1 states:

> Solely for purposes of determining whether a person is a beneficial owner of more than ten percent of any class of equity securities registered pursuant to section 12 of the [1934] Act, the term "beneficial owner" shall mean any person who is deemed a beneficial owner pursuant to section 13(d) of the Act and the rules thereunder . . . .

Id. § 240.16a-1(a)(1). Turning to the rules under § 13(d) of the 1934 Act, we find two relevant provisions. First, a beneficial owner of a security includes any person who has voting power or investment power in relation to the security. *See id.* § 240.13d-3(a). More importantly for our purposes, "[a] person shall be deemed to be the beneficial owner of a security . . . if that person has the right to acquire beneficial ownership of such security, as defined in Rule 13d-3(a) (§ 240.13d-3(a)) within sixty days . . . (B) through the conversion of a security . . . ." *Id.* § 240.13d-3(d)(1)(i)(B). We will refer to this last definition as the "within sixty days" rule.

The district court gave two explanations why it concluded Editek could not prove any set of facts that would make Morgan Capital a beneficial owner before the conversion. The first is based on a misunderstanding of the "within sixty days" rule. From the way the district court applied the rule, the court must have read it as saying the right to acquire beneficial ownership within sixty days through a conversion means the right to acquire this ownership within sixty days of the issuance of the convertible securities. Reading the rule the same way, Editek argued Morgan Capital was a beneficial owner of Editek common stock before the conversion "because [Morgan Capital] had a right to acquire beneficial ownership of Editek Common Stock within sixty days after issuance of [the] Preferred Stock." *Editek*, 974 F. Supp. at 1232 (emphasis and internal quotations omitted). According to Editek's complaint, however, the preferred shares were convertible, not within sixty days of issuance, but beginning sixty days after issuance — that is, on the sixtieth day following the date of issuance. *See id.* at 1233. The district court thus concluded Morgan Capital could not be proven a beneficial owner before the conversion under the "within sixty days" rule. *See id.* The district court rejected Editek's contention that Morgan Capital was a beneficial owner on March 28 because the conversion right was not immediately exercisable on that date. *See id.*

In our view, the district court's interpretation of the "within sixty days" rule is at odds with the rule's purpose. Section 13(d) of the 1934 Act, under which the rule was enacted, requires persons who acquire beneficial ownership of more than five percent of certain classes of securities to report their purchase to the issuer, to the exchanges where the securities are traded, and to the Securities and Exchange Commission (SEC). *See* 15 U.S.C. § 78m(d)(1) (1994). The purpose of this requirement is to alert the issuing company, the market, and the SEC to transactions that might change or influence the control of the company. *See id.* § 78m(d)(6)(D). The "within sixty days" rule should be read with this forward-looking purpose in mind. An illustration will show why. Suppose Morgan Capital's nonvoting preferred stock had been convertible beginning ninety days after issuance. Suppose further that on the first possible conversion date, the preferred stock would be worth more than five percent of Editek's voting common stock. Three days before that date, Morgan Capital sells its preferred stock to a buyer. Under the district court's reading of the "within sixty days" rule, the buyer would have no duty to report its purchase to Editek, the stock exchange, or the SEC, even though the buyer would have a right exercisable in three days to acquire a potentially control-influencing stake in Editek's voting securities.

We think the "within sixty days" rule means just what it says. The SEC does also:

> The Commission is . . . mindful that as the point in time [at] which the right to acquire may come to fruition is extended into the future the . . . right's ability to influence control is correspondingly attenuated. When sixty days or less are left until the right to acquire may be exercised, the Commission believes that the ability of the holder of such right to effect control is sufficient to warrant the imposition of an obligation to file under Rule 13d-1.

Filing and Disclosure Requirements Relating to Beneficial Ownership, Exchange Act Release No. 14,692, [1978 Transfer Binder] Fed. Sec. L. Rep. (CCH) ¶ 81,571, at 80,310 (Apr. 21, 1978). Applied here, the "within sixty days" rule makes Morgan Capital a beneficial owner of Editek common stock on every day within sixty days of every day on which Morgan Capital had the right to acquire Editek common stock through conversion — including March 28. Of course, whether a beneficial owner under the "within sixty days" rule is also a ten percent owner, and thus an insider subject to § 16(b), is a separate matter.

We turn next to the second basis for the district court's conclusion. Noting that the conversion price floated, the district court found relevant the following passage from an SEC release:

> [A] right with a floating exercise price . . . will not be deemed to be acquired or purchased, for Section 16 purposes, until the purchase price of the underlying securities becomes fixed or established, which commonly occurs at exercise. Thus, a right to purchase an equity security is deemed acquired as of the date the exercise or conversion price becomes fixed, and the acquisition, absent an exemption, would be matchable for Section 16(b) purposes with a disposition within six months of the fixing of the price.

[1990-1991 Transfer Binder] Fed. Sec. L. Rep. ¶ 84,709, at 81,265. As we have just explained, under the "within sixty days" rule Morgan Capital's claimed beneficial ownership before the conversion depended on its having a right to acquire such ownership within a stated time. Based on the quoted passage, the district court concluded Morgan Capital did not gain the right referred to in the "within sixty days" rule until the conversion itself, so it could not have been a beneficial owner before the conversion. *See Editek*, 974 F. Supp. at 1233.

Although this conclusion follows logically from the quoted passage, it contradicts the conclusion dictated by the "within sixty days" rule itself, under which Editek's complaint would make Morgan Capital a beneficial owner of Editek common stock well before the conversion date. The quoted language is not at odds with the "within sixty days" rule, however. The SEC is simply talking about something other than determining ten percent beneficial ownership. Again, for those other purposes, the term beneficial owner means a person who has a direct or indirect pecuniary interest in registered equity securities. *See* 17 C.F.R. § 240.16a-1(a)(2). With that in mind, and taking into consideration the quoted passage's context, the SEC's meaning becomes apparent.

The passage is lifted from a lengthy discussion of derivative securities. *See* [1990-1991 Transfer Binder] Fed. Sec. L. Rep. 84,709, at 81,258-81,266. A convertible security is a type of derivative. *See* 17 C.F.R. § 240.16a-1(c). To own a derivative security is to have an indirect pecuniary interest in the underlying security. *See id.* § 240.16a-1(a)(2)(ii)(F). But here is the crucial exception: a derivative with a floating exercise or conversion price is not a derivative security for § 16 purposes. *See id.* § 240.16a-1(c)(6); [1990-1991 Transfer Binder] Fed. Sec. L. Rep. ¶ 84,709, at 81,265. In other words, Morgan Capital, as a holder of floating-price convertible preferred stock, did not own derivative securities, did not have an indirect pecuniary interest in the underlying common stock, and accordingly (assuming Morgan Capital had no other form of pecuniary interest) was not a beneficial owner of the common stock until the conversion — for purposes other than determining ten percent beneficial ownership. It may seem odd that Morgan Capital both was and was not a beneficial owner of Editek common before the conversion, but the SEC has long recognized the two definitions of beneficial owner can result in different determinations of beneficial ownership. See Interpretive Release on Rules Applicable to Insider Reporting and Trading, Release No. 34-18,114, 4 Fed. Sec. L. Rep. (CCH) ¶ 26,062, at 19,063-7 n.17 (Sept. 23, 1981). In sum, the quoted passage has no bearing on whether Morgan Capital was a beneficial owner for the purpose of determining ten percent beneficial ownership before the conversion. That issue is governed by the "within sixty days" rule, not the "pecuniary interest" rule.

The district court held Editek's complaint failed to state a claim based solely on the conclusion that Morgan Capital was not a beneficial owner before the conversion. That conclusion was incorrect, so the district court's ruling cannot stand. On appeal, Morgan Capital has raised two other legal challenges to Editek's complaint. Morgan Capital claims a holder of convertible preferred stock cannot "float" into and out of ten percent ownership of the underlying common stock as the price of the common stock fluctuates. The district court mentioned this issue, but did not resolve it. *See Editek*, 974 F. Supp. at 1233. At oral argument, Morgan Capital argued its stock conversion was not a "purchase" matchable against a later sale, but merely a change in the form of its beneficial ownership. In remanding this case, we express no opinion on these or any other issues, which we leave for the district court to address in the first instance as the parties choose to raise them.

We reverse the judgment of the district court, vacate the district court's order dismissing with prejudice Editek's complaint under Federal Rule of Civil Procedure 12(b)(6), and remand for further proceedings consistent with this opinion.

ENTERRA CORP. v. SGS ASSOCIATES

United States District Court, Eastern District of Pennsylvania
600 F. Supp. 678 (1985)

Broderick, District Judge

The above captioned cases are two related securities actions which arise from an unusual set of factual circumstances and which present some rather novel legal issues. The amended complaint in the *Enterra* case (Civil Action No. 84-2174) alleges, *inter alia*, that the defendant partnership SGS Associates and its individual partners (herein collectively referred to as SGS), which is Enterra Corporation's largest shareholder, violated various federal and state securities laws in connection with the defendants' negotiation, execution, and subsequent alleged violation of a "standstill agreement" with Enterra's Board of Directors ("the Board"). The standstill agreement provided, *inter alia*, that SGS would not purchase or acquire more than 15% of Enterra's outstanding shares and would not make any tender offers to Enterra's shareholders for the purchase of Enterra stock. . . . Enterra seeks, *inter alia*, permanent injunctive relief prohibiting SGS from acquiring or offering to acquire any shares of Enterra stock in violation of the standstill agreement.

SGS (which notwithstanding its standstill agreement with the Board, now desires to have the opportunity to purchase all of Enterra's outstanding shares) filed various counterclaims against Enterra's directors and has moved for a mandatory preliminary injunction against the Board. SGS seeks an order from this Court as follows:

(1) Enjoining the Board to consider the adequacy of any proposal made by the defendants to purchase shares of Enterra;

(2) Enjoining the Board, within ten (10) business days after receipt of a proposal, to disclose in writing to defendants its recommendation regarding the proposal and all of the reasons therefor;

(3) Enjoining the Board, within ten (10) business days after receipt of a proposal and if the Board recommends against acceptance of the proposal, to disclose in writing to defendants all of the reasons for such recommendation, including, without limitation, its view of the adequacy of the proposal from a financial standpoint; and

(4) Enjoining the Board, within ten (10) business days after receipt of a proposal and if the Board recommends against acceptance of the proposal, to disclose in writing to each shareholder of record the fact and terms of the proposal and its recommendation, and to allow each shareholder to decide whether to accept or reject the offer.

In support of its motion for a mandatory preliminary injunction, SGS contends that there exists a common law fiduciary duty owed by the Board to the shareholders which, notwithstanding the standstill agreement, requires the Board to (1) consider the adequacy of any SGS offer to purchase Enterra shares; (2) disclose to shareholders the facts and terms of the offer along with the Board's analysis and decision; and (3) convey the offer to the shareholders and permit the shareholders to accept or reject the SGS offer.

. . .

A. Background

The essential facts with respect to the issues presented are not, for the purposes of the motions for a preliminary injunction, seriously disputed. Enterra is a Pennsylvania corporation with its principal place of business in Radnor, Pennsylvania. Enterra's common stock is traded on the New York and Philadelphia stock exchanges. As of March 30, 1984, Enterra had approximately nine million shares of common stock outstanding held by approximately five thousand shareholders of record. Enterra's Board is composed of seven independent or outside directors and three management or inside directors, including its chairman and president, James Ballengee. The individual defendants in the *Enterra* case, Philip Sassower, James Goren, and Lawrence Schneider (who comprise the SGS Associates partnership) are investors with considerable experience in the field of corporate investment.

In the spring of 1982, Sassower and other members of SGS met with James Ballengee, Enterra's chairman. The SGS group, indicated that its members had accumulated a significant amount (nearly 5%) of Enterra's common stock, and that they desired to purchase additional Enterra shares. Apparently, SGS' purchases had generated significant market interest in Enterra stock, including the anticipation of a possible takeover bid, and the price of Enterra's common stock had increased. This rise in market price, of course, made it more expensive for SGS to acquire additional Enterra shares. At the time of the initial meeting with Ballengee, SGS did not indicate any desire to acquire control of Enterra, but rather expressed an interest in acquiring additional Enterra shares for investment purposes.

Subsequent to this meeting, the parties entered into negotiations which led to the execution of a Standstill Agreement (the Agreement) between Enterra and SGS on November 30, 1982. The Agreement was finalized only after considerable negotiation by counsel representing both parties, and after the preparation and revision of several draft agreements. The Agreement is thirty-four pages in length and provides that it shall remain in effect until November 30, 1992, subject to the occurrence of certain contingencies not applicable here. The provisions of the Agreement pertinent to issues presently before the Court provide that, subject to certain exceptions not applicable here, SGS will not increase its holdings of Enterra voting securities to more than 15% of those outstanding; that SGS will not acquire or offer to acquire any Enterra voting securities by means of a tender offer; that SGS will not publicly suggest or announce its willingness or desire to make or have another party make such a tender offer; that SGS will not assist or participate in such an offer made by any other party, and that SGS will not recommend that any other party commence a tender offer for Enterra voting securities.

The terms of the Agreement were disclosed by Enterra in a press release issued in December of 1982, and in Enterra's 1983 and 1984 proxy statements mailed to shareholders. By February of 1983, SGS had acquired 5% of Enterra's outstanding shares, and filed a Schedule 13D with the Securities and Exchange Commission as required by 17 C.F.R. § 240.13d-1. Attached to the Schedule 13D was a copy of the standstill Agreement. The Schedule 13D stated that the Enterra shares had been acquired for the purpose of investment, and that it was the intention of SGS, subject to the terms of the Agreement, to acquire additional shares of Enterra stock. SGS filed several amendments to its Schedule 13D in 1983 and 1984, reflecting increases in its acquisitions of Enterra shares.

Towards the latter part of 1983, SGS requested Enterra's Board to amend the Agreement in some respects, notably to permit SGS to acquire greater than 15% of the outstanding shares as set forth in the Agreement. The Board declined to amend the Agreement. At this time, the market price of Enterra's shares was declining and relations between SGS and the Board deteriorated thereafter.

In February of 1984, SGS filed an amendment to its Schedule 13D which stated, *inter alia*, that it "had decided to explore other alternatives that may be available." At that time, Enterra's shares were trading at approximately $16 per share. On May 1, 1984, members of the SGS group met with Enterra's chairman and requested that the Agreement be amended to permit acquisition of Enterra shares above the 15% limit, and to permit greater participation by SGS in Enterra's management. When Enterra's chairman stated that the Board's position on amending the Agreement was not favorable, SGS presented him with a letter dated May 1, 1984 which stated, *inter alia:*

The SGS Group, with the approval of the Enterra Corporation, hereby offers to acquire for cash any and all outstanding shares of Enterra at a price of $21 per share. This offer is subject to the approval of the Board of Enterra . . . and execution of an agreement incorporating terms and conditions that would be mutually satisfactory to the SGS Group and Enterra.

The letter requested a response by May 9, 1984. On May 3, 1984, five independent and three management directors of Enterra's Board participated in a meeting and considered the SGS proposal. The Board considered the proposal and declined to approve the offer or to amend the Agreement. That afternoon, after counsel for SGS was informed of the Board's decision, SGS filed an amendment to its Schedule 13D which included a copy of the May 1, 1984 letter offering to acquire all of Enterra's shares. There was an immediate disruption in the trading market for Enterra stock, causing the New York Stock Exchange to halt trading of Enterra shares that day and causing a delay in the opening of trading the following day. On May 4, 1984, Enterra filed the present action against SGS. On May 10, 1984, the entire Board of Enterra met at its regularly scheduled meeting, together with counsel and Enterra's financial advisor, Merrill Lynch. The proposal submitted by SGS again was considered and discussed. Merrill Lynch advised the Board that the $21 per share price offered by SGS was inadequate from a financial point of view. The Board determined that it was not in the best interests of the corporation or the shareholders to accept the SGS proposal at that time or to amend the Agreement.

Currently, SGS owns close to 15% of Enterra's outstanding shares. It is undisputed that if SGS made an offer to purchase all of Enterra's shares directly to Enterra's shareholders, SGS would be in violation of the Agreement. Absent the Agreement, of course, SGS would be free (as is any other party) to make a tender offer for all of Enterra's shares. As of this date, SGS has not made any such offer directly to Enterra's shareholders, presumably because it seeks to avoid the risk of incurring liability for breach of the Agreement. SGS and Wallen now contend, however, that there exists a fiduciary duty on the part of the Board, notwithstanding the Agreement negotiated by SGS, to consider the adequacy of any SGS offer; to relay the terms of the offer and the Board's decision to all shareholders; and most important, to actually *convey* the offer to the shareholders and provide the means by which any shareholder can accept the offer and sell his or her stock to SGS. SGS and Wallen ask this Court to order the Board to do, on *behalf* of SGS, that which SGS contractually obligated itself *not* to do — that is, to make a tender offer for the purchase of all Enterra stock. In effect, granting the preliminary injunction would enable SGS to "have its cake and eat it, too," in that SGS would be permitted to effectively convey its tender offer to Enterra's shareholders, but since the offer to Enterra's shareholders, but since the offer would be extended through the Board and not made directly by SGS, SGS apparently would avoid violating the terms of the Standstill Agreement it signed with the Board.

. . .

C. The Movants' Legal Claims

The implication of the legal theory advanced in support of the motions for a preliminary injunction is that despite the existence of a standstill agreement between a corporation and a substantial shareholder, if at any time the contracting shareholder decides to attempt to acquire an amount of the corporation's stock in excess of the agreed upon limit, the corporation, acting through its board of directors, must nevertheless consider the investor's offer, advise the shareholders of the offer, and give the shareholders the opportunity to accept or reject the offer. The movants' claim thus calls into question whether, notwithstanding the existence of a standstill agreement limiting the percentage of the corporation's stock which the investor may acquire, a board of directors has a fiduciary duty to advise the shareholders of any offer received from the investor to purchase the corporation's stock in excess of the limitation provided in the agreement, and to give the shareholders the opportunity to accept or reject the offer. Before addressing this issue, it is appropriate to review some basic principles of corporate law.

1. Directors' Fiduciary Duty and the Business Judgment Rule

In Pennsylvania, as in most jurisdictions, officers and directors of a corporation stand in a fiduciary relation to the corporation, and must discharge the duties of their positions in good faith and with the diligence, care, and skill which ordinarily prudent persons would exercise under similar circumstances. 15 Pa. Cons. Stat. Ann. § 1404 (Purdon's Supp. 1984); *Brown v. Presbyterian Ministers' Fund*, 484 F.2d 998, 1004 (3d Cir. 1973); *United States v. Gleneagles Investment Co., Inc.*, 565 F. Supp. 556, 589 (M.D. Pa. 1983); *Bellis v. Thal*, 373 F. Supp. 120 (E.D. Pa. 1974); *Wolf v. Fried*, 473 Pa. 26, 373 A.2d 734 (1977). These fiduciary obligations have sometimes been described as the duty of care, i.e., the responsibility of the fiduciary to exercise the care that a reasonably prudent person in a similar position would use under similar circumstances, and the duty of loyalty, i.e., the duty not to take advantage of the fiduciary relationship by engaging in self-dealing. *See Norlin Corporation v. Rooney, Pace Inc., et al.*, 744 F.2d 255, 264 (2d Cir. 1984); *cf. Seaboard Industries, Inc. v. Monaco*, 442 Pa. 256, 276 A.2d 305 (1971).

It is the directors, and not the shareholders, who must manage the business affairs of the corporation, and the directors of a corporation "have the power to bind [the corporation] by any contract which is within its express or implied powers, and which in their judgment is necessary or proper in order to carry out the objectives for which the corporation was created without consulting with or obtaining the consent of the stockholders." 2 W. Fletcher *Cyclopedia of the Law of Private Corporations*, § 505, pp. 515-16 (rev. perm. ed. 1981). *See also, Ashwander v. Tennessee Valley Authority*, 297 U.S. 288, 343, 56 S. Ct. 466, 481, 80 L. Ed. 688 (1936) (Brandeis, J., concurring); *Matter of Penn Central Transportation Co.*, 596 F.2d 1155, 1166 (3d Cir. 1979); *Severance v. Heyl & Patterson*, 123 Pa. Super. 553, 187 A. 53 (1936); *Auerbach v. Bennett*, 47 N.Y.2d 619, 629-31, 419 N.Y.S.2d 920, 393 N.E.2d 994 (1979).

It is an axiomatic principle of corporate law that "[c]ourts are reluctant to interfere in the internal management of a corporation" at the behest of a shareholder, *Wolf v. Fried*, 373 A.2d at 734, and that "[shareholders] cannot secure the aid of a court to correct . . . mistakes of judgment on the part of the [directors]." *Ashwander v. Tennessee Valley Authority*, 297 U.S. at 343, 56 S. Ct. at 481 (Brandeis, J., concurring). In discharging their fiduciary duties to the corporation, the directors are protected against unwarranted interference from complaining shareholders by the "business judgment rule". The business judgment rule provides that directors are not liable to the corporation for mistakes in judgment, whether those mistakes are characterized as mistakes of fact or mistakes of law. *See Briggs v. Spaulding*, 141 U.S. 132, 11 S. Ct. 924, 35 L. Ed. 662 (1891); *Cramer v. General Telephone & Electronics Corp.*, 582 F.2d 259, 274-75 (3d Cir. 1978); *Selheimer v. Manganese Corporation of America*, 423 Pa. 563, 224 A.2d 634 (1966). If the shareholders conclude that the judgment of the directors in pursuing a particular course of action is not sound, their remedy lies in the replacement of the directors through the corporate voting process — they may vote the management out. *See* M. Lipton, *Takeover Bids and the Targets' Boardroom*, 35 Bus. Law. 101, 116 (1979).

One commentator recently has described the business judgment rule as follows:

> Courts review the decisions of corporate directors under the business judgment rule. According to the rule, directors' decisions are presumed to be based on sound business judgment; this presumption can be rebutted only by a showing of fraud, bad faith, or gross overreaching. Courts are willing to defer to directors because it is the board's duty to manage the affairs of the corporation and because courts often consider themselves ill-equipped to second-guess business decisions. The presumption of sound business judgment allows the directors to prevail whenever they can articulate a rational, unselfish business purpose for their actions.

Note, *Protecting Shareholders Against Partial and Two-Tiered Takeovers: The "Poison Pill" Preferred*, 97 Harv. L. Rev. 1964, 1969 (1984) (footnotes omitted) (hereinafter cited as "Harvard L. Rev. Note"). It has been held that the presumption of good faith and sound judgment afforded by the business judgment rule is heightened where the majority of the board consists of independent, outside directors and where the directors have obtained and considered expert legal and business advice. *Panter v. Marshall Field & Co.*, 646 F.2d 271, 277, 294 (7th Cir.), *cert. denied*, 454 U.S. 1092, 102 S. Ct. 658, 70 L. Ed. 2d 631 (1981). *See also* J. Bartlett & C. Andrews, *The Standstill Agreement: Legal and Business Considerations Underlying a Corporate Peace Treaty*, 62 B.U. L. Rev. 143, 150 & n. 25 (1982).

If it is established that a board of directors has acted in fraud, bad faith, or self-interest, the presumption of the business judgment rule does not apply, and the directors bear the burden of showing that the transaction was fair and served a legitimate corporate purpose. Harvard L. Rev. Note, *supra*, 97 Harv. L. Rev. at 1969; *Wolf v. Fried*, 373 A.2d at 736 n. 8. However, as the Third Circuit has noted "by the very nature of corporate life a director has a certain amount of self-interest in everything he does," and that "[the desire to retain] control [of the corporation] is always arguably a motive in any action taken by a director." *Johnson v. Trueblood*, 629 F.2d 287, 292 (3d Cir. 1980), *cert. denied*, 450 U.S. 999, 101 S. Ct. 1704, 68 L. Ed. 2d 200 (1981). Accordingly, in order to overcome the presumption of the business judgment rule, "the plaintiff must make a showing that the sole or primary motive of [the directors] was to retain control." *Id.* at 293 (applying Delaware law). *See also Panter v. Marshall Field & Co.*, 646 F.2d at 294; *Heit v. Baird*, 567 F.2d 1157, 1161 (1st. Cir. 1977); *Warner Communications, Inc. v. Murdoch*, 581 F. Supp. 1482, 1491 (D. Del. 1984). Even those commentators who disagree with the application of the rule's presumption in certain circumstances agree that "[c]urrent case law . . . places the burden on the plaintiff to show that management's sole or primary purpose [in taking the challenged action] was retention of control." Note, *The Standstill Agreement: A Case of Illegal Vote Selling and Breach of Fiduciary Duty*, 93 Yale L.J. 1093, 1110 n. 77 (1984) (hereinafter cited as "Yale L.J. Note"). *See also* Bartlett & Andrews, *supra*, 62 B.U. L. Rev. at 148. Although there appear to be no reported Pennsylvania decisions applying the business judgment rule to "defensive" actions taken by corporate directors in anticipation of or in opposition to a takeover bid, there is no reason to believe (and the parties do not contend) that the Pennsylvania Supreme Court would not follow the prevailing interpretation of the business judgment rule in such circumstances.

A "target" corporation's decision to accept or resist a takeover bid (generally manifested as a tender offer) necessarily rests with the board of directors, since it is the directors, and not the shareholders, who are best able to evaluate the numerous and often complex financial factors which must be considered in determining whether the takeover proposal serves the best interests of the corporation. *See generally* Lipton, *supra*, 85 Bus. Law 101 (1979). *See also* W. Steinbrink, *Management's Response to the Takeover Attempt*, 28 Case. W. Res. L. Rev. 882, 891 (1978). The wave of corporate takeover attempts in recent years has spawned sufficient litigation to establish that the fiduciary duty of corporate directors "to act in the best interests of the corporation's shareholders . . . requires the directors to attempt to block takeovers that would [in their judgment] be harmful to the target company." Harvard L. Rev. Note, *supra,* 97 Harv. L. Rev. at 1968. *See Panter v. Marshall Field & Co.*, 646 F.2d at 299 (directors are obliged to oppose tender offers deemed to be "detrimental to the well-being of the corporation even if that [opposition] is at the expense of the short term interests of individual shareholders."); *Treadway Companies, Inc. v. Care Corp.*, 638 F.2d 357, 381 (2d Cir. 1980); *Heit v. Baird*, 567 F.2d at 1161 ("management has not only the right but the duty to resist by all lawful means persons whose attempt to win control of the corporation, if successful, would harm the corporate enterprise."); *cf. Norlin Corp. v. Rooney, Pace Inc., et al.*, 744 F.2d at 264, 266 (business judgment rule "affords directors wide latitude in devising strategies to resist unfriendly advances," and where the directors determine that the interests of the corporation and its shareholders might be jeopardized, they may take any fair and reasonable actions necessary to thwart an acquisition attempt).

Courts applying the business judgment rule have upheld a wide variety of sometimes drastic defensive tactics undertaken by a target company to prevent a takeover bid, including the sale of large blocks of treasury stock to "friendly" purchasers; acquisitions designed to make the target less attractive or create antitrust obstacles for the offeror; and the institution of antitrust or securities litigation by the target company against the offeror in an effort to block the takeover. Bartlett & Andrews, *supra,* 62 B.U. L. Rev. at 148-50 (citing cases). It is well-established that such "[d]efensive tactics are illegitimate only if a target's management fails to exercise its business judgment and engages in such tactics for the primary purpose of entrenchment." *Warner Communications, Inc. v. Murdoch,* 581 F. Supp. at 1491.

2. The Validity of the Standstill Agreement

With these basic principles of corporate law in mind, the Court will now consider the movant's particular legal claims. Although SGS understandably is reluctant to ask this Court to declare that the standstill agreement which SGS sought, negotiated, and signed with Enterra is invalid and may be disregarded, plaintiff Wallen contends that the Board breached its fiduciary duty to the shareholders in entering into the Agreement, which by its terms restricts SGS' rights to purchase Enterra stock. Wallen contends that a board of directors cannot agree to limit its duty to convey all offers received by the board to purchase the corporation's stock to the shareholders by utilizing the "defensive" mechanism of a standstill agreement.

The use of standstill agreements is a relatively recent corporate development which has received generally favorable reactions from the commentators. *See generally*, Bartlett & Andrews, *supra,* 62 B.U. L. Rev. 143 (1982); K. Bialkin, *The Use of Standstill Agreements in Corporate Transactions*, 373 P.L.I. 91, 94-108 (1981); A. Fleischer & D. Sternberg, *Corporate Acquisitions*, 12 Rev. Sec. Reg. 937 (1979). This Court is advised that standstill agreements have been reached between the board of directors and a substantial investor in approximately fifty publicly-traded corporations in the last several years. The standstill agreement is "in essence, a corporate peace treaty, designed to inject a degree of stability, certainty, and cooperation into the relationship between an issuer and a major investor." Bartlett & Andrews, *supra*, 62 B.U. L. Rev. at 144. The typical standstill agreement serves to relieve the antagonism, suspicion, and hostility which, in this era of corporate takeover bids, often exists between a corporation and a substantial shareholder. The essential provision of a standstill agreement is a limitation, usually expressed as a percentage figure, on the shareholder's holding of the corporation's stock, and generally prohibits the shareholder from making any tender offers for the corporation's stock during the terms of the agreement. Such agreements may also restrict the shareholders' ability to transfer the corporation's shares by affording the corporation a right of first refusal. By entering into such agreements, the directors ensure that the relationship between the corporation and an investor who has been purchasing significant blocks of stock will be clearly governed and defined. Such agreements also serve to avoid the unsettling impact on the corporation's business and workforce which could result from anticipation on the part of customers, shareholders, and employees that a takeover bid may be imminent. The corporation may seek to avert a costly control fight with the contracting shareholder by arriving at a negotiated understanding in advance of an anticipated bid for control. The corporation may also seek to "lock up" a significant block of stock with a "friendly" shareholder in the event that a third party attempts a take over that the board believes is not in the corporation's best interest to accept.

The contracting shareholder, in return, receives assurance that the corporation will not oppose its acquisitions up to the specified limit. Often an investor's substantial purchases of the corporation's stock initially will cause the market price of the stock to rise, and it becomes more costly for the investor to acquire additional stock. The investor may therefore seek to clearly set forth its "investment-only" intentions in order to dispel any anticipation of a tender offer and reduce the market price for the corporation's stock. In entering into a standstill agreement, the investor may seek input into management decisions, and may also obtain certain valuable securities registration rights from the corporation. *See* Bartlett & Andrews, *supra*, 62 B.U. L. Rev. at 144-46; Yale L.J. Note, *supra*, 93 Yale L.J. at 1094-97 and n. 11. Because the primary purpose of a standstill agreement usually is to create a stable and "absolutely certain" relationship between the contracting parties, the "situation . . . calls for a very formal, binding, and judicially enforceable contract." Yale L.J. Note, *supra*, 93 Yale L.J. at 1093 n. 78.

The application of the business judgment rule discussed above leads one to conclude that where "a valid corporate purpose [for executing a standstill agreement] exists and if management has consulted appropriate legal and business advisors before concluding the agreement," courts should not "second-guess management's judgment that the corporation would benefit from an extended period of corporate peace." Bartlett & Andrews, *supra*, 62 B.U. L. Rev. at 150. *See also*, Yale L.J. Note, *supra*, 93 Yale L.J. at 1097, 1112 n. 86 (standstill agreements "are useful in regulating relations between management and a substantial shareholder" and may bring "order and reliability to a relationship that was previously ambiguous and uncertain."). This Court's attention has not been called to any decision challenging the general validity of standstill agreements or the directors' right (indeed, their duty) to execute such an agreement if in their judgment the best interests of the corporation are served thereby. Although this Court would be inclined to challenge the validity of any provision in a standstill agreement requiring the shareholder to vote with management on any material matter, *see* Yale L.J. Note, *supra*, 93 Yale L.J. 1093 (1984), in this case the Agreement's voting provisions are not at issue.

As noted above, no court has determined or even suggested that a standstill agreement such as the one negotiated by Enterra and SGS constitutes a breach of the directors' fiduciary duty to the corporation and the shareholder. In *General Portland, Inc. v. Lafarge Coppee S.A.*, Nos. C.A. 3-81-1060D and C.A. 3-81-1082D, slip op., (N.D. Tex. 1981), *reprinted in* Fed. Sec. L. Rep. (CCH) (¶¶ 99, 148) [1982-83 Transfer Binder at 95, 537], the United States District Court for the Northern District of Texas issued an injunction prohibiting an anticipated tender offer by the defendant on the ground that the corporation was likely to succeed on the merits of its claim that in making its tender offer the defendant would breach a valid, binding, and enforceable standstill agreement. *Id.* at 95, 542.

In *Biechele, et al. v. Cedar Point, Inc., et al.*, 747 F.2d 209 (6th Cir. 1984), the court held that as a matter of law a standstill agreement between the defendant corporation and a "friendly" third party (Pearson) did not constitute an unlawful manipulative device under the federal securities laws, and stated

> The standstill agreement fixed no price for any purchase of Cedar Point stock by Pearson or anyone else . . . There were no competing bidders for the minority interest in Cedar Point which Pearson sought. While the agreement had the practical effect of . . . conditionally ensuring continued control by Cedar Point's board of directors, it would not inhibit third party bidders if they were otherwise interested . . . The effect of the agreement would be to encourage rather than inhibit, competitive bidding.

Biechele, 747 F.2d at 216. *Compare Gearhart Industries, Inc. v. Smith International, Inc.*, 741 F.2d 707 (5th Cir. 1984) (court appeared to assume, without detailed analysis, the general validity of an alleged oral standstill agreement).

As noted above, the actions of a board of directors in managing the affairs of the corporation are governed by the business judgment rule. In the present case, the affidavit submitted by Enterra's chairman sets forth numerous valid corporate purposes supporting the directors' negotiation and approval of the Agreement, which are primarily related to the potential adverse effect upon the corporation which SGS' initial significant purchases of Enterra's stock may have generated. According to the affidavit, the Board, acting in part upon the advice of counsel and Enterra's financial advisors, determined that it was in the best interests of the corporation to execute the Agreement because the stability created by the Agreement would provide numerous benefits to the corporation, including the retention (and recruitment) of key employees; allaying the "takeover" concerns of (and stabilizing relations with) various suppliers, customers, and lenders; settling the trading market for Enterra stock; and preserving the Board's ability to sell the corporation (if at all) at a time and in a manner which is in the best interests of the corporation and all shareholders. At the time the Agreement was negotiated and executed, SGS had not indicated a desire to obtain control of the corporation, nor is there any indication that any third party has at any time been interested in acquiring the corporation. Enterra's shareholders were promptly informed of the existence and substance of the Agreement. Although, as with all actions taken by a board of directors, retention of control arguably was a motive for entering into the Agreement, it is clear that the primary purpose of the Board (which, as noted, includes a majority of independent directors) was to "create a stable, certain, and cooperative relationship between management a substantial shareholder." Yale L.J. Note, *supra*, 93 Yale L.J. at 1096-97. The Board thereafter declined to amend the Agreement to permit SGS to offer to purchase all the shareholders' stock because the Board, in its judgment, considered the offer price financially inadequate. These undisputably are valid business reasons for entering into and declining to amend the Agreement, and, accordingly, this Court has determined that the movants have not demonstrated any reasonable likelihood of success on the merits of their claim that the Board breached its fiduciary duty to the corporation or the shareholders by executing the Agreement with SGS.

3. Alleged Duty to Convey All Offers to Shareholders

As noted above, the movants contend that, notwithstanding the provisions of the standstill Agreement there exists a common law fiduciary duty to (1) consider the adequacy of SGS' offer to buy all of Enterra's shares; (2) communicate that offer to Enterra's shareholders, together with the Board's decision to approve or disapprove the offer and its reasons therefore; and (3) provide some means by which each shareholder actually may accept SGS' offer and sell their shares to SGS. A necessary implication of the movants' claim is that the Agreement negotiated by SGS cannot relieve the Board of its obligation to communicate *and convey SGS'* offer to the shareholders.

At the outset, it appears that SGS may not have standing to assert the *shareholders'* alleged right to be apprised of and to receive the offer presented by SGS to the Board. An alleged breach of fiduciary duty on the part of the directors which is asserted on behalf of all shareholders or the entire corporation (whereby each shareholder suffers an indirect loss in common with other shareholders) must be maintained as a derivative action and cannot be asserted by individual shareholders in their own right. *Davis v. United States Gypsum Co.*, 451 F.2d 659, 662 (3d Cir. 1971); *Fitzpatrick v. Shay*, 314 Pa. Super. 450, 455-56, 461 A.2d 243, 246 (1983). In *Gearhart Industries, Inc. v. Smith International, Inc.*, 741 F.2d 707 (5th Cir. 1984), the court noted that a substantial shareholder who was attempting to purchase a controlling block of the corporation's stock had no standing to assert a breach of fiduciary duty claim against the directors for various actions taken by the directors to oppose the shareholder's takeover bid. The court stated that such claims must be brought by way of a derivative action. 741 F.2d at 721. However, since plaintiff Wallen has brought a derivative action and seeks the same injunctive relief as SGS, this Court will address the merits of their claims.

For the purposes of the motions for a preliminary injunction, it is not disputed that the Board considered the adequacy of the SGS offer (and, necessarily, SGS' request to amend the Agreement), and at oral argument counsel for SGS did not contend that the Board had not properly considered the proposal (Tr. of Oral Argument at 61). The affidavit submitted by the chairman of Enterra's Board states that the SGS offer was considered on two occasions by the Board, and, relying in part upon the advice of Enterra's financial advisor (Merrill Lynch) that the offer was financially inadequate, the Board determined that it was not in the best interests of the corporation to accept the proposal or modify the Agreement. Therefore, assuming that the Board had a fiduciary obligation to the corporation and shareholders to consider in good faith the adequacy of the SGS proposal, it is clear that the Board fulfilled that responsibility. The movants do not contend that the Board's refusal to approve the SGS offer was wrongful or constituted any breach of duty.

The movants also claim that after deciding to reject the SGS proposal, the Board had a fiduciary responsibility to *inform* all shareholders of the terms of the SGS offer and the reasons for the Board's decision not to approve the offer. Ordinarily, of course, an offeror which has been rejected by the board of directors in its efforts to acquire control of the corporation is free to communicate its offer to any and all shareholders by tender offer or otherwise. Thus, ordinarily, there is no need for the directors to disclose the terms of any rejected offer or the substance of any negotiations because the offeror has unfettered access to the shareholders. However, since SGS is restrained by the terms of its Agreement with the Board from approaching the shareholders with an offer to purchase their shares, the movants contend that the Board is under a fiduciary obligation to disclose the terms of the offer (and the Board's decision) to the shareholders. The movants have cited no authority under federal or state law in support of their claim that a board of directors must disclose to all shareholders every offer to purchase all the corporation's shares.

Recently, the Third Circuit has held that there exists no obligation under Section 10(b) of the Securities Exchange Act of 1934 (15 U.S.C. § 78j(b)), and Rule 10b-5 (17 C.F.R. § 240.10b-5) for a "target" corporation to disclose the status of offers or negotiations between the board and a "hostile suitor" attempting to take over the corporation unless and until an "agreement in principle" (e.g., to transfer control or effect a merger) has been reached. *Greenfield v. Heublein, Inc., et al.*, 742 F.2d 751, 756-57 (3d Cir. 1984); *see also Staffin v. Greenberg*, 672 F.2d, 1196 (3d Cir. 1982). No such agreement, of course, was reached in this case. Under the Williams Act, 15 U.S.C. § 78n(d) & (e), Enterra would be required to take certain actions *if* SGS had made a tender offer bid to all shareholders to acquire Enterra's outstanding shares. However, SGS has not made any tender offer, and the provisions of the Williams Act are inapplicable. Indeed, the movants do not contend that the provisions of the Williams Act (or any federal or state securities statute) provide the legal basis of their claim for relief.

Under Pennsylvania law, a corporate board of directors must submit a proposal to merge or consolidate to the shareholders for approval only if the board has approved the proposal. 15 Pa. Cons. Stat. Ann. § 1902 (Purdon's Supp. 1984). In this case, of course, the Board has not approved any SGS proposal. Counsel for Enterra has cited a number of decisions holding that "[d]irectors are under no [fiduciary] duty to reveal [to shareholders] every approach by a would-be acquiror or merger partner." *Panter v. Marshall Field & Co.*, 646 F.2d at 296. *See also Pogostin v. Rice*, 480 A.2d 619 (Del. Supr. Ct. 1984) (directors' refusal to accept tender offer at premium above market price per share, and refusal to negotiate with offeror, does not establish a prima facie case of breach of fiduciary duty). At least one commentator has stated that there is no obligation on the part of directors to pass on to shareholders the right to accept or reject takeover offers submitted to and rejected by the board. Lipton, *supra*, 35 Bus. Law. at 116.

The weight of all these authorities strongly suggests that the Board was under no duty imposed by any federal, state, or common law standard to communicate the terms of the SGS proposal (and the Board's decision to reject it) to Enterra's shareholders. Under the peculiar circumstances of this' case, wherein SGS has bound itself not to present an offer to purchase the corporation's stock in excess of the limit provided for in the Agreement directly to the shareholders, it may well be that there was no obligation on the part of the Board to inform the shareholders of SGS' proposal and the Board's reasons for rejecting it. However, assuming without deciding that the Board was obliged, under the circumstances of this case, to convey this information to the shareholders, the movants' request that this Court order the Board to do so has been rendered moot by Enterra's publication of its 1984 Second Quarterly Report (sent to all shareholders), wherein Enterra's Chairman briefly describes the SGS proposal, the Board's reason for rejecting it, and the status of this litigation.

It is apparent that much of the relief requested by the movants in their motions for a preliminary injunction (i.e., that the Board consider the adequacy of the SGS proposal, and that the Board disclose the terms of the proposal and the basis for its decision to reject it) is no longer at issue. However, although the movants rely heavily upon the shareholders' alleged "right to know" of the Board's determination of the SGS proposal, clearly the movants' primary interest lies in obtaining an order from this Court which would effectively convey SGS' offer to Enterra's shareholders without fear that SGS will incur liability for breach of the standstill agreement. The movants contend that the Board's consideration and disclosure of the SGS proposal are not sufficient, and that the Board itself is obliged to extend, on behalf of SGS, the SGS offer to all of Enterra's shareholders and provide a means by which each shareholder can accept or reject the SGS offer. The movants contend that as an absolute principle of corporate law (and notwithstanding any agreements to the contrary) no board of directors can fail to *convey* to the shareholders an offer received by the board to purchase the shareholders' stock.

The movants have not cited, nor has this Court discovered, any federal or state statute (or any common law authority) which requires the board of directors to *convey* to all shareholders (and permit them to accept or reject) any offer for the purchase of all the shareholders' stock where, as in the present case, the offeror and the corporation have entered into a standstill agreement limiting the percentage of the corporation's stock which the offeror can acquire. As noted above, it may well be that the Board is not even obliged to simply inform the shareholders of the offer. Accordingly, this Court therefore has determined at this stage of the proceedings that no reasonable likelihood of success on the merits of the movants' legal claim has been demonstrated.

This Court has concluded, for all of the reasons set forth above, that the movants have not demonstrated any reasonable likelihood of success on the merits of their legal claims. The motions for preliminary injunctive relief, therefore, must be denied on this basis alone.

. . .

Conclusion

For all of the reasons set forth above, this Court has determined that Wallen and SGS have failed to satisfy the burden necessary to justify the issuance of mandatory injunctive relief. The movants have failed to demonstrate any reasonable likelihood of success on the merits of their legal claims, and have failed to demonstrate the immediate threat of irreparable injury necessary to sustain the grant of a preliminary injunction. Moreover, the Court has determined that the interests of third parties and the public would not be well served by granting the requested injunctive relief. Accordingly, the motions for a preliminary injunction filed by defendant SGS in the *Enterra* case, and by plaintiff Wallen in the *Wallen* case, must be denied.

AMS. MINING CORP. v. THERIAULT

Delaware Supreme Court
2012 Del. LEXIS 459 (Aug. 27, 2012)

Holland, Justice, for the majority.

This is an appeal from a post-trial decision and final judgment of the Court of Chancery awarding more than $2 billion in damages and more than $304 million in attorneys' fees. The Court of Chancery held that the defendants-appellants, Americas Mining Corporation ("AMC"), the subsidiary of Southern Copper Corporation's ("Southern Peru") controlling shareholder, and affiliate directors of Southern Peru (collectively, the "Defendants"), breached their fiduciary duty of loyalty to Southern Peru and its minority stockholders by causing Southern Peru to acquire the controller's 99.15% interest in a Mexican mining company, Minera México, S.A. de C.V. ("Minera"), for much more than it was worth, *i.e.*, at an unfair price.

The Plaintiff challenged the transaction derivatively on behalf of Southern Peru. The Court of Chancery found the trial evidence established that the controlling shareholder, Grupo México, S.A.B. de C.V. ("Grupo Mexico"), through AMC, "extracted a deal that was far better than market" from Southern Peru due to the ineffective operation of a special committee (the "Special Committee"). To remedy the Defendants' breaches of loyalty, the Court of Chancery awarded the difference between the value Southern Peru paid for Minera ($3.7 billion) and the amount the Court of Chancery determined Minera was worth ($2.4 billion). The Court of Chancery awarded damages in the amount of $1.347 billion plus pre- and post-judgment interest, for a total judgment of $2.0316 billion. The Court of Chancery also awarded the Plaintiff's counsel attorneys' fees and expenses in the amount of 15% of the total judgment, which amounts to more than $304 million.

Issues on Appeal

The Defendants have raised [several] issues on appeal . . . . [T]hey contend that the Court of Chancery committed reversible error by failing to determine which party bore the burden of proof before trial. They further claim the Court of Chancery erred by ultimately allocating the burden to the Defendants, because, they submit, the Special Committee was independent, well-functioning, and did not rely on the controlling shareholder for the information that formed the basis for its recommendation . . . [T]hey argue that the Court of Chancery's determination about the "fair" price for the transaction was arbitrary and capricious [and] they assert that the Court of Chancery's award of damages is not supported by evidence in the record, but rather by impermissible speculation and conjecture.

We have determined that all of the Defendants' arguments are without merit. Therefore, the judgment of the Court of Chancery is affirmed.

FACTUAL BACKGROUND

The controlling stockholder in this case is Grupo México, S.A.B. de C.V. The NYSE-listed mining company is Southern Peru Copper Corporation.[26] The Mexican mining company is Minera México, S.A. de C.V.[27]

In February 2004, Grupo Mexico proposed that Southern Peru buy its 99.15% stake in Minera. At the time, Grupo Mexico owned 54.17% of Southern Peru's outstanding capital stock and could exercise 63.08% of the voting power of Southern Peru, making it Southern Peru's majority stockholder.

Grupo Mexico initially proposed that Southern Peru purchase its equity interest in Minera with 72.3 million shares of newly-issued Southern Peru stock. This "indicative" number assumed that Minera's equity was worth $3.05 billion, because that is what 72.3 million shares of Southern Peru stock were worth then in cash. By stark contrast with Southern Peru, Minera was almost wholly owned by Grupo Mexico and therefore had no market-tested value.

Because of Grupo Mexico's self-interest in the merger proposal, Southern Peru formed a "Special Committee" of disinterested directors to "evaluate" the transaction with Grupo Mexico. The Special Committee spent eight months in an awkward back and forth with Grupo Mexico over the terms of the deal before approving Southern Peru's acquisition of 99.15% of Minera's stock in exchange for 67.2 million newly-issued shares of Southern Peru stock (the "Merger") on October 21, 2004. That same day, Southern Peru's board of directors (the "Board") unanimously approved the Merger and Southern Peru and Grupo Mexico entered into a definitive agreement (the "Merger Agreement"). On October 21, 2004, the market value of 67.2 million shares of Southern Peru stock was $3.1 billion. When the Merger closed on April 1, 2005, the value of 67.2 million shares of Southern Peru had grown to $3.75 billion.

This derivative suit was then brought against the Grupo Mexico subsidiary that

---

[26] [3] On October 11, 2005, Southern Peru changed its name to "Southern Copper Corporation" and is currently traded on the NYSE under the symbol "SCCO."

[27] [4] Grupo Mexico held — and still holds — its interest in Southern Peru through its wholly-owned subsidiary Americas Mining Corporation ("AMC"). Grupo Mexico also held its 99.15% stake in Minera through AMC. AMC, not Grupo Mexico, is a defendant to this action, but I refer to them collectively as Grupo Mexico in this opinion because that more accurately reflects the story as it happened.

owned Minera, the Grupo Mexico-affiliated directors of Southern Peru, and the members of the Special Committee, alleging that the Merger was entirely unfair to Southern Peru and its minority stockholders.

The crux of the Plaintiff's argument is that Grupo Mexico received something demonstrably worth more than $3 billion (67.2 million shares of Southern Peru stock) in exchange for something that was not worth nearly that much (99.15% of Minera). The Plaintiff points to the fact that Goldman, which served as the Special Committee's financial advisor, never derived a value for Minera that justified paying Grupo Mexico's asking price, but instead relied on a "relative" valuation analysis that involved comparing the discounted cash flow ("DCF") values of Southern Peru and Minera, and a contribution analysis that improperly applied Southern Peru's own market EBITDA multiple (and even higher multiples) to Minera's EBITDA projections, to determine an appropriate exchange ratio to use in the Merger. The Plaintiff claims that, because the Special Committee and Goldman abandoned the company's market price as a measure of the true value of the give, Southern Peru substantially overpaid in the Merger.

The Defendants remaining in the case are Grupo Mexico and its affiliate directors who were on the Southern Peru Board at the time of the Merger. These Defendants assert that Southern Peru and Minera are similar companies and were properly valued on a relative basis. In other words, the defendants argue that the appropriate way to determine the price to be paid by Southern Peru in the Merger was to compare both companies' values using the same set of assumptions and methodologies, rather than comparing Southern Peru's market capitalization to Minera's DCF value. The Defendants do not dispute that shares of Southern Peru stock could have been sold for their market price at the time of the Merger, but they contend that Southern Peru's market price did not reflect the fundamental value of Southern Peru and thus could not appropriately be compared to the DCF value of Minera.

After this brief overview of the basic events and the parties' core arguments, the Court of Chancery provided the following more detailed recitation of the facts as it found them after trial.

The Key Players

Southern Peru operates mining, smelting, and refining facilities in Peru, producing copper and molybdenum as well as silver and small amounts of other metals. Before the Merger, Southern Peru had two classes of stock: common shares that were traded on the New York Stock Exchange; and "Founders Shares" that were owned by Grupo Mexico, Cerro Trading Company, Inc., and Phelps Dodge Corporation (the "Founding Stockholders"). Each Founders Share had five votes per share versus one vote per share for ordinary common stock. Grupo Mexico owned 43.3 million Founders Shares, which translated to 54.17% of Southern Peru's outstanding stock and 63.08% of the voting power.

Southern Peru's certificate of incorporation and a stockholders' agreement also gave Grupo Mexico the right to nominate a majority of the Southern Peru Board. The Grupo Mexico-affiliated directors who are defendants in this case held seven of the thirteen Board seats at the time of the Merger. Cerro owned 11.4 million Founders Shares (14.2% of the outstanding common stock) and Phelps Dodge owned 11.2 million Founders Shares (13.95% of the outstanding common stock). Among them, therefore, Grupo Mexico, Cerro, and Phelps Dodge owned over 82% of Southern Peru.

Grupo Mexico is a Mexican holding company listed on the Mexican stock exchange. Grupo Mexico is controlled by the Larrea family, and at the time of the Merger defendant Germán Larrea was the Chairman and CEO of Grupo Mexico, as well as the Chairman and CEO of Southern Peru. Before the Merger, Grupo Mexico owned 99.15% of Minera's stock and thus essentially was Minera's sole owner. Minera is a company engaged in the mining and processing of copper, molybdenum, zinc, silver, gold, and lead through its Mexico-based mines. At the time of the Merger, Minera was emerging from — if not still mired in — a period of financial difficulties, and its ability to exploit its assets had been compromised by these financial constraints. By contrast, Southern Peru was in good financial condition and virtually debt-free.

Grupo Mexico Proposes That Southern Peru Acquire Minera

In 2003, Grupo Mexico began considering combining its Peruvian mining interests with its Mexican mining interests. In September 2003, Grupo Mexico engaged UBS Investment Bank to provide advice with respect to a potential strategic transaction involving Southern Peru and Minera.

Grupo Mexico and UBS made a formal presentation to Southern Peru's Board on February 3, 2004, proposing that Southern Peru acquire Grupo Mexico's interest in Minera from AMC in exchange for newly-issued shares of Southern Peru stock. In that presentation, Grupo Mexico characterized the transaction as "[Southern Peru] to acquire Minera [ ] from AMC in a stock for stock deal financed through the issuance of common shares; initial proposal to issue 72.3 million shares." A footnote to that presentation explained that the 72.3 million shares was "an indicative number" of Southern Peru shares to be issued, assuming an equity value of Minera of $3.05 billion and a Southern Peru share price of $42.20 as of January 29, 2004.

In other words, the consideration of 72.3 million shares was indicative in the sense that Grupo Mexico wanted $3.05 billion in dollar value of Southern Peru stock for its stake in Minera, and the number of shares that Southern Peru would have to issue in exchange for Minera would be determined based on Southern Peru's market price. As a result of the proposed merger, Minera would become a virtually wholly-owned subsidiary of Southern Peru. The proposal also contemplated the conversion of all Founders Shares into a single class of common shares.

Southern Peru Forms a Special Committee

In response to Grupo Mexico's presentation, the Board met on February 12, 2004 and created a Special Committee to evaluate the proposal. The resolution creating the Special Committee provided that the "duty and sole purpose" of the Special Committee was "to evaluate the [Merger] in such manner as the Special Committee deems to be desirable and in the best interests of the stockholders of [Southern

Peru]," and authorized the Special Committee to retain legal and financial advisors at Southern Peru's expense on such terms as the Special Committee deemed appropriate. The resolution did not give the Special Committee express power to negotiate, nor did it authorize the Special Committee to explore other strategic alternatives.

The Special Committee's makeup as it was finally settled on March 12, 2004 was as follows:

- Harold S. Handelsman: Handelsman graduated from Columbia Law School and worked at Wachtell, Lipton, Rosen & Katz as an M & A lawyer before becoming an attorney for the Pritzker family interests in 1978. The Pritzker family is a wealthy family based in Chicago that owns, through trusts, a myriad of businesses. Handelsman was appointed to the Board in 2002 by Cerro, which was one of those Pritzker-owned businesses.
- Luis Miguel Palomino Bonilla: Palomino has a Ph.D in finance from the Wharton School at the University of Pennsylvania and worked as an economist, analyst and consultant for various banks and financial institutions. Palomino was nominated to the Board by Grupo Mexico upon the recommendation of certain Peruvian pension funds that held a large portion of Southern Peru's publicly traded stock.
- Gilberto Perezalonso Cifuentes: Perezalonso has both a law degree and an MBA and has managed multi-billion dollar companies such as Grupo Televisa and AeroMexico Airlines. Perezalonso was nominated to the Board by Grupo Mexico.
- Carlos Ruiz Sacristán: Ruiz, who served as the Special Committee's Chairman, worked as a Mexican government official for 25 years before co-founding an investment bank, where he advises on M & A and financing transactions. Ruiz was nominated to the Board by Grupo Mexico.

The Special Committee Hires Advisors and Seeks a Definitive Proposal From Grupo Mexico

The Special Committee began its work by hiring U.S. counsel and a financial advisor. After considering various options, the Special Committee chose Latham & Watkins LLP and Goldman. The Special Committee also hired a specialized mining consultant to help Goldman with certain technical aspects of mining valuation. Goldman suggested consultants that the Special Committee might hire to aid in the process; after considering these options, the Special Committee retained Anderson & Schwab ("A & S").

After hiring its advisors, the Special Committee set out to acquire a "proper" term sheet from Grupo Mexico. The Special Committee did not view the most recent term sheet that Grupo Mexico had sent on March 25, 2004 as containing a price term that would allow the Special Committee to properly evaluate the proposal. For some reason the Special Committee did not get the rather clear message that Grupo Mexico thought Minera was worth $3.05 billion.

Thus, in response to that term sheet, on April 2, 2004, Ruiz sent a letter to Grupo

Mexico on behalf of the Special Committee in which he asked for clarification about, among other things, the pricing of the proposed transaction. On May 7, 2004, Grupo Mexico sent to the Special Committee what the Special Committee considered to be the first "proper" term sheet, making even more potent its ask.

The May 7 Term Sheet

Grupo Mexico's May 7 term sheet contained more specific details about the proposed consideration to be paid in the Merger. It echoed the original proposal, but increased Grupo Mexico's ask from $3.05 billion worth of Southern Peru stock to $3.147 billion. Specifically, the term sheet provided that:

> The proposed value of Minera is US$4, 3 billion, comprised of an equity value of US$3,147 million [sic] and US$1,153 million [sic] of net debt as of April 2004. The number of [Southern Peru] shares to be issued in respect to the acquisition of Minera [ ] would be calculated by dividing 98.84% of the equity value of Minera [by the 20 — day average closing share price of [Southern Peru] beginning 5 days prior to closing of the [Merger].[28]

In other words, Grupo Mexico wanted $3.147 billion in market-tested Southern Peru stock in exchange for its stake in Minera. The structure of the proposal, like the previous Grupo Mexico ask, shows that Grupo Mexico was focused on the dollar value of the stock it would receive.

Throughout May 2004, the Special Committee's advisors conducted due diligence to aid their analysis of Grupo Mexico's proposal. As part of this process, A & S visited Minera's mines and adjusted the financial projections of Minera management (*i.e.*, of Grupo Mexico) based on the outcome of their due diligence.

Goldman Begins To Analyze Grupo Mexico's Proposal

On June 11, 2004, Goldman made its first presentation to the Special Committee addressing the May 7 term sheet. Although Goldman noted that due diligence was still ongoing, it had already done a great deal of work and was able to provide preliminary valuation analyses of the standalone equity value of Minera, including a DCF analysis, a contribution analysis, and a look-through analysis.

Goldman performed a DCF analysis of Minera based on long-term copper prices ranging from $0.80 to $1.00 per pound and discount rates ranging from 7.5% to 9.5%, utilizing both unadjusted Minera management projections and Minera management projections as adjusted by A & S. The only way that Goldman could derive a value for Minera close to Grupo Mexico's asking price was by applying its most aggressive assumptions (a modest 7.5% discount rate and its high-end $1.00/lb long-term copper price) to the unadjusted Minera management projections, which yielded an equity value for Minera of $3.05 billion. By applying the same aggressive assumptions to the projections as adjusted by A & S, Goldman's DCF analysis

[28] [7] At this point in the negotiation process, Grupo Mexico mistakenly believed that it only owned 98.84% of Minera. It later corrects this error, and the final Merger consideration reflected Grupo Mexico's full 99.15% equity ownership stake in Minera.

yielded a lower equity value for Minera of $2.41 billion. Goldman's mid-range assumptions (an 8.5% discount rate and $0.90/lb long-term copper price) only generated a $1.7 billion equity value for Minera when applied to the A & S-adjusted projections. That is, the mid-range of the Goldman analysis generated a value for Minera (the "get") a full $1.4 billion less than Grupo Mexico's ask for the give.

It made sense for Goldman to use the $0.90 per pound long term copper price as a mid-range assumption, because this price was being used at the time by both Southern Peru and Minera for purposes of internal planning. The median long-term copper price forecast based on Wall Street research at the time of the Merger was also $0.90 per pound.

Goldman's contribution analysis applied Southern Peru's market-based sales, EBITDA, and copper sales multiples to Minera. This analysis yielded an equity value for Minera ranging only between $1.1 and $1.7 billion. Goldman's look-through analysis, which was a sum-of-the-parts analysis of Grupo Mexico's market capitalization, generated a maximum equity value for Minera of $1.3 billion and a minimum equity value of only $227 million.

Goldman summed up the import of these various analyses in an "Illustrative Give/Get Analysis," which made patent the stark disparity between Grupo Mexico's asking price and Goldman's valuation of Minera: Southern Peru would "give" stock with a market price of $3.1 billion to Grupo Mexico and would "get" in return an asset worth no more than $1.7 billion.

The important assumption reflected in Goldman's June 11 presentation was that a bloc of shares of Southern Peru could yield a cash value equal to Southern Peru's actual stock market price and was thus worth its market value was emphasized by the Court of Chancery. At trial, the Defendants disclaimed any reliance upon a claim that Southern Peru's stock market price was not a reliable indication of the cash value that a very large bloc of shares — such as the 67.2 million paid to Grupo Mexico — could yield in the market. Thus, the price of the "give" was always easy to discern. The question thus becomes what was the value of the "get." Unlike Southern Peru, Minera's value was not the subject of a regular market test. Minera shares were not publicly traded and thus the company was embedded in the overall value of Grupo Mexico.

The June 11 presentation clearly demonstrates that Goldman, in its evaluation of the May 7 term sheet, could not get the get anywhere near the give. Notably, that presentation marked the *first and last time* that a give-get analysis appeared in Goldman's presentations to the Special Committee.

The Court of Chancery described what happened next as curious. The Special Committee began to *devalue* the "give" in order to make the "get" look closer in value. The DCF analysis of the value of Minera that Goldman presented initially caused concern. As Handelsman stated at trial, "when [the Special Committee] thought that the value of Southern Peru was its market value and the value of Minera was its discounted cash flow value . . . those were very different numbers."

But, the Special Committee's view changed when Goldman presented it with a DCF analysis of the value of Southern Peru on June 23, 2004. In this June 23 presentation, Goldman provided the Special Committee with a preliminary DCF analysis for Southern Peru analogous to the one that it had provided for Minera in the June 11 presentation. But, the discount rates that Goldman applied to Southern Peru's cash flows ranged from 8% to 10% instead of 7.5% to 9.5%. Based on Southern Peru management's projections, the DCF value generated for Southern Peru using mid-range assumptions (a 9% discount rate and $0.90/lb long-term copper price) was $2.06 billion. This was about $1.1 billion shy of Southern Peru's market capitalization as of June 21, 2004 ($3.19 billion). Those values "comforted" the Special Committee.[29]

The Court of Chancery found that "comfort" was an odd word for the Special Committee to use in this context. What Goldman was basically telling the Special Committee was that Southern Peru was being overvalued by the stock market. That is, Goldman told the Special Committee that even though Southern Peru's stock was worth an obtainable amount in cash, it really was not worth that much in fundamental terms. Thus, although Southern Peru had an actual cash value of $3.19 billion, its "real," "intrinsic," or "fundamental" value was only $2.06 billion, and giving $2.06 billion in fundamental value for $1.7 billion in fundamental value was something more reasonable to consider.

The Court of Chancery concluded that the more logical reaction of someone not in the confined mindset of directors of a controlled company may have been that it was a good time to capitalize on the market multiple the company was getting and monetize the asset. The Court of Chancery opined that a third party in the Special Committee's position might have sold at the top of the market, or returned cash to the Southern Peru stockholders by declaring a special dividend. For example, if it made long-term strategic sense for Grupo Mexico to consolidate Southern Peru and Minera, there was a logical alternative for the Special Committee: ask Grupo Mexico to make a premium to market offer for Southern Peru. Let Grupo Mexico be the buyer, not the seller.

In other words, the Court of Chancery found that by acting like a third-party negotiator with its own money at stake and with the full range of options, the Special Committee would have put Grupo Mexico back on its heels. Doing so would have been consistent with the financial advice it was getting and seemed to accept as correct. The Special Committee could have also looked to use its market-proven stock to buy a company at a good price (a lower multiple to earnings than Southern Peru's) and then have its value rolled into Southern Peru's higher market multiple to earnings. That could have included buying Minera at a price equal to its fundamental value using Southern Peru's market-proven currency.

The Court of Chancery was chagrined that instead of doing any of these things, the Special Committee was "comforted" by the fact that they could devalue that currency and justify paying *more* for Minera than they originally thought they should.

---

[29] [8] Tr. at 159 (Handelsman) ("I think the committee was somewhat comforted by the fact that the DCF analysis of Minera [ ] and the DCF analysis of [Southern Peru] were not as different as the discounted cash flow analysis of Minera [ ] and the market value of Southern Peru.").

Special Committee Moves Toward Relative Valuation

After the June 23, 2004 presentation, the Special Committee and Goldman began to embrace the idea that the companies should be valued on a relative basis. In a July 8, 2004 presentation to the Special Committee, Goldman included both a revised standalone DCF analysis of Minera and a "Relative Discounted Cash Flow Analysis" in the form of matrices presenting the "indicative number" of Southern Peru shares that should be issued to acquire Minera based on various assumptions. The relative DCF analysis generated a vast range of Southern Peru shares to be issued in the Merger of 28.9 million to 71.3 million. Based on Southern Peru's July 8, 2004 market value of $40.30 per share, 28.9 million shares of Southern Peru stock had a market value of $1.16 billion, and 71.3 million shares were worth $2.87 billion. In other words, even the highest equity value yielded for Minera by this analysis was short of Grupo Mexico's actual cash value asking price.

The revised standalone DCF analysis applied the same discount rate and long-term copper price assumptions that Goldman had used in its June 11 presentation to updated projections. This time, by applying a 7.5% discount rate and $1.00 per pound long-term copper price to Minera management's projections, Goldman was only able to yield an equity value of $2.8 billion for Minera. Applying the same aggressive assumptions to the projections as adjusted by A & S generated a standalone equity value for Minera of only $2.085 billion. Applying mid-range assumptions (a discount rate of 8.5% and $0.90/lb long-term copper price) to the A & S-adjusted projections yielded an equity value for Minera of only $1.358 billion.

The Special Committee Makes A Counterproposal
Suggests A Fixed-Exchange Ratio

After Goldman's July 8 presentation, the Special Committee made a counterproposal to Grupo Mexico. The Court of Chancery noted it was "oddly" not mentioned in Southern Peru's proxy statement describing the Merger (the "Proxy Statement"). In this counterproposal, the Special Committee offered that Southern Peru would acquire Minera by issuing 52 million shares of Southern Peru stock with a then-current market value of $2.095 billion. The Special Committee also proposed implementation of a fixed, rather than a floating, exchange ratio that would set the number of Southern Peru shares issued in the Merger.

From the inception of the Merger, Grupo Mexico had contemplated that the dollar value of the price to be paid by Southern Peru would be fixed (at a number that was always north of $3 billion), while the number of Southern Peru shares to be issued as consideration would float up or down based on Southern Peru's trading price around the time of closing. But, the Special Committee was uncomfortable with having to issue a variable amount of shares in the Merger. Handelsman testified that, in its evaluation of Grupo Mexico's May 7 term sheet, "it was the consensus of the [Special Committee] that a floating exchange rate was a non-starter" because "no one could predict the number of shares that [Southern Peru] would have to issue in order to come up with the consideration requested."

The Special Committee wanted a fixed exchange ratio, which would set the number of shares that Southern Peru would issue in the Merger at the time of signing. The dollar value of the Merger consideration at the time of closing would vary with the fluctuations of Southern Peru's market price. According to the testimony of the Special Committee members, their reasoning was that both Southern Peru's stock and the copper market had been historically volatile, and a fixed exchange ratio would protect Southern Peru's stockholders from a situation in which Southern Peru's stock price went down and Southern Peru would be forced to issue a greater number of shares for Minera in order to meet a fixed dollar value. The Court of Chancery found that position was hard to reconcile with the Special Committee and Southern Peru's purported bullishness about the copper market in 2004.

Grupo Mexico Sticks to Its Demand

In late July or early August, Grupo Mexico responded to the Special Committee's counterproposal by suggesting that Southern Peru should issue in excess of 80 million shares of common stock to purchase Minera. It is not clear on the record exactly when Grupo Mexico asked for 80 million shares, but given Southern Peru's trading history at that time, the market value of that consideration would have been close to $3.1 billion, basically the same place where Grupo Mexico had started. The Special Committee viewed Grupo Mexico's ask as too high, which is not surprising given that the parties were apparently a full billion dollars in value apart, and negotiations almost broke down.

But, on August 21, 2004, after what is described as "an extraordinary effort" in Southern Peru's Proxy Statement, Grupo Mexico proposed a new asking price of 67 million shares. On August 20, 2004, Southern Peru was trading at $41.20 per share, so 67 million shares were worth about $2.76 billion on the market, a drop in Grupo Mexico's ask. Grupo Mexico's new offer brought the Special Committee back to the negotiating table.

After receiving two term sheets from Grupo Mexico that reflected the 67 million share asking price, the second of which was received on September 8, 2004, when 67 million shares had risen to be worth $3.06 billion on the market, Goldman made another presentation to the Special Committee on September 15, 2004. In addition to updated relative DCF analyses of Southern Peru and Minera (presented only in terms of the number of shares of Southern Peru stock to be issued in the Merger), this presentation contained a "Multiple Approach at Different EBITDA Scenarios," which was essentially a comparison of Southern Peru and Minera's market-based equity values, as derived from multiples of Southern Peru's 2004 and 2005 estimated (or "E") EBITDA.

Goldman also presented these analyses in terms of the number of Southern Peru shares to be issued to Grupo Mexico, rather than generating standalone values for Minera. The range of shares to be issued at the 2004E EBITDA multiple (5.0x) was 44 to 54 million; at the 2005E multiple (6.3x) Goldman's analyses yielded a range of 61 to 72 million shares of Southern Peru stock. Based on Southern Peru's $45.34 share price as of September 15, 2004, 61 to 72 million shares had a cash value of $2.765 billion to $3.26 billion.

The Special Committee sent a new proposed term sheet to Grupo Mexico on

September 23, 2004. That term sheet provided for a fixed purchase price of 64 million shares of Southern Peru (translating to a $2.95 billion market value based on Southern Peru's then-current closing price). The Special Committee's proposal contained two terms that would protect the minority stockholders of Southern Peru: (1) a 20% collar around the purchase price, which gave both the Special Committee and Grupo Mexico the right to walk away from the Merger if Southern Peru's stock price went outside of the collar before the stockholder vote; and (2) a voting provision requiring that a majority of the minority stockholders of Southern Peru vote in favor of the Merger. Additionally, the proposal called for Minera's net debt, which Southern Peru was going to absorb in the Merger, to be capped at $1.105 billion at closing, and contained various corporate governance provisions.

The Special Committee's Proposed Terms Rejected
But the Parties Work Out a Deal

On September 30, 2004, Grupo Mexico sent a counterproposal to the Special Committee, in which Grupo Mexico rejected the Special Committee's offer of 64 million shares and held firm to its demand for 67 million shares. Grupo Mexico's counterproposal also rejected the collar and the majority of the minority vote provision, proposing instead that the Merger be conditioned on the vote of two-thirds of the outstanding stock. Grupo Mexico noted that conditioning the Merger on a two-thirds shareholder vote obviated the need for the walk-away right requested by the Special Committee, because Grupo Mexico would be prevented from approving the Merger unilaterally in the event the stock price was materially higher at the time of the stockholder vote than at the time of Board approval. Grupo Mexico did accept the Special Committee's proposed $1.05 billion debt cap at closing. The Court of Chancery found that was not much of a concession in light of the fact that Minera was already contractually obligated to pay down its debt and was in the process of doing so.

After the Special Committee received Grupo Mexico's September 30 counterproposal, the parties reached agreement on certain corporate governance provisions to be included in the Merger Agreement, some of which were originally suggested by Grupo Mexico and some of which were first suggested by the Special Committee. Without saying these provisions were of no benefit at all to Southern Peru and its outside investors, the Court of Chancery did say that they did not factor more importantly in its decision because they do not provide any benefit above the protections of default law that were economically meaningful enough to close the material dollar value gap that existed.

On October 5, 2004, members of the Special Committee met with Grupo Mexico to iron out a final deal. At that meeting, the Special Committee agreed to pay 67 million shares, dropped their demand for the collar, and acceded to most of Grupo Mexico's demands. The Special Committee justified paying a higher price through what the Court of Chancery described as a series of economic contortions. The Special Committee was able to "bridge the gap" between the 64 million and the 67 million figures by decreasing Minera's debt cap by another $105 million, and by getting Grupo Mexico to cause Southern Peru to issue a special dividend of $100 million, which had the effect of decreasing the value of Southern Peru's stock.

According to Special Committee member Handelsman, these "bells and whistles" made it so that "the value of what was being . . . acquired in the merger went up, and the value of the specie that was being used in the merger went down . . . ," giving the Special Committee reason to accept a higher Merger price.

The closing share price of Southern Peru was $53.16 on October 5, 2004, so a purchase price of 67 million shares had a market value of $3.56 billion, which was higher than the dollar value requested by Grupo Mexico in its February 2004 proposal or its original May 7 term sheet.

At that point, the main unresolved issue was the stockholder vote that would be required to approve the Merger. After further negotiations, on October 8, 2004, the Special Committee gave up on its proposed majority of the minority vote provision and agreed to Grupo Mexico's suggestion that the Merger require only the approval of two-thirds of the outstanding common stock of Southern Peru. Given the size of the holdings of Cerro and Phelps Dodge, Grupo Mexico could achieve a two-thirds vote if either Cerro or Phelps Dodge voted in favor of the Merger.

Multi-Faceted Dimensions of Controlling Power: Large Stockholders Who Want To Get Out Support a Strategic, Long-Term Acquisition as a Prelude to Their Own Exit as Stockholders

One of the members of the Special Committee, Handelsman, represented a large Founding Stockholder, Cerro. The Court of Chancery noted that this might be seen in some ways to have ideally positioned Handelsman to be a very aggressive negotiator. But Handelsman had a problem to deal with, which did not involve Cerro having any self-dealing interest in the sense that Grupo Mexico had. Rather, Grupo Mexico had control over Southern Peru and thus over whether Southern Peru would take the steps necessary to make the Founding Stockholders' shares marketable under applicable securities regulations. Cerro and Phelps Dodge wanted to monetize their investment in Southern Peru and get out.

Thus, while the Special Committee was negotiating the terms of the Merger, Handelsman was engaged in negotiations of his own with Grupo Mexico. Cerro and Phelps Dodge had been seeking registration rights from Grupo Mexico (in its capacity as Southern Peru's controller) for their shares of Southern Peru stock, which they needed because of the volume restrictions imposed on affiliates of an issuer by SEC Rule 144.

The Court of Chancery found that it is not clear which party first proposed liquidity and support for the Founding Stockholders in connection with the Merger. But it is plain that the concept appears throughout the term sheets exchanged between Grupo Mexico and the Special Committee, and it is clear that Handelsman knew that registration rights would be part of the deal from the beginning of the Merger negotiations and that thus the deal would enable Cerro to sell as it desired. The Special Committee did not take the lead in negotiating the specific terms of the registration rights provisions — rather, it took the position that it wanted to leave the back-and-forth over the agreement details to Cerro and Grupo Mexico. Handelsman, however, played a key role in the negotiations with Grupo Mexico on Cerro's behalf.

At trial, Handelsman explained that there were two justifications for pursuing registration rights — one offered benefits exclusive to the Founding Stockholders, and the other offered benefits that would inure to Southern Peru's entire stockholder base. The first justification was that Cerro needed the registration rights in order to sell its shares quickly, and Cerro wanted "to get out" of its investment in Southern Peru. The second justification concerned the public market for Southern Peru stock.

Granting registration rights to the Founding Stockholders would allow Cerro and Phelps Dodge to sell their shares, increasing the amount of stock traded on the market and thus increasing Southern Peru's somewhat thin public float. This would in turn improve stockholder liquidity, generate more analyst exposure, and create a more efficient market for Southern Peru shares, all of which would benefit the minority stockholders. Handelsman thus characterized the registration rights situation as a "win-win," because "it permitted us to sell our stock" and "it was good for [Southern Peru] because they had a better float and they had a more organized sale of shares."

Handelsman's tandem negotiations with Grupo Mexico culminated in Southern Peru giving Cerro registration rights for its shares on October 21, 2004, the same day that the Special Committee approved the Merger. In exchange for registration rights, Cerro expressed its intent to vote its shares in favor of the Merger if the Special Committee recommended it. If the Special Committee made a recommendation against the Merger, or withdrew its recommendation in favor of it, Cerro was bound by the agreement to vote against the Merger.

Grupo Mexico's initial proposal, which Handelsman received on October 18, 2004 — a mere three days before the Special Committee was to vote on the Merger — was that it would grant Cerro registration rights in exchange for Cerro's agreement to vote in favor of the Merger. The Special Committee and Handelsman suggested instead that Cerro's vote on the Merger be tied to whether or not the Special Committee recommended the Merger. After discussing the matter with the Special Committee, Grupo Mexico agreed.

On December 22, 2004, after the Special Committee approved the Merger but well before the stockholder vote, Phelps Dodge entered into an agreement with Grupo Mexico that was similar to Cerro's, but did not contain a provision requiring Phelps Dodge to vote against the Merger if the Special Committee did. By contrast, Phelps Dodge's agreement only provided that, [t]aking into account that the Special Committee . . . did recommend . . . the approval of the [Merger], Phelps Dodge "express[es] [its] current intent, to [ ] submit its proxies to vote in favor of the [Merger]. . . ." Thus, in the event that the Special Committee later withdrew its recommendation to approve the Merger, Cerro would be contractually bound to vote against it, but Grupo Mexico could still achieve the two-thirds vote required to approve the Merger solely with Phelps Dodge's cooperation. Under the terms of the Merger Agreement, the Special Committee was free to change its recommendation of the Merger, but it was not able to terminate the Merger Agreement on the basis of such a change. Rather, a change in the Special Committee's recommendation only gave Grupo Mexico the power to terminate the Merger Agreement.

This issue caused the Court of Chancery concern. Although it was not prepared on this record to find that Handelsman consciously agreed to a suboptimal deal for Southern Peru simply to achieve liquidity for Cerro from Grupo Mexico, it had little doubt that Cerro's own predicament as a *stockholder dependent on Grupo Mexico's whim as a controller for registration rights* influenced how Handelsman approached the situation. The Court of Chancery found that did not mean Handelsman consciously gave in, but it did mean that he was less than ideally situated to press hard. Put simply, Cerro was even more subject to the dominion of Grupo Mexico than smaller holders because Grupo Mexico had additional power over it because of the unregistered nature of its shares.

Most important to the Court of Chancery was that Cerro's desires, when considered alongside the Special Committee's actions, illustrate the tendency of control to result in odd behavior. During the negotiations of the Merger, Cerro had no interest in the long-term benefits to Southern Peru of acquiring Minera, nor did Phelps Dodge. Certainly, Cerro did not want any deal so disastrous that it would tank the value of Southern Peru completely, but nor did it have a rational incentive to say no to a suboptimal deal if that risked being locked into its investments.

The Court of Chancery found that Cerro wanted to *sell* and *sell then and there.* But as a Special Committee member, Handelsman did not act consistently with that impulse for all stockholders. He did not suggest that Grupo Mexico make an offer for Southern Peru, but instead pursued a long-term strategic transaction in which Southern Peru was the buyer. Accordingly, the Court of Chancery concluded that a short-term seller of a company's shares caused that company to be a long-term buyer.

After One Last Price Adjustment, Goldman Makes Its Final Presentation

On October 13, 2004, Grupo Mexico realized that it owned 99.15% of Minera rather than 98.84%, and the purchase price was adjusted to 67.2 million shares instead of 67 million shares to reflect the change in size of the interest being sold. On October 13, 2004, Southern Peru was trading at $45.90 per share, which meant that 67.2 million shares had a dollar worth of $3.08 billion.

On October 21, 2004, the Special Committee met to consider whether to recommend that the Board approve the Merger. At that meeting, Goldman made a final presentation to the Special Committee. The October 21, 2004 presentation stated that Southern Peru's implied equity value was $3.69 billion based on its then current market capitalization at a stock price of $46.41 and adjusting for debt. Minera's implied equity value is stated as $3.146 billion, which was derived entirely from multiplying 67.2 million shares by Southern Peru's $46.41 stock price and adjusting for the fact that Southern Peru was only buying 99.15% of Minera.

No standalone equity value of Minera was included in the Goldman October 21 presentation. Instead, the presentation included a series of relative DCF analyses and a "Contribution Analysis at Different EBITDA Scenarios," both of which were presented in terms of a hypothetical number of Southern Peru shares to be issued to Grupo Mexico for Minera. Goldman's relative DCF analyses provided various matrices showing the number of shares of Southern Peru that should be issued in exchange for Minera under various assumptions regarding the discount rate, the long-term copper price, the allocation of tax benefits, and the amount of royalties that Southern Peru would need to pay to the Peruvian government.

As it had in all of its previous presentations, Goldman used a range of long-term copper prices from $0.80 to $1.00 per pound. The DCF analyses generated a range of the number of shares to be issued in the Merger from 47.2 million to 87.8 million. Based on the then-current stock price of $45.92, this translated to $2.17 billion to $4.03 billion in cash value. Assuming the mid-range figures of a discount rate of 8.5% and a long-term copper price of $0.90 per pound, the analyses yielded a range of shares from 60.7 to 78.7 million.

Goldman's contribution analysis generated a range of 42 million to 56 million shares of Southern Peru to be issued based on an annualized 2004E EBITDA multiple (4.6x) and forecasted 2004E EBITDA multiple (5.0x), and a range of 53 million to 73 million shares based on an updated range of estimated 2005E EBITDA multiples (5.6x to 6.5x). Notably, the 2004E EBITDA multiples did not support the issuance of 67.2 million shares of Southern Peru stock in the Merger. But, 67.2 million shares falls at the higher end of the range of shares calculated using Southern Peru's 2005E EBITDA multiples.

As notable, these multiples were not the product of the median of the 2005E EBITDA multiples of comparable companies identified by Goldman (4.8x). Instead, the multiples used were even higher than Southern Peru's own higher 2005E EBITDA Wall Street consensus (5.5x) — an adjusted version of which was used as the bottom end of the range. These higher multiples were then attributed to Minera, a non-publicly traded company suffering from a variety of financial and operational problems.

Goldman opined that the Merger was fair from a financial perspective to the stockholders of Southern Peru, and provided a written fairness opinion.

Special Committee and Board Approve the Merger

After Goldman made its presentation, the Special Committee voted 3–0 to recommend the Merger to the Board. At the last-minute suggestion of Goldman, Handelsman decided not to vote in order to remove any appearance of conflict based on his participation in the negotiation of Cerro's registration rights, despite the fact that he had been heavily involved in the negotiations from the beginning and his hands had been deep in the dough of the now fully baked deal. The Board then unanimously approved the Merger and Southern Peru entered into the Merger Agreement.

Market Reacts to the Merger

The market reaction to the Merger was mixed and the parties have not presented any reliable evidence about it. That is, neither party had an expert perform an event study analyzing the market reaction to the Merger. Southern Peru's stock price traded down by 4.6% when the Merger was announced. When the preliminary proxy statement, which provided more financial information regarding the Merger terms, became public on November 22, 2004, Southern Peru's stock price again declined by

1.45%. But the stock price increased for two days after the final Proxy Statement was filed.

The Court of Chancery found that determining what effect the Merger itself had on this rise is difficult because, as the Plaintiff pointed out, this was not, as the Defendants contended, the first time that Southern Peru and Minera's financials were presented together. Rather, the same financial statements were in the preliminary Proxy Statement and the stock price fell. However, the Court of Chancery noted that the Plaintiff offered no evidence that these stock market fluctuations provided a reliable basis for assessing the fairness of the deal because it did not conduct a reliable event study.

The Court of Chancery found, in fact, against a backdrop of strong copper prices, the trading price of Southern Peru stock increased substantially by the time the Merger closed. By April 1, 2005, Southern Peru's stock price had a market value of $55.89 per share, an increase of approximately 21.7% over the October 21, 2004 closing price. The Court of Chancery found this increase could not be attributed to the Merger because other factors were in play. That included the general direction of copper prices, which lifted the market price of not just Southern Peru, but those of its publicly traded competitors. Furthermore, Southern Peru's own financial performance was very strong.

Goldman Does Not Update Its Fairness Analysis

Despite rising Southern Peru share prices and performance, the Special Committee did not ask Goldman to update its fairness analysis at the time of the stockholder vote on the Merger and closing — nearly five months after the Special Committee had voted to recommend it. At trial, Handelsman testified that he called a representative at Goldman to ask whether the transaction was still fair, but the Court of Chancery found that Handelsman's phone call hardly constitutes a request for an updated fairness analysis. The Court of Chancery also found that the Special Committee's failure to determine whether the Merger was still fair at the time of the Merger vote and closing was curious for two reasons.

First, for whatever the reason, Southern Peru's stock price had gone up substantially since the Merger was announced in October 2004. In March 2005, Southern Peru stock was trading at an average price of $58.56 a share. The Special Committee had agreed to a collarless fixed exchange ratio and did not have a walk-away right. The Court of Chancery noted an adroit Special Committee would have recognized the need to re-evaluate the Merger in light of Southern Peru's then-current stock price.

Second, Southern Peru's actual 2004 EBITDA became available before the stockholder vote on the Merger took place, and Southern Peru had smashed through the projections that the Special Committee had used for it. In the October 21 presentation, Goldman used a 2004E EBITDA for Southern Peru of $733 million and a 2004E EBITDA for Minera of $687 million. Southern Peru's actual 2004 EBITDA was $1.005 billion, 37% more and almost $300 million more than the projections used by Goldman. Minera's actual 2004 EBITDA, by contrast, was $681 million, 0.8% less than the projections used by Goldman.

The Court of Chancery noted that earlier, in Goldman's contribution analysis it relied on the values (measured in Southern Peru shares) generated by applying an aggressive range of Southern Peru's 2005E EBITDA multiples to Minera's A & S-adjusted and unadjusted projections, not the 2004E EBITDA multiple, and that the inaccuracy of Southern Peru's estimated 2004 EBITDA should have given the Special Committee serious pause. If the 2004 EBITDA projections of Southern Peru — which were not optimized and had been prepared by Grupo Mexico-controlled management — were so grossly low, it provided reason to suspect that the 2005 EBITDA projections, which were even lower than the 2004 EBITDA projections, were also materially inaccurate, and that the assumptions forming the basis of Goldman's contribution analysis should be reconsidered.

Moreover, Southern Peru made $303.4 million in EBITDA in the first quarter of 2005, over 52% of the estimate in Goldman's fairness presentation for Southern Peru's 2005 full year performance. Although the first-quarter 2005 financial statements, which covered the period from January 1, 2005 to March 31, 2005, would not have been complete by the time of the stockholder vote, the Court of Chancery reasonably assumed that, as directors of Southern Peru, the Special Committee had access to non-public information about Southern Peru's monthly profit and loss statements. Southern Peru later beat its EBITDA projections for 2005 by a very large margin, 135%, a rate well ahead of Minera's 2005 performance, which beat the deal estimates by a much lower 45%.

The Special Committee's failure to get a fairness update was even more of a concern to the Court of Chancery because Cerro had agreed to vote against the Merger if the Special Committee changed its recommendation. The Special Committee failed to obtain a majority of the minority vote requirement, but it supposedly agreed to a two-thirds vote requirement instead because a two-thirds vote still prevented Grupo Mexico from unilaterally approving the Merger. This out was only meaningful, however, if the Special Committee took the recommendation process seriously. If the Special Committee maintained its recommendation, Cerro had to vote for the Merger, and its vote combined with Grupo Mexico's vote would ensure passage. By contrast, if the Special Committee changed its recommendation, Cerro was obligated to vote against the Merger.

The Court of Chancery found the tying of Cerro's voting agreement to the Special Committee's recommendation was somewhat odd, in another respect. In a situation involving a third-party merger sale of a company without a controlling stockholder, the third party will often want to lock up some votes in support of a deal. A large blocholder and the target board might therefore negotiate a compromise, whereby the blocholder agrees to vote yes if the target board or special committee maintains a recommendation in favor of the transaction. In this situation, however, there is a factor not present here. In an arm's-length deal, the target usually has the flexibility to change its recommendation or terminate the original merger upon certain conditions, including if a superior proposal is available, or an intervening event makes the transaction impossible to recommend in compliance with the target's fiduciary duties.

Here, by contrast, Grupo Mexico faced no such risk of a competing superior proposal because it controlled Southern Peru. Furthermore, the fiduciary out that the Special Committee negotiated for in the Merger agreement provided only that the Special Committee could change its recommendation in favor of the Merger, not that it could terminate the Merger altogether or avoid a vote on the Merger. The only utility therefore of the recommendation provision was if the Special Committee seriously considered the events between the time of signing and the stockholder vote and made a renewed determination of whether the deal was fair. The Court of Chancery found there is no evidence of such a serious examination, despite important emerging evidence that the transaction's terms were skewed in favor of Grupo Mexico.

Southern Peru's Stockholders Approve the Merger

On March 28, 2005, the stockholders of Southern Peru voted to approve the Merger. More than 90% of the stockholders voted in favor of the Merger. The Merger then closed on April 1, 2005. At the time of closing, 67.2 million shares of Southern Peru had a market value of $3.75 billion.

Cerro Sells Its Shares

On June 15, 2005, Cerro, which had a basis in its stock of only $1.32 per share, sold its entire interest in Southern Peru in an underwritten offering at $40.635 per share. Cerro sold its stock at a discount to the then-current market price, as the low-high trading prices for one day before the sale were $43.08 to $44.10 per share. The Court of Chancery found that this illustrated Cerro's problematic incentives.

Plaintiff Sues Defendants and Special Committee

This derivative suit challenging the Merger, first filed in late 2004, moved too slowly, and it was not until June 30, 2010 that the Plaintiff moved for summary judgment. On August 10, 2010, the Defendants filed a cross-motion for summary judgment, or in the alternative, to shift the burden of proof to the Plaintiff under the entire fairness standard. On August 11, 2010, the individual Special Committee defendants cross-moved for summary judgment on all claims under Southern Peru's exculpatory provision adopted under title 8, section 102(b)(7) of the Delaware Code.

At a hearing held on December 21, 2010, the Court of Chancery dismissed the Special Committee defendants from the case because the plaintiff had failed to present evidence supporting a non-exculpated breach of their fiduciary duty of loyalty. It denied all other motions for summary judgment. The Court of Chancery noted that this, of course, did not mean that the Special Committee had acted adroitly or that the remaining defendants, Grupo Mexico and its affiliates, were immune from liability.

In contrast to the Special Committee defendants, precisely because the remaining directors were employed by Grupo Mexico, which had a self-dealing interest directly in conflict with Southern Peru, the exculpatory charter provision was of no benefit to them at that stage, given the factual question regarding their motivations. At trial, these individual Grupo Mexico-affiliated director defendants made no effort to show that they acted in good faith and were entitled to exculpation despite their lack of independence. In other words, the Grupo Mexico-affiliated directors did nothing to distinguish each other and none of them argued that he should not bear liability for breach of the duty of loyalty if the transaction was unfairly advantageous to Grupo Mexico, which had a direct self-dealing interest in the Merger. Accordingly, the Court of Chancery concluded that their liability would rise or fall with the issue of fairness.

In dismissing the Special Committee members on the summary judgment record, the Court of Chancery necessarily treated the predicament faced by Cerro and Handelsman, which involved facing additional economic pressures as a minority stockholder as a result of Grupo Mexico's control, differently than a classic self-dealing interest. The Court of Chancery continued to hold that view. Although it believed that Cerro, and therefore Handelsman, were influenced by Cerro's desire for liquidity as a stockholder, it seemed counterproductive to the Court of Chancery to equate a legitimate concern of a stockholder for liquidity from a controller into a self-dealing interest.

Therefore, the Court of Chancery concluded that there had to be a triable issue regarding whether Handelsman acted in subjective bad faith to force him to trial. The Court of Chancery concluded then on that record that no such issue of fact existed and even on the fuller trial record (where the Plaintiff actually made much more of an effort to pursue this angle), it still could not find that Handelsman acted in bad faith to purposely accept an unfair deal.

Nevertheless, the Court of Chancery found that Cerro, and therefore Handelsman, did have the sort of economic concern that ideally should have been addressed upfront and forthrightly in terms of whether the stockholder's interest well positioned its representative to serve on a special committee. Thus, although the Court of Chancery continued to be unpersuaded that it could label Handelsman as having acted with the state of mind required to expose him to liability, given the exculpatory charter protection to which he is entitled, it was persuaded that Cerro's desire to sell influenced how Handelsman approached his duties and compromised his effectiveness.

* * *

BURDEN SHIFTING ANALYSIS

The Defendants [argument] on appeal is that the Court of Chancery committed reversible error by failing to determine which party bore the burden of proof before trial. The Defendants submit that the Court of Chancery further erred by ultimately allocating the burden to the Defendants, because the Special Committee was independent, was well-functioning, and did not rely on the controlling shareholder for the information that formed the basis for its recommendation.

When a transaction involving self-dealing by a controlling shareholder is challenged, the applicable standard of judicial review is entire fairness, with the defendants having the burden of persuasion. In other words, the defendants bear the burden of proving that the transaction with the controlling stockholder was entirely fair to the minority stockholders. In the Court of Chancery and on appeal, both the Plaintiff and the Defendants agree that entire fairness is the appropriate standard of judicial review for the Merger.

The entire fairness standard has two parts: fair dealing and fair price.[30] Fair dealing "embraces questions of when the transaction was timed, how it was initiated, structured, negotiated, disclosed to the directors, and how the approvals of the directors and the stockholders were obtained."[31] Fair price "relates to the economic and financial considerations of the proposed merger, including all relevant factors: assets, market value, earnings, future prospects, and any other elements that affect the intrinsic or inherent value of a company's stock."[32]

In *Kahn v. Lynch Communication Systems, Inc.*,[33] this Court held that when the entire fairness standard applies, the defendants may shift the burden of persuasion by one of two means: first, they may show that the transaction was approved by a well-functioning committee of independent directors; or second, they may show that the transaction was approved by an informed vote of a majority of the minority shareholders.[34] Nevertheless, even when an interested cash-out merger transaction receives the informed approval of a majority of minority stockholders or a well-functioning committee of independent directors, an entire fairness analysis is the only proper standard of review.[35] Accordingly, "[r]egardless of where the burden lies, when a controlling shareholder stands on both sides of the transaction the conduct of the parties will be viewed under the more exacting standard of entire fairness as opposed to the more deferential business judgment standard."[36]

In *Emerald Partners v. Berlin*,[37] we noted that "[w]hen the standard of review is entire fairness, *ab initio*, director defendants can move for summary judgment on either the issue of entire fairness or the issue of burden shifting."[38] In this case, the Defendants filed a summary judgment motion, arguing that the Special Committee process shifted the burden of persuasion under the preponderance standard to the Plaintiff. The Court of Chancery found the summary judgment record was insufficient to determine that question of burden shifting prior to trial.

Lynch and its progeny[39] set forth what is required of an independent committee for the defendants to obtain a burden shift. In this case, the Court of Chancery

---

30 [19] Weinberger v. UOP, Inc., 457 A.2d at 711.

31 [20] *Id.*

32 [21] *Id.* (citations omitted).

33 [22] *Kahn v. Lynch Commc'n Sys., Inc.*, 638 A.2d 1110 (Del.1994).

34 [23] *See id.* at 1117 (citation omitted).

35 [24] *Id.*

36 [25] *Kahn v. Tremont Corp.*, 694 A.2d at 428 (citation omitted).

37 [26] *Emerald Partners v. Berlin*, 787 A.2d 85 (Del.2001).

38 [27] *Id.* at 98–99.

39 [28] *See Emerald Partners v. Berlin*, 726 A.2d 1215, 1222–23 (Del.1999) (describing that the special committee must exert "real bargaining power" in order for defendants to obtain a burden shift); *see also Beam v. Stewart*, 845 A.2d 1040, 1055 n. 45 (Del.2004) (noting that the test articulated in *Tremont* requires a determination as to whether the committee members "*in fact*" functioned independently (citing *Kahn v. Tremont Corp.*, 694 A.2d 422, 429–30 (Del.1997)).

recognized that, in *Kahn v. Tremont Corp.*,[40] this Court held that "[t]o obtain the benefit of a burden shifting, the controlling shareholder must do more than establish a perfunctory special committee of outside directors."[41] Rather, the special committee must "function in a manner which indicates that the controlling shareholder did not dictate the terms of the transaction and that the committee exercised real bargaining power 'at an arms-length.' "[42] In this case, the Court of Chancery properly concluded that:

> A close look at *Tremont* suggests that the [burden shifting] inquiry must focus on how the special committee actually negotiated the deal — was it "well functioning"[43] — rather than just how the committee was set up. The test, therefore, seems to contemplate a look back at the substance, and efficacy, of the special committee's negotiations, rather than just a look at the composition and mandate of the special committee.[44]

The Court of Chancery expressed its concern about the practical implications of such a factually intensive burden shifting inquiry because it is "deeply enmeshed" in the ultimate entire fairness analysis.

> Subsuming within the burden shift analysis questions of whether the special committee was substantively effective in its negotiations with the controlling stockholder — questions fraught with factual complexity — will, absent unique circumstances, guarantee that the burden shift will rarely be determinable on the basis of the pretrial record alone.[45] If we take seriously the notion, as I do, that a standard of review is meant to serve as the framework through which the court evaluates the parties' evidence and trial testimony in reaching a decision, and, as important, the framework through which the litigants determine how best to prepare their cases for trial,[46] it is problematic to adopt an analytical approach whereby the burden allocation can only be determined in a post-trial opinion, after all the evidence and all the arguments have been presented to the court.

We agree with these thoughtful comments. However, the general inability to decide burden shifting prior to trial is directly related to the reason why entire fairness remains the applicable standard of review even when an independent committee is utilized, *i.e.*, "because the underlying factors which raise the specter

---

[40] [29] *Kahn v. Tremont Corp.*, 694 A.2d 422 (Del.1997).

[41] [30] *Id.* at 429 (citation omitted).

[42] [31] *Id.* (citation omitted).

[43] [32] *Id.* at 428.

[44] [33] *Accord Kahn v. Lynch Commc'n Sys., Inc.*, 638 A.2d at 1121 ("[U]nless the controlling or dominating shareholder can demonstrate that it has not only formed an independent committee but also replicated a process 'as though each of the contending parties had in fact exerted its bargaining power at arm's length,' the burden of proving entire fairness will not shift." (citing *Weinberger v. UOP, Inc.*, 457 A.2d 701, 709–10 n. 7 (Del.1983)).

[45] [34] *Cf. In re Cysive, Inc. S'holders Litig.*, 836 A.2d 531, 549 (Del. Ch.2003).

[46] [35] *See* William T. Allen et al., *Function Over Form: A Reassessment of Standards of Review in Delaware Corporation Law*, 56 Bus. L. 1287, 1303–04 n. 63 (2001) (noting the practical problems litigants face when the burden of proof they are forced to bear is not made clear until after the trial); *cf. In re Cysive, Inc. S'holders Litig.*, 836 A.2d at 549.

of impropriety can never be completely eradicated and still require careful judicial scrutiny."[47]

This case is a perfect example. The Court of Chancery could not decide whether to shift the burden based upon the pretrial record. After hearing all of the evidence presented at trial, the Court of Chancery found that, although the independence of the Special Committee was not challenged, "from inception, the Special Committee fell victim to a controlled mindset and allowed Grupo Mexico to dictate the terms and structure of the merger." The Court of Chancery concluded that "although the Special Committee members were competent businessmen and may have had the best of intentions, they allowed themselves to be hemmed in by the controlling stockholder's demands."

We recognize that there are practical problems for litigants when the issue of burden shifting is not decided until after the trial.[48] For example, "in order to prove that a burden shift occurred because of an effective special committee, the defendants must present evidence of a fair process. Because they must present this evidence affirmatively, they have to act like they have the burden of persuasion throughout the entire trial court process."[49] That is exactly what happened in this case.

Delaware has long adhered to the principle that the controlling shareholders have the burden of proving an interested transaction was entirely fair.[50] However, in order to encourage the use of procedural devices that foster fair pricing, such as special committees and minority stockholder approval conditions, this Court has provided transactional proponents with what has been described as a "*modest procedural benefit* — the shifting of the burden of persuasion on the ultimate issue of entire fairness to the plaintiffs — if the transaction proponents proved, in a factually intensive way, that the procedural devices had, in fact, operated with integrity."[51] We emphasize that in *Cox*, the procedural benefit of burden shifting was characterized as "modest."

Once again, in this case, the Court of Chancery expressed uncertainty about whether "there is much, if any, practical implication of a burden shift." According to the Court of Chancery, "[t]he practical effect of the *Lynch* doctrine's burden shift is slight. One reason why this is so is that shifting the burden of persuasion under a preponderance standard is not a major move, if one assumes . . . that the outcome of very few cases hinges on what happens if . . . the evidence is in equipoise."[52]

---

[47] [36] *Kahn v. Tremont Corp.*, 694 A.2d at 428 (citing *Weinberger v. UOP, Inc.*, 457 A.2d at 710). *See also In re Cox Commc'ns, Inc. S'holders Litig.*, 879 A.2d 604, 617 (Del. Ch.2005) ("All in all, it is perhaps fairest and more sensible to read *Lynch* as being premised on a sincere concern that mergers with controlling stockholders involve an extraordinary potential for the exploitation by powerful insiders of their informational advantages and their voting clout.").

[48] [37] William T. Allen et al., Function Over Form: A Reassessment of Standards of Review in Delaware Corporation Law, 56 Bus. L. 1287, 1303–04 n. 63 (2001).

[49] [38] *In re Cysive, Inc. S'holders Litig.*, 836 A.2d at 549.

[50] [39] *Kahn v. Tremont Corp.*, 694 A.2d at 428–29.

[51] [40] *In re Cox Commc'ns, Inc. S'holders Litig.*, 879 A.2d at 617 (emphasis added).

[52] [41] In re Cysive, Inc. S'holders Litig., 836 A.2d at 548.

In its post-trial opinion, the Court of Chancery found that the burden of persuasion remained with the Defendants, because the Special Committee was not "well functioning."[53] The trial judge also found, "however, that this determination matters little because I am not stuck in equipoise about the issue of fairness. Regardless of who bears the burden, I conclude that the Merger was unfair to Southern Peru and its stockholders."

Nothing in the record reflects that a different outcome would have resulted if either the burden of proof had been shifted to the Plaintiff, or the Defendants had been advised prior to trial that the burden had not shifted. The record reflects that, by agreement of the parties, each witness other than the Plaintiff's expert was called in direct examination by the Defendants, and then was cross-examined by the Plaintiff. The Defendants have not identified any decision they might have made differently, if they had been advised prior to trial that the burden of proof had not shifted.

The Court of Chancery concluded that this is not a case where the evidence of fairness or unfairness stood in equipoise. It found that the evidence of unfairness was so overwhelming that the question of who had the burden of proof at trial was irrelevant to the outcome. That determination is supported by the record. The Court of Chancery committed no error by not allocating the burden of proof before trial, in accordance with our prior precedents. In the absence of a renewed request by the Defendants during trial that the burden be shifted to the Plaintiff, the burden of proving entire fairness remained with the Defendants throughout the trial.[54] The record reflects that is how the trial in this case was conducted.

Nevertheless, we recognize that the purpose of providing defendants with the opportunity to seek a burden shift is not only to encourage the use of special committees,[55] but also to provide a reliable pretrial guide for the parties regarding who has the burden of persuasion.[56] Therefore, which party bears the burden of proof must be determined, if possible, before the trial begins. The Court of Chancery has noted that, in the interest of having certainty, "it is unsurprising that few defendants have sought a pretrial hearing to determine who bears the burden of persuasion on fairness" given "the factually intense nature of the burden-shifting inquiry" and the "modest benefit" gained from the shift.[57]

The failure to shift the burden is not outcome determinative under the entire

---

[53] [42] *Kahn v. Tremont Corp.*, 694 A.2d at 428.

[54] [43] *Emerald Partners v. Berlin*, 787 A.2d 85, 99 (Del.2001).

[55] [44] *See, e.g., In re Cysive, Inc. S'holders Litig.*, 836 A.2d at 548 ("Because these devices are thought, however, to be useful and to incline transactions towards fairness, the *Lynch* doctrine encourages them by giving defendants the benefits of a burden shift if either one of the devices is employed.").

[56] [45] *See* William T. Allen et al., *Function Over Form: A Reassessment of Standards of Review in Delaware Corporation Law*, 56 Bus. L. 1287, 1297 (2001) (explaining that standards of review should be functional, in that they should serve as a "useful tool that aids the court in deciding the fiduciary duty issue" rather than merely "signal the result or outcome").

[57] [46] *See In re Cysive, Inc. S'holders Litig.*, 836 A.2d at 549 (noting that it is inefficient for defendants to seek a pretrial ruling on the burden-shift unless the discovery process has generated a sufficient factual record to make such a determination).

fairness standard of review. We have concluded that, because the only "modest" effect of the burden shift is to make the plaintiff prove unfairness under a preponderance of the evidence standard, the benefits of clarity in terms of trial presentation outweigh the costs of continuing to decide either during or after trial whether the burden has shifted. Accordingly, we hold prospectively that, if the record does not permit a pretrial determination that the defendants are entitled to a burden shift, the burden of persuasion will remain with the defendants throughout the trial to demonstrate the entire fairness of the interested transaction.

The Defendants argue that if the Court of Chancery rarely determines the issue of burden shifting on the basis of a pretrial record, corporations will be dissuaded from forming special committees of independent directors and from seeking approval of an interested transaction by an informed vote of a majority of the minority shareholders. That argument underestimates the importance of either or both actions to the process component — fair dealing — of the entire fairness standard. This Court has repeatedly held that any board process is materially enhanced when the decision is attributable to independent directors.[58] Accordingly, judicial review for entire fairness of how the transaction was structured, negotiated, disclosed to the directors, and approved by the directors will be significantly influenced by the work product of a properly functioning special committee of independent directors.[59] Similarly, the issue of how stockholder approval was obtained will be significantly influenced by the affirmative vote of a majority of the minority stockholders.[60]

A fair process usually results in a fair price. Therefore, the proponents of an interested transaction will continue to be incentivized to put a fair dealing process in place that promotes judicial confidence in the entire fairness of the transaction price. Accordingly, we have no doubt that the effective use of a properly functioning special committee of independent directors and the informed conditional approval of a majority of minority stockholders will continue to be integral parts of the best practices that are used to establish a fair dealing process.

UNFAIR DEALING PRODUCES UNFAIR PRICE

Although the entire fairness standard has two components, the entire fairness analysis is "not a bifurcated one as between fair dealing and fair price. All aspects of the issue must be examined as a whole since the question is one of entire fairness."[61] In a non-fraudulent transaction, "price may be the preponderant consideration outweighing other features of the merger."[62] Evidence of fair dealing has significant probative value to demonstrate the fairness of the price obtained. The paramount consideration, however, is whether the price was a fair one.[63]

---

[58] [47] *See, e.g., Unocal Corp. v. Mesa Petroleum Co.*, 493 A.2d 946, 955 (Del.1985); Weinberger v. UOP, Inc., 457 A.2d at 709 n. 7.

[59] [48] *Weinberger v. UOP, Inc.*, 457 A.2d at 709 n. 7.

[60] [49] *Id.* at 712, 714.

[61] [50] *Id.* at 711.

[62] [51] *Id.*

[63] [52] *See, e.g., Valeant Pharms. Int'l v. Jerney*, 921 A.2d 732, 746 (Del. Ch. 2007).

The Court of Chancery found that the process by which the Merger was negotiated and approved was not fair and did not result in the payment of a fair price. Because the issues relating to fair dealing and fair price were so intertwined, the Court of Chancery did not separate its analysis, but rather treated them together in an integrated examination. That approach is consistent with the inherent non-bifurcated nature of the entire fairness standard of review.[64]

The independence of the members of the Special Committee was not challenged by the Plaintiff. The Court of Chancery found that the Special Committee members were competent, well-qualified individuals with business experience. The Court of Chancery also found that the Special Committee was "given the resources to hire outside advisors, and it hired not only respected, top tier of the market financial and legal counsel, but also a mining consultant and Mexican counsel." Nevertheless, the Court of Chancery found that, although the Special Committee members had their "hands . . . on the oars[,]" the boat went "if anywhere, backward[.]"

The Special Committee began its work with a narrow mandate, to "evaluate a transaction suggested by the majority stockholder." The Court of Chancery found that "the Special Committee members' understanding of their mandate . . . evidenced their lack of certainty about whether the Special Committee could do more than just evaluate the Merger." The Court of Chancery concluded that, although the Special Committee went beyond its limited mandate and engaged in negotiations, "its approach to negotiations was stilted and influenced by its uncertainty about whether it was actually empowered to negotiate."

Accordingly, the Court of Chancery determined that "from inception, the Special Committee fell victim to a controlled mindset and allowed Grupo Mexico to dictate the terms and structure of the Merger." The Special Committee did not ask for an expansion of its mandate to look at alternatives. Instead, the Court of Chancery found that the Special Committee "accepted that only one type of transaction was on the table, a purchase of Minera by Southern Peru."

In its post-trial opinion, the Court of Chancery stated that this "acceptance" influenced the ultimate determination of unfairness, because "it took off the table other options that would have generated a real market check and also deprived the Special Committee of negotiating leverage to extract better terms." The Court of Chancery summarized these dynamics as follows:

> In sum, although the Special Committee members were competent businessmen and may have had the best of intentions, they allowed themselves to be hemmed in by the controlling stockholder's demands. Throughout the negotiation process, the Special Committee's and Goldman's focus was on finding a way to get the terms of the Merger structure proposed by Grupo Mexico to make sense, rather than aggressively testing the assumption that the Merger was a good idea in the first place.

Goldman made its first presentation to the Special Committee on June 11, 2004. Goldman's conclusions were summarized in an "Illustrative Give/Get Analysis." The Court of Chancery found this analysis "made patent the stark disparity between

---

[64] [53] *Weinberger v. UOP, Inc.*, 457 A.2d at 711.

Grupo Mexico's asking price and Goldman's valuation of Minera: Southern Peru would 'give' stock with a market price of $3.1 billion to Grupo Mexico and would 'get' in return an asset worth no more than $1.7 billion."

According to the Court of Chancery, the Special Committee's controlled mindset was illustrated by what happened after Goldman's initial analysis could not value the "get" — Minera — anywhere near Grupo Mexico's asking price, the "give":

> From a negotiating perspective, that should have signaled that a strong response to Grupo Mexico was necessary and incited some effort to broaden, not narrow, the lens. Instead, Goldman and the Special Committee went to strenuous lengths to equalize the values of Southern Peru and Minera. The onus should have been on Grupo Mexico to prove Minera was worth $3.1 billion, but instead of pushing back on Grupo Mexico's analysis, the Special Committee and Goldman devalued Southern Peru and topped up the value of Minera. The actions of the Special Committee and Goldman undermine the defendants' argument that the process leading up to the Merger was fair and lend credence to the plaintiff's contention that the process leading up to the Merger was an exercise in rationalization.

The Court of Chancery found that, following Goldman's first presentation, the Special Committee abandoned a focus on whether Southern Peru would get $3.1 billion in value in an exchange. Instead, the Special Committee moved to a "relative valuation" methodology that involved comparing the values of Southern Peru and Minera. On June 23, 2004, Goldman advised the Special Committee that Southern Peru's DCF value was $2.06 billion and, thus, approximately $1.1 billion below Southern Peru's actual NYSE market price at that time.

The Court of Chancery was troubled by the fact that the Special Committee did not use this valuation gap to question the relative valuation methodology. Instead, the Special Committee was "comforted" by the analysis, which allowed them to conclude that DCF value of Southern Peru's stock (the "give") was not really worth its market value of $3.1 billion. The Court of Chancery found that:

> A reasonable special committee would not have taken the results of those analyses by Goldman and blithely moved on to relative valuation, without any continuing and relentless focus on the actual give-get involved in real cash terms. But, this Special Committee was in the altered state of a controlled mindset. Instead of pushing Grupo Mexico into the range suggested by Goldman's analysis of Minera's fundamental value, the Special Committee went backwards to accommodate Grupo Mexico's asking price — an asking price *that never really changed.*

The Court of Chancery concluded "[a] reasonable third-party buyer free from a controlled mindset would not have ignored a fundamental economic fact that is not in dispute here — in 2004, Southern Peru stock could have been sold for [the] price at which it was trading on the New York Stock Exchange."

In this appeal, the Defendants contend that the Court of Chancery did not understand Goldman's analysis and rejected their relative valuation of Minera without an evidentiary basis. According to the Defendants, a relative valuation analysis is the appropriate way to perform an accurate comparison of the value of

Southern Peru, a publicly-traded company, and Minera, a private company. In fact, the Defendants continue to argue that relative valuation is the only way to perform an "apples-to-apples" comparison of Southern Peru and Minera.

Moreover, the Defendants assert that Goldman and the Special Committee did actually believe that Southern Peru's market price accurately reflected the company's value. According to the Defendants, however, there were certain assumptions reflected in Southern Peru's market price that were not reflected in its DCF value, *i.e.*, the market's view of future copper price increases. Therefore, the Defendants submit that:

> If the DCF analysis was missing some element of value for [Southern Peru], it would also miss that very same element of value for Minera. In short, at the time that Goldman was evaluating Minera, its analysis of [Southern Peru] demonstrated that mining companies were trading at a premium to their DCF values. The relative valuation method allowed Goldman to account for this information in its analysis and value Minera fairly.

Accordingly, the Defendants argue that the Court of Chancery failed to recognize that the difference between Southern Peru's DCF and market values also implied a difference between Minera's DCF value and its market value.

The Defendants take umbrage at the Court of Chancery's statement that "the relative valuation technique is not alchemy that turns a sub-optimal deal into a fair one." The Court of Chancery's critical comments regarding a relative value methodology were simply a continuation of its criticism about how the Special Committee operated. The record indicates that the Special Committee's controlled mindset was reflected in its assignments to Goldman. According to the Court of Chancery, "Goldman appears to have helped its client rationalize the one strategic option available within the controlled mindset that pervaded the Special Committee's process."

The Defendants continue to argue that the Court of Chancery would have understood that "relative valuation" was the "appropriate way" to compare the values of Southern Peru and Minera if a Goldman witness (Del Favero) had testified at trial. As noted earlier, that argument is inconsistent with the Defendants' post-trial assertion that the record was replete with evidence of what Goldman did (a relative valuation analysis) and why that was done. That argument also disregards the trial testimony of the Defendants' expert witness, Professor Schwartz, who used the same relative valuation methodology as Goldman.

Prior to trial, the Defendants represented that Professor Schwartz would be called at trial to "explain that the most reliable way to compare the value of [Southern Peru] and Minera for purposes of the Merger was to conduct a relative valuation." In their pretrial proffer, the Defendants also represented that Professor Schwartz's testimony would demonstrate that "based on relative valuations of Minera and [Southern Peru] using a reasonable range of copper prices . . . the results uniformly show that the Merger was fair to [Southern Peru] and its stockholders."

At trial, Professor Schwartz attributed the difference between Southern Peru's

DCF value and its market value to the fact that the market was valuing Southern Peru's stock "at an implied copper price of $1.30." Professor Schwartz testified, "if I use $1.30, it gives me the market price of [Southern Peru] and it gives me a market price of Minera Mexico which still makes the transaction fair." In other words, it was fair to "give" Grupo Mexico $3.75 billion of Southern Peru stock because Minera's DCF value, using an assumed long-term copper price of $1.30, implied a "get" of more than $3.7 billion.

The Court of Chancery found that Professor Schwartz's conclusion that the market was assuming a long-term copper price of $1.30 in valuing Southern Peru was based entirely on post-hoc speculation, because there was no credible evidence in the record that anyone at the time of the Merger contemplated a $1.30 long-term copper price. In fact, Southern Peru's own public filings referenced $0.90 per pound as the appropriate long-term copper price. The Court of Chancery summarized its findings as follows:

> Thus, Schwartz's conclusion that the market was assuming a long-term copper price of $1.30 in valuing Southern Peru appears to be based entirely on post-hoc speculation. Put simply, there is no credible evidence of the Special Committee, in the heat of battle, believing that the long-term copper price was actually $1.30 per pound but using $0.90 instead to give Southern Peru an advantage in the negotiation process.

The Court of Chancery also noted that Professor Schwartz did not produce a standalone equity value for Minera that justified issuing shares of Southern Peru stock worth $3.1 billion at the time the Merger Agreement was signed.

The record reflects that the Court of Chancery did understand the Defendants' argument and that its rejection of the Defendants' "relative valuation" of Minera was the result of an orderly and logical deductive reasoning process that is supported by the record. The Court of Chancery acknowledged that relative valuation is a valid valuation methodology. It also recognized, however, that since "relative valuation" is a comparison of the DCF values of Minera and Southern Peru, the result is only as reliable as the input data used for each company. The record reflects that the Court of Chancery carefully explained its factual findings that the data inputs Goldman and Professor Schwartz used for Southern Peru in the Defendants' relative valuation model for Minera were unreliable.

The Court of Chancery weighed the evidence presented at trial and set forth in detail why it was not persuaded that "the Special Committee relied on truly equal inputs for its analyses of the two companies." The Court of Chancery found that "Goldman and the Special Committee went to strenuous lengths to equalize the value of Southern Peru and Minera." In particular, the Court of Chancery found that "when performing the relative valuation analysis, the cash flows for Minera were optimized to make Minera an attractive acquisition target, but no such dressing up was done for Southern Peru."

The Court of Chancery also noted that Goldman never advised the Special Committee that Minera was worth $3.1 billion, or that Minera could be acquired at, or would trade at, a premium to its DCF value if it were a public company. Nevertheless, the Court of Chancery found "the Special Committee did not respond to its intuition that Southern Peru was overvalued in a way consistent with its fiduciary duties or the way that a third-party buyer would have." Accordingly, the Court of Chancery concluded:

> The Special Committee's cramped perspective resulted in a strange deal dynamic, in which a majority stockholder kept its eye on the ball — actual value benchmarked to cash — and a Special Committee lost sight of market reality in an attempt to rationalize doing a deal of the kind the majority stockholder proposed. After this game of controlled mindset twister and the contortions it involved, the Special Committee agreed to give away over $3 billion worth of actual cash value in exchange for something worth demonstrably less, and to do so on terms that by consummation made the value gap even worse, without using any of its contractual leverage to stop the deal or renegotiate its terms. Because the deal was unfair, the defendants breached their fiduciary duty of loyalty.

Entire fairness is a standard by which the Court of Chancery must carefully analyze the factual circumstances, apply a disciplined balancing test to its findings, and articulate the bases upon which it decides the ultimate question of entire fairness.[65] The record reflects that the Court of Chancery applied a "disciplined balancing test," taking into account all relevant factors.[66] The Court of Chancery considered the issues of fair dealing and fair price in a comprehensive and complete manner. The Court of Chancery found the process by which the Merger was negotiated and approved constituted unfair dealing and that resulted in the payment of an unfair price.

The Court of Chancery's post-trial determination of entire fairness must be accorded substantial deference on appeal.[67] The Court of Chancery's factual findings are supported by the record and its conclusions are the product of an orderly and logical deductive reasoning process.[68] Accordingly, the Court of Chancery's judgment, that the Merger consideration was *not* entirely fair, is affirmed.[69]

DAMAGE AWARD PROPER

In the Court of Chancery, the Plaintiff sought an equitable remedy that cancelled or required the Defendants to return to Southern Peru the shares that Southern Peru issued in excess of Minera's fair value. In the alternative, the Plaintiff asked for rescissory damages in the amount of the then present market value of the excess number of shares that Grupo Mexico held as a result of Southern Peru paying an unfair price in the Merger.

---

65 [54] *Cinerama, Inc. v. Technicolor, Inc.*, 663 A.2d 1156, 1179 (Del.1994); *Nixon v. Blackwell*, 626 A.2d 1366, 1373, 1378 (Del.1993); *accord Kahn v. Lynch Commc'n Sys., Inc.*, 638 A.2d at 1120.

66 [55] *See Nixon v. Blackwell*, 626 A.2d at 1373.

67 [56] *Cinerama, Inc. v. Technicolor, Inc.*, 663 A.2d at 1180; *Rosenblatt v. Getty Oil Co.*, 493 A.2d at 937.

68 [57] *Cinerama, Inc. v. Technicolor, Inc.*, 663 A.2d at 1180.

69 [58] *Id.*

In the Court of Chancery and on appeal, the Defendants argue that no damages are due because the Merger consideration was more than fair. In support of that argument, the Defendants rely on the fact that Southern Peru stockholders should be grateful, because the market value of Southern Peru's stock continued on a generally upward trajectory in the years after the Merger. Alternatively, the Defendants argue that any damage award should be at most a fraction of the amount sought by the Plaintiff, and, in particular, that the Plaintiff has waived the right to seek rescissory damages because of "his lethargic approach to litigating the case."

The Court of Chancery rejected the Defendants' argument that the post-Merger performance of Southern Peru's stock eliminates the need for damages. It noted that the Defendants did not "present a reliable event study about the market's reaction to the Merger, and there is evidence that the market did not view the Merger as fair in spite of material gaps in disclosure about the fairness of the Merger." The trial judge was of the opinion that a "transaction like the Merger can be unfair, in the sense that it is below what a real arms-length deal would have been priced at, while not tanking a strong company with sound fundamentals in a rising market, such as the one in which Southern Peru was a participant. That remains my firm sense here. . . ." The Court of Chancery's decision to award some amount of damages is supported by the record and the product of a logical deductive reasoning process.

Nevertheless, the Court of Chancery did agree with the Defendants' argument that the Plaintiff's delay in litigating the case rendered it inequitable to use a rescission-based approach in awarding damages. The Court of Chancery reached that determination because "[r]escissory damages are the economic equivalent of rescission and[,] therefore[,] if rescission itself is unwarranted because of the plaintiff's delay, so are rescissory damages." Instead of entering a rescission-based remedy, the Court of Chancery decided to craft a damage award, as explained below:

> [The award] approximates the difference between the price that the Special Committee would have approved had the Merger been entirely fair (i.e., absent a breach of fiduciary duties) and the price that the Special Committee actually agreed to pay. In other words, I will take the difference between this fair price and the market value of 67.2 million shares of Southern Peru stock as of the Merger date. That difference, divided by the average closing price of Southern Peru stock in the 20 trading days preceding the issuance of this opinion, will determine the number of shares that the defendants must return to Southern Peru. Furthermore, because of the plaintiff's delay, I will only grant simple interest on that amount, calculated at the statutory rate since the date of the Merger.

After determining the nature of the damage award, the Court of Chancery determined the appropriate valuation for the price that the Special Committee *should* have paid. To calculate a fair price for remedy purposes, the Court of Chancery balanced three separate values. The first value was a standalone DCF value of Minera. Using defendant-friendly modifications to the Plaintiff's expert's DCF valuation, the Court of Chancery calculated that a standalone equity value for

Minera as of October 21, 2004 was $2.452 billion. The second value was the market value of the Special Committee's 52 million share counteroffer made in July 2004, "which was sized based on months of due diligence by Goldman about Minera's standalone value, calculated as of the date on which the Special Committee approved the Merger." Because Grupo Mexico wanted a dollar value of stock, the Court of Chancery fixed the value at what 52 million Southern Peru shares were worth as of October 21, 2004, the date on which the Special Committee approved the Merger, at $2.388 billion, giving Minera credit for the price growth to that date. The third value was the equity value of Minera derived from a comparable companies analysis using the companies identified by Goldman. Using the median premium for merger transactions in 2004, calculated by Mergerstat to be 23.4%, and applying that premium to the value derived from the Court of Chancery's comparable companies analysis yielded a value of $2.45 billion.

The Court of Chancery gave those three separate values equal weight in its damages equation: (($2.452 billion+$2.388 billion+$2.45 billion)/3). The result was a value of $2.43 billion. It then made an adjustment to reflect the fact that Southern Peru bought 99.15%, not 100%, of Minera, which yielded a value of $2.409 billion. The value of 67.2 million Southern Peru shares as of the Merger Date was $3.756 billion.[70] Therefore, the base damage award by the Court of Chancery amounted to $1.347 billion.[71] The Court of Chancery then added interest from the Merger Date, at the statutory rate, without compounding and with that interest to run until time of the judgment and until payment.

The Court of Chancery stated that Grupo Mexico could satisfy the judgment by agreeing to return to Southern Peru such number of its shares as are necessary to satisfy this remedy. The Court of Chancery also ruled that any attorneys' fees would be paid out of the award.

The Defendants' first objection to the Court of Chancery's calculation of damages is that its methodology included the Special Committee's counteroffer of July 2004 as a measure of the true value of Minera. The Defendants assert that the counteroffer was "based only on Goldman's preliminary analyses of the companies before the completion of due diligence. And there was no evidence this was anything other than what it appears to be — a negotiating position."

The Court of Chancery explained its reason for including the counteroffer in its determination of damages, as follows:

> In fact, you know, the formula I used, one of the things that I did to be conservative was actually to use a bargaining position of the special committee. And I used it not because I thought it was an aggressive bargaining position of the special committee, but to give the special committee and its advisors some credit for thinking. It was one of the few indications in the record of something that they thought was actually a responsible value.

---

[70] [62] $55.89 closing price x 67,200,000 = $3,755,808,000.

[71] [63] $3.756 billion - $2.409 billion = $1.347 billion.

> And so it was actually not put in there in any way to inflate. It was actually to give some credit to the special committee. If I had thought that it was an absurd ask, I would have never used it. I didn't think it was any, really, aggressive bargaining move. I didn't actually see any aggressive bargaining moves by the special committee. I saw some innovative valuation moves, but I didn't see any aggressive bargaining moves.

The record reflects that the value of Minera pursuant to the counteroffer ($2.388 billion) was very close to the other two values used by the Court of Chancery ($2.452 billion and $2.45 billion). The Court of Chancery properly exercised its discretion — for the reasons it stated — by including the Special Committee's counteroffer as one of the component parts in its calculation of damages. Therefore, the Defendants' argument to the contrary is without merit.

The Defendants also argue that the Court of Chancery "essentially became its own expert witness regarding damages by basing its valuation, at least in part, on its own computer models." In support of that argument, the Defendants rely upon the following statement by the trial judge during oral argument on the fee award: "I'm not going to disclose everything that we got on our computer system, but I can tell you that there are very credible remedial approaches in this case that would have resulted in a much higher award." The Defendants submit that "[i]n the absence of proof from [the] Plaintiff, this speculation and outside-the-record financial modeling is impermissible."

In making a decision on damages, or any other matter, the trial court must set forth its reasons. This provides the parties with a record basis to challenge the decision. It also enables a reviewing court to properly discharge its appellate function.

In this case, the Court of Chancery explained the reasons for its calculation of damages with meticulous detail. That complete transparency of its actual deliberative process provided the Defendants with a comprehensive record to use in challenging the Court of Chancery's damage award on appeal and for this Court to review. Accordingly, any remedial approaches that the Court of Chancery may have considered and rejected are irrelevant.

The Court of Chancery has the historic power "to grant such . . . relief as the facts of a particular case may dictate."[72] Both parties agree that an award of damages by the Court of Chancery after trial in an entire fairness proceeding is reviewed on appeal for abuse of discretion.[73] It is also undisputed that the Court of Chancery has greater discretion when making an award of damages in an action for breach of duty of loyalty than it would when assessing fair value in an appraisal action.[74]

In this case, the Court of Chancery awarded damages based on the difference in

---

[72] [64] *Weinberger v. UOP, Inc.*, 457 A.2d at 714; *see also Glanding v. Industrial Trust Co.*, 45 A.2d 553, 555 (Del.1945) ("[T]he Court of Chancery of the State of Delaware inherited its equity jurisdiction from the English Courts."); 1 Victor B. Woolley, *Woolley on Delaware Practice* § 56 (1906).

[73] [65] *Int'l Telecharge, Inc. v. Bomarko, Inc.*, 766 A.2d 437, 440 (Del. 2000).

[74] [66] *Id.* at 441.

value between what was paid (the "give") and the value of what was received (the "get"). In addition to an actual award of monetary relief, the Court of Chancery had the authority to grant pre- and post-judgment interest, and to determine the form of that interest. The record reflects that the Court of Chancery properly exercised its broad historic discretionary powers in fashioning a remedy and making its award of damages. Therefore, the Court of Chancery's judgment awarding damages is affirmed.

ATTORNEYS' FEE AWARD

The Plaintiff petitioned for attorneys' fees and expenses representing 22.5% of the recovery plus post-judgment interest. The Court of Chancery awarded 15% of the $2.031 billion judgment, or $304,742,604.45, plus post-judgment interest until the attorneys' fee and expense award is satisfied ("Fee Award").

* * *

The record supports its factual findings and its well-reasoned decision that a reasonable attorneys' fee is 15% of the benefit created. Accordingly, we hold that the Fee Award was a proper exercise of the Court of Chancery's broad discretion . . . .

CONCLUSION

The judgment of the Court of Chancery, awarding more than $2 billion in damages and more than $304 million in attorneys' fees, is affirmed.

Berger, Justice, concurring and dissenting:

I concur in the majority's decision on the merits, but I would find that the trial court did not properly apply the law when it awarded attorneys' fees, and respectfully dissent on that issue.

The majority finds no abuse of discretion in the trial court's decision to award more than $304 million in attorneys' fees. The majority says that the trial court applied the settled standards set forth in *Sugarland Industries, Inc. v. Thomas*,[75] and that this Court may not substitute its notions of what is right for those of the trial court. But the trial court did not apply *Sugarland*, it applied its own world views on incentives, bankers' compensation, and envy.

To be sure, the trial court recited the *Sugarland* standards. Its analysis, however, focused on the perceived need to incentivize plaintiffs' lawyers to take cases to trial. The trial court hypothesized that a stockholder plaintiff would be happy with a lawyer who says, "If you get really rich because of me, I want to get rich, too." Then, the trial court talked about how others get big payouts without comment, but that lawyers are not viewed the same way:

> [T]here's an idea that when a lawyer or law firms are going to get a big payment, that there's something somehow wrong about that, just because

---

[75] [133] *Sugarland Indus., Inc. v. Thomas*, 420 A.2d 142 (Del.1980).

> it's a lawyer. I'm sorry, but investment banks have hit it big. . . . They've hit it big many times. And to me, envy is not an appropriate motivation to take into account when you set an attorney fee.

The trial court opined that a declining percentage for "mega" cases would not create a healthy incentive system, and that the trial court would not embrace such an approach. Rather, the trial court repeatedly pointed out that "plenty of market participants make big fees when their clients win," and that if this were a hedge fund manager or an investment bank, the fee would be okay. In sum, the trial court said that the fundamental test for reasonableness is whether the fee is setting a good incentive, and that the only basis for reducing the fee would be envy. That is not a decision based on [precedent].

SCHULWOLF v. CERRO CORP.

New York Supreme Court, New York County
86 Misc. 2d 292 (1976)

Arnold L. Fein, Justice

This is an application, by order to show cause dated February 18, 1976, returnable February 20, 1976 for a temporary injunction enjoining and restraining defendants from directly or indirectly effectuating a merger between defendant Cerro Corporation (Cerro) a New York corporation and defendant Cerro-Marmon Corporation (Cerro-Marmon) a Delaware corporation, pursuant to a Cerro proxy statement dated January 26, 1976, and from doing any act in aid or furtherance of the merger and from holding any stockholders' meetings relating to the merger including the special meeting to approve such merger noticed for February 24, 1976.

Plaintiffs, two of approximately 25,000 shareholders of Cerro, bring this action on behalf of themselves and other shareholders of Cerro similarly situated for a permanent injunction enjoining such merger and for related relief.

Defendant, The Marmon Group, Inc. (Michigan), (Marmon), a Delaware corporation, is a wholly owned subsidiary of GL Corporation (GL), a Delaware corporation, all of the stock of which is owned by defendants Jay A. Pritzker (Jay), Robert A. Pritzker (Robert) and their families. Jay is chairman of the boards of Cerro, Marmon and GL. Robert is president and a director of Cerro, Marmon and GL. The other individual defendants are directors of Cerro. Defendant Cerro-Marmon Corporation (Cerro-Marmon) is a Delaware corporation. Cerro has outstanding approximately 8,000,000 shares of common stock. In early 1974, GL acquired 813,000 shares of Cerro common stock in private and open market purchases. In mid 1974, pursuant to a tender offer to purchase 1,500,000 shares of Cerro common stock at $19 per share, GL purchased 2,773,197 shares of Cerro stock from public stockholders. It then transferred to Marmon all of its holdings of Cerro common stock, totalling 3,586,297 shares, amounting to 45% of all outstanding Cerro common stock. The remaining 55% of Cerro common stock is held by public stockholders including plaintiffs. The purchase of the Cerro stock by GL was financed by borrowings of approximately $68,000,000.

As of January 15, 1976, Cerro, Marmon, Cerro-Marmon and GL entered into an

Exchange Agreement and Cerro-Marmon and Cerro entered into an Agreement and Plan of Merger. These agreements in material part provide for a merger of Cerro into Cerro-Marmon upon the following basis:

> (1) GL, wholly owned by the Pritzkers, will exchange all of the capital stock of Marmon for all of the common stock of Cerro-Marmon, having 82% of the voting rights;
>
> (2) Marmon, which owns 45% of the outstanding common stock of Cerro, will thus become a wholly owned subsidiary of Cerro-Marmon and the Pritzkers will control Cerro-Marmon;
>
> (3) The holders of the remaining 55% of Cerro common stock, being the public stockholders, including plaintiffs, will receive in exchange for each share of common stock held by them one share of Cerro-Marmon $1 per value preferred stock designated as $2.25 Cumulative Series A Preferred Stock, with an annual dividend preference of $2.25 per share and a redemption price and liquidation preference of $22 per share, subject to redemption over 14 years commencing in April 1981 from sinking fund payments, subject to restrictions now in force or to which Cerro- Marmon may become subject from time to time. Such preferred shares will have 18% of the voting rights of Cerro-Marmon, although they will not be entitled to a continuing participation in any possible growth in Cerro-Marmon's earnings or financial well-being, its so-called "residual equity."

Plainly, the arrangement, if approved, will give the Pritzkers control of Cerro-Marmon and all the benefits of its "residual equity."

The proposed transaction is described in careful detail in Cerro's Prospectus and Proxy statement, dated January 26, 1976, part of the notice of special meeting of Cerro stockholders called for February 24, 1976 to consider the merger.

It is undisputed that defendants have meticulously complied with the applicable statutory requirements of New York and Delaware. (New York Business Corporation Law Section 901 *et seq.*). Section 903 thereof, applicable to mergers, requires approval by a vote of 23 of all outstanding shares entitled to vote thereon. The Pritzkers have caused Marmon to agree to be present at the Cerro stockholders' meeting for quorum purposes but to vote its shares of Cerro common stock for the merger *only* if a majority of Cerro's publicly held shares of common stock voting on the merger vote in favor of it. Thus the Pritzkers will partly control the issue as to whether there is to be a merger, which they favor and from which they will reap a substantial benefit.

Does this fact entitle plaintiffs to a temporary injunction, which may be granted only if they have demonstrated a clear legal right to such relief upon undisputed facts, particularly where the relief sought will give them precisely the same relief they might ultimately be granted after a trial?

In essence plaintiffs' position is that they are entitled to injunctive relief, because the facts demonstrate they and other stockholders similarly situated will receive a lesser benefit or sustain a loss due to the merger and the Pritzkers will sustain a substantial benefit therefrom. Until very recently the law has been well settled, particularly in New York, that appraisal and payment is the exclusive remedy of dissenting minority shareholders in a merger, even where there is a "freeze out." However, there is recent authority indicating the emergence of a different rule, at least in cases where there is no clear showing of a proper corporate purpose. In *People v. Concord Fabrics*, 83 Misc. 2d 120, 371 N.Y.S.2d 550, *aff'd.*, 50 A.D.2d 787, 377 N.Y.S.2d 84, a merger was enjoined in a proceeding brought by the Attorney General under the Martin Act (General Business Law Art. 23-A, Section 352).

Concord Fabrics is unlike our case. There was concededly no corporate purpose other than the elimination of minority shareholders under exceedingly unfair terms amounting to a fraudulent practice. Concord was a private company until 1968 when it sold 300,000 common shares at $15 per share. In 1969, the controlling family sold 200,000 shares in a public offering at $20 per share. Listed on the American Stock Exchange, the stock reached a high of $25 per share in 1969. It fell to $1 in 1974, when the original control group, owning 68% of the stock, formed a private corporation to which they transferred their Concord stock. The court enjoined the proposed cash merger agreement which was premised on $3 per share to the public shareholders, who had no say in negotiating the merger agreement or its terms and no power to defeat the merger by vote. In essence, premised on the opinion of an investment banker of dubious independence, the insiders were forcing a private price of 85% below the price at which they had sold stock to the public six years earlier. Moreover, the merger had no other purpose than to give the insiders 100% control of a private corporation constituting the same business enterprise as existed prior to the merger. There was palpably no corporate purpose, and the entire history of the sale of the corporate securities smacked of fraud.

The absence of corporate purpose is manifest in all the other cases relied on by plaintiffs. In *Jutkowitz v. Bourns*, (Cal. Super. Ct., Los Angeles Co., 11/19/75), the opinion states: "Defendants explicitly state that the forced buy-out of the minority shareholders is the only purpose of the whole transaction." Similar are *Bryan v. Brock & Blevins Co., Inc.*, 490 F.2d 563 (5th Cir., 1974, *cert. denied*, 419 U.S. 844, 95 S. Ct. 77, 42 L. Ed. 2d 72), *Albright v. Bergendahl*, 391 F. Supp. 754 (D.C. Utah 1975) and *Berkowitz v. Power Mate Corporation*, 135 N.J. Super. 36, 342 A.2d 566. Moreover in *Berkowitz*, there was evidence of insider self dealing, reducing per share earnings so that the very low merger price appeared attractive.

. . . .

As these and other cases hold, there is no violation of the fiduciary duty owed by the dominant stockholders to the public stockholders if there is a proper corporate purpose for the merger and there has been neither fraud, self dealing nor price manipulation and the alternatives afforded to the public shareholders are a fair price fairly determined or the statutory right to an appraisal. This is particularly so where, as here, the public shareholders can control the issue by voting the merger down. There is no authority for the proposition, apparently contended for by plaintiffs, that no merger of a less than wholly owned subsidiary into its parent can occur, however advantageous to the public shareholders, unless all the public shareholders concur.

The complaint in paragraphs "Forty-Ninth" and "Fiftieth" practically concedes the corporate purposes, set out a pp. iii and 4 of the Proxy Statement and Prospectus:

> (a) to further combine the management and other resources of Cerro and Marmon, thereby allowing inter-company transactions between Cerro and Marmon which could be beneficial to both but which are presently restricted because of possible conflicts of interests and (b) to consolidate Cerro-Marmon and Marmon for financial reporting purposes and consolidate Cerro-Marmon with GL for tax purposes.

It is undisputed that Cerro and Marmon are engaged in related businesses of a substantial character so that combining their management and other resources and providing for inter-company transactions may well benefit both. These appear to be proper corporate business purposes warranting merger. That they will also benefit GL and the Pritzkers is not a ground for enjoining the merger. Nor, in the light of these purposes, is the merger to be enjoined because the public shareholders will not share in future profits if the merger is approved. This is the usual result of such a merger.

Plaintiffs appear to question the procedures by which the merger agreement was worked out and the conclusions of those who participated in the decision and also the means by which the Cerro stock was acquired by GL. Although these allegations appear to be without merit, at best for plaintiffs they would raise triable issues precluding a temporary injunction. Smith, Barney & Co., Incorporated, was retained by Cerro to render an opinion whether Cerro's public stockholders were to receive a fair price. That apparently independent opinion as to price was less than the price set by Cerro as the merger price. If plaintiffs have a basis for a better price, that is a subject for trial not for a temporary injunction. The terms of the merger were worked out, and the negotiations leading to it were conducted by an apparently independent committee, two of whom own or represent substantial blocks of Cerro stock. There is no showing of overreaching. GL and Marmon acquired the bulk of the Cerro shares now held by them by open cash tender offers which were oversubscribed, not by any devious means.

In most respects, the relevant facts are remarkably close to those in *Grimes v. Donaldson, Lufkin & Jenrette, Inc., D.C.*, 392 F. Supp. 1393, C.C.H. Fed. Sec. L. Rep. Par. 94,722 (N.D. Fla. 1974) where the merger was found to have valid business reasons.

In the light of the valid business reasons for the merger, no basis for an injunction is to be found in the fact that Cerro is bearing the $1,500,000 cost of legal, accounting and printing expenses incurred in preparing and mailing the Prospectus & Proxy Statement, the fees paid to Smith, Barney and in holding the meeting. Equally unavailing on the same basis is the fact that Marmon financed its purchase of Cerro stock by borrowing $68,000,000 and that Cerro-Marmon, the merger corporation, will, after the merger, contribute $25,000,000 of "Cerro's money" to Marmon to repay that much of the loan. As long as the merger has a valid corporate purpose and the public shareholders receive a fair price for their stock, this is immaterial. (See Brodsky, Corporate & Securities Litigation, N.Y.L.J., 2/19/76, front page, col. 1, and p. 2, cols. 1 and 3, cited by plaintiffs). Only where the merger is for the sole benefit of the insiders is the use of corporate funds to purchase the stock improper.

The repeated contention by plaintiffs that this is a "freeze-out" is without merit. They are not being offered cash. They will receive a stock interest in the merged corporation, with certain benefits albeit not the so-called "residual equity" benefits of a common shareholder. This is not a freeze-out. Nor is there any evidence to support plaintiffs' contention that they have a right to a continued public market for their stock which will be destroyed because there will be no market for the stock which they will receive. So far as appears, the evidence is to the contrary.

For all of the foregoing reasons, plaintiffs are not entitled to a preliminary injunction.

Although the decision is not so grounded, it must be noted that plaintiffs are chargeable with gross laches. The proposal and its terms were announced publicly on November 19, 1975. The proxy statement was mailed January 27, 1976. Although there was communication between plaintiffs' counsel and Cerro, the order to show cause commencing this action was not obtained and served until February 18, 1976, returnable February 20, four days before the scheduled stockholders' meeting called for February 24, 1976. The intolerable burden such unwarranted delay imposes on defendants and the court would in and of itself warrant denial of the injunction.

Accordingly, the motion for a temporary injunction is in all respects denied. In view of the time exigencies, this decision is deemed the order of the court for all purposes. If the parties are so advised, they may however settle an order on notice.

ALPERT v. 28 WILLIAMS ST. CORP.

New York Court of Appeals
473 N.E.2d 19 (1984)

Chief Judge Cooke.

The subject of contention in this litigation is a valuable 17-story office building, located at 79 Madison Avenue in Manhattan. In dispute is the propriety of a complex series of transactions that had the net effect of permitting defendants, who were outside investors, to gain ownership of the property and to eliminate the ownership interests of plaintiffs, who were minority shareholders of the corporation that formerly owned the building. This was achieved through what is commonly known as a "two-step" merger: (1) an outside investor purchases control of the majority shares of the target corporation by tender offer or through private negotiations; (2) this newly acquired control is used to arrange for the target and a second corporation controlled by the outside investor to merge, with one condition being the "freeze-out" of the minority shareholders of the target corporation by the forced cancellation of their shares, generally through a cash purchase. This accomplishes the investor's original goal of complete ownership of the target corporation.

Since 1955, the office building was owned by 79 Realty Corporation (Realty Corporation), which had no other substantial assets. About two thirds of Realty

Corporation's outstanding shares were held by two couples, the Kimmelmans and the Zauderers, who were also the company's sole directors and officers. Plaintiffs owned 26% of the outstanding shares. The remaining shares were owned by persons who are not parties to this litigation.

Defendants, a consortium of investors, formed a limited partnership, known as Madison 28 Associates (Madison Associates), for the purpose of purchasing the building. In March 1980, Madison Associates began negotiations with the Kimmelmans and the Zauderers to purchase the latter's controlling block of stock at a price equal to its proportion of the building's value, agreed in June 1980 to be $6,500,000. In addition, Madison Associates promised that it would also offer to purchase plaintiffs' stock under the same terms within four months of the closing of the stock purchase agreement in September 1980.

Madison Associates formed a separate, wholly owned company, 28 Williams Street Corporation (Williams Street), to act as the nominal purchaser and owner of the Kimmelman and Zauderer interests. The stock purchase agreement was actually signed by Williams Street and its principal asset was the newly acquired shares of Realty Corporation.

Upon selling their shares, the Kimmelmans and the Zauderers resigned their positions with Realty Corporation and were replaced by four partners of Madison Associates. Now acting as the controlling directors of Realty Corporation on October 17, 1980, the partners of Madison Associates approved a plan to merge Realty Corporation with Williams Street, Realty Corporation being the surviving corporation. Together with a notice for a shareholders meeting to vote on the proposed merger, a statement of intent was sent to all shareholders of Realty Corporation, explaining the procedural and financial aspects of the merger, as well as defendants' conflict of interest and the intended exclusion of the minority shareholders from the newly constituted Realty Corporation through a cash buy-out. Defendants also disclosed that they planned to dissolve Realty Corporation after the merger and thereafter to operate the business as a partnership. The merger plan did not require approval by any of the minority shareholders.

The merger proposed by the directors was approved at the shareholders meeting, held on November 7, 1980. As a result, the office building was owned by the "new" Realty Corporation, which, in turn, was wholly owned by Madison Associates. In accordance with the merger plan, Realty Corporation was dissolved within a month of the merger and its principal asset, title to the building, devolved to Madison Associates.

From the outset, plaintiffs resisted their exclusion from Realty Corporation. First, they rejected overtures by Madison Associates to purchase their shares. Then they unsuccessfully sought to enjoin the sale of the Kimmelman and Zauderer interest to Madison Associates.

The plaintiffs instituted this action on October 31, 1980, initially seeking to enjoin the shareholders meeting called to approve the merger. Failing to temporarily enjoin the Realty Corporation's merger with Williams Street, plaintiffs later amended their complaint to include a request for equitable relief in the form of rescission of the merger.

The propriety of the merger was contested on several grounds. It was contended that the merger was unlawful because its sole purpose was to personally benefit the partners of Madison Associates and that the alleged purposes had no legitimate business benefit inuring to the corporation. Plaintiffs argue that the "business judgment" of the directors in assigning various purposes for the merger was indelibly tainted by a conflict of interest because they were committed to the merger prior to becoming directors and were on both sides of the merger transaction when consummated. Further, they assert that essential financial information was not disclosed and that the value offered for the minority's shares was understated and determined in an unfair manner.

After a trial, Supreme Court held that the merger had been unlawful. It determined that defendants, as directors and majority shareholders of Realty Corporation, had breached their fiduciary duty owed plaintiffs in approving and executing the merger agreement, largely because of defendants' failure to show a "strong and compelling legitimate business purpose" for the merger. The matter was set down for a hearing to determine an appropriate remedy.

The Appellate Division unanimously reversed, on the law and the facts, finding that the trial court's decision was "devoid of factual findings either as to the basis for the conclusion that the shareholders meeting was not lawfully conducted, or whether the entire transaction involved fraud, conflict of interest, or self-dealing" (91 AD2d 530, 531). It rejected the legal standard applied by Supreme Court, holding that the proper standard was that the "[courts] will not interfere with the proper business judgment of directors in the absence of a showing of fraud, illegality, or self-dealing . . . so long as there is some proper corporate purpose for the merger other than the forced buy-out of the minority shares" (*id.*, at p 531). The matter was remanded for a new trial.[76]

Upon retrial, Supreme Court denied plaintiffs' requested relief. It determined that plaintiffs had failed to demonstrate that the merger was not for a legitimate business purpose or that they had been dealt with unfairly and inequitably. The court found that the merger advanced several proper corporate business purposes. It provided a means by which the corporation could attract outside capital investment for extensive repairs and renovations of the building that were needed to produce maximum rents. Certain tax advantages and the distribution of mortgage proceeds would accrue upon the ultimate dissolution of the merged corporation and transfer of the building to the partnership.

The court recognized that because the merger would advance defendants' self-interest and plaintiffs' shares were to be eliminated, it would have been preferable for defendants to have had independent directors or appraisers evaluate whether the merger was fair to all parties. The failure to do so, however, was not deemed fatal to the transaction if, viewed as a whole, it was fair. Thus, the court undertook its own review considering the role that defendants' self-interest played in the merger decision, whether overreaching or bad faith were present, and the

---

[76] [1] Plaintiffs had commenced a separate appraisal proceeding in January 1981, which has been stayed pending resolution of the action for rescission of the merger. The Appellate Division held that the pendency of the appraisal action did not preclude the action for equitable relief.

extent of disclosure of material information to plaintiffs. It also examined how the price for the minority's shares was established and determined that defendants' arrangement with the Kimmelmans and the Zauderers was arrived at through arm's length negotiations and that it reflected the fair market value of the building at the time. In addition, the court noted that the price offered plaintiffs was many times the amount plaintiffs paid for the stock and greatly exceeded the stock's book value and the corporation's past and present earnings. The court concluded that, as a whole, the transaction was fair. As the merger also served a legitimate business purpose and was not tainted by fraud or illegality, plaintiffs' request for rescission was denied. The Appellate Division affirmed the trial court's decision, without opinion.

On this appeal, the principal task facing this court is to prescribe a standard for evaluating the validity of a corporate transaction that forcibly eliminates minority shareholders[77] by means of a two-step merger.[78] It is concluded that the analysis employed by the courts below was correct: the majority shareholders' exclusion of minority interests through a two-step merger does not violate the former's fiduciary obligations so long as the transaction viewed as a whole is fair to the minority shareholders and is justified by an independent corporate business purpose. Accordingly, this court now affirms.

(A)

In New York, two or more domestic corporations are authorized to "merge into a single corporation which shall be one of the constituent corporations", known as the "surviving corporation" (*see* Business Corporation Law, § 901). The statute does not delineate substantive justifications for mergers, but only requires compliance with certain procedures: the adoption by the boards of each corporation of a plan of merger setting forth, among other things, the terms and conditions of the merger; a statement of any changes in the certificate of incorporation of the surviving corporation; the submission of the plan to a vote of shareholders pursuant to notice to all shareholders; and adoption of the plan by a vote of two thirds of the

---

[77] [2] A merger which by majority rule forces the minority interest to give up its equity in the corporation in exchange for cash or senior securities while allowing the controlling interest to retain its equity is commonly referred to as a "freeze-out" merger. It has also been referred to as a "squeeze-out" or a "take-out" merger. Thus, in freeze-outs the danger exists that "a self-interested majority stockholder or control group has ruled unfairly" thus necessitating the need for "safeguards to ensure that minority stockholders receive equal though not identical treatment" (Brudney and Chirelstein, *A Restatement of Corporate Freezeouts*, 87 Yale L.J. 1354, 1358).

[78] [3] It has been observed that corporate freeze-outs of minority interests by mergers occur principally in three distinct manners: (1) two-step mergers, (2) parent/subsidiary mergers, and (3) "going-private" mergers where the majority shareholders seek to remove the public investors (*see* Brudney and Chirelstein, *A Restatement of Corporate Freezeouts*, 87 Yale L.J., at pp 1355-1356). While the final result in a freeze-out merger is the same, it does not necessarily follow that the fiduciary duty owed by the majority to the minority stockholders will be satisfied by the same conduct in each context. Due to differences in the "relative [dangers] of abuse and on the social [values] of the objective served by the elimination of the minority interest" (*id.*, at p 1359) in each of the three merger categories, different protections for the minority and varying notions of fairness may be appropriate for each (*see id.*). This court does not now decide if the circumstances which will satisfy the fiduciary duties owed in this two-step merger will be the same for the other categories.

shareholders entitled to vote on it (*see generally*, Business Corporation Law, §§ 902, 903).

Generally, the remedy of a shareholder dissenting from a merger and the offered "cash-out" price is to obtain the fair value of his or her stock through an appraisal proceeding (*see* Business Corporation Law, § 623). This protects the minority shareholder from being forced to sell at unfair values imposed by those dominating the corporation while allowing the majority to proceed with its desired merger. The pursuit of an appraisal proceeding generally constitutes the dissenting stockholder's exclusive remedy (*see* Business Corporation Law, § 623, subd [k]; *see also Breed v. Barton*, 54 NY2d 82, 85). An exception exists, however, when the merger is unlawful or fraudulent as to that shareholder, in which event an action for equitable relief is authorized (Business Corporation Law, § 623, subd [k]; *see Matter of Willcox v. Stern*, 18 NY2d 195, 204; *Breed v Barton*, 54 NY2d 82, 86, *supra*).[79] Thus, technical compliance with the Business Corporation Law's requirements alone will not necessarily exempt a merger from further judicial review.

(B)

Because the power to manage the affairs of a corporation is vested in the directors and majority shareholders, they are cast in the fiduciary role of "guardians of the corporate welfare" (*Leibert v. Clapp*, 13 NY2d 313, 317). In this position of trust, they have an obligation to all shareholders to adhere to fiduciary standards of conduct and to exercise their responsibilities in good faith when undertaking any corporate action, including a merger. Actions that may accord with statutory requirements are still subject to the limitation that such conduct may not be for the aggrandizement or undue advantage of the fiduciary to the exclusion or detriment of the stockholders.

The fiduciary must treat all shareholders, majority and minority, fairly. Moreover, all corporate responsibilities must be discharged in good faith and with "conscientious fairness, morality and honesty in purpose" (*see Kavanaugh v. Kavanaugh Knitting Co.*, 226 NY 185, 193, *supra*). Also imposed are the obligations of candor (*see Globe Woolen Co. v. Utica Gas & Elec. Co.*, 224 NY 483, 490) and of good and prudent management of the corporation (*see Gordon v. Elliman*, 306 NY 456, 466; *Kavanaugh v. Kavanaugh Knitting Co.*, 226 NY 185, 192, *supra; Weinberger v. UOP, Inc.*, 457 A2d 701, 710 [Del.]). When a breach of fiduciary duty occurs, that action will be considered unlawful and the aggrieved shareholder may be entitled to equitable relief.

---

[79] [4] As the Appellate Division (91 AD2d 530, 531) properly held, there is no bar to a stockholder's institution of an appraisal proceeding in addition to challenging the merger in his individual capacity by an action primarily requesting equitable relief under subdivision (k) of section 623 of the Business Corporation Law on the ground that it is fraudulent or unlawful to the shareholder (*see Breed v. Barton*, 54 NY2d 82, 85-86; *Matter of Weiss v. Summit Organization*, 80 AD2d 526; *Matter of Menschel v. Fluffy Rest.*, 75 AD2d 525). The appraisal action should not be dismissed on the ground that there is "another action pending" (CPLR 3211, subd [a], par 4) because the other action is not "for the same cause of action" (*id.*). The two claims are not identical — one seeks to enforce appraisal rights and the other, equitable relief from the merger (*see Matter of Weiss v. Summit Organization*, 80 AD2d 526, *supra; Matter of Menschel v. Fluffy Rest.*, 75 AD2d 525, *supra*). The appraisal action may be stayed until the equitable action is resolved (*see Matter of Menschel v. Fluffy Rest.*, 75 AD2d 525, *supra*).

(C)

While noting the existence of fiduciary duties is an uncomplicated task, the same may not be said of defining precisely what is proper conduct in the context of a particular corporate transaction. In reviewing a freeze-out merger, the essence of the judicial inquiry is to determine whether the transaction, viewed as a whole, was "fair" as to all concerned. This concept has two principal components: the majority shareholders must have followed "a course of fair dealing toward minority holders" (*Case v. New York Cent. R.R. Co.*, 15 NY2d 150, 156, *supra*; and they must also have offered a fair price for the minority's stock. (*Schulwolf v. Cerro Corp.*, 86 Misc 2d 292, 298).

As a general matter, a principal indicator of fair dealing is the relationship between the parties representing the corporations to be merged (*see Chelrob, Inc. v. Barrett*, 293 NY 442, 460-461). When the directors and majority shareholders of each corporation are independent and negotiate at arm's length, it is more likely that the negotiations will reflect the full exertion of each party's bargaining power and the final terms of the transaction will be the best attainable. When, however, there is a common directorship or majority ownership, the inherent conflict of interest and the potential for self-dealing requires careful scrutiny of the transaction (*see id.*, at pp 461-462; *Everett v. Phillips*, 288 NY 227, 236; *Lirosi v. Elkins*, 89 AD2d 903, 906, *supra*).

Generally, the plaintiff has the burden of proving that the merger violated the duty of fairness, but when there is an inherent conflict of interest, the burden shifts to the interested directors or shareholders to prove good faith and the entire fairness of the merger. The interested parties may attempt to establish this element of fair dealing by introducing evidence of efforts taken to simulate arm's length negotiations. Such steps may have included the appointment of an independent negotiating committee made up of neutral directors or of an independent board to evaluate the merger proposal and to oversee the process of its approval (*see, e.g., Schulwolf v. Cerro Corp.*, 86 Misc 2d 292, 298, *supra; Weinberger v. UOP, Inc.*, 457 A2d 701, 709, n 7 [Del], *supra*). This would tend to negate a finding of self-dealing or overreaching (*see Schulwolf v. Cerro Corp.*, 86 Misc 2d, at p 298, *supra; cf. Tanzer Economic Assoc. v. Universal Food Specialties*, 87 Misc 2d 167, 181).

Fair dealing is also concerned with the procedural fairness of the transaction, such as its timing, initiation, structure, financing, development, disclosure to the independent directors and shareholders, and how the necessary approvals were obtained (*Weinberger v. UOP, Inc.*, 457 A2d 701, 711 [Del], *supra; see Tanzer Economic Assoc. v. Universal Food Specialties*, 87 Misc 2d, at pp 178-179, *supra; Schulwolf v. Cerro Corp.*, 86 Misc 2d, at p 298, *supra*). Basically, the courts must look for complete and candid disclosure of all the material facts and circumstances of the proposed merger known to the majority or directors, including their dual roles and events leading up to the merger proposal.

The fairness of the transaction cannot be determined without considering the component of the financial remuneration offered the dissenting shareholders. When the merger seeks to cancel the minority's shares in exchange for cash, the fiduciaries must ensure that the compensation is equitable. This duty may be satisfied when the cash-out price is reasonably related to the value that might be set by an appraisal proceeding.

In determining whether there was a fair price, the court need not ascertain the precise "fair value" of the shares as it would be determined in an appraisal proceeding. It should be noted, however, that the factors used in an appraisal proceeding are relevant here (*see* Business Corporation Law, § 623; *Klurfeld v. Equity Enterprises*, 79 AD2d 124, 136-137, *supra*). This would include but would not be limited to net asset value, book value, earnings, market value, and investment value (*see Matter of Endicott Johnson Corp. v. Bade*, 37 NY2d 585, 587, *supra*). Elements of future value arising from the accomplishment or expectation of the merger which are known or susceptible of proof as of the date of the merger and not the product of speculation may also be considered (*see* Business Corporation Law, § 623, subd [h], par [4]; *see also Weinberger v. UOP, Inc.*, 457 A2d 701, 713 [Del], *supra*; Note, Reappraising Minority Shareholder Protection in Freezeout Mergers: *Weinberger v. UOP, Inc.*, 58 St John's L Rev 144, 158-161). Evidence that an independent investment firm was retained to render a fairness opinion on the price offered to the minority may be a good means of demonstrating the price which would have been set by arm's length negotiations (*see Tanzer Economic Assoc. v. Universal Food Specialties*, 87 Misc 2d 167, 178, *supra; Schulwolf v. Cerro Corp.*, 86 Misc 2d 292, 298, *supra; Weinberger v. UOP, Inc.*, 457 A2d 701, 712-714 [Del.], *supra*).

(D)

Fair dealing and fair price alone will not render the merger acceptable. As mentioned, there exists a fiduciary duty to treat all shareholders equally (*see Schwartz v. Marien*, 37 NY2d 487, 491-492, *supra*). This duty arises as a concomitant to the power reposed in the majority over corporate governance (*see Case v. New York Cent. R.R. Co.*, 15 NY2d 150, 156-157, *supra*, and cases cited therein). The fact remains, however, that in a freeze-out merger the minority shareholders are being treated in a different manner: the majority is permitted continued participation in the equity of the surviving corporation while the minority has no choice but to surrender their shares for cash. On its face, the majority's conduct would appear to breach this fiduciary obligation. Majority shareholders, however, have an overriding duty to provide good and prudent management, which demands that decisions be made for the welfare, advantage, and best interests of the corporation and the shareholders as a whole. But, it has long been recognized in this State that, under certain circumstances, "the particular interest of the few must give way to the general interest of the many" (*Matter of Niagara Ins. Co.*, 1 Paige Ch 258, 260). Thus, "[departure] from precisely uniform treatment of stockholders may be justified, of course, where a bona fide business purpose indicates that the best interests of the corporation would be served by such departure" (*Schwartz v. Marien*, 37 NY2d 487, 492, *supra*).

In the context of a freeze-out merger, variant treatment of the minority shareholders — i.e., causing their removal — will be justified when related to the advancement of a general corporate interest. The benefit need not be great, but it must be for the corporation. For example, if the sole purpose of the merger is reduction of the number of profit sharers — in contrast to increasing the corporation's capital or profits, or improving its management structure — there will exist no "independent corporate interest" (*see Schwartz v. Marien*, 37 NY2d 487, 492, *supra*). All of these purposes ultimately seek to increase the individual wealth of the remaining shareholders. What distinguishes a proper corporate purpose from an improper one is that, with the former, removal of the minority shareholders furthers the objective of conferring some general gain upon the corporation. Only then will the fiduciary duty of good and prudent management of the corporation serve to override the concurrent duty to treat all shareholders fairly (*see Klurfeld v. Equity Enterprises*, 79 AD2d 124, 136, *supra*). We further note that a finding that there was an independent corporate purpose for the action taken by the majority will not be defeated merely by the fact that the corporate objective could have been accomplished in another way, or by the fact that the action chosen was not the best way to achieve the bona fide business objective.

In sum, in entertaining an equitable action to review a freeze-out merger, a court should view the transaction as a whole to determine whether it was tainted with fraud, illegality, or self-dealing, whether the minority shareholders were dealt with fairly, and whether there exists any independent corporate purpose for the merger.

(E)

As noted, the courts below applied the correct legal standard in concluding that the merger here was proper. Plaintiffs contend that the result is not supported by the record even if that standard is used. Plaintiffs' position, however, relies on weighing the conflicting evidence before the trial court. When this court is confronted by affirmed findings of fact, its scope of review is limited to ascertaining whether there is any evidence in the record to sustain the lower courts' determination (*see Cohen v. Hallmark Cards*, 45 NY2d 493, 499).

Noting that defendants had not employed any neutral committees in negotiating the merger, Supreme Court conducted its own objective review of the transaction. There is evidence in the record to support its conclusion that, viewed as a whole, the transaction was fair. Full disclosure of material information was made in the statement of intent mailed to plaintiffs who also had access to Realty Corporation's books. The stock price was tied to the fair market value of the office building, the corporation's only substantial asset, which was determined in arm's length negotiations.

Without passing on all of the business purposes cited by Supreme Court as underlying the merger, it is sufficient to note that at least one justified the exclusion of plaintiffs' interests: attracting additional capital to effect needed repairs of the building. There is proof that there was a good-faith belief that additional, outside capital was required. Moreover, this record supports the conclusion that this capital would not have been available through the merger had not plaintiffs' interest in the corporation been eliminated. Thus, the approval of the merger, which would extinguish plaintiffs' stock, was supported by a bona fide business purpose to advance this general corporate interest of obtaining increased capital.

Accordingly, the order of the Appellate Division should be affirmed.

JUDGES JASON, JONES, WACHTLER, MEYER, SIMONS and KAYE concur.

Order affirmed, with costs.

WEINBERGER v. UOP, INC.

Delaware Supreme Court
457 A.2d 701 (1983)

MOORE, JUSTICE:

* * *

Finally, we address the matter of business purpose. The defendants contend that the purpose of this merger was not a proper subject of inquiry by the trial court. The plaintiff says that no valid purpose existed — the entire transaction was a mere subterfuge designed to eliminate the minority. The Chancellor ruled otherwise, but in so doing he clearly circumscribed the thrust and effect of *Singer*. *Weinberger v. UOP*, 426 A.2d at 1342-43, 1348-50. This has led to the thoroughly sound observation that the business purpose test "may be . . . virtually interpreted out of existence, as it was in *Weinberger*."[80]

The requirement of a business purpose is new to our law of mergers and was a departure from prior case law. *See Stauffer v. Standard Brands, Inc., supra; David J. Greene & Co. v. Schenley Industries, Inc., supra.*

In view of the fairness test which has long been applicable to parent-subsidiary mergers, *Sterling v. Mayflower Hotel Corp.*, Del. Supr., 93 A.2d 107, 109-10 (1952), the expanded appraisal remedy now available to shareholders, and the broad discretion of the Chancellor to fashion such relief as the facts of a given case may dictate, we do not believe that any additional meaningful protection is afforded minority shareholders by the business purpose requirement of the trilogy of *Singer*, *Tanzer*,[81] *Najjar*,[82] and their progeny. Accordingly, such requirement shall no longer be of any force or effect.

---

[80] [9] Weiss, *The Law of Take Out Mergers: A Historical Perspective*, 56 N.Y.U. L. Rev. 624, 671, n.300 (1981).

[81] [10] *Tanzer v. International General Industries, Inc.*, Del. Supr. 379., 379 A.2d 1121, 1124-25 (1977).

[82] [11] *Roland International Corp. v. Najjar*, Del. Supr., 407 A.2d 1032, 1036 (1979).

IN RE PURE RES., INC., S'HOLDERS LITIG.

Delaware Chancery Court
808 A.2d 421 (2002)

STRINE, VICE CHANCELLOR.

This is the court's decision on a motion for preliminary injunction. The lead plaintiff in the case holds a large block of stock in Pure Resources, Inc., 65% of the shares of which are owned by Unocal Corporation. The lead plaintiff and its fellow plaintiffs seek to enjoin a now-pending exchange offer (the "Offer") by which Unocal hopes to acquire the rest of the shares of Pure in exchange for shares of its own stock.

The plaintiffs believe that the Offer is inadequate and is subject to entire fairness review, consistent with the rationale of *Kahn v. Lynch Communication Systems, Inc.*[83] and its progeny. Moreover, they claim that the defendants, who include Unocal and Pure's board of directors, have not made adequate and non misleading disclosure of the material facts necessary for Pure stockholders to make an informed decision whether to tender into the Offer.

By contrast, the defendants argue that the Offer is a non coercive one that is accompanied by complete disclosure of all material facts. As such, they argue that the Offer is not subject to the entire fairness standard, but to the standards set forth in cases like *Solomon v. Pathe Communications Corp.*,[84] standards which they argue have been fully met.

In this opinion, I conclude that the Offer is subject, as a general matter, to the *Solomon* standards, rather than the *Lynch* entire fairness standard. I conclude, however, that many of the concerns that justify the *Lynch* standard are implicated by tender offers initiated by controlling stockholders, which have as their goal the acquisition of the rest of the subsidiary's shares.[85]

These concerns should be accommodated within the Solomon form of review, by requiring that tender offers by controlling shareholders be structured in a manner that reduces the distorting effect of the tendering process on free stockholder choice and by ensuring minority stockholders a candid and unfettered tendering recommendation from the independent directors of the target board. In this case, the Offer for the most part meets this standard, with one exception that Unocal may cure.

But I also find that the Offer must be preliminarily enjoined because material information relevant to the Pure stockholders' decision-making process has not been fairly disclosed. Therefore, I issue an injunction against the Offer pending an

---

83 [1] 638 A.2d 1110 (Del. 1994).

84 [2] 672 A.2d 35 (Del. 1996).

85 [3] For the purposes of this opinion, my references to tender offers by controlling stockholders mean those tender offers in which the controlling stockholder hopes to acquire all of the remaining shares, in the tender itself, or in combination with a later short-form merger.

alteration of its terms to eliminate its coercive structure and to correct the inadequate disclosures.

I.

These are the key facts as I find them for purposes of deciding this preliminary injunction motion.

A.

Unocal Corporation is a large independent natural gas and crude oil exploration and production company with far-flung operations. In the United States, its most important operations are currently in the Gulf of Mexico. Before May 2000, Unocal also had operations in the Permian Basin of western Texas and southeastern New Mexico. During that month, Unocal spun off its Permian Basin unit and combined it with Titan Exploration, Inc. Titan was an oil and gas company operating in the Permian Basin, south central Texas, and the central Gulf Coast region of Texas. It also owned mineral interests in the southern Gulf Coast.

The entity that resulted from that combination was Pure Resources, Inc. Following the creation of Pure, Unocal owned 65.4% of Pure's issued and outstanding common stock. The remaining 34.6% of Pure was held by Titan's former stockholders, including its managers who stayed on to run Pure. The largest of these stockholders was Jack D. Hightower, Pure's Chairman and Chief Executive Officer, who now owns 6.1% of Pure's outstanding stock before the exercise of options. As a group, Pure's management controls between a quarter and a third of the Pure stock not owned by Unocal, when options are considered.

B.

Several important agreements were entered into when Pure was formed. The first is a Stockholders Voting Agreement. That Agreement requires Unocal and Hightower to vote their shares to elect to the Pure board five persons designated by Unocal (so long as Unocal owns greater than 50% of Pure's common stock), two persons designated by Hightower, and one person to be jointly agreed upon by Unocal and Hightower. Currently, the board resulting from the implementation of the Voting Agreement is comprised as follows:

Unocal Designees:

- Darry D. Chessum — Chessum is Unocal's Treasurer and is the owner of one share of Pure stock.
- Timothy H. Ling — Ling is President, Chief Operating Officer, and director of Unocal. He owns one share of Pure stock.
- Graydon H. Laughbaum, Jr. — Laughbaum was an executive for 34 years at Unocal before retiring at the beginning of 1999. For most of the next three years, he provided consulting services to Unocal. Laughbaum owns 1,301 shares of Pure stock.

- HD Maxwell — Maxwell was an executive for many years at Unocal before 1992. Maxwell owns one share of Pure stock.
- Herbert C. Williamson, III — Williamson has no material ties to Unocal. He owns 3,364 shares of Pure stock.

Hightower Designees:

- Jack D. Hightower — As mentioned, he is Pure's CEO and its largest stockholder, aside from Unocal.
- George G. Staley — Staley is Pure's Chief Operating Officer and also a large stockholder, controlling 625,261 shares.

Joint Designee of Unocal and Hightower:

- Keith A. Covington — Covington's only tie to Unocal is that he is a close personal friend of Ling, having gone to business school with him. He owns 2,401 Pure shares.

As part of the consideration it received in the Titan combination, Unocal extracted a "Business Opportunities Agreement" ("BOA") from Titan. So long as Unocal owns at least 35% of Pure, the BOA limits Pure to the oil and gas exploration and production business in certain designated areas, which were essentially co extensive with the territories covered by Titan and the Permian Basin operations of Unocal as of the time of the combination. The BOA includes an acknowledgement by Pure that it has no business expectancy in opportunities outside the limits set by the contract. This limitation is not reciprocal, however.

By contrast, the BOA expressly states that Unocal may compete with Pure in its areas of operation. Indeed, it implies that Pure board members affiliated with Unocal may bring a corporate opportunity in Pure's area of operation to Unocal for exploitation, but may not pursue the opportunity personally.

Another protection Unocal secured in the combination was a Non Dilution Agreement. That Agreement provides Unocal with a preemptive right to maintain its proportionate ownership in the event that Pure issues new shares or undertakes certain other transactions.

Finally, members of Pure's management team entered into "Put Agreements" with Unocal at the time of the combination. The Put Agreements give the managers — including Hightower and Staley — the right to put their Pure stock to Unocal upon the occurrence of certain triggering events — among which would be consummation of Unocal's Offer.

The Put Agreements require Unocal to pay the managers the "per share net asset value" or "NAV" of Pure, in the event the managers exercise their Put rights within a certain period after a triggering event. One triggering event is a transaction in which Unocal obtains 85% of Pure's shares, which could include the Offer if it results in Unocal obtaining that level of ownership. The NAV of Pure is determined under a complex formula dependent largely on Pure's energy reserves and debt. Notably, Pure's NAV for purposes of the Put Agreement could fall below or exceed the price of a triggering transaction, but in the latter event the triggering transaction would provide the Put holders with the right to receive the higher NAV.

Although it is not clear whether the Put holders can tender themselves into the Offer in order to create a triggering transaction and receive the higher of the Offer price or the NAV, it is clear that the Put Agreements can create materially different incentives for the holders than if they were simply holders of Pure common stock.

In addition to the Put Agreements, senior members of Pure's management team have severance agreements that will (if they choose) be triggered in the event the Offer succeeds. In his case, Hightower will be eligible for a severance payment of three times his annual salary and bonus, or nearly four million dollars, an amount that while quite large, is not substantial in comparison to the economic consequences of the treatment of his equity interest in Pure. Staley has a smaller, but similar package, and the economic consequences of the treatment of his equity also appear to be more consequential than any incentive to receive severance.

II.

A.

With these agreements in mind, I now turn to the course of events leading up to Unocal's offer.

From its formation, Pure's future as an independent entity was a subject of discussion within its board. Although Pure's operations were successful, its status as a controlled subsidiary of another player in the oil and gas business suggested that the day would come when Pure either had to become wholly-owned by Unocal or independent of it.

This reality was made manifest as Pure's management undertook to expand its business. On several occasions, this resulted in requests by Pure for limited waivers of the BOA to enable Pure to take advantage of opportunities beyond the areas designated in that contract. Unocal granted these waivers in each case. Another aspect of this subject also arose, as Unocal considered re entering areas of geographical operation core to Pure's operations. Concerns arose in the minds of Unocal's lawyers about the extent to which the BOA could truly protect those Unocal officers (*i.e.*, Chessum and Ling) who sat on the Pure board from claims of breach of fiduciary duty in the event that Unocal were to pursue, for example, an opportunity in the Permian Basin. Because Unocal owed an indemnification obligation to Chessum and Ling and because it would be difficult to get officers to serve on subsidiary boards if Unocal did not back them, Unocal obviously was attentive to this uncertainty. Stated summarily, some, if not all, the complications that the BOA was designed to address remained a concern — a concern that would be eradicated if Unocal purchased the rest of Pure.

The aggressive nature of Pure's top management also fed this furnace. Hightower is an assertive deal-maker with plans to make Pure grow. To his mind, Unocal should decide on a course of action: either let Pure expand as much as it could profitably do or buy the rest of Pure. In one of the negotiations over a limited waiver of the BOA, Hightower put this choice to Unocal in more or less these terms.

During the summer of 2001, Unocal explored the feasibility of acquiring the rest of Pure. On behalf of Unocal, Pure directors Maxwell and Laughbaum collected non public information about Pure's reserves, production capabilities, and geographic assets and reported back to Unocal. This was done with the permission of Pure's management. By September 2001, it appeared that Unocal might well propose a merger, but the tragic events of that month and other more mundane factors resulted in the postponement of any proposal. Unocal's Chief Financial Officer informed Hightower of Unocal's decision not to proceed and that "all evaluation work on such a transaction ha[d] ceased."[86]

That last statement was only fleetingly true. The record contains substantial evidence that Unocal's management and board soon renewed their consideration of taking Pure private. Pure director Ling knew that this renewed evaluation was going on, but it appears that he never shared that information with his fellow Pure directors. Nor did Unocal ever communicate to Pure that its September 2001 representation that all evaluation work had ceased was no longer correct. Nonetheless, during this period, Unocal continued to have access to non public information from Pure.

Supplementing the pressure for a transaction that was generated by Hightower's expansion plans was a specific financing vehicle that Hightower sought to have the Pure board pursue. In the spring of 2002, Pure's management began seriously considering the creation of a "Royalty Trust." The Royalty Trust would monetize the value of certain mineral rights owned by Pure by selling portions of those interests to third parties. This would generate a cash infusion that would reduce Pure's debt and potentially give it capital to expand. By August of 2002, Hightower was prepared to push hard for this transaction, subject to ensuring that it could be accounted for on a favorable basis with integrity and would not have adverse tax effects.

For its part, Unocal appears to have harbored genuine concerns about the transaction, in addition to its shared concern about the accounting and tax implications of the Royalty Trust. Among its worries was that the Royalty Trust would simply inflate the value of the Put rights of management by delivering Pure (and increasing its NAV) without necessarily increasing its stock price. The Royalty Trust also complicated any future acquisition of Pure because the formation of the Trust would leave Unocal entangled with the third parties who invested in it, who might be classified as holding a form of equity in Pure.

Although the record is not without doubt on the point, it appears that the Pure board decided to pursue consideration of the Royalty Trust during mid-August 2002. During these meetings, however, Chessum raised a host of issues that needed to be resolved favorably before the board could ultimately agree to consummate a Royalty Trust transaction. The plaintiffs argue that Chessum was buying time and trying to throw sand in the gears. Although I believe Unocal was worried about the transaction's effect, I am not prepared to say that Chessum's concerns were illegitimate. Indeed, many of them were shared by Hightower. Nonetheless, what is more evident is that the Royalty Trust discussions put pressure on Unocal to decide whether to proceed with an acquisition offer and that the Royalty Trust was likely

---

[86] [4] Dallas Ex. 1.

not the method of financing that Unocal would use if it wholly owned Pure.[87]

I infer that Hightower knew this. Simultaneous with pushing the Royalty Trust, Hightower encouraged Unocal to make an offer for the rest of Pure. Hightower suggested that Unocal proceed by way of a tender offer, because he believed that his Put rights complicated the Pure board's ability to act on a merger proposal.

B.

Despite his entreaties, Hightower was surprisingly surprised by what came next, as were the members of the Pure board not affiliated with Unocal. On August 20, 2002, Unocal sent the Pure board a letter that stated in pertinent part that:

> It has become clear to us that the best interests of our respective stockholders will be served by Unocal's acquisition of the shares of Pure Resources that we do not already own. . . .
>
> Unocal recognizes that a strong and stable on-shore, North America production base will facilitate the execution of its North American gas strategy. The skills and technology required to maximize the benefits to be realized from that strategy are now divided between Union Oil and Pure. Sound business strategy calls for bringing those assets together, under one management, so that they may be deployed to their highest and best use. For those reasons, we are not interested in selling our shares in Pure. Moreover, if the two companies are combined, important cost savings should be realized and potential conflicts of interest will be avoided.
>
> Consequently, our Board of Directors has authorized us to make an exchange offer pursuant to which the stockholders of Pure (other than Union Oil) will be offered 0.6527 shares of common stock of Unocal for each outstanding share of Pure common stock they own in a transaction designed to be tax-free. Based on the $34.09 closing price of Unocal's shares on August 20, 2002, our offer provides a value of approximately $22.25 per share of Pure common stock and a 27% premium to the closing price of Pure common stock on that date.
>
> Unocal's offer is being made directly to Pure's stockholders. . . .
>
> Our offer will be conditioned on the tender of a sufficient number of shares of Pure common stock such that, after the offer is completed, we will own at least 90% of the outstanding shares of Pure common stock and other customary conditions. . . . Assuming that the conditions to the offer are satisfied and that the offer is completed, we will then effect a "short form" merger of Pure with a subsidiary of Unocal as soon as practicable thereafter. In this merger, the remaining Pure public stockholders will receive the same consideration as in the exchange offer, except for those stockholders who choose to exercise their appraisal rights.

---

[87] [5] Unocal's CFO testified that if Unocal was to buy the rest of Pure, it should do so before the Royalty Trust could be formed. *See* Dallas Dep. at 83-84.

> We intend to file our offering materials with the Securities and Exchange Commission and commence our exchange offer on or about September 5, 2002. Unocal is not seeking, and as the offer is being made directly to Pure's stockholders, Delaware law does not require approval of the offer from Pure's Board of Directors. We, however, encourage you to consult with your outside counsel as to the obligations of Pure's Board of Directors under the U.S. tender offer rules to advise the stockholders of your recommendation with respect to our offer. . . .[88]

Unocal management asked Ling and Chessum to make calls to the Pure board about the Offer. In their talking points, Ling and Chessum were instructed to suggest that any Special Committee formed by Pure should have powers "limited to hiring independent advisors (bank and lawyers) and to coming up with a recommendation to the Pure shareholders as to whether or not to accept UCL's offer; any greater delegation is not warranted."[89]

The next day the Pure board met to consider this event. Hightower suggested that Chessum and Ling recuse themselves from the Pure board's consideration of the Offer. They agreed to do so. After that, the Pure board voted to establish a Special Committee comprised of Williamson and Covington to respond to the Unocal bid. Maxwell and Laughbaum were omitted from the Committee because of their substantial employment histories with Unocal. Despite their work with Unocal in assessing the advisability of a bid for Pure in 2001, however, Maxwell and Laughbaum did not recuse themselves generally from the Pure board's process of reacting to the Offer. Hightower and Staley were excluded from the Committee because there were circumstances in which the Put Agreements could provide them with incentive to support the procession of the Offer, not because the Offer was at the most favorable price, but because it would trigger their right to receive a higher price under the NAV formula in the Put Agreements.

The precise authority of the Special Committee to act on behalf of Pure was left hazy at first, but seemed to consist solely of the power to retain independent advisors, to take a position on the offer's advisability on behalf of Pure, and to negotiate with Unocal to see if it would increase its bid. Aside from this last point, this constrained degree of authority comported with the limited power that Unocal had desired.

During the early days of its operation, the Special Committee was aided by company counsel, Thompson & Knight, and management in retaining its own advisors and getting started. Soon, though, the Special Committee had retained two financial advisors and legal advisors to help it.

For financial advisors, the Special Committee hired Credit Suisse First Boston ("First Boston"), the investment bank assisting Pure with its consideration of the Royalty Trust, and Petrie Parkman & Co., Inc., a smaller firm very experienced in the energy field. The Committee felt that the knowledge that First Boston had gleaned from its Royalty Trust work would be of great help to the Committee,

---

[88] [6] 14D-9 at 17-18.

[89] [7] Chessum Ex. 4.

especially in the short time frame required to respond to the Offer, which was scheduled to expire at midnight on October 2, 2002.

For legal advisors, the Committee retained Baker Botts and Potter Anderson & Corroon. Baker Botts had handled certain toxic tort litigation for Unocal and was active as lead counsel in representing an energy consortium of which Unocal is a major participant in a major piece of litigation. Nonetheless, the Committee apparently concluded that these matters did not materially compromise Baker Botts' ability to act aggressively towards Unocal.

After the formation of the Special Committee, Unocal formally commenced its Offer, which had these key features:

- An exchange ratio of 0.6527 of a Unocal share for each Pure share.
- A non waivable majority of the minority tender provision, which required a majority of shares not owned by Unocal to tender. Management of Pure, including Hightower and Staley, are considered part of the minority for purposes of this condition, not to mention Maxwell, Laughbaum, Chessum, and Ling.
- A waivable condition that a sufficient number of tenders be received to enable Unocal to own 90% of Pure and to effect a short-form merger under 8 Del. C. § 253.
- A statement by Unocal that it intends, if it obtains 90%, to consummate a short-form merger as soon as practicable at the same exchange ratio.

As of this time, this litigation had been filed and a preliminary injunction hearing was soon scheduled. Among the issues raised was the adequacy of the Special Committee's scope of authority.

Thereafter, the Special Committee sought to, in its words, "clarify" its authority. The clarity it sought was clear: the Special Committee wanted to be delegated the full authority of the board under Delaware law to respond to the Offer. With such authority, the Special Committee could have searched for alternative transactions, speeded up consummation of the Royalty Trust, evaluated the feasibility of a self-tender, and put in place a shareholder rights plan (*a.k.a.*, poison pill) to block the Offer.

What exactly happened at this point is shrouded by invocations of privilege. But this much is clear. Having recused themselves from the Pure board process before, Chessum and Ling reentered it in full glory when the Special Committee asked for more authority. Chessum took the lead in raising concerns and engaged Unocal's in house and outside counsel to pare down the resolution proposed by the Special Committee. After discussions between Counsel for Unocal and the Special Committee, the bold resolution drafted by Special Committee counsel was whittled down to take out any ability on the part of the Special Committee to do anything other than study the Offer, negotiate it, and make a recommendation on behalf of Pure in the required 14D-9.

The record does not illuminate exactly why the Special Committee did not make this their Alamo. It is certain that the Special Committee never pressed the issue to a board vote and it appears that the Pure directors never seriously debated the issue at the board table itself. The Special Committee never demanded that Chessum and Ling recuse themselves from consideration of this issue, much less Maxwell and Laughbaum.

At best, the record supports the inference that the Special Committee believed some of the broader options technically open to them under their preferred resolution (*e.g.*, finding another buyer) were not practicable. As to their failure to insist on the power to deploy a poison pill — the by now *de rigeur* tool of a board responding to a third-party tender offer — the record is obscure. The Special Committee's brief suggests that the Committee believed that the pill could not be deployed consistently with the Non Dilution Agreement protecting Unocal, but nowhere indicates how Unocal's contractual right to preserve its 65% position precluded a rights plan designed solely to keep it at that level. The Special Committee also argues that the pill was unnecessary because the Committee's ability to make a negative recommendation — coupled with Hightower's and Staley's by then apparent opposition to the Offer — were leverage and protection enough.

My ability to have confidence in these justifications has been compromised by the Special Committee's odd decision to invoke the attorney-client privilege as to its discussion of these issues. Because the Committee delegated to its legal advisors the duty of negotiating the scope of the Committee's authority and seems to have acquiesced in their acceptance of defeat at the hands of Unocal's lawyers, invocation of the privilege renders it impossible for me know what really went on.[90]

The most reasonable inference that can be drawn from the record is that the Special Committee was unwilling to confront Unocal as aggressively as it would have confronted a third-party bidder. No doubt Unocal's talented counsel made much of its client's majority status and argued that Pure would be on uncertain legal ground in interposing itself — by way of a rights plan — between Unocal and Pure's stockholders. Realizing that Unocal would not stand for this broader authority and sensitive to the expected etiquette of subsidiary-parent relations, the Pure board therefore decided not to vote on the issue, and the Special Committee's fleeting act of boldness was obscured in the rhetoric of discussions about "clarifying its authority."

Contemporaneous with these events, the Special Committee met on a more or less continuous basis. On a few occasions, the Special Committee met with Unocal and tried to persuade it to increase its offer. On September 10, for example, the Special Committee asked Unocal to increase the exchange ratio from 0.6527 to

---

[90] [8] Although time constraints hamper my ability to factor in this issue, in general it seems unwise for a special committee to hide behind the privilege, except when the disclosure of attorney-client discussions would reveal litigation-specific advice or compromise the special committee's bargaining power. In other than those circumstances, the very nature of the special committee process as an integrity-ensuring device requires judicial access to communications with advisors, especially when such committees rely so heavily on these advisors to negotiate and provide expertise in the absence of the unconflicted assistance of management. In other cases, of course, this court has explicitly drawn negative inferences when a board has shielded its actions from view. *See, e.g., Chesapeake Corp. v. Shore*, 771 A.2d 293, 301 (Del. Ch. 2000) (citing *Mentor Graphics Corp. v. Quickturn Design Sys., Inc.*, Del. Ch., C.A. No. 16584, tr. at 505, Jacobs, V.C. (Oct. 23, 1998)).

0.787. Substantive presentations were made by the Special Committee's financial advisors in support of this overture.

After these meetings, Unocal remained unmoved and made no counteroffer.[91] Therefore, on September 17, 2002, the Special Committee voted not to recommend the Offer, based on its analysis and the advice of its financial advisors. The Special Committee prepared the 14D-9 on behalf of Pure, which contained the board's recommendation not to tender into the Offer. Hightower and Staley also announced their personal present intentions not to tender, intentions that if adhered to would make it nearly impossible for Unocal to obtain 90% of Pure's shares in the Offer.

During the discovery process, a representative of the lead plaintiff, which is an investment fund, testified that he did not feel coerced by the Offer. The discovery record also reveals that a great deal of the Pure stock held by the public is in the hands of institutional investors.

III. The Plaintiffs' Demand For A Preliminary Injunction

A. The Merits

The plaintiffs advance an array of arguments, not all of which can be dealt with in the time allotted to me for decision. As a result, I concentrate on those of the plaintiffs' claims that are most important and that might, if meritorious, justify injunctive relief. For the most part, Unocal has taken the lead in responding most comprehensively on behalf of the defendants, who also include all the members of the Pure board. The director-defendants mostly confine themselves to defending their own actions and to responding to the plaintiffs' allegation that Pure's 14D-9 omits and misstates material information.

Distilled to the bare minimum, the plaintiffs argue that the Offer should be enjoined because: (i) the Offer is subject to the entire fairness standard and the record supports the inference that the transaction cannot survive a fairness review; (ii) in any event, the Offer is actionably coercive and should be enjoined on that ground; and (iii) the disclosures provided to the Pure stockholders in connection with the Offer are materially incomplete and misleading.

. . .

B. The Plaintiffs' Substantive Attack on the Offer

1.

The primary argument of the plaintiffs is that the Offer should be governed by the entire fairness standard of review. In their view, the structural power of Unocal over Pure and its board, as well as Unocal's involvement in determining the scope of the Special Committee's authority, make the Offer other than a voluntary, non

---

[91] [9] Earlier, it had made one move: it refused to extend a limited waiver of the BOA allowing Pure to pursue new opportunities outside its core area of operations.

coercive transaction. In the plaintiffs' mind, the Offer poses the same threat of (what I will call) "inherent coercion" that motivated the Supreme Court in *Kahn v. Lynch Communication Systems, Inc.*[92] to impose the entire fairness standard of review on any interested merger involving a controlling stockholder, even when the merger was approved by an independent board majority, negotiated by an independent special committee, and subject to a majority of the minority vote condition.

In support of their argument, the plaintiffs contend that the tender offer method of acquisition poses, if anything, a greater threat of unfairness to minority stockholders and should be subject to the same equitable constraints. More case-specifically, they claim that Unocal has used inside information from Pure to foist an inadequate bid on Pure stockholders at a time advantageous to Unocal. Then, Unocal acted self-interestedly to keep the Pure Special Committee from obtaining all the authority necessary to respond to the Offer. As a result, the plaintiffs argue, Unocal has breached its fiduciary duties as majority stockholder, and the Pure board has breached its duties by either acting on behalf of Unocal (in the case of Chessum and Ling) or by acting supinely in response to Unocal's inadequate offer (the Special Committee and the rest of the board). Instead of wielding the power to stop Unocal in its tracks and make it really negotiate, the Pure board has taken only the insufficient course of telling the Pure minority to say no.

In response to these arguments, Unocal asserts that the plaintiffs misunderstand the relevant legal principles. Because Unocal has proceeded by way of an exchange offer and not a negotiated merger, the rule of Lynch is inapplicable. Instead, Unocal is free to make a tender offer at whatever price it chooses so long as it does not: i) "structurally coerce" the Pure minority by suggesting explicitly or implicitly that injurious events will occur to those stockholders who fail to tender; or ii) mislead the Pure minority into tendering by concealing or misstating the material facts. This is the rule of law articulated by, among other cases, *Solomon v. Pathe Communications Corp.*[93] Because Unocal has conditioned its Offer on a majority of the minority provision and intends to consummate a short-form merger at the same price, it argues that the Offer poses no threat of structural coercion and that the Pure minority can make a voluntary decision. Because the Pure minority has a negative recommendation from the Pure Special Committee and because there has been full disclosure (including of any material information Unocal received from Pure in formulating its bid), Unocal submits that the Pure minority will be able to make an informed decision whether to tender. For these reasons, Unocal asserts that no meritorious claim of breach of fiduciary duty exists against it or the Pure directors.

2.

This case therefore involves an aspect of Delaware law fraught with doctrinal tension: what equitable standard of fiduciary conduct applies when a controlling shareholder seeks to acquire the rest of the company's shares? In considering this issue, it is useful to pause over the word "equitable" and to capture its full import.

---

[92] [11] 638 A.2d 1110 (Del. 1994).

[93] [12] 672 A.2d 35 (Del. 1996).

The key inquiry is not what statutory procedures must be adhered to when a controlling stockholder attempts to acquire the rest of the company's shares. Controlling stockholders counseled by experienced lawyers rarely trip over the legal hurdles imposed by legislation.

Nor is the doctrine of independent legal significance of relevance here. That doctrine stands only for the proposition that the mere fact that a transaction cannot be accomplished under one statutory provision does not invalidate it if a different statutory method of consummation exists. Nothing about that doctrine alters the fundamental rule that inequitable actions in technical conformity with statutory law can be restrained by equity.[94]

This is not to say that the statutory method by which a controlling stockholder proceeds is not relevant to determining the equitable standard of conduct that a court must apply. To the contrary, the structure and statutory rubric employed to consummate transactions are highly influential to courts shaping the common law of corporations. There are good reasons why this is so. A statute's own terms might foreclose (explicitly or implicitly) the application of traditional concepts of fiduciary duty, thereby requiring judges to subordinate default principles of the common law to the superior mandate of legislation.[95] The relevant statutory technique might also be one that does not foreclose common law equitable review altogether, but that has certain characteristics that influence the judiciary's formulation of the extent and nature of the duties owed by the fiduciaries involved in the transaction. Much of the judicial carpentry in the corporate law occurs in this context, in which judges must supplement the broadly enabling features of statutory corporation law with equitable principles sufficient to protect against abuse and unfairness, but not so rigid as to stifle useful transactions that could increase the shareholder and societal wealth generated by the corporate form.

In building the common law, judges forced to balance these concerns cannot escape making normative choices, based on imperfect information about the world. This reality clearly pervades the area of corporate law implicated by this case. When a transaction to buy out the minority is proposed, is it more important to the development of strong capital markets to hold controlling stockholders and target boards to very strict (and litigation-intensive) standards of fiduciary conduct? Or is more stockholder wealth generated if less rigorous protections are adopted, which permit acquisitions to proceed so long as the majority has not misled or strong-armed the minority? Is such flexibility in fact beneficial to minority stockholders because it encourages liquidity-generating tender offers to them and provides incentives for acquirers to pay hefty premiums to buy control, knowing that control will be accompanied by legal rules that permit a later "going private" transaction to

---

[94] [13] *See Schnell v. Chris-Craft Indus., Inc.*, 285 A.2d 437, 439 (Del. 1971) ("[I]nequitable action does not become permissible simply because it is legally possible.").

[95] [14] *See, e.g., In re Unocal Exploration Corp. S'holders Litig.*, 793 A.2d 329, 338 & n. 26 (Del. Ch. 2000) (stating that when controlling stockholder consummates a short-form merger under 8 Del. C. § 253 that is not proceeded by any prior transaction subject to entire fairness review, plaintiff is relegated to the appraisal remedy in the absence of "fraud, gross overreaching, or other such wrongful conduct" or misdisclosures; otherwise, the statute's authorization of a simplified procedure for effecting such mergers would be undermined by the imposition of an equitable requirement of fair process), *aff'd sub nom., Glassman v. Unocal Exploration Corp.*, 777 A.2d 242 (Del. 2001) (same).

occur in a relatively non litigious manner?

At present, the Delaware case law has two strands of authority that answer these questions differently. In one strand, which deals with situations in which controlling stockholders negotiate a merger agreement with the target board to buy out the minority, our decisional law emphasizes the protection of minority stockholders against unfairness. In the other strand, which deals with situations when a controlling stockholder seeks to acquire the rest of the company's shares through a tender offer followed by a short-form merger under 8 Del. C. § 253, Delaware case precedent facilitates the free flow of capital between willing buyers and willing sellers of shares, so long as the consent of the sellers is not procured by inadequate or misleading information or by wrongful compulsion.

These strands appear to treat economically similar transactions as categorically different simply because the method by which the controlling stockholder proceeds varies. This disparity in treatment persists even though the two basic methods (negotiated merger versus tender offer/short-form merger) pose similar threats to minority stockholders. Indeed, it can be argued that the distinction in approach subjects the transaction that is more protective of minority stockholders when implemented with appropriate protective devices — a merger negotiated by an independent committee with the power to say no and conditioned on a majority of the minority vote — to more stringent review than the more dangerous form of a going private deal — an unnegotiated tender offer made by a majority stockholder. The latter transaction is arguably less protective than a merger of the kind described, because the majority stockholder-offeror has access to inside information, and the offer requires disaggregated stockholders to decide whether to tender quickly, pressured by the risk of being squeezed out in a short-form merger at a different price later or being left as part of a much smaller public minority. This disparity creates a possible incoherence in our law.

3.

To illustrate this possible incoherence in our law, it is useful to sketch out these two strands. I begin with negotiated mergers. In *Kahn v. Lynch Communication Systems, Inc.*,[96] the Delaware Supreme Court addressed the standard of review that applies when a controlling stockholder attempts to acquire the rest of the corporation's shares in a negotiated merger pursuant to 8 Del. C. § 251. The Court held that the stringent entire fairness form of review governed regardless of whether: i) the target board was comprised of a majority of independent directors; ii) a special committee of the target's independent directors was empowered to negotiate and veto the merger; and iii) the merger was made subject to approval by a majority of the disinterested target stockholders.[97]

---

[96] [15] 638 A.2d 1110 (Del. 1994).

[97] [16] *Lynch* resolved a split in Court of Chancery authority. One of the Chancery lines of authority presaged the *Lynch* decision. This line conceived of a squeeze-out merger as posing special dangers of overreaching and fear of retribution by the majority. *See Citron v. E.I. DuPont de Nemours & Co.*, 584 A.2d 490, 499-502 (Del. Ch. 1990). The other line advocated the application of the business judgment rule standard of review if the squeeze-out merger was approved by a board comprised of a majority of independent directors, an effective committee of independent directors, or a majority of the minority

The Supreme Court concluded that even a gauntlet of protective barriers like those would be insufficient protection because of (what I will term) the "inherent coercion" that exists when a controlling stockholder announces its desire to buy the minority's shares. In colloquial terms, the Supreme Court saw the controlling stockholder as the 800 pound gorilla whose urgent hunger for the rest of the bananas is likely to frighten less powerful primates like putatively independent directors who might well have been hand-picked by the gorilla (and who at the very least owed their seats on the board to his support).[98]

The Court also expressed concern that minority stockholders would fear retribution from the gorilla if they defeated the merger and he did not get his way.[99] This inherent coercion was felt to exist even when the controlling stockholder had not threatened to take any action adverse to the minority in the event that the merger was voted down and thus was viewed as undermining genuinely free choice by the minority stockholders.[100]

All in all, the Court was convinced that the powers and influence possessed by controlling stockholders were so formidable and daunting to independent directors and minority stockholders that protective devices like special committees and majority of the minority conditions (even when used in combination with the statutory appraisal remedy) were not trustworthy enough to obviate the need for an entire fairness review.[101] The Court did, however, recognize that these safety measures had utility and should be encouraged. Therefore, it held that their deployment could shift the burden of persuasion on the issue of fairness from the controlling stockholders and the target board as proponents of the transaction to shareholder-plaintiffs seeking to invalidate it.[102]

---

shareholders vote. *See In re Trans World Airlines, Inc. S'holders Litig.*, 1988 WL 111271, at *7[, 1998 Del. Ch. LEXIS 139] (Del. Ch. 1988); *Puma v. Marriott*, 283 A.2d 693, 695-96 (Del. Ch. 1971).

98 [17] In this regard, *Lynch* is premised on a less trusting view of independent directors than is reflected in the important case of *Aronson v. Lewis*, 473 A.2d 805 (Del. 1984), which presumed that a majority of independent directors can impartially decide whether to sue a controlling stockholder.

99 [18] *Lynch*, 638 A.2d at 1116 ("Even where no coercion is intended, shareholders voting on a parent subsidiary merger might perceive that their disapproval could risk retaliation of some kind by the controlling stockholder. For example, the controlling stockholder might decide to stop dividend payments or to effect a subsequent cash out merger at a less favorable price, for which the remedy would be time consuming and costly litigation. At the very least, the potential for that perception, and its possible impact upon a shareholder vote, could never be fully eliminated.") (quoting *Citron*, 584 A.2d at 502).

100 [19] *See Citron*, 584 A.2d at 502.

101 [20] Another underpinning of the Lynch line of cases is an implicit perception that the statutory remedy of appraisal is a less than fully adequate protection for stockholders facing Inherent Coercion from a proposed squeeze-out merger. These imperfections have been commented on elsewhere. *See, e.g., Clements v. Rogers*, 790 A.2d 1222, 1238 n. 46 (Del. Ch. 2001); *Andra v. Blount*, 772 A.2d 183, 184 (Del. Ch. 2000); Randall S. Thomas, *Revising the Delaware Appraisal Statute*, 3 Del. L. Rev. 1, 1-2 (2000); Bradley R. Aronstam et al., Delaware's Going Private Dilemma: Fostering Protections for Minority Shareholders in the Wake of Siliconix and Unocal Exploration 33-35 (Aug. 28, 2002) [hereinafter "Aronstam"] (unpublished manuscript).

102 [21] *See Lynch*, 638 A.2d at 1117 ("[A]n approval of the transaction by an independent committee of directors or an informed majority of minority shareholders shifts the burden of proof on the issue of fairness from the controlling or dominating shareholder to the challenging shareholder-plaintiff.").

The policy balance struck in *Lynch* continues to govern negotiated mergers between controlling stockholders and subsidiaries. If anything, later cases have extended the rule in *Lynch* to a broader array of transactions involving controlling shareholders.[103]

4.

The second strand of cases involves tender offers made by controlling stockholders — i.e., the kind of transaction Unocal has proposed. The prototypical transaction addressed by this strand involves a tender offer by the controlling stockholder addressed to the minority stockholders. In that offer, the controlling stockholder promises to buy as many shares as the minority will sell but may subject its offer to certain conditions. For example, the controlling stockholder might condition the offer on receiving enough tenders for it to obtain 90% of the subsidiary's shares, thereby enabling the controlling stockholder to consummate a short-form merger under 8 Del. C. § 253 at either the same or a different price.

As a matter of statutory law, this way of proceeding is different from the negotiated merger approach in an important way: neither the tender offer nor the short-form merger requires any action by the subsidiary's board of directors. The tender offer takes place between the controlling shareholder and the minority shareholders so long as the offering conditions are met. And, by the explicit terms of § 253, the short-form merger can be effected by the controlling stockholder itself, an option that was of uncertain utility for many years because it was unclear whether § 253 mergers were subject to an equitable requirement of fair process at the subsidiary board level. That uncertainty was recently resolved in *Glassman v. Unocal Exploration Corp.*,[104] an important recent decision, which held that a short-form merger was not reviewable in an action claiming unfair dealing, and that, absent fraud or misleading or inadequate disclosures, could be contested only in an appraisal proceeding that focused solely on the adequacy of the price paid.

Before *Glassman*, transactional planners had wondered whether the back end of the tender offer/short-form merger transaction would subject the controlling stockholder to entire fairness review. *Glassman* seemed to answer that question favorably from the standpoint of controlling stockholders, and to therefore encourage the tender offer/short-form merger form of acquisition as presenting a materially less troublesome method of proceeding than a negotiated merger.

Why? Because the legal rules that governed the front end of the tender offer/short-form merger method of acquisition had already provided a more flexible, less litigious path to acquisition for controlling stockholders than the negotiated merger route. Tender offers are not addressed by the Delaware General Corporation Law ("DGCL"), a factor that has been of great importance in shaping the line of decisional law addressing tender offers by controlling stockholders — but not, as I will discuss, tender offers made by third parties.

---

[103] [22] *See, e.g., Emerald Partners v. Berlin*, 787 A.2d 85, 93 n. 52 (Del. 2001); *Kahn v. Tremont Corp.*, 694 A.2d 422, 428 (Del. 1997).

[104] [23] 777 A.2d 242 (Del. 2001).

Because no consent or involvement of the target board is statutorily mandated for tender offers, our courts have recognized that "[i]n the case of totally voluntary tender offers . . . courts do not impose any right of the shareholders to receive a particular price. Delaware law recognizes that, as to allegedly voluntary tender offers (in contrast to cash out mergers), the determinative factors as to voluntariness are whether coercion is present, or whether there are materially false or misleading disclosures made to stockholders in connection with the offer."[105]

In two recent cases, this court has followed *Solomon*'s articulation of the standards applicable to a tender offer, and held that the "Delaware law does not impose a duty of entire fairness on controlling stockholders making a non coercive tender or exchange offer to acquire shares directly from the minority holders."[106]

The differences between this approach, which I will identify with the *Solomon* line of cases, and that of *Lynch* are stark. To begin with, the controlling stockholder is said to have no duty to pay a fair price, irrespective of its power over the subsidiary. Even more striking is the different manner in which the coercion concept is deployed. In the tender offer context addressed by *Solomon* and its progeny, coercion is defined in the more traditional sense as a wrongful threat that has the effect of forcing stockholders to tender at the wrong price to avoid an even worse fate later on, a type of coercion I will call structural coercion.[107] The inherent coercion that found to exist when controlling stockholders seek to acquire the minority's stake is not even a cognizable concern for the common law of corporations if the tender offer method is employed.

This latter point is illustrated by those cases that squarely hold that a tender is not actionably coercive if the majority stockholder decides to: (i) condition the closing of the tender offer on support of a majority of the minority and (ii) promise that it would consummate a short-form merger on the same terms as the tender offer.[108] In those circumstances, at least, these cases can be read to bar a claim against the majority stockholder even if the price offered is below what would be considered fair in an entire fairness hearing ("fair price") or an appraisal action ("fair value"). That is, in the tender offer context, our courts consider it sufficient protection against coercion to give effective veto power over the offer to a majority

---

[105] [24] *Solomon v. Pathe Communications Corp.*, 672 A.2d 35, 39 (Del. 1996) (citations and quotations omitted).

[106] [25] *In re Aquila Inc.*, 805 A.2d 184, 2002 WL 27815, at *5 (Del. Ch. Jan. 3, 2002); *In re Siliconix Inc. S'holders Litig.*, 2001 WL 716787, *6[, 2001 Del. Ch. LEXIS 83] (Del. Ch. June 21, 2001) ("unless coercion or disclosure violations can be shown, no defendant has the duty to demonstrate the entire fairness of this proposed tender transaction"); *see also In re Ocean Drilling & Exploration Co. S'holders Litig.*, 1991 WL 70028, at *5[, 1991 Del. Ch. LEXIS 82] (Del. Ch. Apr. 30, 1991) (taking same basic approach).

[107] [26] *See In re Marriott Hotel Props. II Ltd. P'ship*, 2000 WL 128875, at *18[, 2000 Del. Ch. LEXIS 17] (Del. Ch. Jan. 24, 2000). I include within the concept of structural coercion an offer that is coercive because the controlling stockholder threatens to take action after the tender offer that is harmful to the remaining minority (*e.g.*, to seek affirmatively to delist the company's shares) or because the offer's back-end is so unattractive as to induce tendering at an inadequate price to avoid a worse fate (*e.g.*, a pledge to do a § 253 merger involving consideration in the form of high risk payment-in-kind bonds).

[108] [27] *See, e.g., In re Aquila Inc.*, 2002 Del. Ch. Lexis 5, at *8-*9 (Del. Ch. Jan. 3, 2002).

of the minority.[109] Yet that very same protection is considered insufficient to displace fairness review in the negotiated merger context.

5.

The parties here cross swords over the arguable doctrinal inconsistency between the *Solomon* and *Lynch* lines of cases, with the plaintiffs arguing that it makes no sense and Unocal contending that the distinction is non foolish in the Emersonian sense. I turn more directly to that dispute now.

I begin by discussing whether the mere fact that one type of transaction is a tender offer and the other is a negotiated merger is a sustainable basis for the divergent policy choices made in *Lynch* and *Solomon*? Aspects of this issue are reminiscent of a prominent debate that roared in the 1980s when hostile takeover bids first became commonplace. During that period, one school of thought argued vigorously that target boards of directors should not interfere with the individual decisions of stockholders as to whether to sell shares into a tender offer made by a third-party acquirer. The ability of stockholders to alienate their shares freely was viewed as an important property right that could not be thwarted by the target company's board of directors. In support of this argument, it was noted that the Delaware General Corporation Law provided no requirement for target boards to approve tender offers made to their stockholders, let alone any explicit authority to block such offers. The statute's failure to mention tender offers was argued to be an expression of legislative intent that should be respected by allowing tender offers to proceed without target board interposition.[110]

The debate about that issue was complex and exciting (at least for those interested in corporate law). The arguments of the participants evolved with market practices and results. These arguments ran the gamut from those who argued for total director passivity in the face of structurally non coercive tender offers (*e.g.*, an all-shares, all-cash offer, with the promise to do a back end merger at the same price),[111] to those who advocated for time-limited and methodologically constrained reactions by target boards that would permit the development of higher value opportunities, the negotiation of higher bids, and the provision of full information to target stockholders,[112] and even to those who advocated that target directors could make a good faith decision to "just say no" indefinitely to a bid that they believed was inadequate, but which the stockholders might find attractive.[113]

Many important aspects to that debate remain open for argument. At least one

---

[109] [28] *See, e.g., Siliconix*, 2001 WL 716787 at *8 [, 2001 Del. Ch. LEXIS 83].

[110] [29] Our judiciary has sometimes articulated a somewhat weaker form of this same belief. *See T.W. Services, Inc. v. SWT Acquisition Corp.*, 1989 WL 20290, 1989 Del. Ch. LEXIS 19, at *28-30 (Mar. 2, 1989).

[111] [30] *See generally* Frank H. Easterbrook & Daniel R. Fischel, *The Proper Role of a Target's Management in Responding to a Tender Offer*, 94 Harv. L. Rev. 1161 (1981).

[112] [31] *See generally* Ronald J. Gilson & Reinier Kraakman, *Delaware's Intermediate Standard for Defensive Tactics: Is There Substance to Proportionality Review?*, 44 Bus. Law. 247 (1989).

[113] [32] Martin Lipton is the most prominent spokesman for this position. *See generally* Martin Lipton, *Takeover Bids in the Target's Boardroom*, 35 Bus. Law. 101 (1979).

component of that debate, however, has been firmly decided, which is that the mere fact that the DGCL contemplates no role for target boards in tender offers does not, of itself, prevent a target board from impeding the consummation of a tender offer through extraordinary defensive measures, such as a poison pill, subject to a heightened form of reasonableness review under the so called *Unocal* standard.[114] Indeed, our case law went a step further — it described as an affirmative duty the role of a board of directors whose stockholders had received a tender offer:

> [T]he board's power to act derives from its fundamental duty and obligation to protect the corporate enterprise, which includes stockholders, from harm reasonably perceived, irrespective of its source. Thus, we are satisfied that in the broad context of corporate governance, including issues of fundamental corporate change, a board of directors is not a passive instrumentality.[115]

In the third-party offer context, of course, the controversy was rarely over the need to inspire target directors to erect defenses to tender offers. Instead, the legal battles centered on the extent of the target board's authority to block the bid. It quickly became settled that target boards could employ a poison pill and other defensive measures to deflect a tender offer that was structured in a coercive manner (*e.g.*, a front end loaded, two- tiered tender offer promising junk bonds on the back end).[116]

The extent of a target board's authority to block a tender offer that was not structurally coercive was resolved in a less definitive way. Some argue that a decision of the Delaware Supreme Court — *Paramount Communications, Inc. v. Time Inc.* (" *Time-Warner*")[117] — which did not involve a poison pill — stands for the proposition that a target board may block a fully-funded, all-cash, all-shares tender offer indefinitely so long as it believes in good faith that the offer is inadequate. In such a situation, the threat of yet another kind of coercion — so-called "substantive coercion," (*i.e.*, that stockholders might mistakenly disregard the board's advice not to tender) — is argued by some commentators to justify continuous use of the pill to "just say no."[118] Indeed, the *Time-Warner* decision contains dictum that supports this view and appears to give little, if any, weight to the policy importance of allowing target stockholders to decide for themselves whether to accept a tender offer.[119]

---

[114] [33] *Unocal Corp. v. Mesa Petroleum Co.*, 493 A.2d 946 (Del. 1985).

[115] [34] *Id.* at 954 (citations omitted) (emphasis added).

[116] [35] *See id.* at 956-59.

[117] [36] 571 A.2d 1140 (Del. 1989).

[118] [37] Adherents of this school articulate many reasons for their support of this position. These are well articulated in Martin Lipton & Paul K. Rowe, *Pills, Polls, and Professors: A Reply to Professor Gilson*, 27 Del. J. Corp. L. (forthcoming 2002).

[119] [38] The following language, when accompanied by dictum criticizing *City Capital Assocs. Ltd. P'ship v. Interco Inc.*, 551 A.2d 787 (Del. Ch.), *appeal dismissed*, 556 A.2d 1070 (Del. 1988), arguably communicated this message:

> Delaware law confers the management of the corporate enterprise to the stockholders' duly elected board representatives. The fiduciary duty to manage a corporate enterprise includes the selection of a time frame for achievement of corporate goals. That duty may not

Others, however, believe that the "just say no" question is still an open one and that directors cannot deny their stockholders access to a tender offer solely because of price inadequacy, once they have had an adequate opportunity to develop a higher-value alternative, to provide the stockholders with sufficient information to make an informed decision whether to tender, and perhaps channel the stockholder referendum on the bid into the next election process. Proponents of this view take a less paternalistic approach and believe stockholders, and not the target directors, have the ultimate right to accept a structurally non coercive tender offer.

What is clear, however, is that Delaware law has not regarded tender offers as involving a special transactional space, from which directors are altogether excluded from exercising substantial authority. To the contrary, much Delaware jurisprudence during the last twenty years has dealt with whether directors acting within that space comported themselves consistently with their duties of loyalty and care. It therefore is by no means obvious that simply because a controlling stockholder proceeds by way of a tender offer that either it or the target's directors fall outside the constraints of fiduciary duty law.

In this same vein, the basic model of directors and stockholders adopted by our M & A case law is relevant. Delaware law has seen directors as well-positioned to understand the value of the target company, to compensate for the disaggregated nature of stockholders by acting as a negotiating and auctioning proxy for them, and as a bulwark against structural coercion. Relatedly, dispersed stockholders have been viewed as poorly positioned to protect and, yes, sometimes, even to think for themselves.

6.

Because tender offers are not treated exceptionally in the third-party context, it is important to ask why the tender offer method should be consequential in formulating the equitable standards of fiduciary conduct by which courts review acquisition proposals made by controlling stockholders. Is there reason to believe that the tender offer method of acquisition is more protective of the minority, with the result that less scrutiny is required than of negotiated mergers with controlling stockholders?

Unocal's answer to that question is yes and primarily rests on an inarguable proposition: in a negotiated merger involving a controlling stockholder, the controlling stockholder is on both sides of the transaction. That is, the negotiated merger is a self-dealing transaction, whereas in a tender offer, the controlling stockholder is only on the offering side and the minority remain free not to sell.

As a formal matter, this distinction is difficult to contest. When examined more deeply, however, it is not a wall that can bear the full weight of the *Lynch/Solomon* distinction. In this regard, it is important to remember that the overriding concern of *Lynch* is the controlling shareholders have the ability to take retributive action

---

> be delegated to the stockholders. Directors are not obligated to abandon a deliberately conceived corporate plan for a short-term shareholder profit unless there is clearly no basis to sustain the corporate strategy.

Paramount Communications, Inc., 571 A.2d at 1154 (citations omitted).

in the wake of rejection by an independent board, a special committee, or the minority shareholders. That ability is so influential that the usual cleansing devices that obviate fairness review of interested transactions cannot be trusted. The problem is that nothing about the tender offer method of corporate acquisition makes the 800 pound gorilla's retributive capabilities less daunting to minority stockholders. Indeed, many commentators would argue that the tender offer form is more coercive than a merger vote. In a merger vote, stockholders can vote no and still receive the transactional consideration if the merger prevails.[120] In a tender offer, however, a non tendering shareholder individually faces an uncertain fate. That stockholder could be one of the few who holds out, leaving herself in an even more thinly traded stock with little hope of liquidity and subject to a § 253 merger at a lower price or at the same price but at a later (and, given the time value of money, a less valuable) time. The 14D-9 warned Pure's minority stockholders of just this possibility. For these reasons, some view tender offers as creating a prisoner's dilemma — distorting choice and creating incentives for stockholders to tender into offers that they believe are inadequate in order to avoid a worse fate.[121] But whether or not one views tender offers as more coercive of shareholder choice than negotiated mergers with controlling stockholders, it is difficult to argue that tender offers are materially freer and more reliable measures of stockholder sentiment.

Furthermore, the common law of corporations has long had a structural answer to the formal self-dealing point Unocal makes: a non waivable majority of the minority vote condition to a merger. By this technique, the ability of the controlling stockholder to both offer and accept is taken away, and the sell-side decision-making authority is given to the minority stockholders. That method of proceeding replicates the tender offer made by Unocal here, with the advantage of not distorting the stockholders' vote on price adequacy in the way that a tendering decision arguably does.

Lynch, of course, held that a majority of the minority vote provision will not displace entire fairness review with business judgment rule review. Critically, the *Lynch* Court's distrust of the majority of the minority provision is grounded in a concern that also exists in the tender offer context. The basis for the distrust is the concern that before the fact ("ex ante") minority stockholders will fear retribution after the fact ("ex post") if they vote no — *i.e.*, they will face inherent coercion — thus rendering the majority of the minority condition an inadequate guarantee of fairness. But if this concern is valid, then that same inherent coercion would seem to apply with equal force to the tender offer decision-making process, and be

---

[120] [39] They may or may not receive appraisal rights. In this case, for example, *Unocal* notes that appraisal rights would not be available to dissenters if it had negotiated a merger agreement with Pure. Because it has proceeded by the tender offer route with a hoped-for § 253 merger, such rights will be available even though Unocal is offering widely traded stock, rather than cash, consideration.

[121] [40] *See* Lucian Arye Bebchuk, *Toward Undistorted Choice and Equal Treatment in Corporate Takeovers*, 98 Harv. L. Rev. 1695, 1696 (1985); Lucian Arye Bebchuk, *The Case for Facilitating Competing Tender Offers*, 95 Harv. L. Rev. 1028, 1039-40 (1982); Louis Lowenstein, *Pruning Deadwood in Hostile Takeovers: A Proposal for Legislation*, 83 Colum. L. Rev. 249, 307-09 (1983); Robert A. Prentice & John H. Langmore, *Hostile Tender Offers and the "Nancy Reagan Defense": May Target Boards "Just Say No"? Should They Be Allowed To?*, 15 Del. J. Corp. L. 377, 442 (1990); Aronstam (manuscript at 38-54).

enhanced by the unique features of that process. A controlling stockholder's power to force a squeeze out or cut dividends is no different after the failure of a tender offer than after defeat on a merger vote.[122]

Finally, some of the other factors that are said to support fairness review of negotiated mergers involving controlling stockholders also apply with full force to tender offers made by controlling stockholders. The informational advantage that the controlling stockholder possesses is not any different; in this case, for example, Unocal was able to proceed having had full access to non public information about Pure. The tender offer form provides no additional protection against this concern.

Furthermore, the tender offer method allows the controlling stockholder to time its offer and to put a bull rush on the target stockholders. Here, Unocal studied an acquisition of Pure for nearly a year and then made a "surprise" offer that forced a rapid response from Pure's Special Committee and the minority stockholders.

Likewise, one struggles to imagine why subsidiary directors would feel less constrained in reacting to a tender offer by a controlling stockholder than a negotiated merger proposal. Indeed, an arguably more obvious concern is that subsidiary directors might use the absence of a statutory role for them in the tender offer process to be less than aggressive in protecting minority interests, to wit, the edifying examples of subsidiary directors courageously taking no position on the merits of offers by a controlling stockholder. Or, as here, the Special Committee's failure to demand the power to use the normal range of techniques available to a non controlled board responding to a third-party tender offer.

For these and other reasons that time constraints preclude me from explicating, I remain less than satisfied that there is a justifiable basis for the distinction between the *Lynch* and *Solomon* lines of cases. Instead, their disparate teachings reflect a difference in policy emphasis that is far greater than can be explained by the technical differences between tender offers and negotiated mergers, especially given Delaware's director-centered approach to tender offers made by third-parties, which emphasizes the vulnerability of disaggregated stockholders absent important help and protection from their directors.

7.

The absence of convincing reasons for this disparity in treatment inspires the plaintiffs to urge me to apply the entire fairness standard of review to Unocal's offer. Otherwise, they say, the important protections set forth in the *Lynch* line of cases will be rendered useless, as all controlling stockholders will simply choose to proceed to make subsidiary acquisitions by way of a tender offer and later short-form merger.

I admit being troubled by the imbalance in Delaware law exposed by the *Solomon/Lynch* lines of cases. Under *Solomon*, the policy emphasis is on the right of willing buyers and sellers of stock to deal with each other freely, with only such

[122] [41] A different view might be taken, of course, which recognizes that the constraints of equity and the appraisal statute, when combined, act as a sufficient check on retribution to allow (increasingly sophisticated and active) stockholders to vote on mergers freely. But *Lynch* does not embrace this view.

judicial intervention as is necessary to ensure fair disclosure and to prevent structural coercion. The advantage of this emphasis is that it provides a relatively non litigious way to effect going private transactions and relies upon minority stockholders to protect themselves. The cost of this approach is that it arguably exposes minority stockholders to the more subtle form of coercion that *Lynch* addresses and leaves them without adequate redress for unfairly timed and priced offers. The approach also minimizes the potential for the minority to get the best price, by arguably giving them only enough protection to keep them from being structurally coerced into accepting grossly insufficient bids but not necessarily merely inadequate ones.

Admittedly, the *Solomon* policy choice would be less disquieting if Delaware also took the same approach to third-party offers and thereby allowed diversified investors the same degree of unrestrained access to premium bids by third-parties. In its brief, Unocal makes a brave effort to explain why it is understandable that Delaware law emphasizes the rights of minority stockholders to freely receive structurally, non coercive tender offers from controlling stockholders but not their right to accept identically structured offers from third parties. Although there may be subtle ways to explain this variance, a forest-eye summary by a stockholder advocate might run as follows: As a general matter, Delaware law permits directors substantial leeway to block the access of stockholders to receive substantial premium tender offers made by third-parties by use of the poison pill but provides relatively free access to minority stockholders to accept buy out offers from controlling stockholders.

In the case of third-party offers, these advocates would note, there is arguably less need to protect stockholders indefinitely from structurally non coercive bids because alternative buyers can emerge and because the target board can use the poison pill to buy time and to tell its story. By contrast, when a controlling stockholder makes a tender offer, the subsidiary board is unlikely — as this case demonstrates — to be permitted by the controlling stockholder to employ a poison pill to fend off the bid and exert pressure for a price increase and usually lacks any real clout to develop an alternative transaction. In the end, however, I do not believe that these discrepancies should lead to an expansion of the *Lynch* standard to controlling stockholder tender offers.

Instead, the preferable policy choice is to continue to adhere to the more flexible and less constraining *Solomon* approach, while giving some greater recognition to the inherent coercion and structural bias concerns that motivate the *Lynch* line of cases. Adherence to the *Solomon* rubric as a general matter, moreover, is advisable in view of the increased activism of institutional investors and the greater information flows available to them. Investors have demonstrated themselves capable of resisting tender offers made by controlling stockholders on occasion,[123] and even the lead plaintiff here expresses no fear of retribution. This does not mean that controlling stockholder tender offers do not pose risks to minority stockholders; it is only to acknowledge that the corporate law should not be designed on the assumption that diversified investors are infirm but instead should give great deference to transactions approved by them voluntarily and knowledgeably.

---

[123] [42] Unocal has submitted recent examples of this phenomenon.

To the extent that my decision to adhere to *Solomon* causes some discordance between the treatment of similar transactions to persist, that lack of harmony is better addressed in the *Lynch* line, by affording greater liability-immunizing effect to protective devices such as majority of minority approval conditions and special committee negotiation and approval.[124]

8.

To be more specific about the application of *Solomon* in these circumstances, it is important to note that the *Solomon* line of cases does not eliminate the fiduciary duties of controlling stockholders or target boards in connection with tender offers made by controlling stockholders. Rather, the question is the contextual extent and nature of those duties, a question I will now tentatively,[125] and incompletely, answer.

The potential for coercion and unfairness posed by controlling stockholders who seek to acquire the balance of the company's shares by acquisition requires some equitable reinforcement, in order to give proper effect to the concerns undergirding *Lynch*. In order to address the prisoner's dilemma problem, our law should consider an acquisition tender offer by a controlling stockholder non coercive only when: 1) it is subject to a non waivable majority of the minority tender condition; 2) the controlling stockholder promises to consummate a prompt § 253 merger at the same price if it obtains more than 90% of the shares; and 3) the controlling stockholder has made no retributive threats.[126] Those protections — also stressed in this court's recent *Aquila* decision — minimize the distorting influence of the tendering process on voluntary choice. They also recognize the adverse conditions that confront stockholders who find themselves owning what have become very thinly traded shares. These conditions also provide a partial cure to the disaggregation problem, by providing a realistic non tendering goal the minority can achieve to prevent the offer from proceeding altogether.[127]

The informational and timing advantages possessed by controlling stockholders also require some countervailing protection if the minority is to truly be afforded the opportunity to make an informed, voluntary tender decision. In this regard, the

---

[124] [43] A slight easing of the *Lynch* rule would help level the litigation risks posed by the different acquisition methods, and thereby provide an incentive to use the negotiated merger route. At the very least, this tailoring could include providing business judgment protection to mergers negotiated by a special committee and subject to majority of the minority protection. This dual method of protection would replicate the third-party merger process under 8 Del. C. § 251.

[125] [44] As befits the development of the common law in expedited decisions.

[126] [45] One can conceive of other non-coercive approaches, including a tender offer that was accompanied by a separate question that asked the stockholders whether they wished the offer to proceed. If a majority of the minority had to answer this question yes for the offer to proceed, stockholders could tender their shares but remain free to express an undistorted choice on the adequacy of the offer.

[127] [46] They achieve this at some detriment to individual rights, a detriment that seems justifiable as helping the minority increase its leverage to hold out for a truly attractive offer. This protection still may not render the disaggregated minority capable of extracting the offeror's full reserve price, in contrast to a board with the actual power to stop an offer for at least a commercially significant period of time and to force meaningful give-and-take at the bargaining table, which is not available as an option in the take it-or-leave it tender process.

majority stockholder owes a duty to permit the independent directors on the target board both free rein and adequate time to react to the tender offer, by (at the very least) hiring their own advisors, providing the minority with a recommendation as to the advisability of the offer, and disclosing adequate information for the minority to make an informed judgment.[128] For their part, the independent directors have a duty to undertake these tasks in good faith and diligently, and to pursue the best interests of the minority.[129]

When a tender offer is non coercive in the sense I have identified and the independent directors of the target are permitted to make an informed recommendation and provide fair disclosure, the law should be chary about superimposing the full fiduciary requirement of entire fairness upon the statutory tender offer process. Here, the plaintiffs argue that the Pure board breached its fiduciary duties by not giving the Special Committee the power to block the Offer by, among other means, deploying a poison pill. Indeed, the plaintiffs argue that the full board's decision not to grant that authority is subject to the entire fairness standard of review because a majority of the full board was not independent of Unocal.

That argument has some analytical and normative appeal, embodying as it does the rough fairness of the goose and gander rule.[130] I am reluctant, however, to burden the common law of corporations with a new rule that would tend to compel the use of a device that our statutory law only obliquely sanctions and that in other contexts is subject to misuse, especially when used to block a high value bid that is not structurally coercive. When a controlling stockholder makes a tender offer that is not coercive in the sense I have articulated, therefore, the better rule is that there is no duty on its part to permit the target board to block the bid through use of the pill. Nor is there any duty on the part of the independent directors to seek blocking power.[131] But it is important to be mindful of one of the reasons that make a contrary rule problematic — the awkwardness of a legal rule requiring a board to take aggressive action against a structurally non coercive offer by the controlling stockholder that elects it. This recognition of the sociology of controlled subsidiaries puts a point on the increased vulnerability that stockholders face from controlling stockholder tenders, because the minority stockholders are denied the full range of protection offered by boards in response to third party offers. This factor illustrates

---

[128] [47] This is not to slight the controlling stockholder's fiduciary duty of fair disclosure and its duty to avoid misleading the independent directors and the minority.

[129] [48] Whether a majority stockholder can compose a subsidiary board entirely comprised of persons beholden to itself and use this fact as the reason for depriving the minority of a board recommendation is a question about which I need not speculate, and which recent corporate governance developments suggest will not likely need to be answered definitively.

[130] [49] Management-side lawyers must view this case, and the recent *Digex* case, *see In re Digex Inc. S'holders Litig.*, 789 A.2d 1176 (Del. Ch. 2000), as boomerangs. Decades after their invention, tools designed to help management stay in place are now being wielded by minority stockholders. I note that the current situation can be distinguished from *Digex*, insofar as in that case the controlling stockholder forced the subsidiary board to take action only beneficial to it, whereas here the Pure board simply did not interpose itself between Unocal's Offer and the Pure minority.

[131] [50] If our law trusts stockholders to protect themselves in the case of a controlling stockholder tender offer that has the characteristics I have described, this will obviously be remembered by advocates in cases involving defenses against similarly non-coercive third-party tender offers.

the utility of the protective conditions that I have identified as necessary to prevent abuse of the minority.

9.

Turning specifically to Unocal's Offer, I conclude that the application of these principles yields the following result. The Offer, in its present form, is coercive because it includes within the definition of the "minority" those stockholders who are affiliated with Unocal as directors and officers. It also includes the management of Pure, whose incentives are skewed by their employment, their severance agreements, and their Put Agreements. This is, of course, a problem that can be cured if Unocal amends the Offer to condition it on approval of a majority of Pure's unaffiliated stockholders. Requiring the minority to be defined exclusive of stockholders whose independence from the controlling stockholder is compromised is the better legal rule (and result). Too often, it will be the case that officers and directors of controlled subsidiaries have voting incentives that are not perfectly aligned with their economic interest in their stock and who are more than acceptably susceptible to influence from controlling stockholders. Aside, however, from this glitch in the majority of the minority condition, I conclude that Unocal's Offer satisfies the other requirements of "non coerciveness." Its promise to consummate a prompt § 253 merger is sufficiently specific,[132] and Unocal has made no retributive threats.

Although Unocal's Offer does not altogether comport with the above-described definition of non-coercive, it does not follow that I believe that the plaintiffs have established a probability of success on the merits as to their claim that the Pure board should have blocked that Offer with a pill or other measures. Putting aside the shroud of silence that cloaked the board's (mostly, it seems, behind the scenes) deliberations, there appears to have been at least a rational basis to believe that a pill was not necessary to protect the Pure minority against coercion, largely, because Pure's management had expressed adamant opposition to the Offer. Moreover, the board allowed the Special Committee a free hand: to recommend against the Offer — as it did; to negotiate for a higher price — as it attempted to do; and to prepare the company's 14D-9 — as it did.

For all these reasons, therefore, I find that the plaintiffs do not have a probability of success on the merits of their attack on the Offer, with the exception that the majority of the minority condition is flawed.

C. The Plaintiffs' Disclosure Claims

As their other basis for attack, the plaintiffs argue that neither of the key disclosure documents provided to the Pure stockholders — the S-4 Unocal issued in support of its Offer and the 14D-9 Pure filed in reaction to the Offer — made materially complete and accurate disclosure. The general legal standards that

---

[132] [51] A note is in order here. I believe Unocal's statement of intent to be sufficiently clear as to expose it to potential liability in the event that it were to obtain 90% and not consummate the short-form merger at the same price (*e.g.*, if it made the exchange ratio in the short-form merger less favorable). The promise of equal treatment in short-form merger is what renders the tender decision less distorting.

govern the plaintiffs' disclosure claims are settled.

In circumstances such as these, the Pure stockholders are entitled to disclosure of all material facts pertinent to the decisions they are being asked to make. In this case, the Pure stockholders must decide whether to take one of two initial courses of action: tender and accept the Offer if it proceeds or not tender and attempt to stop the Offer. If the Offer is consummated, the non tendering stockholders will face two subsequent choices that they will have to make on the basis of the information in the S-4 and 14D-9: to accept defeat quietly by accepting the short-form merger consideration in the event that Unocal obtains 90% and lives up to its promise to do an immediate short-form merger or seek to exercise the appraisal rights described in the S-4. I conclude that the S-4 and the 14D-9 are important to all these decisions, because both documents state that Unocal will effect the short-form merger promptly if it gets 90%, and shareholders rely on those documents to provide the substantive information on which stockholders will be asked to base their decision whether to accept the merger consideration or to seek appraisal.

As a result, it is the information that is material to these various choices that must be disclosed. In other words, the S-4 and the 14D-9 must contain the information that "a reasonable investor would consider important in tendering his stock,"[133] including the information necessary to make a reasoned decision whether to seek appraisal in the event Unocal effects a prompt short-form merger.[134] In order for undisclosed information to be material, there must be a "substantial likelihood that the disclosure of the omitted fact would have been viewed by the reasonable stockholder as having significantly altered the 'total mix' of information made available."[135]

The S-4 and 14D-9 are also required "to provide a balanced, truthful account of all matters" they disclose.[136] Related to this obligation is the requirement to avoid misleading partial disclosures. When a document ventures into certain subjects, it must do so in a manner that is materially complete and unbiased by the omission of material facts.[137]

The plaintiffs advance a plethora of disclosure claims, only the most important of which can be addressed in the time frame available to me. I therefore address them in order of importance, as I see them.

1.

First and foremost, the plaintiffs argue that the 14D-9 is deficient because it does not disclose any substantive portions of the work of First Boston and Petrie Parkman on behalf of the Special Committee, even though the bankers' negative views of the Offer are cited as a basis for the board's own recommendation not to tender. Having left it to the Pure minority to say no for themselves, the Pure board

---

[133] [52] *Zirn v. VLI Corp.*, 621 A.2d 773, 779 (Del. 1993).

[134] [53] *See Skeen v. Jo-Ann Stores, Inc.*, 750 A.2d 1170, 1172-73 (Del. 2000).

[135] [54] *Loudon v. Archer-Daniels-Midland Co.*, 700 A.2d 135, 143 (Del. 1997).

[136] [55] *Malone v. Brincat*, 722 A.2d 5, 12 (Del. 1998).

[137] [56] *See Arnold v. Society for Savings Bancorp, Inc.*, 650 A.2d 1270, 1280-82 (Del. 1994).

(the plaintiffs say) owed the minority the duty to provide them with material information about the value of Pure's shares, including, in particular, the estimates and underlying analyses of value developed by the Special Committee's bankers. This duty is heightened, the plaintiffs say, because the Pure minority is subject to an immediate short-form merger if the Offer proceeds as Unocal hopes, and will have to make the decision whether to seek appraisal in those circumstances.

In response, the Pure director-defendants argue that the 14D-9 contains a great deal of financial information, including the actual opinions of First Boston and Petrie Parkman. They also note that the S-4 contains historical financial information about Pure's results as well as certain projections of future results.[138]

As such, they claim that disclosure of more detailed information about the banker's views of value, while interesting, would not have been material. Furthermore, the Special Committee argues that disclosure could be injurious to the minority. Because the Special Committee still hopes to secure a better price at the negotiating table, they are afraid that disclosure of their bankers' range of values will hamper their bargaining leverage. Finally, the director-defendants cite Delaware case law that indicates that a summary of the results of the actual valuation analyses conducted by an investment banker ordinarily need not be disclosed.

This is a continuation of an ongoing debate in Delaware corporate law, and one I confess to believing has often been answered in an intellectually unsatisfying manner. Fearing stepping on the SEC's toes and worried about encouraging prolix disclosures,[139] the Delaware courts have been reluctant to require informative, succinct disclosure of investment banker analyses in circumstances in which the bankers' views about value have been cited as justifying the recommendation of the board.[140] But this reluctance has been accompanied by more than occasional acknowledgement of the utility of such information,[141] an acknowledgement that is understandable given the substantial encouragement Delaware case law has given to the deployment of investment bankers by boards of directors addressing mergers and tender offers.

These conflicting impulses were manifested recently in two Supreme Court opinions. In one, *Skeen v. Jo-Ann Stores, Inc.*,[142] the Court was inclined towards the view that a summary of the bankers' analyses and conclusions was not material to a stockholders' decision whether to seek appraisal. In the other, *McMullin v. Beran*,[143] the Court implied that information about the analytical work of the board's banker could well be material in analogous circumstances.

In my view, it is time that this ambivalence be resolved in favor of a firm

---

[138] [57] Because Pure's historical financial results and projected results were disclosed in the S-4, it would not add materially to the mix of information for the 14D-9 to simply repeat them.

[139] [58] *See, e.g., In re Staples, Inc. S'holders Litig.*, 792 A.2d 934, 954 (Del. Ch. 2001).

[140] [59] Decisions tending towards this view include *Matador Capital Mgmt. v. BRC Holdings*, 729 A.2d 280, 297 (Del. Ch. 1998).

[141] [60] *E.g., Sealy Mattress Co. v. Sealy, Inc.*, 532 A.2d 1324, 1339-40 (Del. Ch. 1987).

[142] [61] 750 A.2d 1170 (Del. 2000).

[143] [62] 765 A.2d 910 (Del. 2000).

statement that stockholders are entitled to a fair summary of the substantive work performed by the investment bankers upon whose advice the recommendations of their board as to how to vote on a merger or tender rely. I agree that our law should not encourage needless prolixity, but that concern cannot reasonably apply to investment bankers' analyses, which usually address the most important issue to stockholders — the sufficiency of the consideration being offered to them for their shares in a merger or tender offer. Moreover, courts must be candid in acknowledging that the disclosure of the banker's "fairness opinion" alone and without more, provides stockholders with nothing other than a conclusion, qualified by a gauze of protective language designed to insulate the banker from liability.

The real informative value of the banker's work is not in its bottom-line conclusion, but in the valuation analysis that buttresses that result. This proposition is illustrated by the work of the judiciary itself, which closely examines the underlying analyses performed by the investment bankers when determining whether a transaction price is fair or a board reasonably relied on the banker's advice. Like a court would in making an after-the-fact fairness determination, a Pure minority stockholder engaging in the before-the-fact decision whether to tender would find it material to know the basic valuation exercises that First Boston and Petrie Parkman undertook, the key assumptions that they used in performing them, and the range of values that were thereby generated. After all, these were the very advisors who played the leading role in shaping the Special Committee's finding of inadequacy.

The need for this information is heightened here, due to the Pure board's decision to leave it up to the stockholders whether to "say no." Had the Pure board taken steps to stop the Offer itself, the Special Committee's desire to conceal the bankers' work during ongoing negotiations might make some sense. But Unocal has not even made a counter-offer to the Committee. Thus, the Special Committee's reserve price is not the issue, it is that of the stockholders that counts, and they deserve quality information to formulate it. Put differently, disclosure of the bankers' analyses will not reveal the stockholders' reserve price, but failure to disclose the information will deprive the stockholders of information material to making an informed decision whether the exchange ratio is favorable to them. In this regard, it is notable that the 14D-9 discloses the Special Committee's overture to increase the exchange ratio. Because this was the Special Committee's first offer, it is likely seen by Unocal as negotiable and as setting a frame on further discussions. Since the Special Committee has already tipped its hand in this way, I fail to see the danger of arming the stockholders who must actually decide on the Offer with the advice of the bankers who were hired at very expensive rates to protect their interests.

Although there are other reasons why I find this type of information material, one final policy reason will suffice for now. When controlling stockholders make tender offers, they have large informational advantages that can only be imperfectly overcome by the special committee process, which almost invariably involves directors who are not involved in the day-to-day management of the subsidiary. The retention of financial advisors by special committees is designed to offset some of this asymmetry, and it would seem to be in full keeping with that goal for the minority stockholders to be given a summary of the core analyses of these advisors in circumstances in which the stockholders must protect themselves in the voting or tender process. That this can be done without great burden is demonstrated by the many transactions in which meaningful summary disclosure of bankers' opinions are made, either by choice or by SEC rule.[144]

For all these reasons, I conclude that the plaintiffs have shown a reasonable probability of success on their claim that the 14D-9 omits material information regarding the First Boston and Petrie Parkman analyses.

2.

The plaintiffs' next claim is easier to resolve. In the 14D-9, the following statement appears:

> On September 11, 2002, Pure's board of directors held a telephonic meeting to discuss the Special Committee's request for a clarification of its purposes, powers, authority and independence. After discussion, Pure's board of directors adopted clarifying resolutions.

This statement is an inaccurate and materially misleading summary of the Pure board's rejection of the Special Committee's request for broader authority. No reasonable reader would know that the Special Committee sought to have the full power of the Pure board delegated to it — including the power to block the Offer through a rights plan — and had been rebuffed. No reasonable reader would know that Chessum and Ling (who just a few pages earlier in the 14D-9 had recused themselves from the Pure board's response to the Offer) had reinserted themselves into the process with Unocal's legal advisors and had beaten back this fit of assertiveness by the Special Committee.

The Pure stockholders would find it material to know that the Special Committee had been denied the powers they sought.[145] As important, they are entitled to a balanced and truthful recitation of events, not a sanitized version that is materially misleading.[146] The plaintiffs have established a probability of success on this issue.

3.

The plaintiffs' next argument has some of the flavor of a "gotcha" claim. In the S-4, the Pure stockholders are told that the Unocal board authorized the Offer at the specific exchange ratio ultimately used in the Offer. That statement is false because the Unocal board actually gave its management authority to make an offer at a greater exchange ratio than was eventually offered.

The plaintiffs argue that this false statement is materially misleading. Moreover, they submit that the specific figure authorized by the Unocal board should have

---

[144] [63] In certain going private transactions, the SEC requires that the entire investment banker board presentation books be made public as an exhibit. This requirement has hardly had a deal-stopping effect.

[145] [65] *Clements v. Rogers*, 790 A.2d 1222, 1242-43 (Del. Ch. 2001) (citing *In re Trans World Airlines, Inc. S'holders Litig.*, 1988 WL 111271, at *5 [, 1988 Del. Ch. LEXIS 139] (Del. Ch. Oct. 21, 1988)).

[146] [66] *Clements*, 790 A.2d at 1242-43; *Matador*, 729 A.2d at 295.

been shared with the Pure board by Ling, since he heard it and yet reinjected himself into the negotiations regarding the Special Committee's powers.

In general, I disagree with the plaintiffs that a controlling stockholder must reveal its reserve price in these circumstances. Our law contemplates the possibility of a price negotiation in negotiated mergers involving a controlling stockholder, a practical impossibility if the reserve price of the controlling stockholder must be revealed. The same is true in the tender offer context.

Furthermore, I do not believe that the mere fact that Ling re entered the Pure board process when the Special Committee sought authority adverse to Unocal's interest means that he had a duty to expose everything he knew about Unocal's negotiating posture. Significant to this conclusion is the absence of any persuasive evidence that the Special Committee was denied any material information from Pure that was available to Unocal in making its bid. Unocal's own subjective reserve price is not such information.

For these reasons, I do not believe the plaintiffs have a reasonable likelihood of success on this issue. Although I am troubled that the S-4 contains a statement that is literally untrue, the statement is not materially misleading because it in no manner conveys the idea that Unocal either lacks the capacity or the willingness to offer more, if the initial Offer does not find favor.

4.

The S-4 contains a section discussing the "Key Factors" motivating Unocal's decision to extend the Offer. The plaintiffs contend that this discussion is materially incomplete and misleading in at least two respects. First, the plaintiffs note that the S-4 has an extensive section on minimizing conflicts of interest, which dilates on the constraints that the BOA imposes on Pure. The plaintiffs argue, and I agree, that the discussion omits any acknowledgement of a very real motivating factor for Unocal's offer — to eliminate the potential exposure to liability Chessum and Ling faced if Unocal began to compete with Pure in Pure's core areas of operation. The record evidence supports the inference that this was a material concern of Unocal. In order for the disclosure that was made not to be misleading, this concern of Unocal's should be disclosed as well.

The plaintiffs' second contention is similar. In its board deliberations on the Offer, Unocal considered a management presentation indicating that Pure was considering "alternative funding vehicles not optimum to Unocal." This appears to be a reference to the Royalty Trust. Although this was highlighted as a concern for its own board, Unocal omitted this motivation from the S-4. This subject is material because the Royalty Trust is an important transaction that could be highly consequential to Pure's future if the Offer does not succeed. The fact that the Royalty Trust's consideration is one of the motivations for Unocal to buy Pure now might factor into a stockholder's determination of whether Unocal has really put its best bid on the table. Moreover, it is necessary to make the rest of the disclosures regarding Unocal's motives not misleading.

5.

The plaintiffs advance an array of additional and cursorily argued disclosure claims. These claims either have been addressed by supplemental disclosures required by the SEC, do not involve materially important issues, or are too inadequately developed to sustain an injunction application.

. . .

V. Conclusion

For all these reasons, the plaintiffs' motion for a preliminary injunction is hereby granted, and the consummation of the Offer is hereby enjoined. IT IS SO ORDERED, and the parties shall submit a more complete preliminary injunction order for entry within the next 48 hours.

SMITH v. VAN GORKOM

Delaware Supreme Court
488 A.2d 858 (1985)

HORSEY, JUSTICE (for the majority):

This appeal from the Court of Chancery involves a class action brought by shareholders of the defendant Trans Union Corporation ("Trans Union" or "the Company"), originally seeking rescission of a cash-out merger of Trans Union into the defendant New T Company ("New T"), a wholly-owned subsidiary of the defendant, Marmon Group, Inc. ("Marmon"). Alternate relief in the form of damages is sought against the defendant members of the Board of Directors of Trans Union, New T, and Jay A. Pritzker and Robert A. Pritzker, owners of Marmon.[147]

Following trial, the former Chancellor granted judgment for the defendant directors by unreported letter opinion dated July 6, 1982.[148] Judgment was based on two findings: (1) that the Board of Directors had acted in an informed manner so as to be entitled to protection of the business judgment rule in approving the cash-out merger; and (2) that the shareholder vote approving the merger should not be set aside, because the stockholders had been "fairly informed" by the Board of Directors before voting thereon. The plaintiffs appeal.

---

[147] [1] The plaintiff, Alden Smith, originally sought to enjoin the merger; but, following extensive discovery, the Trial Court denied the plaintiffs motion for preliminary injunction by unreported letter opinion dated February 3, 1981. On February 10, 1981, the proposed merger was approved by Trans Union's stockholders at a special meeting, and the merger became effective on that date. Thereafter, John W. Gosselin was permitted to intervene as an additional plaintiff; and Smith and Gosselin were certified as representing a class consisting of all persons, other than defendants, who held shares of Trans Union common stock on all relevant dates. At the time of the merger, Smith owned 54,000 shares of Trans Union stock, Gosselin owned 23,600 shares, and members of Gosselin's family owned 20,000 shares.

[148] [2] Following trial, and before decision by the Trial Court, the parties stipulated to the dismissal, with prejudice, of the Messrs. Pritzker as parties defendant. However, all references to defendants hereinafter are to the defendant directors of Trans Union, unless otherwise noted.

Speaking for the majority of the Court, we conclude that both rulings of the Court of Chancery are clearly erroneous. Therefore, we reverse and direct that judgment be entered in favor of the plaintiffs and against the defendant directors for the fair value of the plaintiffs' stockholdings in Trans Union, in accordance with *Weinberger v. UOP, Inc.*, Del. Supr., 457 A.2d 701 (1983).[149]

We hold: (1) that the Board's decision, reached September 20, 1980, to approve the proposed cash-out merger was not the product of an informed business judgment; (2) that the Board's subsequent efforts to amend the Merger Agreement and take other curative action were ineffectual, both legally and factually; and (3) that the Board did not deal with complete candor with the stockholders by failing to disclose all material facts, which they knew or should have known before securing the stockholders' approval of the merger.

I.

The nature of this case requires a detailed factual statement. The following facts are essentially uncontradicted:[150]

-A-

Trans Union was a publicly-traded, diversified holding company, the principal earnings of which were generated by its railcar leasing business. During the period here involved, the Company had a cash flow of hundreds of millions of dollars annually. However, the Company had difficulty in generating sufficient taxable income to offset increasingly large investment tax credits (ITCs). Accelerated depreciation deductions had decreased available taxable income against which to offset accumulating ITCs. The Company took these deductions, despite their effect on usable ITCs, because the rental price in the railcar leasing market had already impounded the purported tax savings.

In the late 1970s, together with other capital-intensive firms, Trans Union lobbied in Congress to have ITCs refundable in cash to firms which could not fully utilize the credit. During the summer of 1980, defendant Jerome W. Van Gorkom, Trans Union's Chairman and Chief Executive Officer, testified and lobbied in Congress for refundability of ITCs and against further accelerated depreciation. By the end of August, Van Gorkom was convinced that Congress would neither accept the refundability concept nor curtail further accelerated depreciation.

Beginning in the late 1960s, and continuing through the 1970s, Trans Union pursued a program of acquiring small companies in order to increase available taxable income. In July 1980, Trans Union Management prepared the annual revision of the Company's Five Year Forecast. This report was presented to the Board of Directors at its July, 1980 meeting. The report projected an annual income

[149] [3] It has been stipulated that plaintiffs sue on behalf of a class consisting of 10,537 shareholders (out of a total of 12,844) and that the class owned 12,734,404 out of 13,537,758 shares of Trans Union outstanding.

[150] [4] More detailed statements of facts, consistent with this factual outline, appear in related portions of this opinion.

growth of about 20%. The report also concluded that Trans Union would have about $195 million in spare cash between 1980 and 1985, "with the surplus growing rapidly from 1982 onward." The report referred to the IT.C. situation as a "nagging problem" and, given that problem, the leasing company "would still appear to be constrained to a tax break even." The report then listed four alternative uses of the projected 1982-1985 equity surplus: (1) stock repurchase; (2) dividend increases; (3) a major acquisition program; and (4) combinations of the above. The sale of Trans Union was not among the alternatives. The report emphasized that, despite the overall surplus, the operation of the Company would consume all available equity for the next several years, and concluded: "As a result, we have sufficient time to fully develop our course of action."

On August 27, 1980, Van Gorkom met with Senior Management of Trans Union. Van Gorkom reported on his lobbying efforts in Washington and his desire to find a solution to the tax credit problem more permanent than a continued program of acquisitions. Various alternatives were suggested and discussed preliminarily, including the sale of Trans Union to a company with a large amount of taxable income.

Donald Romans, Chief Financial Officer of Trans Union, stated that his department had done a "very brief bit of work on the possibility of a leveraged buy-out." This work had been prompted by a media article which Romans had seen regarding a leveraged buy-out by management. The work consisted of a "preliminary study" of the cash which could be generated by the Company if it participated in a leveraged buy-out. As Romans stated, this analysis "was very first and rough cut at seeing whether a cash flow would support what might be considered a high price for this type of transaction."

On September 5, at another Senior Management meeting which Van Gorkom attended, Romans again brought up the idea of a leveraged buy-out as a "possible strategic alternative" to the Company's acquisition program. Romans and Bruce S. Chelberg, President and Chief Operating Officer of Trans Union, had been working on the matter in preparation for the meeting. According to Romans: They did not "come up" with a price for the Company. They merely "ran the numbers" at $50 a share and at $60 a share with the "rough form" of their cash figures at the time. Their "figures indicated that $50 would be very easy to do but $60 would be very difficult to do under those figures." This work did not purport to establish a fair price for either the Company or 100% of the stock. It was intended to determine the cash flow needed to service the debt that would "probably" be incurred in a leveraged buy-out, based on "rough calculations" without "any benefit of experts to identify what the limits were to that, and so forth." These computations were not considered extensive and no conclusion was reached.

At this meeting, Van Gorkom stated that he would be willing to take $55 per share for his own 75,000 shares. He vetoed the suggestion of a leveraged buy-out by Management, however, as involving a potential conflict of interest for Management. Van Gorkom, a certified public accountant and lawyer, had been an officer of Trans Union for 24 years, its Chief Executive Officer for more than 17 years, and Chairman of its Board for 2 years. It is noteworthy in this connection that he was then approaching 65 years of age and mandatory retirement.

For several days following the September 5 meeting, Van Gorkom pondered the idea of a sale. He had participated in many acquisitions as a manager and director of Trans Union and as a director of other companies. He was familiar with acquisition procedures, valuation methods, and negotiations; and he privately considered the pros and cons of whether Trans Union should seek a privately or publicly-held purchaser.

Van Gorkom decided to meet with Jay A. Pritzker, a well-known corporate takeover specialist and a social acquaintance. However, rather than approaching Pritzker simply to determine his interest in acquiring Trans Union, Van Gorkom assembled a proposed per share price for sale of the Company and a financing structure by which to accomplish the sale. Van Gorkom did so without consulting either his Board or any members of Senior Management except one: Carl Peterson, Trans Union's Controller. Telling Peterson that he wanted no other person on his staff to know what he was doing, but without telling him why, Van Gorkom directed Peterson to calculate the feasibility of a leveraged buy-out at an assumed price per share of $55. Apart from the Company's historic stock market price,[151] and Van Gorkom's long association with Trans Union, the record is devoid of any competent evidence that $55 represented the per share intrinsic value of the Company.

Having thus chosen the $55 figure, based solely on the availability of a leveraged buy-out, Van Gorkom multiplied the price per share by the number of shares outstanding to reach a total value of the Company of $690 million. Van Gorkom told Peterson to use this $690 million figure and to assume a $200 million equity contribution by the buyer. Based on these assumptions, Van Gorkom directed Peterson to determine whether the debt portion of the purchase price could be paid off in five years or less if financed by Trans Union's cash flow as projected in the Five Year Forecast, and by the sale of certain weaker divisions identified in a study done for Trans Union by the Boston Consulting Group ("BCG study"). Peterson reported that, of the purchase price, approximately $50-80 million would remain outstanding after five years. Van Gorkom was disappointed but decided to meet with Pritzker nevertheless.

Van Gorkom arranged a meeting with Pritzker at the latter's home on Saturday, September 13, 1980. Van Gorkom prefaced his presentation by stating to Pritzker:

> Now as far as you are concerned, I can, I think, show how you can pay a substantial premium over the present stock price and pay off most of the loan in the first five years. If you could pay $55 for this Company, here is a way in which I think it can be financed.

Van Gorkom then reviewed with Pritzker his calculations based upon his proposed price of $55 per share. Although Pritzker mentioned $50 as a more attractive figure, no other price was mentioned. However, Van Gorkom stated that to be sure that $55 was the best price obtainable, Trans Union should be free to accept any better offer. Pritzker demurred, stating that his organization would

---

[151] [5] The common stock of Trans Union was traded on the New York Stock Exchange. Over the five year period from 1975 through 1979, Trans Union's stock had traded within a range of a high of $3912 and a low of $2414. Its high and low range for 1980 through September 19 (the last trading day before announcement of the merger) was $3814-$2912.

serve as a "stalking horse" for an "auction contest" only if Trans Union would permit Pritzker to buy 1,750,000 shares of Trans Union stock at market price which Pritzker could then sell to any higher bidder. After further discussion on this point, Pritzker told Van Gorkom that he would give him a more definite reaction soon.

On Monday, September 15, Pritzker advised Van Gorkom that he was interested in the $55 cash-out merger proposal and requested more information on Trans Union. Van Gorkom agreed to meet privately with Pritzker, accompanied by Peterson, Chelberg, and Michael Carpenter, Trans Union's consultant from the Boston Consulting Group. The meetings took place on September 16 and 17. Van Gorkom was "astounded that events were moving with such amazing rapidity."

On Thursday, September 18, Van Gorkom met again with Pritzker. At that time, Van Gorkom knew that Pritzker intended to make a cash-out merger offer at Van Gorkom's proposed $55 per share. Pritzker instructed his attorney, a merger and acquisition specialist, to begin drafting merger documents. There was no further discussion of the $55 price. However, the number of shares of Trans Union's treasury stock to be offered to Pritzker was negotiated down to one million shares; the price was set at $38 — 75 cents above the per share price at the close of the market on September 19. At this point, Pritzker insisted that the Trans Union Board act on his merger proposal within the next three days, stating to Van Gorkom: "We have to have a decision by no later than Sunday [evening, September 21], before the opening of the English stock exchange on Monday morning." Pritzker's lawyer was then instructed to draft the merger documents, to be reviewed by Van Gorkom's lawyer, "sometimes with discussion and sometimes not, in the haste to get it finished."

On Friday, September 19, Van Gorkom, Chelberg, and Pritzker consulted with Trans Union's lead bank regarding the financing of Pritzker's purchase of Trans Union. The bank indicated that it could form a syndicate of banks that would finance the transaction. On the same day, Van Gorkom retained James Brennan, Esquire, to advise Trans Union on the legal aspects of the merger. Van Gorkom did not consult with William Browder, a Vice-President and director of Trans Union and former head of its legal department, or with William Moore, then the head of Trans Union's legal staff.

On Friday, September 19, Van Gorkom called a special meeting of the Trans Union Board for noon the following day. He also called a meeting of the Company's Senior Management to convene at 11:00 a.m., prior to the meeting of the Board. No one, except Chelberg and Peterson, was told the purpose of the meetings. Van Gorkom did not invite Trans Union's investment banker, Salomon Brothers or its Chicago-based partner, to attend.

Of those present at the Senior Management meeting on September 20, only Chelberg and Peterson had prior knowledge of Pritzker's offer. Van Gorkom disclosed the offer and described its terms, but he furnished no copies of the proposed Merger Agreement. Romans announced that his department had done a second study which showed that, for a leveraged buy-out, the price range for Trans Union stock was between $55 and $65 per share. Van Gorkom neither saw the study nor asked Romans to make it available for the Board meeting.

Senior Management's reaction to the Pritzker proposal was completely negative. No member of Management, except Chelberg and Peterson, supported the proposal. Romans objected to the price as being too low;[152] he was critical of the timing and suggested that consideration should be given to the adverse tax consequences of an all-cash deal for low-basis shareholders; and he took the position that the agreement to sell Pritzker one million newly-issued shares at market price would inhibit other offers, as would the prohibitions against soliciting bids and furnishing inside information to other bidders. Romans argued that the Pritzker proposal was a "lock up" and amounted to "an agreed merger as opposed to an offer." Nevertheless, Van Gorkom proceeded to the Board meeting as scheduled without further delay.

Ten directors served on the Trans Union Board, five inside (defendants Bonser, O'Boyle, Browder, Chelberg, and Van Gorkom) and five outside (defendants Wallis, Johnson, Lanterman, Morgan and Reneker). All directors were present at the meeting, except O'Boyle who was ill. Of the outside directors, four were corporate chief executive officers and one was the former Dean of the University of Chicago Business School. None was an investment banker or trained financial analyst. All members of the Board were well informed about the Company and its operations as a going concern. They were familiar with the current financial condition of the Company, as well as operating and earnings projections reported in the recent Five Year Forecast. The Board generally received regular and detailed reports and was kept abreast of the accumulated investment tax credit and accelerated depreciation problem.

Van Gorkom began the Special Meeting of the Board with a twenty-minute oral presentation. Copies of the proposed Merger Agreement were delivered too late for study before or during the meeting.[153] He reviewed the Company's ITC and depreciation problems and the efforts theretofore made to solve them. He discussed his initial meeting with Pritzker and his motivation in arranging that meeting. Van Gorkom did not disclose to the Board, however, the methodology by which he alone had arrived at the $55 figure, or the fact that he first proposed the $55 price in his negotiations with Pritzker.

Van Gorkom outlined the terms of the Pritzker offer as follows: Pritzker would pay $55 in cash for all outstanding shares of Trans Union stock completion of which Trans Union would be merged into New T Company, a subsidiary wholly-owned by Pritzker and formed to implement the merger; for a period of 90 days, Trans Union could receive, but could not actively solicit, competing offers; the offer had to be acted on by the next evening, Sunday, September 21; Trans Union could only furnish to competing bidders published information, and not proprietary informa-

---

[152] [6] Van Gorkom asked Romans to express his opinion as to the $55 price. Romans stated that he "thought the price was too low in relation to what he could derive for the company in a cash sale, particularly one which enabled us to realize the values of certain subsidiaries and independent entities."

[153] [7] The record is not clear as to the terms of the Merger Agreement. The Agreement, as originally presented to the Board on September 20, was never produced by defendants despite demands by the plaintiffs. Nor is it clear that the directors were given an opportunity to study the Merger Agreement before voting on it. All that can be said is that Brennan had the Agreement before him during the meeting.

tion; the offer was subject to Pritzker obtaining the necessary financing by October 10, 1980; if the financing contingency were met or waived by Pritzker, Trans Union was required to sell to Pritzker one million newly-issued shares of Trans Union at $38 per share.

Van Gorkom took the position that putting Trans Union "up for auction" through a 90-day market test would validate a decision by the Board that $55 was a fair price. He told the Board that the "free market will have an opportunity to judge whether $55 is a fair price." Van Gorkom framed the decision before the Board not as to whether $55 per share was the highest price that could be obtained, but as to whether the $55 price was a fair price that the stockholders should be given the opportunity to accept or reject.[154]

Attorney Brennan advised the members of the Board that they might be sued if they failed to accept the offer and that a fairness opinion was not required as a matter of law.

Romans attended the meeting as chief financial officer of the Company. He told the Board that he had not been involved in the negotiations with Pritzker and knew nothing about the merger proposal until the morning of the meeting; that his studies did not indicate either a fair price for the stock or a valuation of the Company; that he did not see his role as directly addressing the fairness issue; and that he and his people "were trying to search for ways to justify a price in connection with such a [leveraged buy-out] transaction, rather than to say what the shares are worth." Romans testified:

> I told the Board that the study ran the numbers at 50 and 60, and then the subsequent study at 55 and 65, and that was not the same thing as saying that I have a valuation of the company at X dollars. But it was a way — a first step towards reaching that conclusion.

Romans told the Board that, in his opinion, $55 was "in the range of a fair price," but "at the beginning of the range."

Chelberg, Trans Union's President, supported Van Gorkom's presentation and representations. He testified that he "participated to make sure that the Board members collectively were clear on the details of the agreement or offer from Pritzker;" that he "participated in the discussion with Mr. Brennan, inquiring of him about the necessity for valuation opinions in spite of the way in which this particular offer was couched;" and that he was otherwise actively involved in supporting the positions being taken by Van Gorkom before the Board about "the necessity to act immediately on this offer," and about "the adequacy of the $55 and the question of how that would be tested."

The Board meeting of September 20 lasted about two hours. Based solely upon Van Gorkom's oral presentation, Chelberg's supporting representations, Romans's oral statement, Brennan's legal advice, and their knowledge of the market history

---

[154] [8] In Van Gorkom's words: The "real decision" is whether to "let the stockholders decide it" which is "all you are being asked to decide today."

of the Company's stock,[155] the directors approved the proposed Merger Agreement. However, the Board later claimed to have attached two conditions to its acceptance: (1) that Trans Union reserved the right to accept any better offer that was made during the market test period; and (2) that Trans Union could share its proprietary information with any other potential bidders. While the Board now claims to have reserved the right to accept any better offer received after the announcement of the Pritzker agreement (even though the minutes of the meeting do not reflect this), it is undisputed that the Board did not reserve the right to actively solicit alternate offers.

The Merger Agreement was executed by Van Gorkom during the evening of September 20 at a formal social event that he hosted for the opening of the Chicago Lyric Opera. Neither he nor any other director read the agreement prior to its signing and delivery to Pritzker.

. . . .

On Monday, September 22, the Company issued a press release announcing that Trans Union had entered into a "definitive" Merger Agreement with an affiliate of the Marmon Group, Inc. a Pritzker holding company. Within 10 days of the public announcement, dissent among Senior Management over the merger had become widespread. Faced with threatened resignations of key officers, Van Gorkom met with Pritzker who agreed to several modifications of the Agreement. Pritzker was willing to do so provided that Van Gorkom could persuade the dissidents to remain on the Company payroll for at least six months after consummation of the merger.

Van Gorkom reconvened the Board on October 8 and secured the directors' approval of the proposed amendments — sight unseen. The Board also authorized the employment of Salomon Brothers, its investment banker, to solicit other offers for Trans Union during the proposed "market test" period.

The next day, October 9, Trans Union issued a press release, announcing: (1) that Pritzker had obtained "the financing commitments necessary to consummate" the merger with Trans Union; (2) that Pritzker had acquired one million shares of Trans Union common stock at $38 per share; (3) that Trans Union was now permitted to actively seek other offers and had retained Salomon Brothers for that purpose; and (4) that if a more favorable offer were not received before February 1, 1981, Trans Union's shareholders would thereafter meet to vote on the Pritzker proposal.

It was not until the following day, October 10, that the actual amendments to the Merger Agreement were prepared by Pritzker and delivered to Van Gorkom for execution. As will be seen, the amendments were considerably at variance with Van Gorkom's representations of the amendments to the Board on October 8; and the amendments placed serious constraints on Trans Union's ability to negotiate a better deal and withdraw from the Pritzker agreement. Nevertheless, Van Gorkom

---

[155] [9] The Trial Court stated the premium relationship of the $55 price to the market history of the Company's stock as follows:

> . . . the merger price offered to the stockholders of Trans Union represented a premium of 62% over the average of the high and low prices at which Trans Union stock had traded in 1980, a premium of 48% over the last closing price, and a premium of 39% over the highest price at which the stock of Trans Union had traded any time during the prior six years.

proceeded to execute what became the October 10 amendments to the Merger Agreement without conferring further with the Board members and apparently without comprehending the actual implications of the amendments.

. . . .

Salomon Brothers' efforts over a three-month period from October 21 to January 21 produced only one serious suitor for Trans Union — General Electric Credit Corporation ("GE Credit"), a subsidiary of the General Electric Company. However, GE Credit was unwilling to make an offer for Trans Union unless Trans Union first rescinded its Merger Agreement with Pritzker. When Pritzker refused, GE Credit terminated further discussions with Trans Union in early January.

In the meantime, in early December, the investment firm of Kohlberg, Kravis, Roberts & Co. ("KKR"), the only other concern to make a firm offer for Trans Union, withdrew its offer under circumstances hereinafter detailed.

On December 19, this litigation was commenced and, within four weeks, the plaintiffs had deposed eight of the ten directors of Trans Union, including Van Gorkom, Chelberg and Romans, its Chief Financial Officer. On January 21, Management's Proxy Statement for the February 10 shareholder meeting was mailed to Trans Union's stockholders. On January 26, Trans Union's Board met and, after a lengthy meeting, voted to proceed with the Pritzker merger. The Board also approved for mailing, "on or about January 27," a Supplement to its Proxy Statement. The Supplement purportedly set forth all information relevant to the Pritzker Merger Agreement, which had not been divulged in the first Proxy Statement. . . .

. . . .

On February 10, the stockholders of Trans Union approved the Pritzker merger proposal. Of the outstanding shares, 69.9% were voted in favor of the merger; 7.25% were voted against the merger; and 22.85% were not voted.

II.

We turn to the issue of the application of the business judgment rule to the September 20 meeting of the Board.

The Court of Chancery concluded from the evidence that the Board of Directors' approval of the Pritzker merger proposal fell within the protection of the business judgment rule. The Court found that the Board had given sufficient time and attention to the transaction, since the directors had considered the Pritzker proposal on three different occasions, on September 20, and on October 8, 1980 and finally on January 26, 1981. On that basis, the Court reasoned that the Board had acquired, over the four-month period, sufficient information to reach an informed business judgment on the cash-out merger proposal. The Court ruled:

> . . . that given the market value of Trans Union's stock, the business acumen of the members of the board of Trans Union, the substantial premium over market offered by the Pritzkers and the ultimate effect on the merger price provided by the prospect of other bids for the stock in

> question, that the board of directors of Trans Union did not act recklessly or improvidently in determining on a course of action which they believed to be in the best interest of the stockholders of Trans Union.

The Court of Chancery made but one finding; i.e., that the Board's conduct over the entire period from September 20 through January 26, 1981 was not reckless or improvident, but informed. This ultimate conclusion was premised upon three subordinate findings, one explicit and two implied. The Court's explicit finding was that Trans Union's Board was "free to turn down the Pritzker proposal" not only on September 20 but also on October 8, 1980 and on January 26, 1981. The Court's implied, subordinate findings were: (1) that no legally binding agreement was reached by the parties until January 26; and (2) that if a higher offer were to be forthcoming, the market test would have produced it,[156] and Trans Union would have been contractually free to accept such higher offer. However, the Court offered no factual basis or legal support for any of these findings; and the record compels contrary conclusions.

This Court's standard of review of the findings of fact reached by the Trial Court following full evidentiary hearing is as stated in *Levitt v. Bouvier*, Del. Supr., 287 A.2d 671, 673 (1972):

> [In an appeal of this nature] this court has the authority to review the entire record and to make its own findings of fact in a proper case. In exercising our power of review, we have the duty to review the sufficiency of the evidence and to test the propriety of the findings below. We do not, however, ignore the findings made by the trial judge. If they are sufficiently supported by the record and are the product of an orderly and logical deductive process, in the exercise of judicial restraint we accept them, even though independently we might have reached opposite conclusions. It is only when the findings below are clearly wrong and the doing of justice requires their overturn that we are free to make contradictory findings of fact.

Applying that standard and governing principles of law to the record and the decision of the Trial Court, we conclude that the Court's ultimate finding that the Board's conduct was not "reckless or imprudent" is contrary to the record and not the product of a logical and deductive reasoning process.

The plaintiffs contend that the Court of Chancery erred as a matter of law by exonerating the defendant directors under the business judgment rule without first determining whether the rule's threshold condition of "due care and prudence" was satisfied. The plaintiffs assert that the Trial Court found the defendant directors to have reached an informed business judgment on the basis of "extraneous considerations and events that occurred after September 20, 1980." The defendants deny

---

[156] [10] We refer to the underlined portion of the Court's ultimate conclusion (previously stated):

> that given the market value of Trans Union's stock, the business acumen of the members of the board of Trans Union, the substantial premium over market offered by the Pritzkers and the ultimate effect on the merger price provided by the prospect of other bids for the stock in question, that the board of directors of Trans Union did not act recklessly or improvidently. . . .

that the Trial Court committed legal error in relying upon post-September 20, 1980 events and the directors' later acquired knowledge. The defendants further submit that their decision to accept $55 per share was informed because: (1) they were "highly qualified;" (2) they were "well-informed;" and (3) they deliberated over the "proposal" not once but three times. On essentially this evidence and under our standard of review, the defendants assert that affirmance is required. We must disagree.

Under Delaware law, the business judgment rule is the offspring of the fundamental principle, codified in 8 Del. C. § 141(a), that the business and affairs of a Delaware corporation are managed by or under its board of directors.[157] *Pogostin v. Rice*, Del. Supr., 480 A.2d 619, 624 (1984); *Aronson v. Lewis*, Del. Supr., 473 A.2d 805, 811 (1984); *Zapata Corp. v. Maldonado*, Del. Supr., 430 A.2d 779, 782 (1981). In carrying out their managerial roles, directors are charged with an unyielding fiduciary duty to the corporation and its shareholders. *Loft, Inc. v. Guth*, Del. Ch., 2 A.2d 225 (1938), *aff'd*, Del. Supr., 5 A.2d 503 (1939). The business judgment rule exists to protect and promote the full and free exercise of the managerial power granted to Delaware directors. *Zapata Corp. v. Maldonado, supra* at 782. The rule itself "is a presumption that in making a business decision, the directors of a corporation acted on an informed basis, in good faith and in the honest belief that the action taken was in the best interests of the company." *Aronson, supra* at 812. Thus, the party attacking a board decision as uninformed must rebut the presumption that its business judgment was an informed one. *Id.*

The determination of whether a business judgment is an informed one turns on whether the directors have informed themselves "prior to making a business decision, of all material information reasonably available to them." *Id.*[158]

Under the business judgment rule there is no protection for directors who have made "an unintelligent or unadvised judgment." *Mitchell v. Highland-Western Glass*, Del. Ch., 167 A. 831, 833 (1933). A director's duty to inform himself in preparation for a decision derives from the fiduciary capacity in which he serves the corporation and its stockholders. *Lutz v. Boas*, Del. Ch., 171 A.2d 381 (1961). *See Weinberger v. UOP, Inc., supra; Guth v. Loft, supra.* Since a director is vested with the responsibility for the management of the affairs of the corporation, he must execute that duty with the recognition that he acts on behalf of others. Such obligation does not tolerate faithlessness or self-dealing. But fulfillment of the

---

[157] [11] 8 Del. C. § 141 provides, in pertinent part:

> (a) The business and affairs of every corporation organized under this chapter shall be managed by or under the direction of a board of directors, except as may be otherwise provided in this chapter or in its certificate of incorporation. If any such provision is made in the certificate of incorporation, the powers and duties conferred or imposed upon the board of directors by this chapter shall be exercised or performed to such extent and by such person or persons as shall be provided in the certificate of incorporation.

[158] [12] *See Kaplan v. Centex Corporation*, Del. Ch., 284 A.2d 119, 124 (1971), where the Court stated:

> Application of the [business judgment] rule of necessity depends upon a showing that informed directors did in fact make a business judgment authorizing the transaction under review. And, as the plaintiff argues, the difficulty here is that the evidence does not show that this was done. There were director-committee-officer references to the realignment, but none of these singly or cumulatively showed that the director judgment was brought to bear with specificity on the transactions.

fiduciary function requires more than the mere absence of bad faith or fraud. Representation of the financial interests of others imposes on a director an affirmative duty to protect those interests and to proceed with a critical eye in assessing information of the type and under the circumstances present here. *See Lutz v. Boas, supra; Guth v. Loft, supra* at 510. *Compare Donovan v. Cunningham*, 5th Cir., 616 F.2d 1455, 1467 (1982); *Doyle v. Union Insurance Company*, Neb. Supr., 277 N.W.2d 36 (1979); *Continental Securities Co. v. Belmont*, N.Y. App., 99 N.E.2d 138, 141 (1912).

Thus, a director's duty to exercise an informed business judgment is in the nature of a duty of care, as distinguished from a duty of loyalty. Here, there were no allegations of fraud, bad faith, or self-dealing, or proof thereof. Hence, it is presumed that the directors reached their business judgment in good faith, *Allaun v. Consolidated Oil Co.*, Del. Ch., 147 A. 257 (1929), and considerations of motive are irrelevant to the issue before us.

The standard of care applicable to a director's duty of care has also been recently restated by this Court. In *Aronson, supra*, we stated:

> While the Delaware cases use a variety of terms to describe the applicable standard of care, our analysis satisfies us that under the business judgment rule, director liability is predicated upon concepts of gross negligence. (footnote omitted)

473 A.2d at 812.

We again confirm that view. We think the concept of gross negligence is also the proper standard for determining whether a business judgment reached by a board of directors was an informed one.[159]

In the specific context of a proposed merger of domestic corporations, a director has a duty under 8 Del. C. § 251(b),[160] along with his fellow directors, to act in an

---

[159] [13] Compare *Mitchell v. Highland-Western Glass, supra*, where the Court posed the question as whether the board acted "so far without information that they can be said to have passed an unintelligent and unadvised judgment." 167 A. at 833. Compare also *Gimbell v. Signal Companies, Inc.*, 316 A.2d 599, *aff'd, per curiam* Del. Supr., 316 A.2d 619 (1974), where the Chancellor, after expressly reiterating the *Highland-Western Glass* standard, framed the question, "Or to put the question in its legal context, did the Signal directors act without the bounds of reason and recklessly in approving the price offer of Burmah?" *Id.*

[160] [14] 8 Del. C. § 251(b) provides in pertinent part:

> (b) The board of directors of each corporation which desires to merge or consolidate *shall adopt a resolution approving an agreement of merger* or consolidation. The agreement shall state: (1) the terms and conditions of the merger or consolidation; (2) the mode of carrying the same into effect; (3) such amendments or changes in the certificate of incorporation of the surviving corporation as are desired to be effected by the merger or consolidation, or, if no such amendments or changes are desired, a statement that the certificate of incorporation of one of the constituent corporations shall be the certificate of incorporation of the surviving or resulting corporation; (4) the manner of converting the shares of each of the constituent corporations . . . and (5) such other details or provisions as are deemed desirable. . . . The agreement so adopted shall be executed in accordance with section 103 of this title. *Any of the terms of the agreement of merger or consolidation may be made dependent upon facts ascertainable outside of such agreement, provided that the manner in which such facts shall operate upon the terms of the agreement is clearly and expressly set forth in the agreement of merger or consolidation.*

informed and deliberate manner in determining whether to approve an agreement of merger before submitting the proposal to the stockholders. Certainly in the merger context, a director may not abdicate that duty by leaving to the shareholders alone the decision to approve or disapprove the agreement. *See Beard v. Elster*, Del. Supr., 160 A.2d 731, 737 (1960). Only an agreement of merger satisfying the requirements of 8 Del. C. § 251(b) may be submitted to the shareholders under § 251(c). *See generally Aronson v. Lewis, supra* at 811-13; *see also Pogostin v. Rice, supra.*

It is against those standards that the conduct of the directors of Trans Union must be tested, as a matter of law and as a matter of fact, regarding their exercise of an informed business judgment in voting to approve the Pritzker merger proposal.

III.

The defendants argue that the determination of whether their decision to accept $55 per share for Trans Union represented an informed business judgment requires consideration, not only of that which they knew and learned on September 20, but also of that which they subsequently learned and did over the following four-month period before the shareholders met to vote on the proposal in February, 1981. The defendants thereby seek to reduce the significance of their action on September 20 and to widen the time frame for determining whether their decision to accept the Pritzker proposal was an informed one. Thus, the defendants contend that what the directors did and learned subsequent to September 20 and through January 26, 1981, was properly taken into account by the Trial Court in determining whether the Board's judgment was an informed one. We disagree with this post hoc approach.

The issue of whether the directors reached an informed decision to "sell" the Company on September 20, 1980 must be determined only upon the basis of the information then reasonably available to the directors and relevant to their decision to accept the Pritzker merger proposal. This is not to say that the directors were precluded from altering their original plan of action had they done so in an informed manner. What we do say is that the question of whether the directors reached an informed business judgment in agreeing to sell the Company, pursuant to the terms of the September 20 Agreement presents, in reality, two questions: (A) whether the directors reached an informed business judgment on September 20, 1980; and (B) if they did not, whether the directors' actions taken subsequent to September 20 were adequate to cure any infirmity in their action taken on September 20. We first consider the directors' September 20 action in terms of their reaching an informed business judgment.

-A-

On the record before us, we must conclude that the Board of Directors did not reach an informed business judgment on September 20, 1980 in voting to "sell" the

[Emphasis added.]

Company for $55 per share pursuant to the Pritzker cash-out merger proposal. Our reasons, in summary, are as follows:

The directors (1) did not adequately inform themselves as to Van Gorkom's role in forcing the "sale" of the Company and in establishing the per share purchase price; (2) were uninformed as to the intrinsic value of the Company; and (3) given these circumstances, at a minimum, were grossly negligent in approving the "sale" of the Company upon two hours' consideration, without prior notice, and without the exigency of a crisis or emergency.

As has been noted, the Board based its September 20 decision to approve the cash-out merger primarily on Van Gorkom's representations. None of the directors, other than Van Gorkom and Chelberg, had any prior knowledge that the purpose of the meeting was to propose a cash-out merger of Trans Union. No members of Senior Management were present, other than Chelberg, Romans and Peterson; and the latter two had only learned of the proposed sale an hour earlier. Both general counsel Moore and former general counsel Browder attended the meeting but were equally uninformed as to the purpose of the meeting and the documents to be acted upon.

Without any documents before them concerning the proposed transaction, the members of the Board were required to rely entirely upon Van Gorkom's 20-minute oral presentation of the proposal. No written summary of the terms of the merger was presented; the directors were given no documentation to support the adequacy of $55 price per share for sale of the Company; and the Board had before it nothing more than Van Gorkom's statement of his understanding of the substance of an agreement which he admittedly had never read, nor which any member of the Board had ever seen.

Under 8 Del. C. § 141(e),[161] "directors are fully protected in relying in good faith on reports made by officers." *Michelson v. Duncan*, Del. Ch., 386 A.2d 1144, 1156 (1978); *aff'd, in part and rev'd, in part on other grounds*, Del. Supr., 407 A.2d 211 (1979). *See also Graham v. Allis-Chalmers Mfg. Co.*, Del. Supr., 188 A.2d 125, 130 (1963); *Prince v. Bensinger*, Del. Ch., 244 A.2d 89, 94 (1968). The term "report" has been liberally construed to include reports of informal personal investigations by corporate officers, *Cheff v. Mathes*, Del. Supr., 199 A.2d 548, 556 (1964). However, there is no evidence that any "report," as defined under § 141(e), concerning the Pritzker proposal, was presented to the Board on September 20.[162] Van Gorkom's oral presentation of his understanding of the terms of the proposed Merger

---

[161] [15] Section 141(e) provides in pertinent part:

> A member of the board of directors . . . shall, in the performance of his duties, be fully protected in relying in good faith upon the books of accounts or reports made to the corporation by any of its officers, or by an independent certified public accountant, or by an appraiser selected with reasonable care by the board of directors . . . , or in relying in good faith upon other records of the corporation.

[162] [16] In support of the defendants' argument that their judgment as to the adequacy of $55 per share was an informed one, the directors rely on the BCG study and the Five Year Forecast. However, no one even referred to either of these studies at the September 20 meeting; and it is conceded that these materials do not represent valuation studies. Hence, these documents do not constitute evidence as to whether the directors reached an informed judgment on September 20 that $55 per share was a fair value for sale of the Company.

Agreement, which he had not seen, and Romans' brief oral statement of his preliminary study regarding the feasibility of a leveraged buy-out of Trans Union do not qualify as § 141(e) "reports" for these reasons: The former lacked substance, because Van Gorkom was basically uninformed as to the essential provisions of the very document about which he was talking. Romans's statement was irrelevant to the issues before the Board, since it did not purport to be a valuation study. At a minimum for a report to enjoy the status conferred by § 141(e), it must be pertinent to the subject matter upon which a board is called to act and otherwise be entitled to good faith, not blind, reliance. Considering all of the surrounding circumstances — hastily calling the meeting without prior notice of its subject matter, the proposed sale of the Company without any prior consideration of the issue or necessity therefor, the urgent time constraints imposed by Pritzker, and the total absence of any documentation whatsoever — the directors were duty bound to make reasonable inquiry of Van Gorkom and Romans, and if they had done so, the inadequacy of that upon which they now claim to have relied would have been apparent.

The defendants rely on the following factors to sustain the Trial Court's finding that the Board's decision was an informed one: (1) the magnitude of the premium or spread between the $55 Pritzker offering price and Trans Union's current market price of $38 per share; (2) the amendment of the Agreement as submitted on September 20 to permit the Board to accept any better offer during the "market test" period; (3) the collective experience and expertise of the Board's "inside" and "outside" directors;[163] and (4) their reliance on Brennan's legal advice that the directors might be sued if they rejected the Pritzker proposal. We discuss each of these grounds *seriatim*:

(1)

A substantial premium may provide one reason to recommend a merger, but in the absence of other sound valuation information, the fact of a premium alone does not provide an adequate basis upon which to assess the fairness of an offering price. Here, the judgment reached as to the adequacy of the premium was based on a comparison between the historically depressed Trans Union market price and the amount of the Pritzker offer. Using market price as a basis for concluding that the premium adequately reflected the true value of the Company was a clearly faulty, indeed fallacious, premise, as the defendants' own evidence demonstrates.

The record is clear that before September 20, Van Gorkom and other members of Trans Union's Board knew that the market had consistently undervalued the worth of Trans Union's stock, despite steady increases in the Company's operating income in the seven years preceding the merger. The Board related this occurrence in large part to Trans Union's inability to use its ITCs, as previously noted. Van Gorkom testified that he did not believe the market price accurately reflected Trans Union's true worth; and several of the directors testified that, as a general rule,

[163] [17] We reserve for discussion under Part III hereof, the defendants' contention that their judgment, reached on September 20, if not then informed, became informed by virtue of their "review" of the Agreement on October 8 and January 26.

most chief executives think that the market undervalues their companies' stock. Yet, on September 20, Trans Union's Board apparently believed that the market stock price accurately reflected the value of the Company for the purpose of determining the adequacy of the premium for its sale.

In the Proxy Statement, however, the directors reversed their position. There, they stated that although the earnings prospects for Trans Union were "excellent," they found no basis for believing that this would be reflected in future stock prices. With regard to past trading, the Board stated that the prices at which the company's common stock had traded in recent years did not reflect the "inherent" value of the Company. But having referred to the "inherent" value of Trans Union, the directors ascribed no number to it. Moreover, nowhere did they disclose that they had no basis on which to fix "inherent" worth beyond an impressionistic reaction to the premium over market and an unsubstantiated belief that the value of the assets was "significantly greater" than book value. By their own admission, they could not rely on the stock price as an accurate measure of value. Yet, also by their own admission, the Board members assumed that Trans Union's market price was adequate to serve as a basis upon which to assess the adequacy of the premium for purposes of the September 20 meeting.

The parties do not dispute that a publicly-traded stock price is solely a measure of the value of a minority position and, thus, market price represents only the value of a single share. Nevertheless, on September 20, the Board assessed the adequacy of the premium over market, offered by Pritzker, solely by comparing it with Trans Union's current and historical stock price. (*See supra* n.5)

Indeed, as of September 20, the Board had no other information on which to base a determination of the intrinsic value of Trans Union as a going concern. As of September 20, the Board had made no evaluation of the company designed to value the entire enterprise, nor had the Board ever previously considered selling the company or consenting to a buy-out merger. Thus, the adequacy of a premium is indeterminate unless it is assessed in terms of other competent and sound valuation information that reflects the value of the particular business.

Despite the foregoing facts and circumstances, there was no call by the Board, either on September 20 or thereafter, for any valuation study or documentation of the $55 price per share as a measure of the fair value of the Company in a cash-out context. It is undisputed that the major asset of Trans Union was its cash flow. Yet, at no time did the Board call for a valuation study taking into account that highly significant element of the Company's assets.

We do not imply that an outside valuation study is essential to support an informed business judgment; nor do we state that fairness opinions by independent investment bankers are required as a matter of law. Often insiders familiar with the business of a going concern are in a better position than are outsiders to gather relevant information; and under appropriate circumstances, such directors may be fully protected in relying in good faith upon the valuation reports of their management. *See* 8 Del. C. § 141(e). *See also Cheff v. Mathes, supra.*

Here, the record establishes that the Board did not request its Chief Financial Officer, Romans, to make any valuation study or review of the proposal to determine the adequacy of $55 per share for sale of the Company. On the record before us: The Board rested on Romans's elicited response that the $55 figure was within a "fair price range" within the context of a leveraged buy-out. No director sought any further information from Romans. No director asked him why he put $55 at the bottom of his range. No director asked Romans for any details as to his study, the reason why it had been undertaken or its depth. No director asked to see the study; and no director asked Romans whether Trans Union's finance department could do a fairness study within the remaining 36-hour[164] period available under the Pritzker offer.

Had the Board, or any member, made an inquiry of Romans, he presumably would have responded as he testified: that his calculations were rough and preliminary; and, that the study was not designed to determine the fair value of the Company, but rather to assess the feasibility of a leveraged buy-out financed by the Company's projected cash flow, making certain assumptions as to the purchaser's borrowing needs. Romans would have presumably also informed the Board of his view, and the widespread view of Senior Management, that the timing of the offer was wrong and the offer inadequate.

The record also establishes that the Board accepted without scrutiny Van Gorkom's representation as to the fairness of the $55 price per share for sale of the Company — a subject that the Board had never previously considered. The Board thereby failed to discover that Van Gorkom had suggested the $55 price to Pritzker and, most crucially, that Van Gorkom had arrived at the $55 figure based on calculations designed solely to determine the feasibility of a leveraged buy-out.[165] No questions were raised either as to the tax implications of a cash-out merger or how the price for the one million share option granted Pritzker was calculated.

We do not say that the Board of Directors was not entitled to give some credence to Van Gorkom's representation that $55 was an adequate or fair price. Under § 141(e), the directors were entitled to rely upon their chairman's opinion of value and adequacy, provided that such opinion was reached on a sound basis. Here, the issue is whether the directors informed themselves as to all information that was reasonably available to them. Had they done so, they would have learned of the source and derivation of the $55 price and could not reasonably have relied thereupon in good faith.

None of the directors, Management or outside, were investment bankers or

---

[164] [18] Romans' department study was not made available to the Board until circulation of Trans Union's Supplementary Proxy Statement and the Board's meeting of January 26, 1981, on the eve of the shareholder meeting; and, as has been noted, the study has never been produced for inclusion in the record in this case.

[165] [19] As of September 20 the directors did not know: that Van Gorkom had arrived at the $55 figure alone, and subjectively, as the figure to be used by Controller Peterson in creating a feasible structure for a leveraged buy-out by a prospective purchaser; that Van Gorkom had not sought advice, information or assistance from either inside or outside Trans Union directors as to the value of the company as an entity or the fair price per share for 100% of its stock; that Van Gorkom had not consulted with the Company's investment bankers or other financial analysts; that Van Gorkom had not consulted with or confided in any officer or director of the company except Chelberg; and that Van Gorkom had deliberately chosen to ignore the advice and opinion of the members of his Senior Management group regarding the adequacy of the $55 price.

financial analysts. Yet the Board did not consider recessing the meeting until a later hour that day (or requesting an extension of Pritzker's Sunday evening deadline) to give it time to elicit more information as to the sufficiency of the offer, either from inside Management (in particular Romans) or from Trans Union's own investment banker, Salomon Brothers, whose Chicago specialist in merger and acquisitions was known to the Board and familiar with Trans Union's affairs.

Thus, the record compels the conclusion that on September 20 the Board lacked valuation information adequate to reach an informed business judgment as to the fairness of $55 per share for sale of the Company.[166]

(2)

This brings us to the post-September 20 "market test" upon which the defendants ultimately rely to confirm the reasonableness of their September 20 decision to accept the Pritzker proposal. In this connection, the directors present a two-part argument: (a) that by making a "market test" of Pritzker's $55 per share offer, a condition of their September 20 decision to accept his offer, they cannot be found to have acted impulsively or in an uninformed manner on September 20; and (b) that the adequacy of the $17 premium for sale of the Company was conclusively established over the following 90 to 120 days by the most reliable evidence available — the marketplace. Thus, the defendants impliedly contend that the "market test" eliminated the need for the Board to perform any other form of fairness test either on September 20, or thereafter.

Again, the facts of record do not support the defendants' argument. There is no evidence: (a) that the Merger Agreement was effectively amended to give the Board freedom to put Trans Union up for auction sale to the highest bidder; or (b) that a public auction was in fact permitted to occur. The minutes of the Board meeting make no reference to any of this. Indeed, the record compels the conclusion that the directors had no rational basis for expecting that a market test was attainable, given the terms of the Agreement as executed during the evening of September 20. We rely upon the following facts which are essentially uncontradicted:

The Merger Agreement, specifically identified as that originally presented to the Board on September 20, has never been produced by the defendants, notwithstanding the plaintiffs' several demands for production before as well as during trial. No acceptable explanation of this failure to produce documents has been given to either the Trial Court or this Court. Significantly, neither the defendants nor their counsel have made the affirmative representation that this critical document has been produced. Thus, the Court is deprived of the best evidence on which to judge the merits of the defendants' position as to the care and attention which they gave to the terms of the Agreement on September 20.

Van Gorkom states that the Agreement as submitted incorporated the ingredients for a market test by authorizing Trans Union to receive competing offers over the next 90-day period. However, he concedes that the Agreement which he signed

---

[166] [20] For a far more careful and reasoned approach taken by another board of directors faced with the pressures of a hostile tender offer, see *Pogostin v. Rice*, *supra* at 623-627.

on the evening of September 20 barred Trans Union from actively soliciting such offers and from furnishing to interested parties any information about the Company other than that already in the public domain. Whether the original Agreement of September 20 went so far as to authorize Trans Union to receive competitive proposals is arguable. The defendants' unexplained failure to produce and identify the original Merger Agreement permits the logical inference that the instrument would not support their assertions in this regard. *Wilmington Trust Co. v. General Motors Corp.*, Del. Supr., 51 A.2d 584, 593 (1974); II Wigmore on Evidence § 291 (3d ed. 1940). Van Gorkom, conceding that he never read the Agreement, stated that he was relying upon his understanding that, under corporate law, directors always have an inherent right, as well as a fiduciary duty, to accept a better offer notwithstanding an existing contractual commitment by the Board. (See the discussion *infra*, part III B (3).)

The defendant directors assert that they "insisted" upon including two amendments to the Agreement, thereby permitting a market test: (1) to give Trans Union the right to accept a better offer; and (2) to reserve to Trans Union the right to distribute proprietary information on the Company to alternative bidders. Yet, the defendants concede that they did not seek to amend the Agreement to permit Trans Union to solicit competing offers.

Several of Trans Union's outside directors resolutely maintained that the Agreement as submitted was approved on the understanding that, "if we got a better deal, we had a right to take it." Director Johnson so testified; but he then added, "And if they didn't put that in the agreement, then the management did not carry out the conclusion of the Board. And I just don't know whether they did or not." The only clause in the Agreement as finally executed to which the defendants can point as "keeping the door open" is the following underlined statement found in subparagraph (a) of section 2.03 of the Merger Agreement as executed:

The Board of Directors shall recommend to the stockholders of Trans Union that they approve and adopt the Merger Agreement ('the stockholders' approval') and to use its best efforts to obtain the requisite votes therefor. *GL acknowledges that Trans Union directors may have a competing fiduciary obligation to the shareholders under certain circumstances.*

Clearly, this language on its face cannot be construed as incorporating either of the two "conditions" described above: either the right to accept a better offer or the right to distribute proprietary information to third parties. The logical witness for the defendants to call to confirm their construction of this clause of the Agreement would have been Trans Union's outside attorney, James Brennan. The defendants' failure, without explanation, to call this witness again permits the logical inference that his testimony would not have been helpful to them. The further fact that the directors adjourned, rather than recessed, the meeting without incorporating in the Agreement these important "conditions" further weakens the defendants' position. As has been noted, nothing in the Board's Minutes supports these claims. No reference to either of the so-called "conditions" or of Trans Union's reserved right to test the market appears in any notes of the Board meeting or in the Board Resolution accepting the Pritzker offer or in the Minutes of the meeting itself. That evening, in the midst of a formal party which he hosted for the opening of the

Chicago Lyric Opera, Van Gorkom executed the Merger Agreement without he or any other member of the Board having read the instruments.

The defendants attempt to downplay the significance of the prohibition against Trans Union's actively soliciting competing offers by arguing that the directors "understood that the entire financial community would know that Trans Union was for sale upon the announcement of the Pritzker offer, and anyone desiring to make a better offer was free to do so." Yet, the press release issued on September 22, with the authorization of the Board, stated that Trans Union had entered into "definitive agreements" with the Pritzkers; and the press release did not even disclose Trans Union's limited right to receive and accept higher offers. Accompanying this press release was a further public announcement that Pritzker had been granted an option to purchase at any time one million shares of Trans Union's capital stock at 75 cents above the then-current price per share.

Thus, notwithstanding what several of the outside directors later claimed to have "thought" occurred at the meeting, the record compels the conclusion that Trans Union's Board had no rational basis to conclude on September 20 or in the days immediately following, that the Board's acceptance of Pritzker's offer was conditioned on (1) a "market test" of the offer; and (2) the Board's right to withdraw from the Pritzker Agreement and accept any higher offer received before the shareholder meeting.

(3)

The directors' unfounded reliance on both the premium and the market test as the basis for accepting the Pritzker proposal undermines the defendants' remaining contention that the Board's collective experience and sophistication was a sufficient basis for finding that it reached its September 20 decision with informed, reasonable deliberation.[167] *Compare Gimbel v. Signal Companies, Inc.*, Del. Ch., 316 A.2d 599 (1974), *aff'd, per curiam*, Del. Supr., 316 A.2d 619 (1974). There, the Court of Chancery preliminarily enjoined a board's sale of stock of its wholly-owned subsidiary for an alleged grossly inadequate price. It did so based on a finding that the business judgment rule had been pierced for failure of management to give its board "the opportunity to make a reasonable and reasoned decision." 316 A.2d at 615. The Court there reached this result notwithstanding the board's sophistication and experience; the company's need of immediate cash; and the board's need to act promptly due to the impact of an energy crisis on the value of the underlying assets being sold — all of its subsidiary's oil and gas interests. The Court found those factors denoting competence to be outweighed by evidence of gross negligence; that

---

[167] [21] Trans Union's five "inside" directors had backgrounds in law and accounting, 116 years of collective employment by the Company and 68 years of combined experience on its Board. Trans Union's five "outside" directors included four chief executives of major corporations and an economist who was a former dean of a major school of business and chancellor of a university. The "outside" directors had 78 years of combined experience as chief executive officers of major corporations and 50 years of cumulative experience as directors of Trans Union. Thus, defendants argue that the Board was eminently qualified to reach an informed judgment on the proposed "sale" of Trans Union notwithstanding their lack of any advance notice of the proposal, the shortness of their deliberation, and their determination not to consult with their investment banker or to obtain a fairness opinion.

management in effect sprang the deal on the board by negotiating the asset sale without informing the board; that the buyer intended to "force a quick decision" by the board; that the board meeting was called on only one-and-a-half days' notice; that its outside directors were not notified of the meeting's purpose; that during a meeting spanning "a couple of hours" a sale of assets worth $480 million was approved; and that the Board failed to obtain a current appraisal of its oil and gas interests. The analogy of Signal to the case at bar is significant.

(4)

Part of the defense is based on a claim that the directors relied on legal advice rendered at the September 20 meeting by James Brennan, Esquire, who was present at Van Gorkom's request. Unfortunately, Brennan did not appear and testify at trial even though his firm participated in the defense of this action. There is no contemporaneous evidence of the advice given by Brennan on September 20, only the later deposition and trial testimony of certain directors as to their recollections or understanding of what was said at the meeting. Since counsel did not testify, and the advice attributed to Brennan is hearsay received by the Trial Court over the plaintiffs' objections, we consider it only in the context of the directors' present claims. In fairness to counsel, we make no findings that the advice attributed to him was in fact given. We focus solely on the efficacy of the defendants' claims, made months and years later, in an effort to extricate themselves from liability.

Several defendants testified that Brennan advised them that Delaware law did not require a fairness opinion or an outside valuation of the Company before the Board could act on the Pritzker proposal. If given, the advice was correct. However, that did not end the matter. Unless the directors had before them adequate information regarding the intrinsic value of the Company, upon which a proper exercise of business judgment could be made, mere advice of this type is meaningless; and, given this record of the defendants' failures, it constitutes no defense here.[168]

. . . .

We conclude that Trans Union's Board was grossly negligent in that it failed to act with informed reasonable deliberation in agreeing to the Pritzker merger proposal on September 20; and we further conclude that the Trial Court erred as a matter of law in failing to address that question before determining whether the directors' later conduct was sufficient to cure its initial error.

A second claim is that counsel advised the Board it would be subject to lawsuits if it rejected the $55 per share offer. It is, of course, a fact of corporate life that today when faced with difficult or sensitive issues, directors often are subject to suit, irrespective of the decisions they make. However, counsel's mere acknowledgement

---

[168] [22] Nonetheless, we are satisfied that in an appropriate factual context a proper exercise of business judgment may include, as one of its aspects, reasonable reliance upon the advice of counsel. This is wholly outside the statutory protections of 8 Del. C. § 141(e) involving reliance upon reports of officers, certain experts and books and records of the company.

of this circumstance cannot be rationally translated into a justification for a board permitting itself to be stampeded into a patently unadvised act. While suit might result from the rejection of a merger or tender offer, Delaware law makes clear that a board acting within the ambit of the business judgment rule faces no ultimate liability. *Pogostin v. Rice, supra.* Thus, we cannot conclude that the mere threat of litigation, acknowledged by counsel, constitutes either legal advice or any valid basis upon which to pursue an uninformed course.

Since we conclude that Brennan's purported advice is of no consequence to the defense of this case, it is unnecessary for us to invoke the adverse inferences which may be attributable to one failing to appear at trial and testify.

-B-

We now examine the Board's post-September 20 conduct for the purpose of determining first, whether it was informed and not grossly negligent; and second, if informed, whether it was sufficient to legally rectify and cure the Board's derelictions of September 20.[169]

(1)

First, as to the Board meeting of October 8: Its purpose arose in the aftermath of the September 20 meeting: (1) the September 22 press release announcing that Trans Union "had entered into definitive agreements to merge with an affiliate of Marmon Group, Inc.;" and (2) Senior Management's ensuing revolt.

Trans Union's press release stated:

> FOR IMMEDIATE RELEASE:
>
> CHICAGO, IL — Trans Union Corporation announced today that it had entered into definitive agreements to merge with an affiliate of The Marmon Group, Inc. in a transaction whereby Trans Union stockholders would receive $55 per share in cash for each Trans Union share held. The Marmon Group, Inc. is controlled by the Pritzker family of Chicago.
>
> The merger is subject to approval by the stockholders of Trans Union at a special meeting expected to be held sometime during December or early January.
>
> Until October 10, 1980, the purchaser has the right to terminate the merger if financing that is satisfactory to the purchaser has not been obtained, but after that date there is no such right.
>
> In a related transaction, Trans Union has agreed to sell to a designee of the purchaser one million newly-issued shares of Trans Union common stock at a cash price of $38 per share. Such shares will be issued only if the merger financing has been committed for no later than October 10, 1980, or if the purchaser elects to waive the merger financing condition. In addition,

---

[169] [23] As will be seen, we do not reach the second question.

New York Stock Exchange will be asked to approve the listing of the new shares pursuant to a listing application which Trans Union intends to file shortly.

Completing of the transaction is also subject to the preparation of a definitive proxy statement and making various filings and obtaining the approvals or consents of government agencies.

The press release made no reference to provisions allegedly reserving to the Board the rights to perform a "market test" and to withdraw from the Pritzker Agreement if Trans Union received a better offer before the shareholder meeting. The defendants also concede that Trans Union never made a subsequent public announcement stating that it had in fact reserved the right to accept alternate offers, the Agreement notwithstanding.

The public announcement of the Pritzker merger resulted in an "en masse" revolt of Trans Union's Senior Management. The head of Trans Union's tank car operations (its most profitable division) informed Van Gorkom that unless the merger were called off, fifteen key personnel would resign.

Instead of reconvening the Board, Van Gorkom again privately met with Pritzker, informed him of the developments, and sought his advice. Pritzker then made the following suggestions for overcoming Management's dissatisfaction: (1) that the Agreement be amended to permit Trans Union to solicit, as well as receive, higher offers; and (2) that the shareholder meeting be postponed from early January to February 10, 1981. In return, Pritzker asked Van Gorkom to obtain a commitment from Senior Management to remain at Trans Union for at least six months after the merger was consummated.

Van Gorkom then advised Senior Management that the Agreement would be amended to give Trans Union the right to solicit competing offers through January, 1981, if they would agree to remain with Trans Union. Senior Management was temporarily mollified; and Van Gorkom then called a special meeting of Trans Union's Board for October 8.

Thus, the primary purpose of the October 8 Board meeting was to amend the Merger Agreement, in a manner agreeable to Pritzker, to permit Trans Union to conduct a "market test."[170] Van Gorkom understood that the proposed amendments were intended to give the Company an unfettered "right to openly solicit offers down through January 31." Van Gorkom presumably so represented the amendments to Trans Union's Board members on October 8. In a brief session, the

---

[170] [24] As previously noted, the Board mistakenly thought that it had amended the September 20 draft agreement to include a market test.

A secondary purpose of the October 8 meeting was to obtain the Board's approval for Trans Union to employ its investment advisor, Salomon Brothers, for the limited purpose of assisting Management in the solicitation of other offers. Neither Management nor the Board then or thereafter requested Salomon Brothers to submit its opinion as to the fairness of Pritzker's $55 cash-out merger proposal or to value Trans Union as an entity.

There is no evidence of record that the October 8 meeting had no other purpose; and we also note that the Minutes of the October 8 Board meeting, including any notice of the meeting, are not part of the voluminous records of this case.

directors approved Van Gorkom's oral presentation of the substance of the proposed amendments, the terms of which were not reduced to writing until October 10. But rather than waiting to review the amendments, the Board again approved them sight unseen and adjourned, giving Van Gorkom authority to execute the papers when he received them.[171]

Thus, the Court of Chancery's finding that the October 8 Board meeting was convened to *reconsider* the Pritzker "proposal" is clearly erroneous. Further, the consequence of the Board's faulty conduct on October 8, in approving amendments to the Agreement which had not even been drafted, will become apparent when the actual amendments to the Agreement are hereafter examined.

The next day, October 9, and before the Agreement was amended, Pritzker moved swiftly to off-set the proposed market test amendment. First, Pritzker informed Trans Union that he had completed arrangements for financing its acquisition and that the parties were thereby mutually bound to a firm purchase and sale arrangement. Second, Pritzker announced the exercise of his option to purchase one million shares of Trans Union's treasury stock at $38 per share — 75 cents above the current market price. Trans Union's Management responded the same day by issuing a press release announcing: (1) that all financing arrangements for Pritzker's acquisition of Trans Union had been completed; and (2) Pritzker's purchase of one million shares of Trans Union's treasury stock at $38 per share.

The next day, October 10, Pritzker delivered to Trans Union the proposed amendments to the September 20 Merger Agreement. Van Gorkom promptly proceeded to countersign all the instruments on behalf of Trans Union without reviewing the instruments to determine if they were consistent with the authority previously granted him by the Board. The amending documents were apparently not approved by Trans Union's Board until a much later date, December 2. The record does not affirmatively establish that Trans Union's directors ever read the October 10 amendments.[172]

The October 10 amendments to the Merger Agreement did authorize Trans Union to solicit competing offers, but the amendments had more far-reaching effects. The most significant change was in the definition of the third-party "offer" available to Trans Union as a possible basis for withdrawal from its Merger Agreement with Pritzker. Under the October 10 amendments, a better *offer* was no longer sufficient to permit Trans Union's withdrawal. Trans Union was now permitted to terminate the Pritzker Agreement and abandon the merger only if, prior to February 10, 1981, Trans Union had either consummated a merger (or sale of assets) with a third party or had entered into a "definitive" merger agreement more favorable than Pritzker's and for a greater consideration — subject only to

---

[171] [25] We do not suggest that a board must read *in haec verba* every contract or legal document which it approves, but if it is to successfully absolve itself from charges of the type made here, there must be some credible contemporary evidence demonstrating that the directors knew what they were doing and ensured that their purported action was given effect. That is the consistent failure which cast this Board upon its unredeemable course.

[172] [26] There is no evidence of record that Trans Union's directors ever raised any objections, procedural or substantive, to the October 10 amendments or that any of them, including Van Gorkom, understood the opposite result of their intended effect — until it was too late.

stockholder approval. Further, the "extension" of the market test period to February 10, 1981 was circumscribed by other amendments which required Trans Union to file its preliminary proxy statement on the Pritzker merger proposal by December 5, 1980 and use its best efforts to mail the statement to its shareholders by January 5, 1981. Thus, the market test period was effectively reduced, not extended. (See *infra* note 29.)

In our view, the record compels the conclusion that the directors' conduct on October 8 exhibited the same deficiencies as did their conduct on September 20. The Board permitted its Merger Agreement with Pritzker to be amended in a manner it had neither authorized nor intended. The Court of Chancery, in its decision, overlooked the significance of the October 8-10 events and their relevance to the sufficiency of the directors' conduct. The Trial Court's letter opinion ignores: the October 10 amendments; the manner of their adoption; the effect of the October 9 press release and the October 10 amendments on the feasibility of a market test; and the ultimate question as to the reasonableness of the directors' reliance on a market test in recommending that the shareholders approve the Pritzker merger.

We conclude that the Board acted in a grossly negligent manner on October 8; and that Van Gorkom's representations on which the Board based its actions do not constitute "reports" under § 141(e) on which the directors could reasonably have relied. Further, the amended Merger Agreement imposed on Trans Union's acceptance of a third party offer conditions more onerous than those imposed on Trans Union's acceptance of Pritzker's offer on September 20. After October 10, Trans Union could accept from a third party a better offer only if it were incorporated in a definitive agreement between the parties, and not conditioned on financing or on any other contingency.

The October 9 press release, coupled with the October 10 amendments, had the clear effect of locking Trans Union's Board into the Pritzker Agreement. Pritzker had thereby foreclosed Trans Union's Board from negotiating any better "definitive" agreement over the remaining eight weeks before Trans Union was required to clear the Proxy Statement submitting the Pritzker proposal to its shareholders.

(2)

Next, as to the "curative" effects of the Board's post-September 20 conduct, we review in more detail the reaction of Van Gorkom to the KKR proposal and the results of the Board-sponsored "market test."

The KKR proposal was the first and only offer received subsequent to the Pritzker Merger Agreement. The offer resulted primarily from the efforts of Romans and other senior officers to propose an alternative to Pritzker's acquisition of Trans Union. In late September, Romans's group contacted KKR about the possibility of a leveraged buy-out by all members of Management, except Van Gorkom. By early October, Henry R. Kravis of KKR gave Romans written notice of KKR's "interest in making an offer to purchase 100%" of Trans Union's common stock.

Thereafter, and until early December, Romans's group worked with KKR to develop a proposal. It did so with Van Gorkom's knowledge and apparently grudging consent. On December 2, Kravis and Romans hand-delivered to Van Gorkom a formal letter-offer to purchase all of Trans Union's assets and to assume all of its liabilities for an aggregate cash consideration equivalent to $60 per share. The offer was contingent upon completing equity and bank financing of $650 million, which Kravis represented as 80% complete. The KKR letter made reference to discussions with major banks regarding the loan portion of the buy-out cost and stated that KKR was "confident that commitments for the bank financing . . . can be obtained within two or three weeks." The purchasing group was to include certain named key members of Trans Union's Senior Management, excluding Van Gorkom, and a major Canadian company. Kravis stated that they were willing to enter into a "definitive agreement" under terms and conditions "substantially the same" as those contained in Trans Union's agreement with Pritzker. The offer was addressed to Trans Union's Board of Directors, and a meeting with the Board, scheduled for that afternoon, was requested.

Van Gorkom's reaction to the KKR proposal was completely negative; he did not view the offer as being firm because of its financing condition. It was pointed out, to no avail, that Pritzker's offer had not only been similarly conditioned, but accepted on an expedited basis. Van Gorkom refused Kravis's request that Trans Union issue a press release announcing KKR's offer, on the ground that it might "chill" any other offer.[173] Romans and Kravis left with the understanding that their proposal would be presented to Trans Union's Board that afternoon.

Within a matter of hours and shortly before the scheduled Board meeting, Kravis withdrew his letter-offer. He gave as his reason a sudden decision by the Chief Officer of Trans Union's rail car leasing operation to withdraw from the KKR purchasing group. Van Gorkom had spoken to that officer about his participation in the KKR proposal immediately after his meeting with Romans and Kravis. However, Van Gorkom denied any responsibility for the officer's change of mind.

At the Board meeting later that afternoon, Van Gorkom did not inform the directors of the KKR proposal, because he considered it "dead." Van Gorkom did not contact KKR again until January 20, when faced with the realities of this lawsuit, he then attempted to reopen negotiations. KKR declined due to the imminence of the February 10 stockholder meeting.

GE Credit Corporation's interest in Trans Union did not develop until November; and it made no written proposal until mid-January. Even then, its proposal was not in the form of an offer. Had there been time to do so, GE Credit was prepared to offer between $2 and $5 per share above the $55 per share price which Pritzker offered. But GE Credit needed an additional 60 to 90 days; and it was unwilling to make a formal offer without a concession from Pritzker extending the February 10 "deadline" for Trans Union's stockholder meeting. As previously stated, Pritzker refused to grant such extension; and on January 21, GE Credit terminated further negotiations with Trans Union. Its stated reasons, among others, were its "unwillingness to become involved in a bidding contest with Pritzker in the absence of the

173 [27] This was inconsistent with Van Gorkom's espousal of the September 22 press release following Trans Union's acceptance of Pritzker's proposal. Van Gorkom had then justified a press release as encouraging rather than chilling later offers.

willingness of [the Pritzker interests] to terminate the proposed $55 cash merger."

. . . .

In the absence of any explicit finding by the Trial Court as to the reasonableness of Trans Union's directors' reliance on a market test and its feasibility, we may make our own findings based on the record. Our review of the record compels a finding that confirmation of the appropriateness of the Pritzker offer by an unfettered or free market test was virtually meaningless in the face of the terms and time limitations of Trans Union's Merger Agreement with Pritzker, as amended October 10, 1980.

(3)

Finally, we turn to the Board's meeting of January 26, 1981. The defendant directors rely upon the action there taken to refute the contention that they did not reach an informed business judgment in approving the Pritzker merger. The defendants contend that the Trial Court correctly concluded that Trans Union's directors were, in effect, as "free to turn down the Pritzker proposal" on January 26, as they were on September 20.

Applying the appropriate standard of review set forth in *Levitt v. Bouvier, supra*, we conclude that the Trial Court's finding in this regard is neither supported by the record nor the product of an orderly and logical deductive process. Without disagreeing with the principle that a business decision by an originally uninformed board of directors may, under appropriate circumstances, be timely cured so as to become informed and deliberate, *Muschel v. Western Union Corporation*, Del. Ch., 310 A.2d 904 (1973),[174] we find that the record does not permit the defendants to invoke that principle in this case.

The Board's January 26 meeting was the first meeting following the filing of the plaintiffs' suit in mid-December and the last meeting before the previously-noticed shareholder meeting of February 10.[175] All ten members of the Board and three outside attorneys attended the meeting. At that meeting the following facts, among

---

[174] [28] The defendants concede that Muschel is only illustrative of the proposition that a board may reconsider a prior decision and that it is otherwise factually distinguishable from this case.

[175] [29] This was the meeting which, under the terms of the September 20 Agreement with Pritzker, was scheduled to be held January 10 and was later postponed to February 10 under the October 10 amendments. We refer to the document titled "Amendment to Supplemental Agreement" executed by the parties "as of" October 10, 1980. Under new Section 2.03(a) of Article A VI of the "Supplemental Agreement," the parties agreed, in part, as follows:

> The solicitation of such offers or proposals [i.e., "other offers that Trans Union might accept in lieu of the Merger Agreement"] by TU . . . shall not be deemed to constitute a breach of this Supplemental Agreement or the Merger Agreement provided that . . . [Trans Union] shall not (1) delay promptly seeking all consents and approvals required hereunder . . . [and] shall be deemed [in compliance] if it files its Preliminary Proxy Statement by December 5, 1980, uses its best efforts to mail its Proxy Statement by January 5, 1981 and holds a special meeting of its Stockholders on or prior to February 10, 1981 . . .
>
> . . . .
>
> It is the present intention of the Board of Directors of TU to recommend the approval of the Merger Agreement to the Stockholders, unless another offer or proposal is made which in their opinion is more favorable to the Stockholders than the Merger Agreement.

other aspects of the Merger Agreement, were discussed:

(a) The fact that prior to September 20, 1980, no Board member or member of Senior Management, except Chelberg and Peterson, knew that Van Gorkom had discussed a possible merger with Pritzker;

(b) The fact that the price of $55 per share had been suggested initially to Pritzker by Van Gorkom;

(c) The fact that the Board had not sought an independent fairness opinion;

(d) The fact that, at the September 20 Senior Management meeting, Romans and several members of Senior Management indicated both concern that the $55 per share price was inadequate and a belief that a higher price should and could be obtained;

(e) The fact that Romans had advised the Board at its meeting on September 20, that he and his department had prepared a study which indicated that the Company had a value in the range of $55 to $65 per share, and that he could not advise the Board that the $55 per share offer made by Pritzker was unfair.

The defendants characterize the Board's Minutes of the January 26 meeting as a review of the "entire sequence of events" from Van Gorkom's initiation of the negotiations on September 13 forward.[176] The defendants also rely on the testimony

---

[176] [30] With regard to the Pritzker merger, the recently filed shareholders' suit to enjoin it, and relevant portions of the impending stockholder meeting of February 10, we set forth the Minutes in their entirety:

> The Board then reviewed the necessity of issuing a Supplement to the Proxy Statement mailed to stockholders on January 21, 1981, for the special meeting of stockholders scheduled to be held on February 10, 1981, to vote on the proposed $55 cash merger with a subsidiary of GE Corporation. Among other things, the Board noted that subsequent to the printing of the Proxy Statement mailed to stockholders on January 21, 1981, General Electric Company has indicated that it would not be making an offer to acquire the Company. In addition, certain facts had been adduced in connection with pretrial discovery taken in connection with the lawsuit filed by Alden Smith in Delaware Chancery Court. After further discussion and review of a printer's proof copy of a proposed Supplement to the Proxy Statement which had been distributed to Directors the preceding day, upon motion duly made and seconded, the following resolution was unanimously adopted, each Director having been individually polled with respect thereto:
>
> > RESOLVED, that the Secretary of the Company be and he hereby is authorized and directed to mail to the stockholders a Supplement to Proxy Statement, substantially in the form of the proposed Supplement to Proxy Statement submitted to the Board at this meeting, with such changes therein and modifications thereof as he shall, with the advice and assistance of counsel, approve as being necessary, desirable, or appropriate.
>
> The Board then reviewed and discussed at great length the entire sequence of events pertaining to the proposed $55 cash merger with a subsidiary of GE Corporation, beginning with the first discussion on September 13, 1980, between the Chairman and Mr. Jay Pritzker relative to a possible merger. Each of the Directors was involved in this discussion as well as counsel who had earlier joined the meeting. Following this review and discussion, such counsel advised the Directors that in light of their discussions, they could (a) continue to recommend to the stockholders that the latter vote in favor of the proposed merger, (b) recommend that the stockholders vote against the merger, or (c) take no position with respect to recommending the proposed merger and simply leave the decision to stockholders. After further discussion, it was moved, seconded, and unanimously voted that the Board of Directors continue to recommend that the stockholders vote in favor of the proposed merger, each Director being individually polled with respect to his vote.

of several of the Board members at trial as confirming the Minutes.[177] On the basis of this evidence, the defendants argue that whatever information the Board lacked to make a deliberate and informed judgment on September 20, or on October 8, was fully divulged to the entire Board on January 26. Hence, the argument goes, the Board's vote on January 26 to again "approve" the Pritzker merger must be found to have been informed and deliberate judgment.

On the basis of this evidence, the defendants assert: (1) that the Trial Court was legally correct in widening the time frame for determining whether the defendants' approval of the Pritzker merger represented an informed business judgment to include the entire four-month period during which the Board considered the matter from September 20 through January 26; and (2) that, given this extensive evidence of the Board's further review and deliberations on January 26, this Court must affirm the Trial Court's conclusion that the Board's action was not reckless or improvident.

We cannot agree. We find the Trial Court to have erred, both as a matter of fact and as a matter of law, in relying on the action on January 26 to bring the defendants' conduct within the protection of the business judgment rule.

Johnson's testimony and the Board Minutes of January 26 are remarkably consistent. Both clearly indicate recognition that the question of the alternative courses of action, available to the Board on January 26 with respect to the Pritzker merger, was a legal question, presenting to the Board (*after* its review of the full record developed through pre-trial discovery) *three* options: (1) to "continue to recommend" the Pritzker merger; (2) to "recommend that the stockholders vote against" the Pritzker merger; or (3) to take a noncommittal position on the merger and "simply leave the decision to [the] shareholders."

We must conclude from the foregoing that the Board was mistaken as a matter of law regarding its available courses of action on January 26, 1981. Options (2) and

---

[177] [31] In particular, the defendants rely on the testimony of director Johnson on direct examination:

Q. Was there a regular meeting of the board of Trans Union on January 26, 1981?

A. Yes.

Q. And what was discussed at that meeting?

A. Everything relevant to this transaction.

You see, since the proxy statement of the 19th had been mailed, see, General Electric had advised that they weren't going to make a bid. It was concluded to suggest that the shareholders be advised of that, and that required a supplemental proxy statement, and that required authorization of the board, and that led to a total review from beginning to end of every aspect of the whole transaction and all relevant developments.

Since that was occurring and a supplemental statement was going to the shareholders, it also was obvious to me that there should be a review of the board's position again in the light of the whole record. And we went back from the beginning. Everything was examined and reviewed. Counsel were present. And the board was advised that we could recommend the Pritzker deal, we could submit it to the shareholders with no recommendation, or we could recommend against it.

The board voted to issue the supplemental statement to the shareholders. It voted unanimously — and this time we had a unanimous board, where one man was missing before — to recommend the Pritzker deal. Indeed, at that point there was no other deal. And, in truth, there never had been any other deal. And that's what transpired: a total review of the GE situation, KKR and everything else that was relevant.

(3) were not viable or legally available to the Board under 8 Del. C. § 251(b). The Board could not remain committed to the Pritzker merger and yet recommend that its stockholders vote it down; nor could it take a neutral position and delegate to the stockholders the unadvised decision as to whether to accept or reject the merger. Under § 251(b), the Board had but two options: (1) to proceed with the merger and the stockholder meeting, with the Board's recommendation of approval; *or* (2) to rescind its agreement with Pritzker, withdraw its approval of the merger, and notify its stockholders that the proposed shareholder meeting was cancelled. There is no evidence that the Board gave any consideration to these, its only legally viable alternative courses of action.

But the second course of action would have clearly involved a substantial risk — that the Board would be faced with suit by Pritzker for breach of contract based on its September 20 agreement as amended October 10. As previously noted, under the terms of the October 10 amendment, the Board's only ground for release from its agreement with Pritzker was its entry into a more favorable definitive agreement to sell the company to a third party. Thus, in reality, the Board was not "free to turn down the Pritzker proposal" as the Trial Court found. Indeed, short of negotiating a better agreement with a third party, the Board's only basis for release from the Pritzker Agreement without liability would have been to establish fundamental wrongdoing by Pritzker. Clearly, the Board was not "free" to withdraw from its agreement with Pritzker on January 26 by simply relying on its self-induced failure to have reached an informed business judgment at the time of its original agreement. *See Wilmington Trust Company v. Coulter*, Del. Supr., 200 A.2d 441, 453 (1964), *aff'g Pennsylvania Company v. Wilmington Trust Company* Del. Ch., 186 A.2d 751 (1962).

Therefore, the Trial Court's conclusion that the Board reached an informed business judgment on January 26 in determining whether to turn down the Pritzker "proposal" on that day cannot be sustained.[178] The Court's conclusion is not supported by the record; it is contrary to the provisions of § 251(b) and basic principles of contract law; and it is not the product of a logical and deductive reasoning process.

. . . .

Upon the basis of the foregoing, we hold that the defendants' post-September conduct did not cure the deficiencies of their September 20 conduct; and that, accordingly, the Trial Court erred in according to the defendants the benefits of the business judgment rule.

IV.

Whether the directors of Trans Union should be treated as one or individually in terms of invoking the protection of the business judgment rule and the applicability

[178] [32] To the extent the Trial Court's ultimate conclusion to invoke the business judgment rule is based on other explicit criteria and supporting evidence (i.e., market value of Trans Union's stock, the business acumen of the Board members, the substantial premium over market and the availability of the market test to confirm the adequacy of the premium), we have previously discussed the insufficiency of such evidence.

of 8 Del. C. § 141(c) are questions which were not originally addressed by the parties in their briefing of this case. This resulted in a supplemental briefing and a second rehearing en banc on two basic questions: (a) whether one or more of the directors were deprived of the protection of the business judgment rule by evidence of an absence of good faith; and (b) whether one or more of the outside directors were entitled to invoke the protection of 8 Del. C. § 141(e) by evidence of a reasonable, good faith reliance on "reports," including legal advice, rendered the Board by certain inside directors and the Board's special counsel, Brennan.

The parties' response, including reargument, has led the majority of the Court to conclude: (1) that since all of the defendant directors, outside as well as inside, take a unified position, we are required to treat all of the directors as one as to whether they are entitled to the protection of the business judgment rule; and (2) that considerations of good faith, including the presumption that the directors acted in good faith, are irrelevant in determining the threshold issue of whether the directors as a Board exercised an informed business judgment. For the same reason, we must reject defense counsel's *ad hominem* argument for affirmance: that reversal may result in a multi-million dollar class award against the defendants for having made an allegedly uninformed business judgment in a transaction not involving any personal gain, self-dealing or claim of bad faith.

In their brief, the defendants similarly mistake the business judgment rule's application to this case by erroneously invoking presumptions of good faith and "wide discretion":

> This is a case in which plaintiff challenged the exercise of business judgment by an independent Board of Directors. There were no allegations and no proof of fraud, bad faith, or self-dealing by the directors. . . .
>
> The business judgment rule, which was properly applied by the Chancellor, allows directors wide discretion in the matter of valuation and affords room for honest differences of opinion. In order to prevail, plaintiffs had the heavy burden of proving that the merger price was so grossly inadequate as to display itself as a badge of fraud. That is a burden which plaintiffs have not met.

However, plaintiffs have not claimed, nor did the Trial Court decide, that $55 was a grossly inadequate price per share for sale of the Company. That being so, the presumption that a board's judgment as to adequacy of price represents an honest exercise of business judgment (absent proof that the sale price was grossly inadequate) is irrelevant to the threshold question of whether an informed judgment was reached. *Compare Sinclair Oil Corp. v. Levien*, Del. Supr., 280 A.2d 717 (1971); *Kelly v. Bell*, Del. Supr., 266 A.2d 878, 879 (1970); *Cole v. National Cash Credit Association*, Del. Ch., 156 A. 183 (1931); *Allaun v. Consolidated Oil Co., supra; Allen Chemical & Dye Corp. v. Steel & Tube Co. of America*, Del. Ch., 120 A. 486 (1923).

V.

The defendants ultimately rely on the stockholder vote of February 10 for exoneration. The defendants contend that the stockholders' "overwhelming" vote approving the Pritzker Merger Agreement had the legal effect of curing any failure of the Board to reach an informed business judgment in its approval of the merger.

The parties tacitly agree that a discovered failure of the Board to reach an informed business judgment in approving the merger constitutes a voidable, rather than a void, act. Hence, the merger can be sustained, notwithstanding the infirmity of the Board's action, if its approval by a majority vote of the shareholders is found to have been based on an informed electorate. *Cf. Michelson v. Duncan*, Del. Supr., 407 A.2d 211 (1979), *aff'g in part and rev'g in part*, Del. Ch., 386 A.2d 1144 (1978). The disagreement between the parties arises over: (1) the Board's burden of disclosing to the shareholders all relevant and material information; and (2) the sufficiency of the evidence as to whether the Board satisfied that burden.

On this issue the Trial Court summarily concluded "that the stockholders of Trans Union were fairly informed as to the pending merger. . . ." The Court provided no supportive reasoning nor did the court make any reference to the evidence of record.

The plaintiffs contend that the Court committed error by applying an erroneous disclosure standard of "adequacy" rather than "completeness" in determining the sufficiency of the Company's merger proxy materials. The plaintiffs also argue that the Board's proxy statements, both its original statement dated January 19 and its supplemental statement dated January 26, were incomplete in various material respects. Finally, the plaintiffs assert that Management's supplemental statement (mailed "on or about" January 27) was untimely either as a matter of law under 8 Del. C. § 251(c), or untimely as a matter of equity and the requirements of complete candor and fair disclosure.

The defendants deny that the Court committed legal or equitable error. On the question of the Board's burden of disclosure, the defendants state that there was no dispute at trial over the standard of disclosure required of the Board; but the defendants concede that the Board was required to disclose "all germane facts" which a reasonable shareholder would have considered important in deciding whether to approve the merger. Thus, the defendants argue that when the Trial Court speaks of finding the Company's shareholders to have been "fairly informed" by Management's proxy materials, the Court is speaking in terms of "complete candor" as required under *Lynch v. Vickers Energy Corp.*, Del. Supr., 383 A.2d 278 (1978).

The settled rule in Delaware is that "where a majority of fully informed stockholders ratify action of even interested directors, an attack on the ratified transaction normally must fail." *Gerlach v. Gillam*, Del. Ch., 139 A.2d 591, 593 (1958). The question of whether shareholders have been fully informed such that their vote can be said to ratify director action, "turns on the fairness and completeness of the proxy materials submitted by the management to the . . . shareholders." *Michelson v. Duncan, supra* at 220. As this Court stated in *Gottlieb v. Heyden Chemical Corp.*, Del. Supr., 91 A.2d 57, 59 (1952):

> [T]he entire atmosphere is freshened and a new set of rules invoked where a formal approval has been given by a majority of independent, fully informed stockholders.

In *Lynch v. Vickers Energy Corp., supra,* this Court held that corporate directors owe to their stockholders a fiduciary duty to disclose all facts germane to the transaction at issue in an atmosphere of complete candor. We defined "germane" in the tender offer context as all "information such as a reasonable stockholder would consider important in deciding whether to sell or retain stock." *Id.* at 281. *Accord Weinberger v. UOP, Inc., supra; Michelson v. Duncan, supra; Schreiber v. Pennzoil Corp.,* Del. Ch., 419 A.2d 952 (1980). In reality, "germane" means material facts.

Applying this standard to the record before us, we find that Trans Union's stockholders were not fully informed of all facts material to their vote on the Pritzker Merger and that the Trial Court's ruling to the contrary is clearly erroneous. We list the material deficiencies in the proxy materials:

> (1) The fact that the Board had no reasonably adequate information indicative of the intrinsic value of the Company, other than a concededly depressed market price, was without question material to the shareholder voting on the merger. *See Weinberger, supra* at 709 (insiders' report that cash-out merger price up to $24 was good investment held material); *Michelson, supra* at 224 (alleged terms and intent of stock option plan held not germane); *Schreiber, supra* at 959 (management fee of $650,000 held germane).

Accordingly, the Board's lack of valuation information should have been disclosed. Instead, the directors cloaked the absence of such information in both the Proxy Statement and the Supplemental Proxy Statement. Through artful drafting, noticeably absent at the September 20 meeting, both documents create the impression that the Board knew the intrinsic worth of the Company. In particular, the Original Proxy Statement contained the following:

> Although the Board of Directors regards the intrinsic value of the Company's assets to be significantly greater than their book value . . . , systematic liquidation of such a large and complex entity as Trans Union is simply not regarded as a feasible method of realizing its inherent value. Therefore, a business combination such as the merger would seem to be the only practicable way in which the stockholders could realize the value of the Company.

The Proxy stated further that "[i]n the view of the Board of Directors . . . , the prices at which the Company's common stock has traded in recent years have not reflected the inherent value of the Company." What the Board failed to disclose to its stockholders was that the Board had not made any study of the intrinsic or inherent worth of the Company; nor had the Board even discussed the inherent value of the Company prior to approving the merger on September 20, or at either of the subsequent meetings on October 8 or January 26. Neither in its Original Proxy Statement nor in its Supplemental Proxy did the Board disclose that it had no information before it, beyond the premium-over-market and the price/earnings ratio, on which to determine the fair value of the Company as a whole.

(2) We find false and misleading the Board's characterization of the Romans report in the Supplemental Proxy Statement. The Supplemental Proxy stated:

> At the September 20, 1980 meeting of the Board of Directors of Trans Union, Mr. Romans indicated that while he could not say that $55.00 per share was an unfair price, he had prepared a preliminary report which reflected that the value of the Company was in the range of $55.00 to $65.00 per share.

Nowhere does the Board disclose that Romans stated to the Board that his calculations were made in a "search for ways to justify, a price in connection with" a leveraged buy-out transaction, "rather than to say what the shares are worth," and that he stated to the Board that his conclusion thus arrived at "was not the same thing as saying that I have a valuation of the Company at *X* dollars." Such information would have been material to a reasonable shareholder, because it tended to invalidate the fairness of the merger price of $55. Furthermore, defendants again failed to disclose the absence of valuation information but still made repeated reference to the "substantial premium."

(3) We find misleading the Board's references to the "substantial" premium offered. The Board gave as their primary reason in support of the merger the "substantial premium" shareholders would receive. But the Board did not disclose its failure to assess the premium offered in terms of other relevant valuation techniques, thereby rendering questionable its determination as to the substantiality of the premium over an admittedly depressed stock market price.

(4) We find the Board's recital in the Supplemental Proxy of certain events preceding the September 20 meeting to be incomplete and misleading. It is beyond dispute that a reasonable stockholder would have considered material the fact that Van Gorkom not only suggested the $55 price to Pritzker, but also that he chose the figure because it made feasible a leveraged buy-out. The directors disclosed that Van Gorkom suggested the $55 price to Pritzker. But the Board misled the shareholders when they described the basis of Van Gorkom's suggestion as follows:

> Such suggestion was based, at least in part, on Mr. Van Gorkom's belief that loans could be obtained from institutional lenders (together with about a $200 million equity contribution) which would justify the payment of such price, . . .

Although by January 26 the directors knew the basis of the $55 figure, they did not disclose that Van Gorkom chose the $55 price, because that figure would enable Pritzker to both finance the purchase of Trans Union through a leveraged buy-out and, within five years, substantially repay the loan out of the cash flow generated by the Company's operations.

(5) The Board's Supplemental Proxy Statement, mailed on or after January 27, added significant new matter, material to the proposal to be voted on February 10, which was not contained in the Original Proxy Statement. Some of this new matter was information which had only been disclosed to the Board on January 26; much was information known or reasonably available before January 21 but not revealed in the Original Proxy Statement. Yet, the stockholders were not informed of these facts. Included in the "new" matter first disclosed in the Supplemental Proxy Statement were the following:

(a) The fact that prior to September 20, 1980, no Board member or member of Senior Management, except Chelberg and Peterson, knew that Van Gorkom had discussed a possible merger with Pritzker;

(b) The fact that the sale price of $55 per share had been suggested initially to Pritzker by Van Gorkom;

(c) The fact that the Board had not sought an independent fairness opinion;

(d) The fact that Romans and several members of Senior Management had indicated concern at the September 20 Senior Management meeting that the $55 per share price was inadequate and had stated that a higher price should and could be obtained; and

(e) The fact that Romans had advised the Board at its meeting on September 20 that he and his department had prepared a study which indicated that the Company had a value in the range of $55 to $65 per share, and that he could not advise the Board that the $55 per share offer which Pritzker made was unfair.

The parties differ over whether the notice requirements of 8 Del. C. § 251(c) apply to the mailing date of supplemental proxy material or that of the original proxy material.[179] The Trial Court summarily disposed of the notice issue, stating it was "satisfied that the proxy material furnished to Trans Union stockholders . . . fairly presented the question to be voted on at the February 10, 1981 meeting."

The defendants argue that the notice provisions of § 251(c) must be construed as requiring only that stockholders receive notice of the time, place, and purpose of a meeting to consider a merger at least 20 days prior to such meeting; and since the Original Proxy Statement was disseminated more than 20 days before the meeting, the defendants urge affirmance of the Trial Court's ruling as correct as a matter of statutory construction. Apparently, the question has not been addressed by either the Court of Chancery or this Court; and authority in other jurisdictions is limited. *See Electronics Specialty Co. v. Int'l Controls Corp.*, 2d Cir., 409 F.2d 937, 944 (1969) (holding that a tender offeror's September 16, 1968 correction of a previous misstatement, combined with an offer of withdrawal running for eight days until September, 24, 1968, was sufficient to cure past violations and eliminate any need for rescission); *Nicholson File Co. v. H.K. Porter Co.*, D.R.I., 341 F. Supp. 508, 513-14 (1972), *affd*, 1st Cir., 482 F.2d 421 (1973) (permitting correction of a material misstatement by a mailing to stockholders within seven days of a tender offer withdrawal date). Both *Electronics* and *Nicholson* are federal security cases not arising under 8 Del. C. § 251(c), and they are otherwise distinguishable from this case on their facts.

---

[179] [33] The pertinent provisions of 8 Del. C. § 251(c) provide:

(c) The agreement required by subsection (b) shall be submitted to the stockholders of each constituent corporation at an annual or special meeting thereof for the purpose of acting on the agreement. Due notice of the time, place and purpose of the meeting shall be mailed to each holder of stock, whether voting or non-voting, of the corporation at his address as it appears on the records of the corporation, at least 20 days prior to the date of the meeting. . . .

Since we have concluded that Management's Supplemental Proxy Statement does not meet the Delaware disclosure standard of "complete candor" under *Lynch v. Vickers, supra,* it is unnecessary for us to address the plaintiffs' legal argument as to the proper construction of § 251(c). However, we do find it advisable to express the view that, in an appropriate case, an otherwise candid proxy statement may be so untimely as to defeat its purpose of meeting the needs of a fully informed electorate.

In this case, the Board's ultimate disclosure as contained in the Supplemental Proxy Statement related either to information readily accessible to all of the directors if they had asked the right questions, or was information already at their disposal. In short, the information disclosed by the Supplemental Proxy Statement was information which the defendant directors knew or should have known at the time the first Proxy Statement was issued. The defendants simply failed in their original duty of knowing, sharing, and disclosing information that was material and reasonably available for their discovery. They compounded that failure by their continued lack of candor in the Supplemental Proxy Statement. While we need not decide the issue here, we are satisfied that, in an appropriate case, a completely candid but belated disclosure of information long known or readily available to a board could raise serious issues of inequitable conduct. *Schnell v. Chris-Craft Industries, Inc.*, Del. Supr., 285 A.2d 437, 439 (1971).

The burden must fall on defendants who claim ratification based on shareholder vote to establish that the shareholder approval resulted from a fully informed electorate. On the record before us, it is clear that the Board failed to meet that burden. *Weinberger v. UOP, Inc., supra* at 703; *Michelson v. Duncan, supra.*

. . . .

For the foregoing reasons, we conclude that the director defendants breached their fiduciary duty of candor by their failure to make true and correct disclosures of all information they had, or should have had, material to the transaction submitted for stockholder approval.

VI.

To summarize: we hold that the directors of Trans Union breached their fiduciary duty to their stockholders (i) by their failure to inform themselves of all information reasonably available to them and relevant to their decision to recommend the Pritzker merger; and (2) by their failure to disclose all material information such as a reasonable stockholder would consider important in deciding whether to approve the Pritzker offer.

We hold, therefore, that the Trial Court committed reversible error in applying the business judgment rule in favor of the director defendants in this case.

On remand, the Court of Chancery shall conduct an evidentiary hearing to determine the fair value of the shares represented by the plaintiffs' class, based on the intrinsic value of Trans Union on September 20, 1980. Such valuation shall be made in accordance with *Weinberger v. UOP, Inc., supra* at 712-715. Thereafter, an award of damages may be entered to the extent that the fair value of Trans Union exceeds $55 per share.

Reversed and Remanded for proceedings consistent herewith.

McNeilly, Justice, dissenting:

The majority opinion reads like an advocate's closing address to a hostile jury. And I say that not lightly. Throughout the opinion great emphasis is directed only to the negative, with nothing more than lip service granted the positive aspects of this case. In my opinion Chancellor Marvel (retired) should have been affirmed. The Chancellor's opinion was the product of well reasoned conclusions, based upon a sound deductive process, clearly supported by the evidence and entitled to deference in this appeal. Because of my diametrical opposition to all evidentiary conclusions of the majority, I respectfully dissent.

It would serve no useful purpose, particularly at this late date, for me to dissent at great length. I restrain myself from doing so, but feel compelled to at least point out what I consider to be the most glaring deficiencies in the majority opinion. The majority has spoken and has effectively said that Trans Union's Directors have been the victims of a "fast shuffle" by Van Gorkom and Pritzker. That is the beginning of the majority's comedy of errors. The first and most important error made is the majority's assessment of the directors' knowledge of the affairs of Trans Union and their combined ability to act in this situation under the protection of the business judgment rule.

Trans Union's Board of Directors consisted of ten men, five of whom were "inside" directors and five of whom were "outside" directors. The "inside" directors were Van Gorkom, Chelberg, Bonser, William B. Browder, Senior Vice-President-Law, and Thomas P. O'Boyle, Senior Vice-President-Administration. At the time the merger was proposed, the inside five directors had collectively been employed by the Company for 116 years and had 68 years of combined experience as directors. The "outside" directors were A.W. Wallis, William B. Johnson, Joseph B. Lanterman, Graham J. Morgan and Robert W. Reneker. With the exception of Wallis, these were all chief executive officers of Chicago based corporations that were at least as large as Trans Union. The five "outside" directors had 78 years of combined experience as chief executive officers and 53 years cumulative service as Trans Union directors.

The inside directors wear their badge of expertise in the corporate affairs of Trans Union on their sleeves. But what about the outsiders? Dr. Wallis is or was an economist and math statistician, a professor of economics at Yale University, dean of the graduate school of business at the University of Chicago, and Chancellor of the University of Rochester. Dr. Wallis had been on the Board of Trans Union since 1962. He also was on the Board of Bausch & Lomb, Kodak, Metropolitan Life Insurance Company, Standard Oil and others.

William B. Johnson is a University of Pennsylvania law graduate, President of Railway Express until 1966, Chairman and Chief Executive of I.C. Industries Holding Company, and member of Trans Union's Board since 1968.

Joseph Lanterman, a Certified Public Accountant, is or was President and Chief Executive of American Steel, on the Board of International Harvester, Peoples Energy, Illinois Bell Telephone, Harris Bank and Trust Company, Kemper Insurance Company and a director of Trans Union for four years.

Graham Morgan is a chemist, was Chairman and Chief Executive Officer of U.S. Gypsum, and in the 17 and 18 years prior to the Trans Union transaction had been involved in 31 or 32 corporate takeovers.

Robert Reneker attended University of Chicago and Harvard Business Schools. He was President and Chief Executive of Swift and Company, director of Trans Union since 1971, and member of the Boards of seven other corporations including U.S. Gypsum and the Chicago Tribune.

Directors of this caliber are not ordinarily taken in by a "fast shuffle." I submit they were not taken into this multi-million dollar corporate transaction without being fully informed and aware of the state of the art as it pertained to the entire corporate panorama of Trans Union. True, even directors such as these, with their business acumen, interest and expertise, can go astray. I do not believe that to be the case here. These men knew Trans Union like the back of their hands and were more than well qualified to make on the spot informed business judgments concerning the affairs of Trans Union, including a 100% sale of the corporation. Lest we forget, the corporate world of then and now operates on what is so aptly referred to as "the fast track." These men were at the time an integral part of that world, all professional businessmen, not intellectual figureheads.

The majority of this Court holds that the Board's decision, reached on September 20, 1980, to approve the merger was not the product of an *informed* business judgment, that the Board's subsequent efforts to amend the Merger Agreement and take other curative action were *legally and factually* ineffectual, and that the Board did not deal with complete candor with the stockholders by failing to disclose all material facts, which they knew or should have known, before securing the stockholders' approval of the merger. I disagree.

At the time of the September 20, 1980 meeting, the Board was acutely aware of Trans Union and its prospects. The problems created by accumulated investment tax credits and accelerated depreciation were discussed repeatedly at Board meetings, and all of the directors understood the problem thoroughly. Moreover, at the July, 1980 Board meeting the directors had reviewed Trans Union's newly prepared five-year forecast, and at the August, 1980 meeting Van Gorkom presented the results of a comprehensive study of Trans Union made by The Boston Consulting Group. This study was prepared over an 18 month period and consisted of a detailed analysis of all Trans Union subsidiaries, including competitiveness, profitability, cash throw-off, cash consumption, technical competence and future prospects for contribution to Trans Union's combined net income.

At the September 20 meeting Van Gorkom reviewed all aspects of the proposed transaction and repeated the explanation of the Pritzker offer he had earlier given to senior management. Having heard Van Gorkom's explanation of the Pritzker's offer, and Brennan's explanation of the merger documents, the directors discussed the matter. Out of this discussion arose an insistence on the part of the directors that two modifications to the offer be made. First, they required that any potential competing bidder be given access to the same information concerning Trans Union that had been provided to the Pritzkers. Second, the merger documents were to be modified to reflect the fact that the directors could accept a better offer and would not be required to recommend the Pritzker offer if a better offer was made. The following language was inserted into the agreement:

> Within 30 days after the execution of this Agreement, TU shall call a meeting of its stockholders (the "Stockholder's Meeting") for the purpose of approving and adopting the Merger Agreement. The Board of Directors shall recommend to the stockholders of TU that they approve and adopt the Merger Agreement (the "Stockholders' Approval") and shall use its best efforts to obtain the requisite vote therefor; *provided, however, that GL and NT.C. acknowledge that the Board of Directors of TU may have a competing fiduciary obligation to the Stockholders under certain circumstances.* (Emphasis added)

While the language is not artfully drawn, the evidence is clear that the intention underlying that language was to make specific the right that the directors assumed they had, that is, to accept any offer that they thought was better, and not to recommend the Pritzker offer in the face of a better one. At the conclusion of the meeting, the proposed merger was approved.

At a subsequent meeting on October 8, 1981 the directors, with the consent of the Pritzkers, amended the Merger Agreement so as to establish the right of Trans Union to solicit as well as to receive higher bids, although the Pritzkers insisted that their merger proposal be presented to the stockholders at the same time that the proposal of any third party was presented. A second amendment, which became effective on October 10, 1981, further provided that Trans Union might unilaterally terminate the proposed merger with the Pritzker company in the event that prior to February 10, 1981, there existed a definitive agreement with a third party for a merger, consolidation, sale of assets, or purchase or exchange of Trans Union stock which was more favorable for the stockholders of Trans Union than the Pritzker offer and which was conditioned upon receipt of stockholder approval and the absence of an injunction against its consummation.

Following the October 8 board meeting of Trans Union, the investment banking firm of Salomon Brothers was retained by the corporation to search for better offers than that of the Pritzkers, Salomon Brothers being charged with the responsibility of doing "whatever possible to see if there is a superior bid in the marketplace over a bid that is on the table for Trans Union." In undertaking such a project, it was agreed that Salomon Brothers would be paid the amount of $500,000 to cover its expenses as well as a fee equal to 38ths of 1% of the aggregate fair market value of the consideration to be received by the company in the case of a merger or the like, which meant that in the event Salomon Brothers should find a buyer willing to pay a price of $56.00 a share instead of $55.00, such firm would receive a fee of roughly $2,650,000 plus disbursements.

As the first step in proceeding to carry out its commitment, *Salomon Brothers had a brochure prepared, which set forth Trans Union's financial history, described the company's business in detail and set forth Trans Union's operating and financial projections. Salomon Brothers also prepared a list of over 150 companies which it believed might be suitable merger partners, and while four of such companies, namely, General Electric, Borg-Warner, Bendix, and Genstar, Ltd. showed some interest in such a merger, none made a firm proposal to Trans Union, and only General Electric* showed a substantial interest.[180] As matters transpired, no firm offer which bettered the Pritzker offer of $55 per share was ever made.

On January 21, 1981 a proxy statement was sent to the shareholders of Trans Union advising them of a February 10, 1981 meeting in which the merger would be voted. On January 26, 1981 the directors held their regular meeting. At this meeting the Board discussed the instant merger as well as all events, including this litigation, surrounding it. At the conclusion of the meeting the Board unanimously voted to recommend to the stockholders that they approve the merger. Additionally, the directors reviewed and approved a Supplemental Proxy Statement which, among other things, advised the stockholders of what had occurred at the instant meeting and of the fact that General Electric had decided not to make an offer. On February 10, 1981 the stockholders of Trans Union met pursuant to notice and voted overwhelmingly in favor of the Pritzker merger, 89% of the votes cast being in favor of it.

I have no quarrel with the majority's analysis of the business judgment rule. It is the application of that rule to these facts which is wrong. An overview of the entire record, rather than the limited view of bits and pieces which the majority has exploded like popcorn, convinces me that the directors made an informal business judgment which was buttressed by their test of the market.

At the time of the September 20 meeting the 10 members of Trans Union's Board of Directors were highly qualified and well informed about the affairs and prospects of Trans Union. These directors were acutely aware of the historical problems facing Trans Union which were caused by the tax laws. They had discussed these problems *ad nauseam.* In fact, within two months of the September 20 meeting the board had reviewed and discussed an outside study of the company done by The Boston Consulting Group and an internal five year forecast prepared by management. At the September 20 meeting Van Gorkom presented the Pritzker offer, and the board then heard from James Brennan, the company's counsel in this matter, who discussed the legal documents. Following this, the Board directed that certain changes be made in the merger documents. These changes made it clear that the Board was free to accept a better offer than Pritzker's if one was made. The above facts reveal that the Board did not act in a grossly negligent manner in informing

---

180 [1] Shortly after the announcement of the proposed merger in September, senior members of Trans Union's management got in touch with KKR to discuss their possible participation in a leverage buyout scheme. On December 2, 1980 KKR, through Henry Kravis, actually made a bid of $60.00 per share for Trans Union stock on December 2, 1980, but the offer was withdrawn three hours after it was made because of complications arising out of negotiations with the Reichman family, extremely wealthy Canadians and a change of attitude toward the leveraged buyout scheme, by Jack Kruzenga, the member of senior management of Trans Union who most likely would have been President and Chief Operating Officer of the new company. Kruzenga was the President and Chief Operating Officer of the seven subsidiaries of Trans Union which constituted the backbone of Trans Union as shown through exhaustive studies and analysis of Trans Union's intrinsic value on the market place by the respected investment banking firm of Morgan Stanley. It is interesting to note that at no time during the market test period did any of the 150 corporations contacted by Salomon Brothers complain of the time frame or availability of corporate records in order to make an independent judgment of market value of 100% of Trans Union.

themselves of the relevant and available facts before passing on the merger. To the contrary, this record reveals that the directors acted with the utmost care in informing themselves of the relevant and available facts before passing on the merger.

The majority finds that Trans Union stockholders were not fully informed and that the directors breached their fiduciary duty of complete candor to the stockholders required by *Lynch v. Vickers Energy Corp.*, Del. Supr. 383 A.2d 278 (1978) [Lynch I], in that the proxy materials were deficient in five areas.

Here again is exploitation of the negative by the majority without giving credit to the positive. To respond to the conclusions of the majority would merely be unnecessary prolonged argument. But briefly what did the proxy materials disclose? The proxy material informed the shareholders that projections were furnished to potential purchasers and such projections indicated that Trans Union's net income might increase to approximately $153 million in 1985. That projection, what is almost three times the net income of $58,248,000 reported by Trans Union as its net income for December 31, 1979 confirmed the statement in the proxy materials that the "Board of Directors believes that, assuming reasonably favorable economic and financial conditions, the Company's prospects for future earnings growth are excellent." This material was certainly sufficient to place the Company's stockholders on notice that there was a reasonable basis to believe that the prospects for future earnings growth were excellent, and that the value of their stock was more than the stock market value of their shares reflected.

Overall, my review of the record leads me to conclude that the proxy materials adequately complied with Delaware law in informing the shareholders about the proposed transaction and the events surrounding it.

The majority suggests that the Supplemental Proxy Statement did not comply with the notice requirement of 8 Del. C. § 251(c) that notice of the time, place and purpose of a meeting to consider a merger must be sent to each shareholder of record at least 20 days prior to the date of the meeting. In the instant case, an original proxy statement was mailed on January 18, 1981 giving notice of the time, place and purpose of the meeting. A Supplemental Proxy Statement was mailed January 26, 1981 in an effort to advise Trans Union's shareholders as to what had occurred at the January 26, 1981 meeting, and that General Electric had decided not to make an offer. The shareholder meeting was held February 10, 1981, fifteen days after the Supplemental Proxy Statement had been sent.

All § 251(c) requires is that notice of the time, place and purpose of the meeting be given at least 20 days prior to the meeting. This was accomplished by the proxy statement mailed January 19, 1981. Nothing in § 251(c) prevents the supplementation of proxy materials within 20 days of the meeting. Indeed when additional information, which a reasonable shareholder would consider important in deciding how to vote, comes to light, that information must be disclosed to stockholders in sufficient time for the stockholders to consider it. But nothing in § 251(c) requires this additional information to be disclosed at least 20 days prior to the meeting. To reach a contrary result would ignore the current practice and would discourage the supplementation of proxy materials in order to disclose the occurrence of intervening events. In my opinion, fifteen days in the instant case was a sufficient amount of time for the stockholders to receive and consider the information in the supplemental proxy statement.

CHRISTIE, JUSTICE, dissenting:

I respectfully dissent.

Considering the standard and scope of our review under *Levitt v. Bouvier*, Del. Supr., 287 A.2d 671, 673 (1972), I believe that the record taken as a whole supports a conclusion that the actions of the defendants are protected by the business judgment rule. *Aronson v. Lewis*, Del. Supr., 473 A.2d 805, 812 (1984); *Pogostin v. Rice*, Del. Supr., 480 A.2d 619, 627 (1984). I am also satisfied that the record supports a conclusion that the defendants acted with the complete candor required by *Lynch v. Vickers Energy Corp.*, Del. Supr., 383 A.2d 278 (1978). Under the circumstances, I would affirm the judgment of the Court of Chancery.

NOTE

As a result of the decision in *Smith v. Van Gorkom*, the Delaware General Corporation Law was amended to provide as follows.

> § 102 Contents of Certificate of Incorporation
>
> . . . .
>
> (b) In addition to the matters required to be set forth in the certificate of incorporation by subsection (a) of this section, the certificate of incorporation may also contain any or all of the following matters:
>
> . . . .
>
> (7) A provision eliminating or limiting the personal liability of a director to the corporation or its stockholders for monetary damages for breach of fiduciary duty as a director, provided that such provision *shall not eliminate* or limit the liability of a director (i) for any breach of the director's *duty of loyalty* to the corporation or its stockholders, (ii) for acts or omissions *not in good faith* or which involve *intentional* misconduct or a *knowing* violation of law, (iii) under section 174 of this Title, or (iv) for any transaction from which the director derived an improper personal benefit. No such provision shall eliminate or limit the liability of a director for any act or omission occurring prior to the date when such provision becomes effective. All references in this paragraph to a director shall also be deemed to refer (x) to a member of the governing body of a corporation which is not authorized to issue capital stock, and (y) to such other person or persons, if any, who, pursuant to a provision of the certificate of incorporation in accordance with subsection (a) of § 141 of this title, exercise or perform any of the powers or duties otherwise conferred or imposed upon the board of directors by this title.

LANDRETH TIMBER CO. v. LANDRETH

United States Supreme Court
471 U.S. 681 (1985)

JUSTICE POWELL delivered the opinion of the Court.

This case presents the question whether the sale of all of the stock of a company is a securities transaction subject to the antifraud provisions of the federal securities laws (the Acts).

I

Respondents Ivan K. Landreth and his sons owned all of the outstanding stock of a lumber business they operated in Tonasket, Washington. The Landreth family offered their stock for sale through both Washington and out-of-state brokers. Before a purchaser was found, the company's sawmill was heavily damaged by fire. Despite the fire, the brokers continued to offer the stock for sale. Potential purchasers were advised of the damage, but were told that the mill would be completely rebuilt and modernized.

Samuel Dennis, a Massachusetts tax attorney, received a letter offering the stock for sale. On the basis of the letter's representations concerning the rebuilding plans, the predicted productivity of the mill, existing contracts, and expected profits, Dennis became interested in acquiring the stock. He talked to John Bolten, a former client who had retired to Florida, about joining him in investigating the offer. After having an audit and an inspection of the mill conducted, a stock purchase agreement was negotiated, with Dennis the purchaser of all of the common stock in the lumber company. Ivan Landreth agreed to stay on as a consultant for some time to help with the daily operations of the mill. Pursuant to the terms of the stock purchase agreement, Dennis assigned the stock he purchased to B & D Co., a corporation formed for the sole purpose of acquiring the lumber company stock. B & D then merged with the lumber company, forming petitioner Landreth Timber Co. Dennis and Bolten then acquired all of petitioner's Class A stock, representing 85% of the equity, and six other investors together owned the Class B stock, representing the remaining 15% of the equity.

After the acquisition was completed, the mill did not live up to the purchasers' expectations. Rebuilding costs exceeded earlier estimates, and new components turned out to be incompatible with existing equipment. Eventually, petitioner sold the mill at a loss and went into receivership. Petitioner then filed this suit seeking rescission of the sale of stock and $2,500,000 in damages, alleging that respondents had widely offered and then sold their stock without registering it as required by the Securities Act of 1933, 15 U. S. C. § 77a *et seq.* [15 U.S.C.S. §§ 78a et seq.], (1933 Act). Petitioner also alleged that respondents had negligently or intentionally made misrepresentations and had failed to state material facts as to the worth and prospects of the lumber company, all in violation of the Securities Exchange Act of 1934, 15 U. S. C. § 78a *et seq.* [15 U.S.C.S. §§ 78a et seq.] (1934 Act). Respondents moved for summary judgment on the ground that the transaction was not covered by the Acts because under the so-called "sale of business" doctrine, petitioner had not purchased a "security" within the meaning of those Acts. The District Court granted respondents' motion and dismissed the complaint for want of federal jurisdiction. It acknowledged that the federal statutes include "stock" as one of the instruments constituting a "security," and that the stock at issue possessed all of the characteristics of conventional stock. Nonetheless, it joined what it termed the "growing majority" of courts that had held that the federal securities laws do not apply to the sale of 100% of the stock of a closely held corporation. App. to Pet. for Cert. 13a. Relying on *United Housing Foundation, Inc. v. Forman*, 421 U.S. 837 (1975), 95 S. Ct. 2051, 44 L. Ed. 2d 621 (1975), and *SEC v. W. J. Howey Co.*, 328 U.S. 293, 66 S. Ct. 1100, 90 L. Ed. 1244, 163 A.L.R. 1043 (1946), the District Court ruled that the stock could not be considered a "security" unless the purchaser had entered into the transaction with the anticipation of earning profits derived from the efforts of others. Finding that managerial control of the business had passed into the hands of the purchasers, and thus that the transaction was a commercial venture rather than a typical investment, the District Court dismissed the complaint.

The United States Court of Appeals for the Ninth Circuit affirmed the District Court's application of the sale of business doctrine. 731 F.2d 1348 (1984). It agreed that it was bound by *United Housing Foundation, Inc. v. Forman, supra*, and *SEC v. W. J. Howey Co., supra*, to determine in every case whether the economic realities of the transaction indicated that the Acts applied. Because the Courts of Appeals are divided over the applicability of the federal securities laws when a business is sold by the transfer of 100% of its stock, we granted certiorari. 469 U.S. 1016, 83 L. Ed. 2d 354, 105 S. Ct. 427 (1984). We now reverse.

II

It is axiomatic that "[the] starting point in every case involving construction of a statute is the language itself." *Blue Chip Stamps v. Manor Drug Stores*, 421 U.S. 723, 756 (1975) (POWELL, J., concurring); accord, *Teamsters v. Daniel*, 439 U.S. 551, 558 (1979). Section 2(1) of the 1933 Act, 48 Stat. 74, as amended and as set forth in 15 U. S. C. § 77b(1), defines a "security" as including

> any note, stock, treasury stock, bond, debenture, evidence of indebtedness, certificate of interest or participation in any profit-sharing agreement, collateral-trust certificate, preorganization certificate or subscription, transferable share, investment contract, voting-trust certificate, certificate of deposit for a security, fractional undivided interest in oil, gas, or other mineral rights, . . . or, in general, any interest or instrument commonly known as a "security," or any certificate of interest or participation in, temporary or interim certificate for, receipt for, guarantee of, or warrant or right to subscribe to or purchase, any of the foregoing.[181]

As we have observed in the past, this definition is quite broad, *Marine Bank v.*

---

[181] [1] We have repeatedly ruled that the definitions of "security" in § 3(a)(10) of the 1934 Act and § 2(1) of the 1933 Act are virtually identical and will be treated as such in our decisions dealing with the scope of the term. *Marine Bank v. Weaver*, 455 U.S. 551, 555, n. 3 (1982); *United Housing Foundation, Inc. v. Forman*, 421 U.S. 837, 847, n. 12 (1975).

Weaver, 455 U.S. 551, 556 (1982), and includes both instruments whose names alone carry well-settled meaning, as well as instruments of "more variable character [that] were necessarily designated by more descriptive terms," such as "investment contract" and "instrument commonly known as a 'security.' " *SEC* v. *C. M. Joiner Leasing Corp.*, 320 U.S. 344, 351 (1943). The face of the definition shows that "stock C is considered to be a 'security' within the meaning of the Acts." As we observed in *United Housing Foundation, Inc. v. Forman*, 421 U.S. 837 (1975), most instruments bearing such a traditional title are likely to be covered by the definition. *Id.*, at 850.

As we also recognized in *Forman*, the fact that instruments bear the label "stock" is not of itself sufficient to invoke the coverage of the Acts. Rather, we concluded that we must also determine whether those instruments possess "some of the significant characteristics typically associated with" stock, *id.*, at 851, recognizing that when an instrument is both called "stock" and bears stock's usual characteristics, "a purchaser justifiably [may] assume that the federal securities laws apply," *id.*, at 850. We identified those characteristics usually associated with common stock as (i) the right to receive dividends contingent upon an apportionment of profits; (ii) negotiability; (iii) the ability to be pledged or hypothecated; (iv) the conferring of voting rights in proportion to the number of shares owned; and (v) the capacity to appreciate in value.[182] *Id.*, at 851, 44 L. Ed. 2d 621, 95 S. Ct. 2051.

Under the facts of *Forman*, we concluded that the instruments at issue there were not "securities" within the meaning of the Acts. That case involved the sale of shares of stock entitling the purchaser to lease an apartment in a housing cooperative. The stock bore none of the characteristics listed above that are usually associated with traditional stock. Moreover, we concluded that under the circumstances, there was no likelihood that the purchasers had been misled by use of the word "stock" into thinking that the federal securities laws governed their purchases. The purchasers had intended to acquire low-cost subsidized living space for their personal use; no one was likely to have believed that he was purchasing investment securities. *Ibid.*

In contrast, it is undisputed that the stock involved here possesses all of the characteristics we identified in *Forman* as traditionally associated with common stock. Indeed, the District Court so found. App. to Pet. for Cert. 13a. Moreover, unlike in *Forman*, the context of the transaction involved here — the sale of stock in a corporation — is typical of the kind of context to which the Acts normally apply. It is thus much more likely here than in *Forman* that an investor would believe he was covered by the federal securities laws. Under the circumstances of this case, the plain meaning of the statutory definition mandates that the stock be treated as "securities" subject to the coverage of the Acts.

Reading the securities laws to apply to the sale of stock at issue here comports with Congress' remedial purpose in enacting the legislation to protect investors by "compelling full and fair disclosure relative to the issuance of 'the many types of

---

[182] [2] Although we did not so specify in *Forman*, we wish to make clear here that these characteristics are those usually associated with common stock, the kind of stock often at issue in cases involving the sale of a business. Various types of preferred stock may have different characteristics and still be covered by the Acts.

instruments that in our commercial world fall within the ordinary concept of a security.' " *SEC v. W. J. Howey Co.*, 328 U.S., at 299, 90 L. Ed. 1244, 66 S. Ct. 1100, 163 A.L.R. 1043 (quoting H. R. Rep. No. 85, 73d Cong., 1st Sess., 11 (1933)). Although we recognize that Congress did not intend to provide a comprehensive federal remedy for all fraud, *Marine Bank v. Weaver*, 455 U.S. 551, 556, 102 S. Ct. 1220, 71 L. Ed. 2d 409 (1982), we think it would improperly narrow Congress' broad definition of "security" to hold that the traditional stock at issue here falls outside the Acts' coverage.

III

Under other circumstances, we might consider the statutory analysis outlined above to be a sufficient answer compelling judgment for petitioner.[183] Respondents urge, however, that language in our previous opinions, including *Forman*, requires that we look beyond the label "stock" and the characteristics of the instruments involved to determine whether application of the Acts is mandated by the economic substance of the transaction. Moreover, the Court of Appeals rejected the view that the plain meaning of the definition would be sufficient to hold this stock covered, because it saw "no principled way," 731 F.2d, at 1353, to justify treating notes, bonds, and other of the definitional categories differently. We address these concerns in turn.

A.

It is fair to say that our cases have not been entirely clear on the proper method of analysis for determining when an instrument is a "security." This Court has decided a number of cases in which it looked to the economic substance of the transaction, rather than just to its form, to determine whether the Acts applied. In *SEC v. C. M. Joiner Leasing Corp.*, for example, the Court considered whether the 1933 Act applied to the sale of leasehold interests in land near a proposed oil well drilling. In holding that the leasehold interests were "securities," the Court noted that "the reach of the Act does not stop with the obvious and commonplace." 320 U.S., at 351, 88 L. Ed. 88, 64 S. Ct. 120. Rather, it ruled that unusual devices such as the leaseholds would also be covered "if it be proved as matter of fact that they were widely offered or dealt in under terms or courses of dealing which established their character in commerce as 'investment contracts,' or as 'any interest or instrument commonly known as a 'security.' " *Ibid.*

SEC v. W. J. Howey Co., supra, further elucidated the *Joiner* Court's suggestion that an unusual instrument could be considered a "security" if the circumstances of the transaction so dictated. At issue in that case was an offering of units of a citrus grove development coupled with a contract for cultivating and marketing the fruit and remitting the proceeds to the investors. The Court held that the offering constituted an "investment contract" within the meaning of the 1933 Act because, looking at the economic realities, the transaction "involve[d] an investment of money in a common enterprise with profits to come solely from the efforts of others." 328

---

[183] [3] Professor Loss suggests that the statutory analysis is sufficient. L. Loss, Fundamentals of Securities Regulation 212 (1983). *See infra*, 85 L. Ed. 2d 702.

U.S., at 301, 90 L. Ed. 1244, 66 S. Ct. 1100, 163 A.L.R. 1043.

This so-called "*Howey* test" formed the basis for the second part of our decision in *Forman*, on which respondents primarily rely. As discussed above, see Part II, *supra*, the first part of our decision in *Forman* concluded that the instruments at issue, while they bore the traditional label "stock," were not "securities" because they possessed none of the usual characteristics of stock. We then went on to address the argument that the instruments were "investment contracts." Applying the *Howey* test, we concluded that the instruments likewise were not "securities" by virtue of being "investment contracts" because the economic realities of the transaction showed that the purchasers had parted with their money not for the purpose of reaping profits from the efforts of others, but for the purpose of purchasing a commodity for personal consumption. 421 U.S., at 858, 44 L. Ed. 2d 621, 95 S. Ct. 2051.

Respondents contend that *Forman* and the cases on which it was based[184] require us to reject the view that the shares of stock at issue here may be considered "securities" because of their name and characteristics. Instead, they argue that our cases require us in every instance to look to the economic substance of the transaction to determine whether the *Howey* test has been met. According to respondents, it is clear that petitioner sought not to earn profits from the efforts of others, but to buy a company that it could manage and control. Petitioner was not a passive investor of the kind Congress intended the Acts to protect, but an active entrepreneur, who sought to "use or consume" the business purchased just as the purchasers in *Forman* sought to use the apartments they acquired after purchasing shares of stock. Thus, respondents urge that the Acts do not apply.

We disagree with respondents' interpretation of our cases. First, it is important to understand the contexts within which these cases were decided. All of the cases on which respondents rely involved unusual instruments not easily characterized as "securities." *See* n. 4, *supra*. Thus, if the Acts were to apply in those cases at all, it would have to have been because the economic reality underlying the transactions indicated that the instruments were actually of a type that falls within the usual concept of a security. In the case at bar, in contrast, the instrument involved is traditional stock, plainly within the statutory definition. There is no need here, as there was in the prior cases, to look beyond the characteristics of the instrument to determine whether the Acts apply.

Contrary to respondents' implication, the Court has never foreclosed the possibility that stock could be found to be a "security" simply because it is what it purports to be. In *SEC v. C. M. Joiner Leasing Corp.*, 320 U.S. 344, 64 S. Ct. 120,

---

[184] [4] Respondents also rely on *Tcherepnin v. Knight*, 389 U.S. 332 (1967), 88 S. Ct. 548, 19 L. Ed. 2d 564 (1967), and *Marine Bank v. Weaver*, 455 U.S. 551, 102 S. Ct. 1220, 71 L. Ed. 2d 409 (1982), as support for their argument that we have mandated in every case a determination of whether the economic realities of a transaction call for the application of the Acts. It is sufficient to note here that these cases, like the other cases on which respondents rely, involved unusual instruments that did not fit squarely within one of the enumerated specific kinds of securities listed in the definition. *Tcherepnin* involved withdrawable capital shares in a state savings and loan association, and *Weaver* involved a certificate of deposit and a privately negotiated profit-sharing agreement. See *Marine Bank v. Weaver, supra*, at 557, n. 5, 71 L. Ed. 2d 409, 102 S. Ct. 1220, for an explanation of why the certificate of deposit involved there did not fit within the definition's category "certificate of deposit, for a security."

88 L. Ed. 88 (1943), the Court noted that "we do nothing to the words of the Act; we merely accept them. . . . In some cases, [proving that the documents were securities] might be done by proving the document itself, which on its face would be a note, a bond, or a share of stock." *Id.*, at 355, 88 L. Ed. 88, 64 S. Ct. 120. Nor does *Forman* require a different result. Respondents are correct that in *Forman* we eschewed a "literal" approach that would invoke the Acts' coverage simply because the instrument carried the label "stock." *Forman* does not, however, eliminate the Court's ability to hold that an instrument is covered when its characteristics bear out the label. See *supra*, 85 L. Ed. 2d 697.

Second, we would note that the *Howey* economic reality test was designed to determine whether a particular instrument is an "investment contract," not whether it fits within *any* of the examples listed in the statutory definition of "security." Our cases are consistent with this view.[185] *Teamsters v. Daniel*, 439 U.S., at 558, 58 L. Ed. 2d 808, 99 S. Ct. 790 (appropriate to turn to the *Howey* test to "determine whether a particular financial relationship constitutes an investment contract"); *United Housing Foundation, Inc. v. Forman*, 421 U.S. 837, 95 S. Ct. 2051, 44 L. Ed. 2d 621 (1975); *see supra*, 85 L. Ed. 2d 699. Moreover, applying the *Howey* test to traditional stock and all other types of instruments listed in the statutory definition would make the Acts' enumeration of many types of instruments superfluous. *Golden v. Garafalo*, 678 F.2d 1139, 1144 (CA2 1982). *See Tcherepnin* v. *Knight*, 389 U.S. 332, 343, 88 S. Ct. 548, 19 L. Ed. 2d 564 (1967).

Finally, we cannot agree with respondents that the Acts were intended to cover only "passive investors" and not privately negotiated transactions involving the transfer of control to "entrepreneurs." The 1934 Act contains several provisions specifically governing tender offers, disclosure of transactions by corporate officers and principal stockholders, and the recovery of short-swing profits gained by such persons. *See, e. g.*, 1934 Act, §§ 14, 16, 15 U. S. C. §§ 78n, 78p [15 U.S.C.S. §§ 78n, 78p]. Eliminating from the definition of "security" instruments involved in transactions where control passed to the purchaser would contravene the purposes of these provisions. Accord, *Daily v. Morgan*, 701 F.2d 496, 503 (CA5 1983). Furthermore, although § 4(2) of the 1933 Act, 15 U. S. C. § 77d(2) [15 U.S.C.S. § 77d(2)], exempts transactions not involving any public offering from the Act's registration provisions, there is no comparable exemption from the antifraud provisions. Thus,

---

[185] [5] In support of their contention that the Court has mandated use of the *Howey* test whenever it determines whether an instrument is a "security," respondents quote our statement in *Teamsters v. Daniel*, 439 U.S. 551, 558, n. 11, 99 S. Ct. 790, 58 L. Ed. 2d 808 (1979), that the *Howey* test " 'embodies the essential attributes that run through all of the Court's decisions defining a security' " (quoting *Forman*, 421 U.S., at 852, 44 L. Ed. 2d 621, 95 S. Ct. 2051). We do not read this bit of dicta as broadly as respondents do. We made the statement in *Forman* in reference to the purchasers' argument that if the instruments at issue were not "stock" and were not "investment contracts," at least they were "instrument[s] commonly known as a 'security' " within the statutory definition. We stated, as part of our analysis of whether the instruments were "investment contracts," that we perceived "no distinction, *for present purposes*, between an 'investment contract' and an 'instrument commonly known as a "security.' " 421 U.S., at 852, 44 L. Ed. 2d 621, 95 S. Ct. 2051 (emphasis added). This was not to say that the *Howey* test applied to any case in which an instrument was alleged to be a security, but only that once the label "stock" did not hold true, we perceived no reason to analyze the case differently whether we viewed the instruments as "investment contracts" or as falling within another similarly general category of the definition — an "instrument commonly known as a 'security.' " Under either of these general categories, the *Howey* test would apply.

the structure and language of the Acts refute respondents' position.[186]

B.

We now turn to the Court of Appeals' concern that treating stock as a specific category of "security" provable by its characteristics means that other categories listed in the statutory definition, such as notes, must be treated the same way. Although we do not decide whether coverage of notes or other instruments may be provable by their name and characteristics, we do point out several reasons why we think stock may be distinguishable from most if not all of the other categories listed in the Acts' definition. Instruments that bear both the name and all of the usual characteristics of stock seem to us to be the clearest case for coverage by the plain language of the definition. First, traditional stock "represents to many people, both trained and untrained in business matters, the paradigm of a security." *Daily v. Morgan, supra*, at 500. Thus persons trading in traditional stock likely have a high expectation that their activities are governed by the Acts. Second, as we made clear in *Forman*, "stock" is relatively easy to identify because it lends itself to consistent definition. *See supra*, 85 L. Ed. 2d 697-698. Unlike some instruments, therefore, traditional stock is more susceptible of a plain meaning approach. Professor Loss has agreed that stock is different from the other categories of instruments. He observes that it "goes against the grain" to apply the *Howey* test for determining whether an instrument is an "investment contract" to traditional stock. L. Loss, Fundamentals of Securities Regulation 211-212 (1983). As Professor Loss explains:

> It is one thing to say that the typical cooperative apartment dweller has bought a home, not a security; or that not every installment purchase 'note' is a security; or that a person who charges a restaurant meal by signing his credit card slip is not selling a security even though his signature is an 'evidence of indebtedness.' But stock (except for the residential wrinkle) is so quintessentially a security as to foreclose further analysis.

IV

We also perceive strong policy reasons for not employing the sale of business doctrine under the circumstances of this case.[187] By respondents' own admission,

---

[186] [6] In criticizing the sale of business doctrine, Professor Loss agrees. He considers that the doctrine "comes dangerously close to the heresy of saying that the fraud provisions do not apply to private transactions; for nobody, apparently, has had the temerity to argue that the sale of a *publicly* owned business for stock of the acquiring corporation that is distributed to the shareholders of the selling corporation as a liquidating dividend does not involve a security." L. Loss, Fundamentals of Securities Regulation 212 (1983) (emphasis in original) (footnote omitted).

[187] [7] Justice Stevens dissents on the ground that Congress did not intend the antifraud provisions of the federal securities laws to apply to "the private sale of a substantial ownership interest in [a business] simply because the transaction [w[as] structured as [a] sale of stock instead of assets." 85 L. Ed. 2d 706. Justice Stevens, of course, is correct in saying that it is clear from the legislative history of the 1933 and 1934 Acts that Congress was concerned primarily with transactions "in securities . . . traded in a public market." *United Housing Foundation, Inc. v. Forman*, 421 U.S., 837, 849, 95 S. Ct. 2051, 44 L. Ed. 2d 621 (1975). It also is true that there is no indication in the legislative history that Congress considered the type of transactions involved in this case and in *Gould v. Ruefenach*. The history

application of the doctrine depends in each case on whether control has passed to the purchaser. It may be argued that on the facts of this case, the doctrine is easily applied, since the transfer of 100% of a corporation's stock normally transfers control. We think even that assertion is open to some question, however, as Dennis and Bolten had no intention of running the sawmill themselves. Ivan Landreth apparently stayed on to manage the daily affairs of the business. Some commentators who support the sale of business doctrine believe that a purchaser who has the ability to exert control but chooses not to do so may deserve the Acts' protection if he is simply a passive investor not engaged in the daily management of the business. Easley, Recent Developments in the Sale-of-Business Doctrine: Toward a Transactional Context-Based Analysis for Federal Securities Jurisdiction, 39 Bus. Law. 929, 971-972 (1984); Seldin, When Stock is Not a Security: The "Sale of Business" Doctrine Under the Federal Securities Laws, 37 Bus. Law. 637, 679 (1982). In this case, the District Court was required to undertake extensive factfinding, and even requested supplemental facts and memoranda on the issue of control, before it was able to decide the case. App. to Pet. for Cert. 13a.

More importantly, however, if applied to this case, the sale of business doctrine would also have to be applied to cases in which less than 100% of a company's stock was sold. This inevitably would lead to difficult questions of line-drawing. The Acts' coverage would in every case depend not only on the percentage of stock transferred, but also on such factors as the number of purchasers and what provisions for voting and veto rights were agreed upon by the parties. As we explain more fully in *Gould v. Ruefenacht*, 105 S. Ct. 2308, 85 L. Ed. 2d 708, decided today as a companion to this case, coverage by the Acts would in most cases be unknown and unknowable to the parties at the time the stock was sold. These uncertainties attending the applicability of the Acts would hardly be in the best interests of either party to a transaction. *Cf. Marine Bank v. Weaver*, 455 U.S., at 559, n. 9, 71 L. Ed. 2d 409, 102 S. Ct. 1220 (rejecting the argument that the certificate of deposit at issue there was transformed, chameleon-like, into a "security" once it was pledged).

---

is simply silent — as it is with respect to other transactions to which these Acts have been applied by the Securities and Exchange Commission and judicial interpretation over the half century since this legislation was adopted. One only need mention the expansive interpretation of § 10(b) of the 1934 Act and Rule 10b-5 adopted by the Commission. What the Court said in *Blue Chip Stamps v. Manor Drug Stores*, 421 U.S. 723, 95 S. Ct. 1917, 44 L. Ed. 2d 539 (1975), is relevant:

> When we deal with private actions under Rule 10b-5, we deal with a judicial oak which has grown from little more than a legislative acorn. Such growth may be quite consistent with the congressional enactment and with the role of the federal judiciary in interpreting it, see *J. I. Case Co. v. Borak*, [377 U.S. 426 [84 S. Ct. 1555, 12 L. Ed. 2d 423] (1964)], but it would be disingenuous to suggest that either Congress in 1934 or the Securities and Exchange Commission in 1942 foreordained the present state of the law with respect to Rule 10b-5. It is therefore proper that we consider, in addition to the factors already discussed, what may be described as policy considerations when we come to flesh out the portions of the law with respect to which neither the congressional enactment nor the administrative regulations offer conclusive guidance.

Id., at 737. *See also Ernst & Ernst* v. *Hochfelder*, 425 U.S. 185, 196-197, 96 S. Ct. 1375, 47 L. Ed. 2d 668 (1976). In this case, unlike with respect to the interpretation of § 10(b) in *Blue Chip Stamps*, we have the plain language of § 2(1) of the 1933 Act in support of our interpretation. In *Forman, supra*, we recognized that the term "stock" is to be read in accordance with the common understanding of its meaning, including the characteristics identified in *Forman. See supra*, 85 L. Ed. 2d 697-698. In addition, as stated in *Blue Chip Stamps, supra*, it is proper for a court to consider — as we do today — policy considerations in construing terms in these Acts.

Respondents argue that adopting petitioner's approach will increase the workload of the federal courts by converting state and common-law fraud claims into federal claims. We find more daunting, however, the prospect that parties to a transaction may never know whether they are covered by the Acts until they engage in extended discovery and litigation over a concept as often elusive as the passage of control. Accord, *Golden v. Garafalo*, 678 F.2d, at 1145-1146.

V

In sum, we conclude that the stock at issue here is a "security" within the definition of the Acts, and that the sale of business doctrine does not apply. The judgment of the United States Court of Appeals for the Ninth Circuit is therefore reversed.

Justice Stevens, dissenting.

In my opinion, Congress did not intend the antifraud provisions of the federal securities laws to apply to every transaction in a security described in § 2(1) of the 1933 Act:[188]

> The term 'security' means any note, stock, treasury stock, bond, debenture, evidence of indebtedness, certificate of interest or participation in any profit-sharing agreement, . . . investment contract, voting-trust certificate, . . . or, in general, any interest or instrument commonly known as a 'security.'

15 U.S.C. § 77b(1). See also n. 1, ante. Congress presumably adopted this sweeping definition "to prevent the financial community from evading regulation by inventing new types of financial instruments rather than to prevent the courts from interpreting the Act in light of its purposes." *Sutter v. Groen*, 687 F.2d 197, 201 (CA7 1982). Moreover, the "broad statutory definition is preceded . . . by the statement that the terms mentioned are not to be considered securities if 'the context otherwise requires . . . .' " *Marine Bank v. Weaver*, 455 U.S. 551, 556, 102 S. Ct. 1220, 71 L. Ed. 2d 409 (1982). The legislative history of the 1933 and 1934 Securities Acts makes clear that Congress was primarily concerned with transactions in securities that are traded in a public market. In *United Housing Foundation, Inc. v. Forman*, 421 U.S. 837, 95 S. Ct. 2051, 44 L. Ed. 2d 621 (1975), the Court observed:

> The primary purpose of the Acts of 1933 and 1934 was to eliminate serious abuses in a largely unregulated securities market. The focus of the Acts is on the capital market of the enterprise system: the sale of securities to raise capital for profit-making purposes, the exchanges on which securities are traded, and the need for regulation to prevent fraud and protect the interest of investors. Because securities transactions are economic in

[188] [1] *Cf. Milnarik v. M-S Commodities, Inc.*, 457 F.2d 274, 275-276 (CA7) (Stevens, J., for the court), *cert. denied*, 409 U.S. 887, 93 S. Ct. 113, 34 L. Ed. 2d 144 (1972) ("we do not believe every conceivable arrangement that would fit a dictionary definition of an investment contract was intended to be included within the statutory definition of a security").

> character Congress intended the application of these statutes to turn on the economic realities underlying a transaction, and not on the name appended thereto.

Id., at 849, 44 L. Ed. 2d 621, 95 S. Ct. 2051.

I believe that Congress wanted to protect investors who do not have access to inside information and who are not in a position to protect themselves from fraud by obtaining appropriate contractual warranties.

At some level of analysis, the policy of Congress must provide the basis for placing limits on the coverage of the Securities Acts. The economic realities of a transaction may determine whether "unusual instruments" fall within the scope of the Acts, 85 L. Ed. 2d 700, and whether an ordinary commercial "note" is covered, *id.*, 85 L. Ed. 2d. 701. The negotiation of an individual mortgage note, for example, surely would not be covered by the Acts, although a note is literally a "security" under the definition. *Cf. Chemical Bank v. Arthur Andersen & Co.*, 726 F.2d 930, 937 (CA2), *cert. denied*, 469 U.S. 884, 105 S. Ct. 253, 83 L. Ed. 2d 190 (1984). The marketing to the public of a large portfolio of mortgage loans, however, might well be. See *Sanders v. John Nuveen & Co.*, 463 F.2d 1075, 1079-1080 (CA7), *cert. denied*, 409 U.S. 1009, 93 S. Ct. 443, 34 L. Ed. 2d 302 (1972).

I believe that the characteristics of the entire transaction are as relevant in determining whether a transaction in "stock" is covered by the Acts as they are in transactions involving "notes," "investment contracts," or the more hybrid securities. Providing regulations for the trading of publicly listed stock — whether on an exchange or in the over-the-counter market — was the heart of Congress' legislative program, and even private sales of such securities are surely covered by the Acts. I am not persuaded, however, that Congress intended to cover negotiated transactions involving the sale of control of a business whose securities have never been offered or sold in any public market. In the latter cases, it is only a matter of interest to the parties whether the transaction takes the form of a sale of stock or a sale of assets, and the decision usually hinges on matters that are irrelevant to the federal securities laws such as tax liabilities, the assignability of Government licenses or other intangible assets, and the allocation of the accrued or unknown liabilities of the going concern. If Congress had intended to provide a remedy for every fraud in the sale of a going concern or its assets, it would not have permitted the parties to bargain over the availability of federal jurisdiction.

In short, I would hold that the antifraud provisions of the federal securities laws are inapplicable unless the transaction involves (i) the sale of a security that is traded in a public market; or (ii) an investor who is not in a position to negotiate appropriate contractual warranties and to insist on access to inside information before consummating the transaction. Of course, until the precise contours of such a standard could be marked out in a series of litigated proceedings, some uncertainty in the coverage of the statutes would be unavoidable. Nevertheless, I am persuaded that the interests in certainty and predictability that are associated with a simple "bright-line" rule are not strong enough to "justify expanding liability to reach substantive evils far outside the scope of the legislature's concern."[189] *Sutter v. Groen*, 687 F.2d, at 202.

Both of these cases involved a sale of stock in a closely held corporation. In each case the transaction was preceded by comprehensive negotiations between the buyer and seller. There is no suggestion that the buyers were unable to obtain appropriate warranties or to insist on the exchange and independent evaluation of relevant financial information before entering into the transactions.[190] I do not believe Congress intended the federal securities laws to govern the private sale of a substantial ownership interest in these operating businesses simply because the transactions were structured as sales of stock instead of assets.

I would affirm the judgment of the Court of Appeals in No. 83-1961 and reverse the judgment in No. 84-165.

§ 7.03 CERTAIN ACQUISITION DOCUMENTATION

MBI ACQUISITION PARTNERS, L.P. v. CHRONICLE PUBL'G CO.

United States District Court, Western District of Wisconsin
2001 U.S. Dist. LEXIS 15387 (2001)

CRABB, DISTRICT J.

This is a civil action for monetary relief in which plaintiff MBI Acquisition Partners, L.P., contends that defendants The Chronicle Publishing Company and Richard Suomala committed fraud and fraudulently induced plaintiff to enter into a contract when they failed to disclose the existence of a warehouse that was allegedly leased by defendants to store unprocessed returns, failed to provide accurate financial statements regarding the status of the unprocessed returns and represented expressly that the current level of unprocessed returns was consistent with historical levels. Plaintiff alleges five causes of action: (1) violation of Section 10(b) and 10(b)-5 of the Securities Exchange Act; (2) violation of Wis. Stat. §§ 551.41 (uniform securities law-fraudulent practices: sales and purchase) and 551.59 (uniform securities law-general provisions: civil liabilities); (3) violation of Wis. Stat.

---

189 [2] In final analysis, the Court relies on its own evaluation of the relevant "policy considerations." While I agree that policy considerations are relevant in construing the Securities Acts, I would prefer to rely principally on the policies of Congress as reflected in the legislative history. If extrinsic considerations are to be given effect, I would place a far different evaluation on the weight of the conflicting policies, because I strongly believe that this Court should presume that federal legislation is not intended to displace state authority unless Congress has plainly indicated an intent to do so. *See, e. g., Bennett v. New Jersey*, 470 U.S. 632, 654-655, n. 16, 105 S. Ct. 1555, 84 L. Ed. 2d 572 (1985) (Stevens, J., dissenting); *Garcia v. United States*, 469 U.S. 70, 89-90, 105 S. Ct. 479, 83 L. Ed. 2d 472 (1984) (Stevens, J., dissenting); *Michigan v. Long*, 463 U.S. 1032, 1067, 103 S. Ct. 3469, 77 L. Ed. 2d 1201 (1983) (Stevens, J., dissenting); *United States v. Altobella*, 442 F.2d 310, 316 (CA7 1971) (Stevens, J., for the court). *Cf. Minnesota v. Clover Leaf Creamery Co.*, 449 U.S. 456, 477, 101 S. Ct. 715, 66 L. Ed. 2d 659 (1981) (Stevens, J., dissenting).

190 [3] Indeed, in No. 83-1961, the parties entered into a lengthy Stock Purchase Agreement containing extensive warranties and other protections for the purchasers. App. 206-263.

§ 100.18(1) (marketing; trade practices: fraudulent representations); (4) fraudulent inducement; and (5) violation of Rule 20(a) of the Securities Exchange Act. Subject matter jurisdiction is present, 28 U.S.C. § 1331. Supplemental jurisdiction is present over state law claims. 28 U.S.C. § 1367.

Presently before the court is defendants' motion to dismiss or, in the alternative, to strike plaintiff's claims pursuant to Fed. R. Civ. P. 12(b)(6) and 12(f), respectively. In their motion to dismiss, defendants contend that plaintiff cannot bring its claims because (1) the California choice-of-law provision contained in the purchase agreement bars plaintiff's Wisconsin statutory claims; (2) plaintiff is unable to show reasonable reliance; (3) the "survival," "entire agreement" and "representations and warranties" clauses contained in the purchase agreement bar claims of fraud that occurred outside the purchase agreement; and (4) portions of plaintiff's federal securities claims that rely on representations made outside the purchase agreement are barred because of the "survival" and "representations and warranties" clauses. Because I find that plaintiff has stated claims on which relief can be granted, defendants' motion to dismiss or to strike will be denied.

For the sole purpose of deciding this motion to dismiss, plaintiff's allegations in the complaint are accepted as true.

ALLEGATIONS OF FACT

Plaintiff MBI Acquisition Partners, L.P. is a holding company with its principal place of business in New York, New York. Defendant The Chronicle Publishing Company is a publishing and media holding corporation with its principal place of business in San Francisco, California. Defendant Richard Suomala is a citizen of Minnesota.

Before February 1, 2000, defendant Chronicle owned all of the issued and outstanding capital stock of MBI Publishing Company. Defendant Chronicle retained Donaldson, Lufkin & Jenrette to conduct an auction of MBI. On July 26, 1999, Donaldson, Lufkin & Jenrette invited plaintiff to participate in the auction process. Later that month, it delivered to plaintiff an offering memorandum containing information provided by defendant Chronicle. On August 27, 1999, plaintiff's representatives examined certain financial documents concerning MBI that MBI and defendant Chronicle had assembled at the offices of Donaldson, Lufkin & Jenrette in New York, New York. On September 9, 1999, plaintiff's representatives visited MBI's headquarters in Osceola, Wisconsin.

In early October 1999, plaintiff bid $46 million for MBI. Plaintiff arrived at this offering price by performing calculations that included a discounted cash flow analysis of MBI's operating cash flows based on the current and historical financial information that defendant Chronicle had provided. In late October 1999, defendant Chronicle gave plaintiff a draft share purchase agreement that included disclosure schedules. On November 1, 1999, MBI began leasing a warehouse in which it stored returned product. On November 5, 1999, the parties entered into a purchase agreement whereby plaintiff agreed to pay defendant Chronicle $46 million for all of the outstanding stock of MBI. On November 8-12, 1999, plaintiff's representatives visited MBI's headquarters in Osceola and interviewed members of MBI's management, including defendant Suomala, MBI's chief financial officer, and Ann Eklund, MBI's vice president of operations. Plaintiff's representatives included David Straden and Stephen Walmsley, an employee of plaintiff's accounting and due diligence advisers, Price-WaterhouseCoopers, LLP. In these and subsequent interviews and communications about the business of MBI, defendant Suomala, Eklund and other officers and employees of MBI were acting not only as officers of MBI but as agents of defendant Chronicle in connection with defendant Chronicle's impending sale of MBI. During this visit, Walmsley and others reviewed financial records, including MBI's financial statements as of August 31, 1999, and MBI's general ledger.

Plaintiff's offering price for MBI was reduced subsequently by $4 million on a negotiated basis as a result of MBI's poor performance in October 1999. This poor performance lowered the forecast for MBI's performance for the full year ending December 31, 1999. In January 2000, plaintiff's representatives, including Straden, had numerous telephone conversations with defendant Suomala and representatives from defendant Chronicle regarding MBI's higher than expected levels of accounts receivable. On January 24 and 25, 2000, plaintiff's representatives, including Walmsley, visited MBI's headquarters in Osceola again to check its inventory and accounts receivable. On February 1, 2000, defendant Chronicle sold all of the issued and outstanding capital stock of MBI to plaintiff for $42 million.

Through the disclosure schedules, defendant Chronicle represented that it had disclosed all material contracts to which MBI was a party, including leases for real property, and all real property sites at which MBI's assets were located. These representations were false because the disclosure schedules did not disclose the real property site (a warehouse) at which MBI stored returned product and they did not disclose the lease for this site. Defendant Suomala represented to plaintiff's representatives that the information contained in the financial documents provided to plaintiff reflected MBI's levels of sales returns accurately. This representation was false because the financial documents provided did not disclose that MBI had an additional $1 million in unprocessed customer returns and did not disclose facts about the existence of the warehouse containing unprocessed customer returns.

During the November 1999 visit, officers of MBI, including defendant Suomala and Eklund told Walmsley that (a) MBI's current inventory levels, including unprocessed customer returns, were consistent with MBI's historical levels; (b) MBI's Star Prairie Facility contained only slow moving inventory; and (c) MBI stored unprocessed customer returns only at its Osceola warehouse and nowhere else. These representations were false because MBI's unprocessed return backlog level at that time was ten times higher than the return backlog level at year end 1998 and MBI stored unprocessed customer returns at the Star Prairie facility and at the undisclosed warehouse. In January 2000, plaintiff's representatives asked defendant Suomala and representatives of defendant Chronicle to explain why MBI's receivables were approximately $2 million higher than expected. Defendants offered explanations but failed to disclose that approximately $1 million of the receivables resulted from the backlog of customer returns that had not yet been processed and credited to customers.

During the January 2000 visit, Walmsley asked defendant Suomala and Eklund specifically whether MBI stored returns at any location other than its Osceola warehouse. Both Suomala and Eklund answered this question in the negative. After discovering seven to ten skids of returned product not included by MBI in its inventory count, Walmsley asked defendant Suomala and Eklund specifically whether MBI had any additional unprocessed returns. Suomala and Eklund represented to Walmsley that MBI did not. This statement was false because MBI had additional unprocessed returns at Osceola, the Star Prairie facility and the undisclosed warehouse. Defendant Chronicle made numerous representations and warranties to plaintiff in the purchase agreement, including that (a) MBI's financial statements were accurate; (b) all of MBI's tangible property, including its real property leases, was disclosed; and (c) all of MBI's contracts, including its leases relating to all real property, were disclosed. These representations were false because MBI's financial statements misstated MBI's revenue and profit in that they did not disclose the $1 million in unprocessed returns or include the lease for the undisclosed warehouse.

Plaintiff overvalued MBI on the basis of defendants' misrepresentations and omissions. If the $1 million in unprocessed returns had been reflected in MBI's financial documents, it would have had the effect of reducing its 1999 revenue by $1,039,000, reducing cash flow by $622,000, and would have revealed that MBI's cash flows and profits were in decline. The financial information defendants provided to plaintiff indicated that MBI's cash flows and profits were on the rise. Plaintiff paid $10.4 million more for MBI than it would have paid had it known MBI's true financial condition. Because of defendants' misrepresentations, plaintiff was misled into believing that MBI's revenue and cash flow were much higher than they were. The amount and value of MBI's unprocessed returns at year end 1999 totaled $1 million, a fact that defendants intentionally or recklessly failed to disclose and affirmatively misrepresented. Defendants made affirmative misrepresentations and failed to disclose facts to plaintiff for the purpose of inflating the sales price of MBI.

The purchase agreement contains the following clauses, among others:

> 9.1 Survival. None of the representations and warranties of the Seller, the Company and the Purchaser contained in this Agreement, or in any certificate, instrument or other document delivered by the Seller, the Company or the Purchaser pursuant to this Agreement or in connection with the transactions contemplated hereby, shall survive the Closing. None of the covenants and agreements of the Seller, the Company and the Purchaser contained in this Agreement, or in any certificate, instrument or other documents delivered by the Seller, the Company or the Purchaser pursuant to this Agreement or in connection with the transactions contemplated hereby, shall survive the Closing, except to the extent such covenants and agreements by their terms contemplate performance after the Closing. . . .
>
> 9.6 Entire Agreement. This Agreement, the Confidentiality Agreement and the related documents contained as Exhibits and Schedules hereto or expressly contemplated hereby contain the entire understanding of the parties hereto relating to the subject matter hereof and supersede all prior written or oral and all contemporaneous oral agreements and understand-

ings relating to the subject matter hereof. The Exhibits and Schedules to this Agreement are hereby incorporated by reference into and made a part of this Agreement for all purposes.

9.7 Representations and Warranties Complete. The representations, warranties, covenants and agreements set forth in this Agreement, the Confidentiality Agreement and the Exhibits and Schedules hereto, constitute all the representations, warranties, covenants and agreements of the parties hereto and their respective shareholders, directors, officers, employees, affiliates, advisors (including financial, legal and accounting), agents and representatives and upon which the parties hereto have relied.

9.9 Governing Law. This Agreement will be governed by and construed and interpreted in accordance with the substantive laws of the State of California, without giving effect to any conflicts of law rule or principle that might require the application of the laws of another jurisdiction.

OPINION

. . .

B. Wisconsin State Law Claims

1. Choice-of-law provision

A district court is required to apply the laws of the state in which it sits to resolve conflict of laws questions. *Klaxon Co. v. Stentor Electric Mfg. Co.*, 313 U.S. 487, 61 S. Ct. 1020, 85 L. Ed. 1477 (1941). The first step to resolving a conflict of law is identifying the type of case involved. *Drinkall v. Used Car Rentals, Inc.*, 32 F.3d 329, 331 (8th Cir. 1994). In *Krider Pharmacy v. Medi-Care Data Systems*, 791 F. Supp. 221, 225 (E.D. Wis. 1992), the court held that "Wisconsin law governs the tort aspects of *Krider's* claims . . . because the choice-of-law provision in the sales agreement governs only the parties' contract rights." *See also Smith v. Meadows Mills, Inc.*, 60 F. Supp. 2d 911, 914 (E.D. Wis. 1999) (holding that North Carolina choice-of-law provision "pertains only to the interpretation of the Agreement itself and not to the law surrounding successor liability in the context of tort actions").

Defendants contend that plaintiff's second and third causes of action, which are brought under Wisconsin statutory law, should be dismissed because the choice-of-law provision contained in the purchase agreement states that California law governs "without giving effect to any conflicts of law rule or principle that might require the application of the laws of another jurisdiction." Therefore, defendant contends that the choice-of-law rules, asset out in the purchase agreement, are also governed by California and not Wisconsin law. Plaintiff contends that the purchase agreement choice-of-law provision controls only contract claims and not tort claims.

Plaintiff brought these claims under Wis. Stat. §§ 551.41 (uniform securities law-fraudulent practices: sales and purchase), 551.59 (uniform securities law-general provisions: civil liabilities) and 100.18(1) (marketing; trade practices: fraudulent representations). These fraud claims are tort actions and not breach of contract. *See Jersild v. Aker*, 766 F. Supp. 713, 714 (E.D. Wis. 1991) (noting plaintiffs filed "tort action alleging securities fraud" when plaintiffs filed under Wis. Stat. §§ 551.41, 551.59 and 100.18(1)). *See also Werner v. Pittway Corp.*, 90 F. Supp. 2d 1018, 1033 (W.D. Wis. 2000) (noting plaintiff's claim for fraudulent misrepresentations under § 100.18(1) could fall within a continuing tort theory for statute of limitations purposes); *Wilbur v. Keybank National Assoc.*, 962 F. Supp. 1122, 1132 (N.D. Ind. 1997) (holding that it is "well established that a claim for constructive fraud is a tort action"). Because these are tort claims, I find that the applicable choice-of-law rules are those of Wisconsin law and that Wisconsin law also applies to the substantive claims made by plaintiff.

2. Fraudulent misrepresentations inside the purchase agreement

As to the aspects of plaintiff's second, third and fourth claims that are contained within the purchase agreement itself, defendants argue that plaintiff is required to prove reasonable reliance on the alleged misrepresentations and that plaintiff cannot do so because a finding of reasonable reliance would conflict with the terms of the purchase agreement's "survival," "entire agreement" and "representations and warranties" clauses. Plaintiff asserts that reliance is presumed because its claims are based on fraudulent omissions that contradict the purchase agreement.

In *Affiliated Ute Citizens v. United States*, 406 U.S. 128, 153, 92 S. Ct. 1456, 31 L. Ed. 2d 741 (1972), the Supreme Court found that the defendants had induced holders of stock "to dispose of their shares without disclosing to them material facts that reasonably could have been expected to influence their decisions to sell." The Supreme Court reasoned that "under the circumstances of this case, involving primarily a failure to disclose, positive proof of reliance is not a prerequisite to recovery. All that is necessary is that the facts withheld be material in the sense that a reasonable investor might have considered them important in the making of this decision." *Id.* at 153-54. *See also Harsco Corp. v. Segui*, 91 F.3d 337, 342 n. 5 (2d Cir. 1996) (noting court holding in *Affiliated Ute* and recognizing total non-disclosure of material information as exception to requirement of proving reliance).

The "entire agreement" and "representations and warranties" clauses state that the parties have not relied on any representations other than those contained in the purchase agreement, but plaintiff alleges that numerous false representations were made inside the purchase agreement. For example, plaintiff alleges that the purchase agreement itself states that all financial statements are accurate (when they were not), all of MBI's real property leased are disclosed (when they were not) and all contracts, including real property leases, are disclosed (when they were not). Notwithstanding a "no other representations or warranties" clause, the court held in *Harsco* that any representation within the purchase agreement itself can be the basis of a fraud action against the seller. *Harsco*, 91 F.3d at 344.

Because plaintiff alleges a material omission that a reasonable investor might have considered important, I find that plaintiff is not required to demonstrate reasonable reliance as an element of its state law claims. In addition, the "survival," "entire agreement" and "representations and warranties" clauses do not bar plaintiff from bringing claims of fraud based on misrepresentations made in the purchase agreement itself.

3. Fraudulent misrepresentations outside the purchase agreement

Defendants argue that any claims of misrepresentation brought under state law (the second, third and fourth claims) that occurred outside the purchase agreement should be dismissed or stricken because the purchase agreement contains an integration clause indicating that the agreement survives as evidence of the parties' representations. Plaintiff asserts that the contract language may prevent it from suing under contract law but does not prevent it from suing for the tort of intentional fraudulent conduct. Plaintiff also argues that the Wisconsin law that controls these claims does not allow such contract disclaimers to prevent actions in fraud.

In *Astor Chauffeured Limousine v. Runnfeldt Inv. Corp.*, 910 F.2d 1540, 1545 (7th Cir. 1990), the Court of Appeals for the Seventh Circuit held that an integration clause did not prevent a plaintiff from pursuing securities and common-law fraud claims. In *Astor*, the plaintiff alleged that the written documents did not disclose the truth and that the defendant's oral statements contradicted the written statements. *Id.* Defendants try to differentiate the facts of this case from those in *Astor*, asserting that their integration clause ("entire agreement" and "representations and warranties" clauses collectively) is more substantial than the "wimpy" integration clause in *Astor*. In *Astor*, the integration clause stated "Entire Agreement. This Agreement constitutes the entire agreement between the parties, and may not be amended or supplemented except by written instrument executed by an authorized agent or officer of each of the parties hereto." Defendants argue that their integration clause "specifically provides that there are no other representations and that all representations expire at the time of closing." Dfts.' Reply Br. Mot. to Dismiss, dkt. # 9, at 7-8. But the clause at issue in *Astor* implies that there can be no other representations because the agreement constitutes the entire agreement. Although representations expire at closing, misrepresentations amounting to fraud do not expire at the time of the closing because they are tort claims and are not governed by the contract terms. Plaintiff alleges that the purchase agreement stipulated that all real property leases were disclosed and all financial statements were accurate when, in fact, they were not. The integration clause does not prevent plaintiff from claiming misrepresentations that occurred outside the purchase agreement in order to recover on its state securities fraud claims.

In *Republicbank Dallas v. First Wisconsin Nat'l Bank*, 636 F. Supp. 1470, 1473 (E.D. Wis. 1986), the court held contract disclaimers ineffective to bar intentional fraudulent misrepresentation claims. *See also FS Photo, Inc. v. Picturevision, Inc.*, 61 F. Supp. 2d 473, 481 (4th Cir. 1999) (holding that party to contract may point to contract-inducing representations to prove claim); *Hitachi Credit America Corp. v. Signet Bank*, 166 F.3d 614, 630-31 (4th Cir. 1999) (holding that buyer may recover for fraudulent inducement even where "the contract contains specific disclaimers that do not cover the allegedly fraudulent contract inducing representations"). In this case, plaintiff claims intentional or reckless misrepresentation. Because integration clauses are the functional equivalent of contract disclaimers, defendants cannot escape the conclusion that the integration clause does not bar plaintiff's state law claims.

Defendants assert further that these claims are actually breach of contract claims that plaintiff is merely labeling "fraud." Drawing all inferences in favor of the non-moving party as I must at this stage of the proceedings, I find that plaintiff's characterization of the facts as fraud does not fail to state a claim upon which relief may be granted. Accordingly, I find that in its claims for fraud, plaintiff may rely on defendants' contract-inducing representations in order to prove its claim. Defendants' motion to dismiss plaintiff's state law claims occurring outside the purchase agreement will be denied.

C. Federal Claims: Anti-Waiver Provision of Securities Exchange Act

The anti-waiver provision of the Securities Exchange Act, § 29(a), states that "any condition, stipulation, or provision binding any person to waive compliance with any provision of this chapter or of any rule or regulation thereunder, or any rule of an exchange required thereby shall be void." 15 U.S.C. § 78cc(a). Section 29(a) forbids enforcement of agreements that waive compliance with the provisions of the Securities Exchange Act. *Shearson/American Express Inc. v. McMahon*, 482 U.S. 220, 228, 107 S. Ct. 2332, 96 L. Ed. 2d 185 (1987). Section 29(a) focuses on whether the suspect provision "weakens [plaintiff's] ability to recover under the Exchange Act." *Id.* at 230 (citing *Wilko v. Swan*, 346 U.S. 427, 432, 74 S. Ct. 182, 98 L. Ed. 168 (1953)).

Defendants have moved to dismiss only those portions of the first and fifth federal securities claims that rely on representations made outside the purchase agreement. Specifically, defendants argue for dismissal of allegations that "low-level employees of MBI Publishing allegedly made inaccurate statements about the company's inventory." Dfts.' Reply Br., dkt. # 9, at 11. From the allegations, I assume that defendants are referring to defendant Suomala, the chief financial officer, and Eklund, the vice president of operations, neither of whom appear to be "low-level" employees. In any event, defendants contend that the anti-waiver provision of § 29(a) is not violated by the purchase agreement clauses, which disclaim reliance on any representations made outside the purchase agreement.

Plaintiff argues that the "survival" and "representations and warranties" clauses are void insofar as they violate the § 29(a). Moreover, plaintiff asserts that if the purchase agreement clauses are not void under § 29(a), its federal claims under the Securities Exchange Act would be wholly eliminated. As defendants point out, this seems to be an overstatement because plaintiff would still have an opportunity to prove its federal securities claims based on misrepresentations made inside the purchase agreement. Nevertheless, the question is whether the clauses will "weaken" plaintiff's ability to recover.

Defendants argue that this court should consider the fact that both parties to the purchase agreement are sophisticated and that they mutually negotiated the terms of the purchase agreement. In *Harsco Corp. v. Segui*, 91 F.3d 337, 343 (2d Cir. 1996), the court found that the contested agreement was "a detailed writing developed via negotiations among sophisticated business entities and their advisors. That writing . . . defines the boundaries of the transaction. [The plaintiff] brings this suit principally alleging conduct that falls outside those boundaries." Although the facts suggest that the parties share a high level of sophistication and mutually negotiated the purchase agreement, in *Shearson*, 482 U.S. at 230, the Supreme Court held that "if a stipulation waives compliance with a statutory duty, it is void under § 29(a), whether voluntary or not." Therefore, sophistication of the parties or voluntariness based on mutual negotiation is only part of the equation; the court must also determine whether the disclaimer clauses violate the anti-waiver provision of the Securities Exchange Act.

In *Harsco* the court found for the defendant. With respect to the § 29(a) claim, the court was persuaded by its due diligence investigation, stating that "if [the plaintiff] had been unable to confirm the truth of the representations [in the purchase agreement] during the due diligence period, [it] could have terminated the deal." *Harsco*, 91 F.3d at 344. The court went on to conclude that "there is nothing in the complaint or the Agreement that indicates that [the plaintiff] was duped into waiving the protections of the securities law." *Id.* In this case, plaintiff alleges that it attempted to confirm the truth of the purchase agreement representations but was assuaged with false answers. In short, plaintiff alleges it was duped. According to plaintiff's complaint, from the date of the signing of the purchase agreement, Nov. 5, 1999, until the closing of the stock purchase, Feb. 1, 2000, plaintiff visited MBI several times and made specific inquiries about the status of the returns and accounts receivable, to which defendants responded with misrepresentations. For example, plaintiff alleges that it specifically asked Eklund and defendant Suomala whether the company had any additional unprocessed returns and was falsely told it did not. Plt.'s Cpt., dkt.# 2, at 5-7, 9.

If plaintiff could not rely on these representations made outside the purchase agreement, its ability to recover would be weakened. Accordingly, I find that § 29(a) renders the "survival" and "representations and warranties" clauses void as to the federal securities claims. Therefore, defendants' motion to dismiss those portions of the first and fifth claims that rely on representations made outside the purchase agreement will be denied.

[A] Example of Letter of Intent

[LETTERHEAD OF BUYER, INC.]

Mr. Peter McDermott
Chairman and Chief Executive Officer
Target Inc.
1 Main Street
Home Town, USA

Dear Mr. McDermott:

As you are aware, we have been conducting preliminary investigations of your company with a view toward determining whether an acquisition of your company by Buyer, Inc. would be feasible.

Based upon the results of the preliminary investigations we have conducted, and upon our recent discussions with you and other members of the management of Target, Inc., Buyer, Inc. is now in a position to submit this letter of intent to you, the purpose of which is to set forth the general understanding of ourselves and yourselves with respect to the possible purchase by Buyer, Inc. or by a subsidiary or affiliate of Buyer, Inc., of all of the issued and outstanding shares of common stock, par value $1.00 per share, (the "Stock") of Target, Inc. a Delaware corporation (the "Company").

Subject to the conditions herein, our present tentative understanding is as follows:

1. There are 25,000 shares of Stock outstanding, which are owned as follows:

Peter McDermott	10,000
Maisie Henderson	5,000
Hutch Henderson	5,000
Mac Henderson	5,000

2. At the closing of the contemplated acquisition, which shall be as soon as practicable but not later than the second business day of January 2000 (the "Closing") the undersigned would acquire all such 25,000 shares from such stockholders.

3. The purchase price would be $25.00 per share of Stock; the purchase price will be payable as follows: $10.00 cash per share payable at the closing and an amount equal to $15.00 per share payable in accordance with a five year promissory note of Buyer, Inc. and bearing interest at the rate of 8% per annum.

4. It is understood, of course, since this is only a letter of intent, neither Buyer, Inc. nor any of its stockholders, directors or affiliates, nor Target, Inc., nor any of its stockholders, directors, or affiliates will be bound by its terms. Instead, a detailed agreement between the parties will be prepared for this transaction. The Stock Purchase Agreement will be the binding agreement between the parties with respect to the subject matter of this letter of intent. Unless the Stock Purchase Agreement is entered into (regardless for the reason for the Stock Purchase Agreement not so having been entered into), neither Buyer, Inc., nor any of its stockholders, directors or affiliates, nor Target, Inc., nor any of its stockholders, directors or affiliates shall be under any obligation to each other, irrespective of this letter of intent and irrespective of any negotiations, agreements or undertakings between or actions taken by any of such parties with respect to this letter of intent and/or the transactions contemplated hereby. The Stock Purchase Agreement, if entered into, shall embody the terms of this letter of intent, shall contain representations and warranties of the type customarily made in transactions of this nature and size and provide such other terms, conditions, restrictions and covenants as are customarily used in and reasonably required for transactions of this nature and size. If you desire to pursue the transactions contemplated hereby, please so indicate by Signing and returning a copy of this letter enclosed for that purpose. Upon receipt of a signed copy of the letter from you, we will immediately proceed to complete our investigation of the business and affairs of Target, Inc. and will instruct our attorneys to begin to draft the Stock Purchase Agreement and such other documents as may be necessary to carry out the transactions contemplated hereby.

If, prior to entering into the Stock Purchase Agreement, either of us desires to terminate our negotiations and not proceed with the transactions contemplated hereby, we shall so notify the other party, and this letter of intent shall cease to be effective.

Very truly yours,

BUYER, INC.

By: ____________
Carmel Palen, President

The above is hereby agreed to and accepted.

Peter McDermott
Maisie Henderson
Hutch Henderson
Mac Henderson

[B] Cash for Stock Merger Provisions

Conversion of Securities. At the Effective Time, by virtue of the Merger and without any action on the part of Merger Subsidiary, the Company or the holders of any of the following securities and in accordance with Section 1906 of The Pennsylvania Business Corporation Law ("PBCL"):

a. *Capital Stock of Merger Subsidiary.* Each issued and outstanding share of capital stock of Merger Subsidiary shall be converted into and become one validly issued, fully paid and nonassessable share of common stock, $1.00 par value, of the Surviving Corporation.

b. *Treasury Stock.* Each Share that is owned by the Company or by any subsidiary of the Company, Merger Subsidiary, if any, shall automatically be cancelled and retired and shall cease to exist, and no consideration shall be delivered in exchange therefor.

c. *Conversion of Shares.* Subject to Section 1.07, each Share issued and outstanding (other than Shares to be cancelled in accordance with Section 1.06(b)), shall be cancelled and be converted into the right to receive from the Surviving Corporation an amount equal to $37.00 per share in cash, without interest or dividends, (the "*Merger Consideration*"), upon surrender, in the manner provided in Section 1.08, of the certificate that formerly evidenced such Share. As of the Effective Time, all such Shares shall be cancelled, and when so cancelled, shall no longer be outstanding and shall automatically be retired and shall cease to exist, and each holder of a certificate representing any such Shares shall cease to have any rights with respect thereto, except the right to receive the Merger Consideration for each such Share.

Section 1.07. Dissenting Shares. Notwithstanding anything in this Plan of Merger to the contrary, any issued and outstanding Shares held by a shareholder (a *"Dissenting Shareholder"*) who complies in all respects with Sections 1930 and 1575 through 1580 of the PBCL concerning the right of holders of Shares to require appraisal of their Shares (*"Dissenting Shares"*) shall not be converted as described in Section 1.06(c), but shall become the right to receive payment of the fair value of such Shares in accordance with Sections 1930 and 1575 through 1580 of the PBCL. If, after the Effective Time, a holder of Dissenting Shares withdraws his, her or its demand for appraisal or fails to perfect or otherwise loses his, her or its right of appraisal, in any case pursuant to the PBCL, his, her or its Shares shall be deemed to be converted as of the Effective Time into the right to receive the Merger Consideration for each such Share, without interest or dividends, upon surrender, in the manner provided in Section 1.08, of the certificate or certificates that formerly evidenced such Shares. The Company shall give [the Acquiring Party] prompt notice of any demands for appraisal of Shares received by the Company. The Company shall not, without the prior written consent of [the Acquiring Party], make any payment with respect to, or settle or offer to settle, any such demands.

Section 1.08. Surrender of Shares; Stock Transfer Books.

a. *Paying Agent.* Prior to the Effective Time, a bank or trust company who shall be reasonably satisfactory to the Company shall be designated to act as paying agent in the Merger (the *"Paying Agent"*), and from time to time, on, prior to or after the Effective Time, [the Acquiring Party] shall make available, or cause the Surviving Corporation to make available, to the Paying Agent cash in the amounts necessary for the payment of the Merger Consideration as provided in Section 1.06(c) upon surrender as part of the Merger of certificates formerly representing Shares. Funds made available to the Paying Agent shall be invested by the Paying Agent as directed by [the Acquiring Party] (it being understood that any and all interest or income earned on funds made available to the Paying Agent pursuant to this Agreement shall be turned over to [the Acquiring Party]).

b. *Exchange Procedure.* As soon as reasonably practicable after the Effective Time, the Surviving Corporation shall cause the Paying Agent to mail to each holder of record of a certificate or certificates that immediately prior to the Effective Time represented Shares (the *"Certificates"*), (i) a letter of transmittal (which shall specify that delivery shall be effected, and risk of loss and title to the Certificates shall pass, only upon delivery of the Certificates to the Paying Agent and shall be in a form and have such other provisions as [the Acquiring Party] may reasonably specify) and (ii) instructions for use in effecting the surrender of the Certificates in exchange for the Merger Consideration as provided in Section 1.06. Upon surrender of a Certificate for cancellation to the Paying Agent or to such other agent or agents as may be appointed by [the Acquiring Party], together with such letter of transmittal, duly executed, and such other documents as may reasonably be required by the Paying Agent, the holder of such Certificate shall be entitled to receive in exchange therefor the amount of cash, without interest or dividends, into which the Shares theretofore represented by such Certificate shall have been converted pursuant to Section 1.06(c), and the Certificate so surrendered shall forthwith be cancelled. In the event of a transfer of ownership of Shares that is not registered in the transfer records of the Company, payment may be made to a person other than the person in whose name the Certificate so surrendered is registered, if such Certificate shall be properly endorsed or otherwise be in proper form for transfer and the person requesting such payment shall pay any transfer or other taxes required by reason of the payment to a Person other than the registered holder of such Certificate or establish to the satisfaction of the Surviving Corporation that such tax has been paid or is not applicable. Until surrendered as contemplated by this Section 1.08, each Certificate (other than Certificates representing Dissenting Shares) shall be deemed at any time after the Effective Time to represent only the right to receive upon such surrender the amount of cash, without interest or dividends, into which the Shares of stock theretofore represented by such Certificate shall have been converted pursuant to Section 1.06. No interest shall be paid or shall accrue on the cash payable upon the surrender of any Certificate. [the Acquiring Party] or the Paying Agent shall be entitled to deduct and withhold from the consideration otherwise payable pursuant to this Agreement to any holder of Shares such amounts as [the Acquiring Party] or the Paying Agent is required to deduct and withhold with respect to the making of such payment under the Internal Revenue Code of 1986, as amended, or under any provision of state, local or foreign tax law. To the extent that amounts are so withheld by [the Acquiring Party] or the Paying Agent, such withheld amounts shall be treated for all purposes of this Agreement as having been paid to the holder of the Shares in respect of which such deduction and withholding was made by the [the Acquiring Party] or the Paying Agent.

c. *No Further Ownership Rights in Shares.* All cash paid upon the surrender of Certificates in accordance with the terms of this Plan of Merger shall be deemed to have been paid in full satisfaction of all rights pertaining to the Shares theretofore represented by such Certificates. At the Effective Time, the stock transfer books of the Company shall be closed, and there shall be no further registration of transfers on the stock transfer books of the Surviving Corporation of the Shares that were outstanding immediately prior to the Effective Time. If, after the Effective Time, Certificates are presented to the Surviving Corporation or the Paying Agent for any reason, they shall be cancelled and exchanged as provided in this Article I.

d. *Termination of Payment Fund.* Any portion of the funds made available to the Paying Agent to pay the Merger Consideration which remains undistributed to the holders of Shares for six months after the Effective Time shall be delivered to [the Acquiring Party], upon demand, and any holders of Shares who have not theretofore complied with this Article I and the instructions set forth in the letter of transmittal mailed to such holders after the Effective Time shall thereafter look only to the Surviving Corporation (subject to abandoned property, escheat or other similar laws) for payment of the Merger Consideration to which they are entitled.

[C] Contingent Value Rights

There are instances in which the acquiring party and the target's Board of Directors cannot agree on a per share cash acquisition price. A stalemate can be avoided by utilization of contingent value rights, which provide for a contingent additional cash payment depending upon the target company's financial performance (such as, for example, revenues) for a period of time subsequent to the acquisition. Contingent value rights are unsecured debt obligations of the target company (payable subsequent to the acquisition) and are received by the target's stockholders in the form of a property dividend declared prior to the commencement of the cash tender offer, but payable after the completion of the tender offer. The contingent value rights are not guaranteed or otherwise assumed by the acquiring party. Accordingly, the rights are not "securities" issued by the acquiring party and hence are not required to be registered under the Securities Act of 1933. They are, however, subject to the Trust Indenture Act. Contingent value rights are issued pursuant to a contingent payment rights agreement, which is similar to a trust indenture. Set forth below is an outline of the principal terms of such rights.

PRINCIPAL TERMS OF CONTINGENT PAYMENT RIGHTS

GENERAL:	The Rights will be cash settlement "earn-out" rights which will pay specified amounts if, and only if, (i) a "Change of Control" of the Company occurs prior to December 31, 1998 and (ii) the Company achieves certain levels of Company Sales (as defined below) during the Measurement Period (as defined below). The Rights will be issued by the Company as a dividend on the Common Shares, consisting of one Right per share outstanding on the record date. One Right will also be issued (i) upon exercise of an option outstanding on the record date with respect to each Common Share issued upon exercise thereof and (ii) upon the cash-out of any vested option outstanding on the record date in connection with a "Change of Control" with respect to each Common Share that would have been issuable upon exercise of such vested option. The Rights will be issued pursuant to a Rights Agreement between the Company and a major financial institution, as Rights Agent.
DIVIDEND RECORD DATE:	July _______, 1998 [15 business days after declaration].
DIVIDEND PAYMENT DATE:	September _______, 1998 [60 days after record date].
MEASUREMENT PERIOD:	January 1, 1999 to December 31, 1999.
COMPANY SALES:	All net sales of the Company and its subsidiaries during the Measurement Period, calculated in accordance with generally accepted accounting principles.
CASH PAYMENT AMOUNT:	The payment made per Right will be an amount in cash equal to: (a) $10.00, if Company Sales are $249 million or greater; (b) $6.50, if Company Sales are $241 million; (c) $4.25, if Company Sales are $234 million; (d) $2.00, if Company Sales are $227 million; or (e) $0.00 if less than $222 million. If the Company Sales fall between two of the levels specified above, the amount of the payment made per Right shall be determined by interpolation. No payment shall be made if Company Sales are less than $222 million.
CASH PAYMENT DATE:	March 31, 2000

EXPIRATION DATE:	The Rights shall expire without any payment on December 31, 1998 if no "Change of Control" of the Company has occurred prior to such date. If a "Change of Control" has occurred prior to December 31, 1998, but Company Sales are less than $222 million, the Rights shall expire without any payment on April 1, 2000.
OPTIONAL REDEMPTION:	The Rights may be redeemed at the option of the Company at any time after a "Change of Control" of the Company, in whole or in part, at a redemption price of $10.00 per Right.

[D] Stock-for-Stock Merger Provisions

ARTICLE IV

Each share of the Common Stock, par value $3.33 1/3 per share, of Target which shall be outstanding immediately prior to the effective time of the merger (except any shares of such Common Stock which shall then be held in the treasury of Target and except any shares of Common Stock which shall be held by Surviving Corporation) shall, by virtue of the merger and without any action on the part of the holder thereof, be converted into an exchanged for one share of the $2.25 Cumulative Series A Preferred Stock of Surviving Corporation (the "Series A Preferred Stock"). Each holder of any of such shares of the Common Stock of Target shall, after the effective time of the merger, be entitled on the surrender by such holder to Surviving Corporation or cancellation of the certificate or certificates representing the share or shares thereof held by such holder to receive in exchange therefor a certificate or certificates representing the same number of shares of the Series A Preferred Stock of Surviving Corporation. Until so surrendered, each such outstanding certificate which immediately prior to the effective time of the merger represented shares of the Common Stock of Target shall be deemed for all corporate purposes, subject to the provisions of this Article IV, to evidence the ownership of the shares of the Series A Preferred Stock of Surviving Corporation for which such shares shall have been so exchanged. Unless and until any such certificate shall be so surrendered, dividends payable to the holders of record of shares of the Series A Preferred Stock of Surviving Corporation shall not be paid to the holder of such certificate in respect of the shares of such Series A Preferred Stock represented thereby, but in the case of each such certificate which shall be surrendered as aforesaid there shall be paid to the record holder of the certificate for shares of the Series A Preferred Stock of Surviving Corporation issued in exchange therefor (a) the amount of the dividends which theretofore shall have become payable with respect to the number of shares of the Series A Preferred Stock represented by the certificate issued in exchange upon such surrender, such amount to be paid on the surrender of such certificate, but without interest, and (b) the amount of any dividends with respect to such number of shares, the record date for the determination of the stockholders entitled to which shall be prior to the surrender of such certificate but the payment date of which shall be subsequent to such surrender, such amount to be paid on such payment date.

At the effective time of the merger all shares of the Common Stock of Target held by Acquiring Party immediately prior to the effective time of the merger shall cease to exist and all certificates representing such shares shall be cancelled.

Each share of Common Stock, par value $1.00 per share of the Surviving Corporation which shall be outstanding at the effective time of the merger shall remain unchanged and unaffected by the merger and shall continue as one share of Common Stock par value $1.00 per share, of the Surviving Corporation.

[E] Pre-Filing Clearance Procedure

Many corporate acquisitions and related transactions (such as the creation of a new class of stock to be issued to the holders of the acquired corporation) are not effective until the required documents are filed with the appropriate state authorities. In order to avoid possible last-minute delays (or, heaven forbid, embarrassments) many lawyers obtain prefiling clearance of the documentation by submitting copies thereof to the state offices for their review prior to the time the documents are put in relatively final form, such as being appended to proxy material.

Alexander & Green
299 Park Avenue
New York, N.Y. 10171

August 24, 2012

By Hand

Mr. Joe Mirrione
CT Corporation System
1633 Broadway
New York, NY 10019

RE: Pre-Clearance of Alphatype/New Berthold Agreement of Merger in Delaware

Dear Mr. Mirrione:

Pursuant to our telephone conversation on Friday afternoon, I am enclosing two copies of the Agreement of Merger for the merger of New Berthold, Inc., a Delaware corporation, with and into Alphatype Corporation, also a Delaware corporation. New Berthold, Inc. is a wholly owned subsidiary of Berthold of North America, Inc., a New Jersey corporation.

Would you please arrange to have the Agreement precleared in Delaware as soon as possible? It would be most appreciated if this could be accomplished, as you suggested, by Thursday or Friday of this week.

Best wishes,

Sincerely,
Noel J. Para, A/P

Encl.

TABLE OF CASES

[References are to pages.]

A

B

[References are to pages.]

C

[References are to pages.]

D

E

[References are to pages.]

F

G

[References are to pages.]

H

I

J

K

[References are to pages.]

[References are to pages.]

N

O

P

[References are to pages.]

Q

R

S

[References are to pages.]

T

[References are to pages.]

U

V

W

[References are to pages.]

INDEX

[References are to sections.]

A

B

C

[References are to sections.]

[References are to sections.]

I

L

M

N

P

R

S

[References are to sections.]